STATE CONSTITUTIONAL LAW
THE MODERN EXPERIENCE

Second Edition

■ ■ ■

Randy J. Holland
Justice
Delaware Supreme Court

Stephen R. McAllister
E.S. & Tom W. Hampton Professor of Law
University of Kansas School of Law, and
Solicitor General of Kansas

Jeffrey M. Shaman
Vincent de Paul Professor of Law
DePaul University College of Law

Jeffrey S. Sutton
Judge
United States Court of Appeals for the Sixth Circuit

AMERICAN CASEBOOK SERIES®

WEST
ACADEMIC
PUBLISHING

American Casebook Series is a trademark registered in the U.S. Patent and Trademark Office.

© 2010 Thomson Reuters
© 2016 LEG, Inc. d/b/a West Academic
    444 Cedar Street, Suite 700
    St. Paul, MN 55101
    1-877-888-1330

West, West Academic Publishing, and West Academic are trademarks of West Publishing Corporation, used under license.

Printed in the United States of America

ISBN: 978-1-63459-682-4

Each of the Co-Authors Dedicates This Book as Follows –

Randy J. Holland

To Ilona E. Holland

Ethan, Jennifer, Aurora (Rori), and Chloe

Stephen McAllister

To Suzanne Valdez,

Mara, Fiona, Brett, Isabel, and Sofia

Jeffrey M. Shaman

To Susan Shaman, Craig, and Blair

Jeffrey Sutton

To Peggy Sutton,

Nathaniel, John, and Margaret

FOREWORD

State Constitutional Law – The Modern Experience
Foreword by E. Norman Veasey[*]

As is the case with the weather, lawyers often talk about the constitutions of the various states, but seldom do anything about that subject. Most of the American cases and literature focus on the United States Constitution. State constitutional law is often neglected, but it is a vibrant and significant feature of our jurisprudence. Justice Randy J. Holland, Judge Jeffrey S. Sutton, Professor Steven R. McAllister and Professor Jeffrey M. Shaman have breathed new life into the subject with this outstanding, scholarly casebook.

Lawyers take an oath upon admission to the bar to support the United States Constitution and the constitution of their states of admission. See, e.g., Rule 54, Rules of the Supreme Court of Delaware ("I ... do solemnly swear (or affirm) that I will support the Constitution of the United States and the Constitution of the State of Delaware ..."). But can a lawyer be true to this solemn oath if she has not studied state constitutional law or been examined on her state constitution? Perhaps she can "catch up" in practice with some "on the job training," as the need arises. But that is not a particularly professional approach. This new, epic work on state constitutional law should become an important basis for law school curricula. Moreover, state constitutional law should be considered as a bar examination topic.

The framers of the United States constitution adopted a "'constitutionally mandated balance of power' between the States and the Federal Government ... to ensure the protection of 'our fundamental liberties.'" *Atascadero State Hosp. v. Scanlon*, 473 U.S. 234, 242 (1985) (quoting *Garcia v. San Antonio Metro. Transit Auth.*, 469 U.S. 528 (Powell, J., dissenting)). The preservation of diversity in the legal and governmental systems of each state was expressly contemplated when the United States constitution was framed and adopted. *See* Randy J. Holland, *State Constitutions: Purpose and Function*, 69 Temp. L. Rev. 989, 998-99 (1996). State constitutions are a source of rights independent of the Federal Constitution and may be applied by state courts to grant more extensive protection for individual rights than is recognized under the Federal Constitution.

---

[*] Chief Justice (Ret.) Delaware Supreme Court (1992-2004).

Under the system of dual sovereignty that exists in this nation, a state court is free to interpret its own state constitution in any way it determines, provided it does not contravene federal law. While the Supremacy Clause of the Federal Constitution makes federal law supreme to state law, so long as state constitutional protection does not fall below the federal floor, a state court may interpret its own state constitution as it chooses, irrespective of federal constitutional law. Although decisions of the United States Supreme Court concerning constitutional issues are entitled to respect and may provide guidance on constitutional matters, they are not binding on a state court as it interprets its own state constitutional guarantees. A state court is free as a matter of its own law to grant more expansive rights than those afforded by federal law. The expansion beyond federally guaranteed individual liberties by a state constitution is attributable to a variety of reasons: differences in textual language, legislative history, pre-existing state law, structural differences, matters of particular concern, and state traditions.

As Judge Sutton, one of the co-authors of this work, has written, "… lawyers and clients have two chances, not one, to invalidate [dubious state or local action]. They may invoke the United States Constitution … or that State's Constitution to strike the law. Yet … that is not what most lawyers do." Jeffrey S. Sutton, *Why Teach—and Why Study—State Constitutional Law*, 34 OKLAHOMA CITY UNIVERSITY LAW REVIEW 165, 166 (2009). A lawyer challenging police action or a dubious state statute should welcome the leverage of two arrows in her quiver.

Indeed, lawyers *should*, in many cases, frame their attacks on the constitutions of both sovereigns. Why? "State constitutional law not only gives the client two chances to win, it will also give the client a *better* chance to win." *Id.* at 173. There are many reasons cited by Judge Sutton showing this to be true, but one overarching reason is that a state supreme court's decision that rests on its application of the state constitution is the last word in the case and cannot be countermanded by the United States Supreme Court. As the late Supreme Court Justice William Brennan has written, "Moreover, the state decisions not only cannot be overturned by, they indeed are not even reviewable by, the Supreme Court of the United States." William J. Brennan, Jr., *State Constitutions and the Protection of Individual Rights*, 90 HARV. L. REV. 489, 501 (1977). This principle is based on the established doctrine that "… if a state ground is independent and adequate to support a judgment, the [U.S. Supreme] Court has no jurisdiction at all over the decision despite the presence of federal issues." *Id.* at 501 n.80.

The law concerning unreasonable searches and seizures reflects differing standards between federal and state constitutions and a labyrinth of factual situations. *See United States v. Cortez*, 449 U.S. 411, 417 (1981). A case in point is the 1999 Delaware Supreme Court decision in *Jones v. State*, 745 A.2d 856 (Del. 1999). There the Court held—arguably in the face of contrary federal and Delaware decisions under the United States Constitution adjudicating similarly worded provisions—that the police did not have a reasonable and articulable basis to make a stop of the defendant and the seizure of controlled substances on his person.

In *Jones* the Court framed the issue as "whether the search and seizure language in the Delaware Constitution means the same thing as the United States Supreme Court's construction of *similar* language in the United States Constitution." *Id.* at 495. The Court then analyzed a number of historical references, including those where similar terms had been used, with differing results. *Id.* at 495-506. Noting that the law concerning unreasonable searches and seizures "reflects differing standards between federal and state constitutions and a labyrinth of factual situations," the Court held:

> "If an officer attempts to seize someone before possessing reasonable and articulable suspicion, that person's actions stemming from the attempted seizure may not be used to manufacture the suspicion the police lacked initially."

Id. at 855-56.

State constitutional law, like its federal counterpart, is not limited to issues involving the common law or individual rights. Numerous other areas of law involve the application of state constitutions. The structure and power of state and local governments, the state judicial system, taxation, public finance, and public education are all affected by a state's constitutions and its interpretation. "From its inception of the American republic, federal and state constitutional traditions have been distinct." James E. Henretta, *Foreword: Rethinking the State Constitutional Tradition*, 22 Rutgers L.J. 819, 819-26, 836-39 (1991). The United States Constitution has retained its original character as a document that fixed the basic structure of government and allocated power among its three branches. State constitution-making and amending has been a recurring process within the broader political, social, economic, and historical contexts of time and place. A.E. Dick Howard, *The Values of Federalism*, 1 New. Eur. L. Rev. 241, 145-46 (1993); Lewis B. Kaden, *Politics, Money, and State Sovereignty: The Judicial Role*, 79 Colum. L. Rev. 847-853-57 (1979). *See also* Robert P. Stoker, Reluctant Partners (1991).

This new, richly documented and superbly analyzed casebook by such distinguished legal scholars is destined to be the seminal authority in this vitally important field. For some lawyers, a system of dual sovereignty means that litigants will have two opportunities, not than just one, to invalidate a state law or otherwise halt state action. And for others, our federal system makes state courts accountable for properly interpreting their own constitutions, without regard to whether those interpretations increase or decrease individual liberty and without regard to whether they follow or break from decisions of the U.S. Supreme Court. But for all lawyers, the independence of the sovereignty of the states makes the study and effective use of state constitutional law an imperative in the twenty-first century.

SUMMARY OF CONTENTS

TABLE OF CONTENTS

TABLE OF CASES

Principal cases are in bold type. Non-principal cases are in roman type. References are to Pages.

TABLE OF AUTHORITIES

Books and Articles

Constitutions

Other Sources

EXPLANATORY NOTE

The case book is designed to present a wide variety of materials in an accessible and interesting way. To that end, we have edited the opinions to remove unnecessary discussions, to eliminate unilluminating citations and to omit unhelpful footnotes. Our practice has been to use ellipses only when we have removed language from the opinion in the middle of a paragraph. Otherwise, whenever we have removed paragraphs, citations and footnotes, or even when we have omitted discussions at the beginning or end of a paragraph, we have not used ellipses. As to the (few) footnotes that remain, we have numbered them sequentially within each chapter and, where appropriate, have identified the original number of the footnote in an adjacent bracket. Through it all, the critical point is that we have created these abridged opinions to facilitate teaching an important subject, not to make legal research easier and above all not for the purpose of using the opinions as citations or quotations in legal pleadings. Before citing any of these materials, the lawyer should consult the original opinion or article.

ACKNOWLEDGEMENTS

For this second edition, extra special thanks go to Michele Rutledge, who for the second time took on the herculean task of pulling the draft chapters together, of reorganizing chapters and creating a uniform document, and of putting up with an endless stream of edits and corrections to finalize the chapters and tables in the book.

PERMISSION TO REPRINT

The authors and publishers gratefully acknowledge permission to use excerpts from the following:

Mark Edward DeForrest, *An Overview and Evaluation of State Blaine Amendments: Origins, Scope, and First Amendment Concerns*, 26 Harv. J. L. & Pub. Pol'y. 551 (2003);

Martha Dragich, *State Constitutional Restriction on Legislative Procedure: Rethinking the Analysis of Original Purpose, Single Subject, and Clear Title Challenges*, 38 Harv. J. Legis. 103 (2001);

Peter J. Galie and Christopher Bopst, *The Constitutional Commission in New York: A Worthy Tradition*, 64 Alb. L. Rev. 1285 (2001);

Judith L. Maute, *Selecting Justice in State Courts: The Ballot Box or the Backroom?* 40 S. Tex. L. Rev. 1197 (2000);

Anne Permaloff, *Altering State Constitutions*, 33 Cumb. L. Rev. 217 (2003);

Shannon M. Roesler, *The Kansas Remedy By Due Course Of Law Provision: Defining A Right To A Remedy*, 47 Kan. L. Rev. 655 (1999);

Jeffrey M. Shaman, EQUALITY AND LIBERTY IN THE GOLDEN AGE OF STATE CONSTITUTIONAL LAW (Oxford University Press 2008);

Jeffrey S. Sutton, *Why Teach—and Why Study—State Constitutional Law*, 34 Okla. City Univ. L. Rev. 165 (2009);

Jeffrey S. Sutton, San Antonio Independent School District v. Rodriguez *and Its Aftermath*, 94 Va. L. Rev. 1963 (2008).

STATE CONSTITUTIONAL LAW
THE MODERN EXPERIENCE

Second Edition

CHAPTER I

INTRODUCTION

All law schools in this country offer a course called "Constitutional Law," and virtually all of these courses (and textbooks) teach just half of the story. They teach the course from the perspective of the Federal Constitution, infrequently mentioning, much less explaining, the role of the State Constitutions in our system of government and laws. In one sense, that is quite understandable; it is difficult enough to teach all of *federal* constitutional law in a full-year course. In another sense, it is a missed opportunity, as too many students never learn the full story.

When the Framers "split the atom of sovereignty," *U.S. Term Limits, Inc. v. Thornton*, 514 U.S. 779, 838 (1995) (Kennedy, J., concurring), they created a dual system of government, one with two sets of sovereigns for every corner of the country, not just one. It is a singularly American innovation, the one idea the Framers could have patented because no other government had tried it and no political philosopher had ever proposed it. The American experiment launched a governmental structure with horizontal separation of powers (dividing the executive, legislative, and judicial branches at the national level) *and* vertical separation of powers (dividing the national and the state governments).

In this country, we thus have fifty-one Constitutions—fifty-one charters of government that simultaneously empower and constrain: that give two sets of sovereigns in any one location in the country the power to regulate most areas of American life and that limit those regulations through individual-liberty guarantees and other limitations on the legislative and executive branches. To understand *American* constitutional law, one cannot study federal constitutional law by itself or for that matter state constitutional law by itself. A full understanding of the one cannot be understood without an appreciation of the other. To think otherwise about the matter is akin to taking a course on civil procedure without learning that there are state court procedures as well as federal ones. American constitutional law, like American procedural law, covers both.

Although it is not the objective of this textbook to cover *all* of American constitutional law—to cover the subject from the perspective of all of its federal and state counterparts—it is our mission to correct the imbalance. Our focus is the fifty State Constitutions, yet our method of presentation emphasizes the interrelation of the two sets of constitutions, frequently explaining how the U.S. Constitution deals with an issue before explaining how the State Constitutions handle it or in some instances explaining how the State Constitutions contain provisions that have no parallel in the U.S. Constitution.

Like most torts, property, and contracts textbooks, this casebook is not parochial. It uses decisions from courts throughout the country. It does not focus on the constitution or cases from any one State but surveys the most interesting and thoughtful cases from all of the States.

The book covers several basic topics. The first substantive chapter sets the framework. It explains the interrelation of the State and Federal Constitutions—where federal power is exclusive, where state power is exclusive, and where the two overlap. The next substantive chapter introduces a key theme of the book by discussing why and when state courts may construe guarantees found in their own constitutions more broadly than identical or similarly worded guarantees found in the Federal Constitution. The next several chapters apply these principles to a variety of civil and criminal individual-liberty guarantees of the State Constitutions. Some of the guarantees, as the student will see, have exact counterparts in the U.S. Constitution and indeed often were the models for the first eight provisions of the federal Bill of Rights. Others have similarities to their federal cousins. And still others have no counterparts in the U.S. Constitution. The book then devotes a long chapter to the branches of state government. It considers the grants of authority to each division of state government and the structural limitations placed on that power. The penultimate chapter addresses an issue of considerable import today: the relatively easy amendment process for most State Constitutions, which often require just a majority vote. It might be said that the U.S. Constitution is too difficult to amend, and the State Constitutions are too easy to amend, and we will consider the impact of this salient feature of the state amendment procedures on the development of state constitutional law. The last chapter is historical, starting with the roots of state constitutional law and taking us to the present. It explains the framing of the State Constitutions, discussing the pre-1789 Constitutions and showing how they influenced each other and how they eventually laid the foundation for many components of the U.S. Constitution. It then addresses the later State Constitutions and the waves of amendments to all State Constitutions through different eras in American history.

Why take a class about state constitutional law? A lawyer's duty to a client is a good place to start. Our fifty-one constitutions place two potential sets of constitutional limitations on the validity of every state and local law. Lawyers are problem solvers, and when a state or local law stands in the way of a client's objective, it generally will matter little to the client whether the lawyer manages to invalidate the law on federal or state grounds. A constitutional claimant needs to win just once. No State permits a law invalidated under its constitution to be enforced; and the Supremacy Clause of the U.S. Constitution prohibits any State from enforcing laws invalidated under the Federal Constitution. A necessary consequence of a system of dual sovereignty is that it permits dual claims of unconstitutionality. The first reason for studying state constitutional law, then, is simple: Lawyers are paid to solve problems for their clients, and one way to do that is to win cases. Lawyers paid to help a client win a case will have some explaining to do if they fail to consider taking two shots, rather than just one, at invalidating a state or local law.

State constitutional law not only gives the client two chances to win, but in some settings it may give the client a *better* chance to win. The U.S. Supreme Court is at a disadvantage relative to the state courts when it comes to defining constitutional rights and crafting constitutional remedies in many areas of the law. Because the Supreme Court must announce rights and remedies for fifty States, one National Government, and over 320 million people, it is more constrained than a state supreme court addressing a difficult problem for one State and, say, fifteen million people. That reality begins to explain why, as you will read in Chapter X, the U.S. Supreme Court might reject a constitutional challenge to Texas's system for funding public education, but the Texas Supreme Court later would grant relief in a similar challenge filed under the Texas Constitution. *Compare San Antonio Indep. Sch. Dist. v. Rodriguez*, 411 U.S. 1 (1973), *with Edgewood Indep. Sch. Dist. v. Kirby*, 777 S.W.2d 391 (Tex. 1989). In some settings, the challenge of imposing a constitutional solution on the whole country at once will increase the likelihood that federal constitutional law will be under-enforced or that a "federalism discount" will be applied to the right. State courts face no such problem in construing their own constitutions.

State courts also have a freer hand in doing something the Supreme Court cannot: allowing local conditions and traditions to affect their interpretation of a constitutional guarantee and the remedies imposed to implement that guarantee. The Alaska Supreme Court might gauge privacy issues differently from other States or for that matter the U.S. Supreme Court. The Montana Supreme Court might gauge property rights differently from other States or the U.S. Supreme Court. Or the Utah and Rhode Island Supreme Courts might gauge free-exercise rights differently from other state courts. State constitutional law respects, indeed embraces, differences between and among the States by allowing fifty constitutions to be interpreted differently to account for these differences in culture, geography, and history. In state constitutional law, as in state legislation, the States may be "laboratories of experimentation." *New State Ice Co. v. Liebmann*, 285 U.S. 262, 311 (1932) (Brandeis, J., dissenting).

State constitutional law also holds promise as a way to facilitate the development of *federal* constitutional law. For far too long, we have lived in a top-down constitutional world, in which the U.S. Supreme Court announces a ruling, and the state supreme courts move in lockstep in construing the counterpart guarantees of their own constitutions. Why not do the reverse? That is the way other areas of the law traditionally have developed, be it tort, property, or contract law. In these settings, the state courts are the vanguard—the first ones to decide whether to embrace or reject innovative legal claims. Over time, the market of common law decisions identifies winners and losers. An opinion by a Cardozo or a Traynor might become the benchmark, after which other state courts opt to follow that view or variations on it. Or the state courts might go their separate ways. In either event, the federal courts profit from the experience, as they can choose whether to federalize the issue *after* learning the strengths and weaknesses of the competing ways of addressing the problem.

Once the student learns that State Constitutions are documents of independent force—that the meaning of state guarantees is a matter for the state courts, not the U.S. Supreme Court, to resolve—it opens up a new way of thinking about constitutional law. By the second or third year of law school, most students come to appreciate that many constitutional issues do not lend themselves to one-size-fits-all solutions. It is one thing to apply the requirement that the President be thirty-five years of age, Art. II, § 1, cl. 5, U.S. Const., or a requirement that the Governor of a State be thirty years of age, Ala. Const. Art. V, § 117. But it is quite another to decipher what the more-generalized individual-liberty guarantees—say, due process or free speech—mean when they appear in the State and Federal Constitutions.

As to these vexing areas of the law, the state courts may adopt their own interpretations of parallel (or somewhat parallel) guarantees found in their own constitutions. When difficult areas of constitutional litigation arise, why assume that the U.S. Supreme Court is the only supreme court in the country capable of offering an insightful solution to a difficult problem? Three distinct levels of scrutiny—rational basis, intermediate, or strict—may be the best way to assess equal-protection claims, but they are hardly the self-evident way or the text-ordained way. Rational-basis review may be the best way to assess free-exercise challenges to neutral, generally applicable laws as a matter of national constitutional law, *see Emp't Div. v. Smith*, 494 U.S. 872, 878-79 (1990), but the same may not be true for each state constitution, *see Humphrey v. Lane*, 728 N.E.2d 1039, 1043 (Ohio 2000). A modest standard for enforcing the Takings Clause may work for national taking-of-property claims, *see Kelo v. City of New London*, 545 U.S. 469, 483 (2005), but it is by no means clear that every State should embrace the same approach in addressing similar challenges under its own constitution, *see Bd. of Cty. Comm'rs v. Lowery*, 136 P.3d 639, 652 (Okla. 2006). The more difficult the constitutional question, as these cases show, the more indeterminate the answer may be. In these settings, it may be appropriate to have fifty-one imperfect solutions rather than one imperfect solution—particularly when imperfection may be something we invariably will have to live with in a given area.

In some cases, the *only* way a lawyer can win a case is through the State Constitution because it is the only constitution with a provision on point. State constitutions have a variety of clauses found nowhere in the U.S. Constitution: right-to-remedy clauses, single-subject clauses, uniform-law clauses, to name a few. And some state constitutions have exotic clauses found in few, if any, other state constitutions. The Ohio Constitution, for example, bars the taxation of food sold for human consumption, *see* Ohio Const. Art. XII, § 13, and the Alaska Constitution generally forbids the creation of any "exclusive right or special privilege of fishery" within Alaskan waters, Alaska Const. Art. VIII, § 15.

If ever there were a propitious time for thinking twice about the meaning of American constitutional law—its federal and state components—now may be it. Many of the most ground-breaking constitutional disputes of the day are being waged in the state courts under the State Constitutions. Whether it is school funding, property rights, criminal procedure, religious liberties, or other modern rights disputes, the state courts in recent years have gone from being civil-rights followers to leaders. There is, indeed, a softer side to federalism: A loss in the U.S. Supreme Court no longer inevitably foreshadows a loss in the state courts when the claim is premised on a state constitutional counterpart. As many of these debates confirm, state constitutional litigation can proceed without waiting for, or worrying about, the shadow of federal constitutional law.

Often, indeed, there is a synergy between federal and state constitutional law. It is difficult to imagine *Obergefell v. Hodges*, 135 S. Ct. 2584 (2015), without *Goodridge v. Department of Public Health*, 798 N.E.2d 941 (Mass. 2003). The U.S. Supreme Court recognized as much in *Obergefell*. In establishing a right to same-sex marriage in the Fourteenth Amendment and in overruling its prior contrary decision in *Baker v. Nelson*, 409 U.S. 810 (1972), the Court noted that "the highest courts of many States have contributed to this ongoing dialogue in decisions interpreting their own State Constitutions." *Obergefell*, 135 S. Ct. at 2597. Something similar happened in *Arizona v. Gant*, 556 U.S. 332 (2009), a case about searches incident to arrest. There too the U.S. Supreme Court overruled a prior decision (*New York v. Belton*, 453 U.S. 454 (1981)), and there too the Court recognized that many state courts had not followed *Belton* in construing comparable guarantees in their own constitutions. *Gant*, 556 U.S. at 347 n.8. The influence of state constitutional law on federal constitutional law, moreover, affects originalists and living constitutionalists alike. For originalists, the meaning of the early state constitutions often provides the best evidence of what the Federal Constitution means, particularly when (as is so often the case) the latter was modeled after the former. *See Town of Greece v. Galloway*, 134 S. Ct. 1811 (2014) (construing the First and Fourteenth Amendments); *McDonald v. City of Chicago*, 561 U.S. 742 (2010) (construing the Second and Fourteenth Amendments). For living constitutionalists, developments in state constitutional law often provide the best evidence of evolving social norms. *See Obergefell v. Hodges*.

As all of this suggests and as the rest of the book confirms, no lawyer in the twenty-first century can be a good advocate without appreciating the possibility—the value—of raising state constitutional claims when representing a client. Ask students why they went to law school, and you will find a common answer among many of them: the opportunity to make a difference in the great issues of the day. No lawyer can take advantage of these opportunities without understanding state constitutional law. *See generally* Jeffrey S. Sutton, *Why Teach—and Why Study—State Constitutional Law*, 34 Okla. City U. L. Rev. 165 (2009).

CHAPTER II

DUAL SOVEREIGNTY: THE INTERRELATION OF THE STATE AND FEDERAL CONSTITUTIONS

INTRODUCTION

States operate as true sovereigns within the system created by the federal Constitution. The concept of "federalism," however, is nowhere explicitly written into or defined by the U.S. Constitution. Instead, it is a uniquely American contribution to political theory that is inherent in numerous constitutional provisions. Federalism is a large topic in its own right, one that could easily fill its own casebook. This casebook, with its focus on state constitutional law, is not the proper forum for a lengthy examination of federalism principles.

Instead, this chapter focuses only on some provisions in the U.S. Constitution that tend to bear most directly on state constitutional law, though in some very different ways. The chapter is divided into two major sections: (1) the distribution of federal and state powers under the U.S. Constitution; and (2) federal provisions that limit or influence the content of state constitutions. The second section focuses on Articles VI and IV of the U.S. Constitution. Article VI contains the all-important Supremacy Clause which makes clear that federal law preempts contrary state law, including state constitutional law. Article IV directly addresses a number of matters central to the States' sovereignty and their role in the federal system. The first section examines the relationship between state and federal governmental powers, with attention to the powers exclusive to the federal government, the powers exclusive to the States, and the overlapping powers that the two sovereigns share.

A. THE SOURCES AND NATURE OF FEDERAL AND STATE POWERS

1. Exclusive Federal Powers

a. Article I, § 8

Article I, § 8 of the federal Constitution enumerates the majority of Congress's powers, many of which are exclusive in nature. Such exclusive powers include the power to establish rules of naturalization and immigration, regulate bankruptcy, coin money, establish post offices, protect intellectual property through patent, copyright, and trademark laws, constitute the lower federal courts, regulate and punish piracy, declare war, raise and support an army and a navy, and govern federal territories.

Some Article I powers are theoretically exclusive, but in practice end up intertwined and often overlapping with traditional state police powers, a prime example being Congress's Article I power to regulate commerce "among the several states." In theory, the power to regulate interstate commerce belongs to Congress alone, even to the point of the Supreme Court developing a "Dormant" or "Negative" commerce doctrine which the Court has used to find implied preemption of state police power regulations that, in the Court's view, unduly intrude into matters of interstate commerce. The Court invokes this doctrine in the absence of any Act of Congress either expressly or implicitly requiring such federal preemption. As a practical matter, the dormant commerce power has proven extremely important federal limitation on the States' efforts to regulate a variety of matters.

Thus, the reality is that the federal commerce power in particular has proven particularly difficult to separate from traditional state police powers, even though it is in theory an exclusive federal power. The Supreme Court has at times also attempted to draw lines regarding Congress's affirmative use of this power (in other words when Congress has passed a statute pursuant to its commerce power), though the lines are generally anything but clear. Further, in some contexts, the Court has altogether abandoned any effort to limit Congress's power over interstate commerce insofar as a law is challenged as improperly intruding into the States' sovereignty and government activities. See, e.g., *Garcia v. San Antonio Metropolitan Transit Auth.*, 469 U.S. 528 (1985).

Another potentially important Article I, § 8 power is clause 18, the Necessary and Proper Clause, which receives attention in the context of commerce power cases such as *Gonzales v. Raich* and *NFIB v. Sebelius*, excerpted below.

1. The Commerce Power and the Necessary and Proper Clause

GONZALES v. RAICH
545 U.S. 1 (2005)

STEVENS, J., delivered the opinion of the Court.

California is one of at least nine States that authorize the use of marijuana for medicinal purposes. The question presented in this case is whether the power vested in Congress by Article I, § 8, of the Constitution "[t]o make all Laws which shall be necessary and proper for carrying into Execution" its authority to "regulate Commerce with foreign Nations, and among the several States" includes the power to prohibit the local cultivation and use of marijuana in compliance with California law.

I

In 1996, California voters passed Proposition 215, now codified as the Compassionate Use Act of 1996.[1] The proposition was designed to ensure that "seriously ill" residents of the State have access to marijuana for medical purposes, and to encourage Federal and State Governments to take steps toward ensuring the safe and affordable distribution of the drug to patients in need. The Act creates an exemption from criminal prosecution for physicians, as well as for patients and primary caregivers who possess or cultivate marijuana for medicinal purposes with the recommendation or approval of a physician.

Respondents ... brought this action against the Attorney General of the United States and the head of the DEA seeking injunctive and declaratory relief prohibiting the enforcement of the federal Controlled Substances Act (CSA), 21 U.S.C. § 801 *et seq.* to the extent it prevents them from possessing, obtaining, or manufacturing cannabis for their personal medical use. In their complaint and supporting affidavits, Raich and Monson described the severity of their afflictions, their repeatedly futile attempts to obtain relief with conventional medications, and the opinions of their doctors concerning their need to use marijuana. Respondents claimed that enforcing the CSA against them would violate the Commerce Clause, the Due Process Clause of the Fifth Amendment, the Ninth and Tenth Amendments of the Constitution, and the doctrine of medical necessity.

The question before us ... is not whether it is wise to enforce the statute in these circumstances; rather, it is whether Congress' power to regulate interstate markets for medicinal substances encompasses the portions of those markets that are supplied with drugs produced and consumed locally.

II

Shortly after taking office in 1969, President Nixon declared a national "war on drugs." As the first campaign of that war, Congress set out to enact legislation that would consolidate various drug laws on the books into a comprehensive statute, provide meaningful regulation over legitimate sources of drugs to prevent diversion into illegal channels, and strengthen law enforcement tools against the traffic in illicit drugs. That

---

[1] [3] Cal. Health & Safety Code Ann. § 11362.5 (West Supp. 2005). The California Legislature recently enacted additional legislation supplementing the Compassionate Use Act. §§ 11362.7–11362.9 (West Supp. 2005).

effort culminated in the passage of the Comprehensive Drug Abuse Prevention and Control Act of 1970.

Title II of that Act, the CSA, repealed most of the earlier antidrug laws in favor of a comprehensive regime to combat the international and interstate traffic in illicit drugs. The main objectives of the CSA were to conquer drug abuse and to control the legitimate and illegitimate traffic in controlled substances. Congress was particularly concerned with the need to prevent the diversion of drugs from legitimate to illicit channels.

To effectuate these goals, Congress devised a closed regulatory system making it unlawful to manufacture, distribute, dispense, or possess any controlled substance except in a manner authorized by the CSA. The CSA categorizes all controlled substances into five schedules. The drugs are grouped together based on their accepted medical uses, the potential for abuse, and their psychological and physical effects on the body.

In enacting the CSA, Congress classified marijuana as a Schedule I drug. This preliminary classification was based, in part, on the recommendation of the Assistant Secretary of HEW "that marihuana be retained within schedule I at least until the completion of certain studies now underway." Schedule I drugs are categorized as such because of their high potential for abuse, lack of any accepted medical use, and absence of any accepted safety for use in medically supervised treatment. These three factors, in varying gradations, are also used to categorize drugs in the other four schedules. For example, Schedule II substances also have a high potential for abuse which may lead to severe psychological or physical dependence, but unlike Schedule I drugs, they have a currently accepted medical use. By classifying marijuana as a Schedule I drug, as opposed to listing it on a lesser schedule, the manufacture, distribution, or possession of marijuana became a criminal offense, with the sole exception being use of the drug as part of a Food and Drug Administration preapproved research study.

The CSA provides for the periodic updating of schedules and delegates authority to the Attorney General, after consultation with the Secretary of Health and Human Services, to add, remove, or transfer substances to, from, or between schedules. Despite considerable efforts to reschedule marijuana, it remains a Schedule I drug.

III

Respondents in this case do not dispute that passage of the CSA, as part of the Comprehensive Drug Abuse Prevention and Control Act, was well within Congress' commerce power. Nor do they contend that any provision or section of the CSA amounts to an unconstitutional exercise of congressional authority. Rather, respondents' challenge is actually quite limited; they argue that the CSA's categorical prohibition of the manufacture and possession of marijuana as applied to the intrastate manufacture and possession of marijuana for medical purposes pursuant to California law exceeds Congress' authority under the Commerce Clause.

In assessing the validity of congressional regulation, none of our Commerce Clause cases can be viewed in isolation. As charted in considerable detail in *United States v. Lopez*, our understanding of the reach of the Commerce Clause, as well as Congress' assertion of authority thereunder, has evolved over time. The Commerce Clause emerged as the Framers' response to the central problem giving rise to the Constitution itself: the absence of any federal commerce power under the Articles of Confederation. For the first century of our history, the primary use of the Clause was to preclude the kind of discriminatory state legislation that had once been permissible. Then, in response to rapid industrial development and an increasingly interdependent national economy, Congress "ushered in a new era of federal regulation under the commerce power," beginning with the enactment of the Interstate Commerce Act in 1887, and the Sherman Antitrust Act in 1890.

Cases decided during that "new era," which now spans more than a century, have identified three general categories of regulation in which Congress is authorized to engage under its commerce power. First, Congress can regulate the channels of interstate commerce. Second, Congress has authority to regulate and protect the instrumentalities of interstate commerce, and persons or things in interstate commerce. Third, Congress has the power to regulate activities that substantially affect interstate commerce. Only the third category is implicated in the case at hand.

Our case law firmly establishes Congress' power to regulate purely local activities that are part of an economic "class of activities" that have a substantial effect on interstate commerce. See, e.g., *Wickard v. Filburn*, 317 U.S. 111, 128-129 (1942). Our decision in *Wickard* is of particular relevance. In *Wickard*, we upheld the application of regulations promulgated under the Agricultural Adjustment Act of 1938, which were designed to control the volume of wheat moving in interstate and foreign commerce in order to avoid surpluses and consequent abnormally low prices. The regulations established an allotment of 11.1 acres for Filburn's 1941 wheat crop, but he sowed 23 acres, intending to use the excess by consuming it on his own farm. Filburn argued that even though we had sustained Congress' power to regulate the production of goods for commerce, that power did not authorize "federal regulation [of] production not intended in any part for commerce but wholly for consumption on the farm." Justice Jackson's opinion for a unanimous Court rejected this submission. He wrote:

"The effect of the statute before us is to restrict the amount which may be produced for market and the extent as well to which one may forestall resort to the market by producing to meet his own needs. That appellee's own contribution to the demand for wheat may be trivial by itself is not enough to remove him from the scope of federal regulation where, as here, his contribution, taken together with that of many others similarly situated, is far from trivial."

Wickard thus establishes that Congress can regulate purely intrastate activity that is not itself "commercial," in that it is not produced for sale, if it concludes that failure to regulate that class of activity would undercut the regulation of the interstate market in that commodity.

The similarities between this case and *Wickard* are striking. Like the farmer in *Wickard*, respondents are cultivating, for home consumption, a fungible commodity for which there is an established, albeit illegal, interstate market. Just as the Agricultural Adjustment Act was designed "to control the volume [of wheat] moving in interstate and foreign commerce in order to avoid surpluses ..." and consequently control the market price, a primary purpose of the CSA is to control the supply and demand of controlled substances in both lawful and unlawful drug markets. In *Wickard*, we had no difficulty concluding that Congress had a rational basis for believing that, when viewed in the aggregate, leaving home-consumed wheat outside the regulatory scheme would have a substantial influence on price and market conditions. Here too, Congress had a rational basis for concluding that leaving home-consumed marijuana outside federal control would similarly affect price and market conditions.

More concretely, one concern prompting inclusion of wheat grown for home consumption in the 1938 Act was that rising market prices could draw such wheat into the interstate market, resulting in lower market prices. The parallel concern making it appropriate to include marijuana grown for home consumption in the CSA is the likelihood that the high demand in the interstate market will draw such marijuana into that market. While the diversion of homegrown wheat tended to frustrate the federal interest in stabilizing prices by regulating the volume of commercial transactions in the interstate market, the diversion of homegrown marijuana tends to frustrate the federal interest in eliminating commercial transactions in the interstate market in their entirety. In both cases, the regulation is squarely within Congress' commerce power because production of the commodity meant for home consumption, be it wheat or marijuana, has a substantial effect on supply and demand in the national market for that commodity.

Nonetheless, respondents suggest that *Wickard* differs from this case in three respects: (1) the Agricultural Adjustment Act, unlike the CSA, exempted small farming operations; (2) *Wickard* involved a "quintessential economic activity"—a commercial farm—whereas whereas respondents do not sell marijuana; and (3) the *Wickard* record made it clear that the aggregate production of wheat for use on farms had a significant impact on market prices. Those differences, though factually accurate, do not diminish the precedential force of this Court's reasoning.

The fact that Filburn's own impact on the market was "trivial by itself" was not a sufficient reason for removing him from the scope of federal regulation. That the Secretary of Agriculture elected to exempt even smaller farms from regulation does not speak to his power to regulate all those whose aggregated production was significant, nor did that fact play any role in the Court's analysis. Moreover, even though Filburn was indeed a commercial farmer, the activity he was engaged in—the cultivation of wheat for home consumption—was not treated by the Court as part of his commercial farming operation. And while it is true that the record in the *Wickard* case itself established the causal connection between the production for local use and the national market, we have before us findings by Congress to the same effect.

In assessing the scope of Congress' authority under the Commerce Clause, we stress that the task before us is a modest one. We need not determine whether respondents' activities, taken in the aggregate, substantially affect interstate commerce in fact, but only whether a "rational basis" exists for so concluding. Given the enforcement difficulties that attend distinguishing between marijuana cultivated locally and marijuana grown elsewhere, and concerns about diversion into illicit channels, we have no difficulty concluding that Congress had a rational basis for believing that failure to regulate the intrastate manufacture and possession of marijuana would leave a gaping hole in the CSA. Thus, as in *Wickard*, when it enacted comprehensive legislation to regulate the interstate market in a fungible commodity, Congress was acting well within its authority to "make all Laws which shall be necessary and proper" to "regulate Commerce ... among the several States." U.S. Const., Art. I, § 8. That the regulation ensnares some purely intrastate activity is of no moment. As we have done many times before, we refuse to excise individual components of that larger scheme.

IV

To support their contrary submission, respondents rely heavily on two of our more recent Commerce Clause cases. In their myopic focus, they overlook the larger context of modern-era Commerce Clause jurisprudence preserved by those cases. Moreover, even in the narrow prism of respondents' creation, they read those cases far too broadly.

Those two cases, of course, are *Lopez*, 514 U.S. 549, and *Morrison*, 529 U.S. 598. As an initial matter, the statutory challenges at issue in those cases were markedly different from the challenge respondents pursue in the case at hand. Here, respondents ask us to excise individual applications of a concededly valid statutory scheme. In contrast, in both *Lopez* and *Morrison*, the parties asserted that a particular statute or provision fell outside Congress' commerce power in its entirety. This distinction is pivotal for we have often reiterated that "[w]here the class of activities is regulated and that class is within the reach of federal power, the courts have no power 'to excise, as trivial, individual instances' of the class."

At issue in *Lopez* was the validity of the Gun-Free School Zones Act of 1990, which was a brief, single-subject statute making it a crime for an individual to possess a gun in a school zone. 18 U.S.C. § 922(q)(1)(A). The Act did not regulate any economic activity and did not contain any requirement that the possession of a gun have any connection to past interstate activity or a predictable impact on future commercial activity. Distinguishing our earlier cases holding that comprehensive regulatory statutes may be validly applied to local conduct that does not, when viewed in isolation, have a significant impact on interstate commerce, we held the statute invalid. We explained:

> "Section 922(q) is a criminal statute that by its terms has nothing to do with 'commerce' or any sort of economic enterprise, however broadly one might define those terms. Section 922(q) is not an essential part of a larger regulation of economic activity, in which the regulatory scheme could be undercut unless the intrastate activity were regulated. It cannot, therefore, be sustained under our cases upholding regulations of activities that arise out of or are connected with a commercial transaction, which viewed in the aggregate, substantially affects interstate commerce."

The statutory scheme that the Government is defending in this litigation is at the opposite end of the regulatory spectrum. As explained above, the CSA, enacted in 1970 as part of the Comprehensive Drug Abuse Prevention and Control Act, was a lengthy and detailed statute creating a comprehensive framework for regulating the production, distribution, and possession of five classes of "controlled substances." Our opinion in *Lopez* casts no doubt on the validity of such a program.

Nor does this Court's holding in *Morrison*, 529 U.S. 598. The Violence Against Women Act of 1994 created a federal civil remedy for the victims of gender-motivated crimes of violence. 42 U.S.C. § 13981. The remedy was enforceable in both state and federal courts, and generally depended on proof of the violation of a state law. Despite congressional findings that such crimes had an adverse impact on interstate commerce, we held the statute unconstitutional because, like the statute in *Lopez*, it did not regulate economic activity. We concluded that "the noneconomic, criminal nature of the conduct at issue was central to our decision" in *Lopez*, and that our prior cases had identified a clear pattern of analysis:

"'Where economic activity substantially affects interstate commerce, legislation regulating that activity will be sustained.'".

Unlike those at issue in *Lopez* and *Morrison*, the activities regulated by the CSA are quintessentially economic. The CSA is a statute that regulates the production, distribution, and consumption of commodities for which there is an established, and lucrative, interstate market. Prohibiting the intrastate possession or manufacture of an article of commerce is a rational (and commonly utilized) means of regulating commerce in that product. Because the CSA is a statute that directly regulates economic, commercial activity, our opinion in *Morrison* casts no doubt on its constitutionality.

V

Under the present state of the law … the judgment of the Court of Appeals must be vacated. The case is remanded for further proceedings consistent with this opinion.

SCALIA, J., concurring in the judgment.

I agree with the Court's holding that the Controlled Substances Act (CSA) may validly be applied to respondents' cultivation, distribution, and possession of marijuana for personal, medicinal use. I write separately because my understanding of the doctrinal foundation on which that holding rests is, if not inconsistent with that of the Court, at least more nuanced.

Since *Perez v. United States*, 402 U.S. 146 (1971), our cases have mechanically recited that the Commerce Clause permits congressional regulation of three categories: (1) the channels of interstate commerce; (2) the instrumentalities of interstate commerce, and persons or things in interstate commerce; and (3) activities that "substantially affect" interstate commerce. The first two categories are self-evident, since they are the ingredients of interstate commerce itself. See *Gibbons v. Ogden*, 9 Wheat. 1, 189-190 (1824). The third category, however, is different in kind, and its recitation without explanation is misleading and incomplete.

It is *misleading* because, unlike the channels, instrumentalities, and agents of interstate commerce, activities that substantially affect interstate commerce are not themselves part of interstate commerce, and thus the power to regulate them cannot come from the Commerce Clause alone. Rather, as this Court has acknowledged since at least *United States v. Coombs*, 12 Pet. 72 (1838), Congress's regulatory authority over intrastate activities that are not themselves part of interstate commerce (including activities that have a substantial effect on interstate commerce) derives from the Necessary and Proper Clause. And the category of "activities that substantially affect interstate commerce," is *incomplete* because the authority to enact laws necessary and proper for the regulation of interstate commerce is not limited to laws governing intrastate activities that substantially affect interstate commerce. Where necessary to make a regulation of interstate commerce effective, Congress may regulate even those intrastate activities that do not themselves substantially affect interstate commerce.

II

Today's principal dissent objects that, by permitting Congress to regulate activities necessary to effective interstate regulation, the Court reduces *Lopez* and *Morrison* to little "more than a drafting guide." I think that criticism unjustified. Unlike the power to regulate activities that have a substantial effect on interstate commerce, the power to enact laws enabling effective regulation of interstate commerce can only be exercised in conjunction with congressional regulation of an interstate market, and it extends only to those measures necessary to make the interstate regulation effective. As *Lopez* itself states, and the Court affirms today, Congress may regulate noneconomic intrastate activities only where the failure to do so "could ... undercut" its regulation of interstate commerce. This is not a power that threatens to obliterate the line between "what is truly national and what is truly local."

Lopez and *Morrison* affirm that Congress may not regulate certain "purely local" activity within the States based solely on the attenuated effect that such activity may have in the interstate market. But those decisions do not declare noneconomic intrastate activities to be categorically beyond the reach of the Federal Government. Neither case involved the power of Congress to exert control over intrastate activities in connection with a more comprehensive scheme of regulation; *Lopez* expressly disclaimed that it was such a case, and *Morrison* did not even discuss the possibility that it was. (The Court of Appeals in *Morrison* made clear that it was not. To dismiss this distinction as "superficial and formalistic," is to misunderstand the nature of the Necessary and Proper Clause, which empowers Congress to enact laws in effectuation of its enumerated powers that are not within its authority to enact in isolation. See *McCulloch v. Maryland*, 4 Wheat. 316, 421-422 (1819).

And there are other restraints upon the Necessary and Proper Clause authority. As Chief Justice Marshall wrote in *McCulloch v. Maryland*, even when the end is constitutional and legitimate, the means must be "appropriate" and "plainly adapted" to that end. Moreover, they may not be otherwise "prohibited" and must be "consistent with the letter and spirit of the constitution." These phrases are not merely hortatory. For example, cases such as *Printz v. United States*, 521 U.S. 898 (1997), and *New York v. United States*, 505 U.S. 144 (1992), affirm that a law is not "'*proper* for carrying into Execution the Commerce Clause'" "[w]hen [it] violates [a constitutional] principle of state sovereignty."

III

The application of these principles to the case before us is straightforward. In the CSA, Congress has undertaken to extinguish the interstate market in Schedule I controlled substances, including marijuana. The Commerce Clause unquestionably permits this. The power to regulate interstate commerce "extends not only to those regulations which aid, foster and protect the commerce, but embraces those which prohibit it."

By this measure, I think the regulation must be sustained. Not only is it impossible to distinguish "controlled substances manufactured and distributed intrastate" from "controlled substances manufactured and distributed interstate," but it hardly makes sense to speak in such terms. Drugs like marijuana are fungible commodities. As the Court explains, marijuana that is grown at home and possessed for personal use is never more than an instant from the interstate market—and this is so whether or not the possession is for medicinal use or lawful use under the laws of a particular State. Congress need not accept on faith that state law will be effective in maintaining a strict division between a lawful market for "medical" marijuana and the more general marijuana market.

Finally, neither respondents nor the dissenters suggest any violation of state sovereignty of the sort that would render this regulation "inappropriate,"—except to argue that the CSA regulates an area typically left to state regulation. That is not enough to render federal regulation an inappropriate means. At bottom, respondents' state-sovereignty argument reduces to the contention that federal regulation of the activities permitted by California's Compassionate Use Act is not sufficiently necessary to be "necessary and proper" to Congress's regulation of the interstate market. For the reasons given above and in the Court's opinion, I cannot agree.

O'CONNOR, J., with whom THE CHIEF JUSTICE and Justice THOMAS join as to all but Part III, dissenting.

We enforce the "outer limits" of Congress' Commerce Clause authority not for their own sake, but to protect historic spheres of state sovereignty from excessive federal encroachment and thereby to maintain the distribution of power fundamental to our federalist system of government. One of federalism's chief virtues, of course, is that it promotes innovation by allowing for the possibility that "a single courageous State may, if its citizens choose, serve as a laboratory; and try novel social and economic experiments without risk to the rest of the country." *New State Ice Co. v. Liebmann*, 285 U.S. 262, 311 (1932) (Brandeis, J., dissenting).

This case exemplifies the role of States as laboratories. The States' core police powers have always included authority to define criminal law and to protect the health, safety, and welfare of their citizens. Exercising those powers, California (by ballot initiative and then by legislative codification) has come to its own conclusion about the difficult and sensitive question of whether marijuana should be available to relieve severe pain and suffering. Today the Court sanctions an application of the federal Controlled Substances Act that extinguishes that experiment, without any proof that the personal cultivation, possession, and use of marijuana for medicinal purposes, if economic activity in the first place, has a substantial effect on interstate commerce and is therefore an appropriate subject of federal regulation. In so doing, the Court announces a rule that gives Congress a perverse incentive to legislate broadly pursuant to the Commerce Clause—nestling questionable assertions of its authority into comprehensive regulatory schemes—rather than with precision.

I

In *Lopez*, … [o]ur decision about whether gun possession in school zones substantially affected interstate commerce turned on four considerations. First, we observed that our "substantial effects" cases generally have upheld federal regulation of economic activity that affected interstate commerce, but that § 922(q) was a criminal statute having "nothing to do with 'commerce' or any sort of economic enterprise." In this regard, we also noted that "[s]ection 922(q) is not an essential part of a larger regulation of economic activity, in which the regulatory scheme could be undercut unless the intrastate activity were regulated. It cannot, therefore, be sustained under our cases upholding regulations of activities that arise out of or are connected with a commercial transaction, which viewed in the aggregate, substantially affects interstate commerce." Second, we noted that the statute contained no express jurisdictional requirement establishing its connection to interstate commerce.

Third, we found telling the absence of legislative findings about the regulated conduct's impact on interstate commerce. We explained that while express legislative findings are neither required nor, when provided, dispositive, findings "enable us to evaluate the legislative judgment that the activity in question substantially affect[s] interstate commerce, even though no such substantial effect [is] visible to the naked eye." Finally, we rejected as too attenuated the Government's argument that firearm possession in school zones could result in violent crime which in turn could adversely affect the national economy. The Constitution, we said, does not tolerate reasoning that would "convert congressional authority under the Commerce Clause to a general police power of the sort retained by the States." Later in *Morrison*, we relied on the same four considerations to hold that § 40302 of the Violence Against Women Act of 1994 exceeded Congress' authority under the Commerce Clause.

In my view, the case before us is materially indistinguishable from *Lopez* and *Morrison* when the same considerations are taken into account.

III

We would do well to recall how James Madison, the father of the Constitution, described our system of joint sovereignty to the people of New York: "The powers delegated by the proposed Constitution to the federal government are few and defined. Those which are to remain in the State governments are numerous and indefinite .... The powers reserved to the several States will extend to all the objects which, in the ordinary course of affairs, concern the lives, liberties, and properties of the people, and the internal order, improvement, and prosperity of the State." The Federalist No. 45, pp. 292-293 (C. Rossiter ed.1961).

Relying on Congress' abstract assertions, the Court has endorsed making it a federal crime to grow small amounts of marijuana in one's own home for one's own medicinal use. This overreaching stifles an express choice by some States, concerned for the lives and liberties of their people, to regulate medical marijuana differently. If I were a California citizen, I would not have voted for the medical marijuana ballot initiative; if I were a California legislator I would not have supported the Compassionate Use Act. But whatever the wisdom of California's experiment with medical marijuana, the federalism principles that have driven our Commerce Clause cases require that room for experiment be protected in this case. For these reasons I dissent.

THOMAS, J., dissenting.

Respondents Diane Monson and Angel Raich use marijuana that has never been bought or sold, that has never crossed state lines, and that has had no demonstrable effect on the national market for marijuana. If Congress can regulate this under the Commerce Clause, then it can regulate virtually anything—and the Federal Government is no longer one of limited and enumerated powers.

I

Respondents' local cultivation and consumption of marijuana is not "Commerce ... among the several States." U.S. Const., Art. I, § 8, cl. 3. By holding that Congress may regulate activity that is neither interstate nor commerce under the Interstate Commerce Clause, the Court abandons any attempt to enforce the Constitution's limits on federal power. The majority supports this conclusion by invoking, without explanation, the Necessary and Proper Clause. Regulating respondents' conduct, however, is not "necessary and proper for carrying into Execution" Congress' restrictions on the interstate drug trade. Art. I, § 8, cl. 18. Thus, neither the Commerce

Clause nor the Necessary and Proper Clause grants Congress the power to regulate respondents' conduct.

II

A

The majority holds that Congress may regulate intrastate cultivation and possession of medical marijuana under the Commerce Clause, because such conduct arguably has a substantial effect on interstate commerce. The majority's decision is further proof that the "substantial effects" test is a "rootless and malleable standard" at odds with the constitutional design.

The majority's treatment of the substantial effects test is malleable, because the majority expands the relevant conduct. By defining the class at a high level of generality (as the intrastate manufacture and possession of marijuana), the majority overlooks that individuals authorized by state law to manufacture and possess medical marijuana exert no demonstrable effect on the interstate drug market. The majority ignores that whether a particular activity substantially affects interstate commerce—and thus comes within Congress' reach on the majority's approach—can turn on a number of objective factors, like state action or features of the regulated activity itself. For instance, here, if California and other States are effectively regulating medical marijuana users, then these users have little effect on the interstate drug trade.

The substantial effects test is easily manipulated for another reason. This Court has never held that Congress can regulate noneconomic activity that substantially affects interstate commerce. To evade even that modest restriction on federal power, the majority defines economic activity in the broadest possible terms as "'the production, distribution, and consumption of commodities.'" This carves out a vast swath of activities that are subject to federal regulation. If the majority is to be taken seriously, the Federal Government may now regulate quilting bees, clothes drives, and potluck suppers throughout the 50 States. This makes a mockery of Madison's assurance to the people of New York that the "powers delegated" to the Federal Government are "few and defined," while those of the States are "numerous and indefinite."

* * *

The majority prevents States like California from devising drug policies that they have concluded provide much-needed respite to the seriously ill. It does so without any serious inquiry into the necessity for federal regulation or the propriety of "displac[ing] state regulation in areas of traditional state concern." The majority's rush to embrace federal power "is especially unfortunate given the importance of showing respect for the sovereign States that comprise our Federal Union." Our federalist system, properly understood, allows California and a growing number of other States to decide for themselves how to safeguard the health and welfare of their citizens. I would affirm the judgment of the Court of Appeals.

NATIONAL FEDERATION OF INDEPENDENT BUSINESSES v. SEBELIUS
567 U.S. ___, 132 S. Ct. 2566 (2012)

ROBERTS., C.J.

Today we resolve constitutional challenges to two provisions of the Patient Protection and Affordable Care Act of 2010: the individual mandate, which requires individuals to purchase a health insurance policy providing a minimum level of coverage; and the Medicaid expansion, which gives funds to the States on the condition that they provide specified health care to all citizens whose income falls below a certain threshold. We do not consider whether the Act embodies sound policies. That judgment is entrusted to the Nation's elected leaders. We ask only whether Congress has the power under the Constitution to enact the challenged provisions.

In our federal system, the National Government possesses only limited powers; the States and the people retain the remainder. Nearly two centuries ago, Chief Justice Marshall observed that "the question respecting the extent of the powers actually granted" to the Federal Government "is perpetually arising, and will probably continue to arise, as long as our system shall exist." *McCulloch v. Maryland*, 4 Wheat. 316, 405 (1819). In this case we must again determine whether the Constitution grants Congress powers it now asserts, but which many States and individuals believe it does not possess. Resolving this controversy requires us to examine both the limits of the Government's power, and our own limited role in policing those boundaries.

The Federal Government "is acknowledged by all to be one of enumerated powers." That is, rather than granting general authority to perform all the conceivable functions of government, the Constitution lists, or enumerates, the Federal Government's powers. Congress may, for example, "coin Money," "establish Post Offices," and "raise and support Armies." Art. I, § 8, cls. 5, 7, 12. The enumeration of powers is also a limitation of powers, because "[t]he enumeration presupposes something not enumerated." *Gibbons v. Ogden*, 9 Wheat. 1, 195 (1824). The Constitution's express conferral of some powers makes clear that it does not grant others. And the Federal Government "can exercise only the powers granted to it."

Today, the restrictions on government power foremost in many Americans' minds are likely to be affirmative prohibitions, such as contained in the Bill of Rights. These affirmative prohibitions come into play, however, only where the Government possesses authority to act in the first place. If no enumerated power authorizes Congress to pass a certain law, that law may not be enacted, even if it would not violate any of the express prohibitions in the Bill of Rights or elsewhere in the Constitution.

Indeed, the Constitution did not initially include a Bill of Rights at least partly because the Framers felt the enumeration of powers sufficed to restrain the Government. As Alexander Hamilton put it, "the Constitution is itself, in every rational sense, and to every useful purpose, A BILL OF RIGHTS." The Federalist No. 84, p. 515 (C. Rossiter ed. 1961). And when the Bill of Rights was ratified, it made express what the enumeration of powers necessarily implied: "The powers not delegated to the United States by the Constitution ... are reserved to the States respectively, or to the people." U.S. Const., Amdt. 10. The Federal Government has expanded dramatically over the past two centuries, but it still must show that a constitutional grant of power authorizes each of its actions.

The same does not apply to the States, because the Constitution is not the source of their power. The Constitution may restrict state governments—as it does, for example, by forbidding them to deny any person the equal protection of the laws. But where such prohibitions do not apply, state governments do not need constitutional authorization to act. The States thus can and do perform many of the vital functions of modern government—punishing street crime, running public schools, and zoning property for development, to name but a few—even though the Constitution's text does not authorize any government to do so. Our cases refer to this general power of governing, possessed by the States but not by the Federal Government, as the "police power."

This case concerns two powers that the Constitution does grant the Federal Government, but which must be read carefully to avoid creating a general federal authority akin to the police power. The Constitution authorizes Congress to "regulate Commerce with foreign Nations, and among the several States, and with the Indian Tribes." Art. I, § 8, cl. 3. Our precedents read that to mean that Congress may regulate "the channels of interstate commerce," "persons or things in interstate commerce," and "those activities that substantially affect interstate commerce." The power over activities that substantially affect interstate commerce can be expansive. That power has been held to authorize federal regulation of such seemingly local matters as a farmer's decision to grow wheat for himself and his livestock, and a loan shark's extortionate collections from a neighborhood butcher shop.

Congress may also "lay and collect Taxes, Duties, Imposts and Excises, to pay the Debts and provide for the common Defence and general Welfare of the United States." U.S. Const., Art. I, § 8, cl. 1. Put simply, Congress may tax and spend. This grant gives the Federal Government considerable influence even in areas where it cannot directly regulate. The Federal Government may enact a tax on an activity that it cannot authorize, forbid, or otherwise control. And in exercising its spending power, Congress may offer funds to the States, and may condition those offers on compliance with specified conditions. These offers may well induce the States to adopt policies that the Federal Government itself could not impose.

The reach of the Federal Government's enumerated powers is broader still because the Constitution authorizes Congress to "make all Laws which shall be necessary and proper for carrying into Execution the foregoing Powers." Art. I, § 8, cl. 18. We have long read this provision to give Congress great latitude in exercising its powers: "Let the end be legitimate, let it be within the scope of the constitution, and all means which are appropriate, which are plainly adapted to that end, which are not prohibited, but consist with the letter and spirit of the constitution, are constitutional."

Our permissive reading of these powers is explained in part by a general reticence to invalidate the acts of the Nation's elected leaders. "Proper respect for a coordinate branch of the government" requires that we strike down an Act of Congress only if "the lack of constitutional authority to pass [the] act in question is clearly demonstrated." Members of this Court are vested with the authority to interpret the law; we possess neither the expertise nor the prerogative to make policy judgments. Those decisions are entrusted to our Nation's elected leaders, who can be thrown out of office if the people disagree with them. It is not our job to protect the people from the consequences of their political choices.

Our deference in matters of policy cannot, however, become abdication in matters of law. "The powers of the legislature are defined and limited; and that those limits may not be mistaken, or forgotten, the constitution is written." *Marbury v. Madison*, 1 Cranch 137, 176 (1803). And there can be no question that it is the responsibility of this Court to enforce the limits on federal power by striking down acts of Congress that transgress those limits.

The questions before us must be considered against the background of these basic principles.

I

In 2010, Congress enacted the Patient Protection and Affordable Care Act. The Act aims to increase the number of Americans covered by health insurance and decrease the cost of health care. The Act's 10 titles stretch over 900 pages and contain hundreds of provisions. This case concerns constitutional challenges to two key provisions, commonly referred to as the individual mandate and the Medicaid expansion.

The individual mandate requires most Americans to maintain "minimum essential" health insurance coverage. The mandate does not apply to some individuals, such as prisoners and undocumented aliens. Many individuals will receive the required coverage through their employer, or from a government program such as Medicaid or Medicare. But for individuals who are not exempt and do not receive health insurance through a third party, the means of satisfying the requirement is to purchase insurance from a private company.

Beginning in 2014, those who do not comply with the mandate must make a "[s]hared responsibility payment" to the Federal Government. That payment, which the Act describes as a "penalty," is calculated as a percentage of household income, subject to a floor based on a specified dollar amount and a ceiling based on the average annual premium the individual would have to pay for qualifying private health insurance. In 2016, for example, the penalty will be 2.5 percent of an individual's household income, but no less than $695 and no more than the average yearly premium for insurance that covers 60 percent of the cost of 10 specified services (*e.g.*, prescription drugs and hospitalization). The Act provides that the penalty will be paid to the Internal Revenue Service with an individual's taxes, and "shall be assessed and collected in the same manner" as tax penalties, such as the penalty for claiming too large an income tax refund.

On the day the President signed the Act into law, Florida and 12 other States filed a complaint in the Federal District Court for the Northern District of Florida. Those plaintiffs—who are both respondents and petitioners here, depending on the issue—were subsequently joined by 13 more States, several individuals, and the National Federation of Independent Business. The plaintiffs alleged, among other things, that the individual mandate provisions of the Act exceeded Congress's powers under Article I of the Constitution. The District Court agreed, holding that Congress lacked constitutional power to enact the individual mandate. The District Court determined that the individual mandate could not be severed from the remainder of the Act, and therefore struck down the Act in its entirety. The Court of Appeals for the Eleventh Circuit affirmed in part and reversed in part.

III

The Government advances two theories for the proposition that Congress had constitutional authority to enact the individual mandate.

First, the Government argues that Congress had the power to enact the mandate under the Commerce Clause. Under that theory, Congress may order individuals to buy health insurance because the failure to do so affects interstate commerce, and could undercut the Affordable Care Act's other reforms.

A

The Government's first argument is that the individual mandate is a valid exercise of Congress's power under the Commerce Clause and the Necessary and Proper Clause. According to the Government, the health care market is characterized by a significant cost-shifting problem. Everyone will eventually need health care at a time and to an extent they cannot predict, but if they do not have insurance, they often will not be able to pay for it. Because state and federal laws nonetheless require hospitals to provide a certain degree of care to individuals without regard to their ability to pay, hospitals end up receiving compensation for only a portion of the services they provide. To recoup the losses, hospitals pass on the cost to insurers through higher rates, and insurers, in turn, pass on the cost to policy holders in the form of higher premiums. Congress estimated that the cost of uncompensated care raises family health insurance premiums, on average, by over $1,000 per year.

In the Affordable Care Act, Congress addressed the problem of those who cannot obtain insurance coverage because of preexisting conditions or other health issues. It did so through the Act's "guaranteed-issue" and "community-rating" provisions. These provisions together prohibit insurance companies from denying coverage to those with such conditions or charging unhealthy individuals higher premiums than healthy individuals.

The guaranteed-issue and community-rating reforms do not, however, address the issue of healthy individuals who choose not to purchase insurance to cover potential health care needs. In fact, the reforms sharply exacerbate that problem, by providing an incentive for individuals to delay purchasing health insurance until they become sick, relying on the promise of guaranteed and affordable coverage. The reforms also threaten to impose massive new costs on insurers, who are required to accept unhealthy individuals but prohibited from charging them rates necessary to pay for their coverage. This will lead insurers to significantly increase premiums on everyone.

The individual mandate was Congress's solution to these problems. By requiring that individuals purchase health insurance, the mandate prevents cost-shifting by those who would otherwise go without it. In addition, the mandate forces into the insurance risk pool more healthy individuals, whose premiums on average will be higher than their health care expenses.

This allows insurers to subsidize the costs of covering the unhealthy individuals the reforms require them to accept. The Government claims that Congress has power under the Commerce and Necessary and Proper Clauses to enact this solution.

1

The Government contends that the individual mandate is within Congress's power because the failure to purchase insurance "has a substantial and deleterious effect on interstate commerce" by creating the cost-shifting problem. The path of our Commerce Clause decisions has not always run smooth, but it is now well established that Congress has broad authority under the Clause. We have recognized, for example, that "[t]he power of Congress over interstate commerce is not confined to the regulation of commerce among the states," but extends to activities that "have a substantial effect on interstate commerce." Congress's power, moreover, is not limited to regulation of an activity that by itself substantially affects interstate commerce, but also extends to activities that do so only when aggregated with similar activities of others.

Given its expansive scope, it is no surprise that Congress has employed the commerce power in a wide variety of ways to address the pressing needs of the time. But Congress has never attempted to rely on that power to compel individuals not engaged in commerce to purchase an unwanted product. Legislative novelty is not necessarily fatal; there is a first time for everything. But sometimes "the most telling indication of [a] severe constitutional problem ... is the lack of historical precedent" for Congress's action. At the very least, we should "pause to consider the implications of the Government's arguments" when confronted with such new conceptions of federal power.

The Constitution grants Congress the power to "*regulate* Commerce." Art. I, § 8, cl. 3 (emphasis added). The power to *regulate* commerce presupposes the existence of commercial activity to be regulated. If the power to "regulate" something included the power to create it, many of the provisions in the Constitution would be superfluous. For example, the Constitution gives Congress the power to "coin Money," in addition to the power to "regulate the Value thereof." *Id.*, cl. 5. And it gives Congress the power to "raise and support Armies" and to "provide and maintain a Navy," in addition to the power to "make Rules for the Government and Regulation of the land and naval Forces." *Id.*, cls. 12–14. If the power to regulate the armed forces or the value of money included the power to bring the subject of the regulation into existence, the specific grant of such powers would have been unnecessary. The language of the Constitution reflects the natural understanding that the power to regulate assumes there is already something to be regulated. See *Gibbons*, 9 Wheat., at 188

("[T]he enlightened patriots who framed our constitution, and the people who adopted it, must be understood to have employed words in their natural sense, and to have intended what they have said").

Our precedent also reflects this understanding. As expansive as our cases construing the scope of the commerce power have been, they all have one thing in common: They uniformly describe the power as reaching "activity." It is nearly impossible to avoid the word when quoting them.

The individual mandate, however, does not regulate existing commercial activity. It instead compels individuals to *become* active in commerce by purchasing a product, on the ground that their failure to do so affects interstate commerce. Construing the Commerce Clause to permit Congress to regulate individuals precisely *because* they are doing nothing would open a new and potentially vast domain to congressional authority. Every day individuals do not do an infinite number of things. In some cases they decide not to do something; in others they simply fail to do it. Allowing Congress to justify federal regulation by pointing to the effect of inaction on commerce would bring countless decisions an individual could *potentially* make within the scope of federal regulation, and—under the Government's theory—empower Congress to make those decisions for him.

Applying the Government's logic to the familiar case of *Wickard v. Filburn* shows how far that logic would carry us from the notion of a government of limited powers. In *Wickard*, the Court famously upheld a federal penalty imposed on a farmer for growing wheat for consumption on his own farm. That amount of wheat caused the farmer to exceed his quota under a program designed to support the price of wheat by limiting supply. The Court rejected the farmer's argument that growing wheat for home consumption was beyond the reach of the commerce power. It did so on the ground that the farmer's decision to grow wheat for his own use allowed him to avoid purchasing wheat in the market. That decision, when considered in the aggregate along with similar decisions of others, would have had a substantial effect on the interstate market for wheat.

Wickard has long been regarded as "perhaps the most far reaching example of Commerce Clause authority over intrastate activity," but the Government's theory in this case would go much further. Under *Wickard* it is within Congress's power to regulate the market for wheat by supporting its price. But price can be supported by increasing demand as well as by decreasing supply. The aggregated decisions of some consumers not to purchase wheat have a substantial effect on the price of wheat, just as decisions not to purchase health insurance have on the price of insurance. Congress can therefore command that those not buying wheat do so, just as it argues here that it may command that those not buying health insurance do so. The farmer in *Wickard* was at least actively engaged in the production of wheat, and the Government could regulate that activity because of its effect on commerce. The Government's theory here would effectively override that limitation, by establishing that individuals may be regulated under the Commerce Clause whenever enough of them are not doing something the Government would have them do.

Indeed, the Government's logic would justify a mandatory purchase to solve almost any problem. To consider a different example in the health care market, many Americans do not eat a balanced diet. That group makes up a larger percentage of the total population than those without health insurance. The failure of that group to have a healthy diet increases health care costs, to a greater extent than the failure of the uninsured to purchase insurance. Those increased costs are borne in part by other Americans who must pay more, just as the uninsured shift costs to the insured. Congress addressed the insurance problem by ordering everyone to buy insurance. Under the Government's theory, Congress could address the diet problem by ordering everyone to buy vegetables.

People, for reasons of their own, often fail to do things that would be good for them or good for society. Those failures—joined with the similar failures of others—can readily have a substantial effect on interstate commerce. Under the Government's logic, that authorizes Congress to use its commerce power to compel citizens to act as the Government would have them act.

That is not the country the Framers of our Constitution envisioned. James Madison explained that the Commerce Clause was "an addition which few oppose and from which no apprehensions are entertained." The Federalist No. 45, at 293. While Congress's authority under the Commerce Clause has of course expanded with the growth of the national economy, our cases have "always recognized that the power to regulate commerce, though broad indeed, has limits." The Government's theory would erode those limits, permitting Congress to reach beyond the natural extent of its authority, "everywhere extending the sphere of its activity and drawing all power into its impetuous vortex." The Federalist No. 48, at 309 (J. Madison). Congress already enjoys vast power to regulate much of what we do. Accepting the Government's theory would give Congress the same license to regulate what we do not do, fundamentally changing the relation between the citizen and the Federal Government.

To an economist, perhaps, there is no difference between activity and inactivity; both have measurable economic effects on commerce. But the distinction between doing something and doing nothing would not have been lost on the Framers, who were "practical statesmen," not metaphysical philosophers. As we have explained, "the framers of the Constitution were not mere visionaries, toying with speculations or theories, but practical men, dealing with the facts of political life as they understood them, putting into form the government they were creating, and prescribing in language clear and intelligible the powers that government was to take." The Framers gave Congress the power to *regulate* commerce, not to *compel* it, and for over 200 years both our decisions and Congress's actions have reflected this understanding. There is no reason to depart from that understanding now.

The Government sees things differently. It argues that because sickness and injury are unpredictable but unavoidable, "the uninsured as a class are active in the market for health care, which they regularly seek and obtain." The individual mandate "merely regulates how individuals finance and pay for that active participation—requiring that they do so through insurance, rather than through attempted self-insurance with the back-stop of shifting costs to others."

The Government repeats the phrase "active in the market for health care" throughout its brief, but that concept has no constitutional significance. An individual who bought a car two years ago and may buy another in the future is not "active in the car market" in any pertinent sense. The phrase "active in the market" cannot obscure the fact that most of those regulated by the individual mandate are not currently engaged in any commercial activity involving health care, and that fact is fatal to the Government's effort to "regulate the uninsured as a class." Our precedents recognize Congress's power to regulate "class [es] of *activities*," not classes of *individuals*, apart from any activity in which they are engaged.

The individual mandate's regulation of the uninsured as a class is, in fact, particularly divorced from any link to existing commercial activity. The mandate primarily affects healthy, often young adults who are less likely to need significant health care and have other priorities for spending their money. It is precisely because these individuals, as an actuarial class, incur relatively low health care costs that the mandate helps counter the effect of forcing insurance companies to cover others who impose greater costs than their premiums are allowed to reflect. If the individual mandate is targeted at a class, it is a class whose commercial inactivity rather than activity is its defining feature.

The Government, however, claims that this does not matter. The Government regards it as sufficient to trigger Congress's authority that almost all those who are uninsured will, at some unknown point in the future, engage in a health care transaction. Asserting that "[t]here is no temporal limitation in the Commerce Clause," the Government argues that because "[e]veryone subject to this regulation is in or will be in the health care market," they can be "regulated in advance." Tr. of Oral Arg. 109 (Mar. 27, 2012).

The proposition that Congress may dictate the conduct of an individual today because of prophesied future activity finds no support in our precedent. We have said that Congress can anticipate the *effects* on commerce of an economic activity. But we have never permitted Congress to anticipate that activity itself in order to regulate individuals not currently engaged in commerce. Each one of our cases … involved preexisting economic activity.

Everyone will likely participate in the markets for food, clothing, transportation, shelter, or energy; that does not authorize Congress to direct them to purchase particular products in those or other markets today. The Commerce Clause is not a general license to regulate an individual from cradle to grave, simply because he will predictably engage in particular transactions. Any police power to regulate individuals as such, as opposed to their activities, remains vested in the States.

The Government argues that the individual mandate can be sustained as a sort of exception to this rule, because health insurance is a unique product. According to the Government, upholding the individual mandate would not justify mandatory purchases of items such as cars or broccoli because, as the Government puts it, "[h]ealth insurance is not purchased for its own sake like a car or broccoli; it is a means of financing health-care consumption and covering universal risks." But cars and broccoli are no more purchased for their "own sake" than health insurance. They are purchased to cover the need for transportation and food.

The Government says that health insurance and health care financing are "inherently integrated." But that does not mean the compelled purchase of the first is properly regarded as a regulation of the second. No matter how "inherently integrated" health insurance and health care consumption may be, they are not the same thing: They involve different transactions, entered into at different times, with different providers. And for most of those targeted by the mandate, significant health care needs will be years, or even decades, away. The proximity and degree of connection between the mandate and the subsequent commercial activity is too lacking to justify an exception of the sort urged by the Government. The individual mandate forces individuals into commerce precisely because they elected to refrain from commercial activity. Such a law cannot be sustained under a clause authorizing Congress to "regulate Commerce."

2

The Government next contends that Congress has the power under the Necessary and Proper Clause to enact the individual mandate because the mandate is an "integral part of a comprehensive scheme of economic regulation"—the guaranteed-issue and community-rating insurance reforms. Brief for United States 24. Under this argument, it is not necessary to consider the effect that an individual's inactivity may have on interstate commerce; it is enough that Congress regulate commercial activity in a way that requires regulation of inactivity to be effective.

The power to "make all Laws which shall be necessary and proper for carrying into Execution" the powers enumerated in the Constitution, Art. I, § 8, cl. 18, vests Congress with authority to enact provisions "incidental to the [enumerated] power, and conducive to its beneficial exercise." Although the Clause gives Congress authority to "legislate on that vast mass of incidental powers which must be involved in the constitution," it does not license the exercise of any "great substantive and independent power[s]" beyond those specifically enumerated. Instead, the Clause is "'merely a declaration, for the removal of all uncertainty, that the means of carrying into execution those [powers] otherwise granted are included in the grant.'"

As our jurisprudence under the Necessary and Proper Clause has developed, we have been very deferential to Congress's determination that a regulation is "necessary." We have thus upheld laws that are "'convenient, or useful' or 'conducive' to the authority's 'beneficial exercise.'" But we have also carried out our responsibility to declare unconstitutional those laws that undermine the structure of government established by the Constitution. Such laws, which are not "consist[ent] with the letter and spirit of the constitution," are not "*proper* [means] for carrying into Execution" Congress's enumerated powers. Rather, they are, "in the words of The Federalist, 'merely acts of usurpation' which 'deserve to be treated as such.'" *Printz v. United States*, 521 U.S. 898, 924 (1997) (quoting The Federalist No. 33, at 204 (A. Hamilton)).

Applying these principles, the individual mandate cannot be sustained under the Necessary and Proper Clause as an essential component of the insurance reforms. Each of our prior cases upholding laws under that Clause involved exercises of authority derivative of, and in service to, a granted power. For example, we have upheld provisions permitting continued confinement of those *already in federal custody* when they could not be safely released; criminalizing bribes involving organizations *receiving federal funds*; and tolling state statutes of limitations while cases are *pending in federal court*. The individual mandate, by contrast, vests

Congress with the extraordinary ability to create the necessary predicate to the exercise of an enumerated power.

This is in no way an authority that is "narrow in scope," or "incidental" to the exercise of the commerce power. Rather, such a conception of the Necessary and Proper Clause would work a substantial expansion of federal authority. No longer would Congress be limited to regulating under the Commerce Clause those who by some preexisting activity bring themselves within the sphere of federal regulation. Instead, Congress could reach beyond the natural limit of its authority and draw within its regulatory scope those who otherwise would be outside of it. Even if the individual mandate is "necessary" to the Act's insurance reforms, such an expansion of federal power is not a "proper" means for making those reforms effective.

The Government relies primarily on our decision in *Gonzales v. Raich*. In *Raich*, we considered "comprehensive legislation to regulate the interstate market" in marijuana. Certain individuals sought an exemption from that regulation on the ground that they engaged in only intrastate possession and consumption. We denied any exemption, on the ground that marijuana is a fungible commodity, so that any marijuana could be readily diverted into the interstate market. Congress's attempt to regulate the interstate market for marijuana would therefore have been substantially undercut if it could not also regulate intrastate possession and consumption. Accordingly, we recognized that "Congress was acting well within its authority" under the Necessary and Proper Clause even though its "regulation ensnare[d] some purely intrastate activity." *Raich* thus did not involve the exercise of any "great substantive and independent power," *McCulloch*, of the sort at issue here. Instead, it concerned only the constitutionality of "individual *applications* of a concededly valid statutory scheme."

Just as the individual mandate cannot be sustained as a law regulating the substantial effects of the failure to purchase health insurance, neither can it be upheld as a "necessary and proper" component of the insurance reforms. The commerce power thus does not authorize the mandate.

WYOMING v. OKLAHOMA
502 U.S. 437 (1992)

WHITE, J., delivered the opinion of the Court.

[Although Wyoming is a major coal-producing State, the government of Wyoming does not itself does sell coal, and thus Wyoming is not directly participating in the market for coal. Wyoming law does, however, impose a severance tax on those who extract coal in Wyoming. From 1981 to 1986, four Oklahoma electric utilities purchased virtually 100% of their coal from Wyoming sources, and the Wyoming sellers consequently paid severance taxes on that coal to the State of Wyoming. The Oklahoma Legislature then passed an Act requiring coal-fired electric utilities in Oklahoma to burn a mixture containing at least 10% Oklahoma-mined coal, with the results that the Oklahoma-based utilities reduced their purchases of Wyoming coal in favor of Oklahoma coal and Wyoming's severance tax revenues declined. Wyoming brought an original action in the Supreme Court, alleging that the Oklahoma law violated dormant commerce principles. After deciding both that Wyoming had standing to bring the suit, and that the Supreme Court itself had original jurisdiction over the matter, the Court addressed the merits of the commerce claim.]

III

The Commerce Clause of the United States Constitution provides that "[t]he Congress shall have Power...[t]o regulate Commerce...among the several States...." It is long established that, while a literal reading evinces a grant of power to Congress, the Commerce Clause also directly limits the power of the States to discriminate against interstate commerce. "This 'negative' aspect of the Commerce Clause prohibits economic protectionism—that is, regulatory measures designed to benefit in-state economic interests by burdening out-of-state competitors." When a state statute clearly discriminates against interstate commerce, it will be struck down, unless the discrimination is demonstrably justified by a valid factor unrelated to economic protectionism. Indeed, when the state statute amounts to simple economic protectionism, a "virtually *per se* rule of invalidity" has applied.

The Special Master correctly found that the [Oklahoma] Act, on its face and in practical effect, discriminates against interstate commerce. [T]he Act expressly reserves a segment of the Oklahoma coal market for Oklahoma-mined coal, to the exclusion of coal mined in other States. Such a preference for coal from domestic sources cannot be characterized as anything other than protectionist and discriminatory, for the Act purports to exclude coal mined in other States based solely on its origin. The stipulated facts confirm that from 1981 to 1986 Wyoming provided virtually 100% of the coal purchased by Oklahoma utilities. In 1987 and 1988, following the effective date of the Act, the utilities purchased Oklahoma coal in amounts ranging from 3.4% to 7.4% of their annual needs, with a necessarily corresponding reduction in purchases of Wyoming coal.

Oklahoma attempts to discount this evidence by emphasizing that the Act sets aside only a "small portion" of the Oklahoma coal market, without placing an "overall burden" on out-of-state coal producers doing business in Oklahoma. The volume of commerce affected measures only the *extent* of the discrimination; it is of no relevance to the determination whether a State has discriminated against interstate commerce.

Because the Act discriminates both on its face and in practical effect, the burden falls on Oklahoma "'to justify it both in terms of the local benefits flowing from the statute and the unavailability of nondiscriminatory alternatives adequate to preserve the local interests at stake.'" "At a minimum such facial discrimination invokes the strictest scrutiny of any purported legitimate local purpose and of the absence of nondiscriminatory alternatives." Oklahoma has not met its burden in this respect. In this Court, Oklahoma argues quite briefly that the Act's discrimination against out-of-state coal is justified because sustaining the Oklahoma coal-mining industry lessens the State's reliance on a single source of coal delivered over a single rail line. This justification...is foreclosed by the Court's reasoning in [prior] cases that the State's brief ignores. We have often examined a "presumably legitimate goal," only to find that the State attempted to achieve it by "the illegitimate means of isolating the State from the national economy."

2. The Spending Power

Somewhat obliquely stated in the first clause of Article I, § 8, is a potentially important power that modern Congresses have come to rely upon in many circumstances in order to enact significant legislation. That power is the "spending power," which is essentially the power of Congress to devote federal money to a variety of programs and uses while simultaneously imposing on the recipients of those federal funds a range of conditions and requirements that accompany the funds. This power is sometimes referred to as a "contract" between a State receiving federal funds and the federal government (which is both disbursing those funds and imposing requirements on the States). The Supreme Court's defining case, at least until recently, on the scope of the Spending Power was *South Dakota v. Dole*, 483 U.S. 203 (1987), in which the Court upheld a federal program that required states receiving certain highway funds to raise their minimum drinking age to 21 or else lose a portion of those federal funds. The following case is a more recent and dramatic example of Congress linking substantial new conditions on States with massive amounts of federal funding, funding the States would have lost had they declined to embrace and implement the new program expansion Congress sought.

NATIONAL FEDERATION OF INDEPENDENT BUSINESSES v. SEBELIUS
567 U.S. ___ , 132 S. Ct. 2566 (2012)

Roberts, C.J.

The second provision of the Affordable Care Act directly challenged here is the Medicaid expansion. Enacted in 1965, Medicaid offers federal funding to States to assist pregnant women, children, needy families, the blind, the elderly, and the disabled in obtaining medical care. In order to receive that funding, States must comply with federal criteria governing matters such as who receives care and what services are provided at what cost. By 1982 every State had chosen to participate in Medicaid. Federal funds received through the Medicaid program have become a substantial part of state budgets, now constituting over 10 percent of most States' total revenue.

The Affordable Care Act expands the scope of the Medicaid program and increases the number of individuals the States must cover. For example, the Act requires state programs to provide Medicaid coverage to adults with incomes up to 133 percent of the federal poverty level, whereas many States now cover adults with children only if their income is considerably lower, and do not cover childless adults at all. The Act increases federal funding to cover the States' costs in expanding Medicaid coverage, although States will bear a portion of the costs on their own. If a State does not comply with the Act's new coverage requirements, it may lose not only the federal funding for those requirements, but all of its federal Medicaid funds.

Along with their challenge to the individual mandate, the state plaintiffs in the Eleventh Circuit argued that the Medicaid expansion exceeds Congress's constitutional powers. The Court of Appeals unanimously held that the Medicaid expansion is a valid exercise of Congress's power under the Spending Clause. And the court rejected the States' claim that the threatened loss of all federal Medicaid funding violates the Tenth Amendment by coercing them into complying with the Medicaid expansion.

IV

A

The States ... contend that the Medicaid expansion exceeds Congress's authority under the Spending Clause. They claim that Congress is coercing the States to adopt the changes it wants by threatening to withhold all of a State's Medicaid grants, unless the State accepts the new expanded funding and complies with the conditions that come with it. This, they argue, violates the basic principle that the

"Federal Government may not compel the States to enact or administer a federal regulatory program."

There is no doubt that the Act dramatically increases state obligations under Medicaid. The current Medicaid program requires States to cover only certain discrete categories of needy individuals—pregnant women, children, needy families, the blind, the elderly, and the disabled. There is no mandatory coverage for most childless adults, and the States typically do not offer any such coverage. The States also enjoy considerable flexibility with respect to the coverage levels for parents of needy families. On average States cover only those unemployed parents who make less than 37 percent of the federal poverty level, and only those employed parents who make less than 63 percent of the poverty line.

The Medicaid provisions of the Affordable Care Act, in contrast, require States to expand their Medicaid programs by 2014 to cover *all* individuals under the age of 65 with incomes below 133 percent of the federal poverty line. The Act also establishes a new "[e]ssential health benefits" package, which States must provide to all new Medicaid recipients—a level sufficient to satisfy a recipient's obligations under the individual mandate. The Affordable Care Act provides that the Federal Government will pay 100 percent of the costs of covering these newly eligible individuals through 2016. In the following years, the federal payment level gradually decreases, to a minimum of 90 percent. In light of the expansion in coverage mandated by the Act, the Federal Government estimates that its Medicaid spending will increase by approximately $100 billion per year, nearly 40 percent above current levels.

The Spending Clause grants Congress the power "to pay the Debts and provide for the ... general Welfare of the United States." U.S. Const., Art. I, § 8, cl. 1. We have long recognized that Congress may use this power to grant federal funds to the States, and may condition such a grant upon the States' "taking certain actions that Congress could not require them to take." Such measures "encourage a State to regulate in a particular way, [and] influenc[e] a State's policy choices." The conditions imposed by Congress ensure that the funds are used by the States to "provide for the ... general Welfare" in the manner Congress intended.

At the same time, our cases have recognized limits on Congress's power under the Spending Clause to secure state compliance with federal objectives. "We have repeatedly characterized ... Spending Clause legislation as 'much in the nature of a *contract*.'" The legitimacy of Congress's exercise of the spending power "thus rests on whether the State voluntarily and knowingly accepts the terms of the 'contract.'" Respecting this limitation is critical to ensuring that Spending Clause legislation does not undermine the status of the States as independent sovereigns in our federal system. That system "rests on what might at first seem a counter-intuitive insight, that 'freedom is enhanced by the creation of two governments, not one.'" For this reason, "the Constitution has never been understood to confer upon Congress the ability to require the States to govern according to Congress' instructions." Otherwise the two-government system established by the Framers would give way to a system that vests power in one central government, and individual liberty would suffer.

Permitting the Federal Government to force the States to implement a federal program would threaten the political accountability key to our federal system. "[W]here the Federal Government directs the States to regulate, it may be state officials who will bear the brunt of public disapproval, while the federal officials who devised the regulatory program may remain insulated from the electoral ramifications of their decision." Spending Clause programs do not pose this danger when a State has a legitimate choice whether to accept the federal conditions in exchange for federal funds. In such a situation, state officials can fairly be held politically accountable for choosing to accept or refuse the federal offer. But when the State has no choice, the Federal Government can achieve its objectives without accountability, just as in *New York* and *Printz*. Indeed, this danger is heightened when Congress acts under the Spending Clause, because Congress can use that power to implement federal policy it could not impose directly under its enumerated powers.

Congress may attach appropriate conditions to federal taxing and spending programs to preserve its control over the use of federal funds. In the typical case we look to the States to defend their prerogatives by adopting "the simple expedient of not yielding" to federal blandishments when they do not want to embrace the federal policies as their own. The States are separate and independent sovereigns. Sometimes they have to act like it.

The States, however, argue that the Medicaid expansion is far from the typical case. They object that Congress has "crossed the line distinguishing encouragement from coercion," *New York*, in the way it has structured the funding: Instead of simply refusing to grant the new funds to States that will not accept the new conditions, Congress has also threatened to withhold those States' existing Medicaid funds. The States claim that this threat serves no purpose other than to force unwilling States to sign up for the dramatic expansion in health care coverage effected by the Act.

Given the nature of the threat and the programs at issue here, we must agree. We have upheld Congress's authority to condition the receipt of funds on the States' complying with restrictions on the use of those funds, because that is the means by which Congress ensures that the funds are spent according to its view of the "general Welfare." Conditions that do not here govern the use of the funds, however, cannot be justified on that basis. When, for example, such conditions take the form of threats to terminate other significant independent grants, the conditions are properly viewed as a means of pressuring the States to accept policy changes.

In *South Dakota v. Dole*, we considered a challenge to a federal law that threatened to withhold five percent of a State's federal highway funds if the State did not raise its drinking age to 21. The Court found that the condition was "directly related to one of the main purposes for which highway funds are expended—safe interstate travel." At the same time, the condition was not a restriction on how the highway funds—set aside for specific highway improvement and maintenance efforts—were to be used.

We accordingly asked whether "the financial inducement offered by Congress" was "so coercive as to pass the point at which 'pressure turns into compulsion.'" By "financial inducement" the Court meant the threat of losing five percent of highway funds; no new money was offered to the States to raise their drinking ages. We found that the inducement was not impermissibly coercive, because Congress was offering only "relatively mild encouragement to the States." We observed that "all South Dakota would lose if she adheres to her chosen course as to a suitable minimum drinking age is 5%" of her highway funds. In fact, the federal funds at stake constituted less than half of one percent of South Dakota's budget at the time. In consequence, "we conclude[d] that [the] encouragement to state action [was] a valid use of the spending power." Whether to accept the drinking age change "remain[ed] the prerogative of the States not merely in theory but in fact."

In this case, the financial "inducement" Congress has chosen is much more than "relatively mild encouragement"—it is a gun to the head. Section 1396c of the Medicaid Act provides that if a State's Medicaid plan does not comply with the Act's requirements, the Secretary of Health and Human Services may declare that "further payments will not be made to the State." A State that opts out of the Affordable Care Act's expansion in health care coverage thus stands to lose not merely "a relatively small percentage" of its existing Medicaid funding, but *all* of it. Medicaid spending accounts for over 20 percent of the average State's total budget, with federal funds covering 50 to 83 percent of those costs. In addition, the States have developed intricate statutory and administrative regimes over the course of many decades to implement their objectives under existing Medicaid. It is easy to see how the *Dole* Court could conclude that the threatened loss of less than half of one percent of South Dakota's budget left that State with a "prerogative" to reject Congress's desired policy, "not merely in theory but in fact." The threatened loss of over 10 percent of a State's overall budget, in contrast, is economic dragooning that leaves the States with no real option but to acquiesce in the Medicaid expansion.

Here, the Government claims that the Medicaid expansion is properly viewed merely as a modification of the existing program because the States agreed that Congress could change the terms of Medicaid when they signed on in the first place. The Government observes that the Social Security Act, which includes the original Medicaid provisions, contains a clause expressly reserving "[t]he right to alter, amend, or repeal any provision" of that statute. So it does. But "if Congress intends to impose a condition on the grant of federal moneys, it must do so unambiguously." A State confronted with statutory language reserving the right to "alter" or "amend" the pertinent provisions of the Social Security Act might reasonably assume that Congress was entitled to make adjustments to the Medicaid program as it developed. Congress has in fact done so, sometimes conditioning only the new funding, other times both old and new.

The Medicaid expansion, however, accomplishes a shift in kind, not merely degree. The original program was designed to cover medical services for four particular categories of the needy: the disabled, the blind, the elderly, and needy families with dependent children. Previous amendments to Medicaid eligibility merely altered and expanded the boundaries of these categories. Under the Affordable Care Act, Medicaid is transformed into a program to meet the health care needs of the entire nonelderly population with income below 133 percent of the poverty level. It is no longer a program to care for the neediest among us, but rather an element of a comprehensive national plan to provide universal health insurance coverage.

As we have explained, "[t]hough Congress' power to legislate under the spending power is broad, it does not include surprising participating States with post-acceptance or 'retroactive' conditions." A State could hardly anticipate that Congress's reservation of the right to "alter" or "amend" the Medicaid program included the power to transform it so dramatically.

The Court in *Steward Machine* did not attempt to "fix the outermost line" where persuasion gives way to coercion. The Court found it "[e]nough for present purposes that wherever the line may be, this statute is within it." We have no need to fix a line either. It is enough for today that wherever that line may be, this statute is surely beyond it. Congress may not simply "conscript state [agencies] into the national bureaucratic army," and that is what it is attempting to do with the Medicaid expansion.

b. Fourteenth Amendment Enforcement Powers

Section 5 of the Fourteenth Amendment explicitly grants Congress the power to enforce the protections of Section 1 (privileges or immunities, due process and equal protection) by "appropriate legislation." The Supreme Court has wrestled at times with how expansive the Section 5 power is, and whether there are judicially definable limits. The following case illustrates the challenges and also represents the Court's current view of the scope of the Section 5 power.

CITY OF BOERNE v. FLORES
521 U.S. 507 (1997)

KENNEDY, J., delivered the opinion of the Court.

A decision by local zoning authorities to deny a church a building permit was challenged under the Religious Freedom Restoration Act of 1993 (RFRA or Act), 42 U.S.C. § 2000bb *et seq*. The case calls into question the authority of Congress to enact RFRA. We conclude the statute exceeds Congress' power.

I

Situated on a hill in the city of Boerne, Texas, some 28 miles northwest of San Antonio, is St. Peter Catholic Church. Built in 1923, the church's structure replicates the mission style of the region's earlier history. The church seats about 230 worshippers, a number too small for its growing parish. Some 40 to 60 parishioners cannot be accommodated at some Sunday masses. In order to meet the needs of the congregation the Archbishop of San Antonio gave permission to the parish to plan alterations to enlarge the building.

A few months later, the Boerne City Council passed an ordinance authorizing the city's Historic Landmark Commission to prepare a preservation plan with proposed historic landmarks and districts. Under the ordinance, the commission must preapprove construction affecting historic landmarks or buildings in a historic district.

Soon afterwards, the Archbishop applied for a building permit so construction to enlarge the church could proceed. City authorities, relying on the ordinance and the designation of a historic district (which, they argued, included the church), denied the application. The Archbishop brought this suit challenging the permit denial. The complaint contained various claims, but to this point the litigation has centered on RFRA and the question of its constitutionality. The Archbishop relied upon RFRA as one basis for relief from the refusal to issue the permit. The District Court concluded that by enacting RFRA Congress exceeded the scope of its enforcement power under § 5 of the Fourteenth Amendment. The court certified its order for interlocutory appeal and the Fifth Circuit reversed, finding RFRA to be constitutional. We granted certiorari, and now reverse.

II

Congress enacted RFRA in direct response to the Court's decision in *Employment Div., Dept. of Human Resources of Oregon v. Smith*, 494 U.S. 872 (1990). There we considered a Free Exercise Clause claim brought by members of the Native American Church who were denied unemployment benefits when they lost their jobs because they had used peyote. Their practice was to ingest peyote for sacramental purposes, and they challenged an Oregon statute of general applicability which made use of the drug criminal. In evaluating the claim, we declined to apply the balancing test set forth in *Sherbert v. Verner*, 374 U.S. 398 (1963), under which we would have asked whether Oregon's prohibition substantially burdened a religious practice and, if it did, whether the burden was justified by a compelling government interest. We stated:

> "[G]overnment's ability to enforce generally applicable prohibitions of socially harmful conduct ... cannot depend on measuring the effects of a governmental action on a religious objector's spiritual development. To make an individual's obligation to obey such a law contingent upon the law's coincidence with his religious beliefs, except where the State's interest is 'compelling' ... contradicts both constitutional tradition and common sense."

The application of the *Sherbert* test, the *Smith* decision explained, would have produced an anomaly in the law, a constitutional right to ignore neutral laws of general applicability.

Four Members of the Court disagreed. They argued the law placed a substantial burden on the Native American Church members so that it could be upheld only if the law served a compelling state interest and was narrowly tailored to achieve that end. Justice O'CONNOR concluded Oregon had satisfied the test, while Justice Blackmun, joined by Justice Brennan and Justice Marshall, could see no compelling interest justifying the law's application to the members.

These points of constitutional interpretation were debated by Members of Congress in hearings and floor debates. Many criticized the Court's reasoning, and this disagreement resulted in the passage of RFRA. Congress announced:

> "(1) [T]he framers of the Constitution, recognizing free exercise of religion as an unalienable right, secured its protection in the First Amendment to the Constitution;
>
> "(2) laws 'neutral' toward religion may burden religious exercise as surely as laws intended to interfere with religious exercise;
>
> "(3) governments should not substantially burden religious exercise without compelling justification;

"(4) in *Employment Division v. Smith*, 494 U.S. 872 (1990), the Supreme Court virtually eliminated the requirement that the government justify burdens on religious exercise imposed by laws neutral toward religion; and

"(5) the compelling interest test as set forth in prior Federal court rulings is a workable test for striking sensible balances between religious liberty and competing prior governmental interests."

The Act's stated purposes are:

"(1) to restore the compelling interest test as set forth in *Sherbert v. Verner*, 374 U.S. 398 (1963) and *Wisconsin v. Yoder*, 406 U.S. 205 (1972) and to guarantee its application in all cases where free exercise of religion is substantially burdened; and

"(2) to provide a claim or defense to persons whose religious exercise is substantially burdened by government."

RFRA prohibits "[g]overnment" from "substantially burden[ing]" a person's exercise of religion even if the burden results from a rule of general applicability unless the government can demonstrate the burden "(1) is in furtherance of a compelling governmental interest; and (2) is the least restrictive means of furthering that compelling governmental interest." The Act's mandate applies to any "branch, department, agency, instrumentality, and official (or other person acting under color of law) of the United States," as well as to any "State, or ... subdivision of a State." The Act's universal coverage is confirmed [by the fact that] RFRA "applies to all Federal and State law, and the implementation of that law, whether statutory or otherwise, and whether adopted before or after [RFRA's enactment]." In accordance with RFRA's usage of the term, we shall use "state law" to include local and municipal ordinances.

III

A

Under our Constitution, the Federal Government is one of enumerated powers. *M'Culloch v. Maryland*, 4 Wheat. 316, 405 (1819); see also The Federalist No. 45, p. 292 (C. Rossiter ed. 1961) (J. Madison). The judicial authority to determine the constitutionality of laws, in cases and controversies, is based on the premise that the "powers of the legislature are defined and limited; and that those limits may not be mistaken, or forgotten, the constitution is written." *Marbury v. Madison*, 1 Cranch 137, 176 (1803).

Congress relied on its Fourteenth Amendment enforcement power in enacting the most far-reaching and substantial of RFRA's provisions, those which impose its requirements on the States. The Fourteenth Amendment provides, in relevant part:

"Section 1.... No State shall make or enforce any law which shall abridge the privileges or immunities of citizens of the United States; nor shall any State deprive any person of life, liberty, or property, without due process of law, nor deny to any person within its jurisdiction the equal protection of the laws.

"Section 5. The Congress shall have power to enforce, by appropriate legislation, the provisions of this article."

The parties disagree over whether RFRA is a proper exercise of Congress' § 5 power "to enforce" by "appropriate legislation" the constitutional guarantee that no State shall deprive any person of "life, liberty, or property, without due process of law" nor deny any person "equal protection of the laws."

In defense of the Act, respondent the Archbishop contends, with support from the United States, that RFRA is permissible enforcement legislation. Congress, it is said, is only protecting by legislation one of the liberties guaranteed by the Fourteenth Amendment's Due Process Clause, the free exercise of religion, beyond what is necessary under *Smith*. It is said the congressional decision to dispense with proof of deliberate or overt discrimination and instead concentrate on a law's effects accords with the settled understanding that § 5 includes the power to enact legislation designed to prevent, as well as remedy, constitutional violations. It is further contended that Congress' § 5 power is not limited to remedial or preventive legislation.

All must acknowledge that § 5 is "a positive grant of legislative power" to Congress, *Katzenbach v. Morgan*, 384 U.S. 641, 651 (1966). Legislation which deters or remedies constitutional violations can fall within the sweep of Congress' enforcement power even if in the process it prohibits conduct which is not itself unconstitutional and intrudes into "legislative spheres of autonomy previously reserved to the States."

It is also true, however, that "[a]s broad as the congressional enforcement power is, it is not unlimited." In assessing the breadth of § 5 's enforcement power, we begin with its text. Congress has been given the power "to enforce" the "provisions of this article." We agree with respondent, of course, that Congress can enact legislation under § 5 enforcing the constitutional right to the free exercise of religion. The "provisions of this article," to which § 5 refers, include the Due Process Clause of the Fourteenth Amendment. Congress' power to enforce the Free Exercise Clause follows from our holding in *Cantwell v. Connecticut*, 310 U.S. 296, 303 (1940), that the "fundamental concept of liberty embodied in [the Fourteenth Amendment's Due Process Clause] embraces the liberties guaranteed by the First Amendment."

Congress' power under § 5, however, extends only to "enforc[ing]" the provisions of the Fourteenth Amendment. The Court has described this power as "remedial." The design of the Amendment and the text of § 5 are inconsistent with the suggestion that Congress has the power to decree the substance of the Fourteenth Amendment's restrictions on the States. Legislation which alters the meaning of the Free Exercise Clause cannot be said to be enforcing the Clause. Congress does not enforce a constitutional right by changing what the right is. It has been given the power "to enforce," not the power to determine what constitutes a constitutional violation. Were it not so, what Congress would be enforcing would no longer be, in any meaningful sense, the "provisions of [the Fourteenth Amendment]."

While the line between measures that remedy or prevent unconstitutional actions and measures that make a substantive change in the governing law is not easy to discern, and Congress must have wide latitude in determining where it lies, the distinction exists and must be observed. There must be a congruence and proportionality between the injury to be prevented or remedied and the means adopted to that end. Lacking such a connection, legislation may become substantive in operation and effect. History and our case law support drawing the distinction, one apparent from the text of the Amendment.

B

Respondent contends that RFRA is a proper exercise of Congress' remedial or preventive power. The Act, it is said, is a reasonable means of protecting the free exercise of religion as defined by *Smith*. It prevents and remedies laws which are enacted with the unconstitutional object of targeting religious beliefs and practices. To avoid the difficulty of proving such violations, it is said, Congress can simply invalidate any law which imposes a substantial burden on a religious practice unless it is justified by a compelling interest and is the least restrictive means of accomplishing that interest. If Congress can prohibit laws with discriminatory effects in order to prevent racial discrimination in violation of the Equal Protection Clause, then it can do the same, respondent argues, to promote religious liberty.

While preventive rules are sometimes appropriate remedial measures, there must be a congruence between the means used and the ends to be achieved. The appropriateness of remedial measures must be considered in light of the evil presented. Strong measures appropriate to address one harm may be an unwarranted response to another, lesser one.

A comparison between RFRA and the Voting Rights Act is instructive. In contrast to the record which confronted Congress and the Judiciary in the voting rights cases, RFRA's legislative record lacks examples of modern instances of generally applicable laws passed because of religious bigotry. The history of persecution in this country detailed in the hearings mentions no episodes occurring in the past 40 years. This lack of support in the legislative record, however, is not RFRA's most serious shortcoming. Judicial deference, in most cases, is based not on the state of the legislative record Congress compiles but "on due regard for the decision of the body constitutionally appointed to decide." As a general matter, it is for Congress to determine the method by which it will reach a decision.

Regardless of the state of the legislative record, RFRA cannot be considered remedial, preventive legislation, if those terms are to have any meaning. RFRA is so out of proportion to a supposed remedial or preventive object that it cannot be understood as responsive to, or designed to prevent, unconstitutional behavior. It appears, instead, to attempt a substantive change in constitutional protections. Preventive measures prohibiting certain types of laws may be appropriate when there is reason to believe that many of the laws affected by the congressional enactment have a significant likelihood of being unconstitutional. Remedial legislation under § 5 "should be adapted to the mischief and wrong which the [Fourteenth] [A]mendment was intended to provide against."

RFRA is not so confined. Sweeping coverage ensures its intrusion at every level of government, displacing laws and prohibiting official actions of almost every description and regardless of subject matter. RFRA's restrictions apply to every agency and official of the Federal, State, and local Governments. RFRA applies to all federal and state law, statutory or otherwise, whether adopted before or after its enactment. RFRA has no termination date or termination mechanism. Any law is subject to challenge at any time by any individual who alleges a substantial burden on his or her free exercise of religion.

The reach and scope of RFRA distinguish it from other measures passed under Congress' enforcement power, even in the area of voting rights. In *South Carolina v. Katzenbach*, the challenged provisions were confined to those regions of the country where voting discrimination had been most flagrant, and affected a discrete class of state laws, *i.e.*, state voting laws. Furthermore, to ensure that the reach of the Voting Rights Act was limited to those cases in which constitutional violations were most likely (in order to reduce the possibility of overbreadth), the coverage under the Act would terminate "at the behest of States and political subdivisions in which the danger of substantial voting discrimination has not materialized during the preceding five years. The provisions restricting and banning literacy tests, upheld in *Katzenbach v. Morgan*, 384 U.S. 641 (1966), and *Oregon v. Mitchell*, *supra*, attacked a particular type of voting qualification, one with a long history as a "notorious means to deny and abridge voting rights on racial grounds." In *City of Rome*, *supra*, the Court rejected a challenge to the constitutionality of a Voting Rights Act provision which required certain jurisdictions to submit changes in electoral practices to the Department of Justice for preimplementation review. The requirement was placed only on jurisdictions with a history of intentional racial discrimination in voting. Like the provisions at issue in *South Carolina v. Katzenbach*, this provision permitted a covered jurisdiction to avoid preclearance requirements under certain conditions and, moreover, lapsed in seven years. This is not to say, of course, that § 5 legislation requires termination dates, geographic restrictions, or egregious predicates. Where, however, a congressional enactment pervasively prohibits constitutional state action in an effort to remedy or to prevent unconstitutional state action, limitations of this kind tend to ensure Congress' means are proportionate to ends legitimate under § 5.

The stringent test RFRA demands of state laws reflects a lack of proportionality or congruence between the means adopted and the legitimate end to be achieved. If an objector can show a substantial burden on his free exercise, the State must demonstrate a compelling governmental interest and show that the law is the least restrictive means of furthering its interest. Claims that a law substantially burdens someone's exercise of religion will often be difficult to contest. Requiring a State to demonstrate a compelling interest and show that it has adopted the least restrictive means of achieving that interest is the most demanding test known to constitutional law. If "'compelling interest' really means what it says ..., many laws will not meet the test.... [The test] would open the prospect of constitutionally required religious exemptions from civic obligations of almost every conceivable kind." Laws valid under *Smith* would fall under RFRA without regard to whether they had the object of stifling or punishing free exercise. Even assuming RFRA would be interpreted in effect to mandate some lesser test, say, one equivalent to intermediate scrutiny, the statute nevertheless would require searching judicial scrutiny of state law with the attendant likelihood of invalidation. This is a considerable congressional intrusion into the States' traditional prerogatives and general authority to regulate for the health and welfare of their citizens.

The substantial costs RFRA exacts, both in practical terms of imposing a heavy litigation burden on the States and in terms of curtailing their traditional general regulatory power, far exceed any pattern or practice of unconstitutional conduct under the Free Exercise Clause as interpreted in *Smith*. Simply put, RFRA is not designed to identify and counteract state laws likely to be unconstitutional because of their treatment of religion. In most cases, the state laws to which RFRA applies are not ones which will have been motivated by religious bigotry.

When Congress acts within its sphere of power and responsibilities, it has not just the right but the duty to make its own informed judgment on the meaning and force of the Constitution. This has been clear from the early days of the Republic. In 1789, when a Member of the House of Representatives objected to a debate on the constitutionality of legislation based on the theory that "it would be officious" to consider the constitutionality of a measure that did not affect the House, James Madison explained that "it is incontrovertibly of as much importance to this branch of the Government as to any other, that the constitution should be preserved entire. It is our duty." 1 Annals of Congress 500 (1789). Were it otherwise, we would not afford Congress the presumption of validity its enactments now enjoy.

Our national experience teaches that the Constitution is preserved best when each part of the Government respects both the Constitution and the proper actions and determinations of the other branches. When the Court has interpreted the Constitution, it has acted within the province of the Judicial Branch, which embraces the duty to say what the law is. When the political branches of the Government act against the background of a judicial interpretation of the Constitution already issued, it must be understood that in later cases and controversies the Court will treat its precedents with the respect due them under settled principles, including *stare decisis*, and contrary expectations must be disappointed. RFRA was designed to control cases and controversies, such as the one before us; but as the provisions of the federal statute here invoked are beyond congressional authority, it is this Court's precedent, not RFRA, which must control.

* * *

It is for Congress in the first instance to "determin[e] whether and what legislation is needed to secure the guarantees of the Fourteenth Amendment," and its conclusions are entitled to much deference. Congress' discretion is not unlimited, however, and the courts retain the power, as they have since *Marbury v. Madison*, to determine if Congress has exceeded its authority under the Constitution. Broad as the power of Congress is under the Enforcement Clause of the Fourteenth Amendment, RFRA contradicts vital principles necessary to maintain separation of powers and the federal balance. The judgment of the Court of Appeals sustaining the Act's constitutionality is reversed.

2. Exclusive State Powers

a. Organization of State Government – See Chapter XIV.

Nothing in the federal Constitution or Supreme Court decisions purports to limit or direct the organization of state governments, other than the Article IV promise that the United States shall guarantee to every state in the union a "Republican Form" of government, a provision addressed below and which the Supreme Court has left entirely to the Congress and the President to enforce, if it is to be enforced at all. Also, the Supreme Court has declined to require that state governments follow federal separation of powers principles. Thus, as explored more fully in Chapter XIV, the States may choose, for example, a unicameral rather than bicameral legislature (Nebraska), give their Governors a variety of powers, including some the President of the United States is not permitted, (such as a line item veto), and generally may structure their state court systems as they wish, including the use of elections to select judges. Thus, the organization of state government and the powers accorded the various branches and officials of state government, are a subject about which the federal Constitution has virtually nothing to say and plays essentially no role.

b. Traditional Police Powers

The States, unlike the federal government, are the repository of traditional police powers, understood as a general authority for enacting any and all laws relating to the public health, safety, welfare, and morals. Thus, with the States, the constitutional question generally is not whether they have the authority to pass a particular law but, rather, whether there is any constitutional prohibition on the passing of such a law. This is the opposite of the presumption that applies to Congress, which must point to some enumerated power in the federal Constitution giving Congress the authority to affirmatively legislate on a particular matter.

The result is that the vast majority of criminal law, domestic relations law, tort law, property law, contract law, commercial law, and a host of other traditional areas of the law are dominated by state rather than federal law. Expansion of the understanding of Congress's commerce power has resulted in some regulation by the federal government in areas once exclusively the provinces of the States, but even where that is true (*e.g.*, in the criminal law), the bulk of all criminal law in this country is state law and the vast majority of criminal prosecutions remain state prosecutions.

3. Overlapping and Shared Powers

a. Individual Liberties

With respect to individual liberties, the federal and state constitutions have considerable overlap, though students should not forget that state constitutional liberties predated the federal Constitution's Bill of Rights and the Fourteenth Amendment. Indeed, several revolutionary era state constitutions served as models for the Bill of Rights which James Madison introduced in the first session of Congress.

Not infrequently, state supreme courts have declared that state provisions which are identical or directly analogous to federal provisions are to be interpreted as the Supreme Court of the United States interprets the federal provision (*e.g.*, defining what is an "unreasonable search or seizure under the Fourth Amendment). But in other instances, the States have adopted their own interpretations of such identical or similar provisions. Moreover, there are many state provisions that simply do not have a federal counterpart.

Another important factor in this regard is the federal "incorporation" doctrine which relies on the Due Process Clause of the Fourteenth Amendment and its prohibition on State conduct violative of that provision to "incorporate" against the States most of the individual liberties protected by the federal Bill of Rights. Long ago, the Supreme Court held that the Bill of Rights by its terms only restricts the federal government. *Barron v. Mayor and City Council of Baltimore*, 32 U.S. 243 (1833). But following the Civil War, Reconstruction, and the adoption of the Fourteenth Amendment, the argument was made that "due process of law" necessarily should include the protections of the Bill of Rights, for example liberties such as freedom of speech and religion, the right to bear arms, freedom from unreasonable searches and seizures, the privilege against self-incrimination, the right to counsel and to a jury trial in criminal cases, and freedom from cruel and unusual punishment. Over the course of time, the Supreme Court has held that virtually all of the Bill of Rights protections apply to the States, with the exception of the right to indictment by a grand jury for felonies and the right to a jury trial in civil cases.

Two aspects of the incorporation doctrine are important for purposes of studying state constitutional law. First, if a Bill of Rights protection is incorporated against the States and thus part of the requirement of "due process of law," federal preemption means that the States cannot give such liberties *less* protection than the federal provision requires. Second, the States do have choices, however, in interpreting their own constitutional provisions that may be analogous or identical to federal provisions and certainly can choose to provide *more* protection of such liberties under their own constitutions than the federal provision requires. A recent example of this would be a North Carolina Supreme Court's decision holding that even if the Second Amendment right to keep and bear arms does not apply to the States, the North Carolina Constitution's counterpart provision provides significant protection of this right to North Carolina citizens. *See* Chapter XII.D. Another example is the response of some state supreme courts to a recent Takings Clause decision of the Supreme Court of the United States. *See* Chapter VIII.B.

Another possibility, and one that is not uncommon, is that state supreme courts declare that provisions in their own constitutions will be interpreted to have the same meaning as the Supreme Court of the United States gives to the identical or similar federal provisions. This, of course, results in symmetry in state and federal constitutional law and permits state courts to rely on the decisions of the Supreme Court, both of which may be attractive to state courts. Symmetry may be extremely helpful, for example, in providing law enforcement officials with one clear set of rules to follow, rather than two different sets of rules, one federal and one state. Also, because the Supreme Court decides so many Fourth Amendment cases, for example, there is a wealth of precedent on which to draw in deciding such questions, something that frequently is not the case with respect to decisions interpreting state constitutional provisions in a single state. Of course, there is an argument that too much deference by state courts to the Supreme Court of the United States' decisions abdicates the state courts' duty and responsibility to interpret state constitutions independently of their federal counterpart. *See*, *e.g.*, Stephen R. McAllister, Comment, *Interpreting the State Constitution: A Survey and Assessment of Current Methodology*, 35 Kan. L. Rev. 593 (1987).

b. Criminal Law

The States need no justification for enacting criminal laws other than that such laws serve the general health, welfare, safety and morals of their citizens. Indeed, enacting and enforcing the criminal laws is a core aspect of the States' traditional police powers. The federal government, in contrast, is not given any general power to enact criminal laws. Instead, it must point to powers in Article I, § 8 or elsewhere, that justify the creation of federal crimes, or that in combination with the Necessary and Proper Clause will support such enactments. Perhaps the most frequently invoked federal power to justify the enactment of criminal laws is the power of Congress to regulate commerce "among the Several states." Expansive federal use of this power has caused some controversy and resulted in some important Supreme Court decisions in recent years. An important example follows.

UNITED STATES v. LOPEZ
514 U.S. 549 (1995)

REHNQUIST, C.J., delivered the opinion of the Court.

In the Gun-Free School Zones Act of 1990, Congress made it a federal offense "for any individual knowingly to possess a firearm at a place that the individual knows, or has reasonable cause to believe, is a school zone." The Act neither regulates a commercial activity nor contains a requirement that the possession be connected in any way to interstate commerce. We hold that the Act exceeds the authority of Congress "[t]o regulate Commerce ... among the several States...."

On March 10, 1992, respondent, who was then a 12th-grade student, arrived at Edison High School in San Antonio, Texas, carrying a concealed .38-caliber handgun and five bullets. Acting upon an anonymous tip, school authorities confronted respondent, who admitted that he was carrying the weapon. He was arrested and charged under Texas law with firearm possession on school premises. The next day, the state charges were dismissed after federal agents charged respondent by complaint with violating the Gun-Free School Zones Act of 1990.

A federal grand jury indicted respondent on one count of knowing possession of a firearm at a school zone, in violation of § 922(q). Respondent moved to dismiss his federal indictment on the ground that § 922(q) "is unconstitutional as it is beyond the power of Congress to legislate control over our public schools." The District Court denied the motion, concluding that § 922(q) "is a constitutional exercise of Congress' well-defined power to regulate activities in and affecting commerce, and the 'business' of elementary, middle and high schools...affects interstate commerce." The District Court found [Lopez] guilty of violating § 922(q), and sentenced him to six months' imprisonment and two years' supervised release. The Court of Appeals...reversed respondent's conviction... [holding that the statute] is invalid as beyond the power of Congress under the Commerce Clause."

We start with first principles. The Constitution creates a Federal Government of enumerated powers. As James Madison wrote: "The powers delegated by the proposed Constitution to the federal government are few and defined. Those which are to remain in the State governments are numerous and indefinite." The Federalist No. 45, pp. 292-293 (C. Rossiter ed. 1961). This constitutionally mandated division of authority "was adopted by the Framers to ensure protection of our fundamental liberties." The commerce power "is the power to regulate; that is, to prescribe the rule by which commerce is to be governed. This power, like all others vested in congress, is complete in itself, may be exercised to its utmost extent, and acknowledges no limitations, other than are prescribed in the constitution." The *Gibbons* Court, however, acknowledged that limitations on the commerce power are inherent in the very language of the Commerce Clause.

[E]ven [the Court's] modern-era precedents which have expanded congressional power under the Commerce Clause confirm that this power is subject to outer limits. [W]e have identified three broad categories of activity that Congress may regulate under its commerce power. First,

Congress may regulate the use of the channels of interstate commerce. Second, Congress is empowered to regulate and protect the instrumentalities of interstate commerce, or persons or things in interstate commerce, even though the threat may come only from intrastate activities. Finally, Congress' commerce authority includes the power to regulate those activities having a substantial relation to interstate commerce, *i.e.*, those activities that substantially affect interstate commerce.

We now turn to consider the power of Congress, in the light of this framework, to enact § 922(q). The first two categories of authority may be quickly disposed of: § 922(q) is not a regulation of the use of the channels of interstate commerce, nor is it an attempt to prohibit the interstate transportation of a commodity through the channels of commerce; nor can § 922(q) be justified as a regulation by which Congress has sought to protect an instrumentality of interstate commerce or a thing in interstate commerce. Thus, if § 922(q) is to be sustained, it must be under the third category as a regulation of an activity that substantially affects interstate commerce.

[First,] Section 922(q) is a criminal statute that by its terms has nothing to do with "commerce" or any sort of economic enterprise, however broadly one might define those terms.[2] Section 922(q) is not an essential part of a larger regulation of economic activity, in which the regulatory scheme could be undercut unless the intrastate activity were regulated. It cannot, therefore, be sustained under our cases upholding regulations of activities that arise out of or are connected with a commercial transaction, which viewed in the aggregate, substantially affects interstate commerce.

Second, § 922(q) contains no jurisdictional element which would ensure, through case-by-case inquiry, that the firearm possession in question affects interstate commerce.

[Third,] [a]lthough as part of our independent evaluation of constitutionality under the Commerce Clause we of course consider legislative findings, and indeed even congressional committee findings, regarding effect on interstate commerce, the Government concedes that "[n]either the statute nor its legislative history contain[s] express congressional findings regarding the effects upon interstate commerce of gun possession in a school zone." We agree with the Government that Congress normally is not required to make formal findings as to the

---

[2] [3] Under our federal system, the "'States possess primary authority for defining and enforcing the criminal law.'" The Government acknowledges that § 922(q) "displace[s] state policy choices in…that its prohibitions apply even in States that have chosen not to outlaw the conduct in question."

substantial burdens that an activity has on interstate commerce. But to the extent that congressional findings would enable us to evaluate the legislative judgment that the activity in question substantially affected interstate commerce, even though no such substantial effect was visible to the naked eye, they are lacking here.

The Government's essential contention, *in fine*, is that we may determine here that § 922(q) is valid because possession of a firearm in a local school zone does indeed substantially affect interstate commerce. The Government argues that possession of a firearm in a school zone may result in violent crime and that violent crime can be expected to affect the functioning of the national economy in two ways. First, the costs of violent crime are substantial, and, through the mechanism of insurance, those costs are spread throughout the population. Second, violent crime reduces the willingness of individuals to travel to areas within the country that are perceived to be unsafe. The Government also argues that the presence of guns in schools poses a substantial threat to the educational process by threatening the learning environment. A handicapped educational process, in turn, will result in a less productive citizenry. That, in turn, would have an adverse effect on the Nation's economic well-being.

We pause to consider the implications of the Government's arguments. The Government admits, under its "costs of crime" reasoning, that Congress could regulate not only all violent crime, but all activities that might lead to violent crime, regardless of how tenuously they relate to interstate commerce. Similarly, under the Government's "national productivity" reasoning, Congress could regulate any activity that it found was related to the economic productivity of individual citizens: family law (including marriage, divorce, and child custody), for example. Under the theories that the Government presents…it is difficult to perceive any limitation on federal power, even in areas such as criminal law enforcement or education where States historically have been sovereign. Thus, if we were to accept the Government's arguments, we are hard pressed to posit any activity by an individual that Congress is without power to regulate.

Although Justice BREYER argues that acceptance of the Government's rationales would not authorize a general federal police power, he is unable to identify any activity that the States may regulate but Congress may not. Justice BREYER posits that there might be some limitations on Congress' commerce power, such as family law or certain aspects of education. These suggested limitations, when viewed in light of the dissent's expansive analysis, are devoid of substance.

For instance, if Congress can, pursuant to its Commerce Clause power, regulate activities that adversely affect the learning environment, then, *a fortiori*, it also can regulate the educational process directly. Congress could determine that a school's curriculum has a "significant" effect on the extent of classroom learning. As a result, Congress could mandate a federal curriculum for local elementary and secondary schools because what is taught in local schools has a significant "effect on classroom learning," and that, in turn, has a substantial effect on interstate commerce.

Admittedly, a determination whether an intrastate activity is commercial or noncommercial may in some cases result in legal uncertainty. But…so long as [Congress's] powers are interpreted as having judicially enforceable outer limits,…legislation under the Commerce Clause always will engender "legal uncertainty."

These are not precise formulations, and in the nature of things they cannot be. But we think they point the way to a correct decision of this case. The possession of a gun in a local school zone is in no sense an economic activity that might, through repetition elsewhere, substantially affect any sort of interstate commerce. Respondent was a local student at a local school; there is no indication that he had recently moved in interstate commerce, and there is no requirement that his possession of the firearm have any concrete tie to interstate commerce.

To uphold the Government's contentions here, we would have to pile inference upon inference in a manner that would bid fair to convert congressional authority under the Commerce Clause to a general police power of the sort retained by the States. Admittedly, some of our prior cases have taken long steps down that road, giving great deference to congressional action. The broad language in these opinions has suggested the possibility of additional expansion, but we decline here to proceed any further. To do so would require us to conclude that the Constitution's enumeration of powers does not presuppose something not enumerated, and that there never will be a distinction between what is truly national and what is truly local. This we are unwilling to do.

c. Interstate Compacts – Article I, § 10, cl. 3

An interesting example of overlapping federal and state powers is found in Article I, § 10, cl. 3, which declares that "No State shall, without the Consent of Congress…enter into any Agreement or Compact with another State…." States, of course, do enter into agreements with each other, and sometimes such agreements are essential, for example in resolving a boundary dispute, or allocating water rights in interstate rivers. That said, Congress must give its blessing to such agreements and thus has some leverage to influence the nature and substance of such agreements. Disputes under such compacts sometimes are resolved in original jurisdiction proceedings in the U.S. Supreme Court. *See, e.g., Kansas v. Nebraska and Colorado*, 574 U.S. ___, 135 S.Ct. 1042 (2015) (resolving disputed issues between states under the Republican River Compact).

B. LIMITATIONS ON FEDERAL POWER

1. The Anti-Commandeering Principle

PRINTZ v. UNITED STATES
521 U.S. 898 (1997)

SCALIA, J., delivered the opinion of the Court.

The question presented in these cases is whether certain interim provisions of the Brady Handgun Violence Prevention Act, commanding state and local law enforcement officers to conduct background checks on prospective handgun purchasers and to perform certain related tasks, violate the Constitution.

I

The Gun Control Act of 1968 (GCA), establishes a detailed federal scheme governing the distribution of firearms. It prohibits firearms dealers from transferring handguns to any person under 21, not resident in the dealer's State, or prohibited by state or local law from purchasing or possessing firearms. It also forbids possession of a firearm by, and transfer of a firearm to, convicted felons, fugitives from justice, unlawful users of controlled substances, persons adjudicated as mentally defective or committed to mental institutions, aliens unlawfully present in the United States, persons dishonorably discharged from the Armed Forces, persons who have renounced their citizenship, and persons who have been subjected to certain restraining orders or been convicted of a misdemeanor offense involving domestic violence.

In 1993, Congress amended the GCA by enacting the Brady Act. The Act requires the Attorney General to establish a national instant background-check system by November 30, 1998, and immediately puts in place certain interim provisions until that system becomes operative. Under the interim provisions, a firearms dealer who proposes to transfer a handgun must first: (1) receive from the transferee a statement (the Brady Form), containing the name, address, and date of birth of the proposed transferee along with a sworn statement that the transferee is not among any of the classes of prohibited purchasers; (2) verify the identity of the transferee by examining an identification document; and (3) provide the "chief law enforcement officer" (CLEO) of the transferee's residence with notice of the contents (and a copy) of the Brady Form. With some exceptions, the dealer must then wait five business days before consummating the sale, unless the CLEO earlier notifies the dealer that he has no reason to believe the transfer would be illegal.

The Brady Act creates two significant alternatives to the foregoing scheme. A dealer may sell a handgun immediately if the purchaser possesses a state handgun permit issued after a background check, or if state law provides for an instant background check. In States that have not rendered one of these alternatives applicable to all gun purchasers, CLEOs are required to perform certain duties. When a CLEO receives the required notice of a proposed transfer from the firearms dealer, the CLEO must "make a reasonable effort to ascertain within 5 business days whether receipt or possession would be in violation of the law, including research in whatever State and local recordkeeping systems are available and in a national system designated by the Attorney General." The Act does not require the CLEO to take any particular action if he determines that a pending transaction would be unlawful; he may notify the firearms dealer to that effect, but is not required to do so. If, however, the CLEO notifies a gun dealer that a prospective purchaser is ineligible to receive a handgun, he must, upon request, provide the would-be purchaser with a written statement of the reasons for that determination. Moreover, if the CLEO does not discover any basis for objecting to the sale, he must destroy any records in his possession relating to the transfer, including his copy of the Brady Form. Under a separate provision of the GCA, any person who "knowingly violates [the section of the GCA amended by the Brady Act] shall be fined under this title, imprisoned for not more than 1 year, or both."

Petitioners Jay Printz and Richard Mack, the CLEOs for Ravalli County, Montana, and Graham County, Arizona, respectively, filed separate actions challenging the constitutionality of the Brady Act's interim provisions. In each case, the District Court held that the provision requiring CLEOs to perform background checks was unconstitutional, but concluded that that provision was severable from the remainder of the Act, effectively leaving a voluntary background-check system in place. A divided panel of the Court of Appeals for the Ninth Circuit reversed, finding none of the Brady Act's interim provisions to be unconstitutional.

II

From the description set forth above, it is apparent that the Brady Act purports to direct state law enforcement officers to participate, albeit only temporarily, in the administration of a federally enacted regulatory scheme. Petitioners here object to being pressed into federal service, and contend that congressional action compelling state officers to execute federal laws is unconstitutional. Because there is no constitutional text speaking to this precise question, the answer to the CLEOs' challenge must be sought in historical understanding and practice, in the structure of the Constitution, and in the jurisprudence of this Court. We treat those three sources, in that order, in this and the next two sections of this opinion.

The Government observes that statutes enacted by the first Congresses required state courts to record applications for citizenship, to transmit abstracts of citizenship applications and other naturalization records to the Secretary of State, and to register aliens seeking naturalization and issue certificates of registry. Other statutes of that era apparently or at least arguably required state courts to perform functions...such as resolving controversies between a captain and the crew of his ship concerning the seaworthiness of the vessel, hearing the claims of slave owners who had apprehended fugitive slaves and issuing certificates authorizing the slave's forced removal to the State from which he had fled, taking proof of the claims of Canadian refugees who had assisted the United States during the Revolutionary War, and ordering the deportation of alien enemies in times of war.

These early laws establish, at most, that the Constitution was originally understood to permit imposition of an obligation on state *judges* to enforce federal prescriptions, insofar as those prescriptions related to matters appropriate for the judicial power. That assumption was perhaps implicit in one of the provisions of the Constitution, and was explicit in another. In accord with the so-called Madisonian Compromise, Article III, § 1, established only a Supreme Court, and made the creation of lower federal courts optional with the Congress-even though it was obvious that the Supreme Court alone could not hear all federal cases throughout the United States. And the Supremacy Clause, Art. VI, cl. 2, announced that "the Laws of the United States ... shall be the supreme Law of the Land; and the Judges in every State shall be bound thereby." It is understandable why courts should have been viewed distinctively in this regard; unlike legislatures and executives, they applied the law of other sovereigns all the time. The principle underlying so-called "transitory" causes of action was that laws which operated elsewhere created obligations in justice that courts of the forum State would enforce. The Constitution itself, in the Full Faith and Credit Clause, Art. IV, § 1, generally required such enforcement with respect to obligations arising in other States.

For these reasons, we do not think the early statutes imposing obligations on state courts imply a power of Congress to impress the state executive into its service. Indeed, it can be argued that the numerousness of these statutes, contrasted with the utter lack of statutes imposing obligations on the States' executive (notwithstanding the attractiveness of that course to Congress), suggests an assumed *absence* of such power.

III

A

It is incontestable that the Constitution established a system of "dual sovereignty." *Gregory v. Ashcroft*, 501 U.S. 452, 457 (1991). Although the States surrendered many of their powers to the new Federal Government, they retained "a residuary and inviolable sovereignty," The Federalist No. 39, at 245 (J. Madison). This is reflected throughout the Constitution's text, including (to mention only a few examples) the prohibition on any involuntary reduction or combination of a State's territory, Art. IV, § 3; the Judicial Power Clause, Art. III, § 2, and the Privileges and Immunities Clause, Art. IV, § 2, which speak of the "Citizens" of the States; the amendment provision, Article V, which requires the votes of three-fourths of the States to amend the Constitution; and the Guarantee Clause, Art. IV, § 4, which "presupposes the continued existence of the states and ... those means and instrumentalities which are the creation of their sovereign and reserved rights." Residual state sovereignty was also implicit, of course, in the Constitution's conferral upon Congress of not all governmental powers, but only discrete, enumerated ones, Art. I, § 8, which implication was rendered express by the Tenth Amendment's assertion that "[t]he powers not delegated to the United States by the Constitution, nor prohibited by it to the States, are reserved to the States respectively, or to the people."

This separation of the two spheres is one of the Constitution's structural protections of liberty. The power of the Federal Government would be augmented immeasurably if it were able to impress into its service—and at no cost to itself—the police officers of the 50 States.

B

The dissent perceives a simple answer in that portion of Article VI which requires that "all executive and judicial Officers, both of the United States and of the several States, shall be bound by Oath or Affirmation, to support this Constitution," arguing that by virtue of the Supremacy Clause this makes "not only the Constitution, but every law enacted by Congress as well," binding on state officers, including laws requiring state-officer enforcement. The Supremacy Clause, however, makes "Law of the Land" only "Laws of the United States which shall be made in Pursuance [of the Constitution]," Art. VI, cl. 2, so the Supremacy Clause merely brings us back to the question discussed earlier, whether laws conscripting state officers violate state sovereignty and are thus not in accord with the Constitution.

IV

Finally, and most conclusively in the present litigation, we turn to the prior jurisprudence of this Court. When we were at last confronted squarely with a federal statute that unambiguously required the States to enact or administer a federal regulatory program, our decision should have come as no surprise. At issue in *New York v. United States*, 505 U.S. 144 (1992), were the so-called "take title" provisions of the Low-Level Radioactive Waste Policy Amendments Act of 1985, which required States either to enact legislation providing for the disposal of radioactive waste generated within their borders, or to take title to, and possession of, the waste-effectively requiring the States either to legislate pursuant to Congress's directions, or to implement an administrative solution. We concluded that Congress could constitutionally require the States to do neither. "The Federal Government," we held, "may not compel the States to enact or administer a federal regulatory program."

The Government contends that *New York* is distinguishable on the following ground: Unlike the "take title" provisions invalidated there, the background-check provision of the Brady Act does not require state legislative or executive officials to make policy, but instead issues a final directive to state CLEOs. The Government purports to find support for its proffered distinction of *New York* in our decisions in *Testa v. Katt*, 330 U.S. 386 (1947), and *FERC v. Mississippi*, 456 U.S. 742 (1982). We find neither case relevant. *Testa* stands for the proposition that state courts cannot refuse to apply federal law—a conclusion mandated by the terms of the Supremacy Clause ("the Judges in every State shall be bound [by federal law]"). As we have suggested earlier, that says nothing about whether state executive officers must administer federal law. As for *FERC*, it stated (as we have described earlier) that "this Court never has sanctioned explicitly a federal command to the States to promulgate and enforce laws and regulations," and upheld the statutory provisions at issue precisely because they did *not* commandeer state government, but merely imposed preconditions to continued state regulation of an otherwise pre-empted field....

The dissent makes no attempt to defend the Government's basis for distinguishing *New York*, but instead advances what seems to us an even more implausible theory. The Brady Act, the dissent asserts, is different from the "take title" provisions invalidated in *New York* because the former is addressed to individuals—namely, CLEOs—while the latter were directed to the State itself. That is certainly a difference, but it cannot be a constitutionally significant one. While the Brady Act is directed to "individuals," it is directed to them in their official capacities as state officers; it controls their actions, not as private citizens, but as the agents of the State. To say that the Federal Government cannot control the State, but can control all of its officers, is to say nothing of significance. By resorting to this, the dissent not so much distinguishes *New York* as disembowels it.

Summarizing anti-commandeering principles

We held in *New York* that Congress cannot compel the States to enact or enforce a federal regulatory program. Today we hold that Congress cannot circumvent that prohibition by conscripting the State's officers directly. The Federal Government may neither issue directives requiring the States to address particular problems, nor command the States' officers, or those of their political subdivisions, to administer or enforce a federal regulatory program. It matters not whether policymaking is involved, and no case-by-case weighing of the burdens or benefits is necessary; such commands are fundamentally incompatible with our constitutional system of dual sovereignty.

2. Immunity from Suits under Federal Law

The Eleventh Amendment provides that "[t]he Judicial power of the United States shall not be construed to extend to any suit in law or equity, commenced or prosecuted against one of the United States by Citizens of another State, or by Citizens or Subjects of any Foreign State." Although there is general agreement that this amendment was a reaction to the Supreme Court's decision in *Chisholm v. Georgia*, 2 U.S. 419 (1793), permitting a suit by a citizen of South Carolina to proceed in federal court over Georgia's objections, there is much disagreement about the scope of the constitutional immunity the Eleventh Amendment recognizes.

Importantly, the Supreme Court long ago decided that the immunity is not limited to the diversity jurisdiction-depriving literal terms of the amendment, and instead protects the States more broadly. *Hans v. Louisiana*, 134 U.S. 1 (1890) (holding that the immunity also bars a citizen of a State from suing her own state, even though the literal text does not bar such a suit). Further, the Court in recent years has held that the immunity is from suit under federal law, no matter where the suit is brought, so even a suit in the State's own courts is barred. *Alden v. Maine*, 527 U.S. 706 (1999). This area of the law has been actively litigated the past fifteen years, and many of the cases have produced 5-4 decisions by the Supreme Court. The case below is offered simply to illustrate the questions raised and the nature of the constitutional immunity that the Supreme Court recognizes. Extensive treatment of the States' constitutional immunity must be left to other courses.

ALDEN v. MAINE
527 U.S. 706 (1999)

KENNEDY, J., delivered the opinion of the Court.

In 1992, petitioners, a group of probation officers, filed suit against their employer, the State of Maine, in the United States District Court for the District of Maine. The officers alleged the State had violated the overtime provisions of the Fair Labor Standards Act of 1938 (FLSA), 29 U. S. C. § 201 *et seq.*, and sought compensation and liquidated damages. While the suit was pending, this Court decided *Seminole Tribe of Fla.* v. *Florida*, 517 U. S. 44 (1996), which made it clear that Congress lacks power under Article I to abrogate the States' sovereign immunity from suits commenced or prosecuted in the federal courts. Upon consideration of *Seminole Tribe*, the District Court dismissed petitioners' action, and the Court of Appeals affirmed. Petitioners then filed the same action in state court. The state trial court dismissed the suit on the basis of sovereign immunity, and the Maine Supreme Judicial Court affirmed.

We hold that the powers delegated to Congress under Article I of the United States Constitution do not include the power to subject nonconsenting States to private suits for damages in state courts. We decide as well that the State of Maine has not consented to suits for overtime pay and liquidated damages under the FLSA. On these premises we affirm the judgment sustaining dismissal of the suit.

I

The Eleventh Amendment makes explicit reference to the States' immunity from suits "commenced or prosecuted against one of the United States by Citizens of another State, or by Citizens or Subjects of any Foreign State." U. S. Const., Amdt. 11. We have, as a result, sometimes referred to the States' immunity from suit as "Eleventh Amendment immunity." The phrase is convenient shorthand but something of a misnomer, for the sovereign immunity of the States neither derives from, nor is limited by, the terms of the Eleventh Amendment. Rather, as the Constitution's structure, its history, and the authoritative interpretations by this Court make clear, the States' immunity from suit is a fundamental aspect of the sovereignty which the States enjoyed before the ratification of the Constitution, and which they retain today (either literally or by virtue of their admission into the Union upon an equal footing with the other States) except as altered by the plan of the Convention or certain constitutional Amendments.

A

Although the Constitution establishes a National Government with broad, often plenary authority over matters within its recognized competence, the founding document "specifically recognizes the States as sovereign entities." *Seminole Tribe of Fla.* v. *Florida, supra*, at 71, n. 15; accord, *Blatchford* v. *Native Village of Noatak*, 501 U. S. 775, 779 (1991) ("[T]he States entered the federal system with their sovereignty intact"). Various textual provisions of the Constitution assume the States' continued existence and active participation in the fundamental processes of governance. The limited and enumerated powers granted to the

Legislative, Executive, and Judicial Branches of the National Government, moreover, underscore the vital role reserved to the States by the constitutional design, see, *e.g.*, Art. I, § 8; Art. II, §§ 2-3; Art. III, § 2. Any doubt regarding the constitutional role of the States as sovereign entities is removed by the Tenth Amendment, which, like the other provisions of the Bill of Rights, was enacted to allay lingering concerns about the extent of the national power. The Amendment confirms the promise implicit in the original document: "The powers not delegated to the United States by the Constitution, nor prohibited by it to the States, are reserved to the States respectively, or to the people." U. S. Const., Amdt. 10.

The federal system established by our Constitution preserves the sovereign status of the States in two ways. First, it reserves to them a substantial portion of the Nation's primary sovereignty, together with the dignity and essential attributes inhering in that status. The States "form distinct and independent portions of the supremacy, no more subject, within their respective spheres, to the general authority than the general authority is subject to them, within its own sphere." The Federalist No. 39, p. 245 (C. Rossiter ed. 1961) (J. Madison).

Second, even as to matters within the competence of the National Government, the constitutional design secures the founding generation's rejection of "the concept of a central government that would act upon and through the States" in favor of "a system in which the State and Federal Governments would exercise concurrent authority over the people who were, in Hamilton's words, 'the only proper objects of government.'" In this the Founders achieved a deliberate departure from the Articles of Confederation: Experience under the Articles had "exploded on all hands" the "practicality of making laws, with coercive sanctions, for the States as political bodies." 2 Records of the Federal Convention of 1787, p. 9 (M. Farrand ed. 1911) (J. Madison); accord, The Federalist No. 20, at 138 (J. Madison and A. Hamilton); James Iredell: Some Objections to the Constitution Answered, reprinted in 3 Annals of America 249 (1976).

The States thus retain "a residuary and inviolable sovereignty." The Federalist No. 39, at 245. They are not relegated to the role of mere provinces or political corporations, but retain the dignity, though not the full authority, of sovereignty.

C

The Court has been consistent in interpreting the adoption of the Eleventh Amendment as conclusive evidence "that the decision in *Chisholm* was contrary to the well-understood meaning of the Constitution," *Seminole Tribe*, 517 U. S., at 69, and that the views expressed by Hamilton, Madison, and Marshall during the ratification debates, and by Justice Iredell in his dissenting opinion in *Chisholm*, reflect the original understanding of the Constitution. In accordance with this understanding, we have recognized a "presumption that no anomalous and unheard-of proceedings or suits were intended to be raised up by the Constitution—anomalous and unheard of when the constitution was adopted." As a consequence, we have looked to "history and experience, and the established order of things," rather than "[a]dhering to the mere letter" of the Eleventh Amendment, in determining the scope of the States' constitutional immunity from suit.

Following this approach, the Court has upheld States' assertions of sovereign immunity in various contexts falling outside the literal text of the Eleventh Amendment. In *Hans*, the Court held that sovereign immunity barred a citizen from suing his own State under the federal-question head of jurisdiction. The Court was unmoved by the petitioner's argument that the Eleventh Amendment, by its terms, applied only to suits brought by citizens of other States: Later decisions rejected similar requests to conform the principle of sovereign immunity to the strict language of the Eleventh Amendment in holding that nonconsenting States are immune from suits brought by federal corporations, *Smith* v. *Reeves*, 178 U. S. 436 (1900), foreign nations, *Principality of Monaco, supra*, or Indian tribes, *Blatchford* v. *Native Village of Noatak*, 501 U. S. 775 (1991), and in concluding that sovereign immunity is a defense to suits in admiralty, though the text of the Eleventh Amendment addresses only suits "in law or equity," *Ex parte New York*, 256 U. S. 490 (1921).

These holdings reflect a settled doctrinal understanding, consistent with the views of the leading advocates of the Constitution's ratification, that sovereign immunity derives not from the Eleventh Amendment but from the structure of the original Constitution itself. See, *e.g.*, *Idaho* v. *Coeur d'Alene Tribe of Idaho*, 521 U. S. 261, 267-268 (1997) (acknowledging "the broader concept of immunity, implicit in the Constitution, which we have regarded the Eleventh Amendment as evidencing and exemplifying"); The Eleventh Amendment confirmed, rather than established, sovereign immunity as a constitutional principle; it follows that the scope of the States' immunity from suit is demarcated not by the text of the Amendment alone but by fundamental postulates implicit in the constitutional design.

II

In this case we must determine whether Congress has the power, under Article I, to subject nonconsenting States to private suits in their own courts. As the foregoing discussion makes clear, the fact that the Eleventh Amendment by its terms limits only "[t]he Judicial power of the United States" does not resolve the question. To rest on the words of the Amendment alone would be to engage in the type of ahistorical literalism we have rejected in interpreting the scope of the States' sovereign immunity since the discredited decision in *Chisholm*.

While the constitutional principle of sovereign immunity does pose a bar to federal jurisdiction over suits against nonconsenting States, this is not the only structural basis of sovereign immunity implicit in the constitutional design. Rather, "[t]here is also the postulate that States of the Union, still possessing attributes of sovereignty, shall be immune from suits, without their consent, save where there has been 'a surrender of this immunity in the plan of the convention.'" This separate and distinct structural principle is not directly related to the scope of the judicial power established by Article III, but inheres in the system of federalism established by the Constitution. In exercising its Article I powers Congress may subject the States to private suits in their own courts only if there is "compelling evidence" that the States were required to surrender this power to Congress pursuant to the constitutional design.

In light of history, practice, precedent, and the structure of the Constitution, we hold that the States retain immunity from private suit in their own courts, an immunity beyond the congressional power to abrogate by Article I legislation.

III

The constitutional privilege of a State to assert its sovereign immunity in its own courts does not confer upon the State a concomitant right to disregard the Constitution or valid federal law. The States and their officers are bound by obligations imposed by the Constitution and by federal statutes that comport with the constitutional design. We are unwilling to assume the States will refuse to honor the Constitution or obey the binding laws of the United States. The good faith of the States thus provides an important assurance that "[t]his Constitution, and the Laws of the United States which shall be made in Pursuance thereof ... shall be the supreme Law of the Land." U. S. Const., Art. VI.

Sovereign immunity, moreover, does not bar all judicial review of state compliance with the Constitution and valid federal law. Rather, certain limits are implicit in the constitutional principle of state sovereign immunity.

The first of these limits is that sovereign immunity bars suits only in the absence of consent. Many States, on their own initiative, have enacted statutes consenting to a wide variety of suits. The rigors of sovereign immunity are thus "mitigated by a sense of justice which has continually expanded by consent the suability of the sovereign." Nor, subject to constitutional limitations, does the Federal Government lack the authority or means to seek the States' voluntary consent to private suits. Cf. *South Dakota* v. *Dole*, 483 U. S. 203 (1987).

The States have consented, moreover, to some suits pursuant to the plan of the Convention or to subsequent constitutional Amendments. In ratifying the Constitution, the States consented to suits brought by other States or by the Federal Government. A suit which is commenced and prosecuted against a State in the name of the United States by those who are entrusted with the constitutional duty to "take Care that the Laws be faithfully executed," U. S. Const., Art. II, § 3, differs in kind from the suit of an individual: While the Constitution contemplates suits among the members of the federal system as an alternative to extralegal measures, the fear of private suits against nonconsenting States was the central reason given by the Founders who chose to preserve the States' sovereign immunity. Suits brought by the United States itself require the exercise of political responsibility for each suit prosecuted against a State, a control which is absent from a broad delegation to private persons to sue nonconsenting States.

We have held also that in adopting the Fourteenth Amendment, the people required the States to surrender a portion of the sovereignty that had been preserved to them by the original Constitution, so that Congress may authorize private suits against nonconsenting States pursuant to its § 5 enforcement power. *Fitzpatrick* v. *Bitzer*, 427 U. S. 445 (1976). By imposing explicit limits on the powers of the States and granting Congress the power to enforce them, the Amendment "fundamentally altered the balance of state and federal power struck by the Constitution." When Congress enacts appropriate legislation to enforce this Amendment, see *City of Boerne* v. *Flores*, 521 U. S. 507 (1997), federal interests are paramount, and Congress may assert an authority over the States which would be otherwise unauthorized by the Constitution.

The second important limit to the principle of sovereign immunity is that it bars suits against States but not lesser entities. The immunity does not extend to suits prosecuted against a municipal corporation or other governmental entity which is not an arm of the State. See, *e. g.*, *Lincoln County* v. *Luning*, 133 U. S. 529 (1890). Nor does sovereign immunity bar all suits against state officers. Some suits against state officers are barred by the rule that sovereign immunity is not limited to suits which name the State as a party if the suits are, in fact, against the State. The rule, however, does not bar certain actions against state officers for injunctive or declaratory relief. Compare *Ex parte Young*, 209 U. S. 123 (1908), and *Edelman* v. *Jordan*, 415 U. S. 651 (1974). Even a suit for money damages may be prosecuted against a state officer in his individual capacity for unconstitutional or wrongful conduct fairly attributable to the officer himself, so long as the relief is sought not from the state treasury but from the officer personally. *Scheuer* v. *Rhodes*, 416 U. S. 232, 237-238 (1974);

Ford Motor Co. v. *Department of Treasury of Ind.*, 323 U. S. 459, 462 (1945).

The principle of sovereign immunity as reflected in our jurisprudence strikes the proper balance between the supremacy of federal law and the separate sovereignty of the States. Established rules provide ample means to correct ongoing violations of law and to vindicate the interests which animate the Supremacy Clause. That we have, during the first 210 years of our constitutional history, found it unnecessary to decide the question presented here suggests a federal power to subject nonconsenting States to private suits in their own courts is unnecessary to uphold the Constitution and valid federal statutes as the supreme law.

V

This case at one level concerns the formal structure of federalism, but in a Constitution as resilient as ours form mirrors substance. Congress has vast power but not all power. When Congress legislates in matters affecting the States, it may not treat these sovereign entities as mere prefectures or corporations. Congress must accord States the esteem due to them as joint participants in a federal system, one beginning with the premise of sovereignty in both the central Government and the separate States. Congress has ample means to ensure compliance with valid federal laws, but it must respect the sovereignty of the States.

In an apparent attempt to disparage a conclusion with which it disagrees, the dissent attributes our reasoning to natural law. We seek to discover, however, only what the Framers and those who ratified the Constitution sought to accomplish when they created a federal system. We appeal to no higher authority than the Charter which they wrote and adopted. Theirs was the unique insight that freedom is enhanced by the creation of two governments, not one. We need not attach a label to our dissenting colleagues' insistence that the constitutional structure adopted by the Founders must yield to the politics of the moment. Although the Constitution begins with the principle that sovereignty rests with the people, it does not follow that the National Government becomes the ultimate, preferred mechanism for expressing the people's will. The States exist as a refutation of that concept. In choosing to ordain and establish the Constitution, the people insisted upon a federal structure for the very purpose of rejecting the idea that the will of the people in all instances is expressed by the central power, the one most remote from their control. The Framers of the Constitution did not share our dissenting colleagues' belief that the Congress may circumvent the federal design by regulating the States directly when it pleases to do so, including by a proxy in which individual citizens are authorized to levy upon the state treasuries absent the States' consent to jurisdiction.

The case before us depends upon these principles. The State of Maine has not questioned Congress' power to prescribe substantive rules of federal law to which it must comply. Despite an initial good-faith disagreement about the requirements of the FLSA, it is conceded by all that the State has altered its conduct so that its compliance with federal law cannot now be questioned. The Solicitor General of the United States has appeared before this Court, however, and asserted that the federal interest in compensating the States' employees for alleged past violations of federal law is so compelling that the sovereign State of Maine must be stripped of its immunity and subjected to suit in its own courts by its own employees. Yet, despite specific statutory authorization, see 29 U. S. C. § 216(c), the United States apparently found the same interests insufficient to justify sending even a single attorney to Maine to prosecute this litigation. The difference between a suit by the United States on behalf of the employees and a suit by the employees implicates a rule that the National Government must itself deem the case of sufficient importance to take action against the State; and history, precedent, and the structure of the Constitution make clear that, under the plan of the Convention, the States have consented to suits of the first kind but not of the second. The judgment of the Supreme Judicial Court of Maine is Affirmed.

SOUTER, J., with whom JUSTICE STEVENS, JUSTICE GINSBURG, and JUSTICE BREYER join, dissenting.

In *Seminole Tribe of Fla.* v. *Florida*, 517 U. S. 44 (1996), a majority of this Court invoked the Eleventh Amendment to declare that the federal judicial power under Article III of the Constitution does not reach a private action against a State, even on a federal question. In the Court's conception, however, the Eleventh Amendment was understood as having been enhanced by a "background principle" of state sovereign immunity (understood as immunity to suit), that operated beyond its limited codification in the Amendment, dealing solely with federal citizen-state diversity jurisdiction. To the *Seminole Tribe* dissenters, of whom I was one, the Court's enhancement of the Amendment was at odds with constitutional history and at war with the conception of divided sovereignty that is the essence of American federalism.

Today's issue arises naturally in the aftermath of the decision in *Seminole Tribe*. The Court holds that the Constitution bars an individual suit against a State to enforce a federal statutory right under the Fair Labor Standards Act of 1938, when brought in the State's courts over its objection. In thus complementing its earlier decision, the Court of course confronts the fact that the state forum renders the Eleventh Amendment beside the point, and it has responded by discerning a simpler and more straightforward theory of state sovereign immunity than it found in *Seminole Tribe*: a State's sovereign immunity from all individual suits is a "fundamental aspect" of state sovereignty "confirm[ed]" by the Tenth Amendment. As a consequence, *Seminole Tribe's* contorted reliance on the Eleventh Amendment and its background was presumably unnecessary; the Tenth would have done the work with an economy that the majority in *Seminole Tribe* would have welcomed. Indeed, if the Court's current reasoning is correct, the Eleventh Amendment itself was unnecessary. Whatever Article III may originally have said about the federal judicial power, the embarrassment to the State of Georgia occasioned by attempts in federal court to enforce the State's war debt could easily have been avoided if only the Court that decided *Chisholm* v. *Georgia*, 2 Dall. 419 (1793), had understood a State's inherent, Tenth Amendment right to be free of any judicial power, whether the court be state or federal, and whether the cause of action arise under state or federal law.

The sequence of the Court's positions prompts a suspicion of error, and skepticism is confirmed by scrutiny of the Court's efforts to justify its holding. There is no evidence that the Tenth Amendment constitutionalized a concept of sovereign immunity as inherent in the notion of statehood, and no evidence that any concept of inherent sovereign immunity was understood historically to apply when the sovereign sued was not the font of the law. Nor does the Court fare any better with its subsidiary lines of reasoning, that the state-court action is barred by the scheme of American federalism, a result supposedly confirmed by a history largely devoid of precursors to the action considered here. The Court's federalism ignores the accepted authority of Congress to bind States under the FLSA and to provide for enforcement of federal rights in state court. The Court's history simply disparages the capacity of the Constitution to order relationships in a Republic that has changed since the founding.

On each point the Court has raised it is mistaken, and I respectfully dissent from its judgment.

3. Clear Statement Requirements

GREGORY v. ASHCROFT
501 U.S. 452 (1991)

O'CONNOR, J., delivered the opinion of the Court.

Article V, § 26, of the Missouri Constitution provides that "[a]ll judges other than municipal judges shall retire at the age of seventy years." We consider whether this mandatory retirement provision violates the federal Age Discrimination in Employment Act of 1967 (ADEA or Act), 29

U.S.C. §§ 621-634, and whether it comports with the federal constitutional prescription of equal protection of the laws.

I

Petitioners are Missouri state judges. Judge Ellis Gregory, Jr., is an associate circuit judge for the Twenty-first Judicial Circuit. Judge Anthony P. Nugent, Jr., is a judge of the Missouri Court of Appeals, Western District. Both are subject to the § 26 mandatory retirement provision.

Petitioners and two other state judges filed suit against John D. Ashcroft, the Governor of Missouri...challenging the validity of the mandatory retirement provision. The judges alleged that the provision violated both the ADEA and the Equal Protection Clause of the Fourteenth Amendment to the United States Constitution. The Governor filed a motion to dismiss.

The District Court granted the motion, holding that Missouri's appointed judges are not protected by the ADEA because they are "appointees ... 'on a policymaking level' " and therefore are excluded from the Act's definition of "employee." The court held also that the mandatory retirement provision does not violate the Equal Protection Clause because there is a rational basis for the distinction between judges and other state officials to whom no mandatory retirement age applies.

The United States Court of Appeals for the Eighth Circuit affirmed.

II

The ADEA makes it unlawful for an "employer" "to discharge any individual" who is at least 40 years old "because of such individual's age." 29 U.S.C. §§ 623(a), 631(a). The term "employer" is defined to include "a State or political subdivision of a State." § 630(b)(2). Petitioners work for the State of Missouri. They contend that the Missouri mandatory retirement requirement for judges violates the ADEA.

A

As every schoolchild learns, our Constitution establishes a system of dual sovereignty between the States and the Federal Government. This Court also has recognized this fundamental principle. The Constitution created a Federal Government of limited powers. "The powers not delegated to the United States by the Constitution, nor prohibited by it to the States, are reserved to the States respectively, or to the people." U.S. Const., Amdt. 10. The States thus retain substantial sovereign authority under our constitutional system. The Federal Government holds a decided advantage in this delicate balance: the Supremacy Clause. U.S. Const., Art. VI, cl. 2. As long as it is acting within the powers granted it under the Constitution, Congress may impose its will on the States. Congress may legislate in areas traditionally regulated by the States. This is an extraordinary power in a federalist system. It is a power that we must assume Congress does not exercise lightly.

The present case concerns a state constitutional provision through which the people of Missouri establish a qualification for those who sit as their judges. This provision goes beyond an area traditionally regulated by the States; it is a decision of the most fundamental sort for a sovereign entity. Through the structure of its government, and the character of those who exercise government authority, a State defines itself as a sovereign. "It is obviously essential to the independence of the States, and to their peace and tranquility, that their power to prescribe the qualifications of their own officers...should be exclusive, and free from external interference, except so far as plainly provided by the Constitution...."

Congressional interference with this decision of the people of Missouri...would upset the usual constitutional balance of federal and state powers. For this reason, "it is incumbent upon the federal courts to be certain of Congress' intent before finding that federal law overrides" this balance. We explained recently:

> [I]f Congress intends to alter the 'usual constitutional balance between the States and the Federal Government,' it must make its intention to do so 'unmistakably clear in the language of the statute.' Congress should make its intention 'clear and manifest' if it intends to pre-empt the historic powers of the States....

Will v. Mich. Dept. of State Police, 491 U.S. 58, 65 (1989). This plain statement rule is nothing more than an acknowledgment that the States retain substantial sovereign powers under our constitutional scheme, powers with which Congress does not readily interfere.

These cases stand in recognition of the authority of the people of the States to determine the qualifications of their most important government officials. It is an authority that lies at "the heart of representative government." It is a power reserved to the States under the Tenth Amendment and guaranteed them by that provision of the Constitution under which the United States "guarantee[s] to every State in this Union a Republican Form of Government." U.S. Const., Art. IV, § 4.

B

In 1974, Congress extended the substantive provisions of the ADEA to include the States as employers. At the same time, Congress amended the definition of "employee" to exclude all elected and most high-ranking government officials.

Governor Ashcroft contends that the exclusion of certain public officials also excludes judges, like petitioners, who are appointed to office by the Governor and are then subject to retention election. Governor Ashcroft relies on the plain language of the statute: It exempts persons appointed "at the policymaking level." The Governor argues that state judges, in fashioning and applying the common law, make policy. Missouri is a common law state. The common law, unlike a constitution or statute, provides no definitive text; it is to be derived from the interstices of prior opinions and a well-considered judgment of what is best for the community.

The statute refers to appointees "on the policymaking level," not to appointees "who make policy." It may be sufficient that the appointee is in a position requiring the exercise of discretion concerning issues of public importance. This certainly describes the bench, regardless of whether judges might be considered policymakers in the same sense as the executive or legislature.

Nonetheless, "appointee at the policymaking level," particularly in the context of the other exceptions that surround it, is an odd way for Congress to exclude judges; a plain statement that judges are not "employees" would seem the most efficient phrasing. But in this case we are not looking for a plain statement that judges are excluded. We will not read the ADEA to cover state judges unless Congress has made it clear that judges are *included*. This does not mean that the Act must mention judges explicitly, though it does not. Rather, it must be plain to anyone reading the Act that it covers judges. In the context of a statute that plainly excludes most important state public officials, "appointee on the policymaking level" is sufficiently broad that we cannot conclude that the statute plainly covers appointed state judges. Therefore, it does not.

III

Petitioners argue that, even if they are not covered by the ADEA, the Missouri Constitution's mandatory retirement provision for judges violates the Equal Protection Clause of the Fourteenth Amendment to the United States Constitution. Petitioners contend that there is no rational basis for the decision of the people of Missouri to preclude those aged 70 and over from serving as their judges. They claim that the mandatory retirement provision makes two irrational distinctions: between judges who have reached age 70 and younger judges, and between judges 70 and over and other state employees of the same age who are not subject to mandatory retirement.

Petitioners are correct to assert their challenge at the level of rational basis. This Court has said repeatedly that age is not a suspect classification under the Equal Protection Clause. Nor do petitioners claim that they have a fundamental interest in serving as judges. The State need therefore assert only a rational basis for its age classification. In this case, we are dealing not merely with government action, but with a state constitutional provision approved by the people of Missouri as a whole. This constitutional provision reflects both the considered judgment of the state legislature that proposed it and that of the citizens of Missouri who voted for it. "[W]e will not overturn such a [law] unless the varying treatment of different groups or persons is so unrelated to the achievement of any combination of legitimate purposes that we can only conclude that the [people's] actions were irrational."

The people of Missouri have a legitimate, indeed compelling, interest in maintaining a judiciary fully capable of performing the demanding tasks that judges must perform. It is an unfortunate fact of life that physical and mental capacity sometimes diminish with age. The people may therefore wish to replace some older judges. Voluntary retirement will not always be sufficient. Nor may impeachment—with its public humiliation and elaborate procedural machinery—serve acceptably the goal of a fully functioning judiciary.

The election process may also be inadequate. Whereas the electorate would be expected to discover if their governor or state legislator were not performing adequately and vote the official out of office, the same may not be true of judges. Most voters never observe state judges in action, nor read judicial opinions. State judges also serve longer terms of office than other public officials, making them—deliberately—less dependent on the will of the people. Most of these judges do not run in ordinary elections. The people of Missouri rationally could conclude that retention elections—in which state judges run unopposed at relatively long intervals—do not serve as an adequate check on judges whose performance is deficient. Mandatory retirement is a reasonable response to this dilemma.

The Missouri mandatory retirement provision, like all legal classifications, is founded on a generalization. It is far from true that all judges suffer significant deterioration in performance at age 70. It is probably not true that most do. It may not be true at all. But… [t]he people of Missouri rationally could conclude that the threat of deterioration at age 70 is sufficiently great, and the alternatives for removal sufficiently inadequate, that they will require all judges to step aside at age 70.

IV

The people of Missouri have established a qualification for those who would be their judges. It is their prerogative as citizens of a sovereign State to do so. Neither the ADEA nor the Equal Protection Clause prohibits the choice they have made.

C. FEDERAL LIMITATIONS ON STATE POWER – ARTICLE VI

Article VI may contain the most important provision of all for the States with respect to the effect of federal law on the States. The Supremacy Clause declares that "This Constitution, and the Laws of the

United States which shall be made in pursuance thereof; and all Treaties made, or which shall be made, under the Authority of the United States, shall be the supreme Law of the Land; and the Judges in every State shall be bound thereby, any Thing in the Constitution or Laws of any State to the Contrary notwithstanding." The Supremacy Clause is further bolstered by Article VI's provision that "the Members of the several State Legislatures, and all executive and judicial Officers, both of the United States and of the several States, shall be bound by Oath or Affirmation, to support this Constitution."

These two clauses make clear—in explicit terms—that federal law has primacy over state law, including state constitutions, when there is a conflict between any federal law (constitutional, statutory, or even regulatory) and state law. Although that general principle is quite clear and explicit, the devil is in the details of applying the principle to the innumerable contexts in which claims have arisen that state law is preempted by federal law. Federal preemption doctrine is a complex and intricate area of the law, with outcomes often turning on the specifics of the federal and state laws implicated in a particular case. Thus, the following cases are simply illustrations of situations in which federal law was alleged to preempt state constitutional provisions. In other words, these cases are not offered for the federal substantive principles on which they may be based, such as equal protection, but rather to demonstrate that federal law—both constitutional and statutory—may preempt state constitutional provisions.

Note also that in some of the preemption cases the parties may invoke and the Court may discuss the Tenth Amendment—part of the Bill of Rights—which declares that "[t]he powers not delegated to the United States by the Constitution, nor prohibited by it to the States, are reserved to the States respectively, or to the people." Sometimes resolving preemption questions under Article VI implicates the residual powers of the States, as the argument may be that federal law cannot preempt what has been reserved exclusively to the States. For the most part, however, the Supreme Court has not given the Tenth Amendment substantive meaning, but tended to treat it as a "truism" stating what is essentially fundamental under the federalism the Constitution creates: If the federal government has the power to take certain action, then it necessarily may preempt contrary state law by virtue of the Supremacy Clause, but if the federal government lacks such power, then the power necessarily resides solely in the States.

ROMER v. EVANS
517 U.S. 620 (1996)

KENNEDY, J., delivered the opinion of the Court.

I

The enactment challenged in this case is an amendment to the Constitution of the State of Colorado, adopted in a 1992 statewide referendum. The parties and the state courts refer to it as "Amendment 2." The impetus for the amendment and the contentious campaign that preceded its adoption came in large part from ordinances that had been passed in various Colorado municipalities. For example, the cities of Aspen and Boulder and the city and County of Denver each had enacted ordinances which banned discrimination in many transactions and activities, including housing, employment, education, public accommodations, and health and welfare services. What gave rise to the statewide controversy was the protection the ordinances afforded to persons discriminated against by reason of their sexual orientation. Amendment 2 repeals these ordinances to the extent they prohibit discrimination on the basis of "homosexual, lesbian or bisexual orientation, conduct, practices or relationships."

Yet Amendment 2, in explicit terms, does more than repeal or rescind these provisions. It prohibits all legislative, executive or judicial action at any level of state or local government designed to protect the named class, a class we shall refer to as homosexual persons or gays and lesbians. The amendment reads:

> No Protected Status Based on Homosexual, Lesbian or Bisexual Orientation. Neither the State of Colorado, through any of its branches or departments, nor any of its agencies, political subdivisions, municipalities or school districts, shall enact, adopt or enforce any statute, regulation, ordinance or policy whereby homosexual, lesbian or bisexual orientation, conduct, practices or relationships shall constitute or otherwise be the basis of or entitle any person or class of persons to have or claim any minority status, quota preferences, protected status or claim of discrimination. This Section of the Constitution shall be in all respects self-executing.

Soon after Amendment 2 was adopted, this litigation to declare its invalidity and enjoin its enforcement was commenced in the District Court for the City and County of Denver. Among the plaintiffs (respondents here) were homosexual persons, some of them government employees. They alleged that enforcement of Amendment 2 would subject them to immediate and substantial risk of discrimination on the basis of their sexual orientation. Other plaintiffs (also respondents here) included the three municipalities whose ordinances we have cited and certain other governmental entities which had acted earlier to protect homosexuals from discrimination but would be prevented by Amendment 2 from continuing to do so.

[The Colorado courts declared Amendment 2 unconstitutional under federal law.]

II

The State's principal argument in defense of Amendment 2 is that it puts gays and lesbians in the same position as all other persons. So, the State says, the measure does no more than deny homosexuals special rights. This reading of the amendment's language is implausible. We rely not upon our own interpretation of the amendment but upon the authoritative construction of Colorado's Supreme Court. The state court, deeming it unnecessary to determine the full extent of the amendment's reach, found it invalid even on a modest reading of its implications.

Sweeping and comprehensive is the change in legal status effected by this law. So much is evident from the ordinances the Colorado Supreme Court declared would be void by operation of Amendment 2. Homosexuals, by state decree, are put in a solitary class with respect to transactions and relations in both the private and governmental spheres. The amendment withdraws from homosexuals, but no others, specific legal protection from the injuries caused by discrimination, and it forbids reinstatement of these laws and policies.

III

The Fourteenth Amendment's promise that no person shall be denied the equal protection of the laws must coexist with the practical necessity that most legislation classifies for one purpose or another, with resulting disadvantage to various groups or persons. We have attempted to reconcile the principle with the reality by stating that, if a law neither burdens a fundamental right nor targets a suspect class, we will uphold the legislative classification so long as it bears a rational relation to some legitimate end.

Amendment 2 fails, indeed defies, even this conventional inquiry. First, the amendment has the peculiar property of imposing a broad and undifferentiated disability on a single named group, an exceptional and, as we shall explain, invalid form of legislation. Second, its sheer breadth is so discontinuous with the reasons offered for it that the amendment seems inexplicable by anything but animus toward the class it affects; it lacks a rational relationship to legitimate state interests.

A second and related point is that laws of the kind now before us raise the inevitable inference that the disadvantage imposed is born of animosity toward the class of persons affected. Amendment 2,...in making a general announcement that gays and lesbians shall not have any particular protections from the law, inflicts on them immediate, continuing, and real injuries that outrun and belie any legitimate justifications that may be claimed for it. We conclude that, in addition to the far-reaching deficiencies of Amendment 2 that we have noted, the principles it offends, in another sense, are conventional and venerable; a law must bear a rational relationship to a legitimate governmental purpose, and Amendment 2 does not.

The primary rationale the State offers for Amendment 2 is respect for other citizens' freedom of association, and in particular the liberties of landlords or employers who have personal or religious objections to homosexuality. Colorado also cites its interest in conserving resources to fight discrimination against other groups. The breadth of the amendment is so far removed from these particular justifications that we find it impossible to credit them. We cannot say that Amendment 2 is directed to any identifiable legitimate purpose or discrete objective. It is a status-based enactment divorced from any factual context from which we could discern a relationship to legitimate state interests; it is a classification of persons undertaken for its own sake, something the Equal Protection Clause does not permit. Amendment 2 classifies homosexuals not to further a proper legislative end but to make them unequal to everyone else. This Colorado cannot do. A State cannot so deem a class of persons a stranger to its laws.

NOTE

After the Supreme Court upheld the race-conscious admission program of the Michigan Law School in *Grutter v. Bollinger*, 539 U.S. 306 (2003), Michigan citizens put on the ballot "Proposal 2," and voters approved it by a margin of 58 percent to 42 percent. This enactment became Article I, § 26, of the Michigan Constitution, and provides as follows:

(1) The University of Michigan, Michigan State University, Wayne State University, and any other public college or university, community college, or school district shall not discriminate against, or grant preferential treatment to, any individual or group on the basis of race, sex, color, ethnicity, or national origin in the operation of public employment, public education, or public contracting.

(2) The state shall not discriminate against, or grant preferential treatment to, any individual or group on the basis of race, sex, color, ethnicity, or national origin in the operation of public employment, public education, or public contracting.

(3) For the purposes of this section 'state' includes, but is not necessarily limited to, the state itself, any city, county, any public college, university, or community college, school district, or other political subdivision or governmental instrumentality of or within the State of Michigan not included in sub-section 1.

In *Schuette v. Coalition to Defend Affirmative Action*, 572 U.S. ___, 134 S. Ct. 1623 (2014), the Supreme Court upheld Proposal 2, rejecting the plaintiffs' federal equal protection challenge. Proposal 2 thus is valid and effectively bans the use of affirmative action by state educational institutions in Michigan.

U.S. TERM LIMITS, INC. v. THORNTON
514 U.S. 779 (1995)

STEVENS, J., delivered the opinion of the Court.

The Constitution sets forth qualifications for membership in the Congress of the United States. Article I, § 2, cl. 2, which applies to the House of Representatives, provides: "No Person shall be a Representative who shall not have attained to the Age of twenty five Years, and been seven Years a Citizen of the United States, and who shall not, when elected, be an Inhabitant of that State in which he shall be chosen."

Article I, § 3, cl. 3, which applies to the Senate, similarly provides: "No Person shall be a Senator who shall not have attained to the Age of thirty Years, and been nine Years a Citizen of the United States, and who shall not, when elected, be an Inhabitant of that State for which he shall be chosen."

Today's cases present a challenge to an amendment to the Arkansas State Constitution that prohibits the name of an otherwise-eligible candidate for Congress from appearing on the general election ballot if that candidate has already served three terms in the House of Representatives or two terms in the Senate. The Arkansas Supreme Court held that the amendment violates the Federal Constitution. We agree with that holding. Such a state-imposed restriction is contrary to the "fundamental principle of our representative democracy," embodied in the Constitution, that "the people should choose whom they please to govern them." Allowing individual States to adopt their own qualifications for congressional service would be inconsistent with the Framers' vision of a uniform National Legislature representing the people of the United States. If the qualifications set forth in the text of the Constitution are to be changed, that text must be amended.

I

At the general election on November 3, 1992, the voters of Arkansas adopted Amendment 73 to their State Constitution. Proposed as a "Term Limitation Amendment," its preamble stated:

> The people of Arkansas find and declare that elected officials who remain in office too long become preoccupied with reelection and ignore their duties as representatives of the people. Entrenched incumbency has reduced voter participation and has led to an electoral system that is less free, less competitive, and less representative than the system established by the Founding Fathers.

Therefore, the people of Arkansas, exercising their reserved powers, herein limit the terms of elected officials.

The limitations in Amendment 73 apply to three categories of elected officials. Section 3, the provision at issue in these cases, applies to the Arkansas Congressional Delegation. It provides:

(a) Any person having been elected to three or more terms as a member of the United States House of Representatives from Arkansas shall not be certified as a candidate and shall not be eligible to have his/her name placed on the ballot for election to the United States House of Representatives from Arkansas.

(b) Any person having been elected to two or more terms as a member of the United States Senate from Arkansas shall not be certified as a candidate and shall not be eligible to have his/her name placed on the ballot for election to the United States Senate from Arkansas.

Amendment 73 states that it is self-executing and shall apply to all persons seeking election after January 1, 1993.

On November 13, 1992, respondent Bobbie Hill, on behalf of herself, similarly situated Arkansas "citizens, residents, taxpayers and registered voters," and the League of Women Voters of Arkansas, filed a complaint in the Circuit Court for Pulaski County, Arkansas, seeking a declaratory judgment that § 3 of Amendment 73 is "unconstitutional and void." The State of Arkansas, through its Attorney General, intervened as a party defendant in support of the amendment. Several proponents of the amendment also intervened, including petitioner U.S. Term Limits, Inc.

[Ultimately, the Arkansas Supreme Court held Section 3 to be unconstitutional].

II

As the opinions of the Arkansas Supreme Court suggest, the constitutionality of Amendment 73 depends critically on the resolution of two distinct issues. The first is whether the Constitution forbids States to add to or alter the qualifications specifically enumerated in the Constitution. The second is, if the Constitution does so forbid, whether the fact that Amendment 73 is formulated as a ballot access restriction rather than as an outright disqualification is of constitutional significance.

III

Petitioners argue that the Constitution contains no express prohibition against state-added qualifications, and that Amendment 73 is therefore an appropriate exercise of a State's reserved power to place additional restrictions on the choices that its own voters may make. We disagree for two independent reasons. First, we conclude that the power to add qualifications is not within the "original powers" of the States, and thus is not reserved to the States by the Tenth Amendment. Second, even if States possessed some original power in this area, we conclude that the Framers intended the Constitution to be the exclusive source of qualifications for Members of Congress, and that the Framers thereby "divested" States of any power to add qualifications.

The "plan of the convention" as illuminated by the historical materials, our opinions, and the text of the Tenth Amendment draws a basic distinction between the powers of the newly created Federal Government and the powers retained by the...States.

In short, as the Framers recognized, electing representatives to the National Legislature was a new right, arising from the Constitution itself. The Tenth Amendment thus provides no basis for concluding that the States possess reserved power to add qualifications to those that are fixed in the Constitution. Instead, any state power to set the qualifications for membership in Congress must derive not from the reserved powers of state sovereignty, but rather from the delegated powers of national sovereignty. In the absence of any constitutional delegation to the States of power to add qualifications to those enumerated in the Constitution, such a power does not exist.

Even if we believed that States possessed as part of their original powers some control over congressional qualifications, the text and structure of the Constitution, the relevant historical materials, and, most importantly, the "basic principles of our democratic system" all demonstrate that the Qualifications Clauses were intended to preclude the States from exercising any such power and to fix as exclusive the qualifications in the Constitution. In light of the Framers' evident concern that States would try to undermine the National Government, they could not have intended States to have the power to set qualifications.

Similarly, we believe that state-imposed qualifications, as much as congressionally imposed qualifications, would undermine the second critical idea recognized in [a previous case], that an aspect of sovereignty is the right of the people to vote for whom they wish. Again, the source of the qualification is of little moment in assessing the qualification's restrictive impact.

Finally, state-imposed restrictions...violate a third idea central to this basic principle: that the right to choose representatives belongs not to the States, but to the people. From the start, the Framers recognized that the "great and radical vice" of the Articles of Confederation was "the principle of LEGISLATION for STATES or GOVERNMENTS, in their CORPORATE or COLLECTIVE CAPACITIES, and as contradistinguished from the INDIVIDUALS of whom they consist." The Federalist No. 15, at 108 (Hamilton). Thus the Framers, in perhaps their most important contribution, conceived of a Federal Government directly responsible to the people, possessed of direct power over the people, and chosen directly, not by States, but by the people. The Framers implemented this ideal most clearly in the provision, extant from the beginning of the Republic, that calls for the Members of the House of Representatives to be "chosen every second Year by the People of the several States." Art. I, § 2, cl. 1. Following the adoption of the Seventeenth Amendment in 1913, this ideal was extended to elections for the Senate. The Congress of the United States, therefore, is not a confederation of nations in which separate sovereigns are represented by appointed delegates, but is instead a body composed of representatives of the people.

IV

Petitioners argue that, even if States may not add qualifications, Amendment 73 is constitutional because it is not such a qualification, and because Amendment 73 is a permissible exercise of state power to regulate the "Times, Places and Manner of holding Elections." [Article I, § 4, cl. 1] We reject these contentions.

Unlike §§ 1 and 2 of Amendment 73, which create absolute bars to service for long-term incumbents running for state office, § 3 merely provides that certain Senators and Representatives shall not be certified as candidates and shall not have their names appear on the ballot. They may run as write-in candidates and, if elected, they may serve. Petitioners contend that only a legal bar to service creates an impermissible qualification, and that Amendment 73 is therefore consistent with the Constitution.

In our view, Amendment 73 is an indirect attempt to accomplish what the Constitution prohibits Arkansas from accomplishing directly. As the plurality opinion of the Arkansas Supreme Court recognized, Amendment 73 is an "effort to dress eligibility to stand for Congress in ballot access clothing," because the "intent and the effect of Amendment 73 are to disqualify congressional incumbents from further service." We must, of course, accept the state court's view of the purpose of its own law: We are thus authoritatively informed that the sole purpose of § 3 of Amendment 73 was to attempt to achieve a result that is forbidden by the Federal Constitution. Indeed, it cannot be seriously contended that the intent behind Amendment 73 is other than to prevent the election of incumbents.

Petitioners make the related argument that Amendment 73 merely regulates the "Manner" of elections, and that the amendment is therefore a permissible exercise of state power under Article I, § 4, cl. 1 (the Elections Clause), to regulate the "Times, Places and Manner" of elections. We cannot agree.

A necessary consequence of petitioners' argument is that Congress itself would have the power to "make or alter" a measure such as

Amendment 73. That the Framers would have approved of such a result is unfathomable. As our…discussion above make[s] clear, the Framers were particularly concerned that a grant to Congress of the authority to set its own qualifications would lead inevitably to congressional self-aggrandizement and the upsetting of the delicate constitutional balance. Petitioners would have us believe, however, that even as the Framers carefully circumscribed congressional power to set qualifications, they intended to allow Congress to achieve the same result by simply formulating the regulation as a ballot access restriction under the Elections Clause. We refuse to adopt an interpretation of the Elections Clause that would so cavalierly disregard what the Framers intended to be a fundamental constitutional safeguard.

V

The merits of term limits, or "rotation," have been the subject of debate since the formation of our Constitution, when the Framers unanimously rejected a proposal to add such limits to the Constitution. The cogent arguments on both sides of the question that were articulated during the process of ratification largely retain their force today. Over half the States have adopted measures that impose such limits on some offices either directly or indirectly, and the Nation as a whole, notably by constitutional amendment, has imposed a limit on the number of terms that the President may serve. Term limits, like any other qualification for office, unquestionably restrict the ability of voters to vote for whom they wish. On the other hand, such limits may provide for the infusion of fresh ideas and new perspectives, and may decrease the likelihood that representatives will lose touch with their constituents. It is not our province to resolve this longstanding debate.

We are, however, firmly convinced that allowing the several States to adopt term limits for congressional service would effect a fundamental change in the constitutional framework. Any such change must come not by legislation adopted either by Congress or by an individual State, but rather—as have other important changes in the electoral process—through the amendment procedures set forth in Article V. The Framers decided that the qualifications for service in the Congress of the United States be fixed in the Constitution and be uniform throughout the Nation. That decision reflects the Framers' understanding that Members of Congress are chosen by separate constituencies, but that they become, when elected, servants of the people of the United States. They are not merely delegates appointed by separate, sovereign States; they occupy offices that are integral and essential components of a single National Government. In the absence of a properly passed constitutional amendment, allowing individual States to craft their own qualifications for Congress would thus erode the structure envisioned by the Framers, a structure that was designed, in the words of the Preamble to our Constitution, to form a "more perfect Union."

ARIZONA STATE LEGISLATURE v. ARIZONA INDEP. REDISTRICTING COM'N
135 S. Ct. 2562 (2015)

GINSBURG, J., delivered the opinion of the Court.

This case concerns an endeavor by Arizona voters to address the problem of partisan gerrymandering—the drawing of legislative district lines to subordinate adherents of one political party and entrench a rival party in power. "[P]artisan gerrymanders," this Court has recognized, "[are incompatible] with democratic principles." *Vieth v. Jubelirer*, 541 U.S. 267, 292 (2004) (plurality opinion); *id.*, at 316, 124 S.Ct. 1769 (KENNEDY, J., concurring in judgment). Even so, the Court in *Vieth* did not grant relief on the plaintiffs' partisan gerrymander claim. The plurality held the matter nonjusticiable.

In 2000, Arizona voters adopted an initiative, Proposition 106, aimed at "ending the practice of gerrymandering and improving voter and candidate participation in elections." Proposition 106 amended Arizona's Constitution to remove redistricting authority from the Arizona Legislature and vest that authority in an independent commission, the Arizona Independent Redistricting Commission (AIRC or Commission). After the 2010 census, as after the 2000 census, the AIRC adopted redistricting maps for congressional as well as state legislative districts.

The Arizona Legislature challenged the map the Commission adopted in January 2012 for congressional districts. Recognizing that the voters could control redistricting for state legislators, the Arizona Legislature sued the AIRC in federal court seeking a declaration that the Commission and its map for congressional districts violated the "Elections Clause" of the U.S. Constitution. That Clause, critical to the resolution of this case, provides:

> "The Times, Places and Manner of holding Elections for Senators and Representatives, shall be prescribed in each State by the Legislature thereof; but the Congress may at any time by Law make or alter such Regulations...." Art. I, § 4, cl. 1.

The Arizona Legislature's complaint alleged that "[t]he word 'Legislature' in the Elections Clause means [specifically and only] the representative body which makes the laws of the people,"; so read, the Legislature urges, the Clause precludes resort to an independent commission, created by initiative, to accomplish redistricting. The AIRC responded that, for Elections Clause purposes, "the Legislature" is not confined to the elected representatives; rather, the term encompasses all legislative authority conferred by the State Constitution, including initiatives adopted by the people themselves.

A three-judge District Court held, unanimously, that the Arizona Legislature had standing to sue; dividing two to one, the Court rejected the Legislature's complaint on the merits. We postponed jurisdiction and instructed the parties to address two questions: (1) Does the Arizona Legislature have standing to bring this suit? (2) Do the Elections Clause of the United States Constitution and 2 U.S.C. § 2a(c) permit Arizona's use of a commission to adopt congressional districts? 573 U.S. ___ (2014).

We now affirm the District Court's judgment. We hold, first, that the Arizona Legislature, having lost authority to draw congressional districts, has standing to contest the constitutionality of Proposition 106. Next, we hold that lawmaking power in Arizona includes the initiative process, and that both § 2a(c) and the Elections Clause permit use of the AIRC in congressional districting in the same way the Commission is used in districting for Arizona's own Legislature.

I

C

Proposition 106, vesting redistricting authority in the AIRC, was adopted by citizen initiative in 2000 against a "background of recurring redistricting turmoil" in Arizona. Redistricting plans adopted by the Arizona Legislature sparked controversy in every redistricting cycle since the 1970's, and several of those plans were rejected by a federal court or refused preclearance by the Department of Justice under the Voting Rights Act of 1965.

Aimed at "ending the practice of gerrymandering and improving voter and candidate participation in elections," Proposition 106 amended the Arizona Constitution to remove congressional redistricting authority from the state legislature, lodging that authority, instead, in a new entity, the AIRC. Ariz. Const., Art. IV, pt. 2, § 1, ¶¶ 3–23. The AIRC convenes after each census, establishes final district boundaries, and certifies the new districts to the Arizona Secretary of State. ¶¶ 16–17. The legislature may submit nonbinding recommendations to the AIRC, ¶ 16, and is required to make necessary appropriations for its operation, ¶ 18. The highest ranking officer and minority leader of each chamber of the legislature each select one member of the AIRC from a list compiled by Arizona's Commission on Appellate Court Appointments. ¶¶ 4–7. The four appointed members of the AIRC then choose, from the same list, the fifth member, who chairs the Commission. ¶ 8. A Commission's tenure is confined to one redistricting cycle; each member's time in office "expire[s] upon the appointment of the first member of the next redistricting commission." ¶ 23.

Holders of, or candidates for, public office may not serve on the AIRC, except candidates for or members of a school board. ¶ 3. No more than two members of the Commission may be members of the same political party and the presiding fifth member cannot be registered with any party already represented on the Commission, ¶ 8. Subject to the concurrence of two-thirds of the Arizona Senate, AIRC members may be removed by the Arizona Governor for gross misconduct, substantial neglect of duty, or inability to discharge the duties of office. ¶ 10.

D

On January 17, 2012, the AIRC approved final congressional and state legislative maps based on the 2010 census. Less than four months later, on June 6, 2012, the Arizona Legislature filed suit in the United States District Court for the District of Arizona, naming as defendants the AIRC, its five members, and the Arizona Secretary of State. The Legislature sought both a declaration that Proposition 106 and congressional maps adopted by the AIRC are unconstitutional, and, as affirmative relief, an injunction against use of AIRC maps for any congressional election after the 2012 general election.

A three-judge District Court … unanimously denied a motion by the AIRC to dismiss the suit for lack of standing. The Arizona Legislature, the court determined, had "demonstrated that its loss of redistricting power constitute[d] a [sufficiently] concrete injury." On the merits, dividing two to one, the District Court granted the AIRC's motion to dismiss the complaint for failure to state a claim. Decisions of this Court, the majority concluded, "demonstrate that the word 'Legislature' in the Elections Clause refers to the legislative process used in [a] state, determined by that state's own constitution and laws." As the "lawmaking power" in Arizona "plainly includes the power to enact laws through initiative," the District Court held, the "Elections Clause permits [Arizona's] establishment and use" of the Commission. Judge Rosenblatt dissented in part. Proposition 106, in his view, unconstitutionally denied "the Legislature" of Arizona the "ability to have any outcome-defining effect on the congressional redistricting process."

We … now affirm.

II

[The Court concludes the Arizona Legislature has standing to sue.]

III

On the merits, we instructed the parties to address this question: Do the Elections Clause of the United States Constitution and 2 U.S.C. § 2a(c) permit Arizona's use of a commission to adopt congressional districts?

C

In accord with the District Court, we hold that the Elections Clause permits the people of Arizona to provide for redistricting by independent commission. To restate the key question in this case, the issue centrally debated by the parties: Absent congressional authorization, does the Elections Clause preclude the people of Arizona from creating a commission operating independently of the state legislature to establish congressional districts? The history and purpose of the Clause weigh heavily against such preclusion, as does the animating principle of our Constitution that the people themselves are the originating source of all the powers of government.

We note, preliminarily, that dictionaries, even those in circulation during the founding era, capaciously define the word "legislature." Samuel Johnson defined "legislature" simply as "[t]he power that makes laws." 2 A Dictionary of the English Language (1st ed. 1755); *ibid.* (6th ed. 1785); *ibid.* (10th ed. 1792); *ibid.* (12th ed. 1802). Thomas Sheridan's dictionary defined "legislature" exactly as Dr. Johnson did: "The power that makes laws." 2 A Complete Dictionary of the English Language (4th ed. 1797). Noah Webster defined the term precisely that way as well. Compendious Dictionary of the English Language 174 (1806). And Nathan Bailey similarly defined "legislature" as "the Authority of making Laws, or Power which makes them." An Universal Etymological English Dictionary (20th ed. 1763).

As to the "power that makes laws" in Arizona, initiatives adopted by the voters legislate for the State just as measures passed by the representative body do. See Ariz. Const., Art. IV, pt. 1, § 1 ("The legislative authority of the state shall be vested in the legislature, consisting of a senate and a house of representatives, but the people reserve the power to propose laws and amendments to the constitution and to enact or reject such laws and amendments at the polls, independently of the legislature."). See also *Eastlake v. Forest City Enterprises, Inc.*, 426 U.S. 668, 672 (1976) ("In establishing legislative bodies, the people can reserve to themselves power to deal directly with matters which might otherwise be assigned to the legislature."). As well in Arizona, the people may delegate their legislative authority over redistricting to an independent commission just as the representative body may choose to do.

1

The dominant purpose of the Elections Clause, the historical record bears out, was to empower Congress to override state election rules, not to restrict the way States enact legislation. As this Court explained in *Arizona v. Inter Tribal Council of Ariz., Inc.*, 570 U.S. ——, 133 S.Ct. 2247 (2013), the Clause "was the Framers' insurance against the possibility that a State would refuse to provide for the election of representatives to the Federal Congress."

The Clause was also intended to act as a safeguard against manipulation of electoral rules by politicians and factions in the States to entrench themselves or place their interests over those of the electorate. As Madison urged, without the Elections Clause, "[w]henever the State Legislatures had a favorite measure to carry, they would take care so to mould their regulations as to favor the candidates they wished to succeed." 2 Records of the Federal Convention 241 (M. Farrand rev. 1966).

Arguments in support of congressional control under the Elections Clause were reiterated in the public debate over ratification. ...*** While attention focused on potential abuses by state-level politicians, and the consequent need for congressional oversight, the legislative processes by which the States could exercise their initiating role in regulating congressional elections occasioned no debate. That is hardly surprising. Recall that when the Constitution was composed in Philadelphia and later ratified, the people's legislative prerogatives—the initiative and the referendum—were not yet in our democracy's arsenal. The Elections Clause, however, is not reasonably read to disarm States from adopting modes of legislation that place the lead rein in the people's hands.

2

The Arizona Legislature maintains that, by specifying "the Legislature thereof," the Elections Clause renders the State's representative body the sole "component of state government authorized to prescribe ... regulations ... for congressional redistricting." THE CHIEF JUSTICE, in dissent, agrees. But it is characteristic of our federal system that States retain autonomy to establish their own governmental processes. "Through the structure of its government, and the character of those who exercise government authority, a State defines itself as a sovereign." *Gregory v. Ashcroft*, 501 U.S. 452, 460 (1991). Arizona engaged in definition of that kind when its people placed both the initiative power and the AIRC's redistricting authority in the portion of the Arizona Constitution delineating the State's legislative authority.

This Court has "long recognized the role of the States as laboratories for devising solutions to difficult legal problems." Deference to state lawmaking "allows local policies 'more sensitive to the diverse needs of a heterogeneous society,' permits 'innovation and experimentation,' enables greater citizen 'involvement in democratic processes,' and makes government 'more responsive by putting the States in competition for a mobile citizenry.'"

We resist reading the Elections Clause to single out federal elections as the one area in which States may not use citizen initiatives as an alternative legislative process. Nothing in that Clause instructs, nor has this Court ever held, that a state legislature may prescribe regulations on the time, place, and manner of holding federal elections in defiance of provisions of the State's constitution.

4

Banning lawmaking by initiative to direct a State's method of apportioning congressional districts would do more than stymie attempts to curb partisan gerrymandering, by which the majority in the legislature draws district lines to their party's advantage. It would also cast doubt on numerous other election laws adopted by the initiative method of legislating.

The people, in several States, functioning as the lawmaking body for the purpose at hand, have used the initiative to install a host of regulations governing the "Times, Places and Manner" of holding federal elections. Art. I, § 4. For example, the people of California provided for permanent voter registration, specifying that "no amendment by the Legislature shall provide for a general biennial or other periodic reregistration of voters." The people of Ohio banned ballots providing for straight-ticket voting along party lines. The people of Oregon shortened the deadline for voter registration to 20 days prior to an election. None of those measures permit the state legislatures to override the people's prescriptions. The Arizona Legislature's theory—that the lead role in regulating federal elections cannot be wrested from "the Legislature," and vested in commissions initiated by the people—would endanger all of them.

The list of endangered state elections laws, were we to sustain the position of the Arizona Legislature, would not stop with popular initiatives. Almost all state constitutions were adopted by conventions and ratified by voters at the ballot box, without involvement or approval by "the Legislature." Core aspects of the electoral process regulated by state constitutions include voting by "ballot" or "secret ballot," voter registration, absentee voting, vote counting, and victory thresholds. Again, the States' legislatures had no hand in making these laws and may not alter or amend them.

The importance of direct democracy as a means to control election regulations extends beyond the particular statutes and constitutional provisions installed by the people rather than the States' legislatures. The very prospect of lawmaking by the people may influence the legislature when it considers (or fails to consider) election-related measures. Turning the coin, the legislature's responsiveness to the people its members represent is hardly heightened when the representative body can be confident that what it does will not be overturned or modified by the voters themselves.

Invoking the Elections Clause, the Arizona Legislature instituted this lawsuit to disempower the State's voters from serving as the legislative power for redistricting purposes. But the Clause surely was not adopted to diminish a State's authority to determine its own lawmaking processes. Article I, § 4, stems from a different view. Both parts of the Elections Clause are in line with the fundamental premise that all political power flows from the people. So comprehended, the Clause doubly empowers the people. They may control the State's lawmaking processes in the first instance, as Arizona voters have done, and they may seek Congress' correction of regulations prescribed by state legislatures.

The people of Arizona turned to the initiative to curb the practice of gerrymandering and, thereby, to ensure that Members of Congress would have "an habitual recollection of their dependence on the people." The Federalist No. 57, at 350 (J. Madison). In so acting, Arizona voters sought to restore "the core principle of republican government," namely, "that the voters should choose their representatives, not the other way around." The Elections Clause does not hinder that endeavor.

For the reasons stated, the judgment of the United States District Court for the District of Arizona is *Affirmed*.

ROBERTS, C.J., with whom Justice SCALIA, Justice THOMAS, and Justice ALITO join, dissenting.

Just over a century ago, Arizona became the second State in the Union to ratify the Seventeenth Amendment. That Amendment transferred power to choose United States Senators from "the Legislature" of each State, Art. I, § 3, to "the people thereof." The Amendment resulted from an arduous, decades-long campaign in which reformers across the country worked hard to garner approval from Congress and three-quarters of the States.

What chumps! Didn't they realize that all they had to do was interpret the constitutional term "the Legislature" to mean "the people"? The Court today performs just such a magic trick with the Elections Clause. Art. I, § 4. That Clause vests congressional redistricting authority in "the Legislature" of each State. An Arizona ballot initiative transferred that authority from "the Legislature" to an "Independent Redistricting Commission." The majority approves this deliberate constitutional evasion by doing what the proponents of the Seventeenth Amendment dared not: revising "the Legislature" to mean "the people."

The Court's position has no basis in the text, structure, or history of the Constitution, and it contradicts precedents from both Congress and this Court. The Constitution contains seventeen provisions referring to the "Legislature" of a State, many of which cannot possibly be read to mean "the people." Indeed, several provisions expressly distinguish "the Legislature" from "the People." See Art. I, § 2; Amdt. 17. This Court has accordingly defined "the Legislature" in the Elections Clause as *the representative body* which ma[kes] the laws of the people."

The majority largely ignores this evidence, relying instead on disconnected observations about direct democracy, a contorted interpretation of an irrelevant statute, and naked appeals to public policy. Nowhere does the majority explain how a constitutional provision that vests redistricting authority in "the Legislature" permits a State to wholly exclude "the Legislature" from redistricting. Arizona's Commission might be a noble endeavor—although it does not seem so "independent" in practice—but the "fact that a given law or procedure is efficient, convenient, and useful ... will not save it if it is contrary to the Constitution." No matter how concerned we may be about partisanship in redistricting, this Court has no power to gerrymander the Constitution. I respectfully dissent.

I

The majority begins by discussing policy. I begin with the Constitution. The Elections Clause provides:

> "The Times, Places and Manner of holding Elections for Senators and Representatives, shall be prescribed in each State by the Legislature thereof; but the Congress may at any time by Law make or alter such Regulations, except as to the Places of chusing Senators." Art. I, § 4, cl. 1.

The Elections Clause both imposes a duty on States and assigns that duty to a particular state actor: In the absence of a valid congressional directive to the contrary, States must draw district lines for their federal representatives. And that duty "shall" be carried out "in each State by the Legislature thereof."

In Arizona, however, redistricting is not carried out by the legislature. Instead, as the result of a ballot initiative, an unelected body called the Independent Redistricting Commission draws the lines. The key question in the case is whether the Commission can conduct congressional districting consistent with the directive that such authority be exercised "by the Legislature."

The majority concedes that the unelected Commission is not "the Legislature" of Arizona. The Court contends instead that the people of Arizona as a whole constitute "the Legislature" for purposes of the Elections Clause, and that they may delegate the congressional districting authority conferred by that Clause to the Commission. The majority provides no support for the delegation part of its theory, and I am not sure whether the majority's analysis is correct on that issue. But even giving the Court the benefit of the doubt in that regard, the Commission is still unconstitutional. Both the Constitution and our cases make clear that "the

Legislature" in the Elections Clause is the representative body which makes the laws of the people.

A

The relevant question in this case is how to define "the Legislature" under the Elections Clause. The majority opinion does not seriously turn to that question until page 2671, and even then it fails to provide a coherent answer. The Court seems to conclude, based largely on its understanding of the "history and purpose" of the Elections Clause, that "the Legislature" encompasses any entity in a State that exercises legislative power. That circular definition lacks any basis in the text of the Constitution or any other relevant legal source.

The majority's textual analysis consists, in its entirety, of one paragraph citing founding era dictionaries. The majority points to various dictionaries that follow Samuel Johnson's definition of "legislature" as the "power that makes laws." The notion that this definition corresponds to the entire population of a State is strained to begin with, and largely discredited by the majority's own admission that "[d]irect lawmaking by the people was virtually unknown when the Constitution of 1787 was drafted." Thus, even under the majority's preferred definition, "the Legislature" referred to an institutional body of representatives, not the people at large.

Any ambiguity about the meaning of "the Legislature" is removed by other founding era sources. "[E]very state constitution from the Founding Era that used the term legislature defined it as a distinct multimember entity comprised of representatives." The Federalist Papers are replete with references to "legislatures" that can only be understood as referring to representative institutions. Noah Webster's heralded American Dictionary of the English Language defines "legislature" as "[t]he body of men in a state or kingdom, invested with power to make and repeal laws." 2 An American Dictionary of the English Language (1828). It continues, "The legislatures of most of the states in America ... consist of two houses or branches."

I could go on, but the Court has said this before. As we put it nearly a century ago, "Legislature" was "not a term of uncertain meaning when incorporated into the Constitution.

B

The unambiguous meaning of "the Legislature" in the Elections Clause as a representative body is confirmed by other provisions of the Constitution that use the same term in the same way. When seeking to discern the meaning of a word in the Constitution, there is no better dictionary than the rest of the Constitution itself. Our precedents new and old have employed this structural method of interpretation to read the Constitution in the manner it was drafted and ratified—as a unified, coherent whole.

The Constitution includes seventeen provisions referring to a State's "Legislature." Every one of those references is consistent with the understanding of a legislature as a representative body. More importantly, many of them are only consistent with an institutional legislature—and flatly incompatible with the majority's reading of "the Legislature" to refer to the people as a whole.

Start with the Constitution's first use of the term: "The House of Representatives shall be composed of Members chosen every second Year by the People of the several States, and the Electors in each State shall have the Qualifications requisite for Electors of the most numerous Branch of the State Legislature." Art. I, § 2, cl. 1. This reference to a "Branch of the State Legislature" can only be referring to an institutional body, and the explicit juxtaposition of "the State Legislature" with "the People of the several States" forecloses the majority's proposed reading.

The next Section of Article I describes how to fill vacancies in the United States Senate: "if Vacancies happen by Resignation, or otherwise, during the Recess of the Legislature of any State, the Executive thereof may make temporary Appointments until the next Meeting of the Legislature, which shall then fill such Vacancies." § 3, cl. 2. The references to "the Recess of the Legislature of any State" and "the next Meeting of the Legislature" are only consistent with an institutional legislature, and make no sense under the majority's reading. The people as a whole (schoolchildren and a few unnamed others excepted) do not take a "Recess."

The list goes on. Article IV provides that the "United States shall guarantee to every State in this Union a Republican Form of Government, and shall protect each of them against Invasion; and on Application of the Legislature, or of the Executive (when the Legislature cannot be convened), against domestic Violence." § 4. It is perhaps conceivable that all the people of a State could be "convened"—although this would seem difficult during an "Invasion" or outbreak of "domestic Violence"—but the only natural reading of the Clause is that "the Executive" may submit a federal application when "the Legislature" as a representative body cannot be convened.

Article VI provides that the "Senators and Representatives before mentioned, and the Members of the several State Legislatures, and all executive and judicial Officers, both of the United States and of the several States, shall be bound by Oath or Affirmation, to support this Constitution." Cl. 3. Unless the majority is prepared to make all the people of every State swear an "Oath or Affirmation, to support this Constitution," this provision can only refer to the "several State Legislatures" in their institutional capacity.

Each of these provisions offers strong structural indications about what "the Legislature" must mean. But the most powerful evidence of all comes from the Seventeenth Amendment. Under the original Constitution, Senators were "chosen by the Legislature" of each State, Art. I, § 3, cl. 1, while Members of the House of Representatives were chosen "by the People," Art. I, § 2, cl. 1. That distinction was critical to the Framers. As James Madison explained, the Senate would "derive its powers from the States," while the House would "derive its powers from the people of America."

Before long, reformers took up Wilson's mantle and launched a protracted campaign to amend the Constitution. That effort began in 1826, when Representative Henry Storrs of New York proposed—but then set aside—a constitutional amendment transferring the power to elect Senators from the state legislatures to the people. Over the next three-quarters of a century, no fewer than 188 joint resolutions proposing similar reforms were introduced in both Houses of Congress.

At no point in this process did anyone suggest that a constitutional amendment was unnecessary because "Legislature" could simply be interpreted to mean "people." In fact, as the decades rolled by without an amendment, 28 of the 45 States settled for the next best thing by holding a popular vote on candidates for Senate, then pressuring state legislators into choosing the winner. All agreed that cutting the state legislature out of senatorial selection entirely would require nothing less than to "Strike out" the original words in the Constitution and "insert, 'elected by the people'" in its place.

Yet that is precisely what the majority does to the Elections Clause today—amending the text not through the process provided by Article V, but by judicial decision. The majority's revision renders the Seventeenth Amendment an 86–year waste of time, and singles out the Elections Clause as the only one of the Constitution's seventeen provisions referring to "the Legislature" that departs from the ordinary meaning of the term.

* * *

The constitutional text, structure, history, and precedent establish a straightforward rule: Under the Elections Clause, "the Legislature" is a representative body that, when it prescribes election regulations, may be required to do so within the ordinary lawmaking process, but may not be cut out of that process. Put simply, the state legislature need not be exclusive in congressional districting, but neither may it be excluded.

The majority's contrary understanding requires it to accept a definition of "the Legislature" that contradicts the term's plain meaning, creates discord with the Seventeenth Amendment and the Constitution's many other uses of the term, makes nonsense of the drafting and ratification of the Elections Clause, and breaks with the relevant precedents. In short, the effect of the majority's decision is to erase the words "by the Legislature thereof" from the Elections Clause. That is a judicial error of the most basic order. "It cannot be presumed that any clause in the constitution is intended to be without effect; and therefore such a construction is inadmissible." *Marbury v. Madison*, 1 Cranch 137, 174 (1803).

III

Justice Jackson once wrote that the Constitution speaks in "majestic generalities." In many places it does, and so we have cases expounding on "freedom of speech" and "unreasonable searches and seizures." Amdts. 1, 4. Yet the Constitution also speaks in some places with elegant specificity. A Member of the House of Representatives must be 25 years old. Art. I, § 2, cl. 2. Every State gets two Senators. Art. I, § 3, cl. 1. And the times, places, and manner of holding elections for those federal representatives "shall be prescribed in each State by the Legislature thereof." Art. I, § 4, cl. 1.

For the reasons I have explained, there is no real doubt about what "the Legislature" means. The Framers of the Constitution were "practical men, dealing with the facts of political life as they understood them, putting into form the government they were creating, and prescribing in language clear and intelligible the powers that government was to take." We ought to give effect to the words they used.

The majority today shows greater concern about redistricting practices than about the meaning of the Constitution. I recognize the difficulties that arise from trying to fashion judicial relief for partisan gerrymandering. But our inability to find a manageable standard in that area is no excuse to abandon a standard of meaningful interpretation in this area. This Court has stressed repeatedly that a law's virtues as a policy innovation cannot redeem its inconsistency with the Constitution. "Failure of political will does not justify unconstitutional remedies."

Indeed, the Court has enforced the text of the Constitution to invalidate state laws with policy objectives reminiscent of this one. Two of our precedents held that States could not use their constitutions to impose term limits on their federal representatives in violation of the United States Constitution. *U.S. Term Limits, Inc. v. Thornton*, 514 U.S. 779 (1995). The people of the States that enacted these reforms surely viewed them as measures that would "place the lead rein in the people's hands." Yet the Court refused to accept "that the Framers spent significant time and energy in debating and crafting Clauses that could be easily evaded." The majority approves just such an evasion of the Constitution today.

* * *

The people of Arizona have concerns about the process of congressional redistricting in their State. For better or worse, the Elections Clause of the Constitution does not allow them to address those concerns by displacing their legislature. But it does allow them to seek relief from Congress, which can make or alter the regulations prescribed by the legislature. And the Constitution gives them another means of change. They can follow the lead of the reformers who won passage of the Seventeenth Amendment. Indeed, several constitutional amendments over the past century have involved modifications of the electoral process. Amdts. 19, 22, 24, 26. Unfortunately, today's decision will only discourage this democratic method of change. Why go through the hassle of writing a new provision into the Constitution when it is so much easier to write an old one out?

I respectfully dissent.

D. FEDERAL ARTICLE IV PROVISIONS THAT MAY LIMIT OR INFLUENCE THE CONTENT OF STATE CONSTITUTIONS

Article IV of the U.S. Constitution contains a number of provisions directly relevant to the States and their role in the federal system. In particular, Article IV contains the Full Faith and Credit Clause, the Privileges and Immunities Clause, and the Extradition Clause, all of which essentially require the States to respect other States. (Article IV also includes the Fugitive Slave Clause; a provision superseded and rendered a nullity by the Thirteenth Amendment, which abolished slavery.) Article IV also gives Congress the power to admit new States into the union and includes a provision known as the Guarantee Clause. All of these provisions are addressed in more detail below, using a handful of illustrative cases. Coverage here is intended to introduce the student to some of the important connections between federal constitutional provisions and the States, but the treatment is not intended to be comprehensive.

1. Full Faith and Credit

Section 1 of Article IV provides that "Full Faith and Credit shall be given in each State to the public Acts, Records, and judicial Proceedings of every other State." Complex and difficult questions can and do arise about what judgments of one State must be accorded legal recognition by another State. A common example of applying full faith and credit would be enforcing a civil tort judgment of State A in the courts of State B.

2. Privileges and Immunities

Section 2 of Article IV declares that the "Citizens of each State shall be entitled to all Privileges and Immunities of Citizens in the several States." This Privileges and Immunities Clause (to be distinguished from the Privileges or Immunities Clause of the Fourteenth Amendment) is essentially a non-discrimination principle that protects non-residents of States. See, e.g., *Supreme Court of New Hampshire v. Piper*, 470 U.S. 274 (1985).

3. Extradition

Article IV, section 2 also provides that a fugitive "who shall flee from Justice, and be found in another State, shall on Demand of the executive Authority of the State from which he fled, be delivered up, to be removed to the State having Jurisdiction of the Crime." The Extradition Clause was the subject of a fascinating Supreme Court decision on the eve of the Civil War, see *Kentucky v. Dennison*, 65 U.S. (24 How.) 66 (1861); Stephen R. McAllister, *A Marbury v. Madison Moment on the Eve of the Civil War: Chief Judge Roger Taney and the Kentucky v. Dennison Case*, 14 The Green Bag 2d 405 (2011), resulting in the courts playing a limited role in enforcing the clause for over 125 years until the Supreme Court eventually overruled the earlier case and expanded the courts' ability to require extradition. *Puerto Rico v. Branstad*, 483 U.S. 219 (1987).

4. Congressional Power to Admit New States

An Article IV provision that has at times directly and significantly affected the substantive content of state constitutions is the first clause of Section 3, which provides that "New States may be admitted by the Congress into this Union." This provision has been understood to mean that Congress may impose substantive conditions on new States that require the inclusion, for example, of particular provisions or prohibitions in a State's constitution as a condition for admission to the Union.

COYLE v. SMITH
221 U.S. 559 (1911)

LURTON, J., delivered the opinion of the court.

This is a writ of error to the supreme court of Oklahoma to review the judgment of that court upholding a legislative act of the state, providing for the removal of its capital from Guthrie to Oklahoma City....

The question reviewable under this writ of error, if any there be, arises under the claim set up by the petitioner, and decided against him, that the Oklahoma act of December 29, 1910, providing for the immediate location of the capital of the state at Oklahoma City, was void as repugnant to the enabling act of Congress of June 16, 1906, under which the state was admitted to the Union. The 2d section is lengthy and deals with the organization of a constitutional convention, and concludes in these words: 'The capital of said state shall temporarily be at the city of Guthrie…and shall not be changed therefrom previous to Anno Domini nineteen hundred and thirteen; but said capital shall, after said year, be located by the electors of said state at an election to be provided for by the legislature….' The 22d and last section, applicable to Oklahoma, reads thus: 'That the constitutional convention provided for herein shall by ordinance irrevocably accept the terms and conditions of this act.'

The [Oklahoma] Constitution as framed contains nothing as to the location of the state capital; but the convention which framed it adopted a separate ordinance in these words:

> Enabling act accepted by ordinance irrevocable. Be it ordained by the constitutional convention for the proposed state of Oklahoma, that said constitutional convention do, by this ordinance irrevocable, accept the terms and conditions of an act of the Congress of the United States, entitled, 'An Act to Enable the People of Oklahoma and the Indian Territory to Form a Constitution and State Government, and be Admitted into the Union on an Equal Footing with the Original States….'

The only question for review by us is whether the provision of the enabling act was a valid limitation upon the power of the state after its admission, which overrides any subsequent state legislation repugnant thereto.

The power to locate its own seat of government, and to determine when and how it shall be changed from one place to another, and to appropriate its own public funds for that purpose, are essentially and peculiarly state powers. That one of the original thirteen states could now be shorn of such powers by an act of Congress would not be for a moment entertained. The question, then, comes to this: Can a state be placed upon a plane of inequality with its sister states in the Union if the Congress chooses to impose conditions which so operate, at the time of its admission? The argument is, that while Congress may not deprive a state of any power which it *possesses*, it may, as a condition to the admission of a new state, constitutionally restrict its authority, to the extent, at least, of suspending its powers for a definite time in respect to the location of its seat of government. This contention is predicated upon the constitutional power of admitting new states to this Union, and the constitutional duty of guaranteeing to 'every state in this Union a republican form of government.'

The power of Congress in respect to the admission of new states is found in the 3d section of the 4th article of the Constitution. That provision is that, 'new states may be admitted by the Congress into this Union.' The only expressed restriction upon this power is that no new state shall be formed within the jurisdiction of any other state, nor by the junction of two or more states, or parts of states, without the consent of such states, as well as of the Congress. But what is this power? It is not to admit political organizations which are less or greater, or different in dignity or power, from those political entities which constitute the Union.

The definition of 'a state' is found in the powers possessed by the original states which adopted the Constitution,-a definition emphasized by the terms employed in all subsequent acts of Congress admitting new states into the Union. The first two states admitted into the Union were the states of Vermont and Kentucky, one as of March 4, 1791, and the other as of June 1, 1792. No terms or conditions were exacted from either. Each act declares that the state is admitted 'as a new and *entire member* of the United States of America.' [E]ven stronger was the declaration upon the admission in 1796 of Tennessee as the third new state, it being declared to be 'one of the United States of America,' 'on an equal footing with the original states in all respects whatsoever,'—phraseology which has ever since been substantially followed in admission acts, concluding with the Oklahoma act, which declares that Oklahoma shall be admitted 'on an equal footing with the original states.'

The power is to admit 'new states into *this* Union.' 'This Union' was and is a union of states, equal in power, dignity, and authority, each competent to exert that residuum of sovereignty not delegated to the United States by the Constitution itself. To maintain otherwise would be to say that the Union, through the power of Congress to admit new states, might come to be a union of states unequal in power, as including states whose powers were restricted only by the Constitution, with others whose powers had been further restricted by an act of Congress accepted as a condition of admission.

The argument that Congress derives from the duty of 'guaranteeing to each state in this Union a republican form of government,' power to impose restrictions upon a new state which deprive it of equality with other members of the Union, has no merit. It may imply the duty of such new state to provide itself with such state government, and impose upon Congress the duty of seeing that such form is not changed to one anti-republican, but it obviously does not confer power to admit a new state which shall be any less a state than those which compose the Union.

We come now to the question as to whether there is anything in the decisions of this court which sanctions the claim that Congress may, by the imposition of conditions in an enabling act, deprive a new state of any of those attributes essential to its equality in dignity and power with other states.

As to requirements in such enabling acts as relate only to the contents of the Constitution for the proposed new state, little need[s] to be said. The constitutional provision concerning the admission of new states is not a mandate, but a power to be exercised with discretion. From this alone it would follow that Congress may require, under penalty of denying admission, that the organic law of a new state at the time of admission shall be such as to meet its approval. A Constitution thus supervised by Congress would, after all, be a Constitution of a state, and as such subject to alteration and amendment by the state after admission. Its force would be that of a state Constitution, and not that of an act of Congress.

So far as this court has found occasion to advert to the effect of enabling acts as affirmative legislation affecting the power of new states after admission, there is to be found no sanction for the contention that any state may be deprived of any of the power constitutionally possessed by other states, as states, by reason of the terms in which the acts admitting them to the Union have been framed.

The plain deduction from [the Court's] case[s] is that when a new state is admitted into the Union, it is so admitted with all of the powers of sovereignty and jurisdiction which pertain to the original states, and that such powers may not be constitutionally diminished, impaired, or shorn away by any conditions, compacts, or stipulations embraced in the act under which the new state came into the Union, which would not be valid and effectual if the subject of congressional legislation after admission.

It may well happen that Congress should embrace in an enactment introducing a new state into the Union legislation intended as a regulation of commerce among the states, or with Indian tribes situated within the limits of such new state, or regulations touching the sole care and disposition of the public lands or reservations therein, which might be upheld as legislation within the sphere of the plain power of Congress. But in every such case such legislation would derive its force not from any agreement or compact with the proposed new state, nor by reason of its acceptance of such enactment as a term of admission, but solely because the power of Congress extended to the subject, and therefore would not operate to restrict the state's legislative power in respect of any matter which was not plainly within the regulating power of Congress.

No such question is presented here. The legislation in the Oklahoma enabling act relating to the location of the capital of the state, if construed as forbidding a removal by the state after its admission as a state, is referable to no power granted to Congress over the subject, and if it is to be upheld at all, it must be implied from the power to admit new states. If power to impose such a restriction upon the general and undelegated power of a state be conceded as implied from the power to admit a new state, where is the line to be drawn against restrictions imposed upon new states?

Has Oklahoma been admitted upon an equal footing with the original states? If she has, she, by virtue of her jurisdictional sovereignty as such a state, may determine for her own people the proper location of the local seat of government. She is not equal in power to them if she cannot.

In *Lane County v. Oregon*, 7 Wall. 76 [74 U.S. 71, (1868)], [Chief Justice Chase] said:

> The people of the United States constitute one nation, under one government; and this government, within the scope of the powers with which it is invested, is supreme. On the other hand, the people of each state compose state, having its own government, and endowed with all the functions essential to separate and independent existence. The states disunited might continue to exist. Without the states in union there could be no such political body as the United States.

To this we may add that the constitutional equality of the states is essential to the harmonious operation of the scheme upon which the Republic was organized. When that equality disappears we may remain a free people, but the Union will not be the Union of the Constitution.

NOTE

It is unusual, but occasionally Congress has insisted on a particular substantive provision being included in a new state's constitution as a condition of admission to the Union. One notable example is the anti-polygamy provision in several western state constitutions. *See Romer v Evans*, 517 U.S. 620, 648-649 (1996) (Scalia, J., dissenting) ("The Constitutions of the States of Arizona, Idaho, New Mexico, Oklahoma, and Utah...contain provisions stating that polygamy is "forever prohibited." See Ariz. Const., Art. XX, par. 2; Idaho Const., Art. I, § 4; N.M. Const., Art. XXI, § 1; Okla. Const., Art. I, § 2; Utah Const., Art. III, § 1. The United States Congress...*required* the inclusion of these antipolygamy provisions in the Constitutions of Arizona, New Mexico, Oklahoma, and Utah, as a condition of their admission to statehood. See Arizona Enabling Act, 36 Stat. 569; New Mexico Enabling Act, 36 Stat. 558; Oklahoma Enabling Act, 34 Stat. 269; Utah Enabling Act, 28 Stat. 108. (For Arizona, New Mexico, and Utah, moreover, the Enabling Acts required that the antipolygamy provisions be "irrevocable without the consent of the United States and the people of said State".)

5. The Guarantee Clause

A final Article IV provision that could have had significant influence over the States and the state constitutions is the Guarantee Clause, a provision in Section 4 which declares that the "United States shall guarantee to every State in this Union a Republican Form of Government." As the following cases illustrate, however, the Supreme Court of the United States has not been inclined to give this provision substantive content and instead has tended to treat arguments that the Clause has been violated as raising nonjusticiable, political questions that are not to be answered by the courts.

LUTHER v. BORDEN
48 U.S. (7 How.) 1 (1849)

TANEY, C.J., delivered the opinion of the court.

This case has arisen out of the unfortunate political differences which agitated the people of Rhode Island in 1841 and 1842. It is an action of trespass brought by Martin Luther, the plaintiff in error, against Luther M. Borden and others...for breaking and entering the plaintiff's house. The defendants justify upon the ground that large numbers of men were assembled in different parts of the State for the purpose of overthrowing the government by military force, and were actually levying war upon the State; that, in order to defend itself from this insurrection, the State was declared by competent authority to be under martial law; that the plaintiff was engaged in the insurrection; and that the defendants, being in the military service of the State, by command of their superior officer, broke and entered the house and searched the rooms for the plaintiff, who was supposed to be there concealed, in order to arrest him, doing as little damage as possible. The plaintiff replied that the trespass was committed by the defendants of their own proper wrong, and without any such cause.

The evidence offered by the plaintiff and the defendants...and the questions decided by the Circuit Court, and brought up by the writ of error, are not such as commonly arise in an action of trespass. The existence and authority of the government under which the defendants acted was called in question; and the plaintiff insists, that, before the acts complained of were committed, that government had been displaced and annulled by the people of Rhode Island, and that the plaintiff was engaged in supporting the lawful authority of the State, and the defendants themselves were in arms against it.

This is a new question in this court, and certainly a very grave one; and at the time when the trespass is alleged to have been committed it had produced a general and painful excitement in the State, and threatened to end in bloodshed and civil war.

The evidence shows that the defendants, in breaking into the plaintiff's house and endeavouring to arrest him, as stated in the pleadings, acted under the authority of the government which was established in Rhode Island at the time of the Declaration of Independence, and which is usually called the charter government. For when the separation from England took place, Rhode Island did not, like the other States, adopt a new constitution, but continued the form of government established by the charter of Charles the Second in 1663; making only such alterations, by acts of the legislature, as were necessary to adapt it to their condition and rights as an independent State. It was under this form of government that Rhode Island united with the other States in the Declaration of Independence, and afterwards ratified the Constitution of the United States and became a member of this Union; and it continued to be the established and unquestioned government of the State until the difficulties took place which have given rise to this action.

For some years previous to the disturbances of which we are now speaking, many of the citizens became dissatisfied with the charter government, and particularly with the restriction upon the right of suffrage. Memorials were addressed to the legislature upon this subject, urging the justice and necessity of a more liberal and extended rule. But they failed to produce the desired effect. And thereupon meetings were held and associations formed by those who were in favor of a more extended right of suffrage, which finally resulted in the election of a convention to form a new constitution to be submitted to the people for their adoption or rejection. This convention was not authorized by any law of the existing government. It was elected at voluntary meetings, and by those citizens only who favored this plan of reform; those who were opposed to it, or opposed to the manner in which it was proposed to be accomplished, taking no part in the proceedings. The persons chosen as above mentioned came together and framed a constitution, by which the right of suffrage was extended to every male citizen of twenty-one years of age, who had resided in the State for one year, and in the town in which he offered to vote, for six months, next preceding the election. The convention also prescribed the manner in which this constitution should be submitted to the decision of the people,-permitting everyone to vote on that question who was an American citizen, twenty-one years old, and who had a permanent residence or home in the State.

Upon the return of the votes, the convention declared that the constitution was adopted and ratified by a majority of the people of the State.... The charter government did not, however, admit the validity of these proceedings, nor acquiesce in them. On the contrary, when this new constitution was communicated to the governor, and by him laid before the legislature, it passed resolutions declaring all acts done for the purpose of imposing that constitution upon the State to be an assumption of the powers of government, in violation of the rights of the existing government and of the people at large; and that it would maintain its authority and defend the legal and constitutional rights of the people.

But, notwithstanding the determination of the charter government, and of those who adhered to it, to maintain its authority, Thomas W. Dorr, who had been elected governor under the new constitution, prepared to assert the authority of that government by force, and many citizens assembled in arms to support him. The charter government thereupon passed an act declaring the State under martial law, and at the same time proceeded to call out the militia, to repel the threatened attack and to subdue those who were engaged in it. In this state of the contest, the house of the plaintiff, who was engaged in supporting the authority of the new government, was broken and entered in order to arrest him. The defendants were, at the time, in the military service of the old government, and in arms to support its authority.

The plaintiff contends that the charter government was displaced, and ceased to have any lawful power, after the organization, in May, 1842, of the government which he supported, and although that government never was able to exercise any authority in the State, nor to command obedience to its laws or to its officers, yet he insists that it was the lawful and established government, upon the ground that it was ratified by a large majority of the male people of the State of the age of twenty-one and upwards.

The Circuit Court…instructed the jury that the charter government and laws under which the defendants acted were, at the time the trespass is alleged to have been committed, in full force and effect as the form of government and paramount law of the State, and constituted a justification of the acts of the defendants.

Certainly, the question which the plaintiff proposed to raise by the testimony he offered has not heretofore been recognized as a judicial one in any of the State courts. Undoubtedly the courts of the United States have certain powers under the Constitution and laws of the United States which do not belong to the State courts. But the power of determining that a State government has been lawfully established, which the courts of the State disown and repudiate, is not one of them. Upon such a question the courts of the United States are bound to follow the decisions of the State tribunals, and must therefore regard the charter government as the lawful established government during the time of this contest.

Moreover, the Constitution of the United States, as far as it has provided for an emergency of this kind, and authorized the general government to interfere in the domestic concerns of a State, has treated the subject as political in its nature, and placed the power in the hands of that department. The fourth section of the fourth article of the Constitution of the United States provides that the United States shall guarantee to every State in the Union a republican form of government, and shall protect each of them against invasion; and on the application of the legislature or of the executive (when the legislature cannot be convened) against domestic violence.

Under this article of the Constitution it rests with Congress to decide what government is the established one in a State. For as the United States guarantee to each State a republican government, Congress must necessarily decide what government is established in the State before it can determine whether it is republican or not. And when the senators and representatives of a State are admitted into the councils of the Union, the authority of the government under which they are appointed, as well as its republican character, is recognized by the proper constitutional authority. And its decision is binding on every other department of the government, and could not be questioned in a judicial tribunal.

Congress…by the act of February 28, 1795, provided, that, 'in case of an insurrection in any State against the government thereof, it shall be lawful for the President of the United States, on application of the legislature of such State or of the executive (when the legislature cannot be convened), to call forth such number of the militia of any other State or States, as may be applied for, as he may judge sufficient to sufficient to suppress such insurrection.'

By this act, the power of deciding whether the exigency had arisen upon which the government of the United States is bound to interfere, is given to the President. He is to act upon the application of the legislature or of the executive, and consequently he must determine what body of men constitute the legislature, and who is the governor, before he can act. The fact that both parties claim the right to the government cannot alter the case, for both cannot be entitled to it. If there is an armed conflict, like the one of which we are speaking, it is a case of domestic violence, and one of the parties must be in insurrection against the lawful government. And the President must, of necessity, decide which is the government, and which party is unlawfully arrayed against it.

After the President has acted and called out the militia, is a Circuit Court of the United States authorized to inquire whether his decision was right? If the judicial power extends so far, the guarantee contained in the Constitution of the United States is a guarantee of anarchy, and not of order. No one, we believe, has ever doubted the proposition, that, according to the institutions of this country, the sovereignty in every State resides in the people of the State, and that they may alter and change their form of government at their own pleasure. But whether they have changed it or not by abolishing an old government, and establishing a new one in its place, is a question to be settled by the political power.

PACIFIC STATES TELEPHONE & TELEGRAPH CO. v. OREGON
223 U.S. 118 (1912)

WHITE, C.J., delivered the opinion of the court.

We premise by saying that while the controversy which this record presents is of much importance, it is not novel. It is important, since it calls upon us to decide whether it is the duty of the courts or the province of Congress to determine when a state has ceased to be republican in form, and to enforce the guaranty of the Constitution on that subject. It is not novel, as that question has long since been determined by this court conformably to the practice of the government from the beginning to be political in character, and therefore not cognizable by the judicial power, but solely committed by the Constitution to the judgment of Congress.

The case is this: In 1902 Oregon amended its Constitution. This amendment, while retaining an existing clause vesting the exclusive legislative power in a general assembly consisting of a senate and a house of representatives, added to that provision the following: 'But the people reserve to themselves power to propose laws and amendments to the Constitution, and to enact or reject the same at the polls, independent of the legislative assembly, and also reserve power at their own option to approve or reject at the polls any act of the legislative assembly.' Specific means for the exercise of the power thus reserved was contained in further clauses authorizing both the amendment of the Constitution and the enactment of laws to be accomplished by the method known as the initiative and that commonly referred to as the referendum. In 1903 detailed provisions for the carrying into effect of this amendment were enacted by the legislature.

By resort to the initiative in 1906, a law taxing certain classes of corporations was submitted, voted on, and promulgated by the governor in 1907 as having been duly adopted. By this law telephone and telegraph companies were taxed, by what was qualified as an annual license, 2 per centum upon their gross revenue derived from business done within the state. Penalties were provided for nonpayment, and methods were created for enforcing payment in case of delinquency.

The Pacific States Telephone & Telegraph Company, an Oregon corporation engaged in business in that state, made a return of its gross receipts, as required by the statute, and was accordingly assessed 2 per cent upon the amount of such return. The suit which is now before us was commenced by the state to enforce payment of this assessment and the statutory penalties for delinquency. [The company challenged the tax assessment, lost, and appealed to the Supreme Court.]

The assignments of error...are numerous. The entire matters covered by each and all of them in the argument, however, are reduced to six propositions, which really amount to but one.... In other words, the propositions [of alleged error] each and all proceed alone upon the theory that the adoption of the initiative and referendum destroyed all government republican in form in Oregon. Before immediately considering the text of § 4 of article 4, in order to uncover and give emphasis to the anomalous and destructive effects upon both the state and national governments which the adoption of the proposition implies,...let us briefly fix the inconceivable expansion of the judicial power and the ruinous destruction of legislative authority in matters purely political which would necessarily be occasioned by giving sanction to the doctrine which underlies and would be necessarily involved in sustaining the propositions contended for.

We shall not stop to consider the text [of Article IV, § 4] to point out how absolutely barren it is of support for the contentions sought to be based upon it, since the repugnancy of those contentions to the letter and spirit of that text is so conclusively established by prior decisions of this court as to cause the matter to be absolutely foreclosed. In view of the importance of the subject, the apparent misapprehension on one side and seeming misconception on the other, suggested by the argument as to the full significance of the previous doctrine, we do not content ourselves with a mere citation of the cases, but state more at length than we otherwise would the issues and the doctrine expounded in the leading and absolutely controlling case, *Luther v. Borden*, 7 How. 1 [1849]. [The Court then examines and quotes at length from *Luther*.]

The fundamental doctrines thus so lucidly and cogently announced by the court, speaking through Mr. Chief Justice Taney in [*Luther*], have never been doubted or questioned since, and have afforded the light guiding the orderly development of our constitutional system from the day of the deliverance of that decision up to the present time. It is indeed a singular misconception of the nature and character of our constitutional system of government to suggest that the settled distinction...between judicial authority over justiciable controversies and legislative power as to purely political questions tends to destroy the duty of the judiciary in proper cases to enforce the Constitution. The suggestion but results from failing to distinguish between things which are widely different; that is, the legislative duty to determine the political questions involved in deciding whether a state government republican in form exists, and the judicial power and ever-present duty whenever it becomes necessary, in a controversy properly submitted, to enforce and uphold the applicable provisions of the Constitution as to each and every exercise of governmental power.

How better can the broad lines which distinguish these two subjects be pointed out than by considering the character of the defense in this very case? The defendant company does not contend here that it could not have been required to pay a license tax. It does not assert that it was denied an opportunity to be heard as to the amount for which it was taxed, or that there was anything inhering in the tax or involved intrinsically in the law which violated any of its constitutional rights. If such questions had been raised, they would have been justiciable, and therefore would have required the calling into operation of judicial power. Instead, however, of doing any of these things, the attack on the statute here made is of a wholly different character. Its essentially political nature is at once made manifest by understanding that the assault which the contention here advanced makes is not on the tax as a tax, but on the state as a state. It is addressed to the framework and political character of the government by which the statute levying the tax was passed. It is the government, the political entity, which (reducing the case to its essence) is called to the bar of this court, not for the purpose of testing judicially some exercise of power, assailed on the ground that its exertion has injuriously affected the rights of an individual because of repugnancy to some constitutional limitation, but to demand of the state that it establish its right to exist as a state, republican in form.

As the issues presented, in their very essence, are, and have long since by this court been, definitely determined to be political and governmental, and embraced within the scope of the powers conferred upon Congress, and not, therefore, within the reach of judicial power, it follows that the case presented is not within our jurisdiction, and the writ of error must therefore be, and it is, dismissed for want of jurisdiction.

KERR v. HICKENLOOPER
744 F.3d 1156 (10th Cir. 2014)

LUCERO, C.J.

Article IV, § 4 of the Constitution of the United States of America guarantees to the State of Colorado a "Republican Form of Government." It provides: "The United States shall guarantee to every State in this Union a Republican Form of Government, and shall protect each of them against Invasion; and on Application of the Legislature, or of the Executive (when the Legislature cannot be convened) against domestic Violence." U.S. Const. art. IV, § 4. This right to a republican form of government is further assured and mandated by the enabling act of Congress, Colorado Enabling Act, ch. 139, § 4, 18 Stat. 474 (1875), under which the State was admitted to the Union in 1876.

bound to follow the decisions of the State tribunals." The Court also discussed the Guarantee Clause, labeling the issue of which government was valid as "political in its nature," vested not in the judiciary but in Congress. "Under [the Guarantee Clause] it rests with Congress to decide what government is the established one in a State."

Pacific States involved a fact pattern similar to the one before us, but a much broader legal challenge. Shortly after Oregon amended its state constitution to permit lawmaking by initiative and referendum, the people enacted "a law taxing certain classes of corporations." A corporation affected by the new tax challenged its legitimacy, alleging that "by the adoption of the initiative and referendum, the State violates the right to a republican form of government." "In other words," said the Court, "the propositions [of error in the complaint] each and all proceed alone upon the theory that the adoption of the initiative and referendum destroyed all government republican in form in Oregon." Construing the plaintiff's complaint as an attempt to overturn "not only ... the particular statute which is before us, but ... every other statute passed in Oregon since the adoption of the initiative and referendum," the Justices held "the issues presented, in their very essence, [to be] ... political and governmental, and embraced within the scope of powers conferred upon Congress."

Both the *Luther* and *Pacific States* claims differ from those at bar. Importantly, both cases involved wholesale attacks on the validity of a state's government rather than, as before us, a challenge to a single provision of a state constitution. There can nevertheless be little doubt that these cases include language suggesting that Guarantee Clause litigation is categorically barred by the political question doctrine. In *Luther*, the Court stated that "Congress must necessarily decide what government is established in the State before it can determine whether it is republican or not." And when the *Pacific States* Court faced the question of "whether it is the duty of the courts or the province of Congress to determine when a State has ceased to be republican in form, and to enforce the guaranty of the Constitution on that subject," it declared that the issue was "political in character, and therefore not cognizable by the judicial power, but solely committed by the Constitution to the judgment of Congress."

Had those been the Supreme Court's final words on the justiciability of the Guarantee Clause, a categorical approach might be proper. However, the Court in *Baker* highlighted the proposition that its prior political question cases turned on a number of "attributes which, in various settings, diverge, combine, appear, and disappear in seeming disorderliness" and that much confusion had resulted "from the capacity of the 'political question' label to obscure the need for case-by-case inquiry." After reviewing its prior cases applying the political question doctrine, the Court explained that "several formulations which vary slightly according to the settings in which the questions arise may describe a political question."

Baker then announced six factors that render a case non-justiciable under the political question doctrine:

> [A] textually demonstrable constitutional commitment of the issue to a coordinate political department; or a lack of judicially discoverable and manageable standards for resolving it; or the impossibility of deciding without an initial policy determination of a kind clearly for nonjudicial discretion; or the impossibility of a court's undertaking independent resolution without expressing lack of the respect due coordinate branches of government; or an unusual need for unquestioning adherence to a political decision already made; or the potentiality of embarrassment from multifarious pronouncements by various departments on one question.

"Unless one of these formulations is *inextricable* from the case at bar, there should be no dismissal for nonjusticiability on the ground of a political question's presence."

Given the clarity of this holding, we must agree with the plaintiffs that the six tests identified in *Baker* are the exclusive bases for dismissing a case under the political question doctrine. Furthermore, the *Baker* Court explicitly rejected a categorical Guarantee Clause bar. Immediately after announcing the six political question factors, the Court addressed the argument that the case under its consideration "shares the characteristics of decisions that constitute a category not yet considered, cases concerning the Constitution's guaranty, in Art. IV, § 4, of a republican form of government." It determined that the prior cases in which the Court had considered "Guaranty Clause claims involve those elements which define a 'political question,'" referencing the aforementioned six factors, "*and for that reason and no other*, they are nonjusticiable." "[N]onjusticiability of such claims has nothing to do with their touching upon matters of state governmental organization."

The *Baker* opinion includes a lengthy discussion of *Luther*, ultimately concluding that the decision rested on four of the six previously identified factors:

> the commitment to the other branches of the decision as to which is the lawful state government; the unambiguous action by the President, in recognizing the charter government as the lawful authority; the need for finality in the executive's decision; and the lack of criteria by which a court could determine which form of government was republican.

A reading of *Luther* under which "the political question barrier was ... absolute" was rejected, with the Court continuing that in some circumstances a court could determine "the limits of the meaning of 'republican form,' and thus the factor of lack of criteria might fall away." Even then, however, "there would remain other possible barriers to decision because of primary commitment to another branch, which would have to be considered in the particular fact setting presented." *Id.* In recognizing *Luther* as standing solely for the proposition that "the Guaranty Clause is not a repository of judicially manageable standards which a court could utilize independently in order to identify a State's lawful government," it clarified that it had consistently declined to resort to the clause as a "standard for invalidating state action."

Relying on the Court's directive in *Baker* that "there should be no dismissal for non-justiciability on the ground of a political question's presence" absent one of the specifically identified factors, we reject the proposition that *Luther* and *Pacific States* brand all Guarantee Clause claims as per se non-justiciable.

B

We must yet apply the six-factor test announced in *Baker*.

1

Initially, we consider whether the Guarantee Clause manifests "a textually demonstrable constitutional commitment of the issue to a coordinate political department." The Guarantee Clause provides: "The United States shall guarantee to every State in this Union a Republican Form of Government, and shall protect each of them against Invasion; and on Application of the Legislature, or of the Executive (when the Legislature cannot be convened) against domestic Violence." U.S. Const. art. IV, § 4.

The text of the Guarantee Clause does not mention any branch of the federal government. It commits the "United States"—which would normally be read as including the Article III courts—to the preservation of republican government in the states. The Guarantee Clause is found not in Article I or Article II, where we would expect to find it if its provisions were textually committed to another branch, but in Article IV. Moreover, two other provisions of Article IV specifically empower Congress to act, but the Guarantee Clause does not. The omission of any mention of Congress from the Guarantee Clause, despite Congress' prominence elsewhere in Article IV, indicates there is no "textually demonstrable commitment"—certainly not an inextricable one—barring our review or district court consideration of this case. *Baker*'s refusal to bar Guarantee Clause claims on an "absolute" basis would be rendered a nullity if the clause itself contained a textual commitment to the coordinate political branches.

2

We are similarly unpersuaded that a "lack of judicially discoverable and manageable standards," precludes judicial review of this lawsuit. As construed by *Baker*, the *Luther* decision rested in part on the lack of criteria for determining which government was legitimately republican. We reiterate that this holding rests on the impossibility of applying judicial standards to choose between two governments that each claim to be valid, rather than any extraordinary vagueness in the text of the Guarantee Clause itself. The *Luther* Court asked "by what rule could it have determined the qualification of voters upon the adoption or rejection of the proposed constitution, unless there was some previous law of the State to guide it," and answered: The Court lacks "the right to determine what political privileges the citizens of a State are entitled to, unless there is an established constitution or law to govern its decision." That is not this case.

There is sparse judicial precedent interpreting the Guarantee Clause to aid our analysis. Even Guarantee Clause cases in which the Supreme Court declined to invoke the political question doctrine do not provide much meaningful guidance in this case. "Judicially manageable standards" must include—but cannot be limited to—precedent. We must not "hold[ ] a case nonjusticiable under the second *Baker* test without first undertaking an exhaustive search for applicable standards." *Alperin v. Vatican Bank*, 410 F.3d 532, 552 (9th Cir.2005).

Before the Supreme Court's decision in *District of Columbia v. Heller*, 554 U.S. 570 (2008), there was similarly sparse judicial interpretation of the Second Amendment at both the state and federal levels. Outside the judiciary, historians and law professors studied the meaning of the Amendment, relying on sources typically used to aid constitutional interpretation: dictionaries, ratification history, contemporary treatises, and the like. Meanwhile, states and localities had developed various provisions regulating firearms. There is no evidence that the Court in *Heller* even considered the possibility that the sources available to it could be insufficient for developing judicially discoverable and manageable standards.

As it was with the Second Amendment, so it is with the Guarantee Clause. We are directed, by both parties and by various amici, to sources that courts have relied on for centuries to aid them in constitutional interpretation. Briefing directs us to several of the Federalist Papers, founding-era dictionaries, records of the Constitutional Convention, and other papers of the founders. We have the authority to take judicial notice of other state constitutional provisions regulating the legislature's power to tax and spend. At this stage of the litigation, we must strike a delicate balance between acknowledging that repositories of judicially manageable standards exist and allowing further record development in the district court before the merits of the case are adjudicated.

3

With respect to the third *Baker* test, we conclude that resolving this case will not require the making of a "policy determination of a kind clearly for nonjudicial discretion." TABOR is a hotly contested issue in Colorado that has had a wide-ranging influence on the state's fiscal policy. But the interpretation of constitutional text—even vague constitutional text—is central to the judicial role. We "cannot avoid [our] responsibility merely because the issues have political implications."

Plaintiffs do not ask the court to balance delicate policy matters similar to market conditions, budgeting priorities, or foreign policy concerns. Instead, they seek a ruling as to whether state government under TABOR is republican in form.

If adjudicating this case required us or the district court to determine the wisdom of allocating certain traditionally legislative powers to the people, the third *Baker* factor would dictate dismissal. But deciding whether a state's form of government meets a constitutionally mandated threshold does not require any sort of "policy determination" as courts applying the *Baker* tests have understood that phrase. The case before us requires that we determine the meaning of a piece of constitutional text and then decide whether a state constitutional provision contravenes the federal command.

4

We dispense briefly with the remaining three *Baker* factors: "[4] the impossibility of a court's undertaking independent resolution without expressing lack of the respect due coordinate branches of government; or [5] an unusual need for unquestioning adherence to a political decision already made; or [6] the potentiality of embarrassment from multifarious pronouncements by various departments on one question." These factors are best understood as promoting separation-of-powers principles in cases featuring prior action on an issue by a coordinate branch.

We are aware of no action taken by either Congress or the executive with respect to this litigation specifically or TABOR generally. Both the people and courts of Colorado have made pronouncements on TABOR. However, the possibility that federal judicial decisions will conflict with a state referendum or a state court decision does not implicate the political question doctrine. Such conflicts are an ordinary part of the judicial process.

We thus affirm the district court's conclusion that the specific Guarantee Clause claim asserted in this case is not barred by the political question doctrine.

VI

We emphasize once again that this interlocutory appeal allows us to consider only whether the legislator-plaintiffs have established Article III standing and whether prudential standing jurisprudence or the political question doctrine precludes consideration of their Guarantee Clause and Enabling Act claims. Our answer to those questions completes our role at this stage of the proceedings.

CHAPTER III

THEORIES BY WHICH STATE COURTS MAY CONSTRUE STATE CONSTITUTIONS DIFFERENTLY FROM THEIR FEDERAL COUNTERPARTS

In this chapter, we develop one of the main themes of the textbook: the reasons why state courts might choose to construe a guarantee in their own constitutions differently from a related guarantee in the U.S. Constitution. Before discussing what state courts might do in this respect, it is worth remembering why they may do it. The Supremacy Clause of the U.S. Constitution says that the "Constitution...of the United States...shall be the supreme Law of the Land" and makes "the Judges in every State...bound thereby," notwithstanding any "Thing in the Constitution...of any State to the Contrary." U.S. Const. art. VI. The Clause amounts to a conflict-of-laws provision. Much as the U.S. Constitution governs when it conflicts with a federal statute, *see Marbury v. Madison*, 5 U.S. 137 (1803), so the Supremacy Clause establishes that federal law governs when it conflicts with a state statute or state constitution. In establishing that federal law trumps contrary state law, however, the Supremacy Clause does nothing to limit the force of state law in the absence of a relevant federal provision or decision. That means the state supreme courts not only have the final say over the meaning of their own constitutions, but they also have the final say over the "constitutional" limitations in the State to the extent those limitations exceed any floor set by the U.S. Constitution.

Another way to think about it is this: A litigant challenging the validity of a state or local law may seek relief under the federal or the relevant state constitution. The Framers established a government that features two sets of sovereigns over any given part of the country, that produced fifty-one constitutions, and that in the end places two constitutional limitations on the validity of most state and local laws. The constitutional claimant needs to win just once, and a victory under the one invalidates a local law no less than a victory under the other. One upshot of a federal system of dual sovereignty is that it permits dual claims of unconstitutionality.

To say that a state supreme court *may* invalidate a law under its constitution, however, is not to say that it *should*. The key point of this chapter is to offer reasons why state courts in some areas have charted different paths from the U.S. Supreme Court in construing identical or related constitutional guarantees. The chapter breaks down into four parts. The first considers the reasons why a state court might choose to construe an identically worded guarantee in its own constitution differently from a parallel provision in the U.S. Constitution. The second part considers the state courts' treatment of uniquely worded guarantees. The third part considers two related topics: (1) why a state court might choose not to chart a separate path from the federal constitutional baseline and (2) how one determines whether a state court has relied on an independent and adequate state law ground and thereby insulated its ruling from review by the U.S. Supreme Court. The fourth part addresses a sequencing question that state courts face in resolving every case that raises a state and federal constitutional claim: Which answer comes first? Should the state courts resolve the state claim before resolving the related federal claim? Or should they resolve the federal claims first? Through it all, should the state courts presume that the U.S. Supreme Court's resolution of a federal constitutional claim is presumptively correct when construing similar state guarantees? The chapter is prelude to the next several chapters of the casebook, which develop these themes in the context of specific areas of constitutional law, such as equal protection, due process, property rights, criminal procedure, and many others.

A. SIMILARLY WORDED GUARANTEES

Why might a state supreme court construe an individual-rights guarantee of its state constitution differently from one found in the U.S. Constitution and do so even when the guarantees parallel each other word for word? There are several reasons.

Scope of jurisdiction. The U.S. Supreme Court, in the first place, faces geographical and jurisdictional challenges that the state courts do not. Because the Supreme Court must announce rights and remedies for fifty States, one National Government and over 320 million people, it is far more constrained than a state supreme court addressing a difficult problem for one State and ten million people. All U.S. Supreme Court Justices, no matter the president who appointed them or the worldview they embrace, are sensitive to the risks of issuing rulings that prevent the democratic processes from working in fifty-one different jurisdictions.

New constitutional rights not only require the articulation of a new constitutional theory, they also require the management of a new constitutional right. All judges worry about the next case when they identify a new constitutional right. But U.S. Supreme Court Justices have more to worry about than state court judges in view of the breadth of their jurisdiction and the wider variety of circumstances that each new right will confront. In some settings, the challenge of imposing a constitutional solution on the whole country at once will increase the likelihood that federal constitutional law will be under-enforced or that a federalism discount will be applied to the right. Jeffrey S. Sutton, San Antonio Independent School District v. Rodriguez *and Its Aftermath*, 94 Va. L. Rev. 1963, 1979 (2008). State courts face no such problem in construing their own constitutions.

[handwritten: faster to "correct" state cm law issues]

A mistaken or an ill-conceived constitutional decision is also easier to correct at the state level than it is at the federal level. Not only do the state courts have a narrower jurisdiction and smaller populations that their decisions will affect, but the people at the state level have other remedies at their disposal: an easier constitutional amendment process and, for better or worse, judicial elections. In some settings, these considerations will give state courts more room to innovate—to be the familiar "laboratories of experimentation" that Justice Brandeis envisioned.

Local conditions and traditions. State courts also have a freer hand to do something the Supreme Court cannot: to allow local conditions and traditions to affect their interpretation of a constitutional guarantee and the remedies imposed to implement that guarantee. In one State, the right to privacy may warrant greater protection than in another. In a rural State, individual property rights and the right to bear arms may warrant greater protection than in a State with large suburban and urban populations. Free exercise concerns may resonate differently in some States than in others. And the right to equal protection, and its application to the definition of marriage, may be viewed differently in some States than in others. State constitutional law respects these distinct traditions by allowing the fifty constitutions to be interpreted differently to account for these differences in culture, geography, and history. Through it all, the counterpart guarantees of the U.S. Constitution provide a potential floor in each of these areas.

[handwritten: state courts can carve many cultural decisions]

Indeterminate questions. Another reason why the state courts might not follow the federal courts in construing identical constitutional guarantees is that the legal and equitable complexities of many issues do not lend themselves to one-size-fits-all solutions. Some constitutional issues do not readily submit to a clear answer, and indeterminate legal questions often lead to indeterminate legal answers. The federal courts might apply a balancing test in construing a liberty guarantee, while the state courts might apply a bright-line rule or might adopt a balancing test but balance the competing interests differently. The federal courts might adopt an originalist approach in construing a guarantee, while the state courts might embrace a living constitutionalist approach to the same language. Another protection might be construed in a pragmatic way in the federal courts but construed in a formalistic way in a state court. The more indeterminate the answer to a legal question the more one should expect federal and state court judges of good will, faced with distinct

[handwritten: Trugh as give state courts room to apply diff answers]

geographical limitations on their power, to construe similar language differently.

Disagreement with the U.S. Supreme Court. In some cases, the state court's analysis comes to nothing more than an analytical or policy-based objection to the federal precedent. While these cases may be influenced by the above factors, the theme that dominates the state court's ruling is a fundamental disagreement with the National Court's interpretation of similar language. A system of dual sovereignty contemplates, tolerates, and ultimately embraces state and federal differences of opinion.

In the cases that follow, and in the chapters that follow, ask yourself why the state courts chose to construe the guarantees of their constitutions differently from the similarly worded guarantees of the U.S. Constitution.

SITZ v. DEPARTMENT OF STATE POLICE
506 N.W.2d 209 (Mich. 1993)

BOYLE, J.

The case before us concerns a challenge to the use of sobriety checkpoints by the Michigan State Police. The United States Supreme Court held that the checkpoint scheme does not constitute a violation of the Fourth Amendment of the United States Constitution. *Michigan Dep't of State Police v. Sitz*, 496 U.S. 444 (1990). On remand from that Court, a two-judge majority of the Michigan Court of Appeals determined that sobriety checkpoints violate art. 1, § 11 of the Michigan Constitution. Because there is no support in the constitutional history of Michigan for the proposition that the police may engage in warrantless and suspicionless seizures of automobiles for the purpose of enforcing the criminal law, we hold that sobriety check points violate art. 1, § 11 of the Michigan Constitution.

The first sobriety checkpoint operation was conducted at Dixie Highway and Gretchen Road in Saginaw County on May 17 and 18, 1986. The Saginaw County Sheriff's Department cooperated in the operation which lasted from about 11:45 p.m. to 1:00 a.m. One hundred twenty-six vehicles passed through the checkpoint in that time, with an average delay to motorists of twenty-five seconds or less. Two drivers were retained for sobriety field tests; one was arrested for driving while under the influence of alcohol. A third driver drove through the checkpoint without stopping, was pulled over by an officer in an observation vehicle, and was arrested for driving under the influence.

[The U.S. Supreme Court held] that the Michigan sobriety checkpoint program did not violate the Fourth Amendment of the United States Constitution: "In sum, the balance of the State's interest in preventing drunken driving, the extent to which this system can reasonably be said to advance that interest, and the degree of intrusion upon individual motorists who are briefly stopped, weighs in favor of the state program. We therefore hold that it is consistent with the Fourth Amendment...." *Sitz*, 496 U.S. at 455.

During the decade of United States Supreme Court jurisprudence "commonly characterized as the 'criminal law revolution of the Warren Court,'" the Supreme Court "rapidly extend[ed] the reach of various constitutional provisions applicable to the criminal justice process...." 1 LaFave & Israel, Criminal Procedure, § 2.1, p. 56 and n. 1. Subsequent decisions of the Burger Court were characterized by some commentators as pulling back from, suspending, or weakening the scope of constitutional protections, including the specific guarantees of the Bill of Rights.

Awakened to the potential for a reappraisal of claims based on state constitutional grounds, members of the Michigan bar joined their colleagues across the country in pressing claims seeking interpretations of state law that provided more expansive criminal procedure protections than those recognized under federal law. By 1983, the number of rights-expansive claims based on state law had proliferated to the point that guidance from this Court was deemed both appropriate and necessary.

Thus, in *People v. Nash*, 418 Mich. 196, 341 N.W.2d 439 (1983), the Court conducted the first modern-day comprehensive survey of the circumstances surrounding the creation of Const. 1963, art. 1, § 11 to determine whether our constitution required a higher level of search and seizure protection than the Fourth Amendment of the United States Constitution. Our conclusion in *Nash*, that "[t]he history of Const. 1963, art. 1, § 11, and its plain import, ... suggest that its further expansion ... should occur only when there is a compelling reason to do so" was intended to clarify for the bench and bar that claims that art. 1, § 11 should be interpreted more expansively than the Fourth Amendment must rest on more than a disagreement with the United States Supreme Court.

Our analysis in *Nash* began by noting that the federal and state constitutional provisions that forbid unreasonable searches and seizures are nearly identical.[1]

---

[1]U.S. Const., Am. IV provides:

The right of the people to be secure in their persons, houses, papers, and effects, against unreasonable searches and seizures, shall not be violated, and no Warrants shall issue, but upon probable cause, supported by Oath or affirmation, and particularly describing the place to be searched, and the persons or things to be seized.

Const. 1963, art. 1, § 11 provides:

The person, houses, papers and possessions of every person shall be secure from unreasonable searches and seizures. No warrant to search any place or to seize any person or things shall issue without describing them, nor without probable cause, supported by

The judiciary of this state is not free to simply engraft onto art. 1, § 11 more "enlightened" rights than the framers intended. By the same token, we may not disregard the guarantees that our constitution confers on Michigan citizens merely because the United States Supreme Court has withdrawn or not extended such protection.

The Michigan Declaration of Rights, like the federal Bill of Rights, is "drawn to restrict governmental conduct and to provide protection from governmental infringement and excesses...." *Woodland v. Citizens Lobby*, 423 Mich. 188, 204, 378 N.W.2d 337 (1985). When there is a clash of competing rights under the state and federal constitutions, the Supremacy Clause, art. VI, cl. 2, dictates that the federal right prevails. Where a right is given to a citizen under federal law, it does not follow that the organic instrument of state government must be interpreted as conferring the identical right. Nor does it follow that where a right given by the federal constitution is not given by a state constitution, the state constitution offends the federal constitution. It is only where the organic instrument of government purports to deprive a citizen of a right granted by the federal constitution that the instrument can be said to violate the constitution.

Thus, appropriate analysis of our constitution does not begin from the conclusive premise of a federal floor. Indeed, the fragile foundation of the federal floor as a bulwark against arbitrary action is clearly revealed when, as here, the federal floor falls below minimum state protection. As a matter of simple logic, because the texts were written at different times by different people, the protections afforded may be greater, lesser, or the same.

As long ago as 1889, the justices of this Court stated:

> Personal liberty, which is guaranteed to every citizen under our Constitution and laws, consists of the right of locomotion—to go where one pleases, and when, and to do that which may lead to one's business or pleasure, only so far restrained as the rights of others may make it necessary for the welfare of all other citizens. One may travel along the public highways or in public places; and while conducting themselves in a decent and orderly manner, disturbing no other, and interfering with the rights of no other citizens, there, they will be protected under the law, not only in their persons, but in their safe conduct. The Constitution and the laws are framed for the public good, and the protection of all citizens, from the highest to the lowest; and no one may be restrained of his liberty, unless he has transgressed some law. [*Pinkerton v. Verberg*, 78 Mich. 573, 584, 44 N.W. 579 (1889).]

Our commitment to the protection of liberty was further demonstrated when the Supreme Court of Michigan adopted an exclusionary rule in

---

oath or affirmation. The provisions of this section shall not be construed to bar from evidence in any criminal proceeding any narcotic drug, firearm, bomb, explosive or any other dangerous weapon, seized by a peace officer outside the curtilage of any dwelling house in this state....

1919, forty-two years before it was mandated by federal law. *People v. Marxhausen*, 204 Mich. 559, 171 N.W. 557 (1919). Moreover, as the cases discussed in part IV demonstrate, this Court's "historical general power ... to construe the constitutional provision relating to searches and seizures," *Nash, supra*, 418 Mich. at 214, 341 N.W.2d 439, has been extended to the seizure and search of vehicles.

[T]he history of our jurisprudence conclusively demonstrates that, in the context of automobile seizures, we have extended more expansive protection to our citizens than that extended in *Sitz*. This Court has never recognized the right of the state, without any level of suspicion whatsoever, to detain members of the population at large for criminal investigatory purposes. Nor has Michigan completely acquiesced to the judgment of "politically accountable officials" when determining reasonableness in such a context. *Sitz*, 496 U.S. at 453. In these circumstances, the Michigan Constitution offers more protection than the United States Supreme Court's interpretation of the Fourth Amendment.

In *Roache, supra*, 237 Mich. at 222, this Court showed a marked hostility toward the use of a license check as a pretext to investigate criminal activity. In *Lansing Municipal Judge, supra*, 327 Mich. at 432, we stressed:

> It will be said that no legislature would go so far as to dry up the entire stream of constitutional immunity. But it is not the genius of our system that the constitutional rights of persons shall depend for their efficacy upon legislative benevolence. Rather, the courts are charged with the solemn obligation of erecting around those rights, in adjudicated cases, a barrier against legislative or executive invasion.

The Michigan Constitution has historically treated searches and seizures for criminal investigatory purposes differently than those for regulatory or administrative purposes. These administrative or regulatory searches and seizures have traditionally been regarded as "reasonable" in a constitutional sense. However, seizures with the primary goal of enforcing the criminal law have generally required some level of suspicion, even if that level has fluctuated over the years.

We do not suggest that in a different context we might not reach a similar result under the balancing test of reasonableness employed in *Sitz*. Indeed, our precedent regarding automobiles implicitly incorporates a balancing test that is inherent in assessing the reasonableness of warrantless searches and seizures. We hold only that the protection afforded to the seizures of vehicles for criminal investigatory purposes has both an historical foundation and a contemporary justification that is not outweighed by the necessity advanced. Suspicionless criminal investigatory seizures, and extreme deference to the judgments of politically accountable officials is, in this context, contrary to Michigan constitutional precedent.

NOTES

1. Consider the following excerpts from the U.S. Supreme Court's decision in *Sitz* remanding the case to the Michigan Supreme Court:

> Conversely, the weight bearing on the other scale—the measure of the intrusion on motorists stopped briefly at sobriety checkpoints—is slight. We reached a similar conclusion as to the intrusion on motorists subjected to a brief stop at a highway checkpoint for detecting illegal aliens. We see virtually no difference between the levels of intrusion on law-abiding motorists from the brief stops necessary to the effectuation of these two types of checkpoints, which to the average motorist would seem identical save for the nature of the questions the checkpoint officers might ask. The trial court and the Court of Appeals, thus, accurately gauged the "objective" intrusion, measured by the duration of the seizure and the intensity of the investigation, as minimal.

> [T]he balance of the State's interest in preventing drunken driving, the extent to which this system can reasonably be said to advance that interest, and the degree of intrusion upon individual motorists who are briefly stopped, weighs in favor of the state program. We therefore hold that it is consistent with the Fourth Amendment.

Mich. Dep't of State Police v. Sitz, 496 U.S. 444, 451-52, 455 (1990).

Did the state court simply balance these interests differently? Did it rely on traditions unique to Michigan? Did it simply disagree with the U.S. Supreme Court?

2. One reason that state courts often follow U.S. Supreme Court decisions in construing their own constitutional guarantees is the benefit of uniformity—one standard for state court judges to use and one standard for state officials to follow. But, as Justice Appel of the Iowa Supreme Court points out, such efficiencies may not be consistent with our unique system of federalism: "it is doubtful that uniformity is a constitutional value in a federal system. Indeed, diversity of constitutional analysis is baked into the constitutional cake where states retain sovereign authority over questions not delegated to the federal government by the United States Constitution." *State v. Short*, 851 N.W.2d 474, 487 (Iowa 2014).

STATE v. HEMPELE
576 A.2d 793 (N.J. 1990)

CLIFFORD, J.

The issue in these appeals, argued together, is the constitutionality of warrantless seizures and searches of garbage bags left on the curb for collection.

In *State v. Hempele* a confidential source informed the state police that defendants, Conrad D. Hempele and Sharon Hempele, were distributing illicit drugs from their home at 303 Mill Street in Belvidere. The informant claimed to have seen fifty pounds of marijuana in Conrad's bedroom.

On the basis of that information, a trooper seized the trash sitting in front of 303 Mill Street six months later. 303 Mill Street is one of about ten attached row houses, each with its own front entrance. A short stairway runs from each row house to an eight-foot-wide sidewalk abutting the street. The seized trash was next to the flight of stairs leading to 303 Mill Street. Two weeks later the trooper again seized the garbage in front of the Hempeles' home. On both occasions the trooper removed white plastic trash bags from a plastic garbage can and took the bags to the State Police Tri-Man Unit, where, without a warrant, he opened them and analyzed their contents. He discovered traces of marijuana, cocaine, and methamphetamine in the trash.

A search warrant for defendants' home issued on the basis of the informant's tip and the evidence found in the garbage. When the subsequent search turned up controlled substances and drug paraphernalia, the Hempeles were indicted for drug offenses.

We consider first whether the garbage searches in these two cases violated the United States Constitution.

In *California v. Greenwood*, 486 U.S. 35 (1988), the United States Supreme Court held that the fourth amendment does not prohibit unreasonable searches and seizures of garbage left for collection in an area accessible to the public.... The Supreme Court held that the warrantless searches of Greenwood's garbage "would violate the Fourth Amendment only if respondents [had] manifested a subjective expectation of privacy in their garbage that society accepts as objectively reasonable." Ruling that a privacy expectation in garbage is not reasonable, the Court rejected the defendants' argument.

The Court decided that people lose any reasonable expectation of privacy in their trash by leaving it in bags alongside the street, because such garbage is vulnerable to an unscrupulous person or scavenging animal. Furthermore, garbage is placed on the curb for the specific purpose of having a third party remove it. The defendants should have realized that the trash collector might look through the garbage or allow another person to do so. The Court added that the fourth amendment does not protect what a person knowingly exposes to the public because "the police cannot reasonably be expected to avert their eyes from evidence of criminal activity that could have been observed by any member of the public."

Having decided that an expectation of privacy in trash left for collection in an area accessible to the public is unreasonable, the Court found it unnecessary to determine whether the defendants had manifested a subjective expectation of privacy. The warrantless garbage searches did not violate the fourth amendment.

Under *Greenwood* the issue is whether the garbage was left at a location "accessible to the public."… The Hempeles left their garbage at a location accessible to the public. They cannot escape the force of *Greenwood*.

We now determine whether the New Jersey Constitution protects curbside garbage from unreasonable searches and seizures. Despite the similarity between the text of article I, paragraph 7 of the New Jersey Constitution and the text of the fourth amendment, we have found on several occasions that the former "affords our citizens greater protection against unreasonable searches and seizures than does the fourth amendment."

For most of our country's history, the primary source of protection of individual rights has been state constitutions, not the federal Bill of Rights. The genius of federalism is that the fundamental rights of citizens are protected not only by the United States Constitution but also by the laws of each of the states. The system may be untidy on occasion, but that untidiness invests it with "a vibrant diversity." "As tempting as it may be to harmonize results under the state and federal constitutions, federalism contemplated that state courts may grant greater protection to individual rights if they choose."

Cognizant of the diversity of laws, customs, and mores within its jurisdiction, the United States Supreme Court is necessarily "hesitant to impose on a national level far-reaching constitutional rules binding on each and every state." That Court establishes no more than the floor of constitutional protection. The Supreme Court must be especially cautious in fourth-amendment cases. When determining whether a search warrant is necessary in a specific circumstance, the Court must take note of the disparity in warrant-application procedures among the several states, and must consider whether a warrant requirement in that situation might overload the procedure in any one state. In contrast, we are fortunate to have in New Jersey a procedure that allows for the speedy and reliable issuance of search warrants based on probable cause. A warrant requirement is not so great a burden in New Jersey as it might be in other states.

The Supreme Court itself has implied that garbage searches are an appropriate issue on which state courts may rise above "the lowest common denominator." In holding that the fourth amendment does not protect garbage, the Court suggested that "[i]ndividual States may surely construe their own constitutions as imposing more stringent constraints on police conduct than does the Federal Constitution." *California v. Greenwood*, 486 U.S. at 43.

In determining the reasonableness of an expectation of privacy in curbside garbage left for collection, we start from the premise that "[e]xpectations of privacy are established by general social norms." The "ultimate question" is whether, if garbage searches are "permitted to go unregulated by constitutional restraints, the amount of privacy and freedom remaining to citizens would be diminished to a compass inconsistent with the aims of a free and open society." With that question in mind, we first examine whether it is reasonable for a person to want to keep the contents of his or her garbage private.

privacy based on societal norms

Clues to people's most private traits and affairs can be found in their garbage. "[A]lmost every human activity ultimately manifests itself in waste products and…any individual may understandably wish to maintain the confidentiality of his refuse." A plethora of personal information can be culled from garbage:

> A single bag of trash testifies eloquently to the eating, reading, and recreational habits of the person who produced it. A search of trash, like a search of the bedroom, can relate intimate details about sexual practices, health, and personal hygiene. Like rifling through desk drawers or intercepting phone calls, rummaging through trash can divulge the target's financial and professional status, political affiliations and inclinations, private thoughts, personal relationships, and romantic interests.

Brennan describes how private our trash is.

[*California v. Greenwood*, 486 U.S. at 50 (Brennan, J., dissenting)].

Most people seem to have an interest in keeping such matters private; few publicize them voluntarily. Undoubtedly many would be upset to see a neighbor or stranger sifting through their garbage, perusing their discarded mail, reading their bank statements, looking at their empty pharmaceutical bottles, and checking receipts to see what videotapes they rent. The California Supreme Court commented that it could "readily ascribe many reasons why residents would not want their castaway clothing, letters, medicine bottles or other telltale refuse and trash to be examined by neighbors or others…. Half truths leading to rumor and gossip may readily flow from an attempt to 'read' the contents of another's trash." *People v. Edwards*, 71 Cal.2d 1096, 1104 (1969) (garbage left inside curtilage is constitutionally protected).

Ct suggests that people expect privacy in their garbage

Like the fourth amendment, article I, paragraph 7 "provides protection to the owner of every container that conceals its contents from plain view."…There is no "constitutional distinction between 'worthy' and 'unworthy' containers…." "[P]aper bags, locked trunks, lunch buckets, and orange crates" all receive the same treatment. A privacy expectation does not depend on the value or quality of the container.

Privacy But based on the "value" of the object.

The critical issue is whether the container conceals its contents from plain view. Because ordinary opaque garbage bags conceal their contents from plain view, the presumption is that an expectation of privacy in the contents is reasonable.

The New Jersey Constitution "requires the approval of an impartial judicial officer based on probable cause before most searches may be undertaken." "Any warrantless search is *prima facie* invalid." Those principles certainly apply to opaque containers.

Once the protections of article I, paragraph 7 apply, a lower expectation of privacy is not a sufficient basis on which to carve out an exception to the warrant and probable-cause requirement. We can dispense with that requirement "[o]nly in those exceptional circumstances in which special needs, beyond the normal need for law enforcement, make the warrant and probable cause requirement impracticable...." If a "special need" does exist, we can then make an exception to the requirement only after we "balance the nature and quality of the intrusion on the individual's [article I, paragraph 7] interests against the importance of the governmental interests alleged to justify the intrusion."

Thus, even if garbage searches are only "minimally intrusive" of a person's privacy, the warrant and probable-cause requirement for garbage searches can be scrapped only if a special government interest significantly outweighs those privacy interests.

Because we find no special state interest that makes the warrant requirement impracticable, we hold that the State must secure a warrant based on probable cause in order to search garbage bags left on the curb for collection.

In summary, article I, paragraph 7 applies to the search but not to the seizure of a garbage bag left on the curb for collection. Law-enforcement officials need no cause to seize the bag, but they must have a warrant based on probable cause to search it.

Our decision today does not follow the course set by the Supreme Court because "we are persuaded that the equities so strongly favor protection of a person's privacy interest that we should apply our own standard rather than defer to the federal provision." We are aware that our ruling conflicts not only with *California v. Greenwood* but also with the holdings of virtually every other court that has considered this issue.... Although the weight of the cited authority is impressive, our thorough consideration of the issue leads us to record our respectful disagreement with those courts that have reached a result contrary to ours.

We do concur, however, in the observation that there is no "unique New Jersey state attitude about garbage." Our differences with the cited authority rest on other grounds. As the trial court in *Pasanen* so eloquently put it, "the trouble with those cases is that they are flatly and simply wrong as the matter of the way people think about garbage." Garbage can reveal much that is personal. We do not find it unreasonable for people to want their garbage to remain private and to expect that it will remain private from the meddling of the State.

Article I, paragraph 7 confers "as against the government, the right to be let alone-the most comprehensive of rights and the right most valued by civilized men." *Olmstead v. United States*, 277 *U.S.* 438, 478 (1927) (Brandeis, J., dissenting). Permitting the police to pick and poke their way through garbage bags to peruse without cause the vestiges of a person's most private affairs would be repugnant to that ideal. A free and civilized society should comport itself with more decency.

NOTE

At least one decision since *Hempele* confirms that the decision does not turn on any "unique New Jersey state attitude about garbage," to quote the New Jersey Supreme Court. The New Mexico Supreme Court adopted a similar approach in the context of trash left at a motel. *See New Mexico v. Crane*, 329 P.3d 689 (N.M. 2014) (holding that individual had "a reasonable expectation of privacy in garbage left out for collection in a motel dumpster" under the New Mexico Constitution).

BLUM v. MERRELL DOW PHARMACEUTICALS, INC. (constitutionalism decision)
626 A.2d 537 (Penn. 1993)

NIX, C.J.

The issue before this Court is whether Article I, Section 6 of the Pennsylvania Constitution entitles a party who demands a twelve person jury to a verdict from a jury of twelve persons. For the reasons that follow, [holding] we affirm the Superior Court Order and hold that Section 6 of Article I of the Pennsylvania Constitution entitles a party who properly demands a twelve person jury to a verdict from a jury of twelve persons.

Our starting point must be the decision of the United States Supreme Court in *Williams v. Florida*, 399 U.S. 78 (1970). In *Williams*, the Supreme Court departed from a long history of requiring a twelve person jury as a necessary ingredient of the Sixth Amendment guarantee of trial by jury in all criminal cases. The Supreme Court in *Williams* concluded [SCOTUS precedent] that the "twelve man panel is not a necessary ingredient of 'trial by jury,' and that [Florida's] refusal to impanel more than six members provided for by Florida law did not violate [Williams'] Sixth Amendment rights as applied to the states through the Fourteenth [Amendment]."... We must [QP] now determine whether the *Williams*, *Colgrove* and *Ballew* trilogy, which allows trial by less than twelve member juries in civil cases, is properly part of the jurisprudence of this Commonwealth, by virtue of Section 6 of Article I of the Pennsylvania Constitution.

This Court has emphasized that, in interpreting a provision of the Pennsylvania Constitution, we are not bound by the decisions of the United States Supreme Court which interpret similar federal constitutional provisions. *Commonwealth v. Edmunds*, 526 Pa. 374, 388 (1991).... In *Edmunds*, Mr. Justice Cappy, writing for the majority of the Court, established the following four part framework which we consider in analyzing our State Constitution:

> [L]itigants [must] brief and analyze at least the following four factors:
>
> 1) text of the Pennsylvania Constitutional provision;
>
> 2) history of the provision, including Pennsylvania case law;
>
> 3) related case law from other states;
>
> 4) policy considerations, including unique issues of state and local concern, and applicability within modern Pennsylvania jurisprudence.

The text of Section 6 of Article I of the Pennsylvania Constitution provides as follows:

> "Section 6. Trial by jury shall be as heretofore and the right thereof remain inviolate. The General Assembly may provide, however, by law, that a verdict may be rendered by not less than five-sixths of the jury in any civil case."

On its face, Article I, Section 6 preserves the following two things: the right to trial by jury shall be as heretofore; and the right to trial by jury remains inviolate. The Seventh Amendment to the United States Constitution, although worded differently, is similar to the Pennsylvania provision. On its face, the Seventh Amendment provides the right to trial by jury is preserved and no fact tried by a jury shall be otherwise reexamined other than according to the rules of common law. Although worded differently, both provisions retain the right to trial by jury in civil cases where it existed at common law. Therefore, we must undertake an examination of the history of Section 6 of Article I of our Constitution to determine the meaning of that provision and to decide whether our constitutional scheme is the same as the Federal Constitution or requires a verdict from a twelve member jury in a civil case when a demand for a twelve member jury is properly made.

Before discussing any case law, however, we must give an overview of the concept of juries of twelve members throughout this Commonwealth's history. The Superior Court in this case gave an excellent overview of the twelve member jury concept in this Commonwealth. The Superior Court stated:

> [T]he concept of juries of twelve in this Commonwealth ... has its origin in a document introduced and adopted in Pennsylvania in 1682 by William Penn and known as "Laws Agreed Upon in England." Comment, *The Jury Size Question*

In Pennsylvania: Six Of One And A Dozen Of The Other, 53 Temple L.Q. 89, 100 (1980).

Penn's other writings discussed the evolution of the jury and his belief that it was a "fundamental" part of the government and important to a free society. However, "nowhere did he endeavor to explain why a jury required *twelve* members to fulfill its purpose." *Id.* at 103.

One commentator has observed:

> Penn's own writings and deeds appear to show that his commitment to twelve-member juries was not based on any reasoned notion that twelve was required to assure fairness, but instead stemming from his adherence to traditional common law principles that required twelve member juries.

Id. at 104-105 (footnote omitted). Likewise, there is little information available that casts any light on the intent of the framers of the Pennsylvania Constitution of 1776 regarding the size of juries. *Id.* at 106. The same can be said with regard to the Constitutional Conventions of 1790 and 1838. As for the 1873 Convention, discussion was had on the deletion of the unanimity requirement and the elimination of the term "heretofore." Some saw no problem with this since they *equated a trial by jury with a jury of twelve men*, whereas others believed excising the word "heretofore" would pave the way for a jury of "'three or five or seven ... [or less than twelve] as a constitutional jury....'" *Id.* at 112-113. The proposal was defeated without explanation.

The framers at Pennsylvania's 1968 Convention did not consider the jury provision at all, believing that it was beyond their jurisdiction to affect that right. Even so, our first Constitution of 1776 contained verbiage which has survived and appears in the present-day Article I, § 6. E.g., the 1776 Constitution declared that "trials by jury shall be as *heretofore*." The Constitution of 1790, and the amended ones of 1838, 1873 and 1968, adopted substantially the same provision. Their language was "trial by jury shall be as *heretofore*, the right thereof remain inviolate."

As the Superior Court stated, all of our Constitutions have had the identical language, that being "trial by jury shall be as heretofore." The following language was added to Section 6 of Article I of our Constitution by amendment on May 18, 1971:

> The General Assembly may provide, however, by law, that a verdict may be rendered by not less than five-sixths of the jury in a civil case.

Every Constitution of this Commonwealth has guaranteed to the parties a verdict from a jury of twelve persons where the parties would have had that right at common law. The Constitution, beginning in 1776, has always provided that "trial by jury shall be as heretofore." As stated above, our history and our case law evidence that that language, "trial by jury shall be as heretofore," was understood to guarantee a jury of twelve persons. Thus, Appellants' statement that there is no rationale in 1991 for following *Smith* and the other cases which commented upon the "heretofore" language in our earlier Constitutions is incorrect.

Appellants also argue, assuming *arguendo* that a right to a twelve person jury exists, the 1971 Pennsylvania Constitution and the subsequently enacted five-sixths rule, 42 Pa.C.S. § 5104(b), allow that a decision by ten of twelve jurors constitutes "the verdict of the jury" and it "shall have the same effect as a unanimous verdict of the jury." Therefore, Appellants aver that the decision of ten jurors is always constitutionally sufficient and no constitutional right in this appeal could have been violated where eleven of eleven jurors agree on a verdict.

When the people of this Commonwealth amended Section 6 of Article I of our Constitution in 1971, authorizing the General Assembly to provide for a verdict by not less than five-sixths of the jury in any civil case, they reaffirmed the constitutional right to a jury of twelve persons. A provision of the Constitution will be interpreted, not in a strained or technical manner, but as understood by the people who adopted it. As previously discussed, in this Commonwealth "trial by jury shall be as heretofore" has always required a jury of twelve persons. When the people of this Commonwealth approved the May 18, 1971 amendment to Section 6 of Article I, they understood the reference to "the jury in any civil case" to be to a jury of twelve persons. Thus, the people of this Commonwealth amended only the unanimity feature and reaffirmed that a jury is made up of twelve persons.

The third element we will analyze is the case law from other jurisdictions. Subsequent to the United States Supreme Court decisions, a number of states other than Pennsylvania confronted the issue of whether their state constitutions require a twelve person jury.

Most significantly, after the United States Supreme Court decision in *Williams*, the Supreme Court of Rhode Island, in an advisory opinion to the Senate, held that the jury referred to in Section 15 of Article I of the Rhode Island Constitution requires a panel of twelve. After a thorough analysis of Rhode Island's constitutional history, that court reasoned:

> Although the Supreme Court in *Williams* described the common-law requirement that a petit jury be composed of precisely twelve people as an "historical accident," the Court obviously could not share this observation made in June 1970 with the framers and adopters of the Rhode Island Constitution. Accident or not, it is our firm belief that in 1842 when the draftsmen and the voters said that the right to a jury trial was to remain inviolate, they were extending to an accused, or any litigant who might be entitled to a jury trial, the immutable right to have his case considered in the courts of this state by petit jury composed of exactly twelve persons.

Thus, the Rhode Island Supreme Court, after analyzing its case law and constitutional history, went above the minimum standards set forth by the United States Supreme Court in *Williams* and determined that, under the Rhode Island Constitution, a jury is composed of twelve members.

We similarly conclude that, because of Pennsylvania's history and case law, a jury must be composed of twelve persons where that right existed at common law and the demand for a twelve person jury is properly made. If this Court changed a right that had been understood and guaranteed to the people of this Commonwealth for over 200 years, we would be breaching our duty to speak the will of the people of this Commonwealth. We refuse to breach that duty by allowing a jury to be composed of less than twelve jurors. Only the people of this Commonwealth, by constitutional amendment, may make such a change.

The last prong of the *Edmunds* test is an examination of policy considerations and their applicability within modern Pennsylvania jurisprudence. One policy consideration Appellants request us to consider is the financial burden a jury of twelve persons presents for this Commonwealth.

We find that the most substantial policy consideration is that the people of this Commonwealth have understood since our first Constitution was adopted in 1776 that a "trial by jury" meant a jury composed of twelve persons. Given that understanding of the constitutional right, it is not for the legislative, executive, or judicial branch to change that right; rather, it is exclusively left to the people of this Commonwealth to amend the twelve member jury requirement if they desire that change.

Our constitutional history and case law mandate that we refrain from adopting the United States Supreme Court analysis in *Williams*, *Colgrove*, and *Ballew*, which held that verdicts from juries of less than twelve did not violate the Federal Constitution. This Court is under a duty to guarantee that the intent of the people of this Commonwealth in adopting the Pennsylvania Constitution is carried forward. We are convinced that, when Pennsylvania adopted its first Constitution in 1776, the framers assumed that a jury meant twelve persons. This Court has repeatedly adopted that view. Therefore, even though Section 6 of Article I of the Pennsylvania Constitution does not explicitly state that a jury is constituted of twelve members, our constitutional history and case law make it apparent that "trial by jury" means a jury of twelve persons.

NOTES

1. The Pennsylvania and U.S. Constitutions both preserve the right to "trial by jury." Why does the state court take a different tack in interpreting this language? Does the state court embrace any aspects of the relevant federal decisions?

2. The Delaware Supreme Court, like many state supreme courts, has adopted criteria for determining whether a state constitutional guarantee offers greater protection than a similarly worded federal guarantee. In *Jones v. Delaware*, 745 A.2d 856, 864-65 (Del. 1999), the Court in an

opinion by Chief Justice Veasey used the following criteria in deciding to give the State's search-and-seizure guarantee more protection than the U.S. Supreme Court provided in *California v. Hodari D.*, 499 U.S. 621 (1991):

(1) Textual Language—A state constitution's language may itself provide a basis for reaching a result different from that which could be obtained under federal law.

(2) [Constitutional] History—Whether or not the textual language of a given provision is different from that found in the federal Constitution, legislative history may reveal an intention that will support reading the provision independently of federal law.

(3) Preexisting State Law—Previously established bodies of state law may also suggest distinctive state constitutional rights. State law is often responsive to concerns long before they are addressed by constitutional claims.

(4) Structural Differences—Differences in structure between the federal and state constitutions might also provide a basis for rejecting the constraints of federal doctrine at the state level. The United States Constitution is a grant of enumerated powers to the federal government. Our State Constitution, on the other hand, serves only to limit the sovereign power which inheres directly in the people and indirectly in their elected representatives.

(5) Matters of Particular State Interest or Local Concern—A state constitution may also be employed to address matters of peculiar state interest or local concern.

(6) State Traditions—A state's history and traditions may also provide a basis for the independent application of its constitution.

(7) Public Attitudes—Distinctive attitudes of a state's citizenry may also furnish grounds to expand constitutional rights under state charters. While we have never cited this criterion in our decisions, courts in other jurisdictions have pointed to public attitudes as a relevant factor in their deliberations.

B. DIFFERENTLY WORDED PROVISIONS

When the language of the state constitutional guarantee differs materially from its federal counterpart, the state courts have an additional reason for construing their constitutions differently. That, however, does not diminish the force of the earlier considerations: the scope of jurisdiction of the two courts; the effect of local history (including the history and purpose of the state constitutional provision), local traditions, and local customs; the difficulty of answering some constitutional questions; and disagreement between the two courts. In the following cases, consider the impact of the difference in language between the state and federal guarantees on the courts' decisions relative to the role of these other considerations.

RACING ASSOCIATION OF CENTRAL IOWA v. FITZGERALD
675 N.W.2d 1 (Iowa 2004)

TERNUS, J.

When this case was initially before our court, we held that a statute taxing gross gambling receipts generated at racetracks at a rate nearly twice the rate imposed on gross gambling receipts generated on riverboats violated the United States Constitution and the Iowa Constitution. On certiorari to the United States Supreme Court, that part of our decision holding the statute violated the Equal Protection Clause of the United States Constitution was reversed. The Supreme Court then remanded the case "for further proceedings not inconsistent with [its] opinion." Although this court's ruling that the statute also violated the equality provision contained in the Iowa Constitution was not reviewed by the Supreme Court, we take the opportunity on remand to reconsider our prior decision on the state constitution claim in light of the Court's ruling on the federal constitution issue.   *Court will analyze state con claim*

After giving due consideration to the Court's analysis and decision, we find no basis to change our earlier opinion that the differential tax violates article I, section 6 of the Iowa Constitution. Therefore, we reverse the trial court's contrary ruling and remand this case for a determination of the appropriate relief.   *Holding: State con was violated*

This action was commenced by the appellant, Racing Association of Central Iowa (RACI), to enjoin the collection of that portion of taxes it was required to pay on adjusted gross receipts from gambling in excess of the tax charged to "excursion boats" on such receipts. *See generally* 1989 Iowa Acts ch. 67 (authorizing gambling on "excursion boats"). RACI claimed the tax was unconstitutional under the Equal Protection Clauses of the United States and Iowa Constitutions.   *π's EPC claim*

The tax statute challenged by these parties is Iowa Code section 99F.11 (1999), which imposes a tax "on the adjusted gross receipts received annually from gambling games." The maximum rate is twenty percent. The statute has an exception, however, for the "adjusted gross receipts ... from gambling games at racetrack enclosures." *Id*. The tax rate on racetrack gambling receipts began at twenty-two percent in 1997, and has automatically increased by two percent each year to a maximum rate of thirty-six percent in 2004.

[handwritten margin notes: SC reversed on fed grounds; Statute being challenged]

In our first consideration of this case, we held this differential tax violated the Equal Protection Clause of the United States Constitution and article I, section 6 of the Iowa Constitution.[2]

It is this court's constitutional obligation as the highest court of this sovereign state to determine whether the challenged classification violates Iowa's constitutional equality provision. While the Supreme Court's judgment on the constitutionality of Iowa's disparate tax rates under the federal Equal Protection Clause is persuasive, it is not binding on this court as we evaluate this law under the Iowa Constitution.

The Supreme Court has stated that the Equal Protection Clause "is essentially a direction that all persons similarly situated should be treated alike." Whether this ideal has been met in the context of economic legislation is determined through application of the rational basis test. In its consideration of the case at hand, the Court described the rational basis test as follows:

> "[T]he Equal Protection Clause is satisfied so long as there is a plausible policy reason for the classification, the legislative facts on which the classification is apparently based rationally may have been considered to be true by the governmental decisionmaker, and the relationship of the classification to its goal is not so attenuated as to render the distinction arbitrary or irrational."

The Court has in the past more succinctly stated this standard as "whether the classifications drawn in a statute are reasonable in light of its purpose." It was this enunciation of the rational basis test that our court said in Bierkamp was appropriate for analyzing a claim based on the Iowa equality provision found in article I, section 6 of the Iowa Constitution.

Based on these principles, this court must first determine whether the Iowa legislature had a valid reason to treat racetracks differently from riverboats when taxing the gambling revenue of these businesses. Moreover, the claimed state interest must be *realistically conceivable.* Our court must then decide whether this reason has a basis in fact. Finally, we must consider whether the relationship between the classification, i.e., the differences between racetracks and excursion boats, and the purpose of the classification is so weak that the classification must be viewed as arbitrary?

Our examination of this statute must also be guided by the general legal principles that control a court's review of the constitutionality of a legislative enactment. These tenets are well established. "Statutes are

---

[2]The United States Constitution provides that no state shall "deny to any person within its jurisdiction the equal protection of the laws." U.S. Const. amend. 14. In contrast, article I, section 6 of the Iowa Constitution states: "All laws of a general nature shall have a uniform operation; the general assembly shall not grant to any citizen, or class of citizens, privileges or immunities, which, upon the same terms shall not equally belong to all citizens."

cloaked with a strong presumption of constitutionality." Therefore, a
person challenging a statute shoulders a heavy burden of rebutting this
presumption. This burden includes the task of negating every reasonable
basis that might support the disparate treatment. These rigorous standards
have not, however, prevented this court from finding economic and social
legislation in violation of equal protection provisions. Our prior cases
illustrate that, although the rational basis standard of review is admittedly
deferential to legislative judgment, "'it is not a toothless one'" in Iowa.
Indeed, this court's meaningful review of social and economic legislation
is mandated by our constitutional obligation to safeguard constitutional
values by ensuring all legislation complies with those values.

[margin: Burden on challenger; what they must do]

Although the State has advanced several reasons for the legislative
classification challenged in this case, we focus our discussion primarily on
those found satisfactory by the Supreme Court, as that is the reason for our
reconsideration of the state constitutional claim. The Supreme Court
viewed the issue as whether there was "rational support for the 20
percent/36 percent differential." It then concluded "[t]hat difference" was
helpful to the riverboats because it (1) "encourage[d] the economic
development of river communities [and] promote[d] riverboat history"; (2)
"protect[ed] the reliance interests of riverboat operators" who were
accustomed to a twenty percent tax rate; and (3) "aid[ed] the financial
position of the riverboats." We will address each suggested purpose
separately.

[margin: Ct decides to scrutinize what Scotus found as "rational"]

Our court does not accept the economic development of river
communities and the promotion of riverboat history as a rational basis for
the legislature's distinction between excursion boats and racetracks.
Although these are laudable legislative goals, "the legislative facts on
which the classification is apparently based [cannot] rationally [be]
considered to be true by the governmental decisionmaker," as required by
the Court's articulation of the rational basis test. We note initially that
excursion boat gambling was never anticipated as solely a "river" activity
so as to promote "river communities." When the legislature authorized
gambling on "excursion boats" in 1989, it was envisioned that these boats
would be located on inland waters, such as lakes and reservoirs, as well as
on the Mississippi River and Missouri River, the historical location of
riverboats. Moreover, there is nothing peculiar about racetracks that
prevents their location in river cities. In fact, two of the three communities
in which racetracks are located—Dubuque and Council Bluffs—are river
communities. The Dubuque racetrack is actually on an island in the
Mississippi River. On the other hand, the excursion boat docked near
Osceola, Iowa, is moored on a lake, not a river, and is certainly not located
in a river community. In addition, one river community—Council
Bluffs—has both a racetrack and an excursion boat, only blocks apart. So,

[margin: Ct's reason one. But a rational basis]

[margin: Not solely a river activity]

[bottom margin: Ct's far more nuanced understanding of Iowa's landscape clearly helps analysis]

to justify the differential tax treatment of these enterprises on the supposed connection of excursion boats to river communities and riverboat history and the absence of such a connection by racetracks is illogical.

We acknowledge "the overinclusive-underinclusive dichotomy is usually applied only as part of a strict scrutiny analysis." But our court has stated, in holding legislation violative of the state constitution under the rational basis test, "that as a classification involves extreme degrees of overinclusion and underinclusion in relation to any particular goal, it cannot be said to reasonably further that goal." That is precisely the case here insofar as the differential tax is based on the promotion of river communities and riverboat history. Thus, this legislative purpose cannot withstand review under the rational basis standard.

Even if this court were to take a more expansive view of potential legislative purposes and assume the general assembly sought to promote economic development in general, the taxing scheme still suffers from an irrational classification. There is nothing in the record, nor is it a matter of common knowledge, that excursion boats are a superior economic development tool as compared to racetracks. To the contrary, it appears that both types of gambling enterprises have the potential to enhance the economic climate of the communities in which they are located. If we presume the legislature thought the promotion of gambling was in the economic interests of the general public, then we find no rational basis for distinguishing between gambling that takes place on a floating casino and gambling that occurs at a land-based casino. Regardless of the relative number of such establishments or the size of the city in which they are to be found, excursion boats and racetracks contribute in the same manner to the economy of the local area: they are both gambling enterprises generating gambling receipts that are indistinguishable in terms of the economic benefits to the local community.

Our decision today is a difficult one because we have great respect for the legislature. Notwithstanding our preference to defer to its judgment, we declare the differential tax at issue here invalid under the Iowa Constitution because we are convinced the classifications made in section 99F.11 lack a rational basis in the constitutional sense. Because we are keenly aware of the legislature's constitutional role to make decisions of a policy and political nature, we have not lightly undertaken today's decision. Nonetheless, "[o]ur obligation not to interfere with the legislature's right to pass laws is no higher than our obligation to protect the citizens from discriminatory class legislation violative of the constitutional guaranty of equality of all before the law." Consequently, we decline the opportunity to alter our prior decision that the statutory exception to the twenty percent tax rate on gambling receipts violates article I, section 6 of the Iowa Constitution. We reverse the decision of the district court upholding the higher tax rate on racetracks under the Iowa Constitution and remand for further proceedings.

NOTES

1. Does the Iowa Supreme Court apply the same equal protection test as the U.S. Supreme Court or a different test?   *seems to apply different test*

2. Do you think the U.S. Supreme Court would find the Iowa Supreme Court's most recent decision convincing? Might the Iowa Supreme Court's recent explanation alter the U.S. Supreme Court's analysis under federal law?

STATE v. JORDEN
156 P.3d 893 (Wash. 2007)

BRIDGE, J.

Timothy Jorden appeals his conviction for unlawful possession of cocaine. On March 15, 2003, a Pierce County deputy sheriff conducted a random warrant check of the Golden Lion Motel's guests via the guest registry and discovered Jorden's presence at the Lakewood motel as well as the fact of two outstanding warrants for Jorden's arrest. Deputy sheriffs then entered Jorden's motel room in order to arrest him for the outstanding warrants. Upon entering the room, officers saw cocaine in plain view. Jorden contends that the random check of the motel registry revealing his whereabouts constitutes a violation of his privacy rights under article I, section 7 of the Washington State Constitution.

Claims that privacy was violated

The Pierce County Sheriff's Department takes part in the "Lakewood Crime-Free Hotel Motel Program." 1 Verbatim Report of Proceedings (VRP) at 11. The program offers assistance to motels and hotels that have a history of significant criminal activity, providing training on methods of crime reduction. The program also encourages officers to review the guest registries of hotels and motels on a random basis and without individualized or particularized suspicion. Officers often conduct random criminal checks of the names in guest registries at motels with reputations for frequent criminal activity. When checking into a participating motel, guests are advised that a valid identification is required for check-in and that the identification information is kept on file, but the guests are not told of the possibility for random, suspicionless searches of the registry by law enforcement.   *Guests aren't told of random checks*

Program targets high crime motels/areas

Article I, section 7 of the Washington Constitution provides that "[n]o person shall be disturbed in his private affairs, or his home invaded, without authority of law." "[I]t is well established that article I, section 7 qualitatively differs from the Fourth Amendment and in some areas provides greater protections than does the federal constitution." We must therefore determine "whether article I, section 7 affords enhanced protection in the particular context." Accordingly, we must determine whether that heightened protection is available in these circumstances to Jorden.

Article I, section 7 protects against warrantless searches of a citizen's private affairs. Therefore, a warrantless search is per se unreasonable unless it falls under one of Washington's recognized exceptions. Here, the State does not argue the motel registry review falls into one of the exceptions, but argues that the information in the registry is not a private affair and thus there was no search triggering article I, section 7 protection.

Private affairs are those "'interests which citizens of this state have held, and should be entitled to hold, safe from government trespass.'" In determining whether a certain interest is a private affair deserving article I, section 7 protection, a central consideration is the *nature* of the information sought—that is, whether the information obtained via the governmental trespass reveals intimate or discrete details of a person's life.

In addition, this court has also considered whether there are historical protections afforded to the perceived interest. *McKinney*, 148 Wash.2d at 27. And, where the perceived interest involves the gathering of personal information by the government, this court has also considered the purpose for which the information sought is kept, and by whom it is kept.

Our most important inquiry then becomes whether a random and suspicionless search of a guest registry reveals intimate details of one's life. We first consider that here there is more information at stake than simply a guest's registration information: an individual's very presence in a motel or hotel may in itself be a sensitive piece of information. There are a variety of lawful reasons why an individual may not wish to reveal his or her presence at a motel. As the amicus American Civil Liberties Union (ACLU) points out, couples engaging in extramarital affairs may not wish to share their presence at the hotel with others, just as a closeted same-sex couple forced to meet at the motel also would not. The desire for privacy may extend to business people engaged in confidential negotiations or celebrities seeking respite from life in the public eye. One could also imagine a scenario, as Jorden's trial attorney pointed out during the motion to suppress, where a domestic violence victim flees to a hotel in hopes of remaining hidden from an abuser.

Additionally, we note the sensitivity of the registry information in and of itself. Not only does it reveal one's presence at the motel, it may also reveal co-guests in the room, divulging yet another person's personal or

Ct. resting has intimate details

business associates. Thus, it appears that the information gleaned from random, suspicionless searches of a guest registry may indeed provide "intimate details about a person's activities and associations."

Therefore, the information contained in a motel registry—including one's whereabouts at the motel—is a private affair under our state constitution, and a government trespass into such information is a search. We hesitate to allow a search of a citizen's private affairs where the government cannot express at least an individualized or particularized suspicion about the search subject or present a valid exception to a warrantless search. A random, suspicionless search is a fishing expedition, and we have indicated displeasure with such practices on many occasions.

Consequently, we hold that the practice of checking the names in a motel registry for outstanding warrants without individualized or particularized suspicion violated the defendant's article I, section 7 rights.

Search violated con.

We are not insensitive to the difficulties facing law enforcement in ensuring our motels and hotels remain relatively crime-free, but as a practical matter our holding does not unduly restrict the investigative powers of the police. Random, suspicionless registry checks are but one part of the Lakewood Crime-Free Hotel Motel Program. Law enforcement may continue to randomly run checks of the license plates of cars parked at the motels, provide training to motel owners, and encourage motel owners to be watchful of behavior evincing criminal activity. Reports of such observations may engender the requisite individualized suspicion that is notably missing from current program techniques.

Information contained in a motel registry constitutes a private affair under article I, section 7 of the Washington State Constitution because it reveals sensitive, discrete, and private information about the motel's guest. Absent a valid exception to the prohibition against warrantless searches, random viewing of a motel registry violates article I, section 7 of the Washington State Constitution. The evidence obtained from the registry of the Golden Lion Motel, which led officers to Jorden's room, was obtained through unlawful means and should have been excluded.

C. INDEPENDENT AND ADEQUATE STATE GROUNDS: STATE COURT RULINGS THAT ADDRESS FEDERAL AND STATE BASES FOR DECISION

Given the reality that the state courts may construe a constitutional guarantee in their own constitutions more broadly than one found in the U.S. Constitution, lawyers often will raise both grounds in challenging the validity of a state or local law. When that happens, at least two issues arise: Will the state court rely on just one constitutional guarantee or both of them? And, if it relies on both of them or at least precedents from both jurisdictions, how will the reviewing court—the U.S. Supreme Court—know whether the state court has relied on an independent and adequate state ground, which is insulated from review, or on a federal ground, which is open to review? The answers to both questions have strategic consequences. The losing litigant, for example, will want to show that the state court decision turns on federal law, so that it may seek review in the U.S. Supreme Court. Otherwise, the case is over—unless the litigant can convince the people of the State to amend the state constitution.

In *Michigan v. Long*, 463 U.S. 1032 (1983), the Court provided guidance on these issues. It created a clear-statement rule to the effect that, unless the state court expressly says otherwise, the U.S. Supreme Court would presume that a state court decision dealing with federal and state law issues was based on federal law. Here is how the Court put it:

> Accordingly, when, as in this case, a state court decision fairly appears to rest primarily on federal law, or to be interwoven with the federal law, and when the adequacy and independence of any possible state law ground is not clear from the face of the opinion, we will accept as the most reasonable explanation that the state court decided the case the way it did because it believed that federal law required it to do so. If a state court chooses merely to rely on federal precedents as it would on the precedents of all other jurisdictions, then it need only make clear by a plain statement in its judgment or opinion that the federal cases are being used only for the purpose of guidance, and do not themselves compel the result that the court has reached. In this way, both justice and judicial administration will be greatly improved. If the state court decision indicates clearly and expressly that it is alternatively based on bona fide separate, adequate, and independent grounds, we, of course, will not undertake to review the decision.

Despite this directive from *Michigan v. Long*, state court cases continue to arise in which the ground of decision remains unclear. The next set of decisions presents a case study of this problem—by examining three decisions concerning the same traffic stop, two by the Ohio Supreme Court and one by the U.S. Supreme Court. *Ohio v. Robinette* also considers the other half of the issue this chapter introduces: Why state courts sometimes *resist* relying on independent and adequate state law grounds, even when they have the authority to do so and even when they are expressly told in a given case that they have that authority.

In *Robinette*, the courts dealt with a traffic stop governed by the Fourth Amendment and a virtually identical state guarantee. Section 14 of Article I of the Ohio Constitution provides: "The right of the people to be secure in their persons, houses, papers, and possessions, against unreasonable searches and seizures shall not be violated; and no warrant shall issue, but upon probable cause, supported by oath or affirmation, particularly describing the place to be searched, and the person and things to be seized." The Fourth Amendment, similarly, provides: "The right of the people to be secure in their persons, houses, papers, and effects, against unreasonable searches and seizures, shall not be violated, and no Warrants shall issue, but upon probable cause, supported by oath or affirmation, and particularly describing the place to be searched, and the persons or things to be seized."

OHIO v. ROBINETTE
653 N.E.2d 695 (Ohio 1995)

PFEIFER, J.

The issue in this case is whether the evidence used against Robinette was obtained through a valid search. We find that the search was invalid since it was the product of an unlawful seizure. We also use this case to establish a bright-line test, requiring police officers to inform motorists that their legal detention has concluded before the police officer may engage in any consensual interrogation.

Ct: invalid search.

Rule: cops must inform motorists that

In order to justify any investigative stop, a police officer "must be able to point to specific and articulable facts which, taken together with the rational inferences from those facts, reasonably warrant that intrusion." Absent any additional articulable facts arising after the stop is made, the police officer must tailor his detention of the driver to the original purpose of the stop.   *What cops need for investigative stop*

In this case, Newsome certainly had cause to pull over Robinette for speeding. The question is when the validity of that stop ceased. Newsome testified that from the outset he never intended to ticket Robinette for speeding. When Newsome returned to Robinette's car after checking Robinette's license, every aspect of the speeding violation had been investigated and resolved. All Newsome had to do was to issue his warning and return Robinette's driver's license.   *Stopped for speeding, investigation was completed for speeding*

Instead, for no reason related to the speeding violation, and based on no articulable facts, Newsome extended his detention of Robinette by ordering him out of the vehicle. Newsome retained Robinette's driver's license and told Robinette to stand in front of the cruiser. Newsome then returned to the cruiser and activated the video camera in order to record his questioning of Robinette regarding whether he was carrying any contraband in the vehicle.   *Cop unlawfully extends detention*

When the motivation behind a police officer's continued detention of a person stopped for a traffic violation is not related to the purpose of the original, constitutional stop, and when that continued detention is not based on any articulable facts giving rise to a suspicion of some separate illegal activity justifying an extension of the detention, the continued detention constitutes an illegal seizure.

Rule for an illegal seizure

The entire chain of events, starting when Newsome had Robinette exit the car and stand within the field of the video camera, was related to the questioning of Robinette about carrying contraband. Newsome asked Robinette to step out of his car for the sole purpose of conducting a line of questioning that was not related to the initial speeding stop and that was not based on any specific or articulable facts that would provide probable cause for the extension of the scope of the seizure of Robinette, his passenger and his car. Therefore the detention of Robinette ceased being legal when Newsome asked him to leave his vehicle.

However, this case contains a [unique] feature…: Robinette consented to the search of his vehicle during the illegal seizure. Because Robinette's consent was obtained during an illegal detention, his consent is invalid unless the state proves that the consent was not the product of the illegal detention but the result of an independent act of free will. The burden is on the state to prove that the consent to search was voluntarily given. The factors used in consideration of whether the consent is sufficiently removed from the taint of the illegal seizure include the length of time between the illegal seizure and the subsequent search, the presence of intervening circumstances, and the purpose and flagrancy of the circumstances. *How state can satisfy burden*

In this case there was no time lapse between the illegal detention and the request to search, nor were there any circumstances that might have served to break or weaken the connection between one and the other. The sole purpose of the continued detention was to illegally broaden the scope of the original detention. Robinette's consent clearly was the result of his illegal detention, and was not the result of an act of will on his part. Given the circumstances, Robinette felt that he had no choice but to comply.

This case demonstrates the need for this court to draw a bright line between the conclusion of a valid seizure and the beginning of a consensual exchange. A person has been seized for the purposes of the Fourth Amendment when a law enforcement officer, by means of physical force or show of authority, has in some way restrained his liberty such that a reasonable person would not feel free to walk away.

The transition between detention and a consensual exchange can be so seamless that the untrained eye may not notice that it has occurred. The undetectability of that transition may be used by police officers to coerce citizens into answering questions that they need not answer, or to allow a search of a vehicle that they are not legally obligated to allow.

The present case offers an example of the blurring between a legal detention and an attempt at consensual interaction. Even assuming that Newsome's detention of Robinette was legal through the time when Newsome handed back Robinette's driver's license, Newsome then said,

"One question *before you get gone*: are you carrying any illegal contraband in your car?" (Emphasis added.) Newsome tells Robinette that before he leaves Newsome wants to know whether Robinette is carrying any contraband. Newsome does not ask if he may ask a question, he simply asks it, implying that Robinette must respond before he may leave. The interrogation then continues. Robinette is never told that he is free to go or that he may answer the question at his option.

The "seamless" transition [handwritten margin note]

Most people believe that they are validly in a police officer's custody as long as the officer continues to interrogate them. The police officer retains the upper hand and the accouterments of authority. That the officer lacks legal license to continue to detain them is unknown to most citizens, and a reasonable person would not feel free to walk away as the officer continues to address him.

We are aware that consensual encounters between police and citizens are an important, and constitutional, investigative tool. However, citizens who have not been detained immediately prior to being encountered and questioned by police are more apt to realize that they need not respond to a police officer's questions. A "consensual encounter" immediately following a detention is likely to be imbued with the authoritative aura of the detention. Without a clear break from the detention, the succeeding encounter is not consensual at all.

why a clear break is needed [handwritten margin note]

Therefore, we are convinced that the right, guaranteed by the federal and Ohio Constitutions, to be secure in one's person and property requires that citizens stopped for traffic offenses be clearly informed by the detaining officer when they are free to go after a valid detention, before an officer attempts to engage in a consensual interrogation. Any attempt at consensual interrogation must be preceded by the phrase "At this time you legally are free to go" or by words of similar import.

While the legality of consensual encounters between police and citizens should be preserved, we do not believe that this legality should be used by police officers to turn a routine traffic stop into a fishing expedition for unrelated criminal activity. The Fourth Amendment to the federal Constitution and Section 14, Article I of the Ohio Constitution exist to protect citizens against such an unreasonable interference with their liberty.

OHIO v. ROBINETTE
519 U.S. 33 (1996)

REHNQUIST, C.J.

We are here presented with the question whether the Fourth Amendment requires that a lawfully seized defendant must be advised that he is "free to go" before his consent to search will be recognized as voluntary. We hold that it does not.

We have long held that the "touchstone of the Fourth Amendment is reasonableness." Reasonableness, in turn, is measured in objective terms by examining the totality of the circumstances.

In applying this test we have consistently eschewed bright-line rules, instead emphasizing the fact-specific nature of the reasonableness inquiry. Thus, in *Florida v. Royer*, 460 U.S. 491 (1983), we expressly disavowed any "litmus-paper test" or single "sentence or ... paragraph ... rule," in recognition of the "endless variations in the facts and circumstances" implicating the Fourth Amendment. Then, in *Michigan v. Chesternut*, 486 U.S. 567 (1988), when both parties urged "bright-line rule[s] applicable to all investigatory pursuits," we rejected both proposed rules as contrary to our "traditional contextual approach." And again, in *Florida v. Bostick*, 501 U.S. 429 (1991), when the Florida Supreme Court adopted a *per se* rule that questioning aboard a bus always constitutes a seizure, we reversed, reiterating that the proper inquiry necessitates a consideration of "all the circumstances surrounding the encounter."

We have previously rejected a *per se* rule very similar to that adopted by the Supreme Court of Ohio in determining the validity of a consent to search. In *Schneckloth v. Bustamonte*, 412 U.S. 218 (1973), it was argued that such a consent could not be valid unless the defendant knew that he had a right to refuse the request. We rejected this argument: "While knowledge of the right to refuse consent is one factor to be taken into account, the government need not establish such knowledge as the *sine qua non* of an effective consent." And just as it "would be thoroughly impractical to impose on the normal consent search the detailed requirements of an effective warning," so too would it be unrealistic to require police officers to always inform detainees that they are free to go before a consent to search may be deemed voluntary.

The Fourth Amendment test for a valid consent to search is that the consent be voluntary, and "[v]oluntariness is a question of fact to be determined from all the circumstances." The Supreme Court of Ohio having held otherwise, its judgment is reversed, and the case is remanded for further proceedings not inconsistent with this opinion.

GINSBURG, J., concurring in the judgment.

I write separately...because it seems to me improbable that the Ohio Supreme Court understood its first-tell-then-ask rule to be the Federal Constitution's mandate for the Nation as a whole. "[A] State is free *as a matter of its own law* to impose greater restrictions on police activity than those this Court holds to be necessary upon federal constitutional standards." But ordinarily, when a state high court grounds a rule of criminal procedure in the Federal Constitution, the court thereby signals its view that the Nation's Constitution would require the rule in all 50 States. Given this Court's decisions in consent-to-search cases such as *Schneckloth v. Bustamonte* and *Florida v. Bostick*, however, I suspect that the Ohio Supreme Court may not have homed in on the implication ordinarily to be drawn from a state court's reliance on the Federal Constitution. In other words, I question whether the Ohio court thought of the strict rule it announced as a rule for the governance of police conduct not only in Miami County, Ohio, but also in Miami, Florida.

Formerly, the Ohio Supreme Court was "reluctant to use the Ohio Constitution to extend greater protection to the rights and civil liberties of Ohio citizens" and had usually not taken advantage of opportunities to "us[e] the Ohio Constitution as an independent source of constitutional rights." Recently, however, the state high court declared: "The Ohio Constitution is a document of independent force.... As long as state courts provide at least as much protection as the United States Supreme Court has provided in its interpretation of the federal Bill of Rights, state courts are unrestricted in according greater civil liberties and protections to individuals and groups."

The first-tell-then-ask rule seems to be a prophylactic measure not so much extracted from the text of any constitutional provision as crafted by the Ohio Supreme Court to reduce the number of violations of textually guaranteed rights. In *Miranda v. Arizona*, 384 U.S. 436 (1966), this Court announced a similarly motivated rule as a minimal national requirement without suggesting that the text of the Federal Constitution required the precise measures the Court's opinion set forth. Although all parts of the United States fall within this Court's domain, the Ohio Supreme Court is not similarly situated. That court can declare prophylactic rules governing the conduct of officials in Ohio, but it cannot command the police forces of sister States. The very ease with which the Court today disposes of the federal leg of the Ohio Supreme Court's decision strengthens my impression that the Ohio Supreme Court saw its rule as a measure made for Ohio, designed to reinforce in that State the right of the people to be secure against unreasonable searches and seizures.

The Ohio Supreme Court's syllabus and opinion, however, were ambiguous. Under *Long*, the existence of ambiguity regarding the federal- or state-law basis of a state-court decision will trigger this Court's jurisdiction. *Long* governs even when, all things considered, the more plausible reading of the state court's decision may be that the state court did not regard the Federal Constitution alone as a sufficient basis for its ruling.

It is incumbent on a state court, therefore, when it determines that its State's laws call for protection more complete than the Federal Constitution demands, to be clear about its ultimate reliance on state law. Similarly, a state court announcing a new legal rule arguably derived from both federal and state law can definitively render state law an adequate and independent ground for its decision by a simple declaration to that effect. A recent Montana Supreme Court opinion on the scope of an individual's privilege against self-incrimination includes such a declaration:

> "While we have devoted considerable time to a lengthy discussion of the application of the Fifth Amendment to the United States Constitution, it is to be noted that this holding is also based separately and independently on [the defendant's] right to remain silent pursuant to Article II, Section 25 of the Montana Constitution." *State v. Fuller*, 276 Mont. 155, 167, 915 P.2d 809, 816, cert. denied, 519 U.S. 930 (1996).

An explanation of this order meets the Court's instruction in *Long* that "[i]f the state court decision indicates clearly and expressly that it is alternatively based on bona fide separate, adequate, and independent grounds, [this Court] will not undertake to review the decision."

On remand, the Ohio Supreme Court may choose to clarify that its instructions to law enforcement officers in Ohio find adequate and independent support in state law, and that in issuing these instructions, the court endeavored to state dispositively only the law applicable in Ohio. To avoid misunderstanding, the Ohio Supreme Court must itself speak with the clarity it sought to require of its State's police officers. The efficacy of its endeavor to safeguard the liberties of Ohioans without disarming the State's police can then be tested in the precise way Our Federalism was designed to work.

OHIO v. ROBINETTE
685 N.E.2d 762 (Ohio 1997)

LUNDBERG STRATTON, J.

The first issue that we must determine is whether this court's prior holding should be reaffirmed under the adequate and independent ground of the Constitution of the state of Ohio.

When the United States Supreme Court incorporated the federal Bill of Rights into the Fourteenth Amendment, the United States Constitution became the primary mechanism to safeguard an individual's rights. As a result, state court litigation of constitutional issues was based primarily upon the authority of the United States Constitution.

However, more recently, there has been a trend for state courts to rely on their own constitutions to provide broader protection for individual rights, independent of protections afforded by the United States Constitution. A state may impose greater restrictions on police activity pursuant to its own state constitution than is required by federal constitutional standards. This movement toward enforcing state constitutions independently has been called the "New Federalism."

"New Federalism"; applying state cons

Despite this wave of New Federalism, where the provisions are similar and no persuasive reason for a differing interpretation is presented, this court has determined that protections afforded by Ohio's Constitution are coextensive with those provided by the United States Constitution.

The language of Section 14, Article I of the Ohio Constitution and the Fourth Amendment is virtually identical. Accordingly, this court has interpreted Section 14, Article I of the Ohio Constitution as affording the same protection as the Fourth Amendment. In *Nicholas v. Cleveland* (1932), 125 Ohio St. 474, 484, 182 N.E. 26, 30, [the Court,] in comparing the Fourth Amendment and Section 14, Article I of the Ohio Constitution, stated:

> "While we are not bound by federal decisions upon this feature of the case, since the Bill of Rights in the Constitution of the United States is in almost the exact language of that found in our own, the reasoning of the United States court upon this aspect of the case should be very persuasive. The state courts, however, with practical unanimity, have adopted the same principle as the federal courts."

Thus, case law indicates that, consistent with *Robinette II*, we should harmonize our interpretation of Section 14, Article I of the Ohio Constitution with the Fourth Amendment, unless there are persuasive reasons to find otherwise.

Ohio defaults to fed interpretation, unless given reason otherwise

We will first determine whether Robinette's stop and continued detention were justified. It is undisputed that Officer Newsome's act of stopping Robinette was justified because Robinette was speeding. We also find that Newsome's instruction for Robinette to exit the vehicle was also justified because it was a traffic stop. Once Newsome administered the warning for speeding to Robinette, the reason for the stop ended.

However, Newsome continued to detain Robinette pursuant to a drug interdiction policy. The drug interdiction policy required police officers to ask persons detained during a traffic stop whether they had any contraband and then to ask to search the vehicle.

Royer and *Brown* set out a standard whereby police officers, under certain circumstances, may briefly detain an individual without reasonably articulable facts giving rise to suspicion of criminal activity, if the detention promotes a legitimate public concern, *e.g.*, removing drunk drivers from public roadways or reducing drug trade.

In the case at bar, we find that, pursuant to *Royer* and *Brown*, Officer Newsome was justified in briefly detaining Robinette in order to ask him whether he was carrying any illegal drugs or weapons pursuant to the drug interdiction policy, because such a policy promotes the public interest in quelling the drug trade.

The next issue for our determination is whether the continued detention of Robinette after this point was lawful.

If during the initial detention to ask the contraband question, the officer ascertained reasonably articulable facts giving rise to a suspicion of criminal activity, the officer may then further detain and implement a more in-depth investigation of the individual. For example, at a sobriety checkpoint an officer who detects slurred speech would be justified in detaining the individual to perform a field test.

In the case at bar, Newsome did not have any reasonably articulable facts or individualized suspicion to justify Robinette's further detention in order to ask to search his car. Accordingly, Newsome was not justified in detaining Robinette in order to ask for and execute an intrusive search.

Even though we have determined that Newsome unlawfully detained Robinette to ask for permission to search his car, our analysis is not complete. Voluntary consent, determined under the totality of the circumstances, may validate an otherwise illegal detention and search.

Robinette argues that retention of *Robinette I*'s "free to go" rule would provide predictability in determining whether an individual consented to a search. We find that Robinette's conclusion is based on an oversimplified approach to the issue of consent.

In sum, every search situation is unique unto itself and no set of fixed rules will be sufficient to cover every situation. For that reason, *Bustamonte* utilized the totality-of-the-circumstances test to determine when consent is voluntary. Such a test serves both interests of allowing police to legitimately investigate under varying circumstances while protecting individuals from unreasonable searches and seizures.

In the case at bar, Officer Newsome stopped Robinette for driving sixty-nine miles per hour in a forty-five-mile-per-hour construction zone. Officer Newsome asked Robinette to step to the rear of his (Robinette's) car, which was in front of the patrol car. Newsome returned to his patrol car and turned on a video camera. Newsome gave Robinette a verbal warning *and advised Robinette that he was letting him off with only a verbal warning. But without any break in the conversation* and still in front of the camera, Newsome then asked Robinette, "One question before you get gone: are you carrying any illegal contraband in your car? Any weapons of any kind, drugs, anything like that?" Robinette denied having any contraband in the car. Newsome then immediately asked Robinette if he could search the car. Robinette hesitated, looked at his car, then back at the officer, then nodded his head. Newsome commenced a lengthy search of Robinette's car. During the search Newsome recovered some marijuana and a pill. Robinette was charged with drug abuse.

At the suppression hearing, Robinette provided the following testimony pertaining to the search:

> "Q And did he [Newsome] indicate to you that at that time [when he returned from activating the video camera] that he was giving you a warning and that you were free to go?
>
> "A Yes, he did.
>
> "Q And then at that time, I think, as the tape will reflect, the officer asked you some questions about did you have any weapons of any kind, drugs, anything like that. Do you recall that question?
>
> "A Yes.
>
> " * * *
>
> "Q Did you in fact feel that you were free to leave at that point?
>
> "A I thought I was.
>
> " * * *
>
> "Q The officer then asked if he could search your vehicle. What went through your mind at that point in time?
>
> "A Uhm, I was still sort of shocked and I-I thought-I just automatically said yes.
>
> "Q Did-did you feel that you could refuse the officer?
>
> "A No."

Newsome's words did not give Robinette any indication that he was free to go, but rather implied just the opposite-that Robinette was *not free* to go until he answered Newsome's additional questions. The timing of Newsome's immediate transition from giving Robinette the warning for speeding into questioning regarding contraband and the request to search is troubling. As the majority stated in *Robinette I:*   Under totality, still unionski tutional

When these factors are combined with a police officer's superior position of authority, any reasonable person would have felt compelled to submit to the officer's questioning. While Newsome's questioning was not expressly coercive, the circumstances surrounding the request to search made the questioning impliedly coercive. Even the state conceded, at an oral argument before the United States Supreme Court, that an officer has discretion to issue a ticket rather than a warning to a motorist if the motorist becomes uncooperative. From the totality of the circumstances, it appears that Robinette merely submitted to "a claim of lawful authority" rather than consenting as a voluntary act of free will. Under *Royer*, this is not sufficient to prove voluntary compliance.

We are very mindful that police officers face the enormous and difficult task of fighting crime. Furthermore, we explicitly continue to recognize that officers may conduct checkpoint-type questioning and consensual searches, and may progress to further detention and investigation when individualized suspicion of criminal activity arises during questioning based on reasonably articulable facts. But allowing police officers to do their jobs must be balanced against an individual's right to be free from unreasonable searches. At some point, individual rights must prevail. This is just such a case.

Accordingly, we find that Section 14, Article I of the Ohio Constitution affords protections that are coextensive with those provided by the Fourth Amendment and, therefore, the Ohio Constitution does not require a police officer to inform an individual, stopped for a traffic violation, that he or she is free to go before the officer may attempt to engage in a consensual interrogation. Further, under Section 14, Article I of the Ohio Constitution, we find that the totality-of-the circumstances test is controlling in an unlawful detention to determine whether permission to search a vehicle is voluntary. Once an individual has been unlawfully detained by law enforcement, for his or her consent to be considered an independent act of free will, the totality of the circumstances must clearly demonstrate that a reasonable person would believe that he or she had the freedom to refuse to answer further questions and could in fact leave.

Therefore, pursuant to the totality of the circumstances, we find that Robinette did not voluntarily consent to allow Newsome to search his automobile. As a result, the evidence collected in that search is inadmissible.

NOTES

1. Did the second Ohio Supreme Court decision satisfy *Michigan v. Long*? In other words, does it establish an adequate and independent state law ground? If not, why not?

2. As for the merits, why did the Ohio Supreme Court choose to align the interpretation of its "unreasonable searches and seizures" protection with the similarly worded federal guarantee? Was the initial bright-line rule indefensible as a matter of state law? How was it different from the U.S. Supreme Court's bright-line rule for applying the Fifth Amendment under *Miranda*? What explains the state supreme court's second decision?

D. SEQUENCING: THE ORDER IN WHICH STATE COURTS RESOLVE RELATED STATE AND FEDERAL CLAIMS AND THE PRIORITY GIVEN TO EACH

Michigan v. Long answers one question but leaves open another. After the decision, it is clear that the U.S. Supreme Court will presume that the resolution of state court cases involving federal and state claims turns on federal law unless the state court expressly relies on state law in resolving the claim. But *Michigan v. Long* does not tell state courts whether to prioritize the federal or the related state constitutional argument in resolving dual-claim disputes. That question has led to a vigorous debate among the courts and academics about the appropriate sequence for resolving each claim and the proper weight given U.S. Supreme Court decisions in resolving related state court claims. There are two main approaches to dual-claim cases that appear in the casebooks and the legal literature.

The first goes by the name of the "primacy" approach. It treats state constitutions as the first line of defense in guarding individual liberties and the U.S. Constitution as a backstop in the event the state guarantee does not protect the individual. It requires state courts to resolve the state claims first and to reach the federal claims only if the court does not grant relief based on the state constitution. Another way of putting it is that the "state courts should approach their state constitutions just as the U.S. Supreme Court would approach the federal Constitution—as a unique and highly significant document with a meaning that can and must be derived through independent analysis of the document itself." James A. Gardner, *The Failed Discourse of State Constitutionalism*, 90 Mich. L. Rev. 761, 774 (1992). The leading proponent of the primacy approach is Hans Linde, who argued in favor of it as an academic and later put the theory into practice as a Justice on the Oregon Supreme Court. *See* Hans A. Linde, *Due Process of Lawmaking*, 55 Neb. L. Rev. 197 (1976); Hans A. Linde, *Without "Due Process": Unconstitutional Law in Oregon*, 49 Ore. L. Rev. 125 (1970). In addition to Oregon, other state supreme courts, including Maine and New Hampshire, have used the primacy approach. John W. Shaw, *Principled Interpretations of State Constitutional Law— Why Don't the 'Primacy' States Practice What They Preach?* 54 U. Pitt. L. Rev. 1019, 1025-26 (1993). *See, e.g., State v. Cadman*, 476 A.2d 1148, 1150 (Me. 1984); *State v. Gness*, 85 A.3d 382, 384-85 (N.H. 2014) ("We first address the defendant's claim under the state constitution and rely upon federal law only to aid our analysis."); *State v. Ball*, 471 A.2d 347, 350-51 (N.H. 1983); *Sterling v. Cupp*, 625 P.2d 123 (Or. 1981). Two States apply a variation on this school of thought, the "dual sovereignty" approach, which starts with the state constitution but does not end there; it proceeds to resolve the federal claim independently regardless of whether the court grants relief on the state claim. *See* Shaw, *Principled Interpretations, supra*, at 2028; *see also, e.g., State v. Coe*, 679 P.2d 353 (Wash. 1984); *State v. Badger*, 450 A.2d 336, 346-47 (Vt. 1982).

The second theory goes by a name only an academic would love, the "interstitial" approach, but just as well might be called the "secondary" approach. It treats the U.S. Constitution as the key guardian of individual

Secondary

How NM applies Interstitial framework

rights and the state constitutions as supplemental add-on sources of individual rights. It tells state courts in dual-claim cases to resolve the federal claim first and to reach the state claim only if the court denies relief under the federal claim and, even then, to give considerable deference to U.S. Supreme Court decisions in construing the state constitution. The New Mexico Supreme Court is one of the many state courts that follows this approach:

> Under the interstitial approach, the court asks first whether the right being asserted is protected under the federal constitution. If it is, then the state constitutional claim is not reached. If it is not, then the state constitution is examined. A state court adopting this approach may diverge from federal precedent for three reasons: a flawed federal analysis, structural differences between state and federal government, or distinctive state characteristics. *State v. Sanchez*, 350 P.3d 1169, 1174 (N.M. 2015) (internal quotations omitted).

See also, e.g., Hope Clinic for Women, Ltd. v. Flores, 991 N.E.2d 745 (Ill. 2013) ("[W]hen the language of the provisions within our state and federal constitutions is nearly identical, departure from the United States Supreme Court's construction of the provision will generally be warranted only if we find in the language of our constitution, or in the debates and the committee reports of the constitutional convention, something which will indicate that the provisions of our constitution are intended to be construed differently than are similar provisions in the Federal Constitution.") (quotation omitted); *Right to Choose v. Byrne*, 450 A.2d 925 (N.J. 1982). Most state supreme courts follow the "secondary" approach or variations on it. Joseph Blocher, *Reverse Incorporation of State Constitutional Law*, 84 S. Cal. L. Rev. 323, 339 (2011) ("To this day, most state courts adopt federal constitutional law as their own. Bowing to the nationalization of constitutional discourse, they tend to follow whatever doctrinal vocabulary is used by the United States Supreme Court, discussed in the law reviews, and taught in the law schools.")

Interstitial leads to lockstep

Once a state court opts not to give its constitutional guarantee a meaning independent of the federal counterpart, it tends to proceed in "lockstep" with U.S. Supreme Court decisions construing the linguistically similar guarantee. *See, e.g., State v. Jenkins*, 3 A.3d 806, 839 (Conn. 2010) (holding that "the Connecticut constitution does not provide criminal defendants with greater protections than does the federal constitution in the context of unrelated questioning, including requests for consent to search, made during routine traffic stops"); *State v. Stevens*, 367 N.W.2d 788, 796-97 (Wis. 1985) (holding that search of garbage left out for collection did not violate Wisconsin or Federal Constitutions); *see also People v. Collins*, 475 N.W.2d 684, 691 (Mich. 1991) (stating that the Michigan constitutional provision prohibiting "unreasonable searches and seizures" should "be construed to provide the same protection as that secured by the Fourth Amendment, absent 'compelling reason' to impose a different interpretation"); *State ex rel. Rear Door Bookstore v. Tenth Dist. Court of Appeals*, 588 N.E.2d 116, 123 (Ohio 1992) (declining to find greater free speech guarantees in the Ohio Constitution than the Federal Constitution); *In re F.C. III*, 2 A.3d 1201, 1212 (Pa. 2010) ("[W]e find the due process rights implicated herein under our Constitution to be equal to those under the Fourteenth Amendment of the United States Constitution."); *cf. Am. Atheists, Inc. v. City of Detroit Downtown Dev. Auth.*, 567 F.3d 278, 301 (6th Cir. 2009) (holding that, under Michigan law, the establishment clauses of the Michigan and Federal Constitutions should be interpreted the same way).

A practical consideration affects all dual-claim cases. Unless the parties independently analyze and brief the state constitutional claim, the state court often will be forced to rely on federal law in resolving the state and federal claims. A short coda at the end of an appellate brief to the effect that, if the state court denies relief under the federal claim, it should grant relief under the state constitution, is not apt to convince state courts to take state constitutional claims seriously. Here is an example of how one court dealt with the problem:

> [A]lthough Smallfoot challenges the district court's suppression ruling under both Article I, section 4 of the Wyoming Constitution and the Fourth Amendment to the United States Constitution, he does not provide any legal analysis that the outcome under the Wyoming Constitution would differ from the federal constitution. Smallfoot's state constitutional argument consists of nothing more than recitation of a passage from *O'Boyle v. State* and an assertion that "the warrantless entry and search of [his] residence was not reasonable under all the circumstances." This Court has consistently declined, as a matter of policy, to consider a state constitutional claim in the absence of a sufficient argument supporting "adequate and independent state grounds." *Smallfoot v. State*, 272 P.3d 314, 318 (2012).

See also State v. Short, 851 N.W.2d 474, 491 (Iowa 2014) ("Notwithstanding the development of independent state constitutional law, in many cases lawyers do not advocate an Iowa constitutional standard different from the generally accepted federal standard. As a matter of prudence, we have adopted the approach in these cases that we will utilize the general standard urged by the parties, but reserve the right to apply the standard in a fashion different [from] the federal caselaw.").

Here is one perspective on the risks of the secondary approach and the lockstepping that often goes with it.

Jeffrey S. Sutton, *What Does—and Does Not—Ail State Constitutional Law*
59 Kan. L. Rev. 687 (May 2011)

Some state courts diminish their constitutions by interpreting them in lockstep with the Federal Constitution, occasionally at the beck and call of the state constitution itself.[3] The issue arises when the Federal Constitution and a state constitution contain an identical or similarly worded guarantee and a litigant invokes both of them, by arguing, say, that an arrest violates the federal and state prohibitions on "unreasonable searches and seizures." There is no reason to think, as an interpretive matter, that constitutional guarantees of independent sovereigns, even guarantees with the same or similar words, must be construed the same. Still less is there reason to think that a highly generalized guarantee, such as a prohibition on "unreasonable" searches, would have just one meaning for a range of differently situated sovereigns. Yet in my experience, state and federal courts frequently handle such cases by considering the federal constitutional claim first, after which they summarily announce that the state provision means the same thing.

Why the meaning of a federal guarantee proves the meaning of an independent state guarantee is rarely explained and often seems inexplicable. If the court decisions of another sovereign ought to bear on the inquiry, those of a sister state should have more to say about the point. State constitutions are more likely to share historical and cultural similarities. They necessarily will cover smaller jurisdictions. And in almost all instances they will be construing individual-liberty guarantees that originated in state constitutions, not the Federal Constitution,[4] and

---

[3] [156] *See* Fla. Const. art. I, §§ 12, 17 (requiring that Florida courts construe the state constitutional right against unlawful searches, seizures, and excessive punishments "in conformity with" the Fourth and Eighth Amendments, respectively, as interpreted by the U.S. Supreme Court); *cf.* Cal. Const. art. I, § 7(a) ("A person may not be...denied equal protection of the laws; provided, that nothing...imposes upon the State...any obligations or responsibilities which exceed those imposed by the Equal Protection Clause of the 14th Amendment to the United States Constitution with respect to the use of pupil school assignment or pupil transportation."); *Raven v. Deukmejian*, 801 P.2d 1077, 1089 (Cal. 1990) (striking down a section of Proposition 115 that prevented state courts from construing the California constitution to afford greater rights to criminal defendants than the Federal Constitution).

[4] [159] *See, e.g.*, William J. Brennan, Jr., *State Constitutions and the Protection of Individual Rights*, 90 Harv. L. Rev. 489, 501 (1977) ("Prior to the adoption of the federal Constitution, each of the rights eventually recognized in the federal Bill of Rights had previously been protected in one or more state constitutions."); Randy J. Holland, *State Constitutions: Purpose and Function*, 69 Temp. L. Rev. 989, 997 (1996) ("[S]tate Declarations of Rights were the primary origin and model for the provisions set forth in the Federal Bill of Rights."); Gordon S. Wood, *Foreword: State Constitution-Making in the American Revolution*, 24 Rutgers L.J. 911, 911 (1993) ("The office of our governors,

they indeed will be exercising a power—judicial review—that originated in state constitutional law, not in *Marbury v. Madison*.[5]

Why borrow in particular from the larger, far larger, jurisdiction? Federalism considerations may lead the United States Supreme Court to underenforce (or at least not to overenforce) constitutional guarantees in view of the number of people affected (over 300 million) and the range of jurisdictions implicated (one national government, fifty states, and thousands of local governments). No state supreme court, by contrast, has any reason to apply a "federalism discount" to its decisions, making it odd for state courts to rely exclusively on the meaning of the Federal Constitution in construing their own.

State court decisions of this type not only seem to be prioritizing the wrong decisions in determining the meaning of their own constitutions, but they also seem to be inverting the right sequence for considering state and federal arguments. Federal constitutional avoidance principles would suggest that the state guarantee ought to be considered first. If the state supreme court grants relief to the claimant on the state ground and provides a clear statement that it is doing so, the case is over, and the need to construe the federal constitutional provision disappears with it. No version of the constitutional avoidance doctrine to my knowledge says that courts should consider the claim arising from the larger sovereign before they consider the claim arising from the smaller one.

The nature of a federal constitutional claim points in the same direction. At issue is whether state action violates the Federal Constitution. If the state constitution prohibits the law or conduct at issue, however, there is no work for the Federal Constitution to do. Why not consider that point first, not as a matter of exhaustion, but as a matter of potentially eliminating any ultra vires state action at all and sparing the need to consider the federal claim in the process? By deciding the federal claim first, state courts engage in federal constitutional aggrandizement, not avoidance, and they risk diminishing their state constitutions in the process. By doing the reverse, they claim the rightful independence of their state constitutions.

---

the bicameral legislatures, tripartite separation of powers, bills of rights, and the unique use of constitutional conventions were all born during the state constitution-making period between 1775 and the early 1780s, well before the federal constitution of 1787 was created.").

[5] [160] Joseph Blocher, *Reverse Incorporation of State Constitutional Law*, 84 S. Cal. L. Rev. 323, 334 (2011).

In defense of the state (and federal) courts that take this path, explanations abound. As a matter of history, state constitutional law may have been all that mattered in the country's first 150 years, at least from the perspective of an individual-rights claimant. *See Barron ex rel. Tiernan v. Mayor of Baltimore*, 32 U.S. (7 Pet.) 243 (1833). But the incorporation of most of the Bill of Rights beginning in the 1920s started to change that, and the expansion of federal constitutional protections in the 1950s and 1960s completed the transformation. After the breakthroughs of the Warren Court revolution, who could blame state courts and advocates for relegating state constitutional claims to second-class treatment, if indeed to any treatment at all? A tradition of jurisprudence premised on the predominance of federal rights may not be easy to undo. Even though twenty-first century state courts are as apt to be constitutional innovators as federal courts, decades of state court precedents remain on the books paralleling the federal precedents or at least starting their analyses with them.

Efficiencies also may make a difference. Keep in mind that, by one count, ninety-five percent of the disputes resolved by courts in this country are filed in the state courts, as opposed to the federal ones. Just one of those courts, the California Supreme Court, resolved thirty-seven state constitutional law disputes in 2005, while the United States Supreme Court resolved thirty federal constitutional law disputes that same year. All of this makes it understandable that state courts would keep up with their burgeoning dockets by sticking to the calf-path rather than diverging from it.

Also daunting is the reality, at least the one I have experienced, that many advocates do not press the state arguments on an independent basis. What is argued is not a ground-up assessment of the independent meaning of the state guarantee, premised on its language, its history, or early understandings of its meaning. The point urged instead is that the state courts should construe the state guarantee differently because they can, not because they must, or because the dissent rather than the majority in a U.S. Supreme Court case has the better of the (federal) arguments.

This is the one respect in which Justice Brennan's boundary-crossing 1977 article, *State Constitutions and the Protection of Individual Rights*, 90 Harv. L. Rev. 489, delivered less than it could have for the development of state constitutional law. With the waning of civil rights victories brought by the end of the Warren Court and the beginning of the Burger Court, Justice Brennan pressed the state courts to fortify the breach, to grant relief by another name: a state constitution. "It may not be wide of the mark," he said, "to suppose that...state courts discern, and disagree with, a trend in recent opinions of the United States Supreme Court to pull back from, or at least suspend for the time being, the…application of the federal Bill of Rights and the restraints of the due process and equal protection clauses of the fourteenth amendment." State courts, he thus urged, "cannot rest when they have afforded their citizens the full protections of the federal Constitution," but should grant relief under their own constitutions instead.

In one respect, Justice Brennan was right. Constitutional claimants should prefer two arrows in their quiver—two chances, not just one, to invalidate a state or local law. But the messenger and the message may have helped to perpetuate, if not to create, two damaging myths.

The messenger may have prompted state court advocates and judges to misperceive this option as designed only to be a liberal ratchet, to give just some rights but not others a second chance in the state courts. Yet as shown above, independent state courts (and legislatures) often have protected a range of rights, whether involving liberty, equality, or property, whether before or after the federal courts entered the picture. That the state constitutions provide a second avenue for invalidating a local law says nothing about what kind of law should be, or will be, challenged.

The message pushed one feature of state constitutional law (the authority of the states to construe their constitutions differently) at the expense of another (an independent basis for doing so). The suggested inquiry was not whether state constitutional law demanded a different answer from federal constitutional law based on language, context, and history; it was that, if there is a will, there is now a new way for granting relief. Instead of urging first-principle inquiries into the meaning of the state provisions, the article urged state courts to side with the dissenters in debates already held at the United States Supreme Court—under federal law no less. While state court judges and advocates assuredly have the authority to invoke dissents rather than majority opinions of the United States Supreme Court in construing their own constitutions, heavy reliance on debates about the meaning of a federal guarantee are not apt to dignify the state constitutions as independent sources of law.

The Brennan article thus helped advance state constitutional law in one sense: by reminding advocates, through a prominent Supreme Court Justice, that once-forgotten state constitutional protections remain on the books and that they provide an alternative theory for relief. But in a state constitutional law equivalent of Stockholm syndrome, the article may have advanced the unfortunate myth that federal constitutional law remains front and center—the first line of inquiry—leaving state constitutional law as the quintessential argument of last resort.

Some say that federal claims should be resolved first in cases presenting federal and state contentions because state courts cannot construe their constitutions to offer less protection than the federal guarantee. That is wrong. State courts remain free to construe their constitutional guarantees to offer as little protection as they think appropriate, and only a constitutional amendment can alter that decision. Some state courts have said as much.[6] The only thing state courts cannot do is ignore the independent federal claim. It may be true that a state constitutional ruling that asks less of the government than existing federal constitutional law requires will not impact the parties before the court. But that is not a moot point. Once a state court establishes the interrelation between the two guarantees, it has established that no state constitutional inquiry is needed, a not-unhelpful development for future litigants and courts.

That also is a not-insignificant development for the United States Supreme Court, as it manages and assesses decisions of its own. Some state court rulings directly implicate the meaning of a federal guarantee, such as the Eighth Amendment's prohibition on "cruel and unusual punishment."[7] And some state court rulings may help to inform the original meaning of language in the Federal Constitution that first appeared in the state constitutions or may provide pragmatic reasons for following or steering clear of an approach embraced by the states.[8] Why live in a "top-down constitutional world" when we have the option of allowing the states to be the "vanguard—the first ones to decide whether to embrace or reject innovative legal claims"—and allowing the United States Supreme Court, informed by these experiences, to decide whether to federalize the issue. In a process that Professor Blocher calls "reverse incorporation," the United States Supreme Court remains free, whether on pragmatic or originalist grounds, to learn from and, if appropriate, borrow from the states' experiences.

Perhaps some fear confusion in the bar if the state courts de-link the two constitutional inquiries. After all, the United States Supreme Court's multi-decade experiment with dueling standards for Bill of Rights guarantees applicable to the state and federal governments did not end

---

[6] [165] See e.g., State v. Kennedy, 666 P.2d 1316, 1323 (Or. 1983) ("A state's view of its own guarantee may indeed be less stringent, in which case the state remains bound to whatever is the contemporary federal rule.").

[7] [180] See Roper v. Simmons, 543 U.S. 551, 574 (2005); Atkins v. Virginia, 536 U.S. 304, 312 (2002); Penry v. Lynaugh, 492 U.S. 302, 330-31 (1989); Stanford v. Kentucky, 492 U.S. 361, 369 (1989); Blocher, supra note 3, at 378.

[8] [181] See District of Columbia v. Heller, 554 U.S. 570, 580 n.6, 583 n.7, 584-86, 590 n.13 (2008); New York Times Co. v. Sullivan, 376 U.S. 254, 280 (1964); Davis v. Massachusetts, 167 U.S. 43 (1897); Blocher, supra note 3, at 371, 382.

well, as the Court ultimately collapsed the two. But is confusion really a problem for a single state? If the state courts treat the two guarantees as distinct, the bench, bar, law enforcement, and citizenry still will have to pay attention to just one standard: the more far-reaching of the two.

In the final analysis, there assuredly are historical and practical explanations for linking the meaning of federal and state guarantees and for prioritizing consideration of the federal ones. But continuing to do so in 2011 as a matter of course is increasingly difficult to justify and, worse, all the more likely to deepen the inertia-driven groove that already exists.

CHAPTER IV

EQUALITY

A. INTRODUCTION

Jeffrey M. Shaman, *Equality and Liberty in The Golden Age of State Constitutional Law* (2008) 1-5

Equality is a principle that enjoys a long history in state constitutional law. Some of the earliest state constitutions, which are the oldest political documents in America, proclaimed: "All men are born equally free and independent, and have certain inherent and indefeasible rights."[1] Today, that sentiment can still be found in a number of state constitutions, but is more likely to be expressed as: "All people are created equal and are entitled to equal rights and opportunity under the law."[2] A number of the early state constitutions also contained provisions prohibiting the granting of unequal privileges or immunities. These provisions, too, along with their close counterparts banning special entitlements, can be found in many state constitutions today. After the Civil War and the enactment in the Federal Constitution of the Fourteenth Amendment guaranteeing equal protection of the laws to all persons, some states were moved to follow suit by adding equal protection clauses to their constitutions when the opportunity arose. The civil rights movement of the 1950s and 60s inspired some states to add provisions to their constitutions prohibiting discrimination against persons in the exercise of their civil rights. And after the Equal Rights Amendment (ERA) prohibiting discrimination on the basis of sex failed to gain passage at the federal level, some states adopted their own versions of the ERA. It is worthy of note that long before the conception of the ERA, both Utah and Wyoming enacted state constitutional provisions guaranteeing equal civil, political, and religious rights and privileges for "male and female citizens."

Furthermore, in a number of state constitutions there are provisions that grant specialized protection for various kinds of equality. For instance, a few state constitutions provide for "free and equal elections." There are provisions in three state constitutions that expressly bar segregation. The Alaska constitution states that "No exclusive right or special privilege of fishery shall be created or authorized in the natural waters of the State." Some state constitutions expressly prohibit certain forms of discrimination in the private sector as well as the public one.

---

[1] Pa. Const. art. I, § 1 (1776). *See also* Va. Const. Bill of Rights, § 1 (1776) ("All men are by nature equally free and independent....").

[2] Wis. Const. art. I, § 1 (1982).

Other state constitutions contain so-called "uniformity clauses" that call for taxes to be uniformly levied within the same class of subjects. (See Chapter XIV, sect. E.)

It is important to mention that a number of state constitutions contain a combination of equality provisions. In some cases, the combination of provisions included in a state constitution amounts to a comprehensive mandate for equal treatment under the law. Perhaps the Connecticut constitution contains the most comprehensive protection of equality by declaring that:

> All men when they form a social compact, are equal in rights; and no man or set of men are entitled to exclusive public emoluments or privileges from the community...No person shall be denied the equal protection of the law nor be subjected to segregation or discrimination in the exercise or enjoyment of his or her civil or political rights because of religion, race, color, ancestry, national origin, sex or physical or mental disability.

At the opposite end of the spectrum, there are some state constitutions that contain no language expressly addressing equality or that only briefly refer to it. Nevertheless, other language in those constitutions may be interpreted to encompass a guarantee of equality. The Maryland Court of Appeals, for example, has ruled that although the Maryland Declaration of Rights does not contain an express equal protection clause, the concept of equal protection is embodied in the due process article of the Declaration of Rights. Similarly, the West Virginia Supreme Court of Appeals has held that although the phrase "equal protection" is not found in the state constitution, the principle of equality is an integral part of the state's constitutional law, inherent in the due process clause of the West Virginia Bill of Rights. And the Minnesota Supreme Court has recognized that the law of the land provision in the Minnesota Bill of Rights embraces principles of equality synonymous with the Equal Protection Clause of the Fourteenth Amendment to the Federal Constitution.

The state constitutions, then, are a rich source of protection for equality.

B. RACIAL CLASSIFICATIONS

SHEFF v. O'NEILL
678 A.2d 1267 (Conn. 1996)

PETERS, C.J.

The public elementary and high school students in Hartford suffer daily from the devastating effects that racial and ethnic isolation, as well as poverty, have had on their education. Federal constitutional law provides no remedy for their plight. The principal issue in this appeal is whether, under the unique provisions of our state constitution, the state, which already plays an active role in managing public schools, must take further measures to relieve the severe handicaps that burden these children's education. The issue is as controversial as the stakes are high. We hold today that the needy schoolchildren of Hartford have waited long enough. The constitutional imperatives contained in article eighth, § 1,[3] and article first, §§ 1 and 20,[4] of our state constitution entitle the plaintiffs to relief. At the same time, the constitutional imperative of separation of powers persuades us to afford the legislature, with the assistance of the executive branch, the opportunity, in the first instance, to fashion the remedy that will most appropriately respond to the constitutional violations that we have identified. The judgment of the trial court must, accordingly, be reversed.

The stipulation of the parties and the trial court's findings establish the following relevant facts. Statewide, in the 1991-92 school year, children from minority groups constituted 25.7 percent of the public school population. In the Hartford public school system in that same period, 92.4 percent of the students were members of minority groups, including, predominantly, students who were either African-American or Latino. Fourteen of Hartford's twenty-five elementary schools had a white student enrollment of less than 2 percent. The Hartford public school system currently enrolls the highest percentage of minority students in the state. In the future, if current conditions continue, the percentage of minority students in the Hartford public school system is likely to increase rather than decrease. Although enrollment of African-American students in the twenty-one surrounding suburban towns has increased by more than 60 percent from 1980 to 1992, only seven of these school districts had a minority student enrollment in excess of 10 percent in 1992. Because of the negative consequences of racial and ethnic isolation, a more integrated public school system would likely be beneficial to all schoolchildren.

---

[3] [1] The constitution of Connecticut, article eighth, § 1, provides: "There shall always be free public elementary and secondary schools in the state. The general assembly shall implement this principle by appropriate legislation."

[4] [2] The constitution of Connecticut, article first, § 1, provides: "All men when they form a social compact, are equal in rights; and no man or set of men are entitled to exclusive public emoluments or privileges from the community."

The constitution of Connecticut, article first, § 20, as amended by articles five and twenty-one of the amendments, provides: "No person shall be denied the equal protection of the law nor be subjected to segregation or discrimination in the exercise or enjoyment of his or her civil or political rights because of religion, race, color, ancestry, national origin, sex or physical or mental disability."

A majority of the children who constitute the public school population in Hartford come from homes that are economically disadvantaged, that are headed by a single parent and in which a language other than English is spoken. The percentage of Hartford schoolchildren at the elementary level who return to the same school that they attended the previous year is the lowest such percentage in the state. Such socioeconomic factors impair a child's orientation toward and skill in learning and adversely affect a child's performance on standardized tests. The gap in the socioeconomic status between Hartford schoolchildren and schoolchildren from the surrounding twenty-one suburban towns has been increasing. The performance of Hartford schoolchildren on standardized tests falls significantly below that of schoolchildren from the twenty-one surrounding suburban towns.

The state has not intentionally segregated racial and ethnic minorities in the Hartford public school system. Except for a brief period in 1868, no students in Connecticut have intentionally been assigned to a public school or to a public school district on the basis of race or ethnicity. There has never been any other manifestation of de jure segregation either at the state or the local level. In addition to various civil rights initiatives undertaken by the legislature from 1905 to 1961 to combat racial discrimination, the state board of education was reorganized, during the 1980s, to concentrate on the needs of urban schoolchildren and to promote diversity in the public schools. Since 1970, the state has supported and encouraged voluntary plans for increasing interdistrict diversity.

The state has nonetheless played a significant role in the present concentration of racial and ethnic minorities in the Hartford public school system. Although intended to improve the quality of education and not racially or ethnically motivated, the districting statute that the legislature enacted in 1909, now codified at § 10-240, is the single most important factor contributing to the present concentration of racial and ethnic minorities in the Hartford public school system. The districting statute and the resultant school district boundaries have remained virtually unchanged since 1909. The districting statute is of critical importance because it establishes town boundaries as the dividing line between all school districts in the state.

The defendants maintain that...the plaintiffs are not entitled to judicial relief because the educational disparities of which they complain do not result from the requisite state action. The plaintiffs claim that the state bears responsibility to correct the constitutional violations alleged in their complaint because of the state's failure to "take corrective measures to [e]nsure that its Hartford public schoolchildren receive an equal educational opportunity." That failure is actionable, according to the plaintiffs, because of the state's knowledge of the racial and ethnic isolation in the Hartford schools, combined with the state's extensive involvement in the operations of Connecticut's public schools and the impact of state statutes mandating school attendance within statutorily defined school districts. The defendants maintain, to the contrary, that the state's constitutional duty to provide for the elementary and secondary education of Connecticut schoolchildren is triggered only by state action that is alleged to be intentional state misconduct.

The defendants' argument, derived largely from principles of federal constitutional law, founders on the fact that article eighth, § 1, and article first, §§ 1 and 20, impose on the legislature an affirmative constitutional obligation to provide schoolchildren throughout the state with a substantially equal educational opportunity. It follows that, if the legislature fails, for whatever reason, to take action to remedy substantial inequalities in the educational opportunities that such children are being afforded, its actions and its omissions constitute state action.

The affirmative constitutional obligation that we recognized in *Horton I* and *Horton III*, and reaffirmed recently in *Moore v. Ganim*, 660 A.2d 742 (1995), was not premised on a showing that the legislature had played an active role in creating the inequalities that the constitution requires it to redress. In *Horton I*, we determined that the state's educational financing scheme was unconstitutional even though it was facially nondiscriminatory and even though the disparities resulting therefrom had not been created intentionally by the legislature. These constitutionally unacceptable disparities developed, instead, "from the circumstance that over the years there [had] arisen a great disparity in the ability of local communities to finance local education," and from the legislature's failure to consider "the financial capability of [each] municipality...." In declaring this statutory scheme unconstitutional in *Horton I*, and in requiring further remedial action in *Horton III*, we necessarily determined that the state's failure adequately to address school funding inequalities constituted the state action that is the constitutional prerequisite for affording judicial relief.

The claims now before us likewise implicate the legislature's affirmative constitutional obligation to provide a substantially equal educational opportunity to all of the state's schoolchildren. The plaintiffs document the existence of an extensive statutory system developed in response to the legislature's plenary authority over state public elementary and secondary schools. As a general matter, the plaintiffs challenge the failure of the legislature to address continuing unconstitutional inequities resulting, de facto, from that scheme. The failure adequately to address the racial and ethnic disparities that exist among the state's public school districts is not different in kind from the legislature's failure adequately to address the "great disparity in the ability of local communities to finance local education" that made the statutory scheme at issue in *Horton I* unconstitutional in its application.

The defendants urge us to follow federal precedents that concededly require, as a matter of federal constitutional law, that claimants seeking judicial relief for educational disparities pursuant to the equal protection clause of the fourteenth amendment to the United States constitution must prove intentional governmental discrimination against a suspect class. According to the defendants, because the plaintiffs raise claims of unconstitutional disparities in educational opportunities on the basis of severe racial and ethnic imbalances among school districts, the plaintiffs, too, must prove intentional state action.

For two reasons, we are not persuaded that we should adopt these precedents as a matter of state constitutional law. First and foremost, the federal cases start from the premise that there is no right to education under the United States constitution. Our Connecticut constitution, by contrast, contains a fundamental right to education and a corresponding affirmative state obligation to implement and maintain that right. Second, the federal cases are guided by principles of federalism as "a foremost consideration in interpreting any of the pertinent constitutional provisions under which [a court] examines state action." As the United States Supreme Court noted, "it would be difficult to imagine a case having a greater potential impact on our federal system than the one now before us, in which we are urged to abrogate systems of financing public education presently in existence in virtually every State." Principles of federalism, however, do not restrict our constitutional authority to enforce the constitutional mandates contained in article eighth, § 1, and article first, §§ 1 and 20.

In summary, under our law, which imposes an affirmative constitutional obligation on the legislature to provide a substantially equal educational opportunity for all public schoolchildren, the state action doctrine is not a defense to the plaintiffs' claims of constitutional deprivation. The state had ample notice of ongoing trends toward racial and ethnic isolation in its public schools, and indeed undertook a number of laudable remedial efforts that unfortunately have not achieved their desired end. The fact that the legislature did not affirmatively create or intend to create the conditions that have led to the racial and ethnic isolation in the Hartford public school system does not, in and of itself, relieve the defendants of their affirmative obligation to provide the plaintiffs with a more effective remedy for their constitutional grievances.

Since *Horton I*, it is common ground that the state has an affirmative constitutional obligation to provide all public schoolchildren with a substantially equal educational opportunity. Any infringement of that right must be strictly scrutinized....The issue presented by this case is whether the state has fully satisfied its affirmative constitutional obligation to provide a substantially equal educational opportunity if the state demonstrates that it has substantially equalized school funding and resources. For the purposes of the present litigation, we decide only that the scope of the constitutional obligation expressly imposed on the state by article eighth, § 1, is informed by the constitutional prohibition against segregation contained in article first, § 20. Reading these constitutional provisions conjointly, we conclude that the existence of extreme racial and ethnic isolation in the public school system deprives schoolchildren of a substantially equal educational opportunity and requires the state to take further remedial measures.

Two factors persuade us that it is appropriate to undertake a conjoint reading of these provisions of our state constitution. One is the special nature of the affirmative constitutional right embodied in article eighth, § 1. The other is the explicit prohibition of segregation contained in article first, § 20.

The affirmative constitutional obligation of the state to provide a substantially equal educational opportunity, which is embodied in article eighth, § 1, differs in kind from most constitutional obligations. Organic documents only rarely contain provisions that explicitly require the state to act rather than to refrain from acting. Nothing in the description of the relevant legal landscape in any of our cases suggests that the constitutional right that we articulated in *Horton I* was limited to school financing.

For Connecticut schoolchildren, the scope of the state's constitutional obligation to provide a substantially equal educational opportunity is informed and amplified by the highly unusual[5] provision in article first, § 20, that prohibits segregation not only indirectly, by forbidding discrimination, but directly, by the use of the term "segregation." The section provides in relevant part: "No person shall be denied the equal protection of the law nor be subjected to segregation or discrimination ... because of ... race [or] ... ancestry...."

The express inclusion of the term "segregation" in article first, § 20, has independent constitutional significance. The addition of this term to the text of our equal protection clause distinguishes this case from others in which we have found a substantial equivalence between our equal protection clause and that contained in the United States constitution. Fundamental principles of constitutional interpretation require that "[e]ffect must be given to every part of and each word in our constitution...." In other cases, we have held that, insofar as article first, §

[5] [29] The only other constitutions that explicitly prohibit segregation are those of Hawaii and New Jersey.

20, differs textually from its federal counterpart, its judicial construction must reflect such a textual distinction.

The issue before us, therefore, is what specific meaning to attach to the protection against segregation contained in article first, § 20, in a case in which that protection is invoked as part of the plaintiff school-children's fundamental affirmative right to a substantially equal educational opportunity under article eighth, § 1. In concrete terms, this issue devolves into the question of whether the state has a constitutional duty to remedy the educational impairment that results from segregation in the Hartford public schools, even though the conditions of segregation that contribute to such impairment neither were caused nor are perpetuated by invidious intentional conduct on the part of the state.

Linguistically, the term "segregation" in article first, § 20, which denotes "separation," is neutral about segregative intent. The section prohibits segregation that occurs "because of religion, race, color, ancestry, national origin, sex or physical or mental disability," without specifying the manner in which such a causal relationship must be established.

Whatever this language may portend in other contexts, we are persuaded that, in the context of public education, in which the state has an affirmative obligation to monitor and to equalize educational opportunity, the state's awareness of existing and increasing severe racial and ethnic isolation imposes upon the state the responsibility to remedy "segregation ... because of race [or] ... ancestry...." We therefore hold that, textually, article eighth, § 1, as informed by article first, § 20, requires the legislature to take affirmative responsibility to remedy segregation in our public schools, regardless of whether that segregation has occurred de jure or de facto.

The history of the promulgation of article eighth, § 1, and article first, § 20, supports our conclusion that these constitutional provisions include protection from de facto segregation, at least in public schools. That history includes not only the contemporaneous addition, in 1965, of these two provisions to our constitution, but also the strong commitment to ending discrimination and segregation that is evident in the remarks of the delegates to the 1965 constitutional convention.

Sound principles of public policy support our conclusion that the legislature's affirmative constitutional responsibility for the education of all public schoolchildren encompasses responsibility for segregation to which the legislature has contributed, even unintentionally. The parties agree, as the trial court expressly found, that racial and ethnic segregation is harmful, and that integration would likely have positive benefits for all children and for society as a whole. Further, as the trial court also expressly found, the racial and ethnic isolation of children in the Hartford schools is likely to worsen in the future.

Racial and ethnic segregation has a pervasive and invidious impact on schools, whether the segregation results from intentional conduct or from unorchestrated demographic factors. "[S]chools are an important socializing institution, imparting those shared values through which social order and stability are maintained." *Plyler v. Doe*, 457 U.S. 202, 222 n. 20 (1982). Schools bear central responsibility for "inculcating [the] fundamental values necessary to the maintenance of a democratic political system...." *Ambach v. Norwick*, 441 U.S. 68, 77 (1979). When children attend racially and ethnically isolated schools, these "shared values" are jeopardized: "If children of different races and economic and social groups have no opportunity to know each other and to live together in school, they cannot be expected to gain the understanding and mutual respect necessary for the cohesion of our society." *Jenkins v. Township of Morris School District*, 58 N.J. 483, 498 (1971). "[T]he elimination of racial isolation in the schools promotes the attainment of equal educational opportunity and is beneficial to all students, both black and white." *Lee v. Nyquist*, 318 F. Supp. 710, 714 (W.D.N.Y. 1970), aff'd without opinion, 402 U.S. 935 (1971). Our state constitution, as amended in 1965, imposes on the state an affirmative obligation to respond to such segregation.

It is crucial for a democratic society to provide all of its schoolchildren with fair access to an unsegregated education. As the United States Supreme Court has eloquently observed, a sound education "is the very foundation of good citizenship. Today it is a principal instrument in awakening the child to cultural values, in preparing him for later professional training, and in helping him to adjust normally to his environment. In these days, it is doubtful that any child may reasonably be expected to succeed in life if he is denied the opportunity of an education. Such an opportunity, where the state has undertaken to provide it, is a right which must be made available to all on equal terms." *Brown v. Board of Education*, 347 U.S. at 493. "The American people have always regarded education and [the] acquisition of knowledge as matters of supreme importance.... We have recognized the public schools as a most vital civic institution for the preservation of a democratic system of government ... and as the primary vehicle for transmitting the values on which our society rests.... And these historic perceptions of the public schools as inculcating fundamental values necessary to the maintenance of a democratic political system have been confirmed by the observations of social scientists.... [E]ducation provides the basic tools by which individuals might lead economically productive lives to the benefit of us all. In sum, education has a fundamental role in maintaining the fabric of our society. We cannot ignore the significant social costs borne by our

Nation when select groups are denied the means to absorb the values and skills upon which our social order rests." *Plyler v. Doe*, 457 U.S. at 221.

Our decision to reverse the judgment of the trial court, and to direct that judgment be rendered on behalf of the plaintiffs on the merits of their constitutional claims in the first and second counts of their complaint, requires us to consider what relief may properly be afforded to the plaintiffs.... We have decided...to employ the methodology used in *Horton I*. In that case, the trial court, after having found for the plaintiffs, limited its judgment by granting only declaratory relief but retained jurisdiction to grant consequential relief, if needed, at some future time. *Horton I*. In light of the complexities of developing a legislative program that would respond to the constitutional deprivation that the plaintiffs had established, we concluded, in *Horton I*, that further judicial intervention should be stayed "to afford the General Assembly an opportunity to take appropriate legislative action." Prudence and sensitivity to the constitutional authority of coordinate branches of government counsel the same caution in this case.

In staying our hand, we do not wish to be misunderstood about the urgency of finding an appropriate remedy for the plight of Hartford's public schoolchildren. Every passing day denies these children their constitutional right to a substantially equal educational opportunity. Every passing day shortchanges these children in their ability to learn to contribute to their own well-being and to that of this state and nation. We direct the legislature and the executive branch to put the search for appropriate remedial measures at the top of their respective agendas. We are confident that with energy and good will, appropriate remedies can be found and implemented in time to make a difference before another generation of children suffers the consequences of a segregated public school education.

BORDEN, J., dissenting.

I...agree that racial and ethnic isolation in our public schools is harmful—both to those races and ethnic groups that are so isolated and to the other races and ethnic groups from whom they are isolated. I also agree with the majority's statement, based upon the trial court's finding, that the racial and ethnic isolation of Hartford's schoolchildren is likely to worsen in the future. I agree, furthermore, that racial and ethnic integration of our public schools would be beneficial for all children and society in general. These points of agreement rest on the notions that, as the majority recognizes, schools are important socializing institutions that bear a central responsibility for imparting our shared democratic values to our children, and that the opportunity for children of different races, ethnic backgrounds, economic levels and social groups to get to know each other in school is important if they are to understand and respect each other. Finally, I agree with the majority that the health of the economy of our state requires an educated workforce, which includes "the urban poor as an integral part of our future economic strength." Thus, I agree with the majority on the importance in our state—indeed, in our nation—of finding a way to cross the racial divide.

The majority, however, has transformed a laudable educational philosophy into a constitutional mandate. Thus, the majority has used this court's power to interpret the constitution in order to mandate a vast and unprecedented social experiment.... It is a bedrock principle of our system of government that the legislative branch is the source of the fundamental public policy of the state, and that the courts may invalidate such a policy only where it is established beyond a reasonable doubt that it violates a constitutional right. Not only does the majority fail even to give lip service to this principle, the majority violates it.

NOTE

In *Brown v. Board of Education*, 347 U.S. 483 (1954), the Supreme Court of the United States ruled that racial segregation in public schools violated the Equal Protection Clause of the United States Constitution. In that momentous decision and others adhering to its principles, the Supreme Court rendered classifications based on race constitutionally suspect and subject to strict judicial scrutiny. Since then, litigation concerning racial discrimination has occurred primarily in the federal courts and has been predominantly a matter of federal constitutional law. As illustrated by *Sheff v. O'Neill*, however, in some instances state constitutional provisions may be interpreted to provide more extensive protection for equality than the Federal Constitution provides.

Some years after *Brown*, the Supreme Court drew a distinction between *de jure* and *de facto* racial segregation, ruling that the latter amounted to a violation of the Equal Protection Clause only when proven to be the result of intentional racial discrimination. In California, the state supreme court ruled otherwise, holding in a series of cases that the California equal protection clause prohibited *de facto* as well as *de jure* racial segregation in public schools and that state officials had an affirmative obligation to eradicate all forms of racial segregation in public schools. *Jackson v. Pasadena City School District*, 382 P.2d 878 (Cal. 1963); *San Francisco Unified School District v. Johnson*, 479 P.2d 669 (Cal. 1971); *Crawford v. Board of Education*, 551 P.2d 28 (Cal. 1976). In these cases, the California high court took the position that even in the absence of intentional discriminatory conduct the state constitution required the elimination of racial segregation in public schools. The force of these rulings, though, subsequently was nullified by a ballot initiative amending the state constitution. In contrast, no action has been taken to overrule *Sheff v. O'Neill*, and that decision still stands.

MALABED v. NORTH SLOPE BOROUGH
70 P.3d 416 (Alaska 2003)

BRYNER, J.

In 1997 the North Slope Borough enacted an ordinance that creates a mandatory preference for hiring, promoting, transferring, and reinstating Native Americans in borough government employment. The current version of the preference extends to all Native American applicants who are minimally qualified or meet most minimum job requirements and can meet the remaining requirements during their probationary period of employment; for purposes of the preference, "Native American" is defined to include any person belonging to an Indian tribe under federal law.

The borough enacted this preference after a study of economic conditions showed that the Native American population within the borough, specifically the resident Inupiat Eskimos, was both underemployed and earning substantially less money per capita than borough residents of other races.

Article I, section 1, of the Alaska Constitution guarantees equal protection, providing that "all persons are equal and entitled to equal rights, opportunities, and protection under the law." In addition, Article I, section 3, of the Alaska Constitution categorically prohibits discrimination based on race or national origin: "No person is to be denied the enjoyment of any civil or political right because of race, color, creed, sex, or national origin." The legislature implemented these provisions in part by enacting the Alaska Human Rights Act, which prohibits employment discrimination based on race or national origin, and AS 29.20.630, which specifically prohibits Alaska's municipalities—including home rule municipalities like the North Slope Borough—from engaging in racial and national origin discrimination. In recognition of these requirements, the borough's charter itself prohibits these forms of discrimination: "No person may be discriminated against in any borough employment because of race, age, color, political or religious affiliation, or [national] origin."

Relying on these provisions, Malabed argues that the borough's hiring preference adopts a racial classification or, alternatively, a *classification* based on national origin, in violation of the Alaska Constitution. The borough responds by denying that its preference uses a race-conscious classification; instead, the borough insists, the preference adopts a well-accepted and constitutionally permissible political classification based on membership in federally recognized tribes. In advancing this argument, the borough relies chiefly on *Morton v. Mancari* [, 417 U.S. 535 (1974)].

In *Mancari* the Supreme Court upheld a Bureau of Indian Affairs employment preference for hiring and promoting Native Americans within the BIA. Several non-Native American employees challenged the preference, arguing that the 1972 Equal Employment Opportunity Act had repealed the BIA's statutory authority to grant hiring preferences to Native Americans and that the preference amounted to invidious racial discrimination in violation of their Fifth Amendment due process rights. But the Court found that Congress had not repealed the BIA's authority to prefer Native Americans in hiring. And after analyzing the unique historical relationship between the federal government and Native Americans, the Court concluded that the preference was not only not invidious racial discrimination but was not based on race at all.

The Court pointed out that the disputed BIA preference applied only to members of federally recognized tribes and thus excluded many individuals who were racially Native American. Noting the "unique legal status of Indian tribes under federal law" and the BIA's special interest in furthering Native American self-government, the Court held that the hiring preference was "reasonably and directly related to a legitimate, nonracially based goal."

Assuming for present purposes that the borough's ordinance reflects this kind of political classification and does not discriminate on the basis of race, the ordinance might avoid problems with the Alaska Constitution's bar against racial discrimination. But the political nature of the classification would not necessarily insulate the ordinance from Malabed's equal protection challenge. For the borough, unlike the BIA in *Mancari*, has no obvious governmental interest, as a borough, in furthering Native American self-government; and Native Americans have no explicitly established "unique legal status" under borough law, as *Mancari* found them to have under federal law. Given these disparities between federal and local law, the legitimacy of the borough's hiring preference as a political classification is less apparent than the legitimacy of the BIA's hiring preference in *Mancari*. We must therefore consider whether the ordinance's ostensibly political lines discriminate in a way that offends the Alaska Constitution's guarantee of equal protection.

We have long recognized that the Alaska Constitution's equal protection clause affords greater protection to individual rights than the United States Constitution's Fourteenth Amendment. To implement Alaska's more stringent equal protection standard, we have adopted a three-step, sliding-scale test that places a progressively greater or lesser burden on the state, depending on the importance of the individual right affected by the disputed classification and the nature of the governmental interests at stake: first, we determine the weight of the individual interest impaired by the classification; second, we examine the importance of the purposes underlying the government's action; and third, we evaluate the means employed to further those goals to determine the closeness of the means-to-end fit.

To determine how the borough's hiring preference fares under this standard, we begin by considering the importance of the individual interests implicated by the preference. Here, the borough's hiring preference impairs Malabed's right to seek and obtain employment in his profession. Under similar circumstances, we have declared the right to employment to be an important right. In *State, Departments of Transportation & Labor v. Enserch Alaska Construction, Inc.*, 787 P.2d 624 (Alaska 1989), we reviewed an equal protection challenge to an Alaska statute that provided hiring preferences to residents of economically distressed zones for employment on public works projects. A contractor building a road for the state challenged the preference as a violation of Alaska equal protection. Addressing the first step of Alaska's three-step analysis, we held that the "right to engage in an economic endeavor within a particular industry is an 'important' right for state equal protection purposes."

In the second part of the equal protection analysis we consider the borough's interests, asking whether it had important and legitimate reasons to adopt the hiring preference. The borough offers several reasons supporting its ordinance: reducing unemployment of the largest group of unemployed borough residents—Inupiat Eskimos; strengthening the borough's economy; and training its workforce. But we found comparable governmental interests insufficient in *Enserch*. There the state tried to establish an important and legitimate governmental interest by arguing that the challenged hiring preference reduced unemployment, remedied social harms resulting from chronic unemployment, and assisted economically disadvantaged residents. Though acknowledging these interests as important, we found them to be illegitimate because they favored one class of Alaskans over another:

> While these goals are important, they conceal the underlying objective of economically assisting one class over another. We have held that this objective is illegitimate. In *Lynden Transport, Inc. v. State*, 532 P.2d 700 (Alaska 1975), we ruled that "discrimination between residents and nonresidents based solely on the object of assisting the one class over the other economically cannot be upheld under the equal protection clause." While that case involved discrimination between state residents and nonresidents, the principle is equally applicable to discrimination among state residents. We conclude that the disparate treatment of unemployed workers in one region in order to confer an

economic benefit on similarly-situated workers in another region is not a legitimate legislative goal.

Here, as in *Enserch*, it might seem that "[t]his conclusion essentially ends our inquiry." But the borough nevertheless claims a special interest in preferring to hire Native Americans (an interest not present in *Enserch*).

We reject the notion that the Alaska Constitution radiates implied guardianship powers allowing the state or its boroughs to treat Alaska Natives as if they were wards. To be sure, the United States Supreme Court has recognized implied powers in the United States Constitution that allow Congress broad latitude to legislate on behalf of Native Americans. The borough reasons that the Alaska Constitution must implicitly grant parallel powers to state and municipal governments. But the federal government's implied powers spring directly from the express powers granted to Congress in the United States Constitution's Indian Commerce and Treaty clauses.

In contrast to the federal constitution's provisions dealing with Indian tribes, the Alaska Constitution includes no provisions authorizing state action regarding Alaska Natives and so grants no express powers from which implied powers could arise. To the extent that the Alaska Constitution implies anything concerning the state's relations with Alaska Natives, then, it mirrors the constitutional drafters' well-recognized desire to treat Alaska Natives like all other Alaska citizens. The Alaska Constitution thus implies nothing that would give the borough a legitimate interest in enacting the disputed preference.

We by no means suggest that boroughs are categorically barred from adopting hiring preferences. Nor do we suggest that all state or local legislation pertaining to Alaska Natives or tribal governments should be assumed to establish suspect classifications presumptively barred by equal protection. Our focus is considerably narrower: we simply hold, in keeping with *Enserch*, that the borough has no legitimate basis to claim a general governmental interest in enacting hiring preferences favoring one class of citizens over others; and we find that the borough has failed to identify any source of a legitimate, case-specific governmental interest in the preference it actually adopted—a hiring preference favoring Native Americans. Because the borough is a political subdivision of Alaska, its legitimate sphere of municipal interest lies in governing for all of its people; preferring the economic interests of one class of its citizens at the expense of others is not a legitimate municipal interest, regardless of whether we view its ordinance as drawing distinctions founded on political status or race.

The last step of equal protection analysis under the Alaska Constitution examines the nexus between the state's asserted interests and the means selected to implement those interests. As previously mentioned, even when the state acts for important and legitimate reasons, its action must bear a close connection to those interests to justify impairing an important individual right. Here, of course, because we have found no legitimate borough interest supporting the challenged preference, we need not dwell on the closeness of its means-to-end fit. But a brief comment on the issue is nevertheless important to establish an alternative basis for our equal protection ruling.

For even assuming that the borough had legitimate and important interests in enacting a hiring preference favoring Native Americans, its preference is not closely related to attaining those interests. Addressing a similar situation in *Enserch*, we found a hiring preference in favor of residents of economically distressed areas unconstitutional under Alaska's equal protection guarantee in part because the fit between the preference and its objective was not sufficiently close. We noted that the preference failed to "prioritize relief for those areas most affected by nonresident employment" and that it set no meaningful limits on the state's power to declare any part of Alaska economically distressed at any time.

Here, the nexus between the borough's preference and its stated goals is insufficiently close for comparable reasons. The primary interest asserted by the borough lies in reducing Native American unemployment. But when viewed in light of this purpose, the borough's hiring preference is stunningly broad: it extends borough-wide and to all aspects of borough employment; is potentially limitless in duration; covers not only hiring but also promotions, transfers, and reinstatements; and applies absolutely— even to the extent of requiring Native American applicants without minimum qualifications to be hired over qualified non-Native applicants. Because the borough advances no particular reasons to justify these sweeping provisions, it fails to establish a close fit between its goals and its actions.

We conclude that the borough's hiring preference violates the Alaska Constitution's guarantee of equal protection because the borough lacks a legitimate governmental interest to enact a hiring preference favoring one class of citizens at the expense of others and because the preference it enacted is not closely tailored to meet its goals.

MATTHEWS, J., concurring.

I agree with the opinion of the court that the borough hiring preference violates the equal rights clause of the Alaska Constitution and with much of the court's reasoning. But I prefer to address directly the question whether the ordinance discriminates on the basis of race. I believe that it does, for the reasons that follow.

Inupiat Eskimos are a racial rather than a tribal group. The ordinance frankly acknowledges that its goal is to benefit them. In a prefatory clause the ordinance states "that its purpose in establishing an employment preference for Native Americans is to employ and train its Inupiat Eskimo residents in permanent, full-time positions...." Another clause sounds the same theme: "Whereas, to increase the employment of Inupiat Eskimos, the North Slope Borough would like to give an employment preference to Native Americans...." Similarly, the implementation plan for the ordinance expressly states that its purpose is to employ Inupiat Eskimo residents. Further, at oral argument counsel for the borough explained that one reason the term "Native American" was defined in terms of tribal membership was that it served to distinguish eligible Native Americans from others who are not eligible for benefits under the preference ordinance even though they may have some Native American ancestors. Tribal membership was thus used as a convenient mechanism to describe bona fide Native Americans.

Based on the above we can say with confidence that the purpose of the ordinance was to discriminate on the basis of race. Because by the express terms of the civil rights clause of the Alaska Constitution race is a suspect category, the ordinance must be subjected to strict scrutiny in order to determine whether it is permissible under the equal rights and civil rights clauses. But even if there were no clear indicators of an intent to discriminate on the basis of race, I believe that strict scrutiny would still be required because tribal membership is not only a political category but a racial one.

I reach the conclusion that state or municipal laws that grant individual benefits differentially based on tribal membership should be subject to strict scrutiny for a number of reasons. As noted, this is how we treat all race-based classifications. Further, strict scrutiny is well designed to ensure that laws remain race-neutral, as contemplated by the framers of the Alaska Constitution. This case illustrates that tribal membership readily lends itself to use as a proxy for a racial classification and as a pretext for racial discrimination. An effective tool is necessary to prevent these abuses. In addition, strict scrutiny is the approach taken by some federal courts in tribal classification cases when construing the equal protection clause of the Fourteenth Amendment to the federal constitution. Since the federal constitution contains provisions authorizing legislation on behalf of Native Americans, while the Alaska Constitution presumptively prohibits such legislation, it follows that stronger reasons exist for using the strict scrutiny method for state constitutional questions than for those arising under the federal constitution.

Although strict scrutiny review presents a high barrier, it is a barrier that may be overcome in deserving cases. It is impossible to categorize the kinds of cases that might pass strict scrutiny review. But a federal law calling on the state to give preferential treatment to tribal members would almost certainly present a compelling justification for state legislation. On balance, I believe that strict scrutiny properly accommodates the state's strong interest in preventing discrimination on the basis of race and its relatively rare and limited need to act adjunctively with the federal government in programs that favor tribal members over other state citizens.

The present ordinance does not survive strict scrutiny review. As the opinion of the court establishes, the borough had no legitimate interest, much less a compelling one, in adopting the preference. I believe therefore that the ordinance is prohibited by article I, sections 1 and 3 of the Alaska Constitution.

NOTE

In *Brackett v. Civil Service Commission*, 850 N.E.2d 533 (Mass. 2006), the Supreme Court of Massachusetts upheld an affirmative action program designed to increase the hiring and promotion of women and minorities in the state civil service. In upholding the program, the Court took the position that the standard for equal protection analysis under the Massachusetts Declaration of Rights was the same as the standard under the Federal Constitution. Following the federal standard, the court ruled that the program was justified as a means of remedying the continuing effects of past racial and gender discrimination, and therefore did not violate either the Massachusetts or Federal Constitution.

In recent years, three states—California, Michigan, and Washington—have amended their constitutions to prohibit affirmative action programs. The California Constitution, for example, now provides that:

> The state shall not discriminate against, or grant preferential treatment to, any individual or group on the basis of race, sex, color, ethnicity, or national origin in the operation of public employment, public education, or public contracting.

After enactment of the above provision, the Supreme Court of California found that it was contravened by an outreach program that required contractors bidding on city projects to employ a specified percentage of minority and female subcontractors. *Hi Voltage Wire Works, Inc. v. San Jose*, 12 P.3d 1068 (Cal. 2000).

C. CLASSIFICATIONS BASED ON GENDER

COMMONWEALTH v. PENNSYLVANIA INTERSCHOLASTIC ATHLETIC ASSOCIATION
334 A.2d 839 (Pa. 1975)

BLATT, J.

On November 13, 1973 the Commonwealth of Pennsylvania, acting through its Attorney General initiated suit against the Pennsylvania Interscholastic Athletic Association (PIAA) by filing a complaint in equity in this Court. The PIAA is a voluntary unincorporated association whose members include every public senior high school in this Commonwealth, except for those in Philadelphia. It also includes some public junior high schools as well as some private schools. The PIAA regulates interscholastic competition among its members in the following sports: football, cross-country, basketball, wrestling, soccer, baseball, field hockey, lacrosse, gymnastics, swimming, volleyball, golf, tennis, track, softball, archery and badminton.

The complaint here specifically challenges the constitutionality of Article XIX, Section 3B of the PIAA By-Laws which states: "Girls shall not compete or practice against boys in any athletic contest." The Commonwealth asserts that this provision violates both the equal protection clause of the Fourteenth Amendment to the United States Constitution and also Article I, Section 28 of the Pennsylvania Constitution, the so-called Equal Rights Amendment (ERA), in that it denies to female student athletes the same opportunities which are available to males to practice for and compete in interscholastic sports.

Article I, Section 28 of the Pennsylvania Constitution provides:

Prohibition against denial or abridgment of equality of rights because of sex.

Equality of rights under the law shall not be denied or abridged in the Commonwealth of Pennsylvania because of the sex of the individual.

Since the adoption of the ERA in the Commonwealth of Pennsylvania, the courts of this state have unfailingly rejected statutory provisions as well as case law principles which discriminate against one sex or the other. In *Conway v. Dana*, 318 A.2d 324 (1974) the court cast aside the presumption which had previously existed to the effect that the father, because of his sex, must accept the principal burden of financial support of minor children. The court there indicated that support is the equal responsibility of both parents and that, in light of the ERA, the courts must now consider the property, income, and earning capacity of both in order to determine their respective obligations.

In *Hopkins v. Blanco*, 320 A.2d 139 (1974) the court extended to the wife the right to recover damages for loss of consortium, a right previously available only to the husband. The court there stated: 'The obvious purpose of the Amendment was to put a stop to the invalid discrimination which was based on the sex of the person. The Amendment gave legal recognition to what society had long recognized, that men and women must have equal status in today's world.'

Most recently in *Henderson v. Henderson*, 327 A2d 60 (1974) the section of the Divorce Law which permitted only the wife to receive alimony pendente lite, counsel fees and expenses was ruled unconstitutional. The court in broad terms proclaimed:

> The thrust of the Equal Rights Amendment is to insure equality of rights under the law and to eliminate sex as a basis for distinction. The sex of citizens of this Commonwealth is no longer a permissible factor in the determination of their legal rights and legal responsibilities. The law will not impose different benefits or different burdens upon the members of a society based on the fact that they may be man or woman.

Commonwealth v. Butler, 328 A.2d 851 (1974), filed on the same day as Henderson, held unconstitutional the provision of the Muncy Act which prevented trial courts from imposing a minimum sentence on women convicted of a crime. Only male criminals were subject to the minimum sentence provision.

The PIAA seeks to justify the challenged By-Law on the basis that men generally possess a higher degree of athletic ability in the traditional sports offered by most schools and that because of this, girls are given greater opportunities for participation if they compete exclusively with members of their own sex. This attempted justification can obviously have no validity with respect to those sports for which only one team exists in a school and that team's membership is limited exclusively to boys. Presently a girl who wants to compete interscholastically in that sport is given absolutely no opportunity to do so under the challenged By-Law. Although she might be sufficiently skilled to earn a position on the team, she is presently denied that position solely because of her sex. Moreover, even where separate teams are offered for boys and girls in the same sport, the most talented girls still may be denied the right to play at that level of competition which their ability might otherwise permit them. For a girl in that position, who has been relegated to the "girls' team", solely because of her sex, equality under the law has been denied.

The notion that girls as a whole are weaker and thus more injury-prone, if they compete with boys, especially in contact sports, cannot justify the By-Law in light of the ERA. Nor can we consider the argument that boys are generally more skilled. The existence of certain characteristics to a greater degree in one sex does not justify classification by sex rather than by the particular characteristic. If any individual girl is too weak, injury-prone, or unskilled, she may, of course, be excluded from competition on that basis but she cannot be excluded solely because of her sex without regard to her relevant qualifications. We believe that this is what our Supreme Court meant when it said in *Butler, supra,* that 'sex may no longer be accepted as an exclusive classifying tool.'

Although the Commonwealth in its complaint seeks no relief from discrimination against female athletes who may wish to participate in football and wrestling, it is apparent that there can be no valid reason for excepting those two sports from our order in this case.

For the foregoing reasons, therefore, we issue the following

ORDER

> Now, the 19th day of March --, 1975, the motion of the Commonwealth for summary judgment is granted to the extent that Article XIX, Section 3B of the Pennsylvania Interscholastic Athletic Association is hereby declared unconstitutional, and the Pennsylvania Interscholastic Athletic Association is hereby ordered to permit girls to practice and compete with boys in interscholastic athletics, this order to be effective for the school year beginning in the fall of 1975 and thereafter.

BOWMAN, P.J., dissenting.

The Supreme Court decisions cited and quoted by the majority not only bind me but have my full support and approbation. In my view, however, they do not lend the controlling support attributed to them by the majority as each of said decisions was concerned with either a statute or a previously judicially declared right or duty applicable to one sex to the exclusion of the other. There remains the question of whether the constitutional provision in question is absolute or subject to the concept of rational classification in general contexts excluding or including the role of "state action" as a controlling or influencing factor.

In deciding this case on a motion for summary judgment, the majority, in my view, has acted too soon and gone too far. I would deny plaintiff's motion for summary judgment.

NOTE

In the 1970s the Equal Rights Amendment (ERA), which would prohibit the denial or abridgement of rights on account of sex, failed to gain passage as an amendment to the Federal Constitution. However, between 1970 and 1978 fifteen states adopted constitutional amendments modeled on the ERA. They joined three other states—California, Utah, and Wyoming—whose constitutions have contained provisions expressly banning sexual discrimination since the late 1800's. By now, twenty state constitutions include equality provisions that expressly prohibit discrimination on the basis of sex.

In most states whose constitutions contain a provision expressly proscribing discrimination on the basis of sex, the courts take a strong stance against gender discrimination. The Supreme Court of Washington has taken an especially forceful stance regarding the ERA in declaring that:

> The ERA absolutely prohibits discrimination on the basis of sex and is not subject to even the narrow exceptions permitted under traditional "strict scrutiny"....The ERA mandates equality in the strongest of terms and absolutely prohibits the sacrifice of equality for any state interest, no matter how compelling. *Southwest Washington Chapter, National Electric Contractors Association v. Pierce County*, 667 P.2d 1092, 1102 (Wash. 1983).

A few courts in other states take a nearly absolutist approach to the ERA by ruling that classifications based on gender are prohibited except when necessitated by physical differences between the sexes. Most states that have adopted the ERA, however, take the position that the ERA elevates gender to a suspect classification calling for strict judicial scrutiny of any law that classifies persons on the basis of sex. In one or two states that have adopted a version of the ERA, the courts use an intermediate level of scrutiny to assess gender classifications.

In states whose constitutions do not contain a provision expressly barring sex discrimination, the courts tend to follow the federal approach of using intermediate scrutiny to review classifications based on gender. Some of these states have found that intermediate scrutiny can be an effective means to combat sexual discrimination. For example, in West Virginia, which has not adopted the ERA, the state supreme court used intermediate scrutiny in ruling that the state due process clause, which encompasses an equal protection principle, was violated by a regulation barring girls from playing on high school baseball teams. *Israel v. West Virginia Secondary Schools Activities Commission*, 388 S.E.2d 480 (1989). In striking down the regulation, the court stated that the purpose of the equal protection principle was "to avoid this type of artificial distinction based solely on gender."

Intermediate scrutiny, though, has its limits, and occasionally is used to uphold gender classifications that might be struck down under strict scrutiny. For instance, in *O'Connor v. Board of Education of School Dist. No. 23*, 645 F.2d 578 (7th Cir. 1981), the court employed intermediate scrutiny in upholding a junior high school regulation barring girls from playing on the boys' interscholastic basketball team. Although there was a separate girls' basketball team, it functioned at a lower level of competition than the boys' team and therefore did not offer an equivalent opportunity for the development of athletic skills. Given the substantial disparity between the girls' and boys' teams, it is questionable whether the regulation could have survived strict scrutiny.

GRIFFIN v. CRANE
716 A.2d 1029 (Md. 1998)

BELL, C.J.

James M. Giffin, the petitioner, and Donna L. (Valtri) Crane, the respondent, the parents of two daughters separated in May, 1992, after more than 12 years of marriage. At separation, the petitioner and the parties' two daughters remained in the marital home, while the respondent lived nearby and maintained regular visitation with the children. A year later, the respondent moved to Louisville, Kentucky. Both parties sought to obtain a divorce. The petitioner and the respondent both asked for custody of the two children. The custody and visitation issues were resolved by the parties when they entered into...a written agreement (providing that the petitioner shall have sole physical custody of the children.) The agreement contemplated the possibility of annual reviews of the residential status of the children.

(In 1995, the respondent requested a review of the children's residential status.) A hearing was held on the respondent's motion, during which the court, over a span of six days, received testimony from more than twenty witnesses and viewed a number of exhibits, including private investigators' reports and a videotape. At that hearing, the interests of the children were represented by an attorney appointed by the court. The court granted the respondent's Petition for Modification of Residential Custody, thus modifying the custody agreement by transferring custody of the children from their father to their mother.

The petitioner appealed the judgment to the Court of Special Appeals. He argued in that court that the trial court erred by considering the sex of the parents as a factor in its determination of custody. In an unreported opinion, the intermediate appellate court held, inter alia, that "[t]he consideration of gender was a valid consideration in determining residential custody in this case." In response, the petitioner filed a petition for a writ of certiorari, which this Court granted.

The question that we must decide is whether, in a child custody proceeding, the sex of either parent is a legitimate and proper consideration in determining which of them is the appropriate residential custodian. It is an issue in this case because of some of the language the trial court used to explain its custody decision. As we have seen, the court opined:

> [T]he Court gleans from ... the testimony from at least one expert in this case relative to a girl child having particular need for her mother has seemed to come to the fore and is a necessary factor in my determinations in this case ... The Court feels that the best interests of the children ... as exemplified by the reaching an age where Emily at the very least exemplifies a need for a female hand, causes the Court to come to the conclusion that the children should reside with their mother.

When one considers the trial court's explanation of its decision, it is clear, unambiguously so, that the court was relying on the respondent's gender as the decisive basis for modifying the custody order.

Maryland's Equal Rights Amendment, Article 46 of the Maryland Declaration of Rights, provides: "Equality of rights under the law shall not be abridged or denied because of sex." The words of the Equal Rights Amendment are clear, unambiguous and unequivocal; the Amendment "mandated equality of rights under the law and rendered state-sanctioned sex-based classifications suspect." *State v. Burning Tree Club, Inc.*, 554 A.2d 366, 374 (Md. 1989).

The basic principle of the Maryland Equal Rights Amendment, thus, is that sex is not a permissible factor in determining the legal rights of women, or men, so that the treatment of any person by the law may not be based upon the circumstance that such person is of one sex or the other.... (T)his constitutional provision drastically altered traditional views of the validity of sex-based classifications imposed under the law, and was cogent evidence that the people of Maryland were fully committed to equal rights for men and women. (T)he equality between the sexes demanded by the Maryland Equal Rights Amendment focuses on "rights" of individuals "under the law," which encompasses all forms of privileges, immunities, benefits and responsibilities of citizens. As to these, the Maryland E.R.A. absolutely forbids the determination of such "rights," as may be accorded by law, solely on the basis of one's sex, i.e., sex is an impermissible factor in making any such determination. It is clear, therefore, that the Equal Rights Amendment flatly prohibits gender-based classifications, absent substantial justification, whether contained in legislative enactments, governmental policies, or by application of common law rules.

Although this Court has not had the occasion to address the issue this case presents, our cases since the adoption of the Equal Rights Amendment and the Legislature's action in enacting the Family Law Article make clear what the proper result should be. As we have seen, this Court has interpreted the Amendment's "broad, sweeping mandatory language" as the expression of Maryland's commitment to equal rights for men and women and the statement of its intention to alter traditional attitudes with respect to such rights.

At issue in *Rand v. Rand*, 374 A.2d 900, 904-05 (Md. 1977), was the validity, in light of the Maryland Equal Rights Amendment, of the common law rule that placed the primary liability for the support of minor children on the father. Holding the rule irreconcilable with the E.R.A., we concluded that the "parental obligation for child support is not primarily an obligation of the father, but is one shared by both parents." Another common law rule was at issue in *Kline v. Ansell*, 414 A.2d 929, 933 (Md. 1980), that only men could sue or be sued for criminal conversation. We held that the rule violated the Equal Rights Amendment, explaining that it "provides different benefits for and imposes different burdens upon its citizens based solely upon their sex." In *Condore v. Prince George's Co.*, 425 A.2d 1011 (Md. 1981), we held that the common law doctrine of necessaries, which obligated the husband, but not the wife, to pay for his spouse's necessaries, violated the Equal Rights Amendment. Noting the Court's consistent holdings "that a law that imposes different benefits and different burdens upon persons based solely upon their sex violates the Maryland E.R.A.," this Court, in *Turner v. State*, 474 A.2d 1297, 1302 (Md. 1984), invalidated a criminal statute which prohibited the employment by taverns of so-called female sitters to solicit customers to purchase drinks. We pointed out that, under the statute, a man could be employed as a sitter but a woman could not.

This Court's custody decision in *Elza v. Elza*, 475 A.2d 1180 (Md. 1984), is also instructive, as is the Legislature's recodification, as a part of Code Revision, of former Article 72A § 1. The issue in Elza was the validity of the maternal preference presumption and whether the trial court in a child custody proceeding erred in basing its award of custody to the mother solely on it. Stating that the 1974 amendment to Art. 72A, § 1, by providing, clearly and unambiguously, that "neither parent shall be given preference solely because of his or her sex," expressed the intent of the General Assembly to eradicate sex as a factor in child custody proceedings, this Court abolished the maternal preference doctrine in this State because it permitted custody to be awarded solely on the basis of the mother's sex.

The Pennsylvania Supreme Court, in *Commonwealth ex rel. Spriggs v. Carson*, 368 A.2d 635 (Pa. 1977), held that the "tender years" doctrine, which is Pennsylvania's equivalent of Maryland's maternal preference doctrine, was abolished by that State's E.R.A. The "tender years" doctrine, in essence, maintains that, in a child custody dispute, where a child is of tender years, the mother is presumed to be the more fit parent. The court in *Spriggs* struck down that presumption, stating:

> We ... question the legitimacy of a doctrine that is predicated upon traditional or stereotypic roles of men and women in a marital union. Whether the tender years doctrine is employed to create a presumption which requires the

male parent to overcome its effect by presenting compelling contrary evidence of a particular nature, or merely as a makeshift where the scales are relatively balanced, such a view is offensive to the concept of the equality of the sexes which we have embraced as a constitutional principle within this jurisdiction. Courts should be wary of deciding matters as sensitive as questions of custody by the invocation of 'presumptions'. Instead, we believe that our courts should inquire into the circumstances and relationships of all the parties involved and reach a determination based solely upon the facts of the case then before the Court."

The trial court erred, as a matter of law, in the instant case; it assumed that the respondent necessarily would be a better custodian solely because she has a female hand, and that a girl child of a certain age has a particular and specific need to be with her same sex parent. In so doing, the trial court applied an invalid legal principle. A review of the record of the hearing reveals that, but for the trial court's perception of the need for a female hand for a girl child of Emily's age, that it believed each parent would be a proper and fit custodian. Indeed, that sex-based reason for the custody award to the respondent was the only reason given for the court's decision. Therefore, we will remand the case to the circuit court for further proceedings in that court.... The trial court will be required, of course, on remand once again to consider the best interest of the children in deciding their custody and it must fully set forth and explain the reasons for its decision, consistent with this opinion.

McAULIFFE, J., dissenting.

I cannot agree that the record in this case discloses an impermissible use of gender by the chancellor in the determination of this custody dispute. I would agree that the oral opinion of the chancellor, delivered from the bench after six days of trial, is perhaps inelegant and lacking in as complete a discussion of the rationale for the decision as may have been desired, but viewed in the context of the testimony and of prior statements of the chancellor, it is clear to me that the references to gender related to appropriate considerations.

What is important to understand in this case is that the witnesses were not saying that an adolescent daughter is always better able to communicate with her mother than father, or that there is always an emotional need of a daughter to be with her mother. What was said was in the context of this mother and this daughter, and not some stereotypical figures. In discussing the particular need that existed in this case, the witnesses simply noted that the situation was hardly atypical, and often occurred between a child and the same-sex parent. This is a far cry from establishing a preference or presumption based on gender.

Judges should be precluded from concluding that a special relationship, bonding, or ability to communicate between a parent and a child exists solely on the basis that the parent and child are of the same sex; judges should not be precluded from finding the existence of such a relationship from the facts of the case, even though that relationship may have resulted in part from the reality that the parent and child are of the same sex.

In addition to my disagreement with the interpretation the majority gives to the chancellor's remarks, I dissent because I am concerned that the tone of the majority's opinion may cause trial judges to shy away from perfectly valid and important case-specific findings merely because those findings reflect relationships and needs that are consistent with a particular parent and child being of the same sex.

STATE v. RIVERA
612 P.2d 526 (Haw. 1980)

OGATA, J.

Appellant was convicted of first degree rape under HRS s 707-730 (1976). The applicable statute was amended as of June 26, 1979 and as we understand appellant he would have no equal protection challenge to the new statute. The purpose of the amendment was to restate the statutory provisions in gender-neutral terms.... Appellant challenges the constitutionality of HRS s 707-730 prior to its amendment, and claims that, by its terms, it denied him the equal protection of the law by punishing only men and no women, and protecting only women and no men, thus violating the equal protection guarantees of the Fourteenth Amendment of the United States Constitution and Article I, Section 4 of the Hawaii State Constitution and the equal rights amendment, Article I, Section 21, of the Hawaii State Constitution (ERA).

To withstand judicial scrutiny under the equal protection clause, a sex-based distinction must serve governmental objectives and must be substantially related to achievement of those objectives. Under this principle, the question is whether the sex-based classification in the former rape law served an important governmental objective and was substantially related to achievement of that objective. We find that it plainly met the test.

Although the statute sets up a gender-based classification by defining rape as an offense which can be committed only by a male, it reflects a legislative judgment as to the degree of harm posed to potential victims of nonconsensual intercourse. "While we recognize that it is possible for females to commit a sex offense which might be deemed rape, the fact remains that historically and generally rape is a crime committed by males against females." *Moore v. Cowan*, 560 F.2d 1298, 1303 (6th Cir. 1977).

The legislature chose to selectively deal with the act of forced intercourse by men upon women as a more significant societal problem where the need for proscription was clearest. Protecting women from nonconsensual intercourse is an important legislative objective. And a law which punishes males for nonconsensual intercourse with women against their will is substantially related to that objective. Appellant's contentions might be more persuasive if he had provided us with empirical data tending to show that female rapes of males presented a social problem. In *West Coast Hotel Co. v. Parrish*, 300 U.S. 379 (1937), the United States Supreme Court restated the principle that "(i)f 'the law presumably hits the evil where it is most felt, it is not to be overthrown because there are other instances to which it might have been applied.'" We are dealing with a criminal sex offense statute. We are not dealing with an overbroad generalization based on sex which is entirely irrelevant to any difference between men and women or which demeans the ability or status of the affected class. The courts have been reluctant in striking down criminal sex laws and all have upheld rape statutes against constitutional challenges.

Appellant claims that because Article I, Section 4, now Article I, Section 5, of the Hawaii State Constitution specifically enumerates sex along with race, religion and ancestry, this specific enumeration requires a more stringent test than that required by the Fourteenth Amendment. Moreover, the ERA, which, by its terms forbids classifications based on sex, is said to necessitate a judicial standard of review at least as high as the "strict scrutiny" standard under equal protection analysis.

Not even the ERA, however, forbids all classifications. "The fundamental legal principle underlying the ERA...is that the law must deal with particular attributes of individuals ...." A classification based on a physical characteristic unique to one sex is not an impermissive under- or over-inclusive classification because the differentiation is based on the unique presence of a physical characteristic in one sex and not based on an averaging of a trait or characteristic which exists in both sexes. Two frequently-cited examples are laws relating to wet nurses, which would apply to all or some women but no men; or laws regulating sperm donation which would apply to all or some men, but no women.

Rape was defined in HRS s 707-730 (1976) as a male engaging in "sexual intercourse, by forcible compulsion, with a female." A sex-based distinction existed in the former rape statute but the differentiation in treatment was based upon unique physical characteristics of men and women and the unique characteristics justified the classification. Insofar as rape was defined as forced intercourse by a male with a female, it was based on a physiological characteristic unique to males. Furthermore, as the court stated in *Finley v. State*, 527 S.W.2d at 556 "(h)ymen and uterine injury to female rape victims, the possibility of pregnancy, and the physiological difficulty of a woman forcing a man to have sexual intercourse with her all suggest a justification for the sexual distinction." It has also been said that "(s)o long as the law deals only with a characteristic found in all (or some) women but no men, or in all (or some) men but no women, it does not ignore individual characteristics found in both sexes ...." As such, the statute neither denied equal rights to men nor did it violate the ERA.

D. CLASSIFICATIONS BASED ON AGE

O'NEILL v. BANE
568 S.W.2d 761 (Mo. 1978)

SIMEONE, J.

This is an appeal from a judgment of the Circuit Court of St. Louis County entered on May 4, 1978, holding that s 476.458, RSMo 1976 Supp., requiring mandatory retirement for magistrate and probate judges at age seventy, is unconstitutional as violative of equal protection and due process. Amend. XIV, U.S.Const., Art. I, ss 2 and 10, Mo. Const.... For reasons hereinafter stated, we hold that the statute is not unconstitutional and does not violate equal protection or due process and reverse the judgment of the trial court.

The sole question for our determination is the constitutionality of the mandatory retirement statute relating to magistrate and probate judges embodied in s 476.458 adopted in 1976. In passing, we note that Judge O'Neil has rendered many years of faithful and competent service to the citizens of this state, and especially to the citizens of St. Louis County. He continues to do so. We are aware that although the passage of time has added years to Judge O'Neil's age, it has not lessened his legal abilities. We recognize, as did the several witnesses at the hearing that Judge O'Neil is competent both physically and mentally, that his health is generally good, that he is very competent and that he desires to continue to serve the public.

But those factors do not control the issue. The constitutionality of legislation cannot be determined on an individual basis. The facts are that Judge O'Neil became seventy years of age on November 5, 1977, and has served more than twelve years, and will, on December 31, 1978, complete his term.

In recent years, compulsory retirement systems have come under constitutional attack. Equal protection and due process challenges have been made in a great number of decisions and in a great variety of contexts. In *Massachusetts Bd. of Retirement v. Murgia*, 427 U.S. 307 (1976), the Supreme Court of the United States upheld a Massachusetts compulsory retirement statute relating to a state police officer, which required state police officers to retire at age 50. The Court held (1) that the proper standard of judicial review of the equal protection claim was not "strict scrutiny" but the traditional rational basis test wherein classifications are constitutional if they bear a rational relationship to a permissible state interest; and (2) that the compulsory retirement provision involved satisfied the rational basis standard.... The standard which we must utilize in the instant case is therefore the rational basis test.

Mandatory retirement provisions are recognized by private industry, by state governments and by the federal system under recent legislative amendments. Mandatory retirement systems perform beneficial societal functions. The justification most commonly offered for mandatory retirement schemes is that there is a reasonable connection between increased age and declining job capabilities so that mandatory retirement is a convenient method of insuring an effective and productive work force.

Because there are rational bases for the statute, we hold that s 476.458 is not violative of equal protection or due process.... Several rational bases related to the furtherance of a legitimate state interest are implied in the statute and are clearly recognizable.

First, s 476.458, "marks a stage" in life at which judges must end their regular, daily judicial duties. Judges serve in a sensitive position. Judges' decisions affect many aspects of peoples' lives and property. Judges must be able to adapt to changes in the law and in society. Judges are held to the highest possible standards.

Our citizens are entitled to a judicial system of the highest caliber and to judges with the highest possible mental and physical qualifications. Mandatory judicial retirement is an attempt by the General Assembly to insure the fitness of the judiciary as a whole and to insure the continued competency of the system. The General Assembly in adopting the statute dealt in probabilities. That is all humans can do. There are certain ages in life, learned from experience, at which there is a lessening in mental, physical abilities. If mandatory retirement is invalid at age 70, then at what age 80, 90, or 100? To paraphrase Holmes, in life, one must make choices. That is what the General Assembly did. The statute draws a line at a certain age which attempts to uphold the high competency for judicial posts and which fulfills a societal demand for the highest caliber of judges in the system. The statute is an attempt to insure that, on the whole, only those judges who have the vigor, health and vitality will carry out the public's work in administering justice. The function of mandatory retirement is to permit the withdrawal from the bench that group of judges in which disabilities related to aging are most likely to occur.

Second, the statute which is presumptively valid draws a legitimate line to avoid the tedious and often perplexing decisions to determine which judges after a certain age are physically and mentally qualified and those who are not. A mandatory provision avoids these traumatic and often lengthy hearings.

Third, mandatory retirement increases the opportunity for qualified persons men and women alike to share in the judiciary and permits an orderly attrition through retirement.

Such a provision not only achieves the maximum in qualified judicial personnel, but equally important widens the opportunities for qualified younger members of the Bar to seek a judicial post.... (A) state might prescribe a mandatory retirement for judges in order to "open up" judicial opportunities for younger lawyers and to bring young persons with fresh ideas and techniques into the system.

Fourth, such a mandatory provision also assures predictability and ease in establishing and administering judge's pension plans. The General Assembly, having the constitutional power to do so, has established a comprehensive retirement plan for judges based on retirement at age 70. As a corollary, the General Assembly must be able to plan and determine the amount of appropriations necessary to fulfill the statutory benefits provided for the retirement of judges.

Furthermore, we know that age seventy is an age a time of life which is recognized by society as being "about" the time when the physical and mental processes weaken among many men and women. That recognition is embodied in statutes, in private retirement systems and in the policy of the Congress. All of this, and more, is embodied in the policy of s 476.458.

In sum, we conclude that compulsory retirement of magistrate and probate judges at age seventy embodied in the statute is rationally related to the fulfillment of several legitimate state objectives and hence the statute does not violate equal protection.... (W)e hold that s 476.458 is not violative of the equal protection or due process clauses of the Federal or Missouri Constitutions and hence is constitutional.

In reaching this conclusion we are aware of the substantial contributions that our elderly citizens make to society and "we do not make light of the substantial economic and psychological effects...compulsory retirement can have on an individual...." Retirement can well be a time of life of many useful pursuits. In short "age is not a cage" but a time of life when many new things can be accomplished. But in determining the provisions for mandatory retirement embodied in s

476.458., the General Assembly has weighed these personal considerations against the social goals which compulsory retirement furthers. In this instance we will not intrude into the legislative prerogative and strike down a legislative choice.

NOTES

1. In *Maddux v. Blagojevich*, 911 N.E.2d 979 (Ill. 2009), the Supreme Court of Illinois struck down a state statute mandating the retirement of judges at age 75. Although the state constitution contained a provision authorizing the General Assembly to provide by law for the retirement of judges at a prescribed age, the court nonetheless found that the statute in question violated the constitutional requirement of equal protection of the laws. In striking down the statute, the court noted that it mandated retirement of judges at 75 while other persons 75 and older could run for and hold judicial office:

> Consider the situation of a 76-year-old citizen who has never held judicial office. If that person runs for judicial office and wins, he would *never* face the prospect of compulsory retirement because, under the Act's operation, automatic retirement occurs "at the expiration of the term in which the judge attains the age of 75." There would never be a "term in which" such a judge would "attain the age of 75." (The same would, of course, be true for a judge who left judicial office before turning 75, who then ran for election after turning 76.) The successful candidate in this scenario would fall outside the statute's language and would be eligible for retention at the conclusion of the term. Mandatory retirement would exist for some, but not all, judges because there would exist a class of judges who would be immune from the mandatory retirement envisioned under the Act.

> The Act, therefore, does nothing to advance the goal of insuring a "more vigorous judiciary" since it would allow for people older than 75 years to serve terms of 6 and possibly 10 years. More importantly, the Act creates an irrational classification that could not, in terms of equal protection, withstand scrutiny under our state constitution. Equal protection requires that similarly situated individuals will be treated similarly unless the government can demonstrate an appropriate reason to do otherwise. In cases like this one, where the statutory classification at issue does not involve fundamental rights, courts employ "rational basis scrutiny" to determine whether the classification bears a rational relation to a legitimate purpose.

> There is no rational basis upon which the legislature can prevent 75-year-old or older *former judges* from running in an election, but not citizens 75 years old or older *who were never judges* when the disqualifying characteristic is age. If the legitimate state interest is to insure a "vigorous judiciary," the classification we describe above cannot be deemed rationally related to that purpose. We stress again that if age defines ability (and both the constitutional and legislative history indicate that it was believed that it does), either *all* those 75 years of age or older are unfit or they are not. No presumption of constitutionality could save legislation like this that so blatantly violates equal protection.

Legislation is presumed constitutional and must be construed as not offending the constitution, provided, of course, that the construction is reasonable. This presumption, however, is only the starting point in constitutional analysis; it is not outcome determinative. Thus, notwithstanding a statute's presumption of constitutionality, this court has acknowledged its "power to strike down" legislation when it is "violative of the clear requirements of the constitution."

As we have explained, the judicial article allows for the General Assembly to enact mandatory judicial retirement legislation; however, the plain language of the specific legislation that has been enacted pursuant to the constitution violates equal protection. Moreover, as it is written, it allows certain judges to avoid mandatory retirement. This court is mindful that restraint is called for when presented with challenges to the constitutionality of legislation enacted pursuant to a specific grant of constitutional authority. But we cannot be reluctant to invalidate legislation that either goes beyond the specific grant of authority or is otherwise inconsistent with our constitution....

We have determined that the Act as written is unconstitutional. It is, of course, the General Assembly's prerogative, to attempt to reenact mandatory judicial retirement legislation. Our holding today recognizes this authority. It is also fair to acknowledge, however, the difficulty in exercising that discretion where retirement is linked to age absent a corresponding constitutional age ceiling...which would disqualify a person from running for judicial office.

2. In *Badgley v. Walton*, 10 A.3d 469 (Vt. 2010), the Supreme Court of Vermont ruled that a law requiring all public safety officers to retire at the age of 55 did not violate the common benefits clause of the Vermont Constitution. Adopting a deferential approach, the court concluded that the mandatory retirement law bore a reasonable and just relationship to the legitimate state interest of having a police force that is mentally and physically capable of performing its tasks. While admitting that the law was to some degree an overinclusive means of accomplishing its purpose, the court nonetheless ruled that the law was not so overinclusive as to violate the common benefits clause. The court acknowledged that there were many strong policy arguments for abandoning the mandatory retirement law or raising the retirement age, but the court thought those arguments were more appropriately addressed to the legislature than to the judiciary.

ARNESON v. STATE
864 P.2d 1245 (Mont. 1993)

R.C. McDONOUGH, J.

This is an appeal from the decision of the District Court of the First Judicial District, Lewis and Clark County, concluding that § 19-20-711, MCA) is unconstitutional to the extent that it employed an unreasonable classification in violation of the equal protection clause of the Montana Constitution, Article II, Section 4. We affirm.

In 1989 the legislature passed Chapter 115 Session Laws of 1989 which, for its purpose, provided for a post-retirement adjustment increase in the pensions of the beneficiaries of the Teachers' Retirement System. The law provided that to be eligible for the adjustment, retirees or their beneficiaries must be 55 years of age or older; or, irrespective of age, all those receiving disability or survivorship benefits.

The respondent's benefit was derived from her mother, who was a member of the Teachers' Retirement System, and who had reached retirement age and retired. The mother selected the retirement option that would permit benefits to be paid to her for her lifetime and upon her death continue through the life of her beneficiary (respondent). The mother died shortly after her retirement and the respondent began receiving the benefits. The respondent is 31 years of age.... Being under 55 years of age she did not receive the adjustment. However, if her mother had continued to work and died while working the respondent would be considered a survivor and would receive the adjustment even though she was 31 years of age.

This statute, under the equal protection question, does not come under the strict scrutiny test because strict scrutiny of a legislative classification is required only when the classification impermissibly interferes with the exercise of a fundamental right or operates to a peculiar disadvantage of a suspect class. Here the respondent is not a member of a suspect class nor is a fundamental right involved.

The respondent urges us to adopt the middle-level scrutiny test.... The middle-level scrutiny test has been recently applied by the U.S. Supreme Court in discussing cases involving such things as gender, alienage and illegitimacy, but the court has specifically refused to invoke it involving age and has applied the rational test thereto.... We have previously declined to apply the middle tier scrutiny test to an "age plus" classification, absent a constitutionally based benefit. We also decline to apply it here.... The District Court applied the lowest level of scrutiny, the rational basis test, which determines whether the classification is rationally related to furthering a legitimate state purpose.... We will also apply the rational basis test.

The purpose of this law is to grant to the Retirement System beneficiaries, retirees' survivors, and disabled, an amount to alleviate the eroding effect of inflation on their pension. Both the survivor of an employee and the beneficiary of an employee who has retired, are subject to the effect of inflation. But the classification as to who is to receive the post-retirement adjustment does not include the respondent who is the beneficiary of a former employee who had retired. As a result, this legislation is "under inclusive." This differentiation does not create a reasonable classification between such ultimate adult survivor and adult beneficiary. They are both similarly situated with respect to the purpose of this law.

The respondent states that there is no possible purpose which can be conceived to justify such a classification considering the overall purpose of the legislation of post-retirement adjustment to compensate for inflation. The respondent contends no distinction should be made between a beneficiary of a retired employee and the beneficiary of an employee who died while working when the beneficiaries are both under the age of 55. We agree.

We are unable to find any rational relationship to the purpose of the legislation for the establishment of such a classification. It is wholly arbitrary and an example of the legislature picking and choosing who will receive benefits. Such a classification must distinguish one class from another taking into consideration the purpose of the statute.

The granting of a post-retirement adjustment does not come within the approach of considering whether the enactment is experimental or piecemeal, and therefore applying the legislation to one phase of the problem and not affecting others. As we stated above, the legislature cannot arbitrarily pick and choose. The appellant has made such an argument on a money saving basis, but even if the governmental purpose is to save money, it cannot be done on a wholly arbitrary basis. The classification must have some rational relationship to the purpose of the legislation. There is nothing in the record or by conjecture which would justify the differentiation here.

There is no reasonable basis to the classification which permits an adult beneficiary of a disabled or deceased member to receive the adjustment regardless of age, and deny the adult beneficiary of a deceased service retiree who retired under voluntary or involuntary circumstances the adjustment because the beneficiary is under 55 years of age. The constitutional defect of the statute as applied to respondent is revealed when it is reviewed in light of its practical application. We conclude that its application to this respondent whereby the classification excludes her from receiving the post-retirement adjustment, is unconstitutional and in violation of Article II, Section 4 of the Montana Constitution.

TRIEWEILER, J., concurring.

I rejoice at the majority's re-discovery of the rights provided for in the Equal Protection Clause of Article II, Section 4, of Montana's Constitution. However, I find it peculiar that nowhere in the majority's opinion is any mention made of the majority's decision in *Stratemeyer v. MACO Workers' Compensation Trust* (Mont.1993), 855 P.2d 506. Perhaps that is because the result in this case cannot be reconciled with the majority's decision in *Stratemeyer*. That is because under *Stratemeyer* there is no legislative classification which won't satisfy the toothless rational basis test.

This same majority held in *Stratemeyer* that even where no rational basis for a legislative classification is established by the Legislature or proven in district court, this Court can speculate about why the Legislature acted as it did, and that speculation can serve as the basis for overcoming a constitutional challenge. This Court went on to add that even when the State offers no evidence to justify a legislative classification, a person challenging the legislation has the burden of proving that there is no rational basis. In other words, under the *Stratemeyer* decision, a citizen victimized by legislative discrimination has to, first of all, imagine every conceivable basis for that discrimination about which this Court might speculate and then somehow disprove it. This Court then went on in *Stratemeyer* to conclude that a justification for the classification at issue in that case could have been the Legislature's intention to save money, even though there was no evidence in the record that the classification would save money. This Court held that:

> The exclusion of mental claims rationally relates to the *possible goal* of reducing costs and having a viable program for the State and the enrolled employers and employees in the workers' compensation field. [Emphasis added]. *Stratemeyer*, 855 P.2d at 511.

Certainly, by that standard the classification in this case passes any rational basis test. Who can dispute that discriminating against beneficiaries under a certain age "relates to the possible goal of reducing costs" for the teachers' retirement system?

I, of course, have no regard for the *Stratemeyer* decision. I would not follow it and will urge its early demise at every opportunity.... The majority, however, has neither followed it, distinguished it, nor overruled it. Therefore, its decision in this case is both legally and intellectually inconsistent.

I believe that the right to be free from discrimination based on age is a significant enough right that classifications based on age warrant middle-tier scrutiny.... A need exists to develop a meaningful middle-tier analysis. Equal protection of law is an essential underpinning of this free society. The old rational basis test allows government to discriminate among classes of people for the most whimsical reasons.

According to the laws of Montana, age is a "sensitive" if not "suspect" basis for classification. To hold otherwise would be to ignore the import of the Montana Human Rights Act which provides that "[t]he right to be free from discrimination because of ... age ... is recognized as and declared to be a civil right." Accordingly, I would hold that statutory classifications based upon age involve a sensitive basis for classification and warrant a middle-tier test for determining whether they violate the Equal Protection Clause of Montana's Constitution.

D.P. v STATE
705 So.2d 593 (Fla. 1997)

COPE, J.

Dade County passed a comprehensive anti-graffiti ordinance, which forbids the sale to minors of spray paint cans and broadtipped markers ("jumbo markers"). The ordinance provides that minors can possess spray paint or jumbo markers on public property only if accompanied by a responsible adult. On private property, the minor must have the consent of the property owner, but need not be accompanied by an adult. It is a misdemeanor for a minor to possess spray paint or a jumbo marker without the required supervision or consent. D.P. challenges the facial constitutionality of the provisions of the anti-graffiti ordinance that restrict minors' possession of spray paint or jumbo markers. We conclude that the ordinance is constitutional and affirm the adjudication of delinquency.

D.P. argues that the ordinance violates the due process clauses of the state and federal constitutions because the ordinance imposes a criminal penalty for a minor's possession of spray paint or jumbo markers without the State being required to show that the minor had any criminal intent. D.P. reasons that spray paint and jumbo markers are ordinary household items that have legitimate uses. D.P. urges that it is impermissible for the County to criminalize simple possession of ordinary household objects.

D.P. suggests that in its attack on graffiti, the County has two viable alternatives. First, the County can impose a criminal penalty for possession of spray paint or jumbo markers with intent to make graffiti. The anti-graffiti ordinance already does this. Alternatively, D.P. states that the County could constitutionally place a total ban on possession and sale of spray paint and jumbo markers by anyone, adult or minor. This is an approach that was taken in the City of Chicago and was held constitutional. *See National Paint & Coating Association v. City of Chicago*, 45 F.3d 1124, 1126 (7th Cir. 1995). D.P. reasons that if spray paint and jumbo markers cannot legally be purchased or possessed by anyone, then there would be no such thing as innocent possession of spray paint or jumbo markers. It would follow, therefore, that a criminal penalty could be imposed for possession of the forbidden objects. D.P. reasons, however, that so long as spray paint and jumbo markers are available in households in Dade County (because spray paint and jumbo markers can be lawfully purchased by adults), it follows that the County cannot impose a criminal penalty on minors for possession of the same household objects.

In our view, the anti-graffiti ordinance passes constitutional muster. In the first place, this ordinance does not place an outright ban on possession of spray paint or jumbo markers by minors. The ordinance allows a minor to possess these items on public property, so long as the minor is accompanied by a responsible adult. Possession is allowed on private property so long as the minor has the consent of the owner. Rather than imposing an outright ban, the ordinance simply requires that possession be with supervision.

D.P. concedes that the County could constitutionally pass an ordinance that totally banned all spray paint and jumbo markers. Under this approach, which was taken in Chicago, no one (adult or minor) could buy or possess spray paint or jumbo markers anywhere in Dade County. If a total ban is permissible, then surely it is permissible to take the less extreme measure of prohibiting sales to minors and allowing possession only with supervision.[6]

D.P. suggests that it is impermissible to treat minors differently than adults. That suggestion is clearly incorrect. There are many activities that are legal for adults but prohibited to minors: drinking, and driving under legal age, being the most obvious examples. Some supervisory requirements apply to minors that do not apply to adults, such as compulsory school attendance and the curfew ordinance. In the trial court order holding the ordinance to be constitutional, the Judge Petersen said:

> Having considered the cases and authorities cited by the Juvenile, this Court finds that the analysis under the due process and equal protection provisions of the Florida Constitution do not differ in a manner that changes the result of this case from the analysis under ... the United States constitution. Indeed, the cases cited by the Juvenile referred interchangeably to Florida and Federal due process and equal protection provisions.

No fundamental right is implicated in the possession of spray paint and jumbo markers. Nor is youth a suspect classification. *White Egret Condominium, Inc. v. Franklin*, 379 So.2d 346, 351 (Fla.1979) ("The law is now clear that restriction of individual rights on the basis of age need not pass the strict scrutiny test, and therefore age is not a suspect class."); Metropolitan Dade County v. Pred, 665 So.2d 252 (Fla. 3d DCA 1995)[, review denied, 676 So.2d 413 (Fla. 1996)]. ("[U]nder both the Florida and United States Constitution, children, due to their special nature and vulnerabilities, do not enjoy the same quantum or quality of rights as adults.").

The Court's review is therefore limited to the rational basis test. The rational basis test does not turn on whether this Court agrees or disagrees

---

[6] [1] The trial court noted that based on anecdotal evidence, the graffiti problem appeared to be concentrated in the fifteen-, sixteen-, and possibly seventeen-year-old age group.

with the legislation at issue, and this Court will not attempt to impose on a duly-elected legislative body his reservations about the wisdom of the subject ordinance. Instead, the rational basis test focuses narrowly on whether a legislative body could rationally believe that the legislation could achieve a legitimate government end. The end of controlling the blight of graffiti is obviously legitimate and the Juvenile does not challenge this fact.

In addition, a legislative body could rationally conclude that the subject prohibition of possession by minors of spray paint and jumbo markers without supervision on public property or permission of the private-property owner would serve to control and limit incidences of graffiti. Indeed, the prohibition at issue is less restrictive than the prohibitions on spray paint and jumbo markers upheld in *National Paint*. The Court notes that juveniles can avoid the restrictions at issue by using markers less than one-half inch in [writing surface] or markers that contain water-soluble ink.

For the above reasons, the Court finds that the challenged graffiti ordinance does not offend the due process or equal protection provisions of either the Florida or Federal Constitutions. Accordingly, the Juvenile's Motion to Dismiss is denied.

GREEN, J., dissenting.

Respectfully, I believe that sections 21-30.01(e)(2) and (3) of the Dade County Graffiti Ordinance are facially unconstitutional in that they are violative of the due process clause of both the state and federal constitutions.

I do not believe that it can be realistically maintained, as the state attempts to do on this appeal, that sections 21-30.01(e)(2) and (e)(3) of the graffiti ordinance were enacted for the protection of the public's health, safety, welfare or morals. They were clearly enacted solely for the protection of property within the county. Moreover, the act of criminalizing the possession of spray paint and/or jumbo markers by all unsupervised minors, regardless of their intent, is wholly unreasonable, arbitrary, and capricious and is not reasonably related to the county's legitimate objective in protecting property from graffiti.

We are…confronted in this case with two inherently innocuous items (i.e., spray paint and jumbo markers) that are widely utilized both privately and commercially by minors and adults alike for a variety of innocent purposes as well as to make graffiti. It is true, as a general proposition, that the "[r]egulation of items that have some lawful as well as unlawful uses is not an irrational means of discouraging [criminal behavior]." Although the regulation of such items is not per se irrational, the legislature still has constitutional constraints when enacting a blanket or conditional prohibition on the possession or use of such items. Our state supreme court has said that any prohibition against the possession of objects having a common and widespread lawful use must be "reasonably required as incidental to the accomplishment of the primary purpose of the Act. To be sure, sections 21-30.01(e)(2) and (e)(3) will simplify the state's burden of enforcing the graffiti ordinance against minors, who are deemed to be the primary makers of graffiti. "Expediency, however, is not the test...." I therefore cannot agree that the county can constitutionally criminalize all possession of spray paint and jumbo markers by unsupervised minors on public property, regardless of the circumstances, in the hopes of ensnaring the actual graffiti artists.

The challenged subsections of the graffiti ordinance are virtually indistinguishable from the statutes and ordinances repeatedly struck down under the "innocent acts doctrine" with one exception; the challenged subsections under the graffiti ordinance pertain solely to minors. For this reason, I believe that the central issue in this case is whether minors possess diminished substantive due process rights when it comes to statutes or ordinances that seek to criminalize the possession of inherently innocent items which can be used in criminal endeavors. Neither our state nor the federal supreme court appears to have squarely addressed this issue, but I do not believe that existing law supports the notion that the substantive due process rights of minors are not co-equal to those of adults under the "innocent acts doctrine."

The majority points out that it is not constitutionally impermissible to treat minors differently from adults. While that is certainly true, it is true only in some delineated areas.... The central rationale for finding diminished constitutional rights of minors, in limited circumstances, appears to be for the personal protection of the child or the personal protection of others from the acts of minors. For example, in *T.M. v. State*, 689 So.2d 443 (Fla. 3d DCA 1997), we found section 790.22(9)(a), Florida Statutes, which mandates the imposition of a five day detention period on any juvenile who commits any offense involving the use or possession of a firearm, to be constitutional notwithstanding the fact that an adult who similarly commits any such offense is not subject to the same mandatory incarceration period. The statute in *T.M.*, unlike the graffiti subsections in this case, was attempting to regulate a minor's possession and/or use of an inherently dangerous item. In *Metropolitan Dade County v. Pred*, 665 So.2d 252, 253 (Fla. 3d DCA 1995), we similarly upheld the power of the county to impose a curfew for minors, for the personal well-being of minors. Likewise, the laws which prohibit minors from drinking and driving under the legal age limit are constitutionally permissible because they are for the purpose of protecting minors from inherently dangerous activities.

Thus, although the constitutional rights of minors are not co-equal with those of adults under certain circumstances, I must conclude that those factors which generally tend to support a reduction of the rights of minors are simply not present in this case. The purpose of the challenged subsections of the graffiti ordinance is wholly unrelated to the personal protection of minors or others. The county's sole aim is to protect property from graffiti artists. While that is certainly a legitimate and laudable objective, I do not believe that it can be pursued by the county at the expense and deprivation of fundamental due process rights which both adults and minors share. Because I conclude that minors do not have diminished substantive due process rights under the "innocent acts" doctrine, the challenged subsections of this ordinance are no different than the statutes which have been repeatedly struck down by our supreme court under the "innocent acts" doctrine. For that reason, I believe that the challenged subsections of the graffiti ordinance must suffer the same fate.

E. CLASSIFICATIONS BASED ON SEXUAL ORIENTATION

TANNER v. OREGON HEALTH SCIENCES UNIVERSITY
971 P.2d 435 (Or. Ct. App. 1998)

LANDAU, P.J.

At issue in this case is the lawfulness of Oregon Health Science University's (OHSU) denial of health and life insurance benefits to the unmarried domestic partners of its homosexual employees. Plaintiffs...initiated this action for judicial review of State Employees' Benefits Board (SEBB) orders affirming the lawfulness of the denial.... Plaintiffs contend that OHSU's actions violate...Article I, section 20, of the Oregon Constitution, which prohibits granting privileges or immunities not equally belonging to all citizens.... Before this controversy arose, OHSU provided group health insurance benefits to its employees. In accordance with SEBB eligibility criteria, OHSU permitted employees to purchase insurance coverage for "family members." Under the SEBB criteria, unmarried domestic partners of employees were not "family members" who were entitled to insurance coverage.

Plaintiffs are three lesbian nursing professionals employed by OHSU and their unmarried domestic partners. Each of the couples has enjoyed a long-term and committed relationship, which each wishes to continue for life. Each of the couples would be married if Oregon law permitted homosexual couples to marry.... All three OHSU employees applied for medical and dental insurance benefits for their domestic partners. The OHSU benefits manager refused to process the applications on the ground that the domestic partners of the employees did not meet the SEBB eligibility criteria.

Article I, section 20, prohibits granting privileges or immunities to one citizen or class of citizens that are not equally available to all citizens. That generally is understood to express two separate prohibitions. As the Supreme Court explained in its seminal opinion, *State v. Clark*, 630 P.2d 810 (1981), the clause "forbids inequality of privileges or immunities not available upon the same terms, first, to any citizen, and second, to any class of citizens." In this case, plaintiffs contend that they are members of a class of citizens, homosexual couples, to whom certain privileges, insurance benefits, are not made available.

As used in the Article I, section 20, case law, the term "class" takes on special meaning; only laws that disparately treat a "true class" may violate that section of the constitution. In attempting to describe precisely what is meant by a "true class," the cases draw a distinction between classes that are created by the challenged law or government action itself and classes that are defined in terms of characteristics that are shared apart from the challenged law or action.... The standard example of a nontrue class, drawn from the Supreme Court's decision in Clark, is the classification created by a statute that imposes a filing deadline for filing a petition for review. Such legislation creates two classes of persons: (1) those who timely file petitions for review, and (2) those who do not. Both are "classes" of persons, at least in the colloquial sense of groups having something in common. But in the absence of the statute, they have no identity at all. Legislation that disparately affects such "classes" does not violate Article I, section 20, because of the essentially circular nature of the argument: The legislation cannot disparately affect a class that the legislation itself creates.

In contrast, Article I, section 20, does protect against disparate treatment of true classes, those that have identity apart from the challenged law itself. Various formulations have been used to describe in some affirmative way what a true class is, as opposed to merely what it is not in reference to classes created by the challenged legislation. The cases refer to classification by "ad hominem characteristic," by "personal characteristic," and by "antecedent personal or social characteristics or societal status." Examples of true classes include gender, ethnic background, legitimacy, past or present residency, and military service.

To say that disparately treated true classes are protected by Article I, section 20, does not end the matter. Depending on what type of true class is involved, the legislation or governmental action may or may not be upheld in spite of the disparity. In that regard, the cases draw a distinction between "suspect" classes and other true classes. The former classes are subject to a more demanding level of scrutiny, and legislation or government action disparately treating such classes is much more likely to run afoul of Article I, section 20, than is legislation or government action that disparately treats a nonsuspect class.

The leading opinion on suspect classes is *Hewitt v. SAIF*, 653 P.2d 970 (1982). In that case, the plaintiff, a man, challenged the constitutionality of a statute that permitted an unmarried woman to collect death benefits upon the death of an unmarried man with whom she cohabited for over one year. He contended that the statute, which made no provision for death benefits to an unmarried man who had cohabited with an unmarried woman for the required period, violated Article I, section 20, of the Oregon Constitution. The court held that, under Article I, section 20, disparate treatment of classes that may be regarded as "suspect" is subject to particularly exacting scrutiny. The court did not define precisely what it meant by "suspect" class. It did say that a class is suspect when it is defined in terms of "immutable" characteristics and "can be suspected of reflecting 'invidious' social or political premises, that is to say prejudice or stereotyped prejudgments." The court held that gender constitutes such a class. It then held that the denial of benefits to the plaintiff, a member of the suspect class defined by his male gender, was "inherently suspect." That suspicion, the court held, could be overcome only by evidence that the denial of benefits to him is justified on the basis of "biological differences" between those who are entitled to the benefits under the statute and those who are not. Finding no such justification in the record, the court declared that the statute violated Article I, section 20.

Although the court in *Hewitt* referred to "immutable" characteristics as being sufficient for defining a suspect class under Article I, section 20, subsequent cases make clear that immutability-in the sense of inability to alter or change-is not necessary. The court has since explained that, in addition to gender, such classes as alienage, religious affiliation, race and religion are suspect classes. Both alienage and religious affiliation may be changed almost at will. For that matter, given modern medical technology, so also may gender. We therefore understand from the cases that the focus of suspect class definition is not necessarily the immutability of the common, class-defining characteristics, but instead the fact that such characteristics are historically regarded as defining distinct, socially-recognized groups that have been the subject of adverse social or political stereotyping or prejudice. If a law or government action fails to offer privileges and immunities to members of such a class on equal terms, the law or action is inherently suspect and, as the court made clear in *Hewitt*, may be upheld only if the failure to make the privileges or immunities available to that class can be justified by genuine differences between the disparately treated class and those to whom the privileges and immunities are granted.

Turning to the facts of this case, there is no question but that plaintiffs are members of a true class. That class—unmarried homosexual couples— is not defined by any statute nor by the practices that are the subject of plaintiffs' challenges. Moreover, the class clearly is defined in terms of ad hominem, personal and social characteristics. The question then is whether plaintiffs are members of a suspect class. Here, too, we have no difficulty concluding that plaintiffs are members of a suspect class. Sexual orientation, like gender, race, alienage, and religious affiliation is widely regarded as defining a distinct, socially recognized group of citizens, and certainly it is beyond dispute that homosexuals in our society have been and continue to be the subject of adverse social and political stereotyping and prejudice.

Because plaintiffs are members of a suspect class to which certain privileges and immunities are not made available, we must determine whether the fact that the privileges and immunities are not available to that class may be justified by genuine differences between the class and those to whom the privileges and immunities are made available. Stated perhaps more plainly, we must determine whether the fact that the domestic partners of homosexual OHSU employees cannot obtain insurance benefits can be justified by their homosexuality. The parties have suggested no such justification, and we can envision none.

OHSU's defense is that it determined eligibility for insurance benefits on the basis of marital status, not sexual orientation. According to OHSU, the fact that such a facially neutral classification has the unintended side effect of discriminating against homosexual couples who cannot marry is not actionable under Article I, section 20. We are not persuaded by the asserted defense. Article I, section 20, does not prohibit only intentional discrimination. On point in that regard is the Supreme Court's decision in *Zockert v. Fanning*, 800 P.2d 773 (1990). In that case, the plaintiff parent challenged the constitutionality of a statutory scheme that provided indigent parents court-appointed counsel in parental termination proceedings but did not provide for court-appointed counsel in adoption proceedings that have the effect of terminating parental rights. After concluding that the plaintiff was a member of a true class…it observed that the legislature apparently was unaware of the disparity between the parental termination and adoption proceeding statutes and did not make a conscious policy to treat indigent parents in the two similar proceedings unequally. The court nevertheless concluded that the unintended side effect of providing counsel in termination proceedings was to treat a true class of citizens disparately in violation of Article I, section 20. Intentional conduct, the court held, is not required for discrimination to be actionable under that section of the constitution.

So also in this case, OHSU has taken action with no apparent intention to treat disparately members of any true class of citizens. Nevertheless, its actions have the undeniable effect of doing just that. As in *Zockert*, OHSU's intentions in this case are not relevant. What is relevant is the extent to which privileges or immunities are not made available to all citizens on equal terms.

OHSU insists that in this case privileges and immunities are available to all on equal terms: All married employees—heterosexual and homosexual alike—are permitted to acquire insurance benefits for their spouses. That reasoning misses the point, however. Homosexual couples may not marry. Accordingly, the benefits are not made available on equal terms. They are made available on terms that, for gay and lesbian couples, are a legal impossibility.

We conclude that OHSU's denial of insurance benefits to the unmarried domestic partners of its homosexual employees violated Article I, section 20, of the Oregon Constitution and that the trial court correctly entered judgment in favor of plaintiffs on that ground.

NOTE

Several state courts have addressed the question of whether classifications based on sexual orientation should be considered suspect and therefore reviewed with heightened judicial scrutiny. The results of these cases have been mixed; some courts, like the Oregon Court of Appeals in *Tanner*, have concluded that classifications based on sexual orientation should be reviewed with heightened scrutiny, while other courts have concluded that classifications based on sexual orientation should be reviewed with only minimal scrutiny. E.g., *Singer v. O'Hara*, 522 P.2d 1187 (Wash. Ct. App. 1974).

In *Tanner*, the court ruled that facially neutral laws that have a disparate impact against gay and lesbian persons amount to unconstitutional discrimination on the basis of sexual orientation. Some courts have declined to take this position. For instance, in upholding a rule limiting health insurance coverage to married couples, the Supreme Court of Wisconsin stated, "The challenged rule distinguishes between married and unmarried employees, not between homosexual and heterosexual employees." *Phillips v. Wisconsin Personnel Commission*, 482 N.W.2d 121, 127 (Wis. 1992). Other courts, though, have sided with *Tanner* by striking down laws that deny benefits to same-sex couples that are available to married opposite-sex couples.

In *Baker v. State*, 744 A.2d 864 (Vt. 1999), the Supreme Court of Vermont ruled that by excluding same-sex couples from the legal benefits of marriage, the state marriage laws violated the common benefits clause of the Vermont Constitution, which reads:

> That government is, or ought to be, instituted for the common benefit, protection, and security of the people, nation, or community, and not for the particular emolument or advantage of any single person, family, or set of persons, who are a part only of that community.

The decision in *Baker* extends the legal benefits of marriage, but not the right to marry itself, to same-sex couples. For further discussion of *Baker* and same-sex marriage, see Chapter VI.

F. ECONOMIC RIGHTS

The use of heightened judicial review in cases involving business or economic regulations raises concerns about the revival of "Lochnerism." This refers to the practice, most prominently of the United States Supreme Court in the early part of the 20th Century, of adopting extreme laissez faire economic policy as constitutional doctrine to invalidate remedial statutes regulating wages, prices, or working conditions. The term derives from *Lochner v. New York*, 198 U.S. 45 (1905), in which the Supreme Court ruled that a state statute setting maximum hours of work was a violation of the Due Process Clause of the Fourteenth Amendment. *Lochner* has come to symbolize an era of excessive judicial intervention, during which the Supreme Court combined constitutional doctrine and questionable economic policy to strike down a number of progressive laws regulating business and working conditions.

In the federal court system, minimal judicial scrutiny was devised to counteract Lochnerism by restraining judicial review in economic cases. Since the 1940's, the Supreme Court has consistently used the most minimal form of judicial review in economic cases, granting great deference to the legislature and rarely, if ever, striking down economic legislation.

Many states, also wary of Lochnerism, follow the federal example of applying minimal scrutiny in reviewing economic regulations. In states that adhere to the federal approach, judicial review in cases involving economic matters is extremely reserved, allowing the legislature considerable latitude to regulate economic affairs. Within the confines of minimal judicial scrutiny, economic laws are usually found to be constitutional. While minimal scrutiny of economic legislation represents the norm in state court systems, there are a number of exceptions to this practice. In certain instances, state courts have adopted a less restrained form of scrutiny to assess economic legislation. Using an enhanced variety of judicial review, some state courts have struck down economic legislation on the ground that it runs afoul of an equality provision in the state constitution. The cases that follow in this section illustrate both the deferential approach and the enhanced approach to reviewing economic legislation.

BENSON v. NORTH DAKOTA WORKMEN'S COMPENSATION BUREAU
283 N.W.2d 96 (N.D. 1979)

PEDERSON, J.

The district court of Stark County has twice held in this case that the statute which excludes agricultural service from the mandatory provisions of the Workmen's Compensation Act violates both the Constitution of North Dakota and the Constitution of the United States. When the first holding was appealed to this court, we remanded because of procedural deficiencies and made suggestions as to procedure and issues. On this appeal, we will address the merits of the constitutionality of the agricultural exclusion under the Workmen's Compensation Act.

The record reveals that Benson's scope of employment as an agricultural employee was extremely broad, and included: milking, livestock feeding, equipment operation, cleaning cattle, cleaning barn, hauling silage and grain, assisting in calving, repairing machinery, welding tuning motors, changing oil and greasing machinery, repairing fences and corrals, operating augers, carpentry, driving tractors, trucks and swathers, chopping corn, operating a power saw, painting, and "about anything you could name."

Although North Dakota's Workmen's Compensation Act has been often amended, the stated purpose of the Act has remained essentially as enacted in 1919. The title to the Act clearly discloses that this is an act creating a fund for the benefit of employees injured, and the dependents of employees killed in hazardous employment.

There was no contention by anyone in this case that agricultural employment is not hazardous. By the very nature and scope of tasks required of a general agricultural service employee, such as Benson in the instant case, a jack-of-all-trades develops who may be the master-of-none. While operating a power saw a few minutes during a week, we would not expect Benson to be as proficient or careful as a carpenter helper who operates a power saw forty hours a week. The composite activities of a farmhand are obviously more hazardous than the total of the individual activities when performed full time.

Courts from Montana and Michigan have been the most recent to have considered at least some of the aspects of an agricultural exclusion from workmen's compensation statutes. Both courts expressed some general principles with which we agree…. In *Gutierrez v. Glaser Crandell Company*, 202 N.W.2d 786 (Mich. 1972), out of the seven Michigan justices, four concluded that:

> There is no basis for distinguishing the work of a laborer who drives a truck at a factory from a laborer who drives one on the farm or for any one of numerous other labor activities 'on the farm' as distinguished from the same activity in industry, wholesaling, retailing, or building…. (T)he argument that Section 115(e) is especially tailored to meet the problems of the small farmer and his occasional employees fails to account for the need for similar treatment as to the small businessman grocer, clothier, butcher or as to the small contractor plumber, carpenter, roofer or as to numerous other categories of small employers and their employees who are not accorded this treatment.

Although this court desires to portray an image of intellectual vitality and to display its capacity to identify and evaluate each analytically distinct ingredient of the contending interests, we have a legacy of judicial restraint which we should not cavalierly abandon. Use of judicial restraint, however, does not permit a court to ignore its responsibility. If taken too literally, the rule that a court will not substitute its judgment for that of the legislature could result in the abdication by the court of any authority to review the constitutionality of legislation. The ultimate result would be a destruction of the constitution as a limitation on legislative action. The pendulum could likewise swing too far the other way and the court could become so aggressively creative that the judge's notions as to what is good or bad or necessary or unnecessary could improperly restrict policy-making functions of the legislative branch.

Government could not function without making classifications. The discriminatory effects of classification ordinarily do not violate equal protection as long as there is a basis for disparate treatment that naturally inheres in the subject matter. Any classification can be challenged as denying equal protection; it then becomes the duty of the court to determine the statute's validity and to uphold the classification if it includes all, and only those, persons who are similarly situated with respect to the purpose of the law. Generally, when the legislature has expressed the Purpose of the law, courts need only examine the statute itself in determining whether or not: (1) a particular classification bears some rational relationship to the expressed purpose; (2) the classification is based upon a permissible distinction (that is, are similar things treated similarly); and (3) the classification is clearly arbitrary or unreasonable.

The North Dakota Legislature explicitly expressed the purpose of the Act but the exclusion of agricultural services has no correspondence to that expressed purpose. The legislature made no attempt to express any purpose for the exclusion…. There are four possible purposes for excluding agricultural employees from the benefits offered other employees by the Workmen's Compensation Act:

(1) The purpose of excluding agricultural employees was to overcome political opposition to passage of a workmen's compensation act by a farm-oriented legislature.... (T)his purpose, if we can call it that, only supports a conclusion that agricultural employees had little influence in legislative matters, but supplies no justification for the exclusion in a constitutional sense.

(2) Farm employees should be excluded because their work is not as hazardous as other employment and compulsory coverage for them is not needed. "Least convincing of all is the assertion that farm laborers do not need this kind of protection. Whatever the compensation acts may say, agriculture is one of the most hazardous of all occupations. In 1964, of 4,761,000 agricultural workers, 3,000 were fatally injured, while of 17,259,000 manufacturing employees, the number of fatalities was 2,000." 1B Larson, Workmen's Compensation Law, Farm Labor, s 53:20, p. 9-109.... A conclusion that modern-day farming is nonhazardous defies reality and provides no explanation for the exclusion of agricultural employees from coverage under the Act. It is readily acknowledged that driving cattle on horseback has not become more dangerous than it was in 1919, yet riders employed at sales rings and stockyards have always benefited from coverage while riders employed by farmers and ranchers have not.

(3) Farm employees should be excluded because the "family farm" is a closely knit community of relatives and friends who care for each other's needs and injuries and no other protection is needed.... In this case, Benson's employer, Decker, testified in effect that he thought that he had private insurance that would have taken care of any employee accident. He did carry farm liability coverage which included $2,000 no-fault medical benefits, and these were, in fact, paid to Benson. Decker asserted that he discovered, after the accident, that the coverage he thought he had is not even available from commercial insurance carriers and that it would be "too costly" to carry voluntary workmen's compensation coverage. There may be farmers even more beneficent than Decker but there undoubtedly are many migrant, temporary, part-time employees who have no reason whatsoever to expect to be cared for, if injured, out of any beneficence of their farmer-employer.

(4) Farm employees should be excluded because farm employers cannot afford to pay the premium. We accord this justification considerable weight and perceive more than an element of truth in it. Any addition to the overhead costs of operating a farm threatens the chances of a profitable operation. The latest edition of 1B Larson, Workmen's Compensation Law, s 53:10, indicates that not more than seventeen states have mandatory workmen's compensation coverage for agricultural workers. All other things being equal, there is a recognizable, competitive edge for a farmer who is freed from any item of overhead cost.

We cannot ignore the effect of the exemption upon agricultural employees. When we look at the effect of the agricultural service exclusion, we must focus upon both employer and employee and, although some inequality is permissible, we must balance the benefits against the burdens imposed on each class.... We find unacceptable the suggestion by the attorney general that by excluding farm workers from workmen's compensation coverage, the legislature has, in effect, spread the burden of injured farm workers to the widest possible base to the taxpayers in general because injured farm workers who are poor can receive welfare. The burden still rests entirely upon the injured farm employee, if not economically, surely in the loss of dignity.

We agree with the trial court's conclusion that the exclusion of agricultural employees from the benefits of the Workmen's Compensation Act is unreasonable and contrary to the expressed purpose of the Act. Because of the exclusion, the Act withholds from agricultural employees the sure and certain relief awarded to other wage earners. There is no correspondence between the purpose of the Act and the agricultural classification. There are no proper and justifiable distinctions between agricultural employees and nonagricultural employees in relation to the risk of injury from employment. We hold that the agricultural exemption in the Workmen's Compensation Act violates s 20, Article I, North Dakota Constitution.*

SAND, J., dissenting.

The principal issue is whether or not subdivision (1), the agricultural exemption, is constitutional. In every instance where this question was presented to a court it was upheld. However, in *Gutierrez v. Glaser Crandell Company*, 202 N.W.2d 786 (Mich.1972), the court held invalid a classification within a classification relating to employees engaged in agricultural activities. Numerous court decisions concerned with this topic and the case law, together with the legal rationale, as well as the cases cited in support of the decision overwhelmingly support the validity of the agricultural service exclusion from the Workmen's Compensation Act.

The exclusion of farming and ranching from the Workmen's Compensation Act was challenged in *State of Montana ex rel. Hammond v. Hager*, 503 P.2d 52 (Mont. 1972). In ruling that the exclusion was not arbitrary and unreasonable, the Montana Supreme Court (said):

> Our legislature might have concluded to exclude farming operations because they were hazardous enough that the cost of coverage to the farmer would be an unnecessary and unreasonable burden, particularly since the legislature may not have believed that conditions of farm employment generally were similar to those of the industries the Act did cover. Speculating further, one could as well conclude that the legislature excluded coverage of farmers on the basis, for example, that a great majority of Montana farmers employ too few people to justify the cost and administrative expense required to comply with the Act; that most farm employees are too seasonal or casual to require coverage; or, that

---

* ADDENDUM Since the concurrence of four members of this (five-person) Court is required to declare a statute unconstitutional (Section 88, North Dakota Constitution), and only three member of the Court concur in this opinion, the agricultural exclusion from the Workmen's Compensation coverage is not declared unconstitutional by a sufficient majority.

Montana's farmers should not be put at a competitive disadvantage since most other states also exclude agriculture.

I believe it is common knowledge, or at least well established, that a farmer is not able to pass on the costs to the purchaser or consumer, as is the situation in other commercial enterprises and business. The farmer is required to absorb any additional costs himself. To this should be added that it is common knowledge for farmers to exchange help, particularly with the family farm. Added to this is the further knowledge that minor members of the family, as distinguished from other businesses, perform work as part of the "growing up process" without any given salary, and also exchange services with other family farms. While other businesses also have members of the family working, in most instances they are adults and not minors, as the situation is on the farm.

The majority opinion has not pointed to one single factor why the act is invidiously discriminatory. It simply states so without any support whatsoever. The exclusion does not fall within the suspect class, therefore the need to support the act is not present but it is up to the challengers to clearly illustrate and demonstrate that the act amounts to an invidious discrimination. This has not been done.

COLLINS v. DAY
644 N.E.2d 72 (Ind. 1994)

DICKSON, J.

This case presents a state constitutional challenge to the exclusion of agricultural workers from the coverage of the Indiana Worker's Compensation Statute. The parties have stipulated to the facts. On February 11, 1989, plaintiff-appellant Eugene Collins sustained a broken right leg in an accident in the course of his employment as an agricultural employee of defendant-appellee Glen Day. The defendant denies that any compensable accident occurred under the provisions of the Act and has not paid the plaintiff any worker's compensation benefits. In the plaintiff's application for such benefits, he claims medical expenses of $12,000.00 and average weekly earnings at the time of the accident of $140.00 per week, in addition to the value of the use of a residence.

The full Worker's Compensation Board affirmed the single Hearing Judge's order granting the defendant's Motion to Dismiss, which generally raised the statutory agricultural exemption to the Indiana Worker's Compensation Act, which provides in part that the Act "shall not apply to casual labor ... nor to farm or to agricultural employees, nor to domestic servants, nor to the employers of such persons." The plaintiff appealed, contending that the agricultural exemption violated Article I, Section 23 of the Indiana Constitution (hereafter "Section 23"), which provides:

> The General Assembly shall not grant to any citizen, or class of citizens, privileges or immunities which, upon the same terms, shall not equally belong to all citizens.

In this appeal, the plaintiff argues that the worker's compensation agricultural exemption violates Section 23 because it extends to a special class of employers, an immunity denied to the general class of employers. He further contends that the statutory grant to agricultural employers of the option to elect either to be covered by or to be exempt from the Indiana Worker's Compensation Act is a privilege both denied to a comparable class of agricultural employees and denied to the general class of Indiana employers.

Initially, we must determine whether settled Indiana law forecloses consideration of plaintiff's contention that federal Fourteenth Amendment jurisprudence does not necessarily apply to a claim brought under Section 23 of the Indiana Constitution. During the 143 years since the ratification of Section 23, this Court has assumed various postures with respect to the applicability of federal Fourteenth Amendment standards to Section 23 questions. One such approach suggests that a distinction ought to be drawn between Section 23 and the Fourteenth Amendment. There are striking textual differences between the two provisions. The Fourteenth Amendment prohibits laws which "abridge" privileges or immunities, whereas Section 23 prohibits laws which "grant" unequal privileges or immunities. Many Indiana cases have considered and applied Section 23 separately from the Fourteenth Amendment. For example, in *Graffty v. City of Rushville*, 8 N.E. 609 (Ind. 1886) we noted that Section 23 considerations were to be analyzed independently from the "provisions of the National Constitution." In at least one case, a statute was found to comply with the federal Privileges and Immunities Clause but nevertheless to violate the parallel provision in Indiana's Section 23. *Sperry & Hutchinson Co. v. State*, 122 N.E. 584 (Ind. 1919). Several decisions of this Court have expressly acknowledged that Section 23 "is the antithesis of the 14th amendment to the federal Constitution." Similarly suggesting the distinction between Section 23 and the Fourteenth Amendment, numerous other cases have undertaken the analysis of constitutional claims under first one of the provisions and then the other.

A contrasting line of cases has maintained that Section 23 and the Fourteenth Amendment share substantially the same considerations. In *Dortch v. Lugar*, 266 N.E.2d 25 (Ind. 1971) our opinion noted that Section 23 and the Fourteenth Amendment "concerning the abridging of privileges and immunities of citizens protect substantially identical rights." Other cases have considered the two provisions essentially synonymous.

Numerous cases have treated the two provisions simultaneously, without any explicit statement as to equivalence or separateness.

Notwithstanding that the privileges and immunities cases brought under Section 23 have often assimilated federal equal protection analysis, we are under no obligation to follow Fourteenth Amendment jurisprudence in resolving a Section 23 issue....

We conclude that there is no settled body of Indiana law that compels application of a federal equal protection analytical methodology to claims alleging special privileges or immunities under Indiana Section 23 and that Section 23 should be given independent interpretation and application... Excluding the line of cases which have applied federal equal protection methodology to state Section 23 issues, there exists a considerable body of case law reviewing the state constitutional question, from which a substantially uniform, though still evolving, analytical standard has emerged. Our review discloses several recurrent themes which we now distill into two general factors.

The considerations embodied in the first of the two factors focus upon the nature of the classifications of citizens upon which the legislature is basing its disparate treatment. Numerous cases have stated that the basis of such classification must "inhere in the subject matter." In *Heckler v. Conter*, 187 N.E. 878 (Ind. 1933), we stated that legislative classification must be "based upon substantial distinctions germane to the subject matter and the object to be attained." The distinctions must involve something more than mere characteristics which will serve to divide or identify the class. There must be inherent differences in situation related to the subject-matter of the legislation which require, necessitate, or make expedient different or exclusive legislation with respect to the members of the class.

The significant common theme shared by such formulations is the requirement that, where the legislature singles out one person or class of persons to receive a privilege or immunity not equally provided to others, such classification must be based upon distinctive, inherent characteristics which rationally distinguish the unequally treated class, and the disparate treatment accorded by the legislation must be reasonably related to such distinguishing characteristics. We believe that this requirement incorporates and satisfies the often expressed concerns that such legislative classifications be "just," "natural," "reasonable," "substantial," "not artificial," "not capricious," and "not arbitrary." This requirement, then, comprises the first prong of the two-part Section 23 standard we articulate today.

The second of the two factors embraces concerns, frequently expressed in Section 23 cases, regarding the need for uniformity and equal availability of the preferential treatment for all persons similarly situated.

In *Dixon v. Poe*, 65 N.E. 518 (Ind. 1902), an enactment was invalidated because it failed to "embrace all of the class to which it is naturally related." Section 23 was found to be violated when a law "creates a preference, and establishes an inequality among a class of citizens all of whom are equally meritorious" or which "applies to persons in certain situations, and excludes from effect other persons who are not dissimilar in these respects." Similar considerations are emphasized in numerous cases reviewing Section 23 issues. For example, in *McErlain v. Taylor*, 192 N.E. 260 (Ind. 1934), this Court stated:

> But, if there are other general classes situate[d] in all respects like the class benefitted by the statute, with the same inherent needs and qualities which indicate the necessity or expediency of protection for the favored class, and legislation....withholds the same protection from, the other class or classes in like situation, it cannot stand.

It is important to note that, in applying the two-part standard we articulate today to claims asserted under Section 23, the courts must accord considerable deference to the manner in which the legislature has balanced the competing interests involved. Presuming the statute to be constitutional, courts place the burden upon the challenger "to negative every conceivable basis which might have supported the classification." The question of classification under Section 23 is primarily a legislative question…. In *Sperry & Hutchinson Co.*, 122 N.E. at 587, we said that "[i]f any state of facts within the fair range of probability can be reasonably supposed, which would supply an adequate reason on which to base the classification made, such state of facts will be assumed to have existed when the law was enacted."

To summarize, we hold that Article 1, Section 23 of the Indiana Constitution imposes two requirements upon statutes that grant unequal privileges or immunities to differing classes of persons. First, the disparate treatment accorded by the legislation must be reasonably related to inherent characteristics which distinguish the unequally treated classes. Second, the preferential treatment must be uniformly applicable and equally available to all persons similarly situated. Finally, in determining whether a statute complies with or violates Section 23, courts must exercise substantial deference to legislative discretion.

The resolution of Section 23 claims does not require an analytical framework applying varying degrees of scrutiny for different protected interests. The protections assured by Section 23 apply fully, equally, and without diminution to prohibit any and all improper grants of unequal privileges or immunities, including not only those grants involving suspect classes or impinging upon fundamental rights but other such grants as well. For example, this Court has applied Section 23 to invalidate grants of privilege which were improperly gender-based without using a heightened level of scrutiny. The multiple-level system remains, of course, an integral aspect of the test of a statute's constitutionality under federal Fourteenth Amendment jurisprudence. This Court anticipates that our independent state privileges and immunities jurisprudence will evolve in future cases facing Indiana courts to assure and extend protection to all Indiana citizens in addition to that provided by the federal Fourteenth Amendment.

The plaintiff contends that the exclusion of agricultural employers from the compulsory scope of coverage and the creation of an exclusive privilege for such employers to waive this exclusion each violates Section 23. He contends that the exemption of employers is an immunity extended to one class of employers which is denied to the general class of employers, and that the right to elect coverage is a privilege denied to both agricultural employees and the general class of employers.

We first address whether the treatment of agricultural employers separately from agricultural employees and from the general class of employers is a classification based upon distinctive, inherent characteristics and, if so, whether the unequal treatment is reasonably related to such distinguishing characteristics.

Applying the required deferential standard of review, we find that there are inherent distinctions between these classifications that are reasonably related to the exemption. The legislative classification may have been based upon various features reasonably distinguishing Indiana agricultural employers from other employers, among which are: the prevalence of sole proprietorships and small employment units, including numerous family operations; the distinctive nature of farm work, its attendant risks, and the typical level of worker training and experience; the traditional informality of the agricultural employment relationship and the frequent absence of formal ancillary employee benefit programs; and the peculiar difficulties agricultural employers experience in passing along the additional cost of worker's compensation insurance coverage to the ultimate consumer. Furthermore, we find that within the classification of agricultural employers, the exemption from worker's compensation coverage for employees is uniformly applicable and equally available to all persons who are or may become agricultural employers.

The amicus curiae, Legal Services Organization of Indiana, Inc., through its Migrant Farmworker Project, has submitted a forceful, thorough, and well-documented brief to support its contention that "the nature of agricultural work and the structure of agriculture in 1974 and today is so radically different than in 1915, that the continued exclusion of farmworkers from worker's compensation coverage does not comply with legislat[ive] intent." We do not deny that preferential legislative treatment for a classification which was proper when enacted may later cease to satisfy the requirements of Section 23 because of intervening changes in social or economic conditions. In the present case, however, because we find the plaintiff has failed to carry the burden placed upon the challenger to negative every reasonable basis for the classification, we are not persuaded that the agricultural exemption has become inconsistent with the requirements of Section 23.

We therefore conclude that the statutory agricultural exemption to the Indiana Worker's Compensation Act, Ind. Code § 22-3-2-9(a), does not presently constitute a special immunity in violation of the Indiana Privileges and Immunities Clause, Article I, Section 23 of the Indiana Constitution.

SULLIVAN, J., dissenting without opinion, would deny transfer because he believes the analysis of the Court of Appeals in this case was correct.

CHURCH v. STATE
646 N.E.2d 572 (Ill. 1995)

BILANDIC, C.J.

On April 4, 1988, the plaintiff purchased a private alarm contracting business and began operating the business on a part-time basis. The plaintiff worked approximately 1,000 hours a year leasing, selling and servicing alarm systems. On May 8, 1991, the plaintiff learned that the Private Detective, Private Alarm and Private Security Act of 1983 (Act) required him to obtain a license from the Department before engaging in the private alarm contracting business.

On May 31, 1991, the plaintiff submitted an application for a private alarm contractor's license to the Department. The plaintiff characterized his application as one to obtain a license without examination. As part of his application, the plaintiff informed the Board that he was currently employed as a patrolman for the Petersburg police department, and had been employed in that capacity since 1984, working approximately 1,200 hours a year. The plaintiff also informed the Board that he had 18 years of experience as a police officer. During such period of time, the plaintiff had investigated or assisted in investigating 50 different thefts or burglaries. The plaintiff also informed the Board that his police training included classes and seminars in field sobriety testing, mandatory firearms training, shooting decisions training, police traffic radar certification, use of force/civil liability, legal aspects of deadly force and night firearms, operation scams, domestic violence, criminal law, law for police, interview and interrogation, and an in-service refresher.

On September 12, 1991, the Private Detective, Private Alarm, and Private Security Board (Board) held a meeting where the plaintiff's application was considered. The Board recommended that the application be denied. The Director of the Department approved the Board's recommendation and notified the plaintiff that his application was denied "due to the fact that [his] experience does not meet statutory requirements" under the Act.... At issue in this appeal are the experience requirements set forth in section 14(c)(11)(B) of the Act. That section provides:

> (A)ll persons applying for licensure...shall have a minimum of 3 years experience out of the 5 years immediately preceding his application as a full-time supervisor, manager or administrator or an agency licensed in the State of Illinois as a private alarm contractor agency.

We must now consider the plaintiff's claim that section 14(c)(11)(C), as interpreted by the Department, is unconstitutional because it requires an applicant to have three years of employment with a private alarm contractor as a precondition to licensure. The plaintiff argues that the statute thereby grants members of the private alarm contracting industry an unregulated monopoly over entrance into the private alarm contracting trade. (T)he Department argues that the State, pursuant to its inherent police powers, may regulate businesses for the protection of public health, safety and welfare. The Department notes that the legislature has expressly declared that private alarm contracting is a practice affecting the public health, safety and welfare, and therefore, is subject to regulation.

The fact that the legislature has invoked its police power to regulate a particular trade, however, is not conclusive that such power was lawfully exercised. The means of regulation which the legislature adopts by statute must have a definite and reasonable relationship to the end of protecting the public health, safety and welfare. Here, we must determine whether those portions of the Act relating to the licensing of private alarm contractors bear a reasonable relationship to the legislature's goal of protecting the public from the hazards of incompetent private alarm contractors.

In *People v. Brown*, 95 N.E.2d 888 (Ill. 1950), the court invalidated the 1935 plumbing license statute, which provided that a person could not take the examination to become a licensed master plumber until he had spent five years in the employment of a master plumber as an apprentice and then, spent an additional five years in the employment of a master as a journeyman plumber. The court found the statute unconstitutional, in part, because it gave master plumbers monopolistic control over the avenues of entry into the plumbing business. The court found that no matter how well qualified a person might be by instruction or training, that person could never become a certified registered plumber's apprentice, a journeyman plumber or a master plumber, unless a licensed master plumber so willed. By limiting the manner in which a person could learn the plumbing trade to apprenticeship with a master plumber, when many schools could offer similar instruction, the statute conferred on master plumbers an exclusive monopoly on instruction. The court concluded:

> The legislature conferred a special privilege upon master plumbers, as a class, when it gave them the arbitrary and exclusive right to determine who shall, or shall not, engage in the vocation of learning the trade of journeyman plumber, coupled with their having the sole right, with the uncontrolled exercise thereof, to instruct plumbers' apprentices in that trade.

In *People v. Johnson*, 369 N.E.2d 898 (Ill. 1977) the court invalidated yet another version of the plumbing licensing statute…. The *Johnson* court acknowledged that the legislature may reasonably require an applicant to have practical experience, such as an apprenticeship, as a prerequisite to licensure. The court established a two-part test to determine whether an apprenticeship provision is constitutionally valid: "(1) [the provision] must not have the effect, when implemented, of conferring on members of the trade a monopolistic right to instruct, *and* (2) [it] must be structured in such a way that the apprenticeship it requires is calculated to enhance the…expertise of prospective licensees." (Emphasis added.)

Viewing the instant Act in light of the two-part test established in *Johnson*, we conclude that the licensing scheme for private alarm contractors is unconstitutional. The Act violates the first part of the *Johnson* two-part test, because it grants members of the private alarm contracting trade monopolistic control over individuals who wish to gain entrance into the field. Under the Act, as implemented by the Department, applicants without private alarm contractor experience do not qualify for licensure under the Act. An applicant can gain such experience only by being employed full-time for a licensed private alarm contractor agency or for an entity within the industry for three years in a supervisory or managerial capacity. No matter how well qualified a person may be by instruction, training or prior experience, he or she can never of his or her own free will become a licensed private alarm contractor unless a member of the regulated industry is willing to hire him or her on a full-time basis for the requisite time period in a particular capacity. The Act does not require private alarm contractors to employ a person who wishes to enter the field, nor does the refusal to employ such a person need to be based upon any valid reason. As in *Brown, Schroeder* and *Johnson*, it may be predicated upon an understanding between members of the private alarm contracting industry to limit the number of potential competitors allowed into the trade. In effect, the experience provisions within the Act, as implemented by the Department, give members of the private alarm industry an unregulated and monopolistic right to control entrance to the private alarm business.

The two decisions which the Department cites as authority for the proposition that the Act is constitutional are distinguishable. In *People ex rel. Chicago Dental Society v. A.A.A. Dental Laboratories, Inc.*, 134 N.E.2d 285 (Ill. 1956), the court upheld a portion of the Dental Practice Act that prohibited dental laboratory technician from constructing or repairing dentures, bridges or other replacements for teeth, except when employed to do so by a dentist. The court distinguished the statute from the plumbing license laws invalidated in *Brown, Schroeder* and *Johnson*. The court noted that "[t]here is in the present case no prescribed economic hierarchy, with access to each successive stage controlled by the dominant interest. Any person is free to become a dental laboratory technician. The statute places no artificial restraint upon him." The statute at issue in *A.A.A. Dental Laboratories* did not prohibit access to the industry, but merely prohibited dental technicians from performing certain tasks within the industry unless they were performed under the guidance of a licensed dentist.

The Department's reliance upon *Illinois Polygraph Society v. Pellicano*, 414 N.E.2d 458 (Ill. 1980), is likewise misplaced. In that case, the court upheld a statute which required polygraph examiners to complete a six-month course of study prescribed by the Department of Registration and Education as a prerequisite for licensure. The court rejected an argument that the statute, like the plumbing licensing laws at issue in *Brown, Schroeder* and *Johnson*, was unconstitutional. In upholding the validity of the statute, the *Pellicano* court relied upon several factors that do not exist under the instant statute. The court noted that the statute simply required a certain amount of course study as a prerequisite to licensure and did not require employment for a period of years before an applicant qualified for a license. The *Pellicano* court also noted that any person could obtain an internship license under the statute simply by applying and paying the required fee, and that the courses required by statute were not necessarily taught by licensed examiners. Thus, the court concluded that licensed examiners did not possess a monopolistic right to instruct prospective licensees.

The instant Act also violates the second part of the test set forth in *Johnson*, because there is nothing to suggest that the nature and duration of employment required under the statute are calculated to enhance the expertise of prospective licensees. Section 27 of the Act specifies that employees of a private alarm contractor agency who respond to alarm systems must complete at least 20 hours of classroom training on subject matters related to private security, such as: the law of arrest, search and seizure; civil and criminal liability; the use of force; arrest and control techniques; elements of offenses under the Criminal Code; the law on private police; fire prevention and safety; service of process and report writing; and human and public relations. An agency may, but need not, provide any additional training to employees who respond to alarm systems. Employees who do not respond to alarm systems and employees of other entities within the private alarm field are not required by statute to receive *any* particular training.

Even a cursory review of the plaintiff's application for licensure demonstrates that the plaintiff received training in almost every subject matter listed in section 27 while employed as a police officer. Thus, it appears that the training the plaintiff received outside the private alarm contracting field is at least equal to, if not more extensive than, the limited training statutorily required of employees within the private alarm contracting industry. The Department's brief suggests that the plaintiff lacked sufficient electrical experience to qualify for licensure under the Act. Yet, under the Department's interpretation of the Act, an applicant with the plaintiff's experience and extensive electrical experience would still not qualify for licensure unless he or she was employed full-time for three years in a supervisory capacity within the private alarm contracting field. While the legislature and the Department may have rationally believed that practical experience is necessary to assure competence in the private alarm contracting trade, there is nothing to suggest that the duration and type of experience required under the Act is necessary to enhance the expertise of prospective licensees. There is nothing in the record to suggest that the expertise needed to be a competent private alarm contractor can be provided only by full-time employment as a private alarm contractor for three years in a supervisory capacity. Accordingly, we conclude that the Act, as interpreted by the Department, violates the second prong of the *Johnson* test.

Although we agree with the plaintiff's argument that the experience requirements for private alarm contractors under the Act are invalid, we reject his claim that the circuit court properly ordered the Department to issue him a license. Nothing in the statute or the record before us supports the circuit court's conclusion that the plaintiff is *automatically* entitled to a license.... (S)ection 14(c)(12) of the Act specifically states that the Department "*may* conduct an examination which shall include subjects reasonably related to the activities licensed so as to provide for the protection of the health and safety of the public." (Emphasis added.) Here, the Department determined that the plaintiff was not qualified to sit for the examination, because his experience did not meet statutory requirements. Our conclusion that the statutory experience requirements are invalid does not *ipso facto* lead to the conclusion that the plaintiff is entitled to a license. Rather, we simply reverse the Department's finding that the plaintiff is not qualified to take the licensure examination. For the foregoing reasons, we set aside the decision of the Department, and remand this cause to the Department with directions that the plaintiff shall be allowed to sit for the licensing examination.

G. THE RIGHT TO VOTE

WEINSCHENK v. STATE
203 S.W.3d 201 (Missouri 2006)

Per Curiam:

After a 2006 statute was enacted requiring registered voters to present certain types of state- or federally-issued photographic identification in order to cast regular ballots, Ms. Kathleen Weinschenk and others sued the state to block enforcement of the law on the grounds that it interfered with the fundamental right to vote as protected by the Missouri and United States constitutions. Ms. Weinschenk and the others claimed that the new law required them and other voters—particularly those who are low-income, disabled or elderly and who do not have driver's licenses—to spend money to obtain the necessary documents such as birth certificates in order to obtain the requisite photo ID. The trial court declared the law unconstitutional.

This Court agrees that SB 1014's Photo-ID Requirement violates Missouri's equal protection clause, *Mo. Const. art. I, sec. 2*, and Missouri's constitutional guarantee of the right of its qualified, registered citizens to vote. *Mo. Const. art. I, sec. 25; art. VIII, sec. 2.* While this Court fully agrees with Appellants that there is a compelling state interest in preventing voter fraud, the evidence supports the trial court's conclusion that the Photo-ID Requirement is not narrowly tailored to accomplish that purpose.

SB 1014's Photo-ID Requirement prohibits otherwise qualified and lawfully registered Missourians from voting if they present only out-of-state picture identification, social security cards, utility bills, school or work IDs, or other documents that served as proper identification under the version of section 115.427 in effect prior to the enactment of SB 1014. As amended by SB 1014, section 115.427 now requires that Missourians present as identification a document issued by the state or federal governments that contains the person's name as listed in the voter registration records, the person's photograph, and an expiration date showing that the ID is not expired. In practical effect, the only documents that most Missourians would have that could meet these requirements are a Missouri driver's or non-driver's license or a United States passport.

Both the United States and Missouri constitutions guarantee to their citizens the enjoyment of equal protection of the laws. *U.S. Const. amend. XIV, sec. 1* ("No state shall . . . deny to any person within its jurisdiction the equal protection of the laws"); *Mo. Const. art. I, sec. 2* ("all persons . . . are entitled to equal rights and opportunity under the law").   Courts undertake a two-part analysis to determine the constitutionality of a statute under either the state or federal equal protection clause. The first step is to determine whether the statute implicates a suspect class or impinges upon a fundamental right explicitly or implicitly protected by the Constitution. "If so, the classification is subject to strict scrutiny."   If not, the classification will be subject to rational basis scrutiny. The second step is to apply the appropriate level of scrutiny to the challenged statute. In order to survive strict scrutiny, a limitation on a fundamental right must serve compelling state interests and must be narrowly tailored to meet those interests.

The Missouri Constitution expressly guarantees that "all elections shall be free and open; and no power, civil or military, shall at any time interfere to prevent the free exercise of the right of suffrage." Additionally, rather than leaving the issue of voter qualification to the legislature, the Missouri Constitution has established an exclusive list of qualifications necessary to vote in Missouri. *Mo. Const. art. VIII, sec. 2* ("All citizens of the United States . . . over the age of eighteen who are residents of this state and of the political subdivision in which they offer to vote are entitled to vote at all elections by the people, if . . . they are registered within the time prescribed by law"). These constitutional provisions establish with unmistakable clarity that the right to vote is fundamental to Missouri citizens.

The express constitutional protection of the right to vote differentiates the Missouri constitution from its federal counterpart. Federal courts also have consistently held that the right to vote is equally fundamental under the United States Constitution. But, the right to vote in state elections is conferred under federal law only by implication, not by express guarantee. *See Harper v. Virginia State Bd. Elections, 383 U.S. 663, 665 (1966)* ("the right to vote in state elections is nowhere expressly mentioned" in the United States Constitution). Moreover, the qualifications for voting under the federal system are left to legislative determination, not constitutionally enshrined, as they are in Missouri. Due to the more expansive and concrete protections of the right to vote under the Missouri Constitution, voting rights are an area where our state constitution provides greater protection than its federal counterpart.

The record supports the trial court's determination that SB 1014's Photo-ID Requirement places a burden on the right of Missourians to vote. As set out at length above, it requires each of the individual plaintiffs in this case to present a Missouri driver's license, a Missouri non-driver's license, or a United States passport on election day in order to vote. The record reveals that between 3 and 4 percent of Missouri citizens (estimates vary from 169,215 to 240,000 individuals) lack the requisite photo ID. Appellants concede that many of these citizens, including all of the individual plaintiffs in this case, are eligible to vote and, in many cases, are already registered to vote. Nevertheless, under the new law these eligible registered voters will not be able to cast a regular ballot (or after 2008 any ballot at all) unless they undertake to obtain one of the requisite photo IDs.

Those citizens who do not possess the requisite photo ID, with few exceptions, must expend money to gather the necessary documentation to obtain it in order to exercise their right to vote. Appellants argue that because the documentation-related expenses are one step removed from obtaining the photo ID, which itself is "free," those expenses should not be considered in this Court's analysis. The fact that Missouri has waived collection of costs normally charged to persons seeking a non-driver's license does not make that license "free" if Missourians without certified copies of birth certificates or passports must still expend sums of money to obtain the license. Many voters who presently lack one of the required photo IDs would have to, at the very least, expend money to obtain a birth certificate. In Missouri, obtaining a birth certificate requires at least a $15 payment, which, Appellants conceded at oral argument, is not a *de minimis* cost. If the citizen requires documentation beyond a birth certificate, the costs are greater.

Although this Court has not previously had occasion to evaluate the validity of putting a direct or indirect price or fee on the franchise under the Missouri Constitution, the United States Supreme Court held, in the context of addressing a $1.50 poll tax: "Wealth or fee-paying has . . . no relation to voting qualifications; the right to vote is too precious, too fundamental to be so burdened." *Harper*, *383 U.S. at 670*. While requiring payment to obtain a birth certificate is not a poll tax, as was the $1.50 in *Harper*, it is a fee that qualified, eligible, registered voters who lack an approved photo ID are required to pay in order to exercise their right to free suffrage under the Missouri Constitution. *Harper* makes clear that all fees that impose financial burdens on eligible citizens' right to vote, not merely poll taxes, are impermissible under federal law. There can be no lesser requirement under Missouri law.

Persons who wish to vote who do not already have the requisite photo IDs must arrange to obtain them by presenting a birth certificate or passport and, if necessary, proof of name changes. To do so requires both funds and advance planning to allow for the six to eight weeks that the record shows it takes to obtain a Missouri birth certificate. Once the birth certificate is in hand, the voter must use it to obtain one of the requisite photo IDs. "This is plainly a cumbersome procedure." *Harman v. Forssenius*, 380 U.S. 528, 541 (1965). Those things that require substantial planning in advance of an election to preserve the right to vote can tend to "eliminate from the franchise a substantial number of voters who did not plan so far ahead." *Id.* At 539-40. As it will require payment of money and significant advance planning to obtain necessary documentation, the Photo-ID Requirement is an "onerous procedural requirement which effectively handicap[s] exercise of the franchise." *Lane v. Wilson*, 307 U.S. 268, 275 (1939). This Court agrees with the trial court that the Photo-ID Requirement of SB 1014 represents a heavy and substantial burden on Missourians' free exercise of the right of suffrage.

In light of the substantial burden that the Photo-ID Requirement places upon the right to vote, the statute is subject to strict scrutiny. Missouri's broad interests in preserving the integrity of the election process and combating voter fraud are significant, compelling and important. Yet, Appellants do not demonstrate that SB 1014's requirement of state or federally issued, non-expired photo IDs is strictly necessary or narrowly tailored to accomplish the State's asserted interests. To the contrary, Appellants concede that the only type of voter fraud that the Photo-ID Requirement prevents is in-person voter impersonation fraud at the polling place. It does not address absentee voting fraud or fraud in registration. While the Photo-ID Requirement may provide some additional protection against voter impersonation fraud, the evidence below demonstrates that the Photo-ID Requirement is not "necessary" to accomplish this goal. As the trial court found: "No evidence was presented that voter impersonation fraud exists to any substantial degree in Missouri. In fact, the evidence that was presented indicates that voter impersonation fraud is not a problem in Missouri."

The only evidence that Appellants marshal of voter impersonation fraud occurred *prior* to the enactment of identification requirements in 2002. The 2002 identification law required voters to present some proof of identity or residence when they arrived at the polling place. The list of acceptable identification under the 2002 requirements is much broader than the three types of photo ID that SB 1014 allows and included a utility bill, bank statement, expired passport, out-of-state driver's license, and other commonly available documents of identification. Although Appellants protest that some of the approved identification documents under the 2002 law do not provide proof of eligibility to vote, neither does the Photo-ID Requirement. The Photo-ID Requirement assists in prevention of voter impersonation, but the evidence reveals that the 2002 requirements, which are much less restrictive on the right to vote, have been sufficient to prevent this type of fraud. These facts compel the conclusion that the Photo-ID Requirement is not "necessary to accomplish a compelling state interest."

The conclusion that the Photo-ID Requirement is not necessary to serve the State's asserted end should not be taken as an indication that the State's interest in combating voter fraud is insubstantial.   Indeed, legislative efforts to combat the types of voter fraud and opportunities for voter fraud that persist in Missouri, such as absentee ballot fraud, voter intimidation, and inflated voter registration rolls, should be encouraged. Where the legislature places a heavy burden on the right to vote, however, the Missouri Constitution requires that the burden be justified by a compelling interest and the statute be narrowly tailored or necessary to accomplish the statutory goals.   The Photo-ID Requirement could only prevent a particular type of voter fraud that the record does not show is occurring in Missouri, yet it would place a heavy burden on the free exercise of the franchise for many citizens of this State.

For these reasons, this Court holds that the Photo-ID Requirement violates the equal protection clause of the *Missouri Constitution, article I, section 2*.

Dissenting opinion by Stephen N. Limbaugh, Jr., Judge:

Whatever the deficiencies in the Missouri Voter Protection Act (MVPA), whether real or imagined, the allowance for provisional voting cures all, at least during the two-year transition period before the general election in 2008.   In addition, a determination of the constitutionality of the photo ID provisions of the Act as it applies after the two-year transition period is not yet ripe for adjudication, because it may well be that the General Assembly, in the interim, will act to alleviate the perceived deficiencies.

Because the permanent provisions of the MVPA do not take effect until the general election in November of 2008, any decision on the constitutionality of that part of the Act is premature.   Although the majority is correct that the statute is presently in effect, two years will pass before the parts of the statute the majority finds unconstitutional will be implemented.   Until that time, no harm, real or imagined, will come to any voter.   In the meantime, however, the evidence on which the trial court based its findings and judgment is subject to significant change.   For instance, plaintiffs' primary grievance—that the cost of securing birth certificates or other forms of suitable identification in order to obtain a "free" photo ID is an undue burden on the right to vote—may well be satisfactorily addressed by the General Assembly during its upcoming sessions.   Given the two-year transition period, there is no immediacy to the controversy, no possibility for an accurate determination of the facts, and no way to grant relief specific to the alleged harm.   To declare the statute unconstitutional under these circumstances is a straightforward violation of the ripeness doctrine.

Although I would not reach the merits of the claim against the permanent provisions of the MVPA due to lack of ripeness, I cannot leave unchallenged the majority's incomplete recitation of the facts pertaining to the existence of voter fraud and the need for a photo ID system to combat that fraud. According to the majority, there has been no fraud in the polling places; thus no need to prevent it. But the evidence, in part, is this: In an investigative report issued after the 2000 presidential election by outgoing Secretary of State Rebecca McDowell Cook, and introduced in evidence in this case, "135 people who were not registered to vote were permitted to vote at a polling place without a court order and without apparent authorization from [an election] Board Official." A subsequent report from then Secretary of State Matt Blunt noted, as even the plaintiffs have acknowledged here, that 79 voters registered from vacant lots, 45 people voted twice, and 14 votes were cast by the "dead." Further, as set out in a pending complaint filed in federal court by the United States Department of Justice against the State of Missouri and cited to the trial court and this Court without objection, there is a stunningly large number of duplicate and ineligible voter registrations throughout the state.

NOTE

In his dissenting opinion, Judge Limbaugh states: "According to the majority, there has been no fraud in the polling places; thus no need to prevent it." Is Judge Limbaugh's description of the majority's position correct? Or, is it more accurate to say: "According to the majority, the only evidence of voter impersonation fraud occurred prior to the enactment of the 2002 identification requirements, which are sufficient to prevent voter impersonation fraud and therefore obviate the need for a Photo ID law"? Judge Limbaugh criticizes the majority opinion as an "incomplete recitation of the facts" that neglects to mention two investigative reports documenting numerous instances of voter fraud in the 2000 presidential election. In light of the majority's finding that the evidence shows that the 2002 identification law is sufficient to prevent voter impersonation fraud, are the reports concerning voter fraud in the 2000 election pertinent to the issue at hand? Is it valid to criticize the majority for not specifically mentioning the reports?

LEAGUE OF WOMEN VOTERS OF INDIANA v. ROKITA
929 N.E.2d 758 (Ind. 2010)

DICKSON, J.

The sole plaintiffs in this case, the Indiana State and Indianapolis chapters of the League of Women Voters, brought this action seeking a declaratory judgment that the Indiana Voter ID Law violates Article 2, Section 2, and Article 1, Section 23 of the Indiana Constitution. The trial court granted the defendant's motion to dismiss, concluding that the Voter ID Law did not violate either constitutional provision. The Court of Appeals reversed. We granted transfer, thereby automatically vacating the opinion of the Court of Appeals and accepting jurisdiction over the appeal. Determining that this case presents only facial challenges to the constitutionality of the Voter ID Law, we now affirm the trial court's dismissal of the complaint, but without prejudice to future as-applied challenges by any voter unlawfully prevented from exercising the right to vote.

In 2005, an enactment of the Indiana General Assembly, Public Law 109-2005, referred to by the parties as the Indiana Voter ID Law, made several modifications to Indiana's election and motor vehicle laws. This Law was challenged in federal court where the plaintiffs claimed that it violated the [Equal Protection Clause of the Fourteenth Amendment of the Federal Constitution]. [The U.S. Supreme Court upheld the law by a vote of 6-3, finding no violation of the Equal Protection Clause. *Crawford v. Marion County Election Bd.*, 553 U.S. 181 (2008).]

In both the federal litigation and in the present appeal, the challenges to the Voter ID Law center on its requirement, as summarized by Justice Stevens for the United States Supreme Court, that:

> ...citizens voting in person on election day, or casting a ballot in person at the office of the circuit court clerk prior to election day, [must] present photo identification issued by the government.... [T]he statute applies to in-person voting at both primary and general elections. The requirement does not apply to absentee ballots submitted by mail, and the statute contains an exception for persons living and voting in a state-licensed facility such as a nursing home. A voter who is indigent or has a religious objection to being photographed may cast a provisional ballot that will be counted only if she executes an appropriate affidavit before the circuit court clerk within 10 days following the election. A voter who has photo identification but is unable to present that identification on election day may file a provisional ballot that will be counted if she brings her photo identification to the circuit county clerk's office within 10 days. No photo identification is required in order to register to vote, and the State offers free photo identification to qualified voters able to establish their residence and identity.

The plaintiffs contend that the Voter ID Law violates the Equal Privileges and Immunities Clause of the Indiana Constitution: "The General Assembly shall not grant to any citizen, or class of citizens, privileges or immunities, which, upon the same terms, shall not equally belong to all citizens." Ind. Const. art. 1, § 23. The plaintiffs' complaint alleges two examples of unequal treatment claimed as violations of Section 23: (1) requiring photo identification of in-person but not mail-in absentee voters, and (2) exempting from the photo identification requirement voters residing in state licensed care facilities at which a precinct polling place is located.

In *Collins v. Day*, this Court engaged in a comprehensive review of the history and purposes animating the adoption of Section 23 as part of Indiana's 1851 Constitution and of the subsequent case law, particularly our early decisions that were contemporaneous with its adoption and which were "accorded strong and superseding precedential value." Synthesizing history, text, and subsequent case law, we adopted a superseding analytical formulation that, when statutes grant un-equal privileges or immunities to differing persons or classes of persons, the Equal Privileges and Immunities Clause imposes two requirements: "First, the disparate treatment accorded by the legislation must be reasonably related to inherent characteristics [that] distinguish the unequally treated classes. Second, the preferential treatment must be uniformly applicable and equally available to all persons similarly situated." In addition, "in determining whether a statute complies with or violates Section 23, courts must exercise substantial deference to legislative discretion."

The plaintiffs first compare the classifications of in-person voters with mail-in absentee voters. These two classifications are principally distinguished by the fact that an in-person voter, unlike a mail-in absentee voter, personally appears before election officials who can verify the identity of the person seeking to cast a vote. The plaintiffs urge that the photo identification requirement for in-person voters does not reasonably relate to the inherent differences between in-person voters and mail-in absentee voters. The plaintiffs argue in part that, because the nature of absentee ballots requires a heightened security, the imposition of higher identification security on in-person voters is not reasonably related to the differences between the classifications. This interest in heightened security may be of particular concern in the regulation of absentee voting, but it is not determinative on the issue presented. The plaintiffs argue that the special treatment provided to mail-in absentee voters "do[es] not support the claimed purpose of the Photo ID Law." But such focus on the "purpose" of the Law is not determinative. As we noted in Dvorak v. City of Bloomington, *Collins* "requires only that . . . 'the disparate *treatment* accorded by the legislation,' not the *purposes* of the legislation, 'be reasonably related to the inherent characteristics which distinguish the unequally treated classes.'" More significantly, other critical attributes distinguish the identified disparately treated classes, especially the practicability of requiring and efficaciously utilizing photo identification for mail-in absentee voters, in contrast to in-person voters. For ballots received by mail, there is no opportunity for an election official to personally compare the voter with the voter's photo identification to verify identity. Absentee ballots "reach the hands of election officials outside of the confines of the Election Day polling place." The plaintiffs do not propose any method by which a photo identification requirement could be effectively utilized to verify the identity of a mail-in absentee voter. Legislation is not constitutionally deficient for failing to impose an unenforceable, useless requirement. We find that not requiring photo identification for mail-in absentee voters is reasonably related to the inherent distinctions between such voters and those voting in person. We decline to find that the Voter ID Law's failure to require photo identification of mail-in absentee voters violates the Indiana Equal Privileges and Immunities Clause.

The plaintiffs assert multiple arguments with respect to the Voter ID Law's provision regarding certain voters living and voting in state licensed care facilities. Using the first factor of the *Collins* methodology, the plaintiffs assert that the statute violates Section 23 by permitting residents of state licensed care facilities to vote at their residence without photo identification while requiring such identification as a prerequisite to voting by other seniors living else-where. They argue that "the distinctions between in-person senior citizen voters are not reasonably related to the different treatment accorded by the [Voter ID] Law." The plaintiffs also employ the second *Collins* factor, arguing that the statute grants preferential treatment to residents of certain state licensed care facilities but "does not grant similar relief to the elderly who are able to remain out in the community but who would have the same difficulties in procuring the requisite identification." The plaintiffs thus assert that such privileged classification is not "open to any and all persons who share the inherent characteristics [that] distinguish and justify the classification" nor is the "particular classification . . . extended equally to all such persons."

The relief sought by the plaintiffs is that the entire Voter ID Law be declared unconstitutional, not the overturning of the special exception for voters living in state licensed care facilities that serve as precinct polling places on election day. In light of the relatively extremely small number of voters excluded from the photo identification requirement under this exception, even if arguably violative of Section 23, we find that it represents a minor and insubstantial disparity permissible under Section 23. We explained in Dvorak that, in applying Section 23, "[e]xact exclusion and inclusion is impractical," and noted the following observation from *Collins*:

> It is almost impossible to provide for every exceptional and imaginary case, and a legislature ought not to be required to do so at the risk of having its legislation declared void, even though appropriate and proper as applied to the general subject upon which the law intended to operate.

Applying Dvorak, we find that granting a special privilege to residents of state licensed care facilities to vote at their residence without photo identification constitutes only a minor insubstantial variation that does not render sufficient disparate treatment to warrant judicial invalidation under Section 23.

Finally, in determining whether Section 23 is violated, we "must exercise substantial deference to legislative discretion." Given the scope of the undertaking embraced in the Voter ID Law's efforts in enhancing the integrity of the electoral process and its attempt to tailor its operation to a significant variety of circumstances, we conclude that the possible absence of precise congruity in application to all voters represents a legitimate exercise of legislative discretion warranting our deference.

We conclude that it is clear on the face of the complaint that the plaintiffs, as a matter of law, are not entitled to the relief sought. It is within the power of the legislature to require voters to identify them-selves at the polls using a photo ID.

This result may contrast with a somewhat analogous case in our sister state of Missouri, *Weinschenk v. State*, 203 S.W.3d 201 (Mo. 2006). In that case, particular voters sued to block enforcement of a 2006 Missouri statute requiring registered voters to present certain types of photo ID to vote. Ms. Kathleen Weinschenk and the others claimed that the new law required them and other voters—particularly those who are low-income, disabled, or elderly, and who do not have driver's licenses—to spend money to obtain the necessary documents such as birth certificates in order to obtain the requisite photo ID in violation of the Missouri Constitution's provisions relating to equal protection and the right to vote. The Missouri Supreme Court held that while there is a compelling state interest in preventing voter fraud, the evidence supports the trial court's conclusion that the Photo-ID Requirement is not narrowly tailored to accomplish that purpose. Accordingly, it found the statute unconstitutional.

Not only do the constitutions of Indiana and Missouri vary, but also our statute differs from Missouri's—notably, a requisite photo ID can be obtained from the Indiana Bureau of Motor Vehicles at no cost—and we do not mean to suggest that the facts present in the Missouri case would necessarily warrant declaring the Indiana Voter ID Law unconstitutional. But we do not foreclose such as-applied claims. Here the plaintiffs seek a declaration that it is unconstitutional to require voters to identify themselves at the polls using a photo ID. This is relief to which the plaintiffs are not entitled. But in affirming the trial court, we do so without prejudice to future particularized as-applied claims.

We affirm the judgment of the trial court granting the appellee's motion to dismiss and rejecting the plaintiffs' claims that the Indiana Voter ID Law contravenes Article 2, Section 2 or Article 1, Section 23 of the Indiana Constitution.

Shepard, C.J., and Sullivan and Rucker, JJ., concur. Boehm, J., dissents with separate opinion.

NOTES

1. Two years before the decision of the Indiana Supreme Court in *League of Women Voters of Indiana, Inc. v. Rokita*, the Supreme Court of the United States considered a challenge to the same Indiana Voter ID Law under the Federal Equal Protection Clause. *Crawford v. Marion County Election Board*, 128 S. Ct. 1610 (2008). The high Court upheld the law by a vote of 6-3, finding no violation of the Equal Protection Clause. Justice Stevens' plurality opinion in *Crawford* concluded that the Indiana Voter ID law served the important state interest of preventing voter fraud while imposing only a limited burden on the right to vote. In a dissenting opinion Justice Souter asserted that the Voter ID law imposed a nontrivial burden on tens of thousands of Indiana citizens. He also noted that "the State has not come across a single instance of in-person voter impersonation fraud in all of Indiana's history."

2. A few state constitutions contain provisions expressly guaranteeing "free and equal elections." For example, the Constitution of Delaware states: "All Elections shall be free and equal." Del. Const. art. I, § 3 (1897). *See also* Wyo. Const. art. I, § 27.

3. Other state constitutions contain various provisions guaranteeing the right to vote and setting forth voter qualifications. In *Martin v. Kohls*, 444 S.W.3d 844 (Ark. 2014), the Supreme Court of Arkansas ruled that a Voter ID law violated the right to vote guaranteed by Art. 3 of the Arkansas Constitution by adding a voting qualification other than those listed in the Article itself. In contrast, the Supreme Court of Georgia ruled in *Democratic Party of Georgia, Inc. v. Perdue*, 707 S.E. 2d 67 (Ga. 2011), that a Voter ID law did not violate the right to vote guaranteed by Article 2 of the Georgia Constitution because it was authorized by another provision in the Constitution authorizing the legislature to adopt procedures for the conduct of elections, including methods by which voters were required to prove their identity.

CHAPTER V

DUE PROCESS OF LAW

A. INTRODUCTION

Conferred by King John on the meadow of Runnymede in the year 1215, the Magna Carta proclaimed:

> No Free man shall be taken or imprisoned, or be disseised of his Freehold, or Liberties, or free Customs, or be outlawed, or exiled, or any other wise destroyed; nor will we not pass upon him, nor condemn him, but by lawful judgment of his Peers, or by the Law of the land. We will sell to no man, we will not deny or defer to any man either Justice or Right.

The Magna Carta served as a model for the American colonies, many of which adopted laws based upon the great charter. Shortly after achieving independence, most of the new states enacted constitutional provisions prohibiting the deprivation of life, liberty, or property except by the "law of the land." In time, some states used a somewhat different phraseology, prohibiting the deprivation of life, liberty, or property without "due process of law." Eventually, all of the states enacted either law of the land clauses or due process clauses as part of their state constitutions. According to Thomas Cooley, an eminent constitutional scholar of the late nineteenth century, whichever phrase was used, "the meaning (was) the same in every case." Thomas M. Cooley, A TREATISE ON THE CONSTITUTIONAL LIMITATIONS WHICH REST UPON THE LEGISLATIVE POWER OF THE STATES OF THE AMERICAN UNION 353 (1868).

There are those who argue that the phrase "due process of law" was meant only to refer to the procedures required before a person may be deprived of life, liberty, or property, and did not comprehend judicial authority to invalidate legislation on substantive grounds. Others disagree and believe that due process of law encompassed a substantive component. Beginning in the 1790's an increasing number of state courts gave a substantive content to due process of law in striking down statutes found to arbitrarily divest persons of property rights. By the end of the nineteenth century, an evolving body of law existed that recognized a substantive element to due process of law. See Jeffrey M. Shaman, *On the 100th Anniversary of Lochner v. New York*, 72 Tenn. L. Rev. 455, 476–88 (2005).

Some state constitutions also contain other provisions directed to safeguarding life, liberty, or property. The Kentucky Constitution, for example, states: "Absolute and arbitrary power over the lives, liberty and property of freemen exists nowhere in a republic, not even in the largest majority."[1] In other states, protection for life, liberty, or property has been found implicit in constitutional provisions declaring that "[a]ll persons are by nature free and independent, and have certain natural and inalienable rights"[2] or stating that "[t]he enumeration in this Constitution of certain rights shall not be construed to deny, impair, or disparage others retained by, the people."[3]

As constitutional doctrine evolved, the right of privacy was recognized as a fundamental element of liberty. State constitutional conceptions of the right of privacy first emerged in the early twentieth century, but then fell into quiescence for decades, before being revived for further development. In the meantime, the United States Supreme Court took the lead in formulating a constitutional right of privacy under the Due Process Clause of the Fourteenth Amendment. First, the high Court ruled that the Due Process Clause protects a fundamental right of privacy that encompasses the right to reproductive autonomy. In subsequent decisions, the Court expanded the federal right of privacy to encompass certain family rights and, eventually, a right of intimate association. Yet the Court has placed definitive limits on family and reproductive rights and also has refused to extend the right of privacy to other areas. Over time, the Supreme Court's commitment to the right of privacy has vacillated considerably, leaving the scope of the right of privacy under the Federal Constitution far from certain.

Building on federal doctrine, a number of states have gone on to strengthen the right of privacy by turning to provisions in their state constitutions. Five states—Alaska, California, Florida, Hawaii, and Montana—have amended their constitutions to expressly protect the right of privacy. These express provisions offer a sound textual basis for the expansion of privacy rights. In some states that have no express constitutional protection for privacy, the courts have used more generally worded provisions, such as a due process clause, to recognize and eventually enlarge the right of privacy. Not all states have been willing to join this movement; some state courts have thought it best to recognize no constitutional privacy rights other than those required by the Federal Constitution. But a number of state courts have used their state constitutions to enhance the right of privacy beyond federal dictates.

The guarantee of due process of law mandates that the government follow fair procedures before depriving anyone of life, liberty, or property. The principle of procedural due process applies to all government

---

[1] Ky. Const., Bill of Rights, §2,

[2] N.J. Const., art I, § 1.

[3] Ok. Const., art. II, § 33.

proceedings, both civil and criminal. At its core, the principle of procedural due process requires notice and an opportunity to be heard in a fair proceeding. In some instances, the scope of protection afforded by procedural due process under a state constitution has been extended beyond that provided by the Federal Constitution.

B. REPRODUCTIVE AUTONOMY

DAVIS v. DAVIS
842 S.W.2d 588 (Tenn. 1992)

DAUGHTREY, J.

This appeal presents a question of first impression, involving the disposition of the cryogenically-preserved product of in vitro fertilization (IVF), commonly referred to in the popular press and the legal journals as "frozen embryos." The case began as a divorce action, filed by the appellee, Junior Lewis Davis, against his then wife, appellant Mary Sue Davis. The parties were able to agree upon all terms of dissolution, except one: who was to have "custody" of the seven "frozen embryos" stored in a Knoxville fertility clinic that had attempted to assist the Davises in achieving a much-wanted pregnancy during a happier period in their relationship.

Mary Sue Davis originally asked for control of the "frozen embryos" with the intent to have them transferred to her own uterus, in a post-divorce effort to become pregnant. Junior Davis objected, saying that he preferred to leave the embryos in their frozen state until he decided whether or not he wanted to become a parent outside the bounds of marriage.... We note, in this latter regard, that their positions have already shifted: both have remarried and Mary Sue Davis (now Mary Sue Stowe) has moved out of state. She no longer wishes to utilize the "frozen embryos" herself, but wants authority to donate them to a childless couple. Junior Davis is adamantly opposed to such donation and would prefer to see the "frozen embryos" discarded.

At the outset, it is important to note the absence of two critical factors that might otherwise influence or control the result of this litigation: When the Davises signed up for the IVF program at the Knoxville clinic, they did not execute a written agreement specifying what disposition should be made of any unused embryos that might result from the cryopreservation process. Moreover, there was at that time no Tennessee statute governing such disposition, nor has one been enacted in the meantime. In addition, because of the uniqueness of the question before us, we have no case law to guide us to a decision in this case.

The Right of Procreational Autonomy

The essential dispute here is…whether the parties will become parents. The Court of Appeals held in effect that they will become parents if they both agree to become parents. The Court did not say what will happen if they fail to agree. We conclude that the answer to this dilemma turns on the parties' exercise of their constitutional right to privacy.

[handwritten margin note: Case turns on privacy rights]

The right to privacy is not specifically mentioned in either the federal or the Tennessee state constitution, and yet there can be little doubt about its grounding in the concept of liberty reflected in those two documents…. [I]n the Tennessee Constitution, the concept of liberty plays a central role. Article I, Section 8 provides:

> That no man shall be taken or imprisoned, or disseized of his freehold, liberties or privileges, or outlawed, or exiled, or in any manner destroyed or deprived of his life, liberty or property, but by the judgment of his peers or the law of the land.

[handwritten margin note: Relevant con provision]

Indeed, the notion of individual liberty is so deeply embedded in the Tennessee Constitution that it, alone among American constitutions, gives the people, in the face of governmental oppression and interference with liberty, the right to resist that oppression even to the extent of overthrowing the government. The relevant provisions establishing this distinctive political autonomy appear in the first two sections of Article I of the Tennessee Constitution, its Declaration of Rights:

> Section 1. All power inherent in the people-Government under their control.
>
> That all power is inherent in the people, and all free governments are founded on their authority, and instituted for their peace, safety, and happiness; for the advancement of those ends they have at all times, an inalienable and indefeasible right to alter, reform, or abolish the government in such manner as they may think proper.
>
> Section 2. Doctrine of nonresistance condemned.
>
> That government being instituted for the common benefit, the doctrine of non-resistance against arbitrary power and oppression is absurd, slavish, and destructive of the good and happiness of mankind.

Obviously, the drafters of the Tennessee Constitution of 1796 could not have anticipated the need to construe the liberty clauses of that document in terms of the choices flowing from in vitro fertilization procedures. But there can be little doubt that they foresaw the need to protect individuals from unwarranted governmental intrusion into matters such as the one now before us, involving intimate questions of personal and family concern. Based on both the language and the development of our state constitution, we have no hesitation in drawing the conclusion that there is a right of individual privacy guaranteed under and protected by the liberty clauses of the Tennessee Declaration of Rights.

[handwritten margin note: Tenn has a right of individual privacy]

Undoubtedly, that right to privacy incorporates some of the attributes of the federal constitutional right to privacy and, in any given fact situation, may also share some of its contours. As with other state constitutional rights having counterparts in the federal bill of rights, however, there is no reason to assume that there is a complete congruency. Here, the specific individual freedom in dispute is the right to procreate. In terms of the Tennessee state constitution, we hold that the right of procreation is a vital part of an individual's right to privacy. Federal law is to the same effect.

Right of procreation

In construing the reach of the federal constitution, the United States Supreme Court has addressed the affirmative right to procreate in only two cases. In *Buck v. Bell*, 274 U.S. 200 (1927), the Court upheld the sterilization of a "feebleminded white woman." However, in *Skinner v. Oklahoma*, 316 U.S. 535 (1942), the Supreme Court struck down a statute that authorized the sterilization of certain categories of criminals. The Court described the right to procreate as "one of the basic civil rights of man [sic]," and stated that "[m]arriage and procreation are fundamental to the very existence and survival of the race." In the same vein, the United States Supreme Court has said:

SCOTUS defends right to procreate

> If the right of privacy means anything, it is the right of the *individual*, married or single, to be free from unwarranted governmental intrusion into matters so fundamentally affecting a person as the decision whether to bear or beget a child. *Eisenstadt v. Baird*, 405 U.S. 438 (1972) (emphasis in original).

That a right to procreational autonomy is inherent in our most basic concepts of liberty is also indicated by the reproductive freedom cases, see, e.g., *Griswold v. Connecticut*, 381 U.S. 479 (1965); and *Roe v. Wade*, 410 U.S. 113 (1973), and by cases concerning parental rights and responsibilities with respect to children. See, e.g., *Wisconsin v. Yoder*, 406 U.S. 205 (1972); *Prince v. Massachusetts*, 321 U.S. 158 (1944); *Cleveland Board of Education v. LaFleur*, 414 U.S. 632 (1974); *Pierce v. Society of the Sisters of the Holy Names of Jesus and Mary*, 268 U.S. 510 (1925); and *Bellotti v. Baird*, 443 U.S. 622 (1979). In fact, in *Bellotti v. Baird*, the Supreme Court noted that parental autonomy is basic to the structure of our society because the family is "the institution by which we inculcate and pass down many of our most cherished values, moral and cultural."

More SCOTUS caselaw on procreation autonomy

The United States Supreme Court has never addressed the issue of procreation in the context of in vitro fertilization. Moreover, the extent to which procreational autonomy is protected by the United States Constitution is no longer entirely clear. For the purposes of this litigation it is sufficient to note that, whatever its ultimate constitutional boundaries, the right of procreational autonomy is composed of two rights of equal significance the right to procreate and the right to avoid procreation. Undoubtedly, both are subject to protections and limitations.

2 relevant rights

The equivalence of and inherent tension between these two interests are nowhere more evident than in the context of in vitro fertilization. None of the concerns about a woman's bodily integrity that have previously precluded men from controlling abortion decisions is applicable here. We are not unmindful of the fact that the trauma (including both emotional stress and physical discomfort) to which women are subjected in the IVF process is more severe than is the impact of the procedure on men. In this sense, it is fair to say that women contribute more to the IVF process than men. Their experience, however, must be viewed in light of the joys of parenthood that is desired or the relative anguish of a lifetime of unwanted parenthood. As they stand on the brink of potential parenthood, Mary Sue Davis and Junior Lewis Davis must be seen as entirely equivalent gamete-providers.

It is further evident that, however far the protection of procreational autonomy extends, the existence of the right itself dictates that decisional authority rests in the gamete-providers alone, at least to the extent that their decisions have an impact upon their individual reproductive status.... [N]o other person or entity has an interest sufficient to permit interference with the gamete-providers' decision to continue or terminate the IVF process, because no one else bears the consequences of these decisions in the way that the gamete-providers do.

Further, at least with respect to Tennessee's public policy and its constitutional right of privacy, the state's interest in potential human life is insufficient to justify an infringement on the gamete-providers' procreational autonomy. The United States Supreme Court has indicated in *Webster*, and even in *Roe*, that the state's interest in potential human life may justify statutes or regulations that have an impact upon a person's exercise of procreational autonomy. This potential for sufficiently weighty state's interests is not, however, at issue here, because Tennessee's statutes contain no statement of public policy which reveals an interest that could justify infringing on gamete-providers' decisional authority over the preembryos to which they have contributed.

Tennessee's abortion statute reveals a public policy decision weighing the interests of living persons against the state's interest in potential life. At least during certain stages of a pregnancy, the personal interests of the pregnant woman outweigh the state's interests and the pregnancy may be terminated. Taken collectively, our statutes reflect the policy decision that, at least in some circumstances, the interest of living individuals in avoiding procreation is sufficient to justify taking steps to terminate the procreational process, despite the state's interest in potential life.

Certainly, if the state's interests do not become sufficiently compelling in the abortion context until the end of the first trimester, after very significant developmental stages have passed, then surely there is no state interest in these preembryos which could suffice to overcome the interests of the gamete-providers. The abortion statute reveals that the increase in the state's interest is marked by each successive developmental stage such that, toward the end of a pregnancy, this interest is so compelling that abortion is almost strictly forbidden. This scheme supports the conclusion that the state's interest in the potential life embodied by these four- to eight-cell preembryos (which may or may not be able to achieve implantation in a uterine wall and which, if implanted, may or may not begin to develop into fetuses, subject to possible miscarriage) is at best slight. When weighed against the interests of the individuals and the burdens inherent in parenthood, the state's interest in the potential life of these preembryos is not sufficient to justify any infringement upon the freedom of these individuals to make their own decisions as to whether to allow a process to continue that may result in such a dramatic change in their lives as becoming parents.

The unique nature of this case requires us to note that the interests of these parties in parenthood are different in scope than the parental interest considered in other cases. Previously, courts have dealt with the child-bearing and child-rearing aspects of parenthood. Abortion cases have dealt with gestational parenthood. In this case, the Court must deal with the question of genetic parenthood. We conclude, moreover, that an interest in avoiding genetic parenthood can be significant enough to trigger the protections afforded to all other aspects of parenthood. The technological fact that someone unknown to these parties could gestate these preembryos does not alter the fact that these parties, the gamete-providers, would become parents in that event, at least in the genetic sense. The profound impact this would have on them supports their right to sole decisional authority as to whether the process of attempting to gestate these preembryos should continue. This brings us directly to the question of how to resolve the dispute that arises when one party wishes to continue the IVF process and the other does not.

Balancing the Parties' Interests

Resolving disputes over conflicting interests of constitutional import is a task familiar to the courts. In this case, the issue centers on the two aspects of procreational autonomy-the right to procreate and the right to avoid procreation. Beginning with the burden imposed on Junior Davis, we note that the consequences are obvious. Any disposition which results in the gestation of the preembryos would impose unwanted parenthood on him, with all of its possible financial and psychological consequences. The impact that this unwanted parenthood would have on Junior Davis can only be understood by considering his particular circumstances, as revealed in the record.

Junior Davis testified that he was the fifth youngest of six children. When he was five years old, his parents divorced, his mother had a nervous break-down, and he and three of his brothers went to live at a home for boys run by the Lutheran Church. Another brother was taken in by an aunt, and his sister stayed with their mother. From that day forward, he had monthly visits with his mother but saw his father only three more times before he died in 1976. Junior Davis testified that, as a boy, he had severe problems caused by separation from his parents. He said that it was especially hard to leave his mother after each monthly visit. He clearly feels that he has suffered because of his lack of opportunity to establish a relationship with his parents and particularly because of the absence of his father.

In light of his boyhood experiences, Junior Davis is vehemently opposed to fathering a child that would not live with both parents. Regardless of whether he or Mary Sue had custody, he feels that the child's bond with the non-custodial parent would not be satisfactory. He testified very clearly that his concern was for the psychological obstacles a child in such a situation would face, as well as the burdens it would impose on him. Likewise, he is opposed to donation because the recipient couple might divorce, leaving the child (which he definitely would consider his own) in a single-parent setting.

Balanced against Junior Davis's interest in avoiding parenthood is Mary Sue Davis's interest in donating the preembryos to another couple for implantation. Refusal to permit donation of the preembryos would impose on her the burden of knowing that the lengthy IVF procedures she underwent were futile, and that the preembryos to which she contributed genetic material would never become children. While this is not an insubstantial emotional burden, we can only conclude that Mary Sue Davis's interest in donation is not as significant as the interest Junior Davis has in avoiding parenthood. If she were allowed to donate these preembryos, he would face a lifetime of either wondering about his parental status or knowing about his parental status but having no control over it. He testified quite clearly that if these preembryos were brought to term he would fight for custody of his child or children. Donation, if a child came of it, would rob him twice-his procreational autonomy would be defeated and his relationship with his offspring would be prohibited.

The case would be closer if Mary Sue Davis were seeking to use the preembryos herself, but only if she could not achieve parenthood by any other reasonable means. We recognize the trauma that Mary Sue has already experienced and the additional discomfort to which she would be subjected if she opts to attempt IVF again. Still, she would have a reasonable opportunity, through IVF, to try once again to achieve parenthood in all its aspects-genetic, gestational, bearing, and rearing.

Further, we note that if Mary Sue Davis were unable to undergo another round of IVF, or opted not to try, she could still achieve the child-rearing aspects of parenthood through adoption. The fact that she and Junior Davis pursued adoption indicates that, at least at one time, she was willing to forego genetic parenthood and would have been satisfied by the child-rearing aspects of parenthood alone.

Conclusion

In summary, we hold that disputes involving the disposition of preembryos produced by in vitro fertilization should be resolved, first, by looking to the preferences of the progenitors. If their wishes cannot be ascertained, or if there is dispute, then their prior agreement concerning disposition should be carried out. If no prior agreement exists, then the relative interests of the parties in using or not using the preembryos must be weighed. Ordinarily, the party wishing to avoid procreation should prevail, assuming that the other party has a reasonable possibility of achieving parenthood by means other than use of the preembryos in question. If no other reasonable alternatives exist, then the argument in favor of using the preembryos to achieve pregnancy should be considered. However, if the party seeking control of the preembryos intends merely to donate them to another couple, the objecting party obviously has the greater interest and should prevail.

But the rule does not contemplate the creation of an automatic veto, and in affirming the judgment of the Court of Appeals, we would not wish to be interpreted as so holding. For the reasons set out above, the judgment of the Court of Appeals is affirmed, in the appellee's favor. This ruling means that the Knoxville Fertility Clinic is free to follow its normal procedure in dealing with unused preembryos, as long as that procedure is not in conflict with this opinion. Costs on appeal will be taxed to the appellant.

NOTE

In re Roberto D.B., 923 A.2d 115 (Md. 2007), presented the question of whether a woman who carried and gave birth to twins, but was genetically unrelated to them, must be listed on the birth certificate as the mother of the twins. The twins were conceived through in vitro fertilization when Roberto D.B., who was unmarried, provided his sperm to fertilize eggs from a donor. The fertilized eggs were then implanted in another woman to gestate in her womb. Eight months later, the woman gave birth to twins at a hospital in Silver Spring, Maryland. As required by law, the hospital provides information regarding births to the Maryland Division of Vital Records (MDVR), which issues birth certificates. Unless a court orders otherwise, the hospital will report the gestational carrier as the "mother" of a child to the MDVR. The hospital followed this procedure. Roberto D.B. and the gestational carrier petitioned a circuit court to issue a birth certificate that did not list the gestational carrier as the children's mother. In the petition, they asked the court to declare that Roberto D.B. was the father of the children, and to authorize the hospital to report only the name of the father to the MDVR. Both parties averred that they never intended the gestational carrier to exercise any parental rights over the children and that they agreed that her role in the lives of the children would end upon their birth. The circuit court refused to grant the petition, and an appeal was taken to the Maryland Supreme Court, which ruled that the petition should be granted, allowing the gestational carrier's name to be deleted from the birth certificate.

The court's decision resulted from its construction of a state paternity statute that, as written, provided an opportunity for genetically unrelated males to avoid parentage, while genetically unrelated females did not have the same option. Because the state Equal Rights Amendment prohibited the granting of more rights to one sex than to the other, the court ruled that the paternity statute must be construed to allow genetically unrelated females to have the same right as genetically unrelated males to avoid parentage.

IN RE T.W.
551 So.2d 1186 (Fla. 1989)

SHAW, J.

We have on appeal *In re T.W.*, 543 So.2d 837 (Fla. 5th DCA 1989), which declared unconstitutional section 390.001(4)(a), Florida Statutes (Supp.1988), the parental consent statute. We approve the opinion of the district court and hold the statute invalid under the Florida Constitution.

The procedure that a minor must follow to obtain an abortion in Florida is set out in the parental consent statute and related rules. Prior to undergoing an abortion, a minor must obtain parental consent or, alternatively, must convince a court that she is sufficiently mature to make the decision herself or that, if she is immature, the abortion nevertheless is in her best interests. Pursuant to this procedure, T.W., a pregnant, unmarried, fifteen-year-old, petitioned for a waiver of parental consent under the judicial bypass provision on the alternative grounds that (1) she was sufficiently mature to give an informed consent to the abortion, (2) she had a justified fear of physical or emotional abuse if her parents were requested to consent, and (3) her mother was seriously ill and informing her of the pregnancy would be an added burden. The trial court, after appointing counsel for T.W. and separate counsel as guardian ad litem for the fetus, conducted a hearing within twenty-four hours of the filing of the petition.

The relevant portions of the hearing consisted of T.W.'s uncontroverted testimony that she was a high-school student, participated in band and flag corps, worked twenty hours a week, baby-sat for her mother and neighbors, planned on finishing high school and attending vocational school or community college, had observed an instructional film on abortion, had taken a sex education course at school, would not put her child up for adoption, and had discussed her plans with the child's father and obtained his approval. She informed the court that due to her mother's illness, she had assumed extra duties at home caring for her sibling and that if she told her mother about the abortion, "it would kill her." Evidence was introduced showing that the pregnancy was in the first trimester.

The seminal case in United States abortion law is *Roe v. Wade*, 410 U.S. 113 (1973). There, the Court ruled that a right to privacy implicit in the fourteenth amendment embraces a woman's decision concerning abortion. Autonomy to make this decision constitutes a fundamental right and states may impose restrictions only when narrowly drawn to serve a compelling state interest. The Court recognized two important state interests, protecting the health of the mother and the potentiality of life in the fetus, and ruled that these interests become compelling at the completion of the first trimester of pregnancy and upon viability of the fetus (approximately at the end of the second trimester), respectively. Thus, during the first trimester, states must leave the abortion decision to the woman and her doctor; during the second trimester, states may impose measures to protect the mother's health; and during the period following viability, states may possibly forbid abortions altogether. Subsequent to *Roe*, the Court issued several decisions dealing directly with the matter of parental consent for minors seeking abortions. See *Planned Parenthood Ass'n v. Ashcroft*, 462 U.S. 476 (1983); *City of Akron v. Akron Center for Reproductive Health Inc.*, 462 U.S. 416 (1983); *Bellotti v. Baird*, 443 U.S. 622 (1979) (plurality opinion); *Planned Parenthood v. Danforth*, 428 U.S. 52 (1976).

To be held constitutional, the instant statute must pass muster under both the federal and state constitutions. Were we to examine it solely under the federal Constitution, our analysis necessarily would track the decisions noted above. However, Florida is unusual in that it is one of at least four states having its own express constitutional provision guaranteeing an independent right to privacy, and we opt to examine the statute first under the Florida Constitution. If it fails here, then no further analysis under federal law is required.

As we noted in *Winfield v. Division of Pari-Mutuel Wagering*, 477 So.2d 544 (Fla.1985), the essential concept of privacy is deeply rooted in our nation's political and philosophical heritage. Pursuant to this principle, the United States Supreme Court has recognized a privacy right that shields an individual's autonomy in deciding matters concerning marriage, procreation, contraception, family relationships, and child rearing and education. The Court, however, has made it clear that the states, not the federal government, are the final guarantors of personal privacy: "But the protection of a person's *general* right to privacy-his right to be let alone by other people-is, like the protection of his property and of his very life, left largely to the law of the individual States." *Katz v. United States*, 389 U.S. 347, 350-51 (1967) (emphasis in original). While the federal Constitution traditionally shields enumerated and implied individual liberties from encroachment by state or federal government, the federal Court has long held that state constitutions may provide even greater protection. See, e.g., *Pruneyard Shopping Center v. Robins*, 447 U.S. 74 (1980).

In 1980, Florida voters by general election amended our state constitution to provide:

> Right of privacy.-Every natural person has the right to be let alone and free from governmental intrusion into his private life except as otherwise provided herein. This section shall not be construed to limit the public's right of access to public records and meetings as provided by law. Art. I, §23, Fla. Const.

This Court in *Winfield v. Division of Pari-Mutuel Wagering*, 477 So.2d 544 (Fla. 1985) described the far-reaching impact of the Florida amendment:

> The citizens of Florida opted for more protection from governmental intrusion when they approved article I, section 23, of the Florida Constitution. This amendment is an independent, freestanding constitutional provision which declares the fundamental right to privacy. Article I, section 23, was intentionally phrased in strong terms. The drafters of the amendment rejected the use of the words "unreasonable" or "unwarranted" before the phrase "governmental intrusion" in order to make the privacy right as strong as possible. Since the people of this state exercised their prerogative and enacted an amendment to the Florida Constitution which expressly and succinctly provides for a strong right of privacy not found in the United States Constitution, it can only be concluded that the right is much broader in scope than that of the Federal Constitution. *Winfield*, 477 So.2d at 548.

Consistent with this analysis, we have said that the amendment provides "an explicit textual foundation for those privacy interests inherent in the concept of liberty which may not otherwise be protected by specific constitutional provisions." *Rasmussen v. South Fla. Blood Serv.*, 500 So.2d 533, 536 (Fla.1987). We have found the right implicated in a wide range of activities dealing with the public disclosure of personal matters. See *Barron v. Florida Freedom Newspapers*, 531 So.2d 113 (Fla.1988) (closure of court proceedings and records); *Rasmussen* (confidential donor information concerning AIDS-tainted blood supply); *Winfield* (banking records); *Florida Bd. of Bar Examiners re: Applicant*,

443 So.2d 71 (Fla.1983) (bar application questions concerning disclosure of psychiatric counselling). Florida courts have also found the right involved in a number of cases dealing with personal decisionmaking. See *Public Health Trust v. Wons*, 541 So.2d 96 (Fla.1989) (refusal of blood transfusion that is necessary to sustain life); *Corbett v. D'Alessandro*, 487 So.2d 368 (Fla. 2d DCA) (removal of nasogastric feeding tube from adult in permanent vegetative state); *In re Guardianship of Barry*, 445 So.2d 365 (Fla. 2d DCA 1984) (removal of life support system from brain-dead infant); *see also Satz v. Perlmutter*, 379 So.2d 359 (Fla.1980) (removal of respirator from competent adult, decided prior to passage of privacy amendment under general right of privacy).

The privacy section contains no express standard of review for evaluating the lawfulness of a government intrusion into one's private life, and this Court when called upon, adopted the following standard:

> Since the privacy section as adopted contains no textual standard of review, it is important for us to identify an explicit standard to be applied in order to give proper force and effect to the amendment. The right of privacy is a fundamental right which we believe demands the compelling state interest standard. This test shifts the burden of proof to the state to justify an intrusion on privacy. The burden can be met by demonstrating that the challenged regulation serves a compelling state interest and accomplishes its goal through the use of the least intrusive means. *Winfield*, 477 So.2d at 547.

Florida's privacy provision is clearly implicated in a woman's decision of whether or not to continue her pregnancy. We can conceive of few more personal or private decisions concerning one's body that one can make in the course of a lifetime, except perhaps the decision of the terminally ill in their choice of whether to discontinue necessary medical treatment.

> Of all decisions a person makes about his or her body, the most profound and intimate relate to two sets of ultimate questions: first, whether, when, and how one's body is to become the vehicle for another human being's creation; second, when and how-this time there is no question of "whether"-one's body is to terminate its organic life. L. Tribe, *American Constitutional Law* 1337-38 (2d ed. 1988).

The decision whether to obtain an abortion is fraught with specific physical, psychological, and economic implications of a uniquely personal nature for each woman. The Florida Constitution embodies the principle that "[f]ew decisions are more personal and intimate, more properly private, or more basic to individual dignity and autonomy, than a woman's decision ... whether to end her pregnancy. A woman's right to make that choice freely is fundamental." *Thornburgh v. American College of Obstetricians and Gynecologists*, 476 U.S. 747 (1986).

The next question to be addressed is whether this freedom of choice concerning abortion extends to minors. We conclude that it does, based on the unambiguous language of the amendment: The right of privacy extends to "[e]very natural person." Minors are natural persons in the eyes of the law and "[c]onstitutional rights do not mature and come into being magically only when one attains the state-defined age of majority. Minors, as well as adults…possess constitutional rights." *Danforth*, 428 U.S. at 74. See also *Ashcroft*; *City of Akron*; *H.L. v. Matheson*, 450 U.S. 398 (1981); and *Bellotti*.

Common sense dictates that a minor's rights are not absolute; in order to overcome these constitutional rights, a statute must survive the stringent test announced in Winfield: The state must prove that the statute furthers a compelling state interest through the least intrusive means.

The challenged statute fails because it intrudes upon the privacy of the pregnant minor from conception to birth. Such a substantial invasion of a pregnant female's privacy by the state for the full term of the pregnancy is not necessary for the preservation of maternal health or the potentiality of life. However, where parental rights over a minor child are concerned, society has recognized additional state interests-protection of the immature minor and preservation of the family unit. For reasons set out below, we find that neither of these interests is sufficiently compelling under Florida law to override Florida's privacy amendment.

In evaluating the validity of parental consent and notice statutes, the federal Court has taken into consideration the state's interests in the well-being of the immature minor, *see Ashcroft*; *City of Akron*; *Matheson*; *Bellotti*; *Danforth*, and in the integrity of the family, see *Matheson*; *Bellotti*. In *Bellotti*, the Court set forth three reasons justifying the conclusion that states can impose more restrictions on the right of minors to obtain abortions than they can impose on the right of adults: "[T]he peculiar vulnerability of children; their inability to make critical decisions in an informed, mature manner; and the importance of the parental role in child rearing." *Bellotti*, 443 U.S. at 634. The Court pointed out that "during the formative years of childhood and adolescence, minors often lack the experience, perspective, and judgment to recognize and avoid choices that could be detrimental to them," and that the role of parents in "teaching, guiding, and inspiring by precept and example is essential to the growth of young people into mature, socially responsible citizens." In assessing the validity of parental consent statutes, the federal Court applied a relaxed standard; the state interest need only be "significant," not "compelling," to support the intrusion.

We agree that the state's interests in protecting minors and in preserving family unity are worthy objectives. Unlike the federal Constitution, however, which allows intrusion based on a "significant" state interest, the Florida Constitution requires a "compelling" state interest in all cases where the right to privacy is implicated. We note that Florida does not recognize these two interests as being sufficiently compelling to justify a parental consent requirement where procedures other than abortion are concerned. Section 743.065, Florida Statutes (1987), provides:

> Unwed pregnant minor or minor mother; consent to medical services for minor or minor's child valid.-
>
> (1) An unwed pregnant minor may consent to the performance of medical or surgical care or services relating to her pregnancy by a hospital or clinic or by a physician licensed under chapter 458 or chapter 459, and such consent is valid and binding as if she had achieved her majority.
>
> (2) An unwed minor mother may consent to the performance of medical or surgical care or services for her child by a hospital or clinic or by a physician licensed under chapter 458 or chapter 459, and such consent is valid and binding as if she had achieved her majority.
>
> (3) Nothing in this act shall affect the provisions of s. 390.001 [the abortion statute].

Under this statute, a minor may consent, without parental approval, to any medical procedure involving her pregnancy or her existing child-no matter how dire the possible consequences-except abortion. Under *In re Guardianship of Barry*, 445 So.2d 365 (Fla. 2d DCA 1984) (parents permitted to authorize removal of life support system from infant in permanent coma), this could include authority in certain circumstances to order life support discontinued for a comatose child. In light of this wide authority that the state grants an unwed minor to make life-or-death decisions concerning herself or an existing child without parental consent, we are unable to discern a special compelling interest on the part of the state under Florida law in protecting the minor only where abortion is concerned. We fail to see the qualitative difference in terms of impact on the well-being of the minor between allowing the life of an existing child to come to an end and terminating a pregnancy, or between undergoing a highly dangerous medical procedure on oneself and undergoing a far less dangerous procedure to end one's pregnancy. If any qualitative difference exists, it certainly is insufficient in terms of state interest. Although the state does have an interest in protecting minors, "the selective approach employed by the legislature evidences the limited nature of the ... interest being furthered by these provisions." We note that the state's adoption act similarly contains no requirement that a minor obtain parental consent prior to placing a child up for adoption, even though this decision clearly is fraught with intense emotional and societal consequences.

Based on the foregoing analysis of our state law, we hold that section 390.001(4)(a), violates the Florida Constitution. Accordingly, no further analysis under federal law is required. We expressly decide this case on state law grounds and cite federal precedent only to the extent that it illuminates Florida law. We approve the district court's decision.

GRIMES, J., concurring in part, dissenting in part.

In 1980, the Florida Constitution was amended to specifically guarantee persons the right to privacy. As a consequence, it was thereafter unnecessary to read a right of privacy into the due process provision of Florida's equivalent to the fourteenth amendment. However, this did not mean that Florida voters had elected to create more privacy rights concerning abortion than those already guaranteed by the United States Supreme Court. By 1980, abortion rights were well established under the federal Constitution, and I believe the privacy amendment had the practical effect of guaranteeing these same rights under the Florida Constitution. If the United States Supreme Court were to subsequently recede from *Roe v. Wade*, this would not diminish the abortion rights now provided by the privacy amendment of the Florida Constitution. Consequently, I agree with the analysis contained in parts I and II of the majority opinion, which I read as adopting, for purposes of the Florida Constitution, the qualified right to have an abortion established in *Roe v. Wade*.

In part III, however, the majority opinion interprets the Florida Constitution differently than the United States Supreme Court has interpreted the federal Constitution with respect to a minor's right to an abortion.... [T]he United States Supreme Court has consistently recognized that a state statute requiring parental consent to a minor's abortion is constitutional if it provides a judicial alternative in which the consent is obviated if the court finds that the minor is mature enough to make the abortion decision or, in the absence of the requisite maturity, the abortion is in the minor's best interest.

While purporting to acknowledge the state's interest in protecting minors and in preserving family unity, the majority reaches the conclusion that these interests as reflected in the instant statute must fall in the face of its broad interpretation of the privacy amendment. In effect, the Court has said that the state's interest in regulating abortions is no different with respect to minors than it is with adults. Under this ruling, even immature minors may decide to have an abortion without parental consent. I do not agree with either the majority's broad interpretation of the privacy amendment or its limited view of the state's interest concerning the conduct of minors.

Moreover, I cannot accept the majority's conclusion that section 743.065, which permits an unwed pregnant minor to consent to the performance of medical or surgical care except with respect to abortions, somehow makes the statute under consideration in the instant case unconstitutional. Section 743.065 was designed to permit doctors to avoid liability for providing medical services to minors without parental consent and to ensure that emergency treatment would be available. The decision to have an abortion is clearly different than the decision to undergo other medical or surgical care with respect to pregnancy, and the legislature has a right to determine that different criteria should be followed with respect to consenting to an abortion.

It is this Court's duty to uphold the constitutionality of statutes whenever this can be done consistent with sound legal principles. Clearly, this statute is valid under our federal Constitution as interpreted by the United States Supreme Court. Admittedly, this Court has the authority to give the Florida Constitution a broader interpretation, but there should be a compelling reason for taking such a step.

Here, the legislature has concluded that it is ordinarily desirable that a minor should have the advice and consent of her parents before having an abortion. However, by providing a judicial alternative which is simple, speedy, and confidential, the legislature has also ensured that an abortion will be denied to a minor only when she is too immature to make the decision and when it is against her best interest. Section 390.001(4)(a)(1) reflects a legitimate state concern over the welfare of children and impinges upon the minor's right to privacy in the least intrusive manner. I would uphold the constitutionality of the statute.

NOTE

In 1999, the Florida legislature enacted a statute requiring parental notification (rather than parental consent) before a minor could undergo an abortion. The statute provided for a judicial bypass in lieu of parental notification. Relying on its previous decision in *T.W.*, the Florida Supreme Court ruled that the statute was unconstitutional. *North Florida Women's Health and Counseling Services, Inc. v. State*, 866 So.2d 612 (Fla. 2003). In response, the state legislature proposed a constitutional amendment, adopted by the voters of the state, that counteracted the decision in *North Florida Women's Health and Counseling Services* by specifically authorizing the legislature to require parental notification before a minor has an abortion so long as the legislature also establishes a procedure for judicial bypass of the notification requirement. Fla. Const. art. X, § 22. The amendment did not address parental consent and accordingly had no effect on the ruling in *T.W.*

PLANNED PARENTHOOD v. SUNDQUIST
38 S.W.3d 1 (Tenn. 2000)

ANDERSON, C.J.

This is an appeal from the Circuit Court for Davidson County, which applied an undue burden standard and struck down as unconstitutional the provisions of Tennessee's criminal abortion statutes requiring that physicians inform their patients that "abortion in a considerable number of cases constitutes a major surgical procedure," Tenn. Code Ann. § 39-15-202(b)(4) (1997), and mandating a two-day waiting period requirement, Tenn. Code Ann. § 39-15-202(d)(1). The trial court upheld the second trimester hospitalization requirement, Tenn. Code Ann. § 39-15-201(c)(2), the remaining informed consent requirements, Tenn. Code Ann. § 39-15-202(b)(1)-(3), (b)(5)-(c), and the medical emergency exceptions, Tenn. Code Ann. § 39-15-202(d)(3), (g). The Court of Appeals reversed the judgment of the trial court in part and affirmed in part. The Court of Appeals upheld the following provisions as not imposing an undue burden: the waiting period requirement, based upon the facts of this case; the second trimester hospitalization requirement; and, except for the "major surgical procedure" provision, the remaining informed consent requirements. We granted application for permission to appeal those issues of first impression. We specifically hold that a woman's right to terminate her pregnancy is a vital part of the right to privacy guaranteed by the Tennessee Constitution. We further hold that the right is inherent in the concept of ordered liberty embodied in our constitution and is therefore fundamental. Accordingly, the statutes regulating this fundamental right must be subjected to strict scrutiny analysis. When reviewed under the correct standard, we conclude that none of the statutory provisions at issue withstand such scrutiny. The Court of Appeals' judgment is therefore affirmed in part and reversed in part.

The initial issue which this Court must decide is whether the right of privacy implicated in this case as guaranteed by the Tennessee Constitution is broader than the right as guaranteed by the federal constitution and as construed by the United States Supreme Court. Implicit in this determination is whether the statutes at issue are to be judged under the less demanding undue burden standard, or the more stringent strict scrutiny standard.

United States Supreme Court Cases

In 1973, the United States Supreme Court first recognized a woman's right to terminate her pregnancy in *Roe v. Wade*, 410 U.S. 113, 153 (1973). [In Roe, the United States Supreme Court recognized that a woman has a fundamental right to terminate her pregnancy and that this right is deserving of heightened scrutiny against state restrictions.]

Nineteen years after deciding *Roe*, the Court modified *Roe* in *Planned Parenthood v. Casey*, 505 U.S. 833 (1992). A majority of the Court reaffirmed *Roe*'s holding that the Constitution protects a woman's right to terminate her pregnancy before viability without undue interference from the State. After viability, the state has the power to restrict abortions "if the law contains exceptions for pregnancies which endanger the woman's life or health."

Three justices concluded that the "undue burden standard is the appropriate means of reconciling the State's interest with the woman's constitutionally protected liberty." *Id.* at 876 (joint opinion of O'Connor, Kennedy and Souter, JJ.). Four justices, concurring in part and dissenting in part, criticized the undue burden test. The justices noted that the undue burden approach has no recognized basis in constitutional law. *Id.* at 964 (Rehnquist, C.J., joined by White, Scalia, and Thomas, JJ., concurring in part and dissenting in part).

Most recently, in *Stenberg v. Carhart*, 530 U.S. 914 (2000), a majority of the Court reaffirmed the "undue burden" standard. The Court struck down a statute banning partial birth abortions because it had no exception for the health of the mother and applied to dilation and evacuation abortions as well as to dilation and extraction abortions, thereby constituting an undue burden on the woman's ability to choose an abortion.

Although the United States Supreme Court has now replaced the strict scrutiny standard in the abortion context with the less exacting undue burden standard, this action does not determine the standard which this Court must apply under the Tennessee Constitution. We now turn to the issue of the appropriate standard to apply under our state constitution.

Tennessee Cases

Though we have never before had the abortion issue squarely before us, we have considered the related issue of procreational autonomy. In *Davis v. Davis*, 842 S.W.2d 588 (Tenn. 1992), we first recognized a right to privacy under the Tennessee Constitution. *Davis* involved a divorce dispute over the disposition of seven frozen preembryos the parties had created during their marriage. The husband did not want to become a father outside of the marital relationship and therefore wanted the preembryos destroyed. The wife wanted to donate the preembryos to a childless couple. Our analysis of whether the parties would "become parents" turned on the exercise of the parties' constitutional right to privacy.

After observing that the right to privacy is not specifically mentioned in either the federal or the Tennessee constitutions, we initially reviewed the development of the federal right to privacy for guidance in interpreting our state constitution. We noted that the United States Supreme Court has recognized a federal constitutional right of privacy despite the absence of specific language mentioning such a right in the United States Constitution. We reasoned that, likewise, the "right to privacy, or personal autonomy, while not mentioned explicitly in our state constitution, is nevertheless reflected in several sections of the Tennessee Declaration of Rights." We further reasoned that the drafters of the Tennessee Constitution surely "foresaw the need to protect individuals from unwarranted governmental intrusion into matters…involving intimate questions of personal and family concern." We thus concluded that the Tennessee Constitution protects the individual's right to privacy and explained that:

> the specific individual freedom in dispute is the right to procreate. *In terms of the Tennessee state constitution*, we hold that the right of procreation is a vital part of an individual's right to privacy.

Accordingly, we explicitly relied on the Tennessee Constitution in *Davis* to extend protection to the husband's right to procreational autonomy.

Since the *Davis* decision, we have identified privacy rights in other contexts. We have held that a parent's right to the custody of his or her child implicates a fundamental right of privacy and may not be abridged absent a compelling state interest. The Court of Appeals has relied upon *Davis* to find a privacy interest in consensual adult homosexuality. There is no exhaustive list of activities that fall under the protection of the right to privacy, at either the federal or the state level. However, it is clear that such activities must be of the utmost personal and intimate concern.

We hold that a woman's right to obtain a legal termination of her pregnancy is sufficiently similar in character to those personal and private decisions and activities identified in state and federal precedent to implicate a cognizable privacy interest.

Protections Afforded the Right to Privacy

Determining whether an asserted interest is fundamental is essential because fundamental rights receive special protection under both federal and state constitutions. Federal case law uniformly holds the government regulation of the exercise of fundamental rights is unconstitutional unless the regulations both serve a compelling governmental interest and are narrowly tailored to serve that interest. Tennessee courts have adopted this "strict scrutiny" approach in regard to fundamental rights without exception.

In *Davis*, we found the right to procreational autonomy to be "inherent in our most basic concepts of liberty." That test was essentially a restatement of the fundamental rights approach of *Roe*. Because a woman's right to terminate her pregnancy and an individual's right to procreational autonomy are similar in nature, we find the *Davis* test to be most appropriate here. Thus, a woman's right to terminate her pregnancy is fundamental if it can be said to be inherent in the concept of ordered liberty embodied in the Tennessee Constitution.

Without question, the protections afforded Tennessee citizens by the Tennessee Constitution's Declaration of Rights share the contours of the protections afforded by the United States Constitution's Bill of Rights. This is due, in large part, to affinity of purpose. Both documents were written with the intent to reserve to the people various liberties and to protect the free exercise of those liberties from governmental intrusion.

It is equally without question, however, that the provisions of our Tennessee Declaration of Rights from which the right to privacy emanates differ from the federal Bill of Rights in marked respects. In *Davis*, we found that the right to privacy guaranteed by the Tennessee Constitution sprang from the express grants of rights in article I, sections 3, 7, 19 and 27, and also from the grants of liberty in article I, sections 1, 2 and 8.

These protections contained in our Declaration of Rights are more particularly stated than those stated in the federal Bill of Rights. For example, the explicit guarantee of freedom of worship found under the United States Constitution occupies but sixteen words in an amendment generally guaranteeing freedom of worship, freedom of speech, freedom of the press, the right to assemble, and the right to petition the government for redress of grievances.

In contrast, the guarantee of worship under the Tennessee Constitution exists in its own paragraph constituting eighty-one words. It characterizes mankind's right to worship as "a natural and indefeasible right" and declares "that no human authority can, in any case whatever, control or interfere with the rights of conscience." Tenn. Const. art I, § 3. This Court has said that the language of this section, when compared to the guarantee of religious freedom contained in the federal constitution, is a stronger guarantee of religious freedom.

Tennessee's guarantees of free speech and free press are similarly more descriptive than the federal grant. The verbal expression of these basic freedoms in our constitution is infused with a strong sense of individuality and personal liberty: "The free communication of thoughts and opinions, is one of the invaluable rights of man, and every citizen may freely speak, write and print on any subject, being responsible for the abuse of that liberty." Tenn. Const. art. I, § 19.

This Court is not free to discount the fact that the framers of our state constitution used language different from that used by the framers of the United States Constitution. No words in our constitution can properly be said to be surplusage and differences in expressions of right are particularly relevant to determining the "concept of liberty" embodied in our constitution.

Today, we remain opposed to any assertion that previous decisions suggesting that synonymity or identity of portions of our constitution and the federal constitution requires *this* Court to interpret our constitution as coextensive to the United States Constitution. "Tennessee constitutional standards are not destined to walk in lock step with the uncertain and fluctuating federal standards and do not relegate Tennessee citizens to the lowest levels of constitutional protection, those guaranteed by the national constitution." We have said time and again that:

> The concept of ordered liberty embodied in our constitution requires our finding that a woman's right to legally terminate her pregnancy is fundamental. The provisions of the Tennessee Constitution imply protection of an individual's right to make inherently personal decisions, and to act on those decisions, without government interference. A woman's termination of her pregnancy is just such an inherently intimate and personal enterprise. This privacy interest is closely aligned with matters of marriage, child rearing, and other procreational interests that have previously been held to be fundamental. To distinguish it as somehow non-fundamental would require this Court to ignore the obvious corollary.

The Appropriate Standard

It is well settled that where a fundamental right is at issue, in order for a state regulation which interferes with that right to be upheld, the regulation must withstand strict scrutiny. The State's interest must be sufficiently compelling in order to overcome the fundamental nature of the right.

Other jurisdictions have applied heightened scrutiny of governmental regulation of abortion since *Casey* was decided. Our rejection of the *Casey* standard is similar to the action taken by those state courts. In *Women of the State of Minn. v. Gomez*, 542 N.W.2d 17 (Minn. 1995), the Minnesota Supreme Court considered a complaint for declaratory and injunctive relief challenging the constitutionality of statutes restricting the use of public medical assistance and general assistance funds for abortions. The Court determined that the Minnesota Constitution guaranteed a right of privacy rooted in several provisions of the constitution, including a due process provision, a "law of the land" provision, and a provision protecting against unreasonable searches and seizures. The Court held that the right of privacy includes a woman's right to choose to have an abortion. Stating that it could think of few decisions more intimate, personal and profound than a woman's decision between childbirth and abortion, it held that the case was one of those limited circumstances in which it would interpret the Minnesota Constitution to provide more protection than that afforded under the federal constitution. It subjected the regulations to strict scrutiny because the right of privacy is fundamental.

While the joint opinion in *Casey* adopted the "undue burden" approach, Justice Scalia in a separate dissent and concurrence criticized the so-called standard as being "ultimately standardless." He noted that the undue burden standard was "created largely out of whole cloth" and essentially had no recognized basis in constitutional law.

We agree that the undue burden approach is essentially no standard at all, and, in effect, allows judges to impose their own subjective views of the propriety of the legislation in question. The dissent has criticized the majority for "convert[ing] itself into a roving constitutional convention which is free to strike down the duly enacted laws of the legislature for no other reason than the Court feels they are burdensome and unwise." In fact, that is exactly what the undue burden approach allows. Under that test, the Court is free to determine, under the justices' own subjective opinions as to the wisdom of the legislation, whether the legislation creates an undue burden upon a woman's right to terminate her pregnancy. Application of strict scrutiny, a recognized principle of constitutional law, on the other hand, requires the Court to apply a standard that has been applied repeatedly over the years, and the Court may draw upon that precedent in determining whether the legislation passes muster.

The subjective nature of the undue burden analysis is aptly illustrated by the fact that the majority and the dissent reach diametrically opposed results when applying the analysis. The majority would find each of the challenged abortion statutes to be unconstitutional under *Casey*, while the dissent, applying exactly the same analysis, would reach the opposite result as to each statute, save one.

Thus, the *Casey* test offers our judges no real guidance and engenders no expectation among the citizenry that governmental regulation of abortion will be objective, evenhanded or well-reasoned. This Court finds no justification for exchanging the long-established constitutional doctrine of strict scrutiny for a test, not yet ten years old and applicable to a single, narrow area of the law, that would relegate a fundamental right of the citizens of Tennessee to the personal caprice of an individual judge.

In summary, we hold that a woman's right to terminate her pregnancy is a vital part of the right to privacy guaranteed by the Tennessee Constitution. That right is inherent in the concept of ordered liberty embodied in the Tennessee Constitution and is similar to other privacy interests that have previously been held to be fundamental. We therefore conclude that this specific privacy interest is fundamental. Therefore, the statutory provisions regulating abortion must be subjected to strict scrutiny analysis. After our review of the record and applicable authorities, we conclude that under the Tennessee Constitution, the statutes at issue, Tenn. Code Ann. §§ 39-15-201(c)(2) (the second trimester hospitalization requirement), 39-15-202(b), (c) (the informed consent and physician-only counseling requirements), 39-15-202(d)(1) (the mandatory waiting period requirement), and 39-15-202(d)(3) and (g) (the medical emergency exceptions), are unconstitutional because the statutes are not narrowly tailored to further compelling state interests.

REPRODUCTIVE HEALTH SERVICE OF PLANNED PARENTHOOD OF ST. LOUIS REGION, INC. v. NIXON
185 S.W. 3d 685 (Mo. 2006)

PER CURIAM

Section 188.039, RSMo Supp.2003, creates an informed consent requirement including a 24-hour waiting period before elective abortions may be performed in Missouri. Planned Parenthood argues that the 24-hour waiting provision violates rights of liberty and privacy under the Missouri Constitution.

The Supreme Court of the United States held in *Planned Parenthood v. Casey*, that a 24-hour waiting period does not violate the federal constitution. 505 U.S. 833, 887 (1992). That opinion stated:

> [W]e are not convinced that the 24-hour waiting period constitutes an undue burden.... [T]he right protected by *Roe* is a right to decide to terminate a pregnancy free of undue interference by the State. Because the informed consent requirement facilitates the wise exercise of that right, it cannot be classified as an interference with the right *Roe* protects. The informed consent requirement is not an undue burden on that right.

Despite *Casey*, Planned Parenthood argues that the Missouri constitution should be construed more broadly than the United States constitution.

> The federal due process clause states, in part: "[N]or shall any State deprive any person of life, liberty, or property, without due process of law...." U.S. Const. amend. XIV, sec. 1. The Missouri constitution contains two related clauses. Missouri's due process clause states: "That no person shall be deprived of life, liberty or property without due process of law." Mo. Const. art. I, sec. 10.

Article I, section 2 of the Missouri constitution also states:

> That all constitutional government is intended to promote the general welfare of the people; that all persons have a natural right to life, liberty, the pursuit of happiness and the enjoyment of the gains of their own industry; that all persons are created equal and are entitled to equal rights and opportunity under the law; that to give security to these things is the principal office of government, and that when government does not confer this security, it fails in its chief design.

There is no reason, within the context of this case, to construe this language from the Missouri constitution more broadly than the language used in the United States constitution.

C. THE RIGHT OF INTIMATE ASSOCIATION

STATE v. SAUNDERS
381 A.2d 333 (N.J. 1977)

PASHMAN, J.

Defendant Charles Saunders was indicted along with Bernard Busby on charges of rape, assault with intent to rape and armed robbery. At trial both admitted to having had sexual intercourse with the two complainants, but insisted that the women had participated willingly in exchange for a promise that they would receive "reefers" (marijuana cigarettes) in return. The trial judge, on his own initiative, charged the jury that the defendants could be convicted of the "lesser included offense" of fornication (N.J.S.A. 2A:110-1) if they were found not guilty on the other counts. The jury acquitted the defendants of the charges in the indictment and convicted them of fornication. In charging the jury, the judge defined the crime of fornication as "an act of illicit sexual intercourse by a man, married or single, with an unmarried woman."

Defendant asserts that the instant statute, N.J.S.A. 2A:110-1, is unconstitutional on its face since it generally seeks to outlaw conduct which the State has no power to prohibit.... The right of privacy, upon which defendant bases his attack, is not explicitly mentioned in either the New Jersey or United States Constitutions. However, both documents have been construed to include such a right. On the federal level, the right was first recognized as being of constitutional stature by a majority of the Court in *Griswold v. Connecticut*, 381 U.S. 479 (1965). Subsequent Supreme Court decisions have firmly established the constitutional nature of the right of privacy. In *Roe v. Wade*, 410 U.S. 113 (1973), the Court found that the right of privacy encompassed a woman's decision whether or not to terminate a pregnancy. More recently the right has been recognized in the Court's decisions in *Carey v. Population Services International*, 431 U.S. 678 (1977); *Whalen v. Roe*, 429 U.S. 589 (1977); and *Paul v. Davis*, 424 U.S. 693 (1976).

However, the precise scope of the interests protected by the right of privacy are not easily defined. As the Court noted in *Carey v. Population Services International*, *supra*, the interests which have been held to fall within the protections of the right have been "personal" ones; they have included those "relating to marriage, *Loving v. Virginia*, 388 U.S. 1 (1967); procreation, *Skinner v. Oklahoma*, 316 U.S. 535 (1942); contraception, *Eisenstadt v. Baird*, 405 U.S. 438 (1972);   family relationships, *Prince v. Massachusetts*, 321 U.S. 158, 166 (1944); and child rearing and education, *Pierce v. Society of Sisters*, 268 U.S. 510 (1925);" *Meyer v. Nebraska*, 262 U.S. 390 (1923); *Carey, supra.*

Although the Court in *Carey* observed that the "decision whether or not to beget or bear a child is at the very heart of this cluster of constitutionally protected choices," we believe that the right of privacy is not confined to the private situations involved in each of these decisions. Indeed, the Court's references in *Roe v. Wade* to cases having nothing to do with such decisions should effectively dispel any such notion. While *Carey* certainly emphasizes the importance of a person's choice regarding whether or not to have children, it indicates that the constitutional basis for the protection of such decisions is their relationship to individual autonomy. Mr. Justice Brennan observed that such personal choices concern "the most intimate of human activities and relationships," adding that "decisions whether to accomplish or to prevent conception are among the most private and sensitive." 431 U.S. at 685.

This view of the right of privacy is consistent with the approach taken by this Court in our recent decision in *In re Quinlan*, 355 A.2d 647 (N.J. 1976). There we held, as a matter of State constitutional law, that this important right was broad enough to encompass the freedom to make a personal choice as to the continuance of artificial life-support mechanisms. Though Chief Justice Hughes noted for the Court that the right of privacy had theretofore been primarily associated with decisions involving contraception and family life, he also found that its underlying concern was with the protection of personal decisions, and that it might be included within "the class of what have been called rights of 'personality.'" Our *Quinlan* decision could not have been predicated on privacy grounds if the class of cognizable privacy interests was limited to personal decisions concerning procreative matters.

Any discussion of the right of privacy must focus on the ultimate interest (by) which protection the Constitution seeks to ensure the freedom of personal development. Whether one defines that concept as a "right to 'intimacy' and a freedom to do intimate things," or "a right to the 'integrity' of one's 'personality,'" the crux of the matter is that governmental regulation of private personal behavior under the police power is sharply limited. As Mr. Justice Brandeis stated so eloquently in his dissent in *Olmstead v. United States*, 277 U.S. 438 (1928):

> The makers of our Constitution undertook to secure conditions favorable to the pursuit of happiness. They recognized the significance of man's spiritual nature, of his feelings and of his intellect. They knew that only a part of the pain, pleasure and satisfactions of life are found in material things. They sought to protect Americans in their beliefs, their thoughts, their emotions and their sensations. They conferred, as against the government, the right to be let alone the most valued by civilized men. (277 U.S. at 478.)

We conclude that the conduct statutorily defined as fornication involves, by its very nature, a fundamental personal choice. Thus, the statute infringes upon the right of privacy. Although persons may differ as to the propriety and morality of such conduct and while we certainly do not condone its particular manifestations in this case, such a decision is necessarily encompassed in the concept of personal autonomy which our Constitution seeks to safeguard.

We recognize that the conduct prohibited by this statute has never been explicitly treated by the Supreme Court as falling within the right of privacy. In fact, we note that this question has been specifically reserved by the Court. Nevertheless, our decision today is consistent with the tenor and thrust of the Court's more recent decisions. As we stated earlier, the Court in *Carey* and *Wade* underscored the inherently private nature of a person's decision to bear or beget children. It would be rather anomalous if such a decision could be constitutionally protected while the more fundamental decision as to whether to engage in the conduct which is a necessary prerequisite to child-bearing could be constitutionally prohibited. Surely, such a choice involves considerations which are at least as intimate and personal as those which are involved in choosing whether to use contraceptives. We therefore join with other courts which have held that such sexual activities between adults are protected by the right of privacy. See *State v. Pilcher*, 242 N.W.2d 348 (Iowa 1976).

Finally, we note that our doubts as to the constitutionality of the fornication statute are also impelled by this Court's development of a constitutionally mandated "zone" of privacy protecting individuals from unwarranted governmental intrusion into matters of intimate personal and family concern. It is now settled that the right of privacy guaranteed under the Fourteenth Amendment has an analogue in our State Constitution, *In re Quinlan*, supra, 355 A.2d 647. Although the scope of this State right is not necessarily broader in all respects, the lack of constraints imposed by considerations of federalism permits this Court to demand stronger and more persuasive showings of a public interest in allowing the State to prohibit sexual practices than would be required by the United States Supreme Court.

Yet our inquiry cannot end here. Having found that the statute impinges upon the fundamental right of privacy, we must go on to consider whether that impingement can be justified by some compelling state interest. In an attempt to justify the statute's infringement of protected rights, the State cites its interests in preventing venereal disease and an increase in the number of illegitimate children, and in protecting the marital relationship and public morals by preventing illicit sex.

Perhaps the strongest reason favoring the law is its supposed relationship to the furtherance of the State's salutary goal of preventing venereal disease. We do not question the State's compelling interest in preventing the spread of such diseases. Nor do we dispute the power of the State to regulate activities which may adversely affect the public health. However, we do not believe that the instant enactment is properly designed with that end in mind. First, while we recognize that the statute would substantially eliminate venereal diseases if it could successfully deter people from engaging in the prohibited activity, we doubt its ability to achieve that result. The risk of contracting venereal disease is surely as great a deterrent to illicit sex as the maximum penalty under this act: a fine of $50 and/or imprisonment in jail for six months. As the Court found in *Carey*, absent highly coercive measures, it is extremely doubtful that people will be deterred from engaging in such natural activities. The Court there rejected the assertion that the threat of an unwanted pregnancy would deter persons from engaging in extramarital sexual activities. We conclude that the same is true for the possibility of being prosecuted under the fornication statute.

Furthermore, if the State's interest in the instant statute is that it is helpful in preventing venereal disease, we conclude that it is counter-productive. To the extent that any successful program to combat venereal disease must depend upon affected persons coming forward for treatment, the present statute operates as a deterrent to such voluntary participation. The fear of being prosecuted for the "crime" of fornication can only deter people from seeking such necessary treatment.

We similarly fail to comprehend how the State's interest in preventing the propagation of illegitimate children will be measurably advanced by the instant law. If the unavailability of contraceptives is not likely to deter people from engaging in illicit sexual activities, it follows that the fear of unwanted pregnancies will be equally ineffective. See *Carey*, supra.

The last two reasons offered by the State as compelling justifications for the enactment that it protects the marital relationship and the public morals by preventing illicit sex offer little additional support for the law. Whether or not abstention is likely to induce persons to marry this statute can in no way be considered a permissible means of fostering what may otherwise be a socially beneficial institution. If we were to hold that the State could attempt to coerce people into marriage, we would undermine the very independent choice which lies at the core of the right of privacy. We do not doubt the beneficent qualities of marriage, both for individuals as well as for society as a whole. Yet, we can only reiterate that decisions such as whether to marry are of a highly personal nature; they neither lend themselves to official coercion or sanction, nor fall within the regulatory power of those who are elected to govern.

This is not to suggest that the State may not regulate, in an appropriate manner, activities which are designed to further public morality. Our conclusion today extends no further than to strike down a measure which has as its objective the regulation of private morality. To the extent that N.J.S.A. 2A:110-1 serves as an official sanction of certain conceptions of desirable lifestyles, social mores or individualized beliefs, it is not an appropriate exercise of the police power.

Fornication may be abhorrent to the morals and deeply held beliefs of many persons. But any appropriate "remedy" for such conduct cannot come from legislative fiat. Private personal acts between two consenting adults are not to be lightly meddled with by the State. The right of personal autonomy is fundamental to a free society. Persons who view fornication as opprobrious conduct may seek strenuously to dissuade people from engaging in it. However, they may not inhibit such conduct through the coercive power of the criminal law. As aptly stated by Sir Francis Bacon, "(t)he sum of behavior is to retain a man's own dignity without intruding on the liberty of others." The fornication statute mocks the dignity of both offenders and enforcers. Surely police have more pressing duties than to search out adults who live a so-called "wayward" life. Surely the dignity of the law is undermined when an intimate personal activity between consenting adults can be dragged into court and "exposed." More importantly, the liberty which is the birthright of every individual suffers dearly when the State can so grossly intrude on personal autonomy.

SCHREIBER, J., concurring.

I concur in the result reached by the Court but for different reasons. The majority relies heavily on recent United States Supreme Court decisions involving the right of privacy for its conclusion that the State cannot interfere with the conduct proscribed by the New Jersey fornication statute. I believe they have misgauged the scope of those decisions. For the reasons developed below, I would rest the invalidity of this statute squarely on the ground that it conflicts with Article I, par. 1 of the New Jersey Constitution:

> All persons are by nature free and independent, and have certain natural and unalienable rights, among which are those of enjoying and defending life and liberty and of pursuing and obtaining safety and happiness.

The rights of two adults to make personal decisions are inherent in their freedom of thought. Implementation of those decisions in pursuit of their concept of happiness manifests an exercise of human liberty. Whatever else may be said of happiness, it is best obtained in a climate of free decision where each individual has the choice of consenting or not to acts or events which may affect him. Different persons have differing spiritual and moral views and so long as their personal conduct does not affect others, individuals have freedom to think, decide and act as they see fit. This freedom is an aspect of their right of privacy. Private consensual sexual conduct represents an exercise of that right.

Unlike the United States Constitution, the New Jersey Constitution is not a grant of enumerated powers, but rather a limitation of the sovereign powers of the State vested in the Legislature. That legislative authority is circumscribed by constitutional provisions, including those expressed in Article I, par. 1. Although the Legislature, in exercising its powers, may incidentally affect the natural and unalienable rights of individuals to liberty and the pursuit of happiness which have been recognized in Article I, the validity of any statute directly limiting those rights should be carefully scrutinized in light of its legislative purposes.

At common law fornication was not a crime. As explained by Blackstone:

> In the year 1650, when the ruling power found it for their interest to put on the semblance of a very extraordinary strictness and purity of morals, not only incest and wilful adultery were made capital crimes; but also the repeated act of keeping a brothel, or committing fornication, were (upon a second conviction) made felony without benefit of clergy. But at the restoration, when men, from an abhorrence of the hypocrisy of the late times, fell into a contrary extreme of licentiousness, it was not thought proper to renew a law of such unfashionable rigor. And these offences have been ever since left to the feeble coercion of the spiritual court, according to the rules of the canon law. (W. Blackstone Commentaries, Book IV, Ch. IV, *64-65)

The State rationalizes that the fornication statute is justifiable as a means of preventing the spread of venereal disease and the birth of illegitimate children. As the majority indicates, these grounds are not persuasive. More importantly, there is no evidence that this statute was intended as anything but an attempt to regulate private morality.

The Legislature cannot infringe on the rights of individuals who in private and without affecting others adopt and live by standards which differ from those of society.... It is only when the public interest would be substantially adversely affected by some exercise of the right of privacy or when the public interest would be otherwise substantially promoted by legislation that the Legislature may infringe upon that right.

CLIFFORD, J., dissenting.

I hold to the view (and as I read the other opinions, so do all the other members of this Court) that absent a compelling state interest the State may not regulate a person's private decisions which have merely incidental effects on others. In application that principle leads to the conclusion that if two people freely determine that they wish to have sexual relations in a setting inoffensive to and only incidentally affecting others, the State is without authority to interfere through the criminal process with that decision, despite the fact that such decision may be in violation of conventional community standards of morality. And that includes the grubby little exercise in self-gratification involved here.

But I think we need not, and I would not, get to the constitutional issue, at least not at this point. Rather I would call for the submission of briefs and further argument of counsel on the question whether fornication is a lesser included offense with respect to rape. For several reasons this is the desirable course.

First, there is the sound, oft-expressed principle that constitutional questions should not be reached and resolved unless absolutely imperative in the disposition of the litigation. Inasmuch as there may be another, non-constitutional basis for decision, we should heed that admonition and defer addressing the constitutional question here.

Additionally, the interests of the parties will be amply served by a decision on the narrower "lesser included offense" ground. If fornication is not included in rape, then defendant goes free; certainly Mr. Saunders' interests are fully vindicated, it being neither apparent nor even likely that he has any burning curiosity about, or yearning for resolution of, the constitutional dimensions of the controversy in which he finds himself embroiled. If fornication is a lesser included offense of the crime of rape, then that issue (not heretofore directly presented or authoritatively determined in this State) will have been put to rest, thereby clarifying the law. We would then proceed in the instant case to the constitutional question.

NOTE

In *Commonwealth v. Bonadio*, 415 A.2d 47 (Pa. 1980), the Supreme Court of Pennsylvania struck down a statute that criminalized "deviate sexual intercourse" (defined as oral or anal sex) between persons who were not husband and wife. In the course of its opinion, the court explained that:

> The threshold question in determining whether the statute in question is a valid exercise of the police power is to decide whether it benefits the public generally. The state clearly has a proper role to perform in protecting the public from inadvertent offensive displays of sexual behavior, in preventing people from being forced against their will to submit to sexual contact, in protecting minors from being sexually used by adults, and in eliminating cruelty to animals. To assure these protections, a broad range of criminal statutes constitute valid police power exercises, including proscriptions of indecent exposure, open lewdness, rape, involuntary deviate sexual intercourse, indecent assault, statutory rape, corruption of minors, and cruelty to animals. The statute in question serves none of the foregoing purposes and it is nugatory to suggest that it promotes a state interest in the institution of marriage. The Voluntary Deviate Sexual Intercourse Statute has only one possible purpose: to regulate the private

conduct of consenting adults. Such a purpose, we believe, exceeds the valid bounds of the police power while infringing the right to equal protection of the laws guaranteed by the Constitution of the United States and of this Commonwealth.

With respect to regulation of morals, the police power should properly be exercised to protect each individual's right to be free from interference in defining and pursuing his own morality but not to enforce a majority morality on persons whose conduct does not harm others. "No harm to the secular interests of the community is involved in atypical sex practice in private between consenting adult partners." MODEL PENAL CODE s 207.5 Sodomy & Related Offenses. Comment (Tent. Draft No. 4, 1955). Many issues that are considered to be matters of morals are subject to debate, and no sufficient state interest justifies legislation of norms simply because a particular belief is followed by a number of people, or even a majority. Indeed, what is considered to be "moral" changes with the times and is dependent upon societal background. Spiritual leadership, not the government, has the responsibility for striving to improve the morality of individuals. Enactment of the Voluntary Deviate Sexual Intercourse Statute, despite the fact that it provides punishment for what many believe to be abhorrent crimes against nature and perceived sins against God, is not properly in the realm of the temporal police power.

The concepts underlying our view of the police power in the case before us were once summarized as follows by the great philosopher, John Stuart Mill, in his eminent and apposite work, *On Liberty* (1859):

> (T)he sole end for which mankind are warranted, individually or collectively, in interfering with the liberty of action of any of their number, is self-protection.... (T)he only purpose for which power can be rightfully exercised over any member of a civilised community, against his will, is to prevent harm to others. His own good, either physical or moral is not a sufficient warrant. He cannot rightfully be compelled to do or forbear because it will be better for him to do so, because it will make him happier, because, in the opinions of others, to do so would be wise, or even right. These are good reasons for remonstrating with him, or reasoning with him, or persuading him, or entreating him, but not for compelling him, or visiting him with any evil in case he do otherwise. To justify that, the conduct from which it is desired to deter him must be calculated to produce evil to some one else. The only part of the conduct of any one, for which he is amenable to society, is that which concerns others. In the part which merely concerns himself, his independence is, of right, absolute. Over himself, over his own body and mind, the individual is sovereign.

COMMONWEALTH v. WASSON
842 S.W.2d 487 (Ky. 1992)

LEIBSON, J.

Appellee, Jeffrey Wasson, is charged with having solicited an undercover Lexington policeman to engage in deviate sexual intercourse. KRS 510.100 punishes "deviate sexual intercourse with another person of the same sex" as a criminal offense, and specifies "consent of the other person shall not be a defense." Nor does it matter that the act is private and involves a caring relationship rather than a commercial one. It is classified as a Class A misdemeanor.

The charges were brought in the Fayette District Court where appellee moved to dismiss the charge on grounds that a statute criminalizing deviate sexual intercourse between consenting adults of the same sex, even if the act is committed in the privacy of a home, violates the Kentucky Constitution as: (1) an invasion of a constitutionally protected right of privacy; and (2) invidious discrimination in violation of constitutionally protected rights to equal treatment.

The Fayette District Judge held the statute violated appellee's right of privacy, and dismissed the charge. The Commonwealth appealed to Fayette Circuit Court which affirmed, and further held this statute infringed upon equal protection guarantees found in the Kentucky Constitution. Once more the Commonwealth appealed, and, because of the constitutional issues involved, this Court granted transfer.

Both courts below decided the issues solely on state constitutional law grounds, and our decision today, affirming the judgments of the lower courts, is likewise so limited. Federal constitutional protection under the Equal Protection Clause was not an issue reached in the lower courts and we need not address it. *Bowers v. Hardwick*, 478 U.S. 186 (1986) held federal constitutional protection of the right of privacy was not implicated in laws penalizing homosexual sodomy. We discuss *Bowers* in particular, and federal cases in general, not in the process of construing the United States Constitution or federal law, but only where their reasoning is relevant to discussing questions of state law.

I. RIGHTS OF PRIVACY

No language specifying "rights of privacy," as such, appears in either the Federal or State Constitution. The Commonwealth recognizes such rights exist, but takes the position that, since they are implicit rather than explicit, our Court should march in lock step with the United States Supreme Court in declaring when such rights exist. Such is not the formulation of federalism. On the contrary, under our system of dual sovereignty, it is our responsibility to interpret and apply our state constitution independently. We are not bound by decisions of the United States Supreme Court when deciding whether a state statute impermissibly infringes upon individual rights guaranteed in the State Constitution so long as state constitutional protection does not fall below the federal floor, meaning the minimum guarantee of individual rights under the United States Constitution as interpreted by the United States Supreme Court.

Contrary to popular belief, the Bill of Rights in the United States Constitution represents neither the primary source nor the maximum guarantee of state constitutional liberty. Our own constitutional guarantees against the intrusive power of the state do not derive from the Federal Constitution. The adoption of the Federal Constitution in 1791 was preceded by state constitutions developed over the preceding 15 years, and, while there is, of course, overlap between state and federal constitutional guarantees of individual rights, they are by no means identical. State constitutional law documents and the writings on liberty were more the source of federal law than the child of federal law.... Thus, while we respect the decisions of the United States Supreme Court on protection of individual liberty, and on occasion we have deferred to its reasoning, certainly we are not bound to do so, and we should not do so when valid reasons lead to a different conclusion.

We are persuaded that we should not do so here for several significant reasons. First, there are both textual and structural differences between the United States Bill of Rights and our own, which suggest a different conclusion from that reached by the United States Supreme Court is more appropriate. More significantly, Kentucky has a rich and compelling tradition of recognizing and protecting individual rights from state intrusion in cases similar in nature, found in the Debates of the Kentucky Constitutional Convention of 1890 and cases from the same era when that Constitution was adopted. The judges recognizing that tradition in their opinions wrote with a direct, firsthand knowledge of the mind set of the constitutional fathers, upholding the right of privacy against the intrusive police power of the state.

Kentucky cases recognized a legally protected right of privacy based on our own constitution and common law tradition long before the United States Supreme Court first took notice of whether there were any rights of privacy inherent in the Federal Bill of Rights.... The United States Supreme Court, defining the reach of the zone of privacy in terms of federal due process analysis, limits rights of privacy to "liberties that are 'deeply rooted in this Nation's history and tradition.'" Sodomy is not one of them. *Bowers v. Hardwick* decides that rights protected by the Due Process Clauses in the Fifth and Fourteenth Amendments to the United States Constitution do not "extend a fundamental right to homosexuals to engage in acts of consensual sodomy." See 478 U.S. at 192.

Bowers decides nothing beyond this. But state constitutional jurisprudence in this area is not limited by the constraints inherent in federal due process analysis. Deviate sexual intercourse conducted in private by consenting adults is not beyond the protections of the guarantees of individual liberty in our Kentucky Constitution simply because "proscriptions against that conduct have ancient roots." 478 U.S.

at 192. Kentucky constitutional guarantees against government intrusion address substantive rights. The only reference to individual liberties in the Federal Constitution is the statement in the Preamble that one of the purposes in writing in the Constitution is to "secure the Blessings of Liberty to ourselves and our Posterity." Similarly, the Kentucky Constitution has a Preamble:

> We, the people of the Commonwealth of Kentucky, grateful to Almighty God for the civil, political and religious liberties we enjoy, and invoking the continuance of these blessings, do ordain and establish this Constitution.

But the Kentucky Constitution of 1891 does not limit the broadly stated guarantee of individual liberty to a statement in the Preamble. It amplifies the meaning of this statement of gratitude and purpose with a Bill of Rights in 26 sections, the first of which states:

> § 1. All men are, by nature, free and equal, and have certain inherent and inalienable rights, among which may be reckoned:
>
> > First: The right of enjoying and defending their lives and liberties....
>
> > Third: The right of seeking and pursuing their safety and happiness....
>
> § 2. Absolute and arbitrary power over the lives, liberty and property of freemen exists nowhere in a republic, not even in the largest majority.

[margin note: Ky Con on individual liberty]

The leading case on this subject is *Commonwealth v. Campbell*, 117 S.W. 383 (Ky. 1909). At issue was an ordinance that criminalized possession of intoxicating liquor, even for "private use." Our Court held that the Bill of Rights in the 1891 Constitution prohibited state action thus intruding upon the "inalienable rights possessed by the citizens" of Kentucky. Our Court interpreted the Kentucky Bill of Rights as defining a right of privacy, even though the constitution did not say so in that terminology:

[margin note: State case law defining "right of privacy"]

> Man in his natural state has the right to do whatever he chooses and has the power to do. When he becomes a member of organized society, under governmental regulation, he surrenders, of necessity, all of his natural right the exercise of which is, or may be, injurious to his fellow citizens. This is the price that he pays for governmental protection, but it is not within the competency of a free government to invade the sanctity of the absolute rights of the citizen any further than the direct protection of society requires.... It is not within the competency of government to invade the privacy of a citizen's life and to regulate his conduct in matters in which he alone is concerned, or to prohibit him any liberty the exercise of which will not directly injure society.... [L]et a man therefore be ever so abandoned in his principles, or vicious in his practice, provided he keeps his wickedness to himself, and does not offend against the rules of public decency, he is out of the reach of human laws.

[margin note: rule guarding privacy]

The Court concludes, at p. 387:

> The theory of our government is to allow the largest liberty to the individual commensurate with the public safety, or, as it has been otherwise expressed, that government is best which governs least. Under our institutions there is no room

for that inquisitorial and protective spirit which seeks to regulate the conduct of men in matters in themselves indifferent, and to make them conform to a standard, not of their own choosing, but the choosing of the lawgiver.

The right of privacy has been recognized as an integral part of the guarantee of liberty in our 1891 Kentucky Constitution since its inception. The *Campbell* case is overwhelming affirmation of this proposition:

> [W]e are of the opinion that it never has been within the competency of the Legislature to so restrict the liberty of this citizen, and certainly not since the adoption of the present [1891] Constitution. The Bill of Rights, which declares that among the inalienable rights possessed by the citizens is that of seeking and pursuing their safety and happiness, and that the absolute and arbitrary power over the lives, liberty, and property of freeman exists nowhere in a republic, not even in the largest majority, would be but an empty sound if the Legislature could prohibit the citizen the right of owning or drinking liquor, when in so doing he did not offend the laws of decency by being intoxicated in public...."

At the time Campbell was decided, the use of alcohol was as much an incendiary moral issue as deviate sexual behavior in private between consenting adults is today. Prohibition was the great moral issue of its time.

Nor is the Campbell case an aberration. Subsequent cases cited and followed Campbell. In *Commonwealth v. Smith*, 173 S.W. 340 (Ky. 1915), citing *Campbell*, the Court declared a statute unconstitutional that had led to Smith being arrested for drinking beer in the backroom of an office:

> The power of the state to regulate and control the conduct of a private individual is confined to those cases where his conduct injuriously affects others. With his faults or weaknesses, which he keeps to himself, and which do not operate to the detriment of others, the state as such has no concern.

The holding in Smith is that "the police power may be called into play [only] when it is reasonably necessary to protect the public health, or public morals, or public safety." The clear implication is that immorality in private which does "not operate to the detriment of others," is placed beyond the reach of state action by the guarantees of liberty in the Kentucky Constitution.

In *Hershberg v. City of Barbourville*, 133 S.W. 985 (Ky. 1911), also citing *Campbell*, the Court declared an ordinance which purported to regulate cigarette smoking in such broad terms that it could be applied to persons who smoked in the privacy of their own home "unreasonably interfere[ed] with the right of the citizen to determine for himself such personal matters."

In the area of civil law, Kentucky has been in the forefront in recognizing the right of privacy. In 1909, our Court stepped outside traditional libel law and recognized invasion of privacy as a tort in *Foster-Milburn Co. v. Chinn*, 120 S.W. 364. Then in 1927, in *Brents v. Morgan* 299 S.W. 967, our Court defined this emerging right as "the right to be left alone, that is, the right of a person to be free from unwarranted publicity, or the right to live without unwarranted interference by the public about matters with which the public is not necessarily concerned."

> The right of privacy is incident to the person and not to property.... It is considered as a natural and an absolute or pure right springing from the instincts of nature. It is of that class of rights which every human being has in his natural state and which he did not surrender by becoming a member of organized society. The fundamental rights of personal security and personal liberty include the right of privacy, the right to be left alone.... The right to enjoy life [Ky. Const., § 1, first subpart] in the way most agreeable and pleasant, and the right of privacy is nothing more than a right to live in a particular way.

In the *Campbell* case our Court quoted at length from the "great work" On Liberty of the 19th century English philosopher and economist, John Stuart Mill. We repeat the quote in part:

> The only part of the conduct of anyone, for which he is amenable to society, is that which concerns others. In the part which merely concerns himself, his independence is, of right, absolute.... The principle requires liberty of taste and pursuits; of framing the plan of our life to suit our own character; of doing as we like, subject to such consequences as may follow; without impediment from our fellow creatures, so long as what we do does not harm them, even though they should think our conduct foolish, perverse, or wrong.

[margin: JSM's harm principle]

Mill's premise is that "physical force in the form of legal penalties," i.e., criminal sanctions, should not be used as a means to improve the citizen. The majority has no moral right to dictate how everyone else should live. Public indignation, while given due weight, should be subject to the overriding test of rational and critical analysis, drawing the line at harmful consequences to others. Modern legal philosophers who follow Mill temper this test with an enlightened paternalism, permitting the law to intervene to stop self-inflicted harm such as the result of drug taking, or failure to use seat belts or crash helmets, not to enforce majoritarian or conventional morality, but because the victim of such self-inflicted harm becomes a burden on society. *[margin: Impacts of enlightened paternalism]*

[margin: How "public indignation" should be scrutinized]

Based on the *Campbell* opinion, and on the Comments of the 1891 Convention Delegates, there is little doubt but that the views of John Stuart Mill, which were then held in high esteem, provided the philosophical underpinnings for the reworking and broadening of protection of individual rights that occurs throughout the 1891 Constitution.

We have recognized protection of individual rights greater than the federal floor in a number of cases, most recently: *Ingram v. Commonwealth*, 801 S.W.2d 321 (Ky. 1990), involving protection against double jeopardy and *Dean v. Commonwealth*, 777 S.W.2d 900 (Ky. 1989), involving the right of confrontation. Perhaps the most dramatic recent example of protection of individual rights under the state Constitution

[margin bottom: Ky embraces going ahead of SCOTUS]

where the United States Supreme Court had refused to afford protection under the Federal Constitution, is *Rose v. Council for Better Educ., Inc.,* 790 S.W.2d 186 (Ky. 1989). In *Rose,* our Court recognized our Kentucky Constitution afforded individual school children from property poor districts a fundamental right to an adequate education such as provided in wealthier school districts, even though 16 years earlier the United States Supreme Court held the Federal Constitution provided no such protection in *San Antonio Independent School District v. Rodriguez,* 411 U.S. 1 (1973). The United States Supreme Court found there was no constitutional, or fundamental, right to a particular quality of education which justified invoking the Equal Protection Clause of the Fourteenth Amendment. Our Court found a duty in the Kentucky constitutional requirement that the General Assembly "provide an efficient system of common schools." Ky. Const. Sec. 183.

We view the United States Supreme Court decision in *Bowers v. Hardwick* as a misdirected application of the theory of original intent. To illustrate: as a theory of majoritarian morality, miscegenation was an offense with ancient roots. It is highly unlikely that protecting the rights of persons of different races to copulate was one of the considerations behind the Fourteenth Amendment. Nevertheless, in *Loving v. Virginia,* 388 U.S. 1 (1967), the United States Supreme Court recognized that a contemporary, enlightened interpretation of the liberty interest involved in the sexual act made its punishment constitutionally impermissible.

II. EQUAL PROTECTION

Certainly, the practice of deviate sexual intercourse violates traditional morality. But so does the same act between heterosexuals, which activity is decriminalized. Going one step further, all sexual activity between consenting adults outside of marriage violates our traditional morality. The issue here is not whether sexual activity traditionally viewed as immoral can be punished by society, but whether it can be punished solely on the basis of sexual preference.

We do not speculate on how the United States Supreme Court as presently constituted will decide whether the sexual preference of homosexuals is entitled to protection under the Equal Protection Clause of the Federal constitution. We need not speculate as to whether male and/or female homosexuals will be allowed status as a protected class if and when the United States Supreme Court confronts this issue. They are a separate and identifiable class for Kentucky constitutional law analysis because no class of persons can be discriminated against under the Kentucky Constitution. All are entitled to equal treatment, unless there is a substantial governmental interest, a rational basis, for different treatment. The statute before us is in violation of Kentucky constitutional protection in Section Three that "all men (persons), when they form a social compact, are equal," and in Section Two that "absolute and arbitrary power over the lives, liberty and property of free men (persons) exist nowhere in a republic, not even in the largest majority." We have concluded that it is "arbitrary" for the majority to criminalize sexual activity solely on the basis of majoritarian sexual preference, and that it denied "equal" treatment under the law when there is no rational basis, as this term is used and applied in our Kentucky cases.

Law m a violates EPC

The Commonwealth has tried hard to demonstrate a legitimate governmental interest justifying a distinction, but has failed. Many of the claimed justifications are simply outrageous: that "homosexuals are more promiscuous than heterosexuals, that homosexuals enjoy the company of children, and that homosexuals are more prone to engage in sex acts in public." The only proffered justification with superficial validity is that "infectious diseases are more readily transmitted by anal sodomy than by other forms of sexual copulation." But this statute is not limited to anal copulation, and this reasoning would apply to male-female anal intercourse the same as it applies to male-male intercourse. The growing number of females to whom AIDS (Acquired Immune Deficiency Syndrome) has been transmitted is stark evidence that AIDS is not only a male homosexual disease. The only medical evidence in the record before us rules out any distinction between male-male and male-female anal intercourse as a method of preventing AIDS. The act of sexual contact is not implicated, per se, whether the contact is homosexual or heterosexual. In any event, this statute was enacted in 1974 before the AIDS nightmare was upon us. It was 1982 or 1983 before AIDS was a recognized diagnostic entity.

Ct: state's args about gay people are absurd

Ct mrs states args reasoning

In the final analysis we can attribute no legislative purpose to this statute except to single out homosexuals for different treatment for indulging their sexual preference by engaging in the same activity heterosexuals are now at liberty to perform. By 1974 there had already been a sea change in societal values insofar as attaching criminal penalties to extramarital sex. The question is whether a society that no longer criminalizes adultery, fornication, or deviate sexual intercourse between heterosexuals, has a rational basis to single out homosexual acts for different treatment. Is there a rational basis for declaring this one type of sexual immorality so destructive of family values as to merit criminal punishment whereas other acts of sexual immorality which were likewise forbidden by the same religious and traditional heritage of Western civilization are now decriminalized? If there is a rational basis for different treatment it has yet to be demonstrated in this case. We need not sympathize, agree with, or even understand the sexual preference of

EP! rational basis?

homosexuals in order to recognize their right to equal treatment before the bar of criminal justice.

"Equal Justice Under Law" inscribed above the entrance to the United States Supreme Court, expresses the unique goal to which all humanity aspires. In Kentucky it is more than a mere aspiration. It is part of the "inherent and inalienable" rights protected by our Kentucky Constitution. Our protection against exercise of "arbitrary power over the...liberty...of freemen" by the General Assembly (Section Two) and our guarantee that all persons are entitled to "equal" treatment (in Section Three) forbid a special act punishing the sexual preference of homosexuals. It matters not that the same act committed by persons of the same sex is more offensive to the majority because Section Two states such "power...exists nowhere in a republic, not even in the largest majority."

The purpose of the present statute is not to protect the marital relationship against sexual activity outside of marriage, but only to punish one aspect of it while other activities similarly destructive of the marital relationship, if not more so, go unpunished. Sexual preference and not the act committed, determine criminality, and is being punished. Simply because the majority, speaking through the General Assembly, finds one type of extramarital intercourse more offensive than another, does not provide a rational basis for criminalizing the sexual preference of homosexuals.

LAMBERT, J., dissenting. No specific protections on sex in Con

The issue here is not whether private homosexual conduct should be allowed or prohibited. The only question properly before this Court is whether the Constitution of Kentucky denies the legislative branch a right to prohibit such conduct. Nothing in the majority opinion demonstrates such a limitation on legislative prerogative.

To justify its view that private homosexual conduct is protected by the Constitution of Kentucky, the majority has found it necessary to disregard virtually all of recorded history, the teachings of the religions most influential on Western Civilization, the debates of the delegates to the Constitutional Convention, and the text of the Constitution itself. Rather than amounting to a decision based upon precedent as is suggested, this decision reflects the value judgment of the majority and its view that public law has no right to prohibit the conduct at issue here.... The history and traditions of this Commonwealth are fully in accord with the Biblical, historical and common law view. Since at least 1860, sodomy has been a criminal offense in Kentucky and this fact was well known to the delegates at the time of the 1890 Constitutional Convention.

Embracing "state constitutionalism," a practice in vogue among many state courts as a means of rejecting the leadership of the Supreme Court of the United States, the majority has declared its independence from even the influence of this nation's highest court. The majority cannot, however, escape the logic and scholarship of *Bowers* which reached the conclusion that nothing in the Due Process Clause of the United States Constitution prevented a state from punishing sodomy as a crime. While I do not advocate the view that state courts should march in lock step with the Supreme Court of the United States, on those occasions when state courts depart from that Court's reasoned interpretations, it should be for compelling reasons, usually text or tradition, and only in clearly distinguishable circumstances, none of which are present here.

Perhaps the greatest mischief to be found in the majority opinion is in its discovery of a constitutional right which lacks any textual support. The majority has referred generally to the twenty-six sections in the Bill of Rights of the Kentucky Constitution and quoted § 1 First and Third and § 2. None of the sections cited or quoted contain an inkling of reference to rights of privacy or sexual freedom of any kind. This is conceded by the majority as follows: "No language specifying 'rights of privacy,' as such, appears in either the Federal or State Constitution." The majority opinion is a departure from the accepted methodology of constitutional analysis which requires that text be the beginning point. The majority reasons that differences between the text of the Kentucky Constitution and the United States Constitution free this Court from federal influence, but it fails to explain its discovery of the rights announced here in the absence of any textual basis. This is a dangerous practice. When judges free themselves of constitutional text, their values and notions of morality are given free rein and they, not the Constitution, become the supreme law.

The major premise in the majority opinion is that the Constitution forbids any legal restriction upon the private conduct of adults unless it can be shown that such conduct is harmful to another. This view represents the essence of the philosophy of John Stuart Mill in his essay *On Liberty*. While espousing such a view, however, Mill recognized the difficulty of distinguishing that part of a person's life which affected only himself from that which affected others. He recognized that one who by deleterious vices harmed himself indirectly harmed others and that society suffered indirect harm by the mere knowledge of immoral conduct. Nevertheless, Mill clung to his philosophy by insisting that society was without *power* to punish gambling or drunkenness. He made a ringing defense of the right of persons so disposed to practice polygamy.

Unfortunately for the purposes of the majority, the philosophy of Mill and the views contained in the Campbell case, if logically applied, would necessarily result in the eradication of numerous other criminal statutes. For example, if majoritarian morality is without a role in the formulation of criminal law and the only standard is harm to another, all laws proscribing the possession and use of dangerous or narcotic drugs would fall. Likewise, incest statutes which proscribe sexual intercourse between persons of close kinship regardless of age or consent would be rendered invalid. Laws prohibiting cruelty to animals, the abuse of dead human bodies, suicide and polygamy would be held unconstitutional. Despite the majority's disingenuous departure from Mill based on "an enlightened paternalism" to prevent self-inflicted harm, many prevailing criminal statutes would nevertheless fail the "harm to another" test. While the majority of this Court manifestly sees the proposition otherwise, the Supreme Court of the United States has addressed the role of morality as a rationale to support criminal law and found no impediment.

> The law, however, is constantly based on notions of morality, and if all laws representing essentially moral choices are to be invalidated under the Due Process Clause, the courts will be very busy indeed. *Bowers*, 478 U.S. at 196.

From my study of this case, I have concluded that the privacy right found in the Constitution of Kentucky does not apply to claimed rights not remotely envisioned by the delegates to the Constitutional Convention or reasonably emerging from our history and traditions. As such, the right to determine whether sodomy should be a criminal offense belongs to the people through their elected representatives. We should not deprive the people of that right. As the majority has observed, many states have already decriminalized consensual sodomy. Appellee should take his case to the Kentucky General Assembly and let that branch of government say whether the crime shall remain or be abolished.

To resolve the equal protection issue, one must first review the statute, KRS 510.100. This Act is not limited in its application to persons who consider themselves homosexual nor is it limited to the male or female gender. Any person who engages in deviate sexual intercourse with another person of the same sex is in violation. The statute prohibits conduct and says nothing of the sexual preference or gender of the violator)...There is nothing in the statute by which persons are classified and certainly nothing which accords unequal treatment to persons comprising a recognizable class on factors such as race, gender or ethnic origin.

As persons who engage in homosexual sodomy have never been held to constitute a suspect classification, to be upheld, the statute at issue need only satisfy the lowest level of judicial scrutiny and demonstrate that it bears a rational relationship to a legitimate legislative objective. Protection of public "health, safety and morality" was held to be such an objective in *Bosworth v. City of Lexington*, 125 S.W.2d 995, (Ky. 1930).

I conclude with the view that this Court has strayed from its role of interpreting the Constitution and undertaken to make social policy. This decision is a vast extension of judicial power by which four Justices of this Court have overridden the will of the Legislative and Executive branches of Kentucky State Government and denied the people any say in this important social issue. No decision cited by the majority has ever gone so far and certainly none comes to mind. Where this slippery slope may lead is anybody's guess, but the ramifications of this decision will surely be profound.

NOTE

The majority opinion in *Wasson* discusses and rejects *Bowers v. Hardwick*, 478 U.S. 186 (1986), in which the United States Supreme Court upheld the constitutionality of a Georgia criminal law prohibiting sodomy and ruled that the Due Process Clause of the Federal Constitution does not protect the right of a consenting adult to engage in homosexual conduct. *Bowers* was decided by a 5–4 vote and was overruled seventeen years later in *Lawrence v. Texas*, 539 U.S. 558 (2003). In the seventeen year interim between the two cases, courts in five states—one of which was Georgia—rejected both the reasoning and result of *Bowers* in ruling that criminal laws prohibiting adult consensual homosexual activity violated state constitutional provisions protecting the right of privacy. The first decision of a state supreme court to do so was *Wasson*. The five state decisions rejecting *Bowers* were acknowledged by the Supreme Court in *Lawrence* and apparently played some part in convincing the high Court to overrule *Bowers*. *See* Jeffrey M. Shaman, EQUALITY AND LIBERTY IN THE GOLDEN AGE OF STATE CONSTITUTIONAL LAW 215–22 (2008).

D. CIVIL UNION AND MARRIAGE

BAKER v. STATE
744 A.2d 864 (Vt. 1999)

AMESTOY, C.J.

May the State of Vermont exclude same-sex couples from the benefits and protections that its laws provide to opposite-sex married couples? That is the fundamental question we address in this appeal, a question that the Court well knows arouses deeply-felt religious, moral, and political beliefs. Our constitutional responsibility to consider the legal merits of issues properly before us provides no exception for the controversial case. The issue before the Court, moreover, does not turn on the religious or moral debate over intimate same-sex relationships, but rather on the statutory and constitutional basis for the exclusion of same-sex couples from the secular benefits and protections offered married couples.

The Common Benefits Clause of the Vermont Constitution [Chapter I, Article 7] reads:

> That government is, or ought to be, instituted for the common benefit, protection, and security of the people, nation, or community, and not for the particular emolument or advantage of any single person, family, or set of persons, who are a part only of that community....

[Under the Clause,] plaintiffs may not be deprived of the statutory benefits and protections afforded persons of the opposite sex who choose to marry. We hold that the State is constitutionally required to extend to same-sex couples the common benefits and protections that flow from marriage under Vermont law. Whether this ultimately takes the form of inclusion within the marriage laws themselves or a parallel "domestic partnership" system or some equivalent statutory alternative, rests with the Legislature. Whatever system is chosen, however, must conform with the constitutional imperative to afford all Vermonters the common benefit, protection, and security of the law.

Plaintiffs are three same-sex couples who have lived together in committed relationships for periods ranging from four to twenty-five years. Two of the couples have raised children together. Each couple applied for a marriage license from their respective town clerk, and each was refused a license as ineligible under the applicable state marriage laws.

Assuming that the marriage statutes preclude their eligibility for a marriage license, plaintiffs contend that the exclusion violates their right to the common benefit and protection of the law guaranteed by Chapter I, Article 7 of the Vermont Constitution. They note that in denying them access to a civil marriage license, the law effectively excludes them from a broad array of legal benefits and protections incident to the marital relation, including access to a spouse's medical, life, and disability insurance, hospital visitation and other medical decisionmaking privileges, spousal support, intestate succession, homestead protections, and many other statutory protections.

In considering this issue, it is important to emphasize at the outset that it is the Common Benefits Clause of the Vermont Constitution we are construing, rather than its counterpart, the Equal Protection Clause of the Fourteenth Amendment to the United States Constitution. It is altogether fitting and proper that we do so. Vermont's constitutional commitment to equal rights was the product of the successful effort to create an independent republic and a fundamental charter of government, the Constitution of 1777, both of which preceded the adoption of the Fourteenth Amendment by nearly a century. As we explained in *State v. Badger*, 450 A.2d 336, 347 (Vt. 1982), "our constitution is not a mere reflection of the federal charter. Historically and textually, it differs from the United States Constitution. It predates the federal counterpart, as it extends back to Vermont's days as an independent republic. It is an independent authority, and Vermont's fundamental law."

The words of the Common Benefits Clause are revealing. While they do not, to be sure, set forth a fully-formed standard of analysis for determining the constitutionality of a given statute, they do express broad principles which usefully inform that analysis. Chief among these is the principle of inclusion. As explained more fully in the discussion that follows, the specific proscription against governmental favoritism toward not only groups or "set[s] of men," but also toward any particular "family" or "single man," underscores the framers' resentment of political preference of any kind. The affirmative right to the "common benefits and protections" of government and the corollary proscription of favoritism in the distribution of public "emoluments and advantages" reflect the framers' overarching objective "not only that everyone enjoy equality before the law or have an equal voice in government but also that everyone have *an equal share in the fruits of the common enterprise.*" W. Adams, *The First American Constitutions* 188 (1980) (emphasis added). Thus, at its core the Common Benefits Clause expressed a vision of government that afforded every Vermonter its benefit and protection and provided no Vermonter particular advantage.

We must ultimately ascertain whether the omission of a part of the community from the benefit, protection and security of the challenged law bears a reasonable and just relation to the governmental purpose. Consistent with the core presumption of inclusion, factors to be considered in this determination may include: (1) the significance of the benefits and protections of the challenged law; (2) whether the omission of members of the community from the benefits and protections of the challenged law promotes the government's stated goals; and (3) whether the classification is significantly underinclusive or overinclusive.

The principal purpose the State advances in support of excluding same-sex couples from the legal benefits of marriage is the government's interest in "furthering the link between procreation and child rearing." The State has a strong interest, it argues, in promoting a permanent commitment between couples who have children to ensure that their offspring are considered legitimate and receive ongoing parental support. The State contends, further, that the Legislature could reasonably believe that sanctioning same-sex unions "would diminish society's perception of the link between procreation and child rearing...[and] advance the notion that fathers or mothers...are mere surplusage to the functions of procreation and child rearing." The State argues that since same-sex couples cannot conceive a child on their own, state-sanctioned same-sex unions "could be seen by the Legislature to separate further the connection

between procreation and parental responsibilities for raising children."
Hence, the Legislature is justified, the State concludes, "in using the
marriage statutes to send a public message that procreation and child
rearing are intertwined."

Do these concerns represent valid public interests that are reasonably
furthered by the exclusion of same-sex couples from the benefits and
protections that flow from the marital relation? It is beyond dispute that
the State has a legitimate and long-standing interest in promoting a
permanent commitment between couples for the security of their children.
It is equally undeniable that the State's interest has been advanced by
extending formal public sanction and protection to the union, or marriage,
of those couples considered capable of having children, i.e., men and
women. And there is no doubt that the overwhelming majority of births
today continue to result from natural conception between one man and one
woman.

It is equally undisputed that many opposite-sex couples marry for
reasons unrelated to procreation, that some of these couples never intend
to have children, and that others are incapable of having children.
(Therefore, if the purpose of the statutory exclusion of same-sex couples is
to "further [ ] the link between procreation and child rearing," it is
significantly underinclusive. The law extends the benefits and protections
of marriage to many persons with no logical connection to the stated
governmental goal.

Furthermore, while accurate statistics are difficult to obtain, there is no
dispute that a significant number of children today are actually being
raised by same-sex parents, and that increasing numbers of children are
being conceived by such parents through a variety of assisted-reproductive
techniques. See D. Flaks, et al., Lesbians Choosing Motherhood: A
Comparative Study of Lesbian and Heterosexual Parents and Their
Children, 31 Dev. Psychol. 105, 105 (1995) (citing estimates that between
1.5 and 5 million lesbian mothers resided with their children in United
States between 1989 and 1990, and that thousands of lesbian mothers have
chosen motherhood through donor insemination or adoption); G. Green &
F. Bozett, *Lesbian Mothers and Gay Fathers*, in Homosexuality: Research
Implications for Public Policy 197, 198 (J. Gonsiorek et al. eds., 1991)
(estimating that numbers of children of either gay fathers or lesbian
mothers range between six and fourteen million); C. Patterson, *Children of
the Lesbian Baby Boom: Behavioral Adjustment, Self-Concepts, and Sex
Role Identity*, in Lesbian and Gay Psychology (B. Greene et al. eds., 1994)
(observing that although precise estimates are difficult, number of families
with lesbian mothers is growing); E. Shapiro & L. Schultz, *Single-Sex
Families: The Impact of Birth Innovations Upon Traditional Family
Notions*, 24 J. Fam. L. 271, 281 (1985) ("[I]t is a fact that children are

being born to single-sex families on a biological basis, and that they are being so born in considerable numbers.").

Thus, with or without the marriage sanction, the reality today is that increasing numbers of same-sex couples are employing increasingly efficient assisted-reproductive techniques to conceive and raise children. The Vermont Legislature has not only recognized this reality, but has acted affirmatively to remove legal barriers so that same-sex couples may legally adopt and rear the children conceived through such efforts. See 15A V.S.A. § 1-102(b) (allowing partner of biological parent to adopt if in child's best interest without reference to sex). The state has also acted to expand the domestic relations laws to safeguard the interests of same-sex parents and their children when such couples terminate their domestic relationship. See 15A V.S.A. § 1-112 (vesting family court with jurisdiction over parental rights and responsibilities, parent-child contact, and child support when unmarried persons who have adopted minor child "terminate their domestic relationship").

Therefore, to the extent that the state's purpose in licensing civil marriage was, and is, to legitimize children and provide for their security, the statutes plainly exclude many same-sex couples who are no different from opposite-sex couples with respect to these objectives. If anything, the exclusion of same-sex couples from the legal protections incident to marriage exposes their children to the precise risks that the State argues the marriage laws are designed to secure against. In short, the marital exclusion treats persons who are similarly situated for purposes of the law, differently.

The State also argues that because same-sex couples cannot conceive a child on their own, their exclusion promotes a "perception of the link between procreation and child rearing," and that to discard it would "advance the notion that mothers and fathers…are mere surplusage to the functions of procreation and child rearing" Apart from the bare assertion, the State offers no persuasive reasoning to support these claims. Indeed, it is undisputed that most of those who utilize nontraditional means of conception are infertile married couples, and that many assisted-reproductive techniques involve only one of the married partner's genetic material, the other being supplied by a third party through sperm, egg, or embryo donation. The State does not suggest that the use of these technologies undermines a married couple's sense of parental responsibility, or fosters the perception that they are "mere surplusage" to the conception and parenting of the child so conceived. Nor does it even remotely suggest that access to such techniques ought to be restricted as a matter of public policy to "send a public message that procreation and child rearing are intertwined." Accordingly, there is no reasonable basis to conclude that a same-sex couple's use of the same technologies would undermine the bonds of parenthood, or society's perception of parenthood.

The question thus becomes whether the exclusion of a relatively small but significant number of otherwise qualified same-sex couples from the same legal benefits and protections afforded their opposite-sex counterparts contravenes the mandates of Article 7. We turn, accordingly, from the principal justifications advanced by the State to the interests asserted by plaintiffs.

As noted, in determining whether a statutory exclusion reasonably relates to the governmental purpose it is appropriate to consider the history and significance of the benefits denied. What do these considerations reveal about the benefits and protections at issue here? In *Loving v. Virginia*, 388 U.S. 1, 12 (1967), the United States Supreme Court, striking down Virginia's anti-miscegenation law, observed that "[t]he freedom to marry has long been recognized as one of the vital personal rights." The Court's point was clear; access to a civil marriage license and the multitude of legal benefits, protections, and obligations that flow from it significantly enhance the quality of life in our society.

The Supreme Court's observations in *Loving* merely acknowledged what many states, including Vermont, had long recognized. One hundred thirty-seven years before *Loving*, this Court characterized the reciprocal rights and responsibilities flowing from the marriage laws as "the natural rights of human nature." See *Overseers of the Poor*, 2 Vt. 159. Decisions in other New England states noted the unique legal and economic ramifications flowing from the marriage relation. See, e.g., *Adams v. Palmer*, 51 Me. 480, 485 (1863) ("it establishes fundamental and most important domestic relations"). Early decisions recognized that a marriage contract, although similar to other civil agreements, represents much more because once formed, the law imposes a variety of obligations, protections, and benefits. As the Maine Supreme Judicial Court observed, the rights and obligations of marriage rest not upon contract, "but upon the general law of the State, statutory or common, which defines and prescribes those rights, duties and obligations. They are of law, not of contract." See id. at 483; see also *Ditson v. Ditson*, 4 R.I. 87, 105 (1856) (marriage transcends contract because "it gives rights, and imposes duties and restrictions upon the parties to it"). In short, the marriage laws transform a private agreement into a source of significant public benefits and protections.

While the laws relating to marriage have undergone many changes during the last century, largely toward the goal of equalizing the status of husbands and wives, the benefits of marriage have not diminished in value. On the contrary, the benefits and protections incident to a marriage

license under Vermont law have never been greater. They include, for
example, the right to receive a portion of the estate of a spouse who dies
intestate and protection against disinheritance through elective share
provisions, under 14 V.S.A. §§ 401-404, 551; preference in being
appointed as the personal representative of a spouse who dies intestate,
under 14 V.S.A. § 903; the right to bring a lawsuit for the wrongful death
of a spouse, under 14 V.S.A. § 1492; the right to bring an action for loss of
consortium, under 12 V.S.A. § 5431; the right to workers' compensation
survivor benefits under 21 V.S.A. § 632; the right to spousal benefits
statutorily guaranteed to public employees, including health, life,
disability, and accident insurance, under 3 V.S.A. § 631; the opportunity
to be covered as a spouse under group life insurance policies issued to an
employee, under 8 V.S.A. § 3811; the opportunity to be covered as the
insured's spouse under an individual health insurance policy, under 8
V.S.A. § 4063; the right to claim an evidentiary privilege for marital
communications, under V.R.E. 504; homestead rights and protections,
under 27 V.S.A. §§ 105-108, 141-142; the presumption of joint ownership
of property and the concomitant right of survivorship, under 27 V.S.A. §
2; hospital visitation and other rights incident to the medical treatment of a
family member, under 18 V.S.A. § 1852; and the right to receive, and the
obligation to provide, spousal support, maintenance, and property division
in the event of separation or divorce, under 15 V.S.A. §§ 751-752.

While other statutes could be added to this list, the point is clear. The
legal benefits and protections flowing from a marriage license are of such
significance that any statutory exclusion must necessarily be grounded on
public concerns of sufficient weight, cogency, and authority that the
justice of the deprivation cannot seriously be questioned. Considered in
light of the extreme logical disjunction between the classification and the
stated purposes of the law-protecting children and "furthering the link
between procreation and child rearing"-the exclusion falls substantially
short of this standard. The laudable governmental goal of promoting a
commitment between married couples to promote the security of their
children and the community as a whole provides no reasonable basis for
denying the legal benefits and protections of marriage to same-sex
couples, who are no differently situated with respect to this goal than their
opposite-sex counterparts. Promoting a link between procreation and
childrearing similarly fails to support the exclusion. We turn, accordingly,
to the remaining interests identified by the State in support of the statutory
exclusion.

The State asserts that a number of additional rationales could support a
legislative decision to exclude same-sex partners from the statutory
benefits and protections of marriage. The most substantive of the State's
remaining claims relates to the issue of childrearing. It is conceivable that

the Legislature could conclude that opposite-sex partners offer advantages in this area, although we note that child-development experts disagree and the answer is decidedly uncertain. The argument, however, contains a more fundamental flaw, and that is the Legislature's endorsement of a policy diametrically at odds with the State's claim. In 1996, the Vermont General Assembly enacted, and the Governor signed, a law removing all prior legal barriers to the adoption of children by same-sex couples. At the same time, the Legislature provided additional legal protections in the form of court-ordered child support and parent-child contact in the event that same-sex parents dissolved their "domestic relationship." In light of these express policy choices, the State's arguments that Vermont public policy favors opposite-sex over same-sex parents or disfavors the use of artificial reproductive technologies are patently without substance.

Finally, it is suggested that the long history of official intolerance of intimate same-sex relationships cannot be reconciled with an interpretation of Article 7 that would give state-sanctioned benefits and protection to individuals of the same sex who commit to a permanent domestic relationship. We find the argument to be unpersuasive for several reasons. First, to the extent that state action historically has been motivated by an animus against a class, that history cannot provide a legitimate basis for continued unequal application of the law. See *MacCallum*, 165 Vt. at 459-60, 686 A.2d at 939 (holding that although adopted persons had "historically been a target of discrimination," social prejudices failed to support their continued exclusion from intestacy law). As we observed recently in *Brigham*, 166 Vt. at 267, 692 A.2d at 396, "equal protection of the laws cannot be limited by eighteenth-century standards." Second, whatever claim may be made in light of the undeniable fact that federal and state statutes-including those in Vermont-have historically disfavored same-sex relationships, more recent legislation plainly undermines the contention. See, e.g., Laws of Vermont, 1977, No. 51, §§ 2, 3 (repealing former § 2603 of Title 13, which criminalized fellatio). In 1992, Vermont was one of the first states to enact statewide legislation prohibiting discrimination in employment, housing, and other services based on sexual orientation. See 21 V.S.A. § 495 (employment); 9 V.S.A. § 4503 (housing); 8 V.S.A. § 4724 (insurance); 9 V.S.A. § 4502 (public accommodations). Sexual orientation is among the categories specifically protected against hate-motivated crimes in Vermont. See 13 V.S.A. § 1455. Furthermore, as noted earlier, recent enactments of the General Assembly have removed barriers to adoption by same-sex couples, and have extended legal rights and protections to such couples who dissolve their "domestic relationship." See 15A V.S.A. §§ 1-102, 1-112.

Thus, viewed in the light of history, logic, and experience, we conclude that none of the interests asserted by the State provides a reasonable and just basis for the continued exclusion of same-sex couples from the benefits incident to a civil marriage license under Vermont law. Accordingly, in the faith that a case beyond the imagining of the framers of our Constitution may, nevertheless, be safely anchored in the values that infused it, we find a constitutional obligation to extend to plaintiffs the common benefit, protection, and security that Vermont law provides opposite-sex married couples. It remains only to determine the appropriate means and scope of relief compelled by this constitutional mandate.

We hold only that plaintiffs are entitled under Chapter I, Article 7, of the Vermont Constitution to obtain the same benefits and protections afforded by Vermont law to married opposite-sex couples. We do not purport to infringe upon the prerogatives of the Legislature to craft an appropriate means of addressing this constitutional mandate, other than to note that the record here refers to a number of potentially constitutional statutory schemes from other jurisdictions. These include what are typically referred to as "domestic partnership" or "registered partnership" acts, which generally establish an alternative legal status to marriage for same-sex couples, impose similar formal requirements and limitations, create a parallel licensing or registration scheme, and extend all or most of the same rights and obligations provided by the law to married partners. We do not intend specifically to endorse any one or all of the referenced acts, particularly in view of the significant benefits omitted from several of the laws.

Further, while the State's prediction of "destabilization" cannot be a ground for denying relief, it is not altogether irrelevant. A sudden change in the marriage laws or the statutory benefits traditionally incidental to marriage may have disruptive and unforeseen consequences. Absent legislative guidelines defining the status and rights of same-sex couples, consistent with constitutional requirements, uncertainty and confusion could result. Therefore, we hold that the current statutory scheme shall remain in effect for a reasonable period of time to enable the Legislature to consider and enact implementing legislation in an orderly and expeditious fashion.

The judgment of the superior court upholding the constitutionality of the Vermont marriage statutes under Chapter I, Article 7 of the Vermont Constitution is reversed. The effect of the Court's decision is suspended, and jurisdiction is retained in this Court, to permit the Legislature to consider and enact legislation consistent with the constitutional mandate described herein.

JOHNSON, J., concurring in part and dissenting in part.

I concur with the majority's holding, but I respectfully dissent from its novel and truncated remedy, which in my view abdicates this Court's constitutional duty to redress violations of constitutional rights. I would grant the requested relief and enjoin defendants from denying plaintiffs a marriage license based solely on the sex of the applicants.

In 1948, when the California Supreme Court struck down a state law prohibiting the issuance of a license authorizing interracial marriages, the court did not suspend its judgment to allow the legislature an opportunity to enact a separate licensing scheme for interracial marriages. See *Perez v. Lippold*, 198 P.2d 17, 29 (Calif. 1948) (granting writ of mandamus compelling county clerk to issue certificate of registry). Indeed, such a mandate in that context would be unfathomable to us today. Here, as in *Perez*, we have held that the State has unconstitutionally discriminated against plaintiffs, thereby depriving them of civil rights to which they are entitled. Like the Hawaii Circuit Court in *Baehr v. Miike*, No. 1996 WL 694235, (Haw.Cir.Ct., Dec. 3, 1996), which rejected the State's reasons for excluding same-sex couples from marriage, we should simply enjoin the State from denying marriage licenses to plaintiffs based on sex or sexual orientation. That remedy would provide prompt and complete relief to plaintiffs and create reliable expectations that would stabilize the legal rights and duties of all couples.

During the civil rights movement of the 1960's, state and local governments defended segregation or gradual desegregation on the grounds that mixing the races would lead to interracial disturbances. The Supreme Court's "compelling answer" to that contention was "that constitutional rights may not be denied simply because of hostility to their assertion or exercise." See *Watson*, 373 U.S. at 535. Here, too, we should not relinquish our duty to redress the unconstitutional discrimination that we have found merely because of "personal speculations" or "vague disquietudes." *Id.* at 536. While the laudatory goals of preserving institutional credibility and public confidence in our government may require elected bodies to wait for changing attitudes concerning public morals, those same goals require courts to act independently and decisively to protect civil rights guaranteed by our Constitution.

In our system of government, civil rights violations are remedied by courts, not because we issue "Holy Writ" or because we are "the only repository of wisdom." It is because the courts "must ultimately define and defend individual rights against government in terms independent of consensus or majority will." L. Tribe, *American Constitutional Law* § 15.3, at 896 (1978). Today's decision, which is little more than a declaration of rights, abdicates that responsibility....

This case is undoubtedly one of the most controversial ever to come before this Court. Newspaper, radio and television media have disclosed widespread public interest in its outcome, as well as the full spectrum of opinion as to what that outcome should be and what its ramifications may be for our society as a whole. One line of opinion contends that this is an issue that ought to be decided only by the most broadly democratic of our governmental institutions, the Legislature, and that the small group of men and women comprising this Court has no business deciding an issue of such enormous moment. For better or for worse, however, this is simply not so. This case came before us because citizens of the state invoked their constitutional right to seek redress through the judicial process of a perceived deprivation under state law. The Vermont Constitution does not permit the courts to decline to adjudicate a matter because its subject is controversial, or because the outcome may be deeply offensive to the strongly held beliefs of many of our citizens. We do not have, as does the Supreme Court of the United States, certiorari jurisdiction, which allows that Court, in its sole discretion, to decline to hear almost any case. To the contrary, if a case has been brought before us, and if the established procedures have been followed, as they were here, we must hear and decide it. *State courts can't choose cases, doesn't mean they should be cautious in decisions*

Moreover, we must decide the case on legal grounds. However much history, sociology, religious belief, personal experience or other considerations may inform our individual or collective deliberations, we must decide this case, and all cases, on the basis of our understanding of the law, and the law alone. This must be the true and constant effort of every member of the judiciary. That effort, needless to say, is not a guarantee of infallibility, nor even an assurance of wisdom. It is, however, the fulfillment of our pledge of office.

NOTES

1. In response to the decision in *Baker*, the legislature of Vermont adopted a civil union law granting comprehensive legal benefits (corresponding to marriage rights) to same-sex couples. Ten years later, in 2009 the legislature enacted a law authorizing same-sex marriage, thereby making Vermont the first state to legalize same-sex marriage by statutory enactment without being required to do so by a court ruling. Following the decision in *Baker*, a number of states enacted laws authorizing same-sex civil unions.

2. The opinion in *Baker* mentions *Baehr v. Miike*, No. 1996 WL 694235, (Haw.Cir.Ct., Dec. 3, 1996), a lower court decision ruling that a law limiting marriage to opposite-sex couples violated the Hawaii equal protection clause. Prior to that ruling, the Supreme Court of Hawaii had held that the law in question was presumptively unconstitutional unless the state could show that it was supported by a compelling state interest. *Baehr v. Lewin*, 852 P.2d 44 (Haw. 1993). Upon remand, the circuit court concluded that the law was not supported by a compelling state interest

and therefore was unconstitutional. However, that ruling was superseded by an amendment to the Hawaii Constitution providing that the legislature shall have the power to reserve marriage to opposite-sex couples. Haw. Const. art. I, § 23.

GOODRIDGE v. DEPARTMENT OF PUBLIC HEALTH
798 N.E.2d 941 (Mass. 2003)

MARSHALL, C.J.

Marriage is a vital social institution. The exclusive commitment of two individuals to each other nurtures love and mutual support; it brings stability to our society. For those who choose to marry, and for their children, marriage provides an abundance of legal, financial, and social benefits. In return it imposes weighty legal, financial, and social obligations. The question before us is whether, consistent with the Massachusetts Constitution, the Commonwealth may deny the protections, benefits, and obligations conferred by civil marriage to two individuals of the same sex who wish to marry. We conclude that it may not. The Massachusetts Constitution affirms the dignity and equality of all individuals. It forbids the creation of second-class citizens. In reaching our conclusion we have given full deference to the arguments made by the Commonwealth. But it has failed to identify any constitutionally adequate reason for denying civil marriage to same-sex couples.

We are mindful that our decision marks a change in the history of our marriage law. Many people hold deep-seated religious, moral, and ethical convictions that marriage should be limited to the union of one man and one woman, and that homosexual conduct is immoral. Many hold equally strong religious, moral, and ethical convictions that same-sex couples are entitled to be married, and that homosexual persons should be treated no differently than their heterosexual neighbors. Neither view answers the question before us. Our concern is with the Massachusetts Constitution as a charter of governance for every person properly within its reach. "Our obligation is to define the liberty of all, not to mandate our own moral code." *Lawrence v. Texas*, 123 S.Ct. 2472, 2480 (2003) quoting *Planned Parenthood of Southeastern Pa. v. Casey*, 505 U.S. 833, 850, (1992).

Whether the Commonwealth may use its formidable regulatory authority to bar same-sex couples from civil marriage is a question not previously addressed by a Massachusetts appellate court. It is a question the United States Supreme Court left open as a matter of Federal law in *Lawrence*, where it was not an issue. There, the Court affirmed that the core concept of common human dignity protected by the Fourteenth Amendment to the United States Constitution precludes government intrusion into the deeply personal realms of consensual adult expressions of intimacy and one's choice of an intimate partner. The Court also reaffirmed the central role that decisions whether to marry or have children bear in shaping one's identity. *Id.* at 2481. The Massachusetts Constitution is, if anything, more protective of individual liberty and equality than the Federal Constitution; it may demand broader protection for fundamental rights; and it is less tolerant of government intrusion into the protected spheres of private life.

Barred access to the protections, benefits, and obligations of civil marriage, a person who enters into an intimate, exclusive union with another of the same sex is arbitrarily deprived of membership in one of our community's most rewarding and cherished institutions. That exclusion is incompatible with the constitutional principles of respect for individual autonomy and equality under law.

The plaintiffs are fourteen individuals from five Massachusetts counties. As of April 11, 2001, the date they filed their complaint, the plaintiffs Gloria Bailey, sixty years old, and Linda Davies, fifty-five years old, had been in a committed relationship for thirty years; the plaintiffs Maureen Brodoff, forty-nine years old, and Ellen Wade, fifty-two years old, had been in a committed relationship for twenty years and lived with their twelve year old daughter; the plaintiffs Hillary Goodridge, forty-four years old, and Julie Goodridge, forty-three years old, had been in a committed relationship for thirteen years and lived with their five year old daughter; the plaintiffs Gary Chalmers, thirty-five years old, and Richard Linnell, thirty-seven years old, had been in a committed relationship for thirteen years and lived with their eight year old daughter and Richard's mother; the plaintiffs Heidi Norton, thirty-six years old, and Gina Smith, thirty-six years old, had been in a committed relationship for eleven years and lived with their two sons, ages five years and one year; the plaintiffs Michael Horgan, forty-one years old, and Edward Balmelli, forty-one years old, had been in a committed relationship for seven years; and the plaintiffs David Wilson, fifty-seven years old, and Robert Compton, fifty-one years old, had been in a committed relationship for four years and had cared for David's mother in their home after a serious illness until she died. The plaintiffs include business executives, lawyers, an investment banker, educators, therapists, and a computer engineer. Many are active in church, community, and school groups.

The plaintiffs alleged violation of the laws of the Commonwealth, including but not limited to their rights under arts. 1, 6, 7, 10, 12, and 16, and Part II, c. 1, § 1, art. 4, of the Massachusetts Constitution.[4] The

---

[4] [7] Article 1, as amended by art. 106 of the Amendments to the Massachusetts Constitution, provides: "All people are born free and equal and have certain natural, essential and unalienable rights; among which may be reckoned the right of enjoying and

plaintiffs' claim that the marriage restriction violates the Massachusetts Constitution can be analyzed in two ways. Does it offend the Constitution's guarantees of equality before the law? Or do the liberty and due process provisions of the Massachusetts Constitution secure the plaintiffs' right to marry their chosen partner? In matters implicating marriage, family life, and the upbringing of children, the two constitutional concepts frequently overlap, as they do here. See, e.g., *M.L.B. v. S.L.J.*, 519 U.S. 102 (1996) (noting convergence of due process and equal protection principles in cases concerning parent-child relationships); *Perez v. Sharp*, 198 P.2d 17 (Cal. 1948) (analyzing statutory ban on interracial marriage as equal protection violation concerning regulation of fundamental right). Much of what we say concerning one standard applies to the other.

We begin by considering the nature of civil marriage itself. Simply put, the government creates civil marriage. In Massachusetts, civil marriage is, and since pre-Colonial days has been, precisely what its name implies: a wholly secular institution. See *Commonwealth v. Munson*, 127 Mass. 459, 460-466 (1879) (noting that "[i]n Massachusetts, from very early times, the requisites of a valid marriage have been regulated by

---

defending their lives and liberties; that of acquiring, possessing and protecting property; in fine, that of seeking and obtaining their safety and happiness. Equality under the law shall not be denied or abridged because of sex, race, color, creed or national origin."

Article 6 provides: "No man, nor corporation, or association of men, have any other title to obtain advantages, or particular and exclusive privileges, distinct from those of the community, than what arises from the consideration of services rendered to the public...."

Article 7 provides: "Government is instituted for the common good; for the protection, safety, prosperity, and happiness of the people; and not for the profit, honor, or private interest of any one man, family or class of men: Therefore the people alone have an incontestable, unalienable, and indefeasible right to institute government; and to reform, alter, or totally change the same, when their protection, safety, prosperity and happiness require it."

Article 10 provides, in relevant part: "Each individual of the society has a right to be protected by it in the enjoyment of his life, liberty and property, according to standing laws...."

Article 12 provides, in relevant part: "[N]o subject shall be...deprived of his property, immunities, or privileges, put out of the protection of the law...or deprived of his life, liberty, or estate, but by the judgment of his peers, or the law of the land."

Article 16, as amended by art. 77 of the Amendments, provides, in relevant part: "The right of free speech shall not be abridged." Part II, c. 1, § 1, art. 4, as amended by art. 112, provides, in pertinent part, that "full power and authority are hereby given and granted to the said general court, from time to time, to make, ordain, and establish all manner of wholesome and reasonable orders, laws, statutes, and ordinances, directions and instructions, either with penalties or without; so as the same be not repugnant or contrary to this constitution, as they shall judge to be for the good and welfare of this Commonwealth."

statutes of the Colony, Province, and Commonwealth," and surveying marriage statutes from 1639 through 1834). No religious ceremony has ever been required to validate a Massachusetts marriage. *Id.*

Without question, civil marriage enhances the "welfare of the community." It is a "social institution of the highest importance." Civil marriage anchors an ordered society by encouraging stable relationships over transient ones. It is central to the way the Commonwealth identifies individuals, provides for the orderly distribution of property, ensures that children and adults are cared for and supported whenever possible from private rather than public funds, and tracks important epidemiological and demographic data.

Marriage also bestows enormous private and social advantages on those who choose to marry. Civil marriage is at once a deeply personal commitment to another human being and a highly public celebration of the ideals of mutuality, companionship, intimacy, fidelity, and family. "It is an association that promotes a way of life, not causes; a harmony in living, not political faiths; a bilateral loyalty, not commercial or social projects." *Griswold v. Connecticut*, 381 U.S. 479 (1965). Because it fulfils yearnings for security, safe haven, and connection that express our common humanity, civil marriage is an esteemed institution and the decision whether and whom to marry is among life's momentous acts of self-definition.

Tangible as well as intangible benefits flow from marriage. The marriage license grants valuable property rights to those who meet the entry requirements, and who agree to what might otherwise be a burdensome degree of government regulation of their activities. The benefits accessible only by way of a marriage license are enormous, touching nearly every aspect of life and death. The department states that "hundreds of statutes" are related to marriage and to marital benefits. With no attempt to be comprehensive, we note that some of the statutory benefits conferred by the Legislature on those who enter into civil marriage include, as to property: joint Massachusetts income tax filing; tenancy by the entirety (a form of ownership that provides certain protections against creditors and allows for the automatic descent of property to the surviving spouse without probate); extension of the benefit of the homestead protection (securing up to $300,000 in equity from creditors) to one's spouse and children; automatic rights to inherit the property of a deceased spouse who does not leave a will; the rights of elective share and of dower (which allow surviving spouses certain property rights where the decedent spouse has not made adequate provision for the survivor in a will); entitlement to wages owed to a deceased employee; eligibility to continue certain businesses of a deceased spouse; the right to share the medical policy of one's spouse; thirty-nine week continuation of health coverage for the spouse of a person who is laid off or dies; preferential options under the Commonwealth's pension system; preferential benefits in the Commonwealth's medical program, MassHealth; access to veterans' spousal benefits and preferences; financial protections for spouses of certain Commonwealth employees (fire fighters, police officers, and prosecutors, among others) killed in the performance of duty; the equitable division of marital property on divorce; temporary and permanent alimony rights; the right to separate support on separation of the parties that does not result in divorce; and the right to bring claims for wrongful death and loss of consortium, and for funeral and burial expenses and punitive damages resulting from tort actions.

Exclusive marital benefits that are not directly tied to property rights include the presumptions of legitimacy and parentage of children born to a married couple; and evidentiary rights, such as the prohibition against spouses testifying against one another about their private conversations, applicable in both civil and criminal cases. Other statutory benefits of a personal nature available only to married individuals include qualification for bereavement or medical leave to care for individuals related by blood or marriage; an automatic "family member" preference to make medical decisions for an incompetent or disabled spouse who does not have a contrary health care proxy; the application of predictable rules of child custody, visitation, support, and removal out-of-State when married parents divorce; priority rights to administer the estate of a deceased spouse who dies without a will, and the requirement that a surviving spouse must consent to the appointment of any other person as administrator; and the right to interment in the lot or tomb owned by one's deceased spouse.

Where a married couple has children, their children are also directly or indirectly, but no less auspiciously, the recipients of the special legal and economic protections obtained by civil marriage. Notwithstanding the Commonwealth's strong public policy to abolish legal distinctions between marital and nonmarital children in providing for the support and care of minors, the fact remains that marital children reap a measure of family stability and economic security based on their parents' legally privileged status that is largely inaccessible, or not as readily accessible, to nonmarital children. Some of these benefits are social, such as the enhanced approval that still attends the status of being a marital child. Others are material, such as the greater ease of access to family-based State and Federal benefits that attend the presumptions of one's parentage.

It is undoubtedly for these concrete reasons, as well as for its intimately personal significance, that civil marriage has long been termed a 'civil right.' See, e.g., *Loving v. Virginia*, 388 U.S. 1 (1967) ("Marriage is one of the 'basic civil rights of man,' fundamental to our very existence and survival"), quoting *Skinner v. Oklahoma*, 316 U.S. 535, 541 (1942. The United States Supreme Court has described the right to marry as "of fundamental importance for all individuals" and as "part of the fundamental 'right of privacy' implicit in the Fourteenth Amendment's Due Process Clause." *Zablocki v. Redhail*, 434 U.S. 374 (1978). See *Loving v. Virginia, supra* ("The freedom to marry has long been recognized as one of the vital personal rights essential to the orderly pursuit of happiness by free men").

Without the right to marry—or more properly, the right to choose to marry—one is excluded from the full range of human experience and denied full protection of the laws for one's "avowed commitment to an intimate and lasting human relationship." *Baker v. State*, 744 A.2d 864 (Vt. 1999). Because civil marriage is central to the lives of individuals and the welfare of the community, our laws assiduously protect the individual's right to marry against undue government incursion. Laws may not "interfere directly and substantially with the right to marry." *Zablocki v. Redhail, supra* at 387. See *Perez v. Sharp*, 32 Cal.2d 711, 714 (1948) ("There can be no prohibition of marriage except for an important social objective and reasonable means").

For decades, indeed centuries, in much of this country (including Massachusetts) no lawful marriage was possible between white and black Americans. That long history availed not when the Supreme Court of California held in 1948 that a legislative prohibition against interracial marriage violated the due process and equality guarantees of the Fourteenth Amendment, *Perez v. Sharp*, 198 P.2d 17 (Cal. 1948), or when, nineteen years later, the United States Supreme Court also held that a statutory bar to interracial marriage violated the Fourteenth Amendment, *Loving v. Virginia*, 388 U.S. 1 (1967). As both *Perez* and *Loving* make clear, the right to marry means little if it does not include the right to marry the person of one's choice, subject to appropriate government restrictions in the interests of public health, safety, and welfare. See *Perez v. Sharp, supra* ("the essence of the right to marry is freedom to join in marriage with the person of one's choice"). In this case, as in *Perez* and *Loving*, a statute deprives individuals of access to an institution of fundamental legal, personal, and social significance—the institution of marriage—because of a single trait: skin color in *Perez* and *Loving*, sexual orientation here. As it did in *Perez* and *Loving*, history must yield to a more fully developed understanding of the invidious quality of the discrimination.[5]

---

[5] [17] Recently, the United States Supreme Court has reaffirmed that the Constitution prohibits a State from wielding its formidable power to regulate conduct in a manner that demeans basic human dignity, even though that statutory discrimination may enjoy broad

The Massachusetts Constitution protects matters of personal liberty against government incursion as zealously and often more so, than does the Federal Constitution, even where both Constitutions employ essentially the same language. That the Massachusetts Constitution is in some instances more protective of individual liberty interests than is the Federal Constitution is not surprising. Fundamental to the vigor of our Federal system of government is that "state courts are absolutely free to interpret state constitutional provisions to accord greater protection to individual rights than do similar provisions of the United States Constitution." *Arizona v. Evans*, 514 U.S. 1 (1995).

The individual liberty and equality safeguards of the Massachusetts Constitution protect both "freedom from" unwarranted government intrusion into protected spheres of life and "freedom to" partake in benefits created by the State for the common good. Both freedoms are involved here. Whether and whom to marry, how to express sexual intimacy, and whether and how to establish a family--these are among the most basic of every individual's liberty and due process rights. See, e.g., *Lawrence, supra* at 2481; *Planned Parenthood of Southeastern Pa. v. Casey*, 505 U.S. 833, 851 (1992); *Zablocki v. Redhail*, 434 U.S. 374 (1978); *Roe v. Wade*, 410 U.S. 113, 152-153 (1973); *Eisenstadt v. Baird*, 405 U.S. 438, 453 (1972); *Loving v. Virginia, supra*. And central to personal freedom and security is the assurance that the laws will apply equally to persons in similar situations. "Absolute equality before the law is a fundamental principle of our own Constitution." *Opinion of the Justices*, 98 N.E. 337 (Mass. 1912). The liberty interest in choosing whether and whom to marry would be hollow if the Commonwealth could, without sufficient justification, foreclose an individual from freely choosing the person with whom to share an exclusive commitment in the unique institution of civil marriage.

The Massachusetts Constitution requires, at a minimum, that the exercise of the State's regulatory authority not be "arbitrary or capricious." Under both the equality and liberty guarantees, regulatory authority must, at very least, serve "a legitimate purpose in a rational way"; a statute must "bear a reasonable relation to a permissible legislative objective." Any law failing to satisfy the basic standards of rationality is void.

The plaintiffs challenge the marriage statute on both equal protection and due process grounds. With respect to each such claim, we must first determine the appropriate standard of review. Where a statute implicates a

---

public support. The Court struck down a statute criminalizing sodomy. See *Lawrence, supra* at 2478 ("The liberty protected by the Constitution allows homosexual persons the right to make this choice").

fundamental right or uses a suspect classification, we employ "strict judicial scrutiny." For all other statutes, we employ the "'rational basis' test." For due process claims, rational basis analysis requires that statutes "bear[ ] a real and substantial relation to the public health, safety, morals, or some other phase of the general welfare." For equal protection challenges, the rational basis test requires that "an impartial lawmaker could logically believe that the classification would serve a legitimate public purpose that transcends the harm to the members of the disadvantaged class."

[The department argues that no fundamental right or "suspect" class is at issue here, and rational basis is the appropriate standard of review. For the reasons we explain below, we conclude that the marriage ban does not meet the rational basis test for either due process or equal protection. Because the statute does not survive rational basis review, we do not consider the plaintiffs' arguments that this case merits strict judicial scrutiny.

The department posits three legislative rationales for prohibiting same-sex couples from marrying: (1) providing a "favorable setting for procreation"; (2) ensuring the optimal setting for child rearing, which the department defines as "a two-parent family with one parent of each sex"; and (3) preserving scarce State and private financial resources. We consider each in turn.

The judge in the Superior Court endorsed the first rationale, holding that "the state's interest in regulating marriage is based on the traditional concept that marriage's primary purpose is procreation." This is incorrect. Our laws of civil marriage do not privilege procreative heterosexual intercourse between married people above every other form of adult intimacy and every other means of creating a family. General Laws c. 207 contains no requirement that the applicants for a marriage license attest to their ability or intention to conceive children by coitus. Fertility is not a condition of marriage, nor is it grounds for divorce. People who have never consummated their marriage, and never plan to, may be and stay married. See *Franklin v. Franklin*, 28 N.E. 681 (Mass. 1891) ("The consummation of a marriage by coition is not necessary to its validity"). People who cannot stir from their deathbed may marry. While it is certainly true that many, perhaps most, married couples have children together (assisted or unassisted), it is the exclusive and permanent commitment of the marriage partners to one another, not the begetting of children, that is the sine qua non of civil marriage.

Moreover, the Commonwealth affirmatively facilitates bringing children into a family regardless of whether the intended parent is married or unmarried, whether the child is adopted or born into a family, whether assistive technology was used to conceive the child, and whether the parent or her partner is heterosexual, homosexual, or bisexual. If procreation were a necessary component of civil marriage, our statutes would draw a tighter circle around the permissible bounds of nonmarital child bearing and the creation of families by noncoital means. The attempt to isolate procreation as "the source of a fundamental right to marry," 440 Mass. at 370 (Cordy, J., dissenting), overlooks the integrated way in which courts have examined the complex and overlapping realms of personal autonomy, marriage, family life, and child rearing. Our jurisprudence recognizes that, in these nuanced and fundamentally private areas of life, such a narrow focus is inappropriate.

The "marriage is procreation" argument singles out the one unbridgeable difference between same-sex and opposite-sex couples, and transforms that difference into the essence of legal marriage. Like "Amendment 2" to the Constitution of Colorado, which effectively denied homosexual persons equality under the law and full access to the political process, the marriage restriction impermissibly "identifies persons by a single trait and then denies them protection across the board." *Romer v. Evans*, 517 U.S. 620, 633, (1996). In so doing, the State's action confers an official stamp of approval on the destructive stereotype that same-sex relationships are inherently unstable and inferior to opposite-sex relationships and are not worthy of respect.

The department's first stated rationale, equating marriage with unassisted heterosexual procreation, shades imperceptibly into its second: that confining marriage to opposite-sex couples ensures that children are raised in the "optimal" setting. Protecting the welfare of children is a paramount State policy. Restricting marriage to opposite-sex couples, however, cannot plausibly further this policy. "The demographic changes of the past century make it difficult to speak of an average American family. The composition of families varies greatly from household to household." *Troxel v. Granville*, 530 U.S. 57, 63 (2000). Massachusetts has responded supportively to "the changing realities of the American family," *id.* at 64, and has moved vigorously to strengthen the modern family in its many variations. See, e.g., G.L. c. 209C (paternity statute); G.L. c. 119, § 39D (grandparent visitation statute); *Blixt v. Blixt*, 774 N.E.2d 1052 (Mass. 2002) (same); *E.N.O. v. L.M.M.*, 711 N.E.2d 886 (Mass. 1999) (de facto parent); *Youmans v. Ramos* 711 N.E.2d 165 (Mass. 1999) (same); and *Adoption of Tammy*, 619 N.E.2d 315 (Mass. 1993) (coparent adoption). Moreover, we have repudiated the common-law power of the State to provide varying levels of protection to children based on the circumstances of birth. See G.L. c. 209C (paternity statute); *Powers v. Wilkinson*, 506 N.E.2d 842 (Mass. 1987) ("Ours is an era in which logic and compassion have impelled the law toward unburdening children from the stigma and the disadvantages heretofore attendant upon the status of illegitimacy"). The "best interests of the child" standard does not turn on a parent's sexual orientation or marital status. See e.g., *Doe v. Doe*, 452 N.E.2d 293 (Mass. App. Ct. 1983) (parent's sexual orientation insufficient ground to deny custody of child in divorce action). See also *E.N.O. v. L.M.M.*, 711 N.E.2d 886 (best interests of child determined by considering child's relationship with biological and de facto same-sex parents); *Silvia v. Silvia*, 400 N.E.2d 1330 (Mass. App. Ct. 1980) (collecting support and custody statutes containing no gender distinction).

The department has offered no evidence that forbidding marriage to people of the same sex will increase the number of couples choosing to enter into opposite-sex marriages in order to have and raise children. There is thus no rational relationship between the marriage statute and the Commonwealth's proffered goal of protecting the "optimal" child rearing unit. Moreover, the department readily concedes that people in same-sex couples may be "excellent" parents. These couples (including four of the plaintiff couples) have children for the reasons others do--to love them, to care for them, to nurture them. But the task of child rearing for same-sex couples is made infinitely harder by their status as outliers to the marriage laws. While establishing the parentage of children as soon as possible is crucial to the safety and welfare of children, same-sex couples must undergo the sometimes lengthy and intrusive process of second-parent adoption to establish their joint parentage. While the enhanced income provided by marital benefits is an important source of security and stability for married couples and their children, those benefits are denied to families headed by same-sex couples. While the laws of divorce provide clear and reasonably predictable guidelines for child support, child custody, and property division on dissolution of a marriage, same-sex couples who dissolve their relationships find themselves and their children in the highly unpredictable terrain of equity jurisdiction. Given the wide range of public benefits reserved only for married couples, we do not credit the department's contention that the absence of access to civil marriage amounts to little more than an inconvenience to same-sex couples and their children. Excluding same-sex couples from civil marriage will not make children of opposite-sex marriages more secure, but it does prevent children of same-sex couples from enjoying the immeasurable advantages that flow from the assurance of "a stable family structure in which children will be reared, educated, and socialized." 440 Mass. at 381 (Cordy, J., dissenting).

No one disputes that the plaintiff couples are families, that many are parents, and that the children they are raising, like all children, need and should have the fullest opportunity to grow up in a secure, protected family unit. Similarly, no one disputes that, under the rubric of marriage, the State provides a cornucopia of substantial benefits to married parents and their children. The preferential treatment of civil marriage reflects the Legislature's conclusion that marriage "is the foremost setting for the education and socialization of children" precisely because it "encourages parents to remain committed to each other and to their children as they grow." 440 Mass. at 383, 798 N.E.2d at 996 (Cordy, J., dissenting).... It cannot be rational under our laws, and indeed it is not permitted, to penalize children by depriving them of State benefits because the State disapproves of their parents' sexual orientation.

The third rationale advanced by the department is that limiting marriage to opposite-sex couples furthers the Legislature's interest in conserving scarce State and private financial resources. The marriage restriction is rational, it argues, because the General Court logically could assume that same-sex couples are more financially independent than married couples and thus less needy of public marital benefits, such as tax advantages, or private marital benefits, such as employer-financed health plans that include spouses in their coverage.

An absolute statutory ban on same-sex marriage bears no rational relationship to the goal of economy. First, the department's conclusory generalization—that same-sex couples are less financially dependent on each other than opposite-sex couples—ignores that many same-sex couples, such as many of the plaintiffs in this case, have children and other dependents (here, aged parents) in their care. The department does not contend, nor could it, that these dependents are less needy or deserving than the dependents of married couples. Second, Massachusetts marriage laws do not condition receipt of public and private financial benefits to married individuals on a demonstration of financial dependence on each other; the benefits are available to married couples regardless of whether they mingle their finances or actually depend on each other for support.

The department suggests additional rationales for prohibiting same-sex couples from marrying, which are developed by some amici. It argues that broadening civil marriage to include same-sex couples will trivialize or destroy the institution of marriage as it has historically been fashioned. Certainly our decision today marks a significant change in the definition of marriage as it has been inherited from the common law, and understood by many societies for centuries. But it does not disturb the fundamental value of marriage in our society.

Here, the plaintiffs seek only to be married, not to undermine the institution of civil marriage. They do not want marriage abolished. They do not attack the binary nature of marriage, the consanguinity provisions, or any of the other gate-keeping provisions of the marriage licensing law. Recognizing the right of an individual to marry a person of the same sex will not diminish the validity or dignity of opposite-sex marriage, any more than recognizing the right of an individual to marry a person of a different race devalues the marriage of a person who marries someone of her own race. If anything, extending civil marriage to same-sex couples reinforces the importance of marriage to individuals and communities. That same-sex couples are willing to embrace marriage's solemn obligations of exclusivity, mutual support, and commitment to one another is a testament to the enduring place of marriage in our laws and in the human spirit.

We also reject the argument suggested by the department, and elaborated by some amici, that expanding the institution of civil marriage in Massachusetts to include same-sex couples will lead to interstate conflict. We would not presume to dictate how another State should respond to today's decision. But neither should considerations of comity prevent us from according Massachusetts residents the full measure of protection available under the Massachusetts Constitution. The genius of our Federal system is that each State's Constitution has vitality specific to its own traditions, and that, subject to the minimum requirements of the Fourteenth Amendment, each State is free to address difficult issues of individual liberty in the manner its own Constitution demands.

Several amici suggest that prohibiting marriage by same-sex couples reflects community consensus that homosexual conduct is immoral. Yet Massachusetts has a strong affirmative policy of preventing discrimination on the basis of sexual orientation. See G.L. c. 151B (employment, housing, credit, services); G.L. c. 265, § 39 (hate crimes); G.L. c. 272, '98 (public accommodation); G.L. c. 76, § 5 (public education). See also, e.g., *Commonwealth v. Balthazar*, 366 Mass. 298, 318 N.E.2d 478 (1974) (decriminalization of private consensual adult conduct); *Doe v. Doe*, 452 N.E.2d 293 (Mass. App. Ct. 1983) (custody to homosexual parent not per se prohibited).

The department has had more than ample opportunity to articulate a constitutionally adequate justification for limiting civil marriage to opposite-sex unions. It has failed to do so. The department has offered purported justifications for the civil marriage restriction that are starkly at odds with the comprehensive network of vigorous, gender-neutral laws promoting stable families and the best interests of children. It has failed to identify any relevant characteristic that would justify shutting the door to civil marriage to a person who wishes to marry someone of the same sex.

The marriage ban works a deep and scarring hardship on a very real segment of the community for no rational reason. The absence of any reasonable relationship between, on the one hand, an absolute disqualification of same-sex couples who wish to enter into civil marriage and, on the other, protection of public health, safety, or general welfare, suggests that the marriage restriction is rooted in persistent prejudices against persons who are (or who are believed to be) homosexual. "The Constitution cannot control such prejudices but neither can it tolerate them. Private biases may be outside the reach of the law, but the law cannot, directly or indirectly, give them effect." *Palmore v. Sidoti*, 466 U.S. 429, 433 (1984) (construing Fourteenth Amendment). Limiting the protections, benefits, and obligations of civil marriage to opposite-sex couples violates the basic premises of individual liberty and equality under law protected by the Massachusetts Constitution.

We consider next the plaintiffs' request for relief. We preserve as much of the statute as may be preserved in the face of the successful constitutional challenge.... Here, no one argues that striking down the marriage laws is an appropriate form of relief. Eliminating civil marriage would be wholly inconsistent with the Legislature's deep commitment to fostering stable families and would dismantle a vital organizing principle of our society. We face a problem similar to one that recently confronted the Court of Appeal for Ontario, the highest court of that Canadian province, when it considered the constitutionality of the same-sex marriage ban under Canada's Federal Constitution, the Charter of Rights and Freedoms (Charter). See *Halpern v. Toronto (City)*, 172 O.A.C. 276 (2003). Canada, like the United States, adopted the common law of England that civil marriage is "the voluntary union for life of one man and one woman, to the exclusion of all others." *Id.* at par. (36), quoting *Hyde v. Hyde*, [1861-1873] All E.R. 175 (1866). In holding that the limitation of civil marriage to opposite-sex couples violated the Charter, the Court of Appeal refined the common-law meaning of marriage. We concur with this remedy, which is entirely consonant with established principles of jurisprudence empowering a court to refine a common-law principle in light of evolving constitutional standards.

We construe civil marriage to mean the voluntary union of two persons as spouses, to the exclusion of all others. This reformulation redresses the plaintiffs' constitutional injury and furthers the aim of marriage to promote stable, exclusive relationships. It advances the two legitimate State interests the department has identified: providing a stable setting for child rearing and conserving State resources. It leaves intact the Legislature's broad discretion to regulate marriage....We declare that barring an individual from the protections, benefits, and obligations of civil marriage solely because that person would marry a person of the same sex violates the Massachusetts Constitution.

GREANEY, J. concurring.

The right to marry is not a privilege conferred by the State, but a fundamental right that is protected against unwarranted State interference. See *Zablocki v. Redhail*, 434 U.S. 374, 384 (1978) ("the right to marry is of fundamental importance for all individuals"); *Loving v. Virginia*, 388 U.S. 1, 12, (1967) (freedom to marry is "one of the vital personal rights essential to the orderly pursuit of happiness by free men" under due process clause of Fourteenth Amendment); *Skinner v. Oklahoma*, 316 U.S. 535, 541 (1942) (marriage is one of "basic civil rights of man"). This right is essentially vitiated if one is denied the right to marry a person of one's choice. See *Zablocki v. Redhail, supra* at 384 (all recent decisions of United States Supreme Court place "the decision to marry as among the personal decisions protected by the right of privacy").

A comment is in order with respect to the insistence of some that marriage is, as a matter of definition, the legal union of a man and a woman. To define the institution of marriage by the characteristics of those to whom it always has been accessible, in order to justify the exclusion of those to whom it never has been accessible, is conclusory and bypasses the core question we are asked to decide. This case calls for a higher level of legal analysis. Precisely, the case requires that we confront ingrained assumptions with respect to historically accepted roles of men and women within the institution of marriage and requires that we reexamine these assumptions in light of the unequivocal language of art. 1, in order to ensure that the governmental conduct challenged here conforms to the supreme charter of our Commonwealth.... I do not doubt the sincerity of deeply held moral or religious beliefs that make inconceivable to some the notion that any change in the common-law definition of what constitutes a legal civil marriage is now, or ever would be, warranted. But, as a matter of constitutional law, neither the mantra of tradition, nor individual conviction, can justify the perpetuation of a hierarchy in which couples of the same sex and their families are deemed less worthy of social and legal recognition than couples of the opposite sex and their families.

I am hopeful that our decision will be accepted by those thoughtful citizens who believe that same-sex unions should not be approved by the State. I am not referring here to acceptance in the sense of grudging acknowledgment of the court's authority to adjudicate the matter. My hope is more liberating. The plaintiffs are members of our community, our neighbors, our coworkers, our friends. As pointed out by the court, their professions include investment advisor, computer engineer, teacher, therapist, and lawyer. The plaintiffs volunteer in our schools, worship beside us in our religious houses, and have children who play with our children, to mention just a few ordinary daily contacts. We share a common humanity and participate together in the social contract that is the foundation of our Commonwealth. Simple principles of decency dictate that we extend to the plaintiffs, and to their new status, full acceptance, tolerance, and respect. We should do so because it is the right thing to do.

SPINA, J., dissenting.

What is at stake in this case is not the unequal treatment of individuals or whether individual rights have been impermissibly burdened, but the power of the Legislature to effectuate social change without interference from the courts.... The power to regulate marriage lies with the Legislature, not with the judiciary. Today, the court has transformed its role as protector of individual rights into the role of creator of rights, and I respectfully dissent.

The marriage statutes do not impermissibly burden a right protected by our constitutional guarantee of due process implicit in art. 10 of our Declaration of Rights. There is no restriction on the right of any plaintiff to enter into marriage. Each is free to marry a willing person of the opposite sex. Substantive due process protects individual rights against unwarranted government intrusion.... [T]oday the court does not fashion a remedy that affords greater protection of a right. Instead, using the rubric of due process, it has redefined marriage.

Although this court did not state that same-sex marriage is a fundamental right worthy of strict scrutiny protection, it nonetheless deemed it a constitutionally protected right by applying rational basis review. Before applying any level of constitutional analysis there must be a recognized right at stake. Same-sex marriage, or the "right to marry the person of one's choice" as the court today defines that right, does not fall within the fundamental right to marry. Same-sex marriage is not "deeply rooted in this Nation's history," and the court does not suggest that it is. Except for the occasional isolated decision in recent years, see, e.g., *Baker v. State*, 170 Vt. 194, 744 A.2d 864 (1999), same-sex marriage is not a right, fundamental or otherwise, recognized in this country. In this Commonwealth and in this country, the roots of the institution of marriage are deeply set in history as a civil union between a single man and a single woman. There is no basis for the court to recognize same-sex marriage as a constitutionally protected right.

The remedy that the court has fashioned both in the name of equal protection and due process exceeds the bounds of judicial restraint mandated by art. 30. The remedy that construes gender-specific language as gender-neutral amounts to a statutory revision that replaces the intent of the Legislature with that of the court. Article 30 permits the court...to modify statutory language only if legislative intent is preserved. Here, the alteration of the gender-specific language alters precisely what the

Legislature unambiguously intended to preserve, the marital rights of single men and women. Such a dramatic change in social institutions must remain at the behest of the people through the democratic process.

SOSMAN, J., dissenting.

Based on our own philosophy of child rearing, and on our observations of the children being raised by same-sex couples to whom we are personally close, we may be of the view that what matters to children is not the gender, or sexual orientation, or even the number of the adults who raise them, but rather whether those adults provide the children with a nurturing, stable, safe, consistent, and supportive environment in which to mature. Same-sex couples can provide their children with the requisite nurturing, stable, safe, consistent, and supportive environment in which to mature, just as opposite-sex couples do. It is therefore understandable that the court might view the traditional definition of marriage as an unnecessary anachronism, rooted in historical prejudices that modern society has in large measure rejected and biological limitations that modern science has overcome.

It is not, however, our assessment that matters. Conspicuously absent from the court's opinion today is any acknowledgment that the attempts at scientific study of the ramifications of raising children in same-sex couple households are themselves in their infancy and have so far produced inconclusive and conflicting results. (Notwithstanding our belief that gender and sexual orientation of parents should not matter to the success of the child rearing venture, studies to date reveal that there are still some observable differences between children raised by opposite-sex couples and children raised by same-sex couples.) Interpretation of the data gathered by those studies then becomes clouded by the personal and political beliefs of the investigators, both as to whether the differences identified are positive or negative, and as to the untested explanations of what might account for those differences. (This is hardly the first time in history that the ostensible steel of the scientific method has melted and buckled under the intense heat of political and religious passions.) Even in the absence of bias or political agenda behind the various studies of children raised by same-sex couples, the most neutral and strict application of scientific principles to this field would be constrained by the limited period of observation that has been available. Gay and lesbian couples living together openly, and official recognition of them as their children's sole parents, comprise a very recent phenomenon, and the recency of that phenomenon has not yet permitted any study of how those children fare as adults and at best minimal study of how they fare during their adolescent years. The Legislature can rationally view the state of the scientific evidence as unsettled on the critical question it now faces: are families headed by same-sex parents equally successful in rearing children from infancy to adulthood as families headed by parents of opposite sexes? Our belief that children raised by same-sex couples *should* fare the same as children raised in traditional families is just that: a passionately held but utterly untested belief. The Legislature is not required to share that belief but may, as the creator of the institution of civil marriage, wish to see the proof before making a fundamental alteration to that institution.

As a matter of social history, today's opinion may represent a great turning point that many will hail as a tremendous step toward a more just society. As a matter of constitutional jurisprudence, however, the case stands as an aberration. To reach the result it does, the court has tortured the rational basis test beyond recognition.

CORDY, J., dissenting.

The plaintiffs ground their contention that they have a fundamental right to marry a person of the same sex in a long line of Supreme Court decisions…that discuss the importance of marriage. In context, all of these decisions and their discussions are about the "fundamental" nature of the institution of marriage as it has existed and been understood in this country, not as the court has redefined it today. Even in that context, its "fundamental" nature is derivative of the nature of the interests that underlie or are associated with it. An examination of those interests reveals that they are either not shared by same-sex couples or not implicated by the marriage statutes.

Supreme Court cases that have described marriage or the right to marry as "fundamental" have focused primarily on the underlying interest of every individual in procreation, which, historically, could only legally occur within the construct of marriage because sexual intercourse outside of marriage was a criminal act…. Because same-sex couples are unable to procreate on their own, any right to marriage they may possess cannot be based on their interest in procreation, which has been essential to the Supreme Court's denomination of the right to marry as fundamental.

Supreme Court cases recognizing a right to privacy in intimate decision- making…have also focused primarily on sexual relations and the decision whether or not to procreate, and have refused to recognize an "unlimited right" to privacy…. Although some of the privacy cases also speak in terms of personal autonomy, no court has ever recognized such an open-ended right. "That many of the rights and liberties protected by the Due Process Clause sound in personal autonomy does not warrant the sweeping conclusion that any and all important, intimate, and personal decisions are so protected…." *Washington v. Glucksberg*, 521 U.S. 702, 727 (1997). Such decisions are protected not because they are important, intimate, and personal, but because the right or liberty at stake is "so deeply rooted in our history and traditions, or so fundamental to our concept of constitutionally ordered liberty" that it is protected by due process. *Id.* Accordingly, the Supreme Court has concluded that while the decision to refuse unwanted medical treatment is fundamental, *Cruzan v. Director, Mo. Dep't of Health*, 497 U.S. 261, 278, (1990), because it is deeply rooted in our nation's history and tradition, the equally personal and profound decision to commit suicide is not because of the absence of such roots. *Washington v. Glucksberg, supra.*

While the institution of marriage is deeply rooted in the history and traditions of our country and our State, the right to marry someone of the same sex is not.... Unlike opposite-sex marriages, which have deep historic roots...same-sex relationships, although becoming more accepted, are certainly not so "deeply rooted in this Nation's history and tradition" as to warrant such enhanced constitutional protection.

The burden of demonstrating that a statute does not satisfy the rational basis standard rests on the plaintiffs. It is a weighty one. "[A] reviewing court will presume a statute's validity, and make all rational inferences in favor of it.... The Legislature is not required to justify its classifications, nor provide a record or finding in support of them." The statute "only need[s to] be supported by a conceivable rational basis...."

It is difficult to imagine a State purpose more important and legitimate than ensuring, promoting, and supporting an optimal social structure within which to bear and raise children. At the very least, the marriage statute continues to serve this important State purpose.

The question we must turn to next is whether the statute, construed as limiting marriage to couples of the opposite sex, remains a rational way to further that purpose. Stated differently, we ask whether a conceivable rational basis exists on which the Legislature could conclude that continuing to limit the institution of civil marriage to members of the opposite sex furthers the legitimate purpose of ensuring, promoting, and supporting an optimal social structure for the bearing and raising of children. In considering whether such a rational basis exists, we defer to the decision-making process of the Legislature, and must make deferential assumptions about the information that it might consider and on which it may rely. We must assume that the Legislature (1) might conclude that the institution of civil marriage has successfully and continually provided this structure over several centuries; (2) might consider and credit studies that document negative consequences that too often follow children either born outside of marriage or raised in households lacking either a father or a mother figure, and scholarly commentary contending that children and families develop best when mothers and fathers are partners in their parenting; and (3) would be familiar with many recent studies that variously support the proposition that children raised in intact families headed by same-sex couples fare as well on many measures as children raised in similar families headed by opposite-sex couples; support the proposition that children of same-sex couples fare worse on some measures; or reveal notable differences between the two groups of children that warrant further study.

We must also assume that the Legislature would be aware of the critiques of the methodologies used in virtually all of the comparative studies of children raised in these different environments, cautioning that the sampling populations are not representative, that the observation periods are too limited in time, that the empirical data are unreliable, and that the hypotheses are too infused with political or agenda driven bias.

Taking all of this available information into account, the Legislature could rationally conclude that a family environment with married opposite-sex parents remains the optimal social structure in which to bear children, and that the raising of children by same-sex couples, who by definition cannot be the two sole biological parents of a child and cannot provide children with a parental authority figure of each gender, presents an alternative structure for child rearing that has not yet proved itself beyond reasonable scientific dispute to be as optimal as the biologically based marriage norm. Working from the assumption that recognition of same-sex marriages will increase the number of children experiencing this alternative, the Legislature could conceivably conclude that declining to recognize same-sex marriages remains prudent until empirical questions about its impact on the upbringing of children are resolved.

The fact that the Commonwealth currently allows same-sex couples to adopt, does not affect the rationality of this conclusion. The eligibility of a child for adoption presupposes that at least one of the child's biological parents is unable or unwilling, for some reason, to participate in raising the child. In that sense, society has "lost" the optimal setting in which to raise that child--it is simply not available. In these circumstances, the principal and overriding consideration is the "best interests of the child," considering his or her unique circumstances and the options that are available for that child. The objective is an individualized determination of the best environment for a particular child, where the normative social structure--a home with both the child's biological father and mother--is not an option. That such a focused determination may lead to the approval of a same-sex couple's adoption of a child does not mean that it would be irrational for a legislator, in fashioning statutory laws that cannot make such individualized determinations, to conclude generally that being raised by a same-sex couple has not yet been shown to be the absolute equivalent of being raised by one's married biological parents.

That the State does not preclude different types of families from raising children does not mean that it must view them all as equally optimal and equally deserving of State endorsement and support. For example, single persons are allowed to adopt children, but the fact that the Legislature permits single-parent adoption does not mean that it has endorsed single parenthood as an optimal setting in which to raise children or views it as the equivalent of being raised by both of one's biological parents. The same holds true with respect to same-sex couples--the fact that they may adopt children means only that the Legislature has concluded that they may provide an acceptable setting in which to raise children who cannot be raised by both of their biological parents. The Legislature may rationally permit adoption by same-sex couples yet harbor reservations as to whether parenthood by same-sex couples should be affirmatively encouraged to the same extent as parenthood by the heterosexual couple whose union produced the child.

There is no question that many same-sex couples are capable of being good parents, and should be (and are) permitted to be so. The policy question that a legislator must resolve is a different one, and turns on an assessment of whether the marriage structure proposed by the plaintiffs will, over time, if endorsed and supported by the State, prove to be as stable and successful a model as the one that has formed a cornerstone of our society since colonial times, or prove to be less than optimal, and result in consequences, perhaps now unforeseen, adverse to the State's legitimate interest in promoting and supporting the best possible social structure in which children should be born and raised. Given the critical importance of civil marriage as an organizing and stabilizing institution of society, it is eminently rational for the Legislature to postpone making fundamental changes to it until such time as there is unanimous scientific evidence, or popular consensus, or both, that such changes can safely be made.

While "[t]he Massachusetts Constitution protects matters of personal liberty against government incursion as zealously, and often more so, than does the Federal Constitution," this case is not about government intrusions into matters of personal liberty. It is not about the rights of same-sex couples to choose to live together, or to be intimate with each other, or to adopt and raise children together. It is about whether the State must endorse and support their choices by changing the institution of civil marriage to make its benefits, obligations, and responsibilities applicable to them. While the courageous efforts of many have resulted in increased dignity, rights, and respect for gay and lesbian members of our community, the issue presented here is a profound one, deeply rooted in social policy, that must, for now, be the subject of legislative not judicial action.

NOTES

1. After the decision in *Goodridge*, the Massachusetts Senate requested an advisory opinion from the Massachusetts Supreme Court concerning the constitutionality of a bill pending before the legislature that would prohibit same-sex couples from entering into marriage but allow them to form civil unions with all of the benefits, protections, rights and responsibilities of marriage.[6] In response to the request, the court issued an opinion declaring that civil union was not an adequate substitute for marriage and that to continue to disallow same-sex marriage would be a violation of the state constitution. *Opinion of the Justices to the Senate*, 802 N.E.2d 565 (2004). Excerpts from the court's opinion:

> The same defects of rationality evident in the marriage ban considered in *Goodridge* are evident in, if not exaggerated by, Senate No. 2175. Segregating same-sex unions from opposite-sex unions cannot possibly be held rationally to advance or "preserve" what we stated in *Goodridge* were the Commonwealth's legitimate interests in procreation, child rearing, and the conservation of resources. Because the proposed law by its express terms forbids same-sex couples entry into civil marriage, it continues to relegate same-sex couples to a different status. The holding in *Goodridge*, by which we are bound, is that group classifications based on unsupportable distinctions, such as that embodied in the proposed bill, are invalid under the Massachusetts Constitution. The history of our nation has demonstrated that separate is seldom, if ever, equal.
>
> The bill's absolute prohibition of the use of the word "marriage" by "spouses" who are the same sex is more than semantic. The dissimilitude between the terms "civil marriage" and "civil union" is not innocuous; it is a considered choice of language that reflects a demonstrable assigning of same-sex, largely homosexual, couples to second-class status. The denomination of this difference by the separate opinion of Justice Sosman (separate opinion) as merely a "squabble over the name to be used" so clearly misses the point that further discussion appears to be useless. If, as the separate opinion posits, the proponents of the bill believe that no message is conveyed by eschewing the word "marriage" and replacing it with "civil union" for same-sex "spouses," we doubt that the attempt to circumvent the court's decision in *Goodridge* would be so purposeful. For no rational reason the marriage laws of the Commonwealth discriminate against a defined class; no amount of tinkering with language will eradicate that stain. The bill would have the effect of maintaining and fostering a stigma of exclusion that the Constitution prohibits. It would deny to same-sex "spouses" only a status that is specially recognized in society and has significant social and other advantages. The Massachusetts Constitution, as was explained in the *Goodridge* opinion, does not permit such invidious discrimination, no matter how well intentioned.
>
> We recognize that the pending bill palliates some of the financial and other concrete manifestations of the discrimination at issue in *Goodridge*. But the question the court considered in *Goodridge* was not only whether it was proper

---

[6] The Massachusetts Constitution authorizes the Supreme Court to issue advisory opinions on important questions of law upon the request of either branch of the legislature, the governor, or the executive council. Mass. Const. Part II, c. 3, art. 2

to withhold tangible benefits from same-sex couples, but also whether it was constitutional to create a separate class of citizens by status discrimination, and withhold from that class the right to participate in the institution of civil marriage, along with its concomitant tangible and intangible protections, benefits, rights, and responsibilities. Maintaining a second-class citizen status for same-sex couples by excluding them from the institution of civil marriage is the constitutional infirmity at issue. We are of the opinion that Senate No. 2175 violates the equal protection and due process requirements of the Constitution of the Commonwealth and the Massachusetts Declaration of Rights....The bill maintains an unconstitutional, inferior, and discriminatory status for same-sex couples, and the bill's remaining provisions are too entwined with this purpose to stand independently.

2. In 2004 Massachusetts became the first state to allow same-sex marriage and in May of that year same-sex couples began to marry in Massachusetts. In 2007, the Massachusetts legislature initially voted to amend the state constitution to define marriage as a union between a man and a woman. However, to be effective, constitutional amendments in Massachusetts must be re-approved a second time by the legislature and then submitted to the electorate for a statewide vote. After the initial vote on the amendment, the legislature had a change of heart and voted against the amendment, thereby allowing the continuation of same-sex marriage in the Commonwealth. *See* Jeffrey M. Shaman, EQUALITY AND LIBERTY IN THE GOLDEN AGE OF STATE CONSTITUTIONAL LAW 207 (2008).

3. Since *Goodridge*, other state high courts have addressed the issue of same-sex marriage, with varying results. Some state high courts, in disagreement with *Goodridge*, found nothing unconstitutional about laws limiting marriage to opposite-sex couples. Others, in agreement with *Goodridge*, struck down laws precluding same-sex marriage. *See* Jennifer Friesen, STATE CONSTITUTIONAL LAW: LITIGATING INDIVIDUAL RIGHTS, CLAIMS AND DEFENSES 2–106 (4th ed. 2006), 2009 SUPPLEMENT, 23-5. A similar pattern developed in the federal courts, with some federal courts upholding bans on same-sex marriage, and others striking them down. *See* National Conference of State Legislatures, *Same-Sex Marriage Laws* (3/19/2015), http://www.ncsl.org/research/human-services/same-sex-marriage.aspx.

4. In California, the state supreme court ruled that state laws precluding same-sex marriage violated the equal protection clause of the California Constitution, *In re Marriages Cases*, 183 P.3d 384 (Cal. 2008), but that decision was nullified by Proposition 8, a constitutional amendment adopted by the electorate stating that only marriage between a man and a woman is valid or recognized in California. Cal. Const. art. I, § 7.5. In turn, a federal district court in California ruled that Proposition 8 violated the Due Process and Equal Protection Clauses of the United States

Constitution.   *Perry v. Schwarzenegger*, 704 F.Supp.2d 921 (N.D. Cal. 2010).   State officials decided not to appeal the district court decision, but several backers of Proposition 8 who intervened in the case did appeal to the United States Court of Appeals for the Ninth Circuit, which affirmed the district court decision.   *Perry v. Brown*, 671 F.3d 1052 (9th Cir. 2012.) However, the Court of Appeals decision was vacated by the United States Supreme Court on the ground that the interveners did not have standing to appeal the district court decision.   *Hollingsworth v. Perry*, 133 S. Ct. 265 (2013).   This left the ruling of the district court as the final ruling in the case.

5. At one time, 41 states had adopted statutory or constitutional provisions defining marriage as the union of a man and a woman, thereby precluding same-sex marriage. Jennifer Friesen, 2009 SUPPLEMENT, *supra* note 3, at 22-3. As time progressed, however, state legislatures began to enact laws authorizing same-sex marriage. In some instances these laws were submitted to the voters for their approval or disapproval in state referenda. In 2012 the voters in three states—Maine, Maryland, and Washington— voted in referenda to uphold legislation that had been enacted allowing same-sex marriage. In the same year, the voters of Minnesota rejected a constitutional amendment to prohibit same-sex marriage. The actions taken in these four states reversed a trend of public votes rejecting same-sex marriage; previously voters in 32 states had voted against same-sex marriage. *See* National Conference of State Legislatures, *Same-Sex Marriage Laws* (3/19/2015), http://www.ncsl.org/research/human-services/same-sex-marriage.aspx. By March of 2015, 37 states and the District of Columbia, either by legislation, public vote, or court decision, recognized same-sex marriage. *Id.*

6. On June 26, 2015, the Supreme Court of the United States announced its decision in *Obergefell v. Hodges*, 576 U.S. ___, 135 S. Ct. 2584 (2015), ruling that the right to marry is a fundamental right inherent in the liberty of the person and that under the Due Process and Equal Protection Clauses of the Fourteenth Amendment same-sex couples may not be denied the fundamental right to marry. The decision legalized same-sex marriage throughout the United States and required all states to issue marriage licenses to same-sex couples and to recognize same-sex marriages performed in other states.

The Court's decision in *Obergefell* was by a 5–4 vote. The majority opinion, written by Justice Kennedy, included the following statement:

> No Union is more profound than marriage, for it embodies the highest ideals of love, fidelity, devotion, sacrifice, and family. In forming a martial union, two people become greater than once they were. As some of the petitioners in these cases demonstrate, marriage embodies a love that may endure even past death. It would misunderstand these men and women to say

they disrespect the idea of marriage. Their plea is that they do respect it, respect it so deeply that they seek to fund its fulfillment for themselves. Their hope is not to be condemned to live in loneliness, excluded from one of civilization's oldest institutions. They ask for equal dignity in the eyes of the law. The Constitution grants them that right.

In a dissenting opinion, Chief Justice Roberts made the following observation:

> Although the policy arguments for extending marriage to same-sex couples may be compelling, the legal arguments for requiring such an extension are not. The fundamental right to marry does not include a right to make a State change its definition of marriage. And a State's decision to maintain the meaning of marriage that has persisted in every culture throughout human history can hardly be called irrational. In short, our Constitution does not enact any one theory of marriage. The people of a State are free to expand marriage to include same-sex couples, or to retain the historic definition.

leave the def of marriage to States

E. THE RIGHT OF BODILY INTEGRITY

MATTER OF FARRELL
529 A.2d 404 (N.J. 1987)

GARIBALDI, J.

Although we stated the general principle that competent informed patients have the right to decline life-sustaining treatment in both *In re Quinlan*, 355 A.2d 647 (N.J. 1976) and *In re Conroy*, 486 A.2d 1209 (N.J. 1985), each of those cases involved an incompetent institutionalized patient. In this case we deal for the first time with the right of a competent, terminally-ill adult patient living at home to withdraw a life-sustaining respirator. *Qp*

relevant precedent

Kathleen married Francis Farrell in 1969. They had two children. Prior to her illness, Mrs. Farrell worked as a keypunch operator. In November 1982, she began to experience symptoms associated with ALS, a disorder of the nervous system that results in degeneration of the victim's muscles. Although it eventually renders a patient incapable of movement, ALS does not impair the patient's mental faculties. The cause of the disease is unknown and there is no available treatment or cure. At the time of diagnosis, a victim's life expectancy even with life-sustaining treatment is usually one to three years.

After she became ill, Mrs. Farrell was admitted to a Philadelphia hospital where she underwent a tracheotomy and was connected to a respirator. In the autumn of 1983, she was released from the hospital because it could provide no further help for her condition. She returned home to live with her husband and their two teenage sons. Thereafter Mrs.

Farrell was paralyzed and confined to bed in need of around-the-clock nursing care. Insurance covered all the expenses of this care.

In November 1985, after an experimental program that her husband characterized as "their last hope" had failed, Mrs. Farrell told him that she wanted to be disconnected from the respirator that sustained her breathing. Mr. Farrell told her doctor, John Pino, of her decision. The doctor advised Mrs. Farrell that she would die if her respirator were removed. Dr. Pino arranged for a psychologist, Dr. Jean Orost, to interview Mrs. Farrell. Dr. Orost determined that Mrs. Farrell was not clinically depressed and needed no psychiatric treatment. She concluded that Mrs. Farrell had made an informed, voluntary, and competent decision to remove the respirator. Dr. Orost continued to see Mrs. Farrell on a weekly basis from the time of their first interview in January 1986 until her death the following June.

On June 13, 1986, Francis Farrell filed a Chancery Division complaint seeking his appointment as Special Medical Guardian for his wife with specific authority to disconnect her respirator. He also sought a declaratory judgment that he and anyone who assisted him in disconnecting her respirator would incur no civil or criminal liability.... Part of the trial was conducted at the Farrells' home in order to enable Mrs. Farrell to testify. The court described Mrs. Farrell's medical condition at the time of the trial as follows:

> Mrs. Farrell presently appears to be a very fragile woman, weighing less than 100 pounds. In December 1982 she weighed 161 pounds. She has no control over her hands, arms, feet or legs, is incontinent as to bowel, and has difficulty with bladder function. She has difficulty in swallowing and is fed liquids, such as fruit juices, with a syringe by nurses who attend to her needs 24 hours a day. She is incapable of taking any solid foods by mouth. She is able to open and close her eyes and can see but has difficulty in talking. During her testimony, a court reporter took down what she said, and her husband at times repeated her answers to questions. Her answers were generally limited to yes or no, and at times an alphabet board was used to be certain her answer was understood. Her mouth tended to fill up with saliva and made her answers difficult to understand at times. When her children and better days were discussed with Mrs. Farrell, her eyes filled with tears and her husband assisted her in blowing her nose. She is incapable of moving her head, neck, or any other part of her body. On occasion she is put in a reclining chair and can watch television although she stated she usually falls asleep. She has pain in her arms and back, but medication does relieve it to some extent.

At the trial, Mrs. Farrell testified that she had discussed her decision to withdraw the respirator with her husband, their two sons, her parents, her sister, and her psychologist, Dr. Orost. These discussions had been upsetting, but resulted in open and full communication among all the parties. Mrs. Farrell had also discussed the consequences of her decision with a respiratory specialist, Dr. Sollami. When Mrs. Farrell was asked why she had decided to disconnect her respirator and to let nature take its course, she responded, "I'm tired of suffering." *i. Ans she chose to disconnect from respirator*

After closing arguments on June 23, 1986, the trial court granted all the relief that Mr. Farrell had requested, but stayed his order pending appellate review. On June 29, 1986, Mrs. Farrell died while still connected to the respirator. Despite her death, both the guardian ad litem and Mr. Farrell have urged us to address her case and formulate guidelines that might aid future patients, their loved ones, and their physicians in dealing with similar situations. Because of the extreme importance of the issue and the inevitability of cases like this one arising in the future, we agree to render a decision on the merits.

In resolving this case, as well as the two other cases we decide today, we build on the principles established in *Quinlan* and *Conroy*. Hence, we start by reaffirming the well-recognized common-law right of self-determination that "[e]very human being of adult years and sound mind has a right to determine what shall be done with his own body." *Schloendorff v. Society of New York Hosp.*, 105 N.E. 92, 93 (N.Y. 1914) (Cardozo, J.). In *Conroy*, we stated that "[t]he right of a person to control his own body is a basic societal concept, long recognized in the common law." We explained that the doctrine of "informed consent" was developed to protect the right to self-determination in matters of medical treatment. This doctrine prescribes the "duty of a physician to disclose to a patient information that will enable him to evaluate knowledgeably the options available and the risks attendant upon each before subjecting that patient to a course of treatment." *Common law right to self determination*

As medical technology has been advancing, the doctrine of informed consent has been developing. Thus, in *Conroy* we recognized the patient's right to give an informed refusal to medical treatment as the logical correlative of the right to give informed consent. We stated that "a competent adult person generally has the right to decline to have any medical treatment initiated or continued." *Rule a Unurmy denal of med treatment*

While we held that a patient's right to refuse medical treatment even at the risk of personal injury or death is primarily protected by the common law, we recognized that it is also protected by the federal and state constitutional right of privacy. Numerous other courts have upheld the right of a competent patient to refuse medical treatment even if that decision will hasten his or her death.

Nevertheless, the right to refuse life-sustaining medical treatment is not absolute. The state has at least four potentially countervailing interests in sustaining a person's life:

preserving life, preventing suicide, safeguarding the integrity of the medical profession and protecting innocent third parties. When a party declines life-

4 to right to refuse life sustaining meds
State interests

sustaining medical treatment, (we balance the patient's common-law and constitutional rights against these four state interests) In this case, none of these interests, as we interpreted them in *Conroy*, nor their concert, outweighs Kathleen Farrell's rights to privacy and self-determination.

The state's interest in preserving life embraces "an interest in preserving the life of the particular patient, and an interest in preserving the sanctity of all life." Neither of those interests is compelling in this case. In *Conroy*, we decided that the value of life is desecrated not by a decision to refuse medical treatment but "by the failure to allow a competent human being the right of choice." Thus, "[i]n cases that do not involve the protection of the actual or potential life of someone other than the decisionmaker, the state's indirect and abstract interest in preserving the life of the competent patient generally gives way to the patient's much stronger personal interest in directing the course of his own life."

The next two state interests that we consider in rejection-of-treatment cases, i.e., preventing suicide and safeguarding the integrity of the medical profession, are not threatened by Mrs. Farrell's decision. In *Conroy*, we determined that the State's interest in preventing suicide is "motivated by, if not encompassed within," its interest in preserving life. We explained that declining life sustaining medical treatment may not properly be viewed as an attempt to commit suicide. Refusing medical intervention merely allows the disease to take its natural course; if death were to eventually occur, it would be the result, primarily of the underlying disease, and not the result of a self-inflicted injury.

Courts in other jurisdictions have consistently agreed that refusal of life-supporting treatment does not amount to an attempt to commit suicide. Similarly, medical ethics create no tension in this case. Our review of well-established medical authorities finds them in unanimous support of the right of a competent and informed patient such as Mrs. Farrell to decline medical treatment.... Health care standards are not undermined by the medical authorities that support the right to self-determination that we recognize today. Even as patients enjoy control over their medical treatment, health-care professionals remain bound to act in consonance with specific ethical criteria. We realize that these criteria may conflict with some concepts of self-determination. In the case of such a conflict, a patient has no right to compel a health-care provider to violate generally accepted professional standards.

When courts refuse to allow a competent patient to decline life-sustaining treatment, it is almost always because of the state's interest in protecting innocent third parties who would be harmed by the patient's decision. "[F]or example, courts have required competent adults to undergo medical procedures against their will if necessary to protect the public health,...or to prevent the emotional and financial abandonment of the patient's minor children."

Although Mrs. Farrell left behind two teenage sons, her case is manifestly distinguishable from those in which a parent could be forced to accept treatment because his or her prospect for recovery was good and the parent's death threatened the security of a child or children. Mrs. Farrell did not disregard her children's interest when she decided to withdraw the respirator. In fact, she based her decision in part on her recognition that her medical condition had already put them under extreme stress. Moreover, Mr. Farrell's capacity to care for them in her absence is unquestioned. Therefore the state's interest in protecting innocent third parties does not militate against Mrs. Farrell's decision.

kids not harmed by her choice

The guardian ad litem appointed by the Court to protect the children concluded that they would not be harmed if the court granted relief. His position was based on personal meetings with the children and on a report he received from a psychiatrist who had interviewed them. However, we need not rely on his testimony. Where the evidence reveals a close, loving family like the Farrells, we presume that when the parents make medical decisions, they are concerned about and will protect their children's interests. A guardian ad litem for the children is, therefore, unnecessary in the case of a family like the Farrells.

In light of all of the foregoing, we hold that the state's interests did not outweigh Mrs. Farrell's right to withdraw her respirator. Accordingly, we affirm the judgment of the trial court.

KRISCHER v. McIVER
697 So.2d 97 (Fla. 1997)

GRIMES, J.

Charles E. Hall and his physician, Cecil McIver, M.D., filed suit for a declaratory judgment that section 782.08, Florida Statutes (1995), which prohibits assisted suicide, violated the Privacy Clause of the Florida Constitution and the Due Process and Equal Protection Clauses of the Fourteenth Amendment to the United States Constitution. They sought an injunction against the state attorney from prosecuting the physician for giving deliberate assistance to Mr. Hall in committing suicide. Mr. Hall is thirty-five years old and suffers from acquired immune deficiency syndrome (AIDS) which he contracted from a blood transfusion. The court found that Mr. Hall was mentally competent and that he was in obviously deteriorating health, clearly suffering, and terminally ill.

Alleged state & fed violations

At the outset, we note that the United States Supreme Court recently issued two decisions on the subject of whether there is a right to assisted suicide under the United States Constitution. In *Washington v. Glucksberg*, 521 U.S. 702 (1997), the Court reversed a decision of the Ninth Circuit Court of Appeals which had held that the State of Washington's prohibition against assisted suicide violated the Due Process Clause…. [T]he Court reasoned that the asserted "right" to assistance in committing suicide was not a fundamental liberty interest protected by the Due Process Clause. In the second decision, the Court upheld New York's prohibition on assisted suicide against the claim that it violated the Equal Protection Clause. *Vacco v. Quill*, 521 U.S. 793 (1997).… [T]he Court held that there was a logical and recognized distinction between the right to refuse medical treatment and assisted suicide and concluded that there were valid and important public interests which easily satisfied the requirement that a legislative classification bear a rational relation to some legitimate end.

The remaining issue is whether Mr. Hall has the right to have Dr. McIver assist him in committing suicide under Florida's guarantee of privacy contained in our constitution's declaration of rights. Art. I, § 23, Fla. Const. Florida has no law against committing suicide. However, Florida imposes criminal responsibility on those who assist others in committing suicide. Section 782.08, which was first enacted in 1868, provides in pertinent part that "every person deliberately assisting another in the commission of self murder shall be guilty of manslaughter." See also §§ 765.309, 458.326(4). Thus, it is clear that the public policy of this state as expressed by the legislature is opposed to assisted suicide.

Florida's position is not unique. Forty-five states that recognize the right to refuse treatment or unwanted life support have expressed disapproval of assisted suicide. As of 1994, thirty-four jurisdictions had statutes which criminalized such conduct. Since that date, at least seventeen state legislatures have rejected proposals to legalize assisted suicide.

In 1984, Governor Mario Cuomo convened the New York State Task Force on Life and the Law, a blue ribbon commission composed of doctors, ethicists, lawyers, religious leaders, and interested laypersons, with a mandate to develop public policy on a number of issues arising from medical advances. With respect to assisted suicide and euthanasia, the task force concluded as follows:

> In this report, we unanimously recommend that New York laws prohibiting assisted suicide and euthanasia should not be changed. In essence, we propose a clear line for public policies and medical practice between forgoing medical interventions and assistance to commit suicide or euthanasia. Decisions to forgo treatment are an integral part of medical practice; the use of many treatments would be inconceivable without the ability to withhold or to stop the treatments in appropriate cases. We have identified the wishes and interests of patients as the primary guideposts for those decisions.

Assisted suicide and euthanasia would carry us into new terrain. American society has never sanctioned assisted suicide or mercy killing. We believe that the practices would be profoundly dangerous for large segments of the population, especially in light of the widespread failure of American medicine to treat pain adequately or to diagnose and treat depression in many cases. The risks would extend to all individuals who are ill. They would be most severe for those whose autonomy and well-being are already compromised by poverty, lack of access to good medical care, or membership in a stigmatized social group. The risks of legalizing assisted suicide and euthanasia for these individuals, in a health care system and society that cannot effectively protect against the impact of inadequate resources and ingrained social disadvantage, are likely to be extraordinary.

Set of concerns with assisted suicide.

The Advocacy Center for Persons with Disability, Inc., opposes the legalization of assisted suicide, either by judicial decision negating its prohibition or by legislative enactment. If assisted suicide is permitted in Florida, Floridians will be put on the so-called slippery slope of determining the relative value of life. Floridians with severe physical and mental disabilities, who are particularly vulnerable to being devalued as burdens of society, would be at grave risk.

Fear of putting the weak in harm's way

This Court has also rendered several prior decisions declaring in various contexts that there is a constitutional privacy right to refuse medical treatment. Those cases recognized the state's legitimate interest in (1) the preservation of life, (2) the protection of innocent third parties, (3) the prevention of suicide, and (4) the maintenance of the ethical integrity of the medical profession. However, we held that these interests were not sufficiently compelling to override the patient's right of self-determination to forego life-sustaining medical treatment.

arguments

We cannot agree that there is no distinction between the right to refuse medical treatment and the right to commit physician-assisted suicide through self-administration of a lethal dose of medication. The assistance sought here is not treatment in the traditional sense of that term. It is an affirmative act designed to cause death-no matter how well-grounded the reasoning behind it. Each of our earlier decisions involved the decision to refuse medical treatment and thus allow the natural course of events to occur. *In re Dubreuil*, 629 So.2d 819 (Fla.1993) (due to religious beliefs, individual wanted to refuse blood transfusion); *In re Guardianship of Browning*, 568 So.2d 4 (Fla.1990) (surrogate asserted right of woman who was vegetative but not terminally ill to remove nasogastric feeding tube); *Satz v. Perlmutter*, 379 So.2d 359 (Fla.1980) (individual suffering from Lou Gehrig's disease sought to remove artificial respirator needed to keep him alive).

In the instant case, Mr. Hall seeks affirmative medical intervention that will end his life on his timetable and not in the natural course of events.

There is a significant difference between these two situations. As explained by the American Medical Association:

> When a life-sustaining treatment is declined, the patient dies primarily because of an underlying disease. The illness is simply allowed to take its natural course. With assisted suicide, however, death is hastened by the taking of a lethal drug or other agent. Although a physician cannot force a patient to accept a treatment against the patient's will, even if the treatment is life-sustaining, it does not follow that a physician ought to provide a lethal agent to the patient. The inability of physicians to prevent death does not imply that physicians are free to help cause death. AMA Council on Ethical and Judicial Affairs, Report I-93-8, at 2.

Measured by the criteria employed in our cases addressing the right to refuse medical treatment, three of the four recognized state interests are so compelling as to clearly outweigh Mr. Hall's desire for assistance in committing suicide. First, the state has an unqualified interest in the preservation of life. The state also has a compelling interest in preventing suicide. Finally, the state also has a compelling interest in maintaining the integrity of the medical profession.

We do not hold that a carefully crafted statute authorizing assisted suicide would be unconstitutional. Nor do we discount the sincerity and strength of the respondents' convictions. However, we have concluded that this case should not be decided on the basis of this Court's own assessment of the weight of the competing moral arguments. By broadly construing the privacy amendment to include the right to assisted suicide, we would run the risk of arrogating to ourselves those powers to make social policy that as a constitutional matter belong only to the legislature.

KOGAN, C.J., dissenting.

The notion of "dying by natural causes" contrasts neatly with the word "suicide," suggesting two categories readily distinguishable from one another. How nice it would be if today's reality were so simple. No doubt there once was a time when, for all practical purposes, the distinction was clear enough to all. But that was a time before today, before technology had crept into medicine, when dying was a far more inexorable process. Medicine now has pulled the aperture separating life and death far enough apart to expose a limbo unthinkable fifty years ago, for which the law has no easy description. Dying no longer falls into the neat categories our ancestors knew. In today's world, we demean the hard reality of terminal illness to say otherwise.

The ability of medicine to intrude so profoundly into the act of dying has prompted a rising emphasis on the right of privacy, with its deep concern with self-determination. Since being added to the state Constitution in 1980, Florida's privacy right unquestionably has subtracted certain death-inducing actions from the category of "suicide" as defined at common law. Thus, in *Satz v. Perlmutter*, 379 So.2d 359 (Fla.1980), we upheld the decision of an individual suffering Lou Gehrig's disease to cease artificial respiration needed to keep him alive. In *Public Health Trust v. Wons*, 541 So.2d 96 (Fla.1989), we upheld an individual's right to refuse a blood transfusion needed to save her life even though she had children, where refusal was based on religious beliefs. On similar facts, we reached the same conclusion *In re Dubreuil*, 629 So.2d 819, (Fla.1993), where the State failed to establish the unfitness of the other parent to assume custody of the children. *In re Guardianship of Browning*, 568 So.2d 4 (Fla.1990), we found that the right to refuse treatment could be asserted by a surrogate on behalf of a woman who was vegetative but not terminally ill, but who previously had indicated she wanted life support removed in such circumstances. All of these acts would have been suicide at common law, and the assistance provided by physicians would have been homicide. Today they are not.   *IS: our precedents uphold what would be considered suicide.*

Once Florida had set itself adrift from the common law definition, the problem that immediately arose-that has vexed our courts ever since-is where to draw the new dividing line between improper "suicide" and the emerging "right of self-determination" without simultaneously authorizing involuntary euthanasia. This is no simple task. The majority tries to fix the mark through scrutinizing the means by which dying occurs: Suicide thus is "active" death caused by a "death producing agent," whereas Floridians have a right to choose "passive" death through "natural causes." While language in our prior opinions can be read to support this view, I am not convinced this language can be stretched beyond the differing facts we previously faced.   *Active (banned) v. passive (permitted) deaths*

The issue is different here. In cases of this type, we simply cannot focus on the means by which death occurs, but on the fact that the patient at the time in question has reached the death bed. That is the fact unique in this case that was not present in the earlier cases, and it is the reason why we must use a different analysis. A means-based test works well in the context of refusing medical treatment where life otherwise will continue. It does not work where there is no question death must occur, and must occur painfully.

To my mind, the right of privacy attaches with unusual force at the death bed. This conclusion arises in part from the privacy our society traditionally has afforded the death bed, but also from the very core of the right of privacy-the right of self-determination even in the face of majoritarian disapproval. What possible interest does society have in saving life when there is nothing of life to save but a final convulsion of agony? The state has no business in this arena. Terminal illness is not a portrait in blacks and whites, but unending shades of gray, involving the most profound of personal, moral, and religious questions. Many people can and do disagree over these questions, but the fact remains that it is the dying person who must resolve them in the particular case. And while we certainly cannot ignore the slippery-slope problem, we previously have established fully adequate standards to police the exercise of privacy rights in this context to ensure against abuse.

Finally, I cannot ignore the majority's statement that the issues in this case must be left to the legislature. Such a statement ignores fundamental tenets of our law. Constitutional rights must be enforced by courts even against the legislature's powers, and privacy in particular must be enforced even against majoritarian sentiment. Indeed, the overarching purpose of the Florida Declaration of Rights along with its privacy provision is to "protect each individual within our borders from the unjust encroachment of state authority-from whatever official source-into his or her life.

RAVIN v. STATE
537 P.2d 494 (Alaska 1975)

RABINOWITZ, C.J.

The constitutionality of Alaska's statute prohibiting possession of marijuana is put in issue in this case.... We first address petitioner's contentions that his constitutionally protected right to privacy compels the conclusion that the State of Alaska is prohibited from penalizing the private possession and use of marijuana. Ravin's basic thesis is that there exists under the federal and Alaska constitutions a fundamental right to privacy, the scope of which is sufficiently broad to encompass and protect the possession of marijuana for personal use. Given this fundamental constitutional right, the State would then have the burden of demonstrating a compelling state interest in prohibiting possession of marijuana.

In Alaska this court has dealt with the concept of privacy on only a few occasions. One of the most significant decisions in this area is *Breese v. Smith*, 501 P.2d 159 (Alaska 1972), where we considered the applicability of the guarantee of 'life, liberty, the pursuit of happiness' found in the Alaska Constitution, to a school hairlength regulation. Noting that hairstyles are a highly personal matter in which the individual is traditionally autonomous, we concluded that governmental control of personal appearance would be antithetical to the concept of personal liberty under Alaska's constitution. Subsequent to our decision in *Breese*, a right to privacy amendment was added to the Alaska Constitution. Article I, section 22 reads:

> The right of the people to privacy is recognized and shall not be infringed. The legislature shall implement this section.

The effect of this amendment is to place privacy among the specifically enumerated rights in Alaska's constitution. But this fact alone does not, in and of itself, yield answers concerning what scope should be accorded to this right of privacy. We have suggested that the right to privacy may afford less than absolute protection to "the ingestion of food, beverages or other substances." For any such protection must be limited by the legitimate needs of the State to protect the health and welfare of its citizens.

[I]n our view, the right to privacy amendment to the Alaska Constitution cannot be read so as to make the possession or ingestion of marijuana itself a fundamental right. Nor can we conclude that such a fundamental right is shown by virtue of the analysis we employed in *Breese*. In that case, the student's traditional liberty pertaining to autonomy in personal appearance was threatened in such a way that his constitutionally guaranteed right to an education was jeopardized. Hairstyle, as emphasized in *Breese*, is a highly personal matter involving the individual and his body. Few would believe they have been deprived of something of critical importance if deprived of marijuana, though they would if stripped of control over their personal appearance. Therefore, if we were employing our former test, we would hold that there is no fundamental right, either under the Alaska or federal constitutions, either to possess or ingest marijuana.

The foregoing does not complete our analysis of the right to privacy issues.... Ravin's right to privacy contentions are not susceptible to disposition solely in terms of answering the question whether there is a general fundamental constitutional right to possess or smoke marijuana. This leads us to a more detailed examination of the right to privacy and the relevancy of where the right is exercised. If there is any area of human activity to which a right to privacy pertains more than any other, it is the home. The importance of the home has been amply demonstrated in constitutional law. Among the enumerated rights in the federal Bill of Rights are the guarantee against quartering of troops in a private house in peacetime (Third Amendment) and the right to be "secure in their...houses...against unreasonable searches and seizures..." (Fourth Amendment). The First Amendment has been held to protect the right to "privacy and freedom of association in the home." The Fifth Amendment has been described as providing protection against all governmental invasions "of the sanctity of a man's home and the privacies of life." The protection of the right to receive birth control information in *Griswold v. Connecticut*, 381 U.S. 479 (1965), was predicated on the sanctity of the marriage relationship and the harm to this fundamental area of privacy if police were allowed to "search the sacred precincts of marital bedrooms." And in *Stanley v. Georgia*, 394 U.S. 557 (1969), the Court emphasized the home as the situs of protected "private activities." The right to receive information and ideas was found in *Stanley* to take on an added dimension precisely because it was a prosecution for possession in the home. In a later case, the Supreme Court noted that *Stanley* was not based on the notion that the obscene matter was itself protected by a constitutional penumbra of privacy, but rather was a "reaffirmation that 'a man's home is his castle.'" At the same time the Court noted, "the Constitution extends special safeguards to the privacy of the home, just as it protects other special privacy rights such as those of marriage, procreation, motherhood, child rearing, and education." And as the Supreme Court pointed out, there exists a 'myriad' of activities which may be lawfully conducted within the privacy and confines of the home, but may be prohibited in public.

In Alaska we have also recognized the distinctive nature of the home as a place where the individual's privacy receives special protection. This court has consistently recognized that the home is constitutionally protected from unreasonable searches and seizures, reasoning that the home itself retains a protected status under the Fourth Amendment and Alaska's constitution distinct from that of the occupant's person. The privacy amendment to the Alaska Constitution was intended to give recognition and protection to the home. Such a reading is consonant with the character of life in Alaska. Our territory and now state has traditionally been the home of people who prize their individuality and who have chosen to settle or to continue living here in order to achieve a measure of control over their own lifestyles which is now virtually unattainable in many of our sister states.

The home, then, carries with it associations and meanings which make it particularly important as the situs of privacy. Privacy in the home is a fundamental right, under both the federal and Alaska constitutions. We do not mean by this that a person may do anything at anytime as long as the activity takes place within a person's home. There are two important limitations on this facet of the right to privacy. First, we agree with the Supreme Court of the United States, which has strictly limited the *Stanley* guarantee to possession for purely private, noncommercial use in the home. And secondly, we think this right must yield when it interferes in a serious manner with the health, safety, rights and privileges of others or with the public welfare. No one has an absolute right to do things in the privacy of his own home which will affect himself or others adversely. Indeed, one aspect of a private matter is that it is private, that is, that it does not adversely affect persons beyond the actor, and hence is none of their business. When a matter does affect the public, directly or indirectly, it loses its wholly private character, and can be made to yield when an appropriate public need is demonstrated.

Thus, we conclude that citizens of the State of Alaska have a basic right to privacy in their homes under Alaska's constitution. This right to privacy would encompass the possession and ingestion of substances such as marijuana in a purely personal, non-commercial context in the home unless the state can meet its substantial burden and show that proscription of possession of marijuana in the home is supportable by achievement of a legitimate state interest.

The evidence which was presented at the hearing before the district court consisted primarily of several expert witnesses familiar with various medical and social aspects of marijuana use. Numerous written reports and books were also introduced into evidence. The justifications offered by the State to uphold AS 17.12.010 are generally that marijuana is a psychoactive drug; that it is not a harmless substance; that heavy use has concomitant risk; that it is capable of precipitating a psychotic reaction in at least individuals who are predisposed towards such reaction; and that its use adversely affects the user's ability to operate an automobile. The State relies upon a number of medical researchers who have raised questions as to the substance's effect on the body's immune system, on chromosomal structure, and on the functioning of the brain. On the other hand, in almost every instance of reports of potential danger arising from marijuana use, reports can be found reaching contradictory results. It appears that there is no firm evidence that marijuana, as presently used in this country, is generally a danger to the user or to others. But neither is there conclusive evidence to the effect that it is harmless. The one significant risk in use of marijuana which we do find established to a reasonable degree of certainty is the effect of marijuana intoxication on driving.

Given the evidence of the effect of marijuana on driving, an individual's right to possess or ingest marijuana while driving would be subject to the prohibition provided for in AS 17.12.010. However, given the relative insignificance of marijuana consumption as a health problem in our society at present, we do not believe that the potential harm generated by drivers under the influence of marijuana, standing alone, creates a close and substantial relationship between the public welfare and control of ingestion of marijuana or possession of it in the home for personal use. Thus we conclude that no adequate justification for the state's intrusion into the citizen's right to privacy by its prohibition of possession of marijuana by an adult for personal consumption in the home has been shown. The privacy of the individual's home cannot be breached absent a persuasive showing of a close and substantial relationship of the intrusion to a legitimate governmental interest. Here, mere scientific doubts will not suffice. The state must demonstrate a need based on proof that the public health or welfare will in fact suffer if the controls are not applied.

Interest in privacy works but not enough

The state has a legitimate concern with avoiding the spread of marijuana use to adolescents who may not be equipped with the maturity to handle the experience prudently, as well as a legitimate concern with the problem of driving under the influence of marijuana. Yet these interests are insufficient to justify intrusions into the rights of adults in the privacy of their own homes. Further, neither the federal or Alaska constitution affords protection for the buying or selling of marijuana, nor absolute protection for its use or possession in public. Possession at home of amounts of marijuana indicative of intent to sell rather than possession for personal use is likewise unprotected.

In view of our holding that possession of marijuana by adults at home for personal use is constitutionally protected, we wish to make clear that we do not mean to condone the use of marijuana. The experts who testified below, including petitioner's witnesses, were unanimously opposed to the use of any psychoactive drugs. We agree completely. It is the responsibility of every individual to consider carefully the ramifications for himself and for those around him of using such substances. With the freedom which our society offers to each of us to order our lives as we see fit goes the duty to live responsibly, for our own sakes and for society's. This result can best be achieved, we believe, without the use of psychoactive substances.

NOTES

1. A few years after *Ravin*, the Alaska Supreme Court upheld the constitutionality of a criminal law prohibiting the use and possession of cocaine. *State v. Erickson*, 574 P.2d 1 (Alaska 1978). In upholding the law, the court ruled that the personal use and possession of cocaine in the home was not encompassed within the right of privacy. The court distinguished *Ravin* on the ground that cocaine, unlike marijuana, was shown by scientific evidence to be a serious hazard to health and welfare.

2. Courts in other states have declined to follow *Ravin*. The Supreme Court of Hawaii, for example, refused to allow a right to smoke marijuana, even in the home, notwithstanding that Hawaii's Constitution, like Alaska's, contains a provision expressly protecting the right of privacy. *State v. Mallan*, 950 P.2d 178 (Haw. 1998). The Hawaii high court repudiated *Ravin*, commenting that it was based, at least partially, on social and cultural factors unique to Alaska. Aside from Alaska, no other state has recognized a constitutional right to smoke marijuana.

3. In *Seeley v. State*, 940 P.2d 604 (Wash. 1997), the Supreme Court of Washington refused to approve a right for a terminally ill cancer patient to smoke marijuana for medicinal purposes. The patient averred that marijuana offered the most effective relief from the nausea and vomiting he suffered as a result of chemotherapy. Although the patient claimed only

a limited right to smoke marijuana for medical treatment, the court rejected his claim:

> This court has held that "[t]he right to smoke marijuana is not fundamental to the American scheme of justice, it is not necessary to ordered liberty, and it is not within a zone of privacy." *State v. Smith*, 610 P.2d 869 (Wash. 1980). Other federal and state courts have agreed that possession of marijuana is not a fundamental right guaranteed by the United States Constitution. However, Respondent contends the right infringed is not a general right to smoke marijuana but, rather, a right to have marijuana prescribed as his preferred medical treatment for the nausea and vomiting associated with chemotherapy.

> Here, Respondent asserts a constitutionally protected interest in having his physician prescribe marijuana, an unapproved drug which is regulated as a Schedule I controlled substance, for medical treatment.... (S)cientifically reliable evidence showed that currently available therapies are more effective and do not carry with them the same risks which are attributable to marijuana)... This court and other federal and state courts have reviewed evidence similar to that which has been submitted in this case and have all upheld the constitutionality of marijuana's classification.

> The challenged legislation involves conclusions concerning a myriad of complicated medical, psychological and moral issues of considerable controversy. We are not prepared on this limited record to conclude that the legislature could not reasonably conclude that marijuana should be placed in schedule I of controlled substances. It is clear not only from the record in this case but also from the long history of marijuana's treatment under the law that disagreement persists concerning the health effects of marijuana use and its effectiveness as a medicinal drug. The evidence presented by the Respondent is insufficient to convince this court that it should interfere with the broad judicially recognized prerogative of the legislature. (Respondent has not shown that the legislative treatment of marijuana is "so unrelated" to the achievement of the legitimate purposes of the legislature or that "the facts have so far changed as to render the classification arbitrary and obsolete.) See *Smith*, 610 P.2d 869.

F. PROCEDURAL DUE PROCESS

STATE v. VEALE
972 A.2d 1009 (N.H. 2009)

HICKS, J.

The defendant, Scott W. Veale, appeals orders of the Superior Court relating to its finding that he is incompetent to stand trial. We affirm. The relevant facts are as follows. The defendant is a real estate broker who has been involved in various land and logging disputes for many years. He was indicted in June 2003 for one count of timber trespass and one count of theft by unauthorized taking, after a property owner alleged that he cut and removed oak timber from the owner's property. The court appointed a public defender to represent the defendant. A second public defender entered an appearance to assist in the defense because of his familiarity with real estate issues.

The attorney-client relationship deteriorated over the following months. The defendant believed that he owned the timber and the property. He also believed that local and State authorities prosecuted him as part of an ongoing conspiracy to deprive him of property rights. The public defender conferred with two real estate attorneys to determine whether the defendant's claim had merit. Both concluded that it did not. The defendant, however, continued to insist that the public defenders seek funds for a property survey. Eventually, the defendant accused the public defenders of being part of the conspiracy against him and his family. This severely impaired communication and the public defenders concluded that he was unable to assist in his defense. In July 2004, defense counsel filed a motion to determine competency. Dr. James Adams, a psychiatrist, examined the defendant in November 2004 and ultimately determined that, although the defendant suffered from a paranoid disorder, he was competent to stand trial. Defense counsel moved for, and were granted funds for, a second opinion. Dr. Philip Kinsler, a clinical and forensic psychologist, examined the defendant in March 2005 and concluded that he suffered from a delusional disorder and was incompetent. The defendant filed a *pro se* motion in July 2005 summarizing the breakdown of communication with his appointed counsel, outlining their disagreement over "the need for a mental evaluation," requesting a finding that such evaluation was unnecessary, and requesting new counsel. The clerk refused these pleadings "under Superior Rule 5 for non-compliance with Rule 15."

The Superior Court (*Barry*, J.) held a competency hearing in September 2005, receiving testimony from each doctor. The State conducted the direct examination of Dr. Adams and cross-examination of Dr. Kinsler. The public defender conducted the direct examination of Dr. Kinsler and cross-examination of Dr. Adams. The court also made limited inquiry. The defendant was present at the hearing but did not testify. The court ultimately found the defendant incompetent to stand trial and ruled that he could not be restored to competency. The court later held a hearing on dangerousness, ruled that the defendant was not dangerous and granted the defendant's motion to dismiss the criminal charges.

The defendant filed a *pro se* notice of appeal raising several issues. We appointed the appellate defender to represent him on appeal. The appellate defender moved to withdraw, citing a conflict of interest due to an ineffective assistance of counsel claim alleged against the public defenders. On remand, the trial court appointed the defendant's current counsel. Counsel filed an amended ineffective assistance claim and a motion to vacate the competency finding. The motion alleged a denial of procedural due process. After a hearing, the Trial Court ruled against the defendant on the ineffective assistance of counsel claim and denied his motion to vacate the finding of incompetence. The court noted that defense counsel was ethically bound to raise the competency issue and that such action did not deprive the defendant of procedural due process.

We appointed the defendant's trial counsel to represent him on appeal and granted the appellate defender's motion to withdraw. The defendant appeals only the denial of his motion to vacate, arguing that he was denied due process in the competency determination. He cites the Due Process Clauses of the Fourteenth Amendment to the Federal Constitution and Part I, Article 15 of the State Constitution. We first address this argument under the State Constitution and cite federal opinions for guidance only.

Part I, Article 15 of the State Constitution provides, in relevant part: "No subject shall be...deprived of his property, immunities, or privileges, put out of the protection of the law, exiled or deprived of his life, liberty, or estate, but by the judgment of his peers, or the law of the land...." Law of the land in this article means due process of law. Our threshold determination in a procedural due process claim is "whether the challenged procedures concern a legally protected interest." Undoubtedly, the state constitutional right to due process protects defendants from standing trial if they are legally incompetent. The defendant's due process challenge, however, does not implicate this right. Indeed, the competency proceedings below resulted in a dismissal of the two indictments, and resulted in no confinement because the defendant was found not to be dangerous. The defendant grounds his due process challenge on the stigma attached to his reputation by virtue of the incompetency finding. He argues that, while the competency proceedings may have protected his right not to be tried if incompetent, they erroneously imposed upon him an "indelible stigma" affecting the exercise of various civil rights. It is through this lens that we consider his procedural due process challenge. The State contends that the defendant's asserted reputational interest fails to trigger a due process analysis because he simply "speculates about a number of potential consequences that 'may' or 'can' flow from a finding of incompetence," rendering each "too speculative and remote to constitute the kind of liberty or property interest contemplated by the constitution."

The State would have a stronger argument if we had adopted the analysis in *Paul v. Davis*, 424 U.S. 693 (1976), under our State Constitution. In *Paul*, the Supreme Court coined what would later be known as the "stigma plus" test. The Court noted that "[t]he words 'liberty' and 'property' as used in the Fourteenth Amendment do not in terms single out reputation as a candidate for special protection...." It narrowed its prior holding in *Wisconsin v. Constantineau*, 400 U.S. 433

(1971), by concluding that defamation alone could not constitute an interest triggering due process protection. Instead, the Court read *Wisconsin* as recognizing a cognizable right warranting due process protection where reputational stigma exists in addition to state action altering or extinguishing "a right or status previously recognized by state law." In *Siegert v. Gilley*, 500 U.S. 226 (1991), the Court extended the doctrine by requiring, in addition to the stigma, a contemporaneous tangible loss. We, however, have never adopted the stigma-plus test as the touchstone for procedural due process under the State Constitution. Although other cases have approached the issue, they have merely assumed that state constitutional due process attaches to a reputational right. Accordingly, the issue remains open under the State Constitution.

Although we do not necessarily agree with all of the scholarly criticism of the stigma-plus doctrine, we are mindful that constitutional scholars have not received the doctrine well. By requiring that a separate liberty or property interest accompany the reputational injury, the decision in *Paul* marked a drastic narrowing of its predecessors. In our view, *Paul* effectively relegates the reputational interest to insignificance because the separate injury would, itself, often invoke the Due Process Clause.

Although in interpreting the New Hampshire Constitution we have often followed and agreed with the federal treatment of parallel provisions of the federal document, we never have considered ourselves bound to adopt the federal interpretations." In *Clark v. Manchester*, 305 A.2d 668 (N.H.1973), we concluded that a probationary employee was not entitled to due process, in part, because he failed to show "that the governmental conduct likely will…seriously damage his standing and associations in the community…[or] impose a stigma upon the employee that will foreclose future opportunities to practice his chosen profession." In *Petition of Bagley*, 513 A.2d 331 (N.H. 1986), we stated that "[t]he general rule is that a person's liberty may be impaired when governmental action seriously damages his standing and associations in the community." We also "recognized that the stigmatization that attends certain governmental determinations may amount to a deprivation of constitutionally protected liberty." *Bagley*, 128 N.H. at 284. Thus, we find ample support in our jurisprudence for the proposition that reputational stigma can, by itself, constitute a deprivation of liberty deserving due process.

Accordingly, we hold that competency determinations sufficiently implicate reputational interests to warrant the protection afforded by the State Due Process Clause. Guaranteeing some minimal process guards against the difficulty of undoing harm once visited upon a person's good name. *Cf. Goldberg v. Kelly*, 397 U.S. 254 (1970). In instances such as the present one, a person may not immediately suffer the more tangible effects of such a determination. We have long recognized that some forms of reputational harm can safely be assumed.

Having concluded that competency determinations can potentially damage the protected interest in reputation, we consider what process is required to protect that interest. In so doing, we balance three factors: First, the private interest that will be affected by the official action; second, the risk of an erroneous deprivation of such interest through the procedures used, and the probable value, if any, of additional or substitute procedural safeguards; and finally, the Government's interest, including the function involved and the fiscal and administrative burdens that the additional or substitute procedural requirement would entail.

After balancing the private interest here at issue; the risk of an erroneous deprivation of that interest through the procedures used, and the probable value of additional procedural safeguards; and the Government's interest, we conclude that due process does not require additional process under the State Constitution.

M.E.K. v. R.L.K.
921 So.2d 787 (Fla. App. 2006)

PLEUS, C.J.

The sole issue in this appeal is whether an indigent mother facing involuntary termination of parental rights in an adoption proceeding has a constitutional right to appointment of trial and appellate counsel. We believe she does and therefore reverse the order denying her counsel.

J.L.K. was born in September 2004. A month later, the Department of Children and Families sheltered J.L.K. with his maternal grandmother and initiated dependency proceedings based on allegations that his mother was unable to care for him. Prior to the adjudicatory hearing, J.L.K.'s grandmother moved to dismiss the dependency proceeding on the ground that she would file a separate adoption proceeding pursuant to Chapter 63 and would seek to have the mother's parental rights terminated as part of the adoption. The dependency court abated the dependency proceeding to allow the adoption to proceed.

In March 2005, the grandmother filed a petition for termination of parental rights pending adoption pursuant to Chapter 63 of the Florida Statutes. The lower court terminated the mother's parental rights by default after the mother failed to file a responsive pleading. She was incarcerated at the time. Subsequently, the mother's attorney in the dependency action filed a notice of appearance in the adoption action. He also filed an affidavit of indigency, motion to appoint counsel and motion to vacate the final judgment and set aside default. The mother's appellate attorney appealed the final judgment terminating her parental rights and also filed a motion in the lower court to appoint appellate counsel. The court denied the motions to appoint trial and appellate counsel in the adoption proceeding. The mother appealed this order as well. We consolidated these appeals and temporarily relinquished jurisdiction, after which the lower court approved the parties' stipulation to set aside the final judgment and reinstate the dependency proceedings. Based on this development, we acknowledged dismissal of appeal of the final judgment but agreed to proceed with the appeal of the order denying appointed counsel.

In a 1980 appeal of an order terminating parental rights under Chapter 39, the Florida Supreme Court held that an indigent parent has a right, under both the Florida and United States Constitutions, to appointed counsel in "proceedings involving the permanent termination of parental rights to a child." *In the Interest of D.B.*, 385 So.2d 83 (Fla.1980).

A year later, in *Lassiter v. Dep't of Social Serv. of Durham County, N.C.*, 452 U.S. 18 (1981), the U.S. Supreme Court held that the federal due process clause does not require appointed counsel in every state-initiated termination of parental rights proceeding. Instead, it required trial courts to evaluate the need for counsel on a case-by-case basis. The court noted that it was only determining the minimum due process standard under the federal constitution and that many states have higher standards based on wise public policy. In *O.A.H. v. R.L.A.*, 712 So.2d 4 (Fla. 2d DCA 1998), the second district held that an indigent parent has a constitutional right to appointed counsel in a Chapter 63 involuntary adoption proceeding. It recently reaffirmed that holding in *In the Interest of M.C.*, 899 So.2d 486 (Fla. 2d DCA 2005). Both *O.A.H.* and *M.C.* are similar to the instant case in that they involved indigent parents who did not attend the final hearing in which their parental rights were terminated because they were incarcerated at the time.

In denying the mother's requests for appointed counsel, the lower court declined to follow *O.A.H.* or *M.C.*, stating:

> Ordinarily, the Court would be bound by precedent from another District Court of Appeal in the absence of contrary authority from the Fifth District Court of Appeal. However, the Court in this matter is bound by the U.S. Supreme Court decision in *Lassiter v. Department of Social Services of Durham County, N.C.*

We disagree with this reasoning.... *Lassiter* addressed only the minimum due process requirements under the federal due process clause. The citizens of Florida are also protected by the due process clause in Article 1, section 9 of the Florida Constitution. In our federal system of jurisprudence, the United States Constitution establishes the minimum level of due process protections for all people, but state constitutions and laws may provide additional due process protections.

In the area of termination of parental rights, the Florida due process clause provides higher due process standards than the federal due process clause. Under the federal provision, *Lassiter* does not require appointment of counsel in every case. It only requires a case-by-case determination. But under the state due process clause, *D.B.* requires appointment of counsel in "proceedings involving the permanent termination of parental rights to a child." *D.B.*, 385 So.2d at 90. *O.A.H.* noted that:

> In the years following *Lassiter*, Florida's supreme court has continued to confirm that *D.B.* stands for the proposition that a constitutional right to appointed counsel arises when the proceeding can result in a permanent loss of parental rights.

For these reasons, the lower court should have followed *O.A.H.* and *M.C.* rather than *Lassiter*.

Alternatively, the grandmother argues that even if the trial court was obligated to follow *O.A.H.*, this Court is free to disagree with it. She urges us to reject *O.A.H.*, claiming that it disregards the underlying reasons for appointing counsel and because its broad interpretation of state action creates a slippery slope that will obligate the state to provide counsel in many other types of civil cases. The grandmother is wrong on both counts. In *M.L.B.*, the United States Supreme Court rejected a similar slippery slope argument. *M.L.B.* involved the right of an indigent parent to have the state pay for a transcript of the hearing in an appeal of a private termination of parental rights case. Justice Thomas argued in dissent that extending due process protections found in criminal cases involving the loss of one's liberty to a civil case involving termination of parental rights would create a dangerous precedent used to extend such protections to other civil cases.

The majority rejected this argument, noting that termination of parental rights work "unique kind of deprivation" involving the "awesome authority of the State" to permanently destroy legal recognition of the parental relationship. Therefore, finding certain due process protections applicable in termination of parental rights cases could not be used as precedent to extend such protections to other civil cases. The same analysis is true in the instant case. Finding a right to counsel in a civil termination of parental rights case does not create a dangerous precedent for finding such a right in other civil cases because other civil cases do not involve the same unique deprivation of a fundamental right by the State.

The grandmother also argues that *O.A.H.* ignores the underlying reasons for appointing counsel. She instead urges us to apply the factors found in *Mathews v. Eldridge*, 424 U.S. 319 (1976), for determining whether a right to counsel exists. However, *D.B.* makes clear that in the context of determining whether a right to appointed counsel exists in a case involving the parent-child relationship, Florida courts must weigh the factors enunciated in *Potvin v. Keller*, 313 So.2d 703 (Fla.1975), not *Mathews*. Those factors include: (1) the potential length of parent-child separation, (2) the degree of parental restrictions on visitation, (3) the presence or absence of parental consent, (4) the presence or absence of disputed facts, and (5) the complexity of the proceeding in terms of witnesses and documents. The *D.B.* court further stated that in applying these factors, "counsel will always be required where permanent termination of custody might result, but where there is no threat of permanent termination of parental custody, the test should be applied on a case-by-case basis."

We also note that the first district recently reached the same conclusion in *G.C. v. W.J.*, 917 So.2d 998 (Fla. 1st DCA 2005). G.C. followed *D.B.* and *O.A.H.* in holding that there is a constitutional right to appointed counsel in a Chapter 63 termination of parental rights proceeding.

We therefore hold, as our sister courts have, that article 1, section 9 of the Florida Constitution mandates that counsel be appointed to an indigent parent in an involuntary termination of parental rights proceeding under Chapter 63. Accordingly, we reverse the order denying appointed counsel and remand directing the trial court to enter an order appointing trial and appellate counsel *nunc pro tunc* to the date of the mother's motion to appoint counsel.

PEOPLE v. WASHINGTON
665 N.E.2d 1330 (Ill. 1996)

FREEMAN, J.

The question in this case is whether due process is implicated in a claim of innocence based upon new evidence so as to permit the claim to be raised in a petition under the Post-Conviction Hearing Act. We hold that it is.

In 1982, Kurtis Washington was sentenced to 25 years in prison for murdering Tony Hightie. Hightie had been murdered outside his home in Chicago shortly after 9 p.m. on May 9, 1980. Washington was implicated in the crime by Donna McClure, Hightie's girlfriend, and Ronald Tapes. McClure and Tapes witnessed the murder. At trial, they said that they had been sitting in a parked car near Hightie's home when they were approached by a man. The man said that he was looking for someone named Will. When McClure and Tapes proved no help, the man approached Hightie just as he left his home. Hightie had been wearing a jacket and hat that belonged to Tapes' brother who was named William.

McClure and Tapes said that after a few words with Hightie, the man shot him. The man, McClure and Tapes said, was Washington.

Washington's defense was that he had been at a grocery store at the time of Hightie's murder. The store cashier, a person who had accompanied Washington and Washington's mother all testified to that fact.

The appellate court affirmed the conviction and sentence on direct review. In 1990, Washington filed a post-conviction petition, alleging nine grounds of error, six of which asserted ineffective assistance of trial counsel. One of the grounds was that Washington's trial counsel, a private attorney who also served as Washington's appellate counsel, failed to investigate evidence that someone other than Washington murdered Hightie. The claim was supported with an affidavit of Jacqueline Martin dated March 3, 1990. Evidence was permitted on that as well as the other ineffective-assistance claims.

The trial judge held an in camera hearing in which he considered Martin's testimony. Martin told how Hightie had been shot after having been mistaken for someone else. Martin, who was 16 years old at the time, told how she had been present when Marcus Halsey, then her boyfriend, and Frank Caston had left Halsey's house to revenge an earlier beating of Halsey's brother. She, Halsey, Caston, and Caston's girlfriend drove in a car to an alley in a neighborhood in Chicago. She later learned that it happened to be the neighborhood where Hightie lived. Martin told how, after Halsey and Caston left the car, she had heard two gunshots, and, when the two returned, she had heard Halsey say "it was the wrong guy." Halsey and Caston later changed clothes, discarding in another alley what they had earlier worn. Martin said that they drove to the home of one of Halsey's sisters, where she stayed the rest of the night.

Halsey was questioned by police the next morning. Martin accompanied him to the police station, as did Caston's girlfriend. At the station, Martin found in her pocket bullets that Halsey had handed to her the night before. She said that she threw the bullets away.

Martin said that after the police questioning, Halsey had threatened to kill her if she told anyone what had happened. Halsey's threats continued, Martin said, and so she eventually stopped going to Halsey's house. Some months later, Halsey's brother confronted her as she was walking near a park and forcibly took her to Halsey. She said that she was kept against her will at Halsey's house for three weeks to a month. She eventually escaped with the help of an unnamed acquaintance whom she happened to see while looking out a window. Martin said that she went immediately to her mother's house. That same day she left for Mississippi. She stayed there for six years. Martin told how at the time of the hearing she still feared Halsey.

In view of Martin's in camera testimony, Washington successfully sought to amend his post-conviction petition to add a tenth claim based upon the newly discovered evidence. The trial judge denied relief under the first nine claims Washington asserted, including the ineffectiveness claim which was supported by Martin's affidavit and testimony. Regarding that claim, the judge referred to testimony given by Washington's defense counsel that, in preparation for trial, he had tried to contact Martin. Counsel had also testified that he believed Washington had a strong alibi defense and his strategy was to focus on that rather than to try to prove that someone other than Washington murdered Hightie. However, the trial judge granted a new trial on the ground that Martin's testimony was new evidence which, if believed, would have "had some significant impact" upon the jury. The appellate court affirmed the grant of relief as to the newly discovered evidence claim....

The claim Washington raised is a "free-standing" claim of innocence; unlike the ineffective-assistance claim supported by Martin's testimony, the newly discovered evidence is not being used to supplement an assertion of a constitutional violation with respect to his trial. The issue is not whether the evidence at trial was insufficient to convict Washington beyond a reasonable doubt. The appellate court rejected that challenge on direct appeal. The issue is whether Washington's claim of newly discovered evidence can be raised in a petition under the Post-Conviction Hearing Act to entitle Washington to a new trial. Post-conviction relief is Washington's remaining hope for a judicial remedy, the time limitations of other avenues offering relief for such a claim having lapsed.

To decide the issue, we must see if either a federal or Illinois constitutional right is implicated in such a freestanding claim of innocence, since Post-Conviction Hearing Act relief is limited to constitutional claims. Washington argues that his claim implicates due process protections. The beginning point for addressing that argument is *Herrera v. Collins*, 506 U.S. 390 (1993), where the Supreme Court rejected the contention as a federal constitutional matter. In light of our own constitution's due process guaranty, we must also assess Washington's argument as a matter of Illinois constitutional jurisprudence.

Federal Due Process

The issue in *Herrera* was whether a freestanding claim of innocence following a Texas capital conviction could be raised in a habeas corpus petition in view of either the eighth amendment protection against cruel and unusual punishment or the fourteenth amendment due process clause. Ten years after his conviction, *Herrera* claimed that his brother, who had since died, committed the crimes. The claim was supported by two affidavits. The Court said that the claim implicated neither the eighth nor the fourteenth amendment but also offered that, even if that were not the case, the claim was unpersuasive anyway.

It is no criticism to read *Herrera* as a conflicted decision. As Justice O'Connor said, claims of innocence-even those in noncapital cases-present troubling issues. We are, of course, bound by the Supreme Court's interpretation of the United States Constitution. Conflicted or not, at least for noncapital cases, *Herrera* clearly states, as the Court did in *Townsend v. Sain*, that a freestanding claim of innocence is not cognizable as a fourteenth amendment due process claim. And so Washington's effort to state a federal constitutional due process claim under the Post-Conviction Hearing Act must fail.

Due Process Under the Illinois Constitution

The possibility remains that Washington's claim may be cognizable under the Illinois Constitution's due process protection. That protection is stated as it is in the fourteenth amendment: no person "shall be deprived of life, liberty or property without due process of law." Ill. Const. 1970, art. I, § 2; see U.S. Const., amend. V. The Record of Proceedings of the Constitutional Convention does not reveal anything as to what the drafters intended for the Illinois protection different from the federal counterpart.

Nevertheless, in *People v. McCauley*, 645 N.E.2d 923 (Ill. 1994), we noted that we labor under no self-imposed constraint to follow federal precedent in "lockstep" in defining Illinois' due process protection. In *McCauley*, we looked primarily to how the protection had been interpreted with respect to the issue there presented: police interference with a suspect's right to legal assistance. We found historical support to say that, as a state matter, due process should protect against deliberate attempts to deny legal counsel.

As for Washington's claim here, there are decisions in which this court has perfunctorily evaluated new evidence claims in cases brought under the Post-Conviction Hearing Act. But neither this court nor the appellate court has ever expressly identified the constitutional right implicated in a freestanding claim of innocence based upon new evidence. Again, Post-Conviction Hearing Act relief is impossible if no constitutional right is implicated in the claim asserted. Essentially, then, the issue is the time relativeness of due process as a matter of this State's constitutional jurisprudence; that is, should additional process be afforded in Illinois when newly discovered evidence indicates that a convicted person is actually innocent?

We believe so as a matter of both procedural and substantive due process. In terms of procedural due process, we believe that to ignore such a claim would be fundamentally unfair. Imprisonment of the innocent would also be so conscience shocking as to trigger operation of substantive due process. The conflicted analysis in *Herrera* is some proof of that. Though the Court rejected the application of substantive due process principles as grounds in *Herrera*, the Court nevertheless conceded that "a truly persuasive demonstration of 'actual innocence'" would make a conviction unconstitutional.

We have no difficulty seeing why substantive due process as a matter of Illinois constitutional law offers the grounds for such a conclusion. The Supreme Court rejected substantive due process as means to recognize freestanding innocence claims because of the idea that a person convicted in a constitutionally fair trial must be viewed as guilty. That made it impossible for such a person to claim that he, an innocent person, was unfairly convicted.

We think that the Court overlooked that a "truly persuasive demonstration of innocence" would, in hindsight, undermine the legal construct precluding a substantive due process analysis. The stronger the claim-the more likely it is that a convicted person is actually innocent-the weaker is the legal construct dictating that the person be viewed as guilty. A "truly persuasive demonstration of innocence" would effectively reduce the idea to legal fiction. At the point where the construct falls apart, application of substantive due process principles, as Justice Blackmun favored, is invited. *Herrera*, 506 U.S. at 436, (Blackmun, J., dissenting, joined by Stevens and Souter, JJ.)

We believe that no person convicted of a crime should be deprived of life or liberty given compelling evidence of actual innocence. Given the limited avenues that our legislature has so far seen fit to provide for raising freestanding claims of innocence, that idea-but for the possibility of executive clemency-would go ignored in cases like this one. We therefore hold as a matter of Illinois constitutional jurisprudence that a claim of newly discovered evidence showing a defendant to be actually innocent of the crime for which he was convicted is cognizable as a matter of due process. That holding aligns Illinois with other jurisdictions likewise recognizing, primarily as a matter of state habeas corpus jurisprudence, a basis to raise such claims under the rubric of due process.

That only means, of course, that there is footing in the Illinois Constitution for asserting freestanding innocence claims based upon newly discovered evidence under the Post-Conviction Hearing Act. Procedurally, such claims should be resolved as any other brought under the Act. Substantively, relief has been held to require that the supporting evidence be new, material, noncumulative and, most importantly, "of such conclusive character" as would "probably change the result on retrial."

As for this case, we find neither reason to disagree with the appellate court that those concerns were satisfied nor need to elaborate upon that conclusion.

The judgment of the appellate court is affirmed.

CHAPTER VI

CRIMINAL PROCEDURE

A. RIGHT TO JURY TRIAL

One of the foundations of the American legal system is the common law right to a trial by jury that existed in England prior to the Declaration of Independence. Traditionally, a jury consisted of twelve jurors who had to reach a unanimous verdict. That is no longer the standard provided for in the United States Constitution or the constitutions of many states.

CLAUDIO v. STATE
MAYMI v. STATE
585 A.2d 1278 (Del. 1991)

HOLLAND, J.

The defendants' claim of error presents a novel question in this jurisdiction. The defendants contend that the trial judge improperly substituted an alternate juror for a regular juror after the jury's deliberations had begun. Before the twelve jurors retired to deliberate on the guilt/innocence phase of the trial, the trial judge read his instructions to the twelve regular jurors and the three alternates. When the jury had not reached a verdict at 5:00 p.m., it was sequestered separately as required by title 11, section 4209(b) of the Delaware Code.

The jury began its deliberations at approximately 10:30 a.m. on December 1, 1987. During the first day of deliberations, the jury requested a view of the face of the defendant, Claudio. The trial judge acceded to this request. The twelve jurors and the three alternates were brought back into the courtroom to view Claudio. When the jury had not reached a verdict at 5:00 p.m., it was sequestered for the night.

During the night, one of the regular jurors became ill. The next morning, December 2, he was excused by the trial judge. The trial judge decided to replace the ill juror with one of the alternates, who had been separately sequestered during the first day of deliberations. Defense counsel moved for a mistrial. That motion was denied.

The judge asked the three alternates if they had discussed the case among themselves during their sequestration. The alternates stated they had not discussed the case. The trial judge then permitted the first alternate to become a member of the regular jury in place of the incapacitated juror. Thereafter, the trial judge gave a special instruction to the reconstituted jury. In particular, he instructed the jury to begin its deliberations anew and emphasized the importance of the alternate familiarizing herself with the views of the other eleven jurors.

The reconstituted jury began its deliberations at approximately 9:30 a.m. It deliberated until approximately 5:00 that evening, breaking only for lunch. The jury reconvened at approximately 10:00 a.m. on December 3. It deliberated until it took a break for lunch at noon. The jury continued deliberating after lunch. At approximately 2:00 p.m., the jury indicated that it had arrived at verdicts on all charges. Thus, the jury deliberated six-and-one-half hours prior to the substitution of the alternate juror and the reconstituted jury deliberated "anew" for approximately nine-and-one-half hours.

Claudio and Maymi also contend that the substitution of an alternate juror during the deliberative process violates their right to trial by jury, as it is guaranteed by the Delaware Constitution. The constitutions adopted by the original States and "the constitution of every State entering the Union thereafter, in one form or another," have protected the right to trial by jury in criminal cases. *Duncan v. Louisiana*, 391 U.S. 145, 153 (1968). "The guarantees of jury trial in the Federal and State Constitutions reflect a *profound judgment* about the *way* in which law should be enforced and justice administered."

The Delaware Constitution is not a mirror image of the United States Constitution. The right to a trial by jury in the Delaware Constitution is not phrased identically to its corollary in the original federal Constitution or the federal Bill of Rights. Del. Const. art. I, §§ 4 and 7; U.S. Const. art. III and amend. 6. A review of the history and origin of the right to trial by jury in the Delaware Constitution, *vis-a-vis* the history and origins of that right in the United States Constitution, reveals that the differences in phraseology between the Delaware and the federal right to trial by jury are not merely stylistic. There is, in fact, a significant substantive difference in that historic right, as it has been preserved for Delaware's citizens.

Delaware History of Jury Trials

The right to trial by jury which is provided for in the Delaware Constitution has a long and distinguished historical origin. "Jury trial came to America with English colonists and received strong support from them." *Duncan v. Louisiana*, 391 U.S. at 152. The legal heritage from England was followed in the Delaware courts. It is probable that a jury was empaneled in Delaware as early as 1669. By 1675, trial by jury had become a fixed institution in Delaware.

The American colonies resented royal interference with the right to trial by jury. On October 14, 1774, the First Continental Congress declared:

> That the respective colonies are entitled to the common law of England, and more especially to the great and inestimable privilege of being tried by their peers of the vicinage, according to the course of that law.

The Declaration of Independence stated solemn objections to the King's "depriving us in many cases, of the benefits of Trial by Jury. . . ." *Duncan v. Louisiana*, 391 U.S. at 152.

Following the signing of the Declaration of Independence on July 4, 1776, several states adopted their own constitutions, which included their own "bills of rights." A convention met in Delaware at New Castle on August 27, 1776, to draft a Constitution for Delaware. One of the delegates to that convention was Richard Bassett. The importance of Richard Bassett's participation in framing Delaware's original Constitution, for the purpose of this case, will become apparent.

The Declaration of Rights and Fundamental Rules of the State of Delaware was adopted by the convention on September 11, 1776. Section 13 of that declaration provided: "That trial by jury of facts where they arise is one of the greatest securities of the lives, liberties, and estates of the people."

Shortly thereafter, the first Constitution of the State of Delaware was enacted on September 20, 1776. Article 25 of that first Delaware Constitution stated:

> *The common law of England*, as well as so much of the statute law as have been heretofore adopted in practice in this state, *shall remain in force*, unless they shall be altered by a future law of the Legislature; such parts only excepted as are repugnant to the rights and privileges contained in this constitution and the declaration of rights, & c. agreed to by this convention. (emphasis added).

Thus, Delaware commenced its existence as an independent State with an unambiguous expression of its intention to perpetuate the right to trial by jury, as it had existed at common law, for its citizens.   *Jury right after becomes a state*

During the Revolutionary War, the states governed themselves with virtual autonomy. After securing their freedom from England, the states were reluctant to subject themselves to any other central government, particularly one with substantial powers. Consequently, when the several independent states united following the American Revolutionary War, pursuant to the Articles of Confederation, each state's own sovereignty was made paramount to the national sovereignty. Moreover, since "the Articles of Confederation asserted no authority over individuals," it also afforded no individual protections. Therefore, Delaware's citizens continued to be protected by the Declaration of Fundamental Rights and the Constitution which had been adopted by Delaware in 1776.

Delaware and Debates on the Federal Right to Trial by Jury

When the Constitution of the United States was being considered for ratification in other states, one of the overriding concerns expressed by many was the effect that the presence of a strong central government and the absence of a federal Bill of Rights would have on fundamental rights which had existed at common law, e.g., trial by jury. Article III of the proposed federal Constitution provided that "[t]he Trial of all Crimes…shall be by Jury; and such Trial shall be held in the State where the said Crimes shall have been committed." "The 'very scanty history of this provision in the records of the Constitutional Convention' sheds little light either way on the intended correlation between Article III's 'jury' and the features of the jury at common law." However, in John Dickinson's view, the provision in Article III perpetuated the right to trial by jury as it had existed at common law.

In stating that view in 1788 and urging other states to follow Delaware's lead in ratifying the federal Constitution, John Dickinson described several aspects of the common law right to trial by jury in detail. Dickinson's understanding of Article III and the common law right to trial by jury is particularly instructive in this case.

> It seems highly probable, that those who would reject this labour of public love [the proposed Constitution], would also have rejected the Heaven-taught institution of trial by jury, had they been consulted upon its establishment. Would they not have cried out, that there never was framed so detestable, so paltry, and so tyrannical a device for extinguishing freedom, and throwing unbounded domination into the hands of the king and barons, under a contemptible pretence of preserving it? "What!…Why then is it insisted on; but because the fabricators of it know that it will, and intend that it shall reduce the people to slavery? Away with it—Freemen will never be enthralled by so insolent, so execrable, so pitiful a contrivance."
>
> Happily for us our ancestors thought otherwise. They were not so over-nice and curious, as to refuse blessing, because, they might possibly be abused….
>
> Trial by Jury is our birth-right; and tempted to his own ruin, by some seducing spirit, must be the man, who in opposition to the genius of United American, shall dare to attempt its subversion…
>
> In the proposed confederation, it is preserved inviolable in criminal cases, and cannot be altered in other respects, but when United America demands it.

Despite the assurances from John Dickinson and other Federalist writers, fears had continued to be expressed that Article III's provision failed to preserve *all of the common-law rights* to trial by jury, *e.g.*, the right to be tried by a "jury of the vicinage." That concern, as well as the desire "to preserve the right to jury in civil as well as criminal cases, furnished part of the impetus for introducing amendments to the Constitution that ultimately resulted in the jury trial provisions of the Sixth and Seventh Amendments."

When President George Washington gave his first annual message to Congress in 1789, he noted that demands for amendments to the United States Constitution were widespread. On June 8, 1789, not long after President Washington's first annual message to Congress, James Madison addressed the House of Representatives. The proposed amendments to the United States Constitution, which were described by Madison in that address, covered all of the provisions which eventually became the federal Bill of Rights.

The amendment relating to jury trial in criminal cases, as introduced by James Madison in the House, would have provided that: "The trial of all crimes...shall be by an impartial jury of freeholders of the vicinage, with the requisite of unanimity for conviction, of the right of challenge, and other accustomed requisites." That Amendment passed the House in substantially the same form in which it was submitted. For the purpose of this case, it is important to note the common law form in which the right to trial by jury originally passed in the United States House of Representatives, since John Vining of Delaware was the Chairman of the House Committee Select which had studied Madison's proposals.

After more than a week of debate in the Senate, Madison's proposed amendment with regard to trial by jury was returned to the House in a considerably altered form. "The version that finally emerged from the Committee was the version that ultimately became the Sixth Amendment, ensuring an accused: "the right to a speedy and public trial, by an impartial jury of the State and district wherein the crime shall have been committed, which district shall have been previously ascertained by law." The provisions spelling out such *common-law features* of the jury as "unanimity" or "the accustomed requisites" *were gone.* The "vicinage" requirement had been replaced by wording that reflected a compromise between broad and narrow definitions of that term. Thus, it was left to Congress to determine the actual size of the "vicinage" through the establishment of judicial districts. Significantly, one of Delaware's first two United States Senators during the time of this debate was Richard Bassett. Senator Bassett voted in favor of the common law right to trial by jury, as originally proposed by Madison and recommended by the House Committee Select, chaired by John Vining.

The United States Supreme Court has concluded that three significant features may be observed in the history of the enactment of the United States Constitution's jury trial provisions.

> First, even though the vicinage requirement was as much a feature of the common-law jury as was the twelve-man requirement, the mere reference to "trial by jury" in Article III was not interpreted to include that feature.... Second, provisions that would have explicitly tied the "jury" concept to the "accustomed requisites" of the time were eliminated... Finally, contemporary legislative and

constitutional provisions indicate that where Congress wanted to leave no doubt that it was incorporating existing common-law features of the jury system, it knew how to use express language to that effect. *Williams v. Florida*, 399 U.S. 78, 96 (1970).

Consequently, the United States Supreme Court has concluded that it is not "able to divine precisely what the word 'jury' imported to the Framers, the First Congress, or the States in 1789....But there is absolutely no indication in 'the intent of the Framers' of an explicit decision to equate the [United States] constitutional and common-law characteristics of the jury."

The debates about Madison's proposed amendments to the United States Constitution ended in 1791 with the adoption of the federal Bill of Rights. When the debates about the federal Bill of Rights were over, John Dickinson's interpretation of the phrase "trial by jury" in Article III, as preserving the common law right to trial by jury, had been proven incorrect. Moreover, despite the original urging of James Madison, the subsequent endorsement of that recommendation by the House Committee Select, chaired by Delaware's Congressman John Vining and the support of Senators, such as Delaware's Richard Bassett, the effort to preserve *all* of the common law rights to trial by jury in the federal Bill of Rights had not prevailed. Congress had made an express decision not to preserve all of the features of the common law right to trial by jury, when it could have done so in the Sixth and Seventh Amendments to the United States Constitution.

On September 8, 1791, the Delaware General Assembly called for a state constitutional convention. The Delaware Constitutional Convention "assembled at Dover, on Tuesday, November 29, 1791, and elected John Dickinson, president." Delaware's United States Senator, Richard Bassett, who had been a delegate to the state constitutional convention in 1776 was also a delegate to the Delaware Constitutional Convention in 1791.

John Dickinson's involvement in the debates about the right to trial by jury in Article III, during the ratification process of the United States Constitution in 1788, as well as Congressman John Vining's and Senator Richard Bassett's involvement with the debates on that subject, preceding the enactment of the federal Bill of Rights in 1791, provide important historical insight into what happened in 1791, when Delaware decided to amend its own Constitution. After the debates about the meaning of the term "trial by jury" in Article III and the provisions on that subject to be included in the federal Bill of Rights were finished, Delawareans, especially John Dickinson and Richard Bassett, were acutely aware of the need to set forth an intention to perpetuate fundamental rights, as they had existed at common law, in unambiguous language.

When the amendments to the United States Constitution, which had been proposed by Madison, were being discussed by the House of Representatives Committee Select, John Vining had urged "a plainness and simplicity of style on this and every other occasion, which should be easily understood." John Vining's advice was followed by Dickinson, Bassett, and the other delegates to the 1791 Delaware Constitutional Convention. When the convention concluded its work on December 31, 1791, its draft of the proposed Delaware Constitution provided that "trial by jury shall be as heretofore," i.e., the provision in the 1776 Delaware Constitution perpetuating the guarantee of trial by jury as it existed at common law.

Thus, Delaware's unambiguous commitment to the preservation of the common law right to trial by jury was evidenced with a "simplicity of style." The draft was signed by the members of the Delaware Constitutional Convention on January 12, 1792. The signatures of the long-time champions of the common law right to trial by jury, John Dickinson and Richard Bassett, signify their satisfaction and approval of the provision that "trial by jury shall be as heretofore" in the December 31, 1791, draft. That draft was adopted, without change, as Delaware's Constitution later in 1792.

Delaware's constitutional commitment to continue to guarantee the right to trial by jury for its citizens, as it existed at common law, was expressly recognized in the arguments presented in the earliest reported decision to construe the phrase "trial by jury shall be as heretofore" in the Delaware Constitution of 1792:

> The [Delaware] Constitution is express that "trial by jury shall be as heretofore," plainly intending to secure both the form and the substance, the trial and the constitution of the jury.

> The framers of the [Delaware] Constitution of 1776 were aware of that importance, when they declared it to be a fundamental rule "that trial by jury of facts where they arise is one of the greatest securities of the lives, liberties and estates of the people." The provision in the present Constitution is stronger and more positive, "Trials by jury shall be as heretofore."

> A comparison of the [Delaware] Constitution or System of Government and Declaration of Rights of 1776 with the present Constitution will convince any one, if a doubt exists on the subject, that the Convention of 1792 had the old Constitution before them and made it in fact the groundwork of their labors; for many of its most important provisions are inserted in the present Constitution without the slightest variation even of the expressions, while other principles of the old system are adopted in language differing but little in its terms, and bearing precisely the same purport. The fourteenth section of the Declaration of Rights is made the seventh section of first article of the present [Delaware] Constitution, with this important exception, that it is not provided in the latter, as in the former, that no person shall be found guilty without the unanimous consent of an impartial jury. But are we therefore to suppose that it was intended

to vest the legislature with the power of enacting that a person accused of a criminal offense might be convicted upon the finding of a majority of a jury? By no means. It was considered that this principle was secured by the fourth section, which says that "trial by jury shall be as heretofore," and a repetition of it was deemed unnecessary. *Wilson v. Oldfield*, Clayton 169, 1 Delaware Cases 622, 624-27 (1818).

The teaching of *Oldfield* was ratified and reaffirmed by this Court one hundred and fifty years later:

> It is of course fundamental under our law that the verdict of a jury must be unanimous. This follows from article I, section 4 of the Delaware Constitution, providing that, "The right to trial by jury shall be as heretofore." This provision of our Constitution guarantees the right to trial by jury as it existed at common law....Unanimity of the jurors is therefore required to reach a verdict since such was the common law rule. *Fountain v. State*, 275 A.2d 251 (Del. 1971).

One year earlier, in 1970, the Delaware Constitution Revision Commission had written in its study commentary:

> Article I, section 4, of the present constitution deals with three distinct subjects: (1) Right of trial by jury in civil cases; (2) right of trial by jury in criminal cases; and (3) requirement, composition, and conduct of the grand jury. Since the three types of juries, including special juries, existed at common law, the 1792 Constitution's adoption of the right of trial by jury "as heretofore," and its carryover in successive constitutions to date, brings forward to the present day reliance on the common law as to right of the petit jury in civil and criminal actions, the special jury in civil actions, and the grand jury. Because of this situation, reference must always be made to common law to properly interpret the meaning of the present constitution.

Article I, section 4 of the Delaware Constitution still provides that "[t]rial by jury shall be as heretofore." This language has appeared in article I, section 4 of three successive Delaware constitutions—1792, 1831 and 1897. This language was left unchanged when article I, section 4 was amended as recently as 1984. This Court and the other courts of Delaware have always construed that provision in the Delaware Constitution as "guaranteeing the right to trial by jury as it existed at common law."

In *Williams v. Florida*, when examining the federal Constitutional right to a jury trial, the United States Supreme Court stated:

> While "the intent of the Framers" is often an elusive quarry, the relevant constitutional history casts considerable doubt on the easy assumption in our past decisions that if a given feature existed in a jury at common law in 1789, then it was necessarily preserved in the Constitution.

After an extensive review of the history leading to the actual wording of the right to trial by jury in the federal Bill of Rights, the United States Supreme Court concluded:

> [T]here is absolutely no indication in "the intent of the Framers" of an explicit decision to equate the constitutional and common-law characteristics of the jury.

Accordingly, the United States Supreme Court has turned to other than purely historical considerations to determine which features of the jury system, as it existed at common law, were preserved in the United States Constitution.

Conversely, it is untenable to conclude that the right to trial by jury in the Delaware Constitution means exactly the same thing as that right in the United States Constitution. The history of the right to trial by jury "as heretofore," which has remained unchanged in the Delaware Constitution since 1792, demonstrates an unambiguous intention to equate Delaware's constitutional right to trial by jury with the common law characteristics of that right. Consequently, all of the fundamental features of the jury system, as they existed at common law, have been preserved for Delaware's citizens. Therefore, the proper focus of any analysis of the right to trial by jury, as it is guaranteed in the Delaware Constitution, requires an examination of the common law.

Rule: Del jury rights = common law jury.

At common law, when a member of a jury became ill or died during the trial, the jury was discharged. The other eleven members of the jury were then recalled along with another juror to complete the twelve. The parties were given their full complement of challenges and afforded the opportunity to use them against the reconstituted panel. Once a new jury was selected and sworn, the trial began anew. This was obviously a costly and time consuming process.

What happens in common law after the juror

This Court and others have recognized the validity of implementing procedures which improve the operation of the jury system, as it existed at common law, *without* changing the fundamental common law features of right to trial by jury. For example, in an effort to save scarce judicial resources, statutes and court rules have been enacted which permit the selection of alternate jurors at the beginning of the trial when the regular jurors are selected. Delaware adopted a rule analogous to that used in the federal system. Superior Court Criminal Rule 24(c) permits the selection of up to four alternates along with the regular jury, to "replace jurors who, prior to the time the jury retires to consider its verdict, become or are found to be unable or disqualified to perform their duties."

The present procedure in the Superior Court, which provides for the simultaneous selection of regular and alternate jurors and allows alternate jurors to be substituted prior to the commencement of the jury's deliberations, is the functional equivalent of the common law system. The jurors and the alternates are assiduously instructed not to discuss the case until it has been submitted to them for deliberation.

Alternate juror system is fine w/ common law

The present practice preserves the common law system of submitting the case to twelve persons, who deliberate for the first time, only after all of the evidence has been presented. As one court has stated:

There is no question that the provision for the substitution of alternate jurors prior to the submission of the case to the jury is constitutional. During the course of the trial the 12 regular jurors and the alternate jurors are treated similarly in all respects. And since the jurors are not permitted to discuss the case among themselves until it is submitted to them, there is no way in which the defendants' rights could be prejudiced if 1 or more of the 12 jurors are replaced by an alternate juror. Twelve jurors who hear the evidence and are in all respects treated as jurors participate in the deliberations and render a verdict.

Alt. juror system is constitutional

In fact, the present procedure, pursuant to Superior Court Criminal Rule 24, which provides for the use of alternate jurors and their substitution prior to the commencement of the jury's deliberations has been upheld under the Delaware Constitution by this Court.

Although the substitution of an alternate juror prior to the commencement of the jury's deliberations is the functional equivalent of the practice at common law, the substitution of an alternate juror during the jury's deliberations is the antithesis of the practice at common law. At common law, the commencement of the jury's deliberative process marked a unique and inviolate stage of the trial proceeding. As one commentator notes:

> In 1354, we find among the Parliament Rolls a striking petition,…"that hereafter when any people are at issue and the inquest is charged and sworn, all evidence which is to be said (*totes evidences que sont a dire*) be openly said at the bar, so that after the inquest departs with its charge, no justice or other person have conference (*parlance*) with them to move or procure the said inquest, but that they say the fact upon their own peril and oath." This petition was granted.

In the 18th century, Blackstone wrote:

> Our law has therefore wisely placed this strong and two-fold barrier, of a presentment and a trial by jury, between the liberties of the people, and the prerogative of the crown.…[T]he founders of the English law have with excellent forecast contrived, that…the truth of every accusation, whether preferred in the shape of indictment, information, or appeal, should afterwards be confirmed by the unanimous suffrage of twelve of his equals and neighbours, indifferently chosen and superior to all suspicion.

Blackstone described the jury's deliberative process as follows:

> The jury, after the proofs are summed up, unless the case be very clear, withdraw from the bar to consider of their verdict: and, in order to avoid intemperance and causeless delay, are to be kept without meat, drink, fire, or candle, unless by the permission of the judge, till they are all unanimously agreed.

However, once jury begins deliberating, cannot use alt.

Thus, at common law, once it retired to consider its verdict, "the jury" was irrevocably constituted. The deliberative process was required to continue inviolate by those twelve persons "until they are all unanimously agreed."

All of the fundamental features of the right to trial by jury, as they existed at common law, have been preserved by the Delaware Constitution. This Court has expressly held that under the Delaware

Constitution, unanimity of the jurors is required to reach a verdict since such was the common law rule. It has also been expressly recognized that the Delaware Constitution guarantees the common law right to a trial by a jury of twelve persons in a criminal proceeding. Similarly, the right to trial by jury at common law required a unanimous verdict by the same twelve jurors who retired to deliberate. Thus, that common law characteristic of the right to trial by jury in a criminal proceeding is guaranteed by the Delaware Constitution.   *Rule. Arrived, holding   for Δ.*

At common law, the rule was "[i]f a juror becomes unable to serve after the jury retires to deliberate, a mistrial must be declared if one or both parties refuse to stipulate to a verdict delivered by a jury of less than twelve members." In this case, the substitution of an alternate juror during the deliberative process was in derogation of the common law. Consequently, it was contrary to defendants' right to trial by jury "as heretofore," which has been guaranteed by the Delaware Constitution since 1792.

NOTES

1.   The unanimity requirement of the Delaware Constitution applies to the jury's determination of a statutory aggravating circumstance in the penalty phase of a capital case. *Capano v. State*, 889 A.2d 968 (Del. 2006).

2.   In criminal cases, the Pennsylvania Constitution provides the prosecution "shall have the same right to trial by jury as does the accused." Pa. Const. art. I, § 6; *Commonwealth v. White*, 910 A.2d 648 (Pa. 2006) (prosecution asserted the right).

3.   The Montana Constitution requires the state's consent to waive a jury trial in a criminal case. Mont. Const. art. II, § 26.

4.   The Delaware Constitution provides that "judges shall not charge juries with respect to matters of fact, but may state the questions of fact in issue and declare the law." Del. Const. art. IV, § 19; *Herring v. State*, 805 A.2d 872, 876 (Del. 2002).

5.   Some state constitutions not only specify the number of jurors required in a criminal proceeding but distinguish between the number of jurors needed when the charged offense is either a felony or misdemeanor. Article I, section 16 of the California Constitution provides:

> In criminal actions in which a felony is charged, the jury shall consist of 12 persons. In criminal actions in which a misdemeanor is charged, the jury shall consist of 12 persons or a lesser number agreed on by the parties in open court.

6.   Article I, section 18(a) of the New York Constitution provides:

> The Legislature may provide that in any court of original jurisdiction a jury shall be composed of six or twelve persons . . ., provided, however, that crimes prosecuted by indictment shall be tried by a jury composed of twelve persons, unless a jury trial has been waived.

7. The Utah Constitution requires "jury unanimity" as to a specific crime and as to each element of the crime. *State v. Saunders*, 992 P.2d 951 (Utah 1999).

8. The elimination of jury trial for offenses punishable by less than six months in jail violated the New Hampshire Constitution because the framers intended to guarantee jury trial to all facing the possibility of incarceration. *Opinion of the Justices*, 608 A.2d 202 (N.H. 1992).

B. SELF-INCRIMINATION

The federal Fifth Amendment provides in part: "No person...shall be compelled in any criminal case to be a witness against himself." Textual differences in about twenty state constitutions broaden the scope of the privilege beyond compelled testimonial evidence by providing that: "No person shall be compelled to give evidence against himself." *See* Conn. Const. art. I, § 8; *see also* Pa. Const. art. I, § 9 ("In all criminal prosecutions the accused...cannot be compelled to give evidence against himself. . . ."). The origin of this wording was probably the Virginia provision, *see* Va. Const. art. I, § 8 (The accused "shall not...be compelled in any criminal proceeding to give evidence against himself") or the Massachusetts provision. *See* Mass. Const. pt. I, art. XII ("No subject shall be...compelled to accuse, or furnish evidence against himself."). Other states adopted those models rather than the federal one. *See* Miss. Const. art. III, § 26 ("In all criminal prosecutions the accused...shall not be compelled to give evidence against himself."); Tex. Const. art. I, § 19 ("In all criminal prosecutions the accused...shall not be compelled to give evidence against himself.").

COMMONWEALTH v. MOLINA
104 A.3d 430 (Pa. 2013)

BAER, J.

We granted review in this case to consider whether a defendant's right against self-incrimination, as protected by the federal and Pennsylvania constitutions, is violated when the prosecution utilizes a non-testifying defendant's pre-arrest silence as substantive evidence of guilt. After reviewing this issue of first impression, to which the United States Supreme Court has not definitively spoken, we agree with the Superior Court, as well as several of our sister courts, that the use of pre-arrest silence as substantive evidence of guilt violates a non-testifying defendant's constitutional rights. As discussed below, we would affirm the order of the Superior Court remanding for a new trial. However, given that the status of federal jurisprudence is uncertain, we base our holding upon the right against self-incrimination set forth in Article I, Section 9 of the Pennsylvania Constitution.

In this case, a jury convicted Michael Molina (Defendant) of third degree murder and related crimes resulting from the savage beating of Melissa Snodgrass (Victim), apparently as a result of drug debts owed by Victim to Defendant. On September 7, 2003, Victim told her mother, with whom she lived, that she was leaving the house to run some errands. When she did not return, Victim's mother reported her disappearance to the Missing Persons Unit of the Pittsburgh Police Department. Six months later, her decomposed remains were found under moldy clothing and other debris in the basement of a house in the Spring Garden section of Pittsburgh in which Michael Benintend, one of the prosecution's primary witnesses, resided during the relevant time period.

The issue presented to this Court requires consideration of the Missing Persons Unit detective's testimony and the prosecutor's closing arguments regarding the early days of the investigation into Victim's disappearance. Following a lead that Defendant was holding Victim against her will, the Missing Persons Unit detective assigned to the case went to Defendant's house two days after Victim's disappearance. Pamela Deloe, a second primary prosecution witness, answered the door and asserted that neither Victim nor Defendant were at the house. Accordingly, the detective left her card and asked that Defendant call her. Later that day, Defendant called the detective.

The detective testified regarding the phone call from Defendant:

> I asked him—well, before I could even ask him if he was aware of [Victim] being missing, he stated to me that there were—that he didn't know where she was. It was out on the street that someone said that he was involved in her being missing and it wasn't him.

The detective then inquired as to when Defendant had last seen Victim. He initially responded that he had not seen her for a year and a half, but then he immediately contradicted his statement, claiming instead that he had not seen her for three months. Subsequent to this contradiction, the detective testified that she asked him to come to the police station to speak to her and he refused:

> A. Yes. After he stated that, I asked him if he could come into our office and sit down and talk with me about the case, and he refused. He said he refused to come in.
>
> Q. So this contact that you had with him was over the telephone. Is that what you're saying?
>
> A. Yes, it was over the telephone.

Defense counsel did not object to the reference to Defendant's refusal to come into the office. In due course, the prosecution concluded its questioning of the detective, and defense counsel did not pursue that issue in his cross-examination.

During closing argument, the prosecutor accentuated Defendant's refusal to go to the police station, and when defense counsel objected, the prosecutor stated before the jury that it was not improper to comment on Defendant's pre-arrest silence:

> [Prosecutor:] Look also at what happened in terms of the police investigation in this matter. Three days after this young lady goes missing, three days after she goes missing, detectives are already knocking on the defendant's door because of something they heard, maybe he was holding this person against their [sic] will, and he calls the police back and is very defensive. I mean, before a question's even asked, he denies any knowledge or any involvement with this young lady. He makes contradictory statements to the police about when's the last time that he saw her. First he says, "I saw her a year and a half ago." Then he says, "I saw her three months ago." But most telling, I think, is the fact that the officer invited him. "Well, come on down and talk to us. We want to ask you some more questions about this incident, your knowledge of this young lady," especially because he made these contradictory statements. And what happens? Nothing happens. He refuses to cooperate with the Missing Persons detectives. And why?

> [Defense Counsel]: Your Honor, I have to object to that. That's improper comment, absolutely improper.

> [Prosecutor]: Your Honor, pre-arrest silence is not improper comment at all.

In a brief sidebar discussion, defense counsel requested that the jury be instructed to disregard the statement, which the defense viewed as "absolutely improper;" "If somebody wants to assert their right not to cooperate and talk to the police, that cannot be commented upon." Notably, defense counsel did not seek a mistrial at this juncture. The prosecution responded "there's a sharp line drawn between pre-arrest silence and post-arrest silence." The court allowed the prosecution to proceed without issuing any instructions. The prosecutor further emphasized the silence following the sidebar, stating, "Factor that in when you're making an important decision in this case as well."

The jury found Defendant not guilty of first-degree murder but convicted him of third-degree murder and unlawful restraint based substantially on the eyewitness testimony of Benintend and Deloe, who claimed to have witnessed Defendant brutally beat Victim to death. The trial court sentenced him to twenty to forty years of imprisonment. Defendant appealed the judgment of sentence, raising four issues in his Pa.R.A.P. 1925(b) concise statement of issues presented on appeal, including the claim currently before this Court: whether the trial court erred in not sustaining the objection to the prosecution's reference to Defendant's pre-arrest silence and in not declaring a mistrial.

The Superior Court held that, while the detective's testimony, in and of itself, did not violate the right against self-incrimination, the right was violated when the prosecutor utilized Defendant's refusal to speak further with the detective as substantive evidence of his guilt in his closing argument. The court further concluded that the trial court's error was not harmless. Rather than constituting the overwhelming evidence necessary to meet the Commonwealth's burden of proving harmless error, the Superior Court found the Commonwealth's case to be based upon the testimony of Benintend and Deloe, both of whose credibility was significantly challenged at trial. Accordingly, the Superior Court reversed the convictions and vacated the judgment of sentence.

The Commonwealth filed a petition for allowance of appeal, and this Court granted review to consider whether "the Superior Court err[ed] in ruling that the use by the Commonwealth of a non-testifying defendant's pre-arrest silence as substantive evidence of his guilt infringes upon his constitutional right to be free from self-incrimination?"

I. Salinas v. Texas

In February 2013, we placed the case on hold pending the decision of the United States Supreme Court in *Salinas v. Texas*, which, *inter alia*, raised a claim regarding the use of pre-arrest silence as substantive evidence. As discussed below, the plurality decision of the High Court in that case did not resolve the issue, but instead affirmed the use of the defendant's silence in a fractured decision. Prior to hearing argument, we allowed the parties to submit supplemental briefing addressing *Salinas*.

A search of our caselaw interpreting both the state and federal protections does not reveal any prior insistence by this Court that there be an express invocation of the right against self-incrimination. Instead, our precedent is more aligned with the dissenting four justices in *Salinas*, who concluded that the no ritualistic language is needed but rather found that invocation of the right may be apparent from the circumstances surrounding the defendant's statement.

As applied to this case, we determine that Defendant's actions in affirmatively and definitively refusing to come to the police station and ending the phone call were sufficient to invoke his right against self-incrimination and are distinguishable from Salinas's temporary muteness sandwiched between voluntary verbal responses to police questioning.

II. Constitutionality of the Use of Pre–Arrest Silence as Substantive Evidence

Turning to the issue upon which we granted review, the Commonwealth maintains that the Superior Court erred in concluding that the prosecutor's reference to Defendant's pre-arrest silence violated his right against self-incrimination. The Commonwealth claims that this Court has drawn a line of significance between pre- and post-arrest silence, and that the "privilege against self-incrimination" does not extend backward from the post-arrest period to cover the pre-arrest timeframe scrutinized herein.

Accordingly, we consider whether the trial court committed reversible error in allowing the prosecutor, over defense counsel's objection, to use a non-testifying defendant's pre-arrest silence as substantive evidence of guilt because such use violated the defendant's constitutional right to be protected from self-incrimination. "As this is an issue involving a constitutional right, it is a question of law; thus, our standard of review is de novo, and our scope of review is plenary."

Initially, we recognize that the constitutionality of the use of pre-arrest silence as substantive evidence has split the federal circuit courts and state courts, engendering numerous fractured decisions across the United States. While the United States Supreme Court accepted review of *Salinas* to resolve the issue, it appears to have created a new question regarding the sufficiency of invocation of the right under the Fifth Amendment without resolving whether the Fifth Amendment applies to the use of pre-arrest silence as substantive evidence of guilt, even if properly invoked.

When the federal constitutional jurisprudence has been unclear or in a state of flux, "this Court has not hesitated to render its independent judgment as a matter of distinct and enforceable Pennsylvania constitutional law."

When considering the rights provided by the Pennsylvania Constitution, we are ever cognizant that the federal constitution provides the minimum levels of protection applicable to the analogous state constitutional provision. "[E]ach state has the power to provide broader standards, and go beyond the minimum floor which is established by the federal Constitution." Accordingly, we are not bound by the decisions of the United States Supreme Court on similar constitutional provisions but instead may consider the opinions for their persuasive value.

As we stated in *Pap's A.M.*, we conduct Pennsylvania constitutional analysis consistently with the model set forth in *Edmunds*. "Under *Edmunds*, the Court should consider: the text of the relevant Pennsylvania Constitutional provision; its history, including Pennsylvania case law; policy considerations, including unique issues of state and local concern and the impact on Pennsylvania jurisprudence; and relevant cases, if any, from other jurisdictions."

A. Text

In considering the text of the provisions, we first look to their placement in the larger charter. The structure of the Pennsylvania Constitution highlights the primacy of Pennsylvania's protection of individual rights: "The very first Article of the Pennsylvania Constitution consists of the Pennsylvania Declaration of Rights, and the first section of that Article affirms, among other things, that all citizens 'have certain inherent and indefeasible rights.'" Moreover, our charter further protects the rights detailed in Article I in Section 25, providing, "To guard against transgressions of the high powers which we have delegated, we declare that everything in this article is excepted out of the general powers of government and shall forever remain inviolate." "Unlike the Bill of Rights of the United States Constitution which emerged as a later addendum in 1791, the Declaration of Rights in the Pennsylvania Constitution was an organic part of the state's original constitution of 1776, and appeared (not coincidentally) first in that document." *Edmunds*, 586 A.2d at 896.

One of the rights protected in Article I is Section 9's right against self-incrimination. As is true of most of the provisions of the Pennsylvania Declaration of Rights, Section 9 was adopted in 1776 and served as a model for the protections provided by the Fifth Amendment of the United States Constitution as it predated the federal provision by fifteen years. *See generally id.* at 896 (discussing the historical background of the Pennsylvania Declaration of Rights). Originally, the provision was worded to provide that no "man" can "be compelled to give evidence against himself," with the current wording adopted in 1838. Section 9 currently dictates, "In all criminal prosecutions, the accused ... cannot be compelled to give evidence against himself." This language is very similar to the Fifth Amendment, which provides: "[n]o person ... shall be compelled in any criminal case to be a witness against himself." U.S. CONST. amend. V. While we recognize that "no man" in the federal provision is arguably broader than "the accused" in Pennsylvania's section, we also observe that Pennsylvania's protection against being forced "to give evidence" is potentially more extensive than the federal protection against being "a witness against himself." Given the substantial similarity of the provisions, we do not find the textual differences dispositive. Moreover, "we are not bound to interpret the two provisions as if they were mirror images, even where the text is similar or identical." *Edmunds*, 586 A.2d at 895–96. Indeed, we have previously found Section 9 to provide greater protection than the Fifth Amendment, despite the similar language. *See, e.g., Commonwealth v. Triplett*, 462 Pa. 244, 341 A.2d 62 (1975) (plurality) (holding, in the lead opinion as described below, that under the Pennsylvania Constitution an accused could not be impeached with his prior voluntary, but suppressed, statements; abrogated by subsequent amendment).

The Pennsylvania Constitution also historically contained two exceptions to the right against self-incrimination not present in the federal charter. In 1874, Article III, Section 32 (repealed in 1967) and Article

VIII, Section 10 (now renumbered Article VII, Section 8) were added to allow for compelled testimony regarding cases involving bribery or corrupt solicitations and contested elections, respectively. *See* Ken Gormley, *The Pennsylvania Constitution: A Treatise on Rights and Liberties*, § 12.6(c) at 387 n.318 (2004). The provisions stated that testimony could be compelled but "such testimony shall not afterwards be used against [the witness] in any judicial proceedings except for perjury in giving such testimony." While these provisions provide specific exceptions for when testimony can be compelled, they do not guide our analysis of whether the protections of Section 9 apply to pre-arrest silence.

Given that the textual distinctions between Section 9 and the Fifth Amendment do not definitively speak to the issue before the Court, we find more persuasive our jurisprudence interpreting the provisions, which also incorporates underlying policy considerations.

B. History and Policy Considerations

Our precedent regarding the right against self-incrimination has generally developed in parallel or following the dictates of federal precedent interpreting the Fifth Amendment, particularly after the United States Supreme Court's 1965 decision in *Griffin*, 380 U.S. at 615, 85 S.Ct. 1229 (holding that "the Fifth Amendment, in its direct application to the Federal Government and in its bearing on the States by reason of the Fourteenth Amendment, forbids either comment by the prosecution on the accused's silence or instructions by the court that such silence is evidence of guilt."). On most occasions, we have not considered whether differences exist between the federal and state provisions.

We recognize, however, that this Court has taken inconsistent stances in determining whether the right against self-incrimination under Section 9 exceeds the protections of the Fifth Amendment. At times, we have "stated that, except for the protection afforded by our Commonwealth's Constitution to reputation, the provision in Article I, § 9 which grants a privilege against self-incrimination tracks the protection afforded under the Fifth Amendment." Similarly, we opined generally that we should not extend rights under our Pennsylvania Constitution beyond those in the federal charter absent "a compelling reason to do so." In most of the cases where we have interpreted the rights as coextensive, however, we have indicated that the defendant failed to provide a convincing argument in favor of stronger protection under the Pennsylvania Constitution.

On several occasions, our Court has specifically concluded that the protections of Section 9 exceed those in its federal counterpart. *Swinehart*, 664 A.2d at 969 (addressing immunity and opining that "Article I, Section 9 is, in fact, more expansive than the Fifth Amendment" but not so much as to require greater protection than that provided by the relevant statute); *Turner*, 499 Pa. 579, 454 A.2d 537 (rejecting *Fletcher v. Weir*, 455 U.S. 603, 102 S.Ct. 1309, 71 L.Ed.2d 490, and holding that reference to post-arrest, pre-*Miranda* silence violates Article I, Section 9); *Triplett*, 462 Pa. 244, 341 A.2d 62 (plurality) (diverging, under the lead opinion, from *Harris v. New York*, 401 U.S. 222, 91 S.Ct. 643, 28 L.Ed.2d 1 (1971), and concluding that use of suppressed but voluntary statements to impeach a defendant's testimony violated Article I, Section 9, later abrogated by constitutional amendment). *Cf. Edmunds*, 586 A.2d at 898 (observing in regard to Article I, Section 8 of the Pennsylvania Constitution that from 1961–1973, this Court "tended to parallel the cases interpreting the 4th Amendment," but "beginning in 1973, our case-law began to reflect a clear divergence from federal precedent."). Given the arguably contradictory holdings regarding the interaction between Section 9 and the Fifth Amendment, we must consider our precedent regarding the right against self-incrimination more broadly to determine whether Section 9 protects a defendant's decision to remain silent in the pre-arrest context.

Our jurisprudence regarding references to a defendant's silence is severable into identifiable categories. We initially consider precedent addressing the right against self-incrimination generally. Next, we review those cases where reference to silence is permissible to impeach a defendant who has waived his right by testifying at trial or where counsel has raised an argument necessitating the prosecution's fair response. Additionally, we recognize that courts have created an exception to this general impeachment and fair response rule when the provision of *Miranda* warnings induces a defendant's silence, such that reference to the silence would violate Fourteenth Amendment due process rights, even if it would not violate the Fifth Amendment right against self-incrimination. Finally, in turning to the specific question of pre-arrest silence, we discuss this Court's decision in *Bolus*, which addressed pre-arrest silence in the impeachment context, but specifically left open the question currently before the Court regarding the use of silence as substantive evidence of guilt.

1. General Right Against Self–Incrimination

Similar to the Fifth Amendment, Article I Section 9 dictates that the accused "cannot be compelled to give evidence against himself." The United States Supreme Court has broadly defined the reach of this protection, given its importance in the structure of our judicial system:

> The privilege reflects a complex of our fundamental values and aspirations, and marks an important advance in the development of our liberty. It can be asserted in any proceeding, civil or criminal, administrative or judicial, investigatory or adjudicatory; and it protects against any disclosures which the witness

reasonably believes could be used in a criminal prosecution or could lead to other evidence that might be so used.

Kastigar v. U.S., 406 U.S. 441, 444–45, 92 S.Ct. 1653, 32 L.Ed.2d 212 (1972) (footnotes omitted).

We have acknowledged, however, the "inherent conflict" between the right against self-incrimination and our system's reliance on compelled testimony. While we have credited the "public['s] right to every man's evidence," our courts have emphasized the need for the protection against self-incrimination to avoid the "cruel trilemma of self-accusation, perjury or contempt" that faced those brought before tribunals such as the Star Chamber in England. *Id.* (internal citation omitted). Through forced confession, individuals had to choose whether to incriminate themselves, perjure themselves, or be held in contempt if they remained silent. As Dean Gormley has observed, "the prohibition against conviction by a process of inquisition is the crown jewel" of all rights afforded the accused under federal and state constitutions. Gormley, *The Pennsylvania Constitution*, § 12.6(a), at 386 (internal quotations, citations and footnote omitted).

As the United States Supreme Court did in *Griffin*, this Court has viewed the right against self-incrimination as protecting silence as well as overt self-incrimination. In *Dravecz*, Justice Musmanno explained how silence and self-incrimination are tied:

> Under common law and, of course, this was doubly true in medieval continental Europe, forced confessions were as common as they were cruel and inhuman. The framers of our Bill of Rights were too aware of the excesses possible in all governments, even a representative government, to permit the possibility that any person under the protection of the United States flag could be forced to admit to having committed a crime. In order to make the protection hazard-proof, the framers went beyond coercion of confessions. They used the all-embracive language that no one could be compelled 'to be a witness against himself'. What did the Trial Court in this case do but compel Dravecz to be a witness against himself? Dravecz had said nothing, yet because something was read to him, to which he made no comment, the prosecution insisted that Dravecz admitted guilt. If Dravecz could not be made a self-accusing witness by coerced answers, he should not be made a witness against himself by unspoken assumed answers.

Commonwealth v. Dravecz, 424 Pa. 582, 227 A.2d 904, 907 (1967) (plurality). Our Court took the occasion of the Dravecz case to further explore the ambiguity inherent in silence, as noted above, recognizing that not all those accused of a crime immediately declare their innocence, but some may be made speechless by the accusation. *Id.* Other courts, as did the Superior Court below, have similarly observed that innocent individuals accused of a crime may also remain silent for fear that their explanation will not be believed or to protect another.

Since *Griffin*, the protection of a defendant's silence has become imbedded in our jurisprudence. *See, e.g.*, *Com. v. Wright*, 599 Pa. 270, 961 A.2d 119, 143 (2008) ("[T]his Court vigilantly protects the right to remain silent and recognizes references to an accused's exercise of this right may jeopardize the presumption of innocence in the jury's mind."); *cf. Edmunds*, 586 A.2d at 900 (discussing New Jersey Supreme Court's recognition of a right that is accepted and then becomes imbedded in the state's jurisprudence under a state constitution after twenty-five years of consistent application). Moreover, this Court additionally opined nearly forty years ago that "[t]he prohibition of any reference to an accused's silence reflects the court's desire that an accused not be penalized for exercising his constitutional rights." Accordingly, this Court has long protected a defendant's silence as part of the right against self-incrimination.

2. Permitted Use of Silence as Impeachment Evidence or Fair Response

Under both state and federal precedent, the analysis changes dramatically once a defendant decides to testify because he has waived his right against self-incrimination: "His waiver is not partial; having once cast aside the cloak of immunity, he may not resume it at will, whenever cross-examination may be inconvenient or embarrassing." As the Supreme Court noted in *Jenkins*, it would undermine the fundamental truth-seeking purpose of our adversary system to prevent the prosecution from questioning the validity of the defendant's testimony in an attempt to uncover fabricated defenses: "Once a defendant decides to testify, the interests of the other party and regard for the function of courts of justice to ascertain the truth become relevant, and prevail in the balance of considerations determining the scope and limits of the privilege against self-incrimination." Accordingly, the prosecution may impeach the testifying defendant with his prior statements, actions, or silence, regardless of whether the statements, actions, or silence occurred prior to or after the reading of *Miranda* rights or the defendant's arrest, if the defendant waives his right against self-incrimination by testifying.

The question of whether reference to a non-testifying defendant's pre-arrest silence violates the defendant's right against self-incrimination is now squarely before this Court. As discussed below, we conclude that the timing of the silence, whether it be pre or post-arrest, or pre or post-*Miranda* warnings, is not relevant to the question of whether a prosecutor's use of the silence as substantive evidence of guilt violates an individual's right against self-incrimination. While our courts have found the timing of a defendant's silence in relation to the provision of *Miranda* warnings to be extremely relevant to a defendant's due process rights, *see Doyle*, 426 U.S. 610, 96 S.Ct. 2240, 49 L.Ed.2d 91, the underpinnings of the right against self-incrimination are not based on timing but on whether a person has been compelled to be a witness against himself at a criminal proceeding. Regardless of whether a forced confession is obtained prior to the official act of an arrest or after, it is not admissible at trial as it would result in the defendant being "compelled to give evidence against himself."

Moreover, allowing reference to a defendant's silence as substantive evidence endangers the truth-determining process given our recognition that individuals accused of a crime may remain silent for any number of reasons. As in this case, a defendant's silence in the face of police questioning is "insolubly ambiguous" as it could be indicative of a busy schedule, a distrust of authority, an unwillingness to snitch, as much as it is indicative of guilt. Nonetheless, as we noted in *Turner*, jurors generally view silence as an indication of guilt.

Accordingly, we conclude that our precedent, and the policies underlying it, support the conclusion that the right against self-incrimination prohibits use of a defendant's pre-arrest silence as substantive evidence of guilt, unless it falls within an exception such as impeachment of a testifying defendant or fair response to an argument of the defense.

C. Other jurisdictions

In addition to reviewing the text, history, and policies relating to the Pennsylvania constitutional provisions, under *Edmunds*, we also consider the opinions of our sister states. In so doing, our goal is not to create a "score card," but rather to consider whether the underlying logic of the decisions informs our analysis of the related Pennsylvania provision. We recognize that the First, Sixth, Seventh and Tenth Circuits have concluded that use of pre-arrest silence as substantive evidence of guilt is inadmissible as violative of the right against self-incrimination, while the Fifth, Ninth, and Eleventh have found no constitutional violation, reasoning that the defendant is not subject to government compulsion before he is arrested. Similarly, the question has divided state courts across the nation, through numerous, often, fractured, decisions. Jurists on these courts have ably set forth the competing arguments surrounding the use of pre-arrest silence as substance evidence. We find all of these discussions insightful and helpful to our analysis. However, we ultimately base our decision on the Pennsylvania constitution and our precedent applying the right against self-incrimination.

After reviewing Article I, Section 9 of the Pennsylvania Constitution pursuant to *Edmunds*, we conclude that the factors weigh in favor of diverging from the currently asserted minimum standard of federal protection of the right against self-incrimination in regard to the use of pre-arrest silence as substantive evidence. Specifically, while we recognize the textual similarities with the Fifth Amendment, we conclude that the primacy of the Declaration of Rights to Pennsylvania's charter requires stronger protection of our liberties than under the federal counterpart. More significantly, we emphasize that, while this Court has often tracked federal jurisprudence in regard to the right against self-incrimination, we have interpreted Section 9 to provider a broader right on several occasions, including *Triplett*, *Turner*, and *Swinehart*. We find significant guidance from *Turner* where this Court diverged from federal precedent on an issue closely related to the issue at bar. In *Turner*, we refused to allow the use of a defendant's decision to remain silent post-arrest to impeach the defendant's trial testimony, unless the defendant at trial claims he did not previously remain silent. Accordingly, we hold that Article I, Section 9 is violated when the prosecution uses a defendant's silence whether pre or post-arrest as substantive evidence of guilt.

Turning to the facts of this case, we agree with the Superior Court that the prosecutor violated Defendant's Fifth Amendment right against self-incrimination when he emphasized Defendant's silence as "most telling," by asking "why" Defendant refused to cooperate with the detective, and then instructing the jury to "[f]actor that in when you're making an important decision in this case as well." N.T., Dec. 14–20, 2006, at 581. While the prosecutor's argument is not evidence, the prosecutor used the evidence referencing Defendant's silence to imply his guilt, in essence making him "a witness against himself by unspoken assumed answers." *Dravecz*, 227 A.2d at 907. *Cf. Easley*, 396 A.2d at 1202 (finding a prosecutor's comment on a prior, admitted reference to silence, unconstitutionally "implied to the jury that Easley's silence at the time of arrest was evidence of guilt"). Accordingly, we hold that the prosecutor's use of the properly admitted evidence of Defendant's pre-arrest silence to infer guilt violates Article I, Section 9 of the Pennsylvania Constitution.

COMMONWEALTH v. GELFGATT
11 N.E.3d 605 (Mass. 2014)

SPINA, J.

On May 5, 2010, a State grand jury returned indictments charging the defendant with seventeen counts of forgery of a document, G.L. c. 267, § 1; seventeen counts of uttering a forged instrument, G.L. c. 267, § 5; and three counts of attempting to commit the crime of larceny by false pretenses of the property of another, G.L. c. 274, § 6. The charges arose from allegations that the defendant, through his use of computers, conducted a sophisticated scheme of diverting to himself funds that were intended to be used to pay off large mortgage loans on residential properties. On November 21, 2011, the Commonwealth filed in the

Superior Court a "Motion to Compel the Defendant to Enter His Password into Encryption Software He Placed on Various Digital Media Storage Devices that Are Now in the Custody of the Commonwealth" (motion to compel decryption). The Commonwealth also filed a motion to report a question of law to the Appeals Court prior to trial pursuant to Mass. R.Crim. P. 34, as amended, 442 Mass. 1501 (2004). The question concerned the lawfulness of compelling the defendant to privately enter an encryption key into computers seized from him by the Commonwealth. Following a hearing on January 18, 2012, a judge denied the Commonwealth's motion to compel decryption, but he reported the following question of law:

> "Can the defendant be compelled pursuant to the Commonwealth's proposed protocol to provide his key to seized encrypted digital evidence despite the rights and protections provided by the Fifth Amendment to the United States Constitution and Article Twelve of the Massachusetts Declaration of Rights?"

We transferred the case to this court on our own motion. We now conclude that the answer to the reported question is, "Yes, where the defendant's compelled decryption would not communicate facts of a testimonial nature to the Commonwealth beyond what the defendant already had admitted to investigators." Accordingly, we reverse the judge's denial of the Commonwealth's motion to compel decryption.

The undisputed facts are taken from the parties' submissions to the motion judge.

Beginning in 2009, the defendant, who is an attorney, allegedly orchestrated a scheme to acquire for himself funds that were intended to be used to pay off home mortgage loans. According to the Commonwealth, the defendant identified high-end properties that were listed in an online database as "under agreement." He would research each one at the applicable registry of deeds to determine whether there was a mortgage on the property. If there was, the defendant, purportedly using a computer, would forge an assignment of the mortgage to either "Puren Ventures, Inc." (Puren Ventures) or "Baylor Holdings, Ltd." (Baylor Holdings). He then would record the forged assignment at the applicable registry of deeds and mail a notice to the seller stating that the mortgage on the property had been assigned to one of these sham companies, which he had set up.

The defendant fostered the illusion that Puren Ventures and Baylor Holdings were actual companies by giving each one Internet-based telephone and facsimile numbers. When a closing attorney would contact one of these companies to request a statement documenting the sum necessary to pay off the reassigned mortgage, the attorney would be instructed to send the request to the facsimile number that the defendant had created. Next, the defendant would request an actual payoff figure from the true mortgage holder.   The defendant would transmit this information by Internet facsimile number to the closing attorney, doing so under the guise of the sham company.   The defendant would instruct the closing attorney to send the payoff check to a Boston address where the defendant once had practiced law.   Although ultimately unsuccessful, the defendant purportedly created seventeen fraudulent assignments of mortgages, totaling over $13 million.   According to the Commonwealth, the defendant relied heavily on the use of computers to conceal his identity and perpetrate his alleged scheme.

On December 17, 2009, State police troopers arrested the defendant immediately after he retrieved what he believed to be over $1.3 million in payoff funds from two real estate closings.   They also executed search warrants for his residence in Marblehead and for his vehicle.   During the search of the defendant's residence, troopers observed several computers that were powered on, and they photographed the computer screens.   The troopers seized from the defendant's residence two desktop computers, one laptop computer, and various other devices capable of storing electronic data.   They also seized one smaller "netbook" computer from the defendant's vehicle. Computer forensic examiners were able to view several documents and "bookmarks" to Web sites that were located on an external hard drive.   However, all of the data on the four computers were encrypted with "DriveCrypt Plus" software.

According to the Commonwealth, the encryption software on the computers is virtually impossible to circumvent. Its manufacturer touts the fact that it does not contain a "back door" that would allow access to data by anyone other than the authorized user.   Thus, the Commonwealth states, the files on the four computers cannot be accessed and viewed unless the authorized user first enters the correct password to unlock the encryption.   The Commonwealth believes that evidence of the defendant's purported criminal activities is located on these computers.

On the day of his arrest, the defendant was interviewed by law enforcement officials after having been advised of the Miranda rights. In response to questioning, he said that he had more than one computer in his home.   The defendant also informed the officials that "[e]verything is encrypted and no one is going to get to it."   In order to decrypt the information, he would have to "start the program."   The defendant said that he used encryption for privacy purposes, and that when law enforcement officials asked him about the type of encryption used, they essentially were asking for the defendant's help in putting him in jail.   The defendant reiterated that he was able to decrypt the computers, but he refused to divulge any further information that would enable a forensic search.

On November 21, 2011, the Commonwealth filed its motion to compel decryption pursuant to Mass. R.Crim. P. 14(a)(2), as appearing in 442 Mass. 1518 (2004).   It sought an order compelling the defendant's compliance with a "protocol" that the Commonwealth had established to obtain decrypted digital data.   As grounds for the motion, the Commonwealth stated that compelling the defendant to enter the key to encryption software on various digital media storage devices that had been seized by the Commonwealth was essential to the discovery of "material" or "significant" evidence relating to the defendant's purported criminal conduct.   The Commonwealth further stated that its protocol would not violate the defendant's rights under either the Fifth Amendment to the United States Constitution or art. 12 of the Massachusetts Declaration of Rights.

In denying the Commonwealth's motion to compel decryption, the judge said that, on the one hand, the Commonwealth merely was requesting a sequence of numbers and characters that would enable it to access information on the computers, but that, on the other hand, the Commonwealth was asking for the defendant's help in accessing potentially incriminating evidence that the Commonwealth had seized.   In the judge's view, there was merit to the defendant's contention that production of a password to decrypt the computers constituted an admission of knowledge, ownership, and control.   Further, the judge continued, the scenario presented in this case was far different from compelling a defendant to provide a voice exemplar, a handwriting exemplar, or a blood sample, all of which are deemed to be nontestimonial.   The judge said that the defendant's refusal to disclose the encryption key during his interview with law enforcement officials could be construed as an invocation of his rights under the Fifth Amendment and art. 12.   Finally, it was the judge's understanding that neither the Federal nor the State Constitution requires a defendant to assist the government in understanding evidence that it has seized from a defendant.

Decryption under the Fifth Amendment

The Commonwealth contends that compelling the defendant to enter his encryption key into the computers pursuant to the Commonwealth's protocol would not violate the defendant's Fifth Amendment right against self-incrimination.   In the Commonwealth's view, the defendant's act of decryption would not communicate facts of a testimonial nature to the government beyond what the defendant already has admitted to investigators.   As such, the Commonwealth continues, the defendant's act of decryption does not trigger Fifth Amendment protection.   We agree.

The Fifth Amendment provides that "[n]o person ... shall be compelled in any criminal case to be a witness against himself."   It is well established that "the Fifth Amendment does not independently proscribe the compelled production of every sort of incriminating evidence but applies only when the accused is compelled to make a *testimonial* communication that is incriminating" (emphasis in original). *Fisher v. United States*, 425 U.S. 391, 408, 96 S.Ct. 1569, 48 L.Ed.2d 39 (1976). See *United States v. Hubbell*, 530 U.S. 27, 34, 120 S.Ct. 2037, 147 L.Ed.2d 24 (2000) ("The word 'witness' in the constitutional text limits the relevant category of compelled incriminating communications to those that are 'testimonial' in character"); *Schmerber v. California*, 384 U.S. 757, 761, 86 S.Ct. 1826, 16 L.Ed.2d 908 (1966) ("[T]he privilege protects an accused only from being compelled to testify against himself, or otherwise provide the State with evidence of a testimonial or communicative nature").

Here, the Commonwealth, through its motion, is seeking to compel the defendant to decrypt "all" of the "digital storage devices that were seized from him." Given that the Commonwealth believes that those devices contain information about the defendant's alleged mortgage payoff scheme, the entry of the encryption key or password presumably would be incriminating because "it would furnish the Government with a link in the chain of evidence leading to [the defendant's] indictment." The issue on which this case turns is whether the defendant's act of decrypting the computers is a testimonial communication that triggers Fifth Amendment protection.

Based on our review of the record, we conclude that the factual statements that would be conveyed by the defendant's act of entering an encryption key in the computers are "foregone conclusions" and, therefore, the act of decryption is not a testimonial communication that is protected by the Fifth Amendment.

Massachusetts Constitution

The Commonwealth also contends that compelling the defendant to enter his encryption key pursuant to the Commonwealth's protocol would not violate his privilege against self-incrimination under art. 12 of the Massachusetts Declaration of Rights. We agree.

Article 12 provides that "[n]o subject shall ... be compelled to accuse, or furnish evidence against himself." It is well established that art. 12 affords greater protection against self-incrimination than does the Fifth Amendment in circumstances that are "discrete and well defined." However, as we have explained, "[a]lthough art. 12 demands a more expansive protection, 'it does not change the classification of evidence to which the privilege applies. Only that genre of evidence having a testimonial or communicative nature is protected under the privilege against self-incrimination.'" *Commonwealth v. Burgess, supra,* quoting *Attorney Gen. v. Colleton*, 387 Mass. 790, 796 n. 6, 444 N.E.2d 915

(1982). Like the Federal Constitution, the protection against self-incrimination afforded by art. 12 is unavailable where the government seeks to compel an individual to be the source of real or physical evidence. See *Commonwealth v. Burgess, supra*, and cases cited.

Similarly, we have held that, as is the case under the Federal Constitution, "the act of production, quite apart from the content of that which is produced, may itself be communicative." Where the information conveyed by an act of production "is reflective of the knowledge, understanding, and thoughts of the witness," it is deemed to be testimonial and, therefore, within the purview of art. 12. At the same time, we also have recognized that "[w]hen it is a 'foregone conclusion' that a witness has certain items, and the items themselves are not privileged, the witness has no privilege."

In *Commonwealth v. Burgess*, 426 Mass. at 219, 688 N.E.2d 439, when the court considered the scope of the protection against self-incrimination afforded by both the Federal Constitution and the Massachusetts Declaration of Rights, we pointed out that our analysis under art. 12 need not "merely duplicate our earlier Fifth Amendment analysis." Rather, "[w]e are free to consider certain evidence, considered by the Supreme Court to be insufficiently testimonial for Fifth Amendment purposes, to be sufficiently testimonial for art. 12 purposes." Mindful of this pronouncement, as well as our jurisprudence recognizing the "foregone conclusion" principle, we are not persuaded that the circumstances presented here dictate an analytical departure from the Federal standard. Where the facts that would be conveyed by the defendant through the act of entering an encryption key into the computers seized by the Commonwealth are a "foregone conclusion," his act of production is insufficiently testimonial for art. 12 purposes.

Conclusion

We answer the reported question, "Yes, where the defendant's compelled decryption would not communicate facts of a testimonial nature to the Commonwealth beyond what the defendant already had admitted to investigators." The judge's denial of the Commonwealth's motion to compel decryption is reversed, and this case is remanded to the Superior Court for further proceedings consistent with this opinion.

C. RIGHT TO COUNSEL

BRYAN v. STATE
571 A.2d 170 (Del. 1990)

MOORE, J.

Ransford H. Bryan, III, was convicted by a jury of murder in the first degree, possession of a deadly weapon during the commission of a felony, and theft of over $500 by false pretenses. Bryan contends that the trial court erred in denying his motion to suppress a confession made to police during a custodial interrogation despite his attorney's repeated admonitions not to question the defendant in the absence of counsel. Moreover, the interrogation of Bryan commenced despite the fact that counsel for Bryan had contacted the police investigators following Bryan's arrest and had specifically warned the police not to question the suspect in his absence.

Bryan raises several issues on appeal, but we address only one: Whether a knowing waiver of the right to counsel, guaranteed in Delaware by article I, section 7 of the Constitution of 1897, can occur when the State prevents counsel, whom the State knows has been designated and retained to represent the defendant, from rendering effective legal assistance to his client during a custodial interrogation. In our opinion such police conduct is thoroughly incompatible with fundamental principles of the Delaware Constitution. Accordingly, we reverse.

The defendant was an 18-year-old youth who had had no previous dealings with the criminal justice system. He had just graduated from high school and was living with a friend, Douglas Brockway, Jr.

On October 13, 1987, Brockway told his mother that he believed someone had been stealing money from his bank account using his Money Access Card (MAC). She advised him to contact his bank. The next day, October 14, Brockway went to the bank with his father and signed an affidavit of forgery alleging that money had been withdrawn from his account without his permission on four separate occasions, totaling $810. Later that day, Bryan's mother observed Brockway holding Bryan against a wall and threatening him. He said, "If I find out that you are—that you did this, it is going to be between you and me."

The following day, October 15, Bryan and Brockway told Brockway's mother that they intended to go squirrel hunting. The boys took a twenty-gauge shotgun with them. There is a dispute as to how the gun was removed from the house. Bryan claims that Brockway's gun was passed through the bedroom window, however, Brockway's mother claims that she saw Brockway carrying Bryan's shotgun with shells in hand out of the front door. In any event, the boys left the house together at approximately 6:30 p.m. About 45 minutes later Bryan returned home, alone.

Immediately upon returning Bryan told Brockway's mother that her son had a drug habit and owed $2,000 to a drug dealer. He also stated that he had made the withdrawals from Brockway's account as part of a conspiracy between Brockway and himself to defraud the bank in order to obtain money to pay off the drug debt. He said that Brockway intended to go to the bank and complain about the theft, get reimbursed, and use the proceeds to pay off the drug debt. He further claimed that Brockway had solicited his help to make the withdrawals in an effort not to alert Brockway's mother. During this discussion Bryan also stated that he and Brockway had not gone squirrel hunting, but had instead gone to a shopping center where Brockway, carrying $1,200, met a Mexican drug dealer. Bryan claimed that Brockway talked to the drug dealer, and then told Bryan that he was leaving with him. Bryan said that he saw Brockway drive off with the drug dealer in a red Pontiac.

Detective Warrington of the Delaware State Police began an investigation into the disappearance of Brockway on October 19. He interviewed the victim's mother, father and Bryan at the victim's house. Bryan participated in this interview voluntarily. During the interview Bryan related the Mexican-drug-dealer story. The interviews left Detective Warrington with some suspicions. Specifically, he was concerned first about the inconsistency concerning the removal of the shotgun from the house. Second, he wondered why Bryan related the drug story to the victim's mother and recanted the squirrel hunting story if the purpose of the squirrel hunting story was to cover up the alleged drug involvement. Third, he was concerned about Bryan's denial of knowledge of the $300 of Sussex Trust MAC money found in his wallet.

The following day, October 20, Detective Warrington re-interviewed Bryan and Brockway's family, inquiring into the particular inconsistencies in the defendant's story. Detective Warrington also asked Bryan directly at this time if he knew where Brockway was or had any more information regarding his whereabouts. Bryan denied any such knowledge. However, about this time the police received photographs from Brockway's bank showing Bryan withdrawing money from its MAC machine. The last photo showed defendant withdrawing $300 on October 13. Detective Warrington attempted to get Bryan to take a polygraph test, but his mother stated that retained counsel had advised against it, and that Bryan would not take the test.

On October 21, Bryan's retained counsel, Jack Rubin, a Baltimore lawyer, called Detective Warrington and told him that Bryan would not submit to a polygraph, and that he was not to interrogate Bryan unless there was a warrant for his arrest. Both Bryan and his mother were in Rubin's office during the call. Detective Warrington then told Rubin that he did in fact have a warrant for Bryan's arrest on charges of theft. Rubin then arranged for Bryan to turn himself in the following day and clearly stated to Detective Warrington that he was not to question Bryan and was to deal with the defendant only through counsel.

The following day, October 22, Bryan turned himself in on the theft warrant and was arraigned by a Justice of the Peace. Bryan was accompanied by a local Delaware attorney, who was co-counsel with Rubin. Detective Warrington did not request to question Bryan on this occasion. However, some time later, Detective Warrington telephoned Bryan's Delaware attorney and stated that, as a part of his investigation into Brockway's disappearance, he wanted more information from Bryan. Bryan's Delaware attorney advised Detective Warrington to contact Rubin concerning that request.

Thereafter, Detective Warrington spoke to Rubin, stressing his need for more information. Rubin stated that he would speak with Bryan. On October 27, Detective Warrington called Rubin to see if he had obtained any additional information concerning the whereabouts of Brockway. During that telephone call, Rubin and Detective Warrington scheduled a meeting in Delaware, at the State Police barracks near Lewes, for the following day. At the meeting, Rubin again informed Detective Warrington that the police were not to question Bryan and that all contact between the police and Bryan was to be through Rubin.

In the meantime, a preliminary hearing on the theft charge had been scheduled for October 29. Rubin was becoming concerned that the theft charge and arrest were being used to coerce Bryan into giving a statement regarding the disappearance of Brockway. On October 29, Bryan, accompanied by his Delaware attorney and Rubin, appeared and waived his right to a preliminary hearing. Following Bryan's waiver of a preliminary hearing, Rubin confronted Warrington with his concern. Warrington acknowledged that the theft charge and investigation into Brockway's disappearance were "all interrelated." Consequently, while they were still in the Sussex County Courthouse, Rubin again told Warrington, in Bryan's presence, that Bryan had asserted his right to remain silent and wished to deal with the police only through counsel.

On November 6, two deer hunters found a body in a wooded area near Route 277. The body was clad in a green and white tee shirt matching the description of the tee shirt Brockway was wearing at the time of his disappearance. There were holes in the upper torso of the body consistent with multiple shotgun wounds.

Later that afternoon, Detective Warrington and another police officer went to the defendant's father's residence and informed him that Brockway's body had been found and that they intended to arrest Bryan for murder. Bryan's father was asked to come with them. The reason for this is unclear, however, Detective Warrington testified that Bryan's father agreed to go, and he felt that the father's presence might help "the truth come out." Detective Warrington also testified that they "needed to get the truth out and know exactly what happened that day." When Bryan's father asked Warrington to call Bryan's mother, who had been responsible for hiring Bryan's attorney earlier in the investigation, Warrington indicated that this could be done at the police station.

The police and Bryan's father went to the construction site where Bryan was working. There Bryan was arrested for first degree murder. At the police station Bryan and his father were permitted to talk alone for approximately 30 minutes. During that time the police called Bryan's mother, told her of the arrest, and informed her that Bryan's father was currently talking to her son. Several minutes later Rubin called Detective Warrington and told him again that "you know not to talk to him."

When Bryan's father emerged from the interrogation room he exclaimed, "He says he didn't do it." Two detectives, one of whom was Detective Warrington, immediately entered the room. Bryan was read his *Miranda* warnings but nothing was said to him of Rubin's call. Bryan did not ask for a lawyer and an interrogation ensued, culminating in Bryan making a statement that he accidentally shot Brockway. Bryan then took Detective Warrington to the location where he left the guns and some of the victim's clothing. He acknowledged that his gun inflicted the fatal wounds.

On May 23, 1988, Bryan moved to suppress the statements he made and the tainted evidence flowing from those statements on grounds that the statements were obtained in violation of his rights under the Fourth, Fifth and Sixth amendments to the United States Constitution, and under sections 6 and 7 of the Delaware Constitution of 1897. The motion was denied by the trial court.

Miranda v. Arizona, 384 U.S. 436 (1966), requires that police advise those whom they subject to custodial interrogation of their constitutional rights. Before police may interrogate a suspect in custody, they must obtain a waiver by that suspect of his rights. To be effective, a waiver of rights must be voluntary, knowing and intelligent.

Our decision today examines the prerequisites for a voluntary, knowing and intelligent waiver of the right to counsel in Delaware. Our most recent examination of the issue was in *Weber*.

There, relying in part on article I, section 7 of the Delaware Constitution, we held that:

> To...effectuate the protection given to the accused by *Miranda*, and ensure that a suspect knowingly and intelligently waives his rights, we establish the following rule for the guidance of the trial court: if prior to or during custodial interrogation, and unknown to the suspect, a specifically retained or properly designated lawyer is actually present at the police station seeking an opportunity to render legal advice or assistance to the suspect, and the police intentionally or negligently fail to inform the suspect of that fact, then any statement obtained after the police themselves know of the attorney's efforts to assist the suspect, or any evidence derived from any such statement, is not admissible on any theory that the suspect intelligently and knowingly waived his right to remain silent and his right to counsel as established by *Miranda*.

Weber was decided in the context of a lawyer being present at a police station and attempting to render legal advice to his client.

For purposes of the protections afforded by the Delaware Constitution, there is no distinction between an in-person request by retained counsel to render assistance to his client and a telephonic request by that lawyer. The relevant inquiry is not whether counsel is physically present at the interrogation site, but simply whether specifically retained counsel has made a reasonable, diligent and timely attempt to consult with his client or otherwise render legal services.

The denial of the assistance of counsel is a violation of the due process of law guaranteed by article I, section 7 of the Delaware Constitution. Accordingly, the procedural protections afforded by the Delaware Constitution demand that an accused be afforded the unqualified opportunity to consult with counsel prior to custodial interrogation, provided that (i) the lawyer has clearly made a reasonable, diligent and timely attempt to render legal advice or otherwise perform legal services on behalf of his client, the accused, and (ii) the lawyer has been specifically retained or designated to represent the accused.

Furthermore, when counsel has been specifically designated and retained to represent a suspect and the suspect has clearly made police aware of his desire to deal with police only through his counsel during the investigation leading to the arrest, we impose a heavy presumption against waiver if the lawyer is present and denied access to his client, or, as here, has repeatedly advised the police that no interrogations of the defendant were to occur. We adopt this presumption because an abrupt decision by a suspect to waive his right to counsel without counsel being present, after previously expressing a desire to have his lawyer present, undermines any notion of a knowing, voluntary and intelligent waiver. The Supreme Court has expressed a similar concern: "[T]he accused having expressed his own view that he is not competent to deal with the authorities without legal advice, a later decision at the authorities' insistence to make a statement without counsel's presence may properly be viewed with skepticism."

Although this presumption bears some resemblance to the New York rule, under which a suspect may never waive his right to counsel in the absence of his attorney, we specifically decline to adopt that principle, and reaffirm our decision in *Weber* to that effect. The presumption does not alter the principle that a suspect may knowingly, intelligently and voluntarily waive his right to counsel, even without consulting with his counsel, after first being informed of counsel's efforts. The presumption reflects the additional weight accorded the "factor" or "circumstance" of a consistent prior course of dealing with police under a totality of circumstances analysis, required before a waiver will be considered knowing, voluntary and intelligent. As we have previously held, "the totality of the circumstances include[s] the behavior of the interrogators, the conduct of the defendant, his age, his intellect, his experience, and all other pertinent factors."

In evaluating the totality of the circumstances, a court makes a two-part inquiry. First, the waiver must have been voluntary—it must have been "the product of a free and deliberate choice rather than intimidation, coercion, or deception." Second, the waiver must have been made upon "a full awareness of both the nature of the right being abandoned and the consequences of the decision to abandon it." However, a purported waiver can never satisfy a totality of the circumstances analysis when police do not even inform a suspect that his attorney seeks to render legal advice.

We recognize that a defendant's right to have counsel present during questioning is his own; the decision whether to waive his right can only be made by the defendant and he need not follow the advice of his lawyer. Our holding simply recognizes that to knowingly, voluntarily and intelligently waive this right, a defendant must be informed that his counsel has attempted or is attempting to render legal advice or perform legal services on his behalf. To hold otherwise would be to condone "affirmative police interference in a communication between an attorney and suspect."

In reaching our decision we clarify the confusion in the trial court as to the difference in the protections afforded by article I, section 7 of the Delaware Constitution and by the Fifth Amendment to the United States Constitution. In *Moran v. Burbine*, the United States Supreme Court held that events occurring outside the presence of a suspect have no bearing on his ability to knowingly, voluntarily and intelligently waive his right to counsel under the Fifth Amendment of the United States Constitution. Accordingly, the Supreme Court refused to adopt a rule requiring police to inform a suspect of an attorney's efforts to reach him. Nonetheless, *Moran* invited the States to adopt a more stringent rule under their own constitutions. We do so here on independent State grounds.

Thus, in *Weber* we concluded that "a suspect, who is indifferent to the usual abstract offer of counsel, recited as part of the warnings required by *Miranda*," will not disdain an opportunity to consult with counsel he has specifically retained. It is undisputed that the Delaware Constitution may provide broader protections than the United States Constitution. This principle was expressly recognized in *Moran*: "Nothing we say today disables the States from adopting different requirements for the conduct of its employees and officials as a matter of state law." Accordingly, we decide this issue solely under article I, section 7 of the Delaware Constitution. This is in accord with the holdings of the highest courts of other states when presented with a situation analogous to that in *Moran*.

This brings us to an application of the foregoing legal principles. The trial court's findings of fact reveal deliberate, intentional and willful police conduct intended to subvert the protections afforded by the Delaware Constitution. Under the circumstances, the requirement of a knowing and voluntary waiver of counsel is of paramount importance to any inquiry.

The defendant made police aware of his desire to deal with them only through retained counsel on at least five occasions during the investigation and prior to his arrest. In that period, virtually all of the contact between the investigating officers and the defendant occurred in the presence of counsel. After the defendant's arrest Rubin contacted police and advised them again that they were not to interrogate the defendant in his absence.

Instead, the police disregarded these assertions of the defendant's rights and purportedly obtained a waiver of those rights without informing the defendant of his lawyer's latest attempt to render services on his behalf. The police then immediately interrogated the defendant and obtained a confession. Under such circumstances the defendant could not waive his right to counsel without first being informed that his lawyer was on the phone and was attempting to render legal advice. At a minimum, the defendant had an absolute right to know these facts, and any statement obtained from him violative of this right cannot pass muster under article I, section 7 of the Delaware Constitution.

Accordingly, the use of the confession against Bryan at trial, and evidence derived from it, constituted error. We therefore reverse and order a new trial.

NOTES

1. The Connecticut Constitution requires, as a matter of due process pursuant to article I, section 8, that police promptly inform a suspect of timely efforts by retained counsel to render assistance. *State v. Stoddard*, 537 A.2d 446 (Conn. 1988).

2. The privilege against compelled self-incrimination in the Massachusetts and New Hampshire Constitutions required the rejection of

Moran. State v. Roache, 803 A.2d 572 (N.H. 2002); *Commonwealth v. Mavredakis*, 725 N.E.2d 169 (Mass. 2000). Other states that have declined to follow *Moran* include Illinois, Kentucky, Michigan, Indiana, and New Jersey.

D. CONFRONTATION – FACE TO FACE

COMMONWEALTH v. LUDWIG
594 A.2d 281 (Pa. 1991)

ZAPPALA, J.

We granted review in this case to determine whether the use of closed circuit television testimony by an alleged child victim violates the confrontation clauses of the United States and Pennsylvania Constitutions. We hold that the confrontation clause of the Pennsylvania Constitution does not permit such infringement of a defendant's constitutional right to meet a witness face to face. The use of closed circuit television to transmit the testimony of the witness in this case violates the constitutional protection given to the defendant under article I, section 9 of the Pennsylvania Constitution. Consequently, we reverse the Order of the Superior Court upholding appellant's conviction and sentence.

On August 9, 1984, appellant was charged with rape, involuntary deviate sexual intercourse, incest, indecent assault, corrupting the morals of a minor, and endangering the welfare of children. The alleged victim of these crimes was appellant's five-year-old daughter. At the preliminary hearing, the victim testified that she did not remember what happened with appellant. The victim was unresponsive to further questioning, and the Commonwealth requested a continuance so that it could prepare a petition to the court seeking to use videotaped testimony at the preliminary hearing. The petition was filed by the Commonwealth, and a hearing held. At the hearing, the Commonwealth presented testimony of a psychologist to the effect that the victim had undergone "emotional freezing" at the preliminary hearing and that the condition could occur again. The psychologist also testified that the victim had become withdrawn following the incident, but was now making psychological progress. The psychologist was concerned that the progress might be impaired if the child was forced to testify in court in the physical presence of her father.

The court granted the Commonwealth's petition to the extent that it allowed the child to testify by way of closed circuit television. At the second preliminary hearing, the alleged victim did testify on closed circuit television and the evidence was deemed sufficient to hold the appellant for trial. Notwithstanding appellant's objection, the trial court allowed the same closed circuit television procedures to be employed during the trial itself.

A jury trial began on March 7, 1985. The child testified at the trial via closed circuit television from another room. The child's foster mother was permitted to sit next to the child while the child testified. Also in the room where the child was located was the video camera operator. The courtroom where the judge, prosecutor, defense counsel, appellant and jury were located was linked to the child by microphone. Although the child could not see the people in the courtroom, she could hear them and respond to their questions.

Article I, section 9 of our state constitution guarantees an accused the right to meet his accusers:

> In all criminal prosecutions the accused hath a right to be heard by himself and his counsel, to demand the nature and cause of the accusations against him, to meet the witnesses *face to face*…(emphasis added).

This language is unlike its federal counter-part, the Sixth Amendment, which provides that a defendant in a criminal case "shall enjoy the right…to be confronted with the witnesses against him."

In *Maryland v. Craig*, 497 U.S. 836 (1990), the United States Supreme Court was presented with a challenge to a Maryland statute which permitted closed circuit testimony if a judge determined that the child victim's testimony in the courtroom would result in serious emotional distress and the child's inability to communicate. The trial court rejected the defendant's objection to the procedure as violative of the confrontation clause of the Sixth Amendment to the United States Constitution. The Maryland Court of Appeals reversed, holding that the State did not present sufficient evidence to meet the requirements set forth in *Coy v. Iowa*, 487 U.S. 1012 (1988). The United States Supreme Court reversed in a five to four decision.

Writing for the majority, Justice O'Connor held that in *Coy v. Iowa*, the Court did construe the confrontation clause as guaranteeing the defendant a face to face meeting with witnesses. Since there had been no finding that the particular child witness needed special protection, no reason existed for disallowing face to face confrontation. However, the Court specifically reserved the issue of whether the confrontation clause guarantees an *absolute* right to a face to face meeting.

Reviewing federal case law, the majority held that the purpose of the confrontation clause was to insure that witnesses give testimony under oath, submit to cross-examination and permit observations of witness's demeanor to assist in the assessment of credibility. Thus, federal case law reflects a _preference_ for face to face confrontation, not an absolute guarantee. However, a face to face confrontation may only be dispensed of where denial is necessary to further an important public policy and where the reliability of the testimony is otherwise assured. The Court concluded that a state's interest in the physical and psychological well being of child abuse victims may be sufficiently important to outweigh face to face confrontation.

In a stinging dissent, Justice Scalia, joined in by Justices Brennan, Marshall and Stevens, chastised the majority for applying an interest balancing analysis when the text of the Constitution does not permit it. The Defendant was not requesting an expansive interpretation of the scope of the Sixth Amendment but rather a strict adherence to its words. When a Constitutional guarantee is clear and explicit, as in this instance, an interest balancing analysis is the wrong approach. The confrontation clause does not guarantee reliable evidence but rather it guarantees specific trial procedures that were thought to assure reliable evidence. In effect, the majority subordinated an explicit constitutional protection to "current favored public policy."

Unlike the Sixth Amendment to the United States Constitution, article 1, section 9 of the Pennsylvania Constitution specifically provides for a "face to face" confrontation. We have long held that in interpreting our Constitution we are not bound by the United States Supreme Court's interpretation of similar federal constitutional provisions.

In *Commonwealth v. Sell*, we embraced the admonitions of Justice Brennan of the United States Supreme Court:

> [T]he decisions of the Court are not, and should not be, dispositive of questions regarding rights guaranteed by counter-part provisions of State Law. Accordingly, such decisions are not mechanical applicable to state law issues, and state court judges and the members of the bar seriously err if they so treat them. Rather, state court judges, and also practitioners, do well to scrutinize constitutional decisions by federal courts, for only if they are found to be logically persuasive and well-reasoned, paying due regard to precedent and the policies underlying specific constitutional guarantees, may they properly claim persuasive weight as guide posts when interpreting counter-part state guarantees.

We then refused to adopt the United States Supreme Court's abolition of "automatic standing" under the Fourth Amendment of the United States Constitution reaffirming our holding in *Commonwealth v. Tate* that the:

> State may provide through its constitution a basis for the rights and liberties of its citizens independent from that provided by the federal constitution, and that the rights so guaranteed may be more expansive than their federal counter-parts.

Most recently, in *Commonwealth v. Edmunds*, this Court was again requested to blindly adopt federal jurisprudence to support a "good faith" exception to the exclusionary rule as articulated by the United States Supreme Court in *United States v. Leon*, 468 U.S. 897 (1984). There, after an extensive review of the history of article 1, section 8, our precedents and policy considerations, we determined that adoption of federal jurisprudence was unwarranted.

Unlike its federal counter-part, article 1, section 9 of the Pennsylvania Constitution does not reflect a "preference" but clearly, emphatically and unambiguously requires a "face to face" confrontation. This distinction alone would require that we decline to adopt the United States Supreme Court's analysis and reasoning in *Maryland v. Craig*. However, in addition, we have our own case law which mandates a "face to face" confrontation.

In *Commonwealth v. Russo*, we addressed the "face to face" requirement of article I, section 9 of our Constitution, stating:

> Many people possess the trait of being loose tongued or willing to say something behind a person's back that they dare not or cannot truthfully say to his face or under oath in a courtroom. It was probably for this reason, as well as to give the accused the right to cross-examine his accusers and thereby enable the jury to better determine the credibility of the Commonwealth's witnesses and the strength and truth of its case, that this important added protection was given to every person accused of crime. We have no right to disregard or (unintentionally) erode or distort any provision of the constitution, especially where, as here, its plain and simple language make its meaning unmistakably clear; indeed, because of the times in which we live we have a higher duty than ever before to zealously protect and safeguard the constitution.

Although we were quite emphatic about the importance of this right, no right is absolute. Indeed, the right to confront an accuser is not without exception. In *Commonwealth v. Rodgers*, we permitted the prosecution to use preliminary hearing testimony of a witness at trial when that witness was unavailable. In *Commonwealth v. Stasko*, the prosecutor was permitted to use a videotape deposition of a witness unavailable for trial. In both instances, the original testimony was given in the presence of the defendant with the defendant having the opportunity to face and cross-examine his accuser. However, in each instance, the witnesses' subjective reactions to testifying in the presence of the accused were not a consideration.

Although we have recognized exceptions to the right to confront a witness, the policy reasons underlying those decisions are absent in this case. The witness in this case was neither unavailable nor subjected to cross-examination during prior testimony given in the presence of the accused. In fact, the trial judge instructed the jury that the victim was totally unaware of the existence of the trial itself: "We want [the child] to be as relaxed and casual and normal as possible and she doesn't really know that you are here in this setting. She doesn't really understand that this is all actually a trial. It probably has little significance to her."

Having diluted the significance of her testimony to that extent, it is questionable whether the victim would be testifying under the proper aura.

While we have recognized exceptions to the constitutional right of confrontation, we have done so only in those instances in which the accused has already had the opportunity to confront the witnesses against him face to face. We were satisfied that in those limited instances, the constitutional right to confront the witness had been afforded to the accused. Those decisions cannot be interpreted to permit restrictions on face to face confrontation where the right to confront the witness has *never* been afforded to the accused.

We are cognizant of society's interest in protecting victims of sexual abuse. However, that interest cannot be preeminent over the accused's constitutional right to confront the witnesses against him face to face. The record in this case does not disclose any conduct by the appellant during the proceedings that would give rise to the need to isolate the witness. The subjective fears of the witness, without more, are insufficient to restrict this important constitutional right. Since the trial court relied exclusively upon these fears, its actions cannot be affirmed. The appellant is entitled to face his accusers and the failure to protect that right was error. The appellant is therefore entitled to a new trial during which time the victim must testify in the courtroom before the judge, jury and appellant.

The Order of the Superior Court affirming the Order of the Court of Common Pleas of Monroe County is reversed.

NOTES

1. Following the holding of the Supreme Court of Pennsylvania in *Commonwealth v. Ludwig*, article I, section 9 of the Pennsylvania Constitution was amended.

2. Other states that have rejected as unconstitutional efforts to admit child testimony that was given outside the physical presence of the accused include Hawaii, Illinois, Indiana, New Hampshire, Utah, Texas, and Massachusetts.

3. The constitutions of Idaho, Nevada, and North Dakota do not contain a clause that guarantees the right to confrontation.

E. DUTY TO PRESERVE EVIDENCE

HAMMOND v. STATE
569 A.2d 81 (Del. 1989)

HOLLAND, J.

The defendant-appellant, George M. Hammond, III, was convicted on June 2, 1988, following a jury trial, of two counts of Vehicular Homicide in the First Degree. Hammond was sentenced on August 17, 1988. Hammond filed this appeal on August 18, 1988.

In this appeal, Hammond argues that: the police negligently failed to gather and preserve evidence material to the preparation of his defense.

We find no reversible error. Therefore, the judgments of the Superior Court are affirmed.

Facts

On July 25, 1986, at about 5:00 a.m., Hammond, then age eighteen, Keith Douglas Moore, and Leon Buddy Carter, were involved in a single car accident. They were all occupants in an automobile which left the roadway and came to rest partially imbedded in the foundation of a townhouse that was under construction. The accident resulted in the deaths of Moore and Carter.

Officer William Wayne Walls of the City of Dover Police Department was one of the first persons to reach the accident scene. Walls testified as to what he saw when he arrived. Hammond was in the driver's seat of the vehicle, with his left shoulder against the left door, and his right shoulder against the driver's seat. Hammond's right leg, which was in a cast, was entangled between the accelerator and the brake pedal. Moore was also in the front seat area. Moore's head was on Hammond's chest and his feet were in the passenger's footwell. Carter was slumped over in the left rear seat.

Hammond testified in his own defense. His memory had been "hypnotically refreshed." Hammond stated that he graduated from high school on July 24, 1986, after completing summer courses. Following the graduation ceremony, Hammond and several friends celebrated at Scott William Kisters' apartment. Hammond, Carter, and Moore left Kister's apartment in the early morning hours of July 25, 1986, just prior to the accident. Hammond testified that they had all been drinking and that none of them were in "very good shape." He told the jury that Moore was driving Kisters' car at the time of the accident. According to Hammond's testimony, the force of the collision must have moved him and Moore about within the crash vehicle.

In support of his defense, Hammond presented testimony by Dr. George C. Govatos, a consulting engineer who was qualified as an accident reconstruction expert. Dr. Govatos testified about the kinematics of occupants in a crash vehicle, who are not wearing seatbelts. Dr. Govatos showed the jury a video tape of a test he had performed. The video tape depicted how the impact of a collision could cause the driver and the passenger to be thrown about and come to rest in each other's original seat. Dr. Govatos testified that an examination of the actual vehicle involved in the collision would have been important to his analysis because of the possibility of evidence in the interior of the vehicle that might have been left by the people as they were moved about by the collision, *e.g.*, hair, blood, pieces of clothing, or other physical evidence. Dr. Govatos testified that the existence of such evidence would have helped him to substantiate his opinion on the movement of Hammond and Moore within the crash vehicle. Dr. Govatos also testified that he would have needed the vehicle in order to determine whether mechanical failure could have caused or partially caused the collision.

The crash vehicle was not available to Dr. Govatos because the Dover police no longer had it in their possession when Hammond's attorney filed a discovery request on October 14, 1986. Although the crash vehicle had been towed from the scene and impounded, it was released by the Dover police on August 8, 1986. No evidence was collected from the vehicle by the Dover police before it was released. Hammond moved for a judgment of acquittal, or for a special instruction to the jury, as a result of the State's failure to preserve or to test the crash vehicle. The Superior Court denied both motions.

Right of Access to Evidence

The first issue raised by Hammond on appeal is that the failure of the Dover police to preserve the crash vehicle itself or to gather evidence of blood, clothing, tissue, and fingerprints, from inside of the crash vehicle, violated his constitutionally guaranteed right of access to evidence. This Court has recognized that the "obligation to preserve evidence is rooted in the due process provisions of the Fourteenth Amendment to the United States Constitution and the Delaware Constitution, article I, section 7." *Deberry v. State*, 457 A.2d 744, 751-52 (Del. 1983). The independent and alternative constitutional bases for our holding in *Deberry* is particularly significant in view of the subsequent development of the "access to evidence" doctrine in this Court and the United States Supreme Court. A review of the evolution of these precedents is not only instructive but necessary for a proper evaluation of Hammond's claim.

In *Deberry*, the question presented was "what relief is appropriate when the State had or should have had the requested evidence, but the evidence does not exist when the defense seeks its production?" In answering that inquiry, we held that claims of this type must be examined according to the following paradigm:

> 1) Would the requested material, if extant in the possession of the State at the time of the defense request, have been subject to disclosure under Criminal Rule 16 or *Brady*?
>
> 2) If so, did the government have a duty to preserve the material?
>
> 3) If there was a duty to preserve, was the duty breached, and what consequences should flow from a breach?

The consequences which should flow from a breach of the duty to preserve evidence are determined in accordance with a separate three-part analysis which considers:

1) the degree of negligence or bad faith involved;

2) the importance of the missing evidence considering the probative value and reliability of secondary or substitute evidence that remains available; and

3) the sufficiency of the other evidence produced at the trial to sustain the conviction.

Bailey v. State, 521 A.2d 1069, 1091 (Del. 1987) (citing *Deberry v. State*, 457 A.2d at 752).

In *Deberry*, we concluded "[a] claim that *potentially* exculpatory evidence was lost or destroyed by the State can only be decided after each element of the above analysis has been considered." In *Deberry*, we also noted, for future guidance, the "agencies that create rules for evidence preservation should broadly define discoverable evidence to include any material that *could* be favorable to the defendant."

The year following our decision in *Deberry*, the United States Supreme Court decided *California v. Trombetta*, 467 U.S. 479 (1984). It held:

Whatever duty the Constitution imposes on the States to preserve evidence, that duty must be limited to evidence that might be expected to play a significant role in the suspect's defense. To meet this standard of constitutional materiality, evidence must both possess an exculpatory value that was apparent before the evidence was destroyed, and be of such a nature that the defendant would be unable to obtain comparable evidence by other reasonably available means.

This Court has examined the "access to evidence" doctrine following *Trombetta*. In doing so, we have not limited our inquiry to *Trombetta*'s construction under the United States Constitution. Instead, we have held that "[w]hen a defendant claims that the State has failed to preserve evidence, by losing it after it has been gathered, the analysis which a [Delaware] Court must follow is set forth in *Deberry*." *Bailey v. State*, 521 A.2d at 1090; *see* Del. Const. art I, § 7.

Following our decision in *Bailey*, the United States Supreme Court decided *Arizona v. Youngblood*, 488 U.S. 51 (1988). It held:

The Due Process Clause of the Fourteenth Amendment, as interpreted in *Brady*, makes the good or bad faith of the State irrelevant when the State fails to disclose to the defendant material exculpatory evidence. But we think the Due Process Clause requires a different result when we deal with the failure of the State to preserve evidentiary material of which no more can be said than that it could have been subjected to tests, the results of which might have exonerated defendant....We therefore hold that unless a criminal defendant can show bad faith on the part of the police, failure to preserve potentially useful evidence does not constitute a denial of due process of law.

It appears that, as a matter of federal Constitutional law, the United States Supreme Court has developed a *hybrid approach* when a claim of denial of access to evidence is asserted. The principles of *Trombetta* are applicable to claims relating to a denial of access to *Brady* types of evidence. The "good faith" principles of *Youngblood* are applicable to allegations of a denial of access to potentially favorable types of evidence. However, in *Deberry*, in the event that *either* claim was made, this Court adopted a *unitary* approach.

In Hammond's case, the State has asked this Court to reconsider its decision in *Deberry*, in view of the holding in *Youngblood*. In *Deberry*, the conduct of the State was only one of three factors to be considered when potentially exculpatory evidence had not been preserved. The State argues that *Youngblood* has now established a *single* bright-line "good faith" test which should be applied by this Court in lieu of the *Deberry three-part analysis*, whenever a denial of access is asserted with respect to evidence that *could* be favorable to the defendant.

We remain convinced that fundamental fairness, as an element of due process, requires the State's failure to preserve evidence that could be favorable to the defendant "[to] be evaluated in the context of the entire record." When evidence has not been preserved, the conduct of the State's agents is a relevant consideration, but it is not determinative. Equally relevant is a consideration of the importance of the missing evidence, the availability of secondary evidence, and the sufficiency of the other evidence presented at trial. "[T]here may well be cases which the defendant is unable to prove that the State acted in bad faith but in which the loss or destruction of evidence is nonetheless so critical to the defense as to make a criminal trial fundamentally unfair." *Arizona v. Youngblood*, 488 U.S. at 61.

"Rules concerning [the] preservation of evidence are generally matters of state, not federal constitutional law." *California v. Trombetta*, 467 U.S. at 491. We reaffirm our prior holdings, pursuant to the "due process" requirements of the Delaware Constitution. When the State has failed to preserve evidence that could be favorable to the defendant, the analysis which a court must follow is set forth in *Deberry* and *Bailey*. That analysis draws a balance between the nature of the State's conduct and the degree of prejudice to the accused. In general terms, if the duty to preserve evidence has been breached, a Delaware court must consider: "1) the degree of negligence or bad faith involved; 2) the importance of the missing evidence, considering the probative value and reliability of secondary or substitute evidence that remains available; and 3) the sufficiency of the other evidence used at trial to sustain conviction." We will examine Hammond's contentions in accordance with these principles.

The first step in a *Deberry* evaluation is to determine whether the crash vehicle, if extant in the possession of the State, would have been subject to disclosure under Superior Court Criminal Rule 16 or *Brady*? As we noted in *Deberry*, determining whether the crash vehicle would have been discoverable under *Brady* would be an artificial exercise, since it is no longer available for examination or testing. Therefore, we begin with the provisions of Rule 16.

"[U]nder Superior Court Criminal Rule 16(b), a defendant need only show that an item 'may be material to the preparation of his defense' to be discoverable." This Court has held in another homicide case, that the car which the defendants were using, when the victim was shot and killed, was clearly material to the defense and discoverable under Rule 16. A fortiori, the crash vehicle may clearly be material to the preparation of the defense of a person, such as Hammond, charged with vehicular homicide. Therefore, if the crash vehicle were in the possession of the State, it would have been discoverable under Superior Court Criminal Rule 16.

The second step in a *Deberry* evaluation requires an examination of the State's duty to preserve discoverable evidence. This Court has declined to prescribe the exact procedures that are necessary for the various law enforcement agencies in this State to follow, in order to fulfill their duties to preserve evidence. However, this Court has held that in fulfilling these duties, agencies should create rules for gathering and preserving evidence that are broad enough to include any material that could be favorable to a defendant. In *Deberry*, we observed:

> It is most consistent with the purposes of those safeguards to hold that the duty of disclosure attaches in some form once the Government has first gathered and taken possession of the evidence in question. Otherwise, disclosure might be avoided by destroying vital evidence before prosecution begins or before defendants hear of its existence....Only if evidence is carefully preserved during the early stages of investigation will disclosure be possible later.

We find that the police had a duty to gather and to preserve a crash vehicle which they knew was involved in a fatal accident, when criminal charges were pending and a criminal investigation was continuing.

The record reflects that the crash vehicle was "gathered." It was towed from the scene of the crime and impounded, at the direction of the Dover Police Department, on July 25, 1986. However, the crash vehicle was not preserved. It was released on August 8, 1986. Although Hammond was arrested shortly after the accident, he was not indicted until September 3, 1986. Consequently, when Hammond's attorney filed a discovery request on October 14, 1986, pursuant to Criminal Rule 16, the Dover police no longer had possession of the crash vehicle. The record reflects that the duty to preserve the crash vehicle, at least until the defendant had a reasonable opportunity to inspect it, was breached in Hammond's case.

The final step in a *Deberry* evaluation requires a three-part analysis to determine the consequences which should flow from a breach of the duty to preserve evidence. The first factor to be considered is "the degree of negligence or bad faith involved." Hammond does not contend that the Dover police department released the crash vehicle in bad faith. Hammond does argue that the police were negligent.

The State argues that the police were not negligent in releasing the crash vehicle. When the police arrived, they found the bodies of the accident victims inside of the crash vehicle, in positions which indicated Hammond was the driver. At the hospital, Hammond told one of the investigating police officers that he was the driver. Under these conditions, the State argues that the police had no basis to believe that Hammond would deny being the driver or that the crash vehicle could be material to the preparation of his defense.

The State's argument is addressed to the good faith of the Dover police in releasing the crash vehicle. However, Hammond does not argue that the Dover police acted in bad faith. Hammond's position is that the police were negligent in not preserving the crash vehicle when he was charged with vehicular homicide, since the crash vehicle was the instrumentality of that crime. The Superior Court expressed concern "why a major piece of evidence [the crash vehicle] would not be held at least a little bit longer to give the defendant a chance to look at it." We conclude that the Dover police should have preserved the crash vehicle, for a reasonable time, to permit its inspection by Hammond.

The second factor to be considered in this portion of a *Deberry/Bailey* evaluation is the importance of the missing evidence and the reliability of the secondary or substitute evidence that remains available. Hammond argues that the crash vehicle was important to his case for two separate reasons. First, because evidence of fingerprints, blood, hair, or torn clothing in the interior of the crash vehicle might have established that he was not the driver. Alternatively, because the crash vehicle could have been examined for mechanical failure as a cause of the accident, rather than driver negligence.

The secondary evidence which the State provided to Hammond consisted primarily of photographs of the crash vehicle. The maintenance records of the crash vehicle's owner were also available. Hammond contends that the secondary evidence, especially as it related to his ability to identify the driver, was not a satisfactory substitute. Hammond admits that his expert was able to prepare a video tape of a test, which supported his theory of the hypothetical movement of Hammond and Moore in the vehicle upon impact. However, Hammond argues that without either access to scientific test results or the opportunity to test the interior of the crash vehicle, he was unable to confirm his expert's opinion.

The police found no evidentiary value in the crash vehicle or its contents. In this case, once again, we decline to establish specific procedures which are necessary for law enforcement agencies in this State to fulfill the duty to gather and to preserve evidence. Nevertheless, assuming *arguendo* that there was no duty to gather and test evidence of the interior of the crash vehicle, the crash vehicle in a vehicular homicide should have been preserved. If the crash vehicle itself had been preserved, it would have been available to Hammond for testing. There was little, if any, probative value in the secondary evidence of the crash vehicle's interior that was made available to Hammond, *i.e.*, a single photograph.

The evidence obtained from the interior of the car included the following: torn pieces of clothing found in the car; pieces of car seat fabric; the brake and clutch pads; the steering wheel; test results from blood stains found in the car; test results from arm and head hairs found in the car; and numerous photographs taken from various angles at the scene and at the autobody shop.

The final factor in determining what consequences should flow from the State's breach of the duty to preserve evidence in a *Deberry* evaluation, requires an examination of the sufficiency of the other evidence, which the State presented at trial. In Hammond's case, the State presented eyewitness testimony from another driver, who saw the crash vehicle pass him at a high rate of speed immediately prior to the collision. The record also reflects that the crash vehicle did not turn over and that all of its occupants remained inside. The crash vehicle became lodged in the foundation of a townhouse. Several persons reached the scene of the accident, almost immediately after it occurred. All of them testified that they saw Hammond in the driver's seat. Rescue workers testified that Hammond's leg was in a cast, which was wedged between the accelerator and the brake. The ambulance attendant testified that Hammond told him that he was driving, and that the accident occurred when the cast on his leg caused his foot to slip off of the brake pedal.

The question which must now be answered is what consequences should flow from the failure to preserve the crash vehicle. In the Superior Court, Hammond moved for dismissal or an instruction to the jury that the lost evidence, if available would be exculpatory in nature. In ruling on Hammond's motions, the Superior Court stated it is "clear that the occupants were moved around in the car after the collision." Nevertheless, the Superior Court denied both of Hammond's motions because he had not shown that the evidence, which was not available, would have been conclusively exculpatory to the defendant.

The "conclusively exculpatory" standard, which was applied by the Superior Court, is obviously inconsistent with our holding in *Deberry*. Nevertheless, we find that the State's case against Hammond was strong. Hammond's trial for vehicular homicide, even in the absence of the crash vehicle, was not so fundamentally unfair that his prosecution should have been barred as a denial of due process. Del. Const. art I, § 7. The Superior Court properly denied Hammond's motion to dismiss the State's case.

However, since the State must bear responsibility for the loss of evidence, Hammond was entitled to the inference that the crash vehicle, if available, would have been exculpatory. "Due process" required an appropriate instruction to the jury in a prosecution for vehicular homicide, in the absence of the preservation of the crash vehicle or of secondary evidence having a significant probative value. *See Deberry v. State*, 457 A.2d at 754; Del. Const. art. I, § 7. Such an instruction was given in *Arizona v. Youngblood*, even though no federal Constitutional right was found to have been violated.

More significantly, the trial judge instructed the jury: "If you find that the State has…allowed to be destroyed or lost any evidence whose content or quality are in issue, you may infer that the true fact is against the State's interest." As a result, the uncertainty as to what the evidence might have proved was turned to the defendant's advantage. *Arizona v. Youngblood*, 488 U.S. at 59-60.

We must now determine the effect of the Superior Court's failure to give such an instruction. Hammond's expert witness was able to prepare a video tape of a test supporting Hammond's theory of the hypothetical movement of the crash vehicle's occupants. Although Hammond's request for a jury instruction was denied, the Superior Court permitted Hammond's attorney to make "factual arguments" to the jury about the absence of the crash vehicle or any tests of its interior, and he did so forcefully. Given the strength of the State's case against Hammond, we are convinced beyond a reasonable doubt, that the Superior Court's failure to give a specific instruction was harmless error.

F. DOUBLE JEOPARDY

RICHARDSON v. STATE
717 N.E.2d 32 (Ind. 1999)

DICKSON, J.

With today's decision, we address the application of the Indiana Double Jeopardy Clause in article I, section 14 of the Indiana Constitution as distinct from its federal counterpart in the Fifth Amendment to the United States Constitution.

Prohibitions against double jeopardy protect the integrity of jury acquittals and the finality interest of defendants, shield against excessive and oppressive prosecutions, and ensure that defendants will not undergo the anxiety and expense of repeated prosecution and the increased probability of conviction upon re-prosecution. While double jeopardy provisions are found in both the United States Constitution and the Indiana Constitution, the defendant in this case does not allege any violation of the federal Double Jeopardy Clause. Rather, he claims the protection of the Indiana Double Jeopardy Clause.

Policy benefits of DJ

∆ cites state con

Commentators note that double jeopardy provisions, which appear straightforward and simple, are often extremely difficult to apply and the underlying jurisprudence enormously challenging and complex. Recently, in a series of decisions, this Court acknowledged that some of our decisions during the past twenty years misapplied federal double jeopardy jurisprudence. We did not, however, address whether the Double Jeopardy Clause of the Indiana Constitution provides identical or different protections than its federal counterpart. Today, with our opinions in this case and its companion cases, we address this issue.

QP! Fed = state on DJ?

The Double Jeopardy Clause of the Indiana Constitution

Questions arising under the Indiana Constitution are to be resolved by "examining the language of the text in the context of the history surrounding its drafting and ratification, the purpose and structure of our constitution, and case law interpreting the specific provisions." In construing the Constitution, "a court should look to the history of the times, and examine the state of things existing when the constitution or any part thereof was framed and adopted, to ascertain the old law, the mischief, and the remedy." Because the "intent of the framers of the Constitution is paramount in determining the meaning of a provision," this Court will consider "the purpose which induced the adoption," "in order that we may ascertain what the particular constitutional provision was designed to prevent."

Indiana's framework for interpreting con questions

1) text + history

2) Purpose & structure

3.) case law

When this State was founded in 1816, the framers and ratifiers adopted a double jeopardy provision which provided that, "in all criminal prosecutions, the accused...shall not...be twice put in jeopardy for the same offence." Ind. Const. art 1, § 13 (1816). However, our ability to discern the framers' intentions is limited because the journal of the 1816 Constitutional Convention does not report the delegates' remarks or disclose procedural matters informative to the issue.

original, key text of DJ

Lack of original docs

When the present version of our Constitution was adopted in 1851, the original double jeopardy provision was only slightly modified. Article I, section 14 provides in part: "No person shall be put in jeopardy twice for the same offense." The provision was adopted with no debate and has not been modified to date. The "cardinal principle of constitutional construction [is] that words are to be considered as used in their ordinary sense." Contemporaneous with the adoption of the 1851 Constitution, "offense" was defined as a "crime" or "transgression of law." This definition of "offense," however, does not explain the meaning of "same offense," which has become a term of art. It is not surprising that "[f]or decades, commentators and judges have attempted to define which offenses are the same, and the problem continues to be the focus of much of the contemporary scholarly criticism of double jeopardy doctrine."

Despite the lack of discussion at the 1850-51 Convention regarding Indiana's Double Jeopardy Clause, this Court has recognized that the intent of the framers and ratifiers derived from English common law double jeopardy principles. In *State v. Elder* we explained: "That no person shall be put in jeopardy twice for the same offence is a common-law principle, which, we believe, is incorporated into the constitution of each of the States which compose the United States." With the understanding that the constitutional protection against double jeopardy is one of the "least understood" and "most frequently litigated provisions of the Bill of Rights," "[i]t has always been an accepted judicial technique to have resort to the common law in order to ascertain the true meaning of the double jeopardy clause." Thus, understanding our Double Jeopardy Clause requires that we go beyond its text. The common law is helpful in determining the framers' understanding of the term "same offense."

Scholars trace double jeopardy principles back to ancient Greek, Roman and biblical sources. While some historians trace double jeopardy protections in England to the dispute between King Henry II and Archbishop Thomas à Becket in 1176, the earliest treatise on the English common law, published in the late twelfth century, did not directly mention double jeopardy protections. In the English case reporters between 1290 and 1535, "the word 'jeopardy' occurs only eleven times in reports involving criminal cases, and in only three of these instances was it used in the statement that a man's life shall not be twice 'put in jeopardy' for the same offense."

During the 1600s and 1700s, double jeopardy protections were further examined by Lord Edward Coke and William Blackstone. Lord Coke only found double jeopardy protections in the three pleas of *autrefois acquit* (former acquittal), *autrefois convict* (former conviction), and former pardon. By the late 1700s, a fourth plea of *autrefois attaint* was also recognized. Writing 100 years after Coke, Blackstone began using the phrase "jeopardy" more often, noting that "the plea of *autrefois acquit*, or a former acquittal, is grounded on this universal maxim of the common law of England that no man is to be brought into jeopardy of his life, more than once, for the same offence." *DJ maxim, via BlackStone*

As a further indicator of the framers' understanding of the common law of double jeopardy, we note that the early American colonies departed in some respects from English common law, recognizing broader double jeopardy protections. For example, the bar against double jeopardy for Lord Coke depended on the reasons for the prior acquittal, whereas early American double jeopardy law barred retrial for any prior acquittal. Blackstone described double jeopardy protections as applying only to criminal *felony* prosecutions, whereas early American double jeopardy protections applied to all criminal prosecutions. Under English common law, jeopardy did not attach until a verdict or acquittal was actually rendered, thus allowing retrials following hung juries or mistrials, whereas early American double jeopardy law barred re-prosecution in certain hung jury or mistrial circumstances. Further, early English double jeopardy protections were developed in the context of criminal law practice and procedure different from that which existed and continues to exist in this country. When Coke formulated the double jeopardy prohibition against second prosecutions for the same offense, there did not exist the same number of closely related offenses as we have today. As one commentator has noted, "the law distinguished among rape, arson, and murder, but not between 'intimidating any person from voting' and 'interfering with his right to vote.'" "At the time of Henry III there were only eleven felonies. In Coke's time the number had risen to thirty." By the time the United States Constitution was ratified, England had 160 different felonies. *more "felonies" in America*

Differences showing more expansive DJ in America

Also, early American colonies and states embodied double jeopardy principles in statutory and organic laws, unlike England. In 1641, the Bay Colony of Massachusetts drafted the Body of Liberties, which led to the adoption of the Massachusetts Code of 1648. "The fact that the Bay Colony reduced double jeopardy protection to a written form and expanded it beyond the common law guarantee demonstrates that the colonists regarded the concept to be fundamental." Although New Hampshire was the first (and only) state to include double jeopardy protections in its state constitution *prior* to the ratification of the United States Constitution, almost every state has now included some type of protection against double jeopardy in its state constitution.

As states developed and applied their respective double jeopardy principles, two divergent analyses appeared for determining whether the offenses are the same: (1) the behavioral approach; and (2) the evidentiary approach. The "behavioral approach focuses on the defendant's conduct rather than on the prosecutor's evidence. Courts which use this approach adopt an act, transaction, or intent test." This behavioral approach (also referred to as the same transaction or same conduct approach) was

2 approaches for determining if crime is the same

Behavioral approach

(2nd reflects ILB)

explicitly rejected early by the Indiana Supreme Court. The *Elder* Court noted that two lines of Double Jeopardy Clause interpretation appeared throughout the nation. One line held that state double jeopardy clauses provide "a more liberal rule…in favor of the accused." This more liberal rule was the same transaction/conduct test, which prohibited multiple prosecutions arising out of the "same state of facts, although they may include several offences." Under the other line of interpretation, the evidentiary approach, state double jeopardy clauses "mean no more than the common-law principle." After reviewing Indiana court decisions and the decisions from other state and federal courts, the *Elder* Court rejected the more liberal test, stating that it could "not adopt the rule held in some States, that the accused can not, in any case, be convicted but once upon the same facts when they constitute different offences."

The evidentiary approach (also referred to as the same evidence test) is apparent in the English common law case of *The King v. Vandercomb & Abbot*, 2 Leach 708, 168 Eng. 455 (1796). That court explained the test as follows:

> if crimes are so distinct that evidence of the one will not support the other, it is as inconsistent with reason, as it is repugnant to the rules of law, to say that they are so far the same that an acquittal of the one shall be a bar to a prosecution for the other.

However, American jurisprudence in the last two centuries provides no single, generally accepted articulation of the same evidence test. Rather, the test has assumed three separate formulations: a "required evidence test," an "alleged evidence test," and an "actual evidence test."

In discerning the approach required by the Indiana Constitution, we first note that "[e]arly decisions of this Court interpreting our Constitution…have been accorded strong and superseding precedential value." In seeking the proper interpretation of our Double Jeopardy Clause, we draw from cases involving subsequent prosecutions because double jeopardy claims in multiple punishments cases did not emerge until after 1930, and because this Court has not distinguished between double jeopardy protections in multiple punishment cases and those in subsequent prosecution cases. Our double jeopardy case law appears to fall into five different subsequent prosecution categories—those following a conviction; a mistrial or the discharge of the jury or defendant; a successful appeal; an acquittal; and a civil action.

Our earliest jurisprudence demonstrates that this Court did not limit itself to any single formulation of the evidence test, such as an "actual evidence test," a "required evidence test," or an "alleged evidence test," in determining whether the offenses were the same. In the cases most contemporaneous (1859 to 1884) with the adoption of the 1851 Constitution, this Court did not identify a singular test or restrict the double jeopardy inquiry to the statutory elements or charging instruments, but instead considered all of the circumstances and evidence available to the reviewing court to determine whether the offenses were the same.

Early case law shows no evidence categories

After the ratification of our Constitution in 1851, the Indiana Supreme Court considered whether the convictions were the "same offense" in *Wininger v. State*. In *Wininger*, the defendant was first convicted of assault and battery and then tried for the crime of riot, each arising out of the same event. Noting "conflict in the decisions of some of the sister states," the *Wininger* Court considered whether double jeopardy was violated, holding that "the true rule, in prosecutions for offenses of this character, is, that where the gravamen of the riot consists in the commission of an assault and battery, then, a conviction for that assault, & c., would be a bar to a prosecution for a riot." However, "where the commission of an assault and battery was merely incidental to the riot, then a conviction for the one would not bar a prosecution for the other." Thus, "[t]he question would be, is the one act included in the other?" Looking to the evidence introduced at trial, the Court reversed the second conviction, finding that the Double Jeopardy Clause was violated because "the gravamen of the riot was the assault and battery."

Early rule: for multiple offenses, a yes triggers DJ.

In 1978, the analysis under the Indiana Constitution was merged with the federal constitutional test in *Elmore v. State*: "Now that we are bound by the federal Double Jeopardy Clause, it is more necessary than ever that we be in line with federal standards." Although the *Elmore* Court erroneously concluded that the federal Supremacy Clause required that the federal test govern all Indiana claims, it is clear that this Court, by 1978, considered *both* the Indiana Double Jeopardy Clause and the federal Double Jeopardy Clause to require the same test—a statutory "identity of offense" or "same evidence" test.   During the twenty years following *Elmore*, this Court frequently decided double jeopardy issues by looking to the offenses as charged, believing that this approach was required by federal double jeopardy jurisprudence, and often referring in passing to the Indiana Constitution. We have recently recognized that this methodology is an inaccurate statement of federal double jeopardy law as established by *Blockburger v. United States*, 284 U.S. 299 (1932). Considering *Elmore*'s merger of Indiana double jeopardy law into federal constitutional analysis and its declaration that our state's double jeopardy jurisprudence must "be in line with federal standards," it is not surprising that we did not separately evaluate the Indiana Constitution as an additional, independent source of double jeopardy protection. Instead, we generally addressed double jeopardy claims by applying the prevailing understanding of federal jurisprudence and merely referred to the Indiana Double Jeopardy Clause. This Court today recognizes that these post-*Elmore*, pre-*Games* cases do not constitute precedent regarding the application of the Indiana

By 1978, Ind merges state / Fed tests

Ct: Elmore is wrong! don't merge Fed & state

Double Jeopardy Clause. Our action today should be understood to supercede these cases.

From our review of the constitutional text, the history and circumstances surrounding its adoption, and the earliest cases interpreting and applying the provision, we conclude that Indiana's Double Jeopardy Clause was intended to prevent the State from being able to proceed against a person twice for the same criminal transgression. While none of the early cases presented a comprehensive analysis, a generally articulated test, or a standard of review for double jeopardy claims, the holdings in these decisions do reflect a common theme. A criminal transgression was a person's conduct that violated a statutorily defined crime. In seeking to determine whether two criminal transgressions were the same, this Court in its earliest decisions did not restrict its review only to a comparison of statutory elements of the crime or to an analysis of the language in the charging instruments. Rather, this Court also reviewed the actual evidence presented at trial when available.

Synthesizing these considerations, we therefore conclude and hold that two or more offenses are the "same offense" in violation of article I, section 14 of the Indiana Constitution, if, with respect to *either* the statutory elements of the challenged crimes *or* the actual evidence used to convict, the essential elements of one challenged offense also establish the essential elements of another challenged offense. Both of these considerations, the statutory elements test and the actual evidence test, are components of the double jeopardy "same offense" analysis under the Indiana Constitution.

Because the defendant's convictions for both robbery and battery as a class A misdemeanor, under the circumstances presented, violate the Double Jeopardy Clause of the Indiana Constitution, we vacate the conviction and sentence for battery as a class A misdemeanor. This cause is remanded to the trial court for disposition consistent with this opinion.

NOTE

In 2015, the Indiana Supreme Court held that a defendant's conviction for battery was a violation of the state constitution's prohibition against double jeopardy. The court vacated the defendant's battery conviction but affirmed his criminal confinement conviction. *Hines v. State*, 30 N.E. 3d 1216 (Ind. 2015); decided by the Supreme Court of Indiana.

G. CRUEL AND UNUSUAL PUNISHMENT

STATE v. SANTIAGO
2015 WL 4771974 (Conn. Aug. 25, 2015)

PALMER, J.

Although the death penalty has been a fixture of Connecticut's criminal law since early colonial times, public opinion concerning it has long been divided. In 2009, growing opposition to capital punishment led the legislature to enact Public Acts 2009, No. 09-107 (P.A. 09-107), which would have repealed the death penalty for all crimes committed on or after the date of enactment but retained the death penalty for capital felonies committed prior to that date. Then Governor M. Jodi Rell vetoed P.A. 09-107, however, and it did not become law. Three years later, in 2012, the legislature passed a materially identical act that prospectively repealed the death penalty; see Public Acts 2012, No. 12-5 (P.A. 12-5); and, this time, Governor Dannel P. Malloy signed it into law. During the public hearings on both P.A. 09-107 and P.A. 12-5, supporters argued that the proposed legislation represented a measured and lawful approach to the issue.

Others raised serious concerns, however, as to whether, following a prospective only repeal, the imposition of the death penalty would violate the state constitutional prohibition against cruel and unusual punishment. Perhaps most notably, Chief State's Attorney Kevin T. Kane, who serves as this state's chief law enforcement officer and represents the state in the present case, testified before the legislature that such a statute could not pass constitutional muster. Additionally, the Division of Criminal Justice submitted written testimony, in which it advised the legislature that a prospective only repeal would be a "fiction" and that, "[i]n reality, it would effectively abolish the death penalty for anyone who has not yet been executed because it would be untenable as a matter of constitutional law.... [A]ny death penalty that has been imposed and not carried out would effectively be nullified."

In the present appeal, the defendant, Eduardo Santiago, raises similar claims, contending that, following the decision by the elected branches to abolish capital punishment for all crimes committed *on or after* April 25, 2012, it would be unconstitutionally cruel and unusual to execute offenders who committed capital crimes before that date. Upon careful consideration of the defendant's claims in light of the governing constitutional principles and Connecticut's unique historical and legal landscape, we are persuaded that, following its prospective abolition, this state's death penalty no longer comports with contemporary standards of decency and no longer serves any legitimate penological purpose. For these reasons, execution of those offenders who committed capital felonies prior to April 25, 2012, would violate the state constitutional prohibition against cruel and unusual punishment.

The underlying facts of this case, which are set forth in detail in *Santiago I*, may be summarized briefly as follows. In December, 2000, Mark Pascual agreed to give the defendant a snowmobile from Pascual's repair shop if the defendant would kill the victim, Joseph Niwinski, for whose girlfriend Pascual had developed romantic feelings. That same month, with the assistance of Pascual and another friend, the defendant entered the victim's apartment and shot and killed the victim as he slept. The defendant was charged with, among other things, the capital felony of "murder committed by a defendant who is hired to commit the same for pecuniary gain," in violation of § 53a-54b (2).

Public Act 12-5 not only reflects this state's longstanding aversion to carrying out executions, but also represents the seminal change in the four century long history of capital punishment in Connecticut. Accompanying this dramatic departure are a host of other important developments that have transpired over the past several years. Historians have given us new chronicles of the history and devolution of the death penalty in Connecticut. Legal scholars have provided new understandings of the original meaning of the constitutional prohibition against cruel and unusual punishments. Social scientists repeatedly have confirmed that the risk of capital punishment falls disproportionately on people of color and other disadvantaged groups. Meanwhile, nationally, the number of executions and the number of states that allow the death penalty continue to decline, and convicted capital felons in this state remain on death row for decades with every likelihood that they will not be executed for many years to come, if ever.

Finally, it has become apparent that the dual federal constitutional requirements applicable to all capital sentencing schemes—namely, that the jury be provided with objective standards to guide its sentence, on the one hand, and that it be accorded unfettered discretion to impose a sentence of less than death, on the other—are fundamentally in conflict and inevitably open the door to impermissible racial and ethnic biases. For all these reasons, and in light of the apparent intent of the legislature in prospectively repealing the death penalty and this state's failure to implement and operate a fair and functional system of capital punishment, we conclude that the state constitution no longer permits the execution of individuals sentenced to death for crimes committed prior to the enactment of P.A. 12-5.

Since this court first considered the constitutionality of capital punishment, we have recognized that, "in the area of fundamental civil liberties-which includes all protections of the declaration of rights contained in article first of the Connecticut constitution-we sit as a court of last resort.   In such constitutional adjudication, our first referent is Connecticut law and the full panoply of rights Connecticut citizens have come to expect as their due."

State can prohibits C&U

It is by now well established that the constitution of Connecticut prohibits cruel and unusual punishments under the auspices of the dual due process provisions contained in article first, §§ 8 and 9. Those due process protections take as their hallmark principles of fundamental fairness rooted in our state's unique common law, statutory, and constitutional traditions.   Although neither provision of the state constitution expressly references cruel or unusual punishments, it is settled constitutional doctrine that both of our due process clauses prohibit governmental infliction of cruel and unusual punishments.

In *State* v. *Geisler*, 610 A.2d 1225 (1992), we identified six nonexclusive tools of analysis to be considered, to the extent applicable, whenever we are called on as a matter of first impression to define the scope and parameters of the state constitution: (1) persuasive relevant federal precedents; (2) historical insights into the intent of our constitutional forebears; (3) the operative constitutional text; (4) related Connecticut precedents; (5) persuasive precedents of other states; and (6) contemporary understandings of applicable economic and sociological norms, or, as otherwise described, relevant public policies. These factors, which we consider in turn, inform our application of the established state constitutional standards – standards that, as we explain hereinafter, derive from United States Supreme Court precedent concerning the eighth amendment to the defendant's claims in the present case.

6 factors to apply on matters of 1st impression

Federal Constitutional Standards

The eighth amendment to the federal constitution establishes the minimum standards for what constitutes impermissibly cruel and unusual punishment. Specifically, the United States Supreme Court has indicated that at least three types of punishment may be deemed unconstitutionally cruel: (1) inherently barbaric punishments; (2) excessive and disproportionate punishments; and (3) arbitrary or discriminatory punishments. In *Ross*, we broadly adopted, as a matter of state constitutional law, this federal framework for evaluating challenges to allegedly cruel and unusual punishments.

SCOTUS: 3 types of C&U

Relevant State Constitutional History

We next consider our state's constitutional and pre-constitutional history with respect to the freedom from cruel and unusual punishment. We consider, first, the preconstitutional era and the legal traditions that inform the meaning of the Connecticut constitution and, second, the period leading up to the adoption of the Connecticut constitution of 1818.

Preconstitutional Legal Traditions

We first consider the preconstitutional roots of the freedom from cruel and unusual punishment in Connecticut. As early as 1672, our colonial code, which incorporated a quasi-constitutional statement of individual liberties, provided that, for bodily punishment, none shall be inflicted that are Inhumane, Barbarous or Cruel." The 1672 code also differed from prior Connecticut statutes in that it (1) forbade the use of torture to extract confessions, (2) placed new restrictions on the use of corporal punishment, and (3) afforded novel procedural rights to criminal defendants, especially in capital cases.

In perhaps the most substantial scholarly account of the early legal traditions of the Connecticut colony, William K. Holdsworth offers a window into the original meaning of Connecticut's inceptive prohibition of cruel punishment. Holdsworth describes the years leading up to the adoption of the 1672 code as a key formative period in the colony's legal history. "The decade [of 1662 through 1672] was a watershed in the early history of Connecticut," he explains, "a period of profound intellectual, social, economic, and political change that set the colony on a course of its own." During this period of "extraordinarily rapid and vital change"; a new generation of leaders restructured the colony's political and judicial systems. The legislature "made fairer use of its juries ... gave formal recognition to numerous civil liberties, displayed a greater awareness of individual rights, dealt less severely with most criminal offenders than before, and, either formally or in practice, reduced the penalties for several capital crimes." Id., at pp. 547-48. In the process, Connecticut's new leaders bequeathed to its citizens a "legacy of moderation ..."

"[This unmistakable] tendency toward judicial moderation in the use of physical punishments in the years [1662 through 1675] ... is all the more pronounced when we consider capital crimes and capital punishment." As public attitudes evolved, magistrates grew more reluctant to inflict capital punishment and came to believe that the death penalty should be reserved for only the most heinous and universally condemned offenses. It is apparent from this history that, long before the adoption of either the federal or state constitution, Connecticut citizens enjoyed a quasi-constitutional freedom from cruel punishment, one that reflected our unique social and political traditions and that far exceeded the protections recognized in England at the time. These protections were enshrined in Connecticut's early constitutional statutes and common law, and, from the start, were intimately tied to the principles of due process.

We next consider the historical circumstances leading up to the adoption of the state constitution in 1818. The late eighteenth and early nineteenth centuries witnessed the twilight of a premodern system of criminal justice in the United States. The rapid evolution in penology that occurred in the decades following the founding was especially pronounced in Connecticut. The late eighteenth and early nineteenth centuries in Connecticut witnessed a pronounced liberalization in public, legislative, and judicial attitudes toward crime and punishment The period has been described as one characterized by penological reform, a broader commitment to human rights, and the first serious public questioning of the moral legitimacy of capital punishment This time between the adoption of the federal and state constitutions also saw an emerging awareness of and compassion for "the fate of the condemned perpetrator." These changes coincided with the reopening of the newly established Newgate Prison (Newgate) in 1790, which provided the opportunity to impose incarceration as an alternative to more severe traditional punishments See id., at p. 75.

In summary, it is clear that, from the earliest days of the colonies, and extending until the adoption of the state constitution in 1818, the people of Connecticut saw themselves as enjoying significant freedoms from cruel and unusual punishment, freedoms that were safeguarded by our courts and enshrined in our state's pre-constitutional statutory and common law. That our history reveals a particular sensitivity to such concerns warrants our scrupulous and independent review of allegedly cruel and unusual practices and punishments, and informs our analysis thereof.

Relevant Constitutional Text (3rd because of state's history?)

We next consider the relevant provisions of the state constitution. In light of our state's firm and enduring commitment to the principle that even those offenders who commit the most heinous crimes should not be subjected to inhumane, barbarous, or cruel punishment, the question naturally arises why the framers of the 1818 constitution decided to embed these traditional liberties in our dual due process clauses; see Conn. Const. (1818), art. I, §§ 9 and 10; rather than in an express punishments clause Although there is no indication that that question was debated during the 1818 constitutional convention, we

[Margin handwritten notes:]
18th/19th C & the punishment reforms
#. Prison as alternative to severe punishment
Conn has culture against C&U
Ct: why the DP clauses and not a separate punishment clause?

find guidance in the broader legal history of turn of the century Connecticut.

Connecticut was among three of the original thirteen states that chose not to officially ratify the eighth amendment or, indeed, any of the first ten amendments to the federal constitution. In 1787, the state's representatives to the federal constitutional convention had argued vehemently against the need for a bill of rights. "In Connecticut, unlike those states that had recently been under the domination of royal and proprietary governors and appointed upper houses, limited government was taken for granted. Calvinist theory described limited government, [Connecticut's] Fundamental Orders [of 1639] proclaimed it, the [Connecticut] Charter [of 1662] established it, tradition demanded it, common law enforced it, and frequent elections guaranteed it." During the late eighteenth and early nineteenth centuries, for example, Connecticut courts routinely safeguarded the basic rights enshrined in the federal Bill of Rights on the basis of natural rights or common law, without the need for any formal constitutional sanction. Moreover, there was a particular fear in Connecticut that the adoption of a written bill of rights would imply, by negative inference, that citizens were no longer entitled to unenumerated protections long enshrined in the state's common law. A strong statewide consensus, then, held that no bill of rights was necessary and, indeed, might even limit individual liberty.

Accordingly, in *Moore v. Ganim*, 660 A.2d 742 (1995), we "assume[d] that the framers believed that individuals would continue to possess certain natural rights even if those rights were not enumerated in the written constitution. On the basis of this assumption, we [would] not draw firm conclusions from the silence of the constitutional text.... Rather, in determining whether unenumerated rights were incorporated into the constitution, we must focus on the framers' understanding of whether a particular right was part of the natural law, i.e., on the framers' understanding of whether the particular right was so fundamental to an ordered society that it did not require explicit enumeration. We can discern the framers' understanding, of course, only by examining the historical sources." (Emphasis omitted.)

Relevant Connecticut Precedents

Turning to the next *Geisler* factor, namely, relevant Connecticut precedents, we write on a relatively blank slate with respect to cruel and unusual punishment. Nevertheless, since this court first recognized in *Ross* that our due process clauses independently prohibit cruel and unusual punishment; we have begun to carve out the broad contours of that prohibition.   In *Ross* itself, as we have noted, we adopted the

Ct: adopt fed framework

aforementioned federal framework for evaluating challenges to allegedly cruel and unusual punishments. Specifically, we recognized that, under the state constitution, whether a challenged punishment is cruel and unusual is to be judged according to the "evolving standards of human decency"; and that those standards are reflected not only in constitutional and legislative text, but also "in our history and in the teachings of the jurisprudence of our sister states as well as that of the federal courts." In *Ross*, we also rejected the theory that "article first, § 9, confers the authority to determine what constitutes cruel and unusual punishment solely on the Connecticut legislature and not on the courts." "Although we should exercise our authority with great restraint," we explained, "this court cannot abdicate its nondelegable responsibility for the adjudication of constitutional rights."

Incorporate evolving standards

CL has right to interpret what's C&U

Subsequently, in *Rizzo I*, we characterized it as "settled constitutional doctrine that, independently of federal constitutional requirements, our due process clauses, because they prohibit cruel and unusual punishment, impose constitutional limits on the imposition of the death penalty." In that case, we recognized that there is an "overarching concern for consistency and reliability in the imposition of the death penalty" under our state constitution. Accordingly, in order to avoid having to resolve the state constitutional question raised in that case, we construed General Statutes (Rev. to 1997) § 53a-46a to require that a jury must find beyond a reasonable doubt that the death penalty is the appropriate penalty. *Applying statutes instead.*

Most recently, in *State v. Rizzo*, we engaged in a full analysis of the constitutionality of the death penalty pursuant to the state constitution. At that time, we reiterated that, "in determining whether a particular punishment is cruel and unusual in violation of [state] constitutional standards, we must look beyond historical conceptions to the evolving standards of decency that mark the progress of a maturing society." (Internal quotation marks omitted.) We also "recognize[d] that assessing the propriety of [a punishment] is not exclusively the domain of the legislature, and that this court has an independent duty to determine that the penalty remains constitutionally viable as the sensibilities of our citizens evolve."

1.) evolving standards of decency

2.) ct has its own power to determine C&U

Persuasive Sister State Precedents

The unique structure and text of the Connecticut constitution of 1965, in which the freedom from cruel and unusual punishment is embeded in our dual due process clauses rather than in a distinct punishments clause, mean that sister state authority is less directly relevant than in cases in which we have construed other constitutional provisions. We do agree with our sister courts, however, that, under the

Ct: our con is rare, so other states won't be as helpful

state constitution, the pertinent standards by which we judge the fairness, decency, and efficacy of a punishment are necessarily those of Connecticut.

Conclusion

To summarize our analysis of the first five *Geisler* factors, when construing the state constitutional freedom from cruel and unusual punishment, we broadly adopt the framework that the federal courts have used to evaluate eighth amendment challenges. We apply this framework, however, with respect to the constitutional facts as they exist in Connecticut and mindful of our state's unique and expansive constitutional and preconstitutional history.

We next consider whether the death penalty, as currently imposed in Connecticut, and following the enactment of P.A. 12-5, is so out of step with our contemporary standards of decency as to violate the state constitutional ban on excessive and disproportionate punishment. We conclude that it is.

As we previously noted, both the federal and state constitutions prohibit the imposition of any punishment that is not proportioned and graduated to the offense of conviction. Whether a punishment is disproportionate and excessive is to be judged by the contemporary, "evolving standards of decency that mark the progress of a maturing society." In other words, the constitutional guarantee against excessive punishment is "not fastened to the obsolete but may acquire meaning as public opinion becomes enlightened by a humane justice." *Weems* v. *United States*, 217 U.S. 349 (1910). Because the legal standard is an evolving one, it is both necessary and appropriate for us to consider the issue anew, in light of relevant recent developments, when it is raised.

On only two prior occasions has this court considered in any depth whether capital punishment violates the state constitutional ban on cruel and unusual punishment. In those cases, we considered-and at times blurred the lines between-two distinct constitutional challenges: (1) the claim that capital punishment is inherently barbaric punishment and, therefore, offends the constitution at all times and under all circumstances; and (2) the claim that, although capital punishment may once have comported with constitutional requirements, our state's standards of decency have evolved such that execution now constitutes excessive and disproportionate punishment.

We first take this opportunity to clarify that, although a sudden sea change in public opinion would be sufficient to demonstrate a constitutionally significant shift in contemporary standards of decency, such a dramatic shift is not necessary for us to recognize that a punishment has become repugnant to the state constitution. If the legally salient metaphor is the *evolution* of our standards of decency, then a gradual but inexorable extinction may be as significant as the sociological equivalent of the meteor that, it is believed, suddenly ended the reign of the dinosaurs. In any event, new insights into the history of capital punishment in Connecticut, in tandem with the legislature's 2012 decision to abolish the death penalty prospectively, persuade us that we now have not only a clear picture of the long, steady devolution of capital punishment in our state, and, indeed, throughout New England, but also a dramatic and definitive statement by our elected officials that the death penalty no longer can be justified as a necessary or appropriate tool of justice.

In conclusion, we are aware that the issue of whether the death penalty is an appropriate punishment for the most heinous crimes is one about which people of good faith continue to disagree. Nevertheless, our review of the five objective indicia that have been deemed relevant under both the federal and state constitutions compels the conclusion that, following the enactment of P.A. 12-5, Connecticut's capital punishment scheme no longer comports with our state's contemporary standards of decency. It therefore offends the state constitutional prohibition against excessive and disproportionate punishment.

CHAPTER VII

SEARCH AND SEIZURE

A. INTRODUCTION

The prohibition on unreasonable searches and seizures in many state constitutions is almost identical to the Fourth Amendment of the United States Constitution. However, some state constitutions have textual differences that can be outcome determinative. *See, e.g.*, Haw. Const. art. I, § 7; N.Y. Const. art. I, § 12; La. Const. art. I, § 5. Under the Fourth Amendment, warrantless searches are *per se* unreasonable unless they fall within an exception to the warrant requirement. Some of the exceptions to the Fourth Amendment's warrant requirement are: frisks, inventory searches, searches incident to arrest, consensual searches, automobile searches and searches under exigent circumstances. These and other exceptions are not always permitted in whole or in part by state constitutions.

State constitutions also have been construed to have standards that differ from the Fourth Amendment to determine probable cause and standing. The purpose, policy and operation of the exclusionary rule under state constitutions are frequently different from the federal exclusionary rule.

B. PROBABLE CAUSE

PEOPLE v. GRIMINGER
524 N.E.2d 409 (N.Y. 1988)

TITONE, J.

The primary issue presented is whether the *Aguilar-Spinelli* two-prong test, or the *Gates* totality-of-the-circumstances test, should be employed in determining the sufficiency of an affidavit submitted in support of a search warrant application. *See Illinois v. Gates*, 462 U.S. 213 (1983); *Spinelli v. United States*, 393 U.S. 410 (1969); *Aguilar v. Texas*, 378 U.S. 108 (1964). We conclude that, as a matter of State law, our courts should apply the *Aguilar-Spinelli* test.

Special agents of the United States Secret Service arrested a counterfeiting suspect, and, in the course of interrogation, he signed a detailed statement accusing defendant of keeping large quantities of marihuana and cocaine in his bedroom and adjacent attic. Consequently, one of the agents prepared an affidavit for a warrant to search defendant's home. According to the affidavit, a confidential informant known as source "A" observed substantial quantities of marihuana and quantities of cocaine in defendant's bedroom and attic on numerous occasions, saw defendant sell drugs on numerous occasions, and, as recently as seven days ago, "A" observed 150 to 200 pounds of marihuana in defendant's bedroom and adjacent attic. The affidavit further stated that, pursuant to a consent search, approximately four pounds of marihuana were found in a garbage can at defendant's residence.

Although the agent did not personally know the counterfeiting suspect, his affidavit said that the undisclosed informant was "a person known to your deponent." The agent also omitted the fact that the informant was under arrest when he provided this information. Based solely upon this affidavit, a Federal Magistrate issued the search warrant. On August 26, 1983, the warrant was executed by 2 Federal agents and 6 or 7 Nassau County policemen. The search produced 10 ounces of marijuana, over $6,000 in cash and drug-related paraphernalia. Additionally, the Federal agents turned over the marijuana discovered during the consent search referred to in the warrant to Nassau County law enforcement officials.

Defendant was charged with two counts of criminal possession of marihuana, as well as with criminal sale of marihuana arising out of an unrelated May 1984 incident. Defendant sought to suppress the evidence obtained as a result of the August 26 search, but County Court denied the motion. Although the court found that the agent's affidavit failed to satisfy the "reliability" prong of the *Aguilar-Spinelli* test, it concluded that the *Gates* test should be applied in assessing the sufficiency of a search warrant. Under that test, the court determined that there was probable cause to issue the warrant.

Prior to *Illinois v. Gates*, Federal courts applied the two-pronged *Aguilar-Spinelli* test in probable cause determinations when evaluating hearsay information from an undisclosed informant. Under this test, the application for a search warrant must demonstrate to the issuing Magistrate (i) the veracity or reliability of the source of the information, and (ii) the basis of the informant's knowledge. We adopted this standard as a matter of State constitutional law. In *Illinois v. Gates*, the United States Supreme Court altered its position and adopted the seemingly more relaxed "totality-of-the- circumstances approach."

In *People v. Johnson*, 488 N.E.2d 439 (N.Y. 1985), this court expressly rejected the *Gates* approach for evaluating warrantless arrests. In *People v. Bigelow*, 488 N.E.2d 451 (N.Y. 1985), although the People urged us to adopt the *Gates* test in the search warrant context, we found it unnecessary to decide the question, since "the People's evidence [did] not meet minimum standards of probable cause even if *Gates* was applied." This appeal squarely presents the issue left undecided in *Bigelow*. We are not persuaded, however, that the *Gates* approach provides a sufficient measure of protection, and we now hold that, as a matter of State constitutional law, the *Aguilar-Spinelli* two- prong test should be applied in determining whether there is a sufficient factual predicate upon which to issue a search warrant.

We reaffirm today that in evaluating hearsay information the Magistrate must find some minimum, reasonable showing that the informant was reliable and had a basis of knowledge. Our courts should not "blithely accept as true the accusations of an informant unless some good reason for doing so has been established." The *Aguilar-Spinelli* two-pronged inquiry has proven a satisfactory method of providing reasonable assurance that probable cause determinations are based on information derived from a credible source with firsthand information, and we are not convinced that the *Gates* test offers a satisfactory alternative.

The reasons advanced by the People in support of the *Gates* test are similar to those enunciated by the Supreme Court itself in *Illinois v. Gates*. They contend that the less stringent *Gates* test will encourage the use of warrants, a highly desirable goal. They assert that the *Aguilar-Spinelli* test has been applied in a rigid, inflexible manner to the detriment of law enforcement. The commonsense approach of *Gates*, posit the People, is a more reasonable rule of law, since the hypertechnical two-prong test places an unnecessary burden on law enforcement officers who are not lawyers, but rather public officials "acting under stress and often within the context of a volatile situation."

Although we agree with the People that the use of warrants should be encouraged, there is no reason to believe that police will refrain from obtaining a warrant merely because this State continues to apply the *Aguilar-Spinelli* test. With limited exceptions, carefully circumscribed by our courts, it is always incumbent upon the police to obtain a warrant before conducting a search. Furthermore, whether there was probable cause will generally be raised by the defendant at a suppression hearing. If a Magistrate has already determined that probable cause existed, great deference will be accorded that finding, resulting in far fewer suppression problems. This, in turn, results in a more efficient use of police resources; it is indeed wasteful to make an arrest or conduct a search without a warrant only to have those efforts invalidated by a suppression court.

Nor is the *Aguilar-Spinelli* test a hypertechnical approach to evaluating hearsay information. As we stated in *People v. Hanlon*, "in the real world, we are confronted with search warrant applications which are generally not composed by lawyers in the quiet of a law library but rather by law enforcement officers who are acting under stress and often within the context of a volatile situation. Consequently such search warrant applications should not be read in a hypertechnical manner as if they were entries in an essay contest. On the contrary, they must be considered in the clear light of everyday experience and accorded all reasonable inferences."

In *People v. Johnson*, we recognized that the more structured "bright line" *Aguilar-Spinelli* test better served the highly desirable "aims of predictability and precision in judicial review of search and seizure cases," and that "the protection of the individual rights of our citizens are best promoted by applying State constitutional standards." We find this reasoning equally persuasive in cases involving search warrants. Given the deference paid to the Magistrate's probable cause finding, and given the somewhat subjective nature of the probable cause inquiry, the aims of predictability and precision are again well served by providing the Magistrate with *Aguilar-Spinelli's* concrete, structured guidelines. More importantly, this will also prevent the disturbance of the rights of privacy and liberty upon the word of an unreliable hearsay informant, a danger we perceive under the *Gates* totality-of-the-circumstances test.

The unreliability of the hearsay informant was established by County Court and affirmed by the Appellate Division. We have no basis upon which to review or disturb that finding. The reliability prong of *Aguilar-Spinelli* having not been satisfied, we therefore affirm the Appellate Division order finding the warrant invalid and suppressing the fruits of the search.

COMMONWEALTH v. GRAY
503 A.2d 921 (Pa. 1985)

HUTCHINSON, J.

This case requires us to determine whether the United States Supreme Court's decision in *Illinois v. Gates*, 462 U.S. 213 (1983), adopting a "totality of the circumstances" standard under the federal constitution in analyzing probable cause for search warrants based on information received from confidential informants, also meets the requirements of article I, section 8 of our Pennsylvania Constitution. Appellant was convicted of possession of marijuana with intent to deliver. Superior Court affirmed the conviction and we granted appellant's petition for allowance of appeal.

Several confidential informants told police that appellant and his girlfriend had approximately twenty pounds of marijuana at their residence. On January 27, 1981, the police obtained a search warrant for the premises and two vehicles, one of which was at the home. The probable cause allegations in the accompanying affidavit are the only source of controversy in this case. Because of the importance of this issue we set out those allegations in full:

On 27 January 1981 a confidential informant related the following information to your affiant:

Between 23 January 1981 and 27 January 1981 the confidential informant # 1 was at the residence of Ronald Gray, specifically described above. At the time the informant was present the informant personally saw approximately 20 pounds of marijuana. The informant further related that he had seen marijuana in the automobiles described above.

Your affiant believes the confidential informant to be reliable for the following reasons: Two other confidential informants gave confirming information. In addition Trp. Thomas R. Scales confirmed information.

On 16 January 1981 your affiant spoke with confidential informant # 2. At this time informant # 2 related that RONALD GRAY is one of the major drug distributors in Lycoming County. Informant # 2 is believed to be reliable because he has given information relating to Laughlin Jennings who is presently under criminal charges; Regina Webster and Curtis Missien who are presently under criminal charges; and David Fryday who is presently under criminal charges (the information relating to Fryday confirmed in a statement by Gina Brown who related that she purchased her drugs from Fryday). The informant # 2 stated that Fryday would be found in Wellsboro, Pa. as Fryday had left Williamsport. On 27 January 1981 Fryday was arrested in Wellsboro.

On 18 January 1981 Mr. Brown and Trp. Monahan spoke with confidential informant # 3. At this time confidential informant # 3 related that RONALD GRAY is one of the largest drug dealers in Lycoming County. Informant # 3 related that he had some contact relative to the purchase of drugs with Gray.

On 27 January 1981 Trp. Thomas R. Scales related the following to your affiant:

During the fall of 1978 Trp. Scales had set up a transaction with Gray to purchase (2) cases of morphine from RONALD GRAY. During the course of the transaction, which took place in a cabin off Leg.Rte. 41028, a phone call came stating that there were police in the area. Gray then refused to complete the transaction at that time. This information is contained in P.S.P. reports.

On 27 January 1981 when confidential informant # 1 related the information he was under oath.

On 27 January 1981 Trp. Carey in the presence of Ptl. Mark McCracken (South Williamsport Police) and confidential informant # 1 went to the residence of RONALD GRAY. At that time Trp. Carey located the above described home and the vehicles. The vehicles were present at the location described by the confidential informant.

On 27 January confidential informant # 1 further related that he had contacted Gray concerning the marijuana between 25 January 1981 and 27 January 1981. At this time the informant # 1 stated that Gray said he still had marijuana.

Search Warrant and Affidavit dated January 27, 1981.

The police attempted to obtain appellant's consent to the search by asking him to accompany them while they executed the warrant. After appellant refused, the police went to appellant's home, served the search warrant, and began their search. They uncovered a total of nineteen plastic bags with about one pound of marijuana in each. Drug paraphernalia was found inside the house. The search of the second car produced no evidence used at trial.

Appellant filed an omnibus pre-trial motion in which he asserted that the evidence from this search should have been suppressed because the warrant was defective under the current state of the law. The court denied this portion of the motion, finding that the allegation of probable cause was sufficiently reliable. Appellant was tried and convicted of possession with intent to deliver.

Superior Court affirmed appellant's conviction. It stated that because the allegation of probable cause was sufficient under the relaxed standard of *Illinois v. Gates*, the motion to suppress was properly denied. This appeal followed.

Until 1983, the generally accepted standard for reviewing affidavits of probable cause supporting a search warrant based on information provided by confidential informants came from the United States Supreme Court cases *Aguilar v. Texas* and *Spinelli v. United States*. Those cases required a warrant to pass two specific tests, under which the issuing authority had to be able to see, on the face of the affidavit of probable cause, both the informant's basis for his knowledge and independent facts showing the reliability of the informant.

The warrant in this case fails the *Aguilar-Spinelli* tests because no one of the parts which make up its whole meets both the basis of knowledge test and the test of the particular informant's reliability. The information from Informant No. One satisfies the basis of knowledge test since the affidavit states that this informant "personally saw" marijuana in the cars described in the search warrant. This information was not stale as the drugs were seen during the four-day period immediately preceding the application for the warrant. *See Commonwealth v. Stamps*, 427 A.2d 141 (Pa. 1981) (evidence of possession of large quantities of drugs within fourteen days is not stale).

However, the affidavit does not satisfy the *Aguilar-Spinelli* standards of demonstrating the reliability of this particular informant. It states only that two other confidential informants gave similar information, and that a named trooper confirmed it. Thus, there is no independent demonstration of the reliability of Informant No. One. His reliability is wholly dependent on that of the other informants.

Conversely, Informant No. Two's statement that appellant was a major distributor of drugs in the area does not independently satisfy the basis of knowledge prong of the two-part test. There is no indication that the informant knew about the drugs in appellant's car, and, although he had given credible information regarding other current prosecutions, there is nothing to show any specific information about appellant's current activity. His past reliability is insufficient, by itself, to establish probable cause. Therefore, this informant's statement that appellant is a drug distributor does not independently support a finding of probable cause and does not confirm the other information the affidavit sets out under the *Aguilar-Spinelli* analysis tests, as contrasted with the *Gates* test of synthesis.

Similarly, Informant No. Three does not bolster the credibility of Informant No. One. The application for the warrant states that No. Three knows appellant is a drug distributor, and that he had "some contact relative to the purchase of drugs with [appellant]." This may provide a sufficient basis of knowledge, but it does not demonstrate this third informant's reliability. Consequently, application of the two-pronged *Aguilar-Spinelli* analytical approach to the various pieces of information in the affidavit leaves us without a basis to believe that appellant currently possessed drugs in his car.

Finally, the trooper's statement that he arranged to buy drugs from appellant over two years before does not independently demonstrate the first informant's reliability. These allegations establish only that appellant was a known drug dealer. Only Informant No. One, whose reliability is not independently shown, had direct knowledge of the current possession, and the confirming information by informants whose reliability does appear was as to appellant's status as a drug dealer. That status, standing alone, is insufficient to justify this search.

We therefore turn to the propriety of adopting the standards of *Illinois v. Gates* as sufficient under article I, section 8 of the Pennsylvania Constitution. In *Gates*, the United States Supreme Court decided that its prior holdings creating "tests" for determining whether or not probable cause existed ran contrary to the notion of probable cause as based on "the factual and practical considerations of everyday life on which reasonable and prudent men, not legal technicians, act." The Court also noted that:

> the direction taken by decisions following *Spinelli* poorly serves "the most basic function of any government": "to provide for the security of the individual and of his property." *Miranda v. Arizona*, 384 U.S. 436, 539 (1966). The strictures that inevitably accompany the "two-pronged test" cannot avoid seriously impeding the task of law enforcement....If,...that test must be rigorously applied in every case, anonymous tips would be of greatly diminished value in police work. Ordinary citizens, like ordinary witnesses, *see* Federal Rules of Evidence 701, Advisory Committee Note (1976), generally do not provide extensive recitations of the basis of their everyday observations. Likewise,...the veracity of persons supplying anonymous tips is by hypothesis largely unknown, and unknowable. As a result, anonymous tips seldom could survive a rigorous

application of either of the *Spinelli* prongs. Yet, such tips, particularly when supplemented by independent police investigation, frequently contribute to the solution of otherwise "perfect crimes." While a conscientious assessment of the basis for crediting such tips is required by the Fourth Amendment, a standard that leaves virtually no place for anonymous citizen informants is not.

The Court stated its new test for analyzing warrants:

> The task of the issuing magistrate is simply to make a practical, common-sense decision whether, given all the circumstances set forth in the affidavit before him, including the "veracity" and "basis of knowledge" of persons supplying hearsay information, there is a fair probability that contraband or evidence of a crime will be found in a particular place. And the duty of a reviewing court is simply to ensure that the magistrate had a "substantial basis for…conclud[ing] that probable cause existed."

We have looked at this test before, and have called it "more practical." In addition, we have always held that probable cause determinations must be based on common sense non-technical analysis. Heretofore we have not been presented with a factual background requiring us to determine whether we should reject the *Aguilar-Spinelli* standards. In this case, however, the warrant fails these tests and we must reach the *Gates* issue in order to decide it. This Court is no longer bound by *Aguilar-Spinelli* as a matter of federal constitutional law. Therefore, our prior decisions, based on their two-pronged test, are no longer authoritative. While we can interpret our own constitution to afford defendants greater protections than the federal constitution does, there should be a compelling reason to do so. In *Chandler*, we already noted that the *Gates* analysis appears more practical. That this is so is even more plain on this record. Besides, there is no substantial textual difference between the Fourth Amendment to the United States Constitution and article I, section 8 of the Pennsylvania Constitution that would require us to expand the protections afforded under the federal document.

We do not find persuasive the reasoning applied by other states in rejecting *Gates* and adopting *Aguilar-Spinelli* under state constitutions. *See, e.g., State v. Kimbro*, 496 A.2d 498 (Conn. 1985); *Commonwealth v. Upton*, 476 N.E.2d 548 (Mass. 1985) (on remand from the United States Supreme Court); *State v. Jackson*, 688 P.2d 136 (Wash. 1984). Those cases rejected *Gates* as too amorphous, claiming it was practically equivalent to no standard at all. We, however, believe that a totality of the circumstances approach is as workable here as in those other areas of criminal procedure where a common-sense, practical approach is indicated. Thus, we adopt the *Gates* standard under the Pennsylvania Constitution.

Under the *Gates* totality of the circumstances approach, the warrant in this case is valid. Informant No. One states specifically that he saw a substantial quantity of marijuana in appellant's car within the four-day period preceding the application for the warrant. Although the affidavit does not show on its face that this informant is especially credible or reliable, the whole affidavit contains facts consistent with it. Their total effect confirms it with the ring of truth which is sufficient for men of common sense to conclude that a search is reasonable and justified by probable cause. Three people—one police officer and two confidential informants—have stated that appellant is a known drug dealer. A third confidential informant says he saw twenty pounds of marijuana and that appellant carried this quantity in his car. Viewed together, these allegations raise a fair inference that appellant was in possession of a substantial quantity of a controlled substance. Thus, there was probable cause for the issuance of the search warrant under *Gates*.

Because we hold that article I, section 8 of the Pennsylvania Constitution is satisfied by the *Gates* standard, and because we hold that the warrant in this case satisfied the *Gates* standard, we must affirm appellant's judgment of sentence.

NOTES

1. States that retain, as a matter of state law, the *Aguilar-Spinelli* test or a state variant thereof include: Alaska, Hawaii, Massachusetts, New Mexico, New York, Oregon, Tennessee, and Washington.

2. States that have adopted the *Gates* test are: Colorado, Delaware, Georgia, Iowa, Maine, Michigan, Minnesota, Montana, New Jersey, Nevada, New Hampshire, North Dakota, Pennsylvania, Utah, Texas, and Wyoming.

3. Article I, section 7 of the Tennessee Constitution has been construed to distinguish between information provided by citizen or bystander informants and by an informant from a "criminal milieu." Information from the former is "presumed to be reliable" while information from the latter must be examined by a two-part inquiry adopted in *State v. Jacumin*, 778 S.W.2d 430 (Tenn. 1989), *i.e.*, the affidavit supporting a search warrant must show: (1) the basis for the informant's knowledge and (2) the reliability of the informant or the information. *Accord State v. Williams*, 193 S.W.3d 502 (Tenn. 2006).

C. GOOD FAITH EXCEPTION TO WARRANT REQUIREMENT

STATE v. KOIVU
272 P.3d 483 (Idaho 2012)

EISMANN, J.

This is an appeal asking that we overrule *State v. Guzman*, 842 P.2d 660 (1992), and hold that the *Leon* good-faith exception to the exclusionary rule applies to violations of Article I, section 17, of the Idaho Constitution. Because the State has not shown any ground for doing so, we decline to overrule that case and affirm the order of the district court suppressing evidence obtained incident to an arrest pursuant to a wrongly issued warrant.

Factual Background

Randy Koivu (Defendant) was charged with the crime of possession of methamphetamine in Boundary County. He was found guilty of that crime, and on January 6, 2004, the district court sentenced him to five years in the custody of the Idaho Board of Correction, with three years fixed and two years indeterminate. The court suspended that sentence and placed Defendant on probation for four years. The terms of probation included that Defendant pay a fine of $500.00, court costs of $88.50, public defender reimbursement of $300.00, and restitution of $100.00. Defendant later violated the terms of his probation, and on November 1, 2005, the court entered an order revoking his probation and committing him to the custody of the Idaho Board of Correction. Defendant was released from prison on July 2, 2009.

On March 5, 2010, two sheriff deputies in neighboring Bonner County lawfully stopped a car for speeding. Defendant was the driver of the car. In running a background check of Defendant, the officers were informed that there was a warrant for his arrest out of Boundary County. Reasonably relying upon the validity of the warrant, the deputies arrested Defendant and transported him to the Bonner County jail. Defendant was arrested only because of the warrant; he could not have been arrested for speeding. While searching Defendant at the jail, a baggie of methamphetamine was discovered near his feet.

On March 5, 2010, Defendant was charged in Bonner County with possession of methamphetamine. Defendant waived his right to a preliminary hearing, and on March 17, 2010, the prosecuting attorney filed an information charging Defendant with that crime. The prosecutor also alleged in the information that Defendant was a persistent violator, having had two prior felony convictions.

Has the State Shown that *State v. Guzman* Should Be Overruled?

Article I, section 17, of the Idaho Constitution provides, "The right of the people to be secure in their persons, houses, papers and effects against unreasonable searches and seizures shall not be violated; and no warrant shall issue without probable cause shown by affidavit, particularly describing the place to be searched and the person or thing to be seized." The Idaho Constitution does not specify the remedy for a violation of this provision, nor does the Fourth Amendment to the Constitution of the United States.

In *Weeks v. United States*, 232 U.S. 383 (1914), the United States Supreme Court held for the first time that evidence wrongfully seized by the federal government in violation of a criminal defendant's Fourth Amendment rights could not be used as evidence in the ensuing criminal prosecution. The Court stated that if evidence seized in violation of a defendant's Fourth Amendment rights could be used against him in a criminal prosecution, the protection of the Fourth Amendment would be of no value and it might as well be stricken from the Constitution.

> If letters and private documents can thus be seized and held and used in evidence against a citizen accused of an offense, the protection of the 4th Amendment, declaring his right to be secure against such searches and seizures, is of no value, and, so far as those thus placed are concerned, might as well be stricken from the Constitution. The efforts of the courts and their officials to bring the guilty to punishment, praiseworthy as they are, are not to be aided by the sacrifice of those great principles established be years of endeavor and suffering which have resulted in their embodiment in the fundamental law of the land.

However, the Court held that the Fourth Amendment did not apply to searches and seizures by city police because "[i]ts limitations reach the Federal government and its agencies."

Three and one-half decades later, the Court decided that the Fourth Amendment should apply to the States, and it used the Due Process Clause of the Fourteenth Amendment as the vehicle for doing so. *Wolf v. People of the State of Colorado*, 338 U.S. 25, 27–28 (1949). However, the *Wolf* Court left to the individual States the right to decide whether exclusion of evidence or some other remedy should apply to Fourth Amendment violations. Thus, the Court held "that in a prosecution in a State court for a State crime the Fourteenth Amendment does not forbid the admission of evidence obtained by an unreasonable search and seizure." Under *Wolf*, the Fourth Amendment did not require any particular remedy for its violation. The Court stated that the exclusionary rule announced in *Weeks* "was not derived from the explicit requirements of the Fourth Amendment.... The decision was a matter of judicial implication."

Twelve years later, the Court decided that the exclusionary rule should apply to the States. In *Mapp v. Ohio*, 367 U.S. 643 (1961), the Court held that: (a) "extending the substantive protections of due process to all constitutionally unreasonable searches—state and federal—[ ] was logically and constitutionally necessary," (b) "[t]o hold otherwise is to grant the right but in reality to withhold its privilege and enjoyment," (c) and "the exclusionary rule is an essential part of both the Fourth and Fourteenth Amendments". The Court also stated that reasons for extending the exclusionary rule to the states, included: (a) "the imperative of judicial integrity," (b) "[n]othing can destroy a government more quickly than its failure to observe its own laws, or worse, its disregard of the charter of its own existence," and (c) "it [cannot] lightly be assumed that, as a practical matter, adoption of the exclusionary rule fetters law enforcement". The *Mapp* Court held that the exclusionary rule was required by the Fourth Amendment. It stated, " 'The striking outcome of the *Weeks* case and those which followed it was the sweeping declaration that the Fourth Amendment, although not referring to or limiting the use of evidence in court, really forbade its introduction if obtained by government officers through a violation of the amendment.' " *Id.* at 649. Thus, in *Mapp* the Court reversed direction and held that the exclusionary rule was a personal constitutional right.

The Court's view of the exclusionary rule later changed again. In *Stone v. Powell*, 428 U.S. 465 (1976), the Court held that the exclusionary rule "is not a personal constitutional right," nor is it "calculated to redress the injury to the privacy of the victim of the search or seizure." *Id.* at 486. Rather, "[t]he primary justification for the exclusionary rule ... is the deterrence of police conduct that violates Fourth Amendment rights." *Id.*

In *United States v. Leon*, 468 U.S. 897 (1984), the Court adopted what became known as the *Leon* "good-faith" exception to the exclusionary rule under the Fourth Amendment. In *Leon*, the police had seized evidence acting in reasonable reliance on a search warrant, but the warrant was later determined to have been issued without probable cause. The Court held that the exclusionary rule would not apply to evidence obtained in objectively reasonable reliance on a subsequently invalidated search warrant. The Court also held that "the exclusionary rule is designed to deter police misconduct rather than to punish the errors of judges and magistrates."

The Court has since expanded the good-faith exception to include a search conducted in reasonable reliance upon a subsequently invalidated statute because legislators, like judges, are not the focus of the rule, *Illinois v. Krull*, 480 U.S. 340 (1987); an arrest in reasonable reliance upon information that the arrestee had an outstanding warrant, where the warrant had been quashed but the court clerk had failed to notify the sheriff's office, because applying the exclusionary rule would not deter mistakes made by court employees, *Arizona v. Evans*, 514 U.S. 1 (1995); an arrest in reasonable reliance upon the existence of an outstanding arrest warrant where the officer did not know that the warrant had been recalled due to the negligent failure of a sheriff's employee to update the computer database, *Herring v. United States*, 555 U.S. 135 (2009); and to a search conducted in objectively reasonable reliance upon binding judicial precedent that was later overruled, *Davis v. United States*, —— U.S. —— (2011).

In *Guzman*, the police had obtained evidence pursuant to a search warrant that was later declared invalid because the supporting affidavit alleged only conclusory statements of fact. The trial court applied the good-faith exception under *Leon* and refused to suppress the evidence. This Court declined to apply the good-faith exception to the exclusionary rule under Article I, section 17, of the Idaho Constitution. However, a majority did not agree upon the reasons for doing so. Justice Bistline, the author of *Guzman*, set forth his reasons for applying the exclusionary rule in Part V(A) of his opinion and his criticisms of the *Leon* good-faith exception in Parts V(B) and V(C). *Id.* at 992–97, 842 P.2d at 671–76. Justice Johnson concurred in Part V(A), while Justice McDevitt only concurred in the result in Part V. *Id.* at 998, 842 P.2d at 677. Chief Justice Bakes dissented, and Justice Boyle did not participate due to his resignation. Therefore, a majority rejected the good-faith exception, but a majority did not agree upon the reasons for doing so. Later, a unanimous Court stated that the Court had rejected applying the *Leon* good-faith exception to Article I, section 17, and that the *Guzman* decision would be applied retroactively to all cases that had not become final when *Guzman* was issued.

The State now asks us to revisit the *Leon* good-faith exception and overrule *Guzman*. We would also have to overrule *Arregui* and *Rauch* to the extent that they held that there were reasons supporting the exclusionary rule other than deterring unconstitutional searches and seizures that the law enforcement officers did not reasonably believe were lawful. We will ordinarily not overrule one of our prior opinions unless it is shown to have been manifestly wrong, *Scott v. Gossett*, 66 Idaho 329, 335, 158 P.2d 804, 807 (1945), or the holding in the case has proven over time to be unwise or unjust.

The State also asserts that "[a] review of the authority relied upon by the *Guzman* plurality does not support its analysis or results." It argues that "those cases clearly show that Idaho's exclusionary rule is co-extensive with the exclusionary rule as adopted and applied by the United States Supreme Court." To support that argument, the State writes: "For example, the Court first relied upon *State v. Arregui*, 254 P. 788 (1927), the case adopting the exclusionary rule for Idaho.

There is absolutely nothing in *Arregui* or any other authority relied upon by the *Guzman* Court that commits this Court to construe or apply Article I, section 17, in the same manner as the United States Supreme Court construes or applies the Fourth Amendment. "'The Fourth Amendment and art. 1, § 17 are designed to protect a person's legitimate expectation of privacy, which "society is prepared to recognize as reasonable".' The similarity of language and purpose, however, does not require this Court to follow United States Supreme Court precedent in interpreting our own constitution." *State v. Donato*, 20 P.3d 5, 7 (2001). "Long gone are the days when state courts will blindly apply United States Supreme Court interpretation and methodology when in the process of interpreting their own constitutions." *Id.*

The exclusionary rule is a judicially created remedy for searches and seizures that violate the Constitution. As shown above, courts have disagreed over the years as to whether there should be any remedy for such constitutional violations and, if so, whether it should focus upon redressing the wrong committed against the victim of the unconstitutional search or seizure or only upon deterring future violations of such constitutional rights by law enforcement officials. The holding in *Guzman* was that evidence obtained from a defendant pursuant to a warrant will not be admissible in the defendant's criminal trial if the warrant was issued without probable cause in violation of the Constitution. That holding is not manifestly wrong. It is identical to the holding in *Arregui* and is consistent with the holdings of other courts, including the United States Supreme Court. *Aguilar v. Texas*, 378 U.S. 108 (1964).

The State contends that "[t]he second flaw of Guzman is its contention that the *Leon* good-faith exception to the exclusionary rule is inimical to the values of exclusion unrelated to police deterrence." The State then argues why the *Leon* Court was right and the *Guzman* plurality was wrong. It also asserts that application of the exclusionary rule here would not deter police misconduct because the officers involved simply did what they were required to do—execute an arrest warrant.

This Court's rejection of the *Leon* good-faith exception in *Guzman* was supported by an independent exclusionary rule announced eighty-five years ago in *Arregui*. In *Arregui*, there was no claim of law enforcement misconduct. The officers relied upon the validity of a search warrant that was later held to be invalid due to the lack of a showing of probable cause in the affidavit upon which the warrant was issued. Likewise, in *State v. Oropeza*, 545 P.2d 475 (1976), evidence was suppressed for the same reason. When *Guzman* was decided, "Idaho had clearly developed an exclusionary rule as a constitutionally mandated remedy for illegal searches and seizures in addition to other purposes behind the rule such as recognizing the exclusionary rule as a deterrent for police misconduct." *Donato.*

In some instances, we have construed Article I, section 17, to provide greater protection than is provided by the United States Supreme Court's construction of the Fourth Amendment. "[W]e provided greater protection to Idaho citizens based on the uniqueness of our state, our Constitution, and our long-standing jurisprudence." To overrule *Guzman* and hold that the exclusionary rule's sole purpose is to deter police misconduct, we would also have to overrule *Arregui*, which adopted the exclusionary rule in Idaho in a case in which there was no police misconduct. The State has not pointed to anything in the record showing that during the last eighty-five years *Arregui* has proved to be unwise or unjust. We therefore uphold the district court's order holding that the methamphetamine is not admissible into evidence because the Defendant's arrest pursuant to an invalid warrant of attachment violated his rights under Article I, section 17, of the Idaho Constitution.

COMMONWEALTH v. EDMUNDS
586 A.2d 887 (Pa. 1991)

CAPPY, J.

HISTORY OF THE CASE

The issue presented to this court is whether Pennsylvania should adopt the "good faith" exception to the exclusionary rule as articulated by the United States Supreme Court in the case of *United States v. Leon*, 468 U.S. 897 (1984). We conclude that a "good faith" exception to the exclusionary rule would frustrate the guarantees embodied in article I, section 8 of the Pennsylvania Constitution. Accordingly, the decision of the Superior Court is reversed.

The defendant in the instant case was found guilty after a non-jury trial on August 18, 1987, of criminal conspiracy, simple possession, possession with intent to deliver, possession with intent to manufacture and manufacture of a controlled substance. The conviction was premised upon the admission into evidence of marijuana seized at the defendant's property pursuant to a search warrant, after information was received from two anonymous informants.

The trial court held that the search warrant failed to establish probable cause that the marijuana would be at the location to be searched on the date it was issued. The trial court found that the warrant failed to set forth with specificity the date upon which the anonymous informants observed the marijuana. However, the trial court went on to deny the defendant's motion to suppress the marijuana. Applying the rationale of *Leon*, the trial court looked beyond the four corners of the affidavit, in order to establish that the officers executing the warrant acted in "good faith" in relying upon the warrant to conduct the search. In reaching this conclusion the trial court also decided that *Leon* permitted the court to undercut the language of Pennsylvania Rule of Criminal Procedure 2003, which prohibits oral testimony outside the four corners of the written affidavit to supplement the finding of probable cause.

Rule 2003 provides in relevant part:

(a) No search warrant shall issue but upon probable cause supported by one or more affidavits sworn to before the issuing authority. The issuing authority, in determining whether probable cause has been established, <u>may not consider any evidence outside the affidavits</u>.

(b) At any hearing on a motion for the return or suppression of evidence, or for the suppression of the fruits of the evidence obtained pursuant to a search warrant, <u>no evidence shall be admissible to establish probable cause</u> other than the affidavits provided for in paragraph (a).

The Superior Court in a divided panel decision affirmed the judgment of the trial court, specifically relying upon the decision of the United States Supreme Court in *Leon*. Allocatur was granted by this Court.

The pertinent facts can be briefly summarized as follows. On August 5, 1985, State Police Trooper Michael Deise obtained a warrant from a district magistrate to search a white corrugated building and curtilage on the property of the defendant. As the affidavit of probable cause is central to our decision, we will set it forth in full:

On the date of August 4, 1985, this affiant Michael D. Deise, Penna. State Police, was in contact by telephone with two anonymous Males who were and are members of the community where Louis R. Edmunds resides. Both anonymous males advised the affiant that while checking out familiar hunting areas off Rte. 31, east of Jones Mills and along the south side of Rte. 31. (sic) These men observed growing marijuana near a white corrugated building approximately 20 x 40 feet in a cleared off area. These men looked into the building and observed several plants that appeared to be marijuana. This affiant questioned both of these men as to their knowledge of marijuana. This affiant learned that one of these men saw growing marijuana numerous times while he was stationed in Viet Nam. The other male saw growing marijuana while at a police station. This affiant described a growing marijuana plant and its characteristics and they agreed that what they had viewed agreed with the description and also that it appeared to them to be marijuana as fully described by the affiant. The two males wish to remain anonymous for fear of retaliation or bodily harm. An anonymous male advised this affiant that Louis R. Edmunds lived there. Edmund's description being that of a white male in his middle thirties and he lived at the aforementioned location.

On the 5th of August, 1985, this affiant with the use of a State Police helicopter, flew over the described location and observed the white corrugated building in the mountain area and located as described by the two males. Also on this date this affiant drove past the Rte. 31 entrance and observed a mail box with "Edmunds 228" printed on it.

After obtaining the warrant from the local magistrate, Trooper Deise, accompanied by three other troopers, served the warrant upon the defendant at his residence. Though he did not place the defendant under arrest at this time, the trooper did advise him of his Miranda rights, and had him read the warrant. The trooper also explained to the defendant that the warrant was not for his residence, although the warrant itself included the residence. Rather, the trooper stated that the warrant was meant to relate to the white corrugated building, and that they were searching for marijuana in that building.

After producing the lease which indicated that the white corrugated building was in fact leased to Thomas Beacon, the defendant accompanied the troopers to the building, which was approximately one-quarter of a mile away, up a steep mountainous terrain, on a separate parcel of property owned by Edmunds. The record is devoid of evidence that there was marijuana growing outside the corrugated building. The defendant unlocked the door of the white building and entered with the troopers. Inside the building the troopers discovered seventeen growing marijuana plants, along with gardening implements, high-wattage lights, and a watering system. The marijuana was seized and the charges as recited above were brought against the defendant.

As a preliminary matter, we concur with the inevitable conclusion of the trial court and the Superior Court that probable cause did not exist on the face of the warrant. In *Conner*, this Court made clear that a search warrant is defective if it is issued without reference to the time when the informant obtained his or her information. Coupled with Rule 2003, which mandates that courts in Pennsylvania shall not consider oral testimony outside the four corners of the written affidavit to supplement the finding of probable cause for a search warrant, we are compelled to conclude that the affidavit of probable cause and warrant were facially invalid. As the Superior Court candidly stated, the affidavit in question "did not contain facts from which the date of the hunters' observations could be determined."

QP

The sole question in this case, therefore, is whether the Constitution of Pennsylvania incorporates a "good faith" exception to the exclusionary rule, which permits the introduction of evidence seized where probable cause is lacking on the face of the warrant.

Put in other terms, the question is whether the federal *Leon* test circumvents the acknowledged deficiencies under Pennsylvania law, and prevents the suppression of evidence seized pursuant to an *invalid search warrant*. For the reasons that follow, we conclude that it does not.

Our starting point must be the decision of the United States Supreme Court in *Leon*. In *Leon*, the Supreme Court in 1984 departed from a long history of exclusionary rule jurisprudence dating back to *Weeks v. United States*, 232 U.S. 383 (1914), and *Mapp v. Ohio*, 367 U.S. 643 (1961). The Court in *Leon* concluded that the Fourth Amendment does not mandate suppression of illegally seized evidence obtained pursuant to a constitutionally defective warrant, so long as the police officer acted in good faith reliance upon the warrant issued by a neutral and detached magistrate.

We must now determine whether the good-faith exception to the exclusionary rule is properly part of the jurisprudence of this Commonwealth, by virtue of article 1, section 8 of the Pennsylvania Constitution. In concluding that it is not, we set forth a methodology to be followed in analyzing future state constitutional issues which arise under our own Constitution.

FACTORS TO CONSIDER IN UNDERTAKING PENNSYLVANIA CONSTITUTIONAL ANALYSIS

This Court has long emphasized that, in interpreting a provision of the Pennsylvania Constitution, we are not bound by the decisions of the United States Supreme Court which interpret similar (yet distinct) federal constitutional provisions.

As Mr. Chief Justice Nix aptly stated in *Sell*, the federal constitution establishes certain minimum levels which are "equally applicable to the [analogous] state constitutional provision." However, each state has the power to provide broader standards, and go beyond the minimum floor which is established by the federal Constitution.

The United States Supreme Court has repeatedly affirmed that the states are not only free to, but also encouraged to engage in independent analysis in drawing meaning from their own state constitutions. Indeed, this is a positive expression of the jurisprudence which has existed in the United States since the founding of the nation. Alexander Hamilton, lobbying for the ratification of the United States Constitution in the Federalist Papers over two hundred years ago, made clear that the Supremacy Clause of the Federal Constitution was never designed to overshadow the states, or prevent them from maintaining their own pockets of autonomy. *See* The Federalist No. 33 (A. Hamilton), in *The Federalist Papers* (The New American Library ed.) 204.

Here in Pennsylvania, we have stated with increasing frequency that it is both important and necessary that we undertake an independent analysis of the Pennsylvania Constitution, each time a provision of that fundamental document is implicated. Although we may accord weight to federal decisions where they "are found to be logically persuasive and well reasoned, paying due regard to precedent and the policies underlying specific constitutional guarantees," we are free to reject the conclusions of the United States Supreme Court so long as we remain faithful to the minimum guarantees established by the United States Constitution.

[handwritten margin note: Extent to which state can reject SCOTUS]

The recent focus on the "New Federalism" has emphasized the importance of state constitutions with respect to individual rights and criminal procedure. As such, we find it important to set forth certain factors to be briefed and analyzed by litigants in each case hereafter implicating a provision of the Pennsylvania constitution. The decision of the United States Supreme Court in *Michigan v. Long*, 463 U.S. 1032 (1983), now requires us to make a "plain statement" of the adequate and independent state grounds upon which we rely, in order to avoid any doubt that we have rested our decision squarely upon Pennsylvania jurisprudence. Accordingly, as a general rule, it is important that litigants brief and analyze at least the following four factors:

[handwritten margin note: What ct wants briefed]

[handwritten: text] 1) text of the Pennsylvania constitutional provision;

[handwritten: history] 2) history of the provision, including Pennsylvania case-law;

[handwritten: case law] 3) related case-law from other states;

[handwritten: policy] 4) policy considerations, including unique issues of state and local concern, and applicability within modern Pennsylvania jurisprudence.

Depending upon the particular issue presented, an examination of related federal precedent may be useful as part of the state constitutional analysis, not as binding authority, but as one form of guidance. However, it is essential that courts in Pennsylvania undertake an independent analysis under the Pennsylvania Constitution. Utilizing the above four factors, and having reviewed *Leon*, we conclude that a "good faith" exception to the exclusionary rule would frustrate the guarantees embodied in article I, section 8 of our Commonwealth's constitution.

ANALYSIS

A. *Text*

The text of article 1, section 8 of the Pennsylvania Constitution provides as follows:

Security from Searches and Seizures

Section 8. The people shall be secure in their persons, houses, papers and possessions from unreasonable searches and seizures, and no warrant to search any place or to seize any person or things shall issue without describing them as nearly as may be, nor without probable cause, supported by oath or affirmation subscribed to by the affiant.

Although the wording of the Pennsylvania Constitution is similar in language to the Fourth Amendment of the United States Constitution, we are not bound to interpret the two provisions as if they were mirror images, even where the text is similar or identical. Thus, we must next examine the history of article I, section 8, in order to draw meaning from that provision and consider the appropriateness of a "good faith" exception to the exclusionary rule in the Pennsylvania constitutional scheme.

B. *History*

We have made reference, on repeated occasions, to the unique history of article 1, section 8, as well as other provisions of the Pennsylvania Constitution. As we noted in *Sell:* "constitutional protection against unreasonable searches and seizures existed in Pennsylvania more than a decade before the adoption of the federal Constitution, and fifteen years prior to the promulgation of the Fourth Amendment."

Perhaps the extent of the untapped history of the Pennsylvania Constitution should be underscored. Pennsylvania's Constitution was adopted on September 28, 1776, a full ten years prior to the ratification of the United States Constitution. Like the constitutions of Virginia, New Jersey, Maryland, and most of the original 13 Colonies, Pennsylvania's Constitution was drafted in the midst of the American Revolution, as the first overt expression of independence from the British Crown. *See* W. Adams, *The First American Constitutions* at 61 (1980). The Pennsylvania Constitution was therefore meant to reduce to writing a deep history of unwritten legal and moral codes which had guided the colonists from the beginning of William Penn's charter in 1681. *See* White, *Commentaries on the Constitution of Pennsylvania* (1907). Unlike the Bill of Rights of the United States Constitution which emerged as a later addendum in 1791, the Declaration of Rights in the Pennsylvania Constitution was an organic part of the state's original constitution of 1776, and appeared (not coincidentally) first in that document.

Thus, contrary to the popular misconception that state constitutions are somehow patterned after the United States Constitution, the reverse is true. The federal Bill of Rights borrowed heavily from the Declarations of Rights contained in the constitutions of Pennsylvania and other colonies. For instance, the Pennsylvania Declaration of Rights was the "direct precursor" of the freedom of speech and press. The Delaware Declaration of Rights prohibited quartering of soldiers and ex-post facto laws. North Carolina's Declaration of Rights provided a number of protections to the criminally accused—the right to trial by jury, the privilege against self-incrimination, and others—which later appeared in the United States Constitution.

With respect to article 1, section 8 of the present Pennsylvania Constitution, which relates to freedom from unreasonable searches and seizures, that provision had its origin prior to the Fourth Amendment, in Clause 10 of the original Constitution of 1776. Specifically, the original version of the search and seizure provision reads as follows:

> The people have a right to hold themselves, their houses, papers and possessions free from search and seizure, and therefore warrants without oaths or affirmations first made, affording sufficient foundation for them, and whereby any officer or messenger may be commanded or required to search suspected places, or to seize any person or persons, his or their property, not particularly described, are contrary to that right and ought not be granted.

[handwritten margin note: 3 iterations of Penn's 4th]

The above provision was reworded at the time the Pennsylvania Constitution was revised extensively in 1790, and reappeared as article 1, section 8. The modern version of that provision has remained untouched for two hundred years, with the exception of the words "subscribed to by the affiant," which were added by the Constitutional Convention of 1873.

The requirement of probable cause in this Commonwealth thus traces its origin to its original Constitution of 1776, drafted by the first convention of delegates chaired by Benjamin Franklin. The primary purpose of the warrant requirement was to abolish "general warrants," which had been used by the British to conduct sweeping searches of residences and businesses, based upon generalized suspicions. Therefore, at the time the Pennsylvania Constitution was drafted in 1776, the issue of searches and seizures unsupported by probable cause was of utmost concern to the constitutional draftsmen.

[handwritten margin note: Ct: Penn's 4th was of utmost importance, even early on.]

Moreover, as this Court has stated repeatedly in interpreting article 1, section 8, that provision is meant to embody a strong notion of privacy, carefully safeguarded in this Commonwealth for the past two centuries. As we stated in *Sell:* "the survival of the language now employed in article 1, section 8 through over 200 years of profound change in other areas demonstrates that the paramount concern for privacy first adopted as part of our organic law in 1776 continues to enjoy the mandate of the people of this Commonwealth."

The history of article I, section 8, thus indicates that the purpose underlying the exclusionary rule in this Commonwealth is quite distinct from the purpose underlying the exclusionary rule under the Fourth Amendment, as articulated by the majority in *Leon*.

[handwritten margin note: SCOTUS thinks ex rule is solely to deter cop conduct.]

The United States Supreme Court in *Leon* made clear that, in its view, the *sole purpose* for the exclusionary rule under the Fourth Amendment was to deter police misconduct. The *Leon* majority also made clear that, under the Federal Constitution, the exclusionary rule operated as "a judicially created remedy designed to safeguard Fourth Amendment rights generally through its deterrent effect, rather than a personal constitutional right of the party aggrieved."

This reinterpretation differs from the way the exclusionary rule has evolved in Pennsylvania since the decision of *Mapp v. Ohio* in 1961 and represents a shift in judicial philosophy from the decisions of the United States Supreme Court dating back to *Weeks v. United States*.

Like many of its sister states, Pennsylvania did not adopt an exclusionary rule until the United States Supreme Court's decision in *Mapp* required it to do so. However, at the time the exclusionary rule was embraced in Pennsylvania, we clearly viewed it as a constitutional mandate. This interpretation was in keeping with a long line of federal cases, beginning with *Weeks* in 1914, which viewed the exclusionary rule as a necessary corollary to the prohibition against unreasonable searches and seizures.

As one commentator noted in piecing together the history of the exclusionary rule: "'Deterrence', now claimed to be the primary ground for exclusion, seems to have had no substantial place in any of these conceptions of the practice."

During the first decade after *Mapp*, our decisions in Pennsylvania tended to parallel the cases interpreting the Fourth Amendment. However, beginning in 1973, our case-law began to reflect a clear divergence from federal precedent. The United States Supreme Court at this time began moving toward a metamorphosed view, suggesting that the purpose of the exclusionary rule "is not to redress the injury to the privacy of the search victim (but, rather) to deter future unlawful police conduct." At the same time this Court began to forge its own path under article I, section 8 of the Pennsylvania Constitution, declaring with increasing frequency that article I, section 8 of the Pennsylvania Constitution embodied a strong notion of privacy, notwithstanding federal cases to the contrary. In *Commonwealth v. Platou* and *Commonwealth v. DeJohn*, we made explicit that "the right to be free from unreasonable searches and seizures contained in article I, section 8 of the Pennsylvania Constitution is tied into the implicit right to privacy in this Commonwealth." In *DeJohn*, we specifically refused to follow the United States Supreme Court's decision in *United States v. Miller*, 425 U.S. 435 (1976), which had held that a citizen had no standing to object to the seizure of his or her bank records.

From *DeJohn* forward, a steady line of case-law has evolved under the Pennsylvania Constitution, making clear that article I, section 8 is unshakably linked to a right of privacy in this Commonwealth.

As Mr. Justice Flaherty noted in *Denoncourt v. Commonwealth*, in echoing the wisdom of Justice Brandeis over 60 years ago: "The makers of our Constitution undertook to secure conditions favorable to the pursuit of happiness....They conferred, as against the government, the right to be let alone—the most comprehensive of rights and the right most valued by civilized men."

Most recently, in *Melilli*, this Court cited with approval the decision of the Superior Court in *Commonwealth v. Beauford*, holding that article I, section 8 of the Pennsylvania Constitution was offended by the installation of a pen register device without probable cause. Mr. Justice Papadakos, in rejecting the holding of the United States Supreme Court in *Smith v. Maryland*, 442 U.S. 735 (1979), emphasized that "article I, section 8 of the Pennsylvania Constitution...may be employed to guard *individual privacy* rights against unreasonable searches and seizures more zealously than the federal government does under the Constitution of the United States by serving as an independent source of supplemental rights." Mr. Justice Papadakos went on to conclude that, because a pen register "is the equivalent of a search warrant in its operative effect where the intrusion involves a violation of a privacy interest," the affidavit and order "must comply with the requirements of probable cause required under Pa. Rules of Criminal Procedure Chapter 2000, Search Warrants."

Thus, the exclusionary rule in Pennsylvania has consistently served to bolster the twin aims of article I, section 8; to-wit, the safeguarding of privacy and the fundamental requirement that warrants shall only be issued upon probable cause. As this Court explained in *Commonwealth v. Miller*:

broad protections of exclusionary rule

> The linch-pin that has been developed to determine whether it is appropriate to issue a search warrant is the test of probable cause. It is designed to protect us from unwarranted and even vindictive incursions upon our privacy. It insulates from dictatorial and tyrannical rule by the state, and preserves the concept of democracy that assures the freedom of its citizens. This concept is second to none in its importance in delineating the dignity of the individual living in a free society.

Leon's views on ex rule are irrelevant

Whether the United States Supreme Court has determined that the exclusionary rule does not advance the Fourth Amendment purpose of deterring police conduct is irrelevant. Indeed, we disagree with that Court's suggestion in *Leon* that we in Pennsylvania have been employing the exclusionary rule all these years to deter police corruption. We flatly reject this notion. We have no reason to believe that police officers or district justices in the Commonwealth of Pennsylvania do not engage in "good faith" in carrying out their duties. What is significant, however, is *default assumption of good faith* that our Constitution has historically been interpreted to incorporate a strong right of privacy, and an equally strong adherence to the requirement of probable cause under article 1, section 8. Citizens in this Commonwealth possess such rights, even where a police officer in "good faith" carrying out his or her duties inadvertently invades the privacy or circumvents the strictures of probable cause. To adopt a "good faith" exception to the exclusionary rule, we believe, would virtually emasculate those clear safeguards which have been carefully developed under the Pennsylvania Constitution over the past 200 years.

C. *Related Case-Law From Other States*

A number of states other than Pennsylvania have confronted the issue of whether to apply a "good faith" exception to the exclusionary rule, under their own constitutions, in the wake of *Leon*.

The highest courts of at least two states—Arkansas and Missouri—have seemingly embraced the good faith exception under their own constitutions. *See Jackson v. State*, 722 S.W.2d 831 (Ark. 1987); *State v. Brown*, 708 S.W.2d 140 (Mo. 1986) (en banc). Intermediary appellate courts in at least four other states—Indiana, Kansas, Maryland and Louisiana—have indicated their acceptance of the "good faith" exception. *See Mers v. State*, 482 N.E.2d 778 (Ind. Ct. App. 1985); *State v. Huber*, 704 P.2d 1004 (Kan. Ct. App. 1985); *Howell v. State*, 483 A.2d 780 (Md. Ct. Spec. App. 1984); *State v. Martin*, 487 So.2d 1295 (La. Ct. App.), *writ denied*, 491 So.2d 25 (La. 1986). In virtually all of those states embracing the "good-faith" exception under their own constitutions, however, the reasoning is a simple affirmation of the logic of *Leon*, with little additional state constitutional analysis.

On the other hand, the highest courts of at least four states—New Jersey, New York, North Carolina and Connecticut—have chosen to reject the "good-faith" exception under their own constitutions, with more detailed analysis of state constitutional principles. *See State v. Marsala*, 579 A.2d 58 (Conn. 1990); *State v. Novembrino*, 519 A.2d 820 (N.J. 1987); *People v. Bigelow*, 488 N.E.2d 451 (N.Y. 1985); *State v. Carter*, 370 S.E.2d 553 (N.C. 1988). *See also Mason v. State*, 534 A.2d 242 (Del. 1987) (rejecting good-faith exception as statutory matter); *Commonwealth v. Upton*, 476 N.E.2d 548 (Mass. 1985) (same). The intermediate appellate courts of at least four additional states—Tennessee, Wisconsin, Michigan, and Minnesota—have likewise eschewed the logic of *Leon* under their own state constitutions. *See State v. Taylor*, 763 S.W.2d 756 (Tenn. Crim. App. 1987); *State v. Grawein*, 367 N.W.2d 816 (Wis. Ct. App. 1985); *People v. Sundling*, 395 N.W.2d 308 (Mich. Ct. App. 1986); *State v. Herbst*, 395 N.W.2d 399, 404 (Minn. Ct. App. 1986).

A mere scorecard of those states which have accepted and rejected *Leon* is certainly not dispositive of the issue in Pennsylvania. However, the logic of certain of those opinions bears upon our analysis under the Pennsylvania Constitution, particularly given the unique history of article 1, section 8.

In this respect, we draw support from other states which have declined to adopt a "good faith" exception, particularly New Jersey, Connecticut and North Carolina. In *State v. Novembrino*, the New Jersey Supreme Court found that the "good faith" exception to the exclusionary rule was inconsistent with the New Jersey Constitution, because it would undermine the requirement of probable cause. Although New Jersey, like Pennsylvania, had no exclusionary rule in place prior to *Mapp v. Ohio* in 1961, the New Jersey Court found that it had become "imbedded" in the jurisprudence under that state's constitution. As the New Jersey court wrote in *Novembrino*:

> The exclusionary rule, by virtue of its consistent application over the past twenty-five years, has become an integral element of our state-constitutional guarantee that search warrants will not issue without probable cause. Its function is not merely to deter police misconduct. The rule also serves as the indispensable mechanism for vindicating the constitutional right to be free from unreasonable searches.

Why NJ treats ex rule as constitutional

Similarly, the Connecticut Supreme Court—which most recently rejected the good faith exception on August 7, 1990—concluded that the purpose of the exclusionary rule under article I, section 7 of the Connecticut Constitution, was to "preserve the integrity of the warrant issuing process as a whole." Thus, when evidence was suppressed under this provision due to a defective warrant, "the issuing authority…is not being 'punished' for a mistake, but is, rather, being informed that a constitutional violation has taken place and is also being instructed in how to avoid such violations in the future." *Conn: ex rule preserves warrant requirement*

More directly on point, the North Carolina Supreme Court in *State v. Carter* rejected the "good faith" exception to the exclusionary rule, noting the importance of the privacy rights flowing from the search and seizure provision in the North Carolina Constitution. The court in *Carter* emphasized the need to preserve the integrity of the judiciary in North Carolina, in excluding illegally seized evidence when such important rights of the citizenry were at stake. Wrote the North Carolina Supreme Court: *NC: privacy rights; preserve judicial integrity*

> The exclusionary sanction is indispensable to give effect to the constitutional principles prohibiting unreasonable search and seizure. We are persuaded that the exclusionary rule is the only effective bulwark against governmental disregard for constitutionally protected privacy rights. Equally of importance in our reasoning, we adhere to the rule for the sake of maintaining the integrity of the judicial branch of government.

We similarly conclude that, given the strong right of privacy which inheres in article 1, section 8, as well as the clear prohibition against the issuance of warrants without probable cause, or based upon defective warrants, the good faith exception to the exclusionary rule would directly clash with those rights of citizens as developed in our Commonwealth over the past 200 years. To allow the judicial branch to participate, directly or indirectly, in the use of the fruits of illegal searches would only serve to undermine the integrity of the judiciary in this Commonwealth. From the perspective of the citizen whose rights are at stake, an invasion of privacy, in good faith or bad, is equally as intrusive This is true whether it occurs through the actions of the legislative, executive or the judicial branch of government.

D. *Policy Considerations*

We recognize that, in analyzing any state constitutional provision, it is necessary to go beyond the bare text and history of that provision as it was drafted 200 years ago, and consider its application within the modern scheme of Pennsylvania jurisprudence. An assessment of various policy considerations, however, only supports our conclusion that the good faith exception to the exclusionary rule would be inconsistent with the jurisprudence surrounding article 1, section 8.

First, such a rule would effectively negate the judicially created mandate reflected in the Pennsylvania Rules of Criminal Procedure, in Rules 2003, 2005 and 2006. Specifically, Rule 2003 relates to the requirements for the issuance of a warrant, and provides in relevant part:

> (a) No search warrant shall issue but upon probable cause supported by one or more affidavits sworn to before the issuing authority. The issuing authority, in determining whether probable cause has been established, may not consider any evidence outside the affidavits.

> (b) At any hearing on a motion for the return or suppression of evidence, or for suppression of the fruits of evidence, obtained pursuant to a search warrant, no evidence shall be admissible to establish probable cause other than the affidavits provided for in paragraph (a).

Rule 2003 serves to underscore the incongruity of adopting a good faith exception to the exclusionary rule in Pennsylvania. Although Rule 2003 is not constitutionally mandated by article 1, section 8, as *Milliken* correctly explains, it reflects yet another expression of this Court's unwavering insistence that probable cause exist before a warrant is issued, and only those facts memorialized in the written affidavit may be considered in establishing probable cause, in order to eliminate any chance of incomplete or reconstructed hindsight. It is true, as *Milliken* summarizes, that the history of article 1, section 8 does not itself prohibit the use of oral testimony to establish probable cause, outside the four corners of the warrant. Nonetheless, we have chosen to adopt that Rule as an administrative matter, and that Rule has now stood in Pennsylvania for 17 years.

In the instant case, probable cause—as defined under Pennsylvania law—is lacking. Two lower courts have so held; we concur. Applying the federal *Leon* test would not only frustrate the procedural safeguards embodied in Rule 2003, but would permit the admission of illegally seized evidence in a variety of contexts where probable cause is lacking, so long as the police officer acted in "good faith." In *Leon* itself probable cause was absent entirely, yet illegally seized evidence was admitted into evidence.

We cannot countenance such a wide departure from the text and history of article 1, section 8, nor can we permit the use of a "good faith" exception to effectively nullify Pennsylvania Rule of Criminal Procedure 2003. Our Constitution requires that warrants shall not be issued except upon probable cause. We have specifically adopted Rule 2003 for the purpose of confining the probable cause inquiry to the written affidavit and warrant, in order to avoid any doubt as to the basis for probable cause. We decline to undermine the clear mandate of these provisions by slavishly adhering to federal precedent where it diverges from two hundred years of our own constitutional jurisprudence.

A second policy consideration which bolsters our conclusion is that the underlying premise of *Leon* is still open to serious debate. Although it is clear that the exclusionary rule presents some cost to society, in allowing "some guilty defendants (to)...go free," the extent of the costs are far from clear. A number of recent studies have indicated that the exclusion of illegally seized evidence has had a marginal effect in allowing guilty criminals to avoid successful prosecution. Indeed, the *Leon* decision itself indicates relatively low statistics with respect to the impact of the exclusionary rule in thwarting legitimate prosecutions. Equally as important, the alternative to the exclusionary rule most commonly advanced—*i.e.*, allowing victims of improper searches to sue police officers directly—has raised serious concern among police officers.

A third policy consideration which compels our decisions is that, given the recent decision of the United States Supreme Court in *United States v. Gates* adopting a "totality of the circumstances test" in assessing probable cause, there is far less reason to adopt a "good faith" exception to the exclusionary rule. We have adopted *Gates* as a matter of Pennsylvania law in the recent case of *Commonwealth v. Gray.* As a number of jurists have pointed out, the flexible *Gates* standard now eliminates much of the prior concern which existed with respect to an overly rigid application of the exclusionary rule.

Finally, the dangers of allowing magistrates to serve as "rubber stamps" and of fostering "magistrate-shopping," are evident under *Leon*. As the instant case illustrates, police officers and magistrates have historically worked closely together in this Commonwealth. Trooper Deise and District Justice Tlumac prepared the warrant and affidavit with

Trooper Deise dictating the affidavit while the magistrate typed it verbatim.

There is no suggestion here that Trooper Deise and District Justice Tlumac acted other than in utmost "good faith" when preparing the warrant. Nevertheless, we are mindful of the fact that both state and federal interpretations of the Fourth Amendment require a warrant to be issued by a "neutral and detached magistrate," because as Mr. Justice Papadakos noted, there is a requirement of "an independent determination of probable cause." The reason for this requirement is evident. Would the District Justice act as nothing more than an adjunct of the police department, there would be no opportunity for *review* of the warrant prior to its issuance, and hence, a search warrant would be nothing more than the police's own determination of whether probable cause exists. We cannot countenance such a policy as it clearly runs afoul of our historically based system of government; which requires three *independent* branches.

It must be remembered that a District Justice is not a member of the executive branch—the police—but a member of the judiciary. By falling within the judicial branch of government, the District Justice is thus charged with the responsibility of being the *disinterested* arbiter of disputes and is charged further with acting as the bulwark between the police and the rights of citizens. Unless and until a magistrate independently determines there is probable cause, no warrant shall issue.

This is not to say that we distrust our police or district justices; far from it. We, in fact, have no doubt that police officers and district justices in Pennsylvania are intelligent, committed and independent enough to carry out their duties under the scheme which has evolved over the past thirty years, in order to safeguard the rights of our citizens.

However, requiring "neutral and detached magistrates" furthers the twin aims of safeguarding privacy and assuring that no warrant shall issue but upon probable cause. As such, we see no reason to eliminate this requirement, for if we did, we would eviscerate the purpose of requiring warrants prior to searches. As one member of the Mississippi Supreme Court noted in a similar vein: "If it ain't broke, don't fix it." *Stringer v. State*, 491 So.2d 837, 850 (Miss. 1986).

CONCLUSION

Thirty years ago, when the exclusionary rule was first introduced, police officers were perhaps plagued with ill-defined, unarticulated rules governing their conduct. However, the past thirty years have seen a gradual sharpening of the process, with police officers adapting well to the exclusionary rule.

The purpose of Rule 2003 is not to exclude *bona fide* evidence based upon technical errors and omissions by police officers or magistrates.

Rather, Rule 2003 is meant to provide support for the probable cause requirement of article I, section 8 of the Pennsylvania Constitution by assuring that there is an objective method for determining when probable cause exists, and when it does not.

In the instant case, the evidence seized from defendant Edmunds was the product of a constitutionally defective search warrant. Article I, section 8 of the Pennsylvania Constitution does not incorporate a "good faith" exception to the exclusionary rule. Therefore, the marijuana seized from the white corrugated building, the marijuana seized from Edmund's home, and the written and oral statements obtained from Edmunds by the troopers, must be suppressed. We base our decision strictly upon the Pennsylvania Constitution; any reference to the United States Constitution is merely for guidance and does not compel our decision.

Justice Brandeis, in his eloquent dissent in *Olmstead v. United* States, minded us over a half-century ago:

> In a government of laws, existence of the government will be imperiled if it fails to observe the law scrupulously. Our government is the potent, the omnipresent teacher. For good or for ill, it teaches the whole people by its example. Crime is contagious. If the Government becomes a lawbreaker, it breeds contempt for law; it invites every man to become a law unto himself; it invites anarchy.

Although the exclusionary rule may place a duty of thoroughness and care upon police officers and district justices in this Commonwealth, in order to safeguard the rights of citizens under article I, section 8, that is a small price to pay, we believe, for a democracy.

NOTES

1. In *Leon*, the United States Supreme Court characterized the adoption of the federal exclusionary rule in *Calandra* as a prophylactic measure to deter police conduct and not as a holding that was required by the Fourth Amendment. *United States v. Calandra*, 414 U.S. 338 (1974). This construction permits the Court to recognize exceptions like the "good faith" exception in *Leon*.

2. Although the rationale in *Leon* has been adopted by the majority of state courts in construing state constitutions, 19 states have rejected *Leon* as a matter of state constitutional law.   *Only 19 reject Leon*

3. In rejecting the good faith exception under article I, section 17 of the Idaho Constitution, the Supreme Court of Idaho conducted an extensive analysis and concluded that the policy behind the Idaho exclusionary rule was incompatible with the good faith exception in *Leon* and *Calandra*. *See State v. Guzman*, 842 P.2d 660 (Idaho 1992).

4. The California and Florida Constitutions have been amended to prohibit any state constitutional exclusionary rule, beyond what is required for violations of the Fourth Amendment. *See* Cal. Const. art. I, § 28(d);

Fla. Const. art. I, § 12. Therefore, the California and Florida Constitutions required the adoption of *Leon* because the search and seizure provisions in both constitutions must be construed in lockstep with the Fourth Amendment.

5.   The concurrence in *Utah v. Walker*, 267 P.3d 210 (Utah 2011), shows that a state court theoretically could reject even the exclusionary rule—at least under its own constitution—a theory that would make it unnecessary to consider whether the Leon good-faith exception applies.

D. AUTOMATIC STANDING

STATE v. LAMB
95 A.2d 123 (N.J. 2014)

CUFF, J. (temporarily assigned) delivered the opinion of the Court.
This appeal involves the validity of a warrantless consent search of a house. An investigation of a reported shooting in another part of town led Pennsville police to the house in which police knew defendant Michael W. Lamb had resided at one time. When police arrived, defendant's stepfather emphatically informed police that they were not welcome on his property or in his house.

While defendant's stepfather informed police that they could not enter his home, defendant's girlfriend appeared at the door and left the house. She supplied information to police that provided probable cause for defendant's arrest and confirmed his presence in the house.

Later, defendant's stepfather agreed to leave the house. Soon thereafter, defendant left the house at the insistence of his mother. She remained in the house with three children between the ages of eight months and nine years and a loaded gun.

Defendant's mother permitted police officers to enter the house and agreed to a search of the room where her son and his girlfriend were staying. Police located a loaded handgun and ammunition similar to the equipment used in the earlier shooting.

We conclude that the consent to search provided by defendant's mother was knowing, voluntary, and valid. The absence of defendant and his stepfather from the home permitted defendant's mother to provide or withhold consent. Furthermore, the initial opposition expressed by defendant's stepfather was no longer effective once he was not physically present in his home.

Under the totality of the circumstances, we hold that the warrantless search of defendant's bedroom was solidly anchored to the knowing and voluntary consent to search given by defendant's mother.

Defendant was indicted on two counts of attempted murder, *N.J.S.A.* 2C:5–1, 2C:11–3(a); four counts of aggravated assault, *N.J.S.A.* 2C:12–1(b)(1); one count of unlawful possession of a handgun, *N.J.S.A.* 2C:39–5(b); and one count of possession of a handgun for an unlawful purpose, *N.J.S.A.* 2C:39–4(a).

Defendant filed a motion to suppress the evidence seized from his bedroom. Defendant argued that his mother's will had been overborne by police. He emphasized that she was frightened and believed she had no choice but to consent to a search of her house. Under the circumstances, defendant insisted that her consent to search was not voluntary.

New Jersey has retained the automatic standing rule of *Jones v. United States*, 362 *U.S.* 257 (1960), *overruled by United States v. Salvucci*, 448 *U.S.* 83 (1980). Under the automatic standing rule, virtually all defendants have standing to contest a search or seizure by police where they have either "a proprietary, possessory or participatory interest in either the place searched or the property seized," or if "possession of the seized evidence at the time of the contested search is an essential element of guilt." *Alston*. In this way, our courts have construed the New Jersey Constitution as affording New Jersey citizens greater protection against unreasonable searches and seizures than accorded under the United States Constitution.

The conclusion that a defendant has [automatic] standing to challenge a search on state constitutional grounds is independent of and unrelated to whether that defendant has a reasonable expectation of privacy in the place searched or item seized. The [automatic standing] rule's purpose is to avoid the need to sacrifice a defendant's Fifth Amendment rights and admit to criminal activity in order to assert his Fourth Amendment rights to challenge the search or seizure.

Here, defendant clearly had a possessory interest in the property seized. Possession of the handgun is an essential element of several offenses faced by defendant. Therefore, under New Jersey law, defendant has automatic standing to challenge the search and seizure of the firearm and ammunition.

The focus of this appeal is whether the strenuously expressed statements by defendant's stepfather that the police should remove themselves immediately from the premises overrides the later consent given by defendant's mother. We conclude the rule announced in *Randolph*, does not render the consent given by defendant's mother nugatory and the search unreasonable.

STATE v. BULLOCK
901 P.2d 61 (Mont. 1995)

TRIEWEILER, J.

The defendants, Eddie Peterson and Bill Bullock, were charged in Jefferson County Justice Court with unlawfully killing a game animal and possession of an unlawfully killed animal. The Justice Court suppressed all of the State's evidence pertaining to Peterson, and dismissed the charges against Bullock. The State appealed to the District Court for a trial *de novo*. On appeal, the District Court denied the defendants' motions to dismiss and to suppress evidence. Peterson then pled guilty to unlawfully killing a game animal; Bullock pled guilty to unlawfully possessing a game animal; and both defendants reserved their right to appeal the District Court's order denying their motions to dismiss and suppress evidence. Following two orders by this Court which remanded this case to the District Court for further proceedings, we affirm the District Court's order which denied the defendants' motion to dismiss, and reverse the District Court's order which denied the defendants' motion to suppress evidence.

FACTUAL BACKGROUND

At about 6:30 a.m. on October 31, 1991, while returning home from work, Chuck Wing observed what he estimated was a large six or seven point antlered bull elk on Boulder Hill near Boulder, Montana. He recognized that the elk was in Hunting District 380 where hunters were allowed to shoot only "spikes" unless they had a special permit. As Wing observed the elk, he heard a gunshot, saw the elk fall, and observed two men and a boy standing near a pickup truck in the vicinity of the fallen elk. He believed the pickup belonged to defendant Eddie J. Peterson. He then observed the three people drag the elk to the truck and load it without field-dressing it. Wing reported the incident to Jefferson County Sheriff Tom Dawson, who, in turn, relayed the information to Game Warden Chris Anderson, an employee of the Montana Department of Fish, Wildlife, and Parks. Anderson traveled from Helena to Boulder that morning to investigate the incident.

Anderson first interviewed Wing who related the above information. He then drove to Peterson's home in Boulder, but Peterson was not at home. Anderson returned to the sheriff's office where he learned that Peterson had a cabin in Basin Creek. Rather than try to give directions, Dawson agreed to accompany him to the cabin. To reach Peterson's cabin, it is necessary to travel approximately seven miles on a one-lane forest service road which is bounded by forest on both sides. At least one sign along that road indicates that the road is bordered by private property and advises the public to remain on the road.

Peterson's property is separated from the road by a fence. There is a gate which provides access to his property from the forest service road. "No Trespassing" signs are posted on trees on each side of the gate. His cabin is located at the end of a private road 334 feet from the forest service road. Between the forest service road and Peterson's cabin, the terrain is slightly elevated in a way that conceals Peterson's cabin and the other structures on his property. He moved his cabin beyond the hill at an earlier time so that it would not be evident to passersby.

When Anderson and Dawson reached Peterson's property, the gate was open. They entered the property through the gate and drove approximately 180 feet down Peterson's private road. As they descended the crest of the hill between his cabin and the forest service road, they first observed a large bull elk hanging from a tree in an area about 126 feet from Peterson's cabin. The elk could not be seen from the public road, nor was there evidence that it could be seen from any other public location. Peterson testified that the elk was hanging between his cabin, several vehicles, and a guest sleeping cabin.

The parties agreed that, in the past, anyone who wished to enter Peterson's property or drive on his private road had called to ask permission. In fact, the Jefferson County Sheriff's Office had done so a few days earlier prior to conducting a search for lost hunters. On the date in question, neither Dawson nor Anderson asked or received permission to be on Peterson's property. Neither had they secured a search warrant, in spite of the fact that Anderson testified in Justice Court that he believed there was probable cause that a crime had been committed, that Peterson was involved, and that Peterson still possessed evidence of that crime.

At the hearing held in the District Court pursuant to the defendants' motion to suppress, there was disagreement about exactly what Anderson and Dawson did after observing the elk hanging near Peterson's cabin. However, in stipulations filed with the court earlier, the parties agreed that after observing the elk, Anderson and Dawson went over to examine it. After conducting the examination, Anderson then requested that Peterson take him and Dawson to the place where the elk was killed. Peterson did so, but at the site where the law enforcement officers were taken, there were no elk tracks—only a pile of the elk's entrails. It was apparent to Anderson that the elk had not been killed at that location.

Anderson then confronted Peterson with the information he had received from Wing. Peterson provided him with an explanation that ultimately was found to be inaccurate. Bullock was then questioned, provided responses consistent with Peterson's, and declined the State's offer of immunity in exchange for testimony that would incriminate Peterson.

The following day, Anderson returned to Peterson's cabin and confiscated the elk carcass.

On November 8, 1991, Peterson was charged in Jefferson County Justice Court with unlawfully killing a game animal. Bullock was charged with possession of an unlawfully killed animal. Both defendants pled not guilty to those charges.

Did defendant Bullock have standing to challenge the State's entry upon and search of land owned by Peterson?

The State contends that Bullock has no standing to challenge the legality of the State's entry onto and search of Peterson's land because he had no ownership interest in that land. It contends that pursuant to this Court's recent decisions in *State v. Gonzales* 751 P.2d 1063 (Mont. 1988), and *State v. Powers*, 758 P.2d 761 (Mont. 1988), a party must have some interest in the property searched before he or she can contest the admissibility of evidence gathered during the search.

Bullock responds that he was charged with possessing the elk carcass seized from Peterson's property, and that under our prior decisions, that possessory interest was sufficient to establish standing.

We agree that the State construes our prior decisions regarding standing too narrowly.

Even after the United States Supreme Court retreated from its "automatic standing" rule in cases where a defendant is charged with illegal possession of some item, in *United States v. Salvucci*, 448 U.S. 83 (1980), we held that ownership of the property searched is not necessary to establish standing to object to the legality of a search. *State v. Isom* 641 P.2d 417 (Mont. 1982). We stated:

> Notwithstanding the limitations placed on *Jones* [*v. United States*, 362 U.S. 257 (1960)], the Court in *Rakas* [*v. Illinois*, 439 U.S. 128 (1978)], and again in *Salvucci*, emphasized that ownership is not a key element in determining standing. The test for standing is not to be based on distinctions out of property and tort law: "In defining the scope of that interest, we adhere to the view expressed in *Jones* and echoed in later cases that arcane distinctions in property and tort law between guests, licensees, invitees, and the like ought not to control." The controlling view, then, seems to be that expressed in *Mancusi v. DeForte*, 392 U.S. 364 (1968), in which the Court said that the *Katz* test of "'legitimate expectation of privacy' makes it clear that capacity to claim the protection of the Fourth Amendment depends not upon a property right in the invaded place, but upon whether the area was one in which there was a reasonable expectation of freedom from governmental intrusion."

Following this rationale, we concluded in *Isom* that a defendant who was a guest in his uncle's home at the time that it was searched had standing to object to the government search of that home, even though he had no ownership interest in the premises.

We have since held in both *Gonzales* and *Powers* that a possessory interest in either the premises searched *or the property seized* is sufficient to establish standing. However, we have never modified nor reversed our position in *Isom*.

Other states which have held that a possessory interest in the items seized is sufficient to establish standing to challenge the legality of a search or the property's seizure, have adopted automatic standing rules on independent state grounds where the defendant is charged with unlawfully possessing that item.

For example, in *State v. Alston*, 440 A.2d 1311 (N.J. 1981), the defendants were passengers in a vehicle from which weapons were seized during a search of the vehicle. They were later charged with unlawful possession of the weapons. Pursuant to the defendants' motion, the evidence was suppressed by the trial court, based on the illegality of the police search. On appeal, the state contended that the defendant passengers had no standing to challenge the legality of the search of the vehicle, despite their possessory interest in the weapons which had been seized.

After reviewing the United States Supreme Court's decisions on standing, including *Salvucci*, that court noted an inconsistency in the federal law which appeared to allow prosecutors to assert contradictory positions: "[T]hat the defendant possessed the contraband property for the purposes of proving criminal liability, but that he had insufficient possessory interest in the property for the purposes of defending the legality of the search and seizure." The court pointed out that a basic principle of American federalism confers on state courts the power to afford citizens of each state greater protection against unreasonable searches and seizures than may be required by the Supreme Court's interpretation of the Fourth Amendment, and on that basis, concluded that the *Salvucci* decision afforded inadequate protection against unreasonable searches and seizures.

Finally, the New Jersey Supreme Court concluded that based on its rule of standing which provided that "a criminal defendant is entitled to bring a motion to suppress evidence obtained in an unlawful search and seizure if he has a proprietary, possessory or participatory interest in either the place searched or the property seized," it would retain the automatic standing rule where a defendant is charged with an offense in which possession of the seized evidence at the time of the contested search is an essential element of guilt. It adopted reasoning from former Justice Thurgood Marshall that:

> [t]he automatic standing rule is a salutary one which protects the rights of defendants and eliminates the wasteful requirement of making a preliminary showing of standing in pretrial proceedings involving possessory offenses,

where the charge itself alleges an interest sufficient to support a Fourth Amendment claim.

Other states have also adopted the rule of automatic standing for crimes of possession. *See State v. White*, 574 P.2d 840 (Ariz. Ct. App. 1978); *State v. Alosa*, 623 A.2d 218 (N.H. 1993).

We agree with the reasoning in *Alston*. Based on independent state grounds pursuant to article II, section 11 of the Montana Constitution, we hold that when the charge against the defendant includes an allegation of a possessory interest in the property which is seized, the defendant has standing to object to the prosecutorial use of that evidence based on either the unlawful search of the location where it was found, or its unlawful seizure.

Since Bullock was accused by the State of unlawfully possessing the elk carcass which was found on Peterson's property, we conclude, based on our prior decisions and the logical application of those decisions as set forth above, that he had standing to object to the State's search of Peterson's property and seizure of that carcass.

NOTE

In *United States v. Salvucci*, 448 U.S. 83 (1980), the United States Supreme Court abolished the automatic standing rule for purposes of the Fourth Amendment. As in Montana, a minority of state constitutions are still construed to provide automatic standing for defendants charged with possession of an item seized, without requiring the defendant to assert an ownership or possessory interest. *See, e.g., Commonwealth v. Armendola*, 550 N.E.2d 121 (Mass. 1990); *State v. Evans*, 150 P.3d 105 (Wash. 2007).

E. WARRANT REQUIREMENT

STATE v. EARLS
70 A.3d 630 (N.J. 2013)

RABNER, C.J.

Advances in technology offer great benefits to society in many areas. At the same time, they can pose significant risks to individual privacy rights. This case highlights both principles as we consider recent strides in cell-phone technology. New improvements not only expand our ability to communicate with one another and access the Internet, but the cell phones we carry can also serve as powerful tracking devices able to pinpoint our movements with remarkable precision and accuracy.

In this appeal, we consider whether people have a constitutional right of privacy in cell-phone location information. Cell phones register or identify themselves with nearby cell towers every seven seconds. Cell providers collect data from those contacts, which allows carriers to locate cell phones on a real-time basis and to reconstruct a phone's movement from recorded data. Those developments, in turn, raise questions about the right to privacy in the location of one's cell phone.

Historically, the State Constitution has offered greater protection to New Jersey residents than the Fourth Amendment. Under settled New Jersey law, individuals do not lose their right to privacy simply because they have to give information to a third-party provider, like a phone company or bank, to get service. *See State v. Reid*, 194 *N.J.* 386, 399, 945 *A.*2d 26 (2008). In addition, New Jersey case law continues to be guided by whether the government has violated an individual's reasonable expectation of privacy.

Applying those principles here, we note that disclosure of cell-phone location information, which cell-phone users must provide to receive service, can reveal a great deal of personal information about an individual. With increasing accuracy, cell phones can now trace our daily movements and disclose not only where individuals are located at a point in time but also which shops, doctors, religious services, and political events they go to, and with whom they choose to associate. Yet people do not buy cell phones to serve as tracking devices or reasonably expect them to be used by the government in that way. We therefore find that individuals have a reasonable expectation of privacy in the location of their cell phones under the State Constitution.

We also recognize that cell-phone location information can be a powerful tool to fight crime. That data will still be available to law enforcement officers upon a showing of probable cause. To be clear, the police will be able to access cell-phone location data with a properly authorized search warrant. If the State can show that a recognized exception to the warrant requirement applies, such as exigent circumstances, then no warrant is needed.

Having a clear set of rules serves two key goals. It protects legitimate privacy interests and also gives guidance to law enforcement officials who carry out important public safety responsibilities. Because today's decision creates a new rule of law that would disrupt the administration of justice if applied retroactively, the rule will apply to this defendant and prospective cases only.

The issue before the Court arises in the case of a burglary investigation. In an effort to locate the target and his girlfriend, whose safety was in question, the police obtained cell-phone location information from T–Mobile on three occasions during the same evening—without first getting a court order or a warrant.

We draw the following facts from testimony at the suppression hearing in this case. In January 2006, Detective William Strohkirch of the Middletown Township Police Department was investigating a series of residential burglaries. After a victim told Strohkirch that a cell phone stolen from his home was still active, a court-ordered trace of the phone led the police to a bar in Asbury Park. Strohkirch and two other officers found an individual at the bar with the phone, and they arrested him. He told the police that his cousin, defendant Thomas Earls, had sold him the phone. He added that defendant had been involved in residential burglaries and kept the proceeds in a storage unit that either defendant or his former girlfriend, Desiree Gates, had rented.

At some point on January 26, 2006, the police filed a complaint against defendant for receiving stolen property and obtained an arrest warrant. Strohkirch then began to search for defendant and Gates to ensure her safety and to execute the warrant.

In an effort to locate them, the police contacted T–Mobile, a cell-phone service provider, at about 6:00 p.m. At three different times that evening, T–Mobile provided information about the location of a cell phone the police believed defendant had been using. First, at around 8:00 p.m., T–Mobile told the police that the cell phone in question was in the "general location" of Highway 35 in Eatontown. The police searched the area but did not find defendant or Gates.

Second, at about 9:30 p.m., the police again contacted T–Mobile, which reported that the cell phone was being used in the area of Routes 33 and 18 in Neptune. The police searched that area in response but did not find defendant. Finally, after the police called T–Mobile at around 11:00 p.m., the carrier reported that a cell-site tower in the area of Route 9 in Howell had been used. At no point did the police seek a warrant for the three traces.

Local police departments assisted Strohkirch throughout the evening. At around midnight, the Howell Police Department located defendant's car at the Caprice Motel on Route 9 in Howell. A local officer stayed in the area to watch the car. Meanwhile, Strohkirch and Detective Deickman of the Middletown Police drove to the motel together. When they arrived at about 1:00 a.m., the officer on site reported that he had not seen any movement and that all of the motel rooms were dark.

At about 3:00 a.m., two hours after Strohkirch and Deickman first arrived at the motel, two police officers from Middletown arrived. At that point, Deickman spoke with a clerk in the motel office who confirmed where Gates and defendant were staying. Deickman called their room from the clerk's office to ask Gates to come outside. When defendant and Gates opened the door, the police arrested him. The police saw a flat-screen television and several pieces of luggage on the floor of the room. Inside a closed dresser drawer, the police found a pillowcase tied in a knot.

The police brought defendant and the items to headquarters, where defendant signed consent-to-search forms. Inside the luggage, the police found stolen property and marijuana. The pillowcase contained stolen jewelry.

Defendant filed a motion to suppress. After a three-day hearing, the trial court upheld the seizure of evidence from the storage unit and the motel room, except for the contents of the pillowcase. The court also denied defendant's motion to suppress evidence seized from his car and apartment. Our focus in this appeal is on defendant's arrest, based on the location of the cell phone, and the resulting consequences.

Defendant argues that he had a reasonable expectation of privacy in his cell-phone location information and that a warrant was therefore needed before law enforcement officials could access that information. He submits that technology now allows law enforcement to track the location of cell phones in an intrusive, continuous manner and thereby threatens to erode protected privacy rights. Defendant argues that the traditional distinction between public and private realms is no longer valid because cell-phone tracking monitors a person's movements in and out of both areas.

A basic cell phone operates like a scanning radio. Cell phones use radio waves to communicate between a user's handset and a telephone network. To connect with the local telephone network, the Internet, or other wireless networks, cell-phone providers maintain an extensive network of cell sites, or radio base stations, in the geographic areas they serve.

Whenever a cell phone is turned on, it searches for a signal and automatically registers or identifies itself with the nearest cell site—the one with the strongest signal. The process is automatic. Cell phones re-scan every seven seconds, or whenever the signal strength weakens, even when no calls are made. Cell phones can be tracked when they are used to make a call, send a text message, or connect to the Internet—or when they take no action at all, so long as the phone is not turned off. Today, cell-phone providers can pinpoint the location of a person's cell phone with increasing accuracy. In some areas, carriers can locate cell-phone users within buildings, and even within "individual floors and rooms within buildings."

A recent decision of the United States Supreme Court that rests on principles of trespass has altered the landscape somewhat. *See United States v. Jones*, 132 *S.Ct.* 945 (2012). *Jones* held that the physical installation of a GPS device on a car amounted to a Fourth Amendment search and required a warrant. Federal officers had attached a GPS tracking device to a car, without a valid warrant, and pinpointed the car's movements to within 50 to 100 feet for nearly one month.

The Court unanimously found a violation of the Fourth Amendment but split on the underlying basis. The majority opinion by Justice Scalia, joined by Chief Justice Roberts and Justices Kennedy, Thomas, and Sotomayor, held that the installation of the device constituted a trespass on private property. The decision did not address whether the defendant had a reasonable expectation of privacy that was violated when the police monitored the device.

Article I, Paragraph 7 of the New Jersey Constitution is nearly identical to the Fourth Amendment. Despite the similarity in language, the protections against unreasonable searches and seizures "are not always coterminous." On a number of occasions, this Court has found that the State Constitution provides greater protection against unreasonable searches and seizures than the Fourth Amendment. *See, e.g., Reid*, (recognizing reasonable expectation of privacy in Internet subscriber information); *State v. McAllister* (finding reasonable expectation of privacy in bank records); *State v. Mollica*, (finding privacy interest in hotel-room telephone toll billing records); *State v. Novembrino*, (declining to find good-faith exception to exclusionary rule); *Hunt*, (finding privacy interest in telephone toll billing records).

At the outset, we note that an individual's privacy interest under New Jersey law does not turn on whether he or she is required to disclose information to third-party providers to obtain service. Just as customers must disclose details about their personal finances to the bank that manages their checking accounts, cell-phone users have no choice but to reveal certain information to their cellular provider. That is not a voluntary disclosure in a typical sense; it can only be avoided at the price of not using a cell phone.

When people make disclosures to phone companies and other providers to use their services, they are not promoting the release of personal information to others. Instead, they can reasonably expect that their personal information will remain private. For those reasons, we have departed from federal case law that takes a different approach.

Beyond the question of third-party disclosure, we have examined the expectation of privacy that people reasonably have in various types of personal information. In *Hunt*, this Court observed that people are "entitled to assume that the [telephone] numbers [they dial] in the privacy of [their] home will be recorded solely for the telephone company's business purposes" and not for law enforcement. As the Court explained, a list of phone numbers dialed "'easily could reveal the identities of the persons and the places called, and thus reveal the most intimate details of a person's life.'"

Similarly in *McAllister*, *supra*, the Court noted that bank records "'reveal[ ] many aspects of [a depositor's] personal affairs, opinions, habits and associations. Indeed, the totality of bank records provides a virtual current biography.'"

More recently, in *Reid*, we found that Internet "subscriber information alone can tell a great deal about a person. With a complete listing of IP addresses, one can track a person's Internet usage" and learn where they shop, what political organizations they find interesting, their health concerns, and more.

We also noted how integrally connected all three areas are to essential activities of everyday life. As to each, we found that the State Constitution protects the privacy interest at stake.

We consider the expectation of privacy that should be accorded the location of a cell phone in that context. Using a cell phone to determine the location of its owner can be far more revealing than acquiring toll billing, bank, or Internet subscriber records. It is akin to using a tracking device and can function as a substitute for 24/7 surveillance without police having to confront the limits of their resources. It also involves a degree of intrusion that a reasonable person would not anticipate. Location information gleaned from a cell-phone provider can reveal not just where people go—which doctors, religious services, and stores they visit—but also the people and groups they choose to affiliate with and when they actually do so. That information cuts across a broad range of personal ties with family, friends, political groups, health care providers, and others. In other words, details about the location of a cell phone can provide an intimate picture of one's daily life.

Modern cell phones also blur the historical distinction between public and private areas because cell phones emit signals from both places. In this case, defendant was located in a motel room, not on a public highway. Yet law enforcement had no way of knowing in advance whether defendant's cell phone was being monitored in a public or private space. Cell-phone location information, thus, does more than simply augment visual surveillance in public areas.

Finally, cell-phone use has become an indispensable part of modern life. The hundreds of millions of wireless devices in use each day can often be found near their owners—at work, school, or home, and at events and gatherings of all types. And wherever those mobile devices may be, they continuously identify their location to nearby cell towers so long as they are not turned off.

We analyze those considerations under the State's search-and-seizure jurisprudence. We are required to focus on reasonable expectation of privacy concerns.

As a general rule, the more sophisticated and precise the tracking, the greater the privacy concern. The question before the court, then, is informed by changes in technology, because they affect the level of detail that telephone companies can relay to law enforcement. To be sure, the degree of information available through cell-phone tracking has grown with each passing year. As discussed above, in 2006, cell phones could be tracked to within a one-mile radius or less of the nearest cell tower. Today, that distance has narrowed to the point that cell phones can be pinpointed with great precision—to within feet in some instances. That information is updated every seven seconds through interactions with cell towers, whether the phone is in public or private space. As noted, that continuous process can reveal a great deal of private information about a person's life.

Viewed from the perspective of a reasonable expectation of privacy, what was problematic in 2006 is plainly invasive today. We are not able to draw a fine line across that spectrum and calculate a person's legitimate expectation of privacy with mathematical certainty—noting each slight forward advance in technology. Courts are not adept at that task. Instead, our focus belongs on the obvious: cell phones are not meant to serve as tracking devices to locate their owners wherever they may be. People buy cell phones to communicate with others, to use the Internet, and for a growing number of other reasons. But no one buys a cell phone to share detailed information about their whereabouts with the police. That was true in 2006 and is equally true today. Citizens have a legitimate privacy interest in such information. Although individuals may be generally aware that their phones can be tracked, most people do not realize the extent of modern tracking capabilities and reasonably do not expect law enforcement to convert their phones into precise, possibly continuous tracking tools.

Law and practice have evolved in this area in response to changes in technology. In 2010, a new statute required that police get a court order for cell-site information on a showing of less than probable cause: "specific and articulable facts showing that there are reasonable grounds to believe that the record or other information ... is relevant and material to an ongoing criminal investigation." The statute contains an exception for location information for mobile devices when a "law enforcement agency believes in good faith that an emergency involving danger of death or serious bodily injury to the subscriber or customer" exists. Moreover, as discussed further below, the Attorney General reports that in recent years, many law enforcement officers have obtained warrants based on probable cause before gathering information about the location of a cell phone. We credit the Attorney General's office for that approach.

For the reasons discussed, we conclude that Article I, Paragraph 7 of the New Jersey Constitution protects an individual's privacy interest in the location of his or her cell phone. Users are reasonably entitled to expect confidentiality in the ever-increasing level of detail that cell phones can reveal about their lives. Because of the nature of the intrusion, and the corresponding, legitimate privacy interest at stake, we hold today that police must obtain a warrant based on a showing of probable cause, or qualify for an exception to the warrant requirement, to obtain tracking information through the use of a cell phone.

By providing greater clarity to the law in this area, we strive to meet two aims: to protect the reasonable expectation of privacy that cell-phone users have and, at the same time, to offer clear guidance to law enforcement officials so they may carry out important tasks in the interest of public safety. Both the public and the police will be better served by a clear set of rules. To be sure, law enforcement officials will still be able to turn to cell-phone providers to obtain location information, as long as such requests are accompanied by a warrant issued by a neutral magistrate and supported by probable cause. We emphasize that no warrant is required in emergency situations or when some other exception to the warrant requirement applies.

Our ruling today is based solely on the State Constitution. We recognize that *Jones* and *Smith*, to the extent they apply, would not require a warrant in this case.

STATE v. BRYANT
950 A.2d 467 (Vt. 2008)

SKOGLUND, J.

The issue on this appeal from a conviction for cultivation of marijuana is whether the warrantless aerial scrutiny of defendant's yard, for the purpose of detecting criminal activity by the occupant of the property, violated privacy rights secured by the Vermont Constitution. We hold that Vermont citizens have a constitutional right to privacy that ascends into the airspace above their homes and property. The warrantless aerial surveillance in this case violated that constitutionally protected privacy right. Accordingly, we reverse.

Defendant was charged with felony possession and cultivation of marijuana. He moved to suppress from evidence the marijuana plants discovered growing by his house, alleging a violation of chapter I, article 11 of the Vermont Constitution. The trial court denied the motion. A jury convicted defendant on the cultivation charge, but not on the possession charge. Defendant appeals from the trial court's denial of his motion to suppress. We reverse.

Defendant argues that an unconstitutional aerial surveillance of his property resulted in the issuance of a search warrant that led to the discovery of defendant's marijuana cultivation. At a hearing on the motion to dismiss, the following facts were found by the court or were uncontested. Defendant lives in a remote area on a wooded hill in the town of Goshen, in Addison County. The property is accessible by a locked gate on a Forest Service road to which only defendant, his partner, and the Forest Service have keys. Beyond the gate, the dirt road passes defendant's homestead and continues a short distance into the National Forest, where the road dead-ends. Where the road cuts across defendant's property, the Forest Service has a restricted right-of-way. Defendant has posted prominent no-trespassing signs around his property. Prior to the aerial surveillance, defendant told a local forest official that he did not want the Forest Service or anyone else trespassing on his land.

The local forest official suspected that defendant was responsible for marijuana plants that were reportedly growing in the National Forest (not on defendant's property) because he found defendant's insistence on privacy to be "paranoid." The forest official suggested to the State Police that a Marijuana Eradication Team (MERT) flight over defendant's property might be a good idea. MERT is an anti-drug program, and MERT flights are executed by the Vermont State Police in cooperation with the Army National Guard. A state trooper, scheduled to do a MERT flight, was given the information identifying the defendant's residence as a good target. On August 7, 2003, the state trooper and an Army National Guard pilot flew in a National Guard helicopter to the Goshen area. Having previously located the site on a map, the trooper directed the pilot to defendant's property, where two plots of marijuana were observed growing about 100 feet from the house.

Defendant introduced testimony of several people who witnessed the flight. One witness, who was working outside at the time of the flyover, described the helicopter as being at twice the height of her house, or approximately 100 feet above ground level. She testified that the noise was "deafening." She observed the helicopter spend "a good half-hour" in the area of defendant's residence, where it circled "very low down to the trees." After the flight, the state trooper prepared an application for a search warrant based solely on his observation during the aerial surveillance of what he believed to be marijuana plants. In the application, the trooper characterized the surveillance as having been from "an aircraft at least 500 feet above the ground." The warrant was issued and executed, and three marijuana plots were discovered by defendant's home.

Based on the evidence presented at the suppression hearing, the court found that the helicopter circled defendant's property for approximately fifteen to thirty minutes, well below 500 feet in altitude, and at times as low as 100 feet above the ground. Although both the trooper and the pilot testified that the helicopter remained at least 500 feet off the ground at all times, the court did not find their testimony to be credible. The court further found that pilots doing MERT flights in Vermont are told to stay at least 500 feet above the ground and that, according to a National Guard pilot who testified for the State, the reason MERT pilots are so directed is to avoid invasions of privacy.

TC finds that π flew low

The court, however, denied defendant's motion, holding that defendant had no reasonable expectation of privacy from the sky. The court reasoned that, while helicopter flights over one's property in rural Vermont might be infrequent, a reasonable person would still assume that such flights will happen. The court concluded that the police surveillance was not so intrusive as to violate the Vermont Constitution. We disagree and reverse.

TC: reasonable to expect that helicopter could do this

Article 11 of the Vermont Constitution protects the people's right to be free "from unreasonable government intrusions into legitimate expectations of privacy." When government conducts a warrantless search, the law presumes that the intrusion is unreasonable. The aerial surveillance at issue in this case was warrantless, and therefore presumptively unreasonable. Thus, the sole issue in this case is whether the aerial surveillance constitutes a search under article 11 of Vermont's Constitution? *AR surveillance is search, then Const. violation.*

Rule about warrantless searches

An article 11 search occurs when the government intrudes into "areas or activities" that are the subject of "'legitimate expectations of privacy.'" Under article 11, the question of whether an individual has a legitimate expectation of privacy "'hinges on the essence of underlying constitutional values—including respect for both private, subjective expectations and public norms.'" Therefore, in order to invoke article 11 protection, a person must "exhibit [] an actual (subjective) expectation of privacy…that society is prepared to recognize as reasonable." In other words, article 11 requires an individual to have "conveyed an expectation of privacy in such a way that a reasonable person would conclude that he sought to exclude the public." "Whether the steps taken are adequate for this purpose will depend on the specific facts of each case."

Katz-like formulation of "privacy"

We have often noted the "significance of the home as a repository of heightened privacy expectations," and have deemed those heightened expectations legitimate. Therefore, although we have disagreed amongst ourselves about the extent to which circumstances may alter the general rule, government intrusions into the home are searches for purposes of

Home is different. Don't need to convey privacy expectation.

article 11 even if an individual fails to take affirmative steps to convey his expectation of privacy.

A home's curtilage—the "area outside the physical confines of a house into which the 'privacies of life' may extend"—merits "the same constitutional protection from unreasonable searches and seizures as the home itself." *State v. Rogers*, 638 A.2d 569, 572 (Vt. 1993) (quoting *Oliver v. United States*, 466 U.S. 170, 180 (1984)). However, relying on the principle that there is no invasion of privacy—and therefore no search when government observes that which is willingly exposed to the public, we have consistently held that an individual must take affirmative steps to protect his privacy in his curtilage and his "open fields"—the real property beyond his curtilage. Government does conduct a search when it intrudes onto open fields that a reasonable person would expect to be private. Fences, gates, and no-trespassing signs generally suffice to apprise a person that the area is private.

In this case, we consider whether surveillance from an Army helicopter, circling at 100 feet over defendant's home and garden for fifteen to thirty minutes for the purpose of detecting contraband, violated his legitimate expectations of privacy. Whether and when aerial surveillance constitutes a search are questions that we have not squarely confronted before. We decide this case solely on Vermont Constitutional grounds, but may be guided by decisions of our sister states and the United States Supreme Court on similar questions. We begin our analysis with a survey of those decisions.

The United States Supreme Court has decided three aerial-surveillance cases; the Court ruled in each that the surveillance at issue was not a search within the meaning of the Fourth Amendment. *Florida v. Riley*, 488 U.S. 445, 448 (1989); *Dow Chem. Co. v. United States*, 476 U.S. 227, 239 (1986); *California v. Ciraolo*, 476 U.S. 207, 2014 (1986). For the reasons explained below, we find minimal guidance in these decisions.

It is our opinion that many of the factors relied on by our sister states and the Supreme Court in *Riley* are relevant to evaluating the legitimacy of privacy expectations under article 11 in the context of the aerial surveillance at issue in this case. The legitimacy of an individual's expectation of privacy is a broad question of "'private, subjective expectations and public norms.'" When we declined to adopt the federal open-fields doctrine in *Kirchoff*, we recognized that Vermonters normally expect their property to remain private when posted as such. We have also recognized that Vermonters normally have high expectations of privacy in and around their homes. Therefore, we think it is also likely that Vermonters expect—at least at a private, rural residence on posted land— that they will be free from intrusions that interrupt their use of their property, expose their intimate activities, or create undue noise, wind, or dust.

We are also persuaded that the legality of the altitude at which aerial surveillance takes place can be relevant to the determination of whether an individual has a legitimate expectation of privacy in his real property. Indeed, the citizens of Vermont likely expect that law enforcement personnel as well as other air travelers will abide by safety rules and other applicable laws and regulations when flying over their homes. However, it simply does not follow that whether a member of the public is abiding by the law in occupying a particular spot in the public airspace is an adequate test of whether government surveillance from that same spot is constitutional. Therefore, we disagree with those courts that would use the legality of an aircraft's position alone to evaluate the constitutionality of the surveillance conducted aboard it. *Ct: gov needed to fly legally, but even that isn't enough*

In any event, at least on the facts of this case, no one factor need act as a litmus test of constitutionality, because the surveillance at issue here was a patent violation of defendant's legitimate expectations of privacy. We understand that our abstention from drawing a bright line that makes the legality or frequency of flights at certain altitudes a quick index to the constitutionality of aerial surveillance gives limited guidance to trial courts and law enforcement personnel in the context of other cases. But we are not presented with other cases; we are presented only with this case. In this case, defendant has demonstrated that he has a subjective expectation of privacy in his back yard. He has taken precautions to exclude others from his back yard by posting his land and by communicating to a local forest official that he did not want people *of privacy* trespassing on his land. *Ct: Δ also had a subjectible expectation* ~~of Δ's prop~~

The overriding function of article 11 is to protect personal privacy and dignity against unwarranted intrusion by the state. It requires that the state temper its efforts to apprehend criminals with a concern for the impact of its methods on our fundamental liberties. Principles established in cases such as this delineate the extent to which official intrusion into the privacy of any citizen will be constitutionally permissible.

In *Johnson v. United States*, the Supreme Court wrote that the Fourth Amendment reflects a choice that our society should be one in which citizens "dwell in reasonable security and freedom from surveillance." 333 U.S. 10, 14 (1948). With technological advances in surveillance techniques, the privacy-protection question is no longer whether police have physically invaded a constitutionally protected area. Rather, the inquiry is whether the surveillance invaded a constitutionally protected legitimate expectation of privacy. In this case, the targeted, low-level

↳ How tech has altered the privacy norms.

helicopter surveillance by the police of activities in an enclosed backyard is not consistent with that expectation—not without a warrant.

It may be easy to forget, especially in view of current concerns over drug abuse in our society that the scope of article 11's protection "does not turn on whether the activity disclosed by a search is illegal or innocuous." The interest protected by article 11, like the Fourth Amendment, "is the expectation of the ordinary citizen, who has never engaged in illegal conduct in his life." In his dissent in *White*, Justice Harlan reasoned that the scope of constitutional protection must reflect "the impact of a practice on the sense of security that is the true concern of the [constitution's] protection of privacy." We agree. We protect defendant's marijuana plots against such surveillance so that law-abiding citizens may relax in their backyards, enjoying a sense of security that they are free from unreasonable surveillance.

The aerial surveillance in this case was a warrantless search forbidden by the Vermont Constitution. The warrant authorizing the subsequent search of defendant's premises for marijuana plants was obtained solely on the basis of the aerial observations. The evidence seized upon executing the warrant should therefore have been excluded from defendant's trial. Since the error was clearly prejudicial, his conviction must be overturned.

NOTES

1.   The Vermont Constitution has been construed consistently as having a strong preference for warrants, *i.e.*, "one of the essential checks on unrestrained government determined by the framers…to be necessary to the preservation of individual freedom." *State v. Bauder*, 924 A.2d 38 (Vt. 2007). Under article II of the Vermont Constitution, police must get a search warrant before searching a closed container unless "exceptional" circumstances—risk of undue delay, destruction of evidence or danger to officers—make getting a warrant impracticable. *State v. Neil*, 958 A.2d 1173 (Vt. 2008). Interestingly, article I, section 9 of the Texas Constitution "contains no requirement that a seizure or search be authorized by a warrant, and that a search or seizure that is otherwise reasonable will not be found to be in violation of that section because it was not authorized by a warrant." *Hulit v. State*, 982 S.W.2d 431 (Tex. Crim. App. 1998).

2.   The United States Supreme Court has held that there is no reasonable expectation of privacy in garbage left in a public place with intent to disregard it. Thus, there was no Fourth Amendment search when police officers inspected the contents of opaque plastic bags left out for garbage collection. *California v. Greenwood*, 486 U.S. 35 (1988). Although most state constitutions have been construed to permit a warrantless search of

trash that has been left out for collection, some state constitutions require a warrant. *See State v. Goss*, 834 A.2d 316 (N.H. 2003). *Greenwood* was also rejected on the basis of the greater privacy protection provided by the text in article I, section 7 of the Washington Constitution. *State v. Boland*, 800 P.2d 1112 (Wash. 1990). *See also* Chapter IV.

F. PHYSICAL SEIZURE OF INDIVIDUAL BY POLICE

STATE v. BEAUCHESNE
868 A.2d 972 (N.H. 2005)

DUGGAN, J.

Following a bench trial on stipulated facts, the defendant, John Beauchesne, was convicted of possession of cocaine, possession of marijuana, and resisting detention. On appeal, he challenges his convictions for possession of cocaine and marijuana, arguing that the Superior Court erroneously denied his motion to suppress the cocaine and marijuana. The defendant does not challenge his conviction for resisting detention. We reverse and remand.

On September 27, 2002, Detective Peter Morelli of the Derry Police Department was on duty patrolling downtown Derry. Detective Morelli was in an unmarked cruiser, wearing street clothes and "on the lookout for 'drug crime.'" Although Detective Morelli testified that he previously had investigated drug transactions in the area he was patrolling, he also testified that a drug transaction was no more likely to occur there than any other area in Derry.

At approximately 6:30 p.m., Detective Morelli observed two men standing in an alley off Railroad Avenue. One man was straddling a bike. The defendant was facing the man on the bike. Detective Morelli saw the defendant hand something small and "unidentifiable" to the man straddling the bike, then turn and walk toward the street.

Believing that he had just witnessed a drug transaction, Detective Morelli stopped and exited his cruiser, made eye contact with the defendant and motioned for the defendant to approach him. The defendant did not respond and walked away. Detective Morelli then yelled to the defendant, identifying himself as a police officer and ordering the defendant to stop. The defendant again did not respond and continued walking away.

Detective Morelli followed the defendant on foot. When he saw that the defendant was running away, Detective Morelli again yelled that he was a police officer and ordered the defendant to stop. The defendant continued to run and Detective Morelli followed him. Detective Morelli eventually caught up with the defendant and attempted to grab him. The defendant, however, fell to the ground. During his fall, the defendant either dropped or threw a plastic bag containing a green vegetative matter, which Detective Morelli was able to identify immediately as marijuana. Detective Morelli then fell over the defendant.

Detective Morelli arrested the defendant for resisting detention and possessing marijuana. Detective Morelli subsequently searched the defendant's person and discovered a quantity of cocaine.

The defendant moved to suppress the cocaine and marijuana obtained as a result of the seizure because Detective Morelli lacked reasonable, articulable suspicion when he first ordered the defendant to stop. The trial court denied the motion, ruling that under *California v. Hodari D.*, 499 U.S. 621, 626 (1991), the defendant was not seized until he "fell and thus submitted to the detective's show of authority," at which time Detective Morelli had reasonable, articulable suspicion that the defendant had committed a crime.

On appeal, the defendant argues that the trial court erred in ruling that, under part I, article 19 of the State Constitution, the defendant was not seized until he submitted to Detective Morelli's show of authority. To that end, the defendant argues that we should not adopt the holding in *Hodari D.*, which requires submission to a show of authority, for determining when a seizure occurs under the State Constitution. In addition, the defendant argues that because he was seized for State constitutional purposes when Detective Morelli ordered him to stop, the trial court erred in denying his motion to suppress the cocaine and marijuana because the detective lacked reasonable, articulable suspicion at the time of the seizure.

Seizure

The defendant argues that he was subject to an unlawful seizure because Detective Morelli lacked reasonable suspicion when he first ordered the defendant to stop. Accordingly, the defendant argues that the trial court erred in denying his motion to suppress the cocaine and marijuana as fruits of the unlawful seizure.

It is well settled that "[i]n order for a police officer to undertake an investigatory stop, the officer must have a reasonable suspicion—based on specific, articulable facts taken together with rational inferences from those facts—that the particular person stopped has been, is, or is about to be, engaged in criminal activity." An investigatory stop is a very limited seizure. Thus, in deciding whether Detective Morelli conducted a lawful investigatory stop, we must conduct a two-step inquiry. First, we must determine when the defendant was seized. Second, we must determine whether, at that time, Detective Morelli possessed a reasonable suspicion that the defendant was, had been or was about to be engaged in criminal activity.

The crux of this appeal is the determination of when, under part I, article 19 of the State Constitution, the defendant was seized. The defendant argues that, for State constitutional purposes, he was seized when Detective Morelli first ordered him to stop. The State, relying upon the holding in *Hodari D.*, argues that the defendant was seized when he fell and submitted to Detective Morelli's show of authority.

Not all interactions between the police and citizens involve a seizure of the person. "[A] seizure does not occur simply because a police officer approaches an individual and asks a few questions." *Florida v. Bostick*, 501 U.S. 429 (1991). This is true "[s]o long as a reasonable person would feel free to disregard the police and go about his business." Indeed, the police may request to examine the individual's identification or for consent to search the individual or his belongings. The person stopped, however, is not obliged to answer and the police may not convey a message that compliance with their request is required. Moreover, unless the police officer has reasonable suspicion, the person approached may not be detained.

An interaction between a police officer and a citizen becomes a seizure, however, when a reasonable person believes he or she is not free to leave. *United States v. Mendenhall*, 446 U.S. 544 (1980); *Riley*, 490 A.2d 1362 (adopting the *Mendenhall* definition of seizure). This occurs when an officer, by means of physical force or show of authority, has in some way restrained the liberty of the person. Circumstances indicating a "show of authority" might include the threatening presence of several officers, the display of a weapon by an officer, some physical touching of the person, or the use of language or tone of voice indicating that compliance with the officer's request might be compelled. The analysis is an objective one, requiring a determination of whether the defendant's freedom of movement was sufficiently curtailed by considering how a reasonable person in the defendant's position would have understood his situation.

In *Hodari D.*, the United States Supreme Court addressed the "narrow question...whether, with respect to a show of authority...a seizure occurs even though the subject does not yield." In that case, two police officers on patrol in a high-crime area observed four or five youths, including the defendant, huddled around a car parked at the curb. When the youths saw the police car approach, they ran. One of the officers exited the car and pursued the defendant on foot. As the officer neared, the defendant tossed away what was later determined to be crack cocaine. The Court concluded that the defendant was not seized when the police officer was pursuing him and, thus, the cocaine was admissible because he had not yet been seized when he discarded it. Rather, relying primarily upon the dictionary definition of seizure and the common law of arrest, the Court held that:

> The word "seizure" readily bears the meaning of a laying on of hands or application of physical force to restrain movement, even when it is ultimately unsuccessful. ("She seized the purse-snatcher, but he broke out of her grasp.") It does not remotely apply, however, to the prospect of a policeman yelling "Stop, in the name of the law!" at a fleeing form that continues to flee. That is no seizure.

Accordingly, the Court held that a seizure "requires either physical force…or, where that is absent, submission to the assertion of authority."

Several States have considered whether to adopt the holding in *Hodari D.* for determining when a seizure occurs under their respective state constitutions. Numerous state courts have rejected *Hodari D.* on state constitutional grounds. The Supreme Court of Tennessee summarized the "extensive criticisms" of *Hodari D.* as follows:

> First, the majority's analysis in *Hodari D.* represents a marked departure from the standard the Supreme Court adopted in *United States v. Mendenhall, i.e.,* that a seizure occurs when "in view of all of the circumstances surrounding the incident, a reasonable person would have believed he was not free to leave." Second, the majority's analysis fails to apply common law principles under which an arrest would not be distinguished from an attempted arrest in determining whether a person has been seized. Third, the majority's analysis is flawed for practical reasons and is subject to potential abuse by officers who pursue a subject without reasonable suspicion and use a flight or refusal to submit to authority as reason to execute an arrest or search.

State v. Randolph, 74 S.W.3d 330, 336 (Tenn. 2002); *see also State v. Oquendo*, 613 A.2d 1300, 1310 (Conn. 1992); *Jones v. State*, 745 A.2d 856, 864-66 (Del. 1999) (noting that *Hodari D.* is inconsistent with the State's historic commitment to protecting the privacy of citizens because it "would allow a police officer lacking reasonable suspicion to create that suspicion through an unjustified attempted detention"); *Commonwealth v. Stoute*, 665 N.E.2d 93, 97 (Mass. 1996) (noting that pursuit is no less intrusive on a person's freedom of movement than a stop); *State v. Clayton*, 45 P.3d 30, 33-34 (Mont. 2002) (noting that *Hodari D.* imposes "a subjective element to the traditionally objective test of whether a seizure has occurred" and that utilizing an objective test "allows the police to determine in advance whether the conduct contemplated will implicate [the state constitution] and does not shift the focus of the inquiry to a person's subjective reaction to police conduct"); *State v. Tucker*, 642 A.2d 401, 405 (N.J. 1994) (noting that the Supreme Court's reliance on dictionary definitions of seizure "may be misplaced" because although "[t]he Court correctly states that the officer's chase was not a common-law arrest, [it] fails to point out that this conduct amounted to an attempted arrest, which was also unlawful at common law" (quotation omitted)); *Commonwealth v. Matos*, 672 A.2d 769, 775 (Pa. 1996) (rejecting *Hodari D.* because it is inconsistent with Pennsylvania's recognition that "our citizens enjoy a strong right of privacy, and that our citizens are therefore entitled to broader protection in certain circumstances under our state constitution").

Of the States that have adopted *Hodari D.* under their state constitutions, many do so noting that they do not have a history of providing greater privacy protection to their citizens than the Federal Constitution. *See, e.g., Perez v. State*, 620 So.2d 1256, 1258 (Fla. 1993) (noting that the Florida Constitution specifically prohibits a court from interpreting the Florida Constitution as providing greater protection than the Fourth Amendment to the United States Constitution); *State v. Cronin*, 509 N.W.2d 673, 676 (Neb. 1993) ("Nebraska has neither an explicit constitutional right of privacy nor a history of affording individuals greater rights than are afforded by the federal Constitution.").

In contrast, we have recognized that our State Constitution incorporates a strong right of privacy and provides greater protection for individual rights than the Federal Constitution. *See State v. Canelo*, 653 A.2d 1097 (N.H. 1995). Accordingly, we are persuaded by the reasoning of those States that have declined to adopt the holding in *Hodari D.* for determining when a seizure occurs as a matter of State constitutional law.

We have held that part I, article 19, provides greater protection for individual rights than does the Fourth Amendment. Indeed, we have recognized that "[o]ur Constitution has historically been interpreted to incorporate a strong right of privacy." In *Canelo*, for instance, we adopted the exclusionary rule under the State Constitution because it served to deter police misconduct and "to redress the injury to the privacy of the search victim." We also declined to adopt a good faith exception to the exclusionary rule because it was "incompatible with and detrimental to our citizens' strong right of privacy inherent in part I, article 19."

Likewise, the *Hodari D.* rule is incompatible with the guarantees of part I, article 19. As the Massachusetts Supreme Judicial Court aptly noted:

> [S]tops provoke constitutional scrutiny because they encumber a person's freedom of movement. Pursuit that appears designed to effect a stop is no less intrusive than a stop itself. Framed slightly differently, a pursuit, which, objectively considered, indicates to a person that he would not be free to leave the area (or to remain there) without first responding to a police officer's inquiry, is the functional equivalent of a seizure, in the sense that the person being pursued is plainly the object of an official assertion of authority, which does not intend to be denied, and which infringes considerably on the person's freedom of action.

Commonwealth v. Stoute, 665 N.E.2d 93, 97 (Mass. 1996). Because of the intrusiveness of a police officer's assertion of authority, requiring police officers to possess reasonable suspicion prior to asserting their authority is necessary to adequately protect individual rights under the State Constitution. Thus, under part I, article 19 of the State Constitution, a police officer must possess reasonable suspicion before taking an action that would communicate to a reasonable person that he or she is not free to leave.

Our holding today is supported by sound practical and policy reasons. First, focusing the definition of seizure on the police officer's conduct, and not the individual's conduct, results in the same State constitutional implications for similar police conduct. In this case, for example, Detective Morelli's conduct of identifying himself as a police officer and ordering the defendant to stop is the same, whether or not the defendant submitted to the officer's show of authority. It would be an anomaly to hold that the officer's conduct was a seizure had the defendant submitted, but because the defendant did not submit, the same conduct by the officer was not a seizure. If the officer's attempt to detain the defendant lacks reasonable suspicion, it is unlawful whether or not the defendant submits to the show of authority. Thus, by defining the moment a seizure occurs by the police officer's conduct, "the police [can] determine in advance whether the conduct contemplated will implicate [the state constitution]."

Second, constitutional protections become "meaningful only when it is assured that at some point the conduct of those charged with enforcing the laws can be subjected to the more detached, neutral scrutiny of a judge who must evaluate the reasonableness of a particular search or seizure." *Terry*, 392 U.S. at 21. The *Mendenhall* test achieves this goal by providing an objective standard for judicial review of the seizure. *See Mendenhall*, 446 U.S. at 554. Thus, our holding allows courts to continue to objectively evaluate the reasonableness of the police officer's actions, not the defendant's reaction. Third, we do not write on a blank slate for defining when a seizure occurs. An analysis that focuses exclusively on the conduct of the police is, as several state courts have pointed out, consistent with the well-settled definition of seizure in *Mendenhall*. In *Quezada*, a police officer called to the defendant, "Hey, you, stop," and after the defendant did not respond, called out again, "Hey, I want to speak to you." One of the key factors in our analysis of whether a seizure occurred was that the officer used "language indicating that compliance was not optional." We thus concluded that, "[g]iven the late hour, the absence of other citizens in the vicinity, the presence of two uniformed police officers, and the language of [the officer's] requests, no reasonable person would have believed he was free to ignore the officer and simply walk away." In holding that there was a sufficient "show of authority" to effect a seizure, our analysis focused upon the officer's actions and the other surrounding circumstances. The defendant's reaction was not a part of our seizure analysis.

Finally, our holding serves to effectuate the goal of the exclusionary rule to deter police misconduct. Indeed, one of the primary criticisms of the holding in *Hodari D.* is that it is subject to potential abuse. *See, e.g., Stoute*, 665 N.E.2d at 97-98 (noting that the holding in *Hodari D.* would allow "the police [to] turn a hunch into a reasonable suspicion by inducing the conduct…justifying the suspicion" (quotation omitted)). Thus, because the police are not required to possess reasonable suspicion prior to asserting their authority under *Hodari D.*, that rule "will encourage unlawful displays of force that will frighten countless innocent citizens into surrendering whatever privacy rights they may still have."

Having determined when a seizure occurs under part I, article 19, we must now determine when the defendant was seized. As stated above, a seizure occurs only when a reasonable person believes he is not free to leave because the officer, by means of physical force or show of authority, has in some way restrained the liberty of the person. The analysis is an objective one, requiring a determination of whether the defendant's freedom of movement was sufficiently curtailed by considering how a reasonable person in the defendant's position would have understood his situation.

In this case, although Detective Morelli was in an unmarked cruiser and wearing street clothes, he yelled to the defendant, identified himself as a police officer and ordered the defendant to stop. Detective Morelli then pursued the defendant on foot, again identifying himself as a police officer and ordering the defendant to stop. In view of all the circumstances, the encounter transcended a mere request to communicate. Given Detective Morelli's repeated identification of himself as a police officer and his orders to stop, no reasonable person would have believed he was free to ignore the officer and simply walk away. Thus, the defendant was seized when Detective Morelli first identified himself as a police officer and ordered the defendant to stop.

NOTES

1. Under the New Hampshire Constitution "a seizure occurs when an officer, by means of physical force or show of authority, has in some way restrained the liberty of the person." *State v. Beauchesne*, 868 A.2d 972 (N.H. 2005).

2. The Tennessee Supreme Court held that a defendant was seized, for purposes of the state constitution, "at the moment when the officer pulled up behind the defendant's stopped vehicle and activated his blue emergency lights." *State v. Williams*, 185 S.W.3d 311 (Tenn. 2006).

3. A seizure does not occur under article I, section 6 of the Delaware Constitution when uniformed officers follow a walking pedestrian and request to speak to him, without doing anything more. *Ross v. State*, 925 A.2d 489 (Del. 2007).

4. The rationale of *Hodari D.* was held to be contrary to the unique language in article I, section 8 of the Washington Constitution that restricts police invasions of privacy: "No person shall be disturbed in his private affairs, or his home invaded, without authority of law." *State v. Young*, 957 P.2d 681 (Wash. 1998).

G. WARRANTLESS AUTOMOBILE SEARCH INCIDENT TO ARREST

STATE v. AFANA
233 P.3d 879 (Wash. 2010)

ALEXANDER, J.

Mark Joseph Afana asks this court to reverse a decision of the Court of Appeals in which that court reversed the trial court's suppression of drug evidence found in his car. Afana contends that the warrantless search of his car incident to the arrest of his passenger violated the Fourth Amendment to the United States Constitution and article I, section 7 of the Washington Constitution. Because the arresting officer did not, at the time of the search, have a reasonable basis to believe that the arrestee posed a safety risk or that Afana's car contained evidence of the crime for which the arrest was made, we hold that the trial court properly suppressed the drug evidence as fruit of an unconstitutional search under article I, section 7. In reversing the Court of Appeals, we reject the State's proposed good faith exception to our exclusionary rule.

Facts and Procedural History

At 3:39 a.m. on June 13, 2007, Deputy Sheriff Miller noticed a car parked at the corner of Rimrock and Houston streets in Spokane County. Although the car was legally parked, the deputy's suspicions were aroused and, consequently, he parked behind the car and shined his spotlight on it. The light revealed two people inside the car. Miller then approached the car and asked the occupants what they were doing. The driver said they were watching a movie on his portable DVD (digital video disc) player.

Deputy Miller proceeded to ask both occupants for identification. The driver, Afana, gave the deputy his driver's license; the passenger, Jennifer Bergeron, gave her name. The deputy made a note of both names and handed Afana's license back to him. He then advised Afana and Bergeron that they should find some other place to watch the movie. After returning to his patrol car, Deputy Miller ran warrant checks on both names. The check disclosed that there was an existing warrant for the arrest of Bergeron for the misdemeanor offense of trespass. Because, at this point, Afana and Bergeron were beginning to drive away, the deputy turned on his emergency lights in order to stop the car.

After the car stopped, Miller walked to it and asked Bergeron to step out. When she complied, he placed her under arrest.[1] Deputy Miller then asked Afana to step out of the car. When he did so, Miller proceeded to search the interior of the car. The search turned up a black cloth bag behind the driver's seat with the words "'My Chemical Romance'" on the outside. The bag contained a crystalline substance that the deputy said "looked like Methamphetamine." Marijuana, a glass marijuana pipe, needles, and plastic scales were also found in the bag. The discovery of these items caused Deputy Miller to arrest Afana.

While Afana's petition for review was pending here, the United States Supreme Court issued its decision in *Arizona v. Gant*, 556 U.S. 332 (2009). There, the Court said that "[p]olice may search a vehicle incident to a recent occupant's arrest only if the arrestee is within reaching distance of the passenger compartment at the time of the search or it is reasonable to believe the vehicle contains evidence of the offense of arrest." Upon granting review, we asked the parties to provide supplemental briefing on the effect, if any, of *Gant*. The Washington Defender Association, the American Civil Liberties Union, and the Washington Association of Criminal Defense Lawyers submitted briefs as amici curiae. Prior to oral argument in this case, our court held, consistent with *Gant*, that under article I, section 7 of our state constitution,

> the search of a vehicle incident to the arrest of a recent occupant is unlawful absent a reasonable basis to believe that the arrestee poses a safety risk or that the vehicle contains evidence of the crime of arrest that could be concealed or destroyed, and that these concerns exist at the time of the search.

State v. Patton, 219 P.3d 651 (2009).

Was there authority of law for the search of Afana's car?
Afana contends that the search of his car incident to the arrest of his passenger violated his rights under the Fourth Amendment to the United States Constitution and article I, section 7 of the Washington Constitution. Suppl. Br. of Pet'r at 6. He asserts, therefore, the fruits of this search were properly suppressed by the trial court. "When a party claims both state and federal constitutional violations, we turn first to our state constitution." Article I, section 7 of our state constitution provides: "No person shall be disturbed in his private affairs, or his home invaded, without authority of law." In light of this provision, we must first determine whether Deputy Miller's search constituted a disturbance of Afana's private affairs. We have long recognized a privacy interest in automobiles and their contents.

Thus, the search of Afana's car unquestionably constituted a disturbance of his private affairs.

We must next ask whether the search was justified by authority of law. The "authority of law" requirement of article I, section 7 is satisfied by a valid warrant, subject to a few jealously guarded exceptions. It is always the State's burden to establish that such an exception applies. As we have observed, Deputy Miller did not have a warrant to search Afana's car. Unless it can be shown that the search in question fell within one of the carefully drawn exceptions to the warrant requirement, we must conclude that it was made without authority of law.

The exception at issue here is the automobile search incident to arrest exception. This brings us to a discussion of the aforementioned decision of the United States Supreme Court in *Gant* and this court's decision in *Patton*. In *Gant*, the United States Supreme Court repudiated what it characterized as other courts' "broad reading" of its decision in *New York v. Belton*, 453 U.S. 454 (1981). *Gant*, 129 S.Ct. at 1719. This decision is significant because courts around the country had been of the view that under *Belton* an automobile search did not run afoul of the Fourth Amendment to the United States Constitution as long as it was incident to a recent occupant's arrest, even if there was no possibility of the arrestee gaining access to the automobile at the time the search was conducted. In *Gant*, the Supreme Court, seemingly reining in the reach of *Belton*, held that under the Fourth Amendment "[p]olice may search a vehicle incident to a recent occupant's arrest *only* if the arrestee is within reaching distance of the passenger compartment at the time of the search or it is reasonable to believe the vehicle contains evidence of the offense of arrest." *Gant*, 129 S.Ct. at 1723 (emphasis added).

Following *Gant*, we ruled in *Patton* that article I, section 7 of the state constitution "requires no less" than the Fourth Amendment, and thus

> the search of a vehicle incident to the arrest of a recent occupant is unlawful absent a reasonable basis to believe that the arrestee poses a safety risk or that the vehicle contains evidence of the crime of arrest that could be concealed or destroyed, and that these concerns exist at the time of the search.

In *Buelna Valdez*, a decision handed down shortly after *Patton*, we reiterated that a warrantless search of an automobile is permissible under the search incident to arrest exception only "when that search is necessary to preserve officer safety or prevent destruction or concealment of evidence of the crime of arrest." In view of *Gant* and our recent decisions in *Patton* and *Buelna Valdez*, the question before us, further refined, is whether the search in this case was justified by a concern for the safety of the arresting officer or the concealment or destruction of evidence of the crime of arrest.

Nothing in the record justifies the search that took place here as incident to arrest. We say that because, while the warrant for Bergeron's arrest clearly gave Deputy Miller a valid basis for arresting her, he had no reason to believe that the vehicle in which she was a passenger contained evidence of the crime for which she was being arrested, namely, trespass. Nor did the deputy have reason to believe that the arrestee, Bergeron, posed a safety risk since she was already in custody at the time of the search.

Furthermore, the fact that the driver of the car, Afana, was unsecured at the time of the search does not justify the search. This is so because he was not under arrest at the time the search was conducted and, as we have observed, the United States Supreme Court said in *Gant* that "[p]olice may search a vehicle incident to a recent occupant's arrest only if the *arrestee* is within reaching distance of the passenger compartment at the time of the search." *Gant*, 129 S.Ct. at 1723 (emphasis added). Similarly, in *Patton*, we said that "the search of a vehicle incident to the arrest of a recent occupant is unlawful absent a reasonable basis to believe that the *arrestee* poses a safety risk." When the search that is before us took place, the only arrestee, Bergeron, was in custody and posed no risk. Therefore, under *Patton*, the deputy had no authority of law to search Afana's vehicle because it was out of the reach of the arrestee at the time. Thus, the search violated article I, section 7 of our state constitution.

Should this court recognize a good faith exception to the exclusionary rule under article I, section 7?

The violation of Afana's right of privacy under article I, section 7 automatically implies the exclusion of the evidence seized. Notwithstanding that general principle, the State argues that the evidence should be admissible in Washington under a "good faith" exception to the exclusionary rule. The United States Supreme Court has adopted such an exception to the exclusionary rule for evidence seized in violation of the Fourth Amendment. *See* United States v. Leon, 468 U.S. 897 (1984).

The exception that court recognizes is based on the view that the exclusionary rule is intended simply to deter unlawful police action. Because the exclusionary rule "cannot be expected ... to deter objectively reasonable law enforcement activity," the United States Supreme Court has held that it should not be applied when police have acted in "good faith." By "good faith," the Court means "objectively reasonable reliance" on something that appeared to justify a search or seizure when it was made. Thus, the federal "good faith" exception is applicable when a search or seizure was unconstitutional but the police officer's belief that it was constitutional was objectively reasonable at the time.

Unlike its federal counterpart, Washington's exclusionary rule is "nearly categorical." *State v. Winterstein*, 220 P.3d 1226 (2009). This is due to the fact that article I, section 7 of our state constitution "clearly recognizes an individual's right to privacy with no express limitations." *State v. White*, 640 P.2d 1061 (1982). In contrast to the Fourth Amendment, article I, section 7 emphasizes "protecting personal rights rather than ... curbing governmental actions." This understanding of that provision of our state constitution has led us to conclude that the "right of privacy shall not be diminished by the judicial gloss of a selectively applied exclusionary remedy." Thus, while our state's exclusionary rule also aims to deter unlawful police action, its paramount concern is protecting an individual's right of privacy. Therefore, if a police officer has disturbed a person's "private affairs," we do not ask whether the officer's belief that this disturbance was justified was objectively reasonable, but simply whether the officer had the requisite "authority of law." If not, any evidence seized unlawfully will be suppressed. With very few exceptions, whenever the right of privacy is violated, the remedy follows automatically.

We hold that the search of Afana's car incident to the arrest of his passenger was unconstitutional under *Patton* and *Buelna Valdez*. We also reject the State's request that we adopt a "good faith" exception to the exclusionary rule as incompatible with article I, section 7 and hold that the evidence obtained as a result of this unlawful search must be suppressed. Therefore, we need not address the issue that was determinative for the trial court—i.e., whether the deputy's request for identification from Afana's passenger amounted to a seizure under article I, section 7 of the Washington Constitution.

NOTES

1. Under the Nevada Constitution, "there must exist both probable cause and exigent circumstances for police to conduct a warrantless search of an automobile incident to a lawful custodial arrest." *Camacho v. State*, 75 P.3d 370, 373–74 (Nev. 2003).

2. Under the Wyoming Constitution, a warrantless non-consensual search of a vehicle incident to the defendant's arrest was unreasonable when the operator was arrested for driving with a suspended license and was handcuffed outside the vehicle. *Pierce v. State*, 171 P.3d 525 (Wyo. 2007).

3. Under the Vermont Constitution, the police may not search a vehicle without a warrant after the driver has been arrested, handcuffed, and placed in a police car, unless there is a reasonable need to preserve evidence of a crime or protect the police officer's safety. *State v. Bauder*, 924 A.2d 38 (Vt. 2007).

H. MIRANDA VIOLATION – PHYSICAL EVIDENCE EXCLUDED

The United States Supreme Court held that physical evidence uncovered as a result of *Miranda* violations need not be suppressed. *United States v. Patane*, 542 U.S. 630 (2004). A contrary result has been reached under some state constitutions.

STATE v. PETERSON
923 A.2d 585 (Vt. 2007)

DOOLEY, J.

The issue in this case is the scope of the exclusionary rule in criminal cases, specifically, whether physical evidence obtained as a result of a violation of defendant's *Miranda* rights must be excluded at trial. We conclude that under chapter I, article 10 of the Vermont Constitution and the Vermont exclusionary rule, physical evidence obtained in violation of *Miranda* rights must be suppressed. We reverse in part and remand.

Defendant James Peterson appeals the denial of two suppression motions. Both involve a core set of undisputed facts. Defendant was looking for his girlfriend and drove his car next to a police vehicle so that he and the officer could speak out of their windows. Upon speaking to defendant, the officer smelled marijuana through the vehicle window. During the conversation, defendant admitted that he had been convicted of a drug offense and that he had a marijuana "roach" in his vehicle. The officer then asked defendant to exit the vehicle, which he did.

The officer patted defendant down; he found no weapons, but smelled the odor of marijuana emanating from the front pocket of defendant's sweatshirt. The officer patted the pocket and, feeling nothing, used his flashlight to look inside the pocket, where he saw green flakes of marijuana plant. When asked, defendant admitted he had picked the marijuana earlier that day from a plant or two he had at home for personal use. The officer then asked defendant for consent to search both his vehicle and his home; defendant consented to these searches both verbally and in writing. The written consent form identified defendant's residence to be searched as "3141 Jersey St. & property" in Panton, Vermont.

After searching defendant's vehicle and finding a burned marijuana cigarette as well as a blanket smelling of marijuana, the officer and a state police trooper proceeded to defendant's residence. Defendant was placed in handcuffs for protection of the police, but was advised by the officer that he was not under arrest. The handcuffs were removed upon arrival at defendant's residence and were intermittently taken on and off while the officers conducted the home search. During the home search, the officer located a garbage bag containing a significant amount of marijuana and marijuana paraphernalia. Defendant led the officers to one marijuana plant growing behind his house.

Upon completion of the home search, the officer informed defendant that they would proceed to the Vergennes Police Department for processing. He placed defendant in handcuffs and instructed him to walk in front of the officer. During the walk, the officer expressed that he doubted so much marijuana came from just one plant, and asked defendant whether he had other marijuana plants. He did not inform defendant of his *Miranda* rights. Defendant eventually admitted to the existence of other plants. The officer asked defendant to show him the other plants, and the two men walked through a wooded area with high brush to a plot where twenty-seven growing plants were located. The plot where the twenty-seven plants were growing is not on, nor visible from, defendant's property.

As a result of the search, the police charged defendant with felony possession of more than twenty-five plants of marijuana and felony possession of marijuana consisting of an aggregate weight of one pound or more. Defendant moved to suppress "all evidence obtained by Vermont Law Enforcement Officials subsequent to his being taken into custody," asserting the officers in question violated his rights to be free from self-incrimination and unlawful search and seizure under both the Vermont and United States Constitutions. Defendant's primary argument was that the police had engaged in custodial interrogation, but failed to give defendant the required warnings under *Miranda v. Arizona*, 384 U.S. 436 (1966), and that the finding of the twenty-seven marijuana plants was the result of the unwarned interrogation. The State responded primarily that the search was pursuant to defendant's consent.

Following the testimony and argument on the motion, the court *sua sponte* requested that the parties brief the impact of *United States v. Patane*, 542 U.S. 630 (2004). After receiving the additional briefing, the court denied defendant's motion to suppress, basing its denial on *Patane*. The court concluded that defendant was in custody at the time he was questioned about possible additional marijuana plants, and as such was entitled to *Miranda* warnings at that time prior to further interrogation. Since it was undisputed that the police did not give defendant *Miranda* warnings, the court held that any statements made after defendant was in custody were made in response to interrogation that violated *Miranda*. The court denied the motion to suppress the twenty-seven plants, however, under *Patane*, which held that physical evidence uncovered as a result of a *Miranda* violation need not be suppressed. The court rejected defendant's additional argument that *Patane* is not good law under the Vermont Constitution.

Following the decision, defendant entered into a conditional plea of guilty allowing him to appeal the denial of his motion to suppress. The issue defendant raises on appeal is whether the twenty-seven marijuana plants must be suppressed.

We, therefore, consider the legality of the use of the twenty-seven marijuana plants as evidence and whether we will follow *United States v. Patane* under the Vermont Constitution.

Patane involved an arrest of a convicted felon for violating an abuse prevention order. Without completing *Miranda* warnings, the arresting officer asked the defendant whether he had a gun because gun possession was illegal for a felon, and there was a report that the defendant had a gun. Under persistent questioning, the defendant told the officer that he had a gun in his bedroom and gave permission to retrieve it. When the defendant was charged with illegally possessing a firearm, he moved to suppress the gun as the fruit of a confession given as a result of a custodial interrogation without *Miranda* warnings.

A majority of the United States Supreme Court concluded that the gun was admissible, but it did so in two separate opinions that differed in part. The plurality opinion written by Justice Thomas and joined by Chief Justice Rehnquist and Justice Scalia held:

> [T]he *Miranda* rule is a prophylactic employed to protect against violations of the Self-Incrimination Clause. The Self-Incrimination Clause, however, is not implicated by the admission into evidence of the physical fruit of a voluntary statement. Accordingly, there is no justification for extending the *Miranda* rule to this context. And just as the Self-Incrimination Clause primarily focuses on the criminal trial, so too does the *Miranda* rule. The *Miranda* rule is not a code of police conduct, and police do not violate the Constitution (or even the *Miranda* rule, for that matter) by mere failures to warn. For this reason, the exclusionary rule articulated in cases such as *Wong Sun* does not apply.

The plurality went on to explain that because prophylactic rules "sweep beyond the actual protections of the Self-Incrimination Clause, any further extension of these rules must be justified by its necessity for the protection of the actual right against compelled self-incrimination." It concluded that a "blanket suppression rule could not be justified by reference to the Fifth Amendment goal of assuring trustworthy evidence or by any deterrence rationale," and that such a rule would therefore violate the Court's requirement that it maintain "the closest possible fit...between the Self-Incrimination Clause and any rule designed to protect it."

The concurring opinion of Justices Kennedy and O'Connor accepted part of the plurality's rationale. They concluded that admission of the gun did "not run the risk of admitting into trial an accused's coerced incriminating statements against himself" and went on to state:

In light of the important probative value of reliable physical evidence, it is doubtful that exclusion can be justified by a deterrence rationale sensitive to both law enforcement interests and a suspect's rights during an in-custody interrogation.

Three of the dissenters, Justices Souter, Stevens and Ginsburg, defined the issue as "whether courts should apply the fruit of the poisonous tree doctrine lest we create an incentive for the police to omit *Miranda* warnings before custodial interrogation." They concluded that the majority decision created an "unjustifiable invitation to law enforcement officers to flout *Miranda* when there may be physical evidence to be gained." Justice Breyer joined the dissent except where the failure to give *Miranda* warnings "was in good faith."

In examining whether we should follow *Patane* under the Vermont Constitution, we start with the context of our decision. The right against self-incrimination is guaranteed in the Fifth Amendment to the United States Constitution, which prohibits compelling a criminal defendant to "be a witness against himself." U.S. Const. amend. V. Equivalently, article 10 of the Vermont Constitution prohibits compelling a person "to give evidence against oneself." Vt. Const. ch. I, art. 10. We have held, with respect to adults, that "the article 10 privilege against self-incrimination and that contained in the Fifth Amendment are synonymous." Consistent with this view, we have held that evidence gathered in violation of the prophylactic rules established in *Miranda* is also a violation of article 10. We have not, however, gone beyond *Miranda* and found a violation of the principles of that decision where the United States Supreme Court has not done so.

If this case involved the substance of *Miranda*, for example, the nature of the warnings or the circumstances under which they must be given, the State would have a strong argument that our precedents require that we not go beyond the limits in the decisions of the United States Supreme Court. This, however, is a case in which the district court found a violation of *Miranda* under accepted principles and defendant made a confession to an additional crime under custodial interrogation, a confession that is inadmissible under *Miranda*. The issue is the scope of the remedy for the *Miranda* violation, and on this point our precedents take a different view from that of the United States Supreme Court.

A starting point for examination of this question is *State v. Brunelle*, 534 A.2d 198, 200 (Vt. 1987), where we addressed whether we would follow the decisions in *Harris v. New York*, 401 U.S. 222 (1971), and *United States v. Havens*, 446 U.S. 620 (1980). These decisions allowed the prosecution to impeach a criminal defendant who testifies with statements taken in violation of *Miranda*. We rejected these decisions under the Vermont Constitution because they are inconsistent with the right under article 10 of a defendant "to be heard by himself and his counsel." We held instead that the prosecution can impeach with the suppressed evidence only where "a defendant has testified on direct examination to facts contradicted by previously suppressed evidence bearing directly on the crime charged." Although *Brunelle* is based primarily on a defendant's right to testify, the decision explained its relationship to the right against self-incrimination and *Miranda*. As discussed above, it held that a violation of *Miranda* was also a violation of the article 10 right against self-incrimination. Accordingly, the Court described *Brunelle* as "a limited exception to *State v. Badger*, 450 A.2d 336, 349 (Vt. 1982), which held that '[e]vidence obtained in violation of the Vermont Constitution, or as a result of a violation, cannot be admitted at trial as a matter of state law.'" *Brunelle* necessarily holds that the broad exclusionary rule of *Badger* applies to *Miranda* violations.

Badger is itself an important precedent because it applied a locally-created exclusionary rule to *Miranda* violations to suppress physical evidence, there the defendant's clothing. *Badger* found a violation of article 10 based in part on a failure to give *Miranda* warnings and an invalid waiver under *Miranda*, although it did not explicitly hold that a violation of *Miranda* was a violation of article 10. It went on to develop the broad exclusionary rule for such a violation, because:

> Introduction of such evidence at trial eviscerates our most sacred rights, impinges on individual privacy, perverts our judicial process, distorts any notion of fairness, and encourages official misconduct.

With respect to the clothing at issue, it held that "the seizure of the clothing is too directly connected to the illegal confession to allow" its admission.

Defendant argues with considerable force that *Badger* is directly on point and rejects the *Patane* holding that the exclusionary rule does not extend to physical evidence acquired as a result of a *Miranda* violation. The holding in *Badger* is reinforced by *Brunelle*, and *Brunelle* is independently important because it rejects *Harris* and *Havens* both significant building blocks of the limited exclusionary rule set forth in *Patane* and demonstrates that our adherence to *Miranda* under article 10 does not include adherence to the federal exclusionary rule for *Miranda* violations.

We note that the three state supreme courts that have analyzed *Patane* under their state constitutions have concluded that they cannot adopt it because it undercuts the enforcement of *Miranda*. In *Commonwealth v. Martin*, 827 N.E.2d 198 (Mass. 2005), the Massachusetts Supreme Judicial Court refused to follow *Patane* in enforcing *Miranda* rights through article 12 of the Declaration of Rights of the Massachusetts

Constitution. The court agreed with the observation of Justice Souter, dissenting in *Patane*, that the decision added "'an important inducement for interrogators to ignore the [*Miranda*] rule'" and created "'an unjustifiable invitation to law enforcement officers to flout *Miranda* when there may be physical evidence to be gained.'" It concluded: "To apply the *Patane* analysis to the broader rights embodied in article 12 would have a corrosive effect on them, undermine the respect we have accorded them, and demean their importance to a system of justice chosen by the citizens of Massachusetts in 1780." Thus, it followed earlier decisions in which it had rejected United States Supreme Court rulings weakening the applicability of *Miranda*.

In *State v. Knapp*, 700 N.W.2d 899 (Wis. 2005), the Wisconsin Supreme Court reached the same conclusion under article I, section 8 of the Wisconsin Constitution in a case where the evidence showed that the police had intentionally violated *Miranda*. It relied on the loss of deterrence, the discouragement of police misconduct, and the need to preserve judicial integrity, in deciding to reject *Patane*.

The decisions in *Martin* and *Knapp* were followed under section 10, article I of the Ohio Constitution by the Ohio Supreme Court in *State v. Farris*, 849 N.E.2d 985 (Ohio 2006). Again, the main rationale is the reduction in deterrence of *Miranda* violations:

> We believe that to hold otherwise would encourage law-enforcement officers to withhold *Miranda* warnings and would thus weaken section 10, article I of the Ohio Constitution. In cases like this one, where possession is the basis for the crime and physical evidence is the keystone of the case, warning suspects of their rights can hinder the gathering of evidence. When physical evidence is central to a conviction and testimonial evidence is not, there can arise a virtual incentive to flout *Miranda*. We believe that the overall administration of justice in Ohio requires a law-enforcement environment in which evidence is gathered in conjunction with *Miranda*, not in defiance of it.

We agree with the analysis and result reached in each of these cases.

For the above reasons, we conclude that we will not follow *United States v. Patane* under article 10 of the Vermont Constitution and our exclusionary rule. Physical evidence gained from statements obtained under circumstances that violate *Miranda* is inadmissible in criminal proceedings as fruit of the poisonous tree. Since it is undisputed that the marijuana plants were such fruit in this case, the district court erred in failing to suppress them.

NOTES

1. Under the self-incrimination clause in article I, section 10 of the Ohio Constitution, only evidence "obtained as the direct result of statements made in custody without the benefit of a *Miranda* warning should be excluded." *State v. Farris*, 849 N.E.2d 985 (Ohio 2006).

2. The Massachusetts Supreme Court held that evidence received as the result of a defendant's pre-warning statement to police had to be suppressed as the "fruit" of the detective's unlawful questioning, to safeguard the Massachusetts Constitution's privilege against self-incrimination. *Commonwealth v. Martin*, 827 N.E.2d 198 (Mass. 2005).

CHAPTER VIII

PROPERTY RIGHTS

A. INTRODUCTION

State constitutions and state law protect a variety of property rights. In fact, the U.S. Supreme Court has made clear that, in general, state law (not federal law) primarily determines what constitutes "property" protected by various constitutional provisions: "Because the Constitution protects rather than creates property interests, the existence of a property interest is determined by reference to 'existing rules or understandings that stem from an independent source such as state law.'" *Phillips v. Washington Legal Foundation*, 524 U.S. 156, 164 (1998).

The major section of this chapter focuses on one state constitutional provision that protects property rights and which has a direct federal counterpart. Most, if not all, state constitutions contain "takings clauses" which parallel the Takings Clause in the Fifth Amendment of the U.S. Constitution. With respect to takings law, this chapter covers an interesting story of dynamic federalism, with state courts and legislatures reacting negatively to a U.S. Supreme Court decision that interpreted the federal takings clause in favor of broad governmental power to take private property. Thus, although the state and federal takings clauses generally mirror each other in terms of language, the interpretation of some state takings provisions is significantly different from the U.S. Supreme Court's interpretation of the federal counterpart.

The chapter concludes with a lengthy excerpt from a recent Texas Supreme Court decision in which the Justices debate extensively just how much protection state constitutions should provide to economic rights and interests. This discussion is timely and important, arising in the context of laws requiring "eyebrow threaders" to have a state license that requires hundreds of hours of instruction to obtain. The final case thus raises overarching questions about the protection of economic rights under state constitutions. The case also transcends this chapter in several respects, demonstrating competing approaches to interpreting state constitutions and connecting with both federal due process jurisprudence and the state constitutional right to a remedy / due process of law provisions also considered in Chapter XII.

B. TAKINGS PROVISIONS AND THE POST-*KELO* STORY

Most state constitutions prohibit the government from taking private property for public use, unless just compensation is paid. The U.S. Constitution imposes a similar restraint, declaring "nor shall private property be taken for public use without just compensation." U.S. Const. Amend. V. In *Kelo v. City of New London*, 545 U.S. 469 (2005), the Supreme Court rejected a takings challenge to a city's plan for transferring certain private property obtained through eminent domain to private developers, because the Court held that the plan served a *public purpose* (redeveloping blighted or less valuable property for more valuable uses) and thus satisfied the "public use" requirement.

The *Kelo* prompted responses in many states, with only a handful of states failing to take any action following *Kelo*. In most states, there was strong objection to the notion that taking private property for redevelopment—as opposed to doing so to build schools or public buildings or roads, for example—was constitutional. Some states responded with legislation, others with constitutional amendments, and a few with court decisions favorable to property owners. As one co-author of this book puts it,

> over the last several years, through state legislation, state constitutional amendments and state-court decisions, property-rights advocates have made considerable gains—perhaps obtaining as much as, if not more than, a favorable *Kelo* decision could have offered them. As of today, most States have enacted legislation addressing issues of public use and eminent domain. Seven States have limited the public purposes for which eminent domain is acceptable. Nine States have enacted laws expressly limiting the States' power to exercise eminent domain. Five others have adopted variations on these themes. Some States have sought to reduce the potential abuse of eminent domain by developing procedural changes, requiring state agencies to make stronger showings of public use, requiring agencies to create redevelopment plans, and setting notice and offer requirements to prevent "stealth" condemnation. In other States, court rulings prompted the changes. In 2006, the Ohio and Oklahoma Supreme Courts extended their state constitutional protections against eminent domain beyond the federal baseline by holding that economic benefit alone does not constitutionally justify the exercise of eminent domain. Only a handful of States have not enacted legislation in the wake of *Kelo*.

Jeffrey S. Sutton, *San Antonio Independent School District v. Rodriguez And Its Aftermath*, 94 Va. L. Rev., 1963, 1984–85 (2008) (footnotes omitted).

Following are several state decisions that reject, modify or follow the *Kelo* rule, and illustrate the variety of state responses to *Kelo*.

CITY OF NORWOOD v. HORNEY
853 N.E.2d 1115 (Ohio 2006)

O'CONNOR, J.

We decide the constitutionality of a municipality's taking of an individual's property by eminent domain and transferring the property to a

QP

private entity for redevelopment. In doing so, we must balance two competing interests of great import in American democracy: (the individual's rights in the possession and security of property and the sovereign's power to take private property for the benefit of the community.) Interests in balance

Appropriation cases often represent more than a battle over a plot of cold sod in a farmland pasture or the plat of municipal land on which a building sits. For the individual property owner, the appropriation is not simply the seizure of a house. It is the taking of a home—the place where ancestors toiled, where families were raised, where memories were made. Fittingly, appropriations are scrutinized by the people and debated in their institutions.

Greater, personal significance of appropriation

In reviewing an appropriation similar to that at issue here, a sharply divided United States Supreme Court recently upheld the taking over a federal Fifth Amendment challenge mounted by individual property owners. *Kelo v. New London*, 545 U.S. 469 (2005). (Although it determined that the Federal Constitution did not prohibit the takings, the court acknowledged that property owners might find redress in the states' courts and legislatures, which remain free to restrict such takings pursuant to state laws and constitutions.) Kelo suggested one turn to States

In response to that invitation in *Kelo*, Ohio's General Assembly unanimously enacted 2005 Am.Sub.S.B. No. 167. (The legislature expressly noted in the Act its belief that as a result of *Kelo*, "the interpretation and use of the state's eminent domain law could be expanded to allow the taking of private property that is not within a blighted area, ultimately resulting in ownership of that property being vested in another private person in violation of Sections 1 and 19 of Article I, Ohio Constitution.") Expanded E.D. power from Kelo that state fought

The appellants' property was appropriated by the city of Norwood after the city determined that the appellants' neighborhood was a "deteriorating area," as that term is defined in the provisions governing appropriations in the Codified Ordinances of the City of Norwood ("Norwood Code"). (Although, as we shall discuss below, we have held that a city may take a slum, blighted, or deteriorated property for redevelopment, and suggested that the taking is proper even when the city transfers the appropriated property to a private party for redevelopment) we have never been asked whether a city may appropriate property that the city determines is in an area that may deteriorate in the future.   where rule stops

Rule for takings that's allowed.

We hold that although economic factors may be considered in determining whether private property may be appropriated, the fact that the appropriation would provide an economic benefit to the government and community, standing alone, does not satisfy the public-use requirement of Section 19, Article I of the Ohio Constitution.

I. RELEVANT BACKGROUND

A

Norwood and Its Denizens

The city of Norwood is a modern urban environment. Surrounded by the city of Cincinnati, Norwood was once home to several manufacturing plants and businesses that provided a substantial tax base for the municipality. Despite that industrial component, Norwood was, and for many remains, a desirable place to live. Norwood's neighborhoods were composed of traditional single-family houses and duplexes that provided homes to generations of families and many individuals.

Over the past 40 years, however, Norwood underwent many changes. Like many municipalities in Ohio, Norwood's industrial base eroded, taking with it tax dollars vital to the city. Municipal jobs and many services were eliminated, and the city is millions of dollars in debt. Though the financial outlook of Norwood has been altered greatly over the years, perhaps the most significant change for our purposes here is the physical nature of the city itself.

In the 1960s, property was appropriated from the appellants' neighborhood and used in the construction of a major highway—Interstate 71—through Cincinnati. In the neighborhoods affected, numerous homes were razed and front yards diminished in order to make way for the access roads and ramps to the highway. The streets became busier, creating safety problems for residents who had to back onto busy roadways from their driveways. Residential roads that once ran between major thoroughfares were bisected by the new highway, creating dead-end streets.

Over time, businesses arose in places where houses once stood. The neighborhood became less residential and more commercial. Other changes in the neighborhood's character followed. Traffic increased dramatically due to motorists seeking the highway and businesses in the area. Noise increased, and light pollution became more prevalent.

A private, limited-liability company, Rookwood Partners, Ltd. ("Rookwood"), entered discussions with Norwood about redeveloping the appellants' neighborhood. The preliminary plans for the development call for the construction of more than 200 apartments or condominiums and over 500,000 square feet of office and retail space (all of which would be owned by Rookwood), as well as two large public-parking facilities (which would be owned by Norwood) with spaces for more than 2,000 vehicles. The city expects the redeveloped area to result in nearly $2,000,000 in annual revenue for Norwood.

Norwood, operating with a deficit, was unable to fix the problems or redevelop the appellants' neighborhood on its own …. Discussions between Norwood and Rookwood culminated in a redevelopment contract in which Rookwood agreed to reimburse the city for the expenses of the project, including the costs arising from any need to use eminent domain to appropriate the property necessary for the project.

Rookwood preferred that Norwood acquire the property needed for the project through eminent domain, but Norwood resisted. It encouraged Rookwood to purchase the property through voluntary sales of homes and businesses, without the city's intervention. *E. Dr is enticing private sales*

Rookwood was largely successful; it secured acquisition agreements from a substantial majority of the owners of the property necessary to complete the project. The appellants, however, refused to sell.

Because the appellants refused to sell their property, Rookwood asked Norwood to appropriate the appellants' properties and transfer them to Rookwood. Rookwood, in turn, agreed to raze the existing structures (including the appellants' homes), reconfigure the streets, and redevelop the area. *Adjusted plan for those few who wouldn't sell*

B

The Takings

Norwood used funds provided by Rookwood to retain a consulting firm, Kinzelman Kline Grossman ("KKG"), to prepare an urban-renewal study of the appellants' neighborhood. The study concluded that the construction of I-71 and ensuing conversion of residential and industrial properties to commercial use had led to significant, negative changes in Norwood. Despite acknowledging that many homes were in fair to good condition, KKG concluded that the neighborhood was a "deteriorating area" as that term is defined in the Norwood Code. KKG further determined that the neighborhood would continue to deteriorate and that there would be "continuing piecemeal conversion" of residences to businesses that could be detrimental to the area. *Deterioration is in order*

Highway & businesses harmed Norwood

After public hearings and town meetings were held and the local planning commission recommended approval of the redevelopment plan, Norwood City Council passed a series of ordinances adopting the plan and authorizing the mayor to enter the redevelopment agreement with Rookwood and to appropriate the appellants' property. The city then filed complaints against the appellants to appropriate their properties.

Plan to → Appropriate granted
N) Suit filed to appropriate

At trial, Norwood relied on the testimony of KKG employees to support its conclusion that the appellants' neighborhood was deteriorating. [Ultimately, the trial] concluded … that there was no showing that

Trial ct believes that there was no abuse in deterioration determination

Norwood had abused its discretion in finding that the neighborhood was a "deteriorating area."

II. CONSTITUTIONAL CONSIDERATIONS

A

Individual Property Rights

The rights related to property, i.e., to acquire, use, enjoy, and dispose of property, are among the most revered in our law and traditions. Indeed, property rights are integral aspects of our theory of democracy and notions of liberty.

Believed to be derived fundamentally from a higher authority and natural law, property rights were so sacred that they could not be entrusted lightly to "the uncertain virtue of those who govern." As such, property rights were believed to supersede constitutional principles.

In light of [such] notions of property rights, it is not surprising that the founders of our state expressly incorporated individual property rights into the Ohio Constitution in terms that reinforced the sacrosanct nature of the individual's "inalienable" property rights, Section 1, Article I, which are to be held forever "inviolate." Section 19, Article I.

Ohio has always considered the right of property to be a fundamental right. There can be no doubt that the bundle of venerable rights associated with property is strongly protected in the Ohio Constitution and must be trod upon lightly, no matter how great the weight of other forces.

B

The State's Power of Eminent Domain

There is an inherent tension between the individual's right to possess and preserve property and the state's competing interests in taking it for the communal good. Mindful of that friction and the potential for misuse of the eminent-domain power, James Madison's proposed draft of the Takings Clause included two equitable limitations on its use that were eventually incorporated into the Fifth Amendment: the "public use" requirement and the "just compensation" rule. The amendment confirms the sovereign's authority to take, but conditions the exercise of that authority upon satisfaction of two conjunctive standards: that the taking is for a "public use" and that "just compensation" for the taking is given to the property owner.

Similarly, almost every state constitution eventually included provisions related to eminent-domain powers. Both the Northwest Ordinance and the Ohio Constitution recognized the state's right to take property from an individual, but conditioned the right to take on the equitable considerations of just compensation and public use. Section 19,

Article I requires that the taking be necessary for the common welfare and, to "insure that principle of natural justice," that the persons deprived of their property will be compensated for "every injury resulting from this act," "every infringement on their [property] rights," and "every injurious interference with the control of their own property."

It is axiomatic that the federal and Ohio constitutions forbid the state to take private property for the sole benefit of a private individual, even when just compensation for the taking is provided. A sine qua non of eminent domain in Ohio is the understanding that the sovereign may use its appropriation powers only upon necessity for the common good. *[just compensation; public use; necessity for the common good]*

However, the concept of public use has been malleable and elusive. While broad conceptualizations of public use evolved during the first decades of the 20th century, civic and government leaders became increasingly concerned with living conditions in urban areas and the array of social problems caused by the lack of adequate and safe, affordable housing in cities. The federal government eventually enacted sweeping legislation in an attempt to ameliorate some of those concerns. These modern urban-renewal and redevelopment efforts fostered the convergence of the public-health police power and eminent domain. *[Public health]*

In this paradigm, the concept of public use was altered. Rather than furthering a public benefit by appropriating property to create something needed in a place where it did not exist before, the appropriations power was used to destroy a threat to the public's general welfare and well-being; slums and blighted or deteriorated property. *[from creating to destroying]*

Historic notions equating physical, moral, and social illnesses with slums and blighted areas were reinforced. The term "blight" itself, borrowed from science and connoting an organism that promotes disease, became synonymous with urban decay, and courts were soon invoking the language of disease. Almost all courts, including this one, have consistently upheld takings that seized slums and blighted or deteriorated private property for redevelopment, even when the property was then transferred to a private entity, and continue to do so. These rulings properly employed an elastic public-use analysis to promote eminent domain as an answer to clear and present public-health concerns, permitting razing and "slum clearance."

Inherent in many decisions affirming pronouncements that economic development alone is sufficient to satisfy the public-use clause is an artificial judicial deference to the state's determination that there was sufficient public use. *[Assumption of sufficient public use]*

Although there is merit in the notion that deference must be paid to a government's determination that there is sufficient evidence to support a taking in a case in which the taking is for a use that has previously been determined to be a public use, see *Kelo*, 545 U.S. at 490, (Kennedy, J., concurring), that deferential review is not satisfied by superficial scrutiny. To the contrary, it remains an essential and critical aspect in the analysis of any proposed taking.

There can be no doubt that our role—though limited—is a critical one that requires vigilance in reviewing state actions for the necessary restraint, including review to ensure that the state takes no more than that necessary to promote the public use, and that the state proceeds fairly and effectuates takings without bad faith, pretext, discrimination, or improper purpose. Thus, our precedent does not demand rote deference to legislative findings in eminent-domain proceedings, but rather, it preserves the courts' traditional role as guardian of constitutional rights and limits. Accordingly, "questions of public *purpose* aside, whether…proposed condemnations [are] consistent with the Constitution's 'public use' requirement [is] a constitutional question squarely within the Court's authority."

A court's independence is critical, particularly when the authority for the taking is delegated to another or the contemplated public use is dependent on a private entity. In such cases, the courts must ensure that the grant of authority is construed strictly and that any doubt over the propriety of the taking is resolved in favor of the property owner.

Similarly, when the state takes an individual's private property for transfer to another individual or to a private entity rather than for use by the state itself, the judicial review of the taking is paramount. A primordial purpose of the public-use clause is to prevent the legislature from permitting the state to take private property from one individual simply to give it to another.

Although we have permitted economic concerns to be considered in addition to other factors, such as slum clearance, when determining whether the public-use requirement is sufficient, we have never found economic benefits alone to be a sufficient public use for a valid taking. We decline to do so now.

We hold that an economic or financial benefit alone is insufficient to satisfy the public-use requirement of Section 19, Article I. In light of that holding, any taking based solely on financial gain is void as a matter of law, and the courts owe no deference to a legislative finding that the proposed taking will provide financial benefit to a community.

III. APPLICATION OF THE LAW TO THE FACTS

A

Norwood Code's Use of "Deteriorating Area" as a Standard for a Taking

The takings in the instant cases were based solely on a finding that the neighborhood was a deteriorating area. But what notice does the term "deteriorating area" give to an individual property owner? *[handwritten: QP re: deterrating area]*

As defined by the Norwood Code, a "deteriorating area" is not the same as a "slum or blighted or deteriorated area," the standard typically employed for a taking. And here, of course, there was no evidence to support a taking under that standard. To the contrary, the buildings in the neighborhood were generally in good condition and the owners were not delinquent in paying property taxes. There is no suggestion that the area was vermin-infested or subject to high crime rates or outbreaks of disease, or otherwise posed an impermissible risk to the larger community. *[handwritten: Buildings in Q in good shape]*

Some of the factors upon which the court relied, such as diversity of ownership, could apply to many neighborhoods. And although the term commonly appears in eminent-domain cases and regulations, it is susceptible of many meanings and to manipulation.

Moreover, diversity of ownership is a factor of questionable weight. As seems to have been the case here, diversity of ownership is typically considered to be a negative factor for a neighborhood because it purportedly impedes development. Yet Rookwood was able to secure virtually every property owner's assent to sale without any apparent difficulty. Thus, though diversity of ownership may be a factor to consider in determining whether an area is deteriorated, it is not a compelling one. *[handwritten: why does this cut against gov?]*

In essence, "deteriorating area" is a standardless standard. Rather than affording fair notice to the property owner, the Norwood Code merely recites a host of subjective factors that invite ad hoc and selective enforcement—a danger made more real by the malleable nature of the public-benefit requirement. We must be vigilant in ensuring that so great a power as eminent domain, which historically has been used in areas where the most marginalized groups live, is not abused. *[handwritten: deterorating area isn't a good standard]*

As important, the standard for "deteriorating area" defined in the Norwood Code is satisfied not just upon a finding that a neighborhood *is* deteriorating or *will* deteriorate, but is also satisfied by a finding that it "*is in danger of* deteriorating into a blighted area." The statutory definition, therefore, incorporates not only the existing condition of a neighborhood, but also extends to what that neighborhood might become. But what it *might* become may be no more likely than what *might not* become. Such a speculative standard is inappropriate in the context of eminent domain, even under the modern, broad interpretation of "public use."

[handwritten: Problematic clause]

A fundamental determination that must be made before permitting the appropriation of a slum or a blighted or deteriorated property for redevelopment is that the property, because of its existing state of disrepair or dangerousness, poses a threat to the public's health, safety, or general welfare. Although we adhere to a broad construction of "public use," we hold that government does not have the authority to appropriate private property based on mere belief, supposition, or speculation that the property may pose such a threat in the future. To permit a taking of private property based solely on a finding that the property is deteriorating or in danger of deteriorating would grant an impermissible, unfettered power to the government to appropriate.

Holding!
gov loses

We therefore hold that ... the term "deteriorating area" cannot be used as a standard for a taking, because it inherently incorporates speculation as to the future condition of the property into the decision on whether a taking is proper rather than focusing that inquiry on the property's condition at the time of the proposed taking.

No equitable use?

Because Norwood may not justify its taking of appellants' property on either the basis that the neighborhood was deteriorating or on the basis that the redeveloped area would bring economic value to the city, there is no showing that the taking was for public use. Our conclusion is not altered by the amount of compensation offered to the property owners in this case, even if it was in excess of the fair market value of their property. Though the questions of just compensation and public use are both critical in an eminent-domain analysis, they must be assessed and satisfied independently. Here, there is not an adequate showing that the takings were for a public use.

BD. OF COUNTY COMM'RS OF MUSKOGEE COUNTY v. LOWERY
136 P.3d 639 (Okl. 2006)

LAVENDER, J.

QB

The issues in the present cause are as follows: (1) whether the County's exercise of eminent domain in the instant cases is for public use in accordance with Article 2, § 23 and Article 2, § 24 of the Oklahoma Constitution and (2) whether the County's taking for purposes of economic development of Muskogee County constitutes "public purposes" within the meaning of 27 O.S.2001 § 5 to support such a taking.

No Just compensation?

I

FACTS AND PROCEDURAL HISTORY

Exercise of E.D.

Plaintiff/Appellee County initiated condemnation proceedings against Defendant/Landowners for the purpose of acquiring temporary and permanent right-of-way easements for the installation of three water pipelines. Two of the proposed water pipelines (referred to by the parties and hereinafter collectively referred to as "the Eagle Pipeline") would solely serve Energetix, a privately owned electric generation plant, which was proposed for construction in Muskogee County. By way of the Eagle Pipeline, Energetix's proposed operations would require a maximum of 8,000,000 gallons of water daily for use in cooling towers associated with the operation of an 825 megawatt natural gas-fired power plant.

purpose of EP

what 2 of the pipelines would do

Energetix proposed to build the third water pipeline (hereinafter "the Water District Pipeline") on behalf of the Rural Water District No. 5 (hereinafter "Water District") pursuant to a contract...which expressly provided for Energetix's agreement to build this pipeline at no cost to the Water District "as part of the consideration to induce certain property owners to grant private easements for the Eagle Pipeline." The Water District Pipeline was intended to serve residents of the Water District who were not currently being served and to enhance current water service to residents of the Water District, who were receiving it. *Purpose of WDP*

Landowners filed an answer and counterclaim in each case seeking declaratory and injunctive relief on the basis that the County's proposed taking was an unlawful taking of private property for private use and private purpose of the private company, Energetix, in violation of 27 O.S.2001 § 5 and the eminent domain provisions contained within both the Oklahoma Constitution and the U.S. Constitution. *D's claims (original)*

The Report of Commissioners was thereafter filed, which provided the takings were for a public purpose and established the amount of just compensation to be awarded to Landowners for their respective properties. Landowners filed their respective Exceptions to the Commissioners' Report, objecting primarily on the basis that the takings were not for a valid public purpose, but rather an unlawful taking of private property for private purpose. *D's next set of claims*

w's counter

The trial court ultimately agreed with the County and entered an Order confirming the takings in these cases. Landowners appealed, and the COCA reversed and remanded...[holding] that the takings in the instant cases were unlawful in that they were for the direct benefit of a private company and not for "public purposes" as required.

Procedural posture

II

THE LAW APPLICABLE TO THIS CONDEMNATION PROCEEDING

The Oklahoma General Eminent Domain Statute and Constitutional Eminent Domain Provisions

The County sought to condemn Landowners' private property pursuant to its general eminent domain power granted by 27 O.S.2001 § 5, which provides as follows:

> Any county, city, town, township, school district, or board of education, or any board or official having charge of cemeteries created and existing under the laws of this state, shall have power to condemn lands in like manner as railroad companies, for highways, rights-of-way, building sites, cemeteries, public parks and *other public purposes*.

Additionally, we are guided by the applicable general federal constitutional and state constitutional eminent domain provisions, including and perhaps most notably our special provision concerning the taking of private property. Article 2, § 23 provides as follows:

> No private property shall be taken or damaged for private use, with or without compensation, unless by consent of the owner, except for private ways of necessity, or for drains and ditches across lands of others for agricultural, mining, or sanitary purposes, in such manner as may be prescribed by law.

Our Constitution further generally provides "private property shall not be taken or damaged for public use without just compensation." OKLA. CONST. art. 2, § 24. That constitutional provision additionally states "[in] all cases of condemnation of private property for public or private use, the determination of the character of the use shall be a judicial question." The law is clear that "[p]rivate property may not be taken or damaged by the condemning agency unless the taking or damage is necessary for the accomplishment of a lawful public purpose." [W]e have used the terms "public use" and "public purpose" interchangeably in our analysis of our state constitutional eminent domain provisions, and we therefore view these terms as synonymous.

The Constitutional Limitations and the Framers' Intent

It is settled law that the constitutional eminent domain provisions "are not grants of power, but limitations placed upon the exercise of government power." The framers of the Oklahoma Constitution ... recognized "that to protect both life and property is the first duty of government." In keeping with these principles, we have determined the government's power of eminent domain "lies dormant in the state until the Legislature by specific enactment designates the occasion, modes and agencies by which it may be placed in operation."

"Public Purpose" in the Context of Eminent Domain

[handwritten margin note: E.D. weved in favor of owner, so gov ~~~~ bears burden]

As a general rule, we construe our state constitutional eminent domain provisions "strictly in favor of the owner and against the condemning party." Additionally, Oklahoma eminent domain statutes must conform to the restrictions placed on the exercise of such power by the Oklahoma constitutional eminent domain provisions. We adhere to the strict construction of eminent domain statutes in keeping with our precedent, mindful of the critical importance of the protection of individual private property rights as recognized by the framers of both the U.S. Constitution and the Oklahoma Constitution. If we were to construe "public purpose" so broadly as to include economic development within those terms, then we would effectively abandon a basic limitation on government power by "wash[ing] out any distinction between private and public use of property- and thereby effectively delet[ing] the words 'for public use' from [the constitutional provisions limiting governmental power of eminent domain.]" *Kelo*, 125 S.Ct. at 2671 (O'Connor, J., dissenting). In our view, the power of eminent domain should be exercised with restraint and we therefore construe the term "public purpose" narrowly specifically in this context.

III

AS A MATTER OF OKLAHOMA CONSTITUTIONAL AND STATUTORY LAW, ECONOMIC DEVELOPMENT ALONE IS NOT A PUBLIC PURPOSE TO JUSTIFY THE EXERCISE OF COUNTY'S POWER OF EMINENT DOMAIN

The County's primary argument is that the general eminent domain statute ... authorizes its exercise of eminent domain for the sole purpose of economic development (i.e., increased taxes, jobs and public and private investment in the community) because economic development constitutes a "public purpose" within the meaning of the statute as well as the state constitutional eminent domain provisions.

We recognize the general rule that where legal relief is available on alternative, non-constitutional grounds, we avoid reaching a determination on the constitutional basis. However, the circumstances of this case lead us to the conclusion that it is necessary for us to reach a constitutional determination in addition to our statutory determination. Here, the two determinations are intertwined. The analysis under both the applicable eminent domain statute and under the state constitutional provisions turns on the identical determination of the meaning of the term "public purpose," which we have previously noted ... is synonymous with "public use" as provided in the Oklahoma Constitution. *[handwritten margin note: Why con analysis is necessary]*

Considering the fact that the proposed Eagle Pipeline would be solely dedicated to the purpose of serving a private entity to enable its construction and operation in energy production, it is clear that the County in this case urges a broad interpretation of "public purposes." While arguing the construction of the plant will serve a public purpose by significantly enhancing the economic development of Muskogee County through increased taxes, jobs and public and private investment, County urges our adoption of a rule, which has been applied in other jurisdictions that the exercise of eminent domain for purposes of economic development alone (in the absence of blight) satisfies the constitutional "public use" or "public purpose" requirement. We recognize that the U.S. Supreme Court recently upheld [in *Kelo*] a city's exercise of eminent domain power in furtherance of an economic development plan, holding that economic development satisfied the "public use" restriction in the Fifth Amendment's Takings Clause and finding the city's economic development plan served a "public purpose."

The U.S. Supreme Court expressly limited its holding in *Kelo* as follows: "[t]his Court's authority, however, extends only to determining whether the City's proposed condemnations are for a 'public use' within the meaning of the Fifth Amendment to the Federal Constitution." Notably, the Court in *Kelo* additionally expressly provided as follows:

> We emphasize that nothing in our opinion precludes any State from placing further restrictions on its exercise of the takings power. Indeed, many states already impose "public use" requirements that are stricter than the federal baseline. Some of these requirements have been established as a matter of state constitutional law, while others are expressed in state eminent domain statutes that carefully limit the grounds upon which takings may be exercised.

Contrary to the Connecticut statute applicable in *Kelo*, which expressly authorized eminent domain for the purpose of economic development, we note the absence of such express Oklahoma statutory authority for the exercise of eminent domain in furtherance of economic development in the absence of blight. The statute at issue in the instant cases is a general grant of power that permits condemnation "in like manner as railroad companies, for highways, rights-of-way, building sites, cemeteries, public parks and other public purposes." County here seeks a broad, expansive interpretation of the term "public purpose" to permit the exercise of eminent domain pursuant to the County's general statutory power of eminent domain. However, we have already rejected such a broad interpretation of "public purpose"…[and have held that] "a municipality is not possessed with an unfettered discretion to condemn property for economic redevelopment projects outside of the scope of statutory schemes that the Legislature has provided for removal of blighted property." Accordingly, we hold that economic development alone does not constitute a public purpose and therefore, does not constitutionally justify the County's exercise of eminent domain. Pursuant to our own narrow requirements in our constitutional eminent domain provisions, we view the transfer of property from one private party to another in furtherance of potential economic development or enhancement of a community in the absence of blight as a purpose, which must yield to our greater constitutional obligation to protect and preserve the individual fundamental interest of private property ownership.

To the extent that our determination may be interpreted as inconsistent with the U.S. Supreme Court's holding in *Kelo v. City of New London*, today's pronouncement is reached on the basis of Oklahoma's own special constitutional eminent domain provisions, which we conclude provide private property protection to Oklahoma citizens beyond that which is afforded them by the Fifth Amendment to the U.S. Constitution. In other words, we determine that our state constitutional eminent domain provisions place more stringent limitation on governmental eminent domain power than the limitations imposed by the Fifth Amendment of the U.S. Constitution. We join other jurisdictions including Arizona, Arkansas, Florida, Illinois, South Carolina, Michigan, and Maine, which have reached similar determinations on state constitutional grounds. Other states have similarly restricted the government's eminent domain power through state statute.

[handwritten margin note: the state's rules on takings]

While the Takings Clause of the U.S. Constitution provides "nor shall private property be taken for public use without just compensation," the Oklahoma Constitution places further restrictions by expressly stating "[n]o private property shall be taken or damaged *for private use*, with or without compensation." That constitutional provision additionally expressly lists the exceptions for common law easements by necessity and drains for agricultural, mining and sanitary purposes. The proposed purpose of economic development, with its incidental enhancement of tax and employment benefits to the surrounding community, clearly does not fall within any of these categories of express constitutional exceptions to the general rule against the taking of private property for private use. To permit the inclusion of economic development alone in the category of "public use" or "public purpose" would blur the line between "public" and "private" so as to render our constitutional limitations on the power of eminent domain a nullity. If property ownership in Oklahoma is to remain what the framers of our Constitution intended it to be, this we must not do.

[handwritten margin note: TI's purpose doesn't fit exceptions]

EDMONDSON, J., Dissenting and joined by WINCHESTER, V.C.J.

The Court's decision reflects an understandable sensitivity to the United States Supreme Court's recent approval in *Kelo v. City of New London* of a municipal exercise of eminent domain to take unblighted private residential property and deliver it to a private business in anticipation of public benefits to be derived solely from economic development.

In Oklahoma, our State Constitution extends greater protection to private property than does the Federal Constitution, as the majority opinion ably demonstrates. It also mandates that no private property be taken without just compensation.

However, I do not believe our greater measure of safety for private property was intended to deny non-riparian neighbors access to state water resources; particularly when the water is abundant, access can be achieved merely by taking an easement and is essential to the neighbor's survival, and the purpose is, as here, to expand electrical power resources in an economy in which energy is in critically short supply.

No one should be denied access to public water resources unless it is demonstrated that the access would impair the welfare of the public itself. New generation of electrical power is legislatively favored though it be by a private company and marketed directly to a private consumer, because it contributes to the national energy pool and to the ultimate benefit and security of the public.

GOLDSTEIN v. NEW YORK STATE URBAN DEV. CORP.
921 N.E.2d 165, 13 N.Y.3d 511(2009)

LIPPMAN, C.J.

We are asked to determine whether respondent's exercise of its power of eminent domain to acquire petitioners' properties for purposes of the proposed land use improvement project, known as Atlantic Yards, would be in conformity with certain provisions of our State Constitution. We answer in the affirmative.

On December 8, 2006, respondent Empire State Development Corporation (ESDC) issued a determination pursuant to Eminent Domain Proceedings Law (EDPL) § 204, finding that it should use its eminent domain power to take certain privately owned properties located in downtown Brooklyn for inclusion in a 22-acre mixed-use development proposed, and to be undertaken, by private developer Bruce Ratner and the real estate entities of which he is a principal, collectively known as the Forest City Ratner Companies (FCRC).

The project is to involve, in its first phase, construction of a sports arena to house the NBA Nets franchise, as well as various infrastructure improvements—most notably reconfiguration and modernization of the Vanderbilt Yards rail facilities and access upgrades to the subway transportation hub already present at the site. The project will also involve construction of a platform spanning the rail yards and connecting portions of the neighborhood now separated by the rail cut. Atop this platform are to be situated, in a second phase of construction, numerous high rise

Bk Nets, a platform, high rises, affordable housing

buildings and some eight acres of open, publicly accessible landscaped space. The 16 towers planned for the project will serve both commercial and residential purposes. They are slated to contain between 5,325 and 6,430 dwelling units, more than a third of which are to be affordable either for low and or middle income families.

The project has been sponsored by respondent ESDC as a "land use improvement project" within the definition of Urban Development Corporation Act, upon findings that the area in which the project is to be situated is "substandard and insanitary" or, in more common parlance, blighted. It is not disputed that the project designation and supporting blight findings are appropriate with respect to more than half the project footprint, which lies within what has, since 1968, been designated by the City of New York as the Atlantic Terminal Urban Renewal Area (ATURA). To the south of ATURA, however, and immediately adjacent to the Vanderbilt Rail Yard cut, are two blocks and a fraction of a third which, although within the project footprint, have not previously been designated as blighted. FCRC has purchased many of the properties in this area, but there remain some that it has been unsuccessful in acquiring, whose transfer ESDC now seeks to compel in furtherance of the project, through condemnation. In support of its exercise of the condemnation power with respect to these properties, some of which are owned by petitioners, ESDC, based on studies conducted by a consulting firm retained by FCRC, has made findings that the blocks in which they are situated possess sufficient indicia of actual or impending blight to warrant their condemnation for clearance and redevelopment ... and that the proposed land use improvement project will, by removing blight and creating in its place the above-described mixed-use development, serve a "public use, benefit or purpose."

Blighted land

Not blighted land

Signs of actual or impending blight

Petitioners' initial challenge to ESDC's determination authorizing condemnation of their properties was made in a timely federal court action. The gist of that action was that the disputed condemnation was not supported by a public use and thus violated the Fifth Amendment of the Federal Constitution. Petitioners' federal claims were rejected by the Federal District Court, and the ... judgment dismissing the complaint was affirmed by the Second Circuit. Within six months, petitioners commenced the present proceeding in the Appellate Division ... [and] alleged ... that the proposed taking was not for a "public use" but for the benefit of a private party and thus would be in violation of article I, § 7(a) of the New York State Constitution.

Procedural posture

The Appellate Division ... found for respondent on the merits. It observed that, while the State Constitution, literally read and in its early construction, permitted the taking of property only for "public use," "public use" had since come to be understood as entailing no more than a dominant public purpose. The Court noted that it was well established that the eradication of blight was such a public purpose and found that ESDC's blight findings were supported by the area studies contained in the administrative record.

II

Turning now to the merits, petitioners first contend that the determination authorizing the condemnation of their properties for the Atlantic Yards project is unconstitutional because the condemnation is not for the purpose of putting their properties to "public use" within the meaning of article I, § 7(a) of the State Constitution—which provides that "[p]rivate property shall not be taken for public use without just compensation"—but rather to enable a private commercial entity to use their properties for private economic gain with, perhaps, some incidental public benefit. The argument reduces to this: that the State Constitution has from its inception, in recognition of the fundamental right to privately own property, strictly limited the availability of condemnation to situations in which the property to be condemned will actually be made available for public use, and that, with only limited exceptions prompted by emergent public necessity, the State Constitution's takings clause, unlike its federal counterpart, has been consistently understood literally, to permit a taking of private property only for "public use," and not simply to accomplish a public purpose.

Even if this gloss on this State's takings laws and jurisprudence were correct—and it is not—it is indisputable that the removal of urban blight is a proper, and, indeed, constitutionally sanctioned, predicate for the exercise of the power of eminent domain. It has been deemed a "public use" within the meaning of the State's takings clause at least since *Matter of New York City Housing Authority v. Muller* (270 N.Y. 333 [1936]) and is expressly recognized by the Constitution as a ground for condemnation. Article XVIII, § 1 of the State Constitution grants the Legislature the power to "provide in such manner, by such means and upon such terms and conditions as it may prescribe ... for the clearance, replanning, reconstruction and rehabilitation of substandard and insanitary areas," and section 2 of the same article provides "[f]or and in aid of such purposes, notwithstanding any provision in any other article of this constitution, ... the legislature may ... grant the power of eminent domain to any ... public corporation...." Pursuant to article XVIII, respondent ESDC has been vested with the condemnation power by the Legislature and has here sought to exercise the power for the constitutionally recognized public purpose or "use" of rehabilitating a blighted area.

Petitioners, of course, maintain that the blocks at issue are not, in fact, blighted and that the allegedly mild dilapidation and inutility of the property cannot support a finding that it is substandard and insanitary within the meaning of article XVIII. They are doubtless correct that the conditions cited in support of the blight finding at issue do not begin to approach in severity the dire circumstances of urban slum dwelling described by the *Muller* court in 1936, and which prompted the adoption of article XVIII at the State Constitutional Convention two years later. We, however, have never required that a finding of blight by a legislatively designated public benefit corporation be based upon conditions replicating those to which the Court and the Constitutional Convention responded in the midst of the Great Depression. To the contrary, in construing the reach of the terms "substandard and insanitary" as they are used in article XVIII—and were applied in the early 1950's to the Columbus Circle area upon which the New York Coliseum was proposed to be built—we observed:

> Of course, none of the buildings are as noisome or dilapidated as those described in Dickens' novels or Thomas Burke's 'Limehouse' stories of the London slums of other days, but there is ample in this record to justify the determination of the city planning commission that a substantial part of the area is 'substandard and insanitary' by modern tests. (*Kaskel v. Impellitteri*, 306 N.Y. 73, 78 [1953]).

And, subsequently, in *Yonkers Community Dev. Agency v. Morris* (37 N.Y.2d 478, 481-482 [1975]), in reviewing the evolution of the crucial terms' signification and permissible range of application, we noted:

> Historically, urban renewal began as an effort to remove 'substandard and insanitary' conditions which threatened the health and welfare of the public, in other words 'slums', whose eradication was in itself found to constitute a public purpose for which the condemnation powers of government might constitutionally be employed. Gradually, as the complexities of urban conditions became better understood, it has become clear that the areas eligible for such renewal are not limited to "slums" as that term was formerly applied, and that, among other things, economic underdevelopment and stagnation are also threats to the public sufficient to make their removal cognizable as a public purpose.

It is important to stress that lending precise content to these general terms has not been, and may not be, primarily a judicial exercise. Whether a matter should be the subject of a public undertaking—whether its pursuit will serve a public purpose or use—is ordinarily the province of the Legislature, not the Judiciary, and the actual specification of the uses identified by the Legislature as public has been largely left to quasi-legislative administrative agencies. It is only where there is no room for reasonable difference of opinion as to whether an area is blighted, that judges may substitute their views as to the adequacy with which the public purpose of blight removal has been made out for that of the legislatively designated agencies; where, as here, "those bodies have made their finding, not corruptly or irrationally or baselessly, there is nothing for the courts to do about it, unless every act and decision of other departments of government is subject to revision by the courts."

It is quite possible to differ with ESDC's findings that the blocks in question are affected by numerous conditions indicative of blight, but any such difference would not, on this record, in which the bases for the agency findings have been extensively documented photographically and otherwise on a lot-by-lot basis, amount to more than another reasonable view of the matter; such a difference could not, consonant with what we have recognized to be the structural limitations upon our review of what is essentially a legislative prerogative, furnish a ground to afford petitioners relief.

It may be that the bar has now been set too low—that what will now pass as "blight," as that expression has come to be understood and used by political appointees to public corporations relying upon studies paid for by developers, should not be permitted to constitute a predicate for the invasion of property rights and the razing of homes and businesses. But any such limitation upon the sovereign power of eminent domain as it has come to be defined in the urban renewal context is a matter for the Legislature, not the courts. Properly involved in redrawing the range of the sovereign prerogative would not be a simple return to the days when private property rights were viewed as virtually inviolable, even when they stood in the way of meeting compelling public needs, but a re-weighing of public as against private interests and a reassessment of the need for and public utility of what may now be out-moded approaches to the revivification of the urban landscape. These are not tasks courts are suited to perform. They are appropriately situated in the policy-making branches of government.

The dissenter, after thoughtful review of the evolution of the concept of public use—an evolution that even he acknowledges has sapped the concept of much of its limiting power—urges that there remains enough left in it to require that this case be decided differently. We cannot agree. The Constitution accords government broad power to take and clear substandard and insanitary areas for redevelopment. In so doing, it commensurately deprives the Judiciary of grounds to interfere with the exercise.

While there remains a hypothetical case in which we might intervene to prevent an urban redevelopment condemnation on public use grounds— where "the physical conditions of an area might be such that it would be irrational and baseless to call it substandard or insanitary"—this is not that case. The dissenter looks at the "Blight Study" contained in the administrative record and sees only a "normal and pleasant residential neighborhood," but others, it would appear not irrationally, have come to very different conclusions. This is not a record that affords the purchase necessary for judicial intrusion. The situation in the end is remarkably like ... *Kaskel* where ... the Court said:

> Plaintiff does not dispute with defendants as to the condition of these properties or of the whole area. He is simply opposing his opinion and his judgment to that of public officials, on a matter which must necessarily be one of opinion or judgment, that is, as to whether a specified area is so substandard or insanitary, or both, as to justify clearance and redevelopment under the law. It is not seriously contended by anyone that, for an area to be subject to those laws, every single building therein must be below civilized standards. The statute (and the Constitution), like other similar laws, contemplates that clearing and redevelopment will be of an entire area, not of a separate parcel, and, surely, such statutes would not be very useful if limited to areas where every single building is substandard.

Here too, all that is at issue is a reasonable difference of opinion as to whether the area in question is in fact substandard and insanitary. This is not a sufficient predicate for us to supplant respondent's determination.

SMITH, J., **dissenting**.

The good news from today's decision is that our Court has not followed the lead of the United States Supreme Court in rendering the "public use" restriction on the Eminent Domain Clause virtually meaningless. The bad news is that the majority is much too deferential to the self-serving determination by Empire State Development Corporation (ESDC) that petitioners live in a "blighted" area, and are accordingly subject to having their homes seized and turned over to a private developer. I do not think the record supports ESDC's determination, and I therefore dissent.

I

Article I, § 7(a) of the State Constitution says: "Private property shall not be taken for public use without just compensation."

The words "public use" embody an important protection for property owners. They prevent the State from invoking its eminent domain power as a means of transferring property from one private owner to another who has found more favor with state officials, or who promises to use the land in a way more to the State's liking. They do not require that all takings result in public ownership of the property, but they do ordinarily require that, if the land is transferred to private hands, it be used after the taking in a way that benefits the public directly. A recognized exception permits the transfer of "blighted" land to private developers without so strict a limitation on its subsequent use, but that exception is applicable only in cases in which the use of the land by its original owner creates a danger to public health and safety.

Development of the blight exception

These principles are established by two centuries of New York cases. A line of 19th century decisions made clear that the State could not use the eminent domain power to transfer property from one private owner to another, unless the use to which the second owner put the property would be "public" in some meaningful sense. In the 20th century, an era friendlier to government and less friendly to private property, this rule was diluted, but our cases do not justify the conclusion that the public use limitation was abandoned or rendered trivial. Rather, the 20th century cases created what may be called a "blight exception" to the public use limitation. The critical question on this appeal is whether that exception applies, a question that can be better understood after a more detailed description of the way our "public use" law has developed.

In the early 19th century, New York judges debated whether the eminent domain power could ever be used to transfer property from one private owner to another. Later cases make clear that this debate was settled in favor of the Chancellor's view that certain uses of property by private parties—*e.g.*, for "turnpike and other roads, railways, canals, ferries and bridges"—could be considered public, but that takings in which land was transferred to private hands would be strictly limited to situations in which the public nature of the use was clear. In *Matter of Niagara Falls & Whirlpool Ry. Co.* (108 N.Y. 375, 383 [1888]), we said: "The right of the state to authorize the condemnation of private property for the construction of railroads and to delegate the power to take proceedings for that purpose to railroad corporations, has become an accepted doctrine of constitutional law and is not open to debate." But we held that the proposed taking in the *Niagara* case, which was for a railroad that would serve "the sole purpose of furnishing sight-seers during about four months of the year, greater facilities than they now enjoy for seeing ... part of [the] Niagara river," was not for a public use.

Under the 19th century understanding of public use, the taking at issue in this case would certainly not be permitted. It might be possible to debate whether a sports stadium open to the public is a "public use" in the traditional sense, but the renting of commercial and residential space by a private developer clearly is not.

Our 20th century cases, while not all consistent and containing some confusing language, are best read as modifying, rather than nullifying or abandoning, the established public use limitation. A series of cases upheld takings for what was variously characterized as slum clearance, removal of blight, or correction of unsafe, unsanitary or substandard housing conditions. While these cases undoubtedly expanded the old understanding of public use, they did not establish the general proposition that property may be condemned and turned over to a private developer every time a state agency thinks that doing so would improve the neighborhood.

Muller approved a taking of property where "unsanitary and substandard housing conditions" were found to exist. We observed:

> The public evils, social and economic of such conditions, are unquestioned and unquestionable. Slum areas are the breeding places of disease which take toll not only from denizens, but, by spread, from the inhabitants of the entire city and State. Juvenile delinquency, crime and immorality are there born, find protection and flourish. Enormous economic loss results directly from the necessary expenditure of public funds to maintain health and hospital services for afflicted slum dwellers and to war against crime and immorality. Indirectly there is an equally heavy capital loss and a diminishing return in taxes because of the areas blighted by the existence of the slums.

Awful conditions justifying Muller

Muller did not involve transfer to an ordinary private developer: the property in question was to be rented by the City, or by "limited dividend corporations," to people of low income. In *Muller*, we reiterated the essential principle of the public use limitation:

> Nothing is better settled than that the property of one individual cannot, without his consent, be devoted to the private use of another, even when there is an incidental or colorable benefit to the public. The facts here present no such case.... [T]he public is seeking to take the defendant's property and to administer it as part of a project conceived and to be carried out in its own interest and for its own protection.

Murray, unlike *Muller*, did involve a taking from which a purely private company "may ultimately reap a profit." The need to remedy "conditions in those blighted urban areas where slums exist," conditions that "affect the health, safety and welfare of the public," furnished the reason for upholding the taking.

Our later decision in *Yonkers Community Development* ... does seem to adopt a rather loose interpretation of "substandard" conditions that would justify a taking, but it also says that "courts are required to be more than rubber stamps in the determination of the existence of substandard conditions" and that "in order to utilize the public purpose attached to clearance of substandard land, such clearance must be the primary purpose of the taking, not some other public purpose, however laudable it might be." In *Yonkers*, we found that the agency had not provided factual support for its claim that the land to be taken was substandard, but held that the landowners had failed to raise this issue properly by their pleadings.

Yonkers as cts to be more than rubber stamps

ESDC also relies on *Kaskel v. Impellitteri* (306 N.Y. 73 [1953]), which involved a very questionable "slum clearance" taking, but overlooks an important aspect of that case. The challenge to the governmental action there was brought not by a condemnee, but by a taxpayer suing under General Municipal Law § 51, and we emphasized that in such a case the plaintiff must show corruption, fraud or "a total lack of power ... under the

as: a tax case

law, to do the acts complained of." We implied that the case might be different if the "arbitrary and capricious" standard of an article 78 proceeding were applicable. Even on the stringent section 51 standard, Judges Van Voorhis and Fuld dissented and would have held plaintiff's claim sufficient to withstand summary judgment.

The most troubling cases cited by ESDC are *Cannata v. City of New York* (11 N.Y.2d 210 [1962]) and *Courtesy Sandwich Shop, Inc. v. Port of N.Y. Auth.* (12 N.Y.2d 379 [1963]), which can be read to support an interpretation of "public use" that would permit the transfer by eminent domain of almost anyone's property to a private entity if a state agency thinks the area would benefit from "redevelopment." These cases, however, must be understood in historical context. They were decided after the United States Supreme Court had adopted, in *Berman v. Parker* (348 U.S. 26, 33 [1954]), a "broad and inclusive" definition of public use, to include any "object ... within the authority of Congress." *Berman*, as later cases confirmed, eviscerated the "public use" limitation of the United States Constitution. And at the time of the *Cannata* and *Courtesy Sandwich Shop* decisions, our Court had not adopted the practice, which later became common, of interpreting our state Constitution to afford broader protection to individual rights and liberties than the federal Constitution does. I would view *Cannata* and *Courtesy Sandwich Shop* as mistakenly following *Berman's* lead, and would limit them to their facts or simply reject them.

II

The majority does not wholly reject what I have said in section I of this dissent. Indeed, the majority seems to accept the premise that the Eminent Domain Clause of the New York Constitution has independent vitality, and may offer more protection to property owners than its federal counterpart. I am pleased that the majority does not follow the Supreme Court's decisions in *Berman*, *Midkiff* and *Kelo*, which equate "public use" in the Constitution with public purpose, thus leaving governments free to accomplish by eminent domain any goal within their general power to act. Where I part company with the majority is in its conclusion that we must defer to ESDC's determination that the properties at issue here fall within the blight exception to the public use limitation.

It is clear to me from the record that the elimination of blight, in the sense of substandard and unsanitary conditions that present a danger to public safety, was never the bona fide purpose of the development at issue in this case. Indeed, blight removal or slum clearance, which were much in vogue among the urban planners of several decades ago, have waned in popularity .... It is more popular today to speak of an "urban landscape"—

the words used by Bruce Ratner to describe his "vision" of the Atlantic Yards development in a public presentation in January 2004.

According to the petition in this case, when the project was originally announced in 2003 the public benefit claimed for it was economic development-job creation and the bringing of a professional basketball team to Brooklyn. Petitioners allege that nothing was said about "blight" by the sponsors of the project until 2005; ESDC has not identified any earlier use of the term. In 2005, ESDC retained a consultant to conduct a "blight study." In light of the special status accorded to blight in the New York law of eminent domain, the inference that it was a pretext, not the true motive for this development, seems compelling.

It is apparent from a review of ESDC's blight study that its authors faced a difficult problem. Only the northern part of the area on which Atlantic Yards is to be built can fairly be described as blighted. But the southern part of the project area, where petitioners live, has never been part of ATURA and appears, from the photographs and the descriptions contained in ESDC's blight study, to be a normal and pleasant residential community.

ESDC's consultants did their best. Proceeding lot by lot through the area in which petitioners live, they were able to find that a number of buildings were not in good condition; petitioners claim that this results in large part from the fact that Ratner's plan to acquire the properties and demolish the buildings had been public knowledge for years when the blight study was conducted. Choosing their words carefully, the consultants concluded that the area of the proposed Atlantic Yards development, taken as a whole, was "characterized by blighted conditions." They did not find, and it does not appear they could find, that the area where petitioners live is a blighted area or slum of the kind that prompted 20th century courts to relax the public use limitation on the eminent domain power.

The majority opinion acknowledges that the conditions ESDC relies on here "do not begin to approach in severity the dire circumstances of urban slum dwelling" contemplated by the cases that developed the blight exception. The majority concludes, however, that determining whether the area in question is really blighted is not "primarily a judicial exercise." In doing so, I think, the majority loses sight of the nature of the issue.

The determination of whether a proposed taking is truly for public use has always been a judicial exercise—as the cases cited in section I of this dissent, from *Bloodgood* in 1837 through *Yonkers Community Development* in 1975, demonstrate. The right not to have one's property taken for other than public use is a constitutional right like others. It is hard to imagine any court saying that a decision about whether an utterance is constitutionally protected speech, or whether a search was unreasonable, or whether a school district has been guilty of racial discrimination, is not primarily a judicial exercise. While no doubt some degree of deference is due to public agencies and to legislatures, to allow them to decide the facts on which constitutional rights depend is to render the constitutional protections impotent.

DS: we can't let legislature decide when to take when desirable

The whole point of the public use limitation is to prevent takings even when a state agency deems them desirable. To let the agency itself determine when the public use requirement is satisfied is to make the agency a judge in its own cause. I think that it is we who should perform the role of judges, and that we should do so by deciding that the proposed taking in this case is not for public use.

Some States responded to *Kelo* with statutory enactments, rather than amending their constitution, or adopting a narrower reading of their constitutional provisions parallel to the Fifth Amendment Takings Clause. The following case is an example.

READING AREA WATER AUTHORITY v. SCHUYKILL RIVER GREENWAY ASS'N
100 A.3d 572 (Penn. 2014)

SAYLOR, J.

QP

The primary question raised is whether a municipal authority may exercise its eminent domain powers to condemn an easement over privately-owned land, where the sole purpose of the easement is to supply a private developer with land to install sewer drainage facilities needed for a proposed private residential subdivision.

Δ is a non-profit

The Schuylkill River Greenway Association (the Greenway), a non-profit corporation, owns a strip of land along the west bank of the Schuylkill River in Bern Township, several miles north of the City of Reading. The Greenway and the Township intend to build a public walking/recreational trail on this property as a segment of the larger Schuylkill River Trail. Situated immediately to the west of the Greenway Property is a 58–acre tract owned by Fortune Development, L.P. (Developer), a private developer. Developer seeks to construct a 219–unit adult residential subdivision, known as Water's Edge Village, on this tract.

Development plan

Water's Edge Village would require access to a clean water supply as well as sanitary sewer and stormwater sewer facilities. As for clean water, a water main passing through Ontelaunee (a municipality on the east side of the Schuylkill River) can potentially connect, underneath the Schuylkill River, with a proposed water main on the west side of the river, and then continue west to Water's Edge Village. For this to occur, however, the west-side main would have to run through the Greenway's property. A similar situation exists with regard to sanitary sewer and stormwater sewer outfall, albeit the water would flow in the opposite direction. In particular, treated sewage would combine with stormwater runoff and flow eastward through the Greenway's property, ultimately discharging into the Schuylkill River. The conduits for the clean water and the sewer outfall could be laid side-by-side within a 50-foot-wide underground space on the Greenway's property, connecting the Schuylkill River and Developer's land.

The Reading Area Water Authority (RAWA), a municipal authority created by the City of Reading, supported Developer's planned development and, to that end, tried to purchase an easement across the Greenway Property so that it could supply water to the proposed development. After negotiations with the Greenway failed to produce an agreement, RAWA adopted a resolution in February 2009, authorizing the use of its eminent-domain powers to condemn a utility easement across the Greenway Property connecting Developer's land with the Schuylkill River. The resolution reflected that the easement was to be condemned at Developer's request and that it would be used for water, sewer, and stormwater purposes specifically to enable Developer to build Water's Edge Village. The resolution also stated that Developer would be responsible for initiating eminent domain proceedings in conjunction with RAWA's solicitor, and would be required to pay all costs associated with such proceedings, including just compensation to the Greenway. The City of Reading then passed a resolution approving the RAWA resolution.

In light of the City's approval, in May 2010 RAWA filed a Declaration of Taking Complaint in the Berks County common pleas court, naming the Greenway as the sole defendant and attaching an appraisal, a bond, and a description of the property to be taken. The Complaint requested a decree condemning a 50-foot-wide easement across the Greenway Property, "to construct, maintain, [and] operate utility lines and appurtenance of a water main to be placed under the Schuylkill River for water, sewer and stormwater purposes," and asked that the court value the easement at $3,500 based on the appraisal. According to the attached exhibits, the water main would travel west from Ontelaunee under the Schuylkill River and continue west through the Greenway Property to Developer's property. The sewer main would travel south from a sewage treatment plant on Developer's property and intersect with a pipe which would drain a stormwater retention basin (also on Developer's property). The sewer main and the stormwater pipe would then combine into a single conduit which would travel east under Developer's property, and then continue east through the Greenway Property, within the same 50-foot-wide strip of land, ultimately emerging through a concrete headwall and discharging the effluent onto a six-foot downward slope covered by riprap.[1]

The Greenway filed preliminary objections, alleging that: the taking was invalid under Pennsylvania's Property Rights Protection Act (PRPA), because it was being accomplished solely for the benefit of private enterprise, *see* 26 Pa.C.S. § 204(a) (generally prohibiting the use of eminent-domain powers to take private property "to use it for private enterprise"); and the proposed easement was wider than necessary to accommodate RAWA's water supply line, which the Greenway viewed as the only service legitimately within RAWA's function.

The common pleas court sustained the preliminary objections and dismissed the Complaint. In its opinion, the court explained that the condemnation was effectuated solely to benefit a private commercial developer who had been unable to acquire an easement through private measures and, as such, violated the prohibition on using eminent domain for private purposes ("Under the guise of expanding their customer base and providing water to the public, RAWA is attempting to achieve its true goal and take land from one private owner and give it to another.").

The Commonwealth Court reversed in a published decision, focusing on RAWA's stated purpose—the installation of a water main and utility lines—for which it may exercise eminent domain. In application, the court reasoned that, although the availability of the utilities would make Developer's homes more valuable, this alone would not negate the project's public purpose of providing water, sewer, and stormwater services to citizens in RAWA's service area.

We allowed appeal to consider whether RAWA's actions were legally permissible, particularly in light of recent legislative restrictions on the use of eminent domain to benefit private enterprise.

Appellants (the Greenway and the Township) argue generally that the power of eminent domain may only be exercised for a public purpose. They do not challenge the water easement, opting to focus their advocacy on the drainage easement. Thus Appellants adopt the position that the drainage easement is being taken for the private use of Developer and, as such, it is not authorized by the Pennsylvania Constitution or the Eminent

---

[1] [3] Although the 50–foot–wide strip of land is subsumed within a single utility easement, approximately half of that width would be for water supply and is referred to by the parties as the "water easement," with the other half—the "drainage easement"— being used for sewer outflow. For convenience, we will use this same terminology. Notably, only the drainage easement is at issue in this case, as developed more fully below.

Domain Code, and is affirmatively prohibited by PRPA. *See* Brief for Appellants at 12.

RAWA proffers that there is a public interest in ensuring that homes have running water and access to a sewer line, and that the taking advances this interest regardless of whether Developer will benefit from the availability of such services through its ability to build and sell fully-functioning homes. So long as there is no evidence of corruption, fraud, or malfeasance by the condemnor, RAWA argues, a condemnation for a public purpose should be upheld.

Our resolution of this appeal will ultimately be based on PRPA. However, a review of salient constitutional principles as they apply here is helpful to provide context, particularly in terms of whether the taking is for a public use. The public-use issue is especially relevant because it dovetails to some extent with whether the taking is being accomplished for private enterprise as prohibited by PRPA—although, as will be seen, the correspondence is not exact.

Under the Constitution, land may only be taken without the owner's consent if it is taken for a public use. The question of what constitutes a public use is highly fact-dependent. Although RAWA relies heavily on *Washington Park*, we do not find that decision to be particularly helpful to its position. In *Washington Park*, a private shopping center known as Southgate stood to benefit from the proposed highway exit ramp, and thus, was willing to pay the costs of condemnation. Still, there was no suggestion that the ramp was intended to be owned, co-owned, occupied, or maintained by Southgate, or that its sole purpose was to provide access to Southgate. Here, the record reflects that Developer would not only finance the project, but would acquire exclusive use of the drainage easement to install, operate, and maintain private stormwater and sewage discharge facilities so as to enable it to build a private residential development.

Nevertheless, the present case has added complexion because the drainage easement is to be located side-by-side with the water easement, giving the appearance that the two work in tandem. There is also a natural tendency to regard the two functions as intertwined, at least insofar as the sanitary sewer outfall is concerned, since most of the water that enters a residence ultimately leaves the home through its sewer connection. This lends a certain appeal to the concept that the drainage easement is for a public use—particularly as municipal sewer and drainage systems generally constitute a public use. Furthermore, the drainage easement would, according to Developer's plans, ultimately serve 219 homes in an adult-community residential development. This factor also tends to support the view that the drainage easement is intended for at least a limited public use vis-à-vis the prospective purchasers of the residences, regardless of the identity of the party that constructs, owns, and operates the sewer discharge facilities.

The main difficulty, however, is that there is also a significant private overlay to the taking of the drainage easement: it is, as noted, to be acquired at Developer's behest for the sole use of Developer, and at Developer's sole cost. As well, there is no suggestion that the drainage easement is meant to be used for any purpose broader than servicing the subdivision to be built by Developer. Overall, then, the case involves a mix of public and private purposes working in conjunction with one another. With this in mind, a brief discussion of *Kelo v. City of New London*, its present application, and its legislative aftermath, will be helpful.

At issue in *Kelo* was the taking of private property for economic development and use, *inter alia*, by private commercial interests. The controversy dealt with a city's wide-ranging development project intended "to revitalize the local economy by creating temporary and permanent jobs, generating a significant increase in tax revenue, encouraging spin-off economic activities and maximizing public access to the waterfront[]." *Kelo* was a 5–4 decision in which the majority found that economic development can qualify as a public use for Fifth Amendment purposes even where private enterprise is the engine of such development, and accorded deference to the city's governing body's determination that, although the properties to be taken were not blighted, they were sufficiently distressed that economic rejuvenation of the overall area was in the public interest.

In dissent, Justice O'Connor criticized this level of deference and admonished that, "were the political branches the sole arbiters of the public-private distinction, the Public Use Clause would amount to little more than hortatory fluff." She also expressed that the decision would have a disproportionate impact on the poor, as its beneficiaries would be citizens with substantial influence in the political process, including large corporations and development firms.

The present case is distinguishable from *Kelo* in several respects. First, consistent with the trial court's findings, the taking here has as at least one of its purposes the conferral of a private benefit on a particular, identifiable private party (Developer). Relatedly, there is no evidence of an overall economic development or urban revitalization plan into which this taking fits—above and beyond Developer's own plan for its 58–acre tract.

On the other hand, the scope of the challenged taking is comparatively narrow and, as noted, involves sewer services, which is a more traditional category of public use than the multifaceted, large-scale economic development project at issue in *Kelo*.   *Who can analysis might be needed*

Ultimately, however, we need not decide the constitutional issue because, even if we assume the condemnation can pass Fifth–Amendment scrutiny,[2] to be valid it must also be statutorily permissible. In this regard, it may be observed that, in the wake of *Kelo*, the General Assembly enacted PRPA, which contains a salient, affirmative prohibition on the taking of private property "in order to use it for private enterprise." 26 Pa.C.S. § 204(a).[3]   *PRPA was in response to Kelo*

Notably, PRPA was passed as a direct reaction to *Kelo* to curb what legislators perceived as eminent domain abuse, and with the goal of striking a reasonable balance between (a) the need to defend private property rights from takings accomplished for economic development purposes, and (b) the legitimate needs of urban centers to rehabilitate blighted areas imposing substantial, concrete harm upon the public. Whether or not the *Constitution* viewed as merely "ancillary" the benefits to private enterprise ensuing from a plan to use eminent domain to assist in economic development, in the wake of *Kelo* the *Legislature* began to view such benefits as central and wanted to curtail the ability of condemnors to take others' property for such purposes. Against this backdrop, the legislative body elected to phrase the central prohibition broadly in terms of whether the subject property is being condemned "to use it for private enterprise," rather than "to use it *solely* for private enterprise"—the latter of which, in any event, would have had little effect on the *status quo* since any condemnation accomplished solely for private purposes would likely have failed the constitutional public-use standard.

Legislature uses broader phrase

---

[2] [12] No separate analysis has been advanced in this case to argue that Article I, Section 10 is more restrictive than the federal Takings Clause as interpreted in *Kelo*. [See PA. CONST. art. I, § 10 ("[N]or shall private property be taken or applied to public use, without authority of law and without just compensation being first made or secured."); U.S. CONST. AMEND. V ("[N]or shall private property be taken for public use, without just compensation.").]

[3] [14] Besides Pennsylvania, numerous other jurisdictions reacted to *Kelo* by passing similar legislation with the result that the decision may have led to an overall diminution in takings authority nationwide. See Gregory J. Robinson, *Kelo v. City of New London: Its Ironic Impact on Takings Authority*, 44 URB. LAW. 865, 906 (2012) (concluding that "Kelo has had the ironic effect of setting in motion an overall policy response that, by now, has reduced economic development takings authority below its pre-Kelo level"); Amanda W. Goodin, *Rejecting the Return to Blight in Post–Kelo State Legislation*, 82 N.Y.U. L.REV. 177, 193–94 (2007) (observing that Kelo "provoked fierce public opposition" and that dozens of states reacted by amending their eminent domain laws).

This observation has particular relevance to the present matter because, in spite of the drainage easement's colorable public-use facet as outlined above, RAWA condemned it, in effect, to allow Developer to occupy and use it for private enterprise—namely, to develop a residential subdivision. We therefore conclude that the condemnation of the drainage easement falls within Section 204(a)'s prohibitive scope. Whatever public benefit may ensue from the drainage easement, it is being taken to be used for private enterprise and, as such, is prohibited by Section 204(a).

Accordingly, the order of the Commonwealth Court is reversed, and the matter is remanded to the common pleas court for reinstatement of its order sustaining the preliminary objections and dismissing the Complaint. Although the water easement has not been challenged, the size of the condemned property—the overall utility easement—is in excess of that which is needed for water supply. Hence, RAWA is not entitled to the relief sought in its Complaint.

UTAH DEPT. OF TRANSPORTATION v. CARLSON
332 P.3d 900 (Utah 2014)

LEE, J.

¶ 1 This case presents the question whether the Utah Department of Transportation (UDOT) has the authority to use the power of eminent domain to condemn private property in excess of that needed for a transportation project. The condemnation at issue involved a fifteen-acre parcel owned by Michael Carlson. UDOT condemned the whole parcel despite the fact that it needed only 1.2 acres for its planned project. In so doing, UDOT asserted an interest in avoiding litigation regarding Carlson's severance damages, citing Utah Code section 72–5–113 as the basis for its taking.

¶ 2 In the district court and on appeal, the parties' arguments have focused primarily on a statutory aspect of the question presented— whether section 113 authorizes UDOT's condemnation of excess property. Carlson has also proffered alternative, constitutional grounds for questioning UDOT's authority. Specifically, he advocates for his interpretation of the statute on constitutional avoidance grounds, and asserts that in any event UDOT's taking fails for lack of a "public use" as required under the Takings Clause of the Utah or U.S. Constitution. UTAH CONST. art. 1, § 22; U.S. CONST. amend. V.

¶ 3 The district court ruled in UDOT's favor, but without expressly addressing the constitutional question. Thus, it granted summary judgment for UDOT based on an express agreement with UDOT's construction of the statute (but only an implicit endorsement of the constitutionality of the taking).

¶ 4 We reverse and remand. Although we agree with UDOT's statutory position and thus affirm that aspect of the district court's decision, we reverse and remand for further proceedings on the constitutional question. That question—whether a taking of excess property under Utah Code section 72–5–113 fails for lack of a "public use" under the federal or state Takings Clause—is a serious one. Because we conclude that this issue was properly preserved and should have been addressed expressly by the district court, we reverse and remand to allow that court to address this question....

I

¶ 5 In 2010, the Utah Department of Transportation announced a project involving the construction of a light rail line and expansion of 11400 South in Draper, Utah. As a first step, UDOT initiated an eminent domain action against Michael Carlson, the owner of parcels of property adjacent to 11400 South.

¶ 6 Together, the parcels consist of approximately fifteen acres. Although only 1.2 acres of the property were necessary for the project, UDOT sought to condemn all fifteen acres. UDOT invoked Utah Code section 72–5–113 in support of its statutory authority to "acquire" the full fifteen acres and subsequently to "sell the remainder or ... exchange it for other property needed for highway purposes." It also asserted an interest in avoiding the inconvenience and cost of litigating severance damages in connection with a partial taking of property.

¶ 7 Carlson stipulated that 1.2 acres of his property were necessary for a public use, but opposed condemnation of the rest of his land. As to Utah Code section 72–5–113, Carlson insisted that UDOT's right to "acquire" property was limited to voluntary acquisition and did not extend to the power of eminent domain. In addition, Carlson asserted that UDOT's taking of excess property unnecessary to the completion of a public project—and aimed primarily at avoiding litigation over severance damages—was both statutorily and constitutionally improper.

¶ 8 UDOT filed a motion for partial summary judgment. Although the briefing and argument on the motion focused principally on the question of UDOT's *statutory* authority to condemn excess property, Carlson also raised constitutional concerns. First, he advocated for his interpretation of section 113 on constitutional avoidance grounds. Thus, Carlson urged the rejection of UDOT's statutory position on the ground that it raised serious questions under the Takings Clauses of the Utah and U.S. Constitutions. Second, Carlson asserted an outright challenge to the constitutionality of UDOT's condemnation of excess property. Specifically, he insisted that UDOT had failed to "articulat[e] ... a public use" for the excess property in question, asserting that a mere interest in "avoid[ing] litigat[ion] about a

claim for damages" is insufficient, rendering the statute "[
]constitutionally infirm" as applied here.

¶ 9 In response, UDOT asserted that the transportation project in
general qualified as a public use, and thus the only remaining question was
whether the *amount* of property taken was "necessary" for that public use.
On the question of the amount of property taken, UDOT further asserted
that section 113 granted it discretionary authority to decide whether the
excess property was "necessary" for its project.

¶ 10 The district court entered partial summary judgment for UDOT.
In so doing it expressly endorsed UDOT's construction of Utah Code
section 72–5–113, holding that the statutory authorization for UDOT to
"acquire" excess property was not "ambiguous in this context, and ...
includes condemnation."

II

¶ 12 The parties' ... principal focus ... on appeal concerns the
statutory question whether Utah Code section 72–5–113 authorizes
UDOT's taking of excess property. Yet Carlson also raises constitutional
grounds for reversal, asserting both a constitutional avoidance basis for
rejecting UDOT's statutory position and an outright constitutional
challenge to the statute as applied.

¶ 13 We agree with and uphold the district court's statutory analysis
but remand to allow the court to address Carlson's constitutional challenge
in the first instance.

A. UDOT's Statutory Authority

We find Carlson's construction untenable and thus endorse the reading
advanced by UDOT and adopted by the district court.

C. Carlson's Constitutional Claim

¶ 26 That brings us to Carlson's challenge to the constitutionality of
section 113 as applied in this case. Although Carlson raised this question
in his briefs on appeal, UDOT essentially side-stepped it. It did so on
preservation grounds, asserting that Carlson failed to raise it below. But
our careful review of the record persuades us that Carlson's constitutional
challenge was adequately preserved.

¶ 27 In the district court, the briefing and argument on the
constitutional issue were not extensive. But Carlson did invoke the federal
and state Takings Clauses and cited authority for the proposition that
"private property cannot be taken by the government ... except for
purposes which are of a public character." *Madisonville Traction Co. v. St.
Bernard Mining Co.*, 196 U.S. 239, 251, 25 S.Ct. 251, 49 L.Ed. 462
(1905). At oral argument on the summary judgment motion, moreover,
counsel for Carlson emphasized his client's view that "there has not been

identified [a] public use of" the excess property condemned by UDOT. Continuing, counsel explained Carlson's constitutional challenge as follows:

> There's [only] been an effort to avoid litigating about a claim for damages.... There's been no articulation of a public use that they intend to put to this property. And they just don't. What they've said is we can condemn it because section 72–5–113 gives us the unbridled authority to do so. And I would submit, Your Honor, that interpreted that way, the statute would be unconstitutionally infirm.

¶ 28 In response, the district judge confirmed his understanding of Carlson's argument, as follows: "[Y]our basic argument is to the extent the statute grants condemnation authority beyond what's reasonably necessary for public use, it's in violation of the state constitution?" Carlson's counsel agreed with that restatement of Carlson's claim.

¶ 31 Carlson's constitutional claim raises difficult questions without any clear answers in applicable precedent. The core question is whether UDOT's condemnation of excess property satisfies the "public use" element of the federal and state constitutions. At the federal level, that question has been cued up but not conclusively resolved by the U.S. Supreme Court's decision in *Kelo v. City of New London*, 545 U.S. 469 (2005). *Kelo* reaffirmed the independent vitality of the "public use" element of the federal Takings Clause and marked its outer boundaries. But while *Kelo* declared that purely private takings as well as takings with only a "mere pretext of a public purpose" were unconstitutional, it ultimately "eschewed rigid formulas" for assessing public use and instead "afford[ed] legislatures broad latitude in determining what public needs justify the use of the takings power."

¶ 32 The state-law variant on the "public use" question is even more wide open. In cases involving state takings provisions apparently comparable to Utah's, the courts have adopted a wide range of standards of "public use." In some states, the courts have rejected the *Kelo* standard on the ground that the purpose or original meaning of their state Takings Clauses is incompatible with the notion that "an economic benefit to the government and community, standing alone, does not satisfy the public-use requirement."[4] Other state courts have embraced a standard similar to

---

[4] *City of Norwood v. Horney*, 110 Ohio St.3d 353, 853 N.E.2d 1115, 1123 (2006) (holding that "although economic factors may be considered in determining whether private property may be appropriated, the fact that the appropriation would provide an economic benefit to the government and community, standing alone, does not satisfy the public-use requirement of ... the Ohio Constitution," but stopping short of articulating a test for identifying a public use in contexts that are not purely economic); *see also Cnty. of Wayne v. Hathcock*, 471 Mich. 445, 684 N.W.2d 765, 783 (2004) (holding that condemning property to transfer it to a private entity is only acceptable for one of three traditional "public uses," where the economic benefit is not merely incidental: (1) "where

Kelo's as consistent with their state constitutional provisions,[5] while still others have adopted a variation on *Kelo*.[6]

¶ 34 There is also a second basis for a remand, and that is the lack of any clearly articulated "public use" proffered by UDOT on the record before us. Because the case has proceeded largely on statutory grounds, UDOT appears not to have clearly articulated its anticipated plans or purposes for the excess property at issue. Such an articulation could be crucial to an evaluation of the viability of UDOT's taking under the public-use standard ultimately adopted by the court. Thus, we deem it prudent and appropriate to remand to allow for appropriate consideration of the constitutional question presented in the district court.

[handwritten margin note: Ct: π has explained its public use]

NOTES

1. Why might some state courts be more or less protective of property rights in the context of eminent domain? Could geography or population influence how a court reads a state constitutional takings provision?

2. Can you make arguments for and against a state court reading the state constitution's takings clause differently than the federal Takings Clause? Will different readings cause headaches for local governments and developers?

3. Should state courts interpret the state constitutions to restrict the power of eminent domain, or should that decision be left to each state's political

---

public necessity of the extreme sort requires collective action," such as building infrastructure like railroads; (2) "where the property remains subject to public oversight after transfer to a private entity"; and (3) where the property is selected for condemnation because of "facts of independent public significance," rather than the interests of the eventual private owner, such as where condemnation and razing of a blighted area is itself a public use, not the subsequent rebuilding by a private entity (internal quotation marks omitted)).

[5] *Mayor & City Council of Baltimore City v. Valsamaki*, 397 Md. 222, 916 A.2d 324, 353 (2007) (stating that "economic development [is] a public purpose and constitutionally provides the City with authorization to utilize its power of eminent domain in achieving such development," but finding the facts of the particular case distinguishable and thus not qualifying as a public use).

[6] *R.I. Econ. Dev. Corp. v. The Parking Co.*, 892 A.2d 87, 104 (R.I.2006) (broadly defining public purpose as "public in nature [and] ... designed to protect the public health, safety, and welfare," but holding that this does not go so far as to encompass the condemning authority's "desire for increased revenue" (citation and internal quotation marks omitted)); *Hathcock*, 684 N.W.2d at 786 (holding that the framers of the Michigan constitution did not intend "public use" to include "incidental benefits to the economy," reasoning that "[e]very business ... contribute [s] in some way to the commonwealth"); *Sw. Ill. Dev. Auth. v. Nat'l City Envtl. L.L.C.*, 199 Ill.2d 225, 263 Ill.Dec. 241, 768 N.E.2d 1, 9 (2002) (stating that although "economic development is an important public purpose," it cannot go so far as to take one business's property to allow another to expand).

processes, whether the legislature or public referendum? Some state constitutions expressly provide that "the question whether the contemplated use be really public shall be a judicial question, and determined as such without regard to any legislative assertion that the use is public." Colo. Const. art. II, § 15; *see also* Okla. Const. art. II, § 24 ("In all cases of condemnation of private property for public or private use, the determination of the character of the use shall be a judicial question"); Wash. Const. art. I, § 16 (same language as the Colorado provision quoted above). Does requiring judicial determination ensure greater protection of property rights?

4. Are courts the only or even the best protectors of property rights? Some states responded to the concerns *Kelo* raised by adopting stricter *procedural requirements* for takings that were not for a traditional public use. *See, e.g.*, Fla. Const., art. X, § 6(c) ("Private property taken by eminent domain...on or after January 2, 2007, may not be conveyed to a natural person or private entity except as provided by general law passed by a three-fifths vote of the membership of each house of the Legislature.") Others adopted a flat prohibition that would appear to leave little, if any, room for court interpretation. *See, e.g.*, N.H. Const. pt. 1, art. 12-a ("No part of a person's property shall be taken by eminent domain and transferred, directly or indirectly, to another person if the taking is for the purpose of private development or other private use of the property.")

5. What are the consequences of providing greater protection to property owners under the state constitutions than the federal Takings Clause provides?

Many states permit citizens to initiate constitutional changes directly. The following case could easily fit in Chapter XIII or even Chapter XV of this book, but is included here because the citizens in this instance were attempting to respond to *Kelo* and protect property rights.

NEVADANS FOR THE PROTECTION OF PROPERTY RIGHTS, ET AL. v. HELLER
122 Nev. 894 (2006)

DOUGLAS, J.

In this opinion, we consider the constitutionality of NRS 295.009, which places a single-subject requirement on initiative petitions, and whether the initiative petition at issue in this appeal, the Nevada Property Owners' Bill of Rights, violates that requirement. We conclude that NRS 295.009 is constitutional and that because the Nevada Property Owners' Bill of Rights embraces more than one subject, the initiative violates this statute. Even so, strong public policy favors upholding the initiative power whenever possible, and NRS 295.009 does not prescribe a remedy for single-subject requirement violations. As the initiative includes a severability clause and facially and unequivocally pertains to a primary subject—eminent domain—we are compelled to sever sections 1 and 8, which do not pertain to eminent domain, in lieu of removing the entire initiative from the ballot.

Further, we confirm that initiatives proposing constitutional amendments must propose policy and not direct administrative details. Sections 3, 9, and 10 of the initiative violate this threshold requirement and therefore must be stricken. The rest of the initiative, consisting of sections 2, 4, 5, 6, 7, 11, 12, 13 and 14 shall proceed to the ballot.

BACKGROUND

In September 2005, respondents People's Initiative to Stop the Taking of Our Land (PISTOL), Don Chairez, Kermitt Waters, and Autumn Waters (collectively "the proponents") filed an initiative petition entitled "Nevada Property Owners' Bill of Rights" with the Secretary of State for placement on the November 7, 2006 ballot. The initiative seeks to amend Article 1 of the Nevada Constitution by adding a new section, section 22, consisting of 14 separate provisions. The initiative's provisions are as follows:

1. All property rights are hereby declared to be fundamental constitutional rights and each and every right provided herein shall be self-executing.

2. Public use shall not include the direct or indirect transfer of any interest in property taken in an eminent domain proceeding from one private party to another private party. In all eminent domain actions, the government shall have the burden to prove public use.

3. Unpublished eminent domain judicial opinions or orders shall be null and void.

4. In all eminent domain actions, prior to the government's occupancy, a property owner shall be given copies of all appraisals by the government and shall be entitled, at the property owner's election, to a separate and distinct determination by a district court jury, as to whether the taking is actually for a public use.

5. If a public use is determined, the taken or damaged property shall be valued at its highest and best use without considering any future dedication requirements imposed by the government. If private property is taken for any proprietary governmental purpose, the property shall be valued at the use to which the government intends to put the property, if such use results in a higher value for the land taken.

6. In all eminent domain actions, just compensation shall be defined as that sum of money, necessary to place the property owner back in the

same position, monetarily, without any governmental offsets, as if the property had never been taken. Just compensation shall include, but is not limited to, compounded interest and all reasonable costs and expenses actually incurred.

7. In all eminent domain actions where fair market value is applied, it shall be defined as the highest price the property would bring on the open market.

8. Government actions which result in substantial economic loss to private property shall require the payment of just compensation. Examples of such substantial economic loss include, but are not limited to, the down zoning of private property, the elimination of any access to private property, and limiting the use of private air space.

9. No Nevada state court judge or justice who has not been elected to a current term of office shall have the authority to issue any ruling in an eminent domain proceeding.

10. In all eminent domain actions, a property owner shall have the right to preempt [sic] one judge at the district court level and one justice at each appellate court level. Upon prior notice to all parties, the clerk of that court shall randomly select a currently elected district court judge to replace the judge or justice who was removed by preemption [sic].

11. Property taken in eminent domain shall automatically revert back to the original property owner upon repayment of the original purchase price, if the property is not used within five years for the original purpose stated by the government. The five years shall begin running from the date of the entry of the final order of condemnation.

12. A property owner shall not be liable to the government for attorney fees or costs in any eminent domain action.

13. For all provisions contained in this section, government shall be defined as the State of Nevada, its political subdivisions, agencies, any public or private agent acting on their behalf, and any public or private entity that has the power of eminent domain.

14. Any provision contained in this section shall be deemed a separate and freestanding right and shall remain in full force and effect should any other provision contained in this section be stricken for any reason.

After the necessary signatures were gathered and verified, the Secretary of State determined that the initiative had qualified for placement on the November 2006 ballot. In reviewing the initiative, the Secretary was required to determine whether it complied with Nevada's single-subject requirement, NRS 295.009. The Secretary conducted a "broad" review and concluded, apparently without any analysis, that the initiative "arguably complied with the single subject rule." Appellants, a collection of individuals and government entities opposed to the initiative, then filed a complaint in district court seeking declaratory and extraordinary relief to prevent the initiative from being placed on the ballot. The district court denied all requested relief, ruling that the initiative encompasses only a single subject and is therefore not disqualified from appearing on the ballot. This appeal followed.

DISCUSSION

NRS 295.009, Nevada's recently enacted single-subject requirement for initiatives, is the focal point in this appeal. As the statute's constitutionality has been called into question, we first address this threshold issue. We then discuss the statute's application to the initiative at hand and the remedy, in this case, for a statutory violation. Finally, we analyze the initiative under the threshold requirement that it propose policy.

B. NRS 295.009's single-subject requirement is constitutional

During the 2005 legislative session, the Legislature enacted NRS 295.009, which, among other things, places a single-subject requirement on initiative petitions. Subsection (1)(a) of the statute provides that "[e]ach petition for initiative ... must ... [e]mbrace but one subject and matters necessarily connected therewith and pertaining thereto." Subsection 2 further defines what one subject encompasses.

The proponents challenge the constitutionality of NRS 295.009, under both the Nevada and United States Constitutions. They contend that the Nevada Constitution does not provide the Legislature with the authority to enact a law restricting ballot initiatives to a single subject and that the single-subject requirement places improper limitations on political speech in violation of the First Amendment of the United States Constitution. We conclude that the Legislature properly enacted NRS 295.009 and that since the statute does not place unconstitutional limits on political speech, it does not violate the First Amendment.

1. Nevada Constitution

Nevada Constitution Article 19, Section 2 provides that "the people" reserve unto themselves the power to propose and enact statutes, amendments to statutes, and amendments to the Nevada Constitution by initiative petition. Article 19, Section 5, however, provides that "the legislature may provide by law for procedures to facilitate the operation of [Article 19's provisions]." Thus, the Nevada Constitution explicitly authorizes the Legislature to enact laws regulating the initiative process, so long as those laws facilitate the provisions of Article 19. The proponents fail to address or acknowledge Article 19, Section 5 and its express grant of authority to the Legislature.

By limiting petitions to a single subject, NRS 295.009 facilitates the initiative process by preventing petition drafters from circulating confusing petitions that address multiple subjects.

NRS 295.009's single-subject requirement facilitates the provisions of Article 19. Accordingly, under Article 19, Section 5, the Legislature had the authority to enact this requirement for initiative petitions. The challenge to this statute's constitutionality under the Nevada Constitution therefore necessarily fails.

C. *The initiative fails to satisfy the single-subject requirement*

NRS 295.009(1)(a) provides that "[e]ach petition for initiative or referendum must ... [e]mbrace but one subject and matters necessarily connected therewith and pertaining thereto." Subsection 2 of the statute further defines the "one subject" requirement set forth in subsection (1)(a):

> For the purposes of paragraph (a) of subsection 1, a petition for initiative or referendum embraces but one subject and matters necessarily connected therewith and pertaining thereto, if the parts of the proposed initiative or referendum are functionally related and germane to each other in a way that provides sufficient notice of the general subject of, and of the interests likely to be affected by, the proposed initiative or referendum.

Our preliminary inquiry, then, is whether the initiative's parts are "functionally related" and "germane" to each other.

Although the proponents' attorneys have not been entirely consistent, in either their briefs or during oral argument they have essentially admitted that the initiative originated as a response to the United States Supreme Court's recent decision in *Kelo v. New London*, which concluded that the taking of private property for private development in the context of a redevelopment scheme constituted public use. Indeed, the proponents' briefs point to the *Kelo* majority's statement that "State[s are not precluded] from placing further restrictions on [their] exercise of the takings power" and indicate that the initiative, if enacted, "will do just that." The proponents' attorneys also indicate that the initiative, especially section 2, is designed to prevent the taking of private property by the government through eminent domain for the purposes of transferring that property to a private party.

Proponents' attorneys have also explained, however, that the initiative's provisions go further than simply addressing *Kelo*. At argument, counsel agreed that the initiative is "*Kelo* plus." In fact, counsel made it clear that, with respect to the initiative, "*Kelo* is the tip of the iceberg." And, in their briefs, the proponents' attorneys repeatedly state that the initiative concerns eminent domain. The initiative itself unequivocally sustains these statements, as the vast majority of its provisions address one subject—eminent domain. Indeed, the description of the initiative's effect specifically states that "[t]he following constitutional provisions shall supersede all conflicting Nevada law regarding eminent domain actions." Thus, the primary subject of the initiative is unquestionably eminent domain, with its genesis the Supreme Court's *Kelo* decision. Because each and every provision in the initiative must be "functionally related" and "germane" to one another, it follows that, with respect to this initiative, every provision must be "functionally related" and "germane" to the subject of eminent domain.

Our review of the initiative reveals, however, that, despite the proponents' contentions, not all of the initiative's provisions are "functionally related" and "germane" to the subject of eminent domain. Specifically, we conclude that section 1 and section 8 of the initiative fail to satisfy this requirement. Under section 1, "[a]ll property rights are hereby declared to be fundamental constitutional rights and each and every right provided herein shall be self-executing." Although the proponents insist that this section is "functionally related" and "germane" to the subject of eminent domain because it would require the application of a strict scrutiny standard when property is taken, we disagree. This section is about making all property rights fundamental rights, and thereby creating a broad new class of fundamental rights. It does not deal with the subject of eminent domain. Further, this section's inclusion in an initiative dealing with eminent domain does not provide sufficient notice of the subject addressed in section 1 or the interests likely to be affected by this section.

Section 8 addresses government actions that cause substantial economic loss to property rights. Specifically, section 8 provides that "government actions which result in substantial economic loss to private property shall require the payment of just compensation." This section further provides that "[e]xamples of such substantial economic loss include, but are not limited to, the down zoning of private property, the elimination of any access to private property, and limiting the use of private air space." As a result, this section is extremely broad and concerns any government action that causes substantial economic loss. Although this section would, as the proponents contend, apply to many inverse condemnation cases, which this court has held to be the "constitutional equivalent to eminent domain," it would also apply to myriad other government actions that do not fall even within the most broad definition of eminent domain. As the opponents point out, this provision would require payment of just compensation for, among other things, public construction projects that cause a decrease in business or value while the construction work is ongoing, the creation of new public transportation routes or modification of existing routes when the change negatively impacts property values, and situations in which a zoning change request or special use permit is denied and the party requesting the change or permit would have seen a substantial increase in property value had the request been approved.

To the extent that section 8 would require payment of just compensation for all of the aforementioned government actions if the actions caused substantial economic loss to private property, that section far exceeds the scope of what could, even under an extremely liberal definition, be classified as eminent domain. "Government actions" related to construction projects, public transportation routes, and the denial of requested zoning changes or special use permits are in no way "functionally related" or "germane" to eminent domain, and this section clearly fails to provide sufficient notice of the wide array of subjects addressed in section 8 or the interests likely to be affected by it. Because of the far-reaching impact of this section on government actions completely unrelated to eminent domain, the fact that this section will also affect inverse condemnation is insufficient to render section 8 functionally related or germane to eminent domain. The proponents could easily have phrased section 8 in a way that limited its impact to eminent domain, but instead, they chose to use expansive language addressing government actions far beyond the scope of this subject.

Accordingly, we conclude that although the initiative addresses a primary subject, eminent domain, it embraces more than one subject in light of sections 1 and 8. Because the initiative encompasses more than one subject, it violates NRS 295.009's single-subject requirement. We therefore must determine the appropriate remedy for this violation.

D. *The initiative must be severed to preserve the people's will*

The opponents argue that the initiative should be wholly stricken from the ballot. The proponents, on the other hand, assert that the initiative should be severed and preserved, in major part, for the voters' consideration. For four reasons, severance and preservation is appropriate in this case.

First, and foremost, under the unique circumstances of this case, the initiative, even though it violates the single-subject requirement, is severable, as its primary subject is readily discernable. As discussed above, the vast majority of the initiative's provisions—twelve of fourteen—address eminent domain. Additionally, the proponents have repeatedly stated that the initiative concerns eminent domain. Thus, because the initiative has a single primary subject, it is amenable to severance; the two unrelated sections, 1 and 8, can simply be omitted from the rest of the initiative, so that it may proceed as an eminent domain initiative.

Second, the initiative's section 14 contains a severability clause, which provides that "[a]ny provision contained in this section shall be deemed a separate and freestanding right and shall remain in full force and effect should any other provision contained in this section be stricken for any reason." Thus, the initiative petition's signers have expressed a desire to allow the initiative to proceed even without some sections, and, in severing, this court need not speculate whether the signatories would have signed the petition in its severed form.

Third, NRS 295.009 does not prescribe a remedy for violations of the single-subject requirement. In the absence of a legislative mandate that all violations of the single-subject requirement result in an initiative's disqualification from the ballot, severance is permissible. Severance is routinely employed by courts to address single-subject violations after legislative enactments. Unlike Nevada, most other states' single-subject requirements are included in their constitutions. Because Nevada derives its single-subject requirement from a statute, as opposed to the Constitution, we are not constitutionally mandated to strike the initiative from the ballot.

Fourth, and significantly, our Constitution reserves to the people the initiative power. Although the Legislature has the power to enact laws to facilitate the operation of the initiative process, which includes enacting a single-subject requirement for initiative petitions, this court, in interpreting and applying such laws, must make every effort to sustain and preserve the people's constitutional right to amend their constitution through the initiative process. In this instance, because the Legislature has provided no specific remedy, striking the entire initiative, instead of severing the offending sections and allowing the remaining initiative to be placed on the November ballot, would run counter to the people's right to express their will through the initiative process. We have recognized that "the right to initiate change in this state's laws through ballot proposals is one of the basic powers enumerated in this state's constitution."

For all of these reasons, we conclude that sections 1 and 8 should be severed from the initiative in light of the single-subject violation. Severance eliminates the "Hobson's choice" described by our dissenting colleagues. We also note that the proponents remain free to circulate, in the future, one or more initiative petitions concerning the severed sections.

MAUPIN, J., concurring and dissenting.

I agree with the majority that the single-subject requirement of NRS 295.009 is not constitutionally infirm. I also agree that the initiative petition here violates NRS 295.009 because it contains multiple provisions "functionally related and germane" to more than one subject. I disagree, however, with the majority's remedy for this statutory violation. Thus, I have determined to join Justice Hardesty's dissent with regard to the remedy afforded and agree with him that we should order the petition removed from the November ballot.

HARDESTY, J., concurring in part and dissenting in part.

The majority concludes that the single-subject requirement embodied in NRS 295.009 does not violate the Nevada or federal constitutions, and that, by its plain language, the requirement limits initiative and referendum provisions to those that are "functionally related and germane" to the petition's general subject. The majority further concludes that the initiative at issue in this case, the Nevada Property Owners' Bill of Rights, impermissibly contains provisions functionally related and germane to more than one subject. With these conclusions, I concur. But with regard to the majority's view that, as a consequence of the single-subject requirement violation, this court can and should sever and strike certain provisions from this initiative, I dissent.

C. OTHER PROPERTY-RELATED RIGHTS UNDER STATE CONSTITUTIONS

Of course, States may recognize greater property rights or economic "liberty" interests than the U.S. Constitution would guarantee or protect. Various state constitutional provisions may justify such results, and sometimes state supreme courts may disagree with U.S. Supreme Court doctrine. The following case is a fascinating example of one such situation. Did you know that "eyebrow threading" could be a state constitutional right?

PATEL v. TEXAS DEPT. OF LICENSING
___ S.W.3d ___ (Texas 2015)

JOHNSON, J.

In this declaratory judgment action several individuals practicing commercial eyebrow threading and the salon owners employing them assert that, as applied to them, Texas's licensing statutes and regulations violate the Texas Constitution's due course of law provision. They claim that most of the 750 hours of training Texas requires for a license to practice commercial eyebrow threading are not related to health and safety or what threaders actually do. The State concedes that over 40% of the required hours are unrelated, but maintains that the licensing requirements are nevertheless constitutional.

The trial court and court of appeals agreed with the State. We do not.

Hdcdng: reverse

I. Background

Eyebrow threading is a grooming practice mainly performed in South Asian and Middle Eastern communities. It involves the removal of eyebrow hair and shaping of eyebrows with cotton thread. "Threading," as it is most commonly known, is increasingly practiced in Texas on a commercial basis. Threaders tightly wind a single strand of cotton thread, form a loop in it with their fingers, tighten the loop, and then quickly brush the thread along the skin of the client, trapping unwanted hair in the loop and removing it. In 2011, commercial threading became regulated in Texas when the Legislature categorized it as a practice of "cosmetology." *See* TEX. OCC. CODEE § 1602.002(a)(8) (" '[C]osmetology' means the practice of performing or offering to perform for compensation ... [the] remov[al] [of] superfluous hair from a person's body using depilatories, preparations, or tweezing techniques...."). That categorization and its effects underlie this case.

In order to legally practice cosmetology in Texas a person must hold either a general operator's license or, in certain instances, a more limited but easier-to-obtain esthetician license. *Id.* § 1602.251(a). Licensing requirements for general operators include completing a minimum of 1,500 hours of instruction in a licensed beauty culture school and passing a state-mandated test. Requirements for an esthetician license include completing a minimum of 750 hours of instruction in an approved training program and passing a state-mandated test. Commercial eyebrow threaders must have at least an esthetician license.

The Texas Department of Licensing and Regulation (TDLR or the Department), which is governed by the Texas Commission of Licensing and Regulation (the Commission), is charged with overseeing individuals and businesses that offer cosmetology services. The executive director of TDLR is authorized to impose administrative fines of as much as $5,000 per violation, per day.

In late 2008 and early 2009, TDLR inspected Justringz—a threading business with kiosk locations in malls across Texas—and found Nazira Nasruddin Momin and Vijay Lakshmi Yogi performing eyebrow threading without licenses. TDLR issued Notices of Alleged Violations to them for the unlicensed practice of cosmetology. Minaz Chamadia was also performing threading at Justringz without a license, but she was not cited by TDLR.

Ashish Patel and Anverali Satani own threading salons named Perfect Browz. The State has not taken any administrative action related to Perfect Browz. Satani is the sole owner of another threading business, Browz and Henna. TDLR inspected and investigated Browz and Henna on the basis of complaints filed against it. Although Satani received two warnings for

Browz and Henna employing unlicensed threaders, the Department did not issue a Notice of Alleged Violation.

In December 2009, Patel, Satani, Momin, Chamadia, and Yogi (collectively, the Threaders) brought suit against TDLR, its executive director, the Commission, and the Commission's members (collectively, the State) pursuant to the Uniform Declaratory Judgments Act (UDJA) seeking declaratory and injunctive relief. The Threaders alleged that the cosmetology statutes and administrative rules issued pursuant to those statutes (collectively, the cosmetology scheme) were unreasonable as applied to eyebrow threading and violated their constitutional right "to earn an honest living in the occupation of one's choice free from unreasonable governmental interference." They specifically sought declaratory judgment that, as applied to them, the cosmetology statutes and associated regulations violate the privileges and immunities and due course guarantees of Article I, § 19 of the Texas Constitution. They also sought a permanent injunction barring the State from enforcing the cosmetology scheme relating to the commercial practice of eyebrow threading against them.

In this Court the Threaders argue that (1) the real and substantial test governs substantive due process challenges to statutes and regulations affecting economic interests when the challenges are brought under Article I, § 19 of the Texas Constitution; (2) the cosmetology statutes and rules are unconstitutional as applied to the Threaders because they have no real and substantial connection to a legitimate governmental objective; and (3) even if rational basis review is the correct constitutional test, under the appropriate test, the statutes and regulations are unconstitutional as applied to the Threaders.

The State contends that . . . (5) there is no real difference between the "real and substantial" and "rational relationship" tests for due process concerns; and (6) threading raises public health concerns, implicating valid governmental concerns, thus the challenged licensing statutes and regulations that address these concerns comport with the substantive due process requirements regardless of which test is applied.

III. Constitutionality of the Statutes and Regulations

A. Due Course of Law

Article I, § 19 of the Texas Constitution provides that

> No citizen of this State shall be deprived of life, liberty, property, privileges or immunities, or in any manner disfranchised, except by the due course of the law of the land.

We have at least twice noted that Texas courts have not been entirely consistent in the standard of review applied when economic legislation is challenged under Section 19's substantive due course of law protections. The Threaders go beyond those two cases. They assert that courts considering as-applied substantive due process challenges under Section 19 have mixed and matched three different standards of review through the years. They label those standards as: (1) real and substantial, (2) rational basis including consideration of evidence, and (3) no-evidence rational basis.

The Threaders argue that the first referenced standard—"real and substantial"—is one in which the reviewing court considers whether (1) the legislative purpose for the statute is a proper one, (2) there is a real and substantial connection between that purpose and the language of the statute as the statute functions in practice, and (3) the statute works an excessive or undue burden on the person challenging the statute in relation to the statutory purpose. They argue that the distinguishing characteristic of cases employing the standard is that the courts using it consider evidence concerning both the government's purpose for a law and the law's real-world impact on the challenging party.

The Threaders recognize that the real and substantial test affords less deference to legislative judgments than does the federal rational basis standard. But they point to cases in which this Court specifically said or implied that certain language in the Texas Constitution affords more protection than comparable text in the federal Constitution. They also reference the United States Supreme Court as having noted in *City of Mesquite v. Aladdin's Castle, Inc.*, 455 U.S. 283, 293 (1982), that Article I, § 19 of the Texas Constitution might afford more protections than does the Fourteenth Amendment. They claim that twenty other states utilize the "real and substantial" test.

The Threaders present the second standard—"rational basis including consideration of evidence." Courts applying this test, the Threaders posit, lean heavily on the federal rational basis test and often weigh evidence—including expert testimony—to determine the purpose of a law and whether the law enacted to effect that purpose is reasonable.

The Threaders reference the third standard as "no evidence rational basis." Under the no-evidence version of the rational basis test, they argue, economic regulations do not violate Section 19 if they have any conceivable justification in a legitimate state interest, regardless of whether the justification is advanced by the government or "invented" by the reviewing court, and evidence "seldom" matters.

The Threaders say both the "real and substantial" and "rational basis including consideration of evidence" standards have two prongs, with the first being the primary difference between them. The first prong of the real and substantial standard, they maintain, is whether the challenged statute or regulation has a real and substantial connection to a legitimate governmental objective. They contrast that test with the rational basis including consideration of evidence standard, which they argue is more lenient and favorable toward the government because it asks only whether a statute or regulation arguably *could* bear some rational relationship to a legitimate governmental objective. They further maintain that for both standards the second prong is whether, on balance, the challenged statute or rule imposes an arbitrary or unduly harsh burden on the challenger in light of the government's objective.

B. Development of the Standard

The Declaration of Rights of the 1836 Republic of Texas Constitution included three separate rights guaranteeing "due course of law" or the "due course of the law of the land": (1) the sixth, which (among other protections) prevented an accused in a criminal proceeding from being "deprived of life, liberty, or property, but by due course of law"; (2) the eleventh, which provided that an injured person "shall have remedy by due course of law"; and (3) the seventh, which provided that "[n]o citizen shall be deprived of privileges, outlawed, exiled, or in any manner disenfranchised, except by due course of the law of the land." [3 original DP clauses]

In 1845, a group of delegates met to draft and propose Texas's first state constitution. The committee responsible for drafting the Bill of Rights proposed including two due course of law clauses—not the three clauses in the Declaration of Rights of the 1836 Republic of Texas Constitution. One of the suggested clauses protected an injured party's right to have "remedy by due course of law." The other clause incorporated the criminal due course of law protections from Section 6 of the Republic's Declaration of Rights into a composite due course guarantee: "No citizen of this state shall be deprived of life, liberty, property, or privileges, outlawed, exiled, or in any manner disenfranchised, except by due course of the law of the land." Thus, the committee's proposal added "life, liberty, property" to the existing due course of law guarantee, while removing the same phrase from the protections for the criminally accused. The proposal also added "of this state" after the word "citizen." The proposal was ratified as Article I, § 16 of the Texas Constitution of 1845. [Amendments 9 years later]

The language in the Due Course of Law Clause was not changed in the Texas Constitutions adopted in 1861, 1866, and 1869. But the Constitutional Convention of 1875 reexamined the clause and proposed changing it to its current language. The proposals were adopted, resulting in the clause reading as it now does. [Amend form since 1875]

Texas judicial decisions in the nineteenth and early twentieth century indicated that the Texas Due Course of Law Clause and the federal Due

Process Clause were nearly, if not exactly, coextensive. Such decisions generally tracked the thinking expressed by the Court in *Mellinger v. City of Houston*, 68 Tex. 37, 3 S.W. 249, 252–53 (1887), where the Court held that Article I, § 19 was not violated under the facts of that case because of the United States Supreme Court's interpretation of the Fourteenth Amendment in a similar case. During this period, Texas courts frequently addressed whether a legislative enactment was a proper exercise of the governmental unit's police power, examining justifications for the enactment and typically relying on decisions from the United States Supreme Court as guidance. Occasionally, Texas courts mentioned that a proper review involved examining the enactment for a "real or substantial" relationship to the government's police power interest in public health, morals, or safety—a standard consistent with decisions of the United States Supreme Court.

As to federal due process standards, this period before 1935 is sometimes referred to as the "*Lochner* period" in reference to the United States Supreme Court's decision in *Lochner v. New York*. The Court remained within the bounds charted by *Lochner* for several years. Basically, then, during the "*Lochner* era," substantive due process was a touchstone by which courts analyzed both the purpose and the effect of governmental economic regulation by scrutinizing them with a somewhat equivocal deference to the legislative body's pronounced purpose for a law and its choice of the method embodied in the law to achieve that purpose. The federal landscape changed in 1938. In *United States v. Carolene Products Co.*, 304 U.S. 144 (1938), the Supreme Court pronounced that

> regulatory legislation affecting ordinary commercial transactions is not to be pronounced unconstitutional unless in the light of the facts made known or generally assumed it is of such a character as to preclude the assumption that it rests upon some rational basis.

Texas courts were faced with the question of whether, after *Carolene Products*, to stay the course as to prior decisions interpreting Article I, § 19's due course of law provision, or follow the lead of the United States Supreme Court as to the Fourteenth Amendment's Due Process Clause. That is, Texas courts had to decide whether "due process of law," as used in the Fourteenth Amendment, and "due course of law of the land," as used in Article I, § 19 of the Texas Constitution, remained "in nearly if not all respects, practically synonymous," or whether the meaning of the Texas Constitution remained the same as it had been earlier interpreted because the Constitution's language had not been amended through the political process. As the parties to this case—and numerous Texas courts and commentators—have pointed out, the answer has not been made clear as to substantive due process challenges to governmental regulation of economic interests. As set out more fully above, the Threaders argue that in some cases this Court as well as courts of appeals have continued using a less deferential, heightened-scrutiny standard of review, while in some cases different ones have been applied.

Following the lead of our prior jurisprudence, we conclude that the Texas due course of law protections in Article I, § 19, for the most part, align with the protections found in the Fourteenth Amendment to the United States Constitution. But, that having been said, the drafting, proposing, and adopting of the 1875 Constitution was accomplished shortly after the United States Supreme Court decision in the *Slaughter–House Cases* by which the Court put the responsibility for protecting a large segment of individual rights directly on the states. Given the temporal legal context, Section 19's substantive due course provisions undoubtedly were intended to bear at least some burden for protecting individual rights that the United States Supreme Court determined were not protected by the federal Constitution. That burden has been recognized in various decisions of Texas courts for over one hundred and twenty-five years. We continue to do so today: the standard of review for as-applied substantive due course challenges to economic regulation statutes includes an accompanying consideration as reflected by cases referenced above: whether the statute's effect as a whole is so unreasonably burdensome that it becomes oppressive in relation to the underlying governmental interest.

In sum, statutes are presumed to be constitutional. To overcome that presumption, the proponent of an as-applied challenge to an economic regulation statute under Section 19's substantive due course of law requirement must demonstrate that either (1) the statute's purpose could not arguably be rationally related to a legitimate governmental interest; or (2) when considered as a whole, the statute's actual, real-world effect as applied to the challenging party could not arguably be rationally related to, or is so burdensome as to be oppressive in light of, the governmental interest.

C. Application: The Texas Cosmetology Statutes and Regulations

The Threaders do not contend that the State's licensing of the commercial practice of cosmetology is not rationally related to a legitimate governmental interest. But they strongly urge that the number of hours of training required to obtain even an esthetician license has an arbitrary and unduly burdensome effect as applied to them because the 750–hour requirement has no rational connection to reasonable safety and sanitation requirements, which the State says are the interests underlying its licensing of threaders.

Several statutes address safety standards and sanitary conditions relating to cosmetology. Commission rules also address public safety and sanitary conditions. To address competency of cosmetologists in Texas, the Legislature and Commission have imposed specific educational and training requirements for cosmetologists, estheticians, and salon operators. To become a licensed esthetician, threaders must take at least 750 hours of instruction in a Commission-approved training program and take State-prescribed practical and written examinations. Those training programs must devote at least 225 hours of instruction to facial treatments, cleansing, masking, and therapy; 90 hours to anatomy and physiology; 75 hours to electricity, machines, and related equipment; 75 hours to makeup; 50 hours to orientation, rules, and laws; 50 hours to chemistry; 50 hours to care of clients; 40 hours to sanitation, safety, and first aid; 35 hours to management; 25 hours to superfluous hair removal; 15 hours to aroma therapy; 10 hours to nutrition; and 10 hours to color psychology. Commission-approved beauty schools are not required to teach threading techniques. The schools are required to provide 25 hours of instruction in superfluous hair removal, which encompasses threading, but individual schools decide which techniques to teach. The record reflects that fewer than ten of the 389 Commission-approved Texas beauty schools teach threading techniques, and only one of those devotes more than a few hours to them. Further, threading techniques are not required to be part of the mandated tests. Both the practical and written tests are administered and scored by a third-party testing firm. The firm's testing guidelines show that the practical examination is an hour and thirty minutes in length and includes sanitation, disinfection and hair removal, but does not include threading, although a test-taker may *elect* to remove six hairs from the model's eyebrow using thread instead of tweezers during part of the exam. Nor does the written examination include questions as to threading techniques, although it includes globally relevant questions about sanitation, disinfection, and safety.

As shown above, of the 750 hours of required instruction for an esthetician license, 40 are required to be directly devoted to sanitation, safety, and first aid. But in addition, hygiene and sanitation are covered as they relate to four other portions of the curriculum: facial treatment, anatomy, rules and laws, and superfluous hair removal. Hygiene and sanitation are also addressed in the written and practical licensing exams, along with other topics including disinfection and safety.

One argument the Threaders make, which at its core challenges the rationality of *any* required training, is that the unlicensed practice of eyebrow threading is simply not a threat to public health and safety. In support of the argument they reference their expert witness who submitted a report addressing all of the available medical literature on eyebrow threading, as well as her own empirical analysis of the technique's safety. Based on her investigation and professional experience with eyebrow threading, the expert concluded that threading is safe and, from a medical perspective, requires nothing more than basic sanitation training.

But the Threaders' expert also raised public health concerns during her testimony. She testified that threading may lead to the spread of highly contagious bacterial and viral infections, including flat warts, skin-colored lesions known as mulluscum contagiosum, pink eye, ringworm, impetigo, and staphylococcus aureus, among others. She also agreed that failure to utilize appropriate sanitation practices—for example, proper use of disposable materials, cleaning of work stations, effective hand-washing techniques, and correct treatment of skin irritations and abrasions—can further expose threading clients to infection and disease.

Moving beyond the argument that threading does not pose health risks to begin with, the Threaders contend that as many as 710 of the required 750 training hours for an esthetician license are not related to properly training threaders in hygiene and sanitation, considering the activities they actually perform. The State argues that the Threaders greatly exaggerate the number of unrelated hours, but concedes that as many as 320 of the curriculum hours are not related to activities threaders actually perform.

Both sides disagree as to how many hrs are unnecessary

Differentiating between types of cosmetology practices is the prerogative of the Legislature and regulatory agencies to which the Legislature properly delegates authority. And it is not for courts to second-guess their decisions as to the necessity for and the extent of training that should be required for different types of commercial service providers. But we note in passing that persons licensed to apply eyelash extensions— a specialty involving the use of chemicals and a high rate of adverse reactions—are required to undergo only 320 hours of training. We also note that when the Threaders filed suit, hair braiders were required to undergo only 35 hours of training, 16 of which were in health and safety. Hair braiding, however, has since been deregulated by the Legislature.

The fact that approximately 58% of the minimum required training hours are arguably relevant to the activities threaders perform, while 42% of the hours are not, is determinative of the aspect of the second prong of the as-applied standard which asks whether the effect of the requirements as a whole could be rationally related to the governmental interest. They could be. But the percentage must also be considered along with other factors, such as the quantitative aspect of the hours represented by that percentage and the costs associated with them when determining the other aspect of the second prong—whether the licensing requirements as a whole are so burdensome as to be oppressive to the Threaders. Where the number of hours required and the associated costs are low, the ratio of required hours to arguably relevant hours is less important as to the burdensome question. But its importance increases as the required hours increase. For example, if the statute and Commission's rules required ten hours of training for a threader to be licensed and 58 percent, or 5.8 hours, were arguably relevant to what threaders do, the burden of the irrelevant hours would weigh less heavily in determining whether the effect of the requirements as a whole on aspiring threaders is oppressive. In the case of the Threaders, however, the large number of hours not arguably related to the actual practice of threading, the associated costs of those hours in out-of-pocket expenses, and the delayed employment opportunities while taking the hours makes the number highly relevant to whether the licensing requirements as a whole reach the level of being so burdensome that they are oppressive.

The dividing line is not bright between the number of required but irrelevant hours that would yield a harsh, but constitutionally acceptable, requirement and the number that would not. Even assuming that 430 hours (a number the Threaders dispute) of the mandated training are arguably relevant to what commercial threaders do in practice, that means threaders are required to undergo the equivalent of eight 40–hour weeks of training unrelated to health and safety as applied to threading. The parties disagree about the costs of attending cosmetology training required for a license to practice threading. The Threaders point to evidence that the cost averages $9,000. The State says the $9,000 cost is for private schools while public schools charge only $3,500. Given the record as to the number of hours of training required for subjects unrelated to threading, our decision neither turns on, nor is altered by, the exact cost. But the admittedly unrelated 320 required training hours, combined with the fact that threader trainees have to pay for the training and at the same time lose the opportunity to make money actively practicing their trade, leads us to conclude that the Threaders have met their high burden of proving that, as applied to them, the requirement of 750 hours of training to become licensed is not just unreasonable or harsh, but it is so oppressive that it violates Article I, § 19 of the Texas Constitution.

IV. Response to the Dissents

The dissenting Justices say four things that bear responding to. First, they say that measuring the effects of the provisions by an "oppressive" standard is to measure it by no standard at all. The actuality of the matter is that the standard they propose for measuring the effects of the provisions is for all practical purposes no standard. The only way an enactment could fail the test the dissenters advocate is if the purpose of the enactment were completely mismatched with—that is, it bore no rational relationship to—the provisions enacted to effect it. For example, assume in this case the record demonstrated conclusively, or the State conceded, that the Threaders are right and only 40 hours of the required training are relevant to safety and sanitation in performing threading. It would not matter under the CHIEF JUSTICE'S proposed standard. For under that standard, so long as at least some part of the required training could be rationally related to safety and sanitation, the entire 750 hours are rationally related because the provisions as a whole "might achieve the objective." The logical result of such standard would be that if the State were to require 1,500 or even more hours of training, the increased requirement would pass constitutional muster. Why is that so? Because if 40 hours of training might conceivably effect the Legislature's purpose and be constitutional, then any greater number that included that same 40 hours would also.

Second, the CHIEF JUSTICE references a small minority of other states that require threaders to be licensed either explicitly or by generally requiring licensing of those who commercially remove superfluous hair. But the Threaders neither contest the rationality of the State's requiring them to be licensed, nor the requirement that they take training in subjects such as sanitation and hygiene. What they contest is the excessiveness of the training requirements given the magnitude of the irrelevant training. And whether that excessive requirement violates the Texas Constitution is not determined by the relationship between other states' statutes and regulations and their respective constitutions.

Third, the CHIEF JUSTICE says that articulating and weighing factors such as the cost and relevance of the required training in considering the constitutionality of the provisions is "generally referred to as legislating" and should not be done by judges, and JUSTICE GUZMAN asserts that any line drawing in this case should be done by the Legislature. But providing standards for measuring the constitutionality of legislative enactments is not only a judicial prerogative—it is necessary in order to make the law predictable and not dependent on the proclivities of whichever judge or judges happen to be considering the case. Indeed, the dissenting Justices would reach the result they propose by measuring the licensing provisions against standards—the standards of "rational relationship" jurisprudence—just different standards. Expressing factors by which a statute's constitutionality is to be measured and by which we reach our decision is not legislating; it is judging and providing guidance for courts to use in future challenges to statutes or regulations, which history tells us will come.

Fourth, the CHIEF JUSTICE refers to rediscovering and unleashing "the *Lochner* monster" if legislative enactments are measured against a standard other than the rational relationship standard. But as discussed above, Texas courts, including this Court, have expressed and applied various standards for considering as-applied substantive due process claims for over a century. And it is those decisions on which the standards we set out today are based. Surely if those cases represented a "monster" running amuck in Texas, this Court would have long ago decisively dealt with it.

Courts must extend great deference to legislative enactments, apply a strong presumption in favor of their validity, and maintain a high bar for declaring any of them in violation of the Constitution. But judicial deference is necessarily constrained where constitutional protections are implicated.

V. Conclusion

[handwritten margin note: Holding]

The provisions of the Texas Occupations Code and Commission rules promulgated pursuant to that Code requiring the individual Threaders to undergo at least 750 hours of training in order to obtain a state license before practicing commercial threading violate the Texas Constitution.

WILLETT, J., concurring.

> To understand the emotion which swelled my heart as I clasped this money, realizing that I had no master who could take it from me—*that it was mine—that my hands were my own*, and could earn more of the precious coin.... I was not only a freeman but a free-working man, and no master Hugh stood ready at the end of the week to seize my hard earnings.

[handwritten margin note: Importance of economic liberty]

Frederick Douglass's irrepressible joy at exercising his hard-won freedom captures just how fundamental—and transformative—economic liberty is. Self-ownership, the right to put your mind and body to productive enterprise, is not a mere luxury to be enjoyed at the sufferance of governmental grace, but is indispensable to human dignity and prosperity.

[handwritten margin note: Purpose & Structure]

Texans are doubly blessed, living under two constitutions sharing a singular purpose: to secure individual freedom, the essential condition of human flourishing. In today's age of staggering civic illiteracy—when 35 percent of Americans cannot correctly name a single branch of government—it is unsurprising that people mistake majority rule as America's defining value. But our federal and state charters are not, contrary to popular belief, about "democracy"—a word that appears in neither document, nor in the Declaration of Independence. Our enlightened 18th- and 19th-century Founders, both federal and state, aimed higher, upended things, and brilliantly divided power to enshrine a *promise* (liberty), not merely a *process* (democracy).

One of our constitutions (federal) is short, the other (state) is long—like *really* long—but both underscore liberty's primacy right away. The federal Constitution, in the first sentence of the Preamble, declares its mission to "secure the Blessings of Liberty." The Texas Constitution likewise wastes no time, stating up front in the Bill of Rights its paramount aim to recognize and establish "the general, great and essential principles of liberty and free government." The point is unsubtle and undeniable: Liberty is not *provided* by government; (liberty *preexists* government) It is not a gift from the sovereign; it is our natural birthright. Fixed. Innate. Unalienable.

negative rights

> *Democracy is two wolves and a lamb voting on what to have for lunch. Liberty*
> *is a well-armed lamb contesting the vote.*

This case concerns the timeless struggle between personal freedom and government power. Do Texans live under a presumption of liberty or a presumption of restraint? The Texas Constitution confers power—but even more critically, it constrains power. What *are* the outer-boundary limits on government actions that trample Texans' constitutional right to earn an honest living for themselves and their families? Some observers liken judges to baseball umpires, calling legal balls and strikes, but when it comes to restrictive licensing laws, just how generous is the constitutional strike zone? Must courts rubber-stamp even the most nonsensical encroachments on occupational freedom? Are the most patently farcical and protectionist restrictions nigh unchallengeable, or are there, in fact, judicially enforceable limits?

This case raises constitutional eyebrows because it asks building-block questions about constitutional architecture—about how we as Texans govern ourselves and about the relationship of the citizen to the State. This case concerns far more than whether Ashish Patel can pluck unwanted hair with a strand of thread. This case is fundamentally about the American Dream and the unalienable human right to pursue happiness without curtsying to government on bended knee. It is about whether government can connive with rent-seeking factions to ration liberty unrestrained, and whether judges must submissively uphold even the most risible encroachments.

I recognize the potential benefits of licensing: protecting the public and preventing charlatanism. I also recognize the proven benefits of constitutional constraints: protecting the public and preventing collectivism. Invalidating irrational laws does not beckon a Dickensian world of run-amok frauds and pretenders. The Court's view is simple, and simply stated: Laws that impinge your constitutionally protected right to earn an honest living must not be preposterous.

By contrast, the dissents see government power in the economic realm as infinitely elastic, and thus limited government as entirely fictive, troubling since economic freedom is no less vulnerable to majoritarian oppression than, say, religious freedom—perhaps more so. Exalting the reflexive deference championed by Progressive theorists like Justice Oliver Wendell Holmes, Jr., the dissents would seemingly uphold even the most facially protectionist actions.

The Texas Constitution enshrines structural principles meant to advance individual freedom; they are not there for mere show. Our Framers opted for constitutional—that is, *limited*—government, meaning majorities don't possess an untrammeled right to trammel. The State would have us wield a rubber stamp rather than a gavel, but a written constitution is mere meringue if courts rotely exalt majoritarianism over constitutionalism, and thus forsake what Chief Justice Marshall called their "painful duty"—"to say, that such an act was not the law of the land."

To be sure, the Capitol, not this Court, is the center of policymaking gravity, and judges are lousy second-guessers of the other branches' economic judgments. Lawmakers' policy-setting power is unrivaled—but it is not unlimited. Preeminence does not equal omnipotence. Politicians decide if laws pass, but courts decide if those laws pass muster. Cases stretching back centuries treat economic liberty as constitutionally protected—we crossed that Rubicon long ago—and there is a fateful difference between active judges who defend rights and activist judges who concoct rights. If judicial review means *anything*, it is that judicial restraint does not allow *everything*. The rational-basis bar may be low, but it is not subterranean.

I support the Court's "Don't Thread on Me" approach: Threaders with no license are less menacing than government with unlimited license.

I.

This case lays bare a spirited debate raging in legal circles, one that conjures legal buzzwords and pejoratives galore: activism vs. restraint, deference vs. dereliction, adjudication vs. abdication. The rhetoric at times seems overheated, but the temperature reflects the stakes. It concerns the most elemental—if not elementary—question of American jurisprudence: the proper role of the judiciary under the Constitution.

Judicial duty requires courts to act judicially by adjudicating, not politically by legislating. So when *is* it proper for a court to strike down legislative or executive action as unconstitutional? There are people of goodwill on both sides, and as this case demonstrates, it seems a legal Rorschach test, where one person's "judicial engagement" is another person's "judicial usurpation."

This much is clear: Spirited debates over judicial review have roiled America since the Founding, from *Marbury v. Madison*, to *Worcester v. Georgia* (against which President Jackson bellowed, "John Marshall has made his decision—now let him enforce it."), to the late 19th and early 20th centuries, when Progressives opposed judicial enforcement of economic liberties, all the way to present-day battles over the Patient Protection and Affordable Care Act. In the 1920s and 1930s, liberals began backing judicial protection of *non*economic rights, while resisting similar protection for property rights and other economic freedoms. The Progressives' preference for judicial nonintervention was later embraced by post-New Deal conservatives like Judge Bork. The judicial-review debate, both raucous and reasoned, is particularly pitched today within the broader conservative legal movement. A prominent fault line has opened on the right between traditional conservatives who champion majoritarianism and more liberty-minded theorists who believe robust judicial protection of economic rights is indispensable to limited government.

Today's case arises under the *Texas* Constitution, over which we have final interpretive authority, and nothing in its 60,000—plus words requires judges to turn a blind eye to transparent rent-seeking that bends government power to private gain, thus robbing people of their innate right–antecedent to government—to earn an honest living. Indeed, even if the Texas Due Course of Law Clause mirrored perfectly the federal Due Process Clause, that in no way binds Texas courts to cut-and-paste federal rational-basis jurisprudence that long post-dates enactment of our own constitutional provision, one more inclined to freedom. *Even natural words ≠ lock step*

The test adopted today bears a passing resemblance to "rational basis"-type wording, but this test is rational basis with bite, demanding actual *rationality*, scrutinizing the law's actual *basis*, and applying an actual *test*. In my view, the principal dissent is unduly diffident, concluding the threading rules, while "excessive" and "obviously too much" are not "clearly arbitrary." If these rules are not arbitrary, then the definition of "arbitrary" is itself arbitrary. *Count fl* Without discussing (or even citing) recent federal cases striking down nonsensical licensing rules under the supine federal test, the dissents sever "rational" from "rational basis," loading the dice—relentlessly—in government's favor. Their test is tantamount to no test at all; at most it is pass/fail, and government never fails.

II.

You take my house when you do take the prop /
That doth sustain my house; you take my life /
When you do take the means whereby I live.

Government understandably wants to rid society of quacks, swindlers, and incompetents. And licensing is one of government's preferred tools, aiming to protect us from harm by credentialing certain occupations and activities. You can't practice medicine in Texas without satisfying the Board of Medical Examiners. You can't zoom down SH–130 outside Austin at 85 miles per hour (reportedly the highest speed limit in the Western Hemisphere) without a driver's license. Sensible rules undoubtedly boost our quality of life. And senseless rules undoubtedly weaken our quality of life. Governments at every level—national, state, and local—wield regulatory power, but not always with regulatory prudence, which critics say stymies innovation, raises consumer prices, and impedes economic opportunity with little or no concomitant public benefit. The academic literature has attained consensus: "a licensing restriction can only be justified where it leads to better quality professional services—and for many restrictions, proof of that enhanced quality is lacking."

It merits repeating: Judicial duty does not include second-guessing everyday policy choices, however improvident. The question for judges is not whether a law is sensible but whether it is constitutional. Does state "police power"—the inherent authority to enact general-welfare legislation—*ever* go too far? Does a Texas Constitution inclined to limited government have *anything* to say about government irrationally subjugating the livelihoods of Texans?

A.

The Republic of Texas regulated just one profession: doctors. In 1889, the State of Texas added one more: dentists. Until the mid–20th century, occupational regulation in the Lone Star State was rare (aside from the post-Prohibition alcohol industry) and was generally limited to professions with a clear public-safety impact: nurses, pharmacists, optometrists, engineers, etc.

The Lone Star State is not immune from licensure proliferation. An ever-growing number of Texans must convince government of their fitness to ply their trade, spurring the House Committee on Government Efficiency and Reform in 2013 to lament the kudzu-like spread of licensure: "The proliferation of occupational licensing by the State of Texas can be to the detriment of the very consumer the licensing is professing to protect." Today the number of regulated occupations exceeds 500—about 2.7 million individuals and businesses, roughly one-third of the Texas workforce, higher than the national average—with many restrictions backed by heavy fines and even jail time. Importantly, these statistics reflect state-only regulations; local and federal rules raise the number of must-be-licensed workers higher still.

Unlike some states, Texas doesn't yet require florists, interior designers, horse massagers, ferret breeders, or fortune tellers to get state approval (though the soothsayers would presumably see it coming). But the Lone Star State *does* require state approval to be a shampoo apprentice. And to be an in-person auctioneer (though not to be an *internet* auctioneer). And while you don't need a license to be a bingo caller in Texas, you must be listed on the Registry of Approved Bingo Workers in order to yell out numbers and letters.

B.

As today's case shows, the Texas occupational licensure regime, predominantly impeding Texans of modest means, can seem a hodge-podge of disjointed, logic-defying irrationalities, where the burdens imposed seem almost farcical, forcing many lower-income Texans to face a choice: submit to illogical bureaucracy or operate an illegal business. Licensure absurdities become apparent when you compare the wildly disparate education/experience burdens visited on various professions. The disconnect between the strictness of some licensing rules and their alleged public-welfare rationale is patently bizarre:

> *Emergency Medical Technicians.* EMTs are entrusted with life-and-death decisions. But in Texas, entry-level EMTs need only 140 hours of training before rendering life-saving aid. Contrast that with the radically more onerous education/experience requirements for barbers (300 hours), massage therapists (500 hours), manicurists (600 hours), estheticians (750 hours), and full-service cosmetologists (1,500 hours).

> *Backflow Prevention Assembly Testers.* Of the number of states and the District of Columbia that require licenses for backflow prevention assembly testers, the Lone Star State is the only place where it takes more than two weeks of training/experience—*way* more. Fifty times more. Not two weeks but two *years*.

State licensing impacts our lives from head to toe. Literally. Starting at the top, where does hair end and the beard begin? Texas law has been quite finicky on the matter, leading Texas barbers and cosmetologists to spend years splitting legal hairs and clogging Texas courts. Both of these state-licensed professionals may cut hair, but until 2013 only barbers, not cosmetologists, had state permission to wield a razor blade to shave *facial* hair. Before 2013, if you wanted your beard shaved, you had to visit a barber (probably a man) and not a cosmetologist (probably a woman). And what *is* a "beard" anyway? Why, it's the facial hair below the "line of demarcation" as defined in the Administrative Code. Even the Attorney General of Texas got all shook up wondering whether Elvis's famous sideburns "were hair which a cosmetologist might trim, or a partial beard which could be serviced only [by] a barber."

At the other bodily extreme, what's the demarcation between the foot (which podiatrists can treat) and the ankle (which they can't)? These are high-stakes disputes, and sometimes the licensing bodies have jurisdictional spats with each other, usually over "scope of practice" issues. So where *does* the foot end and the ankle begin?

III.

No man is allowed to be a judge in his own cause, because his interest would certainly bias his judgment, and, not improbably, corrupt his integrity.

Anyone acquainted with human nature understands, as Madison did, that when people, or branches of government, are free to judge their own actions, nothing is prohibited. The Court recognizes that Texans possess a basic liberty under Article I, Section 19 to earn a living. And to safeguard that guarantee, the Court adopts a test allergic to nonsensical government encroachment. I prefer authentic judicial scrutiny to a rubber-stamp exercise that stacks the legal deck in government's favor.

My views are simply stated:

1. *The economic-liberty test under Article I, Section 19 of the Texas Constitution is more searching than the minimalist test under the Fourteenth Amendment to the United States Constitution.*

Even under the lenient rational-basis test—"the most deferential of the standards of review"—the would-be threaders should win this case. It is hard to imagine anything more irrational than forcing people to spend thousands of dollars and hundreds of hours on classes that teach everything they don't do but nothing they actually do. Not one of the 750 required hours of cosmetology covers eyebrow threading. Government-mandated barriers to employment should actually bear some meaningful relationship to reality.

The dissents would subordinate concrete scrutiny to conjectural scrutiny that grants a nigh-irrebuttable presumption of constitutionality. It is elastic review where any conceivable, theoretical, imaginary justification suffices. In my view, Texas judges should instead conduct a genuine search for truth—*as they do routinely in countless other constitutional areas*—asking "What is government actually up to?" When constitutional rights are imperiled, Texans deserve actual scrutiny of actual assertions with actual evidence.

• Should Texas courts reflexively accept disingenuous or smokescreen explanations for the government's actions? No.

• Is government allowed to prevail with purely illusory or pretextual justifications for a challenged law? No.

• Must citizens negate even purely hypothetical justifications for the government's infringement of liberty? No.

• Are Texas courts obliged to jettison their truth-seeking duty of neutrality and help government contrive post hoc justifications? No.

Texas judges should discern whether government is seeking a constitutionally valid end using constitutionally permissible means. And they should do so based on real-world facts and without helping government invent after-the-fact rationalizations. I believe the Texas Constitution requires an earnest search for truth, not the turn-a-blind-eye approach that prevails under the federal Constitution.

2. The Texas Constitution narrows the difference in judicial protection given to "fundamental" rights (like speech or religion) and so-called "non-fundamental" rights (like the right to earn a living).

The jurisprudential fact of the matter is that courts are more protective of some constitutional guarantees than others. One bedrock feature of 20th-century jurisprudence, starting with the U.S. Supreme Court's New Deal-era decisions, was to relegate economic rights to a more junior-varsity echelon of constitutional protection than "fundamental" rights. Nothing in the federal or Texas Constitutions requires treating certain rights as "fundamental" and devaluing others as "non-fundamental" and applying different levels of judicial scrutiny, but it is what it is: Economic liberty gets less constitutional protection than other constitutional rights.

But "economic" and "noneconomic" rights indisputably overlap. As the U.S. Supreme Court has recognized, freedom of speech would be meaningless if government banned bloggers from owning computers. Economic freedom is indispensable to enjoying other freedoms—for example, buying a Facebook ad to boost your political campaign. A decade (and three days) ago in *Kelo v. City of New London*, the landmark takings case that prompted a massive national backlash, Justice Thomas's dissent lamented the bias against economic rights this way: "Something has gone seriously awry with this Court's interpretation of the Constitution. Though citizens are safe from the government in their homes, the homes themselves are not."

Kelo is indeed illustrative, as the rational-basis test applies in eminent-domain cases, too, notwithstanding the assurance in footnote four of *Carolene Products* that alleged violations of the Bill of Rights deserve heightened scrutiny. Even though the Fifth Amendment explicitly protects property, the U.S. Supreme Court has supplanted the *Carolene Products* bifurcation with rational-basis deference in takings cases. The *Kelo* Court stressed its "longstanding policy of deference to legislative judgments," and its unwillingness to "second-guess" the city's determination as to "what public needs justify the use of the takings power." Justice O'Connor's scathing dissent, her final opinion on the Court, forcefully accused her colleagues of shirking their constitutional duty.

I would not have Texas judges condone government's dreamed-up justifications (or dream up post hoc justifications themselves) for interfering with citizens' constitutional guarantees. As in other constitutional settings, we should be neutral arbiters, not bend-over-backwards advocates for the government. Texas judges weighing state constitutional challenges should scrutinize government's *actual* justifications for a law—what policymakers *really* had in mind at the time, not something they dreamed up after litigation erupted. And judges should not be obliged to concoct speculative or far-fetched rationalizations to save the government's case.

3. Texas courts need not turn a blind eye to the self-evident reasons why an increasing number of Texans need a government permission slip to work in their chosen field.

Today's decision recognizes another key contributor to the irrationalities afflicting occupational licensing: the hard-wired inclination to reduce competition. This metabolic impulse—Human Nature 101—has always existed.

Courts need not be oblivious to the iron political and economic truth that the regulatory environment is littered with rent-seeking by special-interest factions who crave the exclusive, state-protected right to pursue their careers. Again, smart regulations are indispensable, but nonsensical regulations inflict multiple burdens—on consumers (who pay more for goods and services, or try to do the work themselves), on would-be entrepreneurs (who find market entry formidable, if not impossible), on lower-income workers (who can't break into entry-level trades), and on the wider public (who endure crimped economic growth while enjoying no tangible benefit whatsoever).

IV.

In Europe, charters of liberty have been granted by power. America has set the example ... of charters of power granted by liberty.

The Founders pledged their lives, fortunes, and sacred honors to birth a new type of nation—one with a radical design: three separate, co-equal, and competing branches. Three rival branches deriving power from three unrivaled words: "We the People." Both the Texas and federal Constitutions presume the branches will be structural adversaries—that legislators, for example, will jealously guard their lawmaking prerogative if the executive begins aggrandizing power. Indeed, inter-branch political competition is a precondition to advancing inter-firm economic competition—that is, the judicial branch asserting judicial power to ensure that the political branches don't arbitrarily insulate established practitioners from newcomers.

A.

As mentioned earlier, the term "judicial activism" is a legal Rorschach test. I oppose judicial activism, inventing rights not rooted in the law. But the opposite extreme, judicial passivism, is corrosive, too—judges who, while not activist, are not *active* in preserving the liberties, and the limits, our Framers actually enshrined. The Texas Constitution is irrefutably framed in proscription, imposing unsubtle and unmistakable limits on government power. It models the federal Constitution in a fundamental way: dividing government power so that each branch checks and balances the others. But as we recently observed, "the Texas Constitution takes Madison a step further by including, unlike the federal Constitution, an explicit Separation of Powers provision to curb overreaching and to spur rival branches to guard their prerogatives." The Texas Constitution constrains government power in another distinctive way: It lacks a Necessary and Proper Clause, often invoked to expand Congress's powers beyond those specifically enumerated. Moreover, as noted above, it contains a Privileges or Immunities Clause that, unlike the federal version, has never been judicially nullified.

As judges, we have no business second-guessing *policy* choices, but when the Constitution is at stake, it is not impolite to say "no" to government. Liberties for "We the People" necessarily mean limits on "We the Government." That's the very reason constitutions are written: to stop government abuses, not to ratify them. Our supreme duty to our dual constitutions and to their shared purpose—to "secure the Blessings of Liberty"—requires us to check constitutionally verboten actions, not rubber-stamp them under the banner of majoritarianism. For people to live their lives as they see fit, a government of limited powers must exercise that power not with force but with reason. And an independent judiciary must *judge* government actions, not merely rationalize them. Judicial restraint doesn't require courts to ignore the nonrestraint of the other branches, not when their actions imperil the constitutional liberties of people increasingly hamstrung in their enjoyment of "Life, Liberty and the pursuit of Happiness."

The power to "protect the public" is a heady and fearsome one. Government is charged with promoting the general welfare, but it must always act within constitutional constraints. Our two constitutions exist to advance two purposes: individual liberty through limited government. Our federal and state Founders saw liberty as America's natural, foundational value, and our rights as too numerous to be exhaustively listed. Liberty both *justifies* government (to erect basic civic guardrails) and *limits* government (to minimize abridgements on human freedom). In other words, our dual constitutional charters exist not to *exalt* majority rule but to protect prepolitical rights that *limit* majority rule. Majoritarianism cannot be permitted to invert our bottom-line constitutional premise. The might of the majority, whatever the vote count, cannot trample individuals' rights recognized in both our federal and state Constitutions, not to mention in our nation's first law, the Declaration.

B.

Our State Constitution, like Madison's Federal handiwork, is infused with Newtonian genius: three rival branches locked in synchronous orbit by competing interests—ambition checking ambition.

Isaac Newton died in 1727, before James Madison, the Father of the U.S. Constitution, was even born, but our Founders, both state and federal, understood political physics: "power seized by one branch necessarily means power ceded by another." Newton's Third Law of Motion, while a physical law, also operates as a political law. When one branch of government exerts a force, there occurs an equal and opposite counterforce. The Laws of Constitutional Motion require these rival branches to stay within their sphere, flexing competing forces so that power is neither seized nor ceded.

Our Framers understood that government was inclined to advance its own interests, even to the point of ham-fisted bullying, which is precisely why the Constitution was written—to keep *government* on a leash, not We the People. But individual liberty pays the price when our ingenious system of checks and balances sputters, including when the judiciary subordinates liberty to the congeries of group interests that dictate majoritarian outcomes.

Police power is undoubtedly an attribute of state sovereignty, but sovereignty ultimately resides in "the people of the State of Texas." The Texas Constitution limits government encroachments, and does so on purpose. "Our Bill of Rights is not mere hortatory fluff; it is a purposeful check on government power." And everyday Texans, and the courts that serve them, must remain vigilant. Government will always insist it is acting for the public's greater good, but as Justice Brandeis warned in his now-celebrated *Olmstead* dissent: "Experience should teach us to be most on our guard to protect liberty when the government's purposes are beneficent."

Government's conception of its own power as limitless is hard-wired. But under the Texas Constitution, government may only pursue constitutionally permissible ends. Naked economic protectionism, strangling hopes and dreams with bureaucratic red tape, is not one of them. And such barriers, often stemming from interest-group politics, are often insurmountable for Texans on the lower rungs of the economic ladder (who unsurprisingly lack political power)—not to mention the harm inflicted on consumers deprived of the fruits of industrious entrepreneurs. Irrational licensing laws oppress hard-working Texans of modest means, men and women struggling to do what Texans of all generations have done: to better their families through honest enterprise.

V.

[W]hile baseball may be the national pastime of the citizenry, dishing out special economic benefits to certain in-state industries remains the favored pastime of state and local governments.

Governments are "instituted among Men" to "secure" preexisting, "unalienable Rights." Our federal and Texas Constitutions are charters of liberty, not wellsprings of boundless government power. Madison adroitly divided political power because he prized a "We the People" system that extolled citizens over a monarchical system of rulers and subjects. The trick was to give government its requisite powers while structurally hemming in that power so that fallible men wouldn't become as despotic as the hereditary monarchs they had fled and fought.

Economic liberty is "deeply rooted in this Nation's history and tradition," and the right to engage in productive enterprise is as central to individual freedom as the right to worship as one chooses. Indeed, Madison declared that "protection" of citizens' "faculties of acquiring property" is the "first object of government," and admonished that a government whose "arbitrary restrictions" deny citizens "free use of their faculties, and free choice of their occupations" was "not a just government." When it comes to occupational licensing—often less about protecting the public than about bestowing special privileges on political favorites—government power has expanded unchecked. But government doesn't get to determine the reach of its own power, something that subverts the original constitutional design of limited government. The Texas Constitution imposes limits, and imposes them intentionally. Bottom line: Police power cannot go unpoliced.

I believe judicial passivity is incompatible with individual liberty and constitutionally limited government. Occupational freedom, the right to earn a living as one chooses, is a nontrivial constitutional right entitled to nontrivial judicial protection. People are owed liberty by virtue of their very humanity—"endowed by their Creator," as the Declaration affirms. And while government has undeniable authority to regulate economic activities to protect the public against fraud and danger, freedom should be the general rule, and restraint the exception.

The Founders understood that a "limited Constitution" can be preserved "no other way than through the medium of courts of justice, whose duty it must be to declare all acts contrary to the manifest tenor of the Constitution void. Without this, all the reservations of particular rights or privileges would amount to nothing." Judicial duty—"so arduous a duty," Hamilton called it—requires courts to be "bulwarks of a limited Constitution against legislative encroachments," including holding irrational anticompetitive actions unconstitutional. Such is life in a constitutional republic, which exalts constitutionalism over majoritarianism precisely in order to tell government "no." That's the paramount point, to tap the brakes rather than punch the gas.

The Court today rejects servility in the economic-liberty realm, fortifying protections for Texans seeking what Texans have always sought: a better life for themselves and their families. There remains, as Davy Crockett excitedly wrote his children, "a world of country to settle."

CHAPTER IX

RELIGION CLAUSES

The First Amendment to the United States Constitution says that "Congress shall make no law…respecting an establishment of religion, or prohibiting the free exercise thereof." Relying on the Due Process Clause of the Fourteenth Amendment and the selective-incorporation doctrine, the United States Supreme Court has extended the restrictions of the Free Exercise and Establishment Clauses to the States. *See Cantwell v. Connecticut*, 310 U.S. 296 (1940) (free exercise clause); *Everson v. Bd. of Educ.*, 330 U.S. 1 (1947) (establishment clause).

Like the United States Constitution, most state constitutions contain religion clauses that prohibit governmental establishments of religion, *see* Jill Goldenziel, *Blaine's Name in Vain?: State Constitutions, School Choice, and Charitable Choice*, 83 Denv. U. L. Rev. 57, 63 (2005), and that provide protection for the free exercise of religious beliefs and practices, *see* Mechthild Fritz, *Religion in a Federal System: Diversity Versus Uniformity*, 38 Kan. L. Rev. 39, 49 (1989). Some of the state guarantees not only pre-date the Bill of Rights, but also were the models for the federal Religion Clauses. *See* Michael W. McConnell, *The Origins and Historical Understanding of Free Exercise of Religion*, 103 Harv. L. Rev. 1409, 1455-58 (1990). We will start with the state freedom of religion clauses, then turn to the state establishment clauses.

A. FREEDOM OF RELIGION

All fifty state constitutions contain provisions that safeguard the rights of their citizens to practice their faith.

Some state guarantees mirror the brief and general language of the national free exercise clause. *See, e.g.*, Mass. Const. art. 46, § 1 ("No law shall be passed prohibiting the free exercise of religion."); Pa. Const. of 1776, art. II, *reprinted in* 2 Federal and State Constitutions, Colonial Charters, and Other Organic Laws of the United States 1328, 1450-1451 (B. Poore ed., 2d ed. 1878) ("free exercise of religious worship"); Va. Bill of Rights of 1776, § 16, *reprinted in* 2 Federal and State Constitutions, Colonial Charters, and Other Organic Laws of the United States 1908-1909 ("all men are equally entitled to the free exercise of religion").

But most of the state guarantees are more specific (and more lengthy). The Ohio Constitution provides a good example:

> All men have a natural and indefeasible right to worship Almighty God according to the dictates of their own conscience. No person shall be compelled to attend, erect, or support any place of worship, or maintain any place of

worship, against his consent; and no preference shall be given, by law, to any religious society; nor shall any interference with the rights of conscience be permitted. No religious test shall be required, as a qualification for office, nor shall any person be incompetent to be a witness on account of his religious belief; but nothing herein shall be construed to dispense with oaths and affirmations. Religion, morality, and knowledge, however, being essential to good government, it shall be the duty of the general assembly to pass suitable laws to protect every religious denomination in the peaceable enjoyment of its own mode of public worship and to encourage schools and the means of instruction.   *What is this clause?*

Ohio Const. art. I, § 7. *See also* Minn. Const. art. I, § 16; Neb. Const. art. I, § 4; Tex. Const. art. I, § 6; Ark. Const. art. II, § 24; N.Y. Const. art. I, § 3 ("The free exercise and enjoyment of religious profession and worship, without discrimination or preference, shall forever be allowed in this state..."); Ill. Const. art. I, § 3; Va. Const. art. I, § 16 ("all men are equally entitled to the free exercise of religion..."). For background on the development and history of state free exercise clauses, see Angela C. Carmella, *State Constitutional Protection of Religious Exercise: An Emerging Post-Smith Jurisprudence*, 1993 BYU L. Rev. 277, 293-305 (1993).

The law in this area has developed considerably in the last few decades—as the state and federal courts and legislatures have reacted to each other through various decisions and legislation. Of particular interest in both court systems has been the vexing problem of regulating religious practices. It is one thing to ensure that citizens may believe whatever they wish. It is quite another to allow them to practice their religion in whatever way they wish. That distinction is at play in the following cases, which present a classic story of federalism, one that starts with a decision by the United States Supreme Court, that leads to a response from Congress, that leads to a second Supreme Court decision, and that ends (for now) with responses from the state supreme courts and the state legislatures.

"classic story of federalism"

EMPLOYMENT DIV., DEP'T OF HUMAN RES. OF OREGON v. SMITH
494 U.S. 872 (1990)

SCALIA, J.

[This case requires us to decide whether the Free Exercise Clause of the First Amendment permits the State of Oregon to include religiously inspired peyote use within the reach of its general criminal prohibition on use of that drug, and thus permits the State to deny unemployment benefits to persons dismissed from their jobs because of such religiously inspired use.]

Respondents Alfred Smith and Galen Black were fired from their jobs with a private drug rehabilitation organization because they ingested peyote for sacramental purposes at a ceremony of the Native American Church, of which both are members. When respondents applied to petitioner Employment Division for unemployment compensation, they were determined to be ineligible for benefits because they had been discharged for work-related "misconduct." ...The Oregon Supreme Court held that respondents' religiously inspired use of peyote fell within the prohibition of the Oregon statute, which "makes no exception for the sacramental use" of the drug. It then considered whether that prohibition was valid under the Free Exercise Clause, and concluded that it was not.

The free exercise of religion means, first and foremost, the right to believe and profess whatever religious doctrine one desires. Thus, the First Amendment obviously excludes all "governmental regulation of religious *beliefs* as such." The government may not compel affirmation of religious belief, impose special disabilities on the basis of religious views, or lend its power to one or the other side in controversies over religious authority or dogma.

But the "exercise of religion" often involves not only belief and profession but the performance of (or abstention from) physical acts: assembling with others for a worship service, participating in sacramental use of bread and wine, proselytizing, abstaining from certain foods or certain modes of transportation. It would be true, we think...that a State would be "prohibiting the free exercise [of religion]" if it sought to ban such acts or abstentions only when they are engaged in for religious reasons, or only because of the religious belief that they display. It would doubtless be unconstitutional, for example, to ban the casting of "statues that are to be used for worship purposes," or to prohibit bowing down before a golden calf.

Respondents in the present case, however, seek to carry the meaning of "prohibiting the free exercise [of religion]" one large step further. They contend that their religious motivation for using peyote places them beyond the reach of a criminal law that is not specifically directed at their religious practice, and that is concededly constitutional as applied to those who use the drug for other reasons. They assert, in other words, that "prohibiting the free exercise [of religion]" includes requiring any individual to observe a generally applicable law that requires (or forbids) the performance of an act that his religious belief forbids (or requires).... We have never held that an individual's religious beliefs excuse him from compliance with an otherwise valid law prohibiting conduct that the State is free to regulate.

Rule

[[Our] decisions have consistently held that the right of free exercise does not relieve an individual of the obligation to comply with a "valid and neutral law of general applicability on the ground that the law proscribes (or prescribes) conduct that his religion prescribes (or proscribes)."

There being no contention that Oregon's drug law represents an attempt to regulate religious beliefs, the communication of religious beliefs, or the raising of one's children in those beliefs, the rule to which we have adhered ever since *Reynolds* plainly controls. "Our cases do not at their farthest reach support the proposition that a stance of conscientious opposition relieves an objector from any colliding duty fixed by a democratic government."

Values that are protected against government interference through enshrinement in the Bill of Rights are not thereby banished from the political process. Just as a society that believes in the negative protection accorded to the press by the First Amendment is likely to enact laws that affirmatively foster the dissemination of the printed word, so also a society that believes in the negative protection accorded to religious belief can be expected to be solicitous of that value in its legislation as well. It is therefore not surprising that a number of States have made an exception to their drug laws for sacramental peyote use. But to say that a nondiscriminatory religious-practice exemption is permitted, or even that it is desirable, is not to say that it is constitutionally required, and that the appropriate occasions for its creation can be discerned by the courts. It may fairly be said that leaving accommodation to the political process will place at a relative disadvantage those religious practices that are not widely engaged in; but that unavoidable consequence of democratic government must be preferred to a system in which each conscience is a law unto itself or in which judges weigh the social importance of all laws against the centrality of all religious beliefs.

religious Exemptions from generally applicable & neutral laws aren't constitutionally required.

Why not implement a balancing act?

NOTES

1. *Smith* limited the reach of *Sherbert v. Verner*, 374 U.S. 398 (1963), which involved a free exercise claim by a man who refused to work on Saturdays due to his religious beliefs and who claimed that the State could not deny him unemployment compensation based on his religious practices. Whereas *Smith* applied rational basis review to a neutral law of general applicability and rejected the free exercise claim, *Sherbert* applied strict scrutiny to the State's unemployment compensation system and granted relief to the religious objector. *Id.* at 406. In *Church of the Lukumi Babalu Aye, Inc. v. Hialeah*, 508 U.S. 520 (1993), the Court followed the *Smith* test, but it applied strict scrutiny because the city had targeted the religious practices of a local religious group for specific regulation.

RB √
95

RFRA to counter Smith

2. Three years after *Smith*, Congress enacted the Religious Freedom Restoration Act (RFRA). Invoking its powers under § 5 of the Fourteenth Amendment, Congress sought to require courts to apply strict scrutiny to claims that state or federal laws burdened the practices of sincere religious adherents. With RFRA, Congress sought to overrule *Smith* legislatively and in the process to extend the *Sherbert* rule to all free exercise claims. Here is the Supreme Court's response.

CITY OF BOERNE v. FLORES
521 U.S. 507 (1997)

KENNEDY, J.

A decision by local zoning authorities to deny a church a building permit was challenged under the Religious Freedom Restoration Act of 1993. The case calls into question the authority of Congress to enact RFRA. *QP: can Congress enact RFRA*

RFRA prohibits "[g]overnment" from "substantially burden[ing]" a person's exercise of religion even if the burden results from a rule of general applicability unless the government can demonstrate the burden "(1) is in furtherance of a compelling governmental interest; and (2) is the least restrictive means of furthering that compelling governmental interest." *RFRA Framework*

Congress relied on its Fourteenth Amendment enforcement power in enacting the most far-reaching and substantial of RFRA's provisions, those which impose its requirements on the States. The Fourteenth Amendment provides, in relevant part:

Section 5. The Congress shall have power to enforce, by appropriate legislation, the provisions of this article. *Power Congress relied upon*

Congress' power under § 5...extends only to "enforc[ing]" the provisions of the Fourteenth Amendment.... The design of the Amendment and the text of § 5 are inconsistent with the suggestion that Congress has the power to decree the substance of the Fourteenth Amendment's restrictions on the States. Legislation which alters the meaning of the Free Exercise Clause cannot be said to be enforcing the Clause. *To alter ≠ to enforce*

Respondent contends that RFRA is a proper exercise of Congress' remedial or preventive power. The Act, it is said, is a reasonable means of protecting the free exercise of religion as defined by *Smith*. It prevents and remedies laws which are enacted with the unconstitutional object of targeting religious beliefs and practices. To avoid the difficulty of proving such violations, it is said, Congress can simply invalidate any law which imposes a substantial burden on a religious practice unless it is justified by a compelling interest and is the least restrictive means of accomplishing that interest. If Congress can prohibit laws with discriminatory effects in order to prevent racial discrimination in violation of the Equal Protection Clause, then it can do the same, respondent argues, to promote religious liberty.

While preventive rules are sometimes appropriate remedial measures, there must be a congruence between the means used and the ends to be achieved. The appropriateness of remedial measures must be considered in light of the evil presented. Strong measures appropriate to address one harm may be an unwarranted response to another, lesser one.

Regardless of the state of the legislative record, RFRA cannot be considered remedial, preventive legislation, if those terms are to have any meaning…. It appears, instead, to attempt a substantive change in constitutional protections. Preventive measures prohibiting certain types of laws may be appropriate when there is reason to believe that many of the laws affected by the congressional enactment have a significant likelihood of being unconstitutional. Remedial legislation under § 5 "should be adapted to the mischief and wrong which the [Fourteenth] [A]mendment was intended to provide against."

The stringent test RFRA demands of state laws reflects a lack of proportionality or congruence between the means adopted and the legitimate end to be achieved. If an objector can show a substantial burden on his free exercise, the State must demonstrate a compelling governmental interest and show that the law is the least restrictive means of furthering its interest. Claims that a law substantially burdens someone's exercise of religion will often be difficult to contest. Requiring a State to demonstrate a compelling interest and show that it has adopted the least restrictive means of achieving that interest is the most demanding test known to constitutional law. If "'compelling interest' really means what it says …, many laws will not meet the test…. [The test] would open the prospect of constitutionally required religious exemptions from civic obligations of almost every conceivable kind." Laws valid under *Smith* would fall under RFRA without regard to whether they had the object of stifling or punishing free exercise. We make these observations not to reargue the position of the majority in *Smith* but to illustrate the substantive alteration of its holding attempted by RFRA…. This is a considerable congressional intrusion into the States' traditional prerogatives and general authority to regulate for the health and welfare of their citizens.

NOTES

1. Although *City of Boerne* invalidated RFRA as applied to the States and local governments, it did not invalidate the law as applied to the

Congress responds to Boerne

National Government. In the aftermath of *City of Boerne*, Congress returned to the drawing board and enacted the Religious Land Use and Institutionalized Persons Act (RLUIPA) of 2000, which applies to state and local governments. The new federal law, as its name suggests, applies only to land-use regulation and prison rules and regulations. RLUIPA, in contrast to RFRA, has withstood at least one constitutional challenge. *See Cutter v. Wilkinson*, 544 U.S. 709 (2005) (holding that RLUIPA does not violate the Establishment Clause).

2. In a federal system, decisions of the United States Supreme Court not only may provoke responses from Congress, but they also may prompt action by the States. The state courts and legislatures have responded to *Smith* and *City of Boerne* in a variety of ways. Some state courts have declined to follow *Smith* as a matter of state constitutional law. And several state legislatures have enacted state-level RFRAs. The following cases explore these approaches.

HUMPHREY v. LANE
728 N.E.2d 1039 (Ohio 2000)

PFEIFER, J.

We hold that under Section 7, Article I of the Ohio Constitution, the standard for reviewing a generally applicable, religion-neutral state regulation that allegedly violates a person's right to free exercise of religion is whether the regulation serves a compelling state interest and is the least restrictive means of furthering that interest. We further hold that the [prison-guard] grooming policy in this case, while in furtherance of a compelling state interest, did not employ the least restrictive means of furthering that interest.

In employing our comparison [to the Free Exercise Clause of the First Amendment,] we are not doing a mere word count, but instead are looking for a qualitative difference. The Ohio Constitution does have an eleven-word phrase that distinguishes itself from the United States Constitution: "nor shall any interference with the rights of conscience be permitted." The United States Constitution states that Congress shall make no law "prohibiting the free exercise [of religion]." We find the phrase that brooks no "interference with the rights of conscience" to be broader than that which proscribes any law prohibiting free exercise of religion. The Ohio Constitution allows no law that even *interferes* with the rights of conscience. The federal Constitution concerns itself with laws that *prohibit* the free exercise of religion. By its nature the federal Constitution seems to target laws that specifically address the exercise of religion, *i.e.*, not those laws that tangentially affect religion. Ohio's ban on any

[margin notes:]
Rule: SS for Smith law

Holding: Uncon because not least restrictive

Ohio has broader F.E.

interference makes even those tangential effects potentially unconstitutional.

The United States Supreme Court's interpretation of the federal Constitution makes it clear that "the right of free exercise does not relieve an individual of the obligation to comply with a 'valid and neutral law of general applicability on the ground that the law proscribes (or prescribes) conduct that his religion prescribes (or proscribes)." Under the standard enunciated by the court in *Smith*, the relevant issues are whether the regulation at issue is religion-neutral and whether it is generally applicable. If those elements are fulfilled, then the regulation does not violate the Free Exercise Clause.

We have made it clear that this court is not bound by federal court interpretations of the federal Constitution in interpreting our own Constitution. As this court held in *Arnold v. Cleveland*:

> "The Ohio Constitution is a document of independent force. In the areas of individual rights and civil liberties, the United States Constitution, where applicable to the states, provides a floor below which state court decisions may not fall. As long as state courts provide at least as much protection as the United States Supreme Court has provided in its interpretation of the federal Bill of Rights, state courts are unrestricted in according greater civil liberties and protections to individuals and groups."

As stated above, the Ohio Constitution's free exercise protection is broader, and we therefore vary from the federal test for religiously neutral, evenly applied government actions. We apply a different standard to a different constitutional protection. We adhere to the standard long held in Ohio regarding free exercise claims—that the state enactment must serve a compelling state interest and must be the least restrictive means of furthering that interest. That protection applies to direct and indirect encroachments upon religious freedom.

To state a prima facie free exercise claim, the plaintiff must show that his religious beliefs are truly held and that the governmental enactment has a coercive affect against him in the practice of his religion. There seems to be no dispute that Humphrey has successfully made those showings in this case.... Forcing Humphrey to cut his hair would certainly infringe upon the free exercise of his religion.

Since Humphrey has made his prima facie case, the burden shifts to the state to prove that the regulation furthers a compelling state interest. Once that aspect has been satisfied, the state must prove that its regulation is the least restrictive means available of furthering that state interest.

We are satisfied that the state does have a compelling interest in establishing a uniform and grooming policy for its guards. Maintenance of a prison system is a central role of government, an area it is uniquely suited for. It is an undertaking essential to justice and to the safety of the

Least restrictive v. narrow tailoring

citizenry, but by its nature is fraught with danger and thus must be tightly controlled. A prison is a dangerous, potentially explosive environment.

The state has sufficiently established that there is a compelling state interest in establishing uniform and grooming policies for prison workers. The state must further prove, however, that the policy is the least restrictive means of furthering that interest....We view the resolution of that issue to be a factual determination. The trial court found as a factual matter that the simple accommodation of allowing Humphrey to wear his hair pinned under his uniform cap was a less restrictive means of furthering [Ohio]'s interest. The trial court saw Humphrey with his hair tucked beneath his cap and found that Humphrey presented the "professional and dignified image" required by the policy.

LR requires facts

The trial judge also considered testimony concerning whether Humphrey's hair affected the attitudes of fellow guards, administrators, and inmates toward him, and viewed with his own eyes whether the accommodation was a practical one. The trial court found that a practical accommodation could be made. We defer to the trial court's factual finding.   *If there's an accommodation, then not LR.*

Therefore, we hold that [Ohio] can further its compelling interest of a uniform grooming policy through a less restrictive means than the policy it currently employs. We accordingly reverse the judgment of the court of appeals and reinstate the trial court's declaratory judgment and injunction.

ATTORNEY GENERAL v. DESILETS
636 N.E.2d 233 (Mass. 1994)

WILKINS, J.

This case involves the tension between a statutory mandate that a landlord not discriminate against unmarried couples in renting accommodations and a landlord's sincerely held religious belief that he should not facilitate what he regards as sinful cohabitation.   *QP*

The defendants have a policy of not leasing an apartment to any person who intends to engage in conduct that violates their religious principles. The defendants' sole reason for declining even to consider Lattanzi and Tarail as tenants was that religion-based policy. The defendants, who are Roman Catholics, believe that they should not facilitate sinful conduct, including fornication. Since developing the policy at least a decade earlier, the defendants have applied it ten or more times to deny tenancies to unmarried couples.   *How often Ds have applied policy*

Δ's policy

General Laws c. 151B, § 4(6)...provided, in part, that it shall be an unlawful practice for the owner of a multiple dwelling "to refuse to rent or lease...or otherwise to deny to or withhold from any person or group of

State statute in question

persons such accommodations because of the race, religious creed, color, national origin, sex, age, ancestry or *marital status* of such person or persons." We shall conclude that the defendants violated the provisions of this statute and that, therefore, we must consider the defendants' argument that enforcement of the statute against them violates their rights under the State…Constitution[.]

Despite the similarity of the [Federal and State[1]] constitutional provisions, this court should reach its own conclusions on the scope of the protections of art. 46, § 1, and should not necessarily follow the reasoning adopted by the Supreme Court of the United States under the First Amendment. Indeed, after the release of our *Nissenbaum* opinion, the Supreme Court substantially altered its standard for determining whether conduct was protected under the free exercise of religion clause by its decision in *Employment Div.*

In interpreting art. 46, § 1, we prefer to adhere to the standards of earlier First Amendment jurisprudence, such as we applied in *Alberts v. Devine, Carroll v. Alberts,* and *Attorney Gen. v. Bailey.* In each opinion, we used the balancing test that the Supreme Court had established under the free exercise of religion clause in *Wisconsin v. Yoder, Sherbert v. Verner,* and subsequent opinions. By applying the balancing test as we do, we extend protections to the defendants that are at least as great as those of the First Amendment. No further discussion of rights under the First Amendment is, therefore, necessary.

The next question is whether the prohibition against discrimination based on marital status substantially burdens the defendants' exercise of their religion…. We first consider whether there is any burden at all on the defendants' free exercise of religion. We have said that the government's failure to provide a child with subsidized transportation to a private sectarian school does not burden the child's free exercise of religion. Here, the situation differs because the government has placed a burden on the defendants that makes their exercise of religion more difficult and more costly. The statute affirmatively obliges the defendants to enter into a contract contrary to their religious beliefs and provides significant sanctions for its violation. Moreover, both their nonconformity to the law and any related publicity may stigmatize the defendants in the eyes of many and thus burden the exercise of the defendants' religion.

The fact that the defendants' free exercise of religion claim arises in a commercial context, although relevant when engaging in a balancing of interests, does not mean that their constitutional rights are not substantially

---

[1] Mass. Const. art. 46, § 1, states: "No law shall be passed prohibiting the free exercise of religion."

burdened. This is not a case in which a claimant is seeking a financial advantage by asserting religious beliefs. ~~If a claim~~ *would financial advantage matter?*

We must, therefore, consider whether the record establishes that the Commonwealth has or does not have an important governmental interest that is sufficiently compelling that the granting of an exemption to people in the position of the defendants would unduly hinder that goal....At the least, the Commonwealth must demonstrate that it has a compelling interest in the elimination of discrimination in housing against an unmarried man and an unmarried woman who have a sexual relationship and wish to rent accommodations to which § 4(6) applies.

Without supporting facts in the record or in legislative findings, we are unwilling to conclude that simple enactment of the prohibition against discrimination based on marital status establishes that the State has such a substantial interest in eliminating that form of housing discrimination that, on a balancing test, the substantial burden on the defendants' free exercise of religion must be disregarded. *Need facts*

We reject any argument that a general rule must be applied because of problems in determining whether religious beliefs sincerely underlie a landlord's refusal to lease. The sincerity of such action assertedly founded on religious beliefs is open to challenge in a free exercise of religion case. We would, moreover, not readily subscribe to a rule that justified the denial of constitutional rights simply because the protection of those rights required special effort. For similar reasons, in the absence of proof, we would not find a compelling State interest in this case simply because other individuals might assert the right to be exempt from this or some other law on religious grounds and in doing so would make enforcement of that law difficult. Yet the practical problems of administering a law with the exemption that the defendants seek may be shown to be such as to make the operation of such an exemption impractical. Finally, the compulsion of the State's interest appears somewhat weakened because the statute permits discrimination by a religious organization in certain respects if to do so promotes the principles for which the organization was established. *State already allows some religious discrimination.* *Can't make a general rule on sincerity*

We are not persuaded on the record that the Commonwealth's interests in the availability of rental housing for cohabiting couples must always prevail over the religion-based practices that people such as the defendants wish to pursue. On the other hand, we cannot say that it is certain that the Commonwealth could not prove in this case that it has some specific compelling interest that justifies overriding the defendants' interests.

The Commonwealth has the task of establishing that it has a compelling interest in eliminating housing discrimination against cohabiting couples that is strong enough to justify the burden placed on the defendants' exercise of their religion. A task of this sort has been carried out successfully in some cases and not in others.

The summary judgment record does not establish that there is no disputed material fact bearing on the compelling State interest question. In that circumstance summary judgment is inappropriate. There are factual circumstances that bear on the question, both as to the existence of a general State interest in the elimination of discrimination in housing based on marital status and as to the existence of a particularized State interest in the Turners Falls area. Uniformity of enforcement of the statute may be shown to be the least restrictive means for the practical and efficient operation of the antidiscrimination law. It should be remembered that the task is to balance the State's interests against the nature of the burden on the defendants and that we are concerned here with the business of leasing apartments, not with participation in a formal religious activity.

Landlords win [handwritten marginal note]

NOTES

1. In *Abdul-Alazim v. Superintendent, Massachusetts Correctional Institution, Cedar Junction*, 778 N.E.2d 946 (Mass. App. Ct. 2002), a Massachusetts appeals court granted relief under *Desilets* to a claim filed by an inmate that prison officials had violated his state-law free exercise rights by prohibiting him from wearing a kufi, a prayer cap used by Muslims during religious worship. *Cf. Holt v. Hobbs*, 135 S. Ct. 853 (2015) (holding that prison-grooming policy violated inmate's free-exercise rights under RLUIPA).

2. In *Swanner v. Anchorage Equal Rights Commission*, 874 P.2d 274 (Alaska 1994), the Court declined to follow the *Smith* test in rejecting a landlord's claim that he had a constitutional right to refuse to rent to unmarried, cohabiting persons of the opposite sex. In doing so, it reasoned as follows:

> Swanner is correct in asserting that a state court may provide greater protection to the free exercise of religion under the state constitution than is now provided under the United States Constitution. Thus, even though the Free Exercise Clause of the Alaska Constitution is identical to the Free Exercise Clause of the United States Constitution, we are not required to adopt and apply the *Smith* test to religious exemption cases involving the Alaska Constitution merely because the United States Supreme Court adopted that test to determine the applicability of religious exemptions under the United States Constitution. We will apply *Frank v. State*, 604 P.2d 1068 (Alaska 1979), to determine whether the anti-discrimination laws violate Swanner's right to free exercise under the Alaska Constitution.
>
> In *Frank v. State*, we adopted the *Sherbert* test to determine whether the Free Exercise Clause of the Alaska Constitution requires an exemption to a facially neutral law. We held that to invoke a religious exemption, three requirements must be met: (1) a religion is involved, (2) the conduct in question is religiously based, and (3) the claimant is sincere in his/her religious belief. Once these three

Cf. we don't have to follow Smith [handwritten marginal note] requirements are met, "[r]eligiously impelled actions can be forbidden only 'where they pose some substantial threat to public safety, peace or order,' or where there are competing governmental interests 'of the highest order and ... [are] not otherwise served....'"

No one disputes that a religion is involved here (Christianity), or that Swanner is sincere in his religious belief that cohabitation is a sin and by renting to cohabitators, he is facilitating the sin…. [But] Swanner… made no showing of a religious belief which requires that he engage in the property-rental business.

Cf. he doesn't have to be a landlord

BARR v. CITY OF SINTON
295 S.W.3d 287 (Texas 2009)

HECHT, J.

The Texas Religious Freedom Restoration Act (TRFRA) provides that "a government agency may not substantially burden a person's free exercise of religion [unless it] demonstrates that the application of the burden to the person…is in furtherance of a compelling governmental interest [and] is the least restrictive means of furthering that interest." TRFRA does not immunize religious conduct from government regulation; it requires the government to tread carefully and lightly when its actions substantially burden religious exercise.

Statute m ⊗ ⊗ question

In this case, a city resident, as part of a religious ministry, offered men recently released from prison free housing and religious instruction in two homes he owned. In response, the city passed a zoning ordinance that not only precluded the use of the homes for that purpose but effectively banned the ministry from the city. The trial court found that the city had not violated TRFRA, and the court of appeals affirmed. We reverse and remand to the trial court for further proceedings.

Facts

RFRA was violated i Holding

In 1998, Pastor Richard Wayne Barr began a religious halfway house ministry through Philemon Restoration Homes, Inc., a nonprofit corporation he directed. The purpose of the ministry was to offer housing, biblical instruction, and counseling to low-level offenders released from prison on probation or parole in transition back into the community…. The guidelines emphasized to prospective residents that Philemon was "a biblical ministry, NOT a social service agency". Each morning began with group prayer and Bible study.

citizens united?

Nonprofit biblical ministry

When Barr began his ministry, the City imposed no zoning or other restrictions on his use of the homes. In January 1999, Barr discussed his ministry with Sinton's mayor, city manager, and police chief, and a few weeks later he presented his ministry before the city council. In response to questions whether Philemon was in compliance with state law, Barr researched the matter and concluded that it was. In April, the city council held a public hearing at which a large number of people expressed both opposition to as well as support of Barr's ministry. A few days later, the city council passed Ordinance 1999-02, which added to the City Code a section that provided as follows:

> "A correctional or rehabilitation facility may not be located in the City of Sinton within 1000 feet of a residential area, a primary or secondary school, property designated as a public park or public recreation area by any governmental authority, or a church, synagogue, or other place of worship."

As the city manager later confirmed, Ordinance 1999-02 targeted Barr and Philemon. The halfway houses they operated were unquestionably within 1,000 feet of a church; indeed, they were across the street from the Grace Fellowship Church, which was helping to support the ministry. But the ordinance was broader, and was intended to be. Because Sinton is small, it would be difficult for a halfway house to be located anywhere within the city limits.

Smith's construction of the Free Exercise Clause does not preclude a state from requiring strict scrutiny of infringements on religious freedom, either by statute or under the state constitution, and many states have done just that, Texas among them. The Texas Legislature enacted TRFRA in 1999, which like RFRA provides in part, that government "may not substantially burden a person's free exercise of religion [unless it] demonstrates that the application of the burden to the person...is in furtherance of a compelling governmental interest; and... is the least restrictive means of furthering that interest." The Act states that "[t]he protection of religious freedom afforded by this chapter is in addition to the protections provided under federal law and the constitutions of this state and the United States."

Applying TRFRA to this case raises four questions, each succeeding question contingent on an affirmative answer to the one preceding:

• Does the City's Ordinance 1999-02 burden Barr's "free exercise of religion" as defined by TRFRA?

• Is the burden substantial?

• Does the ordinance further a compelling governmental interest?

• Is the ordinance the least restrictive means of furthering that interest?

The City argues that Barr's free exercise of religion is not involved because a halfway house need not be a religious operation. But the fact that a halfway house *can* be secular does not mean that it *cannot* be religious. TRFRA defines "free exercise of religion" as "an act or refusal to act that is substantially motivated by sincere religious belief", adding that "[i]n determining whether an act or refusal to act is substantially motivated by sincere religious belief under this chapter, it is not necessary to determine that the act or refusal to act is motivated by a central part or central requirement of the person's sincere religious belief." Not only is such a determination unnecessary, it is impossible for the judiciary. *Ct: we can't do part 1.*

The trial court appears to have been troubled that an operation which can be and often is conducted for purely secular purposes could be entitled to increased protection from government regulation if conducted for religious reasons. But TRFRA guarantees such protection. Just as a Bible study group and a book club are not treated the same, neither are a halfway house operated for religious purposes and one that is not.

The City does not dispute that the purpose of Barr's ministry was to provide convicts a biblically supported transition to civic life. Applicants were required to sign a statement of faith, agree to abide by stated biblical principles, and commit as a group to daily prayer and Bible study. They were specifically told that Barr's halfway house was "a biblical ministry, NOT a social service agency." Barr considered the halfway house a religious ministry, and it appears to have been supported by his church. The record easily establishes that Barr's ministry was "substantially motivated by sincere religious belief" for purposes of the TRFRA.

B   *Burden*

To determine whether a person's free exercise of religion has been substantially burdened, some courts have focused on the burden on the person's religious beliefs rather than the burden on his conduct. Under what have been referred to as the compulsion and centrality tests, the issue is whether the person's conduct that is being burdened is compelled by or central to his religion. The problems with these approaches are the same as those in determining whether conduct is religious. It may require a court to do what it cannot do: assess the demands of religion on its adherents and the importance of particular conduct to the religion. And it is inconsistent with the statutory directive that religious conduct be determined without regard for whether the actor's motivation is "a central part or central requirement of the person's sincere religious belief." These problems are avoided if the focus is on the degree to which a person's religious conduct is curtailed and the resulting impact on his religious expression. The burden must be measured, of course, from the person's perspective, not from the government's. Thus, the United States Court of Appeals for the Fifth Circuit, after surveying decisions by other courts, recently held that under RLUIPA, "a government action or regulation creates a 'substantial burden' on a religious exercise if it truly pressures the adherent to significantly modify his religious behavior and significantly violate his religious beliefs." *a definition of sub burden*

Beliefs v conduct

Ct: we probably can't do pt 2 either

Must focus on individual's perspective

Ordinance 1999-02 prohibited Barr from operating his halfway house ministry in the two homes he owned adjacent to his supporting church, and the city manager testified that it was "a fair statement" that alternate locations were "probably... minimal" and "possibly" "pretty close to nonexistent". The court of appeals stated that "there is nothing in the ordinance that precludes Barr from providing his religious ministry to parolees and probationers, from providing instruction, counsel, and helpful assistance in other facilities in Sinton, or from housing these persons outside the City and providing his religious ministry to them there." But there is no evidence of any alternate location in the City of Sinton where the ordinance would have allowed Barr's ministry to operate, or of possible locations outside the city. Moreover, while evidence of alternatives is certainly relevant to the issue whether zoning restrictions substantially burden free religious exercise, evidence of *some* possible alternative, irrespective of the difficulties presented, does not, standing alone, disprove substantial burden. In a related context, the Supreme Court has observed that "one is not to have the exercise of his liberty of expression in appropriate places abridged on the plea that it may be exercised in some other place." As a practical matter, the ordinance ended Barr's ministry, as the City Council surely knew it would.... [A] burden on a person's religious exercise is not insubstantial simply because he could always choose to do something else.

"To say that a person's right to free exercise has been burdened, of course, does not mean that he has an absolute right to engage in the conduct." The government may regulate such conduct in furtherance of a compelling interest.

Although the government's interest in the public welfare in general, and in preserving a common character of land areas and use in particular, is certainly legitimate when properly motivated and appropriately directed, the assertion that zoning ordinances are per se superior to fundamental, constitutional rights, such as the free exercise of religion, must fairly be regarded as indefensible.

The Supreme Court held in *Smith*, not that the government's interest in neutral laws of general application is always compelling when compared to the people's interest in fundamental rights, but only that the United States Constitution does not require the two interests to be balanced every time they conflict. RFRA, RLUIPA, and TRFRA, as well as laws enacted in other states, now require that balance by statute when government action substantially burdens the free exercise of religion. The government's interest is compelling when the balance weighs in its favor—that is, when the government's interest justifies the substantial burden on religious exercise. Because religious exercise is a fundamental right, that justification can be found only in "interests of the highest order," to quote the Supreme Court in *Yoder*, and to quote *Sherbert*, only to avoid "'the gravest abuses, endangering paramount interest[s].'"

The Sinton City Council's recitation in Ordinance 1999-02—that "the requirements of this section are reasonably necessary to preserve the public safety, morals, and general welfare"—is the kind of "broadly formulated interest[ ]" that does not satisfy the scrutiny mandated by TRFRA. Likewise, the trial court's brief finding—that "[t]he ordinance was in furtherance of a compelling government interest"—falls short of the required scrutiny.

ct: interest has to be more than broadly worded

Although TRFRA places the burden of proving a substantial burden on the claimant, it places the burden of proving a compelling state interest on the government. The City argues that its compelling interest in Ordinance 1999-02 is established by statutes providing that correctional facility regulations presumptively meet strict scrutiny. As we have already explained, however, these statutes are inapplicable.

The City also asserts that Ordinance 1999-02 serves a compelling interest in advancing safety, preventing nuisance, and protecting children. But there is no evidence to support the City's assertion with respect to "the particular practice at issue"—Barr's ministry.

The City's failure to establish a compelling interest in this case in no way suggests that the government never has a compelling interest in zoning for religious use of property or in regulating halfway houses operated for religious purposes. TRFRA guarantees a process, not a result. The City's principal position in this case has been that it is exempt from TRFRA. We do not hold that the City could not have satisfied TRFRA; we hold only that it failed to do so.

No compelling interest

D : Least restrictive

Finally, TRFRA requires that even when the government acts in furtherance of a compelling interest, it must show that it used the least restrictive means of furthering that interest. The City has made no effort to show that it complied with this requirement. Ordinance 1999-02 is very broad. If as the city manager testified, locations in the City of Sinton more than 1,000 feet from a residential area, school, park, recreational area, or church are "pretty close to nonexistent", the ordinance effectively prohibits any private "residential facility...operated for the purpose of housing persons...convicted of misdemeanors...within one...year after having been released from confinement in any penal institution" inside the city limits. Read literally, this would prohibit a Sinton resident from leasing a room to someone within a year of his having been jailed for twice driving with an invalid license. Such restrictions are certainly not the least restrictive means of insuring that religiously operated halfway houses do not jeopardize children's safety and residents' well being.

ct: this law is too broad

We conclude, based on the record before us, that Ordinance 1999-02, as applied to Barr's ministry, violates TRFRA.

CATHOLIC CHARITIES OF THE DIOCESE OF ALBANY v. SERIO
859 N.E.2d 459 (Ct. App. N.Y. 2006)

Whole new rule

R.S. SMITH, J.

QR

Plaintiffs challenge the validity of legislation requiring health insurance policies that provide coverage for prescription drugs to include coverage for contraception. Plaintiffs assert that the provisions they challenge violate their rights under the religion clauses of the federal and state constitutions. We hold that the legislation, as applied to these plaintiffs, is valid. *Holding = Law is valid*

Statute in question

In 2002, the Legislature enacted what is known as the "Women's Health and Wellness Act" (WHWA), mandating expanded health insurance coverage for a variety of services needed by women, including mammography, cervical cytology and bone density screening. At issue here are provisions of the WHWA requiring that an employer health insurance contract "which provides coverage for prescription drugs shall include coverage for the cost of contraceptive drugs or devices."

Provision in question

religious exemption

At the heart of this case is the statute's exemption for "religious employers." Such an employer may request an insurance contract "without coverage for ... contraceptive methods that are contrary to the religious employer's religious tenets." Where a religious employer invokes the exemption, the insurer must offer coverage for contraception to individual employees, who may purchase it at their own expense "at the prevailing small group community rate."

π's claim

Plaintiffs believe contraception to be sinful, and assert that the challenged provisions of the WHWA compel them to violate their religious tenets by financing conduct that they condemn. The sincerity of their beliefs, and the centrality of those beliefs to their faiths, are not in dispute.

Contending that they are constitutionally entitled to be exempt from the provisions of the WHWA providing for coverage of contraceptives, plaintiffs brought this action against the Superintendent of Insurance, seeking a declaration that these portions of the WHWA are invalid, and an injunction against their enforcement. The complaint asserts broadly that the challenged provisions are unconstitutional, but plaintiffs do not argue that they are unenforceable as to employers having no religious objections to contraception; in substance, plaintiffs challenge the legislation as applied to them.

It's an "as-applied" challenge

Article I, § 3 of the New York Constitution provides:

"The free exercise and enjoyment of religious profession and worship, without discrimination or preference, shall forever be allowed in this state to all humankind; and no person shall be rendered incompetent to be a witness on account of his or her opinions on matters of religious belief; but the liberty of conscience hereby secured shall not be so construed as to excuse acts of licentiousness, or justify practices inconsistent with the peace or safety of this state."

In interpreting our Free Exercise Clause we have not applied, and we do not now adopt, the inflexible rule of *Smith* that no person may complain of a burden on religious exercise that is imposed by a generally applicable, neutral statute. Rather, we have held that when the State imposes "an incidental burden on the right to free exercise of religion" we must consider the interest advanced by the legislation that imposes the burden, and that "[t]he respective interests must be balanced to determine whether the incidental burdening is justified." We have never discussed, however, how the balancing is to be performed... We now hold that substantial deference is due the Legislature, and that the party claiming an exemption bears the burden of showing that the challenged legislation, as applied to that party, is an unreasonable interference with religious freedom. This test, while more protective of religious exercise than the rule of *Smith*, is less so than the rule stated (though not always applied) in a number of other federal and state cases.

Since *Smith*, a number of state courts have interpreted their states' constitutions to call for the application of strict scrutiny. Often, however,...the courts rejected claims to religious exemptions, and it is questionable whether the scrutiny applied by those courts is really as strict as their statement of the rule implies.

The apparent reluctance of some courts to pay more than lip service to "strict scrutiny" may be an implicit recognition of what we now explicitly decide. Strict scrutiny is not the right approach to constitutionally-based claims for religious exemptions. Where the State has not set out to burden religious exercise, but seeks only to advance, in a neutral way, a legitimate object of legislation, we do not read the New York Free Exercise Clause to require the State to demonstrate a "compelling" interest in response to every claim by a religious believer to an exemption from the law; such a rule of constitutional law would give too little respect to legislative prerogatives, and would create too great an obstacle to efficient government. Rather, the principle stated by the United States Supreme Court in *Smith*—that citizens are not excused by the Free Exercise Clause from complying with generally applicable and neutral laws, even ones offensive to their religious tenets—should be the usual, though not the invariable, rule. The burden of showing that an interference with religious practice is unreasonable, and therefore requires an exemption from the statute, must be on the person claiming the exemption.

The burden the WHWA places on plaintiffs' religious practices is a serious one, but the WHWA does not literally *compel* them to purchase contraceptive coverage for their employees, in violation of their religious beliefs; it only requires that policies that provide prescription drug coverage include coverage for contraceptives. Plaintiffs are not required by law to purchase prescription drug coverage at all. They assert, unquestionably in good faith, that they feel obliged to do so because, as religious institutions, they must provide just wages and benefits to their employees. But it is surely not impossible, though it may be expensive or difficult, to compensate employees adequately without including prescription drugs in their group health care policies.

It is also important, in our view, that many of plaintiffs' employees do not share their religious beliefs. (Most of the plaintiffs allege that they hire many people of other faiths; no plaintiff has presented evidence that it does not do so.) The employment relationship is a frequent subject of legislation, and when a religious organization chooses to hire nonbelievers it must, at least to some degree, be prepared to accept neutral regulations imposed to protect those employees' legitimate interests in doing what their own beliefs permit. This would be a more difficult case if plaintiffs had chosen to hire only people who share their belief in the sinfulness of contraception.

Finally, we must weigh against plaintiffs' interest in adhering to the tenets of their faith the State's substantial interest in fostering equality between the sexes, and in providing women with better health care. The Legislature had extensive evidence before it that the absence of contraceptive coverage for many women was seriously interfering with both of these important goals. The Legislature decided that to grant the broad religious exemption that plaintiffs seek would leave too many women outside the statute, a decision entitled to deference from the courts. Of course, the Legislature might well have made another choice, but we cannot say the choice the Legislature made has been shown to be an unreasonable interference with plaintiffs' exercise of their religion. The Legislature's choice is therefore not unconstitutional.

NOTES

1.   The U.S. Supreme Court faced a related issue under RFRA in *Burwell v. Hobby Lobby*, 134 S. Ct. 2751 (2014). At issue was the validity of a federal regulation promulgated under the Patient Protection and Affordable Care Act that required for-profit corporations to provide health insurance coverage for contraceptive methods. In invalidating the regulation, the Court reasoned that: (1) for-profit corporations are covered

by RFRA's application to any "person"; (2) the contraceptives mandate substantially burdened the exercise of religion as applied to such corporations; and (3) the mandate failed RFRA's least-restrictive-means requirement.

2. In the quarter century since *Smith*, two things have happened. Most of the *federal* free-exercise enforcement actions have shifted to statutory cases under RFRA with respect to federal laws or under RLUIPA with respect to state land-use and prison-based laws. *See, e.g., Burwell v. Hobby Lobby*, 134 S. Ct. 2751 (2014) (RFRA); *Holt v. Hobbs*, 135 S.Ct. 853 (2015) (RLUIPA); *Gonzales v. O Centro Espirita Beneficente Uniao do Vegetal*, 546 U.S. 418 (2006) (RFRA). And all manner of innovation has occurred at the *state* level, whether under their own Constitutions or under state statutes modeled in part or in whole on RFRA.

B. ESTABLISHMENT OF RELIGION

1. Background

Just as some state freedom of religion clauses mirror their federal counterpart, some state establishment clauses closely resemble the First Amendment of the United States Constitution. All told, eleven States have establishment clauses similar to the First Amendment. Jennifer Friesen, State Constitutional Law: Litigating Individual Rights, Claims and Defenses 4-84 (2006); *see, e.g.,* Cal. Const. art. I, § 4 ("The Legislature shall make no law respecting an establishment of religion."); Fla. Const. art. I, § 3 ("There shall be no law respecting the establishment of religion."); Haw. Const. art. I, § 4 ("No law shall be enacted respecting an establishment of religion."). Thirty-two States have no-preference clauses (two of which, Alabama and California, also have establishment clauses similar to the First Amendment). Friesen, Litigating Individual Rights, Claims and Defenses 4-84; *see, e.g.,* N.J. Const. art. I, § 4 ("There shall be no establishment of one religious sect in preference to another."); Wis. Const. art. I, § 18 ("nor shall…any preference be given to any religious establishments or modes of worship"). And nine States have neither an establishment nor a no-preference clause. Friesen, Litigating Individual Rights, Claims and Defenses 4-84.

Unique to the state constitutions are clauses that expressly limit using public funds to aid religious organizations. Thirty-four States have provisions to this effect. Friesen, Litigating Individual Rights, Claims and Defenses 4-86. As the following excerpt explains, these provisions, often called "Blaine Amendments," have a rich and controversial history.

Mark Edward DeForrest, *An Overview and Evaluation of State Blaine Amendments: Origins, Scope, and First Amendment Concerns*
26 Harv. J.L. & Pub. Pol'y 551 (2003)

The original Blaine Amendment was a proposed amendment to the federal Constitution. The amendment took its name from its sponsor and originator, Representative James Blaine of Maine, who introduced the amendment on December 14, 1875. The text of his proposed amendment reads as follows:

> No State shall make any law respecting an establishment of religion or prohibiting the free exercise thereof; and no money raised by taxation in any State for the support of public schools, or derived from any public fund therefore, nor any public lands devoted thereto, shall ever be under the control of any religious sect, nor shall any money so raised or lands so devoted be divided between religious sects or denominations.

The overarching purpose to the Blaine Amendment, as its plain text demonstrates, was to control the development of government involvement in religious issues at the state level in two critical ways. First, it would have applied the religion clauses of the First Amendment directly to the states. Prior to the development of the incorporation doctrine by the Supreme Court in the twentieth century the provisions of the Bill of Rights (the first ten amendments to the United States Constitution) were not applied to the states by the courts. In Blaine's day, the states were yet to be restrained by the First Amendment; Blaine saw this as a deficiency and sought to remedy this situation by amending the Constitution to directly apply the religion clauses of the First Amendment to the states. The second effect of Blaine's amendment would have been to prohibit state governments from supporting private religious schools with funds from the public treasury.

The Blaine Amendment might have been expected to fade away into oblivion after its rejection by the Senate, but the opposite occurred. After its defeat on the national level, the Blaine Amendment took on new life in the states. Within a year of the defeat of Blaine's proposal, fourteen states had legislation on the books preventing state funds from being used in support of religious schools. By the 1890s, roughly thirty states would incorporate Blaine-style amendments into their constitutions. This trend continued into the twentieth century; even as late as the 1950s, Alaska and Hawaii would incorporate Blaine-style language into their state charters.

Blaine Amendments are found in roughly thirty state constitutions. The language and scope of the state Blaine provisions vary widely, however. Some states adopted Blaine-like provisions prior to the formal proposal of the national Blaine Amendment. Other states, both in the 19th and 20th centuries, willingly adopted Blaine provisions after the national

Blaine Amendment failed. Still other states had Blaine provisions forced upon them as a condition of entering the Union. It should therefore come as no surprise that the Blaine provisions in the states evidence a considerable diversity in language and scope.

The first group of state Blaine provisions to be examined are those that place the narrowest restrictions on state government actions to provide some indirect assistance or aid to private religious or sectarian education. Examples of these kinds of Blaine Amendments can be seen in both New Jersey and Massachusetts. For the most part, these Blaine provisions demonstrate two basic concerns. First, they seek to ensure that primary and secondary public education remains free of sectarian instruction. Second, they usually make certain that public educational funds will not be used to directly support private religious schools. Outside of these two concerns, however, the states with less restrictive Blaine provisions allow some very limited government assistance either with basic transportation or higher education.

Blaine group 1

While the states discussed in the previous [paragraph] have relatively liberal Blaine provisions in their state constitutions, other states have more stringent limitations on government aid to religious schools. While not as permissive as the less restrictive states and not as draconian as the most restrictive states, these states fall into a great middle ground regarding Blaine provisions. Most of these states' Blaine Amendments prohibit direct funding of religious institutions or schools, but leave open, at least within their constitutional texts, the question of whether or not indirect state funding, such as vouchers, are permissible. The language used in this intermediate tier of Blaine states varies considerably from state to state, as even brief examination of the state charters will demonstrate.

Blaine group 2

The Utah Constitution, which reflects church-state concerns unique to that state, contains two provisions dealing with public funding of religious education. The first, found at Article 1, Section 4 of the state charter, mandates that "[n]o public money or property shall be appropriated for or applied to any religious worship, exercise or instruction, or for the support of any ecclesiastical establishment." The second Utah Blaine provision, found at Article 10, Section 9, forbids any direct aid to all religious schools: "[n]either the state of Utah nor its political subdivisions may make any appropriation for the direct support of any school or educational institution controlled by any religious organization." Other states have Blaine-style provisions of similar effect, although the wording is different. Delaware, which in 1897 included a Blaine provision in its state constitution, has an extensive section in its fundamental charter prohibiting direct aid: "No portion of any fund now existing, or which may hereafter be appropriated, or raised by tax, for educational purposes, shall be appropriated to, or used by, or in aid of any sectarian, church or denominational school[.]'"

Alabama, a state of the Old Confederacy, included a Blaine Amendment provision in its state constitution in 1901. This provision prohibits the use of state educational funds to support "any sectarian or denominational school." Kentucky includes a similar provision in its state constitution, but also includes additional language that prohibits the use of money from the state school fund for any purpose other than the "maintenance of the public schools."

The moderate Blaine language used by these states, while varied in expression, affirms the same fundamental principle: direct government aid for expressly sectarian education is prohibited, and for the most part, so is sectarian influence in public educational programs. The strength of this affirmation can be seen in the case of *Fiscal Court of Jefferson County v. Brady*. There, the Kentucky Supreme Court upheld a lower court ruling that struck down a state statute permitting county governments to establish programs to provide for the busing of students in religious or other private schools. Jefferson County had previously instituted a subsidy program that paid a direct sum to private schools to pay for the transportation of students. The private schools funded were overwhelmingly religious in character, and nearly half a million dollars was expended by the county through its subsidy program. The Kentucky Supreme Court found that the private schools involved in the subsidy program combined their own transportation funds with the county subsidy, providing the schools with control over government assets. The court noted specifically that the "financial aid is provided to the school rather than a transportation service to the child," and found that there was a constitutionally significant distinction between providing general transportation for all students and "providing direct payment to selected eligible schools."

The last group of state Blaine provisions to be examined uses language that places the broadest restrictions on government aid to religious schools and organizations. These Blaine provisions often go far beyond the prohibition of direct aid to schools by preventing indirect aid as well. In addition, many of the states include wording in their constitutions prohibiting aid not only to schools, but also to any religious or "sectarian" institution. Florida, for instance, combines a mandate that its state educational fund be used solely for "the support and maintenance of free public schools," with an absolute prohibition on the use of any state revenues "directly or indirectly in aid of any church, sect, or religious denomination or in aid of any sectarian institution." This sterner approach to direct or indirect government aid to religious schools or institutions is paralleled by several other states. Missouri's constitution prohibits the state from giving anything in aid to support:

> [A]ny religious creed, church or sectarian purpose, or to help to support or sustain any private or public school, academy, seminary, college, university, or other institution of learning controlled by any religious creed, church or sectarian denomination whatever; nor shall any grant or donation of personal property or real estate ever be made by the state, or any county, city, town, or other municipal corporation, for any religious creed, church, or sectarian purpose whatever.

Like Florida, Missouri teams an extensive prohibition on government aid to religious bodies and religious schools with another constitutional provision that mandates that the state educational fund be used only for the establishment and maintenance of "free public schools."

While some state Blaine provisions only target education, some go much further. Oklahoma's constitution includes not only the familiar prohibition on support for sectarian educational institutions, but also includes a prohibition on any government aid in support of any "sectarian institution as such." The Indiana Constitution, in a one sentence article, prevents the state from allocating any funds from the treasury "for the benefit of any religious or theological institution." The Georgia State Constitution includes a similar article, expressly mandating that the state refrain from direct or indirect funding "of any sectarian institution." Colorado's state charter, ratified in the same year that the national Blaine Amendment was voted on in the Senate, contains—along with the standard Blaine provisions prohibiting public funding of sectarian schools—a prohibition on state funding for any "charitable, industrial, educational or benevolent purposes" not controlled completely by the state, as well as any "denominational or sectarian institution or association." The Idaho Constitution, ratified in 1890 at the peak of the movement for inclusion of Blaine language in state constitutions, includes a lengthy article banning the allocation of "anything in aid" to religious schools or to religiously-affiliated "literary or scientific institution[s]," while at the same time containing a caveat allowing the state to provide some assistance to non-profit "health facilities" operated by religious groups. Nevada's constitution simply states that the state government cannot provide "funds of any kind or character" for sectarian purposes. The language of all of these provisions extend[s] the standard Blaine provision's prohibition on direct aid to private sectarian schools to include any type of aid to virtually every sort of religiously-controlled institution.

[T]he narrowly-defeated push for a national Blaine Amendment has had a wide-ranging effect on most state constitutions. States, willingly or by command of the federal government, incorporated Blaine provisions into their charters. This move to include Blaine provisions in state constitutions extended into the twentieth century. The overall effect of these Blaine-style provisions, by their express wording or through later judicial interpretations, was usually to preclude both the direct or indirect transfer of state funds to religious or sectarian schools and institutions. The motivation behind the Blaine Amendment was two-fold. First, there was a high degree of hostility towards the teaching and practice of the Roman Catholic Church, and correspondingly there existed a strong desire to ensure that Catholics would be precluded from using the resources of the government to support their parochial schools and other religious institutions. Second, there was an almost imperative desire on the part of the proponents of the Blaine Amendment to protect generic Protestant religiosity in the common schools and the public square. State courts in the twentieth century, with a few exceptions already discussed, rigorously enforced Blaine language to preclude direct, and in many cases indirect, aid and assistance to religious schools or those who wish to attend such schools.

State Blaine provisions do not exist in a constitutional vacuum, however. And while there is no question that states are free to decline to provide money or other forms of aid to private non-governmental entities across the board, there is a significant question as to whether or not the First Amendment allows states to preclude both direct and indirect funding to private religious institutions if those institutions are simply seeking equal access to state funding programs that are open to other private institutions that are of a non-religious character.

2. Cases

Modern disputes about the role of these clauses have focused on governmental programs designed to provide parents (and students) choices outside of the public schools. The issue is whether the programs have the purpose or effect of providing aid to religious schools and other religious organizations on the one hand or of providing aid to the individuals who benefit from them on the other. We start by considering a decision of the United States Supreme Court, *Zelman v. Simmons-Harris*, 536 U.S. 639 (2002), which rejects a federal Establishment Clause challenge to a state voucher program. We then consider several state-court decisions, one that predates *Zelman* and several that follow it.

ZELMAN v. SIMMONS-HARRIS
536 U.S. 639 (2002)

REHNQUIST, C.J.

The State of Ohio has established a pilot program designed to provide educational choices to families with children who reside in the Cleveland

City School District. The question presented is whether this program offends the Establishment Clause of the United States Constitution. We hold that it does not. *Holding: no violation*

There are more than 75,000 children enrolled in the Cleveland City School District. The majority of these children are from low-income and minority families. Few of these families enjoy the means to send their children to any school other than an inner-city public school. *many kids in need*

The program provides two basic kinds of assistance to parents of children in a covered district. First, the program provides tuition aid for students in kindergarten through third grade, expanding each year through eighth grade, to attend a participating public or private school of their parent's choosing. Second, the program provides tutorial aid for students who choose to remain enrolled in public school. *Assistance provided* ~~1) tuition aid~~ ~~2) tutorial aid~~ *(1) Public or private K-8 tuition 2) public tutorial*

The Establishment Clause of the First Amendment, applied to the States through the Fourteenth Amendment, prevents a State from enacting laws that have the "purpose" or "effect" of advancing or inhibiting religion. There is no dispute that the program challenged here was enacted for the valid secular purpose of providing educational assistance to poor children in a demonstrably failing public school system. Thus, the question presented is whether the Ohio program nonetheless has the forbidden "effect" of advancing or inhibiting religion. *QP* → *What Est.C. prevents*

To answer that question, our decisions have drawn a consistent distinction between government programs that provide aid directly to religious schools, and programs of true private choice, in which government aid reaches religious schools only as a result of the genuine and independent choices of private individuals. While our jurisprudence with respect to the constitutionality of direct aid programs has "changed significantly" over the past two decades, our jurisprudence with respect to true private choice programs has remained consistent and unbroken. Three times we have confronted Establishment Clause challenges to neutral government programs that provide aid directly to a broad class of individuals, who, in turn, direct the aid to religious schools or institutions of their own choosing. Three times we have rejected such challenges. *1) How ct assess Est.C. w/ respect to religious schools* *True private choice programs always win*

Mueller, *Witters*, and *Zobrest* … make clear that where a government aid program is neutral with respect to religion, and provides assistance directly to a broad class of citizens who, in turn, direct government aid to religious schools wholly as a result of their own genuine and independent private choice, the program is not readily subject to challenge under the Establishment Clause. A program that shares these features permits government aid to reach religious institutions only by way of the deliberate choices of numerous individual recipients. The incidental advancement of a religious mission, or the perceived endorsement of a *Rule* religious message, is reasonably attributable to the individual recipient, not to the government, whose role ends with the disbursement of benefits.

Respondents…claim that even if we do not focus on the number of participating schools that are religious schools, we should attach constitutional significance to the fact that 96% of scholarship recipients have enrolled in religious schools. They claim that this alone proves parents lack genuine choice, even if no parent has ever said so. We need not consider this argument in detail, since it was flatly rejected in *Mueller*, where we found it irrelevant that 96% of parents taking deductions for tuition expenses paid tuition at religious schools. Indeed, we have recently found it irrelevant even to the constitutionality of a direct aid program that a vast majority of program benefits went to religious schools. The constitutionality of a neutral educational aid program simply does not turn on whether and why, in a particular area, at a particular time, most private schools are run by religious organizations, or most recipients choose to use the aid at a religious school.

In sum, the Ohio program is entirely neutral with respect to religion. It provides benefits directly to a wide spectrum of individuals, defined only by financial need and residence in a particular school district. It permits such individuals to exercise genuine choice among options public and private, secular and religious. The program is therefore a program of true private choice. In keeping with an unbroken line of decisions rejecting challenges to similar programs, we hold that the program does not offend the Establishment Clause.

JACKSON v. BENSON
578 N.W.2d 602 (Wisc. 1998)

STEINMETZ, J.

The next question presented in this case is whether the amended MPCP, [a school voucher program,] violates art. I, § 18 of the Wisconsin Constitution. The Respondents argue, and the court of appeals concluded, that the amended MPCP violates both the "benefits clause" and the "compelled support clause" of art. I, § 18. Upon review, we conclude that the amended MPCP violates neither provision.

The "benefits clause" of art. I, § 18 provides: "nor shall any money be drawn from the treasury for the benefit of religious societies, or religious or theological seminaries." This is Wisconsin's equivalent of the Establishment Clause of the First Amendment. This court has remarked that the language of art. I, § 18, while "more specific than the terser" clauses of the First Amendment, carries the same import; both provisions "are intended and operate to serve the same dual purpose of prohibiting the 'establishment' of religion and protecting the 'free exercise' of religion." Although art. I, § 18 is not subsumed by the First Amendment, we interpret and apply the benefits clause of art. I, § 18 in light of the United States Supreme Court cases interpreting the Establishment Clause of the First Amendment.

Unlike the court of appeals, which focused on whether sectarian private schools were "religious seminaries" under art. I, § 18, we focus our inquiry on whether the aid provided by the amended MPCP is "for the benefit of" such religious institutions. We have explained that the language "for the benefit of" in art. I, § 18 "is not to be read as requiring that some shadow of incidental benefit to a church-related institution brings a state grant or contract to purchase within the prohibition of the section." Furthermore, we have stated that the language of art. I, § 18 cannot be read as being "so prohibitive as not to encompass the primary-effect test." The crucial question, under art. I, § 18, as under the Establishment Clause, is "not whether some benefit accrues to a religious institution as a consequence of the legislative program, but whether its principal or primary effect advances religion."

We find the Supreme Court's primary effect test, focusing on the neutrality and indirection of state aid, is well reasoned and provides the appropriate line of demarcation for considering the constitutionality of neutral educational assistance programs such as the amended MPCP. Since the amended MPCP does not transgress the primary effect test employed in Establishment Clause jurisprudence, we also conclude that the statute is constitutionally inviolate under the benefits clause of art. I, § 18.

This conclusion is not inconsistent with Wisconsin tradition or with past precedent of this court. Wisconsin has traditionally accorded parents the primary role in decisions regarding the education and upbringing of their children. This court has embraced this principle for nearly a century, recognizing that: "parents as the natural guardians of their children [are] the persons under natural conditions having the most effective motives and inclinations and being in the best position and under the strongest obligations to give to such children proper nurture, education, and training."

In this context, this court has held that public funds may be placed at the disposal of third parties so long as the program on its face is neutral between sectarian and nonsectarian alternatives and the transmission of funds is guided by the independent decisions of third parties, and that public funds generally may be provided to sectarian educational institutions so long as steps are taken not to subsidize religious functions.

In *Weiss*, [this] court held that reading of the King James version of the Bible by students attending public school violated the religious benefits clause of art. I, § 18. Although the court's reasoning in *Weiss* may have differed from ours, its holding is entirely consistent with the primary effects test the Supreme Court has developed and we apply today. Requiring public school students to read from the Bible is neither neutral nor indirect. The Edgerton schools reviewed in *Weiss* were directly supported by public funds, and the reading of the Bible was anything but religious-neutral. The program considered in *Weiss* is far different from the neutral and indirect aid provided under the amended MPCP. The holding in *Weiss*, therefore, does not control our inquiry in this case.

The Respondents additionally argue that the amended MPCP violates the "compelled support clause" of art. I, § 18. The compelled support clause provides "nor shall any person be compelled to attend, erect or support any place of worship, or to maintain any ministry without consent...." The Respondents assert that since public funds eventually flow to religious institutions under the amended MPCP, taxpayers are compelled to support places of worship against their consent. This argument is identical to the Respondents' argument under the benefits clause. We will not interpret the compelled support clause as prohibiting the same acts as those prohibited by the benefits clause. Rather we look for an interpretation of these two related provisions that avoids such redundancy.

[T]he amended MPCP does not require a single student to attend class at a sectarian private school. A qualifying student only attends a sectarian private school under the program if the student's parent so chooses. Nor does the amended MPCP force participation in religious activities. On the contrary, the program prohibits a sectarian private school from requiring students attending under the program to participate in religious activities offered at such school. The choice to participate in religious activities is also left to the students' parents. Since the amended MPCP neither compels students to attend sectarian private schools nor requires them to participate in religious activities, the program does not violate the compelled support clause of art. I, § 18.

NOTE

In *Jackson*, the Wisconsin Supreme Court anticipated the U.S. Supreme Court's decision in *Zelman*, both as a matter of federal and state constitutional law. More frequently, state-court individual rights decisions respond to United States Supreme Court decisions, either by following them in lockstep or by reacting against them. It is fair to ask whether constitutional law in general—state and federal—benefits from this top-down approach or whether we would benefit from a bottom-up approach in which the state courts initially wrestle with difficult constitutional issues before the Supreme Court announces the meaning of the relevant federal provision.

TAXPAYERS FOR PUBLIC EDUCATION v. DOUGLAS COUNTY SCHOOL DISTRICT
351 P.3d 461 (Colo. 2015)

RICE, C.J.

Four years ago, the Douglas County School District implemented its Choice Scholarship Pilot Program ("the CSP"), a grant mechanism that awarded taxpayer-funded scholarships to qualifying elementary, middle, and high school students. Those students could use their scholarships to help pay their tuition at partnering private schools, including religious schools.

[margin note: State action in question]

The Colorado Constitution features broad, unequivocal language forbidding the State from using public money to fund religious schools. Specifically, article IX, section 7—entitled "Aid to private schools, churches, sectarian purpose, forbidden"—includes the following proscriptive language:

> Neither the general assembly, nor any county, city, town, township, school district or other public corporation, shall ever make any appropriation, or pay from any public fund or moneys whatever, anything in aid of any church or sectarian society, or for any sectarian purpose, or to help support or sustain any school, academy, seminary, college, university or other literary or scientific institution, controlled by any church or sectarian denomination whatsoever ....

[margin note: This amendment is harsh]

Although this provision uses the term "sectarian" rather than "religious," the two words are synonymous. That section 7 twice equates the term "sectarian" with the word "church" only reinforces this point. Therefore, this stark constitutional provision makes one thing clear: A school district may not aid religious schools.   *[margin note: Rule]*

Yet aiding religious schools is exactly what the CSP does. The CSP essentially functions as a recruitment program, teaming with various religious schools and encouraging students to attend those schools via the inducement of scholarships. To be sure, the CSP does not explicitly funnel money directly to religious schools, instead providing financial aid to students. But section 7's prohibitions are not limited to direct funding. Rather, section 7 bars school districts from "pay[ing] from any public fund or moneys *whatever, anything* in aid of any" religious institution, and from "help[ing] *support or sustain* any school ... controlled by any church or sectarian denomination *whatsoever*" (emphasis added). Given that private religious schools rely on students' attendance (and their corresponding tuition payments) for their ongoing survival, the CSP's facilitation of such attendance necessarily constitutes aid to "support or sustain" those schools.

Respondents point out that the CSP does not *require* scholarship recipients to enroll in a religious school, nor does it force participating Private School Partners to be religious. Respondents thus suggest that the CSP features an element of private choice that severs the link between the District's aid to the student and the student's ultimate attendance at a (potentially) religious school. It is true that the CSP does not *only* partner with religious schools; several Private School Partners are non-religious. The fact remains, however, that the CSP awards public money to students who may then use that money to pay for a religious education. In so doing, the CSP aids religious institutions.

Respondents nevertheless contend that the plain language of section 7 is not plain at all, but that the term "sectarian" is actually code for "Catholic." In so doing, Respondents charge that section 7 is a so-called "Blaine Amendment" that is bigoted in origin. They thus encourage us to wade into the history of section 7's adoption and declare that the framers created section 7 in a vulgar display of anti-Catholic animus.

We need not perform such an exegesis to dispose of Respondents' argument. Instead, we need merely recall that "constitutional provisions must be declared and enforced as written" whenever their language is "plain" and their meaning is "clear." As discussed, the term "sectarian" plainly means "religious." Therefore, we will enforce section 7 as it is written.

[Another Colorado Supreme Court case,] *Americans United*[,] [by contrast] revolved around the Colorado Student Incentive Grant Program, a scholarship for in-state college students. The grant program allowed eligible universities to recommend particular students deserving of scholarships to the Colorado Commission of Higher Education, which in turn administered the grants. The Commission awarded the grant money to the university, which then reduced the student's tuition by the amount of the grant. Although the grant program embraced most colleges and universities, it excluded institutions that were "pervasively sectarian," and it defined six eligibility criteria that schools needed to meet in order *not* to be branded pervasively sectarian.

The First Amendment to the United States Constitution provides in part that "Congress shall make no law respecting an establishment of religion, or prohibiting the free exercise thereof." Respondents contend that several federal cases interpreting the First Amendment constitute binding case law forbidding us from striking down the CSP. In particular, Respondents cite the U.S. Supreme Court's decision in *Zelman v. Simmons-Harris*.... Had Petitioners claimed that the CSP violated the

Establishment Clause, *Zelman* might constitute persuasive authority. But they did not. Rather, Petitioners challenged the CSP under article IX, section 7 of the Colorado Constitution. By its terms, section 7 is far more restrictive than the Establishment Clause regarding governmental aid to religion, and the Supreme Court has recognized that state constitutions may draw a tighter net around the conferral of such aid. As such, *Zelman's* reasoning, rooted in the Establishment Clause, is irrelevant to the issue of whether the CSP violates section 7.

EID, J., concurring in part and dissenting in part.

Today, the plurality interprets article IX, section 7 as prohibiting the expenditure of any state funds that might incidentally or indirectly benefit a religious school. This breathtakingly broad interpretation would invalidate not only the CSP, but numerous other state programs that provide funds to students and their parents who in turn decide to use the funds to attend religious schools in Colorado. The plurality's interpretation barring indirect funding is so broad that it would invalidate the use of public funds to build roads, bridges, and sidewalks adjacent to such schools, as the schools, in the words of the plurality, "rely on" state-paid infrastructure to operate their institutions. Because I fundamentally disagree with the plurality's interpretation, I respectfully dissent from [this part] of its opinion on the following two grounds.

The plurality first takes a wrong turn in interpreting the language of section 7 as invalidating any government expenditure that indirectly benefits religious schools. That is not what the language of section 7 says.

Section 7 bars a government entity from "mak[ing] any appropriation, or pay[ing] from any public fund or moneys whatever ... to help support or sustain any [church or sectarian] school ... whatsoever." This language bars the expenditure of public funds "to help support or sustain" certain schools. But here, the CSP funds are expended not "to help support or sustain" those schools, but rather to help the student recipients. The language does not suggest, as the plurality believes, that government funds that are directed to a student but happen to have an incidental beneficial effect on certain schools are also forbidden. The plurality stresses that the language prohibits a government entity from making such an expenditure "whatever" to certain schools "whatsoever." While these terms reinforce the prohibition on making certain expenditures, they do not modify or expand upon what kind of expenditures are prohibited—that is, expenditures "to support or sustain" a church or sectarian school. In other words, contrary to the plurality's reasoning, these words do not transform the prohibition on expenditures "to support or sustain" certain schools into a prohibition on any expenditures that have the incidental effect of benefiting certain schools.

We elucidated the distinction between direct and indirect assistance in *Americans United*, where we upheld a state grant program that disbursed state grant monies into the school accounts of student grant recipients who attended religious colleges.... We concluded that the program's "primary effect" was not to advance religion because "[t]he design of the statute [was] to benefit the student, not the institution."

The U.S. Supreme Court has recognized this same distinction in its Establishment Clause jurisprudence. In *Zelman*, for example, the Court upheld a program that gave tuition assistance to students from kindergarten to eighth grade in certain districts that could be used to attend any public or private school of their parents' choosing, including religious schools. The Court began by observing that the Establishment Clause prevents states from enacting laws that have the "purpose" or "effect" of advancing or inhibiting religion. There was no dispute that the program had a valid educational (and secular) purpose, and therefore the Court focused on whether it unconstitutionally advanced religion.... The Court relied upon its "consistent and unbroken" line of precedent holding that aid programs generally do not impermissibly "advance religion" when "government aid reaches religious schools only as a result of the genuine and independent choices of private individuals."

Applying this principle to the case before it, the Court concluded that the program was one of "true private choice" and consistent with the Establishment Clause. Significantly, the Court recognized that there may be "incidental advancement of a religious mission" in these sorts of programs. However, such incidental advancement is "reasonably attributable to the individual recipient, not to the government, whose role ends with the disbursement of benefits." Moreover, the Court refused to attach constitutional significance to the fact that ninety-six percent of the aid recipients enrolled in religious schools. According to the Court, "[t]he constitutionality of a neutral educational aid program simply does not turn on whether and why ... most recipients choose to use the aid at a religious school." The point is that aid recipients are the ones to make the choice.

The plurality rejects as "irrelevant" this wealth of Supreme Court precedent that reinforces our reasoning in *Americans United*, pointing out that it interprets the federal Establishment Clause, not section 7. But the plurality's approach is directly contrary to *Americans United*, where, as discussed above, we expressly relied upon our reasoning in considering the Establishment Clause claim in rejecting the section 7 claim. That the aid in question was expended to support students, not the institution, was a critical factor in both our Establishment Clause and section 7 inquiries.

More problematic is the plurality's conclusion that "[b]y its terms, section 7 is far more restrictive than the Establishment Clause regarding governmental aid to religion." The plurality's mistake is to confuse specificity with restriction. Section 7 is certainly more specific than the Establishment Clause, in that it contains a specific prohibition against making public expenditures "to help support or sustain" certain schools. We made a similar point regarding the specificity of article II, section 4 of the Colorado Constitution—which recognizes the "free exercise and enjoyment of religious profession and worship," as well as that "[n]o person shall be required to attend or support any ministry or place of worship"—in *Americans United*, observing that the state provisions are "considerably more specific than the Establishment Clause of the First Amendment." However, far from casting aside the federal counterpart and its accompanying jurisprudence, we declared that the state provisions should be read "to embody the same values of free exercise and government non-involvement secured by the religious clauses of the First Amendment." We reiterated that "although not necessarily determinative of state constitutional claims, First Amendment jurisprudence cannot be totally divorced from the resolution of these claims." Here, the Establishment Clause, as interpreted by the Supreme Court, ends up in the same place as the text of section 7—namely, prohibiting expenditures made to assist institutions, but not prohibiting expenditures made to support students.

A more fundamental problem with the plurality's opinion is that it holds that because section 7 is enforceable on its "plain language," it need not consider whether the provision is in fact enforceable due to possible anti-Catholic animus. As developed above, I believe the plurality is wrong on the plain language. But even if it were right, it would then be obligated to consider whether the language could be enforced to strike down the CSP. In this case, the plurality simply sticks its head in the sand and hopes that because it cannot see the allegations of anti-Catholic bias, no one else will.

The Supreme Court made this point clear in *Lukumi*, where it considered a challenge under the Free Exercise Clause to city ordinances that banned the ritual sacrifice of animals. The City argued that the ordinances were neutral on their face and therefore immune from constitutional scrutiny. The Court rejected this argument, holding instead that "[f]acial neutrality is not determinative" of a Free Exercise claim. According to the Court, "[t]he Free Exercise Clause ... extends beyond facial discrimination.... The [Clause] protects against government hostility which is masked, as well as overt." The court concluded that "[t]he record in this case compels the conclusion that suppression of the central element of the Santeria worship service was the object of the ordinances." Because the ordinances were not neutral, the Court went on to consider whether they were narrowly tailored to advance a compelling state interest. The Court concluded that they were not.

Under *Lukumi*, the plurality cannot begin and end its analysis with the conclusion that the plain language of section 7 is not discriminatory. In fact, the very case upon which the plurality relies for the proposition that states "may draw a tighter net around the conferral of [government] aid" to religion—*Locke v. Davey*—reinforces *Lukumi's* instruction that courts must look behind the text to discover any religious animus. In *Locke*, which involved a Washington state scholarship program that excluded students pursuing a degree in theology, the Court concluded that "[f]ar from evincing the hostility toward religion which was manifest in *Lukumi*, we believe that the [Washington program] goes a long way toward including religion in its benefits." The Court upheld the program against a free exercise challenge only after concluding that it could find nothing "that suggests animus toward religion." The relevant point here is not the Court's conclusion on the matter but that it performed the inquiry in the first place.

Moreover, in this instance, the text of section 7 is not as neutral as the plurality would have it. As noted above, the text bars expenditures "to help support or sustain any school" that is "controlled by any church or sectarian denomination whatsoever." The plurality equates the term "sectarian" with the term "religious," concluding that "the two words are synonymous." But even *Black's Law Dictionary* 1557 (10th ed. 2014), upon which the plurality relies for its conclusion, does not equate the two terms, suggesting that sectarian relates to "*a particular* religious sect." (emphasis added). In fact, in a 1927 case, this court upheld a school board rule requiring Bible reading in public schools against a section 7 challenge on the ground that such activity was not "sectarian"—that is, related to a particular sect. In sum, contrary to the plurality's interpretation, the term "sectarian" refers to a particular religious sect, not to religion generally.

In *Mitchell v. Helms*, 530 U.S. 793, 828 (2000), a plurality of the Court referred to the "shameful pedigree" of anti-sectarian sentiment in the 1870's. According to the plurality:

> Opposition to aid to "sectarian" schools acquired prominence in the 1870's with Congress' consideration (and near passage) of the Blaine Amendment, which would have amended the Constitution to bar any aid to sectarian institutions. Consideration of the amendment arose at a time of pervasive hostility to the Catholic Church and to Catholics in general, and it was an open secret that *"sectarian" was code for "Catholic."* See generally Green, *The Blaine Amendment Reconsidered*, 36 Am. J. Legal Hist. 38 (1992) (emphasis added).

The plurality in this case "decline[s] to ascribe to [*Mitchell*] the force of law" because it is a plurality opinion. But this passage from *Mitchell* is not relevant to this case because it has "the force of law," as the plurality implies; it is relevant for its description of historical context. And while Justice O'Connor, in her separate opinion concurring in the judgment joined by Justice Breyer, objected to the plurality's reasoning in *Mitchell*, she lodged no objection to the plurality's historical description. In fact, Justice Breyer, joined by Justices Stevens and Souter, recounted the same history in his dissent in *Zelman*. As Justice Breyer observed, anti-Catholic sentiment "played a significant role in creating a movement that sought to amend several state constitutions (often successfully), and to amend the United States Constitution (unsuccessfully) to make certain that government would not help pay for '*sectarian*' (*i.e., Catholic*) *schooling for children*."

In the end, the plurality's head-in-the-sand approach is a disservice to Colorado, as it allows allegations of anti-Catholic animus to linger unaddressed. The plurality should squarely address the issue of whether section 7 is enforceable, as this court has done with other provisions of the Colorado Constitution. Because the plurality fails to do so, and because it misinterprets the text of section 7 and ignores relevant Establishment Clause jurisprudence, I respectfully dissent from its opinion. [Justices Coats and Boatright joined Justice Eid's.]

[handwritten: Recounting plurality's deliverers]

CAIN v. HORNE
202 P.3d 1178 (Ariz. 2009)

RYAN, J.

Article 2, Section 12, of the Arizona Constitution provides that "[n]o public money ... shall be appropriated to any religious worship, exercise, or instruction, or to the support of any religious establishment." Article 9, Section 10, of the Arizona Constitution states that "[n]o tax shall be laid or appropriation of public money made in aid of any church, or private or sectarian school, or any public service corporation." The issue before us is whether two state-funded programs violate these provisions of our constitution. *[handwritten: Q P]*

[handwritten margin: 2 relevant provisions]

In 2006, the Legislature enacted two programs that, in part, appropriated state monies to allow students to attend a private school of their choice instead of the public school in the district in which they live. *[handwritten margin: 2 programs]*

The Arizona Scholarships for Pupils with Disabilities Program offers "pupils with disabilities...the option of attending any public school of the pupil's choice or receiving a scholarship to any qualified school of the pupil's choice." Under this program, a public-school student with a disability may transfer to a private primary or secondary school, with the State paying a scholarship up to the amount of basic state aid the student would generate for a public school district. A parent of a disabled student may apply for a scholarship if the pupil attended a public school during *[handwritten margin: What disability program allows]* the prior school year, the parent "is dissatisfied with the pupil's progress," and "[t]he parent has obtained acceptance for admission of the pupil to a qualified school."

The Arizona Displaced Pupils Choice Grant Program allows the State to pay $5,000 or the cost of tuition and fees, whichever is less, for children in foster care to attend the private primary or secondary school of their choice. The program is limited to 500 pupils. A grant school is "a nongovernmental primary school or secondary school or a preschool ... that does not discriminate on the basis of race, color, handicap, familial status or national origin, that maintains one or more grade levels from kindergarten through grade twelve...."

Sectarian and nonsectarian schools may participate in both programs; schools are not required to alter their "creed, practices or curriculum" in order to receive funding. Under both programs, (collectively "the voucher programs") parents or legal guardians select the private or sectarian school their child will attend. The State then disburses a check or warrant to the parent or guardian, who must "restrictively endorse" the instrument for payment to the selected school.

Horne and the intervenors argue that the Aid Clause should be interpreted just as the United States Supreme Court has interpreted the Establishment Clause of the United States Constitution, and that the parental choice involved in signing the state checks over to a private or sectarian school saves the voucher programs from unconstitutionality.

Contrary to Horne's assertion, [our previous cases in] *Kotterman* and *Jordan* do not compel us to interpret the Aid Clause as a mirror image of the Religion Clause or to interpret the Aid Clause as no broader than the federal Establishment Clause. More importantly, both the text and purpose of the Aid Clause support the conclusion that the clause requires a construction independent from that of the Religion Clause.

First, the text of the Aid Clause encompasses more than does the Religion Clause. The Aid Clause prohibits the use of public funds not only to aid *private* or sectarian schools, but to aid public corporations as well. Thus, under the Aid Clause, a statute granting funds to aid a public service corporation engaged exclusively in secular activities might be prohibited; such a statute would pose no difficulties under the Religion Clause, nor could it be readily analyzed under the Supreme Court's Establishment Clause jurisprudence. Likewise, the Religion Clause would prohibit an appropriation to pay for religious instruction in a public school, but the Aid Clause says nothing about such an appropriation, as public schools are not among the forbidden recipients of appropriations under the Aid Clause.

Second, although the two clauses overlap to some extent, they serve different purposes. The Religion Clause appears in Article 2, entitled "Declaration of Rights," and reinforces other provisions in the constitution "dealing with the separation of church and state." The Aid Clause is found in Article 9, entitled "Public Debt, Revenue, and Taxation," and "[u]nlike [Article 2, Section 12]…prohibits public aid to private nonsectarian schools and to public service corporations." The Aid Clause is thus primarily designed to protect the public fisc and to protect public schools.

Both the Aid and Religion Clauses prohibit certain appropriations of public money. In *Kotterman*, this Court addressed whether tax credits for contributions to organizations providing scholarships to students attending non-governmental schools violated the two clauses. We held that neither provision precluded the Legislature from granting a tuition tax credit, because the tax credit was not an appropriation. Because the funds in *Kotterman* were credits against tax liability, not withdrawals from the state treasury, the funds were never in the state's treasury; therefore, the credits did not constitute an appropriation.

Unlike the funds in *Kotterman*, the funds at issue here are withdrawn from the public treasury and earmarked for an identified purpose. Horne and the intervenors do not dispute that the vouchers therefore constitute appropriations of public funds. But ... they argue that the funds do not aid the schools; rather they characterize the funds as aid to students under a "true beneficiary" theory.

Under the true beneficiary theory, individuals benefitted by a government program, rather than the institution receiving the public funds, are characterized as the true beneficiaries of the aid. For example, in *Jordan*, we held that using state funds to partially reimburse the Salvation Army's expenses in providing emergency aid to those in need did not violate the Aid Clause. *Jordan* thus stands for the proposition that an entity covered by the Aid Clause may contract with the State to provide non-religious services to members of the public when such an entity "merely [acts as] a conduit and receives no financial aid or support therefrom."

The voucher programs, however, vary significantly from the program at issue in *Jordan*. In contrast to the program in *Jordan*, the voucher programs do not provide reimbursement for contracted services. In fact, they are designed in such a way that the State does not purchase anything; rather it is the parent or the guardian who exercises sole discretion to contract with the qualified school.

The Aid Clause flatly prohibits "appropriation of public money…in aid of any…private or sectarian school." No one doubts that the clause prohibits a direct appropriation of public funds to such recipients. For all intents and purposes, the voucher programs do precisely what the Aid Clause prohibits. These programs transfer state funds directly from the state treasury to private schools. That the checks or warrants first pass through the hands of parents is immaterial; once a pupil has been accepted into a qualified school under either program, the parents or guardians have no choice; they must endorse the check or warrant to the qualified school.

In sum, the language and purpose of the Aid Clause do not permit the appropriations these voucher programs provide; to rule otherwise would allow appropriations that would amount to "aid of...private or sectarian school[s]," and render the clause a nullity.

MEREDITH v. PENCE
984 N.E.2d 1213 (Ind. 2013)

DICKSON, C.J.

[T]he plaintiffs challenge Indiana's statutory program for providing vouchers to eligible parents for their use in sending their children to private schools. Finding that the challengers have not satisfied the high burden required to invalidate a statute on constitutional grounds, we affirm the trial court's judgment upholding the constitutionality of the statutory voucher program.

To be eligible for the voucher program, a student must live in a "household with an annual income of not more than one hundred fifty percent (150%) of the amount required for the individual to qualify for the federal free or reduced price lunch program." The voucher amount is determined from statutorily defined criteria pegged to the federal free or reduced price lunch program with the maximum voucher being "ninety percent (90%) of the state tuition support amount," designated for the student in the public "school corporation in which the eligible individual has legal settlement."

The fact that a student's family might meet the statutory eligibility qualifications does not require them to participate in the voucher program and to select a program-eligible school. The parents of an eligible student are thus free to select any program-eligible school or none at all. The voucher program does not alter the makeup or availability of Indiana public or charter schools. In accepting program students, eligible schools are free to maintain and apply their preexisting admissions standards except that "[a]n eligible school may not discriminate on the basis of race, color, or national origin." The program statute is silent with respect to religion, imposing no religious requirement or restriction upon student or school eligibility.]

The plaintiffs assert that the school voucher program violates Article 1, Section 4, of the Indiana Constitution. Specifically, the plaintiffs argue that the voucher program is contrary to the decree that "no person shall be compelled to attend, erect, or support, any place of worship, or to maintain any ministry, against his consent." We have previously held that the religious liberty protections in the Indiana Constitution "were not intended merely to mirror the federal First Amendment." When Indiana's present constitution was adopted in 1851, the framers who drafted it and the voters who ratified it did not copy or paraphrase the 1791 language of the federal First Amendment. Instead, they adopted seven separate and specific provisions, Sections 2 through 8 of Article 1, relating to religion.

For the most part, these separate provisions, including Section 4, were adapted from the 1816 Constitution. .... [T]he text of Section 4 is "our primary source for discerning the common understanding of the framers and ratifiers." The plaintiffs' argument under Section 4 focuses on the framers' text declaring that "no person shall be compelled to ... support, any place of worship, or to maintain any ministry, against his consent." Ind. Const. art. 1, § 4 (emphasis added) The word "support," the plaintiffs contend, "includes the compelled payment of taxes that are used for religious purposes," whether the tax is a specific directive (e.g., forced contributions to a religious entity or a direct tax specifically earmarked for religious purposes), or general tax revenues used to "support" religious entities.

This argument improperly expands the language of Section 4 and conflates it with that of Section 6. The former explicitly prohibits a person from being "compelled to attend, erect, or support" a place of worship or a ministry against his consent. This clause is a restraint upon government compulsion of individuals to engage in religious practices absent their consent. To limit the government's taxing and spending related to religious matters, the framers crafted Section 6, which restrains government not as to its compulsion of individuals, but rather its expenditure of funds for certain prohibited purposes ("No money shall be drawn from the treasury, for the benefit of any religious or theological institution." Ind. Const. art. 1, § 6.) The two clauses were drafted to specify separate and distinct objectives in their respective restraints upon government; Section 6 prohibiting expenditures to benefit religious or theological institutions, and Section 4 prohibiting compulsion of individuals related to attendance, erection, or support of places of worship or ministry. ....We view these language distinctions between Sections 4 and 6 to be purposeful. ....The religious liberty protections addressed by Section 4 prohibited government compulsion of individuals and was neither intended nor understood to limit government expenditures, which is addressed by Section 6.

The plaintiffs also assert that the school voucher program violates Article 1, Section 6, of the Indiana Constitution, which provides: "No money shall be drawn from the treasury, for the benefit of any religious or theological institution." In assessing whether the program violates this clause, two issues are potentially implicated: (A) whether the program involves government expenditures for benefits of the type prohibited by Section 6, and (B) whether the eligible schools at which the parents can use the vouchers are "religious or theological institution[s]" as envisioned by Section 6.

[margin handwriting: 2 elements to test m sec. 6]

We first find it inconceivable that the framers and ratifiers intended to expansively prohibit any and all government expenditures from which a religious or theological institution derives a benefit—for example, fire and police protection, municipal water and sewage service, sidewalks and streets, and the like. …. Any benefit to religious or theological institutions in the above examples, though potentially substantial, is ancillary and indirect. We hold today that the proper test for examining whether a government expenditure violates Article 1, Section 6, is not whether a religious or theological institution substantially benefits from the expenditure, but whether the expenditure directly benefits such an institution. To hold otherwise would put at constitutional risk every government expenditure incidentally, albeit substantially, benefiting any religious or theological institution. Such interpretation would be inconsistent with our obligation to presume that legislative enactments are constitutional and, if possible, to construe statutes in a manner that renders them constitutional. Section 6 prohibits government expenditures that directly benefit any religious or theological institution. Ancillary indirect benefits to such institutions do not render improper those government expenditures that are otherwise permissible….

[margin handwriting: Cf: direct benefits? No. Indirect? ✓ fine with us.]

The plaintiffs assert that "the absence of any requirement that participating schools segregate the public funds they receive... necessarily will directly fund the religious activities that take place in these schools," and that the voucher program "substantially" benefits these schools financially and by "promot[ing] these schools' religious mission" by adding to their enrollment students who otherwise would not be able to afford the tuition. We disagree because the principal actors and direct beneficiaries under the voucher program are neither the State nor program-eligible schools, but lower-income Indiana families with school-age children.

[margin handwriting: π: but schools don't have to segregate funds]

[handwriting: Direct beneficiaries are kids]

We find that the only direct beneficiaries of the school voucher program are the participating parents and their children, and not religious schools. The program does not contravene Section 6 by impermissibly providing direct benefits to religious institutions.

In light of the prevailing social, cultural, and legal circumstances when Indiana's Constitution was enacted, we understand Section 6 as not intended to prohibit government support of primary and secondary education which at the time included a substantial religious component. This interpretation is consistent with the presumption of constitutionality which we apply when reviewing a claim of statutory unconstitutionality.

For these reasons, we hold that the phrase "religious or theological institution[s]" in Section 6 of the Indiana Constitution was not intended to, nor does it now, apply to preclude government expenditures for functions, programs, and institutions providing primary and secondary education.... We affirm the grant of summary judgment to the defendants.

CALIFORNIA STATEWIDE COMMUNITY DEVELOPMENT AUTHORITY v. ALL PERSONS INTERESTED IN THE MATTER OF THE VALIDITY OF A PURCHASE AGREEMENT
152 P.3d 1070 (Cal. 2007)

KENNARD, J.

Recognizing that an educated citizenry and workforce are vital to the preservation of the rights and liberties of the people of this state, California in 1879 included in its new Constitution a provision directing the state Legislature to encourage "by all suitable means the promotion of intellectual, scientific, moral, and agricultural improvement." Since 1879, our state Constitution has also included a provision prohibiting state and local governments from granting anything "in aid of any...sectarian purpose, or help[ing] to support or sustain any school, college, university, hospital, or other institution controlled by any...sectarian denomination whatever..."

Against that backdrop, this court in *California Educational Facilities Authority v. Priest* upheld a state bond program funding the construction of educational facilities at religiously affiliated colleges, which were expressly prohibited from using the bond proceeds (paid for by private purchasers of the bonds) for specified religious purposes. We concluded that neither the state nor the federal Constitution prohibited this form of indirect assistance to religiously affiliated colleges, a rule that for more than three decades has allowed California public entities to issue revenue bonds to raise private funds for campus improvements at religiously affiliated colleges. We declined in *Priest*, however, to decide whether that rule would also apply if a college were "pervasively sectarian," a term the United States Supreme Court had used in *Hunt v. McNair* to describe a religiously affiliated school that devotes a substantial portion of its functions to its religious mission.

This case involves bond financing agreements between a public entity and three religiously affiliated schools that, for purposes of this litigation, the parties have assumed to be pervasively sectarian. These schools are thus likely to include a religious perspective in their teachings. (Each agreement expressly prohibits use of the bond proceeds for specified religious purposes). And, as in *Priest*, funds for the projects will not come from any government entity, but from private-sector purchasers of the bonds, and no public entity will have any obligation on the bonds in the event of default by the schools.)

As explained below, in resolving the state constitutional issue we conclude that the pertinent inquiry should center on the substance of the education provided by these three schools, not on their religious character. Therefore, whether the schools are pervasively sectarian (as the parties have assumed) is not a controlling factor in determining the validity of the bond funding program under our state Constitution. Rather, the program's validity turns on two questions: (1) Does each of the recipient schools offer a broad curriculum in secular subjects? (2) Do the schools' secular classes consist of information and coursework that is neutral with respect to religion? This test ensures that the state's interest in promoting the intellectual improvement of its residents is advanced through the teaching of secular information and coursework, and that the expression of a religious viewpoint in otherwise secular classes will provide a benefit to religion that is merely incidental to the bond program's primary purpose of promoting secular education.

(We apply] the following four-part test for determining whether the issuance of government bonds benefiting a religiously affiliated school violates the state constitutional provision in question: (1) The bond program must serve the public interest and provide no more than an incidental benefit to religion; (2) the program must be available to both secular and sectarian institutions on an equal basis; (3) the program must prohibit use of bond proceeds for "religious projects"; and (4) the program must not impose any financial burden on the government. Because the last three requirements can be easily disposed of in this case, we address them first.)

It is undisputed that the Authority has issued tax exempt bonds to encourage private investment in a wide variety of private institutions, secular as well as sectarian. This satisfies *Priest*'s second requirement— that the state bond program not discriminate between secular and sectarian institutions, treating both categories alike.

The bond agreements expressly prohibit each of the three schools from using the bond proceeds to construct or improve any facility for "religious projects," that is "sectarian instruction or as a place for religious worship or in connection with any part of the programs of any school or department of divinity for the useful life of the Project." This satisfies *Priest*'s third requirement.

Because of the utilization of conduit or pass through financing, the capital for the construction projects at the three private schools is funded solely by private-sector purchasers of the bonds. The schools repay the advanced capital plus interest to an independent trustee, who then pays the private bondholders, who have no recourse for nonpayment against the Authority. All of the Authority's costs of issuing the bonds are reimbursed by the schools. Thus, the bond funding places no financial burden on the Authority or any other public entity. This satisfies *Priest's* fourth requirement, that the program not impose a financial burden on the government.

Having concluded that the second, third, and fourth requirements of *Priest* are satisfied, we still need to determine whether the bond program meets *Priest's* first requirement, that the program provide a public benefit and no more than incidentally benefit religion. *Priest* held that the state's issuance of revenue bonds for purchase by private investors to fund construction or improvements of facilities at religiously affiliated colleges benefited the public at large by "'encourag[ing] by all suitable means the promotion of intellectual…improvement'" in California, thus furthering the state constitutional mandate of article IX, section 1, and that it "[did] not have a substantial effect of supporting religious activities."

Here, the proposed state bond program would benefit three schools that the Authority throughout this litigation has described as "pervasively sectarian." Would that bond program satisfy *Priest's* first requirement that the program serve the public interest and no more than incidentally benefit religion? To answer that question, we need to examine the bond program's purpose and effects. The program must have a "primary purpose…to advance legitimate public ends" and its effects may not include a benefit to religious activity that is other than "indirect, remote, [or] incidental" to the primary secular purpose. When a court attempts to determine how, if at all, a bond program would have the effect of supporting religious activity at schools, the characterization of the schools as "pervasively sectarian" does not provide a reliable or satisfactory answer. A more useful and effective approach, we conclude, is to examine the substance of the education that each of these religious schools offers its students.

The goal of the Authority's proposed issuance of revenue bonds here is to enhance the ability of private schools to improve their facilities through funding provided *exclusively by private investors*. By providing a tax exemption on interest earned on the bonds, the government makes the bonds more attractive to private investors and thereby enhances the ability of private institutions to expand their educational facilities. We pointed out in *Priest:* "The framers of [our state] Constitution recognized the importance of education in our social fabric, and imposed a constitutional duty on the Legislature to 'encourage by all suitable means the promotion of intellectual...improvement.'" In the circumstances of that case—a program available to sectarian and nonsectarian schools on an equal basis, in which all aid for religious projects was prohibited, and no financial burden was imposed upon the state—we concluded that the provision of tax exempt bond financing did not violate article XVI, section 5, because "its primary purpose [was] to advance legitimate public ends" and it "d[id] not have a substantial effect of supporting religious activities." Can the same be said of the proposed bond funding in this case with respect to a school that includes a religious perspective in its curriculum? The answer is yes, if certain requirements are met.

First, the school that is the subject of the revenue bond financing arrangement must provide a broad curriculum in secular subjects. When it does, the bond program assists the religious school in providing educational opportunities to California residents, enhancing their employment prospects and deepening their understanding of critical political, social, scientific, and cultural issues. This broad curriculum requirement excludes from the bond funding program religious schools that offer classes in only a few secular subjects, because to provide bond funding for such schools would not sufficiently advance the program's goal of expanding secular educational opportunities for Californians.

We are mindful of the concern that a school with a religious perspective may use the facilities built or improved with the revenue bond proceeds to substantially further its religious mission. Such use would provide more than an incidental benefit to religion, in violation of the principles we enunciated in *Priest.* To ensure that the classes in secular subjects promote the state's interest in secular education and no more than incidentally benefit religion, the religious school must meet a *second* requirement: the information and coursework used to teach secular subjects must be neutral with respect to religion. Of course, religion may be an object of study in classes such as history, social studies, and literature, just as in public schools, in a manner that neither promotes nor opposes any particular religion or religion in general. But a class that includes as part of the instruction information or coursework that promotes or opposes a particular religion or religious beliefs may not be taught in facilities financed through tax exempt bond financing. On remand, in determining religious neutrality, the straightforward assessment for the trial court to make is whether the academic content of a religious school's course in a secular subject such as math, chemistry, or Shakespeare's writings is typical of that provided in nonreligious schools. When a school establishes, through its course descriptions or otherwise, that the academic content of its secular classes is typical of comparable courses at public or other nonreligious schools, it is not necessary to scrutinize the school's day-to-day classroom communications. The circumstance that a teacher may, in addition to teaching a course's religiously neutral content, express an idea or viewpoint that may be characterized as "religious" does not result in a benefit to religion that is more than incidental to the state's primary purpose of enhancing secular education opportunities for California residents.

As we stated in *Priest* in addressing former section 24 of article XIII (the identically phrased predecessor of current section 5 of article XVI of the California Constitution), this "section has never been interpreted...to require governmental hostility to religion, nor to prohibit a religious institution from receiving an indirect, remote, and incidental benefit from a statute which has a secular primary purpose." *Priest* also observed: "'[M]any expenditures of public money give indirect and incidental benefit to denominational schools and institutions of higher learning. Sidewalks, streets, roads, highways, sewers are furnished for the use of all citizens regardless of religious belief.... Police and fire departments give the same protection to denominational institutions that they give to privately owned property and their expenses are paid from public funds.'" Here, we have *no* expenditure of public money, and application of the standards we have set out will ensure that any benefit to religion from the bond funding program is merely incidental.

Uphold

NOTES

1. For an example of another case in which the state supreme court held that the state and federal constitutions were coextensive, see *Anderson v. Town of Durham*, 895 A.2d 944 (Me. 2006), and for an example of another case in which the court held they were not, see *Simmons-Harris v. Goff*, 711 N.E.2d 203 (Ohio 1999) ("There is no reason to conclude that the Religion Clauses of the Ohio Constitution are coextensive with those in the United States Constitution.").

2. For articles dealing with these issues in more depth, see Frank R. Kemerer, *The Constitutional Dimension of School Vouchers*, 3 Tex. F. on C.L. & C.R. 137 (1998); Joseph P. Viteritti, *Blaine's Wake: School Choice, The First Amendment, and State Constitutional Law*, 21 Harv. J.L. & Pub. Pol'y 657 (1998).

CHAPTER X

SCHOOL FUNDING CLAUSES

A. INTRODUCTION

In *Brown v. Board of Education*, 347 U.S. 483, 493 (1954), the Supreme Court observed that "education is perhaps the most important function of state and local governments" before holding that access to public schools "must be made available to all on equal terms." At the same time that *Brown* removed one impediment to equal educational opportunities, it left in place another: the disfiguring effects of wealth on the type of education that American children receive and the challenges that poverty poses for some public schools wishing to provide an education to their students "on equal terms" to the education offered by their wealthier counterparts.

In the late 1960s, while the federal courts faced lawsuits over the pace of the "all deliberate speed" mandate of *Brown II, Brown v. Bd. of Educ.*, 349 U.S. 294, 301 (1955), and related lawsuits premised on removing the vestiges of segregation by requiring school districts to use busing to create racially balanced schools, a new form of institutional litigation related to public education arose—one focused less on the racial makeup of primary and secondary schools and more on the disparities between the quality of education offered to students based on the property wealth of the school districts in which they lived. First in the California state courts, *see Serrano v. Priest*, 5 Cal. 3d 584 (Cal. 1971), and eventually in a federal-court lawsuit filed in Texas, *see Rodriguez v. San Antonio Indep. Sch. Dist.*, 337 F. Supp. 280 (W.D. Tex. 1971), litigants argued that their respective state systems of funding a public education were unconstitutional because they primarily relied on local funding and local control, which permitted wide disparities in the quality of the education that children within the State received based on little more than the property wealth of the school district in which their parents happened to live.

In *Serrano*, the California Supreme Court ruled in favor of the claimants. Relying on the State and Federal Constitutions, the Court made the following points: "the school financing system discriminates on the basis of wealth of a district and its residents," 5 Cal.3d at 604; "the distinctive and priceless foundation of education in our society warrants, indeed compels, our treating it as a 'fundamental interest,'" *id.* at 608-09; the financing system is not necessary to accomplish a compelling state interest, *id.* at 614; and since the funding system "does not withstand 'strict scrutiny,' it denies to the plaintiffs and others similarly situated the equal protection of the laws," *id*. at 614-15.

In *Rodriguez*, the claimants sought to extend *Serrano*'s federal equal-protection holding from California to Texas and eventually to all other States in the country. They premised their lawsuit on two theories of unconstitutionality: that education is a fundamental right and that wealth is a suspect class. Both theories came to the same end, as each would have required Texas (and eventually each State) to satisfy the rigors of strict scrutiny in justifying its system of funding public schools—a test that would force a State to prove that it had done everything within its power to eliminate the marked disparities between the quality of a public education offered to children living in property-rich and property-poor school districts. A three-judge district court ruled for the plaintiffs. It invoked both grounds of unconstitutionality and held that the Equal Protection Clause guaranteed "fiscal neutrality" in Texas's creation and oversight of a school-funding system. 337 F. Supp. at 284, 286.

In a 5–4 decision, the United States Supreme Court reversed. 411 U.S. 1 (1973). In a decision written by Justice Powell, the Court rejected both claims of unconstitutionality. Education is not a fundamental right entitled to strict scrutiny, he wrote, because the Constitution nowhere mentions the topic, precluding fundamental-right status on that basis alone. *Id.* at 35. Nor, he added, do individuals have a fundamental right to a governmental benefit merely because that benefit is significant or even essential. Otherwise, a State's allocation of all manner of public benefits—access to housing, food, health care, to name a few—would face strict scrutiny. *Id.* at 37. In rejecting the contention that wealth was a suspect classification, Justice Powell noted that Texas guaranteed all children a free public education regardless of wealth. It thus had not denied its residents a public benefit on the basis of wealth, but had merely created a system that tolerated a relatively worse public benefit to be provided to some citizens on the basis of wealth. 411 U.S. at 38-39.

Justice Marshall wrote the principal dissent. As the lead advocate for the plaintiffs in *Brown*, Justice Marshall surely understood the stakes of the *Rodriguez* litigation, "including the possibility that the promises of Brown would never be fulfilled unless the courts not only eliminated de jure segregation by race but also curbed the effects of de facto segregation by wealth." Jeffrey S. Sutton, *San Antonio Independent School District v. Rodriguez and Its Aftermath*, 94 Va. L. Rev. 1963, 1970 (2008). He concluded that the plain connection between a meaningful education and other constitutional guarantees made it essential to subject discrimination against a "powerless class[]" over this public benefit to strict scrutiny. *Id.* at 109 (Marshall, J., dissenting).

"For better, for worse or for more of the same, the majority in *Rodriguez* tolerated the continuation of a funding system that allowed serious disparities in the quality of the education a child received based solely on the wealth of the community in which his parents happened to live or could afford to live. Yet even after the Court gave the States the green light to continue relying on that system, they eventually demanded change—in some instances because the political processes prompted it and in other instances because the state courts required it." Sutton, Rodriguez *and Its Aftermath*, 94 Va. L. Rev. at 1971. Thus, although the Supreme Court in *Rodriguez* rejected the California Supreme Court's *federal* equal-protection analysis in *Serrano*, it did not overrule—indeed, it had no power to overrule—*Serrano*'s *state* school-funding ruling or for that matter prevent other States from doing the same under their own constitutions.

This chapter focuses on the aftermath of *Rodriguez*. The state-court litigation that followed *Rodriguez* provides a rich example of the independence of state constitutions (and state legislatures) as a source for protecting rights that the federal constitution (and national legislature) have not protected. In the several decades since the United States Supreme Court's decision in *Rodriguez*, the vast majority of state supreme courts have considered similar claims under their state constitutions, and an increasing majority of them have ruled in favor of the plaintiffs. The purpose of this chapter is to explore the state courts' resolution of these claims—first by considering state constitutional decisions premised on equality theories of unconstitutionality, then by considering state decisions premised on adequacy theories of unconstitutionality, and finally by exploring remedial issues that have arisen in the area.

B. EQUAL PROTECTION DECISIONS

The first wave of state-court decisions after *Rodriguez*, like the *Serrano* decision that preceded *Rodriguez*, principally addressed equal protection claims. As we saw in Chapter 5, many state constitutions (but by no means all of them) contain equal protection clauses. In the immediate aftermath of *Rodriguez*, particularly from 1973 to 1989, many school-finance plaintiffs premised their claims for relief on the equal protection clause, or a comparable reading of another clause, found in the State's constitution. As in *Rodriguez*, the claimants focused on the gap in funding between rich and poor school districts and the challenges faced by property-poor districts in closing the gap. While some of these claims succeeded, most did not. *See e.g.*, *Dupree v. Alma Sch. Dist. No. 30*, 651 S.W.2d 90, 93 (Ark. 1983); *Horton v. Meskill*, 376 A.2d 359, 374 (Conn. 1977); *Pauley v. Kelly*, 255 S.E.2d 859, 878 (W. Va. 1979); *Washakie County Sch. Dist. No. One v. Herschler*, 606 P.2d 310, 333-35 (Wyo.

1980); *see* Molly S. McUsic, *The Future of* Brown v. Board of Education*: Economic Integration of the Public Schools*, 117 Harv. L. Rev. 1334, 1344 (2004) ("Prior to 1989, virtually every school finance case made its equity claim under a state constitution's equal protection clause."). By 1988, the State defendants had prevailed in 15 of the 22 cases in which an equal protection theory of invalidity had been raised. Michael A. Rebell, "Educational Adequacy, Democracy, and the Courts," *in* National Research Council, Achieving High Educational Standards for All: Conference Summary 218, 226-27, n.47 (Timothy Ready et al. eds., 2002).

HORNBECK v. SOMERSET COUNTY BOARD OF EDUCATION
458 A.2d 758 (Md. 1983)

MURPHY, C.J.

This case involves a challenge to the constitutionality of Maryland statutes which govern the system of financing public elementary and secondary schools in the State's twenty-four school districts, *i.e.*, in the twenty-three counties of Maryland and in Baltimore City. The litigation focuses upon the existence of wide disparities in taxable wealth among the various school districts, and the effect of those differences upon the fiscal capacity of the poorer districts to provide their students with educational offerings and resources comparable to those of the more affluent school districts.

The plaintiffs maintain that the lower court correctly held that the Maryland system of public school finance violates the equal protection guarantee of Art. 24 of the Maryland Declaration of Rights. They contend, as the trial judge held, that the right to education, even if it is not fundamental under the federal constitution, is nevertheless of fundamental caliber under the state constitutional provision because, within the formulation of *Rodriguez*, the right is explicitly guaranteed by the state constitution. Plaintiffs seek to buttress their position by referring to the provisions of § 52 of Art. III of the Maryland Constitution which direct in paragraph (4)(f) that the state budget include an "estimate of all appropriations...for the establishment and maintenance throughout the State of a thorough and efficient system of public schools in conformity with Article 8 of the Constitution and with the laws of the State." As paragraph (11) of § 52 directs the Governor to include such estimates for the public schools in the budget "without revision," and because paragraph (6) prohibits the General Assembly from amending the budget to affect the provisions made by the laws of the State for the public school system, the plaintiffs contend that public education is of such high status as to constitute a fundamental right in Maryland. Accordingly, the plaintiffs maintain that the lower court was right in concluding that the State's system of public school financing must be reviewed under the "strict scrutiny" standard, thereby requiring that the State demonstrate that the system promotes a compelling governmental interest—a test with which the Maryland system cannot comply.

While we have not considered the applicability of the *Rodriguez* test in determining whether a right is fundamental for purposes of equal protection review under Art. 24 of the Declaration of Rights, a number of states have considered, and rejected, that test in considering whether education is a fundamental right under state constitutional provisions similar to Art. VIII of the Maryland Constitution. These cases point out that state constitutions, unlike the federal constitution, are not of limited or delegated powers and are not restricted to provisions of fundamental import; consequently, whether a right is fundamental should not be predicated on its explicit or implicit inclusion in a state constitution.

These cases also point out that other public services, such as police, fire, welfare, health care and other social services, which benefit the entire population, are equally as important as education, even though they may not be mentioned in the state constitution. The observation has been made by one court that in terms of "fundamentality" there is little by way of essential difference between any of these vital areas of state concern, so that to apply a strict scrutiny analysis to legislation dealing with any of these "rights" is "to render automatically suspect every statutory classification made by state legislatures in dealing with matters which today occupy a substantial portion of their time and attention." In this regard, it must be noted that many, if not all, of these rights could, within the *Rodriguez* formulation of fundamental rights, be deemed implicitly guaranteed in most state constitutions, thereby requiring application of the strict scrutiny test—a result which the defendants say is certain to wreak havoc with the ability of state legislatures to deal effectively with such critical governmental services. To conclude that education is a right so fundamental as to require strict scrutiny analysis would, the defendants say, likely render unconstitutional a substantial portion of the statutes, bylaws and practices that regulate education in Maryland. The defendants advance the further suggestion that if there must be, as the trial judge held, a compelling State interest that would justify deviation from mathematically exact dollar per pupil equality among all of the school districts, intradistrict disparities between areas, schools and even classes within schools in the same county could not be sustained. Similarly, if the right to education is fundamental, it is suggested that the State would be required to show a compelling interest for maintaining any differences among the State's school districts, even if the differences were not financial.

We recognize, as do all the school finance cases, the vital role public education plays in our society. And we share the view expressed in *Lujan* that education "can be a major factor in an individual's chances for economic and social success as well as a unique influence on a child's development as a good citizen and on his future participation in political and community life." Nevertheless, we conclude that education is not a fundamental right for purposes of equal protection analysis under Art. 24 of the Declaration of Rights.

We decline to adopt the overly simplistic articulation of the fundamental rights test set forth in *Rodriguez*, i.e., that the existence of a fundamental right is determined by whether it is explicitly or implicitly guaranteed in the constitution. Maryland's Constitution explicitly, not to mention implicitly, guarantees rights and interests which can in no way be considered "fundamental."

The directive contained in Article VIII of the Maryland Constitution for the establishment and maintenance of a thorough and efficient statewide system of free public schools is not alone sufficient to elevate education to fundamental status. Nor do the budgetary provisions of § 52 of Article III of the Constitution require that we declare that the right to education is fundamental. The right to an adequate education in Maryland is no more fundamental than the right to personal security, to fire protection, to welfare subsidies, to health care or like vital governmental services; accordingly, strict scrutiny is not the proper standard of review of the Maryland system of financing its public schools.

Plaintiffs next argue that "heightened review" is the appropriate standard for determining the constitutionality of Maryland's system of public school finance under Art. 24 of the Declaration of Rights because the system affects important personal rights to education and significantly interferes with or denies the exercise of such rights. Under this standard, as [another Court of Appeals of Maryland decision] points out, a legislative classification must rest upon some ground of difference having a fair and substantial relationship to the object of the legislation. If this standard of review is applicable, it would, for reasons set forth hereinafter in considering the legislative purpose underlying the Maryland system of public school finance, satisfy the requirements of the "heightened review" test, i.e., the means of financing the public school system do bear a fair and substantial relationship to the legitimate goal of providing an adequate education for all children, while at the same time maintaining the viability of local control. We hold, however, that the heightened review test is not applicable in this case because, as we have already observed, there has been no significant interference with, infringement upon, or deprivation of the underlying right to take advantage of a thorough and efficient education under Art. VIII of the Maryland Constitution.

[handwritten: Sutton is was B a "rule case"]

HORTON v. MESKILL
376 A.2d 359 (Conn. 1977)

[handwritten: sui generis = of its own kind]

HOUSE, C.J.

As other courts have recognized, educational equalization cases are "in significant aspects sui generis" and not subject to analysis by accepted conventional tests or the application of mechanical standards. The wealth discrimination found among school districts differs materially from the usual equal protection case where a fairly defined indigent class suffers discrimination to its peculiar disadvantage. The discrimination is relative rather than absolute. Further, the children living in towns with relatively low assessable property values are afforded public education but, as the trial court found, the education they receive is to a substantial degree narrower and lower in quality than that which pupils receive in comparable towns with a larger tax base and greater ability to finance education. True, the state has mandated local provision for a basic educational program with local option for a program of higher quality but, as the trial court's finding indicates, that option to a town which lacks the resources to implement the higher quality educational program which it desires and which is available to property-richer towns is highly illusory. As Mr. Justice Marshall put it in his dissent in *Rodriguez*: "(T)his Court has never suggested that because some 'adequate' level of benefits is provided to all, discrimination in the provision of services is therefore constitutionally excusable. The Equal Protection Clause is not addressed to the minimal sufficiency but rather to the unjustifiable inequalities of state action. It mandates nothing less than that 'all persons similarly circumstanced shall be treated alike.'" With justification, the trial court found merit to the complaints of the plaintiffs about "the sheer irrationality" of the state's system of financing education in the state on the basis of property values, noting that their argument "'would be similar and no less tenable should the state make educational expenditures dependent upon some other irrelevant factor, such as the number of telephone poles in the district.'"

[handwritten margin note: wealth discrimination is relative not absolute.]

We find our thinking to be substantially in accord with the decisions of the New Jersey Supreme Court in *Robinson v. Cahill* and the California Supreme Court in *Serrano v. Priest*, (*Serrano II*), and whether we apply the "fundamentality" test adopted by *Rodriguez* or the pre-*Rodriguez* test under our state constitution (as the California Supreme Court did in *Serrano II*) or the "arbitrary" test applied by the New Jersey Supreme Court in *Robinson v. Cahill*, we must conclude that in Connecticut the right to education is so basic and fundamental that any infringement of that right must be strictly scrutinized.

[handwritten margin note: Rule: Conn applies strict scrutiny.]

[handwritten: fundamental strict scrutiny]

"Connecticut has for centuries recognized it as her right and duty to provide for the proper education of the young." Education is so important that the state has made it compulsory through a requirement of attendance. The General Assembly has by word, if not by deed, recognized…that it is the concern of the state that "each child shall have…equal opportunity to receive a suitable program of educational experiences." Indeed the concept of equality is expressly embodied in the constitutional provision for distribution of the school fund in the provision (article eighth, s 4) that the fund "shall be inviolably appropriated to the support and encouragement of the public schools throughout the state, and for the equal benefit of all the people thereof."

The present-day problem arises from the circumstance that over the years there has arisen a great disparity in the ability of local communities to finance local education, which has given rise to a consequent significant disparity in the quality of education available to the youth of the state. It was well stated in the memorandum of decision of the trial court, which noted that the "present method (of financing education in the state) is the result of legislation in which the state delegates to municipalities of disparate financial capability the state's duty of raising funds for operating public schools within that municipality. That legislation gives no consideration to the financial capability of the municipality to raise funds sufficient to discharge another duty delegated to the municipality by the state, that of educating the children within that municipality. The evidence in this case is that, as a result of this duty-delegating to Canton without regard to Canton's financial capabilities, pupils in Canton receive an education that is in a substantial degree lower in both breadth and quality than that received by pupils in municipalities with a greater financial capability, even though there is no difference between the constitutional duty of the state to the children in Canton and the constitutional duty of the state to the children in other towns.

We conclude that without doubt the trial court correctly held that, in Connecticut, elementary and secondary education is a fundamental right, that pupils in the public schools are entitled to the equal enjoyment of that right, and that the state system of financing public elementary and secondary education as it presently exists and operates cannot pass the test of "strict judicial scrutiny" as to its constitutionality. These were the basic legal conclusions reached by the court.

While the development of an appropriate legislative plan is not without its complexities, the problem is not insoluble. Nor do we share the alarm expressed in the dissenting opinion at what it concludes are "the implications of the decision" as requiring total state financing of education, loss of local administrative control over educational decisions and the requirement that education in all towns "be brought up to the

Darien standard" which, if it occurred, the trial court found would require an increase of $313,000,000 over the amounts being currently expended. To the contrary, as we have noted, the trial court expressly found that none of these consequences would of necessity follow the adoption by the state of a financing program designed to achieve a substantial degree of equality of educational opportunity and permit all towns to exercise a meaningful choice as to educational services to be offered to students, that the property tax is still a viable means of producing income for education, and that there is no reason why local control needs to be diminished in any degree merely because some system other than the one presently in effect is adopted. We find no reason to reject the validity of these findings. Obviously, absolute equality or precisely equal advantages are not required and cannot be attained except in the most relative sense. Logically, the state may recognize differences in educational costs based on relevant economic and educational factors and on course offerings of special interest in diverse communities. None of the basic alternative plans to equalize the ability of various towns to finance education requires that all towns spend the same amount for the education of each pupil. The very uncertainty of the extent of the nexus between dollar input and quality of educational opportunity requires allowance for variances as do individual and group disadvantages and local conditions.

VINCENT v. VOIGHT
614 N.W.2d 388 (Wis. 2000)

CROOKS, J.

A majority of this court holds that Wisconsin students have a fundamental right to an equal opportunity for a sound basic education. An equal opportunity for a sound basic education is one that will equip students for their roles as citizens and enable them to succeed economically and personally. The legislature has articulated a standard for equal opportunity for a sound basic education in Wis. Stat. §§ 118.30(lg)(a) and 121.02(L) (1997-98) as the opportunity for students to be proficient in mathematics, science, reading and writing, geography, and history, and to receive instruction in the arts and music, vocational training, social sciences, health, physical education and foreign language, in accordance with their age and aptitude. An equal opportunity for a sound basic education acknowledges that students and districts are not fungible and takes into account districts with disproportionate numbers of disabled students, economically disadvantaged students, and students with limited English language skills. So long as the legislature is providing sufficient resources so that school districts offer students the equal opportunity for a sound basic education as required by the constitution, the state school finance system will pass constitutional muster.

We conclude that the school finance system articulated in Wis. Stat. ch. 121 is constitutional under both art. X, § 3 and art. I, § 1 of the Wisconsin Constitution. The Petitioners have not shown beyond a reasonable doubt that the current school financing system violates either art. X, § 3, or art. I, § 1, and therefore, they have not made out a prima facie case in support of their motion for summary judgment.

ABRAHAMSON, C.J., concurring in part and dissenting in part.

The framers of the Wisconsin Constitution recognized the importance of education when they created article X governing the establishment and funding of public schools. Creating a system of free and uniform public schools was considered to be among the most essential of the framers' tasks. Throughout the 1846 and 1848 conventions, the framers expressed the desire that all of Wisconsin's students, rich and poor, would be educated together in the public schools. For example, the requirement in article X, § 4 that localities contribute to school funding was included "directly for the advantage of the poor," because it increased the commitment to local schools. Without local support "the common schools languished, and select schools rose on their ruins."

Article X read as a whole demonstrates that the framers intended to require the legislature to create and finance a school system that is equitable and uniform in character throughout the state and that provides equal educational opportunity for all students.

The constitution "virtually declares that public education is a state power and function, based upon the well-established principle that the whole state is interested in the education of the children of the state and that this function must be exercised by the people as a whole...." The framers believed that the creation of free and uniform public schools was "the only system on which we could depend for the preservation of our liberties." The legislature has recognized that "education is a state function" and that "the state must guarantee that a basic educational opportunity be available to each pupil."

The framers of the Wisconsin Constitution did not intend the school districts' boundaries to be uniform and therefore could not have envisioned the school districts' taxing and spending capacity to be uniform, since taxing and spending ability and school district boundaries are related. But the state school finance system must provide districts and schools with the funding needed to meet the constitutional mandate. The record, which is undisputed, shows that school districts vary widely in the amount spent per student (ranging from $13,534 to $5,301), in the ability to raise dollars for every mill levied, and in the actual levy rates.

The plaintiff-intervenors, the Wisconsin Education Association Council and a number of teachers and school administrators from school districts across the state, assert that the state school finance system is unconstitutional because it does not allow districts with significant numbers of high needs students to offer these students an adequate educational opportunity. High needs students include disabled children, economically disadvantaged children and children with limited skills in the English language. The State's brief concedes, as it must, that it probably costs more per child to educate high needs students.

A non-uniform education can result from treating similarly situated students and school districts differently, but it can also result from treating differently situated students and school districts in the same way. Consequently, to ensure that all students have an opportunity for a sound basic education, school districts with a disproportionate number of high needs students must be provided with extra financial resources to meet the standard that is constitutionally required. *Schools w/more high needs kids need more $*

Because the state school finance system fails to address the costs of educating high needs students, the plaintiff-intervenors argue that schools or school districts with a disproportionate number of such students are not able to provide anywhere near the educational opportunities of other schools or school districts. While the state school finance system especially fails property-poor school districts with disproportionate numbers of high needs students, the plaintiff-intervenors assert that even property-rich school districts that have disproportionate numbers of high needs students, such as Madison, are unable to offer educational opportunities that are uniform with the rest of the state. School districts with large numbers of high needs students may have to divert funds to pay for the higher costs associated with the high needs students, leaving the other students at a disadvantage. *How high needs areas disadvantage kids.*

Although I realize that equal dollars do not necessarily translate to equal educational opportunity, it is clear that substantial funding differences may significantly affect students' opportunities to learn. Money is not the only variable affecting educational opportunity, but it is one that the legislature can equalize.

Both the circuit court and court of appeals acknowledged that they were unable to adequately adjudicate this case because of the lack of a developed standard from this court regarding the requirements of article X, § 3. I would remand the cause to the circuit court for further proceedings in light of the standard the majority opinion sets forth in the present case to determine whether the defendants have met their constitutional obligation.

SYKES, J., concurring in part; dissenting in part.

I agree with the majority's conclusion that the state school finance system is not unconstitutional under Wis. Const. art. X, § 3, the uniformity clause of the education article, or Wis. Const. art. I, § 1, the Equal Protection Clause. Therefore, I join [some] of the [majority] opinion, as well as the decision to affirm. However, I cannot agree with [other parts] of the majority opinion, which announce an expansive new state constitutional right under art. X, § 3 to "an equal opportunity for a sound basic education," defined as an education "that will equip students for their roles as citizens and enable them to succeed economically and personally."

The petitioners allege that the current school finance formula violates the uniformity clause of the education article as well as the Equal Protection Clause of the Wisconsin Constitution by creating or failing to redress alleged educational disparities in so-called "property-poor" districts, districts with many high-needs children, and districts where charter schools and the school choice program decrease the enrollment in the public schools.

Any definition of education or standard for educational adequacy is inherently a political and policy question, not a justiciable one. The people of this state—through their elected representatives in the legislature, the governor's office and local school boards—decide what their schools will teach and how much education is adequate or desirable for their children. What constitutes an "adequate" or "sound" or even "basic" education is most emphatically not a question of constitutional law for this or any other court.

There is certainly nothing in the text of art. X, § 3 to support such a conclusion. Wisconsin Const. art. X, § 3 provides:

> The legislature shall provide by law for the establishment of district schools, which shall be as nearly uniform as practicable; and such schools shall be free and without charge for tuition to all children between the ages of 4 and 20 years.

The newly-minted constitutional right is as follows: "Wisconsin students have a fundamental right to an equal opportunity for a sound basic education. An equal opportunity for a sound basic education is one that will equip students for their roles as citizens and enable them to succeed economically and personally." The new right to education includes "the opportunity for students to be proficient in mathematics, science, reading and writing, geography, and history, and for them to receive instruction in the arts and music, vocational training, social sciences, health, physical education and foreign language, in accordance with their age and aptitude." There is more: "An equal opportunity for a sound basic education acknowledges that students and districts are not fungible and takes into account districts with disproportionate numbers of disabled students, economically disadvantaged students, and students with limited English language skills." And the legislature must henceforward provide "sufficient resources" to meet the new standard; otherwise, it will be in violation of art. X, § 3.

The problem with all of this is that there is no support for it anywhere in the text of the Wisconsin Constitution. It is entirely the product of judicial invention, despite efforts to tie some parts of the standard to particular statutory enactments. This may be fine education policy, and as a parent and a citizen I certainly support the educational aspirations and goals expressed by the new standard, as well as the requirement that schools include instruction in the specified curricular subject areas. But as a judge, I am compelled to say as forcefully as I can that the court's exercise in education clause standard-writing has nothing whatsoever to do with constitutional law.

My conclusion is based upon the text of art. X, § 3, the obvious lack of judicially discoverable or manageable standards for educational adequacy, and the impossibility of deciding the issue without undertaking an initial, clearly nonjudicial policy determination.

NOTE

Whether before 1989 or after, claimants who prevailed on state-law equal protection grounds were the exception that proved the rule. Most of these claims failed. One problem with this theory of unconstitutionality, as with many federal and state equal protection claims, is the all-or-nothing-at-all nature of tiers of review. For many state courts, applying strict or intermediate review to all manner of educational policy decisions—including what subjects are offered, when classes are taught and what sports teams are available—was a bridge too far, establishing a level of scrutiny that was too difficult for States and local governments to satisfy. Yet at the same time, applying rational basis review created a level of scrutiny that was too easy for States to meet. Another problem, one to which we will return at the end of this chapter, concerned remedy. Even when the claimants managed to win under this theory, the courts struggled to identify meaningful and realistic remedies for closing the equity gap. Some remedies effectively required a statewide school-funding system that precluded local school districts from supplementing state aid. Others required a system that came to the same result, one that set a floor and a ceiling on educational spending. Still another obstacle to litigation success in these cases is that state legislatures after *Rodriguez* increasingly removed the most problematic disparity-causing features of their systems of funding public schools. In particular, they adopted school-funding equalization formulas that to one degree or another ameliorated, but did not eliminate, funding disparities.

C. ADEQUACY DECISIONS

The obstacles facing these equal protection challenges prompted a second wave of state-court lawsuits. From 1989 to the present, claimants in this area frequently have seized on a different theory of unconstitutionality. Instead of focusing on equal protection and equity problems, as the claimants in *Rodriguez*, *Serrano*, and the above cases did, these plaintiffs rely on unique state constitutional provisions that have no counterpart in the United States Constitution. Many States for example have provisions in their constitutions requiring the legislature to create a "thorough and efficient system of common schools." *See* Md. Const. art. VIII, § 1; N.J. Const. art. VIII, § 4, ¶ 1; Ohio Const. art. VI, § 2; W. Va Const. art. XII, § 1. Other state constitutions contain similar provisions, requiring the legislature to create a "uniform" system of public schools, *see* N.C. Const. art. IX, § 2; Ind. Const. art. 8, § 1; N.D. Const. § 148; Wis. Const. art. X, § 3, a "quality" system of public schools, *see* Mont. Const. art. X, § 1, cl. 3; Va. Const. art. VIII, § 1, a system of "free instruction," *see* Neb. Const. art. VII, § 1, or free "common schools," *see* Cal. Const. art. IX, § 5; N.Y. Const. art. XI, § 1. While some of the equity decisions looked to these provisions in deciding whether the State recognized a fundamental right to education, they generally did not use the provisions to determine the adequacy of the state system. Relying on these provisions, recent school-funding claimants have placed less emphasis on the equity gap between property-poor and property-wealthy school districts, targeting instead the States' methods for determining the *adequacy* of the education they were guaranteeing to all children and families within their jurisdiction. At the core of these lawsuits is the contention that a State's legislative commitment to equalize educational opportunities by guaranteeing to fund a base-level education, no matter how little revenue a local school district can raise on its own, came to little if the state-guaranteed funding level was too low. The objective of these lawsuits, then, was to rationalize and eventually to increase the state spending floor. In contrast to the first wave of litigation in this area, plaintiffs won nearly two-thirds of these lawsuits between 1989 and 2008. Rebell, at 228. As the following cases illustrate, the principal debate in this litigation turns on whether the States' education clauses amount to mere delegations of authority to the state legislatures or whether they also contain judicially enforceable limits on that authority.

EDGEWOOD INDEPENDENT SCHOOL DISTRICT v. KIRBY
777 S.W.2d 391 (Tex. 1989)

MAUZY, J.

There are approximately three million public school children in Texas. The legislature finances the education of these children through a combination of revenues supplied by the state itself and revenues supplied by local school districts which are governmental subdivisions of the state. Of total education costs, the state provides about forty-two percent, school districts provide about fifty percent, and the remainder comes from various other sources including federal funds. School districts derive revenues from local ad valorem property taxes, and the state raises funds from a variety of sources including the sales tax and various severance and excise taxes.

There are glaring disparities in the abilities of the various school districts to raise revenues from property taxes because taxable property wealth varies greatly from district to district. The wealthiest district has over $14,000,000 of property wealth per student, while the poorest has approximately $20,000; this disparity reflects a 700 to 1 ratio. The 300,000 students in the lowest-wealth schools have less than 3% of the state's property wealth to support their education while the 300,000 students in the highest-wealth schools have over 25% of the state's property wealth; thus the 300,000 students in the wealthiest districts have more than eight times the property value to support their education as the 300,000 students in the poorest districts. The average property wealth in the 100 wealthiest districts is more than twenty times greater than the average property wealth in the 100 poorest districts. Edgewood I.S.D. has $38,854 in property wealth per student; Alamo Heights I.S.D., in the same county, has $570,109 in property wealth per student.

The state has tried for many years to lessen the disparities through various efforts to supplement the poorer districts. Through the Foundation School Program, the state currently attempts to ensure that each district has sufficient funds to provide its students with at least a basic education. Under this program, state aid is distributed to the various districts according to a complex formula such that property-poor districts receive more state aid than do property-rich districts. However, the Foundation School Program does not cover even the cost of meeting the state-mandated minimum requirements. Most importantly, there are no Foundation School Program allotments for school facilities or for debt service. The basic allotment and the transportation allotment understate actual costs, and the career ladder salary supplement for teachers is underfunded. For these reasons and more, almost all school districts spend additional local funds. Low-wealth districts use a significantly greater proportion of their local funds to pay the debt service on construction bonds while high-wealth districts are able to use their funds to pay for a wide array of enrichment programs.

Because of the disparities in district property wealth, spending per student varies widely, ranging from $2,112 to $19,333. Under the existing system, an average of $2,000 more per year is spent on each of the 150,000 students in the wealthiest districts than is spent on the 150,000 students in the poorest districts.

The lower expenditures in the property-poor districts are not the result of lack of tax effort. Generally, the property-rich districts can tax low and spend high while the property-poor districts must tax high merely to spend low.

Property-poor districts are trapped in a cycle of poverty from which there is no opportunity to free themselves. Because of their inadequate tax base, they must tax at significantly higher rates in order to meet minimum requirements for accreditation; yet their educational programs are typically inferior. The location of new industry and development is strongly influenced by tax rates and the quality of local schools. Thus, the property-poor districts with their high tax rates and inferior schools are unable to attract new industry or development and so have little opportunity to improve their tax base.

The amount of money spent on a student's education has a real and meaningful impact on the educational opportunity offered that student. High-wealth districts are able to provide for their students broader educational experiences including more extensive curricula, more up-to-date technological equipment, better libraries and library personnel, teacher aides, counseling services, lower student-teacher ratios, better facilities, parental involvement programs, and drop-out prevention programs. They are also better able to attract and retain experienced teachers and administrators.

Article VII, section 1 of the Texas Constitution provides:

> A general diffusion of knowledge being essential to the preservation of the liberties and rights of the people, it shall be the duty of the Legislature of the State to establish and make suitable provision for the support and maintenance of an efficient system of public free schools.

This is not an area in which the Constitution vests exclusive discretion in the legislature; rather the language of article VII, section 1 imposes on the legislature an affirmative duty to establish and provide for the public free schools. This duty is not committed unconditionally to the legislature's discretion, but instead is accompanied by standards. By express constitutional mandate, the legislature must make "suitable" provision for an "efficient" system for the "essential" purpose of a "general diffusion of knowledge." While these are admittedly not precise terms, they do provide a standard by which this court must, when called upon to do so, measure the constitutionality of the legislature's actions.

There is no reason to think that "efficient" meant anything different in 1875 from what it now means. "Efficient" conveys the meaning of effective or productive of results and connotes the use of resources so as to produce results with little waste; this meaning does not appear to have changed over time. *Defining "efficient" and what it means for education*

If our state's population had grown at the same rate in each district and if the taxable wealth in each district had also grown at the same rate, efficiency could probably have been maintained within the structure of the present system. That did not happen. Wealth, in its many forms, has not appeared with geographic symmetry. The economic development of the state has not been uniform. Some cities have grown dramatically, while their sister communities have remained static or have shrunk. Formulas that once fit have been knocked askew. Although local conditions vary, the constitutionally imposed state responsibility for an efficient education system is the same for all citizens regardless of where they live.

We conclude that, in mandating "efficiency," the constitutional framers and ratifiers did not intend a system with such vast disparities as now exist. Instead, they stated clearly that the purpose of an efficient system was to provide for a "*general* diffusion of knowledge." (Emphasis added.) The present system, by contrast, provides not for a diffusion that is general, but for one that is limited and unbalanced. The resultant inequalities are thus directly contrary to the constitutional vision of efficiency. *Conclusion: what "efficiency" means, and how it's not happening*

The legislature's recent efforts have focused primarily on increasing the state's contributions. More money allocated under the present system would reduce some of the existing disparities between districts but would at best only postpone the reform that is necessary to make the system efficient. A band-aid will not suffice; the system itself must be changed.

We hold that the state's school financing system is neither financially efficient nor efficient in the sense of providing for a "general diffusion of knowledge" statewide and therefore that it violates article VII, section 1 of the Texas Constitution. Efficiency does not require a per capita distribution, but it also does not allow concentrations of resources in property-rich school districts that are taxing low when property-poor districts that are taxing high cannot generate sufficient revenues to meet even minimum standards. There must be a direct and close correlation between a district's tax effort and the educational resources available to it; in other words, districts must have substantially equal access to similar revenues per pupil at similar levels of tax effort. Children who live in poor

Holding: funding model violates constitution.

Rule → substantially equal access to similar revenue per student

districts and children who live in rich districts must be afforded a substantially equal opportunity to have access to educational funds. Certainly, this much is required if the state is to educate its populace efficiently and provide for a general diffusion of knowledge statewide.

Although we have ruled the school financing system to be unconstitutional, we do not now instruct the legislature as to the specifics of the legislation it should enact; nor do we order it to raise taxes. The legislature has primary responsibility to decide how best to achieve an efficient system. We decide only the nature of the constitutional mandate and whether that mandate has been met. Because we hold that the mandate of efficiency has not been met, we reverse the judgment of the court of appeals. The legislature is duty-bound to provide for an efficient system of education, and only if the legislature fulfills that duty can we launch this great state into a strong economic future with educational opportunity for all.

[margin handwriting: What legislature must do.]

[margin handwriting: Policy conclusion]

DeROLPH v. STATE
677 N.E.2d 733 (Ohio 1997)

SWEENEY, J.

Section 2, Article VI of the Ohio Constitution requires the *state* to provide and fund a system of public education and includes an explicit directive to the General Assembly:

> "The general assembly shall make such provisions, by taxation, or otherwise, as, with the income arising from the school trust fund, will secure a thorough and efficient system of common schools throughout the State ...."

The delegates to the 1850-1851 Constitutional Convention recognized that it was the *state's* duty to both present and future generations of Ohioans to establish a framework for a "full, complete and efficient system of public education." Thus, throughout their discussions, the delegates stressed the importance of education and reaffirmed the policy that education shall be afforded to every child in the state regardless of race or economic standing. Furthermore, the delegates were concerned that the education to be provided to our youth not be mediocre but be as perfect as could humanly be devised. These debates reveal the delegates' strong belief that it is the *state's* obligation, through the General Assembly, to provide for the full education of all children within the state.

[margin handwriting: Who can make responsible for education]

In addition to deteriorating buildings and related conditions, it is clear from the record that many of the school districts throughout the state cannot provide the basic resources necessary to educate our youth. For instance, many of the appellant school districts have insufficient funds to purchase textbooks and must rely on old, outdated books. For some classes, there were no textbooks at all.

[margin handwriting: Many districts cant provide basics]

Additionally, many districts lack sufficient funds to comply with the state law requiring a district-wide average of no more than twenty-five students for each classroom teacher. Indeed, some schools have more than thirty students per classroom teacher, with one school having as many as thirty-nine students in one sixth grade class. As the testimony of educators established, it is virtually impossible for students to receive an adequate education with a student-teacher ratio of this magnitude.

All the facts documented in the record lead to one inescapable conclusion—Ohio's elementary and secondary public schools are neither thorough nor efficient. The operation of the appellant school districts conflicts with the historical notion that the education of our youth is of utmost concern and that Ohio children should be educated adequately so that they are able to participate fully in society. Our state Constitution was drafted with the importance of education in mind. In contrast, education under the legislation being reviewed ranks miserably low in the state's priorities. In fact, the formula amount is established after the legislature determines the total dollars to be allocated to primary and secondary education in each biennial budget. Consequently, the present school financing system contravenes the clear wording of our Constitution and the framers' intent.

Furthermore, rather than following the constitutional dictate that it is the *state's* obligation to fund education (as this opinion has repeatedly underscored), the legislature has thrust the majority of responsibility upon local school districts. This, too, is contrary to the clear wording of our Constitution. The responsibility for maintaining a thorough and efficient school system falls upon the state. When a district falls short of the constitutional requirement that the system be thorough and efficient, it is the state's obligation to rectify it.

We also reject the notion that the wide disparities in educational opportunity are caused by the poorer school districts' failure to pass levies. The evidence reveals that the wide disparities are caused by the funding system's overreliance on the tax base of individual school districts. What this means is that the poor districts simply cannot raise as much money even with identical tax effort.

We recognize that disparities between school districts will always exist. By our decision today, we are not stating that a new financing system must provide equal educational opportunities for all. In a Utopian society, this lofty goal would be realized. We, however, appreciate the limitations imposed upon us. Nor do we advocate a "Robin Hood" approach to school financing reform. We are not suggesting that funds be diverted from wealthy districts and given to the less fortunate. There is no "leveling down" component in our decision today.

Ct Isn't asking for spending ceilings?

(Moreover, in no way should our decision be construed as imposing spending ceilings on more affluent school districts.) School districts are still free to augment their programs if they choose to do so. However, it is futile to lay the entire blame for the inadequacies of the present system on the taxpayers and the local boards of education. Although some districts have the luxury of deciding where to allocate extra dollars, many others have the burden of deciding which educational programs to cut or what financial institution to contact to obtain yet another emergency loan. Our state Constitution makes the state responsible for educating our youth. Thus, the state should not shirk its obligation by espousing cliches about "local control."

We recognize that money alone is not the panacea that will transform Ohio's school system into a model of excellence. Although a student's success depends upon numerous factors besides money, we must ensure that there is enough money that students have the chance to succeed because of the educational opportunity provided, not in spite of it. Such an opportunity requires, at the very least, that all of Ohio's children attend schools which are safe and conducive to learning. At the present, Ohio does not provide many of its students with even the most basic of educational needs.

MOYER, C.J., dissenting.

Only infrequently are the members of this court required to balance our appreciation for the principle of separation of powers among the three branches of government against our desire to use the considerable powers of this court to mandate action to improve the imperfect. The issue in this very important case is not whether education in Ohio should be better. All seven members of this court would agree that in an ideal school setting, all children would be taught in well-maintained school buildings by teachers with high salaries and would read from the latest-edition school books. Rather, the question presented is whether specific financing statutes adopted by the Ohio General Assembly violate the words and intent of the Ohio Constitution. By its words, the Constitution requires the General Assembly to "make such provisions, by taxation or otherwise, as...will secure a thorough and efficient system of common schools throughout the state." We find that the statutes withstand plaintiffs' constitutional challenge because, rather than abdicating its duty, the General Assembly has made provisions by the challenged statutes for funding a system of schools with minimum standards throughout the state. The issues of the level and method of funding, and thereby the quality of the system, are committed by the Constitution to the collective will of the people through the legislative branch.

One cannot disagree with the aspirations of the majority to provide a school system that enables children to "participate fully in society," that provides "high quality educational opportunities," and that "allows its citizens to fully develop their human potential." However, the majority relies upon the phrase "thorough and efficient" to declare Ohio's education financing system unconstitutional despite the fact that our Constitution commits the responsibility for ascribing meaning to the phrase "thorough and efficient" to the General Assembly and not to this court. The majority of this court, moreover, apparently interprets the Constitution as requiring that all schools be of the same undefined level of high quality without relying on any supporting text of the Constitution, and equates imperfect schools with an unconstitutional system of funding. We disagree with these conclusions.

We conclude that the question of what level of funding satisfies the constitutional standard of a "thorough and efficient" system of education is a question of quality that revolves around policy choices and value judgments constitutionally committed to the General Assembly. We conclude that defining a "thorough and efficient" system of education financing is a nonjusticiable question.

Such restraint should be exercised only after the court has decided a threshold justiciable issue, that is, whether the General Assembly has made provision by taxation or otherwise to secure a thorough and efficient system of schools. In view of the clear intention of the delegates to the Constitutional Convention of 1851, the words of the Constitution and the agreement among the parties to this case that all plaintiff school districts have met the minimum standards set by the State Department of Education, we conclude that the justiciable question has been answered in favor of the defendants.

Although we may personally favor it, it is not this court's place to order the General Assembly to give education "high priority" in its budget allocations, any more than it is our place to set policy or prioritize the allocation of funds to other state programs. Members of the legislative branch represent the collective will of the citizens of Ohio, and the manner in which public schools are funded in this state is a fundamental policy decision that is within the power of its citizens to change. Under our system of government, decisions such as imposing new taxes, allocating public revenues to competing uses, and formulating educational standards are not within the judiciary's authority.

In that determinations of educational funding adequacy and quality are inherently fluid, we believe that the majority's well-intentioned willingness to enter this fray today will only necessitate more comprehensive judicial involvement tomorrow as educational theories and goals evolve, conditions throughout the state change, and the General Assembly responds. The experiences of other states provide ample proof of the troubled history of litigation that ensues when the judiciary deems itself to be the ultimate authority in setting educational funding mechanisms and standards[.][[Many] cases from other states [confirm] the grim reality of a state supreme court involving itself in setting minimum educational standards, which has resulted in years of protracted litigation, ultimately placing the courts in the position of determining state taxation methods, budgetary priorities, and educational policy.]

Plaintiffs stipulated in the trial court that they were all in compliance with state minimum standards on their most recent scheduled evaluations. In that "an Ohio Administrative Code section is a further arm, extension, or explanation of statutory intent implementing a statute passed by the General Assembly," it follows that those plaintiff schools met the standard of adequacy established by the General Assembly at that time. Plaintiffs did not prove that compliance with the minimum standards then in effect was insufficient to provide an adequate education. Plaintiffs did not attempt to prove that any graduate of any of the plaintiff school districts had been refused entrance to college because his or her diploma was unacceptable. No Ohio school was shown to have been denied accreditation. Plaintiffs did not prove that any Ohio child was without a school to attend.

In the absence of proof of a constitutional violation, the fact that hard problems require hard solutions does not justify judicial second-guessing of the educational funding system established by the General Assembly. Regardless of the appeal of plaintiffs' policy arguments before this court, their arguments are simply addressed to the wrong branch of government. Those who believe that the Education Clause should be changed have procedures available to them by which the Constitution can be amended.

Our dissent should not be viewed as an endorsement of the status quo. However, in the absence of a showing that the statutes in question violate the Constitution, responsibility for correcting the funding of Ohio's educational system does not rest with this court.

DeROLPH v. STATE
754 N.E.2d 1184 (Ohio 2001)

MOYER, C.J.

Since it was first docketed in this court in 1995, this dispute has produced from this court no fewer than three signed majority opinions, a *per curiam* opinion, eleven separate concurrences and dissents, and a number of rulings on motions filed by plaintiffs and defendants. Every justice of the court has expressed her and his views regarding the constitutional issue that once again is presented for our disposition nearly six years after the court exercised its discretionary jurisdiction to review the merits. The written opinions of the justices reflect deeply held beliefs regarding the responsibility of the court as an institution and the principles that define the framework by which each justice decides issues brought to the court. The informal and formal discussions among the justices regarding the jurisdictional and merit issues have been of an intensity and duration unmatched by any other case.

The range of the opinions that reflect the decisional process is broad .... Despite our differences, however, we all agree upon the fundamental importance of education to the children and citizens of this state. Educated, informed citizens sustain the vitality of our democratic institutions.... We agree regarding the goals of public education; we have vigorously disagreed with respect to whether the legislature or the judiciary has the ultimate authority to determine if the goals have been achieved. *Disagreement over who has ultimate authority on determining if goal has been achieved*

The current plan for funding public primary and secondary education adopted by the General Assembly and signed by the Governor is probably not the plan that any one of us would have created were it our responsibility to do so. But that is not our burden, and it is not the test we apply in this decision. None of us is completely comfortable with the decision we announce in this opinion. But we have responded to a duty that is intrinsic to our position as justices on the highest court of the state. Drawing upon our own instincts and the wisdom of Thomas Jefferson, we have reached the point where, while continuing to hold our previously expressed opinions, the greater good requires us to recognize "the necessity of sacrificing our opinions sometimes to the opinions of others for the sake of harmony."

A climate of legal, financial, and political uncertainty concerning Ohio's school-funding system has prevailed at least since this court accepted jurisdiction of the case. We have concluded that no one is served by continued uncertainty and fractious debate. In that spirit, we have created the consensus that [we] should terminate the role of this court in the dispute. *Court: we're done ~~we~~ have ultimate authority.*

Despite the extensive efforts of the defendants to produce a plan that meets the requirements announced by this court, changes to the formula are required to make the new plan constitutional:

Base Cost Formula: H.B. 94 recalculates the cost of providing an adequate education to be $4,814 per student in fiscal year 2002. The base cost formula uses one hundred twenty-seven model school districts as a basis for determining base cost support. That number of school districts is achieved by screening out districts in the top and bottom five percent of all Ohio districts based on income and property wealth from the state's pool of the one hundred seventy top-performing districts. Also included within this number are several districts that did not meet twenty of twenty-seven performance standards, but were included regardless because of a rounding procedure included within H.B. 94. R.C. 3317.012(B)(1), last paragraph. As the plaintiffs note, rounding and wealth screens include districts that should not be considered in the base cost formula and exclude districts that should be considered. Plaintiffs' arguments and our review of the record convince us that the formula must be modified to include the top five percent districts and the lower five percent districts, and by considering only those districts that *actually* meet twenty of twenty-seven performance standards without rounding. We make no determination regarding the time in which the state must calculate and implement actual changes in the amount of funds distributed to each district pursuant to today's order, but the new calculations must be applied retroactive to July 1, 2001, and to the subsequent years designated in R.C. 3317.012. Moreover, in determining future biennial budgets through fiscal year 2007, the rate of millage charged off as the local share of base cost funding under divisions (A)(1) and (2) of R.C. 3317.022 may not be changed from twenty-three mills, irrespective of the language of R.C. 3317.012(D)(4) suggesting such a methodology.

The H.B. 94 model calculates its base cost amount using spending data for FY96, adjusted for inflation, or actual FY99 expenditure data, whichever is lower. The state uses the lower of the two figures to compensate for what it terms an "echo effect," or to adjust for districts that spent more than what was actually needed at the base level, due to line-item expenditures, other state funding outside of the foundation formula, and local enhancement revenues. The model districts subject to lowering of their base cost are those that the state determined to be model districts in 1996. As the plaintiffs' experts observed, there has been insufficient evidence presented by the state to justify lowering the base cost amount to adjust for this supposed echo effect. Accordingly, we are persuaded by the plaintiffs that choosing the lower of FY96 expenditures or FY99 actual expenditures is unsupported by the evidence and should not be used to lower the base cost amount figure.

Parity Aid: The parity aid program is a salutary attempt to provide poorer districts with funds similar to those available to wealthier districts that are used to substantially enhance the educational experience of each student. The plan as adopted would fully fund the parity aid program by fiscal year 2006. We have concluded that the parity aid program must be fully funded no later than the beginning of fiscal year 2004.

To summarize, we observe that the state has chosen to retain a foundation program of funding primary and secondary public education. We find that, having so elected, it must, in order to meet the requirements of *DeRolph I* and *DeRolph II*, formulate the base cost of providing an adequate education by using all school districts meeting twenty of twenty-seven performance standards as set forth by the General Assembly in R.C. 3317.012(B)(1)(a) through (aa), without adjustments to exclude districts based on wealth screens, without rounding adjustments to include additional lower-spending districts, and without use of the "echo effect" adjustment, beginning effective July 1, 2001. In addition, the parity aid program established by the General Assembly must be fully funded no later than July 1, 2003.

plan proposed meets constitutional standards

With full implementation of these modifications to the funding plan adopted by the General Assembly the plan will meet the test for constitutionality created in *DeRolph I* and *DeRolph II.* While the changes will have a fiscal impact, they will not require structural changes to the school foundation program set forth in R.C. Chapter 3317.

One final observation is in order. Historically, the construction and maintenance of school facilities have been considered the responsibility of local school districts. By 1989, the General Assembly had begun addressing school facilities needs and committing funds to construction and repair of school buildings. We have described previously the substantial commitment of the state to the availability of adequate school buildings for every student enrolled in public education. However, the unmet needs are enormous and the time in which it is feasible to meet them is lengthy. We urge the General Assembly to review and consider alternative means of funding school buildings and related facilities.

The state is hereby ordered to implement the changes described above. Because we have no reason to doubt defendants' good faith, we have concluded that there is no reason to retain jurisdiction of the matter before us. If the order receives less than full compliance, interested parties have remedies available to them.

NOTE

Reasonable as this compromise might have seemed, *DeRolph III* did not end the litigation. The State moved for reconsideration of *DeRolph III*, prompting the Court to order the parties to report to a special commissioner to try to settle the case. *DeRolph v. State*, 758 N.E.2d 1113 (Ohio 2001). That did not work either. In response, the Court vacated *DeRolph III* and ordered "a complete systematic overhaul" of the school-funding system. *DeRolph v. State*, 780 N.E.2d 529 (Ohio 2002). After the case was remanded to the trial court and after the trial court tried to enforce the most recent decision, the State successfully filed an original writ of prohibition in the Ohio Supreme Court, prohibiting the trial court from exercising jurisdiction over the case. *State v. Lewis*, 789 N.E.2d 195 (Ohio 2003). As the Court put it, "The duty now lies with the General Assembly to remedy an educational system that has been found by the majority in *DeRolph IV* to still be unconstitutional." *Id.* at 202. In the years since, the Ohio legislature has made changes to its school-funding system, which some claim do not satisfy the requirements of *DeRolph IV* but which no one has challenged in state court.

COLUMBIA FALLS ELEMENTARY SCHOOL DISTRICT NO. 6 v. STATE
109 P.3d 257 (Mont. 2005)

LEAPHART, J.

The State appeals from the District Court's order determining that the State of Montana's public school system violates Article X, Section 1(3), of the Montana Constitution.

Article X, Section 1(3), of the Montana Constitution mandates that "[t]he legislature shall provide a basic system of free quality public elementary and secondary schools…. It shall fund and distribute in an equitable manner to the school districts the state's share of the cost of the basic elementary and secondary school system." As we…stated, the Legislature has made an initial policy determination regarding this language. It has created a public school system and a method of funding the system. Although Article X, Section 1(3), is textually committed to the Legislature in the first instance, once the Legislature acts we are not barred from reaching the question of whether the Legislature has fulfilled its constitutional obligation to "provide a basic system of free quality public elementary and secondary schools."

This funding system is not correlated with any understanding of what constitutes a "quality" education. The evidence for this is two-fold. First, as the State admitted at oral argument, in passing HB 667, the Legislature did not undertake a study of what the Public Schools Clause demands of it. That is, it did not seek to define "quality." As stated above, since the Legislature has not defined "quality" as that term is used in Article X, Section 1(3), we cannot conclude that the current funding system was designed to provide a quality education. Second, as found by the District Court, the Legislature, in creating the spending formula of HB 667, did not link the formula to any factors that might constitute a "quality" education.

The District Court found that the "major problems" with HB 667 were: it provided no mechanism to deal with inflation; it did not base its numbers on costs such as teacher pay, meeting accreditation standards, fixed costs, or costs of special education; increases in allowable spending were not tied to costs of increased accreditation standards or content and performance standards; relevant data was already two years old when the bill was passed; and no study was undertaken to justify the disparity in [certain state-provided] dollars dispensed to high schools as compared to elementary schools. From these credible findings we must conclude that the Legislature did not endeavor to create a school funding system with quality in mind. Unless funding relates to needs such as academic standards, teacher pay, fixed costs, costs of special education, and *[handwritten top margin: Analysis! 4) What legislature made 2) Impact of legislature's law]*

performance standards, then the funding is not related to the cornerstones of a quality education. *[handwritten: Rule about how funding should "look"]*

The above analysis is essentially prospective in nature—that is, it states what the Constitution demands of the Legislature and what the Legislature must do to fashion a constitutional education system. Nonetheless, in order to address the Coalition's claims we have to address the *educational product* that the present school system provides, not just the *manner* in which the Legislature funds that school system. Even given the absence of a definition of "quality" education, the District Court's findings demonstrate that whatever legitimate definition of quality that the Legislature may devise, the educational product of the present school system is constitutionally deficient and that the Legislature currently fails to adequately fund Montana's public school system.

[handwritten right margin: Current system is educationally deficient]

The evidence that the current system is constitutionally deficient includes the following unchallenged findings made by the District Court: school districts increasingly budgeting at or near their maximum budget authority; growing accreditation problems; many qualified educators leaving the state to take advantage of higher salaries and benefits offered elsewhere; the cutting of programs; the deterioration of school buildings and inadequate funds for building repair and for new construction; and increased competition for general fund dollars between special and general education.

[handwritten right margin: Why ct says current system is unconstitutional]

The State counters by arguing that the District Court should have considered output measures, such as test scores, in determining whether the current system is constitutional, and that under such measures Montana compares very favorably with other states. Indeed, Montana's students often do perform quite well on standardized achievement tests. However, current test scores do not tell the whole story. First of all, a "system" of education includes more than high achievement on standardized tests. We have noted elsewhere, for example, that school districts have an interest in integrating their academic programs with extracurricular activities. Secondly, it may be that test scores are not attributable to the current educational system. The voluminous evidence presented at trial … established that although Montana's students are testing well when compared with students in similar states, there are serious concerns as to whether this level of achievement will continue. With the District Court's findings of fact in mind, it may be that the achievement registered by Montana's students is not *because* of the current educational system.

[handwritten right margin: D! but look @ test scores]

[handwritten right margin: ct: scores aren't enough]

[handwritten right margin: ct: test success, but maybe in spite of system.]

Therefore, because the Legislature has not defined what "quality" means we cannot conclude that the current system is designed to provide a "quality" education. Article X, Section 1(3), explicitly requires the

[handwritten bottom margin: Ct! y'all should've defined "quality."]

Legislature to fund a "quality" educational system. Therefore we defer to the Legislature to provide a threshold definition of what the Public Schools Clause requires. We also conclude, however, that given the unchallenged findings made by the District Court, whatever definition the Legislature devises, the current funding system is not grounded in principles of quality, and cannot be deemed constitutionally sufficient.

ABBOTT v. BURKE
971 A.2d 989 (N.J. 2009)

LaVECCHIA, J.

One of the fundamental responsibilities of the State is to provide a public education for its children. The New Jersey Constitution requires that

> [t]he Legislature shall provide for the maintenance and support of a thorough and efficient system of free public schools for the instruction of all the children in the State between the ages of five and eighteen years.

Today we are almost a decade into the twenty-first century, and nearly twenty years have passed since this Court found that the State's system of support for public education was inadequate as applied to pupils in poorer urban districts. Finding that more severely disadvantaged pupils require more resources for their education, the Court held that the State must develop a funding formula that would provide all children, including disadvantaged children in poorer urban districts, with an equal educational opportunity as measured by the Constitution's thorough and efficient clause. A later decision added that the funding needed to be coupled to a set of educational program standards.

Today's decision marks the twentieth opinion or order issued in the course of the Abbott litigation. In the interim, much has changed. There have been significant demographic changes among school districts in terms of the distribution of at-risk pupils and changes in the level of State-provided education funding. The State now maintains that it has heeded our call to create a funding formula based on curriculum content standards and to demonstrate that the formula addresses the needs of disadvantaged students everywhere, thereby achieving constitutional compliance. Therefore, once again we assess the constitutionality of a State school funding system.

This matter is before us on the State's Motion for Review of the Constitutionality of the School Funding Reform Act of 2008 (SFRA). The State's motion seeks a declaration that SFRA's funding formula satisfies the requirements of the thorough and efficient education clause of the New Jersey Constitution and that, therefore, the State is released from the Court's prior remedial orders concerning education funding for students in

Abbott districts. Specifically, the State asks for elimination of the requirements that Abbott districts be provided parity aid and supplemental funding.)   *State's says our Act is satisfactory; free us*

We have reviewed the record, the Special Master's findings and recommendations, and the arguments of the parties. We conclude that SFRA is constitutional, to the extent that this record permitted its review. We therefore hold that SFRA's funding formula may be applied in Abbott districts, with the following caveats. Our finding of constitutionality is premised on the expectation that the State will continue to provide school funding aid during this and the next two years at the levels required by SFRA's formula each year. Our holding further depends on the mandated review of the formula's weights and other operative parts after three years of implementation.)   *We'll review in 3 years*

Ct's con in for now

Our approval of SFRA under the State Constitution relies, as it must, on the information currently available. But a state funding formula's constitutionality is not an occurrence at a moment in time; it is a continuing obligation. Today's holding issues in the good faith anticipation of a continued commitment by the Legislature and Executive to address whatever adjustments are necessary to keep SFRA operating at its optimal level. The three year look-back, and the State's adjustments based on that review, will provide more information about the efficacy of this funding formula. There should be no doubt that we would require remediation of any deficiencies of a constitutional dimension, if such problems do emerge.

With that understanding, SFRA may be implemented as it was designed, as a state-wide unitary system of education funding. The State shall not be required to continue separate funding streams mandated under past remedial orders. During the two-year period until the look-back review occurs, we cannot ignore, as a practical matter, the substantial amount of additional funds that will be available from non-SFRA sources for pupils in Abbott districts. The availability of those funds further cushions the transition to SFRA's funding scheme. In sum, although no prediction is without some uncertainty, the record before us convincingly demonstrates that SFRA is designed to provide school districts in this state, including the Abbott school districts, with adequate resources to provide the necessary educational programs consistent with state standards.)   *SFRA is adequate, even for Abbott districts*

For several decades, this Court has superintended the ongoing litigation that carries the name *Abbott v. Burke*. The Court's one goal has been to ensure that the constitutional guarantee of a thorough and efficient system of public education becomes a reality for those students who live in municipalities where there are concentrations of poverty and crime.

Every child should have the opportunity for an unhindered start in life—an opportunity to become a productive and contributing citizen to our society.

The legislative and executive branches of government have enacted a funding formula that is designed to achieve a thorough and efficient education for every child, regardless of where he or she lives. On the basis of the record before us, we conclude that SFRA is a constitutionally adequate scheme. There is no absolute guarantee that SFRA will achieve the results desired by all. The political branches of government, however, are entitled to take reasoned steps, even if the outcome cannot be assured, to address the pressing social, economic, and educational challenges confronting our state. They should not be locked in a constitutional straitjacket. SFRA deserves the chance to prove in practice that, as designed, it satisfies the requirements of our constitution.

The State's motion, seeking declarations that SFRA satisfies the requirements of the thorough and efficient clause of Article VIII, section 4, paragraph 1 of the New Jersey Constitution and that the funding formula may be implemented in the Abbott districts, and further seeking an order relieving the State from this Court's prior remedial orders concerning funding to the Abbott districts, is granted. Plaintiffs' cross-motion seeking an order preserving and continuing the status quo concerning enforcement of this Court's prior remedial orders addressing funding to Abbott districts is denied.

NOTES

1. The *Abbott* litigation lives on, *see Abbott v. Burke*, 20 A.3d 1018 (N.J. 2011), which to capture the point is known as *Abbott XXI*.

2. For cases in which the courts found claims to be non-justiciable, see *Okla. Educ. Ass'n v. State*, 158 P.3d 1058 (Okla. 2007); *Neb. Coal. for Educ. Equity & Adequacy v. Heineman*, 731 N.W.2d 164 (Neb. 2007); *Ex parte James*, 836 So.2d 813 (Ala. 2002); *Lewis E. v. Spagnolo*, 710 N.E.2d 798 (Ill. 1999); *Coal. for Adequacy & Fairness in Sch. Funding, Inc. v. Chiles*, 680 So.2d 400 (Fla. 1996).

3. For cases in which the courts found claims to be justiciable, see *Abbeville Cty. Sch. Dist. v. South Carolina*, 767 S.E.2d 157 (S.C. 2014); *Gannon v. Kansas*, 319 P.3d 1196 (Kan. 2014); *Brigham v. State*, 889 A.2d 715 (Vt. 2005); *Lake View Sch. Dist. No. 25 v. Huckabee*, 220 S.W.3d 645 (Ark. 2005); *DeRolph v. State*, 677 N.E.2d 733 (Ohio 1997); *Leandro v. State*, 488 S.E.2d 249 (N.C. 1997); *Idaho Schs. for Equal Educ. Opportunity, Inc. v. Evans*, 850 P.2d 724 (Idaho 1993).

4. On the merits, the state supreme courts continue to reach divergent results. Some courts have invalidated school-funding systems in recent years. *See, e.g., Abbeville Cty. Sch. Dist. v. South Carolina*, 767 S.E.2d 157 (S.C. 2014); *Gannon v. Kansas*, 319 P.3d 1196 (Kan. 2014). Others

have rejected such challenges. *See, e.g., Lobato v. Colorado,* 304 P.3d 1132 (Colo. 2013); *Davis v. South Dakota,* 804 N.W.2d 618 (S.D. 2011).

5.   The "thorough and efficient" clauses and similar guarantees placed in most state constitutions point to a conceptual difference between the state constitutions and their federal counterpart. As Emily Zackin explains in *Looking for Rights in All the Wrong Places: Why State Constitutions Contain America's Positive Rights* (Princeton Univ. Press 2013), the States, in contrast to the Federal Government, have a long tradition of placing "positive"—or affirmative—obligations on state and local governments in their constitutions, as opposed to merely "negative" restrictions on government. In support of her thesis, she refers to the state constitutional guarantees dealing with the promise of an adequate system of public schools, the rights of employees, and the guarantee of a safe and healthy environment. *See also* Jeffrey S. Sutton, *Courts as Change Agents: Do We Want More—Or Less?* 127 Harv. L. Rev. 1419 (2014) (reviewing Zackin's book).

D. SCHOOL UNIFORMITY CLAUSES

In addition to containing "thorough and efficient" clauses, some state constitutions contain school "uniformity" clauses. The Florida Constitution, for example, provides: "Adequate provision shall be made by law for a *uniform*, efficient, safe, secure, and high quality system of free public schools." (emphasis added). This next case illustrates how school-uniformity clauses can limit legislative initiatives in the education arena—in this instance, by invalidating a Florida school voucher program.

BUSH v. HOLMES
919 So.2d 392 (Fla. 2006)

PARIENTE, C.J.

Under the [Opportunity Scholarship Program (OSP)], a student from a public school that fails to meet certain minimum state standards has two options. The first is to move to another public school with a satisfactory record under the state standards. The second option is to receive funds from the public treasury, which would otherwise have gone to the student's school district, to pay the student's tuition at a private school. The narrow question we address is whether the second option violates a part of the Florida Constitution requiring the state to both provide for "the education of all children residing within its borders" and provide "by law for a uniform, efficient, safe, secure, and high quality system of free public schools that allows students to obtain a high quality education." Art. IX, § 1(a), Fla. Const.

As a general rule, courts may not reweigh the competing policy concerns underlying a legislative enactment. The arguments of public policy supporting both sides in this dispute have obvious merit, and the Legislature with the Governor's assent has resolved the ensuing debate in favor of the proponents of the program. In most cases, that would be the end of the matter. However, as is equally self-evident, the usual deference given to the Legislature's resolution of public policy issues is at all times circumscribed by the Constitution. Acting within its constitutional limits, the Legislature's power to resolve issues of civic debate receives great deference. Beyond those limits, the Constitution must prevail over any enactment contrary to it.

Our inquiry begins with the plain language of the second and third sentences of article IX, section 1(a) of the Constitution. The relevant words are these: "It is ... a paramount duty of the state to make adequate provision for the education of all children residing within its borders." Using the same term, "adequate provision," article IX, section 1(a) further states: "Adequate provision shall be made by law for a uniform, efficient, safe, secure, and high quality system of free public schools." For reasons expressed more fully below, we find that the OSP violates this language. It diverts public dollars into separate private systems parallel to and in competition with the free public schools that are the sole means set out in the Constitution for the state to provide for the education of Florida's children. This diversion not only reduces money available to the free schools, but also funds private schools that are not "uniform" when compared with each other or the public system. Many standards imposed by law on the public schools are inapplicable to the private schools receiving public monies. In sum, through the OSP the state is fostering plural, nonuniform systems of education in direct violation of the constitutional mandate for a uniform system of free public schools.

In 1998, in response in part to [another Florida Supreme Court case], the Constitutional Revision Commission proposed and the citizens of this state approved an amendment to article IX, section 1 to make clear that education is a "fundamental value" and "a paramount duty of the state," and to provide standards by which to measure the adequacy of the public school education provided by the state:

> The education of children is a *fundamental value of the people of the State of Florida*. It is, therefore, *a paramount duty of the state to make adequate provision for the education of all children residing within its borders*. Adequate provision shall be made by law for a *uniform, efficient, safe, secure, and high quality* system of free public schools that allows students to obtain a high quality education and for the establishment, maintenance, and operation of institutions of higher learning and other public education programs that the needs of the people may require.

Art. IX, § 1(a), Fla. Const. (emphasis supplied).

The provision (1) declares that the "education of children is a fundamental value of the people of the State of Florida," (2) sets forth an education mandate that provides that it is "a paramount duty of the state to make adequate provision for the education of all children residing within its borders," and (3) sets forth *how* the state is to carry out this education mandate, specifically, that "*[a]dequate* provision shall be made by law for a *uniform*, efficient, safe, secure, and *high quality system of free public schools.*"

Article IX, section 1(a) is a limitation on the Legislature's power because it provides both a mandate to provide for children's education and a restriction on the execution of that mandate.

The second sentence of article IX, section 1(a) provides that it is the "paramount duty of the state to make adequate provision for the education of all children residing within its borders." The third sentence of article IX, section 1(a) provides a restriction on the exercise of this mandate by specifying that the adequate provision required in the second sentence "shall be made by law for a uniform, efficient, safe, secure and high quality system of *free public schools.*" (Emphasis supplied.) The OSP violates this provision by devoting the state's resources to the education of children within our state through means other than a system of free public schools.

The Constitution prohibits the state from using public monies to fund a private alternative to the public school system, which is what the OSP does. Specifically, the OSP transfers tax money earmarked for public education to private schools that provide the same service-basic primary education. Thus, contrary to the defendants' arguments, the OSP does not supplement the public education system. Instead, the OSP diverts funds that would otherwise be provided to the system of free public schools that is the exclusive means set out in the Constitution for the Legislature to make adequate provision for the education of children.

Although opportunity scholarships are not now widely in use, if the dissent is correct as to their constitutionality, the potential scale of programs of this nature is unlimited. Under the dissent's view of the Legislature's authority in this area, the state could fund a private school system of indefinite size and scope as long as the state also continued to fund the public schools at a level that kept them "uniform, efficient, safe, secure, and high quality." However, because voucher payments reduce funding for the public education system, the OSP by its very nature undermines the system of "high quality" free public schools that are the sole authorized means of fulfilling the constitutional mandate to provide for the education of all children residing in Florida. The systematic diversion of public funds to private schools on either a small or large scale is incompatible with article IX, section 1(a).

In addition to specifying that a system of free public schools is the means for complying with the mandate to provide for the education of Florida's children, article IX, section 1(a) also requires that this system be "uniform." The OSP makes no provision to ensure that the private school alternative to the public school system meets the criterion of uniformity. In fact, in a provision directing the Department of Education to establish and maintain a database of private schools, the Legislature expressly states that it does not intend "to regulate, control, approve, or accredit private educational institutions." § 1002.42(2)(h), Fla. Stat. (2005). This lack of oversight is also evident in section 1001.21, which creates the Office of Private Schools and Home Education Programs within the Department of Education but provides that this office "ha[s] no authority over the institutions or students served." § 1001.21(1), Fla. Stat. (2005).

Further, although the parent of a student participating in the OSP must ensure that the student "takes all statewide assessments" required of a public school student, § 1002.38(5)(c), the private school's curriculum and teachers are not subject to the same standards as those in force in public schools. For example, only teachers possessing bachelor's degrees are eligible to teach at public schools, but private schools may hire teachers without bachelor's degrees if they have "at least 3 years of teaching experience in public or private schools, or have special skills, knowledge, or expertise that qualifies them to provide instruction in subjects taught." § 1002.38(4)(g), Fla. Stat. (2005).

In addition, public school teachers must be certified by the state. *See* § 1012.55(1), Fla. Stat. (2005). To obtain this certification, teachers must meet certain requirements that include having "attained at least a 2.5 overall grade point average on a 4.0 scale in the applicant's major field of study" and having demonstrated a mastery of general knowledge, subject area knowledge, and professional preparation and education competence. *See* § 1012.56(2)(c), (g)-(i), Fla. Stat. (2005).

Public teacher certification also requires the applicant to submit to a background screening. *See* § 1012.56(2)(d), Fla. Stat. (2005). Indeed, all school district personnel hired to fill positions that require direct contact with students must undergo a background check. *See* § 1012.32(2)(a), Fla. Stat. (2005). This screening is not required of private school employees. *See* § 1002.42(2)(c)(3), Fla. Stat. (2005) (providing that owners of private schools *may* require employees to file fingerprints with the Department of Law Enforcement).

Regarding curriculum, public education instruction is based on the "Sunshine State Standards" that have been "adopted by the State Board of

Education and delineate the academic achievement of students, for which the state will hold schools accountable." § 1003.41, Fla. Stat. (2005). Public schools are required to teach all basic subjects as well as a number of other diverse subjects, among them the contents of the Declaration of Independence, the essentials of the United States Constitution, the elements of civil government, Florida state history, African-American history, the history of the Holocaust, and the study of Hispanic and women's contributions to the United States. *See* § 1003.42(2)(a), Fla. Stat. (2005). Eligible private schools are not required to teach any of these subjects.   *Curriculum requirements not mandated of private*

In addition to being "academically accountable to the parent," a private school participating in the OSP is subject only "to the...curriculum...criteria adopted by an appropriate nonpublic school accrediting body." § 1002.38(4)(f), Fla. Stat. (2005). There are numerous nonpublic school accrediting bodies that have "widely variant quality standards and program requirements." Thus, curriculum standards of eligible private schools may vary greatly depending on the accrediting body, and these standards may not be equivalent to those required for Florida public schools.

In all these respects, the alternative system of private schools funded by the OSP cannot be deemed uniform in accordance with the mandate in article IX, section 1(a).   *Not uniform*

Reinforcing our determination that the state's use of public funds to support an alternative system of education is in violation of article IX, section 1(a) is the limitation of the use of monies from the State School Fund set forth in article IX, section 6. That provision states that income and interest from the State School Fund may be appropriated "only to the support and maintenance of free public schools." Art. IX, § 6, Fla. Const.

In sum, article IX, section 1(a) provides for the manner in which the state is to fulfill its mandate to make adequate provision for the education of Florida's children—through a system of public education. The OSP contravenes this constitutional provision because it allows some children to receive a publicly funded education through an alternative system of private schools that are not subject to the uniformity requirements of the public school system. The diversion of money not only reduces public funds for a public education but also uses public funds to provide an alternative education in private schools that are not subject to the "uniformity" requirements for public schools. Thus, in two significant respects, the OSP violates the mandate set forth in article IX, section 1(a).

2 reasons
OSP
is
unconstitutional

reduces $,
doesn't
promote
uniformity

We do not question the basic right of parents to educate their children as they see fit. We recognize that the proponents of vouchers have a strongly held view that students should have choices. Our decision does not deny parents recourse to either public or private school alternatives to a failing school. Only when the private school option depends upon public funding is choice limited. This limit is necessitated by the constitutional mandate in article IX, section 1(a), which sets out the state's responsibilities in a manner that does not allow the use of state monies to fund a private school education. As we recently explained, "[w]hat is in the Constitution always must prevail over emotion. Our oaths as judges require that this principle is our polestar, and it alone." *Bush v. Schiavo*, 885 So.2d 321, 336 (Fla. 2004).

E. REMEDY

One of the most vexing issues for courts that grant constitutional relief in this area is the question of remedy. It is one thing for a court to recognize an enforceable state constitutional right in this area and even to say that a current school funding system is inadequate. It is quite another to identify what the legislature must do to make its funding system constitutional (and to enforce that order). Claimants frequently seek structural changes to the system and usually demand increased state funding in doing so. The courts have struggled to identify a rationale for deciding how much guaranteed state funding suffices—with some focusing on the cost of certain educational "inputs," some focusing on the costs of certain educational "outputs," and some looking to both.

HOKE COUNTY BOARD OF EDUCATION v. STATE
599 S.E.2d 365 (N.C. 2004)

ORR, J.

The Court now turns its attention to the substantive issues brought forward on appeal by the State. In its first question presented to this Court, the State contends that the trial court erred by applying the wrong standards for determining: (1) when a student has obtained a sound basic education; (2) causation (for a student's failure to obtain a sound basic education); and (3) the State's liability (for a student's failure to obtain a sound basic education). In further support of its initial argument, the State proffers three subarguments, which allege and target specific evidentiary lapses and flaws in the trial court's reasoning. In its argument labeled I(A), the State contends that the trial court erred by using standardized test scores as "the exclusive measure" of whether students were obtaining a sound basic education. In argument I(B), the State argues that the trial court erred by concluding that a denial of the right to a sound basic education could be inferred from the number of socio-economically disadvantaged ("at-risk") students scoring below Level III proficiency on standardized tests. And in argument I(C), the State contends that the trial court erred when it held the State responsible for administrative decisions made by local school boards.

In *Leandro*, this Court decreed that the children of the state enjoy the right to avail themselves of the opportunity for a sound basic education.... Ultimately, the Court defined a sound basic education as one that provides students with at least: (1) sufficient knowledge of fundamental mathematics and physical science to enable the student to function in a complex and rapidly changing society; (2) sufficient fundamental knowledge of geography, history, and basic economic and political systems to enable the student to make informed choices with regard to issues that affect the student personally or affect the student's community, state, and nation; (3) sufficient academic and vocational skills to enable the student to successfully engage in post-secondary education or vocational training; and (4) sufficient academic and vocational skills to enable the student to compete on an equal basis with others in formal education or gainful employment in contemporary society.

[handwritten margin note: Def of a sound basic education]

After declaring a child's constitutional right to the opportunity to receive a sound basic education and defining the elements of such an education, the Court concluded that some of the allegations in plaintiffs' complaint stated claims upon which relief may be granted and ordered the case remanded to the trial court to permit plaintiffs to proceed on such claims.

[handwritten note: What π presented]

At trial, plaintiffs presented evidence that, in accordance with *Leandro*, can be categorized as follows: (1) comparative standardized test score data; (2) student graduation rates, employment potential, post-secondary education success (and/or lack thereof); (3) deficiencies pertaining to the educational offerings in Hoke County schools; and (4) deficiencies pertaining to the educational administration of Hoke County schools. The first two evidentiary categories fall under the umbrella of "outputs," a term used by educators that, in sum, measures student performance. The remaining two evidentiary categories fall under the umbrella of "inputs," a term used by educators that, in sum, describes what the State and local boards provide to students attending public schools. We examine each evidentiary category in turn.

[handwritten margin note: 4 categories π presented]

In its brief, the State contends, at great length, that the trial court erred by using test scores "as the exclusive measure of a constitutionally adequate education." However, as we proceed in our analysis, the Court notes that the record reflects that the trial court considered "output" evidence beyond the realm of test scores, and that evidence such as graduation rates, dropout rates, post-secondary education performance, employment rates and prospects, comports with both this Court's definition of a sound basic education *and* the factors we provided the trial court to consider upon remand. Thus, we reject the State's contention that the trial court used test scores as the "exclusive measure" of a sound basic education.

In continuing our examination of the trial court's order, we move next to the trial court's conclusion that additional "output" evidence—*e.g.*, graduation rates, dropout rates, employment potential, and post-secondary education readiness—further demonstrates that an unacceptably high number of Hoke County students are failing to obtain a sound basic education. In considering evidence concerning dropout and graduation rates, the trial court found that in the mid-1990s only 41% of Hoke County freshmen went on to graduate—a retention rate that was 19% lower than the state average and was the worst retention rate in the state's 100 counties. The trial court went on to conclude that the evidence showed that the primary reason Hoke County's dropout rate was so high was that a great number of Hoke students are "not well prepared for high school" and that "students who do not do well in the early grades are more likely than other students to later drop out of school."

As for the effect of such a high dropout rate, the trial court concluded that the failure of large percentages of Hoke County students to complete high school "not only results in those children who leave having failed to obtain a sound basic education" but is also evidence "of a systematic weakness ... in meeting the needs of many of [Hoke County's] students."

As for those students who did graduate, the trial court's assessment was no less bleak. After considering evidence concerning the employment potential and post-secondary education potential for Hoke County graduates, the trial court concluded that many among the graduates had not obtained a sound basic education in that the evidence showed "they are poorly prepared to compete on an equal basis in gainful employment and further formal education in today's contemporary society." In support of its conclusion, the trial court cited ... numerous examples of Hoke County graduates who pursued employment or who pursued further education at the college level.

In the realm of "outputs" evidence, we hold that the trial court properly concluded that the evidence demonstrates that over the past decade, an inordinate number of Hoke County students have consistently failed to match the academic performance of their statewide public school counterparts and that such failure, measured by their performance while attending Hoke County schools, their dropout rates, their graduation rates, their need for remedial help, their inability to compete in the job markets, and their inability to compete in collegiate ranks, constitute a clear showing that they have failed to obtain a *Leandro*-comporting education. As a consequence of so holding, we turn our attention to "inputs" evidence—evidence concerning what the State and its agents have provided for the education of Hoke County students—in an effort to determine the following two contingencies: (1) Does the evidence support the trial court's conclusion that the State's action and/or inaction has caused Hoke County students not to obtain a sound basic education and, if so; (2) Does such action and/or inaction by the State constitute a failure to meet its constitutional obligation to provide Hoke County students with the opportunity to obtain a sound basic education, as defined in *Leandro*?

It is one thing for plaintiffs to demonstrate that a large number of Hoke County students are failing to obtain a sound, basic public education. It is quite another for plaintiffs to show that such a failure is primarily the result of action and/or inaction of the State, which argues in this appeal that the trial court erred by concluding that a combination of State action and inaction resulted in the systematic poor performance of Hoke County students and graduates.

In defense of its educational offerings in Hoke County at trial, the State attempted to show that its combination of "inputs"—*i.e.*, expenditures, programs, teachers, administrators, etc.—added up to be an aggregate that met or exceeded this Court's definition of providing students with an opportunity for a sound basic education. In addition, both at trial and in this appeal, the State contended that the evidence showed the following: (1) That the educational offerings it provides in Hoke County have improved significantly since the mid-nineties; (2) That such improvements are part and parcel of the State's own recognition of ongoing problems and the need to address them; (3) That if a cognizable group of students within Hoke County are failing to obtain a sound basic education, it is due to factors other than the educational offerings provided by the State; and, (4) That many of the deficiencies that may exist in the educational offerings of Hoke County are due to the administrative shortcomings of the semi-autonomous local school boards.

Plaintiffs, on the other hand, contend that the evidence at trial clearly showed that the State had consistently failed to provide Hoke County schools with the resources needed to provide students with the opportunity to obtain a sound basic education. In addition, plaintiffs argue that the evidence shows that Hoke County students have consistently failed to match the achievements of their statewide counterparts (*see* "outputs" discussion, above) because the State has failed to: (1) provide adequate teachers and/or administrators; (2) provide the funding necessary to offer each student the opportunity to obtain a sound basic education; (3) recognize the failings of Hoke County students as a whole; and (4) implement alternative educational offerings that have and/or would address and correct the problems that have placed and/or place Hoke County students *at risk* of academic failure.

Although the trial court explained that it was leaving the "nuts and bolts" of the educational resources assessment in Hoke County to the other branches of government, it ultimately provided general guidelines for a *Leandro*-compliant resource allocation system, including the requirements: (1) that "every classroom be staffed with a competent, certified, well-trained teacher"; (2) "that every school be led by a well-trained competent principal"; and (3) "that every school be provided, in the most cost effective manner, the resources necessary to support the effective instructional program within that school so that the educational needs of all children, including at-risk children, to have the equal opportunity to obtain a sound basic education, can be met." Finally, the trial court ordered the State to keep the court advised of its remedial actions through written reports filed with the trial court every ninety days.

In our view, the trial court conducted an appropriate and informative path of inquiry concerning the issue at hand. After determining that the evidence clearly showed that Hoke County students were failing, at an alarming rate, to obtain a sound basic education, the trial court in turn determined that the evidence presented also demonstrated that a combination of State action and inaction contributed significantly to the students' failings. Then, after concluding that the State's overall funding and resource provisions scheme was adequate on a statewide basis, the trial court determined that the evidence showed that the State's method of funding and providing for individual school districts such as Hoke County was such that it did not comply with *Leandro*'s mandate of ensuring that all children of the state be provided with the opportunity for a sound basic education. In particular, the trial court concluded the State's failing was essentially twofold in that the State: (1) failed to identify the inordinate number of "at-risk" students and provide a means for such students to avail themselves of the opportunity for a sound basic education; and (2) failed to oversee how educational funding and resources were being used and implemented in Hoke County schools.

In short, the trial court: (1) informed the State what was wrong with Hoke County schools; (2) directed the State to reassess its educational priorities for Hoke County; and (3) ordered the State to correct any and all education-related deficiencies that contribute to a student's inability to take advantage of his right to the opportunity to obtain a sound basic education. However, we note that the trial court also demonstrated admirable restraint by refusing to dictate how existing problems should be approached and resolved. Recognizing that education concerns were the shared province of the legislative and executive branches, the trial court instead afforded the two branches an unimpeded chance, "initially at least," to correct constitutional deficiencies revealed at trial. In our view, the trial court's approach to the issue was sound and its order reflects both findings of fact that were supported by the evidence and conclusions that were supported by ample and adequate findings of fact. As a consequence, we affirm those portions of the trial court's order that conclude that there has been a clear showing of a denial of the established right of Hoke County students to gain their opportunity for a sound basic education and those portions of the order that require the State to assess its education-related allocations to the county's schools so as to correct any deficiencies that presently prevent the county from offering its students the opportunity to obtain a *Leandro*-conforming education.

CLAREMONT SCHOOL DISTRICT v. GOVERNOR
794 A.2d 744 (N.H. 2002)

DUGGAN, J.

The issues before this court are: (1) whether the State's obligation to provide a constitutionally adequate public education requires it to include standards of accountability in the educational system; and, if so, (2) whether existing statutes, regulations and/or rules satisfy this obligation. We hold that accountability is an essential component of the State's duty and that the existing statutory scheme has deficiencies that are inconsistent with the State's duty to provide a constitutionally adequate education.

This litigation began in 1992 when the Claremont School District, along with four other "property poor" school districts, five school children and five taxpayers, filed a petition for declaratory relief in superior court alleging that the system by which the State financed education violated the New Hampshire Constitution. The trial court dismissed the lawsuit, ruling that the New Hampshire Constitution "imposes no qualitative standard of education which must be met" and "imposes no quantifiable financial duty regarding education." The plaintiffs appealed. After examining the meaning of the words used in the Encouragement of Literature Clause at the time the State Constitution was adopted in 1784, historical evidence of the significance of education to the constitutional framers and the interpretation given almost identical language in the Massachusetts Constitution by that State's highest court, this court concluded that Part II, Article 83 requires the State to "provide a constitutionally adequate education to every educable child in the public schools in New Hampshire and to guarantee adequate funding."

In *Claremont I*, we observed that the New Hampshire Constitution "expressly recognizes education as a cornerstone of our democratic system" and the Encouragement of Literature Clause "expressly recognizes that a free government is dependent for its survival on citizens who are able to participate intelligently in the political, economic, and social functions of our system." "Given the complexities of our society today, the State's constitutional duty extends beyond mere reading, writing and arithmetic. It also includes broad educational opportunities needed in today's society to prepare citizens for their role as participants and as potential competitors in today's marketplace of ideas."

This court specifically acknowledged that the task of defining the parameters of the education mandated by the constitution is in the first instance for the legislature and the Governor. That task includes the "responsibility ... to defin[e] the specifics of, and the appropriate means to provide through public education, the knowledge and learning essential to the preservation of a free government."

> Regarding educational adequacy, the opinion underscored that

> > [m]ere competence in the basics—reading, writing, and arithmetic—is insufficient in the waning days of the twentieth century to insure that this State's public school students are fully integrated into the world around them. A broad exposure to the social, economic, scientific, technological, and political realities of today's society is essential for our students to compete, contribute, and flourish in the twenty-first century.

Claremont II also set forth "seven criteria...establishing general, aspirational guidelines for defining educational adequacy." This court deferred, however, in the first instance to the other branches of government to "promptly develop and adopt specific criteria implementing these guidelines."

After considering the pleadings and oral argument, this court decided to exercise its jurisdiction to resolve two specific legal questions:

> (1) Whether the State's obligation to provide a constitutionally adequate public education under part II, article 83 of the New Hampshire Constitution requires the State to include standards of accountability in New Hampshire statutes, regulations and/or rules; and if so

> (2) Whether existing statutes, regulations and/or rules satisfy this obligation.

Accountability is more than merely creating a system to deliver an adequate education. *Claremont I* did not simply hold that the State should deliver a constitutionally adequate education, but in fact held that it is the State's duty under the New Hampshire Constitution to do so. Accountability means that the State must provide a definition of a constitutionally adequate education, the definition must have standards, and the standards must be subject to meaningful application so that it is possible to determine whether, in delegating its obligation to provide a constitutionally adequate education, the State has fulfilled its duty. If the State cannot be held accountable for fulfilling its duty, the duty creates no obligation and is no longer a duty. We therefore conclude that the State's duty to provide a constitutionally adequate education includes accountability.

Having determined that standards of accountability are an essential component of the State's duty to provide a constitutionally adequate education, we must now determine whether the existing statutes, regulations and rules satisfy this obligation. The State argues that these existing laws, which include the definition of an adequate education in RSA 193-E:2; the State's minimum standards for education set forth in the department of education rules, *N.H. Admin. Rules*, Ed ch. 300; and the New Hampshire Education Improvement and Assessment Program (NHEIAP), RSA ch. 193-C (1999), together provide sufficient standards of accountability. According to the State, "it has given detailed curriculum instruction to schools and school boards, created a test to measure student performance, empowered State agencies to review and improve school performance, and enacted literally thousands of pages of other statutes, regulations, and rules to deliver an adequate education."

RSA 193-E:2 sets forth the criteria for an adequate education as follows:

I. Skill in reading, writing, and speaking English to enable them to communicate effectively and think creatively and critically.

II. Skill in mathematics and familiarity with methods of science to enable them to analyze information, solve problems, and make rational decisions.

III. Knowledge of the biological, physical, and earth sciences to enable them to understand and appreciate the world around them.

IV. Knowledge of civics and government, economics, geography, and history to enable them to participate in the democratic process and to make informed choices as responsible citizens.

V. Grounding in the arts, languages, and literature to enable them to appreciate our cultural heritage and develop lifelong interests and involvement in these areas.

VI. Sound wellness and environmental practices to enable them to enhance their own well-being, as well as that of others.

VII. Skills for lifelong learning, including interpersonal and technological skills, to enable them to learn, work, and participate effectively in a changing society.

The State contends that a wide range of satisfactory methods can produce an effective system to deliver what it has defined as an adequate education. The State also asserts that it may choose from a wide array of tools to ensure that school districts are implementing the standards it sets out for the system it chooses. We agree that "there are many different ways that the Legislature could fashion an educational system while still meeting the mandates of the Constitution." The system the State currently has in place appears to use both standards based on what school districts provide (input-based standards) and results that school districts achieve (output-based standards). While minimum standards for school approval set forth what the schools, at the very least, must provide to students, NHEIAP uses curriculum frameworks and mandatory tests to assess what the school districts have achieved.

The State argues that as a central part of the system to deliver a constitutionally adequate education, it "dictates certain school approval standards that schools and school districts must meet. These input based standards are enforceable by the State and extend to virtually every aspect of education, from class size to teacher training to detailed curriculum requirements."

The board of education is required by statute to adopt rules relative to "[m]inimum curriculum and educational standards for all grades of the public schools." These rules are commonly referred to as the State's "minimum standards" or "school approval standards." The minimum standards contain a number of requirements imposed by the State on local school districts so that schools may be approved by the State. For example, the minimum standards set forth the number of days in a standard school year, staff qualifications, maximum class sizes, heating and ventilation requirements, the minimum number of credits required to be offered in certain courses, and the areas of specific substantive materials which must be taught.

The education that the individual schools provide is measured against these standards for approval. If a school does not meet these standards, it can lose its approval. There are four categories of approval: approved with distinction, approved, conditionally approved from one to three years, and unapproved. If a school is unapproved, the department of education is required to work with the local school board to "correct all deficiencies until such time as an unapproved school meets all applicable standards and is designated as an approved school." The purpose of these rules is to hold school districts accountable for providing an adequate education.

Excused noncompliance with the minimum standards for financial reasons alone directly conflicts with the constitutional command that the State must guarantee sufficient funding to ensure that school districts can provide a constitutionally adequate education. As we have repeatedly held, it is the State's duty to guarantee the funding necessary to provide a constitutionally adequate education to every educable child in the public schools in the State.

The responsibility for ensuring the provision of an adequate public education and an adequate level of resources for all students in New Hampshire lies with the State. While local governments may be required, in part, to support public schools, it is the responsibility of the State to take such steps as may be required in each instance effectively to devise a plan and sources of funds sufficient to meet the constitutional mandate.

As noted above, the State may not take the position that the minimum standards form an essential component of the delivery of a constitutionally adequate education and yet allow for the financial constraints of a school or school district to excuse compliance with those very standards. We hold, therefore, that to the extent the minimum standards for school approval excuse compliance solely based on financial conditions, it is facially insufficient because it is in clear conflict with the State's duty to provide a constitutionally adequate education.

State can't allow inadequate finances to be a barrier

NHEIAP, RSA chapter 193-C, is characterized by the State as "[a]nother important element of the State's system for delivering the opportunity for an adequate education." The goals of the program are to define what students should know and be able to do, develop and implement methods for assessing that learning and its application, report assessment results to all citizens of New Hampshire, help to provide accountability at all levels, and use the results, at both the State and local levels, to improve instruction and advance student learning. The department of education pamphlet describes NHEIAP as the "cornerstone of the state's initiatives to continuously improve education for all students."

Admin task

The responsibility for administering NHEIAP lies with the department of education. The commissioner of education is charged with "develop[ing] and implement[ing] this program in conjunction with the state board of education and the legislative oversight committee." In fulfilling its duty pursuant to the statutory framework that makes up NHEIAP, the department of education is directed to develop a program that consists of three interlocking components. The first component is a set of educational standards, RSA 193-C:3, III(a), which the department of education has developed and implemented through curriculum frameworks. The second component is a statewide assessment program, which "shall be [a] valid and appropriate representation[ ] of the standards the students are expected to achieve." The final component is the "local education improvement and assessment plan which builds upon and complements the goals established for [NHEIAP]."

Under RSA 193-C:9, I, however, no school district is required to respond to the assessment results; rather "[e]ach school district in New Hampshire is *encouraged* to develop a local education improvement and assessment plan." This means that even if the assessment results show that all the students in a school are at novice level, neither the school district nor the department of education is required to do anything. Whether an individual school district is providing a constitutionally adequate education or not, it is merely encouraged to develop a local educational improvement plan, and if it opts to do so, the department of education is available to assist. Nothing more is required.

Law provides a directory remedy. BW.

An output-based accountability system that merely encourages local school districts to meet educational standards does not fulfill the State's constitutional duty under Part II, Article 83. While the State may delegate its duty to provide a constitutionally adequate education, the State may not abdicate its duty in the process. The purpose of meaningful accountability is to ensure that those entrusted with the duty of delivering a constitutionally adequate education are fulfilling that duty. When the State chooses to use an output-based tool to measure whether school districts are providing a constitutionally adequate education, that tool must be meaningfully applied. The department of education cannot meaningfully apply the educational standards and assessment tests set out in RSA chapter 193-C when it cannot hold school districts accountable, but instead is limited to using the results to encourage school districts to develop a local education improvement and assessment plan. To the extent the State relies on RSA chapter 193-C to provide for accountability, it must do more than merely encourage school districts to meet the educational standards that are designed to indicate whether students are receiving a constitutionally adequate education.

The State suggests that "[a] student who receives an education of the quality described in [RSA] 193-E:2 and who acquires all of the various skills and types of knowledge expressed there would be well prepared as a citizen to participate in society." While we have no basis to disagree with this statement, the State has not provided a sufficient mechanism to require that school districts actually achieve this goal. We hold that because of deficiencies in the system as set out in this opinion, the State has not met its constitutional obligation to develop a system to ensure the delivery of a constitutionally adequate education.

As the State recognizes, "there are many different ways that the Legislature could fashion an educational system while still meeting the mandates of the Constitution." The development of meaningful standards of accountability is a task for which the legislative branch is uniquely suited. The policy choices to be made are complex, as there are several ways to address this issue. It is for the Governor and the legislature to choose how to measure or evaluate whether a constitutionally adequate education is being provided and what action to take if a school is determined to be deficient. The State's brief describes some of the issues involved:

> Formulating a system for delivery might…require policy choices regarding what sort of standards should exist for teachers, students, schools, and school districts. For example, a delivery system might consist of detailed curriculum rules for each grade and subject area establishing the required substance of each lesson that students must be taught. Other delivery systems might make use of any number of other standards such as class size, graduation rate, college acceptance rate, test scores, or teacher qualifications.

...[D]evising a system to deliver educational services could also require decisions regarding how to implement the standards that are selected. If a school or school district is not meeting applicable standards, what will be the consequence? A system could rely on the Governor to ensure that local school districts are meeting statutory obligations through her power to enforce constitutional and statutory obligations. A different system might enforce standards by rewarding successful schools with increased funding. Alternatively, the system might impose penalties for not meeting standards, such as removing the principal, sending in a team of administrators to take control of the school, or any number of other consequences.

We agree with the State's contention that it may implement a variety of systems. However, when the State chooses a particular method to determine whether those it entrusts with the task are in fact providing a constitutionally adequate education, the State must include meaningful accountability to ensure that the State is fulfilling its constitutional duty.

We conclude that the State "needs to do more work" to fulfill its duty to provide a constitutionally adequate education and incorporate meaningful accountability in the education system. In light of the procedural history of this litigation, including efforts by the executive and legislative branches and their previous statements on this issue, and the application of settled law, this conclusion should be neither surprising nor unanticipated.

We remain mindful that "[w]hile the judiciary has the duty to construe and interpret the word 'education' by providing broad constitutional guidelines, the Legislature is obligated to give specific substantive content to the word and to the program it deems necessary to provide that 'education' within the broad guidelines." We recognize that we are not appointed to establish educational policy and have not done so today.

NEELEY v. WEST ORANGE-COVE CONSOLIDATED INDEPENDENT SCHOOL DISTRICT
176 S.W.3d 746 (Tex. 2005)

HECHT, J.

Under article VII, section 1 of the Constitution of 1876, the accomplishment of "a general diffusion of knowledge" is the standard by which the adequacy of the public education system is to be judged. To achieve such a system, the Legislature has chosen to use local school districts. Borrowing from two statutory pronouncements, the district court concluded:

> To fulfill the constitutional obligation to provide a general diffusion of knowledge, districts must provide "*all Texas children ... access* to a quality education that enables them to achieve their potential and fully participate now and in the future in the social, economic, and educational opportunities of our state and nation." Districts satisfy this constitutional obligation when they

provide all of their students with a *meaningful opportunity* to acquire the essential knowledge and skills reflected in ... curriculum requirements ... such that upon graduation, students are prepared to "continue to learn in postsecondary educational, training, or employment settings."

We agree, with one caveat. The public education system need not operate perfectly; it is adequate if districts are *reasonably* able to provide their students the access and opportunity the district court described.

The system the Legislature has devised prescribes an education curriculum, and by means of accreditation standards, holds schools and districts accountable for teaching it. Schools and districts rated "academically acceptable" provide what we have referred to as an accredited education, and we have presumed, simply in deference to the Legislature, that such an education achieves a general diffusion of knowledge. The district court found that the plaintiffs and intervenors have rebutted this presumption. The court's principal reasons, set out in detailed findings and conclusions, may be summarized as follows:

- TAKS tests (and other such tests) cover only a small part of the prescribed curriculum;

  - the cut scores and passing rates for TAKS tests (or other such tests) are too low and are set, not to reliably measure achievement, but to ensure a low rate of failure;

  - completion and dropout rates are understated and unreliable, in fact fewer than 75% of all students and 70% of minority students complete high school, and this high attrition, worse in larger districts, is unacceptable;

  - other important factors in determining whether a general diffusion of knowledge has been achieved, like college preparedness of graduates, for example, are not considered in rating schools and districts "academically acceptable" and reflect unfavorably on the system;

  - the requirements for an "academically acceptable" rating are set to assure, not that there will be a general diffusion of knowledge, but that almost every district will meet them;

  - the prescribed curriculum and TAKS testing have been made more demanding while funding to satisfy statutory requirements has not kept pace, producing budget pressures that have resulted in—

  - a shortage of qualified teachers, an increase in teachers having to teach outside their fields, and high attrition and turnover rates;

  - difficulty in providing special programs and remediation for students at risk of not completing their education;

  - there has also been a lack of funding to meet increased federal requirements, like the No Child Left Behind Act;

- the changing demographics of the student population—with a majority being economically disadvantaged, 15% having limited proficiency in English, and both groups continuing to grow—have increased education costs while funding has lagged;

• the I/R econometric study correctly shows that the cost of an accredited education exceeds available per-student revenue.

The State defendants contend that the district court focused too much on "inputs" to the public education system—that is, available resources. They argue that whether a general diffusion of knowledge has been accomplished depends entirely on "outputs"—the results of the educational process measured in student achievement. We agree that the constitutional standard is plainly result-oriented. It creates no duty to fund public education at any level other than what is required to achieve a general diffusion of knowledge. While the end-product of public education is related to the resources available for its use, the relationship is neither simple nor direct; public education can and often does improve with greater resources, just as it struggles when resources are withheld, but more money does not guarantee better schools or more educated students. To determine whether the system as a whole is providing for a general diffusion of knowledge, it is useful to consider how funding levels and mechanisms relate to better-educated students. This, we think, is all the district court did.

Con standard
for ed B
based on
outputs

In the extensive record before us, there is much evidence, which the district court credited, that many schools and districts are struggling to teach an increasingly demanding curriculum to a population with a growing number of disadvantaged students, yet without additional funding needed to meet these challenges. There are wide gaps in performance among student groups differentiated by race, proficiency in English, and economic advantage. Non-completion and dropout rates are high, and the loss of students who are struggling may make performance measures applied to those who continue appear better than they should. The rate of students meeting college preparedness standards is very low. There is also evidence of high attrition and turnover among teachers statewide, due to increasing demands and stagnant compensation. But the undisputed evidence is that standardized test scores have steadily improved over time, even while tests and curriculum have been made more difficult. By all admission, NAEP scores, which the district court did not mention, show that public education in Texas has improved relative to the other states. Having carefully reviewed the evidence and the district court's findings, we cannot conclude that the Legislature has acted arbitrarily in structuring and funding the public education system so that school districts are not reasonably able to afford all students the access to education and the educational opportunity to accomplish a general diffusion of knowledge.

LBts may
struggles
of
system

Test scores
are
going up.

NOTE

For more cases dealing with these vexing remedial issues, see *Abbeville Cty. Sch. Dist. v. South Carolina*, 767 S.E.2d 157 (S.C. 2014);

Gannon v. Kansas, 319 P.3d 1196 (Kan. 2014); *Campbell Cty. Sch. Dist. v. State*, 181 P.3d 43 (Wyo. 2008); *Paynter v. State*, 797 N.E.2d 1225 (N.Y. 2003).

CHAPTER XI

THE RIGHT TO A REMEDY AND OPEN COURTS

A. INTRODUCTION AND HISTORICAL BACKGROUND

State constitutions protect a variety of rights. One important provision that most state constitutions include but that the federal constitution does not is often referred to as a "right to a remedy" clause or an "open courts" clause. Such provisions guarantee citizens the right to pursue legal remedies for deprivations of their interests, usually in terms indicating a right to a "remedy by due course of law" or that the courts of the state "shall be open." These provisions often also include language guaranteeing that justice shall be "without denial," "prompt," or "without delay."

The right to a remedy/open courts provisions may limit a state's authority to withdraw or modify existing legal remedies. A frequent area of litigation under these provisions is tort reform, with plaintiffs arguing that damages caps, statutes of repose, worker's compensation systems, and other limitations on various tort actions (*e.g.*, in the malpractice or governmental immunity contexts) violate these state constitutional provisions. There are an abundance of fascinating and challenging state cases interpreting these constitutional provisions, with courts applying various levels of scrutiny and a variety of tests, with a corresponding mix of outcomes regarding the constitutionality of various state statutes that affect legal remedies. This chapter provides several illustrative examples of these cases, but it is by no means exhaustive of this complex and important area of state constitutional law.

Right to a remedy, or open court, provisions have a long historical pedigree. In fact, they predate the U.S. Constitution by centuries, with their roots in the English Magna Carta. Furthermore, even though the right to a remedy principle is explicitly enshrined only in the State constitutions (and not the federal constitution), Chief Justice John Marshall recognized the principle's pedigree more than 200 years ago. In *Marbury v. Madison*, 5 U.S. (1 Cranch) 137, 162-63 (1803), he quoted Blackstone's *Commentaries* for the proposition that "'it is a general and indisputable rule, that where there is a legal right there is also a legal remedy by suit or action at law, whenever that right is invaded.'"

Shannon M. Roesler, *The Kansas Remedy by Due Course of Law Provision: Defining a Right to a Remedy*
47 Kan. L. Rev. 655 (1999) (footnotes omitted)[1]

1. Introduction

The state constitutions of thirty-nine states…contain "remedy by due course of law" provisions. Historically, these provisions were intended as constitutional safeguards of an individual's right to a legal remedy. More than state equivalents of the federal Due Process Clause, these remedy provisions have resulted in a myriad of interpretations by state courts. Plaintiffs generally use state remedy provisions to challenge statutes restricting or eliminating previously established causes of action. In the last few decades, for example, injured parties have used state remedy provisions to challenge tort reform legislation, such as workers' compensation acts and statutory caps on medical malpractice damages.

2. Background

a. The History of the Remedy Clause: The Magna Carta and Sir Edward Coke

Most states with remedy provisions adopted the provision from earlier state constitutions. In constructing the first state constitutions, the colonial and early American writers looked to English law and history, adopting Sir Edward Coke's interpretation of language in the Magna Carta. Like Coke, they sought to protect the judiciary from corruption and to ensure its independence.

The history of the remedy provision…begins with King John in the thirteenth century. King John's courts administered justice for a fee; those seeking access to the courts had to purchase writs, and the more costly writs guaranteed speedier and more successful claims. In response to the Crown's corrupting influence, Chapter 40 of the Magna Carta was written to restore the integrity of the courts by specifically prohibiting the selling of writs: "[t]o no one will we sell, to no one will we refuse or delay, right or justice."

Because the Magna Carta's purpose was to protect the courts from the Crown's corruption, it provided compelling authority for Sir Edward Coke as he battled King James and argued for the supremacy of the common law in the seventeenth century. As an absolutist monarch, King James exercised power over the courts, arguing judges were merely servants of the Crown. Coke, not only argued that the judiciary was independent from the Crown, but also that the King was subject to the common law. In his

---

[1] Copyright © 1999, Kansas Law Review. Reprinted with permission.

crusade to justify the judiciary's independence, Coke wrote the Second Institute; the remedy provision first appears in this context as part of Coke's interpretation of the language in Chapter 40 of the Magna Carta.

Coke expounded on the language in the Magna Carta to fashion a remedy guarantee: "[E]very subject of this Realm, for injury done to him…may take his remedy by the course of the Law, and have justice and right for injury done him, freely without sale, fully without any denial, and speedily without delay." Although commentators have criticized Coke for misreading the Magna Carta, his intent in fashioning the provision, not his accuracy in translation, sheds light on the remedy provision and its historical development. Like the authors of the Magna Carta, he struggled to protect the English court from outside corruption and influence, thereby safeguarding its independence; he did not, however, seek to guarantee the creation of remedies for every injury. The remedy provision was not created, therefore, to address the relationship between the judiciary and the legislature, although this is its context today.

When the remedy provision appeared in…the Delaware Declaration of Rights, Coke's interpretation of Chapter 40 of the Magna Carta was the only textual authority for an independent judiciary. Although the English judiciary's independence was finally recognized in 1701, the colonial courts remained subject to the corrupt devices of the Crown. Thus, shortly before the American Revolution, grievances similar to those of Coke motivated colonists to seek language that would guarantee the integrity of the courts. Not surprisingly, five early bills of rights contain remedy provisions derived from Coke's Second Institute. Moreover, though the federal Bill of Rights does not contain a remedy provision, at least two states, Virginia and North Carolina, argued for the inclusion of remedy language.

b. State Interpretations

The modern context of the remedy provision bears little resemblance to the provision's origins. Litigation involving the remedy provision often surfaces in response to fairly recent areas of law, such as workers' compensation, medical malpractice, and statutes of repose. Though the cases contain similar subject matter from state to state, interpretation of the remedy provision continues to be an area of rich diversity in state constitutional law.

Commentators have categorized the different state interpretations according to various schemes. Often classification schemes draw upon federal equal protection, distinguishing different courts' approaches by varying degrees of judicial scrutiny and by using federal language, such as "fundamental rights."…[One commentator] has divided the varied approaches into two large groups: one group consists of judicially created bright line, or per se, rules while the other group contains ad hoc balancing tests that focus on the particular costs and benefits of a challenged statute.

B. CASES DEFINING THE RIGHT

SMOTHERS v. GRESHAM TRANSFER, INC.,
23 P.3d 333 (Or. 2001)

LEESON, J.

Plaintiff filed this negligence action against defendant, his employer, after an administrative law judge (ALJ) of the Workers' Compensation Board upheld the insurer's denial of plaintiff's workers' compensation claim. The ALJ found that plaintiff's exposure to sulfuric, hydrochloric, and hydrofluoric acid mist and fumes at work was not the "major contributing cause" of plaintiff's respiratory condition and other ailments and, therefore, that plaintiff had not suffered a "compensable injury" under the workers' compensation statutes. Nonetheless, plaintiff believed that he had suffered an injury at work. Accordingly, he brought this action against his employer for negligence. The trial court dismissed plaintiff's complaint for failure to state a claim, reasoning that ORS 656.018 makes workers' compensation law the "exclusive remedy" for work-related injuries, whether or not a claim is compensable. The Court of Appeals affirmed. This court allowed review to address plaintiff's contention that he has been denied a remedy for the injuries that he suffered at work, in violation of the remedy clause in Article I, section 10, of the Oregon Constitution.

I. BACKGROUND

A. *Facts*

Plaintiff's job as a lube technician for defendant's trucking company required him to work in a pit more than four feet deep in a mechanics' shop where trucks were serviced. A truck-washing area was located outside the shop. Defendant's employees cleaned the exteriors of trucks by spraying them with a chemical mixture of diluted sulfuric acid and small amounts of hydrochloric and hydrofluoric acids. When the doors to the shop were open, acid mist and fumes from the truck-washing area drifted into the shop and down into the pit where plaintiff worked. For many months, plaintiff experienced headaches, as well as itching, burning, and watering eyes.

In January 1993, plaintiff contracted an upper respiratory infection that developed into pneumonia. He was hospitalized for five days, and he was unable to work for a month. Plaintiff returned to work, but he suffered another episode of pneumonia in February 1993. In November 1993, his physician diagnosed him with bronchitis. In December 1993, plaintiff's coworkers found him so ill that he was lying on the lunchroom floor. He was sent home, where he was bedridden with bacterial bronchitis for most of the holiday season.

Plaintiff returned to work in January 1994, but his physician expressed concern about his slow rate of recovery. Plaintiff called in sick several times between March and mid-June 1994. In June 1994, claimant stopped working for defendant because of his illness.

Thereafter, plaintiff filed a workers' compensation claim for his lung condition. Defendant's insurer denied plaintiff's claim. At a hearing before an ALJ, the issue was whether plaintiff had a compensable occupational disease. After the hearing, the ALJ upheld the insurer's denial, because plaintiff had failed to prove that his work exposure was the major contributing cause of his lung disorder.

B. *Legal Context for Plaintiff's Negligence Action*

In *Errand v. Cascade Steel Rolling Mills, Inc.* (1995), this court held that the exclusive remedy provisions in ORS 656.018 (1993) did not preclude workers whose workers' compensation claims had been denied from bringing civil actions against their employers in an effort to recover damages for their work-related injuries.

[I]n response to this court's decision in *Errand*, the 1995 Legislature amended ORS 656.018 and added subsection (6) to provide that workers' compensation is the exclusive remedy for work-related injuries, even if a claim is not compensable.

Relying on the "exclusive remedy" provisions of ORS 656.018 (1995), defendant moved to dismiss plaintiff's complaint for failure to state a claim. The trial court granted that motion.

On appeal to the Court of Appeals, plaintiff argued that, although he could not prove that the acid fumes and mist that he had inhaled at work were the *major* contributing cause of his lung condition and other ailments, he nonetheless had been injured at work. Before the 1995 amendments to ORS 656.018, he noted, workers' compensation was the exclusive remedy for only *compensable* work-related injuries. The 1995 amendments to ORS 656.018 made workers' compensation the exclusive remedy for *all* work-related injuries, whether or not a claim is compensable. Those amendments, plaintiff argued, left him with no remedy for the injuries that he had suffered at work, in violation of the remedy clause of Article I, section 10, which guarantees every person a remedy by due course of law for injury to person, property, or reputation. The Court of Appeals rejected plaintiff's argument.

C. *Parties' Arguments*

Before this court, plaintiff repeats his contention that, under the mandate of the remedy clause of Article I, section 10, the legislature may not deprive a person of a remedy for an injury to person, property, or reputation that was recognized at common law, unless the legislature makes available an equivalent remedy. Defendant's response to plaintiff's constitutional argument is twofold. First, defendant contends that the legislature has plenary authority to define what constitutes a cognizable injury to person, property, or reputation. Second, defendant contends that the remedy clause does not limit the legislature's power to modify any common-law or statutory remedy.

In making their arguments, the parties and *amici curiae* assert that this court's remedy clause jurisprudence has not been consistent. Scholars likewise have observed that courts have not adopted a consistent remedy clause jurisprudence. *See, e.g.*, David Schuman, *The Right to a Remedy*, 65 Temp. L. Rev. 1197, 1203 (1992) (courts have adopted a "daunting variety of remedy guarantee interpretations"); Jonathan M. Hoffman, *By the Course of the Law: The Origins of the Open Courts Clause of State Constitutions*, 74 Or. L. Rev. 1279, 1282 (1995) (courts in "total disarray" over how to interpret remedy clauses).

II. REMEDY CLAUSE

A. *Text*

Article I of the Oregon Constitution is Oregon's Bill of Rights. Section 10 provides:

> "No court shall be secret, but justice shall be administered, openly and without purchase, completely and without delay, and every man shall have remedy by due course of law for injury done him in his person, property, or reputation."

Section 10 consists of one sentence that is made up of two independent clauses. The first clause of Article I, section 10, provides that "[n]o court shall be secret" and that justice "shall be administered, openly and without purchase, completely and without delay * * *." That clause prescribes how justice must be administered in Oregon by identifying both a prohibition (no court shall be secret) and a directive (justice must be administered openly, completely, and without purchase or delay).

The second clause mandates that "every man shall have remedy by due course of law for injury done him in his person, property, or reputation." As applicable to modern circumstances, the phrase "every man" means every person. Unlike many provisions in bills of rights, which protect individual rights by prohibiting the legislature from enacting certain laws or prohibiting the government from taking certain actions, the second clause of section 10 protects rights respecting person, property, and reputation by mandating affirmatively that remedy by due course of law be available in the event of injury to those rights.

The key terms in the remedy clause are "remedy," "due course of law," and "injury." [The court reviews various dictionaries of the 19th century].

In summary: Although the text of the remedy clause states in mandatory terms that remedy by due course of law must be available for injury to person, property, or reputation, the clause does not define the terms "remedy," "due course of law," or "injury." Contemporaneous dictionaries provide some definitions, but no definitive picture of the scope or effect of the remedy clause emerges. For further insight into the drafters' intent in writing the remedy clause, we turn to an examination of the historical circumstances relating to that provision.

B. *Historical Circumstances*

1. *Edward Coke's Second Institute*

The principle that the law makes available a remedy for injury to person, property, or reputation comes from the common law. The phrasing of remedy clauses that now appear in the Bill of Rights of the Oregon Constitution and 38 other states traces to Edward Coke's commentary, first published in 1642, on the second sentence of Chapter 29 of the Magna Carta of 1225.

Coke declared that the second sentence of Chapter 29 had evolved into a … guarantee in English law, *viz.*, one involving the rights of subjects in their *private relations* with one another. The assurance that the king would not sell, deny, or defer justice or right had come to mean that

> " * * * *every subject of this realme, for injury done to him in bonis, terris, vel persona, by any other subject*, be he ecclesiastical, or temporall, free, or bond, man, or woman, old, or young, or be he outlawed, excommunicated, or any other without exception, *may take his remedy by the course of the law, and have justice, and right for the injury done to him, freely without sale, fully without any deniall, and speedily without delay*."

Coke, *Second Institute* at 55. In other words, Coke asserted that the common law of England had come to guarantee every subject a legal remedy for injury to goods, lands, or person caused by any other subject. The purpose of the remedial branch of the common law was to discover "that which is tort, crooked, or wrong" and restore "right" or "justice." Coke viewed the remedial branch of the law as the best birthright that English subjects had, because it protected their goods, lands, person, life, honor, and estimation from injury and wrong. *Id.* Coke praised the common law, because it guaranteed both justice ("justitiam") and the means to attain it ("rectum").

Coke's *Second Institute* made its way to the American colonies through a variety of sources.

2. *William Blackstone's Commentaries*

Blackstone's *Commentaries on the Laws of England* is another important source for understanding what the drafters of state constitutions intended when they included in declarations or bills of rights the guarantee of remedy by due course of law for injury to person, property, reputation and, in some instances, liberty. Blackstone's *Commentaries* updated Coke's accounts of the evolution of the common law. The *Commentaries* sold quickly in the American colonies and became one of the principal means of the colonists' information about the state of English law in general.

Blackstone explained that the common law viewed Englishmen as having both absolute and relative rights. Absolute rights are founded on immutable laws of nature and reason, and usually are called liberties. Absolute rights exist in both a state of nature and in civil society, while relative rights, such as those that are based on the marital relationship, are rights that are defined solely by membership in civil society. The principal aim of society is to protect individuals in their enjoyment of absolute rights. The common law recognized three absolute rights: "the right of personal security [including reputation], the right of personal liberty, and the right of private property."

Blackstone described an act that deprives a person of a right as a "wrong." Wrongs can be public (crimes and misdemeanors) or private (civil injuries). *Id.* Blackstone explained that the remedial part of the law provides a method for recovering for deprivations of rights or for redressing wrongs, be they public or private.

Blackstone echoed Coke in stating that it would be "in vain" for the law to recognize rights, if it were not for the remedial part of the law that provides the methods for restoring those rights when they wrongfully are withheld or invaded. To Blackstone, the guarantee of legal remedy for injury "is what we mean properly, when we speak of the protection of the law." Hence, the maxim of English law, *Ubi jus, ibi remedium*: "for every right, there must be a remedy."

4. *Early Remedy Clauses*

The states of Maryland and Delaware were the first to place remedy clauses in their declarations of rights. Both states had been proprietary colonies before the Revolution and, as noted earlier, their governors had guaranteed to the residents of those colonies the rights of Englishmen.

After 1776, the drafters of other state constitutions apparently looked to Maryland and Delaware, if not directly to Coke, Care, or Penn, in crafting their remedy clauses. Clauses guaranteeing remedy for injury to absolute common-law rights became more common after 1780, as constitution writers realized that unrestrained state legislative power was as much a threat to the security of individual rights as unrestrained parliamentary and royal power had been.

As noted, the drafters wrote the Oregon Constitution and its Bill of Rights in 1857. As part of our effort to understand the wording of Oregon's remedy clause in light of the way that wording would have been understood and used by those who wrote the provision, and as a way of bridging the period from the immediate aftermath of the American Revolution to the middle of the nineteenth century, we turn to an examination of the historical evolution of the remedy clause in Indiana, whose constitution of 1851 was the primary source for the Oregon Constitution.

5. *Indiana Remedy Clause*

The territory of Indiana, which had been governed by the Northwest Ordinance of 1787, was admitted into the union in 1816. The Indiana Bill of Rights followed the model of other Midwestern states, such as Ohio and Kentucky. Article I, section 11, of the Indiana Constitution of 1816, provided:

> "That all Courts shall be open, and every person, for an injury done him in his lands, goods, person, or reputation, shall have remedy by the due course of law; and right and justice administered without denial or delay."

The Indiana Constitutional Convention of 1850 ... rewrote various provisions of Indiana's Bill of Rights to assure that the legislature would not invade the rights that were protected therein.

Article I, section 11, of the Indiana Constitution of 1816, was one of the provisions that the convention revised. Renumbered as Article I, section 12, of the Indiana Constitution of 1851, the convention rewrote it to provide:

> "All courts shall be open; and every man, for injury done to him in his person, property, or reputation, shall have remedy by due course of law. Justice shall be administered freely, and without purchase; completely, and without denial; speedily, and without delay."

Unlike the one-sentence version in the 1816 constitution, the 1851 provision consisted of two sentences, each addressing different guarantees. The first sentence guaranteed both open courts and the right to remedy by due course of law for injury to person, property, or reputation. The second sentence prescribed how justice must be administered, and the delegates added requirements that had not been present in the 1816 constitution, including the requirement that justice be administered completely, as well as freely; without purchase; and speedily, without denial or delay.

The decisions to restructure Article I, section 12, to make the remedy clause an independent clause and to add the requirement that justice be administered completely are indications that the drafters of the Indiana Constitution of 1851 intended to secure more firmly than had been done in the 1816 constitution the common-law right to remedy for injury to absolute rights concerning person, property, and reputation. The evolution of the remedy clause in the Indiana Bill of Rights thus indicates that the commitment to protecting absolute common-law rights had strengthened, not waned, with the passage of time.

6. *Commentaries and Case Law from Other Jurisdictions*

The commitment to natural rights was strong in the nineteenth century, just as it had been in the eighteenth century and before. It also was well established in the nineteenth century that, at a minimum, a "remedy" was a means for enforcing a legal right. In *Marbury v. Madison*, 5 U.S. (1 Cranch) 137, 163 (1803), the United States Supreme Court held that the "very essence of civil liberty * * * consists in the right of every individual to claim the protection of the laws, whenever he receives an injury."

In sum, when the Oregon Constitutional Convention convened in 1857, courts and commentators had provided considerable insight into the background and meaning of remedy clauses in state declarations or bills of rights. Those cases and commentaries revealed that the purpose of remedy clauses was to protect "absolute" common-law rights. For injuries to those rights, the remedial side of the common law had provided causes of action that were intended to restore right or justice. Remedy clauses mandated the continued availability of remedy for injury to absolute rights. The requirement that remedy be by due course or due process of law was intended as a limitation on the legislature's authority when it substituted statutory remedies for common-law remedies. It was the duty of courts to enforce those restraints in evaluating whether particular statutory remedies satisfied the requirement that remedy be by "due course of law." With that background, we turn to the drafting and adoption of the remedy clause in Article I, section 10, of the Oregon Constitution.

7. *Oregon Constitutional Convention*

The Oregon Constitutional Convention convened on August 17, 1857 ... [and a] committee recommended the following wording for the provision that became Article I, section 10, of the Oregon Constitution:

> "No tribunal shall be secret, but justice shall be administered openly and without purchase, completely and without delay; and every man shall have remedy by due course of law for injury done him in his person, property, or reputation."

In the final version, the convention substituted the word "court" for the word "tribunal." The convention adopted the Bill of Rights on September 12, 1857.

There is no record of the debates surrounding the changes that the committee on the Bill of Rights made to Article I, section 10. However, in the short time that the committee devoted to drafting the Bill of Rights for the Oregon Constitution, it rewrote Article I, section 12, of the Indiana Constitution of 1851, rather than merely adopting the Indiana provision verbatim. The committee reorganized the provision to express in one clause all the requirements relating to open courts and judicial administration. It expressed in a separate, independent clause the guarantee of remedy by due course of law for injury to person, property, or reputation. The decision to express in a separate, independent clause the guarantee of remedy by due course of law for injury to person, property, or reputation indicates that the drafters of the Oregon Constitution believed that the right to a remedy for injury to those rights needed to be stated clearly and unambiguously in the Oregon Bill of Rights.

Evidence of the scope of the drafters' intent when they wrote the remedy clause in section 10 of the Oregon Bill of Rights admittedly is sketchy. However, we find no indication that the drafters sought to depart from the historical purpose of remedy clauses, which was to mandate the availability of a remedy by due course of law for injury to absolute rights respecting person, property, and reputation. That the drafters of Article I, section 10, of the Oregon Constitution, rewrote and reorganized Article I, section 12, of the Indiana Constitution of 1851, rather than merely adopting that provision verbatim as they did several other provisions of the Indiana Bill of Rights, demonstrates that the drafters gave careful thought to the structure and wording of Article I, section 10. Their choice to express in one clause how justice is to be administered, and to reserve for a separate, independent clause the requirement of remedy by due course of law for injury to person, property, or reputation, indicates that the drafters regarded the remedy clause as providing substantive protection to those absolute common-law rights. Viewed in the context of the historical tradition that gave rise to remedy clauses in other state constitutions, and the mistrust of legislative power that pervaded the mid-nineteenth century, we conclude that the drafters of Article I, section 10, sought to give constitutional protection to absolute rights respecting person, property, and reputation as those rights were understood in 1857, and that the means for doing so was to mandate the availability of remedy by due course of law in the event of injury to those rights. That remedy must be by due course of law is a directive to courts, as the guardians of constitutional rights, to determine the constitutionality of legislatively created remedies respecting such rights.

C. *Oregon Supreme Court Case Law*

This court's case law surrounding Article I, section 10, is extensive. We review that case law first by considering cases analyzing the rights that the remedy clause protects, then cases analyzing its key terms: remedy, due course of law, and injury.

1. *Rights Protected by the Remedy Clause*

This court has stated that the guarantee of remedy by due course of law for injury to person, property, or reputation "is one of the most sacred and essential of all the constitutional guaranties" and that "without it a free government cannot be maintained or individual liberty be preserved." This court also has stated that the purpose of the remedy clause is to make the common-law maxim that there is no wrong without a remedy "a fixed and permanent rule of law in this state." Those statements reflect this court's understanding that certain common-law rights are absolute rights that must be protected from infringement.

Consistent with the foregoing observations, this court for many years held that the purpose of the remedy clause "is to save from legislative abolishment those jural rights which had become well established prior to the enactment of our Constitution."

2. *Remedy*

For rights that are protected by Article I, section 10, this court consistently has held that the law must provide a means for seeking redress for injury. Although this court has held that the remedy clause preserves common-law rights of action, it never has held that the remedy clause prohibits the legislature from changing a common-law remedy or form of procedure, attaching conditions precedent to invoking the remedy, or perhaps even abolishing old remedies and substituting new remedies. That is, the court never has held that the remedy clause freezes in place common-law remedies. However, just as the legislature cannot deny a remedy entirely for injury to constitutionally protected common-law rights, neither can it substitute an "emasculated remedy" that is incapable of restoring the right that has been injured.

3. *Due Course of Law*

For many years, this court viewed the phrase, "due course of law," as a guarantee of "due process of law," like that contained in the Fourteenth Amendment to the United States Constitution. Justice Linde's concurrence in *Davidson v. Rogers*, 574 P.2d 624 (Ore. 1978), set the stage for a different approach. He wrote:

> "The guarantee in article I, section 10, of a 'remedy by due course of law for injury done [one] in his person, property, or reputation' is part of a section dealing with the administration of justice. It is a plaintiffs' clause, addressed to securing the right to set the machinery of the law in motion to recover for harm already done to one of the stated kinds of interest, a guarantee that dates by way of the original state constitutions of 1776 back to King John's promise in Magna Carta chapter 40: 'To no one will We sell, to no one will We deny or delay, right

or justice.' It is concerned with securing a remedy from those who administer the law, through courts or otherwise."

In 1982, in *Cole v. Dept. of Rev.*, 655 P.2d 171 (Ore. 1982), this court adopted Justice Linde's view that the guarantee of remedy by due course of law is not equivalent to the guarantee of due process of law of the Fourteenth Amendment. Unlike the Due Process Clause in the Fourteenth Amendment, which evaluates the adequacy of the processes provided before government deprives a person of life, liberty or property, the remedy clause guarantees remedy by due course of law for injuries to person, property, or reputation that already have occurred.

Our historical inquiry in this case supports this court's holding in *Cole* that the remedy clause of Article I, section 10, is not a due process clause in the sense that due process is used in the Fourteenth Amendment to the United States Constitution. Nonetheless, the mandate in Article I, section 10, that remedy be by due course of law for injury to person, property, or reputation, expresses a limitation on the exercise of legislative power. It is the duty of courts to evaluate the constitutionality of legislative enactments regarding the availability of remedies for injuries to rights that are protected by the remedy clause.

4. *Injury*

Judge Matthew Deady, who had served as the president of the Oregon Constitutional Convention in 1857, provided the first judicial explanation of the meaning of the term "injury" in the remedy clause:

> "[T]he remedy guarantied by [Article I, section 10,] is not intended for the redress of any novel, indefinite, or remote injury that was not then regarded as within the pale of legal redress. But whatever injury the law, as it then stood, took cognizance of and furnished a remedy for, every man shall continue to have a remedy for by due course of law. * * * If [a] then known and accustomed remedy can be taken away in the face of this constitutional provision, what other may not? Can the legislature, in some spasm of novel opinion, take away every man's remedy for slander, assault and battery, or the recovery of a debt?"

Eastman v. County of Clackamas, 32 F. 24, 32 (D.Or. 1887). The word "then" appears to refer to the time when the drafters wrote the Oregon Constitution. Thus, according to Judge Deady, if there was a common-law cause of action for injury to person, property, or reputation in 1857, then the remedy clause mandates the continued availability of remedy for that injury.

This court adopted Judge Deady's view of injury in *Theiler v. Tillamook County*, 146 P. 828 (Ore. 1915). In 1990, in *Sealey*, this court held that the legislature has authority to determine what constitutes a legally cognizable injury. If it were true that the legislature had authority to declare what rights are protected by the remedy clause, then it would follow that the legislature also had plenary authority to define what constitutes a legally cognizable injury to those rights. However, as we have explained above, the remedy clause protects absolute common-law rights respecting person, property, and reputation that existed when the drafters wrote the constitution. If the legislature constitutionally cannot abolish or alter those rights directly, then it cannot abolish them indirectly by defining narrowly what constitutes an injury to those rights. We disavow the holding in *Sealey* that the legislature constitutionally is authorized to define what constitutes an injury to absolute rights respecting person, property, and reputation that are protected by Article I, section 10.

D. *Summary*

Having analyzed the remedy clause ..., we reach the following conclusions. As one of the provisions of the Oregon Bill of Rights, the remedy clause of Article I, section 10, protects rights respecting person, property, and reputation that, in 1857, the common law regarded as "absolute," that is, that derive from nature or reason rather than solely from membership in civil society. By the seventeenth century, the remedial side of the common law had developed to protect those rights in the event of injury by any other subject of the English realm. The function of common-law causes of action was to restore "justice" or "right" following injury. "Injury" at common law meant any harm or wrong to absolute rights for which a cause of action existed.

Drafters of remedy clauses in state constitutions sought to protect absolute common-law rights by mandating that a remedy always would be available for injury to those rights. The drafters of the Oregon remedy clause identified absolute rights respecting person, property, and reputation as meriting constitutional protection under the remedy clause. As to those rights, the remedy clause provides, in mandatory terms, that remedy by due course of law shall be available to every person in the event of injury. The word "remedy" refers both to a remedial process for seeking redress for injury and to what is required to restore a right that has been injured. Injury, in turn, is a wrong or harm for which a cause of action existed when the drafters wrote the Oregon Constitution in 1857. A common-law cause of action is a constitutionally adequate remedy for seeking redress for injury to protected rights. However, the remedy clause does not freeze in place common-law causes of action that existed when the drafters wrote the Oregon Constitution in 1857. The legislature may abolish a common-law cause of action, so long as it provides a substitute remedial process in the event of injury to the absolute rights that the remedy clause protects. At a minimum, to be remedy by due course of law, the statutory remedy must be available for the same wrongs or harms for which the common-law cause of action existed in 1857. That is, if the common law provided a cause of action for an injury to one of the rights that the remedy clause protects, then a legislatively substituted remedial process must be available for that injury.

It follows from the foregoing that, in analyzing a claim under the remedy clause, the first question is whether the plaintiff has alleged an injury to one of the absolute rights that Article I, section 10 protects. Stated differently, when the drafters wrote the Oregon Constitution in 1857, did the common law of Oregon recognize a cause of action for the alleged injury? If the answer to that question is yes, and if the legislature has abolished the common-law cause of action for injury to rights that are protected by the remedy clause, then the second question is whether it has provided a constitutionally adequate substitute remedy for the common-law cause of action for that injury.

E. *Analysis of This Case*

At the outset, we emphasize that the issue is a narrow one. Plaintiff does not challenge the constitutionality of the workers' compensation system as a whole. Neither does he contend that the "exclusive remedy" provisions of ORS 656.018 (1995) *per se* are unconstitutional. Thus, plaintiff here does not assert that substituting the workers' compensation remedial process for the common-law cause of action by an employee against an employer for negligence violates Article I, section 10.

The narrow issue in this case is whether the exclusive remedy provisions of ORS 656.018 (1995) are unconstitutional under the remedy clause to the extent that there now is a category of workers who have been injured at work but receive no compensation benefits, because they cannot prove that the work-related incident was the *major* contributing cause of their injury or disease. From the perspective of the workers' compensation system, such workers are deemed to have suffered no injury and therefore are not entitled to compensation benefits. At common law, by contrast, injury was understood to be any wrong or harm to person, rights, reputation, or property.

We turn to the facts of this case. Plaintiff contends that he was injured at work, that is, that he suffered a harm to his person in the form of severe and progressive respiratory problems, as well as other physical ailments, after he inhaled sulfuric, hydrochloric, and hydrofluoric acid mist and fumes while working in the pit in defendant's shop. Before his exposure, plaintiff had not experienced any of his symptoms. Because plaintiff was unable to prove that his work exposure was the major contributing cause of his disabling lung condition, however, he did not have a compensable injury under present workers' compensation law. Moreover, as we have explained, under ORS 656.018 (1995), workers' compensation purports to be the exclusive remedy for work-related injuries, whether or not a claim is a compensable claim. Thus, under present workers' compensation law, plaintiff was left with no means for seeking redress for the injuries that he alleges that he suffered at work and for which a common-law cause of action would have been available before the advent of the workers' compensation system.

The first question is whether plaintiff has alleged an injury to one of the rights for which the remedy clause mandates that a remedy be available by due course of law. Plaintiff's complaint alleges that he suffered permanent injury to his lungs and that he suffers other physical ailments, because defendant negligently permitted mist and fumes from sulfuric, hydrochloric, and hydrofluoric acid to drift into the shop area and pit where plaintiff worked, was aware that exposure to them could cause harm to plaintiff, failed to provide plaintiff with proper safety instructions or protection from the chemicals, and failed to warn plaintiff that he would be exposed to the chemicals. To answer the first question, we must decide whether, when the drafters wrote the Oregon Constitution, the common-law of Oregon would have recognized an action for negligence under the circumstances of this case. We conclude that it would.

Our next, more specific, inquiry is whether at common law in Oregon in 1857, an employee would have had a cause of action against an employer for failure to provide a safe workplace and failure to warn of dangerous working conditions to which the employee would be exposed. That is, and unlike most other exercises in constitutional construction, the substantive content of the constitutional right can be established only by identifying the content of the common law in 1857. Although no Oregon cases addressed the common-law rights of employees to bring such negligence actions against their employers in the years immediately surrounding the creation of the Oregon Constitution, the content of the common law in 1857 may be divined from a wide range of sources. Cases from other jurisdictions, as well as Oregon cases decided within a relatively short period after 1857, are instructive.

We conclude that, in 1857, the common law of Oregon would have recognized that a worker had a cause of action for negligence against his employer for failing to provide a safe workplace and failing to warn of the dangerous conditions to which the worker would be exposed at work.

The next question is whether there is a remedial process available to plaintiff for seeking redress for the injuries that he alleges that he suffered to his lungs and other parts of his body when he was exposed to acid mist and fumes at work. As we have explained, when the drafters wrote the Oregon Constitution, plaintiff would have had a negligence cause of action against his employer for his alleged injuries. However, in 1913, the Oregon Legislature adopted the "Workmen's Compensation Act," which … provided, in part:

"Every workman subject to this Act * * * who, * * * while so employed sustains personal injury by accident arising out of and in the course of his employment and resulting in his disability * * * shall be entitled to receive from the Industrial Accident Fund hereby created the sum or sums hereinafter specified and the right to receive such sum or sums shall be in lieu of all claims against his employer on account of such injury or death except as hereinafter specifically provided * * *."

When the workers' compensation program was adopted, and for almost 70 years thereafter, the statutory scheme provided that a work-related injury was a "compensable injury" if the worker could show, as a plaintiff had been required to show at common law, that the work-related incident was a contributing cause of the injury. Moreover, this court held that the word "injury" in the workers' compensation statutes was to be given "broad and liberal construction in view of the remedial and humanitarian purposes of the [Workers'] Compensation Law."

Under current workers' compensation law, an occupational disease generally is considered to be an injury. However, as we have explained, workers' compensation law now provides that occupational diseases and some injuries are "compensable" injuries only if the worker can prove that the work-related incident was the major contributing cause of the disease or injury. The major contributing cause standard means a cause, or combination of causes, that contributes more to the injury for which the worker seeks compensation than all other causes combined, or most of the cause. The major contributing cause standard did not exist at common law. Thus, for those workers' compensation claims that are subject to the major contributing cause standard, workers' compensation law does not provide compensation for a work-related incident that was only a contributing cause of the workers's injury. Therefore, workers' compensation law no longer provides a remedy for some wrongs or harms occurring in the workplace for which a common-law negligence cause of action had existed when the drafters wrote the Oregon Constitution in 1857. Nevertheless, under ORS 656.018 (1995), workers' compensation law purports to be the exclusive remedy for work-related injuries, whether or not a claim is compensable.

Based on our analysis of the remedy clause of Article I, section 10, we conclude that determining whether the exclusive remedy provisions of ORS 656.018 (1995) violate that clause involves a case-by-case analysis. The first inquiry is whether a workers' compensation claim alleges an injury to an "absolute" common-law right that the remedy clause protects. If it does, and the claim is accepted and the worker receives the benefits provided by the workers' compensation statutes, then the worker cannot complain that he or she has been deprived of a remedial process for seeking redress for injury to a right that the remedy clause protects. Neither can the worker complain that he or she has been deprived of a remedial process if a compensation claim is denied because the worker is unable to prove that the work-related incident was a contributing cause of the alleged injury, which is what a plaintiff would have had to prove in a common-law cause of action for negligence. However, if a workers' compensation claim for an alleged injury to a right that is protected by the remedy clause is denied because the worker has failed to prove that the work-related incident was the major, rather than merely a contributing, cause of the injury, then the exclusive remedy provisions of ORS 656.018 (1995) are unconstitutional under the remedy clause, because they leave the worker with no process through which to seek redress for an injury for which a cause of action existed at common law.

In this case, as noted, plaintiff alleges that he suffered injuries to his lungs and other ailments when he was exposed to sulfuric, hydrochloric, and hydrofluoric acid mist and fumes at work. As we have explained, for those injuries, he would have had a common-law cause of action when the drafters wrote the Oregon Constitution in 1857. However, plaintiff followed the procedures prescribed by Oregon statutes and first filed a workers' compensation claim. The ALJ held that plaintiff had not suffered a compensable injury because, although the work exposure might have contributed to his injuries, plaintiff could not prove that the work exposure was the major contributing cause of his injuries.

As we have explained, plaintiff believed that he had suffered *an* injury at work, albeit not a *compensable* injury as defined under present workers' compensation law. Therefore, after his workers' compensation claim was denied, plaintiff filed this action to seek redress for his injuries. For the reasons that we have explained, the remedy clause mandates that a remedy be available to all persons-including workers-for injuries to "absolute" common-law rights for which a cause of action existed when the drafters wrote the Oregon Constitution in 1857. Having alleged an injury of the kind that the remedy clause protects, and having demonstrated that there was no remedial process available under present workers' compensation laws, plaintiff should have been allowed to proceed with his negligence action.

The judgment of the circuit court is reversed, and the case is remanded to that court for further proceedings.

ARBINO v. JOHNSON & JOHNSON
880 N.E.2d 420 (Ohio 2007)

MOYER, C.J.

I. Introduction

Petitioner Melisa Arbino initiated a products-liability action against respondents Johnson & Johnson, Ortho-McNeil Pharmaceutical, Inc., and Johnson & Johnson Pharmaceutical Research & Development, L.L.C. (collectively, "Johnson & Johnson") in 2006. She alleges that she suffered blood clots and other serious medical side effects from using the Ortho Evra Birth Control Patch, a hormonal birth-control medication that Johnson & Johnson created.

The case was filed in the United States District Court for the Southern District of Ohio. Arbino's complaint contains challenges to the constitutionality of four tort-reform statutes…[The District Court] certified four questions of state law for review.

II. Tort Reform in Ohio and Stare Decisis

Before engaging in a specific analysis of these issues, it is necessary to briefly review the major tort-reform laws enacted by the General Assembly in recent history. Doing so provides the proper context for our decision and frames the necessary discussion of stare decisis.

Since 1975, the General Assembly has adopted several so-called tort-reform acts, which were inevitably reviewed by this court. In the course of this review, we have examined several specific provisions that are similar in language and purpose to those at issue here; all of these similar statutes have been declared unconstitutional.

The first reform provision we reviewed was former R.C. 2307.43, which was passed in the Ohio Medical Malpractice Act of 1975. This statute placed a $200,000 cap on general medical-malpractice damages not involving death, with no exceptions for those suffering severe injuries. The General Assembly passed this legislation to combat a perceived malpractice-insurance crisis. Although it took several years for a challenge to be raised, we ultimately held that R.C. 2307.43 violated the due-process protections of the Ohio Constitution.

The General Assembly's next major enactment was the Tort Reform Act of 1987, which sought to change civil-justice and insurance law to alleviate another "insurance crisis." In *Sorrell v. Thevenir* (1994), 69 Ohio St.3d 415, 419-420, we examined one facet of this law, R.C. 2317.45, which placed a significant limitation on the collateral-source rule adopted in *Pryor v. Webber* (1970), 23 Ohio St.2d 104. The H.B. 1 version of R.C. 2317.45 required the trial court to subtract certain collateral benefits from a plaintiff's final award of compensatory damages. We held that this mandatory deduction of collateral benefits violated the right to a jury trial, due process, equal protection, and the right to a remedy.

In *Galayda v. Lake Hosp. Sys., Inc.* (1994), 71 Ohio St.3d 421, we reviewed…another tort-reform statute. This statute required trial courts to order awards of future damages in excess of $200,000 in medical-malpractice actions to be paid in a series of periodic payments upon the motion of any party. We deemed that statute unconstitutional as a violation of the right to a jury trial and of the Due Process Clause of the Ohio Constitution.

In *Zoppo v. Homestead Ins. Co.* (1994), 71 Ohio St.3d 552,…we examined [a] statute [that] required a trial judge to determine the amount of punitive damages to be awarded in a tort action, even when the trier of fact was a jury. We struck this section as a violation of the right to a jury trial in the Ohio Constitution.

Finally, the General Assembly passed substantial reforms in 1997. Among other things, it modified the collateral-source rule in tort actions to require the trier of fact to consider but not automatically set off collateral benefits, capped punitive damages and allowed the trier of fact to determine damages up to the cap in tort and products-liability claims, and capped noneconomic damages at different levels, with higher limits for permanent injuries.

The protracted interbranch tension on this subject establishes at least two key points. First, tort reform has been a major issue of concern in this state over the past several decades and remains one today. Ohio is hardly unique in this regard, as such reforms have been raised in nearly every state in the nation. State legislatures and judiciaries have differed widely in their responses to this issue, and a definite split in authority is clear. The federal judiciary has been drawn to the issue as well, with the United States Supreme Court offering guidance on several key issues over the past few years, most notably regarding punitive-damages awards.

A fundamental principle of the constitutional separation of powers among the three branches of government is that the legislative branch is "the ultimate arbiter of public policy." It necessarily follows that the legislature has the power to continually create and refine the laws to meet the needs of the citizens of Ohio. The fact that the General Assembly has repeatedly sought to reform some aspects of the civil tort system for over 30 years demonstrates the continuing prominence of this issue.

Second, even considering the numerous opinions by this court on this issue, the basic constitutionality of tort-reform statutes is hardly settled law. Our prior review has focused on certain unconstitutional facets of the prior tort-reform laws that can be addressed to create constitutionally valid legislation. We have not dismissed all tort reform as an unconstitutional concept.

III. Standard of Review

A. Limits on Noneconomic Damages in R.C. 2315.18

The first certified question concerns the constitutionality of R..C. 2315.18. The statute provides a basic procedure for the imposition of damages in certain tort actions. After a verdict has been reached for the plaintiff in one of the specified tort actions, the court (in a bench trial) will enter findings of fact or the jury (in a jury trial) will return a general verdict accompanied by answers to interrogatories. [T]hese findings or interrogatories will specify both the total compensatory damages recoverable by the plaintiff and the portions of those damages representing economic and noneconomic losses.

Thereafter, the court must enter judgment for the plaintiff for the amount of economic damages, without limitation. For noneconomic damages, the court must limit recovery to the greater of (1) $250,000 or (2) three times the economic damages up to a maximum of $350,000, or $500,000 per single occurrence. [T]hese limits on noneconomic damages do not apply if the plaintiff suffered "[p]ermanent and substantial physical deformity, loss of use of a limb, or loss of a bodily organ system," or "[p]ermanent physical functional injury that permanently prevents the injured person from being able to independently care for self and perform life-sustaining activities."

2.   Open Courts and Right to a Remedy

Arbino…argues that R.C. 2315.18 violates Ohio's "open courts" and "right to a remedy" provisions. The Constitution provides: "*All courts shall be open*, and every person, for an injury done him in his land, goods, person, or reputation, *shall have remedy* by due course of law, and shall have justice administered without denial or delay." (Emphasis added.) Section 16, Article I, Ohio Constitution.

The definition of these rights is well settled. "When the Constitution speaks of remedy and injury to person, property, or reputation, it requires an opportunity granted at a meaningful time and in a meaningful manner." We have interpreted this provision to prohibit statutes that effectively prevent individuals from pursuing relief for their injuries.

A statute need not "completely abolish the right to open courts" to run afoul of this section. Any enactment that eliminates an individual's right to a judgment or to a verdict properly rendered in a suit will also be unconstitutional. Thus, we struck down the statute in *Sorrell* under circumstances "where the collateral source benefits reduce *the entire jury award*." When an individual is wholly foreclosed from relief after a verdict is rendered in his or her favor, the rights to "a meaningful remedy and open courts become hollow rights hardly worth exercising."

Arbino states that R.C. 2315.18 violates this provision because it "denies *any* recovery for noneconomic damages for the increment of harm greater than $250,000." We disagree.

Although R.C. 2315.18 does limit certain types of noneconomic damages, those limits do not wholly deny persons a remedy for their injuries. Injured persons not suffering the catastrophic injuries (for which there are no damages limits) may still recover their full economic damages and up to $350,000 in noneconomic damages, as well as punitive damages. These available remedies are "meaningful" ones under the Constitution. While the statute prevents some plaintiffs from obtaining the same dollar figures they may have received prior to the effective date of the statute, it neither forecloses their ability to pursue a claim at all nor "completely obliterates the entire jury award." Therefore, R.C. 2315.18 does not violate the right to a remedy or the right to an open court under Section 16, Article I of the Ohio Constitution.

C. Punitive-Damages Limits in R.C. 2315.21

The third certified question concerns the constitutionality of R.C. 2315.21, which limits the recovery of punitive damages in certain tort actions. The S.B. 80 amendments to this section included a procedure for bifurcation of proceedings for compensatory and punitive damages and a limitation on the amount of punitive damages recoverable in tort actions. Arbino has not challenged the bifurcation process, instead focusing her attack on the punitive-damages limitations.

The statute limits punitive damages in tort actions to a maximum of two times the total amount of compensatory damages awarded to a plaintiff per defendant. However, these limitations do not apply if the defendant committed a felony in causing the injury, one of the elements of the felony is that it was committed purposely or knowingly, and the defendant was convicted of or pleaded guilty to the felony.

If the limitations do apply, punitive damages may be limited further if the defendant is a "small employer" or an individual. In that case, the punitive damages may not exceed "the lesser of two times the amount of the compensatory damages awarded to the plaintiff from the defendant or ten percent of the employer's or individual's net worth when the tort was committed, up to a maximum of three hundred fifty thousand dollars."

Additionally, punitive damages may not be awarded more than once against the same defendant for the same act or course of conduct once the maximum amount of damages has been reached. However, this restriction can be overcome if the plaintiff offers new and substantial evidence of previously undiscovered behaviors for which punitive damages are appropriate or the prior awards against the defendant were "totally insufficient" to punish the defendant.

2. Right to a Remedy and Right to an Open Court

Arbino also argues that R.C. 2315.21 violates the right to a remedy in an open court. This right protects against laws that completely foreclose a cause of action for injured plaintiffs or otherwise eliminate the ability to receive a meaningful remedy.

Like the noneconomic-damages limits, the punitive-damages limits...do not deny plaintiffs the right to seek a remedy for their tort claims. Further, they do not eliminate the ability to seek a "meaningful" remedy for their injuries, primarily because punitive damages "are not compensation for injury. Instead, they are private fines levied by civil juries to punish reprehensible conduct and to deter its future occurrence."

Because punitive damages are separate and apart from any remedy for a plaintiff's injuries, and because [the statute] does not prevent potential plaintiffs from bringing a successful cause of action for their injuries, it does not violate Section 16, Article I of the Ohio Constitution.

IV. Conclusion

The decision in this case affirms the General Assembly's efforts over the last several decades to enact meaningful tort reforms. It also places Ohio firmly with the growing number of states that have found such reforms to be constitutional.[2] However, the issue remains a contentious one across the nation, with several states finding such statutes unconstitutional.[3]

We appreciate the policy concerns Arbino and her amici have raised. However, the General Assembly is responsible for weighing those concerns and making policy decisions; we are charged with evaluating the constitutionality of their choices. Issues such as the wisdom of damages limitations and whether the specific dollar amounts available under them best serve the public interest are not for us to decide.

---

[2] [8] {¶ a} As of the date of this opinion, courts have upheld limits on noneconomic damages in at least 19 other jurisdictions. {¶ b} At least ten states have upheld limitations on punitive damages, including provisions requiring that a certain percentage of awards be allotted to a designated public fund.

[3] [9] Among those finding such attempts at reform unconstitutional are Illinois; New Hampshire; North Dakota; South Dakota; and Wisconsin.

RUTHER v. KAISER
983 N.E.2d 291 (Ohio 2012)

LANZINGER, J.

I. Background

{¶ 2} R.C. 2305.113(C) sets a four-year statute of repose for medical-malpractice claims. Except for minors or those of unsound mind, a person must file a medical claim no later than four years after the alleged act of malpractice occurs or the claim will be barred. Limited exceptions also exist for malpractice discovered during the fourth year after treatment and for malpractice that leaves a foreign object in a patient's body. R.C. 2305.113(D)(1) and (2). Those exceptions allow one additional year after discovery of an injury to file suit.

{¶ 3} This case involves a medical-malpractice claim filed well after the statute of repose set forth in R.C. 2305.113(C), and no statutory exception applies. Timothy Ruther developed abdominal pains that led to a diagnosis of a liver lesion and hepatitis C in December 2008.

{¶ 4} Around this time, Timothy Ruther's wife, appellee Tracy Ruther reviewed medical records detailing appellant Dr. George Kaiser's care of her husband. These records showed elevated liver-enzyme levels in July 1995, May 1997, and October 1998. Although the parties contest the length of time Mr. Ruther received treatment at Dr. Kaiser's practice, appellant Warren County Family Practice Physicians, Inc., it is not disputed that Dr. Kaiser stopped treating Mr. Ruther years before he complained of abdominal pain.

{¶ 5} In May 2009, the Ruthers sued Dr. Kaiser and Warren County Family Practice Physicians, Inc., for medical malpractice. The Ruthers claimed that Dr. Kaiser had failed "to properly assess, evaluate and respond to abnormal laboratory results including, but not limited to, very high liver enzymes." Mr. Ruther died while the case was pending. Mrs. Ruther then amended the complaint to add a claim for wrongful death and sought a declaratory judgment that R.C. 2305.113(C), as applied to her husband, violates the United States and Ohio constitutions.

{¶ 6} Dr. Kaiser and the medical practice moved for summary judgment, asserting that the statute of repose found in R.C. 2305.113(C) barred the amended complaint, having been brought more than ten years after the alleged act of malpractice. The trial court, however, denied the motion, concluding that applying the statute of repose in this case would violate the Ohio Constitution, Article 16, Section 1.

{¶ 7} The Twelfth District Court of Appeals affirmed the trial court's denial of summary judgment. Like the trial court, the appellate court concluded that the statute, as applied to Mrs. Ruther's medical-malpractice claim, "bars her claim after it had already vested, but before she or the decedent knew or reasonably could have known about the claim[,] [thereby constituting] a violation of the right-to-a-remedy provision of Section 16, Article I of the Ohio Constitution."

{¶ 8} We granted Dr. Kaiser's request for discretionary review. The sole proposition of law reads: "The medical malpractice statute contained in O.R.C. § 2305.113(C) does not violate the open courts provision (Section 16, Article I) and is therefore constitutional."

II. Analysis

1. Right to Remedy

{¶ 10} The constitutional provision at issue in this case, Ohio Constitution, Article I, Section 16, guarantees that "[a]ll courts shall be open, and every person, for an injury done him in his land, goods, person, or reputation, shall have remedy by due course of law, and shall have justice administered without denial or delay." This one provision contains many important constitutional principles—"open courts," "right to remedy," and "due course of law."

{¶ 12} A plain reading of Article I, Section 16 reveals that it does not provide for remedies without limitation or for any perceived injury. Rather, the right-to-remedy clause provides that the court shall be open for those to seek remedy "by *due course of law*." (Emphasis added.) Article I, Section 16 does not prevent the General Assembly from defining a cause of action.

{¶ 13} We have previously stated that the right-to-remedy provision applies only to existing, vested rights and that the legislature determines what injuries are recognized and what remedies are available. "No one has a vested right in rules of the common law. * * * The great office of statutes is to remedy defects in the common law as they are developed, and to adapt it to new circumstances."

{¶ 14} Thus, the General Assembly has the right to determine what causes of action the law will recognize and to alter the common law by abolishing the action, by defining the action, or by placing a time limit after which an injury is no longer a legal injury.

{¶ 15} The question remains whether R.C. 2305.113(C) is a valid exercise of the General Assembly's authority to define or limit a cause of action.

2. No Extinguishment of Vested Right

{¶ 16} The Twelfth District Court of Appeals declared R.C. 2305.11(C) unconstitutional as applied, reasoning that the statute extinguishes the right to remedy for a vested claim, relying in a large part on *Hardy*. The error in *Hardy*, repeated by the appellate court, is that there is no actual examination of when a medical-malpractice claim vests. *Hardy* mistakenly appears to conclude that a medical-malpractice claim arises (becomes "actionable") immediately upon the breach of the standard of care—i.e., the negligent act or omission. And yet a cause of action for negligence does not arise until there is "the existence of a duty, a breach of that duty and injury resulting proximately therefrom."

{¶ 17}   To be actionable, then, the claim for medical negligence requires an injury. We have clearly stated that it is when a patient discovers or in the exercise of reasonable care and diligence should have discovered the resulting injury that a cause of action for medical malpractice accrues, or, in other words, vests. If indeed an action immediately accrues upon a negligent act or omission, then the one-year statute of limitations for filing all medical-malpractice claims would begin to run immediately.

{¶ 18}   But the General Assembly recognized in R.C. 2305.113 that in some cases, an injury may not manifest itself within one year of a breach of a duty of care and so has provided the general discovery period of four years. Within that boundary, when the patient discovers or should have discovered the injury, or when the relationship with the doctor terminates, whichever is later, the one-year statute of limitations begins to run. R.C. 2305.113(C) does not bar a vested cause of action, but prevents a cause of action from vesting more than four years after the breach of the duty of care. Therefore, it is a true statute of repose.

3. Rational Basis for R.C. 2305.113(C)

{¶ 19}   Many policy reasons support this legislation. Just as a plaintiff is entitled to a meaningful time and opportunity to pursue a claim, a defendant is entitled to a reasonable time after which he or she can be assured that a defense will not have to be mounted for actions occurring years before. The statute of repose exists to give medical providers certainty with respect to the time within which a claim can be brought and a time after which they may be free from the fear of litigation.

{¶ 20}   Forcing medical providers to defend against medical claims that occurred 10, 20, or 50 years before presents a host of litigation concerns, including the risk that evidence is unavailable through the death or unknown whereabouts of witnesses, the possibility that pertinent documents were not retained, the likelihood that evidence would be untrustworthy due to faded memories, the potential that technology may have changed to create a different and more stringent standard of care not applicable to the earlier time, the risk that the medical providers' financial circumstances may have changed—i.e., that practitioners have retired and no longer carry liability insurance, the possibility that a practitioner's insurer has become insolvent, and the risk that the institutional medical provider may have closed.

{¶ 21} Responding to these concerns, the General Assembly made a policy decision to grant Ohio medical providers the right to be free from litigation based on alleged acts of medical negligence occurring outside a specified time period. This decision is embodied in Ohio's four-year statute of repose for medical negligence, set forth in R.C. 2305.113(C). The statute establishes a period beyond which medical claims may not be brought even if the injury giving rise to the claim does not accrue because it is undiscovered until after the period has ended.

C. Upholding the Statute of Repose Is Consistent with the Majority View

{¶ 32} The Supreme Court of Wisconsin faced a similar right-to-remedy challenge to its statute of repose. The medical claim involved a child whose congenital condition that later caused blindness was discovered sometime after her tenth birthday. A lawsuit on her behalf was filed three years later against the doctor who had treated her as a newborn. The Wisconsin statutes of limitations and repose granted one year from discovery to file suit, as long as five years had not passed since the act or omission that was the basis of the claim, or until the minor's tenth birthday. The court recognized that some claims would be foreclosed before a plaintiff had an opportunity to know that an injury occurred, stating:

> [T]he legislature may sever a person's claim by a statute of limitations or a statute of repose when the person has had no possibility of discovering the injury—when the person has been blameless in every respect. These decisions represent judicial deference to the stated policy of the legislature. Protecting the interests of those who must defend claims based on old acts or omissions is a policy concern that legislative bodies have weighed for centuries.

The court concluded:

> We find [the statutes of limitations and repose] constitutional, despite the harsh results they yield in this case. We hold that [the statutes] do not violate the right-to-remedy clause because a prospective claimant does not have a legislative right to pursue a medical malpractice action if the injury is discovered after the statutory time limitation period elapses.

{¶ 33} Thirty-two states have such statutes in existence. *See* Robin Miller, Validity of Medical Malpractice Statutes of Repose, 5 A.L.R.6th 133 (2011). And of that number, at least 16 statutes of repose have been upheld as constitutional against challenges similar to that of the open-courts or right-to-remedy provisions.

III. Conclusion

{¶ 35} A plaintiff like Mrs. Ruther, whose cause of action for medical malpractice does not accrue until after the statute of repose has expired pursuant to R.C. 2305.113(C), is not deprived of a vested right. Because R.C. 2305.113(C) is a valid exercise of the General Assembly's authority to limit a cause of action, Mrs. Ruther failed to present clear and convincing evidence that the statute is unconstitutional as applied to her claim. We therefore hold that the medical-malpractice statute of repose found in R.C. 2305.113(C) does not extinguish a vested right and thus does not violate the Ohio Constitution, Article I, Section 16.

PFEIFER, J., dissenting.

{¶ 40} Early in law school, every student is introduced to the rich historical tradition and critical importance of the common law in our nation's development. Today, American judges and attorneys are invited to assist both developed and developing countries in applying our common-law traditions, which date back centuries in England, to their efforts in empowering their courts to protect basic and constitutional human rights without interference from political leaders and legislative bodies or their military establishment. The power of every citizen in the United States to seek redress in our open courts for injury done, be it by our government, another citizen, or a large corporation, is a source of some amazement and great envy in many parts of the world. That the resulting decisions by judges and juries are respected and enforced without police or military intervention is incomprehensible in some quarters. Protecting our citizens' individual fundamental constitutional rights from attack by the government is the proud duty of the American judiciary and a part of our oath.

{¶ 42} The sweeping language employed by the majority in this case is the crescendo in our court's decade-long deference to, and acceptance of, the General Assembly's assault on our citizens' right to remedy set forth, without alteration, for over two centuries in the Ohio Constitution.

{¶ 43}   When is a fundamental right, contained in the Ohio Constitution and Bill of Rights since 1802, no longer the individual right of an Ohio citizen? According to this court, whenever the Ohio General Assembly chooses to extinguish the right, it will no longer exist, period. The majority writes:

> A plain reading of Article I Section 16 reveals that it does not provide for remedies without limitation or for any perceived injury. Rather, the right-to-remedy clause provides that the court shall be open for those to seek remedy "by *due course of law*." (Emphasis added.) Article I, Section 16 does not prevent the General Assembly from defining a cause of action.

In case the reader did not understand the breadth of the majority's devastating proclamation, it continues: "Thus, the General Assembly has the right to determine what causes of action the law will recognize and to alter the common law by abolishing the action, by defining the action, or by placing a time limit after which an injury is no longer a legal injury."

{¶ 44}   Under *Ruther*, we now fully abdicate our solemn duty to enforce and protect constitutional rights afforded citizens since the beginning of statehood. If the General Assembly abolishes a remedy, including those recognized at common law when the constitution was written, it is now clearly within its power. We will afford "great deference" in presuming constitutionality of any act of the General Assembly limiting or abolishing a cause of action.

{¶ 45}   Continued erosion of the venerable right of every citizen to a remedy in open court for injury done will inevitably flow from the General Assembly. It may come in small drips or in tidal waves, but it will come. The economic interests pushing limitations on causes of action are just too powerful and too seductive for the General Assembly to resist. We have now removed the Assembly's only dam against the onslaught: this court's previous vigorous enforcement of the "right to remedy" constitutional protections.

{¶ 46}   When Timothy and Tracy Ruther sought a remedy in open court for injuries suffered because of a doctor's failure to properly respond to three elevated liver-enzyme tests taken more than a decade before Timothy developed a fatal liver lesion and hepatitis C, they could never have envisioned the damage their case would ultimately cause for generations of Ohioans yet to be injured. Their personal tragedy has evolved into a undiscovered nightmare for legions of Ohioans who will find the courthouse doors barred for the presentation of their future legitimate injury claims.

McINTOSH v. MELROE CO.
729 N.E.2d 972 (Ind. 2000)

BOEHM, J.

This case deals with the validity of the provision in the Product Liability Act that bars product liability claims for injuries sustained more than ten years after the product is delivered to its "initial user or consumer." The plaintiffs argue that this provision violates their constitutional right under Article I, Section 12 of the Indiana Constitution to a remedy by due course of law.

FACTUAL AND PROCEDURAL BACKGROUND

On June 9, 1993, James McIntosh was injured in an accident involving a Clark Bobcat skid steer loader manufactured by Melroe. McIntosh and his wife filed suit alleging that his injuries and her resulting loss of companionship were caused by a defect in the loader. Melroe responded with a motion for summary judgment based on the ten-year statute of repose, Indiana Code § 34-20-3-1(b). That section provides that "a product liability action must be commenced...within ten (10) years after the delivery of the product to the initial user or consumer." Melroe designated evidence establishing that the loader had been delivered to its initial user on September 9, 1980, almost thirteen years before the accident. The McIntoshes did not dispute this evidence, but replied that the statute of repose violated their rights under Article I, Sections 12...of the Indiana Constitution.

I. Article I, Section 12

Article I, Section 12 of the Indiana Constitution provides, in relevant part: "All courts shall be open; and every person, for injury done to him in his person, property, or reputation, shall have remedy by due course of law." The McIntoshes argue that the statute of repose violates Section 12 because it "abrogates all of the tort protections provided by common law," and these are claimed to be guaranteed by the "due course of law" provision of Section 12.

Melroe contends that this case is governed by our decision in *Dague v. Piper Aircraft Corp.*, 418 N.E.2d 207, 213 (Ind. 1981), which held that the statute of repose does not violate Section 12. The McIntoshes assert that *Dague* addressed only the provision in Section 12 that "all courts shall be open" and did not deal with the provision that "every person, for injury done to him in his person...shall have remedy by due course of law."

A. Methodology

We agree with the dissent that the various frequently invoked constitutional talismans—constitutional text, history of the times, intent of the framers, etc.—are proper keys to the interpretation of Article I, Section 12. But apart from the text itself, precedents of this Court, and precedents from other states with similar provisions, we find no relevant guideposts on this point. In particular, there appears to be no unique Indiana history surrounding the adoption of this Clause in 1816 or its redrafting in 1851.

B. The Branches of Federal Due Process and State Article I, Section 12 Doctrine

By 1986, this Court could correctly observe that there was a "substantial line of cases treating the 'due process' clause of the federal constitution and the 'due course' clause of the Indiana Constitution as interchangeable." The two constitutional provisions do share certain commonalities. Both prohibit state action that deprives a person of a protectable interest without a fair proceeding. Both also require, as a threshold matter, that the claimant have a "protectable interest."

This is not to say, however, that the "open courts" or "remedies" clause of Article I, Section 12 is in all applications to be equated with the due process provisions of the Fifth and Fourteenth Amendments. In broad brush, the federal provisions guarantee procedural and substantive due process rights. Procedural rights ensure, for example, that a party will be given "the opportunity to be heard 'at a meaningful time and in a meaningful manner.'" *Mathews v. Eldridge*, 424 U.S. 319, 333 (1976). Procedural rights are found in both the civil context, where due process imposes requirements of notice, a right to a hearing, etc., as well as the criminal context, where it is the source of an array of criminal procedural rights, either directly through the Due Process Clause of the Fifth Amendment or via the Due Process Clause of the Fourteenth Amendment.

The "substantive" due process strain declares some actions so outlandish that they cannot be accomplished by any procedure. In earlier times, this took the form of preservation of property and contractual rights. It reached a highwater mark in cases invalidating progressive era and New Deal legislation, most notably the now discredited *Lochner v. New York*, 198 U.S. 45 (1905), which struck down a state law limiting the work week to sixty hours. This doctrine remains today as a constitutional bar to actions that "shock the conscience," *see County of Sacramento v. Lewis*, 523 U.S. 833, 846 (1998), despite the recognition that "guideposts for responsible decisionmaking in this uncharted area are scarce and open-ended." *Collins v. City of Harker Heights*, 503 U.S. 115, 125 (1992).

Article I, Section 12 of our State Constitution also has multiple strains, but they are not the same as the federal pair. [T]he remedies clause prescribes procedural fairness. It guarantees a "remedy by due course of law" for injuries to "person, property, or reputation." Section 12 also differs from the due process clauses by providing that the courts "shall be open," a requirement that seems meaningful only to civil litigants.

In the context of a procedural right to "remedy by due course of law" in a civil proceeding, the Indiana Constitution has developed a body of law essentially identical to federal due process doctrine. [T]here also is a strain of Article I, Section 12 doctrine that is analogous to federal substantive due process. As elaborated below, in general this doctrine imposes the requirement that legislation interfering with a right bear a rational relationship to a legitimate legislative goal, but does not preserve any particular remedy from legislative repeal.

To presage and capsulize our conclusions under these differing lines of Section 12 doctrine, the Product Liability Act statute of repose is consistent with each. In terms of pure civil procedural due process analysis, there is no issue. The bar of the statute of repose in the Product Liability Act does not purport to regulate the procedure in the courts. Nor is the open courts requirement violated because, as *Dague* held, it remains the province of the General Assembly to identify legally cognizable claims for relief. If the law provides no remedy, denying a remedy is consistent with due course of law. Finally, there is no state constitutional "substantive" due course of law violation because this legislation has been held to be, and we again hold it to be, rationally related to a legitimate legislative objective. It is debatable whether the Product Liability Act eliminated a common law remedy, but even if it did, there is no substantive constitutional requirement that bars a statute from accomplishing that.

C. The Constitution Did Not Freeze the Common Law

The McIntoshes argue that they have a constitutional right to a remedy for their injuries because the framers of the 1851 Constitution "decided not to give the General Assembly broad powers to abolish the common law." From this they suggest that they have a protectable constitutional right to the remedy provided by the common law for product liability injuries. This amounts to a claim that common law remedies may not be abolished. It is fundamentally a claim that these remedies constitute a protected species similar to the rights thought embedded in the constitution by substantive due process. Although *Dague* did not address this contention in the context of upholding the Product Liability Act's statute of repose, precedent strongly rejects it. This Court has long recognized the ability of the General Assembly to modify or abrogate the common law. "Indiana courts have uniformly held that in cases involving injury to person or property, Article I, § 12 does not prevent the legislature from modifying or restricting common law rights and remedies." In sum, the courts of this State, like those of most others, "generally agree that the constitutional assurance of a remedy for injury does not create any new substantive rights to recover for particular harms. Rather, the clause promises that, for injuries recognized elsewhere in the law, the courts will be open for meaningful redress." Jennifer Friesen, *State Constitutional Law* § 6-2(c) (2d ed. 1996).

Although there is a significant split in other states as to whether provisions similar to our "remedy by due course" provision permit the legislature to impose a statute of repose in product liability cases, we agree with the Supreme Court of Oregon that "[t]he legislature has the authority to determine what constitutes a legally cognizable injury." Indeed, we believe that there is a very powerful reason that the General Assembly must have the authority to determine what injuries are legally cognizable, i.e., which injuries are wrongs for which there is a legal remedy. A contrary view implies a static common law that is inconsistent with the evolution of legal doctrine before and after 1851. Perhaps equally important, if we are to find some remedies chiseled in constitutional stone, we wander into the area of "scarce and open-ended" guideposts for identifying which remedies are of constitutional dimension, and which are not.

We have long held that the General Assembly has the authority to modify the common law and that there is no "fundamental right" to bring a particular cause of action to remedy an asserted wrong. Rather, because individuals have "no vested or property right in any rule of common law," the General Assembly can make substantial changes to the existing law without infringing on citizen rights. Because no citizen has a protectable interest in the state of product liability law as it existed before the Product Liability Act, the General Assembly's abrogation of the common law of product liability through the statute of repose does not run afoul of the "substantive" due course of law provision of Article I, Section 12.

D. If "Due Course of Law" Provides No Remedy, None Is Required by the Constitution

In this case, the General Assembly has determined that injuries occurring ten years after the product was delivered to a user are not legally cognizable claims for relief. Accordingly, the McIntoshes are not entitled to a "remedy" under Section 12. Thus, the statute of repose "'does not bar a cause of action; its effect, rather, is to prevent what might otherwise be a cause of action from ever arising.... The injured party literally has *no* cause of action. The harm that has been done is *damnum absque injuria*— a wrong for which the law affords no redress.'"

Although the state constitution requires courts to be open to provide remedy by due course of law, legislation by rational classification to abolish a remedy is consonant with due course of law. If the law provides no remedy, Section 12 does not require...one.

Finally, the dissent concludes that Article I, Section 12 guarantees to each citizen "a substantive right to remedy for injuries suffered." We think this confuses "injury" with "wrong." There is not and never has been a right to redress for every injury, as victims of natural disasters or faultless accidents can attest. Nor is there any constitutional right to any particular remedy. Indeed, as we have pointed out, some forms of "wrong" recognized at common law have long since been abolished by the legislature without conflict with the Indiana Constitution. Ironically, the wrong the dissent contends in this case to be preserved by the constitution against legislative interference, strict liability for product flaws, did not exist in 1851; it was adopted as part of the Product Liability Act in 1978. It is true, as the dissent notes, that the concept of strict liability did not originate with the Product Liability Act. Although strict liability did not exist in 1851, by the 1970s, it had become a recognized theory of recovery. This further underscores the point that the common law was not frozen in 1851 and is not chiseled in stone today.

E. The Statute Is A Rational Means of Achieving a Legitimate Legislative Goal

Although we reject the McIntoshes' [challenge], the legislature's authority is not without limits. Section 12 requires that legislation that deprives a person of a complete tort remedy must be a rational means to achieve a legitimate legislative goal. [W]e also [have held] that, as applied to the individual case, the limitation must not be an unreasonable impediment to the exercise of an otherwise valid claim.

The Product Liability Act meets both tests. The statute of repose represents a determination by the General Assembly that an injury occurring ten years after the product has been in use is not a legally cognizable "injury" that is to be remedied by the courts. This decision was based on its apparent conclusion that after a decade of use, product failures are "due to reasons not fairly laid at the manufacturer's door." The statute also serves the public policy concerns of reliability and availability of evidence after long periods of time, and the ability of manufacturers to plan their affairs without the potential for unknown liability. It provides certainty and finality with a bright line bar to liability ten years after a product's first use. It is also rationally related to the General Assembly's reasonable determination that, in the vast majority of cases, failure of products over ten years old is due to wear and tear or other causes not the fault of the manufacturer, and the substantial interests already identified warrant establishing a bright line after which no claim is created.

In sum, the McIntoshes do not have a vested interest in the state of the common law as it existed before the Product Liability Act was passed. The General Assembly has made the permissible legislative choice to limit product liability actions to the first ten years of a product's use. Accordingly, the McIntoshes' injuries, which occurred after the ten-year statute of repose ended, were not legally cognizable injuries for which a remedy exists and the statute of repose does not violate Section 12.

DICKSON, J., dissenting.

This case presented us with an opportunity to restore to Indiana's jurisprudence important principles of our state constitution. By doing so, we could have vividly exemplified the Rule of Law notwithstanding the allure of pragmatic commercial interests. We should hold that the ten-year statute of repose provision in the Indiana Products Liability Act violates [] the Right to Remedy Clause[] of the Indiana Constitution.

Right to Remedy Clause

Within the Bill of Rights of the Indiana Constitution, Section 12 provides in relevant part: All courts shall be open; and every person, for injury done to him in his person, property, or reputation, shall have remedy by due course of law.[4] The majority today holds that the statute of repose in the Indiana Products Liability Act, which denies remedy to citizens injured by defective products that happen to be more than ten years old, does not violate this provision. Noting prior cases that have considered the Due Course of Law Clause of the Indiana Constitution analogous to the Due Process Clause of the U.S. Constitution, the majority correctly acknowledges that the two provisions are not synonymous, but nevertheless finds the statute of repose provision proper because it concludes that there is no constitutional right to remedy in Indiana. I disagree.

Thirty-seven other state constitutions also include a "remedies" provision. These provisions trace their roots to chapter 40 of the Magna Carta: "To no one will we sell, to no one will we deny, or delay right or justice." It is this assurance of access to justice that is embodied in our Right to Remedy Clause.

Applying our well-established methodology of constitutional interpretation, I conclude that Section 12 provides separate and distinct protections and is not coextensive with federal due process jurisprudence. I am also convinced that Section 12 ensures not only that procedures must comply with due course of law, but further that both the text and the history provide strong support for understanding Section 12 of Indiana's Bill of Rights to provide a substantive right to remedy for injuries suffered.

The legislature has the authority to modify or abrogate common law rights as long as such change does not interfere with constitutional rights. Although constitutional rights may be subjected to legislative restraints and burdens necessitated by the State's exercise of its police power to promote the peace, safety, and well-being of the public, this police power is not unlimited: "[T]here is within each provision of our Bill of Rights a cluster of essential values which the legislature may qualify but not alienate." "A right is impermissibly alienated when the State materially burdens one of the core values which it embodies." The right to remedy for injury is such a core value.

While legislative qualifications of this right may be enacted under the police power, the total abrogation of an injured person's right to remedy is an unacceptable material burden. The statute of repose provision in the Products Liability Act is no mere qualification. It does not merely limit the time within which to assert a remedy, nor does it merely modify the

---

[4] [1] The full provision states: "All courts shall be open; and every person, for injury done to him in his person, property, or reputation, shall have remedy by due course of law. Justice shall be administered freely, and without purchase; completely, and without denial; speedily, and without delay." IND. CONST. art. I, § 12.

procedure for enforcing the remedy. Nor is it a narrow, limited immunity necessitated by police power. On the contrary, the repose provision completely bars the courthouse doors to all persons injured by products over ten years old, even for claims alleging negligence, and even where the products were designed, built, sold, and purchased with the expectation of decades of continued use. Although this provision denies all Indiana citizens access to justice ensured by the Right to Remedy Clause, it is especially pernicious to those economically disadvantaged citizens who must rely on older or used products rather than new ones.

I would find that the Products Liability Act repose provision violates our Right to Remedy Clause.

IEROPOLI v. AC&S CORP.
842 A.2d 919 (Pa. 2004)

CAPPY, C.J.

In this appeal, we review the order of the court of common pleas granting summary judgment to Appellee Crown Cork & Seal Company, Inc. ("Crown Cork") pursuant to the newly enacted statute ("Statute") that limits the successor asbestos-related liabilities of certain Pennsylvania corporations. For all the reasons that follow, we hold that the Statute is unconstitutional as applied under Article I, Section 11 of the Pennsylvania Constitution.

On December 19, 2000, Appellants, Frank and Margaret Ieropoli, commenced a civil action, filing a complaint against Crown Cork and twenty-four other defendants. In their complaint, Appellants alleged that Frank Ieropoli was exposed to defendants' respective asbestos products while working as a machinist with General Electric from 1947 until 1979...Appellants asserted several causes of action against Crown Cork sounding in tort or contract. For the most part, Appellants asserted these same causes of action against Crown Cork's co-defendants. Appellants requested that a judgment for compensatory damages, punitive damages...be entered against Crown Cork and its co-defendants individually, and jointly and severally, where appropriate.

The Statute was passed by the General Assembly, signed into law on December 17, 2001, and made immediately effective. The Statute limits the asbestos-related liabilities of corporations incorporated in Pennsylvania before May 1, 2001 that arise out of mergers or consolidations. The Statute provides:

§ 1929.1. Limitations on asbestos-related liabilities relating to certain mergers or consolidations.-

(a) Limitation on successor asbestos-related liabilities.

(1) Except as further limited in paragraph (2) the cumulative successor asbestos-related liabilities of a domestic business corporation that was incorporated in this Commonwealth prior to May 1, 2001, shall be limited to the fair market value of the total assets of the transferor determined as of the time of the merger or consolidation, and such corporation shall have no responsibility for successor asbestos-related liabilities in excess of such limitation.

On February 7, 2002, Crown Cork filed a [motion for summary judgment]…requesting that judgment be entered in its favor in several hundred asbestos cases pending against it in the Court of Common Pleas in Philadelphia County. In its Motion, Crown Cork set forth the following undisputed, material facts of record: Crown Cork is a Pennsylvania business corporation and a manufacturer of beverage cans; Crown Cork purchased a majority of the stock of Mundet Cork Corporation ("Mundet Cork") in November 1963; Mundet Cork had a division that made, sold and installed asbestos insulation; Crown Cork never operated the insulation division; Crown Cork sold the insulation division 90 days after acquiring Mundet Cork's stock; Crown Cork acquired all of Mundet Cork's stock and merged with Mundet Cork on February 10, 1996; the value of Mundet Cork's assets at the time of the merger was in the range of $11 to $12 million; the value of Mundet Cork's assets at the time of the merger adjusted for inflation was in the range of $50 to $55 million; Crown Cork was reincorporated in Pennsylvania on March 30, 1996; Crown Cork was sued in asbestos-related cases solely as a successor to Mundet Cork; and Crown Cork has paid out $336 million on asbestos-related claims.

Based on these facts, Crown Cork asserted that because all of the cases that are the subject of its Motion come within the Statute's definition of "asbestos claims"; because it has already paid an amount in excess of the limit on liability created by the Statute; and because Appellants no longer have a damages remedy for the claims they asserted against it, the Statute required that its Motion be granted.

Appellants argued that application of the Statute in this case is unconstitutional under Article I, Section 11 of the Pennsylvania Constitution. More specifically, Appellants asserted that Article 1, Section 11 was violated because application of the Statute in this case serves to extinguish accrued causes of action. The trial court rejected Appellants' argument. While acknowledging that the Appellants' causes of action against Crown Cork accrued prior to the Statute's enactment, the trial court concluded that the Statute did not extinguish any cause of action.

We begin with a discussion of Article 1, Section 11 of the Pennsylvania Constitution. Article I, Section 11 has been in the Pennsylvania Constitution since 1790, and is part of the Constitution's Declaration of Rights. Article I, Section 11 states:

§ 11. Courts to be open; suits against the Commonwealth

All courts shall be open; and every man for an injury done him in his lands, goods, person or reputation shall have remedy by due course of law, and right and justice administered without sale, denial or delay. Suits may be brought against the Commonwealth in such manner, in such courts and in such cases as the legislature may by law direct.

The constitutions of thirty-nine states contain a provision that is substantially similar to that part of Article 1, Section 11 that is highlighted. This provision, commonly referred to as the "open courts" or "remedies" clause, is derived from Magna Carta and Sir Edward Coke's Seventeenth Century commentary on the Great Charter, which was relied upon by the drafters of early American state constitutions.

Turning to the respective arguments the parties have presented, Appellants assert that as a general proposition, Article 1, Section 11 does not prevent the General Assembly from enacting a statute that eliminates a cause of action that exists at common law. Appellants contend that what Article 1, Section 11 precludes is the elimination of accrued causes of action by newly-enacted legislation. According to Appellants, the application of the Statute to the causes of action they brought against Crown Cork violates this rule.

Crown Cork…contends that the Statute merely varies the remedy that was available to Appellants [and]…the fact that Appellants have collected settlement monies or will recover damages from its co-defendants shows that Article 1, Section 11 is not violated. Finally,…Crown Cork asserts that because the Statute only alters the allocation of damages among multiple defendants, Article 1, Section 11 is not implicated.

We begin our analysis of Appellant's constitutional challenge to the Statute by determining what the Statute's application in this case means for Crown Cork. This determination is a matter of statutory construction. Through the causes of action they brought against Crown Cork, Appellants seek a payment of damages from the company for the losses they allegedly sustained as a result of Frank Ieropoli's exposure to certain asbestos products that Crown Cork's merger partner manufactured and sold. Because Crown Cork has met § 1929.1(a)(1)'s limit, however, the Statute provides that Crown Cork "shall have no responsibility for cumulative successor asbestos-related liabilities…." Under § 1929.1(e)'s definition, "successor asbestos-related liabilities" are "[a]ny liabilities, whether known or unknown, asserted or unasserted, absolute or contingent, accrued or unaccrued, liquidated or unliquidated or due or to become due, related in any way to asbestos claims", and include payments made "in connection with settlements, judgments or other discharges in this Commonwealth or another jurisdiction." Under that same definition, an "asbestos claim" is "[a]ny claim, wherever or whenever made for damages, losses, indemnification, contribution or other relief arising out of, based on or in any way related to asbestos."

In our view, the Statute is clear and unambiguous as to the protection the General Assembly intended to give to Crown Cork. The words of the Statute state that a qualified corporation is not responsible for any liability that is related to any claim for relief related to asbestos. Thus, in the present case, the Statute protects Crown Cork from any liability to Appellants on the causes of action they brought against it.

It now remains to determine whether the protection from liability on Appellants' causes of action that the Statute gives to Crown Cork affects those causes of action in a way that Article 1, Section 11 prohibits. For this, we begin with the meaning of the phrase "cause of action". In this case, "cause of action" relates to remedy. It is the vehicle by which a person secures redress from another person for the consequences of an event that is a legal injury. Moreover, as we have seen, a cause of action that has accrued takes on an even greater meaning. It is a vested right, which under Article 1, Section 11, may not be eliminated by subsequent legislation.

In light of these principles, the violation of Article 1, Section 11 that the Statute's application occasions in this case is clear. Before the Statute's enactment, each cause of action that Appellants brought against Crown Cork was a remedy—it was the vehicle by which Appellants lawfully pursued redress, in the form of damages, from Crown Cork for an alleged legal injury. But under the Statute, Appellants cannot obligate Crown Cork to pay them damages on those causes of action. In this way, each cause of action has been stripped of its remedial significance, as it can no longer function as the means by which Appellants may secure redress from Crown Cork. As a remedy, each cause of action has been, in essence, extinguished. Under Article 1, Section 11, however, a statute may not extinguish a cause of action that has accrued.

By way of conclusion, we in the majority point out that we are as concerned with the heavy toll that asbestos litigation is visiting upon certain Commonwealth corporations as are our respected colleagues in the dissent. Nevertheless, any statutory effort aimed at reformation must not offend the Remedies Clause, if it is to pass constitutional muster. That Clause, which binds both the legislature and the courts, provides that an accrued cause of action is a vested right and as such, cannot be eliminated by subsequent legislation. This is the basic and undeniable principle that applies here. We know of no authority that supports the proposition that an accrued cause of action that is the subject of a merger does not receive the Remedies Clause's full protection. Likewise, we know of no authority (separate from the Statute) that would in these circumstances, override the general tenet of corporate law that states that the corporation that absorbs another corporation in a merger becomes legally responsible in every sense of the word for the latter's liabilities and debts.

Thus, for all of the foregoing reasons, we hold that the Statute as applied in this case is unconstitutional under Article 1, Section 11.

NEWMAN, J., **dissenting**.

The majority finds Section 1929.1 repugnant to Article I, Section 11 of the Pennsylvania Constitution, which states that "[a]ll courts shall be open; and every man for an injury done him in his lands, goods, person or reputation **shall have remedy by due course of law**, and right and justice administered without sale, denial or delay." (emphasis added). We have explained that this provision of our state Constitution ensures "that the Legislature may not extinguish a right of action which has already accrued to a claimant."

The problem in the instant case is the identification of the party legally responsible for the injuries suffered by the Ieropolis. The responsible party in the instant case is not Crown; rather it is Mundet Cork. My point in this regard is not intended to undo a century of successor liability law, but to acknowledge the artifice of deeming a successor corporation responsible for the injury. The cause of action in this case does not accrue against Crown; more accurately, it accrues against Mundet Cork and, pursuant to its status as successor, Crown steps into the shoes of Mundet Cork to ensure that, as between a blameless plaintiff and a corporation that has succeeded a corporation responsible for an injury, the successor corporation, not the blameless plaintiff, is responsible for the acts of the tortfeasor. Successor liability is an important tenet of our system of jurisprudence, but it is not one protected by Article I, Section 11 of the Pennsylvania Constitution. Causes of action in tort do not accrue in a vacuum—rather, they arise against an entity for a wrong done at the time an injury is incurred. Article I, Section 11 forecloses retroactive elimination or limitation of the liability of the tortfeasor.

Conceived of in this way, Section 1929.1 does not extinguish a vested right or an accrued cause of action. Neither does it eliminate a right to a remedy. Instead, Section 1929.1 limits the amount of liability that successor corporations can be made to be accountable for and, ultimately, limits the class of entities who can be made to bear the burden of that right. This is not to say that the legislature could constitutionally provide that all pending asbestos cases are summarily dismissed—this would extinguish vested causes of action against entities responsible for injuries. But the constitutional provision with which we are concerned, Article I, Section 11, does not estop the General Assembly from limiting (or eliminating) the effect of successor liability, even retroactively. Section

1929.1 does not retroactively limit or extinguish the liability because the successor corporation (in the case *sub judice*, Crown) is not the tortfeasor.

It is conceivable, although unlikely, that at some point in the future a plaintiff in a pending asbestos case could, by virtue of Section 1929.1, be denied any recovery. That would be an unfortunate result of my position in this case, but that potentiality should not enter into the consideration of a court of last resort charged with determining whether the statute passes constitutional muster.

NOTES

1.   What level of scrutiny do the courts apply when evaluating claims that a statutory enactment has violated the right to a remedy or open courts provisions? Does the standard resemble any standard applied in other state or federal contexts, *e.g.*, in federal equal protection or due process analysis?

2.   Is the "right to a remedy by due course of law" a procedural guarantee? A substantive protection? Or both?

3.   Does it matter to the courts whether a challenged limitation affects only a common law claim? A statutory claim? Is there justification for treating statutory and common law claims differently?

LANEY v. FAIRVIEW CITY
57 P.3d 1007 (Utah 2002)

DURHAM, C.J.

This case addresses whether Utah Code Ann. § 63-30-2(4)(a) violates the "open courts" clause, of the Utah Constitution. The district court held that Fairview City (the City) is immune from suit for its alleged negligence under the Utah Governmental Immunity Act. We hold that the 1987 amendment, declaring all acts of municipalities to be governmental functions, is unconstitutional as applied to municipalities operating electrical power systems.

BACKGROUND

On September 16, 1991, John Laney was electrocuted and killed while moving irrigation pipe. The thirty-foot aluminum water irrigation pipe that Laney was carrying came into contact with, or within arcing distance of, high voltage power lines. The power lines were owned by the City.

Accordingly, Laney's wife and children brought a wrongful death action against the City claiming, inter alia, that the City was negligent for failing to maintain the power lines in a safe condition. The Laneys complain that the power lines did not meet minimum safety standards because they were too low to the ground. They also allege that the lines were unsafe because they were not insulated and did not contain warnings.

The City moved for summary judgment asserting that the decision whether or not to improve the power lines was a discretionary function entitled to immunity under Utah Code Ann. § 63-30-10(1) (1997). Discretionary function immunity is an exception to a waiver of sovereign immunity within the Utah Governmental Immunity Act. The Utah Governmental Immunity Act declares that all governmental entities are immune from suit for any injury which results from the exercise of a "governmental function." The term governmental function is broadly defined in section 63-30-2(4)(a), and by virtue of that broad definition, the statute cloaks governmental entities with immunity for a wide range of activities. However, Utah Code Ann. § 63-30-10 waives sovereign immunity "for injury proximately caused by a negligent act or omission." Then, subsection (1) creates an exception to this waiver for negligence and immunizes governmental entities for "the exercise or performance or the failure to exercise or perform a discretionary function...."

The district court agreed that the City was entitled to immunity for its decision to not improve the power lines and granted the City's motion for summary judgment.

Plaintiffs appeal, claiming that Utah Code Ann. § 63-30-2(4)(a) is unconstitutional because it violates article I, section 11, the open courts clause, of the Utah Constitution.

ANALYSIS

CONSTITUTIONALITY OF UTAH CODE ANN. § 63-30-2(4)(a)

Because we find that the City's maintenance of the power lines constitutes a discretionary function within the meaning of the Governmental Immunity Act, we must address the plaintiffs' [constitutional] challenge. Article I, section 11 of the Utah Constitution provides:

> All courts shall be open, and every person, for an injury done to him in his person, property, or reputation, shall have remedy by due course of law, which shall be administered without denial or unnecessary delay; and no person shall be barred from prosecuting or defending before any tribunal in this state, by himself or counsel any civil cause to which he is a party.

Plaintiffs argue that the Act deprives them of their rights guaranteed by the open courts clause.

A. Berry v. Beech Aircraft Analysis

The State urges this court to abandon nearly a century of precedent, arguing for an interpretation that would virtually write article I, section 11 out of the Utah Constitution. Specifically, the State asks the court to overrule *Berry v. Beech Aircraft Corp.*, 717 P.2d 670 (Utah 1985), and the principles explained therein. As early as 1915, only twenty years after Utah's constitution was adopted, this court acknowledged that article I, section 11 placed "a limitation upon the Legislature to prevent that branch of the state government from closing the doors of the courts against any person who has a legal right which is enforceable in accordance with some known remedy."

1.   Plain Meaning and Historical Purpose

In arguing for article I, section 11 to be treated solely as a procedural right, the State disregards the plain meaning and historical purpose of Utah's open courts provision. Throughout our state's history, this court has consistently recognized that the plain meaning of the guarantee "impose[s] some *substantive* limitation on the legislature to abolish judicial remedies in a capricious fashion."

[O]pen courts provisions in Utah and other states have served two principal purposes:

> First, they were intended to help establish an independent foundation for the judiciary as an institution. Second, open courts or remedies clauses were intended to grant individuals rights to a judicial remedy for the protection of their person, property, or reputation from abrogation and *unreasonable limitation by economic interests that could control state legislatures.*

Although some states with open courts provisions have construed them to guarantee only procedural rights and court access, such a construction has never been accepted in Utah. Article I, section 11's constitutional guarantee has been interpreted to protect substantive rights to remedies throughout our state's history. The open courts provision was adopted, as part of the original Constitution itself, at the end of the nineteenth century, during a period when abuse had generated concern and distrust of the legislative branch in numerous states. That abuse included misuse of political influence by railroads and other corporate interests, who convinced state legislators to favor private interests through legislative enactments insulating them from the general laws.

Focusing entirely on the "procedural" content of the language found in section 11, as the State does, is misleading. Constitutional language must be viewed in context, meaning that its history and purpose must be considered in determining its meaning. The language that a remedy shall be had by "due course of law" describes the law by which the remedy is secured, as well as the procedural guarantees also protected by this section. Article I, section 7 already contains a due process provision guaranteeing procedural rights. Thus, if the State's reading of section 11 is correct, section 11 is redundant and mere surplusage—it has no constitutional role or function that is not already performed by section 7. That view has never been embraced by any Utah decision.

B. Application of Berry to Subsection 63-30-2(4)(a)

We now turn to the analysis of the constitutionality of subsection 63-30-2(4)(a) using the test set forth in *Berry*. A legislative enactment that does not eliminate a remedy is not unconstitutional under the open courts provision. Therefore, we must first determine whether a cause of action has been abrogated by the legislative enactment. If no remedy was eliminated, there is no need to proceed with the *Berry* test.

1. Abrogation of Remedy

The State argues in this case that no remedy was abrogated because the 1987 amendment to the Governmental Immunity Act had been enacted four years before Mr. Laney was electrocuted in 1991. The issue under the open courts provision, however, is not whether a statute has already been enacted before a claim arises, but rather whether the statute abrogates a cause of action existing at the time of its enactment. Thus, the State's argument that there is no abrogation of a remedy if a statute is already in effect at the time a cause of action arises is inapplicable.

Plaintiffs assert that the 1987 amendment abrogated a remedy because the law in effect prior to the amendment provided individuals negligently injured by municipality-operated power lines with a cause of action against the municipality. Prior to the amendment, the scope of sovereign immunity depended on whether the governmental activity complained of was found to be a "governmental function" or a "proprietary function." Only those activities determined to be governmental functions were afforded immunity. The Act did not define what constituted a governmental function, therefore this court established a standard whereby a function could be considered a governmental function. This definition of governmental function was used to determine whether an activity was covered by the Act until the legislature redefined the term in 1987.

Plaintiffs argue that the City's operation and maintenance of a municipal electrical power system would not have been a governmental function under [this Court's] standard because maintaining power lines is not "of such a unique nature that it can only be performed by a governmental agency or that...is essential to the core of governmental immunity." We agree.

Prior to the 1987 amendment, the operation of an electrical power system was considered a proprietary function, which was not entitled to immunity under the Act. Under the 1987 amendment, however, a claim against a municipality for negligent maintenance of power lines can be barred by the scope of immunity protection afforded the City. Although the Act waives immunity for governmental functions if there is negligence involved, a plaintiff suing a municipality is now subject to the exceptions to the waiver of immunity. By defining a governmental function as *any* act of a governmental entity, whether or not the activity is characterized as governmental or proprietary, the 1987 amendment effectively grants immunity protection for some activities that...formerly...were not entitled to immunity. Therefore, we find that the 1987 amendment partially abrogated a remedy for a municipality's negligence. Because a remedy has been abrogated, we proceed with the *Berry* test to determine the constitutionality of the amendment under the open courts provision.

2.   No Reasonable Alternative Remedy

Under the first prong of the *Berry* analysis, when a remedy has been abrogated, this court first determines whether the legislature has provided a "reasonable alternative remedy 'by due course of law' for vindication of [a plaintiff's] constitutional interest." In *Berry*, we held that the substitute benefit "must be substantially equal in value or other benefit to the remedy abrogated in providing essentially comparable substantive protection to one's person, property, or reputation, although the form of the substitute remedy may be different...." In the instant case, we find no indication that the legislature provided any substitute remedy, nor does the State make this argument. Therefore, we must turn to the second prong of the *Berry* test.

3.   Elimination of Clear Social or Economic Evil

The State contends that even if a remedy was abrogated, the amendment is constitutional under the second prong of the *Berry* test, which provides that where no alternative remedy has been provided, "abrogation of the remedy or cause of action may be justified only if there is a clear social or economic evil to be eliminated and the elimination of an existing legal remedy is not an arbitrary or unreasonable means for achieving the objective."

Cases involving statutes of limitation and statutes of repose have come before this court with mixed results. In an early case, we held that article I, section 11, did not preclude the legislature from prescribing a one-year statute of limitations for the time within which to assail the regularity or organization of an irrigation district. In three cases, statutes of repose were struck down because they barred actions without regard to the occurrence of an injury and did not provide a reasonable amount of time to file a lawsuit. No effective and reasonable alternative was provided, and the abrogation of the remedy was held to be arbitrary and unreasonable.

In the only case that we have found which did *not* involve an act of the legislature, this court abolished the common law tort of criminal conversation and justified its abolition under the open courts provision on the ground that the cause of action was "unfair and bad policy," "serve[d]" no useful purpose, was subject to abuse, and protected interests that were already adequately served by the tort of alienation of affections.

Recently, in *Day v. State*, 980 P.2d 1171 (Utah 1999), we relied on the open courts provision to strike down a statute granting immunity for negligent operation of an emergency vehicle in circumstances where immunity had not previously existed. We declared the statute unconstitutional because the legislature was not acting to obviate a "clear social evil" in this state. The sponsor of the legislation had explained that the statute was necessary because of a rash of frivolous lawsuits, "especially in California." We noted that on its face, the sponsor's statement did not identify any social, economic, or any other evil in Utah.

With that backdrop ..., we turn to the instant case. The 1987 amendment eliminates the appellants' right to sue for Mr. Laney's wrongful death. The statutory amendment thus sharply limited instances where municipalities operating a power system could be held liable for their negligence.

According to the legislative history, the 1987 amendment [was proposed] in the "hope that passage of these bills will make it easier or cheaper for a government entity to obtain liability insurance." Thus the legislative objective appears to have been to make liability insurance more affordable for government entities by reducing liability risks. While that objective is worthy, the legislature swept too broadly when it severely curtailed negligence actions against municipalities operating power systems. The legislative concern about increased damage awards against governmental entities is stated in very general terms; no specifics are given. We do not know whether any municipality in this state operating an electrical system has sustained a large damage award. We do know that only a small fraction operate municipal power systems. The general nature of the legislative findings do not show that large damage awards have been made against municipalities in connection with their operation of an electrical power system, or that such operation has been affected in any way by potential liability.

The City generates an annual profit operating its electrical power system. It is not an operation subsidized by tax dollars. The cost of liability insurance, therefore, might not even be paid for by the taxpayers of the City, but rather by consumers of the electrical power, some of whom may live outside the City. If the City cannot afford to purchase reasonable amounts of liability insurance to meet its high standard of care, rate increases may be justified and necessary.

Equally disturbing is the broad sweep that the legislature took to meet its objective. In the instant case, the legislature has defined *all* activities of municipalities as governmental action, regardless of their nature. In its sweep, the operation of both a sewer system and a golf course is governmental, along with the operation of a municipal electrical power system, even though the potential for negligently causing death by the municipality is vastly greater in the latter activity.

If large verdicts are vexatious to cities, a reasonable approach might be to create very limited immunities to address specific problems, or to place "caps" on the amount of damages, as the legislature has done elsewhere in the Governmental Immunity Act. This court has, for example, upheld statutory caps on judgments for damages for personal injury against a governmental entity.

We therefore hold that the 1987 amendment is unconstitutional as it applies to municipalities operating electrical power systems. No clear social or economic evil has been specifically identified, and the broad sweep of the amendment is arbitrary and unreasonable when applied to the operation of a municipal electrical power system, where a high duty of care is imposed. We express no opinion on the constitutionality of the amendment as applied to other municipal activities since a lower standard of care may apply and different considerations may be relevant.

WILKINS, J., concurring and dissenting:

In my opinion, section 63-30-2(4)(a) of the Utah Governmental Immunity Act, does not violate article I, section 11 of the Utah Constitution, the Open Courts Clause. In my view, the Legislature acted within its constitutional authority in setting forth the current scheme of sovereign immunity in Utah. Under the statute, Fairview City should be entitled to immunity for its omissions, to not raise the height of, insulate, or provide further warnings on its power lines, a discretionary function within the discretionary function exception of the Utah Governmental Immunity Act.

In the recent past, the Open Courts Clause has been interpreted in such a way that it limits the legislature's ability to alter, modify, or eliminate the law by requiring legislation to meet this court's approval through the *Berry* test. In *Berry*, prior members of this court admittedly "broke new ground and read article I, section 11 ... as imposing a strong substantive limitation on the legislature's ability to limit or eliminate a cause of action for, or the remedies available for [personal injury]."

In my view, [the *Berry*] test permits a majority of this court to substitute its judgment of what constitutes good public policy for the judgment of the legislature, the branch of government that is not only best suited to determine and implement public policy under our system of government, but constitutionally obligated to do so. I am of the opinion that whether a substitute remedy is of "substantially equal value or other benefit to the remedy abrogated," and whether there is a clear social or economic evil to be eliminated, are two questions that should be answered by the legislature, not this court, and that we overstep our bounds in so doing. I agree that the Open Courts Clause limits legislative authority. Numerous constitutional provisions prevent the legislative branch from eliminating constitutional or inalienable rights. I do not think, however, that the Open Courts Clause guarantees one the right to a judicial remedy for every injury done to one's person, property, or reputation.

The first *Berry* assumption with which I disagree is the assumption that those who suffer because of legislation preventing recovery for personal injury are individuals who are somehow part of a minority that is not represented or underrepresented in the political process. [I]ndividuals who suffer injury to their person, property, or reputation are not a discreet and insular minority. All persons, regardless of ethnic background, economic background, gender, religious persuasion, or other affiliations, may suffer injury. Viewing an injured individual or group retrospectively, after they have suffered injury, they may very well be unable to rally the political process. Prospectively, however, all of us as citizens, regardless of status, are subject to legislation limiting our ability to recover for personal injury. No group is singled out by legislation that limits the ability to recover for personal injuries. All citizens face the possibility of personal injury, even those who are generally visible in society that belong to what we may think are privileged, identifiable groups. Those thwarted by the Utah Governmental Immunity Act, those who have suffered personal injuries at the hands of the government, may be any of us; they do not comprise a distinct and insular group whose voice may not be heard through the political process.

Second, *Berry* assumes that the Open Courts Clause contains language which should be interpreted to protect against majoritarian abuse. I disagree. Other provisions in our constitution are more suited to protecting against majoritarian abuse. They contain language which more specifically implies protection for political minorities, and these provisions have also been interpreted to protect groups and individuals that are isolated from the political process. [T]he language of the Open Courts Clause is ill-suited to protect against majoritarian abuse.

The real danger presented by the *Berry* test is that of majoritarian abuse by the members of this court. The risk, in my mind, lies in requiring that new legislation satisfy the policy predilections of a majority of the members of this court by providing, in the eyes of this court, an adequate alternative remedy; or by eliminating what is viewed as a clear social or economic evil by this court. The constitution vests power in the legislature to implement, as law, the will of the majority of the citizens of this State.

Third, the *Berry* interpretation assumes that each individual who suffers an injury to his or her person, property, or reputation, is constitutionally entitled to a remedy. The idea that a remedy can be fashioned for every injury is optimistic and well-intentioned, but, as a practical matter, impossible. The law cannot, and therefore does not, guarantee a remedy for every injury.

Individuals who have been injured in their persons, property, or reputation, are entitled to a remedy only when the law, statutory or common, recognizes an injury and permits a remedy. The Open Courts Clause should not be interpreted to provide a right to a remedy. It should be interpreted to guarantee *access* to seek a judicial determination as to whether the law grants a remedy for the injury suffered. The courts, through the common law, may create remedies when public policy dictates that certain interests are worthy of protection and the legislature has not spoken. Likewise, the legislature creates remedies when it determines, as a matter of public policy, that certain interests are worthy of protection. If the law provides for a remedy, then the Open Courts Clause guarantees the right to seek that permitted remedy through the courts.

The *Berry* test places this court in the position of sitting as a second legislature, re-weighing the social or economic policy, instead of analyzing, as other methods of constitutional analysis do, whether the law is rationally related to its avowed purpose. Substitution of the policy of three or more judges for the policy of the legislature, absent specific constitutional authority, is contrary to our system of government.

TINDLEY v. SALT LAKE CITY SCHOOL DISTRICT,
116 P.3d 295 (Utah 2005)

PARRISH, J.

¶ 1 This appeal concerns the constitutionality of section 63–30–34 of the Utah Governmental Immunity Act, which limits the damages recoverable in actions against the state or its political subdivisions. Plaintiffs brought this action against the Salt Lake City School District (the "District"), asserting that the limitation violates both the Utah and the United States Constitutions. The District successfully moved for summary judgment. Plaintiffs appealed. We affirm.

BACKGROUND

¶ 2 David Smith was employed by the District as a teacher and debate team coach at Highland High School in Salt Lake City, Utah. Smith selected eight students, including Erin Anderson, Matt Ehrman, Brian and Jeff Horman, and Eric Sabodski, to compete in a debate tournament at the University of Southern California ("USC"). The tournament began on Friday, November 3, 2000, and concluded the following Sunday. Each student competing in the tournament paid a portion of the costs to attend, with the remaining costs paid by funds raised through the high school debate club.

¶ 3 Intending to drive the team to USC, Smith reserved a fifteen-passenger van from a rental agency. When Smith arrived at the rental agency, however, he learned that the van he had reserved was unavailable. Consequently, Smith rented two minivans to transport the students to the competition. District employee and assistant debate team coach Christian Bradley drove one of the vans, while Smith drove the other.

¶ 4 The debate team arrived at USC and participated in both the preliminary and the elimination rounds of the competition. Following the elimination rounds on Sunday afternoon, the team began the return trip to Salt Lake City. Bradley left at approximately 1:00 p.m., driving one of the rented minivans, with Eric, Jeff, Erin, Brian, and Matt as passengers. Smith followed shortly thereafter with the remaining students. Late that evening, while traveling through Millard County, Utah, Bradley lost control of the minivan due to his own negligence. The vehicle flipped several times, ejecting Eric, Jeff, and Erin.

¶ 5 Eric and Jeff were killed in the accident, and the remaining three students were seriously injured. Erin sustained numerous injuries, including a severe traumatic brain injury. Brian's injuries included crushed vertebrae and a fractured hand and foot, and Matt suffered an injury to his knee, as well as multiple contusions and abrasions. It is uncontested that plaintiffs' aggregate damages exceeded $500,000.

¶ 6 Recognizing its liability for Bradley's negligence, the District and its insurer, the Utah State Division of Risk Management, entered into a settlement agreement with plaintiffs Erin, Brian, Matt, and the parents and estates of Eric and Jeff. Under the settlement agreement, the District agreed to pay plaintiffs collectively $500,000, the maximum amount then recoverable under the Utah Governmental Immunity Act. In exchange, plaintiffs agreed to relinquish their rights to pursue any claims against the District or its employees, but reserved the right to challenge the constitutionality of the damage cap imposed by the Governmental Immunity Act.

¶ 7 In accordance with the settlement agreement, plaintiffs filed suit in district court, alleging that the cap violates several provisions of the Utah Constitution, including the open courts clause, as well as the provisions guaranteeing due process, uniform operation of laws, and the right to recover damages for injuries resulting in death.

ANALYSIS

¶ 9 Historically, the ability to sue the State of Utah or one of its political subdivisions rested on a determination of whether the governmental entity was protected by the common law doctrine of sovereign immunity. That changed in 1965, when the Utah Legislature enacted the Utah Governmental Immunity Act (the "Act"), which barred all causes of action against the state and its political subdivisions unless expressly authorized by statute. Specifically, the Act provided that "all governmental entities," including school districts, "are immune from suit for any injury which results from the exercise of a governmental function." Utah Code Ann. §§ 63–30–2(3), (7), –3(1) (1997 & Supp.2000). Despite its broad grant of immunity, the Act expressly waived immunity for "injury proximately caused by a negligent act or omission of an employee committed within the scope of employment." *Id.* § 63–30–10 (1997). Judgments obtained pursuant to this waiver, however, were limited. The Act provided that

> if a judgment for damages for personal injury against a governmental entity, or an employee whom a governmental entity has a duty to indemnify, exceeds $250,000 for one person in any one occurrence, or $500,000 for two or more persons in any one occurrence, the court shall reduce the judgment to that amount.

¶ 10 Plaintiffs argue that this statutory limitation on judgments violates article I, section 11 of the Utah Constitution, commonly referred to as the open courts clause.

I. THE OPEN COURTS CLAUSE:

ARTICLE I, SECTION 11 OF THE UTAH CONSTITUTION

¶ 12 We first address plaintiffs' claim that the cap violates the open courts clause found in article I, section 11 of the Utah Constitution. That provision provides:

> All courts shall be open, and every person, for an injury done to him in his person, property or reputation, shall have remedy by due course of law, which shall be administered without denial or unnecessary delay; and no person shall be barred from prosecuting or defending before any tribunal in this State, by himself or counsel, any civil cause to which he is a party.

¶ 13 The open courts clause is not merely a procedural protection. Rather, this court has held that the open courts clause provides citizens of Utah the "right to a remedy for an injury." In *Laney v. Fairview City*, we declared that "the plain meaning of the [open courts clause] 'imposes some *substantive* limitation on the legislature['s ability] to abolish judicial remedies in a capricious fashion.'" In *Berry ex rel. Berry v. Beech Aircraft Corp.*, 717 P.2d 670 (Utah 1985), we stated that

> the basic purpose of Article I, section 11 is to impose some limitation on [the legislature's] power for the benefit of those persons who are injured in their persons, property, or reputations since they are generally isolated in society, belong to no identifiable group, and rarely are able to rally the political process to their aid.

In other words, the open courts clause provides more than procedural protections; it also secures substantive rights, thereby restricting the legislature's ability to abrogate remedies provided by law.

¶ 17 Although the open courts clause protects both substantive and procedural rights, the clause is not an absolute guarantee of all substantive rights. Rather, it applies only to legislation which "abrogates a cause of action existing at the time of its enactment." The legislature thus remains free to abrogate or limit claims that could not have been brought under then-existing law. Claims barred by the doctrine of governmental immunity are an example of this principle. In *DeBry v. Noble*, 889 P.2d 428 (Utah 1995), we noted that "the scope of the protections afforded by article I, section 11 [have] to be viewed in light of the immunities that were recognized when the Utah Constitution was adopted," including "governmental immunity."

¶ 18 In addition, the mere fact that legislation abrogates an existing legal remedy does not render it impermissible under the open courts clause. Such legislation is acceptable under *Berry* so long as it either "provides an injured person an effective and reasonable alternative remedy" or seeks to eliminate "a clear social or economic evil." With respect to the second alternative, "the [abrogation] of an existing legal remedy [cannot be] an arbitrary or unreasonable means for achieving the objective."

¶ 19 The District argues that the doctrine of sovereign immunity rendered it immune from suit prior to the passage of the Act. Accordingly, it reasons that the Act could not have abrogated any "existing remedy" in violation of the open courts clause. Plaintiffs urge us to reject this conclusion for two reasons. First, plaintiffs argue that the doctrine of sovereign immunity was not part of Utah law at the time the Utah Constitution was adopted. Second, even assuming that sovereign immunity was part of Utah law, they assert that it protected governmental entities only when those entities were performing activities constituting a governmental function, and that transporting students to an out-of-state, extracurricular debate tournament does not qualify as such. We decline plaintiffs' invitation to revisit the historical evolution of sovereign immunity under Utah law because we conclude that the District would have been entitled to immunity for its activity in this case prior to the adoption of the Act.

¶ 21 The 1987 amendment substantively expanded the scope of immunity established by the Act, providing immunity for activities that were once deemed proprietary and, therefore, had not been covered by immunity under the common law. Accordingly, to determine whether the Act, or its 1987 amendment, "abrogates a cause of action existing at the time of its enactment," we must determine whether plaintiffs would have had a right to bring their cause of action against the District at any time prior to 1987. If not, the Act does not abrogate an existing remedy, thereby terminating our analysis. If, however, plaintiffs would have been able to bring suit against the District prior to 1987, we must then determine whether the Act's abrogation of that cause of action is permissible under *Berry*.

¶ 24 We have long recognized the essential nature of public schools' educational activities. While the act of providing classroom instruction lies at the heart of a school district's function, any supplemental activities that are necessary to sustain this function must similarly be subject to the same rule. This principle is consistent with our previous recognition that the scope of a school board's immunity, prior to the enactment of the Act, extended to its operation of an incinerator to dispose of garbage collected on school grounds.

¶ 25 Here, we are unwilling to conclude that a school's operation of an extracurricular student debate team, including its transport of the team to and from out-of-state competitions, falls outside the realm of a school district's core activities. Such an activity clearly benefits student education and is unlikely to be available to public school students if not offered through their schools. Moreover, imposing tort liability on a school district for the operation of such activities is more likely to deter schools from offering them than to promote public safety. We note that other jurisdictions have consistently held that similar extracurricular activities fall within the scope of a public school's traditional governmental immunity. *See, e.g., Yanero v. Davis*, 65 S.W.3d 510, 527 (Ky. 2001) (interscholastic athletics); *Churilla v. Sch. Dist.*, 306 N.W.2d 381, 381 (Mich. App. 1981) (football program); *McManus v. Anahuac Indep. Sch. Dist.*, 667 S.W.2d 275, 278 (Tex. Ct. App. 1984) (school-sponsored bonfire and pep rally).

¶ 26 We conclude that school districts have always enjoyed governmental immunity for the operation of such programs as the one at issue. Thus, the Act did not in any way limit or abrogate a right to recover from the District.

CONCLUSION

¶ 37 In conclusion, we hold that section 63–30–34 of the Utah Code is constitutional as applied to plaintiffs. Specifically, the limitation on damages found in the Utah Governmental Immunity Act does not violate the open courts clause ....

NOTES

1. Are right to a remedy/open courts provisions substantive, procedural, or both? What does "substantive" and "procedural" mean in this context?

2. How difficult is it for the courts to give content and meaning to right to a remedy/open courts provisions without usurping the legislative function? Are the separation of powers considerations in this context similar to or different from such concerns generally?

MELLO v. BIG Y FOODS
826 A.2d 1117 (Conn. 2003)

BORDEN, J.

The two issues in this reservation are, first, whether the plaintiff's claim for permanent and significant scarring on her foot and ankle is barred by...the exclusive remedy provision of the Workers' Compensation Act (act), [and second, if] so, whether that bar violates article first, § 10, of the constitution of Connecticut. We answer the first question in the affirmative and the second question in the negative.

The parties stipulated to the following facts. The plaintiff was employed by the defendant. On July 3, 1998, during the course of and in the scope of her employment, the plaintiff sustained a compensable burn injury to her right foot and ankle, which later resulted in permanent and significant scarring. The plaintiff filed a claim pursuant to chapter 568 of the General Statutes seeking workers' compensation benefits, including a claim for benefits for permanent and significant scarring .... The defendant accepted the compensability of the plaintiff's underlying injury to her foot by way of voluntary agreement, and paid for medical treatment and indemnity benefits for missed work, and for a 3 percent permanent disability to her right foot. The defendant denied compensability, however, for the scarring to the plaintiff's foot and ankle. Thereafter, the commissioner found that there was no scarring to the plaintiff's face, head or neck, and that the scarring to her foot and ankle did not interfere with her ability to obtain or continue work. Accordingly, the commissioner denied the plaintiff's claim for scarring to her foot and ankle.

I

THE PLAINTIFF'S CLAIM IS BARRED BY THE ACT'S
EXCLUSIVITY PROVISIONS

We begin by addressing the first reserved question: whether the plaintiff's claim is barred by the exclusivity provision of the act.

We conclude that the plaintiff's claim that her scarring should be actionable against her employer outside the workers' compensation system is inconsistent with the act. In place of the trade-offs provided by the act would be a situation in which employees could seek compensation for those aspects of their compensable injuries that are specifically enumerated in the act, while seeking damages in tort against their employers for those aspects of their injuries not specifically enumerated. Such a result would, in many cases, including the present action, expose employers to liability under both the act and the common law. The costs and the lack of predictability that would result from such a rule would be unreasonable in light of the legislature's endeavor to reduce the costs of the system and in light of the public policy behind the act, which seeks to afford remedies quickly and efficiently to injured employees.

II

THE EXCLUSIVITY BAR, AS APPLIED TO THE FACTS OF THIS CASE, DOES NOT VIOLATE ARTICLE FIRST, § 10, OF THE CONNECTICUT CONSTITUTION

Having answered the first question in the affirmative, we now turn to the second question: whether the exclusivity provision, as applied to the facts of this case, violates article first, § 10, of the constitution of Connecticut. That is, is the act's exclusivity provision unconstitutional, as applied to the facts of this case, because it precludes the plaintiff from exercising her preexisting common-law right to bring an action in negligence seeking damages for her scarring? We conclude that it is not.

Article first, § 10, of the constitution of Connecticut provides that "[a]ll courts shall be open, and every person, for an injury done to him in his person, property or reputation, shall have remedy by due course of law, and right and justice administered without sale, denial or delay." "This provision appears in the constitution of 1818 and in its several revisions and reenactments, and has been referred to as the right to redress." It is settled law that this provision restricts the power of the legislature to abolish a legal right existing at common law prior to 1818 without also establishing a "reasonable alternative to the enforcement of that right." In order to be reasonable, however, an alternative need not be the *exact* equivalent of the abolished common-law right or its remedy. "Thus for each remedy or item of damage existing under the prior fault system, it is not required that that item be duplicated under the [alternative] act but that the bulk of remedies under the act be of such significance that a court is justified in viewing this legislation on the whole as a substitute, the benefits from which are sufficient to tolerate the removal of the prior cause of action." In other words, in determining whether an alternative is reasonable, a court need only consider the aggregated benefits of the legislative alternative and assess whether those aggregated benefits reasonably approximate the rights formerly available under the common law.

We have concluded that the act is a reasonable alternative to claims in tort for damages that existed at common law as actions for trespass on the case. In *Daily*, the principal plaintiff claimed that the injury to his hand, sustained during routine maintenance of a precision machine, was actionable under a product liability theory, despite the fact that he was entitled to and had been receiving benefits under the act. We disagreed and concluded, instead, that through "the aggregate benefits associated with the workers' compensation laws...the legislature provided a 'reasonable alternative' to workers having product liability claims and that [it], as a result, did not enact legislation violative of article first, § 10, of the Connecticut constitution."

We conclude...that the act's rights and remedies provide a reasonable alternative to the plaintiff's common-law right to bring a negligence action for damages resulting from her scarring. The plaintiff has been compensated, through the act, for all compensable losses associated with the injury she sustained to her foot. This compensation included medical costs, lost wages and a permanent disability payment of 3 percent. Under the terms of the act, the plaintiff received these benefits without the delay of filing an action and the burden of proving negligence. This is the exchange offered by the act; workers forego certain damages and remedies available to them under common law, but they gain a predictable, reliable, speedy and inexpensive means of obtaining compensation. [T]he rights and remedies available under a legislative "'reasonable alternative'" need not equate, in every respect and detail, the superseded common-law rights and remedies. The aggregated benefits need only reasonably approximate the former right.

NOTES

1. Right to a remedy/open courts provisions have been litigated in a variety of contexts, as the cases illustrate. Should all contexts be treated the same for constitutional purposes? Or are there reasons to evaluate damages caps, repose periods, defenses, workers' compensation, or procedural limitations differently? Note that such cases might also arise in the criminal context. *See, e.g., Dorsey v. State*, 716 A.2d 807 (Del. 2000) (declaring a state constitutional right to a suppression of evidence remedy in the context of an unconstitutional search).

2. How do the standards the state courts use in evaluating right to a remedy/open courts provisions compare to federal due process and equal protection standards? Are they the same, similar, or distinctly different? Do right to a remedy provisions serve the same purposes as the Fourteenth Amendment's Due Process and Equal Protection Clauses?

3. For additional reading on state constitutional right to remedy/open courts provisions, see David Schuman, *The Right To A Remedy*, 65 Temple L. Rev. 1197 (1992); Jonathan M. Hoffman, *Questions Before Answers: The Ongoing Search to Understand the Origins of the Open Courts Clause*, 32 Rutgers L.J. 1005 (2001). *See also* John C. P. Goldberg, *The Constitutional Status of Tort Law: Due Process and the Right to a Law for the Redress of Wrongs*, 115 Yale L.J. 524 (2005).

CHAPTER XII

OTHER STATE INDIVIDUAL RIGHTS

A. PRIVACY

The right of privacy is a broad concept, used to refer to a variety of claims or entitlements. Professor Friesen notes that:

> The right of privacy under state constitutions potentially embraces at least three distinct types of interests: (1) the right to be free of unreasonable government (or, sometimes, private) surveillance; (2) the right to prevent the accumulation or dissemination of certain kinds of information (sometimes called "informational" privacy); and (3) the right to make important choices about personal or family life free of state coercion (sometimes called "autonomy" rights). Jennifer Friesen, *State Constitutional Law: Litigating Individual Rights, Claims and Defenses* § 2.01 (4th ed. LexisNexis 2006).

The right of an individual to make personal decisions free from government control is covered in Chapter V. At this point, the focus is on the right to be free from unreasonable governmental surveillance.

While the United States Constitution does not contain an express right of privacy, there is an explicit enumerated right to privacy in the state constitutions of Alaska, California, Florida, Hawaii, and Montana. Alaska Const. art. I, § 22; Cal. Const. art. I, § 1; Fla. Const. art. I, § 23; Haw. Const. art. I, § 6; Mont. Const. art. II, § 10. The privacy provision in the Florida Constitution states:

> Every natural person has the right to be let alone and free from governmental intrusion into the person's private life except as otherwise provided herein. This section shall not be construed to limit the public's right of access to public records and meetings as provided by law. Fla. Const. art I, § 23.

Six other state constitutions, although not having a separate right to privacy, protect forms of privacy through the "search and seizure" sections of the state constitution.

YORK v. WAHKIAKUM SCHOOL DISTRICT NO. 200
178 P.3d 995 (Wash. 2008) (*en banc*)

SANDERS, J.

The question before us is whether random and suspicionless drug testing of student athletes violates article I, section 7 of the Washington State Constitution.

The Wahkiakum School District ("school district") randomly drug tests all student athletes under the authority of Wahkiakum School Board Policy No. 3515 ("policy 3515"). Aaron and Abraham York and Tristan

Schneider played sports for Wahkiakum High School, agreed to the policy, and were tested. Their parents ("York and Schneider parents") sued the school district alleging its drug testing policy violated article I, section 7 of the Washington State Constitution. The school district claims random drug testing, without any individualized suspicion, is constitutional. The superior court agreed. We accepted direct review.

The school district asks us to adopt a "special needs" exception to the warrant requirement to allow random and suspicionless drug testing. But we do not recognize such an exception and hold warrantless random and suspicionless drug testing of student athletes violates the Washington State Constitution.

Wahkiakum requires its student athletes to refrain from using or possessing alcohol or illegal drugs. Beginning in 1994, the school district implemented myriad ways to combat drug and alcohol use among the student population. Nevertheless, drug and alcohol problems persisted. Acting independently of the school district, the Wahkiakum Community Network (community network) began surveying district students. From these surveys, the community network ranked teen substance abuse as the number one problem in Wahkiakum County. As reiterated by the trial court, the community network's surveys showed that in 1998, 40 percent of sophomores reported previously using illegal drugs and 19 percent of sophomores reported illegal drug use within the previous 30 days, while 42 percent of seniors reported previously using illegal drugs and 12.5 percent reported illegal drug use within the previous 30 days. In 2000, 50 percent of student athletes self-identified as drug and/or alcohol users.

As a result, the school district decided to implement random drug testing where all students may be tested initially and then subjected to random drug testing during the remainder of the season. The school district formed the Drug and Alcohol Advisory Committee (now the "Safe and Drug Free Schools Advisory Committee") to help deal with the student substance abuse problems. The committee evaluated the effectiveness of its previous programs, such as D.A.R.E. (Drug Abuse Resistance Education) and support groups, and contemplated adopting policy 3515, which would require random drug testing of student athletes. The trial court found:

> Based upon the evidence of substantial alcohol and drug use among students and pursuant to the School District's statutory authority and responsibility to maintain order and discipline in its schools, to protect the health and safety of its students, and to control, supervise and regulate interschool athletics, the Board of Directors adopted the policy.

As part of the policy, all student athletes must agree to be randomly drug tested as a condition of playing extracurricular sports. The drug testing is done by urinalysis, with the student in an enclosed bathroom stall and a health department employee outside. The sample is then mailed to Comprehensive Toxicology Services in Tacoma, Washington. If the results indicate illegal drug use, then the student is suspended from extracurricular athletic activities; the length of suspension depends on the number of infractions and whether the student tested positive for illegal drugs or alcohol. Also, the school district provides students with drug and alcohol counseling resources. The results are not sent to local law enforcement or included in the student's academic record. And the student is not suspended from school, only extracurricular sports.

During the 1999-2000 school year, Aaron York and Abraham York played sports and were tested under the policy. And Tristan Schneider was tested under the policy during the 2000-2001 year. The York and Schneider parents brought suit arguing the school district's policy violated the Washington State Constitution. Their motion for a preliminary injunction was denied by superior court Judge Penoyar, and the Court of Appeals dismissed the petition as moot. The trial court then held that while the school district's policy "approached the tolerance limit" of our constitution, the policy was nevertheless constitutional and narrowly tailored to reach a compelling government end.

The York and Schneider parents sought and obtained direct review in our court of a summary judgment order and ask us to determine whether the school district's policy 3515 is constitutional.

We are aware there are strong arguments, policies and opinions marshaled on both sides of this debate, but we are concerned only with the policy's constitutionality. And while we are loath to disturb the decisions of a local school board, we will not hesitate to intervene when constitutional protections are implicated. No matter the drawbacks or merits of the school district's random drug testing, we cannot let the policy stand if it offends our constitution. Students "do not 'shed their constitutional rights' at the schoolhouse door."

The question before us is narrow: Whether Wahkiakum School District's blanket policy requiring student athletes to submit to random drug testing is constitutional. The United States Supreme Court has held such activity does not violate the Fourth Amendment to the federal constitution. But we have never decided whether a suspicionless, random drug search of student athletes violates article I, section 7 of our state constitution. Therefore, we must decide whether our state constitution follows the federal standard or provides more protection to students in the state of Washington.

*May Wahkiakum School District Perform Suspicionless, Random Drug
Tests of Student Athletes?*

a.   *Federal cases concerning public school searches*

The school district argues we should follow federal cases and allow suspicionless, random drug testing of its student athletes. Two federal cases are apposite to our consideration. These cases, while helpful, do not control how we interpret our state constitution. There are stark differences in the language of the two constitutional protections; unlike the Fourth Amendment, article I, section 7 is not based on a reasonableness standard.

The United States Supreme Court has held public school searches presented a "special need," which allowed a departure from the warrant and probable cause requirements. *New Jersey v. T.L.O.*, 469 U.S. 325 (1985). The *T.L.O.* Court held school teachers and administrators could search students without a warrant if: (1) there existed "reasonable grounds for suspecting that the search will turn up evidence that the student has violated or is violating either the law or the rules of the school," and (2) the search is "not excessively intrusive in light of the age and sex of the student and the nature of the infraction."

Next, in *Vernonia School District 47J v. Acton*, 515 U.S. 646 (1995), a public school district implemented a random drug testing of school athletes, similar to the one at issue here. Each student athlete was tested at the beginning of the season and then each week 10 percent were randomly selected for testing. Most critics of *Acton* are not persuaded the majority's analysis justifies a suspicionless search of the student athletes. But the *Acton* majority claimed individualized suspicion would unduly interfere with the government's goals and might actually make the situation worse. Its reasoning was based primarily on three rationales: (1) individualized suspicion would "transform[] the process into a badge of shame," where teachers could claim any troublesome student was abusing drugs; (2) teachers and student officials are neither trained nor equipped to spot drug use; and (3) individualized suspicion creates an unnecessary loss of resources in defending claims and lawsuits against arbitrary imposition, when students and parents will inevitably challenge whether reasonable suspicion did indeed exist.

But these arguments were unpersuasive several years earlier when the Court applied an individualized suspicion standard to public schools in *T.L.O.* The *Acton* majority never adequately explained why individual suspicion was needed in *T.L.O.* but not in *Acton.* Justice O'Connor spent much of her dissent taking issue with this standard:

> [N]owhere is it *less* clear that an individualized suspicion requirement would be
> ineffectual than in the school context. In most schools, the entire pool of

potential search targets—students—is under constant supervision by teachers and administrators and coaches, be it in classrooms, hallways, or locker rooms.

> The great irony of this case is that most (though not all) of the evidence the District introduced to justify its suspicionless drug testing program consisted of first- or second-hand stories of particular, identifiable students acting in ways that plainly gave rise to reasonable suspicion of in-school drug use—and thus that would have justified a drug-related search under our *T.L.O.* decision.

The Wahkiakum School District modeled its policy after the one used by the Vernonia School District. But simply passing muster under the federal constitution does not ensure the survival of the school district's policy under our state constitution. The Fourth Amendment provides for "[t]he right of the people to be secure in their persons, houses, papers, and effects, against unreasonable searches and seizures." Therefore, a Fourth Amendment analysis hinges on whether a warrantless search is reasonable, and it is possible in some circumstances for a search to be reasonable without a warrant. But our state constitutional analysis hinges on whether a search has "authority of law" – in other words, a warrant. Wash. Const. art. I, § 7.

b. Search and seizure analysis under article I, section 7

Our state constitution provides: "No person shall be disturbed in his private affairs, or his home invaded, without authority of law." Wash. Const. art. I, § 7. It is well established that in some areas, article I, section 7 provides greater protection than its federal counterpart – the Fourth Amendment. When determining whether article I, section 7 provides greater protection in a particular context, we focus on whether the unique characteristics of the constitutional provision and its prior interpretations compel a particular result. We look to the constitutional text, historical treatment of the interest at stake, relevant case law and statutes, and the current implications of recognizing or not recognizing an interest.

This requires a two-part analysis. First, we must determine whether the state action constitutes a disturbance of one's private affairs. Here that means asking whether requiring a student athlete to provide a urine sample intrudes upon the student's private affairs. Second, if a privacy interest has been disturbed, the second step in our analysis asks whether authority of law justifies the intrusion. The "authority of law" required by article I, section 7 is satisfied by a valid warrant, limited to a few jealously guarded exceptions. Because the Wahkiakum School District had no warrant, if we reach the second prong of the analysis we must decide whether the school district's activity fits within an exception to the warrant requirement. Relying on federal law, the school district claims there is a "special needs" exception to the warrant requirement that we should adopt. The York and Schneider parents point out we have not adopted such an exception and urge us not to do so here.

Suspicionless, Random Drug Testing Disturbs a Student Athlete's Private Affairs.

When inquiring about private affairs, we look to "'those privacy interests which citizens of this state have held, and should be entitled to hold, safe from governmental trespass absent a warrant.'" This is an objective analysis.

The private affair we are concerned with today is the State's interference in a student athlete's bodily functions. Specifically, does it intrude upon a privacy interest to require a student athlete to go into a bathroom stall and provide a urine sample, even against that student's protest? Federal courts and our court both agree the answer is an unqualified yes, such action intrudes into one's reasonable expectation of privacy. Indeed, we offer heightened protection for bodily functions compared to the federal courts.

Because we determine that interfering with a student athlete's bodily functions disturbs one's private affairs, we must address the second prong of the article I, section 7 analysis: does the school district have the necessary authority of law to randomly drug test student athletes?

Under Article I, Section 7 There Is No Authority of Law That Allows a School District to Conduct Random Drug Tests.

We have long held a warrantless search is *per se* unreasonable, unless it fits within one of the "'jealously and carefully drawn exceptions.'" These exceptions include exigent circumstances, consent, searches incident to a valid arrest, inventory searches, the plain view doctrine, and *Terry* investigative stops. Any exceptions to the warrant requirement must be rooted in the common law. And it is always the government's burden to show its random drug testing fits within one of these narrow exceptions. Today the school district asks us to accept an analog to the federal special needs doctrine to justify its drug testing policy. The York and Schneider parents point out we have never formally adopted a special needs exception and therefore claim no exception to the warrant requirement exists here.

a.   Federal special needs exception

Before addressing whether we have adopted or will adopt such a special needs exception, it is helpful to briefly examine the federal exception to understand both its requirements and its breadth. The United States Supreme Court has held there are certain circumstances when a search or seizure is directed toward "'special needs, beyond the normal need for law enforcement" and "the warrant and probable-cause requirement [are] impracticable.'" For there to be a special need, not only must there be some interest beyond normal law enforcement but also any evidence garnered from the search or seizure should not be expected to be used in any criminal prosecution against the target of the search or seizure. The Court has applied such reasoning to administrative searches, border patrols, and prisoners and probationers.

The United States Supreme Court has also held drug testing presents a special need and may be done under certain circumstances without a warrant or individualized suspicion. In *Skinner v. Railway Labor Executives' Assoc.*, 489 U.S. 602, 634 (1989), the Court upheld warrantless and suspicionless blood and urine testing of railroad employees following major train accidents. The Court applied similar reasoning in *National Treasury Employees Union v. Von Raab*, 489 U.S. 656 (1989), when it held immigration officials may be subjected to random drug testing.

   b. Is there a Washington State special needs exception?

We have never adopted a special needs exception but have looked to federal special needs cases when dealing with similar issues. In cases concerning administrative searches, border patrols, and prisoners and probationers, our courts have departed from the warrant requirement in similar, but not always identical, ways.

We cannot countenance random searches of public school student athletes with our article I, section 7 jurisprudence. As stated earlier, we require a warrant except for rare occasions, which we jealously and narrowly guard. We decline to adopt a doctrine similar to the federal special needs exception in the context of randomly drug testing student athletes. In sum, no argument has been presented that would bring the random drug testing within any reasonable interpretation of the constitutionally required "authority of law."

Accordingly, we hold the school district's policy 3515 is unconstitutional and violates student athletes' rights secured by article I, section 7. Therefore we reverse the superior court. The York and Schneider parents shall recover their costs.

NOTE

The "special needs" rationale was adopted by the Supreme Court of New Jersey and led it to hold that the search and seizure protection in the state constitution did not prohibit a drug testing program in a public high school. The school's policy provided for the random, suspicionless drug and alcohol testing of all students who engaged in an extracurricular activity or who possessed a parking permit. *Joye v. Hunterdon Cent. Reg'l High Sch. Bd. of Educ.*, 826 A.2d 624 (N.J. 2003).

B. FREE SPEECH AND EXPRESSION

Although the texts of state constitutions regarding freedom of speech are quite similar to each other, they are different from the language in the First Amendment. The origins of the provisions in state constitutions can be traced to William Blackstone's Commentaries:

> Every freeman has an undoubted right to lay what sentiments he pleases before his public; to forbid this, is to destroy the freedom of the press: but if he publishes what is improper, mischievous, or illegal, he must take the consequences of his own temerity. William Blackstone, 4 Commentaries 152.

The first time that Blackstone's "abuse" qualification appeared in an American Constitution was the text of the Pennsylvania Constitution of 1790:

> The free communication of thoughts and opinions is one of the invaluable rights of man; and every citizen may freely speak, write, and print on any subject, being responsible for the abuse of that liberty. Pa. Const. art. IX, § 7 (1790).

Today, protections for speech, expression and the press are found in more than forty state constitutions. The provision in the New York Constitution is typical:

> Every citizen may freely speak, write and publish his or her sentiments on all subjects, being responsible for the abuse of that right; and no law shall be passed to restrain or abridge the liberty of speech or of the press. N.Y. Const. art. I, § 8.

The free speech provisions in state constitutions generally have two components. The first part describes the protected right and the responsibility for the abuse of those rights. The second part prohibits laws that abridge the protected rights.

FASHION VALLEY MALL v. NATIONAL LABOR RELATIONS BOARD
172 P.3d 742 (Cal. 2007)

MORENO, J.

We granted the request of the United States Court of Appeals for the District of Columbia Circuit to decide whether, under California law, a shopping mall may enforce a rule prohibiting persons from urging customers to boycott a store in the mall. For the reasons that follow, we hold that the right to free speech granted by article I, section 2 of the California Constitution includes the right to urge customers in a shopping mall to boycott one of the stores in the mall.

On October 4, 1998, thirty to forty Union members had distributed leaflets to customers entering and leaving the Robinsons-May store at the Mall. The leaflets stated that Robinsons-May advertises in the Union-

Tribune, described several ways that the newspaper allegedly treated its employees unfairly, and urged customers who believed "that employers should treat employees fairly" to call the newspaper's "CEO," listing his name and telephone number. The administrative law judge concluded: "From all indications, the leafleters conducted their activity in a courteous and peaceful manner without a disruption of any kind and without hindrance to customers entering or leaving" the store.

Within fifteen or twenty minutes, Mall officials "arrived on the scene to stop the leafleting," notifying the Union members that they were trespassing because they had not obtained a permit from the Mall "to engage in expressive activity," and warning them that they "would be subject to civil litigation and/or arrest if they did not leave." A police officer appeared and, following a brief argument, the Union members moved to public property near the entrance to the Mall and continued distributing leaflets briefly before leaving the area.

The Mall has adopted rules requiring persons who desire to engage in expressive activity at the Mall to apply for a permit five business days in advance. The applicant "must agree to abide by" the Mall's rules, including rule 5.6.2, which prohibits "impeding, competing or interfering with the business of one or more of the stores or merchants in the shopping center by:...[u]rging, or encouraging in any manner, customers not to purchase the merchandise or services offered by any one or more of the stores or merchants in the shopping center."

The administrative law judge found that the Union "was attempting to engage in a lawful consumer boycott of Robinsons-May because Robinsons-May advertised in the Union-Tribune newspaper" and further found "that it would have been utterly futile for the Union to have followed [the Mall]'s enormously burdensome application-permit process because its rules contained express provisions barring the very kind of lawful conduct the Union sought to undertake at the Mall." The administrative law judge thus ordered the Mall to cease and desist prohibiting access to the Union's "leafleters for the purpose of engaging in peaceful consumer boycott handbilling."

Article I, section 2, subdivision (a) of the California Constitution declares: "Every person may freely speak, write and publish his or her sentiments on all subjects, being responsible for the abuse of this right. A law may not restrain or abridge liberty of speech or press." Nearly 30 years ago, in *Robins v. PruneYard Shopping Center*, 592 P.2d 341 (Cal. 1979), *aff'd*, 447 U.S. 74 (1980), we held that this provision of our state Constitution grants broader rights to free expression than does the First Amendment to the United States Constitution by holding that a shopping mall is a public forum in which persons may exercise their right to free speech under the California Constitution. We stated that a shopping center "to which the public is invited can provide an essential and invaluable forum for exercising [free speech] rights." We noted that in many cities the public areas of the shopping mall are replacing the streets and sidewalks of the central business district which, "have immemorially been held in trust for the use of the public and, time out of mind, have been used for purposes of assembly, communicating thoughts between citizens, and discussing public questions." Because of the "growing importance of the shopping center[,]…to prohibit expressive activity in the centers would impinge on constitutional rights beyond speech rights," particularly the right to petition for redress of grievances. Accordingly, we held that the California Constitution "protect[s] speech and petitioning, reasonably exercised, in shopping centers even when the centers are privately owned." We added the caveat in *PruneYard* that "[b]y no means do we imply that those who wish to disseminate ideas have free rein," noting our previous "endorsement of time, place, and manner rules."

The Mall in the present case generally allows expressive activity, as mandated by the California Constitution, but requires persons wishing to engage in free speech in the Mall to obtain a permit. Under rule 5.6.2, the Mall will not issue a permit to engage in expressive activity unless the applicant promises to refrain from conduct "[u]rging, or encouraging in any manner, customers not to purchase the merchandise or services offered by any one or more of the stores or merchants in the shopping center." We must determine, therefore, whether a shopping center violates California law by banning from its premises speech urging the public to boycott one or more of the shopping center's businesses.

The idea that private property can constitute a public forum for free speech if it is open to the public in a manner similar to that of public streets and sidewalks long predates our decision in *PruneYard*. The United States Supreme Court recognized more than half a century ago that the right to free speech guaranteed by the First Amendment to the United States Constitution can apply even on privately owned land. In *Marsh v. Alabama*, 326 U.S. 501 (1946), the high court held that a Jehovah's Witness had the right to distribute religious literature on the sidewalk near the post office of a town owned by the Gulf Shipbuilding Corp., because the town had

> all the characteristics of any other American town…. In short, the town and its shopping district are accessible to and freely used by the public in general, and there is nothing to distinguish them from any other town and shopping center except the fact that the title to the property belongs to a private corporation.

The high court stated: "The more an owner, for his advantage, opens up his property for use by the public in general, the more do his rights become circumscribed by the statutory and constitutional rights of those who use it."

Our decision that the California Constitution protects the right to free speech in a shopping mall, even though the federal Constitution does not, stems from the differences between the First Amendment to the federal Constitution and article I, section 2 of the California Constitution. We observed in *Gerawan Farming, Inc. v. Lyons*, 12 P.3d 720 (Cal. 2000), that the free speech clause in article I of the California Constitution differs from its counterpart in the federal Constitution both in its language and its scope:

> It is beyond peradventure that article I's free speech clause enjoys existence and force independent of the First Amendment's. In section 24, article I states, in these very terms, that "[r]ights guaranteed by [the California] Constitution are not dependent on those guaranteed by the United States Constitution." This statement extends to all such rights, including article I's right to freedom of speech. For the California Constitution is now, and has always been, a "document of independent force and effect particularly in the area of individual liberties."

> As a general rule...article I's free speech clause and its right to freedom of speech are not only as broad and as great as the First Amendment's, they are even "broader" and "greater."

In *PruneYard*, high school students in the mall were prohibited from soliciting support for their opposition to a United Nations resolution against Zionism. We held that the mall could not prohibit the students' efforts despite the fact that this free speech activity was unrelated to the business of the center. In so holding, we relied upon our earlier decision in *Schwartz-Torrance*, which, we noted, "held that a labor union has the right to picket a bakery located in a shopping center." We cautioned, however, that we did not "imply that those who wish to disseminate ideas have free rein," noting our previous "endorsement of time, place, and manner rules." We also repeated Justice Mosk's observation in his dissent in *Diamond II* that compelling a shopping center to permit "[a] handful of additional orderly persons soliciting signatures and distributing handbills in connection therewith, under reasonable regulations adopted by defendant to assure that these activities do not interfere with normal business operations would not markedly dilute defendant's property rights."

The Mall argues that its rule banning speech that advocates a boycott is a "reasonable regulation" designed to assure that free expression activities "do not interfere with normal business operations" within the meaning of our decision in *PruneYard*. According to the Mall, it "has the right to prohibit speech that interferes with the intended purpose of the Mall," which is to promote "the sale of merchandise and services to the shopping public." We disagree.

It has been the law since we decided *Schwartz-Torrance* in 1964, and remains the law, that a privately owned shopping center must permit peaceful picketing of businesses in shopping centers, even though such picketing may harm the shopping center's business interests. Our decision in *Diamond* recognized that citizens have a strengthened interest, not a diminished interest, in speech that presents a grievance against a particular business in a privately owned shopping center, including speech that advocates a boycott.

The level of scrutiny with which we review a restriction of free speech activity depends upon whether it is a content-neutral regulation of the time, place, or manner of speech or restricts speech based upon its content. A content-neutral regulation of the time, place, or manner of speech is subjected to intermediate scrutiny to determine if it is "(i) narrowly tailored, (ii) serves a significant government interest, and (iii) leaves open ample alternative avenues of communication." A content-based restriction is subjected to strict scrutiny. "[D]ecisions applying the liberty of speech clause [of the California Constitution], like those applying the First Amendment, long have recognized that in order to qualify for intermediate scrutiny (*i.e.*, time, place, and manner) review, a regulation must be 'content neutral,' and that if a regulation is content based, it is subject to the more stringent strict scrutiny standard."

Prohibiting speech that advocates a boycott is not a time, place, or manner restriction because it is not content neutral. The Mall's rule prohibiting persons from urging a boycott is improper because it does not regulate the time, place, or manner of speech, but rather bans speech urging a boycott because of its content. Restrictions upon speech "that by their terms distinguish favored speech from disfavored speech on the basis of the ideas or views expressed are content based."

The Mall argues that its rule prohibiting speech that urges a boycott is "a 'content-neutral' restriction under California law because it applies to any and all requests for a consumer boycott of the Mall's merchants…regardless of the subject matter or viewpoint of the speaker advocating the boycott." The Mall is mistaken. The Mall's rule prohibiting all boycotts may be viewpoint neutral, because it treats all requests for a boycott the same way, but it is not content neutral, because it prohibits speech that urges a boycott while permitting speech that does not.

The rule at issue here prohibiting speech that advocates a boycott cannot similarly be justified by legitimate concerns that are unrelated to content. Peacefully urging a boycott in a mall does not by its nature cause congestion, nor does it promote fraud or duress. "[T]he boycott is a form of speech or conduct that is ordinarily entitled to protection under the First and Fourteenth Amendments." Our California Constitution provides greater, not lesser, protection for this traditional form of free speech. Unlike the ordinance in *Alliance*, the Mall's rule in the instant case is not concerned with the inherently intrusive nature of such speech, but rather with the impact such speech may have on its listeners. "Handbills…'depend entirely on the persuasive force of the idea.' The loss of customers because they read a handbill urging them not to patronize a business…is the result of mere persuasion." The Mall is concerned that the speech may be effective and persuade customers not to patronize a store. But "[l]isteners' reaction to speech is not a content-neutral basis for regulation." The Mall seeks to prohibit speech advocating a boycott solely because it disagrees with the message of such speech, which might persuade some potential customers not to patronize the stores in the Mall.

The Mall's rule prohibiting speech that advocates a boycott cannot withstand strict scrutiny. The Mall's purpose to maximize the profits of its merchants is not compelling compared to the Union's right to free expression. Urging customers to boycott a store lies at the core of the right to free speech. "The safeguarding of these rights to the ends that men may speak as they think on matters vital to them and that falsehoods may be exposed through the processes of education and discussion is essential to free government. Those who won our independence had confidence in the power of free and fearless reasoning and communication of ideas to discover and spread political and economic truth." The fact that speech may be convincing is not a proper basis for prohibiting it. The right to free speech "extends to more than abstract discussion, unrelated to action." The First Amendment is a charter for government, not for an institution of learning. "Free trade in ideas" means free trade in the opportunity to persuade to action, not merely to describe facts. The Mall cites no authority, and we are aware of none, that holds that a store has a compelling interest in prohibiting this traditional form of free speech.

A shopping mall is a public forum in which persons may reasonably exercise their right to free speech guaranteed by article I, section 2 of the California Constitution. Shopping malls may enact and enforce reasonable regulations of the time, place and manner of such free expression to assure that these activities do not interfere with the normal business operations of the mall, but they may not prohibit certain types of speech based upon its content, such as prohibiting speech that urges a boycott of one or more of the stores in the mall.

We hold that, under California law, Fashion Valley Mall may not maintain and enforce against the Union its rule 5.6.2, which prohibits "[u]rging, or encouraging in any manner, customers not to purchase the merchandise or services offered by any one or more of the stores or merchants in the shopping center."

NOTE

The United States Supreme Court decided one of the seminal cases involving state constitutional rights in *PruneYard Shopping Center v. Robins*, 447 U.S. 74 (1980). The issue before it was framed as "whether state constitutional provisions, which permit individuals to exercise free speech and petition rights on the property of a privately owned shopping center to which the public is invited, violate the shopping center owner's property rights under the Fifth and Fourteenth Amendments or his free speech rights under the First and Fourteenth Amendments." *Id.* at 76. The California Supreme Court held that article 1, sections 2 and 3 of the California Constitution "protects speech and petitioning, reasonably exercised, in shopping centers even when the centers are privately owned" and have a policy not to permit *any* publicly expressive activity, that is strictly enforced in a non-discriminatory fashion. *Robins v. PruneYard Shopping Center*, 592 P.2d 341, 347 (Cal. 1979).

In *Lloyd Corp. v. Tanner*, 407 U.S. 551 (1972), the United States Supreme Court had considered a similar issue in the context of First Amendment rights. In *Lloyd*, the court held that when a shopping center owner opens its private property to the public for the purpose of shopping, the First Amendment of the United States Constitution does not create individual rights in expression beyond those already existing under applicable law. *See PruneYard Shopping Center v. Robins*, 447 U.S. at 81. In *PruneYard*, the court's holding in *Lloyd* was distinguished on the basis that it did "not *ex proprio vigore* limit the authority of the State to exercise its police power or its sovereign right to adopt in its own Constitution individual liberties more expansive than those conferred by the Federal Constitution." *Id.*

The United States Supreme Court then pointed out that in *Lloyd*, unlike the situation presented in *PruneYard*, "there was no state constitutional or statutory provision that had been construed to create rights to the use of private property by strangers, comparable to those found to exist by the California Supreme Court." *Id.* The Supreme Court then addressed the argument that the rights conferred by the California Constitution, if exercised at the private shopping center, would constitute a taking of property without just compensation in violation of the Fifth and Fourteenth Amendments:

> It is true that one of the essential sticks in the bundle of property rights is the right to exclude others. And here there has literally been a "taking" of that right to the extent that the California Supreme Court has interpreted the State Constitution to entitle its citizens to exercise free expression and petition rights on shopping center property. But it is well established that "not every destruction or injury to property by governmental action has been held to be a 'taking' in the constitution sense."

> Here the requirement that appellants permit appellees to exercise state-protected rights of free expression and petition on shopping center property clearly does not amount to an unconstitutional infringement of appellants' property rights under the Taking Clause. There is nothing to suggest that preventing appellants from prohibiting this sort of activity will unreasonably impair the value or use of their property as a shopping center. The PruneYard is a large commercial complex that covers several city blocks, contains numerous separate business establishments, and is open to the public at large. The decision of the California Supreme Court makes it clear that PruneYard may restrict expressive activity by adopting time, place, and manner regulations that will minimize any interference with its commercial functions. Appellees were orderly, and they limited their activity to the common areas of the shopping center. In these circumstances, the fact that they may have "physically invaded" appellants' property cannot be viewed as determinative.

Id. at 82-84. Accordingly, the unique right of petition afforded by the California Constitution prevailed in *PruneYard* even though the assertion of a First Amendment right had not succeeded in *Lloyd*, despite an almost identical factual context.

The United States Constitution does not confer a general right to free speech in a privately owned shopping center. Most state constitutions have been construed the same way. The state constitutions of California, Oregon, Massachusetts, New Jersey and Colorado have been interpreted to confer certain rights of expression at privately owned shopping centers. Only California, however, has held that the free speech protection in its state constitution applies to both private and state action.

STATE v. STUMMER
194 P.3d 1043 (Ariz. 2008)

BERCH, V. C.J.

Petitioners Hubert August Stummer and Dennis Allen Lumm were charged with violating section 13-1422 of the Arizona Revised Statutes, which forbids adult bookstores from remaining open during certain early morning hours. We have been asked to determine whether the hours of operation provision of section 13-1422 violates the free speech provision of the Arizona Constitution.

Petitioners operate adult-oriented businesses in Phoenix that sell sexually explicit books and magazines. They were charged with violating section 13-1422(A), which requires adult bookstores to close for fifty-three hours each week: from 1 a.m. to 8 a.m., Monday through Saturday, and from 1 a.m. to noon on Sunday.

Petitioners moved to dismiss the charges, citing *Empress Adult Video & Bookstore v. City of Tucson*, 59 P.3d 814, 823-24 (Ariz. Ct. App. 2002), which held the hours of operation provision in section 13-1422(A) unconstitutional. Bound by *Empress*, the superior court granted the motion. The State appealed, arguing that *Empress* was wrongly decided.

Section 13-1422 limits the hours an adult bookstore may remain open:

> An adult arcade, adult bookstore or video store, adult cabaret, adult motion picture theater, adult theater, escort agency or nude model studio shall not remain open at any time between the hours of 1:00 a.m. and 8:00 a.m. on Monday through Saturday and between the hours of 1:00 a.m. and 12:00 noon on Sunday.

The Arizona Legislature enacted section 13-1422 in response to complaints from citizens and local businesses that "adult" businesses were causing negative effects, including increased prostitution and sexually oriented litter, in the surrounding communities. These negative effects were alleged to be more prevalent during the early morning hours and the proponents therefore urged the legislature to restrict the operating hours of these businesses to reduce the problems.

These negative effects are byproducts or "secondary effects" of speech. The legislature purportedly designed section 13-1422(A) to suppress these secondary effects, not to suppress the speech itself. Although such regulations necessarily affect speech, restrictions on secondary effects have received less exacting scrutiny under the Federal Constitution than have laws designed to directly curtail speech. We must decide what level of scrutiny Arizona courts should apply when determining the constitutionality, under article 2, section 6 of the Arizona Constitution, of content-based secondary effects regulations.

Analysis of Section 13-1422 Under the First Amendment

Under the First Amendment, regulations that target speech based on its content are typically subject to strict scrutiny. The federal courts, however, have carved out an exception to this rule: Certain time, place, and manner restrictions designed to address the secondary effects of speech are subject to intermediate scrutiny.

Finding such regulations justified by the goal of reducing secondary effects rather than suppressing speech, the Supreme Court initially characterized such regulations as content neutral. More recently, however, federal courts have begun to acknowledge that secondary effects laws directed exclusively at adult businesses are not truly content neutral.

Nonetheless, the federal courts continue to apply a form of intermediate scrutiny. Under the federal test, a "statute will be upheld if it is designed to serve a substantial government interest, is narrowly tailored to serve that interest, and does not unreasonably limit alternative avenues of communication."

Applying this test, several federal courts have upheld statutes imposing hours of operation restrictions on sexually oriented businesses against First Amendment challenges.

Soon after section 13-1422 became effective, a coalition of adult businesses challenged the statute in federal court, asserting that its hours provision violates the First Amendment. Applying the *Renton* test, the district court upheld section 13-1422 and denied injunctive relief. Affirming, the Ninth Circuit found the intermediate scrutiny test satisfied. It concluded that section 13-1422 serves a substantial government interest; is narrowly tailored because "Arizona's interest in ameliorating secondary effects 'would be achieved less effectively absent the regulation,'" and leaves open alternative channels for communication by allowing stores to remain open "seventeen hours per day Monday through Saturday, and thirteen hours on Sunday."

Interpreting Article 2, § 6 of the Arizona Constitution

The issue presented in this case is not...whether section 13-1422 violates the First Amendment to the United States Constitution, but rather whether it passes muster under article 2, section 6 of the Arizona Constitution. Both the First Amendment and article 2, section 6, protect speech from abridgment by the government. The First Amendment does so by restraining government interference with speech rights. It provides that "Congress shall make no law...abridging the freedom of speech, or of the press." U.S. Const. amend. I. Arizona's free speech provision, in contrast, guarantees each individual's right to speak freely. It states that "[e]very person may freely speak, write, and publish on all subjects, being responsible for the abuse of that right." Ariz. Const. art. 2, § 6.

The encompassing text of article 2, section 6 indicates the Arizona framers' intent to rigorously protect freedom of speech. In addressing censorship, we have said that the words of Arizona's free speech provision "are too plain for equivocation. The right of every person to freely speak, write and publish may not be limited."

Arizona courts have had few opportunities to develop Arizona's free speech jurisprudence. With regard to unprotected speech, Arizona courts construing article 2, section 6 have followed federal interpretations of the United States Constitution. For example, in being "responsible for the abuse" of the right to speak, write, and publish on "all subjects," one may be held liable for defamation, notwithstanding the right to "freely speak."

We have also stated that article 2, section 6 has "greater scope than the First Amendment." This is not a case, however, in which we need to determine the boundaries of Arizona's free speech provision. The State does not argue that the books and magazines in Petitioners' bookstores are obscene. Thus in selling those materials, Petitioners are engaging in protected speech under article 2, section 6. We need only decide whether and to what extent the State may curtail this protected speech in order to reduce secondary effects.

Our opinion in *Mountain States Telephone & Telegraph Co. v. Arizona Corporation Commission*, 773 P.2d 455 (Ariz. 1989), is the starting point for our analysis of this issue. That case involved the regulation of "ScoopLines": pay-per-call telephone numbers that provided customers with messages on a variety of topics, such as sports and weather. In response to consumer complaints, the Arizona Corporation Commission ordered Mountain States to block ScoopLines and "to propose a presubscription plan for the Commission's approval." Mountain States sought relief from this Court, arguing that the Commission's order violated article 2, section 6.

There, as here, the government argued that the regulation was intended to accomplish a goal unrelated to the suppression of protected speech and that any effect on speech rights was "incidental and permissible." Although we concluded that the Commission could impose content-neutral "time, place, and manner" regulations, we cautioned that, "given Arizona's constitutional protections, when dealing with regulations that affect speech, the [government] must regulate with narrow specificity so as to affect as little as possible the ability of the sender and receiver to communicate."

In *Empress*, the court of appeals interpreted *Mountain States*' "narrow specificity" language as requiring that the regulation "affect *as little as possible* the ability of the sender and receiver to communicate." The court of appeals thus effectively adopted a "least restrictive means" standard. Applying this standard, the court concluded that section 13-1422 violated the Arizona Constitution because closing adult businesses for at least seven hours a day was not the least restrictive means of addressing the secondary effects of adult businesses.

The booksellers here urge that we adopt the *Empress* standard. We conclude, however, that such a standard is not appropriate for judging the constitutionality of secondary effects regulations. When a regulation is content based, but directed at addressing the secondary effects of speech, the legislative choice is entitled to more deference than the strict scrutiny test permits. The government may have a substantial interest in addressing certain secondary effects of speech, and applying strict scrutiny may effectively preclude regulations designed to prohibit such effects.

The State urges us instead to apply the federal intermediate scrutiny standard articulated by the Supreme Court in *Renton* and *Alameda Books*, as did the Ninth Circuit in *Center for Fair Public Policy* and the court of appeals panel in this case. We decline to strictly apply the federal test because it is inconsistent with the broad protection of speech afforded by the Arizona Constitution. Because Arizona's speech provision safeguards the right to speak freely on all topics, our test must more closely scrutinize laws that single out speech for regulation based on its disfavored content. We thus turn to the question of the appropriate test for determining the constitutionality, under article 2, section 6, of secondary effects regulations.

The appropriate test for measuring the constitutionality of content-based secondary effects regulations must vindicate the constitutional right to free speech, yet accommodate the government's interest in protecting the public health, safety, and welfare. The test has two phases. First, to qualify for intermediate scrutiny, the State must demonstrate that a content-based regulation is directed at ameliorating secondary effects, not at suppressing protected speech. Second, to survive intermediate scrutiny, the State must show that, in addressing the secondary effects, the regulation does not sweep too broadly.

In the first phase, the challenger must demonstrate that the challenged provision interferes with the right to freely speak, write, or publish. Once the challenger has shown that a content-based or content-correlated regulation affects free expression, the State bears the burden of demonstrating that the enacting body had a reasonable basis for believing that the speech singled out for regulation created secondary effects different from or greater than the effects of speech generally, and that the challenged regulation was designed to suppress those secondary effects, not to suppress the speech itself.

The State may carry that burden by demonstrating to the court that, on the basis of the evidence before it, the enacting body might reasonably believe that the regulated speech created negative secondary effects greater than those created by speech generally and that the regulation would address those effects. If the State meets this burden of showing that the legislative body enacted the challenged regulation to respond to secondary effects rather than disfavored speech, we will address the challenged regulation under a form of intermediate scrutiny.

In the second phase of the inquiry for determining the constitutionality of a content-based secondary effects regulation, the court must examine whether the regulation protects substantial government interests and whether it significantly reduces secondary effects without unduly interfering with protected speech. The deference afforded at the first phase, in which the court determines whether intermediate scrutiny applies, does not extend to the second phase, in which the court assesses the effects of the challenged law. For the regulation to survive, its proponent must show that the government has a substantial interest, that the regulation significantly furthers that interest, and that the challenged regulation does not unduly burden speech. To establish or disprove these prongs, the challenger and the proponent of the regulation may bring forth pre- and post-enactment evidence.

In applying the phase-two test, the court must first assess the importance of the government's asserted interest. Regulations designed to reduce crime, protect children, or safeguard constitutional rights, for example, may justify some infringement on speech rights. Lesser concerns, such as the abatement of mere litter or governmental convenience, will not justify suppression of speech.

If the government advances a substantial interest, the court must then determine whether the regulation significantly furthers that interest. A court may find this prong satisfied if the regulation substantially reduces or has a significant ameliorative impact on secondary effects. In this analysis, the court must consider the likelihood that the regulation will achieve its intended result. For example, the court may consider how much sex-related crime occurs during the hours of forced closure. The answer to this inquiry may elucidate whether the regulation is designed to significantly reduce such negative secondary effects and thus whether it may achieve its intended result.

Finally, the third prong—whether the regulation unduly burdens speech—may be satisfied by establishing that the government's substantial interest would be less effectively achieved without the regulation and ample alternative means of communication exist. Although the test does not require the least restrictive means possible, the proponent must show a close fit or nexus between the ends sought and the means employed for achieving those ends.

In analyzing the facts of this case under the first phase of Arizona's secondary effects test, we conclude that the Petitioners have established that their protected speech is burdened by a content-based regulation. The State, in turn, has met its burden of demonstrating that the hours provision of section 13-1422 was designed to curb the secondary effects of speech, not to prohibit the speech itself. The State adduced evidence that the legislature reasonably believed that adult businesses encourage criminal activity and sexually oriented litter, that these effects were worse in the nighttime hours, and that the statute at issue would ameliorate those effects. We therefore turn to the second phase of the inquiry, application of the three-part test: whether the government's interests are substantial, whether the regulation significantly furthers those interests, and whether the regulation unduly burdens speech.

In the second phase, the court must first assess the significance of the government's interests. The existence of mere litter is not by itself sufficiently important to permit a substantial restriction on speech. As we stated in *New Times, Inc. v. Arizona Board of Regents*, 519 P.2d 169, 174 (Ariz. 1974), "minor matters of public inconvenience or annoyance cannot be transformed into substantive evils of sufficient weight to warrant the curtailment of liberty of expression." Combating criminal activity such as prostitution and public indecency, however, is a substantial governmental interest. We therefore move to the second and third prongs of the phase-two analysis.

As to the second prong, whether the statute significantly furthers the government's interest, the record is devoid of evidence that secondary effects are greater during the hours of forced closure. The record reflects only two pieces of evidence on this point. One was the testimony of a representative of the City of Phoenix who testified that the city could *not* show a relationship between the hours of operation and the incidence of crime. The other was a study from Glendale, Colorado, finding that *fewer* police calls or incidents arose from a particular adult business during the late night hours than during other times. Neither piece of evidence supports the assertion that the effects are greater during the hours of forced closure. Without such a showing, the State may have difficulty establishing that closure is an appropriate remedy—that is, that this statute significantly furthers the government's interest in reducing secondary effects. The government must establish that, during their early morning operation, adult bookstores disproportionately cause negative secondary effects and that these negative effects are or will be significantly lessened by closure during those hours.

Finally, regarding the third prong, the State has not shown that any substantial interests would be achieved less effectively without the bookstores' closure for fifty-three hours each week. The record also does not contain evidence regarding the availability of alternative channels of communication during the hours of closure.

In short, because this case was decided on a motion to dismiss, the record contains no evidence of the significance of the infringement on speech, the effectiveness of the statute in reducing negative secondary effects, the nexus between the ends sought and the means employed, or the availability of alternative measures.

Because no court below has had the opportunity to apply the test we formulate today for evaluating the constitutionality of content-based secondary effects regulations, we conclude that all parties should have the opportunity to present additional evidence supporting their positions, and the trial court should have the opportunity to apply .the test for constitutionality detailed above. We therefore remand this case to the superior court for further proceedings consistent with this opinion.

We vacate the opinion of the court of appeals and remand this case to the trial court.

NOTES

1. The federal secondary effects standards have been adopted in construing the constitutions of some states. *See People v. Superior Court*, 774 P.2d 769 (Cal. 1989); *DiRaimo v. City of Providence*, 714 A.2d 554 (R.I. 1998).

2. The Tennessee Supreme Court held that a state obscenity statute, based upon the *Miller* test, did not violate the state constitution's guarantee in article I, section 19 of free communications of thoughts and opinions. *Tennessee v. Marshall*, 859 S.W.2d 289 (Tenn. 1993). The states of Maryland, Minnesota, Ohio, Texas and Washington have followed the First Amendment jurisprudence on obscenity even when there have been differences in the text of the state constitution.

C. CIVIL JURY TRIAL

Although the Sixth Amendment right to trial by jury in a criminal proceeding has been made binding upon the states by virtue of the Fourteenth Amendment, *Duncan v. Louisiana*, 391 U.S. 145, 156 (1968), the United States Supreme Court has thus far declined to hold that the Seventh Amendment right to trial by jury in a civil proceeding is binding upon the states. *See Minneapolis & St. Louis R.R. Co. v. Bombolis*, 241 U.S. 211 (1916). Accordingly, the right to a jury trial in civil proceedings has always been and remains exclusively protected by provisions in the constitution of each state.

SOFIE v. FIBREBOARD CORP.
771 P.2d 711 (Wash. 1989)

UTTER, J.

Austin and Marcia Sofie challenge the constitutionality of section 4.56.250 of the Washington Code. This statute, part of the 1986 tort reform act, places a limit on the noneconomic damages recoverable by a personal injury or wrongful death plaintiff. The Sofies brought a direct appeal to this court after the trial judge in their tort action, under the direction of the statute, reduced the jury's award of noneconomic damages. The respondents subsequently cross-appealed to the Court of Appeals, raising several issues of trial court error, issues we consider here.

The Sofies argue that section 4.56.250 violates their constitutional rights to trial by jury, equal protection, and due process. We find that the statute's damages limit interferes with the jury's traditional function to determine damages. Therefore, section 4.56.250 violates article 1, section

21 of the Washington Constitution, which protects as inviolate the right to a jury. Because the statute is unconstitutional on this basis, we do not consider its constitutionality under the latter two doctrines raised by appellants, although we briefly survey the equal protection issues. Respondents' arguments concerning trial court error are without merit.

The Washington Legislature passed section 4.56.250 in 1986 partly as a response to rising insurance premiums for liability coverage. The damages limit that the statute creates operates on a formula based upon the age of the plaintiff. As a result, the older a plaintiff is, the less he or she will be able to recover in noneconomic damages. The trial judge applies the limit to the damages found by the trier of fact. If the case is tried before a jury, the jury determines the amount of noneconomic damages without knowledge of the limit. The jury goes about its normal business and the judge reduces, according to the statute's formula and without notifying the jury, any damage verdicts that exceed the limit.

In September 1987, the Sofies sued Fibreboard Corp. and other asbestos manufacturers for the harm caused to Mr. Sofie by their asbestos products. Mr. Sofie, then aged 67, was suffering from a form of lung cancer—mesothelioma—caused by exposure to asbestos during his career as a pipefitter. At trial, Mr. Sofie's attorneys presented evidence of the extreme pain he experienced as a result of the disease. The testimony indicated that Mr. Sofie spent what remained of his life waiting for the next "morphine cocktail," for the next hot bath, for anything that would lessen his consuming physical agony.

At the end of the trial, the jury found the defendants at fault for Mr. Sofie's disease. They returned a verdict of $1,345,833 in favor of the Sofies. Of this amount, $1,154,592 went to compensate noneconomic damages: $477,200 for Mr. Sofie's pain and suffering and $677,392 for Mrs. Sofie's loss of consortium. While the trial judge specifically found the jury's finding of damages reasonable, he indicated he was compelled under the damages limit to reduce the noneconomic portion of the verdict to $125,136.45, resulting in a total judgment of $316,377.45.

The dispositive issue of this case is the right to a jury trial. This court has long approached the review of legislative enactments with great care. The wisdom of legislation is not justiciable; our only power is to determine the legislation's constitutional validity. In matters of economic legislation, we follow the rule giving every reasonable presumption in favor of the constitutionality of the law or ordinance. We employ this caution to avoid substituting our judgment for the judgment of the Legislature.

Other courts, faced with unconstitutional tort damage limits, have adhered to similar principles when reviewing those legislative actions. The Kansas Supreme Court put it well:

> This court is by the Constitution not made the critic of the legislature, but rather, the guardian of the Constitution. The constitutionality of a statute is presumed, and all doubts must be resolved in favor of its validity. Before a statute may be stricken down, it must clearly appear the statute violates the Constitution. Moreover, it is the court's duty to uphold the statute under attack, if possible, rather than defeat it, and if there is any reasonable way to construe the statute as constitutionally valid, that should be done. *Kansas Malpractice Victims Coalition v. Bell*, 757 P.2d 251, 256-57 (Kan. 1988).

To determine the extent of the right to trial by jury as it applies here, we must first identify the source of the constitutional protection. The seventh amendment to the United States Constitution does not apply through the Fourteenth Amendment to the states in civil trials. The right to jury trial in civil proceedings is protected solely by the Washington Constitution in article 1, section 21. Therefore, the relevant analysis must follow state doctrine; our result is based entirely on adequate and independent state grounds.

Article 1, section 21 states:

> The right of trial by jury shall remain inviolate, but the legislature may provide for a jury of any number less than twelve in courts not of record, and for a verdict by nine or more jurors in civil cases in any court of record, and for waiving of the jury in civil cases where the consent of the parties interested is given thereto.

Our basic rule in interpreting article 1, section 21 is to look to the right as it existed at the time of the constitution's adoption in 1889. We have used this historical standard to determine the scope of the right as well as the causes of action to which it applies. These two issues, scope and the applicable causes of action, merit separate discussion.

State ex rel. Mullen v. Doherty, 47 P. 958 (1897), being close in time to 1889, provides some contemporary insight on the scope issue. In *Mullen*, we cited section 248 of the Code of 1881, in force at the time of the constitution's passage, to determine the jury's role in the constitutional scheme: "either party shall have the right in an action at law, upon an issue of fact, to demand a trial by jury." Subsequent cases underscore the jury's fact finding province as the essence of the right's scope.

At issue in the present case is whether the measure of damages is a question of fact within the jury's province. Our past decisions show that it is indeed. The constitutional nature of the jury's damage-finding function is underscored by *Baker v. Prewitt*, 19 P. 149 (Wash. 1888). In that case, the territorial Supreme Court stated:

> Sections 204 and 289 of the [territorial] Code seem to require that in all actions for the assessment of damages the intervention of a jury must be had, save

> where a long account may authorize a referee, etc. This statute is mandatory, and
> we are satisfied that where the amount of damages is not fixed, agreed upon, or
> in some way liquidated, a jury must be called, unless expressly waived.

If our state constitution is to protect as inviolate the right to a jury trial at least to the extent as it existed in 1889, then *Baker*'s holding provides clear evidence that the jury's fact-finding function included the determination of damages. This evidence can only lead to the conclusion that our constitution, in article 1, section 21, protects the jury's role to determine damages.

The present case is not the first time we have recognized the constitutional nature of the jury's damage-determining role. In *James v. Robeck*, 490 P.2d 878 (Wash. 1971), we stated: "To the jury is consigned under the constitution the ultimate power to weigh the evidence and determine the facts-and the amount of damages in a particular case is an ultimate fact."

The jury's role in determining noneconomic damages is perhaps even more essential. In *Bingaman v. Grays Harbor Comm'ty Hosp.*, 699 P.2d 1230 (Wash. 1985), the husband of a woman who died painfully 35 hours after giving birth, the result of medical malpractice, brought a wrongful death and survival action. The only issue before this court was whether the trial judge had properly reduced the jury's damage verdict of $412,000 for the woman's pain and suffering. In resolving the issue in the plaintiff's favor, we stated: "The determination of the amount of damages, *particularly in actions of this nature*, is primarily and peculiarly within the province of the jury, under proper instructions."

United States Supreme Court jurisprudence on the Seventh Amendment's scope in [federal] civil trials, while not binding on the states, also provides some insight. In *Dimick v. Schiedt*, 293 U.S. 474 (1935), the Court used historical analysis to determine whether the Seventh Amendment allowed additur. Citing cases and treatises dating from the time of the amendment's adoption, the Court found that determining damages, as an issue of fact, was very much within the jury's province and therefore protected by the Seventh Amendment. The Court also indicated that a judge should give more deference to a jury's verdict when the damages at issue concern a noneconomic loss. The Court quoted the English case of *Beardmore v. Carrington*, 2 Wils. 244, 248:

> There is great difference between cases of damages which [may] be certainly
> seen, and such as are ideal, as between assumpsit, trespass for goods where the
> sum and value may be measured, and actions of imprisonment, malicious
> prosecution, slander and other personal torts, where the damages are matter of
> opinion, speculation, ideal...

The Court clarified the implications of the difference between these two classes of actions by quoting from Mayne's Treatise on Damages, at 571:

"'in cases where the amount of damages was uncertain their assessment was a matter so peculiarly within the province of the jury that the Court should not alter it.'"

A method of historical analysis used by the United States Supreme Court in *Tull v. United States*, provides further insight. The *Tull* Court looked for proceedings analogous to the enforcement action under the federal clean water act which were contemporary with the Seventh Amendment's adoption. Finding that the common law proceeding of debt, in which the litigants had a right to a jury, was analogous to the clean water act enforcement action, the Court applied the Seventh Amendment right to the modern action. Without stretching the analogy as far as the Supreme Court did, it is logical to apply the more recent tort theories by analogy to the common law tort actions that existed in 1889. We note again that we reach our result today on adequate and independent state grounds. The holding in *Tull*, like all United States Supreme Court precedent in the civil trial area of the Seventh Amendment, is not binding on the states and merely serves as an example to us. It does not compel the result we reach.

Ultimately, there is not even an issue whether the right to a jury attaches to the Sofies' case. While they asserted "newer" tort theories in their complaint, the heart of the appellants' cause of action centered on negligence and willful or wanton misconduct resulting in personal injury. These basic tort theories are the same as those that existed at common law in 1889. Subsequent cases and statutes have recognized newer theories of recovery within the framework of these basic tort actions, but the basic cause of action remains the same. Therefore, the right to trial by jury—with its scope as defined by historical analysis—remains attached here.

The potential impact of the constitution's language was not lost on the Legislature. During the floor debates on the Tort Reform Act, the legislators were warned of the possible constitutional problems with their new legislation. Senator Talmadge stated:

> The Constitution of this state in Article I, Section 21, talks about the right to trial by jury being inviolate, not being something that we can invade as members of the Legislature, and when you start to put limitations on what juries can do, you have, in fact, invaded the province of the jury and have not preserved the right to a trial by jury inviolate.

Senate Journal, 49th Legislature (1986), at 449.

It is highly persuasive that in Kansas, Texas, Ohio, and Florida, states that have found the damages limit unconstitutional, the operative language of the right to jury trial provisions in those states' constitutions is nearly identical to our own. *See* Kan. Const. Bill of Rights § 5 ("The right of trial by jury shall be inviolate"); Tex. Const. art. I, § 15 ("The right of trial by jury shall remain inviolate"); Ohio Const. art. I, § 5 ("The right of trial by jury shall be inviolate"); Fla. Const. art. I § 22 ("The right of trial by jury shall be secure to all and remain inviolate").

The weight of authority from other states, both numerically and persuasively, supports the conclusion that Washington's damages limit violates the right to trial by jury.

McCOOL v. GEHRET
657 A.2d 269 (Del. 1995)

HOLLAND, J.

This is an appeal from the Superior Court. In their original complaint, the plaintiffs-appellants, Paul and Tammera McCool (the "McCools") alleged medical negligence by the defendant-appellee, John Gehret, M.D. ("Dr. Gehret"), and certain other health care providers. The complaint was amended to allege tortious interference by Dr. Gehret with the plaintiffs' medical expert witness, Robert Dein, M.D. ("Dr. Dein"). Over the plaintiffs' objection, the Superior Court granted Dr. Gehret's motion to sever the trial of the McCools' claim for medical malpractice from the trial of their claim for tortious interference.

A jury trial was held on the medical malpractice claim only, beginning on January 18, 1994. The jury returned a verdict in favor of Dr. Gehret on January 26, 1994. On February 3, 1994, the plaintiffs filed a motion for a mistrial or, in the alternative, a new trial.

On April 20, 1994, a one-day bench trial was held regarding the tortious interference claim. This bench trial was held before a different Superior Court judge than the one who had presided at the malpractice trial.

The McCools contend that forcing them to proceed with a bench trial on their tortious interference claim, despite their objection, violated their Delaware Constitutional right to have a trial by jury in that civil proceeding. The historical origins of the right to trial by jury, which is provided for in the Delaware Constitution, was reviewed by this Court in *Claudio v. State*, 585 A.2d 1278 (Del. 1991). In *Claudio*, this Court noted that when Delaware adopted its Constitution in 1792, notwithstanding the ratification of the first ten amendments or federal Bill of Rights in 1791, it did not create "a mirror image of the United States Constitution" with regard to trial by jury.

When the Delaware Constitution of 1792 was adopted, the right to trial by jury set forth in the federal Bill of Rights as the Sixth and Seventh Amendments to the United States Constitution was only a protection against action by the federal government. Following the adoption of the Fourteenth Amendment to the United States Constitution, the Sixth

Amendment right to trial by jury in *criminal* proceedings has been deemed to have been incorporated by the Due Process clause and now also provides protection against state action. Nevertheless, the United States Supreme Court has not held that the Seventh Amendment's guarantee of jury trials in *civil* proceedings was made applicable to the states by the incorporation doctrine with the adoption of the Fourteenth Amendment to the United States Constitution.

Accordingly, the right to a jury trial in civil proceedings has always been and remains exclusively protected by provisions in the Delaware Constitution. Delaware adopted its first Constitution in 1776, which provided, in pertinent part:

> The common law of England, as well as so much of the statute law as have been heretofore adopted in practice in this state, shall remain in force, unless they shall be altered by a future law of the Legislature; such parts only excepted as are repugnant to the rights and privileges contained in this constitution and the declaration of rights, & c. agreed to by this convention. Del. Const. of 1776, art. 25.

Delaware also adopted its own *Declaration of Rights* in 1776, which guaranteed the right to trial by jury to all citizens of the State of Delaware and included a statement "[t]hat trial by jury of facts where they arise is one of the greatest securities of the lives, liberties and estates of the people."

When Delaware adopted its next Constitution in 1792, its citizens were guaranteed the right to trial by jury "as heretofore." Consequently, since its inception in 1776, the Delaware Constitution has afforded its citizens the right to trial by jury in both criminal and civil proceedings. In doing so, the Delaware Constitution has expressly preserved all of the fundamental features of the jury system as they existed at common law.

A *sine qua non* of that common law jurisprudence is the principle that either party shall have the right to demand a jury trial upon an issue of fact in an action at law. As previously noted, the 1776 Delaware *Declaration of Rights*, which was preserved by the "heretofore" text in the 1792 Constitution, referred to the right to trial by jury regarding factual issues as "one of the greatest securities of the lives, liberties and estates of the people." Similarly, in a letter to Pierre S. DuPont, Thomas Jefferson described the fact finding function of jurors as:

> the very essence of a Republic.... We of the United States...think experience has proved it safer for the mass of individuals composing the society to reserve to themselves personally the exercise of all rightful powers to which they are competent....

> Hence, with us, the people...being competent to judge of the facts occurring in ordinary life,...have retained the functions of judges of facts under the name of jurors....

> I believe…that action by the citizens, in person in affairs within their reach and competence, and in all others by representatives chosen immediately and removable by themselves, constitutes the essence of a Republic.

Letter from Thomas Jefferson to Pierre S. DuPont (April 4, 1816).

In 1855, the Delaware General Assembly enacted a statute that purportedly allowed judges to decide issues of fact without a jury in actions at law, with the agreement of all the parties. Nevertheless, because the Delaware Constitution preserved the right to trial by jury as "heretofore," Delaware judges took the position that, absent constitutional amendment, the General Assembly could not alter the right by statute. Therefore, notwithstanding the enactment of the 1855 statute by the General Assembly, Delaware judges remained reluctant to decide issues of fact in an action at law because they concluded that the Delaware Constitution required a jury to decide such questions.

When the present Delaware Constitution was rewritten in 1897, the General Assembly included several significant provisions regarding the right to trial by jury. Article I of the 1897 Delaware Constitution was denominated for the first time as the "Bill of Rights." Section 4 of that article provided for the right to trial by jury as "heretofore." Article IV, section 19 was a new addition in the 1897 Constitution and provided: "Judges shall not charge juries with respect to matters of fact, but may state the questions of fact in issue and declare the law." Del. Const. art. IV, § 19. The reason given during the Constitutional debates for the adoption of section 19 was to ensure "that Judges shall confine themselves to their business, which is to adjudge the law and leave juries to determine the facts."

In *Storey*, this Court characterized section 19 as perpetuating Delaware's commitment to trial by jury in civil actions at law with regard to issues of fact. In examining when a trial judge may set aside a jury verdict, this Court described Delaware's long history of commitment to trial by jury. We explained that section 19 reaffirmed Delaware's commitment to the common law principles regarding trial by jury:

> In the policy of the law of this state, declared by the courts in numberless decisions, the jury is the sole judge of the facts of a case, and so jealous is the law of this policy that by express provision of the Constitution the court is forbidden to touch upon the facts of the case in its charge to the jury.

In 1897, another new section was added to article IV of Delaware's Constitution. Article IV, section 20 provides that, "[i]n civil causes where matters of fact are at issue, if the parties agree, such matters of fact shall be tried by the court, and judgment rendered upon their decision thereon as upon a verdict by a jury." Del. Const. art. IV, § 20. According to the Constitutional debates, the purpose of the new section was to address the concerns of Delaware's jurists about the constitutionality of the 1855 statutory authorization for litigants to waive a trial by jury in an action at law on an issue of fact.

In this case the McCools specifically demanded a jury trial on their medical malpractice claim and their tortious interference claim. When the jury that heard their medical malpractice claim was discharged, the McCools agreed to waive their right to a jury trial regarding their tortious interference claim only because the original trial judge offered to decide the remaining claim as a bench trial. The record contains the following statement by the McCools' attorney to the second trial judge:

> For practical reasons, the [medical malpractice] trial went a bit longer than we expected. Because of the two-week period of the jury panel, [the original trial judge] explained to us that it did not appear we would be able to get the same jury.

> Discussing this in chambers as well as I think in the courtroom,...[the original trial judge] proposed [to personally hear] this count...[as] a bench trial, [the] benefit being, again, that even though we don't have the jury, at least we have a judge who did have the benefit of hearing all the testimony.

When the original trial judge subsequently declined to hear the tortious interference claim, the McCools objected to proceeding with a bench trial before another judge. Their attorney advised the second judge:

> Based on our understanding that the matter would be heard on the bench trial before [the original trial judge], my clients and I agreed to have it heard that way rather than [by] jury trial. [I] just want to go on record that is their position. They still are opposed to...the assignment of your honor.

Although a party has no right to insist on a bench trial before a particular judge, the record reflects that the McCools' waiver of their right to a jury trial was, in fact, permitted to be premised upon such a condition. The McCools only waived their right to a jury trial on the condition that the bench trial would be held before the original judge who had heard the medical malpractice claim and was familiar with much of the evidence relevant to the tortious interference claim. When the original trial judge, who had induced the McCools to waive their right to a jury trial, refused to hear their tortious interference claim, the condition upon which the McCools' waiver had been predicated ceased to exist.

This Court has recognized that the right to a trial by jury, as guaranteed by the Delaware Constitution, may be relinquished pursuant to a valid waiver. Under the circumstances presented in this case, however, the McCools could not be forced to proceed with a bench trial before a second judge, in the absence of an unconditional waiver of their fundamental right to a trial by jury. Consequently, the bench trial of the tortious interference claim that proceeded, without the McCools' express and unconditional waiver of a jury trial, violated article IV, section 20 and article I, section 4 of the Delaware Constitution.

NOTES

1. Article I, § 13 the Illinois Constitution of 1970 states: "The right of trial by jury as heretofore enjoyed shall remain inviolate." Ill. Const. (1970), art. I, § 13. The meaning of this provision has been explained as follows:

> The constitutional provision that "the right of trial by jury as heretofore enjoyed shall remain inviolate" means that the right to a jury trial shall continue in all cases where such right existed at common law at the time the Constitution was adopted, but that constitutional provision has never been held to prohibit the legislature from creating new rights unknown to the common law and provide for their determination without a jury.

Standidge v. Chicago Rys. Co., 98 N.E. 963 (Ill. 1912).

Therefore, the right to a jury trial under the Illinois Constitution is not guaranteed in any action that did not exist at common law, even if the action is legal in nature. However, the right to a jury trial continues in all civil cases where the right existed at common law at the time the federal Bill of Rights was adopted. In addition, it has been recognized that the Illinois General Assembly may create an action unknown at common law and provide a right to a trial by jury.

2. In civil cases, the Kentucky Constitution has been construed as recognizing exceptions to the right to a jury trial, including causes of action at common law that would have been regarded as equitable.

3. The Pennsylvania Constitution was amended to provide that a verdict may be rendered by not less than five-sixths of the jury in any civil case. Subject to that amendment, however, the right to trial by jury remained "as heretofore" and "inviolate." Pa. Const. art. I, § 6. In a civil case, twelve jurors retired to deliberate but one juror did not complete the deliberations. After the plaintiff-appellant's motion for a mistrial was denied, the eleven remaining jurors returned a unanimous verdict. The Pennsylvania Supreme Court reversed and held that the parties were entitled to a verdict of twelve jurors, notwithstanding the fact that the unanimous verdict of eleven jurors was greater than five-sixths of twelve. *See Blum v. Merrell Dow Pharmaceuticals, Inc.*, 626 A.2d 537 (Pa. 1993).

D. RIGHT TO BEAR ARMS

JANE DOE v. WILMINGTON HOUSING AUTHORITY
88 A.3d 654 (Del. 2014)

RIDGELY, J.

In this certified question proceeding, we address whether lease provisions for apartments of a Delaware public housing authority that restrict when residents, their household members, and their guests may carry and possess firearms in the common areas violate the right to keep and bear arms guaranteed by Article I, Section 20 of the Delaware Constitution. We accepted two questions of state law from the United States Court of Appeals for the Third Circuit ("Third Circuit"). Pending before the Third Circuit is an appeal from a judgment of the United States District Court for the District of Delaware in *Doe. v. Wilmington Housing Authority*. The District Court found no violation of the Second Amendment or the Delaware Constitution. The certified questions are:

> 1. Whether, under Article I, § 20 of the Delaware Constitution, a public housing agency such as the WHA may adopt a policy prohibiting its residents, household members, and guests from displaying or carrying a firearm or other weapon in a common area except when the firearm or other weapon is being transported to or from a resident's housing unit or is being used in self-defense.

> 2. Whether, under Article I, § 20 of the Delaware Constitution, a public housing agency such as the WHA may require its residents, household members, and guests to have available for inspection a copy of any permit, license, or other documentation required by state, local, or federal law for the ownership, possession, or transportation of any firearm or other weapon, including a license to carry a concealed weapon, as required by Del. Code Ann. tit. 11, § 1441, on request when there is reasonable cause to believe that the law or policies have been violated.

We answer both certified questions in the <u>negative</u>.

Facts and Procedural History

Appellants Jane Doe and Charles Boone ("Residents") filed suit in the Delaware Court of Chancery against the Wilmington Housing Authority (WHA), a nonprofit agency of the State of Delaware that provides housing to low-income individuals and families, and against WHA's Executive Director, Frederick Purnell. Jane Doe lived in the Park View, a <u>privately</u> owned housing facility managed by the WHA. Doe's lease required her to follow the "House Rules." The original version of House Rule 24, in effect when the suit was filed, stated, "Tenant is not permitted to display or use any firearms, BB guns, pellet guns, slingshots, or other weapons on the premises." Charles Boone lived in the Southbridge Apartments, a <u>public</u> housing facility owned and operated by the WHA. Boone's lease stated that residents are "not to display, use, or possess ... any firearms, (operable or inoperable) or other dangerous instruments or deadly weapons as defined by the laws of the State of Delaware anywhere on the property of the Authority." Residents were subject to eviction if they, their household members, or their guests violated the lease provisions and rules.

Doe and Boone alleged that the restrictions on gun use and possession violated their right to bear arms as provided in the Second Amendment to the United States Constitution and in Article I, Section 20 of the Delaware Constitution. They also alleged that the WHA firearms rules and policies were preempted by Delaware law and that the WHA exceeded its statutory authority by enacting them.

The defendants removed the case to the United States District Court for the District of Delaware on June 1, 2010. On June 28, 2010, the Supreme Court of the United States decided *McDonald v. City of Chicago*, holding that the Second Amendment applies to the states through the Due Process Clause of the Fourteenth Amendment. The defendants informed the District Court that they were reevaluating the constitutionality of the WHA firearm rules and policies in light of *McDonald*.

On October 25, 2010, the WHA adopted a new firearms policy (the "Revised Policy") for its public housing units, including Southbridge. The Revised Policy provides, in full:

Lease Modification (Replaces Lease Part I § DC.P.):

> Ownership, possession, transportation, display, and use of firearms and weapons is governed by the Wilmington Housing Authority Firearms and Weapons Policy which is incorporated into and made a part of this lease.
>
> Wilmington Housing Authority Firearms and Weapons Policy:
>
> WHA recognizes the importance of protecting its residents' health, welfare, and safety, while simultaneously protecting the rights of its residents to keep and bear arms as established by the federal and state constitutions. WHA therefore adopts the following Firearms and Weapons Policy. Residents, members of a resident's household, and guests:
>
> > 1. Shall comply with all local, state, and federal legal requirements applicable to the ownership, possession, transportation, and use of firearms or other weapons. The term "firearm" includes any weapon from which a shot, projectile or other object may be discharged by force of combustion, explosive, gas and/or mechanical means, whether operable or inoperable, loaded or unloaded, and any weapon or destructive device as defined by law.
> >
> > 2. Shall not discharge or use any firearm or other weapons on WHA property except when done in self-defense.
> >
> > 3. Shall not display or carry a firearm or other weapon in any common area, except where the firearm or other weapon is being transported to or from the resident's unit, or is being used in self-defense.
> >
> > 4. Shall have available for inspection a copy of any permit, license, or other documentation required by state, local, or federal law for the ownership, possession, or transportation of any firearm or other weapon, including a license to carry a concealed weapon as required by 11 Del C. § 1441, upon request, when there is reasonable cause to believe that the law or this Policy has been violated.
> >
> > 5. Shall exercise reasonable care in the storage of loaded or unloaded firearms and ammunition, or other weapons.

6. Shall not allow a minor under 16 years of age to have possession of a firearm, B.B. gun, air gun, or spear gun unless under the direct supervision of an adult.

7. Shall not give or otherwise transfer to a minor under 18 years of age a firearm or ammunition for a firearm, unless the person is that child's parent or guardian, or unless the person first receives the permission of the minor's parent or guardian.

Violation of this Policy by any resident or member of the resident's household shall be grounds for immediate Lease termination and eviction. In addition, a resident or member of the resident's household who knowingly permits a guest to violate this Policy shall be subject to immediate Lease termination and eviction.

On December 13, 2010, the WHA replaced the Park View's House Rule 24 with amended Rule 24, which was substantively identical to the Revised Policy.

Residents filed an amended complaint challenging only paragraph 3, the Common Area Provision, and paragraph 4, the Reasonable Cause Provision, of the Revised Policy. The parties filed cross-motions for summary judgment.

The District Court granted the summary judgment motion filed by the WHA and denied the motion filed by Residents. The District Court found no Second Amendment violation, and no appeal was taken from that ruling. The District Court applied the same analysis to the challenge under Article I, Section 20 of the Delaware Constitution ("Section 20") and found no violation. The District Court found no legal merit to the preemption and scope-of-authority challenges. The questions on which the Third Circuit seeks guidance concern the Section 20 analysis.

In addressing the Section 20 claims, the District Court noted that "[t]here is scant judicial authority interpreting Delaware's constitutional right to bear arms, and none is directly relevant to the issue now before this Court." The District Court granted summary judgment on the Section 20 claims for the same reasons it granted summary judgment on the Second Amendment claims.

The District Court analyzed the Second Amendment issues under recent Supreme Court decisions, including *District of Columbia v. Heller*, and *McDonald*. The District Court also examined the circuit court cases applying *Heller* and *McDonald*, including the Third Circuit's opinion in *United States v. Marzzarella*. The District Court noted that all had adopted a form of intermediate rather than strict scrutiny to analyze laws and policies that restrict firearm possession in public spaces as opposed to in the home.

The District Court followed *United States v. Marzzarella*, examining:

> whether the challenged law imposes a burden on conduct falling within the
> scope of the Second Amendment's guarantee. If it does not, our inquiry is
> complete. If it does, we evaluate the law under some form of means-end
> scrutiny. If the law passes muster under that standard, it is constitutional. If it
> fails, it is invalid.

Applying this analysis, the District Court first assumed that the Revised
Policies fell within the Second Amendment's scope, then applied
intermediate scrutiny to assess the constitutionality of paragraphs 3 and 4
of the Revised Policy. The District Court applied intermediate scrutiny on
the basis that those policies do not prohibit residents from possessing
firearms in their homes, but rather regulate "the manner in which Plaintiffs
may lawfully exercise their Second Amendment rights." The District
Court concluded that the two challenged paragraphs of the Revised
Policies were reasonably related to important government interests in
promoting and protecting the safety of public housing residents, guests,
and employees. The District Court also found a reasonable fit between the
Common Area Provision and the promotion of safety in shared areas of
public housing complexes. The District Court further found a reasonable
fit between the Reasonable Cause Provision and the promotion of safety
because obtaining a concealed-weapon permit requires training in gun
safety and is a "reasonable mechanism for assisting with enforcement of
the Common Area Provision." Doe and Boone did not appeal the District
Court's ruling dismissing their Second Amendment claims. Therefore, the
Second Amendment analysis remains the law of the case.

[margin note: D.C. found provisions reasonable]

[margin note: Fed Issue resolved]

The District Court dismissed the claims under the Delaware
Constitution, Article I, Section 20 for the same reasons it dismissed the
Second Amendment claim after applying the same analysis. Doe and
Boone timely appealed the District Court's rulings on their state
constitutional claims to the Third Circuit, which thereafter certified the
two questions now before us.   [margin/inline note: Appeal on State Issue]

Discussion

The acceptance of certified questions of law under Article IV, Section
11 of the Delaware Constitution and Supreme Court Rule 41 is entirely
within the discretion of this Court. We review a certified question in the
context in which it arises. We have the discretion to reformulate or
rephrase the question of law certified. Questions of law and constitutional
claims are decided *de novo*.

We begin by noting that the Declaration of Rights in the Delaware
Constitution has not always been interpreted identically to the counterpart
provisions in the federal Bill of Rights. As we have previously explained:

> The Declaration of Rights in the Delaware Constitution is not a mirror image of
> the federal Bill of Rights. Consequently, Delaware judges cannot faithfully

discharge the responsibilities of their office by simply holding that the Declaration of Rights in Article I of the Delaware Constitution is necessarily in "lock step" with the United States Supreme Court's construction of the federal Bill of Rights.

To determine whether a state constitutional provision is substantively identical to an analogous provision of United States Constitution, this Court considers the list of nonexclusive factors originally articulated in the concurring opinion of Justice Handler of the New Jersey Supreme Court in *State v. Hunt*. The *Hunt* factors provide a framework to determine whether a state constitutional provision affords an independent basis to reach a different result than what could be obtained under federal law. The seven factors include:

(1) Textual Language—A state constitution's language may itself provide a basis for reaching a result different from that which could be obtained under federal law. Textual language can be relevant in either of two contexts. First, distinctive provisions of our State charter may recognize rights not identified in the federal constitution.... Second, the phrasing of a particular provision in our charter may be so significantly different from the language used to address the same subject in the federal Constitution that we can feel free to interpret our provision on an independent basis....

(2) Legislative History—Whether or not the textual language of a given provision is different from that found in the federal Constitution, legislative history may reveal an intention that will support reading the provision independently of federal law....

(3) Preexisting State Law—Previously established bodies of state law may also suggest distinctive state constitutional rights. State law is often responsive to concerns long before they are addressed by constitutional claims. Such preexisting law can help to define the scope of the constitutional right later established.

(4) Structural Differences—Differences in structure between the federal and state constitutions might also provide a basis for rejecting the constraints of federal doctrine at the state level. The United States Constitution is a grant of enumerated powers to the federal government. Our State Constitution, on the other hand, serves only to limit the sovereign power which inheres directly in the people and indirectly in their elected representatives. Hence, the explicit affirmation of fundamental rights in our Constitution can be seen as a guarantee of those rights and not as a restriction upon them.

(5) Matters of Particular State Interest or Local Concern—A state constitution may also be employed to address matters of peculiar state interest or local concern. When particular questions are local in character and do not appear to require a uniform national policy, they are ripe for decision under state law. Moreover, some matters are uniquely appropriate for independent state action....

(6) State Traditions—A state's history and traditions may also provide a basis for the independent application of its constitution....

(7) Public Attitudes—Distinctive attitudes of a state's citizenry may also furnish grounds to expand constitutional rights under state charters. While we have

never cited this criterion in our decisions, courts in other jurisdictions have pointed to public attitudes as a relevant factor in their deliberations.

"The[se] enumerated criteria, which are synthesized from a burgeoning body of authority, are essentially illustrative, rather than exhaustive." But those criteria do "share a common thread—that distinctive and identifiable attributes of a state government, its laws and its people justify recourse to the state constitution as an independent source for recognizing and protecting individual rights."

This case concerns the right to keep and bear arms under Article I, Section 20 of the Delaware Constitution. Although Section 20 was not enacted until 1987, Delaware has a long history, dating back to the Revolution, of allowing responsible citizens to lawfully carry and use firearms in our state. The parties agree, as does this Court, that Delaware is an "open carry" state. Like the citizens of our sister states at the founding, Delaware citizens understood that the "right of self-preservation" permitted a citizen to "repe[l] force by force" when "the intervention of society in his behalf, may be too late to prevent an injury." An individual's right to bear arms was "understood to be an individual right protecting against both public and private violence." The right to keep and bear arms was also understood to exist for membership in the militia and for hunting.

In 1791, Delaware delegates to the state constitutional convention were unable to agree on the specific language that would codify in our Declaration of Rights the right to keep and bear arms in Delaware. After several attempts, the effort was abandoned. Concerns over groups of armed men stood in the way of an agreement even though there was an apparent consensus among the delegates on an individual's right to bear arms in self-defense.

Not until almost 200 years later did the Delaware General Assembly agree on the language to be used. Article I, Section 20 provides: "A person has the right to keep and bear arms for the defense of self, family, home and State, and for hunting and recreational use." The General Assembly's stated purpose in enacting the constitutional amendment was to "explicitly protect[ ] the traditional right to keep and bear arms," which it defined in the text of the amendment. By including the right to keep and bear arms in the Delaware Constitution, the General Assembly has recognized this right as fundamental.

Contentions of the Parties

Residents argue that we should answer both questions in the negative. The WHA argues for an affirmative answer to both. Residents contend that Article I, Section 20 is not a mirror image of the Second Amendment, that the protections it provides are not limited to the home, and that the

WHA Revised Policy cannot withstand strict scrutiny, intermediate scrutiny, or the *Hamdan* test that we utilized in *Griffin v. State*. WHA replies that: (1) the rights protected by Section 20 are coextensive with those protected by the Second Amendment because hunting and recreational use are not in issue, (2) intermediate scrutiny applies, (3) as a landlord WHA may adopt reasonable policies for the protection of residents, and (4) its Revised Policy is narrowly tailored to advance the compelling interest in assuring the safety of its tenants.

Article I, Section 20 of the Delaware Constitution Is an Independent Source for Recognizing and Protecting the Right to Keep and Bear Arms

This Court has previously addressed the application of Article I, Section 20 of the Delaware Constitution on four occasions. In *Short v. State*, we held that 11 *Del. C.* § 1448, which prohibits felons from possessing a deadly weapon, does not violate Section 20. In *Smith v. State*, we held that Section 20, when enacted, did not alter the then-existing law pertaining to the crime of carrying a concealed deadly weapon without a license and the statutory privilege to carry a concealed deadly weapon with a license. In *Dickerson v. State*, we affirmed a conviction for carrying a concealed weapon without a license outside of the home. And most recently in *Griffin v. State*, we considered an as-applied challenge to a conviction for carrying a concealed deadly weapon without a license in the home. In *Griffin*, we explained that although the right to bear arms "is not absolute," "Griffin's constitutional right to bear arms authorized his carrying a concealed knife in his home." That did not end the inquiry, because after the police arrived "the balance between [Griffin's] interest in carrying a concealed weapon in his home and the State's interest in public safety shifted in favor of the State."

In all of these cases but one, no federal Second Amendment jurisprudence was cited. Although both Section 20 and the Second Amendment share a similar historical context that informs our analysis, the interpretation of Section 20 is not dependent upon federal interpretations of the Second Amendment. The text of Section 20, enacted in 1987, and the Second Amendment, effective beginning in 1791, is not the same. On its face, the Delaware provision is intentionally broader than the Second Amendment and protects the right to bear arms outside the home, including for hunting and recreation. Section 20 specifically provides for the defense of self and family *in addition to* the home. Accordingly, our interpretation of Section 20 is not constrained by the federal precedent relied upon by the WHA, which explains that at the core of the Second Amendment is the right of law abiding, responsible citizens to use arms in defense of "hearth and home." We agree with Residents that

Article I, Section 20 is not a mirror image of the Second Amendment and that the scope of the protections it provides are not limited to the home.

Our conclusion that the interpretation of Article I, Section 20 is a source, independent from the Second Amendment, for recognizing and protecting individual rights, is supported by the *Hunt* factors. The distinctive language of Section 20 and the legislative history demonstrates the General Assembly's intent to provide a right to keep and bear arms independent of the federal right. Moreover, public attitudes, as reflected in the laws passed by the General Assembly, and Delaware's long tradition of allowing responsible, law-abiding citizens to keep and bear arms outside of the home, favor recognizing an independent right under the Delaware Constitution. Two *Hunt* factors—the structural differences in constitutional provisions and matters of particular state interest—do not require that Section 20 be interpreted coextensively with the Second Amendment. In summary, Article I, Section 20 of the Delaware Constitution is an independent source for recognizing and protecting the right to keep and bear arms.

2 relevant Hunt factors [handwritten margin note]

Intermediate Scrutiny Applies

In *Griffin v. State*, this Court applied the three-part analysis adopted from the Wisconsin Supreme Court's decision in *State v. Hamdan*, in deciding whether an individual has a right to carry a concealed deadly weapon in the home. We held that:

> First, the court must compare the strength of the state's interest in public safety with the individual's interest in carrying a concealed weapon. Second, if the individual interest outweighs the state interest, the court must determine, "whether an individual could have exercised the right in a reasonable, alternative manner that did not violate the statute." Third, the individual must be carrying the concealed weapon for a lawful purpose.

Analytical framework [handwritten margin note]

Our analysis employed heightened scrutiny in the context of a prosecution for carrying a concealed deadly weapon.

Where government action infringes a fundamental right, Delaware courts will apply a heightened scrutiny analysis. The parties have not argued otherwise here. Where heightened scrutiny applies, the State has the burden of showing that the state action is constitutional. Here, the parties differ on the appropriate heightened scrutiny analysis, Residents argue for strict scrutiny and the WHA argues for intermediate scrutiny. Both sides also argue that under strict scrutiny, intermediate scrutiny, or the *Hamdan* test, the result is in their favor. For the reasons which follow, we conclude that intermediate scrutiny is the proper level of constitutional review.

"A governmental action survives strict scrutiny only where the state demonstrates that the test is narrowly tailored to advance a compelling government interest." "[S]trict scrutiny is a tool to determine whether there is a cost-benefit justification for governmental action that burdens interests for which the Constitution demands unusually high protection." In contrast, intermediate scrutiny requires more than a rational basis for the action, but less than strict scrutiny. Intermediate scrutiny seeks to balance potential burdens on fundamental rights against the valid interests of government. To survive intermediate scrutiny, governmental action must "serve important governmental objectives and [must be] substantially related to [the] achievement of those objectives." The governmental action cannot burden the right more than is reasonably necessary to ensure that the asserted governmental objective is met.

Although the right to bear arms under the Delaware Declaration of Rights is a fundamental right, we have already held that it is not absolute. The General Assembly that enacted Article I, Section 20 left in place a series of statutes affecting the right to keep and bear arms in Delaware. Our prior cases so recognized and found no legislative intent (for example) to invalidate laws prohibiting felons from possessing deadly weapons or prohibiting (with certain exceptions) the carrying of a concealed deadly weapon outside the home without a license. The General Assembly's careful and nuanced approach supports an intermediate scrutiny analysis that allows a court to consider public safety and other important governmental interests. Accordingly, we agree with the WHA that paragraphs 3 and 4 of the Revised Policy should be subject to intermediate scrutiny.

Under Intermediate Scrutiny the Common Area Provision Is Overbroad

It is undisputed that Residents are subject to eviction under the WHA lease provision and rules if they, their household members, or their guests violate the Common Area Provision that restricts the possession of firearms in the common areas of the WHA properties where the Residents and their household members live. That restriction infringes the fundamental right of responsible, law-abiding citizens to keep and bear arms for the defense of self, family, and home. WHA therefore has the burden to demonstrate that its governmental action passes intermediate scrutiny.

To satisfy its burden, WHA argues that it has an important governmental interest in protecting the health, welfare, and safety of all WHA residents, staff, and guests who enter onto WHA property. WHA argues that an accidental discharge of a firearm may have serious fatal consequences and that dangers inherent in the increased presence of firearms. But these same concerns would also apply to the area within any apartment—interior locations where the WHA concedes it cannot restrict the possession of firearms for self-defense. The Revised Policy does more than proscribe the unsafe *use* of a firearm. It also prohibits *possession* in the public housing common areas except where the firearm is being transported to or from an apartment. In this context, WHA must show more than a general safety concern and it has not done so.

In *Griffin v. State* we explained that an individual's interest in the right to keep and bear arms is strongest when "the weapon is in one's home or business and is being used for security." Residents have a possessory interest in both their apartments and the common areas. And although Residents cannot exclude other residents or the public from the common areas, their need for security in those areas is just as high for purposes of Section 20 as it would be inside their apartment or business. The common areas are effectively part of the residences. The laundry rooms and TV rooms are similar to those typically found in private residences; and the Residents, their families, and their guests will occupy them as part of their living space.

With the Common Area Provision in force under penalty of eviction, reasonable, law-abiding adults become disarmed and unable to repel an intruder by force in any common living areas when the intervention of society on their behalf may be too late to prevent an injury. Even active and retired police officers who are residents, household members, or guests are disarmed by the Common Area Provision. They are restricted in possessing firearms in the public housing common areas of the apartment buildings despite their exemption by the General Assembly from concealed-carry license requirements.

Nor is the Common Area Provision sustainable under intermediate scrutiny because the WHA owns the property and is a landlord. WHA contends that it is acting as a landlord and not as a sovereign. We recognize that where the government is a proprietor or employer, it has a legitimate interest in controlling unsafe or disruptive behavior on its property. But WHA has conceded that after *McDonald*, as a landlord it may not adopt a total ban of firearms. Thus, occupying the status of government landlord, alone and without more, does not control. How the property is used must also be considered. Public housing is "a home as well as a government building." The WHA is different from other public agencies in that it essentially replicates for low-income families services similar to those provided by a private landlord. The individual's need for defense of self, family, and home in an apartment building is the same whether the property is owned privately or by the government.

Unlike a state office building, courthouse, school, college, or university, the services provided by the WHA in the common areas are not the services typically provided to the public on government property. They are limited to supplying adequate housing for low-income families and individuals and to maintaining the grounds and buildings for the residents. Some regulation of possessing firearms on WHA property could pass intermediate scrutiny, for example prohibiting possession in offices where state employees work and state business is being done. Here, however, the restrictions of the Common Area Provision are overbroad and burden the right to bear arms more than is reasonably necessary. Indeed, the Common Area Provision severely burdens the right by functionally disallowing armed self-defense in areas that Residents, their families, and guests may occupy as part of their living space. Section 20 of the Delaware Constitution precludes the WHA from adopting such a policy.

Accordingly, we answer the first certified question in the negative.

The Reasonable Cause Provision Is Overbroad

The record before us shows that the Revised Policy was adopted by the WHA during the litigation before the District Court and after the United States Supreme Court decision in *McDonald v. City of Chicago*. The WHA "suspended, reviewed, and replaced" its original policies banning all firearms on its property pursuant to "the HUD-mandated procedure for doing so ... in view of the Supreme Court's holding in *McDonald*." The Reasonable Cause Provision of the Revised Policy requires the production upon request by a resident, household member, or guest of

> a copy of any permit, license, or other documentation required by state, local, or federal law for the ownership, possession, or transportation of any firearm or other weapon, including a license to carry a concealed weapon as required by 11 *Del. C.* § 1441, upon request, when there is reasonable cause to believe that the law *or this Policy* has been violated.

By it terms, the Reasonable Cause Provision exists, as least in part, to enforce compliance with the Common Area Provision, which we have found to be overbroad and unconstitutional.

Where a statute, regulation, or state action faces a constitutional challenge, "a Court may preserve its valid portions if the offending language can lawfully be severed." But where it is evident that the remaining provisions would not have been enacted without the unconstitutional provision, a court should invalidate the entire provision. The Reasonable Cause Provision was enacted, together with the Common Area Provision, by the WHA in response to *McDonald*. Because the unconstitutional Common Area Provision is not severable as a matter of Delaware law, the Reasonable Cause Provision which enforces it is unconstitutional and overbroad as well. For that reason, we answer the second certified question in the negative.

Conclusion

We answer both certified questions in the negative. The Clerk is directed to transmit this opinion to the Third Circuit.

NOTES

1. The Second Amendment to the United States Constitution reads: "A well regulated militia being necessary to the security of a free State, the right of the people to keep and bear arms shall not be infringed." The United States Supreme Court recently construed that language in *District of Columbia v. Heller*, 128 S.Ct. 2783 (2008), holding that the amendment protects an *individual* right to bear arms.

2. In *Heller*, the Supreme Court declared that felon-in-possession statutes are permitted by the United States Constitution. In *Britt v. State*, 681 S.E. 2d 320 (N.C. 2009), however, the North Carolina Supreme Court held that its state constitutional right to bear arms precluded the state from imposing a ban on a non-violent felon possessing a firearm. Thus, the North Carolina Constitution provides greater protection than the Second Amendment.

3. The Constitutions of forty-four states contain a provision that protects the right to bear arms. The texts of those state constitutional guarantees are often different from the Second Amendment. For example, the New Hampshire Constitution provides: "All persons have the right to keep and bear arms in defense of themselves, their families, their property and the state." N.H. Const. pt. 1, art. 2-a.

E. EXCESSIVE FINES – PUNITIVE DAMAGES

COLONIAL PIPELINE CO. v. BROWN
365 S.E.2d 827 (Ga. 1988)

SMITH, J.

This appeal consolidates two related cases stemming from the destruction of a bulldozer after it hit and ruptured Colonial Pipeline's underground petroleum pipeline. The owner of the bulldozer, Wright Contracting Company, sued Colonial, Baxter Brown, the real estate developer who hired Wright to do grading work, and Malcolm Burnsed, the surveyor who did the grading plan.

Case No. 44926 is Colonial's appeal from a jury verdict awarding Wright $52,728.46 actual damages, $304.75 consequential damages and $5,000,000 punitive damages. We affirm in part and reverse in part case No. 44926—the punitive damages award is reversed.

Colonial purchased a right-of-way easement from Reese W. Cross and Eloise H. Cross in 1976. Colonial's pipeline was to be installed on part of their property that faced Westover Road, and it was to run parallel to the road. The property subject to the easement was higher than the road, and the easement required Colonial to bury the pipeline at least thirty inches below the grade of Westover Road.

Baxter Brown, an experienced real estate broker, purchased five acres of land out of a larger parcel owned by the Crosses. The five acres Mr. Brown purchased were subject to Colonial's recorded easement.

Mr. Brown hired Malcolm Burnsed, a registered land surveyor, to survey the property and prepare a boundary line survey and a grading plan.

Although a preliminary title opinion was prepared four days prior to the purchase of the property in December 1981, Mr. Brown asserted that he had not seen it prior to the date the pipeline was ruptured on June 15, 1982. Both the preliminary title opinion and the final title opinion contained identical language: "Right-of-way easement from REESE WILSON CROSS and ELOISE HUCKABEE CROSS to COLONIAL PIPELINE COMPANY, A DELAWARE CORPORATION, dated August 26, 1976, and recorded in Deed Book 568, pages 329-330, in the aforesaid Clerk's Office."

Neither the boundary line survey nor the grading plan prepared by Mr. Burnsed contained a hint of Colonial's easement. Mr. Burnsed found a warranty deed dated 1966 from L.W. Cross to R.W. Cross in the court records. Because the deed stated that it was "[s]ubject to easements of record," Mr. Burnsed used the grantor/grantee index to determine if there was an easement prior to 1966. He testified that he had looked at the property and did not see any physical evidence of a pipeline, therefore, he had no reason to check to see if an easement had been conveyed after 1966. Mr. Burnsed testified that he did not know that the pipeline was under the property he had surveyed until the pipeline was ruptured.

Mr. Burnsed testified that he did not obtain a copy of the title opinion in preparing his boundary line survey and admitted that the Rules of State Board of Registration for Professional Engineers and Land Surveyors, Section 180-7-.02 provides: "The surveyor prior to making [a boundary line survey] shall acquire all necessary data, including deeds, maps, *certificates of title.*" (emphasis supplied).

David James, the area manager for Wright Contracting Company, testified that he did not see any evidence of the pipeline on the property that Wright was hired to grade. He further testified that he did not see the Colonial Pipeline marker that was located 670 feet south of the property. He did indicate that he knew that the pipeline was in the area, but he did not know that it was under the property.

Mr. James stated that if he had known about the pipeline he would not have relied upon the terms of the easement, he would have called Colonial and they would have located the pipeline for him.

The Wright Contracting Company "Safety Rules Procedure" manual provides in part: "Construction Practices...*Excavating and Trenching* operations will include proper safeguards and inspections to *determine location and extent of underground utilities.*" (Emphasis supplied.)

An expert witness, Mr. John Sperry, testified that if he were going to cut a five acre tract out of a larger tract and provide a boundary line survey, he would look *forward* from the 1966 deed to see if any parcels or easements had been deeded out of the property. (If the surveyor had looked forward, he would have found the easement.) In answer to another question, Mr. Sperry testified that if he was hired to do a grade plan and topographical survey that he would ask for the title opinion. (If the surveyor had obtained the title opinion he would have found the easement.) Mr. Sperry indicated that there is no difficulty in securing a map from Colonial Pipeline that shows the location of the pipeline. He testified that the general standards by which one should conform as a surveyor are in Section 180-7-.02 of the Rules of State Board of Registration for Professional Engineers and Land Surveyors.

The bulldozer operator was grading between eight and nine inches below the level specified in the grading plan when the pipeline was ruptured.

Federal regulations require Colonial to conduct an aerial inspection of the entire pipeline every fourteen days to discover unusual activities. Colonial had contracted with a new aerial patrol contractor on May 1, 1982. He had difficulty finding the line from the air; as a result, only two partial inspections were conducted in the fourteen days preceding the occurrence. The red clay field where Wright was grading was observed by a Colonial employee on a June 11, 1982, flight, but he assumed the activity was farming and failed to report it.

The pipeline was installed approximately 48 inches below the surface of the land; however, it was approximately one and three-quarter inches above the center of Westover Road. Although a marker was located 1,120 feet south of the ruptured line and 670 feet south of the property line and another 2,245 feet north of the rupture at the intersection of Old Dawson Road and Westover Road, there were no markers on the property at the time of the rupture. The distance between the two markers was 3,358 feet. Federal law requires that "[e]ach operator shall place and maintain line markers over each buried line in accordance with the following: (1) Markers must be located at each public road crossing, at each railroad crossing and in sufficient number along the remainder of each buried line so that the location is accurately known."

There was also evidence that six years earlier another construction worker had hit a portion of the pipeline that was on property that was unmarked, but there were no damages.

The jury's verdict exonerated Mr. Brown and Mr. Burnsed and awarded Wright $52,728.46 actual damages, $304.75 consequential damages, and $5,000,000 punitive damages.

The appeal of the punitive damages award raises several issues. One is whether or not the complaint sounds in contract or tort. We hold that it sounds in tort, and inasmuch as we are reversing on the punitive damages phase of the case, we will not go into detail as to that point.

Colonial challenges the punitive damages element of this case on two grounds, due process and the Eighth Amendment prohibition against excessive fines contending that this prohibition applies to civil as well as criminal cases. Colonial then asserts that five million dollars in punitive damages violates this amendment. Because we are reversing this case under the excessive fines clause of the Georgia Constitution, article I, section I, paragraph XVII, we are not going to address the due process argument.

Ingraham v. Wright, 430 U.S. 651 (1977), has been relied upon to find that the Eighth Amendment does not apply to civil cases. But, *Ingraham* dealt only with the cruel and unusual punishment clause of the Eighth Amendment, it did not concern the excessive fines clause. It cannot be viewed as excluding punitive damages from scrutiny under the excessive fines clause of the Eighth Amendment. Moreover, even if *Ingraham* had held that the Eighth Amendment of the United States Constitution applied only to criminal cases, there would be nothing to prevent the application of the excessive fines clause of article I, section I, paragraph XVII of the 1983 Georgia Constitution to civil cases, thereby affording greater protection under state law.

Punitive damages "are private fines levied by civil juries to punish reprehensible conduct and to deter its future occurrence." In Georgia, when the tortious conduct amounts to "wilful misconduct, malice, fraud, wantonness, or oppression, or that entire want of care which would raise the presumption of a conscious indifference to consequences," punitive damages are allowed pursuant to section 51-12-5 of the Georgia Code to deter the wrongdoer from repeating his wrongful acts. Punitive damages cannot be imposed without a finding of some form of culpable conduct. Negligence, even gross negligence, is inadequate to support a punitive damage award. Punitive damages, although civil in nature, nonetheless serve the criminal law goal of deterrence rather than the traditional compensatory goal of civil law.

"The applicability of the Eighth Amendment always has turned on its original meaning, as demonstrated by its historical derivation." *Ingraham*, 430 U.S. at 670-71 n.39. A review of the history of the excessive fines clause of the Eighth Amendment indicates that it has an origin that was not limited to criminal cases.

Prior to 1215 a system developed whereby a monetary penalty was demanded from one who engaged in either criminal or civil misconduct. The penalty was called an "amercement." The amercement was not levied according to any fixed schedule but was imposed arbitrarily at the discretion of the court. Abuses in the use of "amercements" flourished. The abuses were so pervasive that a great deal of space was devoted to them in the Magna Carta:

> Chapter 20 of the Great Charter, the king was made to concede that: A freeman shall not be amerced for a slight offense, except in accordance with the degree of the offense; and for a grave offense he shall be amerced in accordance with the gravity of the offense, yet saving always his "contenement;" and a merchant in the same way, saving his "merchandise;" and a villein shall be amerced in the same way, saving his "wainage"—if they have fallen into our mercy; and none of the aforesaid amercements shall be imposed except by the oath of honest men of the neighbourhood.

> From these three provisions of Magna Carta, two related protections emerge. First, there is a requirement of reasonableness, of proportionality, of sensible relation between punishment and offense. Second, the penalty inflicted should not, in any event, destroy the offender's means of making a living in his particular trade or calling. Magna Carta guaranteed not just bare survival, but continued productive economic viability.

The United States Constitution as originally submitted to the states was criticized for its failure to include a declaration of rights. "Magna Carta and the English Bill of Rights were invoked as models of what was required, and a tacit understanding was reached that some such provisions would be added by way of amendment." "The Eighth Amendment was based directly on Art. I, Sec. 9, of the Virginia Declaration of Rights (1776)...[which] in turn...adopted verbatim the language of the English Bill of Rights. There can be no doubt that the Declaration of Rights guaranteed at least the liberties and privileges of Englishmen."

We hold that the excessive fines clause of article I, section I, paragraph XVII of the Georgia Constitution applies to the imposition of punitive damages in civil cases because, "the purpose of the deprivation is among those ordinarily associated with punishment, such as retribution, rehabilitation, or deterrence," *Ingraham*, 430 U.S. at 687-88 (White, J., dissenting.), and because the Eighth Amendment excessive fines clause of the United States Constitution was intended as a protection from all excessive monetary penalties.

In order to decide what fines are excessive under the excessive fines clause of the Georgia Constitution, article I, section I, paragraph XVII, a look into the history of torts is necessary.

"Broadly speaking, a tort is a civil wrong, other than breach of contract, for which the court will provide a remedy in the form of an action for damages." W.L. Prosser and W.P. Keeton, *Prosser & Keeton, Handbook on the Law of Torts*, p. 2 (5th ed., 1984).

> In the early English law, after the Norman conquest, remedies for wrongs were dependent upon the issuance of writs to bring the defendant into court. In the course of the thirteenth century the principle was established that no one could bring an action in the King's common law courts without the King's writ. As a result of the jealous insistence of the nobles and others upon the prerogatives of their local courts, the number of writs which the King could issue was limited, and their forms were strictly prescribed. There were, in other words, "forms of action," and unless the plaintiff's claim could be fitted into the form of some established and recognized writ, he was without a remedy in the King's courts. The result was a highly formalized system of procedure, which governed and controlled the law as to the substance of the wrongs which might be remedied.

> The writs which were available for remedies that were purely tortious in character were two-the writ of trespass, and the writ of trespass on the case.

> The form of action in trespass had originally a criminal character. It would lie only in cases of forcible breaches of the King's peace, and it was only on this basis that the royal courts assumed jurisdiction over the wrong. The purpose of the remedy was at first primarily that of punishment of the crime; but to this there was added later the satisfaction of the injured party's claim for redress. If the defendant was found guilty, damages were awarded to the successful plaintiff, and the defendant was imprisoned, and allowed to purchase his release by payment of a fine. What similarity remains between tort and crime is to be traced to this common beginning. *See* Woodbine, *The Origin of the Action of Trespass* 33 Yale L.J. 799 (1923), 34 Yale L.J. 343 (1934); Maitland, *The Forms of Action at Common Law* (1941) 65.

W.L. Prosser, *Cases and Materials on Torts*, p. 2 (6th ed., 1976).

> Originally the two remedies [criminal and tort] were administered by the same court, and in the same action. Tort damages were at first awarded to the injured individual as an incident to an criminal prosecution; and as late as 1694 the defendant to a writ of trespass was still theoretically liable to a criminal fine and imprisonment. Because of this common origin, it is not unusual for a tort and a crime to bear the same name, such as "assault," "battery," "trespass," or "libel," and often enough such terms will refer to the same conduct. But tort and criminal law have developed along different lines, with different ends in view, and so it does not necessarily follow that the term has the same meaning in both. Thus it is entirely possible that an act may be a tort, but not a crime of the same name, or that it may amount to the crime and not the tort....

> The idea of punishment, or of discouraging other offenses, usually does not enter into tort law, except in so far as it may lead the courts to weight the scales somewhat in favor of the plaintiff's interests in determining that a tort has been committed in the first place. In one rather anomalous respect, however, the ideas underlying the criminal law have invaded the field of torts. Where the

defendant's wrongdoing has been intentional and deliberate, and has the character of outrage frequently associated with crime, all but a few courts have permitted the jury to award in the tort action "punitive" or "exemplary" damages, or what is sometimes called "smart money." Such damages are given to the plaintiff over and above the full compensation for the injuries, for the purpose of punishing the defendant, of teaching the defendant not to do it again, and of deterring others from following the defendant's example....

Something more than the mere commission of a tort is always required for punitive damages. There must be circumstances of aggravation or outrage, such as spite or "malice," or a fraudulent or evil motive on the part of the defendant, or such a conscious and deliberate disregard of the interests of others that the conduct may be called willful or wanton. There is general agreement that, because it lacks this element, mere negligence is not enough, even though it is so extreme in degree as to be characterized as "gross," a term of ill-defined content, which occasionally, in a few jurisdictions, has been stretched to include the element of conscious indifference to consequences, and so to justify punitive damages. Still less, of course, can such damages be charged against one who acts under an innocent mistake in engaging in conduct that nevertheless constitutes a tort.

Typical of the torts for which such damages may be awarded are assault and battery, libel and slander, deceit, seduction, alienation of affections, malicious prosecution, and intentional interferences with property such as trespass, private nuisance, and conversion. *But it is not so much the particular tort committed as the defendant's motives and conduct in committing it which will be important as the basis of the award.*

W.L. Prosser and W.P. Keeton, supra, pp. 8-11 (citations omitted) (emphasis supplied).

Thus it can be seen that the tort law grew out of the criminal law and as such retains some of the elements thereof, to-wit, punitive damages. The word punitive means to inflict punishment.

The statute in Georgia that allows an assessment of punitive damages is section 51-12-5. This statute authorizes a jury to award additional damages to "deter the wrongdoer from repeating the trespass"—the basis upon which the award was made in this case. The code section states that in every tort there may be aggravating circumstances, either in "the act or the intention" in which event additional or punitive damages may be awarded.

In a punitive damage case, the trier of fact must determine: First, was a personal injury or death involved or mere damage to property; and second, was the negligence active or passive. The next step in the determination as to whether punitive damages should be awarded is to decide if there was any evidence of wilful misconduct, malice, fraud, wantonness or oppression, or that entire want of care which would raise the presumption of a conscious indifference to consequences.

This case involved personal property damage only. The bulldozer was in an open field, not near any building or residence, and there was no bodily injury to this plaintiff. There was constructive notice to the landowner that Colonial's pipeline was under his property. The surveyor failed to discover the recorded easement, and the bulldozer operator was grading approximately eight or nine inches below the level specified in the grading plan when the pipeline was ruptured. The punitive damages awarded are approximately one hundred times the total of actual and consequential damages.

The trial court erred in denying the motion for new trial as to punitive damages. We, therefore, reverse the $5,000,000 award as being excessive because (1) any negligence present was passive; (2) there was no bodily injury to this plaintiff, and the award does not bear a rational relationship to the actual damages award; (3) there is no rational relationship between the offense and the punishment in that the punitive damage award was 100 times the property damage award.

NOTES

1. The United States Supreme Court held that awards of punitive damages in state private party civil cases are not covered by the Eighth Amendment's prohibition against "excessive fines." *Browning-Ferris Indus. v. Kelco Disposal, Inc.*, 492 U.S. 257 (1989).

2. The majority of state constitutions have been interpreted to apply excessive fine prohibitions only to penalties imposed for criminal offenses and not to an arguably excessive civil damage award.

3. In Ohio, a statute giving the judge, rather than the jury, authority to award punitive damages was held to violate the state constitutional guarantee to a jury trial. *Zoppo v. Homestead Ins. Co.*, 644 N.E.2d 397 (Ohio 1994). However, in Kansas, a statute that gave the judge power to set the amount of punitive damages, after the jury concluded punitive damages should be awarded, did not violate the state constitutional right to a jury trial. *Smith v. Printup*, 866 P.2d 985 (Kan. 1993).

4. In Montana, punitive damages were held to be civil actions under the "trial by jury" provision of the state constitution and, therefore, a two-thirds vote of the jury had the effect of unanimity. *Finstad v. W.R. Grace & Co.*, 8 P.3d 778 (Mont. 2000); Mont. Const. art. II § 26.

F. CRIME VICTIMS' RIGHTS

SCHILLING v. CRIME VICTIMS RIGHTS BOARD
692 N.W.2d 623 (Wis. 2005)

ROGGENSACK, J.

The first sentence of article I, section 9m of the Wisconsin Constitution states: "This state shall treat crime victims, as defined by law, with fairness, dignity and respect for their privacy." We recognize that according crime victims fairness, dignity and respect is very important to a just enforcement of the criminal code of the State of Wisconsin. The legislature has recognized the importance of victims' rights as well, by enacting section 950.04 of the Wisconsin Statutes. However, because we conclude that this constitutional provision is a statement of purpose that describes the policies to be promoted by the State and does not provide an enforceable, self-executing right, we affirm the circuit court decision reversing the private reprimand of District Attorney Patrick Schilling issued by the Crime Victims Rights Board under section 950.09(2)(a).

BACKGROUND

Jennifer Hansen Marinko (Hansen) was murdered in Price County in October 1999. She was survived by her two children, her mother and nine siblings. Patrick Schilling, District Attorney for Price County, prosecuted Daniel Marinko (Marinko) in connection with her death, and on March 8, 2001, Marinko was convicted of both first-degree intentional homicide and armed burglary with a dangerous weapon.

At the sentencing hearing held on April 12, 2001, Schilling played part of the tape of the 911 telephone call that Hansen's son had made to the police after discovering his mother dead. While Schilling made sure that Hansen's children would not be present at the sentencing hearing, he did not inform other family members that he was going to play the tape or otherwise give them an opportunity to leave the courtroom before he played it. Schilling turned off the tape before it had finished playing because he recognized that it was having a dramatic effect on the family members.

In July 2001, five of Hansen's survivors (collectively "complainants") filed a complaint against Schilling with the Crime Victims Rights Board (Board). After determining that there was probable cause to believe that Schilling had violated the complainants' crime victims' rights, the Board held an evidentiary hearing on May 30 and 31, 2002.

In a written decision, the Board found that the tape of the 911 call was "highly upsetting" and that "Schilling knew of the tape's powerful emotional content...[which] was the reason for its presentation at the sentencing hearing." The Board further found that "Schilling intended to create an emotional event at the sentencing hearing for the purpose of influencing the sentencing decision, which, unfortunately, was at the expense of [Hansen's] family."

Citing article I, section 9m of the Wisconsin Constitution and section 950.01 of the Wisconsin Statutes for the principle that "[v]ictims of crime are entitled to be treated with fairness, dignity, respect, courtesy and sensitivity," the Board found that the complainants had "met their burden to prove by clear and convincing evidence that [] Schilling failed to treat them with fairness, dignity, respect, courtesy and sensitivity on April 12, 2001, when he played the 911 tape made on the day of [Hansen's] death at the sentencing hearing." Citing its authority under section 950.09(2)(a) of the Wisconsin Statutes, the Board ordered a private reprimand of Schilling "for violating the complainants' rights to be treated with fairness, dignity, respect and sensitivity in the playing of the 911 tape at the April 12, 2001, sentencing hearing."

Schilling sought judicial review of the Board's decision pursuant to sections 227.52, 227.53 and 227.57 of the Wisconsin Statutes in the circuit court for Dane County. The circuit court, the Honorable Michael N. Nowakowski presiding, reversed the Board's decision. The Board then appealed to the court of appeals, and we granted the court of appeals' certification.

DISCUSSION

Pursuant to section 950.09(2)(a) of the Wisconsin Statutes, the Board may "[i]ssue private and public reprimands of public officials, employees or agencies that violate the rights of crime victims provided under this chapter, ch. 938, and article I, section 9m, of the Wisconsin constitution." At issue in this case is whether the first sentence of article I, section 9m of the Wisconsin Constitution, which reads, "This state shall treat crime victims, as defined by law, with fairness, dignity and respect for their privacy," creates a "right" that the Board may enforce under section 950.09(2)(a) of the Wisconsin Statutes, or whether it is descriptive of policies to be furthered by the State.

The Board argues that the first sentence of article I, section 9m of the Wisconsin Constitution is self-executing and thereby provides crime victims an enforceable right to be treated with fairness, dignity and respect for their privacy. Schilling counters that the language in question instead serves to articulate general policies and does not create enforceable rights. We conclude that the constitutional language in question is a statement of purpose that describes the policies to be promoted by the State and does not create an enforceable, self-executing right.

Interpreting Article I, Section 9m of the Wisconsin Constitution

The Wisconsin Constitution was amended in 1993 to include article I, section 9m. We have explained that the purpose of construing a constitutional amendment is "to give effect to the intent of the framers and of the people who adopted it." The question presented in the present case is whether the first sentence of article I, section 9m of the Wisconsin Constitution was intended as a statement of purpose that articulates the importance of recognizing crime victim rights, or whether it was intended to provide crime victims with an enforceable right that is self-executing.

Like statutes, constitutional provisions may include statements of purpose that use broad language. As with a statute's statement of purpose, a constitutional section's statement of purpose does not provide for an independent, enforceable claim, as it is not in itself substantive. Such a statement of purpose is instead instructive of intent and guides implementation.

We have also explained that "[a] constitutional provision is self-executing if no legislation is necessary to give effect to it, and if there is nothing to be done by the legislature to put it in operation." However, a statement of purpose, policy or principle is not self-executing.

To ascertain whether the first sentence of article I, section 9m of the Wisconsin Constitution was intended to serve as a statement of purpose or was intended to provide an enforceable, self-executing right requires constitutional interpretation. We examine three sources in interpreting a constitutional provision: "the plain meaning of the words in the context used; the constitutional debates and the practices in existence at the time of the writing of the constitution; and the earliest interpretation of the provision by the legislature as manifested in the first law passed following adoption." We have broadly understood the second of these sources, the constitutional debates and practices in existence contemporaneous to the writing, to include the general history relating to a constitutional amendment.

Applying this analysis, we note first that the plain meaning of the first sentence of article I, section 9m of the Wisconsin Constitution in context indicates that it serves as a statement of purpose and does not create enforceable, self-executing rights. Article I, section 9m of the Wisconsin Constitution provides:

> This state shall treat crime victims, as defined by law, with fairness, dignity and respect for their privacy. This state shall ensure that crime victims have all of the following privileges and protections as provided by law: timely disposition of the case; the opportunity to attend court proceedings unless the trial court finds sequestration is necessary to a fair trial for the defendant; reasonable protection from the accused throughout the criminal justice process; notification of court proceedings; the opportunity to confer with the prosecution; the opportunity to

make a statement to the court at disposition; restitution; compensation; and information about the outcome of the case and the release of the accused. The legislature shall provide remedies for the violation of this section. Nothing in this section, or in any statute enacted pursuant to this section, shall limit any right of the accused which may be provided by law.

The provision in question, "This state shall treat crime victims, as defined by law, with fairness, dignity and respect for their privacy," opens the section. It uses very broad terms to describe how the State must treat crime victims. The subsequent sentence requires the State to "ensure" that crime victims have a number of "privileges and protections," which are articulated in detail. This structure, opening the section with broad indications of how crime victims should be treated, followed by a detailed list of privileges and protections to which victims are entitled, shows that the first sentence was intended to serve as a general guide or statement of policy regarding victims' rights, whereas the second sentence was intended to provide an outline of the specific rights that the State shall afford crime victims.

Next, we examine the constitutional amendment's history. In an early attempt to secure the initial legislative approval needed to adopt a state constitutional victims' rights amendment, Senator Barbara Ulichny introduced 1989 Senate Joint Resolution 94. With her drafting request to the Legislative Reference Bureau (LRB), Senator Ulichny attached two articles written by other states' attorneys general as background material for the drafter that provide some evidence of the legislature's intent. *See* Don Siegelman & Courtney W. Tarver, *Victims' Rights in State Constitutions*, 1 Emerging Issues in St. Const. L. 163 (1988); Ken Eikenberry, *Victims of Crime/Victims of Justice*, 34 Wayne L. Rev. 29 (1987); Legislative Reference Bureau Drafting Record for 1989 S.J.R. 94.

From this background material, we learn that 1989 Senate Joint Resolution 94 was introduced in the midst of a larger, nationwide movement to recognize the rights of crime victims, particularly through the amendment of state constitutions. The materials note that crime victims were being treated insensitively and with a lack of consideration, even by well-meaning public agencies. Moreover, it was believed that rights of crime victims needed to be addressed both out of a sense of fundamental fairness and justice to victims, as well as to enhance the effectiveness of the criminal justice system, because the cooperation of crime victims and witnesses was understood to be central to law enforcement, Lois Haight Herrington, who chaired a presidential task force on victims of crime, explained that her task force concluded that:

> the treatment of crime victims in America was a national disgrace. Ignored, mistreated, or blamed, the innocent victims had been handled like photographs or fingerprints—mere evidence to be manipulated at the criminal justice system's convenience. By the end of the ordeal, many victims vowed that they

would never again become embroiled in the system, and that they would tell their friends and loved ones to stay away from the courts. Just as a pebble dropped in a pool causes rippling all across the water, the mistreatment of victims spread resentment and distrust of the justice system throughout entire communities. *We saw that this insensitivity toward victims was not only unjust, it was unwise.* The criminal justice system is absolutely dependent upon the cooperation of crime victims to report and testify. Without their help, the system cannot hold criminals accountable and stem the tide of future crime.

Eikenberry, *supra*, at 30 (emphasis added).

With this background established, we turn to the history of the actual language adopted. The legislature considered and rejected identical language for article I, section 9m of the Wisconsin Constitution in 1991 Assembly Joint Resolution 4 and 1989 Assembly Joint Resolution 138, both of which included a right to fairness and respect in a list of specifically enumerated rights:

> The rights of victims of crime shall be defined and protected by law and shall include: *the right to be treated with fairness and respect for their dignity and privacy throughout the criminal justice process;* the right to timely disposition of the case following arrest of the accused; the right to be reasonably protected from the accused throughout the criminal justice process; the right to notification of court proceedings; the right to attend trial and all other court proceedings that the accused has the right to attend; the right to confer with the prosecution; the right to make a statement to the court at sentencing; the right to restitution and compensation; and the right to information about the disposition of the case, including the conviction, sentence, imprisonment and release of the accused.

1991 A.J.R. 4 (emphasis added); 1989 A.J.R. 138 (emphasis added). The legislature rejected this language, deciding to remove the reference to fairness, dignity and respect from the list of enumerated rights and move it to a separate sentence. *See* Wis. Const. art. I, § 9m. We infer from that decision that the broad language of fairness, dignity and respect in the amendment's first sentence was intended to have a different significance than the language specifically articulating rights in the second sentence.

The statutory structure that was in place prior to the adoption of article I, section 9m of the Wisconsin Constitution provides evidence of the manner in which the amendment's first and second sentences were intended to differ in significance. The legislature had created Chapter 950, "Rights of victims and witnesses of crimes," in 1980. On its face, article I, section 9m of the Wisconsin Constitution appears to have adopted the structure of the pre-amendment codification of victims' rights. Section 950.01 of the Wisconsin Statutes of 1991-1992, entitled "Legislative intent," read in language very similar to the first sentence of article I, section 9m of the Wisconsin Constitution: "[T]he legislature declares its intent, in this chapter, to ensure that all victims...of crime are treated with dignity, respect, courtesy and sensitivity." Then, at section 950.04 of the

Wisconsin Statutes of 1991-1992, entitled "Basic bill of rights for victims and witnesses," specific rights of victims and witnesses were enumerated in detail, as they are in the second sentence of article I, section 9m of the Wisconsin Constitution.

Not only is the structure of the constitutional amendment on its face parallel to the pre-existing codification, the Legislative Reference Bureau (LRB) has explained that the constitutional amendment was adopted with the Chapter 950 provisions in mind. A LRB publication regarding the amendment explained that advocates of the amendment believed it was "necessary to give weight to the statutory language" and included a rationale for the amendment given by Eau Claire County Supervisor Gerald L. Wilkie in 1990 that refers to the pre-existing codification of victim rights:

> Though we have a comprehensive set of victim rights, the real problem is that these laws carry little weight.... A constitutional amendment is important because it would permanently ensure the rights will be honored and it will give our courts a constitutional basis for recognizing the victim's interest.

As article I, section 9m of the Wisconsin Constitution was adopted to give weight to chapter 950 and parallels that statutory scheme's structure, our conclusion that the opening sentence of article I, section 9m of the Wisconsin Constitution was meant to be a statement of purpose, set apart from and then followed by the enumeration of the specific enforceable rights crime victims are afforded in the second sentence, is further reinforced.

We turn next to the legislature's earliest interpretation of article I, section 9m of the Wisconsin Constitution, as manifested in 1997 Wis. Act 181, the first significant law passed regarding the rights of crime victims following the amendment's adoption. With 1997 Wis. Act 181, the legislature retained the pre-amendment statutory structure of providing for rights in detail in a provision entitled "Basic bill of rights for victims and witnesses." Further, 1997 Wis. Act 181 created a subsection at section 950.04(1v) entitled "Rights of victims," which enumerated crime victim rights, none of which make reference to fairness, dignity or respect for privacy. Instead, the legislature retained the broad language referring to fairness and dignity in the provision entitled "Legislative intent" at section 950.01 of the Wisconsin Statutes.

Moreover, subsequent to the adoption of 1997 Wis. Act 181, the LRB explained that article I, section 9m of the Wisconsin Constitution "recognizes specified privileges and protections for crime victims and directs the legislature to provide remedies for violations of those rights." Thus, the amendment apparently was intended to require remedies, such as the private reprimand at issue in this case, only for violations of the "privileges and protections" enumerated in the second sentence of article

I, section 9m of the Wisconsin Constitution. The LRB further noted that 1997 Wis. Act 181 lists "the rights of crime victims as protected by the Wisconsin Constitution and statutory law" in section 950.04(1v) of the Wisconsin Statutes, which, because section 950.04(1v) does not list rights of fairness, dignity or respect for privacy, further supports our conclusion.

The LRB's analysis of Engrossed 1997 Assembly Bill 342, which created 1997 Wis. Act 181, also suggests that the legislature did not interpret article I, section 9m of the Wisconsin Constitution to provide a separate enforceable right to fairness, dignity and respect for privacy. The LRB's analysis lists the rights that the state constitution provides to crime victims, without including the right to fairness, dignity and respect for privacy in the list.

In sum, based on our examination of the plain meaning of article I, section 9m of the Wisconsin Constitution, which is affirmed by the history of and the legislature's earliest interpretation of that amendment, we conclude that the first sentence of article I, section 9m of the Wisconsin Constitution does not provide a self-executing right that the Board is empowered to enforce via private reprimand pursuant to section 950.09(2)(a) of the Wisconsin Statutes. However, we recognize that crime victims, by virtue of the crimes they suffer, experience profound tragedy before they encounter the criminal justice system. While every act of insensitivity towards a crime victim may not constitute a violation of a right enforceable under section 950.09(2)(a), we believe that justice requires that all who are engaged in the prosecution of crimes make every effort to minimize further suffering by crime victims. Accordingly, we encourage officials within the criminal justice system, including prosecuting attorneys and their staffs, to establish effective lines of communication and good rapport with crime victims to the furthest extent possible.

Moreover, this holding is not to be construed as rendering the first sentence of article I, section 9m of the Wisconsin Constitution without meaning or to minimize the importance of the rights of crime victims in this state. Rather, the first sentence of article I, section 9m of the Wisconsin Constitution is a constitutional mandate. It articulates this State's policy regarding the treatment of crime victims. It also functions to guide Wisconsin courts' interpretations of the state's constitutional and statutory provisions concerning the rights of crime victims.

CONCLUSION

The first sentence of article I, section 9m of the Wisconsin Constitution states: "This state shall treat crime victims, as defined by law, with fairness, dignity and respect for their privacy." We recognize that according crime victims fairness, dignity and respect is very important to a just enforcement of the criminal code of the State of Wisconsin. The legislature has recognized the importance of victims' rights as well, by enacting section 950.04 of the Wisconsin Statutes. However, because we conclude that this constitutional provision is a statement of purpose that describes the policies to be promoted by the State and does not provide an enforceable, self-executing right, we affirm the circuit court decision reversing the private reprimand of District Attorney Patrick Schilling issued by the Crime Victims Rights Board under section 950.09(2)(a) of the Wisconsin Statutes.

The decision of the circuit court is affirmed.

NOTES

1. In 1982, California was the first state to pass a victims' rights amendment to its constitution. *See* Timothy A. Razel, Note, *Dying to Get Away with It: How the Abatement Doctrine Thwarts Justice—And What Should be Done Instead*, 75 Fordham L. Rev. 2193, 2207 (2007); *see also* Alice Kosklea, Comment, *Victim's Rights Amendments: An Irresistible Political Force Transforms the Criminal Justice System*, 34 Idaho L. Rev. 157, 165 (1997). The provision, approved by the California electorate, gave victims the right to "restitution, safe schools, consideration of public safety when setting bail, and an unrestricted admissibility of prior felony convictions," as well as "the absolute right to appear at sentencing and parole proceedings." Cal. Const. art. I, § 28. Florida and Michigan followed with voter-approved amendments in 1988. That same year, the states of Arizona and Washington attempted, but failed, to pass victims' rights amendments to their constitutions. Washington and Texas passed victims' rights amendments in 1990. By 1996, twenty-eight states had victims' rights constitutional amendments. Today, thirty-two states have victims' rights constitutional amendments.

2. The victims' rights amendments vary by state, but all seek to achieve one or more of the following objectives: (1) make the victim whole economically; (2) develop administrative sensitivity to the distress of the victim; (3) respect the victim's privacy; (4) provide protection against potential victim intimidation; (5) reduce the burdens on victims willing to assist with the prosecution of the defendant; (6) increase victim participation in the prosecution beyond simply appearing as a witness. *See* Jay M. Zitter, Annotation, *Validity, Construction, and Application of State Constitutional or Statutory Victims' Bill of Rights*, 91 A.L.R.5th 343 § 2[a] (2008); LaFave *et al*, 1 Criminal Procedure § 1.4(k) (2d ed. 2004).

3. Although Montana does not have a victims' rights amendment, in 1998, the voters approved a constitutional amendment that expanded the purpose of the criminal justice system to include restitution to crime victims. Mont. Const. art. II, § 28(1) ("Laws for the punishment of crime

shall be founded on the principles of prevention, reformation, public safety, and restitution for victims.").

4.   A victims' right that has been the subject of case law in various states is the right to be present at trial. *See, e.g.*, Ariz. Const. art. II, § 2.1(A)(3) (giving victims of crimes the right "to be present at...all criminal proceedings where the defendant has the right to be present"); Utah Const. art. I, § 28 (stating that the victim has the right "to be present at...important criminal justice hearings related to the victim"). The victim's presence at trial has been argued to be prejudicial to the defendant because the victim hears the testimony of the other witnesses before testifying against the defendant. *See Gore v. State*, 599 So.2d 978 (Fla. 1992) (holding that the trial court's excusal of the murder victim's stepmother from the rule of witness sequestration because she was a relative of the victim and had the right to be present in the courtroom during trial did not prejudice the defendant). Some constitutional provisions try to balance the rights of the victim with the rights of the defendant by permitting the victim to be present at trial only where it does not interfere with the defendant's rights. Fla. Const. art. I, § 16(b) (giving victims of crimes "the right to...be present...at all crucial states of criminal proceedings, to the extent that these rights do not interfere with the constitutional rights of the accused").

CHAPTER XIII

STATE CONSTITUTIONAL PROVISIONS WITH NO FEDERAL COUNTERPARTS

A. INTRODUCTION

There is a wide variety of state constitutional provisions, some of which have no counterparts in the Federal Constitution. For example, while the Federal Constitution makes no mention of education, all state constitutions contain education articles that guarantee the right to a free public education. These constitutional guarantees of a free public education are discussed in Chapter XI. Many state constitutions contain provisions guaranteeing a right to a remedy or open courts; these provisions, which also have no federal counterparts, are covered in Chapter XII. A growing number of state constitutions contain provisions directing the legislature to protect the environment or guaranteeing public rights to a clean and healthy environment. *See* Barton H. Thompson, Jr., *The Environment and Natural Resources* (Chapter Ten) in G. Alan Tarr & Robert E. Williams (eds.) STATE CONSTITUTIONS IN THE 21st CENTURY (2006). A few state constitutions include provisions mandating aid for the needy. The Montana Constitution, for instance, states that: "The legislature shall provide such economic assistance and social and rehabilitative services as may be necessary for those inhabitants who, by reason of age, infirmities, or misfortune may have need for the aid of society." Montana Const. art. XII, § 3(3). Turning to another subject, the New Jersey Constitution guarantees employees in the private sector the right to "organize and bargain collectively." N.J. Const. art. I, § 19. As noted in the Introduction, some state constitutions have exotic provisions with no federal counterparts, such as article XII, § 13 of the Ohio Constitution, which bars the taxation of food sold for human consumption, or article VIII, § 15 of the Alaska Constitution, which forbids the creation of any "exclusive right or special privilege of fishery" within Alaskan waters.

In this Chapter, the focus is on state constitutional provisions with no federal counterparts that place limits on legislative authority. Three areas will be covered: single subject and clear title rules; public policy requirements, and uniformity clauses.

As their name suggests, single subject rules require that each bill considered by the legislature address but one subject. Clear title rules require that the subject of each bill be clearly expressed in its title. These types of provisions first began to appear around the end of the eighteenth century to counteract corruption and undue influence of special interest groups in state legislatures. *See* Millard H. Ruud, *No Law Shall Embrace More than One Subject*, 42 Minn. L. Rev. 389, 414-452 (1958). Today, they are included in the vast majority of state constitutions as a means to bring transparency, order, and fairness to the legislative process.

Some state constitutions include provisions requiring that public funds be spent only for public purposes. The Illinois Constitution, for example, states that "Public funds, property or credit shall be used only for public purposes." Ill. Const. art. VIII, § 1 (1970). A public policy requirement also may be found underlying state constitutional provisions that prohibit the granting of special privileges or immunities. By banning special entitlements, state constitutions imply that legislation must be for the benefit of the public. *See* Jeffrey M. Shaman, EQUALITY AND LIBERTY IN THE GOLDEN AGE OF STATE CONSTITUTIONAL LAW 28-33 (2008). In other states, notwithstanding the absence of an express constitutional mandate, the courts have read a "public purpose doctrine" into their state constitutions. In Wisconsin, for instance, the public purpose doctrine is a well-established constitutional principle, even though it is not recited in any specific clause of the state constitution. *State ex rel. Warren v. Nusbaum*, 208 N.W.2d 780, 795 (Wis. 1973). Whether explicit or implicit, the tenet that public funds be spent only for public purposes is an important requirement of state constitutional law.

A number of state constitutions contain so-called "uniformity clauses" that require taxes to be uniformly levied upon the same class of subjects. Some uniformity clauses apply only to property taxes, while others apply to all taxes. In reviewing the constitutionality of tax laws under uniformity clauses, some state courts adopt a deferential stance that affords a fair degree of latitude that enables the legislature to make classifications for taxing purposes, so long as they are not unduly arbitrary or unreasonable. In other states, however, the courts are not so deferential to the legislature in reviewing tax laws under uniformity clauses. In these states, the courts apply more rigorous scrutiny to evaluate tax laws challenged as violating the constitutional requirement of uniformity.

B. SINGLE SUBJECT AND CLEAR TITLE RULES

Martha Dragich, *State Constitutional Restriction on Legislative Procedure: Rethinking the Analysis of Original Purpose, Single Subject, and Clear Title Challenges*
38 Harv. J. Legis. 103 (2001)

State constitutions contain a variety of provisions governing legislative procedures. Unlike substantive limits, procedural restrictions regulate only the process by which legislation is enacted. Common examples are original purpose, single subject, and clear title restrictions. Original purpose clauses prohibit the amendment of a bill so "as to change its original purpose." Single subject rules limit each bill to one subject. Clear title rules require that the subject of the bill be clearly expressed in the bill's title. These provisions are designed to eradicate perceived abuses in the legislative process, such as hasty, corrupt, or private interest legislation. They are intended to promote open, orderly, and deliberative legislative processes, and can be found in almost all state constitutions.

The genesis of state constitutional restrictions on legislative procedure has been recounted elsewhere. The clear title rule, for example, was first adopted in 1798 in Georgia and the single subject rule first appeared in 1818 in Illinois. Most other states followed suit in the mid-nineteenth century. Constitutional restrictions on legislative procedure have survived and have been re-adopted in modern constitutions despite criticism that they allow the invalidation of legislation on "technical" grounds.

State constitutional restrictions on legislative procedure, unlike legislative rules adopted by the two houses of Congress, provide an avenue for challenging statutes, and such litigation is fairly common. The large number of procedural challenge cases seems surprising since State courts consistently proclaim that statutes are presumed constitutional. The Missouri Supreme Court, for example, has long insisted that "[t]he use of these procedural limitations to attack the constitutionality of statutes is not favored. A statute has a presumption of constitutionality. We interpret procedural limitations liberally and will uphold the constitutionality of a statute against such an attack unless the act *clearly and undoubtedly* violates the constitutional limitation. The burden of establishing [a statute's] unconstitutionality rests upon the party questioning it."

Other states likewise favor a liberal construction of procedural restrictions. Courts have used a variety of phrases to express the high standard to be applied in these cases, stating that statutes will be held unconstitutional, for example, only if "clearly, plainly and palpably so," only if shown "beyond a reasonable doubt" to violate the constitution, or only in case of a "manifestly gross and fraudulent violation." As a result of these high standards, state courts uphold legislation against procedural challenges "more often than not." The Minnesota Supreme Court observed that from the late 1970s until 2000, it had decided five single subject/clear title cases, upholding the statute in every case. In 1984, a Missouri judge indicated that the Missouri Supreme Court had not sustained a procedural challenge in twenty years.

Why, then, do litigants continue to raise original purpose, single subject, and clear title claims? One explanation of this behavior is that "[s]uch challenges are easy to make because all that is necessary is reference to the face of the statute." Another explanation is that each of these cases, depending as it does on the specific text of a particular enactment, is sui generis. As such, there is always a chance that a court will sustain a challenge to one piece of legislation even though it has rejected challenges to many other statutes. A more cynical explanation is that procedural challenges offer litigants one last chance to attack legislation they were unable to defeat during the legislative process.

Whatever their motivations, these claims have begun to pay off. The Minnesota Supreme Court, for example, "sound[ed] an alarm that [it] would not hesitate to strike down" legislation violating single subject and clear title provisions. The Missouri Supreme Court has heard ten procedural challenge cases since 1994, finding violations in five of them. The Illinois Supreme Court sustained only one single subject challenge from 1970 to 1996, but it has sustained four challenges since 1997.

A recent Illinois decision led to a nationally publicized furor in the Illinois legislature. In *People v. Cervantes*, the Illinois Supreme Court struck down the Safe Neighborhoods Law for violation of the single subject restriction. The law had been in effect nearly five years at the time of the decision. The scope of the Illinois court's ruling-striking down the entire enactment-is important. The court found that the Safe Neighborhoods Law was intended to address neighborhood safety problems relating to "gangs, drugs, and guns." Two portions of the law were found to constitute separate subjects: provisions amending the WIC (Women, Infants, and Children nutrition program) Vendor Management Act, and provisions relating to the licensing of secure residential youth care facilities. The Illinois Supreme Court discerned "no natural and logical connection" between these provisions and neighborhood safety. The portion of the Safe Neighborhoods Law challenged in *Cervantes* related not to the WIC vendor management program or the licensing of residential youth care facilities, but to weapons. Because the entire act was ruled unconstitutional, however, the defendant's gunrunning charge was dismissed. In fact, prosecutors were "forced to dismiss" firearms charges against numerous defendants. Five years after initial passage of the Safe Neighborhoods Law, the Illinois legislature found itself sharply divided on the merits of reenacting the gun control provisions. The measure has not been reenacted even though the Governor called a special session of the legislature for that purpose.

The Safe Neighborhoods Law exemplifies one consistent thread among recent procedural challenge cases: major changes were introduced into the challenged bills very late in the legislative process. This type of legislative procedure runs directly counter to the open, rational, and deliberative model the constitutional restrictions contemplate. Bills enacted in a hasty, apparently deceptive, or ill-considered process thus

seem to invite procedural challenges. To return to *Cervantes*, the original
Senate bill, relating to community service sentencing, was amended in the
House so as to replace its entire contents with new provisions, now
described as the "Safe Neighborhoods Law." The Senate refused to concur
with the House amendment. A conference committee was formed, and that
body deleted the entire House amendment and substituted another entirely
new bill, 157 pages long and containing three components. That version
then passed the Senate and the House and was signed by the governor.
Similarly, in a Missouri case, *St. Louis Health Care Network v. State*, a
substitute bill was offered on the last day of the legislative session for a
bill originally relating to the Missouri Family Trust. The substitute bill
contained provisions relating to nonprofit corporations, charitable gift
annuities, and same-sex marriages. In both cases, the timing and scope of
the changes raised suspicion.

Court suspects foul play?

A court's description of the legislative procedure leading to passage of
the bill at issue sometimes indicates that the court's willingness to
overturn the law is based on a suspicion that the process was tainted. For
example, the Maryland Court of Appeals described the
"transmogrifi[cation]" of a one-page bill concerning a specific tax into
"lengthy emergency legislation" extending to government ethics and
county taxing authority. Similarly, the Supreme Court of Appeals of West
Virginia explained how a bill on thoroughbred racing became "an omnibus
bill which encompassed authorization for all agency rules considered that
year."

§ Sub can be a hook for overturning law

1. Original Purpose

Missouri's original purpose provision is typical. It reads in pertinent
part:

> No law shall be passed except by bill, and *no bill shall be so amended in its
> passage through either house as to change its original purpose.* Bills may
> originate in either house and be amended or rejected by the other. Every bill
> shall be read by title on three different days in each house.

By its text, section 21 not only establishes the original purpose rule, but
also implies a limitation of the rule and hints at the rule's underlying
rationale. The text makes clear that the original purpose rule does not
prohibit amendments to a bill during the course of its consideration and
passage. In fact, it explicitly permits either house to amend bills
originating in the other house. The Missouri Supreme Court has indicated
that "Article III, § 21 was not designed to inhibit the normal legislative
processes, in which bills are combined and additions necessary to comply
with the legislative intent are made." At least one other state agrees that
the original purpose rule should not be applied in such a way as to "unduly
hamper the legislature."

Original purpose rule/procedure rationale

In essence, the original purpose rule is "designed to prevent the enactment of ... statutes in terms so blind that legislators themselves ... [would fail] to become apprised of the changes in the laws." The final sentence of section 21 supports this rationale. It provides for the reading by title of each bill on three different days in each house. The rule protects the legislative process by allowing bills to be read and monitored by title alone. That is, a legislator is entitled to read bills as originally introduced and to decide, on that basis, how extensively to monitor each bill's progress. Legislators are assured that the purpose of a bill will not have changed dramatically following its introduction. This same reasoning serves to provide adequate notice to members of the public who wish to monitor pending legislation.

The original purpose rule also reinforces the deadline for introduction of new bills by preventing legislators from disguising new bills as amendments to existing bills. Accordingly, the original purpose rule is concerned with *changes* in content of the bill. By aiding legislators in monitoring hundreds of bills introduced in each legislative session, the original purpose rule helps legislators to represent the desires of their constituents.

Though only a few of the recent cases involve original purpose claims, the outcomes are instructive. In *Barclay v. Melton*, a bill that "had as its sole purpose the creation of a tax credit for dependents" was amended by deleting all of the provisions contained in the introduced version and replacing them with new contents. As passed, the bill "assess[ed] a tax surcharge against ... residents of [certain] school districts." The Arkansas Supreme Court concluded that the change from a tax credit to a tax surcharge was a change in the bill's original purpose.

Changes less extreme than this about-face seem not to trigger invalidation on original purpose grounds. *Advisory Opinion No. 331* appears to be unusual in this regard. There, the Alabama Supreme Court ruled that a bill whose original purpose was "to make appropriations for the ordinary expenses of ... the government" was unconstitutionally altered so as to change its original purpose when provisions limiting the powers of government officials to make necessary expenditures were added. According to the court, the purpose of the bill changed "from one of making general appropriations ... to one of ... repealing and changing other provisions of law ...." This bill represents a more subtle change. As finally passed, it contained two contradictory elements: provisions authorizing expenditures and provisions limiting the same expenditures. This case adds credence to the notion that a change in direction is fundamental in establishing an original purpose violation.

2. Single Subject and Clear Title

In most states, the single subject and clear title rules are combined in one section of the constitution. The combined rule is commonly phrased: "[n]o bill shall contain more than *one subject*, which shall be *clearly expressed* in its title." In some states, a bill must embrace "one subject, and matters properly connected therewith." Exceptions are commonly made for certain types of bills, such as "general appropriation bills, which may embrace the various subjects and accounts for which moneys are appropriated," and bills revising or codifying the law. It is well-established that even when combined, the single subject/clear title provision sets forth two independent requirements-that a bill have only one subject, and that the bill's title clearly express that subject. The common phrasing of the rule suggests that clear title analysis cannot proceed until the subject of the bill has been determined and found to be "single."

a. Single Subject

How broad can the subject be?

Two reasons are thought to support the single subject requirement: the prevention of logrolling and the preservation of a meaningful role for the governor. Simply stated, the single subject rule exists "to secure to every distinct measure of legislation a separate consideration and decision, dependent solely upon its individual merits." One leading commentator observed, "limiting each bill to a single subject" allows legislators to "better grasp[] and more intelligently discuss[]" the issues presented by each bill. Without the rule, the danger is that "several minorities [may combine] their several proposals as different provisions of a single bill and thus consolidat[e] their votes so that a majority is obtained for the omnibus bill where perhaps no single proposal...could have obtained majority approval separately."

S.sub allows more clarity & better focus

minorities can gain a majority w/out S. sub.

Furthermore, the single subject rule protects the governor's veto prerogative by "prevent[ing] the legislature from forcing the governor into a take-it-or-leave-it choice when a bill addresses one subject in an odious manner and another subject in a way the governor finds meritorious." The rule is "intended to prohibit [] anti-majoritarian tactic[s]." In a word, the single subject rule protects the *decision* of the legislators and governor on each individual legislative proposal.

Save govs from "all or nothing" choices

Hammerschmidt v. Boone County is a classic case of a single subject violation. Two very narrow bills relating to the conduct of elections were combined, and thereafter provisions relating to the form of county governance were added. There was no "rational unity" between the provisions relating to election procedures and those relating to county governance, and no reason except "tactical convenience" for combining them in a single bill. Election procedures and county governance cannot

seems like there's a unnecessarily unprincipled argument for multi subject

Is there "rational unity"? or is it just tactical convenience?

be reconciled as parts of any single subject. No title could be written to express a single subject incorporating both of these elements.

Another good example is *People v. Cervantes*, an Illinois case. A bill originally relating to community service sentencing was amended several times during the course of its consideration. As passed, the bill expanded the offenses for which a minor can be tried as an adult, permitted longer sentences for felonies committed in furtherance of the activities of a gang, amended sentences for driving while intoxicated, adjusted sentences for drug offenses, and amended various other sentencing provisions. All of these provisions were found to be related to the amended bill's subject matter, neighborhood safety. Portions of the bill relating to the licensing of youth correctional facilities and welfare program vendor fraud, however, were held to relate to other subjects unconnected with neighborhood safety.

b. Clear Title

Two distinct purposes support the clear title requirement. Most importantly, the requirement "is designed to assure that the people are fairly apprised...of the subjects of legislation that are being considered in order that they have [an] opportunity of being heard thereon." Secondarily, by requiring the title to express the whole subject of the bill, the rule "defeats surprise within the legislative process" and prohibits a legislator from "surreptitiously inserting unrelated amendments into the body of a pending bill." These two purposes reflect a widespread concern with special interest legislation in the nineteenth century. The clear title rule, properly understood, safeguards openness and honesty in the legislative process and facilitates public participation.

There are two common variations of clear title violations: overly broad, "amorphous" titles and under-inclusive titles. *St. Louis Health Care Network v. State* is a paradigmatic case of an amorphous title so broad that it gave no notice of the contents of the bill. This Article classifies *St. Louis Health Care Network* as a clear title case rather than a single subject case precisely because the title is so vague that one cannot discern from it what the bill itself provides. Clear title is properly the basis on which this case was resolved.

National Solid Waste Management Ass'n v. Director, Department of Natural Resources is a paradigmatic case of an under-inclusive title. The title-"relating to solid waste management"-accurately described the subject of most of the bill's provisions, but failed to give any hint of its application to hazardous waste. As a result, the title failed to provide notice of a portion of the bill's subject. The court assumed that the bill's two aspects, solid waste and hazardous waste, could be reconciled as part

[handwritten margin note: Invalidating the law because of an insufficient title]

of a broader subject, but because the title failed to express the full extent of the bill's subject, the court invalidated the law.

The preceding analysis demonstrates that the original purpose, single subject, and clear title provisions, though related, are distinct. The original purpose requirement allows legislators to monitor vast numbers of bills by reference to their titles, confident that each bill's original purpose will remain reasonably constant throughout the process of consideration. It also secures adequate time for the consideration of each proposal by preventing late amendments that drastically alter the bill. The single subject rule assures that legislators and the governor can make a choice based upon the merits of legislation on each subject by preventing them from having to swallow unrelated bitter provisions with the sweet. Finally, the clear title rule protects the right of the public to know the subjects of legislation being considered and to voice opinions on measures of concern to them, and protects against fraudulent or surreptitious legislation.

McINTIRE v. FORBES
909 P.2d 846 (Or. 1996)

GRABER, J.

Petitioners challenge the constitutionality of the light rail funding provisions of Senate Bill 1156 (SB 1156 or the Act), enacted by the Oregon legislature in special session in August 1995. They assert that sections 1 to 17 of the Act (the substantive provisions relating to light rail funding) are invalid for a number of reasons. We conclude that sections 1 to 17 of the Act are invalid because the legislative act in which they are contained violates the "one-subject" requirement of Article IV, section 20, of the Oregon Constitution.

Article IV, section 20, of the Oregon Constitution, provides in part:

"Every Act shall embrace but one subject, and matters properly connected therewith, which subject shall be expressed in the title. But if any subject shall be embraced in an Act which shall not be expressed in the title, such Act shall be void only as to so much thereof as shall not be expressed in the title."

At the outset, we will be mindful of this court's caution:

"The constitutional provision prohibiting a statute from containing more than one subject or object should not be technically, strictly, or narrowly, but reasonably, fairly, broadly, and liberally construed, with due regard to its purpose. It should not be so construed so as to hamper or cripple legislation, or render it oppressive or impracticable, by a strictness unnecessary to the accomplishment of the beneficial purpose for which it was adopted, or to make laws unnecessarily restrictive in their scope and operation, or to multiply the number of laws unnecessarily, or to promote controversy in regard to the validity of legislative enactments." *Garbade and Boynton v. City of Portland,* 214 P.2d 1000 (1950) (quoting 50 Am.Jur., Statutes, § 194, p. 175).

[handwritten margin note: How S-sub rule should be applied. As against mandatory]

The principal purpose for the title requirement of Article IV, section 20, is to provide fair notice to legislators (and to others) of the contents of a bill:

> "The constitutional restriction on titles of legislative acts was designed to prevent the use of the title as a means of deceiving members of the legislature and other interested persons as the bill moved through the legislative process. The restriction was intended to assure those who could not examine the body of the act itself that the act did not deal with more than its title disclosed." *Warren v. Marion County et al.*, 353 P.2d 257 (1960).

Those persons who may wish to follow legislation as it moves through the legislative process may include members of the public, the Governor, local government officials, and others.

The principal purpose for the one-subject requirement of Article IV, section 20, for the body of an act is to guard against logrolling. *Nielson (v. Bryson*, 477 P.2d 714 [1970]) reiterates that "one of the principal objects was to 'prevent the combining of incongruous matters and objects totally distinct and having no connection or relation with each other in one and the same bill.'" *Nielson* also defines logrolling as "combining subjects representing diverse interests, in order to unite the members of the legislature who favored either, in support of all."

The Oregon appellate courts have adjudicated at least 90 cases under Article IV, section 20, although none since 1970. The cases are not always clear or consistent in analytical approach. However, several cases examine the body of an act, the title of the act, and the relationship between the body and the title…. After considering the foregoing sources, we conclude that the appropriate analysis of a one-subject challenge to the body of an act, made under Article IV, section 20, should proceed in these steps:

> (1) Examine the body of the act to determine whether (without regard to an examination of the title) the court can identify a unifying principle logically connecting all provisions in the act, such that it can be said that the act "embrace[s] but one subject."

> (2) If the court has not identified a unifying principle logically connecting all provisions in the act, examine the title of the act with reference to the body of the act. In a one-subject challenge to the body of an act, the purpose of that examination is to determine whether the legislature nonetheless has identified, and expressed in the title, such a unifying principle logically connecting all provisions in the act, thereby demonstrating that the act, in fact, "embrace[s] but one subject."

Petitioners have summarized the contents of SB 1156 as follows:

> "SB 1156…(1) provides state funding [and land use procedures] for light rail, (2) expands the availability of card-lock service stations, (3) promotes 'regional problem solving' in land use matters, (4) regulates confined animal feeding, (5) preempts local pesticide regulation, (6) adopts new timber harvesting rules, (7) grants immunity to shooting ranges for 'noise pollution,' and (8) protects salmon from cormorants."

We are unable to discern a principle unifying those eight topics. Neither are we able to perceive among the parts of the Act some logical connection relating each to the others. That being so, we move to the next step. We consider whether the legislature nonetheless has identified a unifying principle, logically connecting all provisions in the Act, that we do not yet perceive. If it has, and if the title discloses that unifying principle, then the Act, in fact, embraces but one subject.

In approaching this question, we focus on the title's "relating" clause ("Relating to the activities regulated by state government"), because that is what serves the constitutional function of the title. It is, for example, the relating clause that informs the President of the Senate and the Speaker of the House what amendments to a bill are germane.

The relating clause in the title in this case—the statement that the Act is one "[r]elating to the activities regulated by state government"—fails to identify and express a unifying principle logically connecting all provisions in the Act. It fails to perform that function, because—in this extreme case—the relating clause is so global that it does little more than define the universe with respect to which the legislature is empowered to act.

Respondents argue, however, that the relating clause is not global. They suggest that "the activities regulated" should be read to mean activities already regulated and that "state government" means that activities regulated by local governments are not included.

The "limits" suggested by respondents are illusory. The relating clause for SB 1156, even thus limited, is still so broad and general that it logically connects all provisions in the Act only in the meaningless sense that it announces a connection among nearly all things in the legislative universe. The title does not, in the constitutional sense, express a unifying principle. The phrase "[r]elating to the activities regulated by state government" is too broad and general to unify the disparate topics embraced by SB 1156.

Senate Bill 1156 embraces more than one subject. That being so, a guarantee of Article IV, section 20, was not met, and the process for enacting that legislation was fundamentally flawed. The court is obliged to consider and to remedy violations of Article IV, section 20. In this case, we hold that SB 1156 violates Article IV, section 20, of the Oregon Constitution. That being so, and consistent with the limited grant of jurisdiction in this case, we hold that sections 1 to 17 of SB 1156 are void.

TURNBULL v. FINK
668 A.2d 1370 (Del. 1995)

[handwritten margin note: US M? one -sub as as procedural hook to fgbt law?]

HARTNETT, J.

This is an Interlocutory Appeal. The Plaintiffs-Appellants challenge pre-trial rulings of the Superior Court as to the extent to which the State waived its sovereign immunity by the purchase of commercial liability insurance covering accidents involving two buses operated by the Delaware Administration for Regional Transit ("DART"). The issue presented to the Superior Court was which statute controls these proceedings: 2 Del.C. § 1329, enacted by 66 Del.Laws C. 360 ("1989 Bond Act"), or 18 Del.C. § 6511. Title 2, Del.C. § 1329 waives the State's sovereign immunity, as to DART, up to a maximum of $300,000 for each occurrence, if DART has in place the commercial insurance coverage authorized to be purchased by the 1989 Bond Act. Title 18, Del.C. § 6511 waives sovereign immunity generally, up to the limit of insurance coverage, if there is in place the insurance authorized to be purchased under that Section.

[handwritten margin note: Did discrepancies between the statutes?]

The Superior Court held that, as between 18 Del.C. § 6511 and 2 Del.C. § 1329, Section 1329 was the more specific and later enacted statute and, therefore, its provisions control. Consequently, the Superior Court determined that 2 Del.C. § 1329 limits the State's waiver of sovereign immunity, as to accidents involving DART, to the lesser of the amount of applicable insurance coverage, or $300,000.

In this Court, Appellants raise for the first time a claim that Section 68 of the 1989 Bond Act, which enacted 2 Del.C. § 1329, is unconstitutional. Specifically, they assert that the Act violated Article II, Section 16 of the Delaware Constitution because it contained more than one subject and that the subject "waiver of sovereign immunity" was not set forth in the title to the bill. The text of Article II § 16 of the Delaware Constitution precludes Appellant's argument. It states: "No bill or joint resolution, except bills appropriating money for public purposes, shall embrace more than one subject, which shall be expressed in its title." Delaware courts have consistently followed the "plain meaning rule" for construction of statutes or the Delaware Constitution. One formulation used by this Court in stating the "plain meaning rule" is: "In the absence of any ambiguity, the language of the statute must be regarded as conclusive of the General Assembly's intent. The judicial role is then limited to an application of the literal meaning of the words."

[handwritten margin note: Subject & title claims confined upon bills?]

[handwritten margin note: Textual interpretation. Tools of users]

As noted by Millard H. Ruud in his article *No Law Shall Embrace More than One Subject*, 42 Minn. L .Rev. 389, 414-452 (1959), the text of the Delaware Constitution is more permissive than any other state constitution because it provides that a bill of the Delaware General

Del exception to one subject rule

Assembly which appropriates money for public purposes is free of the restraint that it be limited to one subject. As Professor Ruud points out, in 1958 18 states had adopted constitutional provisions specifically dealing with the limitation of contents of bills making appropriations-both general appropriations bills and other appropriation bills. The Constitutions of seven of those 18 states (including Pennsylvania) expressly excepted only general appropriation bills from the one subject restriction. There are only four states, including Delaware, in which a "one subject" limitation provision in the State's Constitution is exempted as to all appropriation bills. Of these four states only the Delaware Constitution provides that any bill appropriating money for public purposes is excepted from the one-subject and title requirements.

The 1989 Bond Act is clearly a bill appropriating money for public purposes and its provision relating to the waiver of sovereign immunity in Section 68 relates to the insurance authorized to be purchased in the Act. The 1989 Bond Act is similar to the Annual Budget Act and differs only as to the number of appropriations and its source of funds. The 1989 Bond Act makes over 130 separate appropriations and the money appropriated has several sources including the General Fund, general obligation bonds, revenue bonds, funds made available from the repeal of prior appropriations not yet expended, and certain special funds. As a bill appropriating money for public purposes, the 1989 Bond Act clearly falls within the exception in Article II, § 16 of Delaware Constitution. No other provision in the Delaware Constitution requires a one-subject limitation or a requirement for a title for a bill appropriating money for public purposes. There is, therefore, no requirement in the Delaware Constitution that the 1989 Bond Act be limited to one subject that is expressed in its title. The framers of the Delaware Constitution undoubtedly recognized, even in 1897, the difficulties in limiting an appropriation bill to one subject or setting forth its provisions in a title.   *So... can't argue substantively, Thus, attack*

procedurally.

Appellants do not assert that they have been mislead or prejudiced by any deficiencies in the 1989 Bond Act. To the contrary, they are benefitted by the enactment of Section 68 that enacted 2 Del.C. § 1329 because it waives the constitutional doctrine of sovereign immunity, up to $300,000 per occurrence, if DART has in place the insurance coverage authorized to be purchased by the Act. Without Section 68, Appellants would not have the benefit of this waiver.   *Section 68 benefits π*

For the foregoing reasons, the pre-trial rulings of the Superior Court that 2 Del.C. § 1329, enacted by Section 68 of the 1989 Bond Act, applies to this lawsuit and that it limits any recovery to $300,000 per occurrence are AFFIRMED and this proceeding is REMANDED for further action.

HOLLAND, J., dissenting.

[handwritten: Limiting bills to one subject won't stop legislative confusion]

[handwritten margin: Summarizing TI's argument +]

The interlocutory judgments of the Superior Court which determined that 2 Del.C. § 1329, rather than 18 Del.C. § 6511, applies to these proceedings and limits any recovery to $300,000 per occurrence should be reversed because § 1329 is unconstitutional....The appellants contend that 2 Del.C. § 1329 is violative of the Delaware Constitution because it was enacted as Section 68 of the 1989 Bond and Capital Improvements Act ("1989 Bond Act"). In support of that contention, the appellants assert that the title of the 1989 Bond Act gave no indication its purpose was to alter the doctrine of sovereign immunity and that it was improper to include substantive legislation in an appropriation bill.

The Single-Subject and Title Rules

The two general provisions in Article II, § 16 of the Delaware Constitution, that a bill contain only one subject and that the title of the bill express its subject, are distinct requirements. Each has different historical origins. Nevertheless, these two requirements are often combined in a single provision, such as Article II, § 16 of the Delaware Constitution, to achieve a common purpose. Before examining the exception for appropriation bills, it is important to understand the history and purpose of the two general requirements.

[handwritten margin: Key policy reason for sub./title requirements]

The potential problem caused by an omnibus bill, which includes unrelated provisions on heterogeneous matters, is an uninformed legislative vote. This was recognized by the Romans. In 98 B.C., the Lex Caecilia Didia was enacted to prohibit the adoption of laws which contained unrelated provisions—the lex satura. The omnibus bill continued to be a cause for concern in colonial America prior to the Revolutionary War. Consequently, the constitution of nearly every state now contains a general requirement that legislation be limited to a single subject.

[handwritten margin: Fear of the "omnibus" sub. bused]

The other general requirement in Article II, § 16, that the subject matter of a bill be expressed in its title, originated with the Georgia Constitution of 1798. In 1795, the Georgia legislature passed the Yazoo Act, which made grants to private persons that were not reflected in the statute's title. The Georgia Constitution was amended in 1798. The constitution of almost every state now requires that the title of a bill adequately express its subject matter. These provisions are also intended to insure informed legislative action, as the 1897 debates on the Delaware Constitution reflect:

[handwritten margin: Don't sign something you don't understand. Won't shift to read — read]

> Oftentimes bills have been introduced in the Legislature with very harmless titles, but amendments have been added to those bills and when they have passed both Houses, they are entirely different from what they were originally. Delaware Constitutional Debates 1897, Vol. 1, p. 264.

Consistent with the foregoing historical background, this Court has recognized that the two general requirements of Article II, § 16 were included in the Delaware Constitution of 1897 in order to "prevent deception of the general public and the members of the General Assembly by titles to bills which give no adequate information of the subject matter of the bills." The single-subject and title provisions in Article II, § 16 are intended to assure sufficient notice that "legislation, the content of which was inadequately brought to the public attention, or so-called sleeper legislation" does not slip through the General Assembly. If a bill contains multiple subjects or the title of the bill is such that it would "trap the unwary into inaction," it must be struck down as a violation of this section of the Delaware Constitution.

Nevertheless, appropriation bills have traditionally been conditionally exempted from both of the general requirements, the single-subject and the title provisions, in state constitutions. In view of the historical fear of omnibus legislation, which led to the constitutional proscriptions against bills with multiple subjects or nondescript titles, however, the exceptions for appropriation bills are always narrow. The condition for exemption is usually a limitation that the provisions in an appropriation bill relate only to appropriations.

While appropriation bills must contain no other substantive provisions than appropriations matters, this does not mean that an appropriation bill must merely be a list of monetary appropriations and respective recipients. Rather, appropriation bills may contain substantive language which relates to the specific appropriations in the appropriation bill. Such language may be found to be "conditional" or "incidental" to an appropriation and, therefore, properly included in an appropriation bill. Factors which indicate that language in an appropriation bill is not merely "conditional" or "incidental," but rather is improperly substantive are: first, the provision is not germane to any appropriation in the appropriation bill; second, the provision amends or repeals an already existing law; and third, the provision is permanent in nature, extending beyond the life of the appropriation act. If an appropriation act contains substantive, non-financial legislation, it then becomes precisely the kind of omnibus bill the single-subject and title rules were meant to prohibit. Accordingly, an appropriation act is an improper place for an enactment of matters unrelated to appropriations. Otherwise, the purpose behind the single-subject and title rules would be meaningless, since they could be circumvented simply by putting a substantive change into legislation otherwise primarily devoted to appropriations. Consequently, those courts which have considered the issue all conclude:

> While under the Constitution general appropriation bills are exempted from the
> general constitutional provision which requires that all bills must contain but

one subject, which must be clearly expressed in the title it does not follow that general laws may be amended, modified, or repealed by a general appropriation act under such a general title)…

During the debates on the 1897 Delaware Constitution, Edward G. Bradford proposed that appropriation bills be excluded from the constitutional provision which provided that no bill should embrace more than one subject expressed in its title (the single-subject and title rules)…. During the discussion on this proposal, the Pennsylvania Constitution was cited as one of its origins and as persuasive authority for its adoption. In 1894, three years prior to the Delaware constitutional debates, two similar provisions in the Pennsylvania Constitution, along with a provision giving the governor line-item veto power over appropriations, were interpreted by the Pennsylvania Supreme Court to have the same purpose, *i.e.*, to prevent the passage of extraneous matters in appropriation bills. With the benefit of the Pennsylvania Supreme Court's interpretation of its constitutional provisions regarding: appropriation bills; the single-subject rule; and the line-item veto, the drafters of the Delaware Constitution understood that excluding appropriation bills from the single-subject rule meant that such bills would not contain substantive provisions other than appropriations matters.

The narrow exemption for appropriation bills in Article II, § 16 is similar to the limited authorization for the gubernatorial line-item veto in Article III, § 18. In construing the latter provision, this Court has recognized the distinction between bills which have the fundamental purpose of appropriating money for public purposes, and bills which are fundamentally substantive in nature, but which also include an appropriation relating to the substantive issues. As to the former type of bill, the Governor has line-item veto power, but as to the latter, the Governor may only approve or veto the bill in its entirety.

Accordingly, this Court has interpreted the Governor's line-item veto power, as set forth in Article III, § 18 of the Delaware Constitution, to extend "only to a bill containing more than one appropriation and 'embracing distinct items,'" and not to "bills which contain only a single item of appropriation" among other substantive provisions.

The provisions in Article II, § 16 and Article III, § 18 of the Delaware Constitution, when viewed in historical context and read in para materia, reflect that to be an appropriation bill the provisions in the legislation must all relate to appropriations. The purpose of exempting appropriation bills from the single-subject and title rules of Article II, § 16 was to allow appropriation bills to designate money for more than one purpose without running afoul of the constitutional mandate that a bill embrace only the one subject expressed in its title. The exception for appropriation bills in

Article II, § 16 was not intended to allow substantive provisions other than money appropriations to be included in appropriation bills.

Similarly, the constitutional authority for a line-item veto in Article III, § 18 was limited to appropriation bills only, not legislation that related to substantive subjects and also included appropriations.

Section 68 of 1989 Bond Act Violates Appropriation Exception

Although Article II, § 16 of the Delaware Constitution specifically excludes appropriation bills from its purview, Section 68 of the 1989 Bond Act does not fall within that exclusion. The Constitutional Debates of 1897 reflect that the purpose of excluding appropriation bills from this section was to allow the legislature to make appropriations for many different purposes at once. Those debates also reflect the drafters of Article II, § 16 did not intend to permit the passage of "sleeper" legislation by including substantive non-monetary enactments in an appropriation bill.

Relying on the debates to flesh out purpose of provision

Section 68 of the 1989 Bond Act, through which 2 Del.C. § 1329 was enacted, is the type of legislation that was intended to be prevented by Article II, § 16 of the Delaware Constitution. Section 68 of the 1989 Bond Act amends Title 2 of the Delaware Code to waive the State's sovereign immunity for DART operations that are covered by commercial insurance and to impose a liability cap of $300,000. This is a substantive enactment of a permanent nature, which is improper in a bill otherwise completely devoted to "appropriating money for public purposes." Del. Const. art. II, § 16. There is also no indication in the title of the 1989 Bond Act that any change was to be made in the substantive law relating to sovereign immunity. Consequently, as a substantive change to the law of sovereign immunity, which was part of an appropriation bill, Section 68 violated Article II, § 16 of the Delaware Constitution.

Why is court call the provision unconstitutional

Severability provisions

What are the ramifications of concluding that Section 68 of the 1989 Bond Act is unconstitutional? The other sections of the 1989 Bond Act are unaffected because of the severability provision in Section 73.

> Section 73. Severability. If any section, part, phrase, or provision of this Act or the application thereof be held invalid by any court of competent jurisdiction, such judgment shall be confined in its operation to the section, part, phrase, provision, or application directly involved in the controversy in which such judgment shall have been rendered and shall not affect or impair the validity of the remainder of this Act or the application thereof.

Therefore, although Section 68 is unconstitutional, it does not invalidate the remaining provisions of the 1989 Bond Act. See 66 Del. Laws c. 360, § 73.

Does the DS rule the same w/out the severability provision?

GREGORY v. SHURTLEFF
299 P.3d 1098 (Utah 2013)

[The Appellants are a group of current and former legislators, other elected and unelected government officials, and self-described "good citizens." They brought suit to enjoin the enforcement of Senate Bill 2 (the Bill), which contains some fourteen items relating to education, establishing new programs and amending existing programs, and funding provisions for some programs. The Appellants claim that the Bill violates Article VI, Section 22 of the Utah Constitution, which provides that "no bill shall be passed containing more than one subject, which shall be clearly expressed in its title."]

DURHAM, J., opinion of the Court:

A. The Complaint did not State a Violation of the Single-Subject Rule

Appellants argue that the Bill treats too many separate aspects of the public education system to pass muster under the single-subject rule. In their complaint, Appellants supported this claim by extensive reference to the legislative history of the items contained in the Bill. They point out that, when introduced as separate items, some had failed on a floor vote, some passed in one chamber but were held in committee in the other, and some were never submitted for even committee consideration as individual items. They further assert that popular bills were "used as hostages to extort or compel enactment of the less popular bills."

Almost a century ago, this court opined that while the single-subject rule is mandatory and binding alike upon the courts and the Legislature, yet it should be liberally construed in favor of upholding a law, and should be so applied as to effectuate its purpose in preventing the combination of incongruous subjects neither of which could be passed when standing alone. A too strict application of the provision might, however, result in hampering wholesome legislation upon any comprehensive subject rather than in preventing evils. Furthermore, while bills must address a single subject, "[t]here is no constitutional restriction as to the *scope or magnitude* of the single subject of a legislative act." "A liberal view should be taken of both the act and the constitutional provisions so as not to hamper the law making power, but to permit the adoption of comprehensive measures covering a whole subject."

Examined on its face, under this liberal standard the Bill does not violate the single-subject rule. All its provisions deal with public education. It is easy to imagine a law that all would agree violates the single-subject rule. For instance, a bill dealing with pet licenses, mining regulation and beekeeping could not be plausibly argued to fit under any all-encompassing rubric less general than "legislation," or at the most specific "safety" (assuming that the pet licensing regime had that as its purpose). Similarly, one can imagine items of legislation so targeted that no plausible argument could be made that they violate the single-subject rule. Most actual legislation, of course, falls somewhere in between, and while the single-subject rule is mandatory and must be policed by this court, under our tradition of liberal construction a bill addressing even a relatively large number of educational programs does not violate that rule. *Cf. Akin v. Dir. of Revenue* (Mo. 1996) (holding that a bill containing some twenty enactments and thirty-eight reenactments in the area of education, along with various revenue mechanisms to fund those laws, does not violate the single-subject rule because it contains only one subject, education.).

In addition to their general argument that the Bill contains too many disparate subjects, Appellants argue that it violates the single-subject rule for two specific reasons. First, they argue that it combines substantive law and appropriations measures, and that such a combination is a per se violation of the rule. Second, they include in their complaint a detailed legislative history of the components of the Bill, and argue that the fact that some of these components were rejected by the legislature as individual bills, while others passed committee or a floor vote in one house but were then held and combined with the rest of the Bill's components, demonstrates that the Bill constitutes impermissible "bundling" and "log-rolling" in violation of the spirit of the single-subject rule.

Appellants urge us to adopt what they represent as the rule of *Washington State Legislature v. State* (Wash. 1999): a bright-line test holding that the combination in one bill of substantive and appropriations measures violates the single-subject rule. But it is not clear to us that *Washington State Legislature* establishes any such bright-line test. We are unpersuaded by the other cases cited by Appellants in their urging us to establish a rule that the combination of substantive and appropriations measures always violates the single-subject rule. We therefore decline to adopt such a rule. As explained above, the Bill on its face treats a single, albeit broad, subject: education. The presence in the Bill of funding measures directed towards education programs does not render it unconstitutional. We are left, then, with Appellants' remaining argument on this point: that the legislative history of the items in the Bill reveal that it is the product of impermissible "log-rolling," and that it therefore violates the single-subject rule.

In Appellants' description, the Bill is the sum of 14 bills, all of which started as single subject measures. All initially were introduced, reviewed, considered, and debated as separate, stand-alone legislation. Two of these bills were defeated by majority vote in the House. Two others lacked sufficient merit to survive committee hearings. These failed bills were revived and, through bundling were allowed to ride "piggy-back" on popular legislation and money measures to enactment at the eleventh hour of the 2008 general session.

For three reasons, however, we conclude that these facts—even taken at face value, as we do when reviewing the grant of a motion to dismiss—do not state a claim that the Bill violates the single-subject rule. First, the text of Article VI, Section 22 speaks to the contents and title of the Bill itself; it makes no reference to legislative motive. We have determined that the Bill itself, in treating multiple programs related to education, handles a "single subject"; we further determine that an itemized list of those programs is a clear expression of the Bill's content, which is what the clear-title rule requires. It is true that in *Wilson* we identified the "purpose" of the single-subject rule as "preventing the combination of *incongruous subjects* neither of which could be passed when standing alone." But in light of our tradition of liberally construing the single-subject rule, we already concluded that the subjects in the Bill are *not* incongruous in the constitutional sense. Therefore, even taking at face value Appellants' assertions that portions of the Bill "could [not] be passed when standing alone," *Wilson* neither requires nor empowers us to find them unconstitutional solely on that basis if we have not determined that they are "incongruous." While the prevention of "log-rolling" may be a *purpose* of the single-subject rule, the *text* of that rule requires us to focus on a bill's contents, rather than conducting a review of a law's "backstory" as revealed in legislative history.

Second, Appellants have not identified—and we have not independently found—any prior opinion of this court that analyzes a single-subject claim by reference to the legislative history of the bill at issue. Appellants cite *McGuire v. Univ. of Utah Med. Ctr.* (Utah 1979) and *Jensen v. Matheson*, (Utah 1978), for the proposition that this court has previously examined legislative journals in its Article VI, Section 22 jurisprudence. This is true, but those cases dealt with other provisions of the section: respectively, the clear-title rule and a voting/recordation provision. These cases do not establish the propriety of undertaking an extensive search of legislative history in the application of the single-subject rule, and we are not persuaded that we should depart from an examination of the Bill on its face, at least absent any ambiguity or other interpretive problems revealed by such a facial examination. To do so would put us in the position of examining the motives and strategies of the Legislature, rather than its acts.

Finally, where a bill has not been shown to violate the single-subject rule, separation-of-powers considerations make us hesitate to inquire into the internal process that led to the bill's passage. Sometimes we are required to, as it were, "pierce the veil" of the legislative text—for

Respecting separation of powers

instance, when a facially neutral bill is alleged to have some impermissible invidious motive. And allegations of outright illegality, in the form of bribery or the like, have their remedy elsewhere in the law. But the line between forbidden "log-rolling" and mere "horse-trading" may be a fine one, and we are not confident in our ability—or even our constitutional power—to police it in the manner which Appellants ask of us.

How do you separate logrolling from horse trading?

B. The Complaint did not State a Violation of the Clear–Title Rule

The Bill was entitled "MINIMUM SCHOOL PROGRAM BUDGET AMENDMENTS." Under this title came a caption identifying the session in which the Bill was submitted and its chief sponsor and sponsor in the House. Under this caption came a double line, then the following: "LONG TITLE. General Description: This bill provides funding for the Minimum School Program and other education programs. Highlighted Provisions: This bill: [followed by a bullet-pointed list of short descriptions of the various components of the bill]." Appellants argue that the Bill violates the clear-title rule for two reasons. First, they argue that the "short title" is under-inclusive and misleading. Second, they argue that the "long title" does not cure the constitutional defect.

πs 2 args

This court considered the clear-title rule in Utah's first year of statehood. *Ritchie v. Richards* (1896). There, we held that a bill entitled "An act relating to and making sundry provisions concerning *elections*," could not constitutionally contain a provision governing the *appointment* of persons to vacated positions. "This section," we determined, "does not relate to elections, nor does it concern elections. Therefore the title does not embrace it." A more recent opinion saw the purpose of the clear-title rule as ensuring that "the legislators will be advised of the subject and purpose of the act in order that there be no misunderstanding, omitting, nor burying or obscuring of what is being proposed."

Purpose of clear title

Here, the bill's "long title" informs the reader that "[t]his bill provides funding for the Minimum School Program and other education programs," proceeding to give a full list of those programs in bullet-point format. This is constitutionally sufficient—*if* the "long title" can be considered part of the "title" which the constitution says must clearly express the bill's "subject."

πs argue against multiple titles

Appellants insist it cannot be so considered. First, they observe that Article VI, Section 22 speaks of the bill's "title" in the singular. Second, they argue that our case law has treated additional or supplementary titles of laws as unnecessary surplusage. Third, they argue that the clear-title rule is intended to benefit the public and that the public is less likely than the legislators to notice the presence of such additional titles.

Appellees and Amicus counter that a "long title" is an acceptable manner of observing the constitutional clear-title rule, and that in this case the Bill's "long title," as the constitution requires, clearly expresses the Bill's subject. We agree that the "long title" of this Bill is its title for purposes of Article VI, Section 22 and that it clearly expresses the Bill's subject. The Bill therefore does not violate the clear-title rule.

First, the fact that Article VI, Section 22 speaks of a bill's "title" in the singular is not dispositive. The Bill before us *has* a singular title. That title, it is true, is divided into a five-word header ("MINIMUM SCHOOL PROGRAM BUDGET AMENDMENTS") and a longer title, which is in turn divided into a "General Description" and a list of "Highlighted Provisions." But the text of Section 22 does not indicate how long or detailed a bill's "title" must be, or whether it may be divided into sub-parts. As we have interpreted and applied it above, the single-subject rule permits one bill to treat multiple aspects of the public education system. Accordingly, a title such as the one this Bill has is arguably the fairest way of putting legislators and citizens on notice of what the Bill contains. If the Bill's contents are constitutional in scope—and we have determined that they are—then an itemized description of them is a constitutionally acceptable way to clearly express those contents.

Appellants cite *Edwards* in support of their argument that "the use of a second title may be constitutionally improper." The case is inapposite. In *Edwards*, we determined that certain "extraneous matter added to what constitutes the actual title is *harmless*. ... [and] wholly unnecessary, and the elimination of this surplus matter is ... required of us in order to preserve" an otherwise constitutional law. But here we have, if anything, the opposite situation. By itself, "MINIMUM SCHOOL PROGRAM BUDGET AMENDMENTS" might well be unconstitutionally under-inclusive. The "long title," with its list of programs contained in the Bill, removes the cloud over the Bill's constitutionality.

Third and finally, we disagree that the "long title" is of use only to legislators. It is not written in technical or misleading language. It puts anyone reading it, whether they be a member of the legislature or of the general public, on notice of the Bill's contents. For all these reasons, we determine that the full title of the Bill comports with the constitutional requirement that it "clearly express[ ]" the subject of the Bill.

NOTE

In cases where a single subject or clear title violation is found, a question may arise concerning the proper remedy for the violation. Should the violation be remedied by severing the offending provisions and allowing the remainder of the statute to stand, or should the entire statute be stricken as unconstitutional? Some state constitutional provisions provide an answer to this question themselves by opting for severability. For example, the constitutions of both Iowa and Oregon state that "If any subject shall be embraced in an act which shall not be expressed in the title, such act shall be void only as to so much thereof as shall not be expressed in the title." Iowa Const. art III, § 29; Oregon Const. art. IV, §20. In other states where constitutional provisions do not specify a remedy, some courts, as a matter of statutory interpretation, have followed a general preference for severability rather than striking down an entire statute. In *Hammerschmidt v. Boon County*, 877 S.W.2d 98 (Mo. 1994), the Supreme Court of Missouri set forth the following criteria for severability:

> Under the usual circumstances, this Court bears an obligation to sever unconstitutional provisions of a statute unless the valid provisions of the statute are so essentially and inseparably connected with, and so dependent upon, the void provision that it cannot be presumed the legislature would have enacted the valid provisions without the void one; or unless the court finds that the valid provisions, standing alone, are incomplete and are incapable of being executed in accordance with the legislative intent.

> Where, as here, the procedure by which the legislature enacted a bill violates the Constitution, severance is a more difficult issue. When the Court concludes that a bill contains more than one subject, the entire bill is unconstitutional unless the Court is convinced beyond reasonable doubt that one of the bill's multiple subjects is its original, controlling purpose and that the other subject is not. In reaching this determination, the Court will consider whether the [additional subject]...is essential to the efficacy of the...[bill], whether it is a provision without which the...[bill] would be incomplete and unworkable, and whether the provision is one without which the...[legislators] would not have adopted the...[bill].

> Where the Court is convinced that the bill contains a "single central [remaining] purpose", we will sever that portion of the bill containing the additional subject(s) and permit the bill to stand with its primary, core subject intact. In determining the original, controlling purpose of the bill for purposes of determining severance issues, a title that "clearly" expresses the bill's single subject is exceedingly important. *Id.* at 103 (citations omitted).

The Supreme Court of Pennsylvania has pointed out that there are significant policy justifications militating against severance in cases where logrolling may have occurred. *Pennsylvanian Against Gambling Expansion Fund, Inc. v. Commonwealth*, 877 A.2d 383, 403, n.14 (Pa. 2005). The practice of logrolling—combining unrelated subjects in one bill in order to obtain majority approval of the entire bill—does not comport with the fair and deliberative process anticipated by single subject and clear title provisions. Where logrolling occurs, the entire law in question may be tainted, and arguably should be struck down in its entirety.

Still, striking down an act in its entirety is a drastic measure that can have serious consequences. In that regard, re-consider the discussion of

People v. Cervantes in the excerpt from Professor Dragich's article at the beginning of this section.

C. PUBLIC PURPOSE REQUIREMENTS

MAREADY v. CITY OF WINSTON-SALEM
467 S.E.2d 615 (N.C. 1996)

WHICHARD, J.

Plaintiff-appellant, William F. Maready, instituted this action against the City of Winston-Salem, its Board of Aldermen, Forsyth County, its Board of Commissioners, and Winston-Salem Business, Inc. Plaintiff contends that N.C.G.S. § 158-7.1, which authorizes local governments to make economic development incentive grants to private corporations, is unconstitutional because it violates the public purpose clause of the North Carolina Constitution and because it is impermissibly vague, ambiguous, and without reasonably objective standards. Plaintiff also argues that the local governing bodies violated the State's Open Meetings Law by voting on and deciding grant matters in closed sessions.

Following a three-day evidentiary hearing and oral argument, the trial court found N.C.G.S. § 158-7.1 unconstitutional, enjoined defendants from making further incentive grants or otherwise committing public funds pursuant to that statute.

This action challenges twenty-four economic development incentive projects entered into by the City or County pursuant to N.C.G.S. § 158-7.1. The projected investment by the City and County in these projects totals approximately $13,200,000. The primary source of these funds has been taxes levied by the City and County on property owners in Winston-Salem and Forsyth County. City and County officials estimate an increase in the local tax base of $238,593,000 and a projected creation of over 5,500 new jobs as a result of these economic development incentive programs. They expect to recoup the full amount of their investment within three to seven years. The source of the return will be revenues generated by the additional property taxes paid by participating corporations. To date, all but one project has met or exceeded its goal.

The typical procedures the City and County observe in deciding to make an economic development incentive expenditure are as follows: A determination is made that participation by local government is necessary to cause a project to go forward in the community. Officials then apply a formula set out in written guidelines to determine the maximum amount of assistance that can be given to the receiving corporation. The amounts actually committed are usually much less than the maximum. The expenditures are in the form of reimbursement to the recipient for purposes such as on-the-job training, site preparation, facility upgrading, and parking. If a proposal satisfies the guidelines as well as community needs, it is submitted to the appropriate governing body for final approval at a regularly scheduled public meeting. If a project is formally approved, it is administered pursuant to a written contract and to the applicable provisions and limitations of N.C.G.S. § 158-7.1.

Article V, Section 2(1) of the North Carolina Constitution provides that "[t]he power of taxation shall be exercised in a just and equitable manner, for public purposes only." In *Mitchell v. North Carolina Indus. Dev. Fin. Auth.*, 273 N.C. 137, 159 S.E.2d 745 (1968), Justice (later Chief Justice) Sharp, writing for a majority of this Court, stated:

> The power to appropriate money from the public treasury is no greater than the power to levy the tax which put the money in the treasury. Both powers are subject to the constitutional proscription that tax revenues may not be used for private individuals or corporations, no matter how benevolent.

In determining whether legislation serves a public purpose, the presumption favors constitutionality. Reasonable doubt must be resolved in favor of the validity of the act. The Constitution restricts powers, and powers not surrendered inhere in the people to be exercised through their representatives in the General Assembly; therefore, so long as an act is not forbidden, its wisdom and expediency are for legislative, not judicial, decision.

In exercising the State's police power, the General Assembly may legislate for the protection of the general health, safety, and welfare of the people. It may "experiment with new modes of dealing with old evils, except as prevented by the Constitution." The initial responsibility for determining what constitutes a public purpose rests with the legislature, and its determinations are entitled to great weight.

The enactment of N.C.G.S. § 158-7.1 leaves no doubt that the General Assembly considers expenditures of public funds for the promotion of local economic development to serve a public purpose.... When making amendments to chapter 158 and adding other provisions designed to promote economic development, the General Assembly mandated: "This act, being necessary for the prosperity and welfare of the State and its inhabitants, shall be liberally construed to effect these purposes." The General Assembly has further demonstrated its commitment to economic development by enacting several other statutes that permit local governments to appropriate and spend public funds for such purposes.... These enactments clearly indicate that N.C.G.S. § 158-7.1 is part of a comprehensive scheme of legislation dealing with economic development whereby the General Assembly is attempting to authorize exercise of the power of taxation for the perceived public purpose of promoting the general economic welfare of the citizens of North Carolina.

While legislative declarations such as these are accorded great weight, ultimate responsibility for the public purpose determination rests with this Court. If an enactment is for a private purpose and therefore inconsistent with the fundamental law, it cannot be saved by legislative declarations to the contrary. It is the duty of this Court to ascertain and declare the intent of the framers of the Constitution and to reject any act in conflict therewith.

This Court has addressed what constitutes a public purpose on numerous occasions. It has not specifically defined "public purpose," however; rather, it has expressly declined to "confine public purpose by judicial definition [, leaving] 'each case to be determined by its own peculiar circumstances as from time to time it arises.'" As summarized by Justice Sharp in *Mitchell*:

> A slide-rule definition to determine public purpose for all time cannot be formulated; the concept expands with the population, economy, scientific knowledge, and changing conditions. As people are brought closer together in congested areas, the public welfare requires governmental operation of facilities which were once considered exclusively private enterprises, and necessitates the expenditure of tax funds for purposes which, in an earlier day, were not classified as public. Often public and private interests are so co-mingled that it is difficult to determine which predominates. It is clear, however, that for a use to be public its benefits must be in common and not for particular persons, interests, or estates; the ultimate net gain or advantage must be the public's as contradistinguished from that of an individual or private entity.

Plaintiff also argues, and the trial court apparently agreed, that this question falls squarely within the purview of *Mitchell v. North Carolina Industrial Development Financing Authority*. There we held unconstitutional the Industrial Facilities Financing Act, a statute that authorized issuance of industrial revenue bonds to finance the construction and equipping of facilities for private corporations. The suit was filed as a test case, before any bonds were issued, to enjoin the appropriation of $37,000 from the State Contingency and Emergency Fund for the purpose of enabling the Authority to organize and begin operations. We find Mitchell distinguishable.

One of the bases for the *Mitchell* decision was that the General Assembly had unenthusiastically passed the enacting legislation, declaring it to be bad policy. The opinion stated:

> At the time the General Assembly passed the Act, it declared in Resolution No. 52 that it considered the Act bad public policy. It explained that it felt compelled to authorize industrial revenue bonds in order to compete for industry with neighboring states which use them. As proof of its reluctance to join the industry-subsidizing group of states, the General Assembly requested the

President and the other forty-nine states to petition Congress to make the interest on all such bonds thereafter issued subject to all applicable income-tax laws.

The resolution recited that the General Assembly passed the act reluctantly, with reservations, and as a defensive measure. The Assembly's obvious apprehension over using public funds to benefit private entities in this manner clearly served to undermine the Court's confidence in the constitutionality of the legislation. The converse is true here in that the Assembly has unequivocally embraced expenditures of public funds for the promotion of local economic development as advancing a public purpose.

Further, and more importantly, the holding in Mitchell clearly indicates that the Court considered private industry to be the primary benefactor of the legislation and considered any benefit to the public purely incidental. Notwithstanding its recognition that any lawful business in a community promotes the public good, the Court held that the "Authority's primary function, to acquire sites and to construct and equip facilities for private industry, is not for a public use or purpose." The Court rightly concluded that direct state aid to a private enterprise, with only limited benefit accruing to the public, contravenes fundamental constitutional precepts... Thus, the Court implicitly rejected the act because its primary object was private gain and its nature and purpose did not tend to yield public benefit.

This Court most recently addressed the public purpose question in *Madison Cablevision v. City of Morganton*, 325 N.C. 634, 386 S.E.2d 200, where it unanimously held that N.C.G.S. § 160A, art. 16, part 1, which authorizes cities to finance, acquire, construct, own, and operate cablevision systems, does not violate the public purpose clause of Article V, Section 2(1). The Court stated that "[t]wo guiding principles have been established for determining that a particular undertaking by a municipality is for a public purpose: (1) it involves a reasonable connection with the convenience and necessity of the particular municipality; and (2) the activity benefits the public generally, as opposed to special interests or persons." Application of these principles here mandates the conclusion that N.C.G.S. § 158-7.1 furthers a public purpose and hence is constitutional.

As to the first prong, whether an activity is within the appropriate scope of governmental involvement and is reasonably related to communal needs may be evaluated by determining how similar the activity is to others which this Court has held to be within the permissible realm of governmental action. We conclude that the activities N.C.G.S. § 158-7.1 authorizes are in keeping with those accepted as within the scope of permissible governmental action.

Economic development has long been recognized as a proper governmental function. In *Wood v. Commissioner of Oxford*, 97 N.C. 227, 2 S.E. 653, this Court upheld the statutory, voter-approved borrowing of money for the purchase of railroad capital stock and donations by towns located along a privately owned, for-profit railroad.

Even subsequent to *Mitchell*, this Court declared that stimulation of the economy involves a public purpose. *State ex rel. Util. Comm'n v. Edmisten*, 294 N.C. 598, 242 S.E.2d 862 (1978), involved a challenge to Utilities Commission approval of a rate increase to subsidize exploration for natural gas by private companies. In upholding the Commission's action, the Court said:

> Stimulation of the economy is an essential public and governmental purpose and the manner in which this purpose is to be accomplished is, within constitutional limits, exclusively a legislative decision.

Further, the activities N.C.G.S. § 158-7.1 authorizes invoke traditional governmental powers and authorities in the service of economic development. For example, subsections 158-7.1(b)(5) and (6) authorize economic development expenditures in connection with local government operation of water, sewer, and other utility systems, matters long considered a proper role of government. Likewise, the power under (b)(1) to acquire land for an industrial park, develop it for its intended use, and then convey it is analogous to the powers granted by the Urban Redevelopment Law (chapter 160A, article 22), which this Court has consistently upheld as meeting the public purpose test. Urban redevelopment commissions have power to acquire property, clear slums, and sell the property to private developers. In that instance, as here, a private party ultimately acquires the property and conducts activities which, while providing incidental private benefit, serve a primary public goal.

As to the second prong of the *Madison Cablevision* inquiry, under the expanded understanding of public purpose, even the most innovative activities N.C.G.S. § 158-7.1 permits are constitutional so long as they primarily benefit the public and not a private party. "It is not necessary, in order that a use may be regarded as public, that it should be for the use and benefit of every citizen in the community." Moreover, an expenditure does not lose its public purpose merely because it involves a private actor. Generally, if an act will promote the welfare of a state or a local government and its citizens, it is for a public purpose.

Viewed in this light, section 158-7.1 clearly serves a public purpose. Its self-proclaimed end is to "increase the population, taxable property, agricultural industries and business prospects of any city or county." However, it is the natural consequences flowing therefrom that ensure a net public benefit. The expenditures this statute authorizes should create a more stable local economy by providing displaced workers with continuing employment opportunities, attracting better paying and more highly skilled jobs, enlarging the tax base, and diversifying the economy. Careful planning pursuant to the statute should enable optimization of natural resources while concurrently preserving the local infrastructure. The strict procedural requirements the statute imposes provide safeguards that should suffice to prevent abuse.

The public advantages are not indirect, remote, or incidental; rather, they are directly aimed at furthering the general economic welfare of the people of the communities affected. While private actors will necessarily benefit from the expenditures authorized, such benefit is merely incidental. It results from the local government's efforts to better serve the interests of its people. Each community has a distinct ambience, unique assets, and special needs best ascertained at the local level. Section 158-7.1 enables each to formulate its own definition of economic success and to draft a developmental plan leading to that goal. This aim is no less legitimate and no less for a public purpose than projects this Court has approved in the past.

Finally, while this Court does not pass upon the wisdom or propriety of legislation in determining the primary motivation behind a statute, it may consider the circumstances surrounding its enactment. In that regard, a Legislative Research Commission committee made a report to the 1989 General Assembly, warning that:

> The traditional foundations of North Carolina's economy--agriculture and manufacturing--are in decline. And, the traditional economic development tool--industrial recruitment--has proven inadequate for many of North Carolina's communities. Low wages and low taxes are no longer sufficient incentives to entice new industry to our State, especially to our most remote, most distressed areas.

In the economic climate thus depicted, the pressure to induce responsible corporate citizens to relocate to or expand in North Carolina is not internal only, but results from the actions of other states as well. To date, courts in forty-six states have upheld the constitutionality of governmental expenditures and related assistance for economic development incentives.... Thus, by virtue of the trial court's ruling, North Carolina currently stands alone in so holding. Considered in this light, it would be unrealistic to assume that the State will not suffer economically in the future if the incentive programs created pursuant to N.C.G.S. § 158-7.1 are discontinued. As Chief Justice Parker noted in his dissent in *Mitchell*:

> North Carolina is no longer a predominantly agricultural community. We are developing from an agrarian economy to an agrarian and industrial economy.

North Carolina is having to compete with the complex industrial, technical, and scientific communities that are more and more representative of a nation-wide trend. All men know that in our efforts to attract new industry we are competing with inducements to industry offered through legislative enactments in other jurisdictions as stated in the legislative findings and purposes of this challenged Act. It is manifest that the establishment of new industry in North Carolina will enrich a whole class of citizens who work for it, will increase the per capita income of our citizens, will mean more money for the public treasury, more money for our schools and for payment of our school teachers, more money for the operation of our hospitals like the John Umstead Hospital at Butner, and for other necessary expenses of government. This to my mind is clearly the business of government in the jet age in which we are living. Among factors to be considered in determining the effect of the challenged legislation here is the aggregate income it will make available for community distribution, the resulting security of their [sic] income, and the opportunities for more lucrative employment for those who desire to work for it.

The General Assembly thus could determine that legislation such as N.C.G.S. § 158-7.1, which is intended to alleviate conditions of unemployment and fiscal distress and to increase the local tax base, serves the public interest. New and expanded industries in communities within North Carolina provide work and economic opportunity for those who otherwise might not have it. This, in turn, creates a broader tax base from which the State and its local governments can draw funding for other programs that benefit the general health, safety, and welfare of their citizens. The potential impetus to economic development, which might otherwise be lost to other states, likewise serves the public interest. We therefore hold that N.C.G.S. § 158-7.1, which permits the expenditure of public moneys for economic development incentive programs, does not violate the public purpose clause of the North Carolina Constitution. Accordingly, the decision of the trial court on this issue is reversed.

ORR, J., dissenting.

At issue in this case is the City of Winston-Salem and Forsyth County's authorization, pursuant to N.C.G.S. § 158-7.1, to expend public funds directly to, and for the benefit of, selected private businesses as an inducement to these businesses to either expand or locate in the community. The majority opinion sanctions this practice on the theory that since jobs were created and the tax base increased by virtue of the inducements, the expenditures, totalling $13.2 million for the twenty-four challenged projects, were for a public purpose as required by Article V, Section 2 of the North Carolina Constitution. As a result, it appears to me that little remains of the public purpose constitutional restraint on governmental power to spend tax revenues collected from the public. Because I believe that the majority's holding in this case is (1) based on a theory unsupported by the evidence, and (2) contrary to established precedent interpreting the intent of the North Carolina Constitution, I respectfully dissent.

The logic upon which the majority opinion rests its conclusion that the expenditure of these funds was for a public purpose can be stated as follows: The creation of new jobs and an increase in the tax base ipso facto benefits the general public. Therefore, local government expenditure of tax dollars to a private business for its private benefit in order to induce the business to either expand or locate in the community is for a public purpose if it creates new jobs and increases the tax base.

The fallacy of this reasoning begins with the assumption that new jobs and a higher tax base automatically result in significant benefit to the public.... No evidence was presented that incentives paid or committed by the City and County improved the unemployment rate or that they otherwise resulted in meaningful economic enhancement. No evidence was presented that the incentive grants made by the City and County reduced the net cost of government or resulted in a reduction in the amount or rate of property taxes paid by, or the level of services rendered to, the citizens of Winston-Salem and/or Forsyth County.

Although there is undoubtedly some benefit to the general public, as noted with approval in the majority opinion, "direct state aid to a private enterprise, with only limited benefit accruing to the public, contravenes fundamental constitutional precepts." As Justice Sharp (later Chief Justice) stated in *Mitchell v. North Carolina Indus. Dev. Fin. Auth.*, 273 N.C. 137, 159 S.E.2d 745 (1968):

> It is clear, however, that for a use to be public its benefits must be in common and not for particular persons, interests, or estates; the ultimate net gain or advantage must be the public's as contradistinguished from that of an individual or private entity.

In examining the stated purposes of the grants, it is obvious that the $13.2 million was authorized for the specific benefit of the companies in question. The money expended was directly for the use of these private companies to pay for such activities as on-the-job training for employees, road construction, site improvements, financing of land purchases, upfitting of the facilities, and even spousal relocation assistance. In weighing these direct "private benefits" paid for by the taxpayers against the limited "public benefits," only one conclusion can be reached—that the trial court correctly held that the expenditures in question were not for a public purpose. The opposite conclusion reached by the majority can be reached only by ignoring the weight of the private benefits and relying instead on the assumption that simply creating new jobs and increasing the tax base is a public purpose that justifies the payment of tax dollars to the private sector. As previously noted, there is simply no evidence to support such a conclusion, and the majority's position must fail.

The majority also relies on a "changing times" theory to ignore the law as set forth in Mitchell and Stanley. While economic times have changed and will continue to change, the philosophy that constitutional interpretation and application are subject to the whims of "everybody's doing it" cannot be sustained.

Finally, many of the arguments presented to this Court rest on public policy. Advocates for these business incentives contend that without them, North Carolina will be at a significant competitive disadvantage in keeping and recruiting private industry. They further contend that the economic well-being of our state and its citizens is dependent on the continued utilization of this practice. These arguments are compelling, and even plaintiff admits that a public purpose is served by general economic development and recruitment of industry. However, plaintiff and those supporting his point of view argue that direct grants to specific, selected businesses go beyond the acceptable bounds of public purpose expenditures for economic development. Instead, they say that this is selected corporate welfare to some of the largest and most prosperous companies in our State and in the country. Moreover, these opponents contend that the grants are not equitably applied because they generally favor the larger companies and projects and, in this case, under the County's Economic Incentives Program Guidelines, completely eliminate retail operations from being considered. In challenging the actual public benefit, a question also is raised about the economic loss and devastation to smaller North Carolina communities that lose valued industry to larger, wealthier areas. For example, the move of Southern National Bank headquarters from Lumberton to Winston-Salem undoubtedly adversely affected Lumberton.

Also troubling is the question of limits under the majority's theory. If it is an acceptable public purpose to spend tax dollars specifically for relocation expenses to benefit the spouses of corporate executives moving to the community in finding new jobs or for parking decks that benefit only the employees of the favored company, then what can a government not do if the end result will entice a company to produce new jobs and raise the tax base? If a potential corporate entity is considering a move to Winston-Salem but will only come if country club memberships are provided for its executives, do we sanction the use of tax revenue to facilitate the move? I would hope not, but under the holding of the majority opinion, I see no grounds for challenging such an expenditure provided that, as a result of such a grant, the company promises to create new jobs, and an increased tax base is projected.

HOPPER v. CITY OF MADISON
256 N.W.2d 139 (Wis. 1977)

This is an action by the plaintiff, a resident and taxpayer of the city of Madison, for a permanent injunction enjoining the city of Madison and its officials from expending certain funds appropriated for the year 1975. A number of appropriations were challenged by the appellant's action, but only three are involved upon this appeal. They are: (1) $10,000 to the budget of the City Planning Department for human resource services to be provided by the Madison Tenant Union (MTU); (2) $14,000 to the budget of the City Planning Department for human resource services to be provided by the Spanish-American Organization (SAO); and (3) $81,517 to the budget of the City Department of Public Health for a day care program.

The complaint alleged that the appropriations for services provided by MTU and SAO were made contrary to the law because they are to private organizations which benefit only certain citizens and because once the funds are delivered to these organizations, the city will lose all control over their expenditure and use. The complaint further alleged that the appropriation for a day care program was made contrary to the law in that no program outlining the purposes and administration of those funds has been established.

HANLEY, J.

Three issues are presented on appeal:

1. Does the appropriation for services to be provided by the Madison Tenant Union constitute the expenditure of public funds for other than a public purpose?

2. Does the appropriation for services to be provided by the Spanish-American Organization constitute the expenditure of public funds for other than a public purpose?

3. Does the appropriation to the public health department for a day care program constitute the expenditure of public funds for other than a public purpose?

Although not established by any specific clause in the state constitution, the public purpose doctrine is a well-established constitutional tenet. "Public funds may be expended for only public purposes. An expenditure of public funds for other than a public purpose would be abhorrent to the constitution of Wisconsin." This rule applies to the expenditure of public funds by municipalities.

What constitutes public purpose is in the first instance a question for the legislature to determine and its opinion should be given great weight. This court, however, is not bound by the legislature's enactment or declarations regarding its purpose, for it is the court's constitutional burden to examine the challenged legislation and assess its realistic operation.

In so examining a legislative expenditure of public funds, there is a strong presumption that a legislature's acts are constitutional, and it is the duty of this court, if possible, to construe a legislative enactment as to find it in harmony with constitutional principles. In *Hammermill* the court stated, 58 Wis.2d at page 46, 205 N.W.2d at page 792:

> It is not enough that respondent establish doubt as to the act's constitutionality nor is it sufficient that respondent establish the unconstitutionality of the act as a probability. Unconstitutionality of the act must be demonstrated beyond a reasonable doubt. Every presumption must be indulged to sustain the law if at all possible and, wherever doubt exists as to a legislative enactment's constitutionality, it must be resolved in favor of constitutionality.

The court is not concerned with the wisdom, merits or practicability of the legislature's enactment, but only with its validity in light of specific constitutional principles. It is constitutionally sufficient if any public purpose can be conceived which might reasonably be deemed to justify or serve as a basis for the expenditure. "A court can conclude that no public purpose exists only if it is 'clear and palpable' that there can be no benefit to the public."

To sustain a public purpose, the benefit to the public must be direct and not merely indirect or remote. However, the fact that the appropriation is made to a private agency does not render it unconstitutional. If an appropriation is designed in its principle parts to promote a public purpose so that its accomplishment is a reasonable probability, private benefits which are necessary and reasonable to the main purpose are permissible.

Appropriation for Services of Madison Tenant Union

The city council appropriated $10,000 to the budget of the City Planning Department to be granted to MTU in exchange for services to be performed pursuant to the terms of a written agreement between the city and MTU. Under this contract, MTU is obligated to "perform services for the City as outlined in the attached Human Resources Funding Application Form and any amendments thereto." MTU's application form describes the service to be provided generally as an information and grievance service for tenants, designed to inform tenants of their rights and assist them with problems in the landlord-tenant relationship. This service will be provided by grievance workers who will answer telephone inquiries and meet with individual tenants. These workers will be familiar with the applicable statutory law and the entire situation of tenants in Madison.

The appellant also contends this appropriation lacks a public purpose generally. In support of this position, the appellant argues that only that part of the city comprised of tenants could benefit from the services purchased from MTU. Although the number of beneficiaries is a pertinent factor in determining whether an appropriation has a public purpose, this court has stated many times "the fact the (appropriation) may benefit certain individuals or one particular class of people, more immediately than other individuals or classes does not necessarily deprive the (appropriation) of its public purpose."

The appellant also makes the argument that the trial court, in concluding the MTU appropriation was for a public purpose, only considered the grievance operation in the most favorable light and failed to consider what MTU would in fact do with the appropriation. The appellant claims evidence of certain MTU activities demonstrates that MTU is not concerned with promoting peaceful and equitable landlord-tenant relations, the adherence to local and state laws controlling these relations, or understanding by tenants of the rights and problems of landlords. The evidence referred to, appellant claims, shows that MTU's only interest is in furthering tenants' rights against those of landlords in any possible manner, including the promotion of rent strikes, picketing, boycotts, and blacklisting of selected landlords. Appellant argues that there is no reason to believe that the Tenant Union would act any differently in the future, simply because it is being subsidized by the city, than it has in the past.

However, the appropriated funds may be used only as provided in the contract between the city and MTU. This contract does not include any of the above-mentioned activities.

The record shows that of all housing units in the city, 49.3 percent are occupied by tenants. MTU's application for funding states that MTU receives approximately 75 telephone calls concerning landlord-tenant problems each week. A community with such a significant tenant segment has an interest in equitable landlord-tenant relations. These relations are a matter of public welfare. The expenditure for informational and grievance services for tenants who lack the expertise held by landlords in landlord-tenant law promotes such equitable relations. This program will also promote adherence to local and state laws governing landlord-tenant relations. Upon this record, it is not clear and palpable that there can be no benefit to the public by this expenditure. It has not been established beyond a reasonable doubt that no public purpose can be conceived which might reasonably justify this expenditure. It is not, therefore, unconstitutional.

Appropriation to Spanish-American Organization

The city appropriated $14,000 to SAO for its program, a bilingual multi-service center. SAO's application, which outlines the services purchased under SAO's contract with the city, states that SAO will provide:

"(1) bi-lingual outreach and referral services to Spanish-speaking residents of Madison and Spanish-speaking migratory farm workers;

"(2) employment and educational counseling for migrant workers in the transitional process of resettlement;

"(3) in cooperation with the Area Technical College, courses in adult basic education and English as a second language;

"(4) temporary accommodations for migrant families in the process of resettlement and assistance in locating adequate permanent housing; (and)

"(5) in cooperation with the Wisconsin State Employment Service, bi-lingual job counseling, development and placement services to Spanish-speaking residents."

The appellant further claims that the SAO expenditure generally lacks a public purpose because only a small number of persons will benefit and because some of the persons served will be migrant workers who are not residents of the city. As stated above in respect to the MTU appropriation, the fact a certain group of persons are the immediate beneficiaries of the appropriation does not necessarily deprive the appropriation of its public purpose.

In its application for funding, SAO stated:

The 1970 U.S. Census indicates that there are over 2,200 residents in Dane County whose principal language is Spanish. The area Spanish-speaking community is one of the fastest growing sub-communities in the State of Wisconsin and in Madison. With the gradual decline of the migrant labor market, many former migrant families, a majority of who are Chicano, have chosen to resettle in Wisconsin. Although the greater share of resettlement has taken place in the State's south-eastern counties, Madison continues to receive an additional 10 to 20 families each year. 1973-74 public school enrollment data shows that the Spanish-speaking community of Madison is the 5th largest in the State. In addition, nearby food processing plants annually attract several hundred Spanish-speaking migratory workers who travel through Madison on their way to other jobs or in the resettlement process.

The services to be provided under the contract between SAO and the city seek to assist these persons in solving their various problems caused in large part by their language barrier. A community center which provides such assistance serves a public purpose. In the absence of such services, the public may be harmed by the recognized social consequences of poverty and illiteracy. It is a reasonable conclusion that these services will enable Spanish-speaking persons to contribute economically and culturally to the community. These matters are within the objective of the public welfare, the promotion of which will benefit the community as a whole.

In regard to the services provided by SAO to persons in the migrant stream, the citizenry receives the benefit of satisfaction from fulfilling a perceived moral duty by providing temporary assistance to these shelterless, needy persons. Such temporary accommodations also avoid the problem of these persons having nowhere but the streets to go. These benefits are certainly not as significant as those received by the public when the persons receiving the service are residents of the city, and it would be difficult to find a constitutionally sufficient public purpose served by an expenditure for service only for migrants. However, in this case, services provided to migrant workers are only a portion, the record shows, of all the services to be provided by SAO under its program. The SAO program, as a whole, promotes a public purpose, and therefore the expenditure to purchase services provided by that program is constitutional.

Appropriation for Day Care

The city appropriated a total of $198,000 to the budget of the City Department of Public Health for various day care services. $117,000 of this money was designated as tuition aids to be distributed based upon standards of family need. These standards had not been established by the city council at the time of the commencement of the action, and the trial court therefore granted summary judgment to the defendant in respect to this portion of the appropriation for the reason that it could not be determined what persons would be served by the funds. The appellant does not challenge the trial court's decision in respect to this $117,000 appropriation for a day care tuition aids program.

The appellant does claim, however, that the trial court erred in not finding the appropriation of the remaining approximately $81,000 to be for other than a public purpose. Generally stated, these funds are to be allocated for two operations: (1) administration of the city's day care program, which includes salaries and benefits for city employees overseeing the program, and (2) direct aid to day care centers to improve their quality.

The appellant's major challenge to this expenditure for day care is that it lacks a public purpose because it is not to be limited for the benefit of poor and needy families, and therefore will aid families who do not need assistance.

The city's expenditure to ensure the availability of quality day care benefits the community as a whole. The record reasonably supports the conclusion that there is a need for improved day care service. The report of the City Committee on Day Care shows that in the city over 35 percent of women with children under the age of six are in the labor force. The report further states that less than half the children under the age of six who require out of home care may be accommodated in the presently available facilities. The vast majority of children in grades kindergarten through fifth who need extended care are not provided for. The two aspects of the day care program which are challenged here are to a great degree intertwined with the tuition aids program, which provides relief to poor and needy families, enabling the parents to work and contribute economically to the city.

It may not be seriously questioned that the care and supervision of the city's children is a matter of public health and welfare. It is reasonable to conclude that the city's program to improve and make more available day care service promotes these objectives. The appellant's claim that present day care facilities are adequate goes to the wisdom of the legislation, not whether it serves a public purpose.

We conclude that the challenged appropriations were not made contrary to the law. They constituted expenditure of funds for public purposes by promoting the health and general welfare of the public. The trial court correctly granted the defendants' motion for summary judgment dismissing the plaintiff's action.

TOWN OF BELOIT v. COUNTY OF ROCK
657 N.W.2d 344 (Wis. 2003)

CROOKS, J.

Belle Zyla, Marvin Prothero, and the Green-Rock Audubon Society (Intervenors) petitioned for review of a court of appeals decision, which reversed and remanded the decision of the Circuit Court for Rock County, William D. Johnston, Circuit Court Judge. The court of appeals held that the Town of Beloit (town) has the statutory authority to spend public tax monies to develop and sell property in the Heron Bay subdivision, and that the town's goals in developing the subdivision constitute legitimate and valid public purposes.

We affirm the court of appeals decision. In *Libertarian Party of Wisconsin v. State*, 199 Wis.2d 790, 809, 546 N.W.2d 424 (1996), this court held that creating jobs and enhancing the tax base were legitimate and valid reasons, along with others, for finding a legislative public purpose in the expenditure of public funds to build the Milwaukee Brewers' Miller Park. Accordingly, we hold that the combination of the town's enunciated goals of creating jobs, promoting orderly growth, increasing the tax base, and preserving and conserving an environmentally sensitive area for the benefit of the citizens of the town is a legitimate and valid public purpose under Wisconsin statutes, case law, and the United States and Wisconsin Constitutions.

This case involves a question of whether the Town of Beloit violated the public purpose doctrine. Although there is no specific clause in the

Wisconsin Constitution establishing the public purpose doctrine, this court has recognized that the doctrine is firmly accepted as a basic constitutional tenet of the Wisconsin Constitution and the United States Constitution, mandating that public appropriations may not be used for other than public purposes. Courts are to give great weight and afford very wide discretion to legislative declarations of public purpose, but are not bound by such legislative expressions. It is the duty of this court to determine whether a public purpose can be conceived, which might reasonably be deemed to justify the basis of the duty.... Under the public purpose doctrine, "[w]e are not concerned with the wisdom, merits or practicability of the legislature's enactment. Rather we are to determine whether a public purpose can be conceived which might reasonably be deemed to justify or serve as a basis for the expenditure."

Consequently, a conclusion that no public purpose exists can be determined only if it is "clear and palpable" that there can be no benefit to the public. In *State ex rel. Warren v. Reuter*, 44 Wis.2d 201, 211, 170 N.W.2d 790 (1969), this court described the public purpose concept as fluid:

> [T]he concept of public purpose is a fluid one and varies from time to time, from age to age, as the government and its people change. Essentially, public purpose depends on what the people expect and want their government to do for the society as a whole and in this growth of expectation, that which often starts as hope ends in entitlement.

Although courts are not bound by legislative expressions of public purposes, they nevertheless have a constitutional burden to examine legislative actions for the existence of a public purpose pursuant to the Wisconsin Constitution. However, the court's duties are limited to determining whether the legislation contravenes the provisions of the constitution. The presumption of constitutionality is applicable in making such a determination. As such, courts are to give great weight to the opinion of the legislative body, and "[i]f any public purpose can be conceived which might rationally justify the expenditure, the constitutional test is satisfied." Consequently, a court will conclude that there is no public purpose only if it is "clear and palpable that there can be no benefit to the public."

Because of the accepted view that local governments are often in the best position to determine the needs of the public in that locality, Wisconsin municipalities have traditionally been given wide discretion to determine whether a public expenditure is warranted due to public necessity, convenience, or welfare. As such, the public purpose doctrine has been broadly interpreted.

A review of Wisconsin case law illustrates that the trend of Wisconsin courts is to extend the concept of public purpose. In *Bowman*, 34 Wis.2d at 64-65, 148 N.W.2d 683, the industrial development through the creation of separate county agencies and bond issues, pursuant to Wis. Stat. § 59.071, was determined to be a valid constitutional enactment as it related to a declaration of public purpose. In *West Allis v. Milwaukee County*, 39 Wis.2d 356, 159 N.W.2d 36 (1968), construction of incinerators and waste disposal facilities was considered a public purpose. In addition, financial aid to the Marquette School of Medicine (now the Medical College of Wisconsin), a private nonprofit corporation, was upheld on the premise that public health is a public purpose. This court upheld the industrial bonding law under Wis. Stat. § 66.521 (1969), as a public purpose, because the protection of the economic interests of the general public fell within the scope of promotion of the general welfare. Similarly, the elimination of unsafe, unsanitary and overcrowded housing was found to promote the overall public purpose of providing stable residences for those of lower income.

A few years later, this court upheld the creation and operation of the Wisconsin solid waste recycling authority, in part because "recycling can be defined as a means of garbage collection, and, as such, has been denominated as clearly a matter justifying expenditure of public funds."

Wisconsin courts have continued the liberal application of the public purpose doctrine. In 2001, the court of appeals held that the construction of a parking lot to promote rehabilitation of the downtown area was held to be a public purpose. In a similar vein, a city's expenditure of funds to increase the tax base and generally enhance the economic climate of the community was held to satisfy the public purpose doctrine.

Most significantly, this court was recently presented with the question of whether the expenditure of public funds for the construction of the new Milwaukee Brewers' Miller Park satisfied the public purpose doctrine. The purported goals of creating jobs and enhancing the tax base were held to be valid reasons, along with other reasons, by this court. In our analysis, we recognized that enhancing the tax base and creation of new jobs are legitimate and valid public purposes, and held that:

> The purpose of the Stadium Act is to promote the welfare and prosperity of this state by maintaining and increasing the career and job opportunities of its citizens and by protecting and enhancing the tax base on which state and local governments depend upon. It is clear that the community as a whole will benefit from the expenditures of these public funds. Creation of new jobs is of vital importance to the State of Wisconsin and economic development is a proper function of our government. *Libertarian Party*, 199 Wis.2d at 826.

Accordingly, the goal of increasing the tax base, as well as creation of new jobs, has been recognized by this court, and other Wisconsin courts to be a legitimate and valid public purpose justifying the expenditure of public funds.

The record is replete with references to the underlying reasons for the town's decision to develop the Heron Bay Subdivision. In particular, the town was motivated to develop the land by its desire to create jobs, expand the tax base and create an orderly growth of single family housing for the benefit of members of the community.

The town was also concerned with the environmental impact that a subdivision would have in this ecologically sensitive area. As a result of that concern, the town ultimately determined that it was its duty to ensure that an ecologically fragile area was properly developed and that the best way to accomplish this goal was to carry out the development itself.

Thus, contrary to the Intervenors' argument...the record clearly indicates that the town acted on behalf of the public welfare.... Finally, as noted by the town, any profit realized from the sale of the subdivision would in fact benefit the Town of Beloit in that the profit would go into the Town Treasury and ultimately benefit all of the citizens of the town by way of decreased taxes and reduced debt.

In summary...this court has recognized, pursuant to our decision in *Libertarian Party*, that purposes for legislative action such as increasing the tax base and creation of new jobs, along with other reasons, are legitimate public purposes justifying the expenditure of public funds. This court holds that the combination of goals here of creating jobs, promoting orderly growth, enhancing the tax base, and preserving and conserving environmentally sensitive lands is a legitimate and valid public purpose justifying the expenditure of public funds by the Town of Beloit. Accordingly, we affirm the court of appeals decision.

ABRAHAMSON, C.J., dissenting.

I would affirm the order of the circuit court granting summary judgment to the intervenors on the ground that the town's proposed expenditure for the development of the subdivision did not serve a public purpose.

An expenditure is for a public purpose if it provides a direct advantage or benefit to the public at large. It is not for a public purpose if the advantage to the public is indirect, remote, or uncertain. The constitutional public purpose test is satisfied when the purposes expressed by the legislative body or "conceived" by the court rationally justify the expenditure. In determining whether a public purpose exists the judiciary accords the legislative branch deference and thus plays a limited role. Nevertheless, the court does not merely rubber-stamp government expenditures. The state and federal constitutions demand that courts perform their independent function to assess the realistic operation of the law to protect the public. A court "is not bound by the legislature's enactment or declarations regarding its purpose, for it is the court's constitutional burden to examine the challenged legislation and assess its realistic operation."

The combination of goals enunciated by the majority opinion as constituting a legitimate and valid public purpose for the Town of Beloit's expenditures properly includes a list of benefits that might conceivably, in some circumstances, provide a direct benefit to taxpayers and thereby satisfy the public purpose doctrine. An expenditure of funds that is legitimately designed to create jobs, promote orderly growth, increase the tax base, and preserve an environmentally sensitive area is made for a public purpose.

I dissent in this case, however, to express my conviction that some of the goals on which the majority opinion rests its conclusion are merely assertions unsupported by the facts of this case while others are admittedly hoped for but distant outcomes, not justifications. The public purpose doctrine becomes a charade if a town may justify expenditures by merely offering enough of the proper buzzwords, "job creation," "orderly growth," "increasing the tax base," and "environment concerns," without any facts to back up the assertions. Moreover, judicial review cannot begin and end simply with the recitation of those buzzwords, without any analysis.

I dissent because I conclude on the basis of this record that it is clear beyond a reasonable doubt that the taxpayers of the Town of Beloit will be paying taxes to support the sale of lots for the future construction of private housing from which any benefit to the taxpayers is indirect, remote, and uncertain.

This case is before the court on summary judgment and so our analysis is based upon stipulated facts and affidavits. The parties' stipulation regarding the public purpose states only that the development is based on a policy decision that the town will be able to sell the lots to private individuals, realize a profit, expand the town's tax base, and open up the northwest side of the town in an orderly planned manner. The affidavits do not discuss any particular public purpose except in passing and in conclusory terms. Indeed, analysis of the record exposes the town's asserted justifications and those conceived of by the majority of this court as nothing more than a recitation of buzzwords.

I begin by looking at the four justifications upon which the majority opinion rests its holding: job creation, expanding the tax base, promoting orderly growth, and environmental conservation.

The majority opinion lists job creation as an express goal of the town's expenditure in this case, despite the fact that the town did not articulate that benefit as a goal in its stipulation, brief, or oral argument. Indeed, there is no evidence in the record that the Town of Beloit ever intended the expenditure of monies to develop and sell property in the Heron Bay subdivision to create jobs, let alone that the expenditure would in fact create jobs.

The majority opinion includes this noble public goal based solely upon a single affidavit from the town's attorney, asserting in broad terms, not necessarily related to this subdivision development, that "the Town of Beloit has a history of leading development for the benefit of its citizens. The purpose of development has been to develop jobs, a greater tax base for the community and places for citizens to live."

No evidence appears in the record of the types of jobs that would be created in this case, who would receive those jobs, or how long those jobs would last. The only jobs immediately on the horizon may be jobs related to development of the subdivision. If homes are constructed in the future, one-time construction jobs might be made available in the community. A public purpose cannot rest on conjecture alone.

The court's emphasis on the public purpose of preservation of an environmentally sensitive strip of land along the Rock River also amounts to reliance on buzzwords.... In any event, it is unclear why any expenditure of funds for subdivision improvement is necessary for environmental protection of land the town owns along the river. The monies expended go to the development of the sites, not the creation or enforcement of any environmental easement or covenant. According to the parties' stipulation, the public can access these lands for recreation and enjoyment at the present time. To conclude that the town is justified in expending funds for sewer, water, roads, gas, electricity, storm sewer management and any other appurtenances necessary for development of the subdivision for sale for homes because the public would benefit from no development on a particular strip of town-owned land is doublespeak.

The two other goals in the combination of objectives the majority opinion says supports the expenditures for a public purpose are the promotion of orderly growth and increasing the tax base. The town, however, makes no showing of the relationship of the subdivision to orderly growth. Orderly growth is accomplished by a master plan, zoning codes, and regulation of private land developers. The Town of Beloit has such a master plan in place. How the town is promoting orderly growth by development of the subdivision is therefore unclear. The majority opinion appears to have accepted the town's mere suggestion of promoting orderly growth. It certainly cannot base its conclusion on facts because the record is devoid of any such facts.

The final objective of the expenditures is to increase the tax base. The tax base will increase if the lots are sold and houses are constructed. Yet the stipulation states that the "Town has not sold any portion of the Heron

Bay Lands as of this date [December 7, 1999]. The Town has no guarantee that anyone will purchase any of the future residential lots...."

The majority opinion's combination of goals justifying the expenditures in this case thus boils down to this: the expenditure serves an acceptable public purpose because the town's tax base might be enhanced. I disagree with this position. An enhanced tax base from the sale of land and the construction of homes is an indirect, remote, and uncertain benefit of the expenditure in the present case and is not a sufficient public purpose to justify the town's running a for-profit real estate development business and engaging in the non-traditional enterprise of building residential home sites.

Next we turn to the two additional goals the town asserted as justifications for the expenditure in this case that the majority opinion rightly ignores. Both of them are similarly indirect, remote, and too uncertain to constitute public purposes.

First, the town freely admits in the stipulation that it is acting with the hope of making a profit. The town has the power to sell property. The majority opinion goes to great length to explain this statutory authority. Even where a government entity acts pursuant to a valid law, however, it is still subject to the constitution and the public purpose doctrine. The issue in this case is whether the town may expend funds for subdivision development to make a bigger profit on the sale. No evidence was presented analyzing either the expected revenue or market demand for the lots. The justification of a hoped-for profit, pursued to its logical end, would justify the expenditure of public funds for any potentially profitable endeavor in which the town seeks to engage. That cannot be what the public purpose doctrine means.

Second, the affidavit from the town attorney asserts in broad terms, not necessarily related to this subdivision development, that development in the town is to provide places for citizens to live. Nothing in the record evidences a need for single-family residential housing or the lack of private capital to develop such housing. Several private ventures proposed development of the land, but the Town rejected the proposals. In *Heimerl v. Ozaukee County*, 256 Wis. 151, 40 N.W.2d 564 (1949), the court held that building private driveways was not "allied with a public purpose" and declared the expenditures unconstitutional. Similarly, the development of river front lots in and of itself is not allied with a public purpose.

The public purpose doctrine demands deference to the legislative branches of government. Nevertheless, the court must examine the operational facts concerning government expenditures in order to determine whether a direct benefit to the public results. No facts exist in the record in the present case or can be conceived by the court to support a public purpose. I therefore conclude, as did the circuit court, that the possibility of public benefit is too indirect, remote, and uncertain to sustain the expenditures.

D. UNIFORMITY CLAUSES

ALLEGHENY PITTSBURGH COAL v. WEBSTER COUNTY
488 U.S. 336 (1989)

REHNQUIST, C.J.

The West Virginia Constitution guarantees to its citizens that, with certain exceptions, "taxation shall be equal and uniform throughout the State, and all property, both real and personal, shall be taxed in proportion to its value...." Art. X, § 1. The Webster County tax assessor valued petitioners' real property on the basis of its recent purchase price, but made only minor modifications in the assessments of land which had not been recently sold. This practice resulted in gross disparities in the assessed value of generally comparable property, and we hold that it denied petitioners the equal protection of the laws guaranteed to them by the Fourteenth Amendment.

Between 1975 and 1986, the tax assessor for Webster County, West Virginia, fixed yearly assessments for property within the county at 50% of appraised value. She fixed the appraised value at the declared consideration at which the property last sold. Some adjustments were made in the assessments of properties that had not been recently sold, although they amounted to, at most, 10% increases in 1976, 1981, and 1983 respectively.

Each year, petitioners pursued relief before the County Commission of Webster County sitting as a review board. They argued that the assessment policy of the Webster County assessor systematically resulted in appraisals for their property that were excessive compared to the appraised value of similar parcels that had not been recently conveyed. Each year the county commission affirmed the assessments, and each year petitioners appealed to the state Circuit Court. A group of these appeals from Allegheny and its successor in interest, Kentucky Energy, were consolidated by the West Virginia Circuit Court and finally decided in 1985. Another group of appeals from Shamrock and Oneida were consolidated and decided by the West Virginia Circuit Court early the next year.

The judge in both of these cases concluded that the system of real property assessment used by the Webster County assessor systematically and intentionally discriminated against petitioners in violation of the West

Virginia Constitution and the Fourteenth Amendment's Equal Protection Clause. He ordered the county commission to reduce the assessments on petitioners' property to the levels recommended by the state tax commissioner in his valuation guidelines published for use by local assessors. Underlying the judge's conclusions were findings that petitioners' tax assessments over the years were dramatically in excess of those for comparable property in the county. He found that "the assessor did not compare the various features of the real estate to which the high assessment was applied with the various features of land assessed at a much lower rate." "The questioned assessments were not based upon the presence of economically minable or removable coal, oil, gas or harvestable timber in or upon petitioners' real estate, as compared to an absence of the same in or upon [neighboring] properties." Nor were they "based upon present use or immediately foreseeable economic development of petitioners' real estate." Rather, "[t]he sole basis of the assessment of petitioners' real estate was, according to the assessor, the consideration declared in petitioners' deeds."

This approach systematically produced dramatic differences in valuation between petitioners' recently transferred property and otherwise comparable surrounding land. For the years 1976 through 1982, Allegheny was assessed and taxed at approximately 35 times the rate applied to owners of comparable properties. After purchasing that land, Kentucky Energy was assessed and taxed at approximately 33 times the rate of similar parcels. From 1981 through 1985, the county assessed and taxed the Shamrock-Oneida property at roughly 8 to 20 times that of comparable neighboring coal tracts. These disparities existed notwithstanding the adjustments made to the assessments of land not recently conveyed. In the case of the property held by Allegheny and Kentucky Energy, the county's adjustment policy would have required more than 500 years to equalize the assessments.

On appeal, the Supreme Court of Appeals of West Virginia reversed. It found that the record did not support the trial court's ruling that the actions of the assessor and board of review constituted "intentional and systematic" discrimination. It held that "assessments based upon the price paid for the property in arm's length transactions are an appropriate measure of the 'true and actual value' of...property." That other properties might be undervalued relative to petitioners' did not require that petitioners' assessments be reduced: "Instead, they should seek to have the assessments of other taxpayers raised to market value." We granted certiorari to decide whether these Webster County tax assessments denied petitioners the equal protection of the law and, if so, whether petitioners could constitutionally be limited to the remedy of seeking to raise the assessments of others.

We agree with the import of the opinion of the Supreme Court of Appeals of West Virginia that petitioners have no constitutional complaint simply because their property is assessed for real property tax purposes at a figure equal to 50% of the price paid for it at a recent arm's-length transaction. But their complaint is a comparative one: while their property is assessed at 50% of what is roughly its current value, neighboring comparable property which has not been recently sold is assessed at only a minor fraction of that figure. We do not understand the West Virginia Supreme Court of Appeals to have disputed this fact. We read its opinion as saying that even if there is a constitutional violation on these facts, the only remedy available to petitioners was an effort to have the assessments on the neighboring properties raised by an appropriate amount. We hold that the assessments on petitioners' property in this case violated the Equal Protection Clause of the Fourteenth Amendment to the United States Constitution, and that petitioners may not be remitted to the remedy specified by the Supreme Court of Appeals of West Virginia.

The county argues that its assessment scheme is rationally related to its purpose of assessing properties at true current value: when available, it makes use of exceedingly accurate information about the market value of a property-the price at which it was recently purchased. As those data grow stale, it periodically adjusts the assessment based on some perception of the general change in area property values. We do not intend to cast doubt upon the theoretical basis of such a scheme. That two methods are used to assess property in the same class is, without more, of no constitutional moment. The Equal Protection Clause "applies only to taxation which in fact bears unequally on persons or property of the same class." The use of a general adjustment as a transitional substitute for an individual reappraisal violates no constitutional command. As long as general adjustments are accurate enough over a short period of time to equalize the differences in proportion between the assessments of a class of property holders, the Equal Protection Clause is satisfied. Just as that Clause tolerates occasional errors of state law or mistakes in judgment when valuing property for tax purposes, it does not require immediate general adjustment on the basis of the latest market developments. In each case, the constitutional requirement is the seasonable attainment of a rough equality in tax treatment of similarly situated property owners.

But the present action is not an example of transitional delay in adjustment of assessed value resulting in inequalities in assessments of comparable property. Petitioners' property has been assessed at roughly 8 to 35 times more than comparable neighboring property, and these discrepancies have continued for more than 10 years with little change. The county's adjustments to the assessments of property not recently sold are too small to seasonably dissipate the remaining disparity between these assessments and the assessments based on a recent purchase price.

The States, of course, have broad powers to impose and collect taxes. A State may divide different kinds of property into classes and assign to each class a different tax burden so long as those divisions and burdens are reasonable. It might, for example, decide to tax property held by corporations, including petitioners, at a different rate than property held by individuals. In each case, "[i]f the selection or classification is neither capricious nor arbitrary, and rests upon some reasonable consideration of difference or policy, there is no denial of the equal protection of the law."

But West Virginia has not drawn such a distinction. Its Constitution and laws provide that all property of the kind held by petitioners shall be taxed at a rate uniform throughout the State according to its estimated market value. There is no suggestion in the opinion of the Supreme Court of Appeals of West Virginia, or from any other authoritative source, that the State may have adopted a different system in practice from that specified by statute; we have held that such a system may be valid so long as the implicit policy is applied even-handedly to all similarly situated property within the State. We are not advised of any West Virginia statute or practice which authorizes individual counties of the State to fashion their own substantive assessment policies independently of state statute. The Webster County assessor has, apparently on her own initiative, applied the tax laws of West Virginia in the manner heretofore described, with the resulting disparity in assessed value of similar property. Indeed, her practice seems contrary to that of the guide published by the West Virginia Tax Commission as an aid to local assessors in the assessment of real property.

"[I]ntentional systematic undervaluation by state officials of other taxable property in the same class contravenes the constitutional right of one taxed upon the full value of his property." "The equal protection clause ... protects the individual from state action which selects him out for discriminatory treatment by subjecting him to taxes not imposed on others of the same class." We have no doubt that petitioners have suffered from such "intentional systematic undervaluation by state officials" of comparable property in Webster County. Viewed in isolation, the assessments for petitioners' property may fully comply with West Virginia law. But the fairness of one's allocable share of the total property tax burden can only be meaningfully evaluated by comparison with the share of others similarly situated relative to their property holdings. The relative undervaluation of comparable property in Webster County over time therefore denies petitioners the equal protection of the law.

NORDLINGER v. HAHN
505 U.S. 1 (1992)

BLACKMUN, J.

In 1978, California voters staged what has been described as a property tax revolt by approving a statewide ballot initiative known as Proposition 13. The adoption of Proposition 13 served to amend the California Constitution to impose strict limits on the rate at which real property is taxed and on the rate at which real property assessments are increased from year to year. In this litigation, we consider a challenge under the Equal Protection Clause of the Fourteenth Amendment to the manner in which real property now is assessed under the California Constitution.

As enacted by Proposition 13, Article XIIIA of the California Constitution caps real property taxes at 1% of a property's "full cash value." § 1(a). "Full cash value" is defined as the assessed valuation as of the 1975-1976 tax year or, "thereafter, the appraised value of real property when purchased, newly constructed, or a change in ownership has occurred after the 1975 assessment." § 2(a). The assessment "may reflect from year to year the inflationary rate not to exceed 2 percent for any given year." § 2(b).

In short, Article XIIIA combines a 1% ceiling on the property tax rate with a 2% cap on annual increases in assessed valuations. The assessment limitation, however, is subject to the exception that new construction or a change of ownership triggers a reassessment up to current appraised value. Thus, the assessment provisions of Article XIIIA essentially embody an "acquisition value" system of taxation rather than the more commonplace "current value" taxation. Real property is assessed at values related to the value of the property at the time it is acquired by the taxpayer rather than to the value it has in the current real estate market.

Over time, this acquisition-value system has created dramatic disparities in the taxes paid by persons owning similar pieces of property. Property values in California have inflated far in excess of the allowed 2% cap on increases in assessments for property that is not newly constructed or that has not changed hands. As a result, longer term property owners pay lower property taxes reflecting historic property values, while newer owners pay higher property taxes reflecting more recent values. For that reason, Proposition 13 has been labeled by some as a "welcome stranger" system—the newcomer to an established community is "welcome" in anticipation that he will contribute a larger percentage of support for local government than his settled neighbor who owns a comparable home. Indeed, in dollar terms, the differences in tax burdens are staggering. By 1989, the 44% of California homeowners who have owned their homes since enactment of Proposition 13 in 1978 shouldered only 25% of the more than $4 billion in residential property taxes paid by homeowners statewide. If property values continue to rise more than the annual 2% inflationary cap, this disparity will continue to grow.

According to her amended complaint, petitioner Stephanie Nordlinger in November 1988 purchased a house in the Baldwin Hills neighborhood of Los Angeles County for $170,000. The prior owners bought the home just two years before for $121,500. In early 1989, petitioner received a notice from the Los Angeles County Tax Assessor, who is a respondent here, informing her that her home had been reassessed upward to $170,100 on account of its change in ownership. She learned that the reassessment resulted in a property tax increase of $453.60, up 36% to $1,701, for the 1988-1989 fiscal year.

Petitioner later discovered she was paying about five times more in taxes than some of her neighbors who owned comparable homes since 1975 within the same residential development. For example, one block away, a house of identical size on a lot slightly larger than petitioner's was subject to a general tax levy of only $358.20 (based on an assessed valuation of $35,820, which reflected the home's value in 1975 plus the up-to-2% per year inflation factor). According to petitioner, her total property taxes over the first 10 years in her home will approach $19,000, while any neighbor who bought a comparable home in 1975 stands to pay just $4,100. The general tax levied against her modest home is only a few dollars short of that paid by a pre-1976 owner of a $2.1 million Malibu beachfront home.

After exhausting administrative remedies, petitioner brought suit against respondents in Los Angeles County Superior Court. She sought a tax refund and a declaration that her tax was unconstitutional. Respondents demurred. By minute order, the Superior Court sustained the demurrer and dismissed the complaint without leave to amend. The California Court of Appeal affirmed [and] the Supreme Court of California denied review. We granted certiorari.

The appropriate standard of review is whether the difference in treatment between newer and older owners rationally furthers a legitimate state interest. In general, the Equal Protection Clause is satisfied so long as there is a plausible policy reason for the classification, the legislative facts on which the classification is apparently based rationally may have been considered to be true by the governmental decisionmaker, and the relationship of the classification to its goal is not so attenuated as to render the distinction arbitrary or irrational. This standard is especially deferential in the context of classifications made by complex tax laws. "[I]n structuring internal taxation schemes 'the States have large leeway in making classifications and drawing lines which in their judgment produce reasonable systems of taxation.'"

We have no difficulty in ascertaining at least two rational or reasonable considerations of difference or policy that justify denying petitioner the benefits of her neighbors' lower assessments. First, the State has a legitimate interest in local neighborhood preservation, continuity, and stability. The State therefore legitimately can decide to structure its tax system to discourage rapid turnover in ownership of homes and businesses, for example, in order to inhibit displacement of lower income families by the forces of gentrification or of established, "mom-and-pop" businesses by newer chain operations. By permitting older owners to pay progressively less in taxes than new owners of comparable property, the Article XIIIA assessment scheme rationally furthers this interest.

Second, the State legitimately can conclude that a new owner at the time of acquiring his property does not have the same reliance interest warranting protection against higher taxes as does an existing owner. The State may deny a new owner at the point of purchase the right to "lock in" to the same assessed value as is enjoyed by an existing owner of comparable property, because an existing owner rationally may be thought to have vested expectations in his property or home that are more deserving of protection than the anticipatory expectations of a new owner at the point of purchase. A new owner has full information about the scope of future tax liability before acquiring the property, and if he thinks the future tax burden is too demanding, he can decide not to complete the purchase at all. By contrast, the existing owner, already saddled with his purchase, does not have the option of deciding not to buy his home if taxes become prohibitively high. To meet his tax obligations, he might be forced to sell his home or to divert his income away from the purchase of food, clothing, and other necessities. In short, the State may decide that it is worse to have owned and lost, than never to have owned at all.

Petitioner argues that Article XIIIA cannot be distinguished from the tax assessment practice found to violate the Equal Protection Clause in *Allegheny Pittsburgh*. Like Article XIIIA, the practice at issue in *Allegheny Pittsburgh* resulted in dramatic disparities in taxation of properties of comparable value. But an obvious and critical factual difference between this case and *Allegheny Pittsburgh* is the absence of any indication in *Allegheny Pittsburgh* that the policies underlying an acquisition-value taxation scheme could conceivably have been the purpose for the Webster County tax assessor's unequal assessment scheme. In the first place, Webster County argued that "its assessment scheme is rationally related to its purpose of assessing properties at true current value" Moreover, the West Virginia "Constitution and laws provide that all property of the kind held by petitioners shall be taxed at a rate uniform throughout the State according to its estimated market value," and the Court found "no suggestion" that "the State may have adopted a different system in practice from that specified by statute."

Even if acquisition-value policies had been asserted, the assertion would have been nonsensical given its inherent inconsistency with the county's principal argument that it was in fact trying to promote current-value taxation. *Allegheny Pittsburgh* was the rare case where the facts precluded any plausible inference that the reason for the unequal assessment practice was to achieve the benefits of an acquisition-value tax scheme. By contrast, Article XIIIA was enacted precisely to achieve the benefits of an acquisition-value system. *Allegheny Pittsburgh* is not controlling here.

Article XIIIA is not palpably arbitrary, and we must decline petitioner's request to upset the will of the people of California. The judgment of the Court of Appeal is affirmed.

STEVENS, J., dissenting.

During the two past decades, California property owners have enjoyed extraordinary prosperity. As the State's population has mushroomed, so has the value of its real estate. Between 1976 and 1986 alone, the total assessed value of California property subject to property taxation increased tenfold. Simply put, those who invested in California real estate in the 1970's are among the most fortunate capitalists in the world.

Proposition 13 has provided these successful investors with a tremendous windfall and, in doing so, has created severe inequities in California's property tax scheme. As a direct result of this windfall for [prior purchasers], later purchasers must pay far more than their fair share of property taxes. In my opinion, such disparate treatment of similarly situated taxpayers is arbitrary and unreasonable.

Nor can *Allegheny Pittsburgh* be distinguished because West Virginia law established a market-value assessment regime. Webster County's scheme was constitutionally invalid not because it was a departure from state law, but because it involved the relative "systematic undervaluation...[of] property in the same class" (as that class was defined by state law). Our decisions have established that the Equal Protection Clause is offended as much by the arbitrary delineation of classes of property (as in this case) as by the arbitrary treatment of properties within the same class (as in *Allegheny Pittsburgh*). Thus, if our unanimous holding in *Allegheny Pittsburgh* was sound—and I remain convinced that it was-it follows inexorably that Proposition 13, like Webster County's assessment scheme, violates the Equal Protection Clause. Indeed, in my opinion, statewide discrimination is far more invidious than a local aberration that creates a tax disparity.

BETTIGOLE v. ASSESSORS OF SPRINGFIELD
178 N.E.2d 10 (Mass 1961)

CUTTER, J.

These two bills in equity present questions about the validity of the proposed 1961 assessment of property taxes in Springfield. They have been argued together. The Bettigole case is brought by individual, fiduciary, and corporate owners of multi-family dwellings, commercial real estate, and other property in Springfield which it is alleged 'will be in 1961 and subsequent years...deliberately...over-valued and over-assessed both in relation to other classes of taxable real estate for which assessed valuations have been established at lower percentages of fair cash value and in relation to the general average or ratio of valuations to fair cash value of taxable real estate in' Springfield. It is alleged that the board of assessors (the board) has for many years established assessed valuations for different classes of real estate in the city at widely differing percentages of the full fair cash value of such real estate and plans to do so for 1961. The bill seeks a declaration as to the 'lawfulness under the Constitution and laws of [t]he Commonwealth of the policy and practice' just described, and also injunctive relief (a) against continuance of this assessment practice by the assessors, and (b) against action to send out bills for, and to collect, the taxes so assessed.

By August 1, 1961, the board "had determined the sound value [a term used by the board as equivalent to fair cash value] of each parcel of taxable real estate in the [c]ity as of January 1, 1961, and the fair cash value of the personal property owned by each [taxable] person." The board had also classified all parcels of real estate into six categories, set out below, and a majority had voted on September 8 and 15, 1961, "to establish...[1961] assessed valuations of all taxable property in the [c]ity by applying the following percentages to the sound value determined by the...[board] for the following classes of property," respectively, viz., (1) single family residences—50%; (2) two family residences—60%; (3) three family residences—65%; (4) four or more family residences—70%; (5) property of public utilities and commercial and industrial properties—85%; (6) farms, vacant land, and other real estate—70%. Personal property subject to local taxation was to be assessed at 85% of the fair cash value thereof previously determined by the board.

"The [b]oard determined assessed valuations for 1960 in substantially the same manner as it intends to use in 1961 and 1962 and the board's practice of applying varying percentages of sound or fair cash value of different classes of property in arriving at assessed valuations was deliberate and intentional." A table, made a part of each statement of agreed facts...shows, for example, that the fair cash (sound) value of

22,005 parcels of single family residence property was $266,285,568, but that these parcels were assessed at an aggregate of $133,142,792 for only 50% of their fair cash (sound) value. The table indicates that, if all taxable property in the city had been assessed at 100% of fair cash value, these 22,005 parcels would have been subjected to aggregate taxes of $11,223,937 at a tax rate of $42.15 per $1,000 of valuation, whereas they were in fact taxed only $8,601,024 under a tax rate of $64.60. The table also shows that 2,521 parcels of public utility, commercial and industrial properties, assessed at 85% of fair cash value, were in fact taxed $9,602,217, whereas, if all taxable property in the city had been assessed at 100% of fair cash value, the aggregate tax on these 2,521 parcels would have been only $7,370,792. This is the most striking comparison revealed by Annex A, and (although this is not done in the statements of agreed facts) its effect can be shown in tabular form (by a simple mathematical calculation from Annex A) as follows:

	(A) Approximate percentage of total fair cash value of all taxable property	(B) Approximate percentage of all property taxes assessed on non-uniform basis
22,005 single family residence parcels	43%	33%
2,521 public utility, commercial and industrial parcels	28%	37%

It thus appears that 43% of the total fair cash value of taxable property in Springfield is paying only 33% of the property taxes, whereas 28% of the total is paying 37% of the property taxes. The somewhat lesser disparity, produced by the board's assessment method, among various other classes of property is equally susceptible of mathematical demonstration.

The plaintiffs are owners of properties within the classes of four and more family residences, commercial and industrial properties, and farms, vacant land and other real estate, listed in detail in annexes to the bills. Because "they own such property [each of the plaintiffs will] pay substantially more in taxes for 1961 if the [board's assessing] practice described [earlier in this opinion] is followed than if the assessed valuations of all taxable property in Springfield were the fair cash value of such property."

The plaintiffs "insist that, in accordance with the [C]onstitution and laws of the Commonwealth, the assessed valuations of all taxable property in...Springfield should be the fair cash value of such property." A majority of the board insists "upon following...[the above described] practice...and have refused to establish assessed valuations...at the fair cash value of...property."

These cases continue property tax controversies which have existed in Springfield in recent years. The bills present for consideration, upon very complete, precise statements of agreed facts, the question whether the whole 1961 property tax assessment scheme violates the Constitution of the Commonwealth (Part II, c. 1, § 1, art. 4) which empowers the General Court "to impose and levy proportional and reasonable assessments, rates, and taxes, upon all the inhabitants of, and persons resident, and estates lying, within the said commonwealth...." (emphasis supplied). See also art. 10 of the Declaration of Rights, which reads, "Each individual...has a right to be protected...in the enjoyment of his life, liberty and property, according to standing laws. He is obliged, consequently, to contribute his share to the expense of this protection..." (emphasis supplied). It is well settled that the words "his share" in art. 10 of the Declaration of Rights 'forbid the imposition upon one taxpayer of a burden relatively greater or relatively less than that imposed upon other taxpayers.' Similarly, "the expression 'proportional and reasonable' [in Part II, c. 1, § 1, art. 4] forbids the imposition of taxes upon one class of persons or property at a different rate from that which is applied to other classes." This interpretation of these constitutional provisions has been unvarying "from the early days of the Commonwealth to the present time." In *Cheshire v. County Commrs. of Berkshire*, 118 Mass. 386, 389, this court said that the constitutional provision for "proportional and reasonable" taxes "forbids their imposition upon one class of persons or property at a different rate from that which is applied to other classes, whether that discrimination is effected directly in the assessment or indirectly through arbitrary and unequal methods of valuation." The court there recognized that "[p]ractically it is impossible to secure exact equality or proportion in the imposition of taxes" but it pointed out that the statutory "aim [should] be towards that result, by approximation at least." The statements of agreed facts negate any suggestion of "equality or proportion" in the 1961 Springfield assessments, for it is established that disproportion, rising to a maximum of the difference between 50% and 85% of fair cash value, "was deliberate and intentional" and that personal property and one class of real estate was thus to be assessed 170% (85/50) of the level of assessment of another class of real estate. This is not even equality by "approximation," which, at the least, requires attempted equality of assessment in absolute good faith and to the best of the abilities of the public officers charged with making valuations.

Upon the basis of the foregoing authorities, there can be no doubt that the board's proposed 1961 assessment scheme is a complete, widespread, and fundamental failure to comply with either the constitutional or the statutory requirements for proportional assessment.

TOPEKA CEMETERY ASSOCIATION v. SCHNELLBACHER
542 P.2d 278 (Kan. 1975)

PRAGER, J.

This is an action by a taxpayer attacking a statutory tax exemption on the ground that it is discriminatory and hence in violation of the Kansas Constitution. The facts in the case have been stipulated and essentially are as follows: The Topeka Cemetery Association, plaintiff-appellee, is a Kansas cemetery corporation created pursuant to statute. The cemetery association owns property in Topeka which has been platted and dedicated exclusively as a cemetery. The Topeka Cemetery Association has been in existence for many years. The great majority of the lots have been sold to provide individual or family burial lots. A number of the lots have not been sold and are owned by the corporation and available for future sale. The unsold cemetery lots, driveways, lawns, and areas used for maintenance of the cemetery are dedicated to burial purposes and under the association's charter cannot be used for any other purpose.

Prior to 1969 the legislature by statute exempted from taxation all lands used exclusively as graveyards. (K.S.A.1968 Supp. 79-201 Second.) In 1969 the legislature by Chapter 429, Laws of 1969, amended 79-201 Second to provide as follows:

> 79-201.... That the property described in this section, to the extent herein limited, shall be exempt from taxation:
>
>> Second. All lots or tracts of land located within cemeteries, which have been purchased by individual owners and are used or to be used exclusively as a grave site or sites by said individual owner or the family thereof.

Section 3 of Chapter 429 repealed K.S.A.1968 Supp. 79-201 along with other statutes. The effect of the statute was to classify cemetery lands into two groups for tax purposes. Lots or tracts of land owned by individual owners for present or future use as grave sites are declared exempt from ad valorem taxation. Lots or tracts of land owned by a cemetery corporation are not exempt from ad valorem taxation and are required to be assessed and taxed by state taxing officials.

The sole issue presented on this appeal is one of law and simply stated is as follows: Is K.S.A. 79-201 Second unconstitutional as a violation of Article 11, Section 1, of the Kansas Constitution? At the time the case was tried Article 11, Section 1, provided as follows:

> System of taxation; classification; exemption. The legislature shall provide for a uniform and equal rate of assessment and taxation, except that mineral products, money, mortgages, notes and other evidence of debts may be classified and taxed uniformly as to class as the legislature shall provide. All property used exclusively for state, county, municipal, literary, educational, scientific, religious, benevolent and charitable purposes, and all household goods and personal effects not used for the production of income, shall be exempted from taxation.

This section of the constitution was amended in 1974 but such amendment did not affect the issue presented to the court in this case. The exceptions mentioned in the section are not applicable in the present case and will not be discussed. Specifically, the Topeka Cemetery Association contends the K.S.A. 79-201 Second violates that portion of Article 11, Section 1, which requires the legislature to provide for a uniform and equal rate of assessment and taxation.

This constitutional provision has been before this court for interpretation on many occasions since the provision was adopted as a part of the original constitution of Kansas. It would be helpful to consider some of the general principles of law which this court has followed in applying the constitutional provision to specific taxing statutes enacted by various state legislatures down through the years. As a general proposition all property is subject to taxation except property which is specifically exempted either by the constitution or by statute. Constitutional and statutory provisions exempting property from taxation are to be strictly construed and the burden of establishing exemption from taxation is upon the one claiming it. The constitutional exemptions provided for in Article 11, Section 1, of the Kansas Constitution extend to all property used exclusively for state, county, municipal, literary, educational, scientific, religious, benevolent and charitable purposes and all household goods and personal effects not used for the production of income. We have held that the constitutional exemptions depend solely upon the exclusive use made of the property and not upon the ownership or the character, charitable or otherwise, of the owner.

The legislature has the authority to provide that property other than that named in the constitution may be exempt from taxation, but this exemption must have a public purpose and be designed to promote the public welfare. Some statutory exemptions have been based upon public ownership of property by the United States government. Without congressional action there is immunity from state and local taxation, implied from the United States Constitution itself, of all properties, functions and instrumentalities of the federal government. Statutory exemptions also have been created to apply to property owned by the state or one of its political subdivisions. In *City of Harper v. Fink*, supra, this court stated that under statutes granting tax exemptions to city property, ownership rather than exclusive use is the test of exemption from taxation. It is obvious that statutory exemptions based upon Public ownership of property may have a rational basis and that a public purpose may be served thereby.

Throughout our judicial history a different test has been applied in situations where public property is not involved and where the statutory tax exemption pertains to property owned by private individuals or corporations. We have consistently held that where public property is not involved, a tax exemption must be based upon the use of the property and not on the basis of ownership alone. The reason for the rule is that a classification of private property for tax purposes based solely upon ownership unlawfully discriminates against one citizen in favor of another and therefore is a denial of equal protection of the law. In *Associated Rly. Equipment Owners v. Wilson*, 167 Kan. 608, 208 P.2d 604, we stated that the equal protection clause of the federal constitution and state constitutional provisions pertaining to equality and uniformity of taxation are substantially similar and that, in general, what violates one will contravene the other and vice versa. In 1887 it was held in *M. & M. Rly. Co. v. Champlin, Treas.*, 37 Kan. 682, 16 P. 222 that a distinction made in the taxation of property in a township belonging to residents and nonresidents was unconstitutional and void and in violation of Article 11, Section 1, of the Kansas Constitution.

The term 'equality' and 'uniformity' were explained in *Wheeler v. Weightman*, 96 Kan. 50, 149 P. 977, where the court stated as follows:

> The essentials are that each man in city, county, and state is interested in maintaining the state and local governments. The protection which they afford and the duty to maintain them are reciprocal. The burden of supporting them should be borne equally by all, and this equality consists in each one contributing in proportion to the amount of his property. To this end all property in the state must be listed and valued for the purpose of taxation; the rate of assessment and taxation to be uniform and equal throughout the jurisdiction levying the tax. The imposition of taxes upon selected classes of property to the exclusion of others and the exemption of selected classes to the exclusion of others, constitute invidious discriminations which destroy uniformity.

In *Voran v. Wright*, 129 Kan. 1, 281 P. 938, it is declared that the classification permitted by Section 1 of Article 11 of the Kansas Constitution applies to property and not to owners thereof. At page 606 of the opinion on rehearing it is stated: "...A classification as to owners is not now permissible...."

The rule of uniformity may be violated as effectively by arbitrary exemptions from taxation as by arbitrary impositions. In *Mount Hope Cemetery Co. v. Pleasant*, 139 Kan. 417, 32 P.2d 500, this court has before it a factual situation and a statute quite similar to that presented in this case. In that action the Mount Hope Cemetery Co. brought an original proceeding in mandamus in the supreme court to require the state tax commission to order stricken from the tax rolls of Shawnee county certain land lying near Topeka which had been conveyed to the cemetery in trust for cemetery purposes. Prior to 1931 it was provided by statute that all lands used exclusively as graveyards shall be exempt from taxation. In 1931 the legislature enacted R.S.1933 Supp. 17-1314 which reads:

> All lands held and owned by cemetery corporations or associations shall be subject to assessment and taxation: Provided, That where lands are held or owned by municipal corporations for cemetery purposes, such lands shall be exempt from taxation: And provided further, Where such lands are divided or platted in burial lots and the same have been sold to a person for burial purposes, such lot or lots shall be exempt from assessment and taxation, and also shall not be subject to attachment or execution.

This court held that that portion of the statute of 1931 which sought to subject plaintiff's public cemetery to taxation on the ground of corporation ownership of the fee title to the property violated those provisions of the state and federal constitutions which guarantee to all persons, corporate and individual, within the jurisdiction of the state the equal protection of the law, and which forbid unjust discrimination among individuals and corporations in respect to taxation of their properties. In the later case of *Mount Hope Cemetery Co. v. City of Topeka*, 190 Kan. 702, 378 P.2d 30, the earlier case of *Mount Hope Cemetery Co. v. Pleasant*, supra, is cited and it is stated in syllabus 3 that ownership is not the test of whether property is liable to taxation but rather the uses to which property is devoted may exempt it therefrom.

When we turn to the undisputed facts and the statute under consideration in this case and apply the principles of law discussed above, we are compelled to conclude that the statutory classification contained in K.S.A. 79-201 Second is discriminatory and unconstitutional as a violation of Article 11, Section 1, of the Kansas Constitution. All lots and tracts of land contained within the boundaries of a cemetery platted by a cemetery corporation are dedicated exclusively for burial purposes and cannot be used for any other purpose. Since all lands in the cemetery are dedicated exclusively for burial purposes, we find no rational basis for treating differently land owned by individuals and that owned by the corporation, except ownership, which is not a permissible basis for classification. In our judgment the rationale of *Mount Hope Cemetery Co. v. Pleasant*, supra, is controlling in this case.

Since we have determined that the 1969 amendment to 79-201 Second is unconstitutional, we must next determine whether or not the statutory exemption which prior law granted all lands used exclusively as graveyards stands repealed by the repealing clause contained in Section 3 of Chapter 429, Laws of 1969. In this regard the general rule is stated in *City of Kansas City v. Robb*, 164 Kan. 577, 190 P.2d 398, to be as follows:

> Where a legislative act expressly repealing an existing statute, and providing a substitute therefor, is invalid, the repealing clause is also invalid unless it appears that the legislature would have passed the repealing clause even if it had not provided a substitute for the statute repealed.

In applying this rule we must determine whether the legislature would have passed the repealing clause even if it had not provided a substitute for the act repealed. We have concluded that that question must be answered in the negative. We think it highly questionable that the legislature would have completely wiped out the statutory exemption heretofore provided for land used exclusively as graveyards. *Mount Hope Cemetery Co. v. Pleasant*, supra, contains a history of the statutory exemption for burial grounds in this state. In the opinion Mr. Justice Dawson points out that from the formation of the state, burial grounds have been exempted from taxation. The underlying philosophy for the statutory exemption for burial grounds is that provision for the decent interment of the dead and for the seemly and dignified maintenance of property set apart for its accomplishment is a public purpose. We have concluded that it is highly unlikely that the legislature would have totally repealed the tax exemption for burial grounds contained in K.S.A.1968 Supp. 79-201 Second without providing a substitute. Hence we hold that the attempted repeal of K.S.A. 1968 Supp. 79-201 Second by Section 3, Chapter 429, Laws of 1969, must fall along with the attempted amendment of said section by Section 1 of Chapter 429. We wish to make it clear that our decision here does not affect in any way other provisions of Chapter 429 which have to do with statutory tax exemptions not involved in this case. We therefore hold that the statutory exemption for lands used exclusively as graveyards as provided by K.S.A.1968 Supp. 79-201 Second as it existed prior to the attempted amendment in 1969 was still in full force and effect for the tax years involved in this case and that the lots and tracts of land owned by Topeka Cemetery Association in its platted cemetery are exempted from ad valorem taxation.

LEONARD v. THORNBURGH
489 A.2d 1349 (Pa. 1985)

FLAHERTY, J.

This is an appeal from an order of the Commonwealth Court which declared unconstitutional Section 359(b) of the Tax Reform Code of 1971, known as the Philadelphia Non-Resident Wage Tax Cap, and Philadelphia Ordinance No. 1716. The Non-Resident Wage Tax Cap limits to 4 5/16% the rate at which non-residents can be taxed by the City of Philadelphia upon income earned in Philadelphia. Ordinance No. 1716, effective July 1, 1983, amended the City's Wage and Net Profits Tax so as to levy the tax at the rates of 4 5/16% upon non-residents, and 4 96/100% upon residents. Commonwealth Court, in declaring these provisions unconstitutional, reasoned that the differing tax rates applicable to residents and non-residents of the City of Philadelphia violated the Uniformity Clause of the Pennsylvania Constitution, Article VIII, Section I, which provides:

> All taxes shall be uniform, upon the same class of subjects, within the territorial limits of the authority levying the tax, and shall be levied and collected under general laws.

The appellant, Secretary of Revenue James I. Scheiner, contends that the tax provisions in question comport with constitutional requirements, under the Uniformity Clause of the Pennsylvania Constitution, supra, as well as under the equal protection clause of the Fourteenth Amendment. The appellee, Kathleen Leonard, a resident of Philadelphia who is aggrieved by having been assessed higher wage taxes than would have been payable had she not been a resident of Philadelphia, argues that the Uniformity Clause, rather than the Fourteenth Amendment, is the relevant constitutional standard, and that under that standard the tax provisions are invalid. It is well established, however, that in matters of taxation both constitutional standards are relevant, and that allegations of violations of the equal protection clause, and of the Uniformity Clause, are to be analyzed in the same manner.

The principles which govern the analysis of claims of non-uniform taxation are well established. The legislature possesses wide discretion in matters of taxation. The burden is upon the taxpayer to demonstrate that a classification, made for purposes of taxation, is unreasonable. *Amidon v. Kane*, 279 A.2d 53, 60 (1971) ("[T]he challengers of the constitutionality of state or local taxation bear a heavy burden...."). Indeed, tax legislation will not be declared unconstitutional unless it "*clearly, palpably,* and *plainly* violates the Constitution.*"

Under the equal protection clause, and under the Uniformity Clause, absolute equality and perfect uniformity in taxation are not required. In cases where the validity of a classification for tax purposes is challenged, the test is whether the classification is based upon some legitimate distinction between the classes that provides a non-arbitrary and "reasonable and just" basis for the difference in treatment. Stated alternatively, the focus of judicial review is upon whether there can be discerned "some concrete justification" for treating the relevant group of taxpayers as members of distinguishable classes subject to different tax burdens. When there exists no legitimate distinction between the classes, and, thus, the tax scheme imposes substantially unequal tax burdens upon persons otherwise similarly situated, the tax is unconstitutional.

Applying these principles to the instant case, we find that the tax scheme in question meets constitutional requirements, for there exists the requisite basis for treating residents and non-residents of Philadelphia as separate classes of wage earners subject to different tax rates. The legitimate distinction between those classes rests not upon the superficial fact that one class resides in Philadelphia while the other resides elsewhere, but rather, at a deeper level of analysis, upon significant differences between the two classes of wage earners that provide reasonable and concrete justifications for their being taxed at different rates.

This is not a case, therefore, where mere residence, uncorrelated with concrete justifications related to the situs of residence, has been relied upon by the taxing authority as an asserted basis for differential tax treatment. In the past, it has been held that residence alone is an insufficient basis upon which to sustain differential tax treatment, absent further justifications which correlate with the status of residency. See *Columbia Gas Corp. v. Commonwealth*, 360 A.2d at 595-597 (disparate rates of tax on foreign and domestic corporations invalid where Commonwealth offered no justification for taxing foreign corporations more heavily than domestic ones); *Danyluk v. Johnstown*, 178 A.2d 609 (1962) (city's capitation tax on non-residents held unauthorized and invalid, with dictum indicating that an occupation tax levied only against non-residents would violate constitutional uniformity standards); *Carl v. Southern Columbia Area School District*, 400 A.2d 650 (1979) (school district's tax invalid where, without reasonable justification, taxpayers residing in different counties were charged different amounts for precisely the same educational services).

In the instant case, it may clearly be presumed that non-resident wage earners utilize services provided by the City of Philadelphia to a lesser extent than do residents. Rather than benefit from twenty-four hour and seven day per week availability of such services, non-resident wage earners avail themselves of such services primarily during an eight hour workday on a five day per week basis. Though the exact proportions of the services used by the two classes are not quantifiable, it is clear that differences in the levels of service utilization must necessarily exist. This is true of city-provided services offered to residents and non-residents alike, such as police, fire, sanitation, and other services. As to each of these, the residents' needs are essentially full-time, while the non-residents' needs are merely part-time. These services receive funding from the City of Philadelphia's General Fund, and it is into the General Fund that wage tax revenues are deposited. Further, there are certain services, funded by the General Fund, that are offered only to residents, such as public schools, mental health and retardation services, and child and family welfare services. In short, residents and non-residents are not similarly situated with respect to their needs for services provided by the City of Philadelphia.

An additional justification for differentiating the tax treatment of residents and non-residents is to be found in the extent of the political representation the two classes enjoy. The legislature, in capping the wage tax rate applicable to non-residents, afforded protection to persons who are subject to city wage taxes but who have no voice in the city council. In contrast, residents of the city have recourse through their own elected representatives, the members of city council, in the event that they believe their tax rates are excessive.

We conclude that valid reasons have been offered for imposing a higher tax rate on resident wage earners of the City of Philadelphia than is imposed upon non-resident wage earners. The wage tax scheme in question is, therefore, in compliance with constitutional requirements governing uniformity of taxation. Accordingly, the order of the Commonwealth Court, declaring the tax provisions in question unconstitutional, is reversed.

ALLEGRO SERVICES, LTD. v. METROPOLITAN PIER AND EXPOSITION AUTHORITY
665 N.E. 2d 1246 (Ill. 1996)

NICKELS, J.

This appeal represents our second encounter with the program of taxes imposed by defendant, the Metropolitan Pier and Exposition Authority (Authority), to finance the renovation and expansion of McCormick Place and related infrastructure improvements. In *Geja's Cafe v. Metropolitan Pier & Exposition Authority*, 606 N.E.2d 1212 (1992), this court upheld a retailers' occupation tax imposed by the Authority on certain food and beverage sales. In the instant case we consider the constitutionality of an airport departure tax imposed by the Authority on providers of ground transportation services from Chicago's O'Hare and Midway Airports. Plaintiffs include several suburban and out-of-state businesses which provide bus, van or limousine transportation from the airports, but which do not serve destinations within the City of Chicago. Plaintiffs brought this action in the circuit court of Cook County on behalf of themselves and all others similarly situated, challenging the constitutionality of the tax under the commerce clause and the equal protection clause of the United States Constitution (U.S. Const., art. I, § 8; amend. XIV) and the uniformity clause of the Illinois Constitution of 1970 (Ill. Const.1970, art. IX, § 2). The trial court entered judgment on the pleadings or summary judgment in the Authority's favor on each of the counts in plaintiffs' class action complaint.

In 1992, the General Assembly enacted the Metropolitan Pier and Exposition Authority Act (Act) to provide for a project to renovate and expand McCormick Place (the expansion project). The expansion project includes plans for the renovation of McCormick Place's existing facilities and the construction of a new exhibition hall with a concourse to the existing facilities. It is anticipated that the expanded and improved McCormick Place facilities will lead to a significant increase in tourism to Chicago, thereby boosting certain sectors of the local and regional economy.

To finance the expansion project, the Authority was granted power to issue bonds in an amount not to exceed $937 million. In turn, under section 13 of the Act the Authority is directed to levy a series of local taxes in order to repay the bonds. Section 13(f) provides that "[b]y ordinance the Authority shall...impose an occupation tax on all persons, other than a governmental agency, engaged in the business of providing ground transportation for hire to passengers in the metropolitan area...."

The Authority enacted an ordinance imposing the airport departure tax in accordance with section 13(f), and plaintiffs brought this lawsuit as a class action seeking, inter alia, a declaratory judgment that the airport departure tax is invalid. The trial court conditionally certified four classes of plaintiffs who provide airport transportation service exclusively to destinations outside the City of Chicago. Classes A and C consist of operators of taxicabs or limousines based in Illinois (Class A) or outside the State (Class C) that, from time to time, depart from the airports with passengers for hire, but are not licensed by the City of Chicago to operate within its city limits. Class E consists of all operators of buses or vans regulated by the Interstate Commerce Commission that provide scheduled service from the airports with no destinations within the City of Chicago. Class F consists of bus and van operators providing charter or other unscheduled passenger service from the airports to destinations outside the City of Chicago. Vehicle operators with vehicle licenses issued by the City of Chicago who pay the tax are not included in the plaintiff classes.

Plaintiffs' class action complaint, as amended, consists of 13 counts challenging the airport departure tax under a variety of theories. Several counts raise the theory that, as applied to the members of the plaintiff classes, the airport departure tax violates the constitutional guarantees of equal protection and uniformity in nonproperty taxation because only those vehicle operators serving destinations in Chicago stand to benefit economically from increased tourism related to the expansion and renovation of McCormick Place....

Plaintiffs first contend that the trial court erred in denying their summary judgment motion and granting the Authority's motion on those counts alleging that the airport departure tax violates the equal protection clause of the United States Constitution and the uniformity clause of the Illinois Constitution. The uniformity clause provides:

> In any law classifying the subjects or objects of non-property taxes or fees, the classes shall be reasonable and the subjects and objects within each class shall be taxed uniformly. Exemptions, deductions, credits, refunds and other allowances shall be reasonable. Ill. Const. 1970, art. IX, § 2.

The uniformity clause imposes more stringent limitations than the equal protection clause on the legislature's authority to classify the subjects and objects of taxation. *Geja's Cafe v. Metropolitan Pier & Exposition Authority*, 153 Ill.2d 239, 247, 606 N.E.2d 1212 (1992); *Searle Pharmaceuticals, Inc. v. Department of Revenue*, 117 Ill.2d 454, 467-68, 512 N.E.2d 1240 (1987). "If a tax is constitutional under the uniformity clause, it inherently fulfills the requirements of the equal protection clause." *Geja's Cafe*, 153 Ill.2d at 247. Accordingly, we need only consider the validity of the airport departure tax under the uniformity clause.

To survive scrutiny under the uniformity clause, a nonproperty tax classification must be based on a real and substantial difference between the people taxed and those not taxed, and the classification must bear some reasonable relationship to the object of the legislation or to public policy. The uniformity requirement, as traditionally understood, may be violated by classifications which are either "underinclusive" or "overinclusive." Although the uniformity clause imposes a more stringent standard than the equal protection clause, the scope of a court's inquiry under the uniformity clause remains relatively narrow. Statutes bear a presumption of constitutionality, and broad latitude is afforded to legislative classifications for taxing purposes. One challenging a nonproperty tax classification has the burden of showing that it is arbitrary or unreasonable, and if a state of facts can reasonably be conceived that would sustain the classification, it must be upheld.

In the case at bar, the common characteristic linking the vehicle operators in the plaintiff classes—and forming the basis of plaintiffs' uniformity clause challenge—is that although they provide ground transportation service departing from the airports, they do not transport airport passengers for hire into the City of Chicago. Some of the class members are prohibited by Chicago's ground transportation licensing ordinance from transporting passengers from the airports to destinations in Chicago. Under the ordinance, a Chicago vehicle license is required to provide transportation service wholly within the city. Other class members provide scheduled airport service along routes which do not include destinations in the City of Chicago. Plaintiffs maintain that in terms of the economic impact of the McCormick Place expansion project, there is a real and substantial difference between the vehicle operators in the plaintiff classes and their city-licensed counterparts, because only the operators of city-licensed vehicles enjoy the opportunity to transport passengers from the airports to McCormick Place or nearby downtown hotels. Plaintiffs contend that any positive economic impact from the expansion project for class members is too indirect to support taxing them in the same manner as those operators providing airport transportation to destinations in Chicago, who enjoy a direct benefit by virtue of an increased demand for transportation to McCormick Place and nearby hotels.

Plaintiffs rely on *Geja's Cafe*, where, as previously noted, this court upheld the food and beverage tax imposed by the Authority in connection with the McCormick Place expansion project. The tax applied to certain types of food and beverage sales within a geographic subdistrict in Chicago. One of the arguments raised by its opponents was that pursuant to the uniformity requirement, the tax should have been imposed on food and beverage sales throughout Cook County. This court rejected the argument, finding that "[t]he General Assembly could reasonably conclude that the direct beneficiaries [of the expansion project's economic impact] would be those within the taxing subdistrict, and plaintiffs have not produced anything to suggest that narrowing the taxed area in this fashion was unreasonable." Plaintiffs contend that, like the food and beverage tax in Geja's Cafe, the Authority's airport departure tax should also be limited to the subclass of vehicle operators who benefit most directly from the expansion project.

In response, the Authority notes that in *Geja's Cafe* this court merely held that it was permissible to limit the tax to the geographic subdistrict; the court did not hold or suggest that a more broadly applicable tax would necessarily be unconstitutional. The Authority's observation underscores a basic flaw in plaintiffs' analysis. Plaintiffs' argument rests largely on their understanding that a "real and substantial difference" between the vehicle operators in the plaintiff classes and those who transport passengers from the airports into Chicago would necessarily be fatal to a tax scheme imposing the same taxes on both groups of operators. While *Geja's Cafe* and other decisions under the uniformity clause hold that there must be a real and substantial difference between the people taxed and those not taxed, we are aware of no authority for a converse rule that there may be no real and substantial difference among those taxed. As this court observed in *Geja's Cafe*, "[t]he uniformity clause was not designed as a straitjacket for the General Assembly. Rather, the uniformity clause was designed to enforce minimum standards of reasonableness and fairness as between groups of taxpayers." Accordingly, the "real and substantial difference" standard merely represents the minimum level at which the differences among groups are of a sufficient magnitude to justify taxing the groups differently. However, just because the differences between groups reach this minimum level, it does not follow that identical tax treatment would necessarily be unreasonable.

To apply the real and substantial difference test in the manner plaintiffs propose would transform the uniformity requirement from a minimum standard of reasonableness and fairness to a precise formula for drawing tax lines. Under the analysis that plaintiffs advocate, the relative tax treatment of any two groups of potential taxpayers would be preordained by the existence or nonexistence of a real and substantial difference between the groups. Under such an analysis, the taxing body would be deprived of any range of options in the formulation of tax classifications. We reject such a rigid rule. Instead, we adhere to the view that the existence of a real and substantial difference between groups of taxpayers only establishes that differential taxation may be permissible, not that it is constitutionally essential.

Plaintiffs cite *Northwestern University v. City of Evanston*, 221 Ill.App.3d 893 (1991), in support of their understanding of the real and substantial difference requirement. Plaintiffs' reliance on that decision is misplaced. In *Northwestern*, the appellate court held that pursuant to the uniformity clause, a local hotel-motel tax could not constitutionally be applied to an educational facility simply because the facility included several floors of sleeping rooms primarily for use by students. As we read *Northwestern*, the ratio decidendi was that "[a] taxing body is...prohibited under the uniformity provisions of the Illinois Constitution from defining statutory terms contrary to their common meaning." We express no opinion on the quality of this reasoning. Suffice it to say that the decision has no application here.

We agree with plaintiffs that at some point the differences among taxpayers may be so profound that taxing them as a single class would violate the uniformity requirement. In our view, however, this limitation is embraced within the uniformity clause test's second and more general requirement that tax classifications must bear some reasonable relationship to the object of the legislation or to public policy. In other words, the relevant question here is not whether the differences among vehicle operators serving the airports are "real and substantial," but whether the differences are so great that the General Assembly's decision to tax all such operators as a single class bears no reasonable relationship to the object of the tax. We turn to that question below.

The parties agree that in enacting the scheme of taxation to finance the McCormick Place expansion project, the General Assembly sought to impose the tax burden on certain industries that could be expected to realize significant economic benefits from the large number of visitors the project is expected to bring to the Chicago area. The Authority contends that while not all ground transportation providers who serve the airports will necessarily benefit in precisely the same way or to the same extent, it was still reasonable for the General Assembly to treat all providers as a single class for tax purposes based on anticipated benefits flowing to the class as a whole. The Authority maintains that by focusing exclusively on a limited sector of the market for ground transportation services—the market for transportation from the airports to downtown Chicago— plaintiffs have ignored the broader positive economic impact for the industry in general resulting from the expansion project. Plaintiffs respond that the specific benefits the Authority claims the vehicle operators in the plaintiff classes will enjoy are either nonexistent or "drastically attenuated" and do not support industry wide taxation.

As a prelude to consideration of these arguments, we digress briefly to address certain procedural matters. First, we note that in *Geja's Cafe*, this court clarified the burdens borne by the parties in litigation involving a uniformity clause challenge. While a classification will be upheld if a state of facts can reasonably be conceived to sustain it, the opponent of a tax is not required to come forward with any and all conceivable explanations for the tax and then prove each one to be unreasonable. Rather, upon a good-faith uniformity challenge, the taxing body bears the initial burden of producing a justification for the classifications. Once the taxing body has provided a sufficient justification, the opponent has the burden of persuading the court that the justification is unsupported by the facts.

We also take note of the procedural posture of this case, which is before us on the trial court's ruling in favor of the Authority on the parties' cross-motions for summary judgment. Summary judgment is appropriate where "the pleadings, depositions, and admissions on file, together with the affidavits, if any, show that there is no genuine issue as to any material fact and that the moving party is entitled to a judgment as a matter of law." The purpose of summary judgment is not to try a question of fact, but to determine whether one exists. Plaintiffs are not required to prove their case at the summary judgment stage. However, to survive a motion for summary judgment, the nonmoving party must present a factual basis which would arguably entitle him to a judgment. Accordingly, in the present case, to the extent the Authority has produced a legally sufficient justification for its tax classification, plaintiffs would then be required to present a factual basis negating the asserted justification to survive defendant's motion for summary judgment. Conversely, if the Authority has failed to produce a legally sufficient justification for the classification, plaintiffs would be entitled to a judgment as a matter of law.

Applying these principles, we conclude that the Authority has submitted a legally sufficient justification for imposing the airport departure tax on the members of the plaintiff classes who operate taxicab or limousine services from the airports to destinations outside the City of Chicago (Classes A and C). First, the Authority notes that while suburban and out-of-state operators are precluded from making trips into Chicago, Chicago-licensed operators are permitted to operate outside the city. Hence, both categories of operators compete for the business in taking travellers from the airports to suburban and out-of-state destinations. The Authority maintains that the generally increased demand for transportation from the airports into the city owing to the McCormick Place expansion project will take many city-licensed operators out of competition for the suburban/out-of-state market, thereby increasing the share of this market served by suburban and out-of-state taxicab and limousine operators. In other words, the increased demand for the city market will allow operators without Chicago licenses to take up the slack in the market for airport transportation to destinations outside the city.

Second, the Authority contends that the demand for downtown hotel rooms during major McCormick Place events is likely to divert other visitors to hotels in the suburbs, thereby increasing the demand for transportation from the airports to those hotels. The Authority notes the findings of a marketing study conducted by the firm of KPMG Peat Marwick in conjunction with the McCormick Place expansion project:

> A poorly documented but real effect is the ripple effect. When a large event comes to Chicago, demand currently accommodated in an area may be displaced into outlying areas. A convention oriented hotel which has a strong commercial base may displace regular corporate demand to outlying hotels. Meeting events in Chicago regularly have room in the O'Hare, Oakbrook and Rosemont areas. As delegates stay in these hotels, regular business may be displaced to further outlying areas. In this way the outlying areas are getting demand associated with McCormick Place, but it is not from visitors attending McCormick Place events directly.

Plaintiffs contend that their own informal survey shows that, at present, visitors attending McCormick Place events rarely stay in suburban hotels. However, plaintiffs have offered no evidence contradicting the assertion that McCormick Place events displace other visitors to outlying areas. Nor have plaintiffs offered any evidence to refute the Authority's theory that suburban and out-of-state taxicab and limousine operators will benefit from decreased competition in the market they serve. In essence, plaintiffs simply protest that these benefits are too indirect in comparison with the benefits to city-licensed operators. Be that as it may, the benefits identified are nonetheless tangible and would appear to represent reasonable conclusions about the dynamics of related market forces in the local economy. In this regard, we agree with the observation of our appellate court in *Forsberg v. City of Chicago*, 151 Ill.App.3d 354, 365, 502 N.E.2d 283 (1986), cited by the Authority, that "not all persons burdened by a tax must be benefited in the same way." We cannot say as a matter of law that the inclusion of these vehicle operators bears no reasonable relationship to the object of the tax.

The Authority also points out several potential benefits to the members of the plaintiff classes operating bus or van services (Classes E and F). First, bus and van operators are permitted to transport passengers into Chicago from points outside the city, and do in fact operate both scheduled and charter services with stops in Chicago. The Authority notes deposition testimony that an estimated 30% of the charter business conducted by Sam Van Galder, Inc. (Van Galder)—a Wisconsin-based bus company which is the parent company of plaintiff Alco Bus Corporation (Alco)—consists of trips to museums, baseball games and civic events in Chicago. Thus, the Authority maintains that the expansion project will create new opportunities for bus operators to transport passengers who reside in the suburbs and neighboring states to events at McCormick Place. Moreover, the expansion project includes plans to reroute the northbound lanes of Lake Shore Drive in a manner designed to enhance access to the Field Museum, the Shedd Aquarium and the Adler planetarium, thereby increasing the market for charter services to these already popular attractions. The Authority further notes that bus companies throughout the area enjoy a substantial volume of business as subcontractors in connection with the market for shuttle service between hotels and conventions held at McCormick Place. Business records of one of the major prime contractors for convention shuttle service show subcontracts to suburban and out-of-state companies for over 1,400 buses during a 17-month period.

Plaintiffs' principal objection to the Authority's reasoning is that the particular examples of charter service that the Authority cites involve separately incorporated affiliates of certain plaintiffs rather than the plaintiffs themselves. For instance, plaintiffs dispute the relevance of the charter business conducted by Van Galder, the parent company of plaintiff Alco. Plaintiffs note that Van Galder's charter business is entirely separate from Alco's airport transportation operation and potential benefits to Van

Galder cannot justify imposition of the airport departure tax on Alco. This argument is unpersuasive. The General Assembly cannot be charged with knowledge of the corporate structure of every firm in the ground transportation industry. In formulating tax classifications, the General Assembly is entitled to make reasonable assumptions about the characteristics of the industries subjected to taxation. In this regard, we think it was reasonable for the General Assembly to consider bus companies as integrated enterprises for purposes of appraising the economic impact of McCormick Place and the expansion project.

Plaintiffs also dispute the Authority's contention that suburban and out-of-state bus companies benefit from subcontracting opportunities related to convention shuttle service. Plaintiffs insist that under recent amendments to applicable Chicago ordinances, city-licensed charter operators are prohibited from "affiliating" with unlicensed operators. The provisions that plaintiffs have identified do not resemble the propositions for which they have been cited. We further note that Chicago has provided by ordinance that temporary permits may be issued to operators of licensed charter/sightseeing vehicles for the operation of additional vehicles as charter/sightseeing vehicles. Thus, there is no reason to believe subcontracting opportunities have ceased to exist or will in the future. Plaintiffs' argument is without merit.

As with the taxicab and limousine operators, we conclude that the Authority has submitted a legally sufficient justification for imposition of the bus and van operators in the plaintiff classes. Plaintiffs have not introduced evidence showing that the asserted justifications for taxing the members of the four plaintiff classes are factually erroneous. Accordingly, the trial court properly granted the Authority's motion for summary judgment on the counts brought under the uniformity and equal protection clauses.

For the foregoing reasons, the judgment of the circuit court of Cook County is affirmed.

CHAPTER XIV

ORGANIZATION OF STATE GOVERNMENTS

A. INTRODUCTION

The Supreme Court of the United States has made clear on several occasions that the U.S. Constitution has nothing to say about the structure and organization of state governments. *See, e.g., Sweezy v. New Hampshire*, 354 U.S. 234, 255 (1957) ("[T]his Court has held that the concept of separation of powers embodied in the United States Constitution is not mandatory in state governments."); *Highland Farms Dairy v. Agnew*, 300 U.S. 608, 612 (1937) ("How power shall be distributed by a state among its governmental organs is commonly, if not always, a question for the state itself."). Thus, the federal constitution does not compel states to allocate certain powers to particular branches of government or, indeed, even to have the traditional three federal branches. As a result, though many state government systems bear significant similarities to the federal government's structure and organization, there also are significant and interesting differences between the organization of the state governments and the federal system. This chapter explores some of those differences.

B. LEGISLATIVE POWER

1. Introduction

State legislative organization and power generally is defined at some length in state constitutions. All states but Nebraska have a bicameral legislature, not unlike the federal Congress, though the state legislatures vary in their specifics. Generally, state legislatures have responsibility for all lawmaking and exercise traditional police powers, meaning that their actions are limited only by political will and constitutional constraints such as may be found in the federal or relevant state constitution. Thus, state legislatures can and do legislate on a wide array of topics and subject matters. Important topics for legislation in most states include taxation and spending, criminal law, domestic relations, education, and infrastructure such as roads and transportation.

This chapter focuses on one potentially significant way in which the States and local governments may differ from the federal Congress—the imposition of term limits.

2. Term Limits for State and Local Officials

The Supreme Court of the United States held in *U.S. Term Limits, Inc. v. Thornton*, 514 U.S. 779 (1995) (excerpted in Chapter III, above), that the States may not impose term limits on their members of Congress, because the Qualifications Clauses in the federal constitution provide the exclusive credentials for determining those qualified to sit in Congress. Thus, there are no enforceable state term limits for U.S. Senators and members of the U.S. House of Representatives.

But there is no federal constraint on the imposition of term limits on members of state legislatures, state executive officials such as governors and attorneys general, local government bodies, or even potentially state judges. Thus, the States have been a fertile laboratory with respect to the adoption and constitutionality of measures limiting the terms of various state and local government officials. Several states have adopted such limits and, in many cases, though not all, term limits have withstood challenge under state constitutions. Below are two examples of state supreme courts interpreting such provisions and assessing their validity under state law.

HOERGER v. SPOTA
997 N.E.2d 1229, 21 N.Y.3d 549 (N.Y. 2013)

PER CURIAM.

At issue in this appeal is the validity of Suffolk County's term limit law pertaining to the office of district attorney. Petitioners allege that, as a consequence of such local law, respondent District Attorney Thomas J. Spota III is ineligible to hold the office he seeks. We conclude that the County is without the power to regulate the number of terms the district attorney may serve, and therefore we affirm the order finding the designating petitions valid.

The Suffolk County Legislature imposed term limits on county officials, including the district attorney. After approval by public referendum, the measure was added to the Suffolk County Charter, which specifies that "[n]o person shall serve as District Attorney for more than 12 consecutive years." Respondent, who was elected district attorney in 2001, will have served three full four-year terms (or 12 consecutive years) as of December 31, 2013. Spota, however, has been designated as a candidate in the upcoming primary election for the Democratic, Republican, Independence and Conservative Parties.

Petitioner Raymond G. Perini is a candidate for district attorney in the Republican Party primary. Petitioners-objectors are registered voters who filed objections to respondent's designating petitions with the Suffolk

County Board of Elections. They commenced this special proceeding seeking to invalidate the designating petitions.

The State Constitution requires that "[i]n each county a district attorney shall be chosen by the electors once in every three or four years as the legislature shall direct" (NY Const, art XIII, § 13 [a]). For counties outside of New York City, the state legislature has determined that the term of office shall be four years. In addition, a district attorney is subject to removal from office, not by county officials, but by the Governor (see NY Const, art XIII, § 13 [b]). The Governor is likewise vested with the authority to fill a vacancy existing in that office.

We have therefore recognized that "a [d]istrict [a]ttorney is a constitutional officer chosen by the electors of a county." In other words, although the district attorney may be an officer serving a county, the office and its holder clearly implicate state concerns. For example, there is a strong state interest in establishing adequate salaries for district attorneys, as the representatives of the People of the State of New York responsible for enforcing the Penal Law at the local level.

Existing law further illustrates the necessity of statewide uniformity of qualifications for district attorneys. An individual must be at least 18 years old, a resident of the county and a citizen of the United States. We have also mandated that a district attorney must be an attorney admitted to practice in order to properly fulfill the duties of the office and that a county may not alter that prerequisite even in the face of major practical obstacles (see Matter of Curry v Hosley, 86 NY2d 470, 475 [1995] ["The possible practical difficulties that might ensue given the few admitted lawyers in Hamilton County cannot override the important legal principle, *applicable throughout the State*, that the nature of the District Attorney's duties and responsibilities to the public require the officeholder to be an attorney"]). The office of district attorney is plainly subject to comprehensive regulation by state law, leaving the counties without authority to legislate in that respect. In this light, we view the limitation on the length of time a district attorney can hold office to be an improper imposition of an additional qualification for the position (see generally U.S. Term Limits, Inc. v Thornton, 514 US 779 [1995]).

Permitting county legislators to impose term limits on the office of district attorney would have the potential to impair the independence of that office because it would empower a local legislative body to effectively end the tenure of an incumbent district attorney whose investigatory or prosecutorial actions were unpopular or contrary to the interests of county legislators. The state has a fundamental and overriding interest in ensuring the integrity and independence of the office of district attorney.

SMITH, J., dissenting.

I dissent, because I see nothing in the State Constitution or any state statute that prevents Suffolk County from imposing a limit on the number of consecutive years that a district attorney may serve. On the contrary, article IX, § 2 (c) (ii) (1) of the Constitution and Municipal Home Rule Law § 10 (1) (ii) (a) (1) empower local governments to adopt local laws relating to the "qualifications" and "terms of office" of their "officers and employees," in the absence of inconsistent state legislation, and no state legislation that is inconsistent with Suffolk County Local Law No. 27-1993 exists.

It is irrelevant that, as the majority notes, a district attorney is "a constitutional officer" as well as a county officer and that the office of district attorney is a subject of statewide concern. These premises lead, at most, to the conclusion that the state has the power to prohibit the limitation of district attorneys' terms—a proposition petitioners do not contest. The issue is whether the state has exercised that power; the majority cites no statute in which it has done so. Nor can it fairly be said that there is a "*necessity* of statewide uniformity" on this issue. No calamity will occur if some counties have term limits for district attorneys and others do not. Perhaps statewide uniformity is desirable, but that is for the state legislature, not this Court, to decide.

TELLI v. BROWARD COUNTY
94 So.3d 504 (Fla. 2012)

PER CURIAM.

This case is before the Court for review of the decision of the Fourth District Court of Appeal in *Snipes v. Telli*, 67 So.3d 415 (Fla. 4th DCA 2011), which held that the Florida Constitution permits Broward County to impose term limits on the office of county commissioner. [W]e approve the Fourth District's decision and hold that Broward County's term limits do not violate Florida's Constitution.

I. BACKGROUND

In 2000, Broward County voters approved an amendment to the Broward County charter providing for term limits on county commissioners. The charter, as amended, limited county commissioners to no more than three consecutive four-year terms:

Effective with the terms of the Commissioners that commenced in November 2000, an individual shall not be eligible for election as a Commissioner for more than three consecutive four-year terms. Service as a Commissioner prior to the terms that commenced in November 2000 shall not be considered in applying the term limitations of this Section. Service of a two-year term, or any other partial term subsequent to November 2000, shall not be considered in applying the term limitation provisions of this Section.

In February 2010, William Telli filed a complaint against Broward County for declaratory relief, arguing that the term limits were unconstitutional under the Florida Constitution. The [trial court] found that this Court's decision[s] required a determination that Broward County's term limits for commissioners were unconstitutional. The Fourth District [Court of Appeals] reversed the circuit court's judgment.

II. ANALYSIS

Provisions throughout the Florida Constitution impose or specifically delegate imposition of "qualifications" for specific offices.[1] But in *Cook v. City of Jacksonville*, 823 So.2d 86 (Fla. 2002), this Court held that term limit provisions imposed disqualifications from office, and that article VI, section 4, of the Florida Constitution, entitled "Disqualifications," "provides the exclusive roster of those disqualifications which may be permissibly imposed." Article VI, section 4, provides:

(a) No person convicted of a felony, or adjudicated in this or any other state to be mentally incompetent, shall be qualified to vote or hold office until restoration of civil rights or removal of disability.

(b) No person may appear on the ballot for re-election to any of the following offices:

(1) Florida representative,

(2) Florida senator,

(3) Florida Lieutenant governor, [or]

(4) any office of the Florida cabinet, [2]

if, by the end of the current term of office, the person will have served (or, but for resignation, would have served) in that office for eight consecutive years.

At the time article VI was amended to include section 4(b), separate constitutional provisions already imposed term limits on the governor, art. IV, § 5(b), and age limits on justices and judges, art. V., § 8. Not allowing Broward County in this case to decide whether its county commissioners

---

[1] [3] See, e.g., art. II, § 5, Fla. Const. (public officers); art. III, §§ 5, 15, Fla. Const. (legislators); art. IV, § 5, Fla. Const. (governor, lieutenant governor, and cabinet members), art. IV, § 8, Fla. Const. (Parole and Probation Commission); art. V, § 8, Fla. Const. (justices and judges); art. V, § 12(a), Fla. Const. (Judicial Qualifications Commission); art. V, § 18, Fla. Const. (public defenders).

[2] [4] Subsections (5) and (6), imposing the same term limits on U.S. Representatives and Senators from Florida, have been omitted. This Court's decision in Ray v. Mortham, 742 So.2d 1276 (Fla.1999), severed subsections (5) and (6) and rendered them unenforceable as violative of the Qualifications Clause of the Tenth Amendment to the United States Constitution.

should be subject to term limits brings into focus the broad implication of the Court's prior ruling in *Cook*, and the limitation it has on the exercise of Florida counties' home rule power as authorized by the Florida Constitution.

In *Cook*, this Court reviewed two consolidated cases in which county charters were amended to impose term limits on, among other officers, those county officers listed in article VIII, section 1(d), of the Florida Constitution: sheriff, tax collector, property appraiser, supervisor of elections, and clerk of the circuit court. This Court in *Cook* ... conclude[ed] that the county charter-imposed term limits on those offices were unconstitutional:

> [A]rticle VI, section 4, Florida Constitution, provides the only disqualifications which may be imposed upon offices authorized by the constitution. Clearly, by virtue of article VI, section 4(b), the Florida Constitution contemplates that term limits may be permissibly imposed upon certain offices authorized by the constitution. By the constitution identifying the offices to which a term limit disqualification applies, we find that it necessarily follows that the constitutionally authorized offices not included in article VI, section 4(b), may not have a term limit disqualification imposed. If these other constitutionally authorized offices are to be subject to a term limit disqualification, the Florida Constitution will have to be amended to include those offices.

This Court further noted in *Cook* that the "the broad authority granted to charter counties" does not include the authority to impose additional "disqualifications which pertain to these offices authorized by the constitution."

Justice Anstead dissented. He analyzed the broad home rule authority granted ... under the Florida Constitution:

> This broad language was obviously intended to allow charter counties wide latitude in acting regulations governing the selection and duties of county officers.... The term limit provisions in the charters in these cases are not inconsistent with any provision of general law relating to elected county officers. Given this grant of broad authority and consistency with general law, I can find no legal justification for concluding that charter counties should not be allowed to ask their citizens to vote on eligibility requirements of local elected officials, including term limits, since they could abolish the offices completely or decide to select the officers in any manner of their choosing.

Justice Anstead also disagreed with the majority's position that article VI, section 4(b), Florida Constitution, listing the state elected offices with mandatory term limits, somehow excluded charter counties from imposing term limits. He pointed out that there was "no wording in article VI, section 4(b) (or anywhere else in the Florida Constitution or the Florida Statutes) that indicates that the named officers in article VI, section 4(b) are subject to term limits *to the exclusion of all other government officers, state or local*, in the State of Florida." The "disqualification" distinction was not persuasive to him because regardless of whether it is called a "qualification" or "disqualification," it determines whether someone will hold office. "[T]he reference to term limits as a 'disqualification' cannot logically be stretched to mean that the absence of a reference to county offices in article VI, section 4(b) *precludes* term limits from being enacted at the county level." *Ah Feas*

This Case

The implied prohibition in *Cook* against term limits for county officers and county commissioners from the lack of inclusion in article VI, section 4, of the Florida Constitution overly restricts the authority of counties pursuant to their home rule powers under the Florida Constitution. Because we now agree with Justice Anstead's dissenting opinion, and recede from *Cook*, we need not reach the issue of whether the office of county commissioner is one of those constitutional offices to which *Cook* applies.

Holding: Cook overly restricts

Policy: Cook undermined county authority

In this case, the prior opinion in *Cook* undermines the ability of counties to govern themselves as that broad authority has been granted to them by home rule power through the Florida Constitution. Interpreting Florida's Constitution to find implied restrictions on powers otherwise authorized is unsound in principle.

Receding from the *Cook* decision will promote stability in the law by allowing the counties to govern themselves, including term limits of their officials, in accordance with their home rule authority. Because the qualifying deadlines have not occurred, there are no reliance issues implicated by this ruling.

III. CONCLUSION

Based on the foregoing, we recede from *Cook* and the rationale it relied upon .... Therefore, we hold that the term limits provided in Broward County's charter do not violate the Florida Constitution ...., and approve the Fourth District on different grounds.

LORTON v. JONES
322 P.3d 1051 (Nev. 2014)

Same body but diff positions? Ban applies

HARDESTY, J.

Article 15, Section 3(2) of the Nevada Constitution prohibits an individual from being "elected to any state office or local governing body [if he or she] has served in that office, or at the expiration of his [or her] current term [he or she] will have served, 12 years or more." The parties do not dispute that the "local governing body" of the City of Reno, Nevada, is the city council, which is made up of six council members and the mayor of Reno. The issue we must decide is whether an individual who has served for 12 years or more as a council member is thereafter prohibited, by the limitations imposed under Article 15, Section 3(2), from running for mayor of Reno. Because the Reno City Charter makes the mayor a member of the city's "local governing body" for all purposes, we conclude that Article 15, Section 3(2) bars a term-limited council member from thereafter being elected mayor of Reno.

BACKGROUND

The City of Reno is a municipal corporation, organized and existing under the laws of the State of Nevada through a charter approved by the Legislature. Under the Reno City Charter, the legislative power of the city is vested in the city council, which consists of six city council members and the mayor. The mayor and one of the city council members represent the city at large, while the remaining city council members each represent one of Reno's five wards.

In this matter, real party in interest Jessica Sferrazza served on the Reno city council as the representative for Ward 3 for 12 years, ending in 2012. Real party in interest Dwight Dortch is currently serving on the Reno city council as the representative for Ward 4. When his term ends in 2014, he will also have served on the city council for 12 years. Both Sferrazza and Dortch have publicly expressed an intention to run for mayor of Reno in the 2014 election.

Petitioner George "Eddie" Lorton, a citizen of Reno who also intends to run for mayor, filed this writ petition seeking extraordinary relief preventing respondents Reno City Clerk Lynette Jones and Washoe County Registrar and Chief Elections Officer Dan Burk from taking the steps necessary to include either Sferrazza or Dortch on the 2014 ballot for the mayoral race. Lorton asserts that both Sferrazza and Dortch are ineligible to run for mayor under Article 15, Section 3(2) of the Nevada Constitution by virtue of their 12 years of service as city council members.

DISCUSSION

Article 15, Section 3(2) of the Nevada Constitution provides, in full, that

> No person may be elected to any state office or local governing body who has served in that office, or at the expiration of his [or her] current term if he [or she] is so serving will have served, 12 years or more, unless the permissible number of terms or duration of service is otherwise specified in this Constitution.

It is undisputed that, under this provision, an individual may not serve in the same state office or position on a local governing body for more than 12 years. The question here is, when a local governing body includes multiple positions, such as when a city council is made up of both city council members and the city's mayor, does Article 15, Section 3(2) also prevent an individual who has served for 12 years in one position on that local governing body from then serving additional terms in a different position on the same body?

Article 15, Section 3(2)

Article 15, Section 3(2) states that "[n]o person may be elected to any state office or local governing body who has served in *that office*" for 12 years or more. Nev. Const. art. 15, § 3(2) (emphasis added). In this context, the word "*that*" is used to modify the general term "*office*" in order to refer to a particular office. Specifically, "that office" appears to refer to both the term "state office" and the phrase "local governing body." Put differently, the sentence may properly be read as saying that "[n]o person may be elected to any state office ... who has served in that office" for 12 years or more, and that "[n]o person may be elected to any ... local governing body who has served in that office" for 12 years or more.

As to a state office, the effect of Article 15, Section 3(2) is clear insofar as the word "office" is used in both parts of the phrase. So if a person has served in a particular state office for 12 years or more, that person may not serve any additional terms in that specific state office. The effect of the portion of the provision referring to a "local governing body" is less clear because the words "office" and "local governing body" have different meanings, as an "office" is "[a] position of duty, trust, or authority, esp[ecially] one conferred by a governmental authority for a public purpose," *Black's Law Dictionary* 1190 (9th ed.2009), while a "governing body" refers to "[a] group of ... officers or persons having ultimate control."

Context within Article 15, Section 3(2)

Before looking outside the language of the provision, we note that, although the text is ambiguous, the drafters' word choice may still provide some indications as to the proper interpretation of the provision. On this point, it is significant that the drafters chose to use different terms in addressing how term limits apply in state and local elections by saying that a person may not be elected to a "state office or local governing body." *See* Antonin Scalia & Bryan A. Garner, *Reading Law: The Interpretation of Legal Texts* 170 (2012). To illustrate, the drafters could have used "state governing body" and "local governing body" to indicate the bodies as a whole. Or they could have used "state office" and "local office" to refer to individual positions. Instead, they chose the distinct terms "state office" and "local governing body," which indicates that, at the state level, the drafters intended to prevent election to a specific office, but at the local level, the intent was to preclude continuing service on the governing body generally.

Purpose and public policy

Outside of the text, the purpose of the provision and public policy are relevant to our interpretation of Article 15, Section 3(2), and these considerations further support the conclusion that the limitations apply to the local governing body as a whole. Article 15, Section 3(2)'s limitations provision was enacted by the voters through the ballot initiative process following its approval at the 1994 and 1996 elections. When the question was presented to voters, the proponents stated that its purpose was to "stop career politicians" by preventing them from holding office for an excessive number of terms. Nevada Ballot Questions 1994, 1996, Nevada Secretary of State, Question No. 9. The objective of limiting career politicians in order to promote a government of citizen representatives has been recognized as a legitimate state interest validating the imposition of term limits.

With regard to city council members, prohibiting reelection to the "local governing body" as a whole is in line with this goal given that a local governing body may be made up of members who represent different wards, and thus arguably hold different offices, but whose roles are essentially the same. In light of this structure, prohibiting a city council member who is term limited in one ward from being elected to what is essentially the same position in a different ward serves the purpose of preventing one person from holding the same political position for excessive years.

Sferrazza and Dortch argue that this purpose would not be undermined under their interpretation of Article 15, Section 3(2) because their interpretation would not allow a council member to serve for more than 12 years by representing multiple wards. They say that this is so because the council members collectively serve in one office within the city council, while the mayor serves in a separate office on that body. Building on this foundation, Sferrazza's counsel asserted at oral argument that Article 15, Section 3(2) is "office based," in that it precludes reelection to the same office, as opposed to being "body based" and precluding reelection to the body as a whole. But as discussed above, Article 15, Section 3(2) does not say that a term-limited individual is precluded from reelection to "an office on a local governing body." Instead, it says that the person may not be reelected to the "local governing body."

In further evaluating the "office based" versus "body based" distinction, the term-limits provisions related to the Nevada Legislature provide helpful context. In particular, Article 4, Section 3(2) of the Nevada Constitution provides that "[n]o person may be elected or appointed as a member of the Assembly who has served in that Office ... 12 years or more, *from any district of this State*." Similarly, Article 4, Section 4(2) states that "[n]o person may be elected or appointed as a Senator who has served in that Office ... 12 years or more, *from any district of this State*." In these two provisions, "that office" refers to the office of "member of the Assembly" and the office of "Senator," respectively. In the absence of clarifying language, these provisions could have been interpreted to mean that a Senator representing a specific district could not serve for more than 12 years as the representative of that district. But the drafters included the phrase "from any district of this state" to preclude any question as to whether the provisions prevented reelection only to the specific seat or to the Assembly or Senate respectively. While Article 15, Section 3(2) does not include the same language as Article 4, Section 3(2) and Article 4, Section 4(2), it does provide that the person may not be elected to the "local governing body," again indicating an intent to preclude election to the body as a whole, which is consistent with the term-limit provisions governing elections to the Legislature.

Based on these considerations, we conclude that the drafters intended to preclude reelection to the local governing body as a whole when a member has served on that body for 12 years or more in any capacity. Thus, the question that remains is whether the mayor of Reno is sufficiently distinct from the city council to preclude application of Article 15, Section 3(2) to council members who may seek to run for mayor.

Article 15, Section 11 and the Reno City Charter

In construing constitutional provisions, we must read those provisions in harmony with each other whenever possible. Under Article 15, Section 11 of the Nevada Constitution, the provisions of a legally adopted charter control with regard to "the tenure of office or the dismissal from office" of any municipal officer or employee. Reading that provision in conjunction with Article 15, Section 3(2), this court must give effect to any charter provisions that shed light on the extent to which the mayor is part of the local governing body, and thus, is subject to Article 15, Section 3(2)'s limitations. As a result, we must look to the Reno City Charter in order to determine whether, in Reno, a council member who has served for 12 years or more is precluded from being elected as the mayor of Reno.

Notably, the Reno City Charter states that the city council is Reno's governing body. And the charter expressly provides that the mayor is a member of the city council, which in turn means that the mayor is a member of the local governing body. We recognize that the mayor is identified in the charter as a separate elective officer from the other six council members, and that the mayor has additional duties that do not fall on the other council members. But these additional responsibilities do not divest the mayor of his or her full and equal membership on the city council.

Furthermore, a review of the charter demonstrates that the mayor's primary function relates to his or her service on the city council. The mayor of Reno is not the chief executive and administrative officer, as that role is filled by the city manager, *see* Reno City Charter, Art. III, §

3.020(1), and the mayor has no administrative duties. The mayor is the head of the city government for ceremonial purposes only. While the Reno City Charter may assign additional duties to the Reno mayor, none of those added duties change the equality of all of the members of the city council or provide a basis for the unequal application of the limitations provision to all members of the "local governing body."

Thus, based on the provisions of the Reno City Charter, we conclude that the Reno mayor is a member of the "local governing body," subject to the same limitations that apply to the other city council members. Accordingly, because Sferrazza and Dortch each will have served on the Reno city council for 12 years by the end of the current term, they are ineligible to be elected as Reno's mayor.

SAITTA, J., with whom PARRAGUIRRE, J., agrees, dissenting,

I would deny the petition for a writ of mandamus or prohibition. Although the majority frames the issue in terms of whether Article 15, Section 3(2) of the Nevada Constitution prohibits reelection to a local governing body as a whole, the effect of the court's conclusion is to find that the Reno mayor is essentially just a seventh city council member with a few minor additional responsibilities thrown in to his or her job description. This conclusion gives short shrift to both the language of the constitutional provision and the role of the Reno mayor. To reach its result, the court focuses on the "local governing body" language and discounts the phrase "that office." To me, it is the "that office" language that determines the provision's operation here.

The majority recognizes that its governing body-based interpretation necessitates construing "that office" to mean either "that local governing body" or "any office within that local governing body." Such a construction, however, is contrary to our well-established rules of construction, which charge this court with giving words their usual and natural meaning. A "governing body," on the other hand, encompasses a group of officers. Thus, an office cannot be equated to a governing body. Moreover, the drafters used the word "that" to modify the word "office," which demonstrates that the phrase "that office" refers to a specific office, not to any particular governing body as a whole. Undeniably, the words "that office," as used in Article 15, Section 3(2), cannot be read as meaning "that local governing body" or "any office within that local governing body."

As used in Article 15, Section 3(2), "that office" identifies the specific position that the person at issue has held for 12 or more years. And for the phrase to have any significance within the term-limits provision, "that office" must be the office to which the person is ineligible for election.

Here, the Reno City Charter explains that the Reno city council is made up of two separate elective offices: mayor and city council member. In this context, no one disputes that the six city council members all hold the same office, that of city councilman or city councilwoman. Indeed, the charter does not distinguish them from one another and they are all granted the same duties and powers.   *fair counter*

But the mayor is different. The mayor is elected to the office of mayor, not to the office of city council member. Bob Cashell is formally recognized as Mayor Cashell, not Councilman Cashell. Further, the mayor's responsibilities are set out distinctly in the part of the charter governing the executive department, Reno City Charter, Art. III, § 3.010(1), while the city council members' duties are included in the article governing the legislative department. And unlike the council members, the mayor is the public figurehead of the Reno city government.

Quite significantly, the mayor alone is charged with protecting the public peace and suppressing riots, and section 3.010(1)(f) authorizes him or her to declare emergencies and empowers the mayor to take immediate protective actions such as establishing a curfew, barricading streets and roads, and redirecting funds for emergency use. And finally, the mayor is responsible for appointing certain commission and committee members. These duties are among those that set the mayor apart from the six city council members, establishing the office of mayor as a separate and distinct office. As a result, a person who has served for 12 years as a city council member has not served in the office of mayor, and thus, is not precluded by Article 15, Section 3(2) from holding "that office."

NOTES

1. Probably more state cases uphold term limits than strike them down. For other examples of such litigation, see *Massey v. Secretary of State*, 579 N.W.2d 862 (Mich. 1998) (upholding Michigan term limits); *Bailey v. County of Shelby*, 188 S.W.3d 539 (Tenn. 2006) (upholding term limits imposed on county officials); *Child v. Lomax*, 188 P.3d 1103 (Nev. 2008).

2. Should it matter how the term limits are imposed? In some states, it has been done by constitutional amendment, whether by popular initiative or otherwise, while in others it has been done by statute.

3. Do term limits make more sense for certain officials but perhaps not others? For example, are the arguments for or against term limits stronger depending on whether the limited officials are state legislators, state-wide executive officers such as the governor, attorney general, or secretary of state, or local officials such as county or city commissioners, or even local mayors?

4. Should some officials be "off limits" in this context? What about state judges? Colorado had a vigorous public debate several years ago and defeated a proposal to limit the terms of state judges.

5. Can you identify the policy arguments in favor of and against term limits?

C. EXECUTIVE POWER

1. The Selection and Organization of the Executive

The federal constitution deposits all executive authority in the President of the United States. As a result, the President nominates his cabinet members, including the Attorney General, the Secretary of State, and the Secretary of the Treasury. In a real sense, this is a "unitary" executive model, because the President retains control over the important executive branch officials. As one legal scholar recently observed, "[m]any states, however, have diverged from the federal model by having other elected statewide officials, particularly an independently elected state attorney general. Which model is better: the federal or the state? Is a unitary executive optimal in a democracy like ours, or would an unbundled plural executive be better?" Steven G. Calabresi, *The Fatally Flawed Theory of the Unbundled Executive*, 93 Minn. L. Rev. 1696, 1697 (2009).

Thus, although the executive power in the States is often the same or similar to the power exercised in the federal system (with some potentially significant exceptions such as line item veto power, which is addressed in the next section), it is frequently exercised by multiple state officials all of whom are elected, with the result that such officials are not necessarily beholden to the Governor nor subject to the Governor's control and supervision. Indeed, it is quite common for a state to elect its Attorney General, its Secretary of State, and its Treasurer. Such a system obviously can at times lead to conflict between the Governor and these officials. Further complicating the situation, in many states these elected executive officials may to some extent be subject to the will and supervision of the legislature, rather than the Governor, and in some instances may by statute or constitution supersede the Governor's power in some respects.

For example, in some states, the Attorney General may be required to take particular legal action at the direction of the Legislature. Indeed, a legislature may even direct the Attorney General to sue the Governor! *See, e.g., State of Kansas ex rel. Stephan v. Finney*, 836 P.2d 1169) (Kan. 1992) (at the legislature's direction, the Attorney General sued the Governor in a mandamus action in the state supreme court seeking a determination whether the Governor had the constitutional authority to enter into a binding gaming compact with an Indian tribe without approval of the legislature).

Also, in states that elect their Attorney General, it is quite typical that the Attorney General alone (to the exclusion of the Governor) has the constitutional authority to represent the State in court proceedings. Thus, a Governor may even be forced to hire or retain separate counsel to assert the Governor's position in a particular matter in a case of conflict with the Attorney General.

Further, many states do not follow anything like the federal constitution's distinctions between "principal" and "inferior" executive officers, with the corresponding consequence that many executive officials who would be appointed by the President in the federal system are not appointed at all or at least are not appointed by the Governor, nor are many state appointments (such as to the state supreme court) subject to some kind of legislative confirmation process, in contrast to the federal system that requires Senate confirmation of all Article III judges.

The issues here are numerous and sometimes complex, and the variations among states are significant. Our purpose in this section is only to highlight the fact that the executive powers may be exercised by different officials in the States than would be the case in the federal system, with some resulting complications (such as pitting the Governor against the Attorney General) that do not arise in the federal system. One example of such complexities follows.

PERDUE v. BAKER
586 S.E.2d 606 (Ga. 2003)

FLETCHER, C.J.

Governor Sonny Perdue filed a petition for writ of mandamus seeking to compel Attorney General Thurbert Baker to dismiss an appeal filed on behalf of the State of Georgia in a case involving legislative reapportionment under the Voting Rights Act. The trial court denied the Governor's petition, ruling that the Attorney General had exclusive authority to decide whether to continue the State's efforts to enforce a law enacted by the General Assembly and signed by the Governor. The issue presented here is whether the Attorney General has the authority under state law to appeal a court decision invalidating a state redistricting statute despite the Governor's order to dismiss the appeal. Because there is constitutional authority for the General Assembly to vest the Attorney General with specific duties and a state statute vested the Attorney General with the authority to litigate in the voting rights action, we hold that the Attorney General had the power to seek a final determination on the validity of the State Senate redistricting statute under the federal Voting Rights Act.

PRIOR PROCEEDINGS

Following the 2000 decennial census, the General Assembly enacted a bill that reapportioned State Senate districts and Governor Roy Barnes signed the bill into law…. The State then filed a civil action in the United States District Court for the District of Columbia seeking preclearance of the Senate redistricting plan under Section 5 of the Voting Rights Act, a prerequisite to enforcing the law. The State sought a declaratory judgment that the plan did not have the purpose or effect of "'denying or abridging the right to vote on account of race or color' or membership in a language minority group." Denying the State's request for a declaratory judgment, the district court held that the State failed to meet its burden of proof under Section 5 that the State Senate redistricting plan did not have a retrogressive effect on the voting strength of African-American voters in Georgia. It denied preclearance.

The General Assembly enacted a revised Senate redistricting plan, Act 444, and the State submitted the new plan to the district court for preclearance. In June 2002, the three-judge district court approved the revised Senate redistricting plan. Act 444, which was not codified into law, expressly provides that its senatorial districts are contingent and shall take effect only if the original Senate redistricting plan cannot lawfully be implemented under the federal Voting Rights Act. To obtain a final determination, the Attorney General filed a direct appeal in July 2002 to the United States Supreme Court challenging the federal district court's order rejecting the original Senate redistricting plan. The Supreme Court granted review in January 2003.

Ten days later, soon after being installed into office, Governor Perdue requested that Attorney General Baker dismiss the appeal. The Governor contended that the Georgia Constitution vests his office with the chief executive powers to dismiss an appeal pending in the U.S. Supreme Court when the State of Georgia is the sole-named appellant. The Attorney General disagreed, citing constitutional provisions that vest his office with exclusive authority in all legal matters related to the executive branch in state government. Faced with this refusal, the Governor sought a writ of mandamus to require the Attorney General to dismiss the pending appeal in the Supreme Court.

ALLOCATION OF EXECUTIVE POWERS

1. Both the Governor and Attorney General are elected constitutional officers in the executive branch of state government, which is responsible for enforcing state statutes. The Georgia Constitution provides that the

Governor is vested with the chief executive powers. Among those powers is the responsibility to see that the laws are faithfully executed. Other executive officers, including the Attorney General, are vested with the powers prescribed by the constitution and by law. The constitution states that the Attorney General "shall act as the legal advisor of the executive department, shall represent the state in the Supreme Court in all capital felonies and in all civil and criminal cases in any court when required by the Governor, and shall perform such other duties as shall be required by law."

Within the executive branch, both the Governor and Attorney General have statutory authority to direct litigation on behalf of the State of Georgia. Under the State Government Reorganization Act of 1931, which established the Department of Law, the Governor "shall have power to direct the Department of Law, through the Attorney-General as head thereof, to institute and prosecute in the name of the State such matters, proceedings, and litigations as he shall deem to be in the best interest of the people of the State." The Governor also has the power to provide for the defense of any action in which the State has an interest.

OCGA § 45-15-3 sets out the Attorney General's general responsibilities. It repeats his constitutional duties to serve as the executive branch's legal adviser, represent the State in all capital felony appeals, and represent the State in all civil and criminal actions when required by the Governor; it further provides that the Attorney General may give written legal opinions to state departments on request and prepare all state contracts when advisable. Of primary relevance in this case are the last two duties specified in the code section. Subsection (6) gives the Attorney General independent authority to represent the State in any civil action without the Governor's request: "It is the duty of the Attorney General...[t]o represent the state in all civil actions tried in any court." The final subsection is a catch-all phrase similar to the language in the constitution, giving the Attorney General authority to perform "other services as shall be required of him by law."

Construed together, these constitutional provisions and statutes do not vest either officer with the exclusive power to control legal proceedings involving the State of Georgia. Instead, these provisions suggest that the Governor and Attorney General have concurrent powers over litigation in which the State is a party. Both executive officers are empowered to make certain that state laws are faithfully enforced; both may decide to initiate legal proceedings to protect the State's interests; both may ensure that the State's interests are defended in legal actions; and both may institute investigations of wrongdoing by state agencies and officials. Thus, they share the responsibility to guarantee that the State vigorously asserts and defends its interests in legal proceedings.

As a result, we reject the broader claim by each officer that he has the ultimate authority to decide what is in the best interest of the people of the State in every lawsuit involving the State of Georgia. By giving both the Governor and Attorney General the responsibility for enforcing state law, the drafters of our constitutions and the General Assembly have made it less likely that the State will fail to forcefully prosecute or defend its interests in a court of law or other legal proceeding. This overlapping responsibility is also consistent with the existing practice in state government. Most important, it provides a system of checks and balances within the executive branch so that no single official has unrestrained power to decide what laws to enforce and when to enforce them.

We also reject the dissent's narrow characterization of the Attorney General's role as merely that of legal counsel to the Governor. To imply that the Georgia Rules of Professional Conduct control the Attorney General's relationship to the Governor ignores the important and independent role assigned to the Attorney General under our constitution. Accepting the dissent's argument would eviscerate the Attorney General's separate constitutional role.

The State of Georgia is not one branch of government, one office, or one officer. The State's authority resides with the people who elect many officers with different responsibilities under valid law.

2. Our conclusion that both officers have the duty to enforce state laws is consistent with the language and legislative history of article V of the 1983 Georgia Constitution. The first paragraph on the Governor's duties and powers in the Executive Article states the following: "The chief executive powers shall be vested in the Governor. The other executive officers shall have such powers as may be prescribed by this Constitution and by law."

The Committee to Revise Articles IV and V intended for this paragraph to explain the allocation of powers within the executive branch of state government. First, the drafters wanted to provide a clear statement that the Governor was the chief executive in relationship to other executive officers, both elected and appointed. This clarification was necessary to address the past assertions of some constitutional officers that as elected officers they were not subject to the Governor's power. Second, the drafters wanted to indicate that the Governor had not only express powers, but also had reserved powers. Finally, the drafters wanted to ensure that the Governor did not possess unlimited authority over other executive officers. Immediately after granting executive powers to the Governor, the 1983 Constitution places a restraint on those powers: it grants to the other executive officers "such powers as may be prescribed by this Constitution and by law." This provision means that the other constitutionally elected officers possess powers granted to them by the constitution and other laws.

3. To support his claim that "the Governor, and the Governor alone" is authorized to make decisions related to litigation filed in the State's name, the Governor relies on the constitutional provision describing the Attorney General's duties and a [statute]. The 1983 Constitution, like all the constitutions since 1868, provides that the Attorney General "shall represent the state ... in all civil and criminal cases in any court when required by the Governor." In addition, OCGA § 45-15-35 vests the Governor with the power to direct the Department of Law to institute and prosecute litigation in the name of the State. The Governor contends that this language means the Attorney General must follow his orders to dismiss or withdraw an appeal in any case regardless of the circumstances.

Contrary to the Governor's contention, we do not read these constitutional or statutory provisions as denying power to the Attorney General in representing the State, but instead interpret them as granting additional power to the Governor. As a result, we decline to address the Governor's contention, adopted by the dissent, that his express right to initiate litigation always includes the implicit right to end any lawsuit. Rather, the dispositive issue is whether any laws of this State grant the Attorney General independent authority to continue the litigation in this case. To decide whether the Governor's powers as chief executive include the absolute right to direct the Attorney General to dismiss the State's appeal, we look to the powers and duties of the Attorney General as prescribed under the Georgia Constitution and statutory law.

[handwritten margin note: the gov's right to initiate doesn't mean a right to end any suit]

THE ATTORNEY GENERAL'S DUTIES

4. The Attorney General is a state executive officer elected at the same time and holding office for the same term as the Governor. As an elected state constitutional officer, the Attorney General has the powers prescribed to him by the 1983 Constitution, statutes, and case law. The General Assembly has given the Attorney General specific authority to act independently on behalf of the State in a variety of civil and criminal cases. For example, the code chapter on the Attorney General empowers that officer to represent the State in all capital felony actions before this Court, prosecute any person for violating a criminal statute while dealing with the State, represent the State in all civil actions in any court, file and prosecute civil recovery actions against any person who violates a statute in dealing with the State, represent the state authorities that are instrumentalities of the State, represent the Comptroller General in collecting or securing any state claim, and represent the State before the United States Supreme Court.

[handwritten margin note: AG's range of independent authority]

In 1975, there were two changes in the law related to the Attorney General's duties that made explicit what had previously been only implicit: the Attorney General has the power to represent the State in civil actions independently of the Governor's direction. First, this Court held in *Coggin v. Davey* that the Attorney General was authorized to represent legislators in legal actions arising out of their official duties in the General Assembly. Three months later, the General Assembly amended Ga.Code Ann. § 40-1602 (OCGA § 45-15-3) to expressly grant the Attorney General the authority to represent the State in civil actions without any request from the Governor. The 1975 amendment was enacted "to clarify the duties of the Attorney General and the circumstances under which the Attorney General shall act at the direction of the Governor." Prior to the amendment, the caption of § 40-1602 describing the Attorney General's duties was entitled "Duties required by Governor." The first sentence began, "It is the duty of the Attorney General when required so to do by the Governor," and then listed six separate duties of the State's chief legal officer. The 1975 amendment deleted the words "by Governor" from the caption, "when required so to do by the Governor" in the first sentence, and "when required by the Governor" in subparagraph 6.

Thus, this 1975 amendment resolved, at least in part, the broader issue of the Attorney General's powers that this Court declined to address in *Coggin v. Davey.* The amended code section provides authority for the Attorney General to represent legislators and other state officials "on his own motion" without any request, requirement, or direction from the Governor. We need not decide, however, the full extent of the Attorney General's power to represent the State under this statute or the circumstances, if any, under which the Governor may compel the Attorney General to end his representation. In this case, a more narrowly drawn statute provides authority for the Attorney General to continue the voting rights litigation despite the Governor's order to dismiss the appeal.

ACT 444

5. Act 444 was enacted after the federal district court had denied preclearance to the original Senate redistricting plan, but before the State filed an appeal of that decision to the U.S. Supreme Court. By its terms, Act 444 expresses the legislature's intent that the original redistricting plan for the State Senate should be followed if allowed by federal law. Section 1(d) states that the original plan's provisions are "suspended" until the State can obtain a final determination on the legality of the original plan under the federal Voting Rights Act. At the time the General Assembly enacted Act 444, the first step in the process for the State to obtain a "final determination" on its ability to enforce the reapportionment

plan under the federal Voting Rights Act was to file a direct appeal with the Supreme Court seeking to reverse the district court's opinion.

As the State's chief legal officer, the Attorney General is the official charged with representing the State in reapportionment cases. Before any change affecting voting qualifications, standards, practices, and procedures may take effect, the State must obtain preclearance of the change under Section 5 of the Voting Rights Act. One way to obtain preclearance is by instituting a declaratory judgment action in the United States District Court for the District of Columbia. If preclearance is declined, the State's only remedy is to file a direct appeal to the United States Supreme Court. OCGA § 45-15-9 provides that the Attorney General "shall represent the State in all actions before the Supreme Court."

Accordingly, after the three-judge court denied preclearance, the Attorney General appealed to the Supreme Court. By appealing, the Attorney General was fulfilling his general duty as chief legal officer to execute state law and his specific duty to defend the reapportionment law as enacted by the General Assembly.

SEPARATION OF POWERS

6. We next consider whether Act 444 violates the doctrine of separation of powers by directing that it takes effect only after a final determination is made regarding the enforceability of the provisions of Act 1EX6 under the Voting Rights Act. Because Act 444 does not impermissibly encroach on the power of the executive branch to control litigation, but instead is a proper assertion of legislative power to determine reapportionment, we conclude that it does not violate separation of powers.

A legislative enactment violates separation of powers when it increases legislative powers at the expense of the executive branch, or when the enactment "'prevent[s] the Executive Branch from accomplishing its constitutionally assigned functions,'" even if it does not increase legislative powers. Thus, this Court must examine the respective roles of the legislative and executive branches and determine whether Act 444 inappropriately intrudes upon executive branch powers and functions.

The core legislative function is the establishment of public policy through the enactment of laws. Thus, the expressed intent of the legislative body to prefer one reapportionment scheme over another is plainly proper and within the sphere of legislative power. Nothing prevents the legislature from expressing this intent through a fallback or contingency provision.

On the other hand, the executive branch generally has the power and authority to control litigation as part of its power to execute the laws, and a law that removes from the executive branch sufficient control of litigation may well violate separation of powers. However, the executive branch does not have the authority to decline to execute a law under the guise of executing the laws: "To contend that the obligation imposed…to see the laws faithfully executed, implies a power to forbid their execution, is a novel construction of the Constitution and entirely inadmissible." The power to forbid the execution of the laws would enable the executive branch to nullify validly enacted statutes. In that situation, the executive branch would encroach upon the legislative power to repeal statutes or upon the judicial branch's power of judicial review. What the executive branch cannot do directly, it cannot do indirectly. Thus, even though the executive branch generally has the power and authority to control litigation, it cannot exercise this power in order to prevent the execution of a law.   *Gov. can't prevent the execution of law.*

Balancing these principles in light of this case, we conclude that the legislature may require an appeal to the U.S. Supreme Court so that the legislature's preferred reapportionment scheme be implemented. The intrusion by the legislature into the executive branch function of control of litigation is justified by the limited nature of the encroachment—pursuit of one case—and by the subject matter of the litigation-legislative reapportionment.

Legislature acting within its bounds

Because the legislative encroachment into the executive power of controlling litigation is limited to carrying out the legislature's chosen reapportionment plan, it does not impermissibly intrude into executive branch functions and does not constitute a separation of powers violation. The dissent's dire prediction of a political and constitutional crisis is possible only because it ignores the uniqueness of legislative reapportionment.

CONCLUSION

The Constitution mandates that the Attorney General perform "such other duties as shall be required by law." Act 444 suspends the operation of the new redistricting provisions "pending a final determination of their enforceability under the federal Voting Rights Act of 1965," which requires federal court resolution. Accordingly, when the Attorney General declined to dismiss the appeal, he was fulfilling a duty required by Act 444. Because the Attorney General was acting consistently with his constitutional and statutory duties, we conclude that the Governor does not have a clear legal right to compel the Attorney General to dismiss the appeal or case from the courts. Therefore, the Governor is not entitled to the writ of mandamus.

2. The "Line Item" Veto Power

In *Clinton v. City of New York*, 524 U.S. 417 (1998), the Supreme Court of the United States struck down an Act of Congress that had been described as giving the President a "line item" veto power, in other words giving the President power to strike or cancel individual items within a bill presented for his signature. The Constitution, art. I, § 7, cl. 2, provides no such power to the President explicitly, but instead declares in the Presentment Clause as follows: "Every Bill which shall have passed the House of Representatives and the Senate, shall, before it becomes a Law, be presented to the President of the United States; If he approve he shall sign it, but if not he shall return it, with his Objections...." The Supreme Court held that the law Congress passed purporting to give the President the power to strike particular items from a bill while permitting the remainder of the bill to become law violated the Presentment Clause.

Interestingly, line item veto powers in state constitutions were not present in the colonial charters but instead appeared much later, notably in the Confederacy's constitution during the Civil War and as late as the 20th century. Well over 40 states now give their Governors such authority. The line item veto provisions vary in their nature and scope, with some being limited only to appropriations measures while others authorize broad line item vetoes regarding any legislation and for any reason. Further, the States' line item veto measures have proven a not infrequent source of litigation between Governors and legislatures or legislators, the latter of whom often have been granted standing by state courts to challenge gubernatorial exercises of the power (contrasted with the Supreme Court of the U.S. which held, prior to *Clinton v. City of New York* that individual members of Congress had no standing to challenge the President's exercise of such authority. *Raines v. Byrd*, 521 U.S. 811 (1997)).

Following are three examples of state court litigation over a Governor's exercise of the line item veto power. Note carefully the contexts in which the disputes arise and the parties.

ST. JOHN'S WELL CHILD AND FAMILY CENTER v. SCHWARZENEGGER
50 Cal.4th 960 (Cal. 2010)

GEORGE, C.J.,

We granted review in this original writ proceeding to address the propriety of the Governor's use of the so-called "line-item veto" under the asserted authority of article IV, section 10, subdivision (e) of the California Constitution, to further reduce funding that already had been reduced by the Legislature in its midyear adjustments to the Budget Act of 2009.

I.

Although the current economic downturn affects all Californians, many persons are particularly vulnerable because they receive essential health and welfare assistance from agencies dependent upon state tax revenues. In this setting, government must choose between and among equally needy groups, knowing that many of those groups not fully funded may be devastated.

In the context of the constitutionally prescribed budget process, the power to *appropriate* public funds belongs exclusively to the Legislature. With respect to a bill containing appropriations, the Governor has three options: (1) to sign the bill, (2) to veto the measure in its entirety (Cal. Const., art. IV, § 10, subd. (a)), or (3) to *"reduce or eliminate one or more items of appropriation"* (*id.*, subd. (e) (hereafter article IV, section 10(e)), italics added). The question posed by this case is whether the Governor exceeded his limited powers under article IV, section 10(e), by using his line-item authority to further reduce funding levels set forth in midyear reductions that the Legislature had made to the Budget Act of 2009, thereby imposing a reduction of appropriated sums greater than the reduction made by the Legislature.

Petitioners include St. John's Well Child and Family Center, a nonprofit network of five community health centers and six school-based clinics in medically underserved areas of Los Angeles County, and other entities and individuals located throughout the state whose programs and lives will be drastically affected by the further reductions here at issue.

Respondents are Arnold Schwarzenegger, the Governor of the State of California, and John Chiang, who, as the Controller of the State of California, is responsible for the administration of the state's finances, including disbursement of funds appropriated by law. The Controller does not take a position on the merits of this litigation.

Interveners are Darrell Steinberg, in his official capacity as President pro Tempore of the California State Senate, and in his personal capacity as a resident and taxpayer of Sacramento County, and John Pérez, in his official capacity as Speaker of the California Assembly. Several amici curiae have filed briefs supporting the various parties.

Petitioners and interveners contend that the action taken by the Governor exceeded constitutional limits, because the individual budget cuts he made were not imposed on "items of appropriation" (art. IV, § 10(e)) that could be individually vetoed or reduced. They further contend that, in taking this action, the Governor purported to exercise authority belonging solely to the Legislature, in violation of article III, section 3 of the California Constitution.

II.

On February 20, 2009, the Governor signed into law the 2009 Budget Act, which set forth various appropriations of state funds for the 2009–2010 fiscal year. Thereafter, California's economy worsened; the revenue assumptions upon which the 2009 Budget Act was based proved to be far too optimistic, and the state's overall cash-flow positions continued to deteriorate. The Governor, pursuant to California Constitution, article IV, section 10, subdivision (f) proclaimed a fiscal crisis, and the Legislature assembled in special session to address the fiscal emergency. Following months of negotiations, the Legislature passed Assembly Bill 4X 1 on July 23, 2009. The final revised budget package enacted as Assembly Bill 4X 1 consisted of 547 pages, set forth in 583 sections, and represented an effort to address more than $24 billion in budget shortfalls, including $15.6 billion in cuts, nearly $4 billion in additional revenues, more than $2 billion in borrowing, approximately $1.5 billion in fund shifts, and more than $1 billion in deferrals and other adjustments.

On July 28, 2009, the Governor exercised his line-item authority to reduce or eliminate several items contained in Assembly Bill 4X 1, and then signed the measure into law. The Governor eliminated numerous separate line items contained in various sections of Assembly Bill 4X 1. The effect of these reductions was to further decrease the total amount appropriated in the 2009 Budget Act by more than $488 million. Many of the items reduced by the Governor already had been reduced by the Legislature in Assembly Bill 4X 1 from the amounts appropriated in the 2009 Budget Act. The Governor's signing message explained that his cuts to the spending bill were for the most part designed "to increase the reserve and to reduce the state's structural deficit."

III.

The question presented by this case as a matter of first impression is whether, after the Legislature has made midyear reductions to appropriations that originally appeared in the 2009 Budget Act, the Governor's line-item power encompasses the authority to make further reductions.

"The California Constitution declares that the legislative power of the state is vested in the Legislature and the executive power [is vested] in the Governor. Unless permitted by the Constitution, the Governor may not exercise legislative powers. He may veto a bill 'by returning it with any objections to the house of origin,' and it will become law only if 'each house then passes the bill by rollcall vote ... two thirds of the membership concurring....' If the Governor fails to act within a certain period of time, the measure becomes law without his signature. The Governor's veto power is more extensive with regard to appropriations. He may 'reduce or *eliminate one or more items of appropriation while approving other portions of a bill.'* Such items may be passed over his veto in the same manner as vetoed bills."

"In California, the Constitution of 1849 included a gubernatorial veto provision similar to that contained in the United States Constitution. The Constitution of 1879 added the item veto power, allowing the Governor to 'object to one or more items' of appropriation in a bill which contained several 'items of appropriation.' By constitutional initiative in 1922, the Governor was empowered *not only to eliminate 'items of appropriation' but to reduce them*, while approving other portions of a bill. The 1922 amendment also directed the Governor to submit a budget to the Legislature containing his recommendation for state expenditures.

Neither the so-called "item veto," nor the "line-item veto" allowing the Governor to eliminate or reduce items of appropriation, confers the power to selectively veto *general* legislation. The Governor has no authority to veto part of a bill that is not an "item of appropriation." "[A]rticle III, section 3 provides that one branch of government may not exercise the powers granted to another 'except as permitted by this Constitution.' Case law, commentators, and historians have long recognized that in exercising the veto the Governor acts in a legislative capacity. It follows that in exercising the power of the veto the Governor may act only as permitted by the Constitution. That authority is to veto a 'bill' or to 'reduce or eliminate one or more items of appropriation.'"

The dispositive issue, then, is whether the funding in question—specified in the seven sections of Assembly Bill 4X 1 that the Governor further reduced—encompassed "items of appropriation" (Cal. Const., art. IV, § 10(e)) as to which the Governor could exercise his line-item authority.

IV.

Petitioners and interveners contend that, because the items at issue in Assembly Bill 4X 1 *reduced* the amounts previously appropriated in the 2009 Budget Act, these items were not "appropriations." They maintain that a "reduction" cannot be an "appropriation," and observe that there are no instances in which a California governor previously has exercised line-item authority in this manner.

B.

Petitioners, interveners, and their amici curiae insist that only an *increase* in spending authority can constitute an appropriation. They emphasize that none of the definitions of "item of appropriation" contained in the cases refer to a *decrease* in the spending authorized by a previously enacted budget, and they maintain that such a reduction may not be deemed an item of appropriation. They further argue that because the 2009 Budget Act *already* had set aside sums of money to be paid by the treasury for specific purposes, those items and the sections of Assembly Bill 4X 1 that proposed only reductions to existing, previously enacted appropriations did not satisfy the requirement of money set aside for a particular purpose. The argument, in other words, is that a reduction in a set-aside cannot itself be considered a set-aside or an appropriation. We disagree.

The cases do not require, as petitioners and interveners suggest, that *solely* items that add amounts to funds already provided can constitute "items of appropriation." ***Whether spending authority is increased or decreased, it still fundamentally remains spending authority. Although described as reductions in specified items and sections, each of the provisions at issue in Assembly Bill 4X 1 nevertheless directs the "specific setting aside of an amount, not exceeding a definite fixed sum, for the payment of certain particular claims or demands." The items in Assembly Bill 4X 1 that were eliminated or further reduced by the Governor's exercise of line-item authority *capped* the spending authority at an amount less than that set forth in the 2009 Budget Act. The Controller could not thereafter disburse, nor could the recipients of the funds thereafter draw upon, any amount larger than that set aside by the Legislature for the specified purposes.

There is no substantive difference between a Governor's reduction of an item of appropriation in the original 2009 Budget Act, to which interveners and petitioners raise no objection, and a Governor's reduction of that same item in a subsequent amendment to the 2009 Budget Act— that is, Assembly Bill 4X 1. Both actions involve changes in authorized spending.

Interveners insist in their reply brief that the Governor was entitled, in essence, to only one bite at the budget apple. They concede that although he "had the authority to reduce or eliminate each of the items of appropriation at issue here when they were first passed in February, 2009," he nevertheless did not possess that same authority a few months later with regard to "the legislative reductions made in July." We discern no reason why the Governor should have the power to reduce items of appropriation when first enacted, and yet not retain that same power when the Legislature, in response to changed circumstances, sees fit to amend those same appropriations.

Adoption of the view advanced by petitioners, interveners, and their amici curiae that the legislative provisions at issue were not "items of appropriation" would permit the Legislature, in a single bill, to selectively make multiple reductions in previous appropriations, leaving the Governor only the power to veto the entire bill—a limitation that the 1922 amendment to article IV of the California Constitution specifically was designed to eliminate. Indeed, as we earlier observed, that amendment was promoted in order to permit the Governor to "*reduce an appropriation to meet the financial needs of the treasury*," and we are unaware of any evidence or authority suggesting that the drafters of that measure and the voters who enacted article IV, section 10(e) intended that the Governor should be precluded from exercising such line-item authority in order to further reduce authorized funding following a legislative act that itself reduced such funding in response to an ongoing and mounting fiscal crisis. Moreover, if spending reductions are not considered to be items of appropriation (and hence are not subject to a two-thirds vote requirement), a simple legislative majority would be able to overturn a two-thirds vote on the annual budget act. We decline to construe the phrase "items of appropriation" in such a manner.

V.

Interveners' contention that the amounts designated by the items of Assembly Bill 4X 1 at issue should not be reducible by the Governor is based in part upon a separation-of-powers theory, also advanced by amici curiae SEIU California State Council et al. This claim is premised upon (1) the absence in California's Constitution of explicit gubernatorial authority to increase or decrease the size of spending cuts made by the Legislature in response to a declaration of fiscal emergency, and (2) language in *Harbor*, *supra*, 742 P.2d 1290, emphasizing that, as interveners put it, "the power to veto, reduce or eliminate is not the power to create or increase." Specifically, interveners cite our observations in *Harbor* that "[t]he word 'veto' means 'I forbid' in Latin" and that "the effect of the veto [is] negative, frustrating an act without substituting anything in its place."

In the view of interveners, when undertaking the challenged line-item reductions, "the Governor sought to use his power to *increase* what the Legislature had done. The Legislature had made a policy determination regarding how much state spending had to be cut in response to the fiscal crisis and where those spending cuts were to be made. The Governor, however, disagreed with the Legislature's policy determinations. He wanted to make *more* cuts in order to keep a larger budget reserve." According to interveners, the Governor's preference for a larger budget reserve is a policy determination belonging to the legislative, not the executive, branch.

The determination whether the items in Assembly Bill 4X 1 at issue constitute appropriations cannot be made by characterizing the Governor's use of line-item authority as "increasing" the Legislature's reductions and then categorizing that act as impermissibly affirmative or "creative." Treating the exercise of line-item authority as an *increase in the reduction*, rather than as a *decrease in the appropriation* is as arbitrary as differentiating between the description of a glass of water as half full and a description of the same vessel as half empty. By increasing the Legislature's reduction, the Governor decreases the size of the appropriation. What matters is not whether the Governor's act is seen as being affirmative or negative, but rather its purpose and practical effect.

Interveners' separation-of-powers argument thus begs the question. True, the Governor's challenged acts were legislative in nature and, "[a]s an executive officer, [the Governor] is forbidden to exercise any legislative power or function *except as the Constitution expressly provide*[*s*]." Thus, the question before us is not whether the gubernatorial act at issue was legislative in nature, but whether it was constitutionally authorized. As we earlier explained, the act undertaken by the Governor was authorized by the opening sentence of article IV, section 10(e) of our Constitution: "The Governor may reduce or eliminate one or more *items of appropriation* while approving other portions of a bill." (Italics added.)

Similarly, as discussed above, we conclude there is no persuasive reason to hold that the Governor is prevented from exercising line-item authority with respect to *changes* that the Legislature has made to items of appropriation. [T]he Governor's line-item power does not give him the last word. The Legislature retains the ability to override the Governor's reduction of items of appropriation in the same manner as other bills, by separately reconsidering and passing them by a two-thirds majority of each house.

JACKSON v. SANDFORD
398 S.C. 580 (2011)

KITTREDGE, J.

Petitioner Darrick Jackson, Mayor of the Town of Timmonsville, brought this action seeking a declaratory judgment in the Court's original jurisdiction that Governor Sanford's veto of certain appropriations to the State Budget and Control Board was unconstitutional.

I.

The annual appropriations bill for fiscal year 2010–2011 allocated $248,882,042 to the State Budget and Control Board ("the Board"), $25,234,009 of which was to be drawn from the General Fund. Some of the Board's expenditures were to be financed entirely from the General Fund, while other expenditures were financed using other sources or a combination of sources. The bill set aside the amounts to be drawn from the General Fund in a separate column. In another column, the bill listed the total appropriation for each expenditure, reflecting both General Funds and funds from other sources. The bill did not include separate columns delineating the amounts to be drawn from each of the other sources.

In his Veto 52, Governor Sanford purported to veto the entire amount of General Funds appropriated to the Board. In his accompanying veto message, Governor Sanford stated the Board had "over $1 billion in carry-forward funds" and could use "available funds and ... cost-cutting measures" to "sustain [the] agency ... over the next fiscal year." The House of Representatives sustained this veto.

Petitioner brought this action seeking a declaratory judgment that the Governor's Veto was invalid ....

II.

Article IV, section 21 of the South Carolina Constitution provides in relevant part:

> Every bill or joint resolution which shall have passed the General Assembly ... shall, before it becomes a law, be presented to the Governor, and if he approves he shall sign it; if not, he shall return it, with his objections, to the house in which it originated, which shall enter the objections at large on its Journal and proceed to reconsider it....

> Bills appropriating money out of the Treasury shall specify the objects and purposes for which the same are made, and appropriate to them respectively their several amounts in distinct items and sections. If the Governor shall not approve any one or more of the items or sections contained in any bill appropriating money, but shall approve of the residue thereof, it shall become a law as to the residue in like manner as if he had signed it. The Governor shall then return the bill with his objections to the items or sections of the same not approved by him to the house in which the bill originated, which house shall enter the objections at large upon its Journal and proceed to reconsider so much of the bill as is not approved by the Governor....

"The veto power can be exercised only when clearly authorized by the constitution, and the language conferring it is to be strictly construed." The veto power is "a negative power to void a distinct item. In *Drummond v. Beasley*, we explained that the Governor may not "modify legislation rather than nullify legislation" by removing conditions and restrictions on expenditures while leaving the expenditures themselves intact. The Florida Supreme Court has explained:

> [T]he veto power is intended to be a negative power, the power to nullify ... legislative intent. It is not designed to alter or amend legislative intent.... [T]he veto must, in effect, destroy the fund. Otherwise, the governor could legislate by altering the purpose for which the money was allocated.

We apply a "common sense construction" when interpreting the General Assembly's obligation to organize appropriation bills into "distinct items or sections" and when interpreting the power of the Governor to veto such "items or sections."

III.

The dispositive question before the Court may be framed in one of two ways, either of which compels a finding of an unconstitutional veto. First, a Governor is constitutionally permitted to veto an item in its entirety, but not partially. Stated differently, we must determine whether Veto 52 was a nullification of legislation or a modification of legislation. Putting these concepts together, the rule of law is that a veto of an item in its entirety is a nullification, while a veto of only part of an item is a modification. If a nullification, Veto 52 is constitutional; if a modification, Veto 52 is unconstitutional.

Rule

We begin with defining an "item" for constitutional purposes. Our constitution uses the term "item" to embrace a specified sum of money together with the "object and purpose" for which the appropriation is made. Our case law is in accord. Other jurisdictions have employed similar definitions for the term "item."

Petitioner's first argument focuses on the spatial format of the appropriations bill into *columns* as opposed to *lines*. Petitioner contends the Governor could veto only *lines* of an appropriation bill, not *columns*. This argument appears to be premised on the notion of a Governor's "line item veto." To be sure, the phrase "line item veto" has currency as a colloquial expression, but it is not part of our constitutional framework. Our constitution permits the Governor to veto "items or sections" of bills that appropriate money, but it does not require that these items or sections be organized into lines. Thus, we reject Petitioner's argument and agree with the Governor that the spatial arrangement of numbers on the page does not dictate the definition of an "item."

line v column

"spatial" considerations gotta go

While we agree that the arrangement of information in a column, rather than in a line, is irrelevant, we disagree with Governor Sanford and Respondent Eckstrom that the column designating the amount of General Funds to be expended was a standalone "item" that could be vetoed without vetoing the objects and purposes to which those General Funds were devoted. The Governor vetoed one source of appropriated funds while leaving the remainder of the total appropriation, and the specified "objects and purposes" of the appropriation, intact.

The Governor attempted to veto funds arising from a particular source, but he did not veto the purpose to which those funds were allocated. The net result, then, was that the total appropriation for each of the Board's programs, positions, and expenses was reduced by the amount the General Assembly had designated to be drawn from the General Fund, but the

How the veto impacted funds

programs, positions, and expenses themselves were not eliminated. This was an improper modification of legislation.

The net effect of Veto 52 was a veto of *part* of an item, resulting in modification of legislation, which is an unconstitutional exercise of the veto power.*** The Governor seeks refuge in the contention that Veto 52 is consistent with the historical practice of South Carolina Governors. Because other Governors have exercised their veto authority in a similar manner, the argument goes, the Court should defer to the historical practice. The Governor's position has ostensible merit, for "[l]ong established practice has great weight in interpreting constitutional provision[s] relative to executive veto power." However, we are not persuaded that the practice of vetoing only one of several sources of funds without vetoing the corresponding objects and purposes is as well rooted in our history as the Governor suggests. The Governor cites in his brief to vetoes in 1935 and 1948 as similar to Veto 52. We do not read the cited 1935 and 1948 vetoes as similar. The acts at issue did not list General Funds separately from any other funds. These examples and others present vetoes of the total funding and the corresponding objects and purposes. Thus, we are not convinced that the interpretation advanced by the Governor is as "long established" as he contends. In any event, a veto of only one of several sources of funds is patently in conflict with the Governor's authority under our constitution.

IV.

We find the Governor's veto of only the General Fund portion of the appropriation to the Budget and Control Board was unconstitutional because it exceeded the authority granted to him by article IV, section 21 of the South Carolina Constitution. The Governor is empowered to veto "items," which comprise both the designated funds and the objects and purposes for which the appropriation is intended. By vetoing only one of several sources of funds, the Governor vetoed only part of an item, rendering the veto unconstitutional. Having declared Veto 52 unconstitutional, we hold the General Assembly's appropriation of General Funds to the Budget and Control Board is effective and has the force of law.

HOMAN v. BRANSTAD
812 N.W.2d 623 (Iowa 2012)

WATERMAN, J.

This appeal requires our court to resolve another dispute between the executive and legislative branches of our state government over the scope of the Governor's item veto power. On July 27, 2011, Governor Terry E. Branstad item vetoed several provisions in Senate File 517, an appropriations bill passed in the final days of the Eighty-fourth General Assembly. Primarily at issue is $8.66 million the legislature appropriated in section 15(3) for the operation of Iowa Workforce Development (IWD) field offices. The Governor, without vetoing that appropriation, item vetoed section 15(3)(c), prohibiting the closure of field offices, and section 15(5), defining "field office" to require the presence of a staff person. His accompanying item-veto message noted his purpose was to provide "enhanced benefits through maximum efficiencies" by replacing staffed field offices with numerous additional "virtual access point [computer] workstations" for the delivery of employment services to Iowans throughout our state. The Governor also item vetoed section 20, which restricts IWD from spending any appropriated funds on the National Career Readiness Certificate Program, without item vetoing any of the several appropriations to IWD in Senate File 517. And, the Governor item vetoed similar provisions in the bill for the following fiscal year.

We must decide whether the Governor's item vetoes comply with article III, section 16 of our state constitution, the item-veto amendment ratified by the people of Iowa in 1968. Plaintiffs, Danny Homan, the president of Iowa Council 61 of the American Federation of State County and Municipal Employees, a state-employee union, and William A. Dotzler, Jr., Bruce Hunter, David Jacoby, Kirsten Running–Marquardt, and Daryl Beall, legislators in the Eighty-fourth General Assembly, filed this action in district court alleging the Governor unconstitutionally item vetoed "conditions or restrictions" on the appropriations.

This is not an easy case. The legislature failed to use language in section 15(3) expressly conditioning the $8.66 million appropriation on the restrictions against closing staffed field offices. Nonetheless, we conclude the definition of "field office" in section 15(5) qualifies or restricts the $8.66 million appropriation in section 15(3)(b) "for the operation of field offices." Accordingly, the Governor could not veto section 15(5) without vetoing the accompanying appropriation in section 15(3). We further conclude the Governor impermissibly item vetoed the restriction in section 20 on use of IWD appropriations for the national certificate program.

Simply stated, the legislature appropriated funds to IWD with strings attached, and our constitution does not permit the Governor to cut the strings and spend the money differently.

Holdins

I. Background Facts and Proceedings.

The Eighty-fourth General Assembly of Iowa passed Senate File 517, "The Economic Development Appropriations Bill," on June 27, 2011. The bill was sent to Governor Branstad three days later, on the last day of the legislative session. On July 27, Governor Branstad item vetoed sections 15(3)(c) and 15(5), as follows:

> Sec. 15. DEPARTMENT OF WORKFORCE DEVELOPMENT. There is appropriated from the general fund of the state to the department of workforce development for the fiscal year beginning July 1, 2011, and ending June 30, 2012, the following amounts, or so much thereof as is necessary, for the purposes designated:
>
> ....
>
> 3. WORKFORCE DEVELOPMENT OPERATIONS
>
> a. For the operation of field offices, the workforce development board, and for not more than the following full-time equivalent positions:
>
> $8,671,352
>
> .... FTEs 130.00
>
> b. Of the moneys appropriated in paragraph "a" of this subsection, the department shall allocate $8,660,480 for the operation of field offices.
>
> ——— c. The department shall not reduce the number of field offices below the number of field offices being operated as of January 1, 2009.

Governor Branstad's transmittal letter to Secretary of State Schultz explained:

> I am unable to approve the item designated Section 15, subsection 3, paragraph c, in its entirety. This item would prohibit Iowa Workforce Development ("IWD") from putting forth an enhanced delivery system that broadens access to Iowans across the state in fiscal year 2012. In order to develop a sustainable delivery system, in light of continually fluctuating federal funding, the department must put forth a system that embraces the use of technology while providing enhanced benefits through maximum efficiencies. At this time, IWD has over one hundred ninety virtual access point workstations in over sixty new locations throughout the state in order to increase access to these critical services. Iowans are already utilizing expanded hours of operations, six days a week. At my direction, IWD will have hundreds of additional virtual access points by the end of fiscal year 2012.
>
> I am unable to approve the item designated as Section 15, subsection 5 in its entirety. This item attempts to define a delivery system in such a way as to prevent growth and progress in serving Iowans in fiscal year 2012. IWD has recognized the necessity of delivering services through multiple streams, including technology. As such, IWD is putting forth a plan that delivers more services to Iowans while streamlining government.

Sections 17, 18, and 19 appropriated additional funds to IWD. Section 20 restricts IWD from using appropriated funds for the National Career Readiness Certificate Program. Governor Branstad item vetoed section 20 as follows:

> Sec. 20. APPROPRIATIONS RESTRICTED. The department of workforce development shall not use any of the moneys appropriated in this division of this Act for purposes of the national career readiness certificate program.

The Governor's transmittal letter to Secretary Schultz explained:

> I am unable to approve the item designated as Section 20 in its entirety. This item would prohibit IWD from using the National Career Readiness Certificate program in fiscal year 2012. The National Career Readiness Certificate program is an Iowa-based product which is an assessment and skill development tool that has been embraced by over 400 Iowa employers as an exceptional tool for demonstrating skills for a potential employee. It is nationally recognized by both the Executive Office of the President and the U.S. Department of Labor as a reliable and portable tool for job seekers to present and certify their skills. I cannot agree with the denial to IWD of the potential use of this program.

Plaintiffs … alleged these item vetoes exceeded Governor Branstad's constitutional authority and sought a declaratory ruling the vetoes were void and that Senate File 517 became law as presented to the Governor.

II. Standard of Review.

Whether the Governor properly exercised his item veto power "'is an issue of constitutional analysis which presents a question of law for the courts.'"

III. Analysis.

"Our opinion concerning the wisdom of either the original enactment or the vetoes does not enter into our judicial evaluation of the legality of the Governor's action." The elected branches decide how best to deliver employment services to Iowans; our role as the third branch is to decide this constitutional case.

The Governor's item-veto power is set forth in article III, section 16 of the Iowa Constitution, which provides in pertinent part:

> *The governor may approve appropriation bills in whole or in part, and may disapprove any item of an appropriation bill;* and the part approved shall become a law. Any item of an appropriation bill disapproved by the governor shall be returned, with his objections, to the house in which it originated, or shall be deposited by him in the office of the secretary of state in the case of an appropriation bill submitted to the governor for his approval during the last three days of a session of the general assembly, and the procedure in each case shall be the same as provided for other bills. Any such item of an appropriation bill may be enacted into law notwithstanding the governor's objections, in the same manner as provided for other bills.

In construing the item-veto provision, our mission "'is to ascertain the intent of the framers.'"

"[T]he purpose of the item veto provision of our constitution [is to] give [ ] the governor a larger role in the state budgetary process." In *Rants*, we further observed "the item veto power developed 'to control logrolling, or the legislators' practice of combining in a single bill provisions supported by various minorities in order to create a legislative majority.'" * * * "[T]he item veto power grants the governor a limited legislative function in relation to appropriation bills." "'[W]hatever the veto's successes in dealing with budget problems, by empowering the executive to veto a part of a bill, the item veto opens up a set of knotty legal and conceptual difficulties.'"

Defining the scope of an "item" subject to veto has proven difficult. By its terms, article III, section 16 permits the Governor to "disapprove any item of an appropriation bill." "This language—particularly the term 'item'—has caused this court and other courts their greatest interpretive difficulty." Separate policy items placed in an appropriation bill may be the subject of item veto—the item itself need not appropriate money. *** In *Welden v. Ray*, however, we held "that if the Governor desires to veto a legislatively-imposed qualification upon an appropriation, he must veto the accompanying appropriation as well." We have used the terms "proviso," "restriction," "qualification," "limitation," and "condition" interchangeably to "denote[] 'a provision in a bill that limits the use to which an appropriation may be put.'" The point is this: when the legislature makes a specific appropriation for a specific purpose, the Governor can veto the appropriation as an item, but cannot veto the purpose and use the appropriation for a different purpose. We must decide whether the provisions vetoed by Governor Branstad in Senate File 517 are separate items subject to veto, or rather, conditions or qualifications upon an item of appropriation that could not be vetoed without vetoing the appropriation.

B. The Validity of the Item Veto of Section 15(5). We ... address whether the Governor constitutionally could item veto the definition of "field office" in section 15(5) without vetoing the $8.66 million appropriation "for the operation of field offices" in section 15(3)(b). The district court ruled this item veto was unconstitutional, stating:

> Read in the context in which they were enacted, the legislative limitations embodied in the definitions contained in the vetoed provisions were clearly intended by the legislature to apply directly to the funds appropriated "for the operation of field offices." With the use of the phrase "in this section" the legislature evinced an intent to place restrictions on the use of the appropriations it made earlier in the section.

We agree. Section 15(5), entitled "DEFINITIONS," begins by stating, "For purposes of this section...." The provision then defines "field office" as requiring the physical presence of an employee at each field office. This definition applies throughout section 15 and, thus, controls the meaning of "field office" in section 15(3)(b), which appropriates $8.66 million "for the operation of field offices." The legislature textually linked section 15(5) to the appropriation in section 15(3). Reading the provisions together, as the legislature directed, makes clear that each "field office" funded in section 15(3)(b) is to be staffed with an IWD employee. That is, a location with a computer workstation but no employee physically present is not a "field office" within the meaning of the appropriation provision.

We have cautioned the item veto cannot be used to strike a provision that is "inextricably linked" to or an "integral part" of an appropriation. We see these provisions as inseparable and inextricably linked. The funds appropriated for field offices were for those defined in section 15(5) to require the physical presence of a staff person. The definition of "field office" is an integral part of the appropriation for the operation of field offices. Definitions can impose conditions; this one did. The $8.66 million appropriation had strings attached, tying the funds to the requirement that state employees staff the field offices. The fiscal wisdom of this requirement is not for our court to decide. But our constitution does not permit the Governor to cut the strings and keep the money.

In *Rants*, we reiterated the following admonition:

> [I]f the removal of the provision would permit the governor to "legislate by striking qualifications [on appropriations] in a manner which distorts legislative intent" or to "divert money appropriated by the legislature for one purpose so that it may be used for another," we consider it an inseparable statement of the legislature's will, impervious to an item veto unless both the condition and the appropriation to which it is related are item vetoed together. *Rush*, 362 N.W.2d at 482 ("The vetoed language created conditions, restricting the use of the money to the stated purpose. It is not severable, because upon excision of this language, the rest of the legislation is affected.")....

To allow the Governor to veto the definition in section 15(5) without vetoing the accompanying appropriation in section 15(3)(b) would impermissibly "distort[ ] legislative intent" or "divert money appropriated by the legislature for one purpose so that it may be used for another." Specifically, the Governor would be disregarding the express legislative direction requiring staffed field offices and diverting the money appropriated for a different purpose—unmanned computer kiosks. We conclude section 15(5) is impervious to an item veto without a veto of section 15(3).

We therefore hold the Governor's item veto of section 15(5) was unconstitutional.

C. The Validity of the Item Veto of Section 20. We now turn to the cross-appeal. The district court upheld the validity of Governor Branstad's item veto of section 20, which states:

> Sec. 20. APPROPRIATIONS RESTRICTED. The department of workforce development shall not use any of the moneys appropriated in this division of this Act for purposes of the national career readiness certificate program.

The district court ruled that section 20 is a rider subject to item veto:

> Although this provision places explicit qualifications and limitations on the use of the appropriated funds, it is overly broad in the appropriated funds to which it

is attached. It therefore must be considered to be a rider, and not an item, for item veto analysis purposes. Accordingly, Governor Branstad's item vetoes of Division I, Section 20 and of Division IV, Section 66, were effective and should be upheld.

We disagree. We have cautioned the legislature cannot tie unrelated provisions in a bill together to frustrate the Governor's item-veto power. But, the fact IWD received appropriations through four different provisions of Senate File 517, specifically sections 15, 17, 18, and 19, does not make the express restriction on use of the money in section 20 overly broad or a rider subject to item veto. A "rider" is "an unrelated substantive piece of legislation incorporated in the appropriation bill." Section 20 is not "unrelated" to the IWD appropriations. To the contrary, section 20 explicitly restricts the use of IWD's appropriations, and that is all it does.

"Inherent in the power to appropriate is the power to specify how the money shall be spent." We have held provisions restricting executive branch agencies from spending appropriated money for nonspecified purposes are conditions not subject to independent veto. Section 20 precludes IWD from spending any of its appropriations on the national certificate program. Without this restriction, IWD could transfer funds appropriated for another purpose to the program. Like the provisions in *Rush*, section 20 is an appropriately tailored "outgrowth of the legislature's power to appropriate funds."

Section 20 uses the type of "phraseology" that, according to *Turner*, identifies a condition. Section 20 constitutes a "condition," that is, "a provision in a bill that limits the use to which an appropriation may be put." Accordingly, Governor Branstad could not item veto section 20 without also vetoing the IWD appropriations in sections 15, 17, 18, and 19.

We hold the Governor's item veto of section 20 was <u>unconstitutional.</u>

D. The Remedy. We now turn to the remedy required by our holdings that the Governor's item vetoes of section 15(5) and section 20 were unconstitutional. The district court granted the remedy sought by plaintiffs in their petition and declared that "Senate File 517 became law as if the Governor had not exercised the item vetoes which were herein determined to be void." Governor Branstad argues on appeal the proper remedy for an invalid veto of a condition on an appropriation is to invalidate the entire item containing the appropriation. The Governor is correct on this point. This remedy is required by article III, section 16, which provides in relevant part:

> Any bill submitted to the governor for his approval during the last three days of a session of the general assembly, shall be deposited by him in the office of the

secretary of state, within thirty days after the adjournment, with his approval, if approved by him, and with his objections, if he disapproves thereof.

> The governor may approve appropriation bills in whole or in part, and may disapprove any item of an appropriation bill; and the part approved shall become a law.

Iowa Const. art. III, § 16.

Senate File 517 is an appropriation bill that was presented to the Governor on June 30, 2011, the last day of the legislative session. Bills presented to the Governor during "the last three days of a session of the general assembly" do not become law without the Governor's affirmative approval. The Governor has thirty days to approve or disapprove the bill. This is known as the "pocket veto" period because the bill fails if the Governor takes no action. In this case, Governor Branstad's timely transmittal letter to Secretary of State Schultz stated, "Senate File 517 is approved on this date with the following exceptions, which I hereby disapprove." The letter went on to identify the provisions the Governor disapproved by exercising his item veto.

In *Rants*, Governor Vilsack item vetoed parts of a nonappropriations bill presented to him during the last three days of the session. We held his item vetoes were invalid and as a result the entire bill failed. We stated, "[N]o portion of HF 692 became law because the entire bill did not receive the affirmative approval of both the Legislature and Governor...." This result was required because nonappropriations bills must be approved or disapproved in their *entirety*, and an invalid item veto cannot constitute approval.

By contrast, our constitution provides the Governor "may approve appropriation bills in whole or in part, and may disapprove any item of an appropriation bill; and the part approved shall become law." Iowa Const. art. III, § 16. Because the Governor may approve or disapprove any *item* in an appropriation bill, an ineffective item veto is not fatal to the entire bill, but only to the affected items.

We hold that, when the Governor impermissibly item vetoes a condition on an appropriation during the pocket veto period, the appropriation item fails to become law. This result is mandated by our constitutional requirement that enactments do not become law without the approval of both elected branches except when a legislative supermajority overrides a veto. Here, the Governor did not approve the IWD appropriations with the conditions. Yet, the legislature did not pass the appropriations without the conditions. Thus, the IWD appropriations without the conditions could not become law because the approval of both elected branches was lacking.

Specifically, the Governor failed to effectively approve section 15(3), containing the $8.66 million appropriation for the operation of field offices because he failed to approve the accompanying condition defining field offices in section 15(5). The Governor's affirmative approval of section 15(3) was required during the pocket veto for it to become law. Section 15(3) fails for this reason.

Section 20 is a restriction on IWD appropriations. Those appropriations are found in sections 15(1)–(4), 17, 18, and 19. Governor Branstad's approval of those sections was ineffective in light of his failure to approve the accompanying condition in section 20. Accordingly, those sections did not become law. The remaining sections of Senate File 517, affirmatively approved by Governor Branstad, became law.

NOTES

1. Is the question whether the Governor has properly exercised a line item veto a "legal" rather than "political" question? Can you articulate the arguments for and against the courts' involvement?

2. Who should have "standing" to challenge a Governor's line item veto? The Legislature? Individual legislators? Citizens or entities actually affected by the veto, such as those who would have received state funds but for the Governor's veto?

3. How difficult is it to define what constitutes an "appropriation" measure for line item veto purposes? What if the Governor vetoes a particular tax deduction or exemption provisions in a major tax system overhaul bill? Or vetoes a provision eliminating mandatory retirement for judges at age 70 (on the ground that the provision will permit judges to serve longer and thus accrue larger retirement benefits that the State will be obligated to pay)? Or vetoes a provision requiring local sheriffs' departments to conduct background checks on all firearms purchases in their counties (on the ground that such a requirement will require more state funding for sheriffs)?

4. For additional commentary on this topic, see Richard Briffault, *The Item Veto In State Courts*, 66 Temple L. Rev. 1171 (1993); Winston David Holliday, Jr., *Tipping the Balance of Power: A Critical Survey of the Gubernatorial Line Item Veto*, 50 S.C. L. Rev. 503 (1999) (discussing South Carolina's experience and comparing it with Iowa, Wisconsin, and Virginia).

D. JUDICIAL POWER

By now, you are familiar with one of the essential tasks of the state judiciary: interpreting the state constitution. That of course is not all that state court judges do. They interpret legislation and regulations (federal and state); they develop state evidentiary, criminal, civil and appellate rules; they regulate the practice of law in their States; and, through their supreme courts, they exercise supervisory authority over the lower state courts.

This section considers three important differences between the federal and state judicial branches: (1) the election of most state court judges; (2) the authority of state court judges to issue advisory opinions; and (3) the authority of federal judges to certify questions of state law to the state supreme courts. And it ends by addressing an issue common to the state and federal courts: implied constitutional remedies.

1. The Election of Judges

One of the key distinctions between the federal and state judiciaries is their manner of selection and tenure of service. Under the United States Constitution, the President nominates federal judges, and the Senate confirms them. Once confirmed, federal judges serve for life or, as Article III puts it, during "good behavior." As the excerpt from the following article shows, that is a distant cry from the way most States choose their judges.

Judith L. Maute, *Selecting Justice in State Courts: The Ballot Box or the Backroom?*
41 South Texas Law Review 1197 (Fall 2000)

Popular election of judges was virtually unheard of until the early Nineteenth Century. On the federal level, the United States Constitution dictated both the manner of appointment and lifetime tenure without reduction of salary. Andrew Jackson's presidency triggered a new wave of populism which advocated voter control over all aspects of government. Thereafter, several states amended their constitutions, providing for selection by election, or partisan challenges to incumbent judges. Newer states tended to follow uncritically the populist electoral model based on the idea that courts should have some accountability to the electorate. This transformation was achieved "almost completely without regard for the particular considerations of policy and principle which arise out of the nature and functions of the judicial arm of the government." The pendulum swung back towards appointment starting in the 1920s. Missouri was the first state to implement what became known as "merit selection" in 1940.

Currently, there are four basic systems of judicial selection in the United States. Judges are chosen through either partisan or nonpartisan elections in twenty-one states; eleven additional states use elections for some judgeships, usually the lower courts. What has become known as merit selection is the sole selection method in fourteen states. Seven jurisdictions use a combination of merit and election methods with the remaining states using a combination of merit and appointive systems. At present, twenty-two states use merit selection for at least their highest appeals courts. This figure can be misleading. Approximately eighty-seven percent of all state court judges are selected or retained on the basis of popular elections, although about eighty percent of all judicial offices are initially filled by appointment to compete unexpired terms.

A. Appointment

The oldest method of judicial selection in the United States is appointment. In the original thirteen states, to avoid giving exclusive power to one individual, the legislature, or the governor with legislative approval, appointed judges. Today, most states use various combinations of the appointive system. California judges, except for superior court judges, are appointed by the governor, and must then be approved by a commission on judicial appointments. New Hampshire uses an elected executive council to approve appointments by the governor. In New York, only court of appeals judges are appointed by the governor with the consent of the senate, while the remaining judges are chosen in partisan elections. Most states fill interim vacancies by gubernatorial appointment.

B. Partisan Elections

Partisan election of judges began after Andrew Jackson's populist presidency. Some authorities believe the move to elections was a response to widespread dissatisfaction with the perceived elitism of judges. Proponents maintain that judicial elections assure accountability to the people and are the only reliable method for removing judges whose decisions are unacceptable to the populace. Voters may have little information on the individual judicial candidates. Partisan elections can cue voters on a candidate's ideology through the identification of political affiliation. The political party of the judicial candidate can be used for screening purposes. "Although it has been proven otherwise in some cases, it was thought that with the party 'footing the bill' for and controlling recruitment, special interests would be kept at arm's length from the process."

Some voters favor judicial elections because it gives them a choice between parties and a voice in the system. There is a greater electoral turnout when voters have more information on which to make a decision, such as political party cues. One unfortunate method of increasing voter participation is the heightened negativity of judicial campaigns. Wisconsin Supreme Court Justice Shirley Abrahamson faced blistering campaign attacks by opponent Sharren Rose in the 1999 race. Critics of partisan judicial elections claim that increased costs of campaigning and problematic funding sources create an image of justice going to the highest bidder. Special interest groups try to help elect judges favorable to their cause by pouring money into those judges' campaign coffers. Six candidates spent almost six million dollars in 1990 Texas judicial campaigns. Abrahamson and Rose spent over one million dollars on their campaigns.

Another cost of judicial elections is time spent campaigning for office instead of fulfilling the judge's duties. Successful lawyers may be reluctant to run for office, investing their reputation, time, money and effort seeking a job that is neither guaranteed nor highly paid. Additionally, having to answer to political parties and vocal contributors can deter qualified individuals from running for a judicial position.

It is debatable whether partisan elections in fact make judges accountable to the public. Most judges are initially appointed to fulfill vacant positions by the state governor, and run unopposed in the next periodic election. This scenario effectively removes the voter from the equation. Even when there is opposition in a judicial race, voter turnout is typically low. Unless the judicial election takes place during the general election and has become a hotly contested race, most voters either do not vote for the judicial offices or vote with little information, evidenced by the fact that they cannot remember who they voted for immediately afterwards.

C. Nonpartisan Elections

Thirteen states use nonpartisan elections for judicial offices, and seven additional states use it only for selected judicial offices. Ohio is unique in that it nominates judicial candidates in partisan primaries and then places them on a nonpartisan ballot for the general election. Supporters claim that nonpartisan elections remove the problem of politics entailed by partisan elections while keeping accountability to the voters. Adopted in response to the problem of judges controlled by party politics, nonpartisan elections were intended to involve voters in the process and exclude politics and special interests.

"[M]ost commentators contend that, far from being an improvement upon partisan elections, nonpartisan elections are an inferior alternative to partisan elections because they possess all of the vices of partisan elections and none of the virtues." Voters lose their main cue for information on who to vote for and, lacking more relevant information on individual candidates, rely on other factors such as ballot position or name recognition. Candidates who served in prior political offices as prosecutor, legislator or county commissioner, have greater name recognition which helps them in later campaigns for judicial office. Voter apathy may be greater in nonpartisan elections, with lower turn-outs and voter roll-off (not voting in certain races), so that the judicial incumbents usually win. To counter this information problem, some jurisdictions print and distribute voter pamphlets, which greatly increases the election costs. Nonpartisan elections are becoming increasingly expensive and involve many of the same problems with campaign contributions as partisan elections. The most obvious example is the highly politicized, nasty and expensive battle between Ohio Supreme Court incumbent Justice Alice Robie Resnick, a Democrat, and her Republican challenger District Court of Appeals Judge Terrence O'Donnell. Business and insurance groups, with generous backing from the Chamber of Commerce, targeted Resnick for defeat because of her votes in two controversial cases. While ultimately unsuccessful, the bruising fight has prompted state leaders to reconsider selection methods.

D. Merit Selection

Albert Kales, Northwestern University law professor, first called for merit selection of judges in 1914 when the American Judicature Society was founded.

> Kales' plan called for (1) the nomination of judicial candidates based solely on merit by a commission of presiding judges, (2) the selection of judges from this list of nominees by an elected chief justice, and (3) retention elections conducted on a noncompetitive...basis. In 1926, British political scientist Harold Laski suggested that the Kales plan be modified in certain respects. Laski recommended that the Governor rather than the chief justice appoint judges and that the advisory committee consist of a judge or judges from the state supreme court, the attorney general, and the president of the state bar association.

California was the first state to adopt a type of merit plan for its supreme court and intermediate courts; it is still in use today. The governor makes nominations to fill vacant positions which must be approved by a commission including the chief justice, a present justice of the court of appeals and the attorney general. After confirmation, the judges must stand for retention at regular intervals. California is also noteworthy for having been the first state in which hotly contested retention elections resulted in the ouster of judges because of their unpopular decisions.

The most widely known merit selection plan, the "Missouri Plan," was first adopted in 1940. A judicial nominating committee makes recommendations to the governor who then chooses one of the nominees to fill a vacancy. Like many other states, Missouri now uses a "modified" merit system, in which appellate and metropolitan trial courts use a merit appointment process, but elections select the trial bench in rural areas. The judge must thereafter stand for retention at regular intervals. Missouri continues to use this system for its supreme court, courts of appeals and its trial courts in large metropolitan areas such as Kansas City and St. Louis. Three separate nominating commissions are used in Missouri: one for the appellate courts, and one each for Jackson county and St. Louis county circuit courts. Although repeal measures have been regularly introduced, the plan has yet to be revoked. All other state judges are selected in partisan elections.

Alaska was the first state to enact a merit plan for all state judges, in 1959. Rhode Island is the latest state to change to the merit plan for its trial judges in 1994. Delaware, Hawaii, Massachusetts, and Nebraska are the only other states which use merit selection for all judicial appointments.

Judicial nomination committees are composed of lawyers and laypersons. Some jurisdictions require the nominating commission be divided between political parties. Arizona dictates that the names submitted to the governor must be balanced based on political parties. According to Sheldon and Maule, the nomination committee lessens the political pressure on the appointing authority, usually the governor, so that the most qualified persons are submitted as finalists.

Merit selection proponents maintain that it: 1) removes politics from the selection process as much as possible, especially when there are effective controls for politics in the selection of nomination committee members; 2) removes the need to campaign for office and raise contributions; 3) results in more qualified applicants and selections; 4) removes the issue of voter apathy and the problem with ethical restrictions on judicial campaign speech; 5) allows accountability to voters by using retention elections to remove bad judges; and 6) increases minority representation on the bench. They contend it is the best method to reduce the influence of politics in judicial selection.

Opponents disagree with most of these assertions. They contend merit selection is elitist and merely moves the politics outside the light of the electoral system and into the backroom, allowing for private decisionmaking by politically-appointed nomination committees. They assert that retention elections are undemocratic, misleading to voters, and allow little meaningful choice. Campaign contributions must still be addressed if a judge up for retention is targeted by a special interest group based on an unpopular decision. A courageous judge may have a difficult time defending her record against an anonymously funded soft money campaign. In contested judicial elections, at least the voters are presented with a known alternative to the incumbent, enabling them to vote in a more meaningful way.

E. *Hybrid Selection*

Eight states use some combination of merit selection, appointment, or elections to fill their judicial positions. In South Carolina, for instance, a merit commission nominates candidates, but the judge is elected by the legislature. The legislature also elects the judges in Virginia. In Maine, judges are confirmed by the Senate after being appointed by the governor. In New Hampshire, judges are appointed by the governor, then confirmed by an elected five member executive council. Floridians recently amended their constitution to provide for counties to vote on whether to "opt-in" to selecting trial court judges through the merit system.

NOTES

1.   Some see the election of judges to a term of years as a threat to judicial independence. How can popularly elected judges, who often must raise considerable campaign funds to win elections, maintain the independence of mind to rule fairly on the issues that come before them? And even when that is not a problem, how can majoritarian-elected judges be entrusted to enforce the counter-majoritarian guarantees of the state constitution. *See* Sandra Day O'Connor, "The Threat to Judicial Independence," The Wall Street Journal, A18 (Sept. 27, 2006); Sandra Day O'Connor, "Judicial Independence and Civics Education," Utah Bar Journal (July 18, 2009). Others see the election of judges in Jacksonian terms—as the only way to place a check on the judiciary, particularly at a time when so many of the most important issues of the day are coming before the courts.

2.   State judicial elections may implicate questions of *federal* constitutional law. For example, the free-speech guarantees of the First Amendment may place restrictions on the capacity of state judicial ethics codes to restrict what candidates may say in running for judicial office, e.g., *Republican Party of Minnesota v. White*, 536 U.S. 765 (2002) (the First Amendment does not permit the Minnesota Supreme Court to prohibit candidates for judicial election in that State from announcing their views on disputed legal and political issues), or they may not. *Williams-Yulee v. Florida Bar*, 575 U.S. ___ (2015) (state bar can prohibit candidates for judicial office from making personal solicitations for donations to the candidate's campaign, because elected judges are different than other elected officials, and must maintain the public's confidence that they will be fair and impartial). Also, the substantive due process guarantees of the Fourteenth Amendment require judges to recuse themselves in some settings, most notably when they have directly or indirectly received considerable campaign funds from a party to a case before the judge. *See Caperton v. A.T. Massey Coal Co.*, 556 U.S. 868 (2009).

2. Justiciability: Standing, Mootness and Political Questions

GREGORY v. SHURTLEFF
299 P.3d 1098 (Utah 2013)

DURHAM, J.

INTRODUCTION

¶ 1 Appellants brought suit to enjoin the enforcement of a law, claiming that the law violated the state constitution in four respects. On appeal, we consider whether Appellants had standing to bring these claims in the first place. We hold that, although they lacked the personal injury required for traditional standing, Appellants had public-interest standing to bring the first two claims. We also hold that they did not have standing to bring the second two claims under either the traditional or the public-interest doctrine of standing.

BACKGROUND

¶ 2 In March 2008, the legislature enacted Senate Bill 2 (the Bill). The Bill contained some fourteen items relating to education, establishing new programs and amending existing programs; it also contained funding provisions for some programs.

¶ 3 Appellants are a group of current and former legislators, other elected and unelected government officials, and self-described "good citizens." They include current and former members of the Utah State Board of Education (the Board). However, they appear in their individual capacities, and the Board itself is not a party to this litigation. In May 2008, Appellants filed suit in district court against the State's Attorney General, its Treasurer, and the Executive Director of the Department of Human Resources (collectively, Appellees), seeking a declaration that the Bill was unconstitutional and an injunction against its implementation, as well as an award of costs and fees.

¶ 4 Appellants claimed the Bill was unconstitutional in four respects. The first two claims fall under Article VI, Section 22 of the Utah Constitution, which provides that "no bill shall be passed containing more than *one subject*, which shall be *clearly expressed* in its title." (Emphasis added.) Appellants argue that the Bill as a whole violates this provision in two respects: first, they argue that it contained "more than one subject"; second, that its subject was not "clearly expressed in its title" (collectively, the Article VI Claims). The second two claims fall under Article X, Section 3 of the Utah Constitution, which provides that "[t]he general control and supervision of the public education system shall be vested in a State Board of Education." Appellants argue that two items of the Bill violate this provision: first, the item that delegates the administration of the Teacher Salary Supplement Program to the Department of Human Resources; second, the item that delegates textbook approval to private entities (collectively, the Article X Claims).

¶ 5 Appellees moved to dismiss the Article VI Claims pursuant to rule 12(b)(6) of the Utah Rules of Civil Procedure. They subsequently moved to dismiss the Article X Claims for lack of standing and moved in the alternative for partial summary judgment on those claims. The district court granted Appellees' motion to dismiss the Article VI Claims for failure to state a claim, and later granted the State's motion for summary judgment on the Article X Claims. It did not rule on the alternative motion to dismiss those claims for lack of standing.

ANALYSIS

¶ 9 Since standing is a jurisdictional requirement, we first must determine whether Appellants have standing to bring any of their claims. Unlike in the federal system, our law recognizes that appropriate plaintiffs without individualized injury may nevertheless possess standing to bring certain claims treating issues of great public importance. We determine that the issues underlying the Article VI Claims rise to this level and that Appellants are appropriate parties to bring these claims; Appellants therefore have standing to raise the Article VI Claims. The issues underlying the Article X claims, however, do not rise to this level, and furthermore Appellants are not appropriately situated to bring them. Accordingly, they do not have standing to raise the Article X claims.

¶ 10 On the merits of the district court's dismissal of the Article VI Claims, we hold that even on the facts alleged by Appellants, the Bill does not violate either the single-subject or clear-title rules of Article VI, Section 22. Accordingly, the dismissal is affirmed.

I. STANDING

¶ 11 "[I]n Utah, as in the federal system, standing is a jurisdictional requirement." Furthermore, "[s]tanding is an issue that a court can raise sua sponte at any time."

A. Utah Recognizes Public–Interest Standing in Matters of Great Constitutional or Public Importance

¶ 12 "Unlike the federal system, the judicial power of the state of Utah is not constitutionally restricted by the language of Article III of the United States Constitution requiring 'cases' and 'controversies,' since no similar requirement exists in the Utah Constitution." While it is "the usual rule that one must be personally adversely affected before he has standing to prosecute an action .... it is also true this Court may grant standing where matters of great public interest and societal impact are concerned."

¶ 13 "[D]espite our recognition of this Court's power to grant standing where matters of great public interest and societal impact are concerned," however, "this Court will not readily relieve a plaintiff of the salutory requirement of showing a real and personal interest in the dispute." Therefore,

> we engage in a three-step inquiry in reviewing the question of a plaintiff's standing to sue. The first step in the inquiry will be directed to the *traditional criteria* of the plaintiff's personal stake in the controversy.... If the plaintiff does not have standing under the first step, we will then address the question of *whether there is anyone who has a greater interest* in the outcome of the case than the plaintiff. If there is no one, and if the issue is unlikely to be raised at all if the plaintiff is denied standing, this Court will grant standing.... The Court will deny standing when a plaintiff does not satisfy the first requirement of the analysis and there are potential plaintiffs with a more direct interest in the issues who can more adequately litigate the issues. The third step in the analysis is to decide if the issues raised by the plaintiff are of *sufficient public importance* in and of themselves to grant him standing.

¶ 14 In a more recent case, we summarized this alternative basis for standing as follows: "[T]he statutory and the traditional common law tests are not the only avenues to gain standing; Utah law also allows parties to gain standing if they can show that they are *an appropriate party* raising issues of significant public importance.

¶ 16 Our public-interest standing doctrine is not unusual in state jurisprudence. Numerous other states, mindful that their constitutions do not impose the same restrictions on their judicial power that the federal constitution imposes on federal courts, have similarly established (under various names) a doctrine of public-interest standing.

¶ 17 The case of Michigan is particularly illuminating. Recently, the Supreme Court of that state overruled a line of cases which "departed dramatically from Michigan's historical approach to standing." In restoring Michigan's traditional approach to standing, the *Lansing* court explained that "[t]here is no support in either the text of the Michigan Constitution or in Michigan jurisprudence ... for recognizing standing as a constitutional requirement or for adopting the federal standing doctrine." The same is true of Utah's constitution and jurisprudence.

B. Appellants Do Not Meet the Traditional Standing Criteria of Having a "Personal Stake in the Controversy" for Any of Their Four Claims

¶ 21 Appellants argue that they have traditional standing to bring the Article X Claims for two reasons. First, they argue that the challenged provisions of the Bill deny "plaintiffs as voters ... their political prerogative, implicit in Article 10, Section 3, to hold Board members politically accountable by a meaningful exercise of the right to vote." This argument is not persuasive. To the extent that one's status as a voter in itself ever gives one a right to challenge legislation, it can only be through some form of an *alternative* form of standing, such as our public-interest doctrine. It does not constitute a "personal stake in [a] controversy."

¶ 22 Appellants' second argument is that they have traditional standing to bring the Article X Claims because six of them are members of the Board. They argue that the Salary Supplement Program and the Textbook Approval Program "positively forbid the members of [the Board] from exercising their Article 10, Section 3 powers respecting those programs .... mak[ing] it impossible for them to fulfill their oaths of office ... and impair[ing] their ability, as candidates, in seeking re-election to office." This argument is similarly unconvincing. Appellants cite no authority for the proposition that elected officials have a vested interest in reelection sufficient to satisfy the traditional test for standing. And while it is true that elected officials who take oaths of office should take those oaths seriously, they likewise cite no authority establishing that taking such an oath gives them standing to challenge a law which they assert will infringe on their ability to faithfully execute it. Appellants are, in essence, asking that we view those who were members of the Board at the time they brought suit as being localized attorneys general, charged with constitutional authority to prosecute alleged violations of their portion of the constitution. This we decline to do.

¶ 23 For similar reasons, we determine that Appellants lack standing to bring those claims under the traditional doctrine of standing. As explained below, we conclude that they do have public-interest standing to bring the Article VI Claims. But that is only because we determine that violations of the provisions at issue in those claims are of sufficient public importance that they give Appellants standing to raise such violations in their role as citizens.

¶ 24 In previous cases where this court has reviewed the merits of a claim that either or both the single-subject and clear-title rules of Article VI, Section 22 have been violated, the plaintiffs alleged a direct and personal injury sufficient to satisfy the traditional standing test. While we determine below that the Article VI Claims treat issues of public significance and that Appellants are appropriately situated to bring them, comparison with the cases cited above clarifies that Appellants have standing to bring those claims only under the alternative public-interest doctrine. They do not have a "personal stake in the controversy."

C. The Article VI Claims Rise to the Level of Great Constitutional Importance, and Appellants are Appropriately Situated to Raise Them

¶ 25 As explained above, Appellants do not meet the traditional requirements for standing on any of their four claims. We therefore consider whether they meet the requirements for public-interest standing.

First, we examine their Article VI Claims, and determine that they do meet those requirements.

¶ 26 Article VI, Section 22 of the Utah Constitution provides: "Except general appropriation bills and bills for the codification and general revision of laws, no bill shall be passed containing more than one subject, which shall be clearly expressed in its title." These provisions, we have observed, "reflect[ ] an intent to limit legislative power and prevent special interest abuse" and are "clearly motivated by a wariness of unlimited legislative power."

¶ 27 The restrictions placed on legislative activity by Article VI, Section 22 of the Utah Constitution are part of the fundamental structure of legislative power articulated in our constitution. They are accordingly of sufficient importance and general interest that claims of their violation may be brought even by plaintiffs who lack standing under the traditional criteria.[14] Not every constitutional provision, to be sure, is of such importance that a claim of its violation will necessarily rise to the level of "significant public importance" required for public-interest standing under the formulation of *Cedar Mountain*, 2009 UT 48, ¶ 8, 214 P.3d 95. Our discussion below reveals, for instance, that delegations of particular functions to specific executive agencies may not rise to that level. But today we hold that the single-subject and clear-title rules of Article VI, Section 22 do.

¶ 28 Under *Cedar Mountain*, the importance of the issue by itself is not enough to give parties public-interest standing. One must also be "an appropriate party." "[A]n appropriate party .... has the interest necessary to effectively assist the court in developing and reviewing all relevant legal and factual questions ...." To demonstrate that it is an "appropriate party," a plaintiff must further show that "the issues are unlikely to be raised if the party is denied standing."

¶ 29 First, Appellants are "appropriate parties" with "the interest necessary to effectively assist the court in developing and reviewing all relevant legal and factual questions" with respect to the Article VI Claims. The "appropriateness" of a party under the public-interest standing doctrine is a question of *competency*. In the *Sierra Club* case, we determined that the Club "would have standing under the alternative [public-interest] test" due to its policy concerns and status as an "entity focused on protecting the environment." The coalition of Appellants in the instant case is not as well-established or long-standing as the Sierra Club, but it similarly has policy concerns and has come together to "focus[ ] on" the instant constitutional challenge. Further, Appellants have shown themselves able to "effectively assist the court" in its consideration of the Article VI Claims. While the district court dismissed those claims, and we affirm that dismissal, Appellants have nevertheless done an admirable job of briefing the facts and controlling law. That their complaint ultimately failed to state a claim does not mean that they were not appropriate parties to bring it. While we hold today that the Bill does not violate the clear-title and single-subject rules of Article VI, Section 22, Appellants have caused this court to consider those rules and clarify the standards they impose for the first time in decades, and that in itself is a considerable achievement.

¶ 30 Second, *Sierra Club* requires that "the issues [be] unlikely to be raised if the party is denied standing." *Id.* ¶ 36 (internal quotation marks omitted). We can certainly construct hypothetical plaintiffs who might be seen to have traditional standing to bring at least some of Appellant's claims. For instance, a teacher whose colleagues' salaries were raised under the Teacher Salary Supplement Program, but whose own salary was left unchanged, might invoke direct economic interests. Similarly, we can imagine a suit brought by a textbook publisher whose materials were rejected pursuant to the Textbook Approval Program. But our inquiry is not whether some hypothetical plaintiff can be imagined; it is whether "the issues are *unlikely* to be raised if the party is denied [public-interest] standing." Here, where the Board itself is silent and no other plaintiff has emerged in the years since the Bill's passage, we think that is indeed unlikely.

¶ 31 One more feature of our prior statements on public-interest standing deserves mention. In *Sierra Club*, we observed that a court's recognition that a party has public-interest standing analysis

> requires the court to determine not only that the issues are of a sufficient weight but also that they are not more appropriately addressed by another branch of government pursuant to the political process. The *more generalized* the issues, the more likely they ought to be resolved in the legislative or executive branches.

Id. ¶ 39. But Article VI, Section 22 places restrictions on the legislative process itself. Where the legislature has passed a bill and the governor has signed it, we cannot assume that either of those branches are appropriate parties to whom to entrust the prosecution of a claim that the bill violates the strictures of Article VI, Section 22. And "more generalized" in this context speaks not to the general nature of the *interest*—for that is inherent in every issue of "sufficient weight" to justify the recognition of public-interest standing—but rather to the generalized nature of the *issue itself*. In other words, public-interest standing should not be used by courts to engage in review of nonjusticiable political questions. Here, Appellants' claims do not raise that type of question. Rather, they seek to enforce an explicit and mandatory constitutional provision dealing primarily with questions of form and process.

¶ 32 We conclude that Appellants satisfy the requirements of the public-interest standing doctrine with respect to the Article VI Claims.

LEE, J., concurring in part and dissenting in part

¶ 63 In the past several decades, this court's standing jurisprudence has strayed further and further from its traditional mooring in the judicial power clause of the Utah Constitution. Thus, although we have long recognized a "traditional" conception of standing requiring individualized injuries sustaining private rights of action, our more recent decisions have exhibited increasing willingness to overlook that requirement under a "public interest" exception. That exception, as reconceived by the court today, stretches the principle of standing beyond recognition.

¶ 64 I respectfully dissent from the majority's invocation—and extension—of this "public interest" exception to the traditional requirement of standing. Its methodology is incompatible with the judicial power clause in Article VIII of the Utah Constitution. That clause limits our authority to the resolution of cases that fall within the traditional conception of the judicial power. In overriding these constraints, the majority robs the constitutional limits on our power of meaningful content. It does so to uphold standing for the Article VI claimants in this case on public interest grounds, thereby subjecting the standing inquiry to the arbitrary discretion of the court, under a standardless "test" that is little more than a post-hoc justification for a preferred result. Under this test, the standing question is left to a subjective, case-by-case assessment of a majority of the court as to whether the claims seem sufficiently "important" to merit review.

¶ 65 Instead of expanding the public interest exception, I would repudiate our prior dicta on this point and reject the exception altogether. And I would resolve the case under a traditional formulation of standing—one requiring an assertion of injury sustaining a private action. That formulation, in my view, requires dismissal of all of the claims at issue in this case, including the Article VI claims the majority reaches on public interest grounds.

I. STANDING AS A CONSTITUTIONAL COMPONENT OF THE JUDICIAL POWER

¶ 66 Standing is not a judge-made principle of judicial restraint subject to common-law evolution over time. It is an essential element of the constitutional provisions defining and limiting the judicial power. Such an element requires careful definition, rooted in an interpretation of the binding text of our constitution. We assail the very principle of constitutionalism when we ignore that interpretive role and opt instead to invoke and refine standardless "exceptions" justifying (but failing to explain) our case-by-case preferences to exercise jurisdiction in some cases but not in others.

¶ 70 Thus, I cannot accept the "public interest" test invoked by the court. I would instead interpret Article VIII of our constitution to confine the authority of the Utah courts to hear cases filed by private plaintiffs only where they vindicate "private rights," as that term was historically understood at the time of the framing of the Utah Constitution. That standard requires dismissal of all claims in this case for lack of standing.

¶ 71 In the sections that follow, I set forth the historical basis for the standard I would adopt, show that this standard is compatible with most all of the holdings (but not some of the dicta) from our court on the law of standing, and explain why the citizen-plaintiffs in this case lack standing.

II. THE TRADITIONAL CONCEPTION OF STANDING

¶ 72 [W]e must take seriously our role of interpreting the judicial power clause of Article VIII. And in interpreting that clause, we must examine the traditional understanding of the judicial power, identifying limits on the judicial power in established case law and in our constitutional history. If the traditional standing requirement is rooted in the constitution, it cannot be seen as a mere salutary invention of this court or as a matter within our power to "relieve" a plaintiff of fulfilling. Instead, it must be understood as a constraint on the exercise of judicial power that we are duty-bound to follow—just as we are with any provision of the constitution—unless and until the people repeal or amend the terms of Article VIII. As detailed below, I would find that the standing limits on our judicial power are indeed constitutionally rooted. This conclusion necessarily forecloses the majority's approach—of announcing an evolving set of discretionary standards endorsing claimants we deem "appropriate" or claims we find within the "public interest."

¶ 73 The starting point for this analysis, of course, is the text of Article VIII. That provision confers on our courts the "judicial power," and it speaks of our authority to issue "writs" and to decide "cases." UTAH CONST. art. VIII, §§ 1, 3, 5. These are definite terms with fixed content that place meaningful restrictions on the exercise of judicial power. First, because the power we wield must be "judicial," we are foreclosed from making law or announcing our views in an advisory or other non-judicial posture. And second, our exercise of the judicial power must be in the context of the issuance of "writs" or in our resolution of "cases," a formulation that implies a particular form for exercising the judicial power.

¶ 74 Our interpretation of Article VIII, then, must be informed by an analysis of the traditional nature of the judicial power and of the types of writs and cases traditionally resolved in the courts. And in my view, the relevant history is clear. Established case law in Utah and elsewhere has long limited the judicial power to the resolution of suits brought by private parties in cases involving so-called "private rights."

¶ 75 Eighteenth- and nineteenth-century precedent established important limitations on the sorts of writs and cases that could be initiated by private parties and entertained by courts. The traditional formulation in the case law uniformly held that suits involving "public rights"—interests held by the public generally and not by individuals—could not be initiated by private plaintiffs. Specifically, in actions involving criminal prosecutions, public nuisances, and writs of mandamus, the courts held that private individuals could not maintain actions vindicating public rights. For me, these cases establish a key element of the doctrine of standing as a gateway to the invocation of the judicial power: Private parties lack standing to sue to vindicate public rights, which must be asserted by government representatives and not by private individuals.

III. PUBLIC INTEREST STANDING IN UTAH CASES

¶ 93 Our modern standing cases do not foreclose the approach I advocate; they leave plenty of room for faithful adherence to the traditional standing formulation. Prior to today's decision, our cases have only occasionally adverted to a "public interest" notion of standing, and almost always in dicta (as an alternative to traditional standing). Today the court crosses a significant, problematic line. It extends the dicta in our cases to a square holding, and does so in a manner that deprives the limits of the public interest exception of any meaningful content.

A. The Private Right Limitation in Our Law

¶ 94 The holdings in most of our cases (if not always the dicta) have effectively maintained traditional limitations on standing. In *Jenkins v. Swan*, for example, we foreclosed standing in cases where "other potential plaintiffs with a more direct interest in [the] particular question" exist. This holding appropriately prefers parties that meet traditional standing requirements.

¶ 95 We departed from that approach to some extent in *Utah Chapter of the Sierra Club v. Utah Air Quality Board*, 2006 UT 74, 148 P.3d 960, where we outlined the parameters of an expanded "public right" standing. But that discussion was dicta and not controlling. Because the plaintiff satisfied traditional standing requirements, the court did not need to opine about an alternative (public right) standing test.

¶ 96 To my knowledge, we have only once employed the *Sierra Club* dicta in a case where we found traditional standing lacking: in *City of Grantsville v. Redevelopment Agency of Tooele City*. In that case, we upheld a municipality's "alternative" standing to litigate a contract matter involving a claim for breach of a development agreement. *Id.* Yet although the *City of Grantsville* opinion upholds Grantsville City's standing on public interest grounds, *id.*, that conclusion was again unnecessary. The city, after all, was a signatory to the agreement with an express right to receive proceeds of the development, and as such it was unquestionably a third-party beneficiary with a traditional, private-right interest in the contract dispute.

¶ 97 In *City of Grantsville* the court claimed not to reach the third-party beneficiary basis for standing. But in my view the court necessarily (if implicitly) relied on this ground, as Grantsville City's third-party beneficiary status is the only plausible legal basis for its standing.

¶ 99 And in my view the court must have relied on that status in its decision. A complete stranger to a contract would never be granted standing to sue to enforce it. And the enforcement of a mere contract is not a matter of fundamental public importance; surely it is less so than the constitutional claims under Article X deemed insufficient by the majority today. So even the *City of Grantsville* opinion is not really authority for public interest standing generally (and certainly not public interest standing in contract actions brought by third parties); it is better viewed as endorsing the standing of a named third-party beneficiary who failed to press a third-party beneficiary argument.

¶ 100 This case is thus a significant milestone. It marks the first time the court has endorsed a general theory of public interest standing in a square holding. That holding is problematic on many levels. In addition to ignoring the traditional limits on our authority under Article VIII, the public interest exception undermines at least two strands of our case law requiring a real party in interest to bring its own claims.

¶ 101 First, rule 17 of the Utah Rules of Civil Procedure requires that "[e]very action shall be prosecuted in the name of the real party in interest." Standing overlaps with the real party in interest requirement "inasmuch as both terms are used to designate a plaintiff who possesses a sufficient interest in the action to be entitled to be heard on the merits Courts generally define a real party in interest as "the person who is the true owner of the right sought to be enforced." So, even if a merely "competent" or "appropriate" party could establish standing under the proposed "public interest" principle, it would have to satisfy other rules governing parties in dispute, including the requirement that it be the true owner of the right sought to be enforced.

¶ 102 Second, we have traditionally limited a litigant's ability to assert a third party's rights. Third-party vindication of another's rights is generally proper only if "some substantial relationship between the claimant and the third parties [exists]," if it is impossible for the rightholders to assert their own constitutional rights, and if the third parties' constitutional rights would be diluted "were the assertion of jus tertii not permitted."

¶ 103 We have recognized these limitations for good reason. As the U.S. Supreme Court has explained, " 'courts should not adjudicate [a third party's] rights unnecessarily," as "it may be that in fact the holders of those rights ... do not wish to assert them' " and the "third parties themselves usually will be the best proponents of their own rights." Thus, courts "should prefer to construe legal rights only when the most effective advocates of those rights are before them."

¶ 104 I dissent because I see no basis in our precedent or elsewhere for abandoning these principles. I find no comfort in the fact that the approach embraced by the majority today "is not unusual in state jurisprudence." That is apparently true. But it is also beside the point if the trends in caselaw outside of Utah are incompatible with the provisions of the law that we are bound to enforce. And that is exactly how I see the authority before us.

¶ 105 The state precedent cited by the majority rests entirely on the faulty premise of "standing" as a judge-made principle of prudential restraint. In adopting a public interest conception of standing, these state courts have routinely ignored the governing constitutional language—with the dismissive assertion that the federal "case or controversy" limitation is not a part of the state judicial power clause. For reasons I've explained above, the conclusion (of unbridled, common-law power) does not at all follow from the premise (the lack of a "case or controversy" clause). Thus, the court may find persuasive the notion of standing in state court as "'a self-imposed rule of restraint'" or a "'judge-made doctrine'" that " 'free[s]'" state courts to "'reject procedural frustrations in favor of' " their own subjective sense of what is a " 'just and expeditious.'" But I find them helpful only in highlighting the problematic foundation of the public interest doctrine of standing. We should reject that doctrine and instead follow the traditional formulation of standing that is deeply rooted in the holdings of our cases and in the text of Article VIII.

B. The Majority's Eradication of a Meaningful "Public Interest" Standard

¶ 106 In upholding plaintiffs' standing to assert their Article VI claims in this case, the court not only invokes the "public interest" exception in a square holding; it stretches the exception in a manner that erases all meaningful limits on the doctrine of standing. The majority heralds its intent to preserve "strict standards" in a manner that "avoid[s] the temptation to apply a judge's own beliefs and philosophies to a determination of what questions are of great public importance." Yet the court's variation on the public interest standard eliminates any real limits, strict or otherwise, leaving the applicability of the exception to the court's unbridled discretion.

¶ 107 First, in repudiating any requirement that the plaintiff be a traditional claimant with an individual injury—or even the "*most* appropriate party," as our prior dicta sometimes suggested[25]—the court effectively abandons any threshold limitation based on the plaintiff's stake in the outcome of the case. The court articulates this element in terms that require a determination that the plaintiff is "'an appropriate party.'" But this inquiry is hardly a "test." It seems to me that it is more of a post-hoc passing grade—one crafted to justify the court's ultimate determination to reach the merits of the case.

¶ 108 That becomes clear when the court actually applies the test. In deeming plaintiffs "appropriate," the court says nothing that couldn't be said about any litigant with the resources to hire effective counsel (and with even the most remote interest). Perhaps it's true that plaintiffs have "done an admirable job of briefing the facts and controlling law" in this case, but that is no meaningful gateway to standing. Nor is the fact that the plaintiffs have "policy concerns" and are "focus[ed] on the instant constitutional challenge." We should require (and almost always have required) more from litigants than a showing that they are deeply worried about the case before us. Finally, the fact that plaintiffs "have caused this court to consider" the Article VI issues they have raised and to "clarify the standards they impose for the first time in decades" may ultimately be an "achievement." But if so, it is a circular achievement of the court's own making. The fact that the court ultimately considered the issues presented cannot itself be a justification for agreeing to consider the issues. Plaintiffs have achieved standing only because we granted it to them. It is a bootstrap to commend that "achievement" as a *basis* for upholding standing.

¶ 109 The court cements the circularity of its test in its articulation of the second step of the analysis. While acknowledging the existence of plaintiffs with concrete interests in suing to challenge SB 2 (such as teachers who fail to qualify for a salary supplement under the statute or textbook publishers whose books are not approved by the statutory approval program), the court dismisses these "hypothetical" plaintiffs as irrelevant—asserting that their failure to file suit to date is enough to render "unlikely" a lawsuit by these parties. This is a striking—and deeply troubling—step in our public interest standing jurisprudence. Before today, the question was not whether directly affected parties had filed suit, but whether they existed. If the failure of real parties in interest to file suit is enough to sustain recognition of a member of the general public to step in as an "appropriate" party, we have defined the gateway to the judicial power out of existence. We have assured that the jurisdictional threshold to the Utah courts depends only our subjective determination to hear a case even absent the presence of the claimant with a traditional stake in filing it.

¶ 110 Finally, the court's test is also circular in its assessment of the ultimate question of whether the Article VI claims asserted by plaintiffs are "of sufficient importance and general interest that claims of their violation may be brought even by plaintiffs who lack standing under the traditional criteria." Except to conclude that the Article VI issues are "part of the fundamental structure of legislative power articulated in our constitutionthe court offers no justification for deeming this element satisfied. And the court's further explication of the point only confirms its analytical emptiness. I see no rational, articulable basis for deeming the Article VI issues sufficiently important while rejecting the Article X issues on this score.

¶ 111 It is hardly an answer to note that "[n]ot every constitutional provision" is sufficiently important. That only begs the question of which ones clear the bar—and of the theoretical basis for setting the bar, or the level at which it is set. In begging these questions, the court has evaluated the importance element entirely within the confines of a black box. That not only deprives the parties in this case of an understanding of the basis of the court's decision; it also withholds from lower courts the tools needed to make these determinations going forward.

¶ 112 The hollow nature of the majority's standing analysis is confirmed by the court's ultimate rejection of public interest standing for the Article X claims. The court's proffered rationale—that the Article VI claims involve "restrictions which must be observed every time the legislature exercises its core function of passing laws" while the Article X claims involve a mere "a delegation of a defined subject to particular agency,"—is misdirection at best. Surely abiding by the constitution's power-allocation scheme is part of the legislature's "core function" that must be considered each time a law is passed. And the majority's refusal to "conclude that such questions can *never* be appropriate ones in which to employ the public-interest standing doctrine" only bears that out and emphasizes the standardless quality of this doctrine. Either the violation of a constitutional provision is important or it is not. Its importance cannot depend on the identity of the plaintiffs or the circumstances of each case, as the majority implies.

¶ 113 In all, the majority's distinction between the Article VI and Article X claims does not spring from meaningful analysis. It is an attempt to paper over an ultimate conclusion—the court's preference for reaching one set of claims (under Article VI) while declining to reach others (under Article X).

¶ 114 The exercise of unfettered discretion is troubling, especially on a matter constituting a limit on our power under the Utah Constitution. As we explained in *Utah Transit Authority*, "on matters affecting the scope of our own power or jurisdiction, our duty to vigilantly follow the strictures of the constitution is a matter of great significance." We ignore that responsibility when we treat the constitutional limits on our power as "mere matter[s] of convenience or judicial discretion." And we undermine the fundamental notion of a written constitution when we adopt jurisdictional standards that show no fidelity to that document and seize unbridled "discretion to decide which cases should be spun out and which cut off based on some vague sense of fairness or importance of the issue."

¶ 115 The public interest notion of standing cannot stand in the face of these principles. The court's extension of this doctrine here is particularly problematic, as it cements the public interest exception in a square holding, and in a manner that assures arbitrariness in its application going forward.

IV. THE TRADITIONAL STANDING TEST APPLIED HERE

¶ 116 For all these reasons, we should reinforce the constitutional basis for our traditional conception of standing and repudiate the public interest exception as incompatible with our constitutional tradition. And we should vacate and dismiss this case for lack of standing.

¶ 117 The Article VI claims at issue here are prototypical, generalized grievances. Plaintiffs have asserted no injury peculiar to them—no interest or stake beyond that of all Utah citizens. They are complaining about the *process* that resulted in the enactment of SB 2—a process allegedly lacking the clear title and single subject required by the Utah Constitution—and not an unlawful impact of the legislation on them as private individuals.

¶ 118 Thus, plaintiffs are not individuals or entities with a direct stake in challenging SB 2, like the affected teachers or book publishers identified by the majority. They are Utah taxpayers asserting a generalized challenge to the propriety of the legislative process culminating in SB 2. Their standing cannot be upheld under our historical standing caselaw without doing serious violence to their core principle. They lack standing on that basis, and their case should be dismissed.

¶ 121 The bounds of our judicial power cannot accommodate the kind of expansion that "public right" standing for merely "competent" plaintiffs involves. We cannot properly allow less than directly interested parties to litigate before us. To do so risks unrestrained decision-making based on underdeveloped facts and law and ultimately against the will and rights of those directly harmed. It also risks invasion of the province of the legislature. Public dispute resolution is beyond our constitutional authority in a case filed by private plaintiffs.

COUEY v. ATKINS
357 Ore. 460 (Ore. 2015)

LANDAU, J.

ORS 250.048(9) provides that a person who is registered with the Secretary of State to collect initiative petition signatures for pay may not, "at the same time, obtain signatures on a petition or prospective petition for which the person is not being paid." Plaintiff initiated this action against the Secretary of State, challenging the constitutionality of that statute. At the time he initiated the action, he had registered to collect initiative petition signatures for pay and had been hired to do just that. At the same time, he wanted to collect signatures on other measures on a volunteer basis. He contended that ORS 250.048(9) violated his constitutional rights of freedom of expression and association.

During the pendency of the litigation, however, plaintiff stopped working as a paid signature collector, and his registration expired. The secretary moved for summary judgment on the ground that the action had become moot. Plaintiff opposed the motion, submitting an affidavit stating that he intended to work as a paid signature collector in the future and that he might be interested in collecting signatures on a volunteer basis on other measures at the same time. He also argued that, even if his action had become moot, the action nevertheless should proceed because it is "likely to evade judicial review in the future," and ORS 14.175 expressly authorizes courts to adjudicate such cases.

The trial court entered summary judgment dismissing the action on the ground that the action had become moot. The court concluded that, because plaintiff had failed to ask for expedited consideration, his is not the sort of case that is likely to evade review under ORS 14.175. The Court of Appeals affirmed, and we accepted plaintiff's petition for review.

On review, the case presents the following issues for us to resolve: (1) whether the averments in plaintiff's affidavit are sufficient to establish that his action is not moot; (2) even if the action is moot, whether it is nevertheless justiciable under ORS 14.175 because it is likely to evade review within the meaning of that statute; and (3) if it is subject to ORS 14.175, whether the legislature possessed the constitutional authority to enact it. The case thus requires us to examine the subject of justiciability—in terms of this court's own jurisprudence on the rule against deciding moot cases, the intended meaning of the statutory exception to that rule, and the legislature's constitutional authority to enact such a law. It does not require us to reach the merits.

For the reasons that follow, we conclude that: (1) plaintiff's affidavit is insufficient to establish that his action is not moot; (2) the action nevertheless is likely to evade judicial review under the standard set out in ORS 14.175, because it is not necessary to request expedited consideration to meet its terms; and (3) the legislature does possess the constitutional authority to enact the statute. Accordingly, because we conclude that the case is justiciable under ORS 14.175, we reverse the decision of the Court of Appeals, reverse the decision of the trial court, and remand for further proceedings.

I. BACKGROUND

A. *Regulatory context*

We begin with a brief summary of the regulation of the initiative petition signature collection process to provide context for our discussion of the relevant facts. The powers of initiative and referendum reserved by the people in Article IV, section 1, of the Oregon Constitution allow them to enact statutes, adopt or reject bills passed by the legislature, and adopt amendments to the state constitution. The parties who seek to place a statewide initiative measure on an election ballot, known as the chief petitioners, must submit to the Secretary of State the text of the proposed measure along with the required number of sponsorship signatures. There follows the certification of a ballot title, an impartial summary of the proposed measure. Once the ballot title has been certified, the chief petitioners are responsible for collecting signatures from registered voters who support placing the measure on an upcoming election ballot. Depending on whether the measure proposes to enact a statute or to adopt a constitutional amendment, the number of required signatures varies from six to eight percent of the total votes cast for governor at the last election. Chief petitioners have a limited time to collect those signatures, which must be submitted to the Secretary of State at least four months before the date of the next regularly scheduled general election.

The process of collecting initiative petition signatures is regulated by statute and by administrative rules promulgated by the Secretary of State. Chief petitioners are authorized to hire paid signature collectors. But they must notify the Secretary of State of their intention to do that, and the petition itself must include a statement that one or more persons is being paid to collect signatures. Before a person may be paid to collect initiative petition signatures, he or she must register with the Secretary of State, specify for which measures signatures will be collected, and complete a training program prescribed by rule by the secretary. That registration remains in effect for a limited time; it expires four months before the next general election, when initiative petition signatures are due.

A registered paid initiative petition signature collector may not collect signatures on other measures on a volunteer basis. ORS 250.048(9) provides: "A person registered under this section [to be a paid collector] may not obtain signatures on a petition or prospective petition for which the person is being paid and, at the same time, obtain signatures on a petition or prospective petition for which the person is not being paid." The statute further provides that the Secretary of State may not count any signatures that were collected in violation of that restriction.

II. ANALYSIS

A. *Is plaintiff's action moot?*

[The Court concludes that it is moot, under traditional principles].

B. *If moot, is plaintiff's action nevertheless justiciable under* ORS 14.175?

Plaintiff argues that, if we conclude that his action is moot, it is nevertheless justiciable under ORS 14.175. That statute provides:

> "In any action in which a party alleges that an act, policy or practice of a public body ... is unconstitutional or is otherwise contrary to law, the party may continue to prosecute the action and the court may issue a judgment on the validity of the challenged act, policy or practice even though the specific act, policy or practice giving rise to the action no longer has a practical effect on the party if the court determines that:
>
> > "(1) The party had standing to commence the action;
> >
> > "(2) The act challenged by the party is capable of repetition, or the policy or practice challenged by the party continues in effect; and
> >
> > "(3) The challenged policy or practice, or similar acts, are likely to evade judicial review in the future."

Thus, ORS 14.175 provides that, if a judgment in a case "no longer has a practical effect on the party" who initiated it—that is, if a case has become moot—the court is nevertheless authorized to issue such a judgment if the party can meet each of the three stated requirements. In this case, the parties agree that plaintiff satisfied the first two requirements of the statute. They dispute whether he satisfied the third, that is, that the challenged policy or practice is "likely to evade judicial review in the future."

Plaintiff contends that ORS 14.175 requires only that it is "likely" that such challenges as the one that he has initiated will evade review in the future. Election law challenges, he contends, are not likely to be adjudicated to final judgment within the short, two-year election cycle that the law provides. Indeed, plaintiff notes that in this case, the time between the date the law went into effect and the end of the election cycle was even shorter: six months. Under the circumstances, it was extremely unlikely that his claim would not evade review. Plaintiff observes that ORS 14.175 adopts the "capable of repetition, yet evading review" exception to the rule against deciding moot cases, which federal courts have embraced for many years. Because of that borrowing, he argues, federal cases are especially relevant. And those federal cases make clear that election cases such as this one are precisely the sort of cases that come within the exception.

The Secretary of State insists that two years is adequate time to resolve claims such as plaintiff's. According to the secretary, plaintiffs advancing such claims may take advantage of statutory opportunities to request expedited consideration or certification directly to this court.

This time, we agree with plaintiff. Whether such challenges as plaintiff's are "likely to evade judicial review" is a question of statutory construction, which we examine by applying familiar principles. We review the text of the statute, in context, along with any relevant legislative history and settled rules of construction.

ORS 14.175 applies when it is "likely" that challenges such as the one before the court will evade review in the future. The term is undefined in the statute. Under the circumstances, we assume that the legislature intended the term to convey its ordinary meaning. The ordinary meaning of the adjective "likely" is "of such a nature or so circumstanced as to make something probable." *Webster's Third New Int'l Dictionary* 1310 (unabridged ed 2002). The word "probable," in turn, is defined as something "that is based on or arises from adequate fairly convincing ... evidence or support."

Thus, on the bare face of things, it appears that the statute applies when it is probable that a similar challenge will evade judicial review in the future. Certainty is not required. Nothing in the context of the statute suggests a contrary meaning.

There is a wealth of case law concerning the capable of repetition rule. In that regard, federal law has long been settled that the capable of repetition exception applies to election-related challenges. State courts, likewise, apply the exception to election cases.

The settled case law concerning the capable of repetition exception persuades us that ORS 14.175 applies to election cases such as the one before us. We find no indication from the text of the statute or its history that the legislature intended to include a requirement that the plaintiffs in each case exhaust every possible avenue of expedition as a predicate to invoking the statutory exception to the rule against deciding moot cases. We therefore conclude that the trial court and the Court of Appeals erred in holding that plaintiff is not entitled to proceed under ORS 14.175.

C. *Is ORS 14.175 constitutional?*

That brings us to the "obvious question," as the Court of Appeals phrased it: whether the statute violates the Oregon Constitution because it runs afoul of this court's decision in *Yancy*, which held that the "judicial power" that Article VII (Amended), section 1, of the Oregon Constitution confers on the courts does not include the authority to decide moot cases and, in addition, does not include the authority to recognize any exceptions to that limitation, including an exception for controversies that are capable of repetition, yet evade review. The secretary argues that *Yancy* held only that *the courts* lack authority to decide moot cases, not that *the legislature* cannot confer such authority. In the secretary's view, nothing in *Yancy* forecloses the legislature from enacting ORS 14.175.

In particular, this court's decisions in *Yancy* and *Kellas v. Dept. of Corrections*, 341 Or. 471, 145 P.3d 139 (2006), have caused uncertainty about the extent to which the state constitution imposes justiciability limitations on the exercise of judicial power by the courts. The problem lies in the fact that *Yancy* and *Kellas* reflect two starkly different—and irreconcilable—views of the power conferred by Article VII (Amended), section 1.

In *Yancy*, the court addressed whether it should recognize an exception to the doctrine that the court lacks constitutional authority to decide moot cases. The court explained that such issues as standing, ripeness, and mootness are all aspects of justiciability—that is, the authority of the court to exercise "judicial power" as authorized by Article VII (Amended), section 1, of the state constitution. The court noted that the relevant test of justiciability has always been whether "'the court's decision in the matter will have some practical effect on the rights of the parties to the controversy.'" The court discussed the historical context of the original judicial power provision of the state constitution, including decisions of the United States Supreme Court on the authority of federal courts under Article III of the federal constitution. The court concluded that, although it could not derive from that research a "definitive conclusion regarding the scope of judicial power under the Oregon Constitution," it nevertheless believed that "the prevailing view throughout the American legal landscape in 1857 was that the constitutional grant of judicial power did not include the power to decide cases that had become moot ."

Then–Associate Justice (now Chief Justice) Balmer specially concurred, explaining that he found nothing in the text, context, or historical background of the constitution to suggest that the framers intended courts to lack *authority* to decide moot cases, particularly those that involve events that are so brief that they inevitably conclude before the courts can render a final decision. In Justice Balmer's view, the relevant history and prior case law reflect a prevailing view of "the contours of mootness as a *prudential*, rather than a constitutional, matter."

In *Kellas*, the court took a completely different approach to justiciability—one easier to reconcile with Justice Balmer's specially concurring opinion in *Yancy* than with the majority opinion in that case. At issue in *Kellas* was the constitutionality of a statute that conferred on "any person" standing to challenge the validity of administrative rules, regardless of whether those persons would be affected by those rules. Given *Yancy's* explanation that standing is an aspect of constitutional justiciability—which the court said requires a judicial decision to have a "practical effect on the rights of the parties"—the answer would seem to have been straightforward: Regardless of an absence of legislative standing requirements, the constitution does not permit courts to decide cases unless a judicial decision would have a practical effect on the rights of the parties. But that is not how *Kellas* was decided.

In *Kellas*, the court cautioned against reading into the judicial power clause of Article VII (Amended), section 1, "constitutional barriers to litigation with no support in either the text or history of Oregon's charter of government." The court noted that the "cases" or "controversies" clause of Article III, section 2, of the United States Constitution had given rise to an extensive body of case law regarding the justiciability of disputes in federal court, which includes such matters as standing, mootness, and ripeness. But, the court observed, "The Oregon Constitution contains no 'cases' or 'controversies' provision." *Id.* For that reason, the court concluded, "we cannot import federal law regarding justiciability into our analysis of the Oregon Constitution." *Id.* The court noted that, historically, Oregon courts have avoided imposing justiciability barriers to litigation and have, instead, left such matters to legislative prerogative. In the end, the court found no constitutional impediment to the legislature granting any person the right to challenge administrative rules, regardless of whether a judicial decision on the matter would affect them.

The fact of the matter is that none of the aspects of justiciability that the majority in *Yancy* listed—standing, mootness, or ripeness—finds the sort of direct textual support that *Kellas* suggests is required to support a "constitutional barrier to litigation." The two decisions cannot be reconciled.

1. *Constitutional text*

The "judicial power" vested in the judicial branch was first described in two provisions of the original 1857 state constitution. Article VII, section 1, provided:

> "The Judicial power of the State shall be vested in a Supr[e]me Court, Circuit[ ] Courts, and County Courts, which shall be Courts of Record having general jurisdiction, to be defined, limited, and regulated by law in accordance with this Constitution."

And Article VII, section 9, provided:

> All judicial power, authority, and jurisdiction not vested by this constitution or by laws consistent therewith, exclusively in some other Court shall belong to the Circuit Courts, and they shall have appellate jurisdiction, and supervisory authority over the County Courts, and all other inferior Courts, Officers, and tribunals.

From the bare text of those provisions, at least two things are noteworthy. First, nothing in the text of the constitution itself defined the term "judicial power." Second, nothing in the text of the constitution itself imposed any limitations on its exercise. Neither of the judicial-power provisions was patterned after the judicial-power provisions of the federal constitution, which expressly limited the exercise of judicial power by federal courts to specifically enumerated categories of "cases" and "controversies." To the contrary, the 1857 constitution vested "*[a]ll* judicial power" in the courts, without limitation or qualification.

That departure from the federal pattern was apparently deliberate. The original Article VII, in fact, was one of the few provisions of the 1857 constitution to have been largely drafted from scratch. In 1910, the voters amended the constitution, approving a new Article VII, which addressed a number of different issues pertaining to the courts—in particular, judicial elections and terms of office, jury verdicts in civil cases, grand juries, and the standard of review of jury verdicts. The new Article VII also eliminated the original Article VII, section 9, and reworded section 1 to provide that "[t]he judicial power of the state shall be vested in one supreme court and in such other courts as may from time to time be created by law."

As with the original Article VII, section 1, the new version referred to the "judicial power" of the state, but did not define or otherwise delineate it. Importantly, Article VII (Amended), section 1—like its predecessor—did not include any limitations on the "judicial power" that the courts are authorized to exercise. In particular, like the original, the 1910 judicial power provision omitted any reference to the sort of "case or controversy" limitations that appear in Article III of the federal constitution.

2. *Historical context*

Because the text of Article VII (Amended), section 1, offers little help in discerning what its framers understood "judicial power" to mean, we must examine the historical context ….

g. Significance of the historical context

The foregoing examination of the historical context—of the 1857 constitution and, particularly, of the 1910 amendments—shows a complete absence of evidence that the framers would have understood the "judicial power" conferred in either 1857 or in 1910 to have been limited to what we now term "justiciable" cases. To the contrary, the relevant case law shows that courts permitted persons with no personal stake in the outcome to initiate "public actions" and that, while moot cases could be dismissed, the decision to do so was one of judicial discretion and could depend on whether the issues were of particular public importance. Federal case law was entirely consistent with that state law practice, culminating in the explicit recognition of exceptions to the mootness doctrine for cases of public interest and cases that are capable of repetition, yet evade review. The notion that federal courts are without constitutional authority to decide "nonjusticiable" cases did not emerge until well into the twentieth century.

To recap the bidding so far, then: Nothing in the text of Article VII, section 1, or Article VII (Amended), section 1, imposes any limitations on the exercise of "judicial power." In particular, there are no "case or controversy" limitations of the sort that are imposed under Article III of the United States Constitution. Nor are there any explicit references to a lack of constitutional authority to hear cases initiated by parties lacking a personal stake in the outcome. Moreover, nothing in the historical context of either provision of the Oregon Constitution lends support for the notion that the framers would have understood them to have included such limitations implicitly because of the very nature of the term "judicial power," at least not in public action cases or those involving issues of "public importance."

3. *Later Oregon case law*

We turn, then, to an examination of Oregon cases decided after the adoption of the 1910 amendments. As we have noted, the court has not been consistent in its views of justiciability generally, and mootness particularly. Rather, over the course of the last 100 years, the cases have veered back and forth between regarding justiciability as a constitutional imperative and treating it as a prudential consideration.

4. *Reassessing justiciability*

We are left with essentially two competing conceptions of justiciability in our case law. On the one hand, we have *Yancy*, which viewed justiciability as a constitutional requirement inherent in the nature of "judicial power" conferred under Article VII (Amended), section 1, of the state constitution. On the other hand, we have *Kellas*, which concluded that nothing in the text or historical context of Article VII (Amended), section 1, suggests such limitations on the exercise of judicial power.

In light of our reexamination of the text, historical context, and case law relevant to the adoption of Article VII (Amended), section 1, we conclude that *Kellas* has the better of the argument, at least to the extent that courts are presented with "public actions" or cases involving matters of "public interest." *Kellas* correctly observed that nothing in the text imposes any limits on the exercise of "judicial power" under Article VII (Amended), section 1.

The same cannot be said of *Yancy*. *Yancy* began by acknowledging that the text of Article VII (Amended), section 1, says nothing about justiciability, standing, mootness, ripeness, or any other limitation on the judicial power exercised by the courts of this state. The court nevertheless concluded that the very nature of the "judicial power" itself implicitly includes such limitations. The court based that conclusion on an analysis of the historical context of Article VII (Amended), section 1. Unfortunately, that analysis was seriously incomplete.

Yancy claimed support for its interpretation of "judicial power" in essentially three places. First, it relied on the several instances in which the justices of the United States Supreme Court declined to issue advisory opinions, in particular, *Hayburn's Case*. But those instances concerned the exercise of judicial power under the federal constitution, which, as we have noted, is subject to limitations not present in Article VII (Amended), section 1. Moreover, the cases involved particular institutional concerns that inhere in requests for judicial decisions that either are reviewable by other branches of government or involved requests for advice outside the context of a judicial proceeding. As a result, as we have noted, those cases were construed in the nineteenth century to apply to those circumstances and were viewed as turning on separation of powers principles; the notion that the cases stood for broader conceptions of justiciability did not surface until the twentieth century and well after the adoption of the 1910 amendments to the Oregon Constitution.

Second, *Yancy* claimed support from more recent federal court case law arising under But, as we have noted, federal justiciability case law is not predicated on the meaning of "judicial power" *simpliciter*, but on the case-or-controversy *limitations* on the judicial power.

Third, *Yancy* claimed support from one early Oregon decision, *Burnett*. As *Yancy* characterized it, *Burnett* stands for the proposition that, to be a proper exercise of the judicial power, proper parties with a personal stake in the outcome must appear before the court. That, however, is not what *Burnett* stands for. As we have explained, *Burnett* first noted that, ordinarily, a writ of review will not issue unless the challenged order was judicial in nature. In that context, the court said that "judicial" orders are those involving proper parties with a personal stake. The court then noted that, notwithstanding that ordinary rule, challenged orders of a more "general" character—operating "in a very general manner upon the entire body of the taxpayers of the county"—still are justiciable, even though no party had a personal stake in the outcome. According to the court, "[i]n all cases where the proceeding sought to be reviewed involves a matter of public interest affecting a great number of persons, the allowance of the writ is in the sound discretion of the court." Thus, directly contrary to the way that *Yancy* characterized it, *Burnett* is consistent with the general practice of courts in the nineteenth century to review actions involving public rights.

In short, *Yancy's* analysis is undercut by significant omissions and by misinterpretations of the historical evidence of what the framers likely would have understood of the "judicial power" conferred by the constitution. The decision must be disavowed in favor of *Kellas*.

In disavowing the justiciability analysis of *Yancy*, we do not hold that the state constitution imposes no constraints on the exercise of judicial power. This case does not require such a broad holding. Rather, we hold that, based on the foregoing analysis of the text, historical context, and case law interpreting Article VII (Amended), section 1, there is no basis for concluding that the court lacks judicial power to hear public actions or cases that involve matters of public interest that might otherwise have been considered nonjusticiable under prior case law. Whether that analysis means that the state constitution imposes no such justiciability limitations on the exercise of judicial power in other cases, we leave for another day.

We also do not hold that moot cases will no longer be subject to dismissal. We hold only that Article VII (Amended), section 1, does not *require* dismissal in public actions or cases involving matters of public interest. In a similar vein, we emphasize that, merely because there are no justiciability limitations on the exercise of judicial power in public actions or cases involving matters of public interest does not mean that the reference to "judicial power" in Article VII (Amended), section 1, is an empty vessel to be filled as it pleases the legislature. Separation of powers principles make clear that there are limits to what constitutes the "judicial power" that courts may exercise.

This case does not require us to define the boundaries of the judicial function. It suffices at this juncture to make the point that, even though such justiciability doctrines as mootness and standing are not implicit in Article VII (Amended), section 1—at least not in public action cases or those involving matters of public importance—there remain other limitations on the "judicial power" that may be exercised under the state constitution.

5. *Application*

We turn to the question whether the legislature acted within its authority in enacting ORS 14.175. Under *Kellas*, the legislature's authority to enact legislation is "plenary, subject only to limitations that arise either from the Oregon Constitution or from a source of supreme federal law."

We are aware of no limitation on the legislature's authority to enact legislation authorizing litigants to maintain an action that, although otherwise moot, is capable of repetition, yet evading review. Such legislation purports to confer no more authority than what we have just concluded the courts possess under Article VII (Amended), section 1. As our analysis demonstrates, judicial determination of such cases is consistent with centuries of historical practice and the sound prudential exercise of judicial power, at least as to public action cases or cases involving matters of public interest.

IN RE GUARDIANSHIP OF TSCHUMY
853 N.W.2d 728 (Minn. 2014)

GILDEA, C.J.

The question presented in this case is whether court approval is required before a guardian who has the power to consent to necessary medical treatment for a ward under Minn.Stat. § 524.5–313(c)(4)(i) (2012), may consent to remove the ward from life-sustaining treatment when all the interested parties agree that such removal is in the ward's best interests. The district court held that a guardian who possesses the medical-consent power under Minn.Stat. § 524.5–313(c)(4)(i), cannot consent to the removal of a ward's life support without prior court approval. The court of appeals reversed, holding that unless otherwise limited by court order, a guardian given the statutory medical-consent power has the authority to consent to the removal of life-sustaining treatment without a separate order from the district court. Because we conclude that the guardian did not need further court approval, we affirm.

On September 24, 2007, a social worker at appellant Jeffers Tschumy's nursing facility filed a petition asking the Hennepin County District Court to appoint a guardian for Tschumy. The social worker said 53–year–old Tschumy was "an incapacitated person" who "lack[ed] sufficient understanding or capacity to make or communicate responsible decisions concerning his person." According to the social worker, Tschumy was "facing multiple medical issues" and was "unable to make informed medical decisions."

After a hearing, the district court appointed Tschumy's then conservator to be his guardian. The court found "clear and convincing evidence" that Tschumy was "an incapacitated person" who needed a guardian. The court made several findings of fact regarding Tschumy's needs at the time, many of which referred to his inability to make medical decisions for himself. The court said Tschumy needed assistance providing for his "health care, housing, food, transportation, and finances," and acknowledged that Tschumy did not appropriately manage his diabetes. The court also found that Tschumy was "incapable" of exercising certain "rights and powers," including the ability to consent to necessary medical care. In the letters of guardianship, the court gave the guardian the authority to, among other things, "[g]ive any necessary consent to enable, or to withhold consent for, the Ward to receive necessary medical or other professional care, counsel, treatment or service."

On April 15, 2012, Tschumy choked on a sandwich and went into respiratory and cardiac arrest. Tschumy lost his pulse, and the group home staff administered CPR. Doctors at Abbott Northwestern Hospital were able to remove fragments of the sandwich, but a CT scan showed Tschumy had an "anoxic brain injury." In a report later filed with the district court, Tschumy's attorney laid out a dire prognosis for Tschumy. He said that since Tschumy had been in the hospital, "his conditions of severe and irreversible anoxic encephalopathy, continuous seizures, and respiratory failure have not improved." Initial opinions of the doctors regarding Tschumy's "dismal prognosis for return of meaningful neurologic recovery" were confirmed as time passed, "as his seizures [could not] be controlled without deep sedation" and seizure medication. Tschumy's treatment team was in "unanimous agreement that this unfortunate man [had] suffered irreversible brain damage and [could not] survive."

On April 23, 2012, Allina Health System, d/b/a Abbott Northwestern Hospital, filed a motion asking the Hennepin County District Court to amend the successor letters of general guardianship to "specifically authorize the guardian to request removal of life support systems." The district court held a hearing the next day. Vogel opposed the motion to amend the successor letters, arguing that he already had the authority to approve the removal of life support. The court appointed attorney Michael Biglow to represent Tschumy, investigate what Tschumy would want, and make a recommendation to the court.

In an order filed May 11, 2012 ("May order"), the district court authorized the guardian and the hospital to remove Tschumy's life support systems. The court held that the medical power granted to a guardian does not grant the guardian the unrestricted authority to direct the removal of life support but said it would explain that holding in a later order, so as not to postpone Tschumy's removal from life support. Tschumy was removed from life support, and he died soon thereafter. On May 17, 2012, the court discharged Vogel as Tschumy's guardian.

Vogel appealed the district court's … order. The court of appeals asked the parties to file "informal memoranda" addressing three questions: whether the district court's October order was independently appealable, whether Vogel had standing to appeal, and whether the appeal was moot. After the parties filed their informal memoranda, the court found that the appeal was timely, Vogel had standing to appeal, and the case was not moot because it was "capable of repetition, yet evad[ed] review" and involved an important public issue of statewide significance.

I.

We turn first to the question of whether we have jurisdiction to decide this case. The parties do not contend that we lack jurisdiction. But the existence of a justiciable controversy is essential to our exercise of jurisdiction, so we can raise the issue on our own.

A.

There are several interrelated, potential jurisdictional problems in this case. Tschumy has died, and no ruling we make will affect him. Vogel has been discharged as Tschumy's guardian, and similarly, no ruling we make will affect the scope of his guardianship over Tschumy. As a result, there are questions about the parties' continuing interest in this case, as well as questions about Vogel's standing to appeal the district court's October order and Tschumy's standing to appeal the court of appeals decision.

We have dismissed appeals for lack of jurisdiction where the issues in the case were moot. We do so because courts are designed to decide actual controversies. We will also dismiss cases as moot if we are unable to grant effective relief.

We have not previously considered whether we should dismiss an appeal that arises in the unusual context presented here. Several states have addressed the mootness issue in this context, however, and almost all of them have concluded that even though the person on life support had died pending an appeal, the appellate court should still resolve issues over the authority to order the discontinuation of life-sustaining treatment. These cases recognize that an appellate court has the authority to decide the question presented as an exception to the mootness doctrine.

Our precedent similarly permits us to exercise our discretion to consider a case that might be technically moot as an exception to our mootness doctrine. We have said that we have authority to decide cases that are technically moot when those cases are functionally justiciable and present important questions of statewide significance. Our mootness doctrine therefore is flexible and discretionary; it is not a mechanical rule that we invoke automatically. Our precedent illustrates our careful analysis of all aspects of the issues presented before we determine whether to dismiss the case or exercise our discretion to consider the appeal as an exception to the mootness doctrine.

B.

With these cases in mind, we turn to the jurisdictional question presented here. The question of whether a guardian needs prior court approval to consent to the removal of life-sustaining treatment is functionally justiciable. The question was ably briefed and argued by the parties and the record contains the factual information necessary for a decision. In addition, there was thoughtful and informative amicus support for the position that each party advocated.

In addition, this case presents an important public issue of statewide significance. The impact of uncertainty on such an important question also counsels in favor of exercising our discretion to resolve this issue in this case. The district court's May order notes "that there are thousands of guardians in Minnesota holding the same power that Mr. Vogel has." And in her amicus brief, the Attorney General represents that there are over 12,000 wards under State supervision in Minnesota. A decision from our court will help clarify for the guardians and their wards the scope of the guardians' authority to make one of life's most fundamental decisions.

We acknowledge the possibility that the issue presented here could arise in a future case. Because this case is functionally justiciable and the issue presented is one of public importance and statewide significance that we should decide now, our precedent provides us with the authority to decide this case even though it is technically moot. [T]here are no countervailing constitutional and prudential considerations warranting a decision not to exercise jurisdiction in this case. The prudential considerations weigh heavily in favor of exercising jurisdiction in the unusual context presented here, given that it is our obligation to afford paramount consideration to the "welfare" of the ward. We therefore hold that we have jurisdiction and turn to the merits of the case.

STRAS, J., dissenting.

If the caption of this case accurately reflected the nature of this appeal, it would say *In re the Interpretation of Minn.Stat. § 524.5–313(c)(4)(i)*, rather than *In re the Guardianship of: Jeffers J. Tschumy, Ward.*

The reason is that this appeal has little to do with Jeffers Tschumy. When Tschumy was alive, Abbott Northwestern Hospital sought and obtained a court order to cease providing life-sustaining medical treatment to Tschumy, who died shortly thereafter. At that point, there was nothing left for the district court, or any other court, to decide in order to resolve the parties' dispute. It is now more than two years after the cessation of treatment and Tschumy's death, and the parties to the original dispute have received exactly the relief that they requested. Yet the parties in this appeal still seek an answer to the question of whether a court order was required to remove life support, a controversial and difficult legal question that is purely academic at this point.

The parties' request strikes at the very heart of judicial power. For nearly 150 years, we have consistently declined to answer purely academic questions, no matter how interesting or important they are, because courts do "not issue advisory opinions or decide cases merely to make precedent[ ]." Yet despite our longstanding prohibition on advisory opinions, the plurality is ready and willing to answer the parties' question because, in its view, the case is functionally justiciable and the legal issue is sufficiently important. I respectfully dissent because the plurality's approach casts aside the fundamental limitations on our authority and aggrandizes judicial power at the expense of the Legislature—the branch of government that the Minnesota Constitution vests with the authority to address abstract policy questions. Minn. Const. arts. III, § 1, IV, § 1.

II.

It is still unclear why, or how, this case is before us, and on whose behalf the two parties are acting. For its part, the plurality asserts that the legal issue in this case is important and the case is functionally justiciable, so we should just go ahead and decide it. The problem is that this case has *all* of the hallmarks of a nonjusticiable controversy. The parties appealed from an advisory opinion of the district court, the same pot of money is paying for the legal fees incurred by both parties, and there is no way to order meaningful relief for anyone in this litigation regardless of the legal conclusion that we reach. Under these circumstances, in which there is no case or controversy, it is our duty under the Minnesota Constitution to dismiss the appeal.

A.

The Minnesota Constitution does not grant us the authority to "decide cases merely to make precedents." Rather, "[w]e make precedents only as incident to the determination of actual controversies." As we recognized in 1865, only 8 years after Minnesota became a state, requiring judges to decide legal questions in the absence of an actual controversy is "inconsistent with judicial duties" and would set "a dangerous precedent."

We are not a junior-varsity legislature. The parties ask us to decide a legal question that is completely disconnected from any case or controversy and to make a pure policy decision about how guardians *should* act in the future when making life-ending decisions for a ward. Instead of reiterating the longstanding principle that we do not decide cases merely to make precedent and recognizing that pure policy decisions are for the Legislature to make, the plurality would adopt what is, in essence, a different rule: we do not decide cases merely to make precedent, unless we say differently. However, the plurality's rule would itself set a "dangerous precedent" and "[t]he evils which might result to the people from such a source will suggest themselves on a moment's reflection."

[T]he controversy between *Tschumy and the Hospital*—neither of which has any interest in the proceedings before this court—was justiciable at its inception. When the district court authorized Tschumy's removal from life support in May 2012, however, the controversy ended and there was nothing left to decide. The Hospital, which had commenced the litigation, received the court authorization that it sought and advised the district court that it did not seek any other relief. In fact, the Hospital's attorney told the district court that "the decision about Mr. Tschumy can be made without [addressing the broader legal question] at all, and may[ ]be [it] should be." Tschumy also received the relief that he, as represented by Vogel (his guardian) and Biglow (his court-appointed attorney), had sought: authorization for the cessation of life-sustaining treatment. Yet, nearly 5 months later, the district court issued a second order, in which it broadly concluded that guardians do not have the authority to unilaterally withdraw life-sustaining medical treatment from a ward under the guardianship statutes, even though by the time of the second order, the case had long been moot.

The only person left unsatisfied by the district court's decision was Vogel. In his capacity as Tschumy's guardian, Vogel received exactly the relief he sought, and he has never contended otherwise. However, in his *personal* capacity as a professional guardian—entirely separate from his role in this particular case—Vogel would have preferred to win in a different way. Instead of obtaining court approval to withdraw treatment, Vogel wanted a court order saying that he already had the authority to direct the withdrawal of life support. Vogel made his opinion clear when he said that, if the district court decided to say (as it eventually did) that court approval was required to terminate treatment, such a ruling would be "an awful precedent."

Vogel's position, which the plurality must necessarily view as sufficient to create a justiciable controversy, suffers from several problems. First, Vogel's standing in this litigation has always been derivative of Tschumy's interests, and he has thus lacked standing throughout the appellate process, both because neither Tschumy nor his estate has any further interest in the case, and because Vogel is no longer serving as Tschumy's guardian. To my knowledge, we have never held that a person who had a purely representational interest in the district court can assert a personal interest on appeal. There is, after all, a reason why the caption of this case says *In re the Guardianship of: Jeffers J. Tschumy, Ward*, rather than *In re the Personal Interests of: Joseph Vogel, Professional Guardian*.

Second, even if Vogel could now assert a purely personal interest on appeal, "[y]ou cannot persist in suing after you've won." Once a litigant has obtained the relief that he or she requested below, the fact that the litigant wishes the court had said something different in its opinion does not provide a sufficient continuing interest for an appeal. In other words, justiciability focuses on "whether the relief sought would, if granted, make a difference to the legal interests of the parties (as distinct from their psyches, which might remain deeply engaged with the merits of the litigation)."

Third, the personal interest asserted by Vogel on appeal—that the district court adopted the wrong legal rule—is clearly insufficient in light of the fact that district court orders have no precedential value and govern *only* the rights of the parties to the litigation. It is difficult to understand how Vogel could retain a sufficient continuing interest, even in his personal capacity, in seeking the reversal of a legal rule adopted in a nonprecedential opinion that, by definition, applied only to Tschumy and the Hospital. Such an interest is at best hypothetical, and most likely fictional.

Fourth, it is questionable whether there are any adverse parties in this case at all. Vogel, ostensibly acting as Tschumy's guardian, is depleting the funds in Tschumy's estate in an effort to obtain a non-"awful precedent" from this court. But Tschumy's estate is also paying the legal fees incurred by the other side—represented by Biglow, the court-appointed attorney who ostensibly represents Tschumy in this appeal—to advocate against Vogel's position. Tschumy's estate cannot simultaneously have an interest in two totally opposite rules: on the one hand, a rule that a court order is not required to remove life support (advanced by Vogel), and on the other, a rule that a court order is required to remove life support (advanced by Biglow). In short, there is good reason to doubt that the parties are truly adverse when the same pot of money is funding the litigation expenses of both sides.

What is clear, therefore, is that Vogel and Biglow seek an advisory opinion—that is, they do not truly wish to resolve a current dispute, but instead seek our advice, as they sought the advice of the court of appeals, on an abstract legal question.

[N]o one is asserting a legally cognizable interest on appeal. Vogel's only interest in the appeal is his dissatisfaction with what he perceives to be an "awful" rule from a nonprecedential district court opinion. Biglow, for his part, does not articulate any continuing interest in this "dispute," let alone a legally cognizable one. Even aside from the fact that Tschumy, whom Biglow ostensibly represents, no longer has any interest in this case, Biglow is not a professional guardian, and he has never asserted that the outcome of this case will have any impact on his legal practice. In fact, at oral argument, Biglow all but acknowledged that the driving force for his legal position on appeal has been taking a position opposite to Vogel, rather than a personal or professional interest in obtaining a particular result. [T]here is insufficient adversity in this case because Tschumy's estate is paying the legal fees of both sides, and it is not clear why, or to what extent, either side is opposing the other. [A]s stated above, our judgment in this case (as well as that of the court of appeals) is meaningless, other than as an attempt to create precedent. Thus, even though this case presents a legal issue with statewide importance, the Minnesota Constitution requires us to exercise restraint and await a different case—one with a justiciable controversy—to decide the issue.

The requirement of a justiciable controversy is not an excuse for courts to decline to decide tough or important questions. Rather, it is a constitutional constraint on the authority of the judiciary. The Minnesota Constitution divides the powers of the government into three "distinct departments," and provides that "[n]o person or persons belonging to or constituting one of these departments shall exercise any of the powers properly belonging to either of the others except in the instances expressly provided in this constitution." Minn. Const. Art. III, § 1. The judiciary is limited to "judicial act[s]." The resolution of an abstract legal question outside of the context of a justiciable controversy is not a "judicial act," it is a legislative act, and I cannot subscribe to the plurality's approach because it requires us to act as legislators, not as judges.

It should be clear at this point, as the district court's language in its second order implicitly acknowledged, that this case no longer involves any real controversy between the parties. It is now a manufactured controversy involving an abstract and hypothetical legal question that the parties, if the question is still sufficiently important to them, should direct to the Legislature. Accordingly, rather than adopting an approach that would expand our own power at the Legislature's expense, I would instead follow precedent and dismiss the appeal in this case for lack of subject matter jurisdiction.

B.

Not only does this case fail to satisfy our general definition of a justiciable controversy, which alone warrants dismissal, it is also moot. A case becomes moot when "the court is unable to grant effectual relief." The plurality concludes, and I agree, that this case is moot because we are unable to grant effective relief to anyone, much less Tschumy. Nevertheless, the plurality would decide the case anyway because, in its view, it "presents an important public issue of statewide significance" and it is "functionally justiciable."

It is true, as the plurality notes, that courts in other jurisdictions have decided controversies that are similar to this one. But these foreign cases were all decided under different constitutions—some of which permit advisory opinions in certain circumstances—and in the face of different facts—none of which required an appellate court to review what was itself an advisory opinion. Most importantly, these other courts have adopted an approach that is inconsistent with this court's interpretation of Article III, Section 1 of the Minnesota Constitution.

III.

The scope of a guardian's authority to make end-of-life decisions for a ward is, without question, an exceedingly important question. But it is a bedrock constitutional principle that Minnesota courts lack the authority to decide *any* legal question, even an exceedingly important one, in the absence of a justiciable controversy. When a justiciable controversy is missing, as it is here, and as it was in the court of appeals, it is our constitutional duty to dismiss the case. In the absence of a justiciable controversy, it is the Legislature's job, not ours, to clarify the scope of a guardian's authority in making end-of-life decisions for a ward. To reach any other conclusion would violate Article III, Section 1 of the Minnesota Constitution. For these reasons, I would vacate the decision of the court of appeals and remand with instructions to dismiss the appeal for lack of subject matter jurisdiction.

PAGE, J., joins the dissent of Justice Stras.

BERRY v. CRAWFORD
990 N.E.2d 410 (Ind. 2013)

DICKSON, C.J.

With this case we confront whether the judicial branch may, consistent with the Indiana Constitution, review actions of and intervene in the internal management of the legislative branch, specifically the decision of the House of Representatives to collect fines from House members who left the state to prevent the formation of a quorum. We hold that when, as here, the Indiana Constitution expressly assigns certain functions to the legislative branch without any contrary constitutional qualification or limitation, challenges to the exercise of such legislative powers are nonjusticiable and the doctrine of separation of powers precludes judicial consideration of the claims for relief, and the defendants' request for dismissal of the plaintiffs' claims should have been granted in full.

During the 2011 legislative session, members of the Indiana House of Representatives Democratic Caucus left the House Chambers and the state to prevent the formation of a quorum in order to block a vote on impending legislation. Members of the House Republican Caucus imposed, by motion, fines on the absent legislators. The Speaker of the House, Brian Bosma, then directed the Principal Clerk, M. Caroline Spotts, to submit payroll grids to the Auditor of State, Tim Berry, withholding the fines from legislative pay. The plaintiffs, affected members of the House Democratic Caucus, brought suit in Marion Superior Court seeking to recover the withheld pay and enjoin future action to recover the fines.

On December 6, 2011, the trial court granted the defendants' motion to dismiss in part, finding that the determination of the fine was within the House's "exclusive constitutional authority" and thus outside the court's jurisdiction, but denied it in part, finding that review of the collection of fines was within the court's jurisdiction. ("*Berry I*").

During the 2012 legislative session, members of the House Democratic Caucus again absented themselves from the House Chambers in order to block a vote on impending legislation. House Republicans again passed motions to compel and fine the absent members. The trial court consolidated the trial on the merits with the previous hearing on the motion for preliminary injunction and entered final judgment for the plaintiffs ("*Berry II*"). The court ordered return of the withheld amounts and issued a permanent injunction preventing future withholding, finding that the seizure of the members' pay in satisfaction of the legislative fines violated the Indiana Wage Payment Statutes. The defendants appeal.

In granting the defendants' motion to dismiss in part, the trial court found that it could not "interfere with the House's 'exclusive constitutional authority' to compel attendance or determine a fine, even if it violates [statutory law] when doing so." We agree. For courts to get involved in such a legislative function would amount to the type of "constitutionally impermissible judicial interference with the internal operations of the legislative branch" which we have rejected in the past. Yet, in denying the motion with regard to review of the collection of the legislative fines, the trial court found that "the House's 'exclusive constitutional authority' to compel attendance does not preclude Indiana courts from otherwise interpreting and enforcing applicable Indiana statutes—which is the courts' 'exclusive constitutional authority.'" Thus, the trial court concluded, it was not precluded from deciding plaintiffs' Indiana wage claims and Indiana constitutional claims relating to the collection of the fines. This is incorrect.

The defendants assert that "[t]he Indiana Constitution commits legislative discipline exclusively to the respective houses of the General Assembly, and discipline of members is not subject to judicial review." In support, the defendants cite various provisions of Article 4 of the Indiana

Constitution, which delineate the powers of the legislative department. Article 4, Section 10, states, in relevant part, "Each House, when assembled, shall choose its own officers...; judge the elections, qualifications, and returns of its own members; determine its rules of proceeding, and sit upon its own adjournment." Ind. Const. art. 4, § 10. The defendants also rely on Article 4, Section 11,

> Two-thirds of each House shall constitute a quorum to do business; but a smaller number may meet, adjourn from day to day, and *compel the attendance of absent members*. A quorum being in attendance, if either House fail to effect an organization within the first five days thereafter, the members of the House so failing, shall be entitled to no compensation, from the end of the said five days until an organization shall have been effected.

Finally, the defendants cite Article 4, Section 14, relating to discipline of members: "Either House *may punish its members for disorderly behavior*, and may, with the concurrence of two-thirds, expel a member; but not a second time for the same cause." Therefore, the defendants argue, the trial court, in reviewing the plaintiffs' claims and entering final judgment for the plaintiffs, acted in violation of the principles of separation of powers decreed by the Indiana Constitution.

The separation of powers doctrine is embodied in Article 3, Section 1, of the Indiana Constitution, which states,

> The powers of the Government are divided into three separate departments; the Legislative, the Executive including the Administrative, and the Judicial: and no person, charged with official duties under one of these departments, shall exercise any of the functions of another, except as in this Constitution expressly provided.

While the Constitution of the United States implicitly mandates the separation of powers at the federal level, the constitutions of Indiana and many other states clearly and explicitly command that each branch of state government respect the constitutional boundaries of the coordinate branches.

Article 7, Section 1, of the Indiana Constitution vests the judicial power of the state in the courts. The circuit courts exercise jurisdiction "as may be prescribed by law," Ind. Const. art. 7, § 8, and the intermediate appellate courts and Supreme Court "shall exercise appellate jurisdiction" as specified by rules promulgated by the Supreme Court, *id.* art. 7, §§ 4, 6. Although jurisdiction is granted to the courts by the Constitution, such jurisdiction is neither absolute nor unlimited. Our cases have repeatedly held that prudential concerns may render a dispute nonjusticiable by the courts. The distinction between jurisdiction and justiciability is a fine one and has been confused in the past. It is necessary here to clearly explain this distinction. Jurisdiction is defined as "[a] court's power to decide a case or issue a decree." Black's Law Dictionary 927 (9th ed. 2009). It is the power in the first instance for a court to exercise authority over and rule on a dispute. Justiciability, on the other hand, is "[t]he quality or state of being appropriate or suitable for adjudication by a court." Accordingly, prudential concerns over the appropriateness of a case for adjudication may preclude the courts from deciding a dispute on the merits.

Traditionally, the justiciability discussion under Indiana law has focused on questions of standing and mootness. However, a separate justiciability concern arises when courts are asked to review internal matters of a coordinate branch of government. In such situations, although the courts have jurisdiction to review the case in the first instance, justiciability concerns stemming from Article 3, Section 1, caution the courts to intervene only where doing so would not upset the balance of the separation of powers. Thus, the decree issued by a court pursuant to its lawful *jurisdiction* may, on occasion, state that, for prudential reasons, the issues in the case at hand are *nonjusticiable*.

Article 4, Section 1, of the Indiana Constitution vests the legislative power in the General Assembly, consisting of the Senate and the House of Representatives. Ind. Const. art. 4, § 1. Article 4, Section 10, directs each house of the legislature to determine its own rules of proceeding. Pursuant to this directive, the House of Representatives passes, in every General Assembly, House Rules which serve to govern the internal operations of the House. Here, the plaintiffs' fines were imposed pursuant to two House Rules: Rule 36, which requires members' attendance at legislative session, and Rule 4, which authorizes House leadership to enforce Rule 36 by compelling attendance of members. These rules were unanimously adopted by the House on Organization Day of the 117th General Assembly, and are further justified by provisions in Article 4, Section 11 ("Two-thirds of each House shall constitute a quorum to do business; but a smaller number may meet, adjourn from day to day, and compel the attendance of absent members."), and Article 4, Section 14 ("Either House may punish its members for disorderly behavior...."). Much like the constitutional grant of jurisdiction to the General Assembly over "the elections, qualifications, and returns of its own members," the constitutional grant of jurisdiction to the legislature over its internal proceedings and the discipline of its members is exclusive. Sections 10, 11, and 14 of Article 4 represent an express constitutional commitment to the legislature. Absent any further express constitutional limitation or qualification on this grant of authority, the plaintiffs' claims are nonjusticiable.

Plaintiffs put forth two constitutional bases which they contend support their challenge to the imposition and collection of fines for their nonattendance: Article 4, Section 26, the right to protest, and Article 4, Section 29, the right to compensation for services. However, neither of these provisions provides an express constitutional limitation to the right of each respective house to determine its rules of proceedings, compel the attendance of absent members, and punish its members for disorderly conduct.

As longstanding precedent makes clear, "It is settled that the Legislature, if not restrained by some provision of the Constitution, has the power to increase or diminish the compensation of public officers during the term for which they were elected." Here, the provision of Article 4, Section 29, on its face, does restrain the legislature from *increasing* the compensation of its members "during the session at which such increase may be made," but it does not expressly restrain the legislature from *diminishing* members' compensation for any reason. The constitutional provision of Article 4, Section 29, restraining the Legislature from increasing compensation, does not present a constitutional limitation on the power of each house to compel attendance and punish disorderly conduct of its members, by the collection of fines.

The plaintiffs further allege that the provisions of the Indiana Wage Payment Statutes act as a statutory limitation on the defendants' actions in collecting the legislative fines. We disagree. To apply the provisions of the Indiana Wage Payment Statutes to the House of Representatives in this action would be to undermine the constitutional authority of the House over the imposition and enforcement of legislative discipline and vest it in the courts, in contradiction of the separation of powers doctrine. This purported *statutory* limitation cannot serve as a means for the courts to consider challenges to legislative action to compel attendance and punish disorderly members where there exists no *constitutional* limitation on the House's express constitutional power to take such actions. Thus, although the legislature has authorized the courts to enforce the Indiana Wage Payment Statutes, here, application to members of the House of Representatives would violate the separation of powers and is therefore constitutionally impermissible.

The plaintiffs in this case were disciplined for their nonattendance and resulting obstruction to the formation of a quorum necessary for conducting the regular business of the House of Representatives, a core legislative function. In fact, plaintiffs themselves declare that "[b]etween February 22, 2011, and March 27, 2011, the Democratic Representatives caucused each day in Illinois and engaged in activities related to their membership in the Indiana House of Representatives," and frame the act of quorum breaking as "a time-honored fulfillment of [legislative] obligations." Be that as it may, it is not within the constitutional authority of the courts to determine what constitutes proper discipline under Article 4, nor to limit the House of Representatives' enforcement of legislative discipline as it relates to this core legislative function. The issues are nonjusticiable, and, as a constitutional and prudential matter, it is improper for the judicial branch to entertain consideration of the plaintiffs' requests for relief.

This is not to say that any or all disputes within a political branch of government fall outside the purview of the judicial authority. If House leadership attempted to discipline members for actions that were outside the "core legislative function," the courts could more readily take action. If the method of legislative discipline took the form of criminally punishable action, the courts could certainly entertain criminal prosecution of the offenders. But the actions taken here were within the authority granted both in the Indiana Constitution and in the House Rules passed pursuant to constitutional authority. Thus, there is no constitutional basis on which the plaintiffs' claims are justiciable in Indiana courts.

Conclusion

Although courts in general have the power to determine disputes between citizens, even members of the Indiana General Assembly, we hold that where a particular function has been expressly delegated to the legislature by our Constitution without any express constitutional limitation or qualification, disputes arising in the exercise of such functions are inappropriate for judicial resolution. The case before us involves such nonjusticiable claims for relief on which the judicial branch must decline to pass judgment. The trial court erred in ruling on the merits of this dispute. Both the issuance and collection of fines as legislative discipline are functions constitutionally committed to the legislative branch without express limitation or qualification by our Constitution.

RUCKER, J., dissenting.

As I understand the majority's position, this Court has the authority to decide the issue presented to us today, but for matters of "prudence" the Court declines to exercise that authority. And in determining whether prudence demands this Court should not intervene, the majority adopts a test that finds no support in our long standing case authority. That is, an "*express* constitutional *limitation*" on an otherwise constitutionally sanctioned legislative act. In other words, according to the majority, so long as a particular constitutional provision permits the Legislature to take certain action, then the Court will not intervene unless *another* constitutional provision expressly limits the legislature from taking that action. We have never adopted such a test, which in my view would effectively preclude review of almost any legislative act. Instead this Court's jurisprudence teaches that an issue is nonjusticiable only when "[o]n its face [the Legislature] was acting pursuant to specific constitutional authority and not contrary thereto...." Here, in my view, the Legislature appears to have been acting contrary to specific constitutional authority. And thus the issue before us does not support the "prudence" the majority invokes.

Discussion

I.

To begin, it is important to note this controversy is not about the ability of the Legislature to discipline its members, including the assessment of fines and penalties. "Either House may punish its members for disorderly behavior, and may, with the concurrence of two-thirds, expel a member; but not a second time for the same cause." Ind. Const. art. 4, § 14. Further, the Constitution provides that when a quorum is not present to do business: "a smaller number [of House members] may meet, adjourn from day to day, and compel the attendance of absent members." Ind. Const. art. 4, § 11. Instead, what is at stake is the ability of the Legislature to collect the fines it imposed by withholding wages and the per diem payments of some of its members to which those members are entitled.

There is specific Indiana constitutional authority addressing legislative pay. Article 4, Section 29 declares: "The members of the General Assembly *shall receive for their services a compensation to be fixed by law;* but no increase of compensation shall take effect during the session at which such increase may be made." Under our longstanding and traditional approach in addressing issues of justiciability, the question before us is straightforward, namely: whether the majority caucus "on its face" was "acting ... contrary" to this constitutional authority. It appears plain to me—without engaging in excessive formalism—that by reducing the compensation to which the minority caucus members were entitled, the majority caucus at the very least was acting "on its face" contrary to Article 4, Section 29. This is so because the phrase "fixed by law" must be given meaning. Article 4, Section 1 of the Indiana Constitution provides:

> The Legislative authority of the State shall be vested in the General Assembly, which shall consist of a Senate and a House of Representatives. The style of every law shall be: "Be it enacted by the General Assembly of the State of Indiana"; and *no law shall be enacted, except by bill.*

In interpreting Section 29's mandate, it appears to me that a legislator's compensation must be set by a bill enacted by the General Assembly, and not by a rule of one chamber. Thus the issue before us deserves full consideration by this Court and should not be avoided for an alleged lack of justiciability.

II.

In the case before us the majority abandons this Court's own authority on the question of when an issue is or is not justiciable in favor of a test apparently endorsed in other jurisdictions. I make two observations. First, if the Article 4, Section 29 directive that legislative compensation "shall ... be fixed by law" does not in the majority's view provide an "express constitutional limitation" on the legislature's power to discipline its members by withholding compensation, I am hard pressed to discern what might so qualify. Second, the authority on which the majority relies actually supports the view that the issue before us passes the justiciability test.

Conclusion

In sum, I would hold that Indiana's Wage Payment Statute applies squarely to these facts. The House's constitutionally-granted Legislative discretion to punish its members does not include the discretion to reduce its members' compensation. Defendants' actions are in direct conflict with Article 4, Section 29 of the Indiana Constitution.

3. Advisory Opinions

The "case" and "controversy" requirement of Article III of the United States Constitution prohibits federal courts from issuing advisory opinions to the other branches of government. Many states take the same view under their state constitutions (even without a "case or controversy" requirement) but other states have different rules. Thus, some state constitutions—permit their state supreme courts, in appropriate circumstances, to issue advisory opinions about the validity of existing laws or those under consideration. The following cases offer a small sample of the types of issues that may arise in this area.

STATE OF KANSAS EX REL. MORRISON v. SEBELIUS
179 P.3d 366 (Kan. 2008)

LUCKERT, J.

During the 2007 Kansas legislative session, the legislature passed and the governor signed [an Act] regulating the time and place of protests at funerals. [I]n a section the parties refer to as the judicial trigger provision, the legislature provided that the funeral protest provisions of the new legislation would not become operative unless and until this court or a federal court determined the funeral protest provisions were constitutional. In another provision, referred to as the judicial review provision, the legislature directed the attorney general to file a lawsuit challenging the constitutionality of the funeral protest provisions.

This lawsuit is not the action suggested in those provisions, however. In this action, the attorney general challenges the constitutionality of the judicial trigger provision, arguing the legislature violated the separation of powers doctrine by directing the attorney general to file the lawsuit contemplated in the provision. This argument is constructed on two premises. First, according to the attorney general, the legislature usurped or intruded into executive and judicial powers by ordering the attorney general to file a lawsuit he believes would seek an unconstitutional remedy and, as a result, would lack merit. Second, the attorney general's conclusion regarding the merits of the suit is based upon an argument that the judicial trigger lawsuit would require a court to provide advice to the legislature as to whether the funeral protest provisions are constitutional and should become operative; he notes that courts do not have the judicial power to provide advisory opinions. If we agree with the attorney general on these points, he requests an order severing the judicial trigger provision from the Kansas Funeral Privacy Act.

Statutory Provisions

In arguing a present controversy exists, the governor's argument is based, in part, upon section 6 of the Kansas Funeral Privacy Act, which provides the Act shall "take effect and be in force from and after its publication in the statute book."

The impact of this provision is diluted by the so-called judicial trigger, which makes some of the Act's provisions inoperative. The judicial trigger provision states:

"(i) Amendments by this act to this section *shall be applicable* on and after whichever of the following dates is applicable:

(1) If the action authorized by K.S.A.2007 Supp. 75–702a, and amendments thereto, is decided in Kansas state court, amendments by this act to this section shall be applicable from and after the date the Kansas supreme court upholds the constitutionality thereof.

(2) If the action authorized by K.S.A.2007 Supp. 75–702a, and amendments thereto, is decided in federal court, amendments by this act to this section shall be applicable from and after the date of the judgment of the court upholding the constitutionality thereof."

Among the provisions that are not operative because of the judicial trigger are those which make it unlawful to demonstrate "at any public location within 150 feet of any entrance to a cemetery, church, mortuary, or other location where a funeral is held or conducted, within one hour prior to the scheduled commencement of a funeral, during a funeral or within two hours following the completion of a funeral" or to interfere with a funeral procession or anyone's ability to exit or enter a funeral.

Section 3 states:

"In accordance with K.S.A. 75–702, and amendments thereto, the attorney general shall seek judicial determination of the constitutionality of K.S.A. 21– 4015. If the action authorized by this section is brought in a district court of this state, then the judgment of that district court shall be appealed directly to the Kansas supreme court as a matter of right."

The combined effect ... is that the attorney general is under a current statutory obligation to challenge the constitutionality of the Kansas Funeral Privacy Act. This obligation creates a current controversy regarding whether the legislature's directive violates the separation of powers doctrine.

Separation of Powers Doctrine

The separation of powers doctrine is not expressly stated in either the United States or Kansas Constitutions. The basic contours of the separation of powers doctrine are easily stated. Each of the three branches of our government—the legislative, judicial, and executive branches—is given the powers and functions appropriate to it.

As we apply these principles to this case, we begin with a presumption that the judicial trigger and review provisions are constitutional. Next, we must examine the powers of each branch in the context of the issues before this court. First, is there a significant usurpation or intrusion into the powers of the attorney general and the courts through the legislative directive to file a judicial trigger lawsuit which the attorney general believes lacks merit? Second, does the judicial trigger provision purport to make either a federal court or this court an advisor to the legislature on whether inoperative funeral protest provisions are facially constitutional and, therefore, should be allowed to become operative?

Legislative Directive to File Suit

Regarding the essential nature of the power of the attorney general and of the legislature with respect to the attorney general, the Kansas Constitution designates the attorney general as an executive officer in Article 1, § 1. The Kansas Constitution does not define the attorney general's duties, however. In the absence of constitutional definition of powers, the legislature has the power to define the attorney general's duties.

In defining the attorney general's duties, the legislature obligated the attorney general to "give his or her opinion in writing, without fee, upon all questions of law submitted to him or her by the legislature, or either branch thereof." This power is consistent with the long-held view that the giving of advisory opinions is an executive, not a judicial, power.

The legislative record regarding the Kansas Funeral Privacy Act reveals the attorney general advised the legislature regarding the constitutionality of the Act and, consistent with his argument before this court, opined the funeral protest provisions are laudable, important, and constitutional. The legislature apparently wanted a second opinion and directed the attorney general to seek that opinion by filing the judicial trigger lawsuit.

Additionally, the legislature imposed a duty upon the attorney general to file and defend lawsuits involving the State when directed to do so by the legislature or the governor. The duty is imposed by K.S.A.2007 Supp. 75–702, which states:

> The attorney general shall appear for the state, and prosecute and defend all actions and proceedings, civil or criminal, in the supreme court, in which the state shall be interested or a party, and shall also, when required by the governor or either branch of the legislature, appear for the state and prosecute or defend, in any other court or before any officer, in any cause or matter, civil or criminal, in which this state may be a party or interested or when the constitutionality of any law of this state is at issue and when so directed shall seek final resolution of such issue in the supreme court of the state of Kansas.

This provision is not under attack in this suit. Nor does the attorney general argue the judicial review provision in the Kansas Funeral Privacy Act, which draws authority from K.S.A.2007 Supp. 75–702, is unconstitutional by itself. Rather, he argues the unconstitutionality arises when the judicial review provision of the Kansas Funeral Privacy Act is combined with the judicial trigger provision, because the result is a directive from the legislature requiring the attorney general to take action contrary to the Kansas Constitution and, therefore, lacking merit.

[T]he legislature, like the governor, lacks constitutional authority to intrude into the attorney general's duties as an officer of the court. The legislature cannot override an attorney's ethical duties to not "bring or defend a proceeding, or assert or controvert an issue therein, unless there is a basis for doing so that is not frivolous, which includes a good faith argument for an extension, modification or reversal of existing law." Moreover, the attorney general is duty bound to uphold the constitution. Consequently, the legislature cannot direct the attorney general to file an action if the attorney general has a good faith belief that the action seeks an unconstitutional remedy.

The attorney general does not suggest this conclusion ends our analysis. Nor does he argue his conclusion regarding the merits of a judicial trigger action should not be tested. Indeed, the point of this action is to seek an adjudication that an action attacking the inoperative Kansas Funeral Privacy Act's funeral protest provisions would necessarily seek a remedy that is constitutionally prohibited—*i.e.*, an advisory opinion.

Legislative Directive for An Advisory Opinion

Unquestionably, courts have the power to determine whether a statute is constitutional. This power arises, however, only when the question is presented in an actual case or controversy between parties; courts do not have the power to issue advisory opinions. As the United States Supreme

Court explained in *Muskrat v. United States*, 219 U.S. 346, 357-358 (1911), which is often cited as the classic case stating the rule against advisory opinions:

> In [*Marbury v. Madison*] Chief Justice Marshall, who spoke for the court, was careful to point out that the right to declare an act of Congress unconstitutional could only be exercised when a proper case between opposing parties was submitted for judicial determination; that there was no general veto power in the court upon the legislation of Congress; and that the authority to declare an act unconstitutional sprang from the requirement that the court, in administering the law and pronouncing judgment between the parties to a case, and choosing between the requirements of the fundamental law established by the people and embodied in the Constitution and an act of the agents of the people, acting under authority of the Constitution, should enforce the Constitution as the supreme law of the land.

Kansas courts have followed the same rule as federal courts.

Advisory Opinions and Federal Separation of Powers

The prohibition against advisory opinions is imposed by the United States and Kansas Constitutions. [T]he antithesis of a justiciable controversy—i.e., those having definite and concrete issues arising between parties with adverse legal interests that are immediate, real, and amenable to conclusive relief—is a case seeking an advisory opinion.

The issues presented in the judicial trigger suit contemplated by the Act would be hypothetical, essentially asking: If the provisions were being enforced, would they infringe on any constitutional right? The parties and the court would speculate on what rights an aggrieved party might assert as having been violated, and those issues would be considered in the abstract without actual facts to inform the court's analysis and resolution of the questions.

We, therefore, conclude the lawsuit contemplated by the judicial trigger provision, K.S.A. 21–4015(i), would not satisfy federal standards used to determine whether an actual case or controversy exists and under federal law would be considered a provision calling for an impermissible advisory opinion from the courts.

Advisory Opinions and Kansas Separation of Powers

Despite Kansas' earlier adherence to the rule of *Muskrat*, application of the federal principles does not automatically lead to the conclusion that the Act's judicial trigger could not be activated in Kansas. State courts are not bound by the prohibition against advisory opinions found in the Constitution of the United States or by federal justiciability requirements. The United States Constitution's prohibition arises solely from Article III.

Hence, each state is free to define the judicial powers of its courts. Speaking generally, most state constitutions, including our Kansas Constitution, vary from the Constitution of the United States in three substantive ways that affect judicial power: (1) the inherent remedial role of state courts differs because of the nature of rights accorded by state constitutions; (2) jurisdiction of state courts differs from that of federal courts; and (3) the text of the judicial article in state constitutions often does not refer to the necessity of cases or controversies.

First, regarding the difference in the inherent remedial powers of the courts, the distinction arises because the Constitution of the United States grants what are referred to as negative rights—*i.e.*, rights which the government may not infringe. If a court finds an infringement of such a right—whether the infringement arises from an unconstitutional statute or through the actions of a government official—the remedy is to stop the infringement by striking the offending statute, prohibiting and punishing the action, and suppressing fruits obtained from the unconstitutional act.

Similarly, state constitutions, including Kansas', grant negative rights, and judicial remedies for violations of those rights are consistent with remedies allowed in federal courts. The difference in the inherent remedial power of state courts arises because all state constitutions also grant positive rights, *i.e.*, rights that entitle individuals to benefits or actions by the state. When a positive right has been violated, the typical remedy imposed for protecting negative rights—prohibiting government action— exacerbates the problem that arose when the government failed to act and fulfill its duties. To enforce a positive right, courts must mandate a positive remedy by requiring the state government to act and thereby fulfill the constitutional right.

The second substantive difference between judicial power provisions in state constitutions and the provisions in the Constitution of the United States is found in the delineation of jurisdiction. Each state is free to determine the jurisdictional limits of its courts in any respect not preempted by federal jurisdiction. State constitutions contain unique jurisdictional features. For example, Article 3, § 3 of the Kansas Constitution grants this court original jurisdiction of this and similar quo warranto actions and mandamus actions.

The Kansas Constitution's jurisdictional provisions do not vary from those in the United States Constitution as drastically as other states' constitutions. Several states have explicitly empowered state courts to give advisory opinions. Kansas is not one of those jurisdictions.

The final distinction between the provisions regarding judicial power in the United States and Kansas Constitutions is a difference in how the judicial power is phrased. Article 3, § 1 of the Kansas Constitution grants the "judicial power" exclusively to the courts just as Article III, § 1 of the United States Constitution establishes the separation of powers parameter in the federal government. But, Article 3 of the Kansas Constitution, like parallel provisions of many other state constitutions, does not include the "case" or "controversy" language found in Article III, § 2 of the United States Constitution.

Nevertheless, Kansas courts have repeatedly recognized that the "judicial power" is the "power to hear, consider and determine controversies between rival litigants." In recognizing a constitutional case-or-controversy requirement, Kansas courts have relied solely on the separation of powers doctrine embodied in the Kansas constitutional framework.

Like federal decisions, this court's decisions note the policy considerations that underlie the requirement of justiciability and the prohibition against advisory opinions: controversies provide factual context, arguments are sharpened by adversarial positions, and judgments resolve disputes rather than provide mere legal advice. As in federal court, less rigorous requirements have been imposed in declaratory judgment cases; yet, actual cases and controversies are still required.

Thus, despite the differences between our Kansas Constitution and the Constitution of the United States, both limit the judicial power to actual cases and controversies. The judicial power granted by Article 3 of the Kansas Constitution does not include the power to give advisory opinions. A Kansas court issuing an advisory opinion would violate the separation of powers doctrine by exceeding its constitutional authority.

Advisory Opinions Regarding Legislation

The constitutional prohibition against advisory opinions applies to all cases, whether involving legislation or not. Where, as here, the lawsuit would request an opinion regarding the constitutionality of inoperative legislation, an additional separation of powers issue is presented: Does the judicial trigger provision abdicate legislative power by seeking advice regarding the constitutionality of inoperative legislation?

Article 2 of the Kansas Constitution gives the legislature the exclusive power to pass, amend, and repeal statutes. It is universally recognized that "'the essential of the legislative function is the determination of the legislative policy and its formulation and promulgation as a defined and binding rule of conduct within the limitations laid down by the constitution.'" The separation of powers doctrine, therefore, prohibits either the executive or judicial branches from assuming the role of the legislature.

Broadly speaking, where the legislature looks to the future and changes existing conditions by making a new rule to be applied thereafter, by contrast "the judiciary investigates, declares, and enforces liabilities as they stand on present or past facts, under laws supposed *already to exist*." Consequently, when the legislature is considering legislation, a court cannot enjoin the legislature from passing a law. "This is true whether such action by the legislature is in disregard of its clearly imposed constitutional duty or is the enactment of an unconstitutional law."

Power is shifted away from the legislature when the legislature does not reach its own independent conclusion, albeit preliminary, regarding the constitutionality of a statute. Consequently, the giving of a judicial opinion regarding the constitutionality of pending legislation "violates the principle of separation of powers by facilitating abdication by the legislature of its duty to make a judgment on the constitutionality of a pending statute independent of that made by the justices."

The fact that the legislature has requested the advice does not cure the constitutional problems. "[A] power or duty forbidden by the Constitution cannot be conferred on the court by the Legislature, and cannot be exercised by the court or its members." Consistent with this conclusion, Kansas cases, although not addressing the specific circumstance of legislation authorizing advisory opinions, have held that while the legislature may enact laws that confer jurisdiction or impose judicial functions on a court, it cannot impose a legislative or executive function on courts, except for functions relating to court administration. To do so would constitute a violation of the separation of powers doctrine by the legislature because it would be requiring the judicial branch to exercise legislative or executive power.

Moreover, it is widely recognized that such advisory opinions regarding the constitutionality of legislation would have little effect. Such decisions relate to the facial constitutionality of the statute, having little impact if the statute is attacked on an "as applied" basis, and do not directly affect the rights of nonparties who have a due process right to be heard.

The governor does not dispute these authorities but suggests a different situation is presented because the attorney general would not be seeking an opinion regarding pending legislation. Rather, the Kansas Funeral Privacy Act will not be further considered by the legislature; once this court renders a decision regarding the constitutionality of the substantive provisions of the Act, those provisions would become operative without further legislative action. Consequently, she suggests this case is more similar to three decisions in which the United States Supreme Court has considered the constitutionality of legislation that is not operative.

The attorney general disagrees, suggesting that because the substantive provisions are inoperative the legislature has requested advice on whether the provisions should become operative rather than making that decision as a legislative body. Additionally, the attorney general notes that the governor's arguments ignore the justiciability requirements that are inherent in the constitutional requirements.

We agree with the attorney general on this point. A review of each of the cited cases reveals that the cases involved actual controversies, parties with conflicting positions and a stake in the litigation, and a factual framework for consideration. In contrast, none of these attributes would be present in a suit brought by the attorney general pursuant to the Kansas Funeral Privacy Act's directive.

[T]he Kansas Funeral Privacy Act provisions criminalizing funeral protests are not in effect. Additionally, ... the Kansas Funeral Privacy Act repealed the Funeral Picketing Act. In other words, there would be no effective statute to consider in the judicial trigger lawsuit, and any arguments regarding the constitutionality of the provision would not be tied to the resolution of an actual dispute; both the governor and the attorney general believe the funeral protest provisions are constitutional. Thus, the litigation would lack adversarial sharpening of issues. Finally, the judgment would not have binding effect of any sort.

Consequently, we conclude the judicial trigger provision seeks an unconstitutional remedy that would violate the separation of powers doctrine in two respects. First, a lawsuit filed pursuant to the provision would not present an actual case or controversy. It would seek an advisory opinion, and a court would not have the judicial power to grant the remedy. Second, the provision purports to make the Kansas Supreme Court an advisor to the legislature on whether the inoperative funeral protest provisions are facially constitutional and should be allowed to become operative. A court issuing such an opinion would usurp the legislature's duty to make a preliminary judgment on the constitutionality of inoperative legislative provisions.

Hence, we hold the legislature violated the separation of powers doctrine by directing the attorney general to file an action challenging the constitutionality of the funeral protest provisions of the Kansas Funeral Privacy Act.

In re OPINION OF THE JUSTICES (APPOINTMENT OF CHIEF JUSTICE OF THE SUPREME COURT)
842 A.2d 816 (N.H. 2003)

To His Excellency the Governor and the Honorable Council:

The undersigned justices of the supreme court have considered the questions submitted in your resolution adopted December 3, 2003, and filed on December 9, 2003. You requested our reply on an expedited basis, and, if possible, before December 31, 2003. Time limitations prevented us from complying with our usual practice of allowing interested parties an opportunity to provide memoranda on the questions presented. As time is of the essence, therefore, in response to this resolution, we submit the following:

We have in the past asked to be excused from answering inquiries when they are beyond the spirit or letter of the constitutional provision for advisory opinions. We respectfully ask to be excused from answering the present inquiries.

Part II, Article 74 of the State Constitution empowers the justices of the supreme court to render advisory opinions, outside the context of concrete, fully-developed factual situations and without the benefit of adversary legal presentations, only in carefully circumscribed situations. Part II, Article 74 permits the justices of the supreme court to render advisory opinions only "upon important questions of law and upon solemn occasions" when asked to do so by the legislature or the Governor and Council on matters relating to their official duties. When we issue such opinions, we act not as a court, but as individual constitutional advisors to the legislative or executive branches.

With respect to issuing advisory opinions about existing statutes, as we are asked to do here, our constitutional authority is especially limited. We have no authority under Part II, Article 74 to issue advisory opinions to either branch of the legislature regarding existing legislation. That authority extends only to proposed legislation.

There are occasions where the Governor and Council are entitled to advisory opinions as to their official duty and authority under existing law. This is not such an occasion because there are limitations in the operation of Part II, Article 74. To express our views about the constitutionality of RSA 490:1 would be expressing our views upon questions involving private rights. It would also place us in the position of giving advice in matters that may come before the court for decision.

As we have previously explained, "Where the constitutionality of existing law is ... brought in question, those who may deem their rights infringed...may have recourse to our courts for the protection of their supposed privileges."

In addition, the unusual nature of the private rights involved in this situation make the questions posed particularly ill-suited for an advisory opinion. Among "those who may deem their rights infringed" could be one of our colleagues or one of us. Because of this, we are disqualified from reaching the merits of the questions. Such being the case, the question of whether replacement justices may be appointed under RSA 490:3 arises. That question is addressed by the Chief Justice in his separate opinion.

The justices of the supreme court rarely decline to answer questions posed pursuant to Part II, Article 74. We do so now only after carefully considering our constitutional duties and based upon long-established prior decisions.

For these reasons, we respectfully request to be excused from answering the questions posed.

BROCK, C.J., Separate Opinion.

I write separately to explain why I conclude that I am not authorized to appoint replacement justices in this matter. Part II, Article 74 of the New Hampshire Constitution vests in "the justices of the supreme court" the exclusive authority to render advisory opinions upon questions posed by the legislature or the Governor and Council "upon important questions of law." Part II, Article 74 does not vest the authority to issue advisory opinions with the supreme court, as an institution, but rather with the individual supreme court justices. When the justices of the supreme court give an advisory opinion pursuant to Part II, Article 74, they do not act as a court, but as constitutional advisors to the legislative or executive branches.

Only sitting supreme court justices are "justices of the supreme court" for Part II, Article 74 purposes; only sitting supreme court justices may act as constitutional advisors to co-equal branches of the government. Justices appointed to replace sitting members of the court pursuant to RSA 490:3 are not "justices of the supreme court." As we [have] explained a justice appointed to sit in a specific matter pursuant to RSA 490:3 does not become a supreme court justice. A justice appointed to a specific case is "merely enabled to use his power as a judicial officer on a temporary basis, according to RSA 490:3."

Furthermore, RSA 490:3 does not accord a judge assigned to sit temporarily on the supreme court all of the powers of a sitting supreme court justice, but rather only the authority to "hear arguments, render decisions, and file opinions" in one specific matter. In context, the reference to filing an "opinion" does not refer to an advisory opinion, but rather refers to an opinion in a justiciable controversy.

NOTE

The situation on which an advisory opinion was sought in this case was resolved in *In Re Petition of Governor*, 846 A.2d 1148 (N.H. 2004), excerpted below at page 932.

4. Certified Questions

Although federal courts are courts of limited jurisdiction, they frequently entertain questions of state law under their diversity jurisdiction and pendent jurisdiction. When an outcome-dispositive state law question arises in a federal-court case, one or both litigants may wish to ask the court to certify the question to the relevant state supreme court—so that the final dispositor of state law may resolve the question. The process is regulated by the state supreme courts, which generally retain authority to accept or reject the invitation. For like reasons, a federal court on its own initiative may seek to certify the question.

LEHMAN BROTHERS v. SCHEIN
416 U.S. 386 (1974)

DOUGLAS, J.

The Court of Appeals by a divided vote reversed the District Court. While the Court of Appeals held that Florida law was controlling, it found none that was decisive. So it then turned to the law of other jurisdictions, particularly that of New York, to see if Florida "would probably" interpret *Diamond* to make it applicable here. The Court of Appeals concluded that the defendants had engaged with Chasen "to misuse corporate property," and that the theory of *Diamond* reaches that situation, "viewing the case as the Florida court would probably view it." There were emanations from other Florida decisions that made the majority on the Court of Appeals feel that Florida would follow that reading of *Diamond*. Such a construction of *Diamond*, the Court of Appeals said, would have "the prophylactic effect of providing a disincentive to insider trading." And so it would. Yet under the regime of *Erie R. Co. v. Tompkins*, 304 U.S. 64 (1938), a State can make just the opposite her law, providing there is no overriding federal rule which pre-empts state law by reason of federal curbs on trading in the stream of commerce.

The dissenter on the Court of Appeals urged that that court certify the state-law question to the Florida Supreme Court as is provided in Fla.Stat.Ann. s 25.031 and its Appellate Rule 4.61. That path is open to this Court and to any court of appeals of the United States. We have, indeed, used it before, as have courts of appeals.

Here resort to it would seem particularly appropriate in view of the novelty of the question and the great unsettlement of Florida law, Florida being a distant State. When federal judges in New York attempt to predict uncertain Florida law, they act, as we have referred to ourselves on this Court in matters of state law, as "outsiders" lacking the common exposure to local law which comes from sitting in the jurisdiction.

The judgment of the Court of Appeals is vacated and the cases are remanded so that that court may reconsider whether the controlling issue of Florida law should be certified to the Florida Supreme Court pursuant to Rule 4.61 of the Florida Appellate Rules.

REHNQUIST, J., concurring.

I agree with [the Court], but think it appropriate to emphasize the scope of the discretion of federal judges in deciding whether to use such certification procedures.

Petitioners here were defendants in the District Court. That court, applying applicable New York choice-of-law rules, decided that Florida law governs the case and, finding that the respondents' complaint requested relief which would extend the substantive law even beyond New York's apparently novel decision in *Diamond v. Oreamuno*, 24 N.Y.2d 494 (1969), dismissed the complaint on the merits. The Court of Appeals agreed that Florida law applied, but held that Florida law would permit recovery on the claim stated by respondents. The opinion of the dissenting judge of the Court of Appeals, disagreeing with the majority's analysis of Florida law, added in a concluding paragraph that in light of the uncertainty of Florida law, the Florida certification procedure should have been utilized by the Court of Appeals. On rehearing, petitioners requested the Court of Appeals to utilize this procedure, but they concede that this is the first such request that they made. Thus petitioners seek to upset the result of more than two years of trial and appellate litigation on the basis of a point which they first presented to the Court of Appeals upon petition for rehearing.

The authority which Congress has granted this Court to review judgments of the courts of appeals undoubtedly vests us not only with the authority to correct errors of substantive law, but to prescribe the method by which those courts go about deciding the cases before them. But a sensible respect for the experience and competence of the various integral parts of the federal judicial system suggests that we go slowly in telling the courts of appeals or the district courts how to go about deciding cases where federal jurisdiction is based on diversity of citizenship, cases which they see and decide far more often than we do.

This Court has held that a federal court may not remit a diversity plaintiff to state courts merely because of the difficulty in ascertaining local law; it has also held that unusual circumstances may require a federal court having jurisdiction of an action to nonetheless abstain from deciding doubtful questions of state law. In each of these situations, our decisions have dealt with the issue of how to reconcile the exercise of the jurisdiction which Congress has conferred upon the federal courts with the important considerations of comity and cooperative federalism which are inherent in a federal system, both of which must be subject to a single national policy within the federal judiciary.

At the other end of the spectrum, however, I assume it would be unthinkable to any of the Members of this Court to prescribe the process by which a district court or a court of appeals should go about researching a point of state law which arises in a diversity case. Presumably the judges of the district courts and of the courts of appeals are at least as capable as we are in determining what the Florida courts have said about a particular question of Florida law.

State certification procedures are a very desirable means by which a federal court may ascertain an undecided point of state law, especially where, as is the case in Florida, the question can be certified directly to the court of last resort within the State. But in a purely diversity case such as this one, the use of such a procedure is more a question of the considerable discretion of the federal court in going about the decisionmaking process than it is a question of a choice trenching upon the fundamentals of our federal-state jurisprudence.

While certification may engender less delay and create fewer additional expenses for litigants than would abstention, it entails more delay and expense than would an ordinary decision of the state question on the merits by the federal court. The Supreme Court of Florida has promulgated an appellate rule, which provides that upon certification by a federal court to that court, the parties shall file briefs there according to a specified briefing schedule, that oral argument may be granted upon application, and that the parties shall pay the costs of the certification. Thus while the certification procedure is more likely to produce the correct determination of state law, additional time and money are required to achieve such a determination.

If a district court or court of appeals believes that it can resolve an issue of state law with available research materials already at hand, and makes the effort to do so, its determination should not be disturbed simply because the certification procedure existed but was not used. The question of whether certification on the facts of this case, particularly in view of the lateness of its suggestion by petitioners, would have advanced the goal of correctly disposing of this litigation on the state law issue is one which I would leave, and I understand that the Court would leave, to the sound judgment of the court making the initial choice. But since the Court has today for the first time expressed its view as to the use of certification procedures by the federal courts, I agree that it is appropriate to vacate the judgment of the Court of Appeals and remand the cases in order that the Court of Appeals may reconsider certification in light of the Court's opinion.

HALEY v. UNIVERSITY OF TENNESSEE-KNOXVILLE
188 S.W.3d 518 (Tenn. 2006)

E. RILEY ANDERSON, J.

In addition to the dispute that is the basis of the certified question, the parties have also raised the question of whether the Supreme Court has the authority to answer the certified question. We address that issue first.

Certified Questions

Rule 23 of the Tennessee Rules of the Supreme Court provides:

> The Supreme Court may, at its discretion, answer questions of law certified to it by the Supreme Court of the United States, a Court of Appeals of the United States, a District Court of the United States in Tennessee, or a United States Bankruptcy Court in Tennessee. This rule may be invoked when the certifying court determines that, in a proceeding before it, there are questions of law of this state which will be determinative of the cause and as to which it appears to the certifying court there is no controlling precedent in the decisions of the Supreme Court of Tennessee.

Tenn. Sup.Ct. R. 23, § 1. This Court adopted Rule 23 in 1989 and has since accepted and answered numerous certified questions from the federal courts. In spite of the fact that the rule has been in place for seventeen years, U.T. argues that it is unconstitutional and that this Court lacks jurisdiction to decide the certified question. For the following reasons, we reject U.T.'s argument.

A certification procedure permits a state's highest court to accept and answer a question of state law certified to it by the federal court to assist the federal court in deciding a question of state law. A majority of states have in place a procedure similar to our Rule 23. As the United States Supreme Court recognized in *Erie Railroad Co. v. Tompkins*, 304 U.S. 64, 78 (1938), "[e]xcept in matters governed by the Federal Constitution or by Acts of Congress, the law to be applied in any case [in federal court] is the law of the state." In cases where the "law of the state" is unclear, absent a certification procedure the federal court must either "(1) guess at the law and risk laying down a rule which may later prove to be out of harmony with state decisions...or (2) abstain from deciding the case until the state courts pass upon the point of law involved." Certification procedures assist the federal courts in correctly disposing of state law issues without incurring the delay inherent in the abstention process. Certification thus "save[s] time, energy, and resources and helps build a cooperative judicial federalism." *Lehman Bros. v. Schein*, 416 U.S. 386, 391 (1974).

More importantly, the certification procedure protects states' sovereignty. "To the extent that a federal court applies different legal rules than the state court would have, the state's sovereignty is diminished [because] the federal court has made state law." Such an impact on state sovereignty "is no small matter, especially since a federal court's error may perpetuate itself in state courts until the state's highest court corrects it."

Notwithstanding the strong policy arguments weighing in favor of a certification procedure, U.T. argues that because this Court's jurisdiction is limited by the Tennessee Constitution to appellate jurisdiction, the Court lacks jurisdiction to answer certified questions. Article VI, section 2 of the Tennessee Constitution provides that the jurisdiction of the Supreme Court "shall be appellate only, under such restrictions and regulations as may from time to time be prescribed by law; but it may possess such other jurisdiction as is now conferred by law on the present Supreme Court."

We have consistently held that Article VI, section 2's grant of power limits this Court to adjudicating appellate matters only. In construing the scope of our jurisdiction under Article VI, section 2, however, we have in the past been concerned exclusively with the Court's authority to adjudicate, that is, to finally settle, disputes before this Court. Because answering a certified question is not an adjudicative function, it is not an exercise of this Court's jurisdiction and is not prohibited by Article VI, section 2.

Our power to answer certified questions comes, then, not from the Tennessee Constitution's grant of jurisdiction. Rather, our power to answer certified questions is grounded in Article VI, section 1 of the Constitution. That section provides that "[t]he judicial power of this State shall be vested in one Supreme Court and in such Circuit, Chancery and other inferior Courts as the Legislature shall from time to time, ordain and establish; in the Judges thereof, and in Justices of the Peace." As the head of the judiciary, this Court is "the repository of the inherent power of the judiciary in this State." As an exercise of that inherent power, it is within the realm of the Court's authority to answer questions certified to us by the federal courts.

We have stated that answering certified questions not only furthers judicial efficiency and comity, but also protects this state's sovereignty against encroachment from the federal courts. Answering certified questions thus protects the "dignity, independence and integrity" of not only this Court but of the state as a whole and is therefore within the inherent power of this Court. As a sovereign state, Tennessee has "the power to exercise and the responsibility to protect" the sovereignty granted to it by the United States Constitution.

We therefore hold that we may answer certified questions consistent with the inherent power of this Court and with our responsibility to protect the sovereignty of the state.

5. Implied Constitutional Remedies

KATZBERG v. REGENTS OF THE UNIV. OF CALIFORNIA
58 P.3d 339 (Cal. 2002)

GEORGE, C.J.

We granted review in this matter…to consider whether an individual may bring an action for money damages on the basis of an alleged violation of a provision of the California Constitution, in the absence of a statutory provision or an established common law tort authorizing such a damage remedy for the constitutional violation. In the present case, plaintiff seeks, among other relief, monetary damages based upon defendant's alleged violation of his due process "liberty" interest under article I, section 7, subdivision (a), of the California Constitution (hereafter article I, section 7(a)), by failing to provide him with a timely "name-clearing" hearing after his removal as department chairman at a university medical center. We conclude that an action for damages is not available.[3]

I.

In 1991, plaintiff Richard W. Katzberg was appointed professor of medicine at the University of California at Davis Medical School and Chairperson of the Department of Radiology at the University of California Davis Medical Center. In July 1995, the university commenced an investigation concerning alleged mishandling of funds by the department of radiology. In February 1996, the university issued a press release regarding the investigation, and the Sacramento District Attorney's Office thereafter announced that it would initiate a criminal investigation.

The investigation concerned approximately $250,000 that allegedly had been placed inappropriately in radiology accounts to be used for payment of department expenses. Most of this money came from rebates provided by medical equipment vendors. There never has been any allegation that plaintiff made any personal use of the challenged funds.

---

[3] [1] We do not here consider the propriety of actions such as those based upon grounds established under common law tort principles-for example, actions for false arrest, false imprisonment, wrongful termination based upon violation of public policy, or the like. In such actions, a breach of duty or violation of public policy may be established by demonstrating a violation of a constitutional provision, and damages properly may be awarded to remedy the tort. We consider here only whether an action for damages is available to remedy a constitutional violation that is not tied to an established common law or statutory action.

Instead, the alleged improprieties related to placement of funds in the department's account rather than in the medical center's general funds.

In March 1996, the university announced that "appropriate personnel actions" had been initiated, but did not name any specific employee. Later that month, plaintiff was removed as chairperson of the department. He remained a tenured professor at the medical school and a staff physician at the medical center.

Plaintiff sued various defendants on numerous grounds, and the resulting litigation has moved back and forth between state and federal courts. For present purposes, it is sufficient to note that plaintiff's third amended complaint—the one here at issue—named as defendants the Regents of the University of California (the Regents) and the Chancellor of the University of California at Davis, Larry N. Vanderhoef (hereafter collectively, defendants). The complaint alleged that by making stigmatizing statements about plaintiff in the course of removing him from his position as department chairperson, defendants violated the *liberty* interest of plaintiff protected under article I, section 7(a).

Although the department chairmanship was an at-will position, terminable without cause at the discretion of the chancellor of the Davis campus (and hence plaintiff concedes that he had no due process *property* right to that position), it is well established that "an at-will [public] employee's *liberty* interests are deprived when his discharge is accompanied by charges 'that might seriously damage his standing and associations in his community' or 'impose[ ] on him a stigma or other disability that foreclose[s] his freedom to take advantage of other employment opportunities.'" When such a liberty deprivation occurs, a party has a right to a "name-clearing hearing." The third amended complaint alleged that plaintiff had not been provided with such a hearing at which he could defend himself, either prior to, or since, his removal. The complaint also sought a variety of relief, including an injunction, damages, attorney fees, and costs.

The trial court granted defendants' motion to strike the prayer for relief.

In this court, plaintiff contends that article I, section 7(a) affords him a right to damages for the asserted violation of his due process liberty interest. By contrast, defendants assert that a name-clearing hearing is the sole remedy that a court should impose for the alleged constitutional violation. For purposes of analyzing the damages issue upon which we granted review, we shall assume, as did the Court of Appeal, that the facts alleged in the third amended complaint are sufficient to establish a violation of the due process liberty interest under the state Constitution's due process clause.

II.

Article I, section 26 of the California Constitution states: "The provisions of this Constitution are mandatory and prohibitory, unless by express words they are declared to be otherwise." Under this provision, "all branches of government are required to comply with constitutional directives or prohibitions." As we observed more than a century ago, "[e]very constitutional provision is self-executing to this extent, that everything done in violation of it is void."

Accordingly, the question posed in this case is not whether article I, section 7(a) is "self-executing." It is clear that the due process clause of article I, section 7(a) *is* self-executing, and that even without any effectuating legislation, all branches of government are required to comply with its terms. Furthermore, it also is clear that, like many other constitutional provisions, this section supports an action, brought by a private plaintiff against a proper defendant, for declaratory relief or for injunction. The question presented here is whether, assuming the complaint states a violation of plaintiff's due process liberty interest, plaintiff may maintain an action for *monetary damages* to remedy the asserted violation of his due process liberty interests under article I, section 7(a), on the facts alleged.

III.

More than 30 years ago in *Bivens v. Six Unknown Fed. Narcotics Agents*, 403 U.S. 388 (1971), the United States Supreme Court recognized the right of a party to recover damages for the violation of a constitutional right [the Fourth Amendment protection against unreasonable searches and seizures] in an action against federal agents. The court in *Bivens* did not approach the issue as posing a question whether the Fourth Amendment was *intended* to provide an action for damages, or whether such an intent could be *inferred* from that provision; instead, the court viewed the matter as posing a question whether the court should create a cause of action for damages—in effect, a constitutional tort—to remedy a Fourth Amendment violation, even though Congress had not specifically provided such a remedy and even though the Fourth Amendment does not provide for enforcement by an award of damages. The high court reasoned that as a general proposition "'federal courts may use any available remedy to make good the wrong done.'" In support of its conclusion that a damages remedy was warranted, the court emphasized that (i) there existed "no special factors counseling hesitation" to recognize such a right; (ii) there was no equally effective alternative remedy; and (iii) there was no "explicit congressional declaration that persons injured by a federal officer's violation of the Fourth Amendment may not recover money damages from the agents."

Subsequent to *Bivens*, the United States Supreme Court has considered numerous cases in which plaintiffs have sought money damages under a constitutional cause of action premised upon the asserted violation of various federal constitutional provisions. After twice following the lead of *Bivens*, and recognizing the availability of a constitutional tort action for damages on the strength of the considerations set out above, *Davis v. Passman*, 442 U.S. 228, 245 (1979) (*Davis*) (damages allowed to remedy violation by former congressman of equal protection component of Fifth Amendment due process clause); *Carlson v. Green*, 446 U.S. 14, 18-23 (1980) (*Carlson*) [damages allowed to remedy Eighth Amendment violations by prison officials]), the high court for the past two decades repeatedly has refused to recognize a federal constitutional tort action for money damages in cases presenting that issue. *Chappell v. Wallace*, 462 U.S. 296, 305 (1983) (*Chappell*) [alleged equal protection violations by superior officer in United States military]; *Bush v. Lucas*, 462 U.S. 367 (1983) (*Bush*) [alleged First Amendment violation against federal agency employee by superiors]; *United States v. Stanley*, 483 U.S. 669 (1987) [alleged due process violations by military personnel during the course of active military service]; *Schweiker v. Chilicky*, 487 U.S. 412 (1988) (*Schweiker*) [alleged due process violation by government officials, resulting in deprivation of Social Security benefits]; *FDIC v. Meyer*, 510 U.S. 471 (1994) (*Meyer*) [alleged due process violation concerning employment termination by federal agency]; *Correctional Services Corp. v. Malesko*, 534 U.S. 61, 68 (2001) (*Malesko*) [alleged Eighth Amendment violation by private operator of federal prison halfway house].)

In each of these more recent cases, the high court found that the first *Bivens* consideration mentioned above—"special factors" that "counsel hesitation" by a court in recognizing a constitutional tort damages remedy—militated against recognition of that remedy. And in these recent cases, the court also substantially retreated from, and reformulated, the other *Bivens* considerations mentioned above. The court has found that the absence of a "complete" alternative remedy will not support an action for damages, so long as a "meaningful" alternative remedy in state or federal law is available, and it has implicitly discarded the proposition, mentioned in *Bivens*, and emphasized in *Davis* and *Carlson*, that money damages are *presumptively* available unless Congress prohibits that remedy.[4]

The experience in other jurisdictions has been similar. Some out-of-state decisions, often relying upon a combination of (i) the jurisdiction's indigenous common law antecedents, (ii) special legislative history, and

---

[4] [7] Although the high court has declined to extend *Bivens,* it has not abandoned the core holding of that case, and has recognized the continuing validity of that decision and its progeny.

(iii) the Restatement Second of Torts section 874A, have recognized a constitutional tort cause of action and corresponding right to be awarded money damages for various state constitutional violations.[5] A greater number of cases, however, often tracking the reasoning of the most recent United States Supreme Court decisions or pointing to the absence of any historical basis for implying a damages action, have declined to recognize such a constitutional tort or implied damages remedy in a variety of circumstances.[6]

---

[5] [9] See *Brown v. State of New York*, 674 N.E.2d 1129 (N.Y. 1996) (damages allowed for violation of state's search and seizure and equal protection provisions, based upon Restatement Second of Torts, § 874A, early New York case authority recognizing a right to damages for such violations, and the absence of adequate alternative remedies); *Widgeon v. Eastern Shore Hosp. Center*, 479 A.2d 921, 923-925 (Md. 1984) (damages allowed for violation of state's search and seizure provision, based in part upon well-established English and early Maryland common law antecedents); *Moresi v. Dept. of Wildlife & Fisheries*, 567 So.2d 1081, 1091-1093 (La. 1990) (damages permissible to remedy illegal search and seizure, based in part upon English common law); see also *Binette v. Sabo*, 710 A.2d 688, 699 (Conn. 1998) (damages allowed for state constitution search and seizure violation; court found this remedy supported by "compelling policy considerations" and the absence of any special factors counseling against recognition of such an action); *Corum v. University of North Carolina*, 413 S.E.2d 276, 289-291 (N.C. 1992) (suggesting that damages may be allowed to remedy state free speech violation, based upon state common law authority, but noting that courts must defer to alternative remedies); *Old Tuckaway v. City of Greenfield*, 509 N.W.2d 323, 328 n. 4 (Wisc. 1993) (suggesting in dictum that damages may be allowed to remedy violations of state due process clause); see also *Walinski v. Morrison & Morrison*, 377 N.E.2d 242, 243-245 (Ill. App. 1978) (damages allowed to remedy violation of constitutional antidiscrimination clause; court found the drafters of the provision intended to create a right enforceable through damages).

[6] [10] See *Dick Fischer Dev. v. Dept. of Admin.*, 838 P.2d 263, 268 (Alaska 1992) (no damages allowed for asserted violation of state due process provision, based in part upon availability of alternative remedies); *Board of County Com'rs v. Sundheim*, 926 P.2d 545, 549-553 (Colo. 1996) (no damages allowed for asserted violation of state due process provision, based in part upon availability of alternative remedies); *Kelley Property Dev. v. Town of Lebanon*, 627 A.2d 909, 923-924 (Conn. 1993) (no damages allowed for asserted violation of state due process provision, based in part upon availability of alternative remedies and special factors counseling hesitation to recognize such a right); *Garcia v. Reyes*, 697 So.2d 549, 551 (Fla. App. 1997) (summarily holding there is no right to money damages for violation of state due process guarantee); *77th Dist. Judge v. State*, 438 N.W.2d 333, 339-340 (Mich. App. 1989) (no damages for violation of state equal protection rights; court noted, among other things, the availability of alternative relief and deference to legislative policy making expertise); *Moody v. Hicks*, 956 S.W.2d 398, 402 (Mo. App. 1997) (no damages for asserted violation of state search and seizure rights; court noted, among other things, the availability of alternative relief and deference to legislative policy making expertise); *Rockhouse Mountain Prop. v. Town of Conway*, 503 A.2d 1385, 1388-1389 (N.H. 1986) (no damages for alleged state due process and equal protection violations, based in part upon availability of alternative remedies); *Augat v. State* (A.D.1997), 666 N.Y.S.2d 249, 251-252 (N.Y. App. Div. 1997) (declining to extend *Brown, supra*, to allow damages for asserted violation of due process and freedom

California decisions have followed a similar trend. Putting aside cases recognizing an inverse condemnation action for damages to remedy a violation of the state just compensation clause (a constitutional provision that clearly contemplates an award of damages determined in a judicial proceeding, see Cal. Const., art. I, § 19), only two decisions, each filed two decades ago, have recognized an action for damages to remedy a violation of the state Constitution. All subsequent decisions addressing the issue have declined to find such an action for damages.

IV.

We conclude it is appropriate to employ the following framework for determining the existence of a damages action to remedy an asserted constitutional violation. First, we shall inquire whether there is evidence from which we may find or infer, within the constitutional provision at issue, an affirmative intent either to authorize or to withhold a damages action to remedy a violation. In undertaking this inquiry we shall consider the language and history of the constitutional provision at issue, including whether it contains guidelines, mechanisms, or procedures implying a monetary remedy, as well as any pertinent common law history. If we find any such intent, we shall give it effect.

Second, if no affirmative intent either to authorize or to withhold a damages remedy is found, we shall undertake the "constitutional tort" analysis adopted by *Bivens* and its progeny. Among the relevant factors in this analysis are whether an adequate remedy exists, the extent to which a constitutional tort action would change established tort law, and the nature and significance of the constitutional provision. If we find that these factors militate against recognizing the constitutional tort, our inquiry

---

of association rights, based upon availability of alternative remedies); *Hanton v. Gilbert*, 486 S.E.2d 432, 438-439 (N.C. App. 1997) (no damages for alleged violation of state due process clause, based in part upon availability of alternative remedies and deference to legislature); *Provens v. Stark Cty. Bd. of Mental Ret.*, 594 N.E.2d 959, 963-965 (Ohio 1992) (no damages for alleged state free speech violation, based in part upon availability of alternative remedies and deference to legislature); *Hunter v. City of Eugene*, 787 P.2d 881, 883-884 (Ore. 1990) (no damages for alleged state "free expression" violations based in part upon absence of textual or historic basis for implying such a right; court concluded that creation of such a right is a task properly left to legislature); *City of Beaumont v. Bouillion*, 896 S.W.2d 143, 148-150 (Tex. 1995) (no damages for alleged state free speech and assembly violations; court noted there was no evidence that violations of the provisions were intended to be remedied by damages, and observed that there was no historical or common law basis for recognizing a damages action); *Spackman ex rel. Spackman v. Board of Educ.*, 16 P.3d 533, 537-539 (Utah 2000) (no damages for asserted state due process and "open education" violations, based in part upon availability of alternative remedies and deference to legislature); *Shields v. Gerhart*, 658 A.2d 924, 929-934 (Vt. 1995) (no damages for asserted state free speech and due process violations, based in part upon availability of alternative remedies).

ends. If, however, we find that these factors favor recognizing a constitutional tort, we also shall consider the existence of any special factors counseling hesitation in recognizing a damages action, including deference to legislative judgment, avoidance of adverse policy consequences, considerations of government fiscal policy, practical issues of proof, and the competence of courts to assess particular types of damages.

V.

In sum, we discern no evidence from which to infer within article I, section 7(a), an intent to afford a right to seek damages to remedy the asserted violation of the due process liberty interest alleged in this case. We also find no basis upon which to recognize a constitutional tort action for such damages.

NOTES

1. Could the plaintiff have argued that a state constitutional "right to a remedy" provision supported his claim for damages as a remedy for a constitutional violation?

2. Should state courts should look to analogous federal doctrines when interpreting state constitutions, as the court does in this case when it relies heavily on the federal *Bivens* line of cases? Are there reasons why the U.S. Constitution and state constitutions might be (or even should be) interpreted differently in this regard?

3. Do you see a separation of powers argument lurking in this case? One could ask the question *which branch* of state government—the courts or the state legislature—should determine what remedies, if any, are to be available for violations of state-created legal rights and interests? That proposition has been raised and discussed explicitly in the federal *Bivens* cases, with the Court and individual Justices more than once arguing that the creation of any federal remedy in a particular circumstance should be left to Congress to decide, rather than the Court.

E. SEPARATION OF POWERS

IN RE PETITION OF GOVERNOR
846 A.2d 1148 (N.H. 2004)

PER CURIAM.

Craig Benson as Governor of the State of New Hampshire, and the Executive Council of the State of New Hampshire, petitioned this court...to exercise original jurisdiction and rule that RSA 490:1...is unconstitutional. The Office of the Attorney General appeared in opposition. The President of the New Hampshire Senate and the Speaker of the New Hampshire House of Representatives filed *amicus* briefs defending the constitutionality of the statute.

The justices of this court recused themselves from participating in the case. In accordance with RSA 490:3 (1997), this panel was assembled, and convened...to hear the matter. The statute in dispute, RSA 490:1 (Supp.2003), provides:

> The supreme court shall consist of 5 justices appointed and commissioned as prescribed by the constitution. On the effective date of this section, the administrative position of chief justice shall be held by the justice with the most seniority on the court for a period of up to 5 years. Each succeeding chief justice shall serve for a period of up to 5 years and shall be the justice with the most seniority of service on the court who has not yet served as chief justice. A justice may decline to serve as chief justice; however, no justice shall be permitted to serve successive terms as chief justice. In the event that all 5 justices have served a term as chief justice, succeeding chief justices shall serve rotating 5-year terms based on seniority.

The petitioners submit two arguments in support of their []position that RSA 490:1 is unconstitutional. First, the petitioners argue [it] is unconstitutional because the legislative branch lacks the requisite constitutional authority to prescribe the method of selection of judicial officers and impermissibly limits the chief justice's term of office. The petitioners advance two sub-arguments in support of that proposition.

First, they argue the legislature does not have any power with respect to the appointment of judicial officers as that power has been expressly committed to the executive branch [in the New Hampshire Constitution]. Part II, Article 46 provides: "All judicial officers ... shall be nominated and appointed by the governor and council[.]" The petitioners contend the legislature is without power to alter this constitutionally prescribed method of selection of judicial officers.

Second, the petitioners claim the chief justice position on the supreme court is a separate and distinct office from that of associate justice. The petitioners argue that, if the term "judicial office" is understood to include administrative functions, the legislature would be without authority to enact RSA 490:1, as the power to appoint the chief justice would lie exclusively with the executive branch pursuant to Part II, Article 46. While the petitioners acknowledge both the chief justice and associate justices have the same adjudicatory powers in common, they submit their judicial powers are not limited to adjudication and in particular that the chief justice has enhanced judicial powers by way of additional and unique constitutionally delegated duties.

> The chief justice of the supreme court shall be the administrative head of all the courts. He shall, with the concurrence of a majority of the supreme court justices, make rules governing the administration of all courts in the state and

the practice and procedure to be followed in all such courts. The rules so promulgated shall have the force and effect of law.

There is no dispute that the constitution explicitly reserves the power of appointment of all judicial officers to the executive branch. Nor can it be disputed that the chief justice is a judicial officer. To say otherwise defies logic, reason and tradition. While there is nothing in the constitution that specifically creates or defines the office of chief justice of the supreme court, the position is assumed to exist as evidenced by Articles 40 and 73-a. Similarly, there is nothing in the United States Constitution which specifically sets out a citizen's right of privacy. Yet, that right is now deeply rooted in federal constitutional law. Like the right of privacy under the federal constitution, the traditional appointment of the chief justice by the governor and council for over two hundred years has effectively rooted that power in our state constitution.

The respondents' position is that the chief justice is not a discrete judicial officer requiring nomination and appointment by the governor and council. This argument is dependent upon the view that the only constitutional duties of a judicial officer are adjudicative. To that end, because the chief justice's adjudicatory duties do not differ from the adjudicatory duties of the associate justices, the respondents contend that the chief justice position is not separate and distinct. The respondents' argument is further dependent upon the view that the chief justice's constitutionally prescribed administrative and legislative duties are not part of his or her judicial duties, but rather are auxiliary and independent.

In *In re Mone*, 719 A.2d 626, 633 (N.H. 1998), we determined that, a statute removing the responsibility for court security from the judiciary and vesting it with the executive branch, violated the separation of powers doctrine because it encroached upon the judiciary's inherent power to control courtroom functions and ensure the fair adjudication of controversies. In discussing the origin of the judiciary's administrative powers, we observed: "Although not specifically set forth in the constitution, *powers reserved for the judiciary arise from its most fundamental duty to interpret and administer the law.*" *Id.* at 631 (emphasis added). We noted that the judiciary's exercise of administrative powers to control its courtrooms specifically did not interfere with the separation of powers doctrine because "security is an integral part of the essential adjudicatory function of the courts." Accordingly, we concluded in that instance the judiciary's administrative powers derived from its adjudicatory powers.

While the respondents attempt to draw a distinction between "judicial" duties and the administrative or legislative duties granted separately to the chief justice, we are not convinced that such a distinction exists in fact or in law. We have consistently reiterated that "this court has the responsibility to protect and preserve the judicial system. We have the *inherent authority* to take whatever action is necessary to effectuate this responsibility." This inherent judicial authority includes the use of superintendent powers that flow from and support our essential adjudicatory functions.

Whether the statutory mechanism of rotating 5-year terms for the chief justice position better serves the public than executive nomination and appointment is not a question for this court to consider. The question before us is whether the legislature is empowered by the constitution to declare it so. Our answer to this question is that the legislature is not so empowered. Part II, Article 46 of the New Hampshire Constitution emphatically provides: "*All* judicial officers…shall be nominated and appointed by the governor and council[.]" (emphasis added). There have been no exceptions to this mandatory language. The legislative branch is no less constrained than the other branches of government to stay within the limitations of the constitution. Even if constitutional language appears to leave a vacuum, it does not necessarily follow, as night the day, that the legislature is empowered to fill it.

Because there is no basis for a distinction between this court's adjudicatory duties and its administrative or legislative duties when considering the composition of "judicial power," we agree with the petitioners that the chief justice position is a discrete judicial office. Based on Articles 40 and 73-a, the chief justice inescapably holds separate and unique *judicial powers.* Accordingly, the constitution requires that the chief justice position be filled by executive nomination and appointment, as the separate commissioning of the chief justice historically reflects.

We also agree with petitioners that RSA 490:1 violates the separation of powers doctrine …. There is no doubt that pursuant to Part II, Article 4 of the constitution, the legislature has "full power and authority to erect and constitute judicatories and courts of record[.]" The appointment of judicial officers, however, is strictly reserved for the executive branch …. For over two centuries, governors and executive councils have utilized their Article 46 executive powers to nominate and appoint the chief justice of the supreme court. RSA 490:1 for the first time invades this right of the governor and executive council by categorizing the chief justice as solely an "administrative position." This usurpation of an exclusively executive function violates the separation of powers doctrine.

Moreover, RSA 490:1 impermissibly encroaches upon the prerogative of the judicial branch. While a complete and total separation of powers is neither possible nor contemplated by the constitution, encroachment by one branch into the essential powers of another is impermissible. Here, the legislature impermissibly encroaches on the position of chief justice and upon the independence of the judiciary. First, the constitution specifically conveys upon *all* judicial officers a lifetime appointment to their respective positions, conditioned only upon good behavior and requiring retirement at the age of seventy. RSA 490:1 divests the chief justice position of this lifetime appointment and replaces it with a rotating 5-year term based on seniority. Because the chief justice position is a discrete one, the legislature's enactment of RSA 490:1 is unconstitutional in that it divests the chief justice of the constitutional right to lifetime tenure (subject to the age limitations set forth in Part II, Article 78). Absent a constitutional amendment, the legislature is without authority to do so.

Second, as the petitioners warn, upholding RSA 490:1 would effectively grant the legislature free license to alter the means of appointment and the term of the chief justice based upon the politics of the moment. There is simply nothing to prevent the legislature from further amending the statute at any time to provide for other terms or means of selection of the chief justice by the legislature or otherwise, or to preclude a particular justice from succeeding to the chief justice position. This method of indirectly "addressing" judges out of office, while different in form, is not unfamiliar in theory to the judiciary. In fact, the arbitrary removal of judges from the bench prompted the reforms in 1784 that granted all judges the constitutional right to permanent and honorable salaries and lifetime tenure conditioned only upon good behavior.

While the legislature can no longer abolish the judiciary as a whole, or arbitrarily remove a sitting justice from office, RSA 490:1 would effectively allow it to control the judiciary by manipulating the statute and the chief justice position to its advantage.

IN RE REQUEST FOR ADVISORY OPINION FROM HOUSE OF REPRESENTATIVES
961 A.2d 930 (R.I. 2008)

To the Honorable, the House of Representatives of the State of Rhode Island and Providence Plantations:

We have received your request seeking the advice of the justices of this Court, in accordance with the provisions of article 10, section 3 of the Rhode Island Constitution, concerning legislation (2007-H 6266) that is presently pending before the House of Representatives. The questions propounded are as follows:

"(1) Would the proposed act, if duly enacted into law, which permits members of the General Assembly to sit as members of the Coastal Resources Management Council (CRMC)...violate the constitutional amendment to Article IX, Section 5, so called Separation of Powers Amendment, passed by the electorate on November 2, 2004...?

"(2) Would the proposed act, if duly enacted into law, permit the Speaker of the House to appoint public members to the Coastal Resources Management Council (CRMC)...?

Pursuant to the provisions of article 10, section 3 of the Rhode Island Constitution it is our duty to issue an advisory opinion at the request of the House of Representatives when the question concerns the constitutionality of pending legislation.

I

The Separation of Powers Amendments

In November of 2004, the electorate of the State of Rhode Island approved the so-called separation of powers amendments. These amendments ushered in four fundamental changes to the Rhode Island Constitution and, for the first time in Rhode Island's history, clearly and explicitly established three separate and distinct departments of government. Those fundamental changes may be summarized as follows:

(1) Article 3, section 6 was amended to preclude legislators from serving on state boards, commissions, or other state or quasi-public entities that exercise executive power;

(2) Article 5 was amended to provide that the powers of the Rhode Island government are distributed into "three separate and distinct departments";

(3) Article 6, section 10, which had vested broad "continuing powers" in the General Assembly, was repealed; and

(4) Article 9, section 5 was amended to give the Governor appointment power with respect to members of any state or quasi-public entities exercising executive power, subject to the advice and consent of the Senate.

The doctrine of separation of powers, which is now expressly established in the Rhode Island Constitution, declares that governmental powers at the state level are divided among "three separate and distinct departments." In practice, this doctrine operates to confine legislative powers to the legislature, executive powers to the executive department, and judicial powers to the judiciary, precluding one branch of the government from usurping the powers of another.

While there can be no doubt that the separation of powers amendments constitute an important recalibration of the system of checks and balances within our state government, we do not view the amendments as effectuating a wholesale reallocation of power among the executive and the legislative departments. We emphasize, however, that the pendulum has not now swung to the opposite extreme with the adoption of the 2004 constitutional amendments. While the formal incorporation of the doctrine of separation of powers into the Constitution has established a somewhat different balance of power among the departments from that which existed previously, it would be overly simplistic and patently erroneous to view the amendments as somehow *subordinating* the role of the legislative branch to that of the executive.

It is incontestably true that, for most of its history, the Rhode Island General Assembly enjoyed significantly more power than did the legislatures of most of our sister states. "Unlike the United States Congress, the Rhode Island General Assembly does not look to our State Constitution for grants of power.... Accordingly, this court has consistently adhered to the view that the General Assembly possessed all of the powers inhering in sovereignty other than those which the constitution textually commits to the other branches of our state government and that those that are not so committed...are powers reserved to the General Assembly."

The proponents and drafters of the constitutional amendments, which were designed to bring about a greater degree of separation of powers in Rhode Island's governmental structure, manifestly carried out their task with precision. Certain powers of the General Assembly were explicitly curtailed, while others were left largely or entirely unaffected by the amendments.

III

Appointments to the CRMC

The doctrine of separation of powers does not prohibit some overlapping of functions. The resolution of the problems with which government must grapple requires a certain degree of pragmatism; we are not in the pristine realm of algebraic equations, but rather in the complex and infinitely nuanced real world. Accordingly, administrative agencies may combine, to a certain extent, the functions of all three departments of government.

Nevertheless, as the United States Supreme Court has noted, the principle of separation of powers will be violated where the legislative department tries to control the execution of its enactments directly, instead of indirectly by passing new legislation. Direct legislative control of executive powers would be an impermissible usurpation of the central function of a coordinate branch.

Given the language of the separation of powers amendments, it is now our task to ascertain whether or not the CRMC exercises executive power. If it does exercise such power to any meaningful degree, then, pursuant to the plain language of the separation of powers amendments, two significant conclusions ineluctably result: (1) no member of the General

Assembly nor an appointee of that body may sit on the CRMC; and (2) appointments to the CRMC are to be made exclusively by the Governor (in the exercise of his or her constitutionally conferred appointment power) with the advice and consent of the Senate.

Upon examination of the CRMC's organic statute, chapter 23 of title 46, it appears that the CRMC combines functions that must properly be characterized as executive with functions that are quasi-legislative and quasi-judicial in nature. This is so even though the CRMC is an independent body not subject to direct gubernatorial supervision or control. The CRMC's organic statute … states that its provisions "shall be enforced by the coastal resources management council." The CRMC is authorized to "administer…programs" developed pursuant to its quasi-legislative power to develop policy and adopt regulations.

It is clear to us that the above-summarized powers and functions of the CRMC are manifestly executive in nature. To state that *all* of the CRMC's powers and functions are legislative would be to blind oneself to that reality. To do so would be to willfully ignore the language of article 5 of the Rhode Island Constitution, which expressly requires the three departments of government to be "separate and distinct." The duties and functions to be conferred on the CRMC pursuant to the proposed legislation are not unconstitutional; the CRMC may constitutionally combine functions that may best be described as quasi-legislative, executive, and quasi-judicial in nature.

In our opinion, the proposed CRMC legislation, which is the subject of the questions posed to us, cannot be reconciled with our Constitution to the extent that it would permit sitting legislators to serve on the CRMC and would allow the General Assembly to make some appointments to that body. In other words, in view of the fact that the CRMC exercises executive power, the Governor has the right to appoint its members with the advice and consent of the Senate.

Without retreating from the foregoing views with respect to the effect of the separation of powers amendments on the appointment process, we would also emphasize that the General Assembly remains fully empowered to carry out its constitutional duty to protect the natural environment of the state through the vigorous and proactive exercise of its legislative powers. Nothing written in this advisory opinion should be construed as implying that the General Assembly does not retain the fullness of its constitutionally bestowed fact-finding powers and oversight responsibility with respect to the protection of the natural environment. We also note that the legislative branch of our state government also retains an important role in the appointment process due to the fact that the Senate may approve or reject gubernatorial appointments.

It is also important to note that the General Assembly retains without diminution its vast constitutional power to enact, revise, or repeal laws concerning coastal management and preservation of natural resources. In the course of exercising its plenary legislative power, the General Assembly may, for example, (1) provide specific criteria with respect to CRMC membership composition and qualifications; (2) narrow or expand the mandate of the CRMC; (3) adopt more elaborate oversight procedures and safeguards; (4) mandate training for new CRMC members; (5) require periodic reports on CRMC activities; (6) retain the right to review CRMC decisions in discrete areas relating to budget or revenue; (7) create a joint subcommittee to oversee coastal resources management; (8) create procedures for the thorough and rigorous vetting of CRMC nominees (including disclosure statements); (9) limit the Governor's removal power; (10) assume performance of the CRMC's rulemaking functions; or (11) restructure the CRMC in to one or more bodies exercising either purely quasi-legislative or purely executive functions.

We conclude by respectfully urging the Governor and the General Assembly to discuss the various subjects addressed in this advisory opinion with the goal of reaching a mutually satisfactory agreement regarding the rights and duties conferred upon each department by the terms of our Constitution.

CHAPTER XV

AMENDMENT AND REVISION OF STATE CONSTITUTIONS

A. INTRODUCTION

Thomas Jefferson suggested that constitutions should provide each generation with an opportunity to choose its own form of government:

> Let us provide in our Constitution for its revision at stated periods. What these periods should be, nature herself indicates. By the European tables of mortality, of the adults living at any one moment of time, a majority will be dead in about nineteen years. At the end of that period then, a new majority is come into place, or, in other words, a new generation. Each generation is as independent as the one preceding, as that was of all which had gone before. It has then, like them, a right to choose for itself the form of government it believes most promotive of its own happiness; ... and it is for the peace and good of mankind, that a solemn opportunity of doing this every nineteen or twenty years, should be provided by the constitution.[1]

That opportunity has been provided for in all state constitutions. Although most state constitutions have not been completely revised every generation, the process of periodic amendments between replacements has been constant for two centuries.

The malleability of state constitutions is a sharp contrast to the stability of the United States Constitution. It has been estimated that between 1776 and 1991 more than 5,800 amendments to state constitutions have been adopted.[2] By 1964, it was estimated that:

> the existing state constitutions had been modified ... some 3,718 times—South Carolina with 250, California with 350, Louisiana with 439—to cite a few of the worst offenders. The constitutions of Alabama, Florida, New Hampshire, New York, Oregon, South Carolina and Texas had each been amended over ninety times. The average number of amendments for each state was seventy-eight.[3]

---

[1] Jefferson to Samuel Kercheval, July 12, 1816, in Thomas Jefferson, Writings: Autobiography; A Summary View of the Rights of British American; Notes on the State of Virginia; Public Papers; Addresses, Messages, and Replies; Miscellany; Letters (New York: Library of America, 1984), 1402.

[2] See Donald S. Lutz, *Toward a Theory of Constitutional Amendment* 88, American Political Science Review 359 (1994). See also James A. Henretta, Foreword: Rethinking the State Constitutional Tradition, 22 RUTGERS L.J. 819, 829 (1991).

[3] W. Brooke Graves, State Constitutional Law: A Twenty-Five Year Summary, 8 WM. & MARY L. REV. 1, 36 (1966).

The writing and amending of state constitutions has been of a distinctively populist and political nature.[4] As of January 1995,

> the American states had held over 230 constitutional conventions and adopted 146 constitutions. They had also adopted over 6,000 statewide amendments to their current constitutions. This last figure, of course, substantially understates the frequency of state constitutional amendment, since it excludes both purely local amendments and amendments to the states' previous constitutions.[5]

Thus, since 1776, the fifty states have had at least 146 constitutions, with thirty-one states having had two or more constitutions.[6] The continual process of state constitution-making has transformed the short, principle-oriented charters of the early republic into "super-legislative" documents.[7] In 1776, state constitutions contained an average of about 7,150 words. In 1985, the average state constitution contained 26,150 words and the longest, the Alabama Constitution, was almost ten times greater than the national average.[8]

State constitutions usually contain common themes: structure of government, separation of powers, individual rights, and responsibilities or limitations on the state in specific subject areas. The solutions to the particular issues raised by those themes are frequently varied and often unique. The differences are attributable to the text and context of each state's historical legal, social, political, and economic landscape.[9]

State constitutions have been the laboratories where many issues have been introduced that were either fused or fractured by the principles of a federal republican democracy. Just as the first state constitutions provided guidance for the United States Constitution, subsequent state constitutions have continued to provide positive and negative examples for each other and the nation. State constitutions pioneered provisions regarding "popular election of judges, women's suffrage, equal rights for women, black

---

[4] James A. Henretta, Foreword: Rethinking the State Constitutional Tradition, 22 RUTGERS L.J. 819, 829 (1991).

[5] G. Alan Tarr, Constitutional Politics in the States, Contemporary Controversies and Historical Patterns, p. 3 (Greenwood Press 1996).

[6] Kermit L. Hall, "Mostly Anchor and Little Sail: The Evolution of American State Constitutions," in Paul Finkelman and Stephen E. Gottlieb, eds., Toward a Usable Past: Liberty Under State Constitutions (Athens: University of Georgia Press, 1991), pp. 394-95.

[7] James A. Henretta, Foreword: Rethinking the State Constitutional Tradition, 22 RUTGERS L.J. 819, 829 (1991).

[8] Kermit L. Hall, "Mostly Anchor and Little Sail" The Evolution of American State Constitutions" in Paul Finkelman and Stephen E. Gottlieb, eds., Toward a Usable Past: Liberty Under State Constitutions (Athens: University of Georgia Press, 1991), pp. 388.

[9] See Truax v. Corrigan, 257 U.S. 312, 344 (1921) (Holmes, J., dissenting).

disfranchisement and suffrage, the income tax," prohibition, the line-item veto, and balanced budget requirements.[10]

Early state constitutions were relatively succinct frameworks of government. Current state constitutions, like Delaware's 1897 Constitution, "contain many of the provisions adopted during the various 'waves' of state constitution-making."[11] Two exceptions are Vermont and Massachusetts, which have kept their state constitutions of 1793 and 1780, respectively.[12] Another exception is the 1784 New Hampshire Constitution. Accordingly, most other state constitutions reflect a "layering" of the concerns of successive generations.[13]

This evolutionary process was never intended for and has not taken place with regard to the United States Constitution. James Madison had argued, in THE FEDERALIST No. 49, that frequent constitutional amendments would be inimical to the national government's stability.[14] According to Madison, the longevity of the United States Constitution, basically as it was enacted originally, would lead to the veneration of its principles and structure.[15]

In a nineteenth century treatise, which was commented upon favorably by Chief Justice John Marshall, Justice Joseph Story, and Chancellor James Kent, it was written:

> The [constitutional] convention did not suppose that their production was perfect.... Changes in the circumstances of the country, might require corresponding alterations in the government.... The Framers of the Constitution were aware of this, and, therefore, wisely provided a method, by which it may be amended, without disturbances of the public tranquility, or injury to the general system.

> [The Constitution] contains within itself a provision for amendment, by which to remedy any defects in its original structure, or such as may occur in process of time. But this power should be used with great caution; and always with the

---

[10] Kermit L. Hall, "Mostly Anchor and Little Sail," The Evolution of American and State Constitutions *in* Paul Finkelman and Stephen E. Gottlieb, eds., *Toward a Usable Past: Liberty Under State Constitutions*, p. 394-95 (Athens: University of Georgia Press, 1991).

[11] Robert F. Williams, State Constitutional Law: Cases and Materials 19 (2d ed., 1993).

[12] Paul Finkleman and Stephen E. Gottlieb, editors *Toward a Usable Part: Liberty Under State Constitutions* (Athens: University of Georgia Press 1991) p. 14 n.19.

[13] Robert F. Williams, State Constitutional Law: Cases and Materials 19 (2d ed., 1993).

[14] The Federalist No. 49, at 340 (Jacob E. Cooke ed., Middletown, Conn.: Wesleyan University Press, 1961).

[15] *Id.*

conviction, that *stability* is an important requisite of good government; and that frequent changes are destructive of its utility.[16]

In fact, as a result of the requirements in Article V, the United States Constitution has proven to be difficult to amend.[17] The first ten amendments to the United States Constitution, the Bill of Rights, were submitted collectively and became operative with Virginia's ratification in 1791. Following the ratification of the Twelfth Amendment in 1804, the United States Constitution was not amended again until 1865. It has been estimated that approximately 10,000 amendments to the United States constitution have been proposed.[18] To date, however, there have only been a total of twenty-seven amendments to the United States Constitution and it contains a total of only approximately 7300 words.

B. ALTERING STATE CONSTITUTIONS

Anne Permaloff, *Methods of Altering State Constitutions*
33 Cumb. L. Rev. 217 (2003)[19]

All of the 50 state constitutions in the United States contain provisions outlining the manner in which they may be altered or revised. State constitutions may be altered through legislatively proposed amendments, constitutional conventions, constitutional initiatives, constitutional commissions, and judicial interpretation. This paper examines the methods of alteration that include direct public representation and involvement at some stage in the alteration process, thus limiting the discussion to the first four methods listed.

There is considerable variation among the states in terms of which methods of alteration are allowed by their existing state constitutions. Furthermore, each method varies greatly in terms of the procedures required for its use. This paper will identify and discuss the variations within each method of alteration, which states use a given method, and the positive and negative factors associated with its use. Some of the philosophical, political, and cultural factors that influenced adoption of specific methods will be discussed as well. Finally, the paper will consider which methods might be appropriate for Alabama and for inclusion in a new Alabama constitution.

---

[16] James A. Bayard, A Brief Exposition of the Constitution of the United States 3 (2d ed. 1838), 135-36, 160 (emphasis in Bayard's text).

[17] Donald S. Lutz, *Toward a Theory of Constitutional Amendment,* 88 American Political Science Review 355 (1994).

[18] Richard B. Bernstein with Agel, Jerome, Amending America xii (New York: Times Books 1993).

[19] Reprinted with permission.

1. The Idea that Constitutions May Be Altered Is Not New

Popular sovereignty or the idea that government is based on popular consent served as the foundation for the Declaration of Independence, the original state constitutions, as well as the U.S. Constitution. Donald S. Lutz who has studied early state constitutional development indicates that an evolutionary process resulted in the gradual adoption of the idea, "… that a doctrine of popular sovereignty required that constitutions be written by popularly selected convention, rather than the legislature, and then ratified by a process that elicited popular consent ideally in a referendum."

Lutz notes that this notion quickly led to American expansion of John Locke's concept that replacement of government and the contract upon which it was based (a constitution) could occur only if those exercising power breached their contract. The American version held that if the public created the governing document and could alter its content by amendment, it also could replace the document at any time.

Lutz and others suggest that at least three other ideas reinforced this conception of constitutional change: human nature though imperfect is educable; faith that deliberative processes of decision-making will lead to the public good; and distinct differences between fundamental or constitutional law and legislative enactments.

Popular sovereignty implies that all constitutional matters should be based upon some form of popular consent, which in turn implies a formal, public process. Human fallibility implies the need for some method of altering or revising the constitution. A distinction between normal and constitutional matters implies that constitutional matters require a distinctive, highly deliberative process and thus implies the need for an amendment procedure more difficult than that used for normal legislation. Together these premises require that the procedure be neither too easy nor to difficult.

Robert F. Williams writes of another basis for the notion that constitutions may be altered—the idea that each generation should have the opportunity to refashion government to meet its needs. He and others quote Thomas Jefferson's views on this point for Jefferson not only advocated amending constitutions through convention, he advocated periodic revisions within set time frames:

> Some men look at constitutions with sanctimonious reverence, and deem them like the arc of the covenant, too sacred to be touched. They ascribe to the men of the preceding age a wisdom more than human, and suppose what they did to be beyond amendment. I knew that age well; I belonged to it, and labored with it. It deserved well of its country. It was very like the present, but without the experience of the present…I am certainly not an advocate for frequent and untried changes in laws and constitutions…. But I know also that laws and

institutions must go hand in hand with the progress of the human mind. Let us, as our sister States have done, avail ourselves of our reason and experience, to correct the crude essays of our first and unexperienced, although wise, virtuous, and well-meaning councils. And lastly, let us provide in our constitution for its revision at stated periods.... Each generation is as independent as the one preceding, as that was of all which had gone before. It has then, like them, a right to choose for itself the form of government it believes most promotive of its own happiness; consequently, to accommodate to the circumstances in which it finds itself, that received from its predecessors; and it is for the peace and good of mankind, that a solemn opportunity of doing this every nineteen or twenty years, should be provided by the constitution; so that it may be handed on, with periodic repairs, from generation to generation, to the end of time, if anything human can so long endure.

Jefferson wrote this passage in response to questions about a constitutional convention to revise the original Virginia constitution. Similar comments from other original signers of the U.S. Constitution could be cited to make the point that from the beginning of this nation's history trust in the public and its ability to grow and learn served as the basis of the argument that constitutions should change over time.

Other contemporaries of Jefferson's such as James Madison and John Adams believed in the ability to alter constitutions by amendment, but they believed that constitutions should not be altered easily. They did not support automatic periodic revision. For Madison the danger to be avoided was use of the amending process to foster factional (interest group) objectives. He believed constitutional change should be reserved for important matters such as the protection of basic rights. He was the major champion of the first amendments to the U.S. Constitution which were proposed by the very first Congress, the Bill of Rights.

Alan Tarr, one of the best known scholars on the development of state constitutions writes:

> The United States has not one constitution but fifty-one. These constitutions were drafted at various stages in the nation's history, and their contents (not surprisingly) reflect the constitutional thought regnant at the time of their adoption. The political theory underlying state constitutions has often diverged from the perspective of 1787.

For Tarr, the states have their own constitutional tradition which encompasses not only the constitutional amendment and constitutional convention processes but constitutional initiative as well:

> First, the initiative and direct democracy more generally fit comfortably within the state constitutional tradition. Second, this compatibility derives from the belief, basic to the state constitutional tradition, that the primary danger facing republican government is minority faction—power wielded by the wealthy or well-connected few—rather than majority faction. Third, the state tradition's divergence from Federalist #10's diagnosis of the threats to republican government is paralleled by a skepticism about the "republican remedies"

proposed in The Federalist Papers. More specifically, the state constitutional tradition is characterized by a distrust of government by elected representatives representation not only fails to solve the problems afflicting republican government, but it may even aggravate those problems by empowering minority factions. If this is so, of course, then direct democracy—or mechanisms designed to approximate it—become much more attractive.

Tarr also reminds us that:

State constitutions of the eighteenth and early nineteenth centuries tended to concentrate power in the state legislature. In addition to enacting laws and imposing taxes, the legislatures in most states selected the governor and state judges and appointed other state officials (and oftentimes local officials as well). Legislators could also remove officials by impeachment and require the removal of judges by address. Moreover, these broad powers existed virtually without check.

The legislative authority was based on the fact that the legislature was considered the only institution that directly represented the citizenry. Even more important, ... state constitution-makers sought to approximate direct democracy in their systems of representative government.

2. Legislatively Proposed Amendments

State constitutions are altered most frequently through legislatively proposed amendments. This process first appeared in state constitutions in the 1770s and was a well established principle by the 1780s. Today all 50 state constitutions allow for such amendment. All but one state (Delaware) requires that amendments proposed by the legislature be ratified by a vote of the electorate. Research has repeatedly tied frequent use of the amendment process to the length of a constitution. The longer the constitution, the more it is amended.

Conditions of legislative passage vary from state to state. Seventeen states require that the proposal pass by a simple majority of the membership of each house or 50% plus one. Alabama and seven other states set the bar higher at three-fifths or 60% of the membership of each house while 18 states require a two-thirds vote or 67%. Additional requirements may also apply.

Twelve states (Delaware, Indiana, Iowa, Massachusetts, Nevada, New York, Rhode Island, South Carolina, Tennessee, Virginia, and Wyoming) require that the amendment proposal be passed at two or more separate sessions of the legislature. The conditions of the vote may be different for each session. For example, Connecticut sets the vote at three-fourths (75%) of each house in the first session of passage and then requires passage in two more sessions at a majority level. And, a general election must occur between the two final sessions. South Carolina, Virginia and Tennessee, the only southern states that require passage in two sessions, differ in their procedures. Virginia requires a majority vote in both sessions. In South Carolina, initial passage is set at two-thirds of the membership; second passage is set at a majority but occurs only after ratification of the amendment by the electorate. In Tennessee the number on first passage is set at two-thirds of the senate and a majority of the house and then on second passage the figure is set at two-thirds of both houses.

Only six states place limits on the number or types of amendments that may be presented to the electorate. Arkansas, Kansas and Kentucky limit amendments on a ballot to three, five, and four respectively. In Colorado no more than six articles of the constitution may have amendments proposed in the same legislative session. New Jersey does not limit the number of proposed amendments on the ballot, but a proposal that has been defeated by the electorate may not be put on the ballot until three general elections have passed.

State constitutions either set a specified time and type of election for popular ratification (for example, the next general election) or allow the timing of the vote to be determined by the legislature itself. When the legislature is given the power to determine the timing of the vote as it is in Alabama, the type of election at which the vote occurs (for example, primary vs. general election, presidential election year vs. off-year election, regularly scheduled election vs. a special election) and factors such as likely turnout level and the disposition of voters likely to vote may influence the decision-making. High or low turnout may be the goal depending upon the purpose as well as the beneficiaries of the proposal.

Because legislatively proposed amendments are not normal legislation, they are not sent to the governor for signature or veto. The governor is important to the process, however. As a political party leader, she may work with legislative leaders to facilitate or block passage. Easy access to the media and interest groups may be part of this effort, particularly in attempting to activate supporters or opponents in legislative lobbying efforts. Sometimes governors lead election style campaigns aimed at activating the electorate to vote. Governors engaged in such campaigns may find their potential opponents working the other side of the issue while testing the waters for the next election.

Almost all (44 out of 49) of the state constitutions require a majority popular vote for ratification of an amendment. Most require a majority vote of those voting on the amendment. Three require a majority of those voting in the election while New Hampshire requires a two-thirds vote of those voting on the amendment. Illinois requires a two-thirds vote on the amendment or a majority of those voting in the election. States may add other requirements to these numbers. For example, in Florida any amendment creating a new tax or fee not in effect on November 7, 1994 must pass by a two-thirds vote, and Louisiana requires that amendments that impact five or fewer political subdivisions (for example, parishes or counties) must pass by a majority vote at the state level and a majority in each impacted subdivision. In New Mexico some amendment votes dealing with the right to vote and with education must be approved by 75% of the electorate; they reach the ballot only after 75% of each house have agreed to the proposals. Georgia's current constitution allows only for amendments that are of a general and uniform applicability throughout the state. This eliminates local purpose amendments and keeps the number of amendments down.

3. Constitutional Conventions

The constitutional convention is the oldest and traditional method used for creating constitutions and making major changes in existing constitutions. The convention is often referred to as the most democratic of the alteration procedures because it involves the electorate to the greatest extent.

Tarr, in outlining the Nineteenth Century experience with constitutional conventions, suggests at least three ways in which constitutional conventions then (and now) approximate direct democracy:

> First, the membership of state constitutional conventions tended to mirror the populace of the states. Convention delegates were—like state legislators— elected by the people, but unlike legislators, they did not tend to be professional politicians.... Second, the people exercised control over the calling of conventions. Whereas the legislature met regularly, a convention came into being only by popular vote, when the people wanted fundamental political issues addressed. Thus when convention delegates met, they had a ready-made agenda of popular concerns to guide their deliberations.... Third, ratification by referendum afforded the people an opportunity to approve or reject the measures proposed by constitutional conventions—not an approximation of direct democracy but the real thing.... Usually voters considered the proposed constitution as a whole rather than voting on particular provisions. Yet in at least some states the practice developed of submitting controversial proposals as separate items, lest opposition to them doom the entire document.

Tarr also writes that often constitutional conventions were initiated in the 1800s in order to create a balance between the branches of government. As legislative bodies came to be viewed as dominated by specific interest groups, the conventions were used to enhance gubernatorial and judicial authority in order to protect the public. Constitutional initiatives which will be addressed in a later section were also used to return power to the people.

4. Constitutional Convention Procedures Today

Forty-two of the 50 states make provisions in their constitutions for constitutional conventions. Generally legislatures are given the right to initiate the constitutional convention call. That call usually requires voter approval. Then, the electorate selects the delegates to the convention using procedures outlined by the state constitution or by the legislature in enabling legislation. The enabling legislation may be outlined to the electorate at the time of its vote on the convention call. The electorate generally must ratify any document or alterations in the existing constitution that are proposed by the convention. As with the amending process, however, there are many variations in this overall pattern.

The standard convention call requirements are a majority vote or a two-thirds (67%) vote of both houses. South Dakota and Illinois require three-quarters (75%) of each house to call a convention.

Fourteen states require an automatic periodic vote by the electorate on whether to hold a convention. New York's 1846 constitution was the first to include such a mandatory referendum provision. Eight states (Connecticut, Illinois, Maryland, Missouri, Nebraska, New York, Ohio, and Oregon) mandate a vote every 20 years. Michigan requires a vote every 16 years. Four states (Alaska, Iowa, New Hampshire, and Rhode Island) use a 10 year cycle while Hawaii's vote must occur every 9 years. For many of these states if a vote for a convention has been called during the interim period, the mandatory vote cycle starts from the date of that vote.

An important factor to be considered in relation to the mandatory vote is whether the constitution includes a self-executing clause for any convention voted for by the electorate. Self-executing clauses may set up procedures for calling the convention, outline delegate selection procedures and delegate requirements, provide for convention location and staff support as well as operating funds all with no action required by the legislature. Without self-execution clauses, the voters may authorize a convention only to find that the legislature may then fail to enact the enabling legislation required, thus forcing the electorate to seek judicial remedies.

State constitutions vary greatly on whether a popular vote is required to ratify the recommendations made by a constitutional convention. When popular ratification procedures are specified in the constitution, the standard requirement for passage is a majority vote of those voting on the proposal. Nine states including Alabama, Florida, Mississippi, and West Virginia do not have specific ratification requirements in their constitutions. The convention call proposal itself usually outlines the procedures to be used for ratification, but the conditions of the ratification vote may also be left to the determination of the convention itself. Seven state constitutions including Kentucky's make no provision at all for popular ratification.

Conventions often are called during crisis periods or periods of major change. For example, the 1968 Florida Constitution was written by a convention called for by the first legislature to take office after reapportionment on a one-person, one-vote basis. One set of political issues its members had to deal with were the tensions between North Florida and South Florida. These tensions not only reflected differences in political party orientations but differences in their economic base. They also were tied to North Florida's domination of the state legislature due to the several decades long failure of the legislature to reapportion itself as the population base grew in South Florida. Similar regional tensions tied to legislative malapportionment aided in making the 1960s the last major decade for state constitutional conventions and total rewriting of state constitutions. The last constitutional convention which was successful in winning voter approval of its recommendations was held in Louisiana in 1974.

5. Strengths and Weaknesses

The greatest strength of the legislatively called convention process is that it maximizes direct citizen participation in the revision process. Citizens are indirectly represented at the legislative vote stage because they decided through the election process who votes on the proposal. They then vote directly on the proposal. They vote again to select convention delegates. Finally, recommendations from the convention must be ratified by the electorate. There is the potential for increasing citizen attention and interest in politics, governmental problems, and possible solutions. There is also the potential for increasing knowledge levels and developing a true public dialogue and debate process.

Several weaknesses or problems with the convention approach to revision are cited by opponents. First, many recent attempts to call conventions have failed due to public suspicion and distrust of politicians and the political process. Second, interest group activity is likely to be high and to create a divisive atmosphere at the delegate selection stage, during convention operations, and at ratification. Some groups will seek to preserve the protected position they have in the current constitution; they will be competing with those who have a vested interest in seeking special treatment for themselves. This is, of course, the democratic process at work. Third, many fear that the ability to spend money or to attract money from interest groups, not competence or concern for the public interest, will drive delegate selection. Others fear that unless specifically barred by the enabling legislation or the constitution, legislators and other elected officials will predominate among the delegates. The previously mentioned items are viewed as reinforcing this possibility.

A major problem exists in the manner by which conventions usually originate by legislative proposal. If the legislature has been captured by interests seeking to preserve the status quo (for example, rural Alabama's dominance of the legislature until the late 1960s), a proposal for a convention will not pass the legislature, and the will of the people may be thwarted. This is precisely the argument advanced by Progressive and Populist reformers during the late 1800s and early 1900s to justify the use of constitutional initiative as a revision method. An automatic periodic vote to determine if a convention should be held is another mechanism for bypassing a recalcitrant legislature.

6. Constitutional Initiatives

An initiative is a form of direct legislation that allows individuals and/or groups to propose public policy through the creation of a constitutional amendment. Currently, 18 states have constitutional initiative powers that allow the public to propose amendments to their constitutions and then submit them to the electorate for ratification. In Florida this process may be used to call a constitutional convention.

Constitutional initiative proposals usually are restricted to single topics and may generally deal with only one article of the constitution. Exceptions include situations where change in one article impacts another article; both may then be changed by the amendment. The general procedures for initiatives begin with the filing of the proposed amendment with the required state office. That office must determine that the amendment and petition meets legal requirements. The sponsors then circulate the petition within the electorate. Numbers of petition signatures required usually are tied to a percentage of the total votes cast in the last gubernatorial election. Currently the numbers range from 3% to 15%. When the requisite number of registered voters have signed the petitions, they are filed with the appropriate state office for review and certification. If the petitions meet all legal requirements, the proposed amendment is placed on the ballot for a vote.

Other requirements than the general format listed above may be set. For example, Mississippi requires petition signatures to be collected within a 12 month period, be equal to at least 12% of the votes for governor in the last gubernatorial election, and have no more than one-fifth (20%) of the signatures from any one congressional district. If a congressional district represents more than one-fifth of the signatures, the Mississippi Secretary of State who must determine whether the petition qualifies for the ballot must eliminate the excess signatures from the signature count.

7. Direct Initiative

Sixteen states, including Arkansas, Florida and Oklahoma use the direct constitutional initiative process. There is no legislative review or revision of the proposed amendment. Once legal requirements are met, the proposed amendment must be placed on the ballot. The timing of the vote is set by the constitution in relation to the date of formal certification of the petitions as legal. The election is usually specified as a general election. In Nevada passage of the constitutional initiative requires a majority vote of the electorate in two successive elections. This provision was established in 1962 with voter acceptance of a legislatively proposed amendment that created the process while simultaneously repealing Nevada's use of the indirect constitutional initiative which will be discussed below.

Many of the direct constitutional initiative states have requirements that specify that if two conflicting amendment proposals pass in the same election, the one with the highest number of votes will go into effect. The effective date of a newly passed amendment may be immediately or 30 days after the official certification of election results or a constitutionally specified day of the year such as January 1 or July 1, the first day of the budget year for most states.

8. Indirect Initiative

Two states, Mississippi and Massachusetts, use the indirect constitutional initiative. Indirect initiatives require that once the petition process is complete and certified as meeting all legal requirements, the proposed amendment must be submitted to the legislature for review. (The Nevada version which was abolished in 1962 in favor of a restrictive direct initiative process required that the proposed amendment also be sent to the governor for review.)

Mississippi's legislature receives constitutional initiative proposals on the first day of the legislative session. The legislature has several options available to it in its review process, but it must act within a four month deadline or the proposed amendment automatically goes on the ballot. The legislature's first option is to accept the proposal by a majority vote of each house; the proposal then goes on the ballot. If the legislature finds the amendment unacceptable and rejects it but without offering an alternative, the proposed amendment is placed on the ballot. If the legislature amends the proposal, both the original proposal and the legislative alternative will appear on the ballot for separate votes. If the proposal is rejected by the legislature which then passes an alternative, a complicated method of presentation and vote counting is specified in the Mississippi constitution:

> both such measures shall be printed on the official ballots that a voter can express separately two (2) preferences: First by voting for the approval of either measure or against both measures, and secondly, by voting for one measure or the other measure. If the majority of those voting on the first issue is against both measures, then both measures fail, but in that case the vote on the second issue nevertheless shall be carefully counted and made public. If the majority voting on the first issue is for the approval of either measure, then the measure receiving a majority of the votes on the second issue and also receiving not less than forty percent (40%) of the total votes cast at the election at which the measure was submitted for approval shall be law. Any person who votes for the ratification of either measure on the first issue must vote for one (1) of the measures on the second issue in order for the ballot to be valid. Any person who votes against both measures on the first issue may vote but shall not be required to vote for any of the measures on the second issue in order for the ballot to be valid.

All proposals on the ballot carry with them a fiscal analysis outlining their likely financial impacts.

In Mississippi passage of proposed amendments requires a majority of those voting on the proposal. That majority vote count must represent at least 40% of the votes cast in the election. No more than five proposals are allowed on the ballot in any one election, and defeated proposals may not be reconsidered until two years have elapsed.

Massachusetts requires a constitutional initiative to be presented to a joint session of the legislature and to be approved by 25% of the legislature in two successive sessions before it may go on the ballot. If it fails to get the necessary 25%, it will not go to the ballot. During the first review the legislature may amend the proposal if 75% of the legislators vote to do so. The second legislative session may not amend the proposal. Another option available to the legislature is to pass a substitute version of the amendment. The original proposal and the clearly identified legislative alternative then go to the electorate for a vote.

The Massachusetts process has led to legislative approval of only three amendments. The first two were approved by the voters in 1938 and 1974. The third, a 1994 proposal to establish a graduated income tax, failed to receive voter approval.

9. Limitations on Constitutional Initiatives

Constitutional initiatives may be limited by specific provisions of a constitution. What, if any, limitations exist varies greatly from state to state. For example, the Massachusetts constitution places specific restrictions on what portions of the constitution may not be amended through the initiative process. It states that basic citizen rights such as the right to a jury trial, freedom of speech, freedom of the press, the right to peacefully assembly, and religious matters are excluded from initiative action as are some election related matters. The Massachusetts constitution also protects the independence of the judiciary by disallowing constitutional initiatives that alter judicial appointment procedures, judicial qualifications, and the tenure and removal processes for judges. In addition, constitutional initiatives are barred from creating specific appropriations from the state treasury. Illinois's constitution limits constitutional initiatives to structural and procedural subjects found in the Legislative article. The Mississippi constitution states that the initiative may not be used to alter or repeal the following: the Bill of Rights; Mississippi Public Employees' Retirement System (and laws related to it); right to work provisions; or the constitutional initiative process. California requires that all initiatives must apply to all political subdivisions and be applicable to all subdivisions even if a majority in that jurisdiction voted against the ratified initiative.

Some states may require review of a constitutional initiative by the attorney general of the state for its legality. The opinion that results may be merely advisory in nature or may be given the force of law. Some reviews are accomplished at an initial notice filing that precedes circulation of the petition. This review determines whether all legal requirements have been met for the petition itself including proper format, especially improper or unclear ballot language; it may also determine whether the proposal itself meets constitutional muster. Both federal and state constitutional issues may be involved. Some states require the reviews at the time signed petitions have been filed. These reviews may be undertaken by a state's supreme court. The proposals may become the subject of court cases both before and after they have been approved by the electorate.

10. Strengths and Weaknesses

The constitutional initiative process, particularly in the direct initiative form, returns the power to act to the public. This power may be exercised even when a legislature or one of its houses has been captured by interest groups and blocks all efforts to institute a constitutional convention or to propose amendments. For example, the Oklahoma initiative was created to thwart the power that the railroads held over the state legislature. It is often viewed as a form of direct grass roots democracy.

Weaknesses cited for the initiative process are numerous. One set of complaints focuses on the procedures involved in the petition process. Because states may set the number of required signatures high, require signatures from registered voters, and often limit the time period within which the signatures must be collected, organized groups with large memberships and/or money rather than individual citizens have a distinct advantage. Those with the money are increasingly employing professionals who may not even live in the state to generate and circulate the petitions. In other instances, groups from outside the state that have a national agenda may go into several states with their initiative campaigns. At least one state has attempted to deal with these issues by restricting the right to file and circulate petitions to those who are registered voters in the state. Some states passed laws to make the paying of those who circulate a petition illegal, but a Colorado law to this effect was declared unconstitutional by the U.S. Supreme Court in a unanimous vote. Another problem is that unless the statutory or constitutional requirements require a clear and concise petition statement summarizing the proposal and give a court or the attorney general the authority to police these factors, confusing and purposively misleading information may be disseminated. A similar problem can exist for ballot summaries. Another concern is that majorities voting on initiatives may not be sensitive to minority rights. Both conservative rural interests and African American groups in Mississippi opposed the initiative process on this ground. Minority rights issues are one reason state constitutions may specify that basic rights found in their bill of rights are not alterable by initiative. Constitutions are supposed to serve as the fundamental law of the state. Amendment added by initiative increasingly represent policy issues normally dealt with by legislatures using their lawmaking powers.

A final issue centers around extraordinary majorities; it often is cited by those who are concerned by minority rights. A state that uses constitutional initiative may require a majority vote for passage of the initiative or for passage of a legislatively proposed amendment. An initiative proposal may include within it restrictions on how the proposal once adopted may be changed by future initiatives or amendments. The popular restriction is to require a two-thirds or three-fifths vote. Future generations must come to higher levels of agreement to change proposals made today by a majority vote. They lose the flexibility to create change that was part of the original argument for creation of constitutional initiative authority. A constitutional initiative also may be used to place restrictions on how certain laws may be passed by the legislature. An example is the Florida requirement that new tax proposals pass the legislature by super majority.

11. Constitutional Commissions

Constitutional commissions serve two major purposes: (1) studying the constitution and proposing changes and (2) preparing for a constitutional convention. They have also been used by legislatures as devices to forestall constitutional convention calls.

Commissions may be authorized by law or state constitution to meet on a periodic basis. They may be established by law, executive order, or other means (for example, the Alabama Citizens Commission on Constitutional Reform) to meet for a specified period. They generally report the results of their work to the governor, legislature, or other public authority. In the 1990s both California and New York used the commission system. New York's governor in 1992 created the Temporary New York State Commission on Constitutional Reform to prepare for a convention should the public agree to the automatic convention call set for 1997. The electorate rejected the convention call. California used an executively created commission to make recommendations to the legislature and governor.

One example of the successful use of a commission as an advisory group charged with making recommendations to the legislature may be found in Florida in the 1960s. In 1964 a legislatively proposed amendment received majority support from the Florida electorate. The amendment specified:

> Either branch of the legislature, at any regular session, or at any special or extraordinary session called for the purposes, may propose by joint resolution a revision of the entire constitution or a revision or amendment of any portion or portions thereof and may direct and provide for an election thereon.

The Florida legislature used its new authority to create a revision commission by statute. It met in 1965-1966 and submitted proposals for major revisions of the constitution to the legislature in 1966. These proposals together with legislative revisions were submitted to the voters in the 1968 general election. On passage they became the 1968 Florida Constitution. This new constitution added not only constitutional initiative but a revision commission unlike that used to develop the new constitution. The Florida Constitutional Review Commission is the only constitutionally established commission with the authority to report its recommendations directly to the electorate for a vote.

12. Strengths and Weaknesses

The commission system allows for study and careful deliberation. Its work can be done transparently so that the public is fully informed of all its activities and has numerous opportunities to contribute their concerns and recommendation. If the commission must report to the legislature, its recommendations must be translated into legislatively proposed amendments. Only Florida has a commission that reports recommendations directly to the public. Even when the public has voted against this commission's recommendations, public debate has been increased and change has been generated through later legislative actions.

If commissions are dependent upon legislatures or governors for their call rather than automatically established on a periodic basic, they may never be called into existence. Or if called by a governor, the legislature might ignore their work for partisan reasons. A periodic cycle for automatically calling a commission into session can insure that constitutional reviews are accomplished.

A major problem may be that enabling legislation is not accounted for in the commission process. The Florida CRC worked well in 1998 because of the cooperative efforts of politicians, not existing law.

There are those that critique Florida's CRC and who urge its abolition. For example, Joseph Little finds that the appointment process created the gift of a rich political plum to the politicians who happened to be the incumbents in the designated offices when the time for appointing…rolled abound. He believes the appointees support the political and agendas of those they represent, not the public. In addition, he argues that the public's presentations at the public hearings represent statements of an ideological bent or served as mechanisms for venting displeasure with legislative actions. Little believes that the authority given the CRC is too great, that its proposed amendments often deal with policy issues best handled by the legislature, and that its packaging of recommendations together for a single vote by the electorate forces it to accept revisions it does not want in order to get that does want.

13. Conclusion

Selection of one revision method over another should be based on at least two criteria: an examination of the basic underlying values each reflects and the administrative and political problems associated with each. Some of the administrative problems may be handled through careful constitutional wording and enabling legislation.

Direct democracy and participation by the public is maximized through the use of the constitutional convention. Direct constitutional initiative and required periodic votes by the electorate on whether a constitutional convention should be held also value direct democracy.

Indirect or representative democracy is maximized by legislative involvement in the revisions process. The amendment process usually begins with legislative proposals. Legislatures also serve as the major initiators of constitutional conventions, and in Mississippi and Massachusetts the legislature also reviews constitutional initiatives from the public.

Should a constitutional convention be held in Alabama, the Commission might give consideration to recommending that a new constitution require periodic public votes on whether a constitutional convention should be held. The Florida Constitutional Revision Commission approach should be examined carefully. It combines elements of indirect democracy (appointment of members by public officials) with elements of direct democracy (automatic periodic creation, required public hearing, and sending of recommendations to the public for a vote without legislative intervention). Many of the administrative problems faced by the commission could be overcome through enabling provisions written into the constitution.

C. INITIATIVE

CARTER v. LEHI CITY
269 P.3d 141 (Utah 2012)

LEE, J.

This case presents questions concerning the scope of the people's initiative power under article VI of the Utah Constitution. Petitioners are Lehi City voters who sought to place on the municipal ballot initiatives regulating salaries and residency requirements for certain city employees. The City refused to accept the initiatives, and this litigation ensued.

Our consideration of this matter has caused us to reexamine our precedents defining the nature and extent of the people's power to legislate by initiative. The framework embraced in those precedents has prompted some misgivings over the years. At the core of our concern has been the difficulty of applying the test in our cases predictably and consistently.

This concern is particularly troubling in a field that implicates the constitutional power of the people to initiate legislation. That power is a fundamental guardian of liberty and an ultimate protection against tyranny. Its preservation cannot be left to the whims of a doctrine whose invocation turns on the discretionary decrees of the judicial branch. Of all the branches of government, we are least suited to decide on the wisdom of allowing the people to supplant their representatives in a particular field of regulation. We are the least representative branch of government. There is a troubling irony in our making discretionary calls on the propriety of acts by the ultimate repository of regulatory power. We must assure that our decisions on such vital matters are dictated by law, not by our individual preferences.

With this in mind, we return to first principles to examine the nature and scope of the people's initiative power. In the paragraphs below, we evaluate the text and structure of article VI of the Utah Constitution and analyze its meaning in historical perspective. From those materials we develop a legal framework for delineating the people's initiative power that is consistent with the text and original meaning of article VI.

This page of history outweighs the volume of logic in our existing precedent. Thus, we abandon the framework set forth in *Citizen's Awareness Now v. Marakis*, 873 P.2d 1117 (Utah 1994), and refined in subsequent cases, replacing it with a standard that defines the people's initiative power on the basis of the nature of the power to effect "legislation," as that term is traditionally understood.

In so doing, we do not envision a fundamental change in the ultimate breadth of the initiative power. Our new framework is not aimed at overturning the results of most of our prior decisions in this area. We aim to clarify the law and to bring it in line with the text and original meaning of the constitution, not to overrule the results of many of our cases. Thus, our decision today is sensitive to and ultimately consistent with the doctrine of stare decisis. That doctrine recognizes that "people should know what their legal rights are as defined by judicial precedent, and having conducted their affairs in reliance on such rights, ought not to have them swept away by judicial fiat." *Austad v. Austad*, 2 Utah 2d 49, 269 P.2d 284, 290 (1954). A decision to clarify unworkable precedent does not undermine but advances that goal, particularly where we preserve the results of most of our prior cases. *See id.*

Applying our new standard, we uphold the initiatives proposed by petitioners as properly legislative and reject Lehi City's various objections to placing them on the ballot.

In December 2010, a group of Lehi City voters sought to amend two city ordinances by submitting to the city recorder two voter initiatives for inclusion in the 2011 municipal election ballot. Initiative One sought to set "maximum salary and total compensation limits" on all salaried city employees. Initiative Two sought to impose a city residency requirement for certain city employees. Each initiative garnered more than the minimum number of registered voter signatures required by statute, and it is undisputed that the initiatives otherwise complied with title 20A, chapter 7 of the election code, which governs the manner and conditions for proposing citizen initiatives.

In a May 2011 council meeting, the Lehi City Council determined that the proposed amendments were not valid exercises of the voters' power to initiate legislation, and adopted a resolution directing the city recorder to refuse to place them on the November 2011 election ballot. The resolution stated the council's conclusions that "both initiatives are legally insufficient in that they: i) are not the proper subject of an initiative petition because they are administrative in nature; ii) may be an unconstitutional impairment of contract; [and] iii) conflict with state law."

Upon learning of the council's decision, three of the initiatives' sponsors filed a petition for writ of extraordinary relief directly in this court as authorized by Utah Code section 20A–7–507. The petitioners contend that Initiatives One and Two are proper exercises of initiative power under article VI of the Utah Constitution and that the initiatives should be submitted for voter approval in the next municipal election. We agree with the petitioners: The subject matter of Initiatives One and Two is legislative in nature; the initiatives do not conflict with state law because Utah Code section 10–3–818, invoked by the City, does not apply to voter initiatives; and the City's remaining arguments are not ripe for review.

Lehi City's central contention is that Initiatives One and Two are "administrative in nature" and thus not "appropriate for voter participation." We disagree with Lehi and hold that Initiatives One and Two are proper exercises of the people's legislative power.

Article VI, section 1 of the Utah Constitution vests "Legislative power" in "the people of the State of Utah" and provides for its exercise through ballot initiatives and referenda. Under this provision, our cases have long recognized a general limit on the people's initiative power. An initiative is appropriate if it is "legislative," but *ultra vires it* it is "administrative." *Citizen's Awareness Now v. Marakis*, 873 P.2d 1117, 1122 (Utah 1994). This legislative/administrative distinction is a reflection of our constitution's explicit and strict separation of powers, which is set forth in article V.

Under article V of the Utah Constitution,

> The powers of the government of the State of Utah shall be divided into three distinct departments, the Legislative, the Executive, and the Judicial; and no person charged with the exercise of powers properly belonging to one of these departments, shall exercise any functions appertaining to either of the others, except in the cases herein expressly directed or permitted.

We begin with some fundamental principles that are evident in the text, structure, and history of our constitution. First, the initiative power of the people is parallel to and coextensive with the power of the state legislature. Second, the constitution accords a similar initiative power to the people on a local level, to be exercised within counties, cities, and towns. From these principles, it follows that the question courts should ask in evaluating the propriety of a proposed initiative is whether the initiative would be a proper exercise of legislative power if enacted by the state legislature.

"The government of the State of Utah was founded pursuant to the people's organic authority to govern themselves." As reinforced in our constitution, "[a]ll political power is inherent in the people; and all free governments are founded on their authority." Utah Const. art. I, § 2.

Under this basic premise, upon which all our government is built, the people have the inherent authority to allocate governmental power in the bodies they establish by law.

Acting through the state constitution, the people of Utah divided their political power, vesting it in the various branches of government. Article VI vests "The Legislative power of the State" in two bodies: (a) "the Legislature of the State of Utah," and (b) "the people of the State of Utah as provided in Subsection (2)." *Id.* art. VI, § 1(1). On its face, article VI recognizes a single, undifferentiated "legislative power," vested both in the people and in the legislature. Nothing in the text or structure of article VI suggests any difference in the power vested simultaneously in the "Legislature" and "the people." The initiative power of the people is thus parallel and coextensive with the power of the legislature. This interpretation is reinforced by the history of the direct-democracy movement, by constitutional debates in states with constitutional provisions substantially similar to Utah's article VI, and by early judicial interpretations of those provisions.

Utah amended its constitution to provide for ballot initiatives in 1900, the second of twenty-four states to do so. At the time, a Progressive movement had gained widespread support, based on the premise that "only free, unorganized individuals could be trusted and that any intermediary body such as politicians, political parties and legislative bodies were inherently corrupt and distorted the public interest." The thrust of the initiative movement was a sentiment that the people should flex the muscles of their organic governmental power and reserve for themselves the legislative power that had previously been vested solely in the state legislatures. Only by wielding the legislative power could the people govern themselves in a democracy unfettered by the distortions of representative legislatures.

The Progressive movement's nationwide force impelled many states to consider constitutional amendments that provided for direct democracy in the form of initiatives and referenda. These debates addressed the nature of the legislative power that would be exercised directly by the people. Although the legislative history of Utah's initiative amendment is limited, the debates in other states inform the scope of the people's legislative power as it was originally understood.

For example, throughout the debates in Massachusetts and Ohio, delegates acknowledged that the people are the ultimate source of sovereign power and spoke of the initiative amendments as reservations of the same power delegated to the legislature. Indeed, the delegates took for granted that the governmental power to be reserved by the people was legislative power and focused their arguments on the wisdom of sharing that power between the people and the legislature.

The adoption of initiative and referendum amendments raised questions in many state courts regarding the power allocated between the people and the legislature. In early judicial interpretations of article VI and similar constitutional provisions in other states, courts generally understood that the people and the legislature hold parallel and coextensive power.

In one of the first Utah cases interpreting article VI, Justice Larson explained that through ballot initiative, the people are a "legislative body coequal in power" with the legislature. The Supreme Court of Washington stated that "[t]he passage of an initiative measure as a law is the exercise of the same power of sovereignty as that exercised by the Legislature in the passage of a statute." *Love v. King Cnty.*, 44 P.2d 175, 178 (1935). Likewise, soon after becoming the first state to pass an initiative amendment, the North Dakota Supreme Court recognized that "the Legislative Assembly and the people are in effect coordinate legislative bodies with coextensive legislative power." *State v. Houge*, 271 N.W. 677, 680 (1937). And the Oregon Supreme Court, explaining that the initiative power is parallel to the legislature's power, stated that "[l]aws proposed and enacted by the people under the initiative ... are subject to the same constitutional limitations as other statutes, and may be amended or repealed by the Legislature at will." *Kadderly v. City of Portland*, 74 P. 710, 720 (1903).

The people's legislative power may be exercised at either a statewide or local level. Article VI, section 1(2) distinguishes statewide and local initiatives but affirms that the initiative power at both levels is coextensive with the power vested in the legislature.

Under subsection (2)(a), "legal voters of the State" are authorized to "initiate *any desired legislation* and cause it to be submitted to the people for adoption," subject only to the "conditions," "manner," and "time provided by statute." UTAH CONST. art. VI, § 1(2)(a) (emphasis added). Subsection (2)(b) recognizes parallel power of "legal voters of any county, city, or town"—to "initiate *any desired legislation* and cause it to be submitted to the people of the county, city, or town for adoption," again subject only to the "conditions," "manner," and "time provided by statute." *Id.* § (2)(b) (emphasis added).

These two provisions recognize a relatively unlimited legislative power reserved by the people. Whether on a statewide or local basis, the people may propose any measure that is "desired"—so long as it is "legislation," and so long as the people follow the conditions and manner prescribed by statute. And though the legislature may prescribe the "manner" and "conditions" for exercising initiative power, article VI nowhere indicates that the scope of the people's initiative power is less than that of the legislature's power, or that the initiative power is derived from or delegated by the legislature. Instead, "[u]nder our constitutional assumptions, all power derives from the people, who can delegate it to representative instruments which they create." Therefore a "referendum [or initiative] cannot ... be characterized as a delegation of power." And in exercising the initiative power, the people do not act under the authority of the legislature.

Yet while article VI, subsection (2) authorizes the people to exercise their full legislative power by proposing "any desired legislation," its division between statewide and local authority necessarily implies a geographical limit on local initiative power. The voters of a municipality could not adopt, for example, a statewide traffic law. Otherwise, however, the people's legislative power is the same—and is coextensive with the power delegated to the legislature—regardless of whether that power is wielded on a statewide or local level. Therefore, when courts must determine the propriety of a voter initiative, the relevant inquiry must look to the nature and limits of legislative power. The people's initiative power reaches to the full extent of the legislative power, but no further.

The conclusion that the people hold retained, coextensive power to adopt "legislation" leaves unresolved the question of the nature and extent of the legislative power. It may not be possible to mark the precise boundaries of that power with bright lines. But we can describe the essential hallmarks of such power, and in so doing we can prescribe a working standard for judging the propriety of ballot initiatives under the Utah Constitution.

The starting point in our analysis is the constitutional separation of legislative, executive, and judicial powers. *See* UTAH CONST. art. V. Our understanding of the legislative power is informed by its placement in relation to—and separation from—the executive and judicial power. Thus, we proceed to identify the hallmarks of legislative power and to describe its boundaries in part by its separation from the executive and the judicial power.

In the paragraphs that follow, we identify two key hallmarks of legislative power as it has historically been understood. Legislative power generally (a) involves the promulgation of laws of general applicability; and (b) is based on the weighing of broad, competing policy considerations. This power is different from the executive power, which encompasses prosecutorial or administrative acts aimed at applying the law to particular individuals or groups based on individual facts and circumstances. It is also distinguished from the judicial power, which involves the application of the law to particular individuals or groups based on their particularized circumstances.

In light of the foregoing, a ballot initiative should be deemed an appropriate legislative act where it proposes a law of general applicability. Laws that prescribe rules of conduct for the general population are squarely within the ambit of generally applicable rules, and ballot initiatives proposing such laws are per se legislative.

General application to the population as a whole is a sufficient condition to sustain the legislative propriety of a ballot initiative. But it is not a necessary condition. Legislation usually applies to "more than a few people," but there are circumstances where legislation may properly extend to only one or a few individuals. Such a law could still be "legislative" where it (1) is based on general policy concerns rather than individual circumstances and (2) governs "all future cases falling under its provisions" and not just specified individuals.

In questionable cases at the margins of these standards, it may be useful to consult historical examples of traditional exercises of legislative power. Thus, if a particular initiative seems close to a blurry part of the doctrinal line between the legislative and the executive, a court's decision may be informed by history. An initiative that finds longstanding parallels in statutes enacted by legislative bodies, for example, may be deemed legislative on that basis, while initiatives that seem more like traditional executive acts may be deemed to fall on that side of the line.

Our decision today adopts a new paradigm for evaluating the propriety of ballot initiatives under our constitution. In so doing, however, we do not intend to signal an abrupt change in the scope of the initiative power or in the results that we foresee in the cases that come before us. In fact, the framework articulated above preserves the results of many of our prior cases in this field and is even consistent with some of our prior analysis.

We turn, finally, to the initiatives at issue in this case. In our view, Initiatives One and Two fall comfortably within the constitutional framework set forth above. Initiative One sets salary limits on all city officials who are ineligible for overtime pay. If passed, this initiative would apply generally to any person fitting the definition of a city employee who is ineligible for overtime. All current and future employees coming within the initiative's terms would be subject to the initiative. Rather than applying to one specific person, the salary limits apply generally to the entire class of persons specified by the proposed law. The adoption of salary limits for city offices, moreover, is based on broad policy considerations pertinent to the offices, not the specific circumstances of individual, identified employees. This is classic legislation possessing all of the hallmarks of the legislative power.

Initiative Two is likewise legislative. It imposes a residency requirement for eighteen city officials. This requirement is generally applicable because, for each listed official, all present and future individuals obtaining that office would be subject to the residency requirement. Like the salary cap, the residency requirement applies generally to an entire class of persons, not a specific person. And again a decision whether to impose a residency requirement is based on broad policy considerations pertinent to the office, not the specific circumstances of individual officers. This, too, is classic legislative action within the people's initiative power.

If there were any doubt about the legislative nature of these initiatives, it could easily be resolved by reference to historical uses of similar government power. Here again, history confirms our theoretical analysis. Residency and salary restrictions are hardly novel exercises of legislative power. In fact, the legislature has long adopted residency requirements for various county and municipal government offices by legislation.

As for salaries for government offices, our state constitution tasks the legislature with setting many such salaries, including "[t]he Governor, Lieutenant Governor, State Auditor, State Treasurer, Attorney General, and any other state officer as the Legislature may provide." Utah Const. art. VII, § 18. Following this constitutional mandate, the legislature has— since the founding of our state—enacted legislation setting the extent and limits of public-employee compensation.

This historical pattern confirms that public-employee compensation and residency requirements are subject matters appropriate for legislative control. Initiatives One and Two are properly legislative and should have been accepted by the Lehi City recorder for placement on the municipal ballot.

ARIZONA STATE LEGISLATURE v. ARIZONA INDEPENDENT REDISTRICTING COMMISSION, ET AL.
135 S.Ct. 2652 (2015)

GINSBURG, J.

This case concerns an endeavor by Arizona voters to address the problem of partisan gerrymandering—the drawing of legislative district lines to subordinate adherents of one political party and entrench a rival party in power.

In 2000, Arizona voters adopted an initiative, Proposition 106, aimed at "ending the practice of gerrymandering and improving voter and candidate participation in elections." Proposition 106 amended Arizona's Constitution to remove redistricting authority from the Arizona

Legislature and vest that authority in an independent commission, the Arizona Independent Redistricting Commission (AIRC or Commission). After the 2010 census, as after the 2000 census, the AIRC adopted redistricting maps for congressional as well as state legislative districts.

The Arizona Legislature challenged the map the Commission adopted in January 2012 for congressional districts. Recognizing that the voters could control redistricting for state legislators, the Arizona Legislature sued the AIRC in federal court seeking a declaration that the Commission and its map for congressional districts violated the "Elections Clause" of the U.S. Constitution. That Clause, critical to the resolution of this case, provides:

"The Times, Places and Manner of holding Elections for Senators and Representatives, shall be prescribed in each State by the Legislature thereof; but the Congress may at any time by Law make or alter such Regulations...." Art. I, § 4, cl. 1.

The Arizona Legislature's complaint alleged that "[t]he word 'Legislature' in the Elections Clause means [specifically and only] the representative body which makes the laws of the people," so read, the Legislature urges, the Clause precludes resort to an independent commission, created by initiative, to accomplish redistricting. The AIRC responded that, for Elections Clause purposes, "the Legislature" is not confined to the elected representatives; rather, the term encompasses all legislative authority conferred by the State Constitution, including initiatives adopted by the people themselves.

We hold that lawmaking power in Arizona includes the initiative process, and that both § 2a(c) and the Elections Clause permit use of the AIRC in congressional districting in the same way the Commission is used in districting for Arizona's own Legislature.

Direct lawmaking by the people was "virtually unknown when the Constitution of 1787 was drafted." Donovan & Bowler, An Overview of Direct Democracy in the American States, in Citizens as Legislators 1 (S. Bowler, T. Donovan, & C. Tolbert eds. 1998). There were obvious precursors or analogues to the direct lawmaking operative today in several States, notably, New England's town hall meetings and the submission of early state constitutions to the people for ratification. But it was not until the turn of the 20th century, as part of the Progressive agenda of the era, that direct lawmaking by the electorate gained a foothold, largely in Western States.

The two main "agencies of direct legislation" are the initiative and the referendum. Munro, Introductory, in IRR 8. The initiative operates entirely outside the States' representative assemblies; it allows "voters [to] petition to propose statutes or constitutional amendments to be adopted or rejected by the voters at the polls." While the initiative allows the electorate to adopt positive legislation, the referendum serves as a negative check. It allows "voters [to] petition to refer a legislative action to the voters [for approval or disapproval] at the polls." "The initiative [thus] corrects sins of omission" by representative bodies, while the "referendum corrects sins of commission."

In 1898, South Dakota took the pathmarking step of affirming in its Constitution the people's power "directly [to] control the making of all ordinary laws" by initiative and referendum. In 1902, Oregon became the first State to adopt the initiative as a means, not only to enact ordinary laws, but also to amend the State's Constitution. By 1920, the people in 19 States had reserved for themselves the power to initiate ordinary lawmaking, and, in 13 States, the power to initiate amendments to the State's Constitution. Those numbers increased to 21 and 18, respectively, by the close of the 20th century.

For the delegates to Arizona's constitutional convention, direct lawmaking was a "principal issu[e]." By a margin of more than three to one, the people of Arizona ratified the State's Constitution, which included, among lawmaking means, initiative and referendum provisions. In the runup to Arizona's admission to the Union in 1912, those provisions generated no controversy.

In particular, the Arizona Constitution "establishes the electorate [of Arizona] as a coordinate source of legislation" on equal footing with the representative legislative body. The initiative, housed under the article of the Arizona Constitution concerning the "Legislative Department" and the section defining the State's "legislative authority," reserves for the people "the power to propose laws and amendments to the constitution." Art. IV, pt. 1, § 1. The Arizona Constitution further states that "[a]ny law which may be enacted by the Legislature under this Constitution may be enacted by the people under the Initiative." Art. XXII, § 14. Accordingly, "[g]eneral references to the power of the 'legislature' in the Arizona Constitution "include the people's right (specified in Article IV, part 1) to bypass their elected representatives and make laws directly through the initiative." Leshy xxii.

Proposition 106, vesting redistricting authority in the AIRC, was adopted by citizen initiative in 2000 against a "background of recurring redistricting turmoil" in Arizona. Redistricting plans adopted by the Arizona Legislature sparked controversy in every redistricting cycle since the 1970's, and several of those plans were rejected by a federal court or refused preclearance by the Department of Justice under the Voting Rights Act of 1965.

Aimed at "ending the practice of gerrymandering and improving voter and candidate participation in elections," Proposition 106 amended the Arizona Constitution to remove congressional redistricting authority from the state legislature, lodging that authority, instead, in a new entity, the AIRC. Ariz. Const., Art. IV, pt. 2, § 1.   The AIRC convenes after each census, establishes final district boundaries, and certifies the new districts to the Arizona Secretary of State. The legislature may submit nonbinding recommendations to the AIRC, and is required to make necessary appropriations for its operation. The highest ranking officer and minority leader of each chamber of the legislature each select one member of the AIRC from a list compiled by Arizona's Commission on Appellate Court Appointments. The four appointed members of the AIRC then choose, from the same list, the fifth member, who chairs the Commission. A Commission's tenure is confined to one redistricting cycle; each member's time in office "expire[s] upon the appointment of the first member of the next redistricting commission."

Holders of, or candidates for, public office may not serve on the AIRC, except candidates for or members of a school board. No more than two members of the Commission may be members of the same political party, *ibid.*, and the presiding fifth member cannot be registered with any party already represented on the Commission. Subject to the concurrence of two-thirds of the Arizona Senate, AIRC members may be removed by the Arizona Governor for gross misconduct, substantial neglect of duty, or inability to discharge the duties of office.

Several other States, as a means to curtail partisan gerrymandering, have also provided for the participation of commissions in redistricting. Some States, in common with Arizona, have given nonpartisan or bipartisan commissions binding authority over redistricting.   The California Redistricting Commission, established by popular initiative, develops redistricting plans which become effective if approved by public referendum. Still other States have given commissions an auxiliary role, advising the legislatures on redistricting, or serving as a "backup" in the event the State's representative body fails to complete redistricting. Studies report that nonpartisan and bipartisan commissions generally draw their maps in a timely fashion and create districts both more competitive and more likely to survive legal challenge.

In sum, our precedent teaches that redistricting is a legislative function, to be performed in accordance with the State's prescriptions for lawmaking, which may include the referendum and the Governor's veto. The exercise of the initiative, we acknowledge, was not at issue in our prior decisions. But as developed below, we see no constitutional barrier to a State's empowerment of its people by embracing that form of lawmaking.

Banning lawmaking by initiative to direct a State's method of apportioning congressional districts would do more than stymie attempts to curb partisan gerrymandering, by which the majority in the legislature draws district lines to their party's advantage. It would also cast doubt on numerous other election laws adopted by the initiative method of legislating.

The list of endangered state elections laws, were we to sustain the position of the Arizona Legislature, would not stop with popular initiatives. Almost all state constitutions were adopted by conventions and ratified by voters at the ballot box, without involvement or approval by "the Legislature." Core aspects of the electoral process regulated by state constitutions include voting by "ballot" or "secret ballot," voter registration, absentee voting, vote counting, and victory thresholds. Again, the States' legislatures had no hand in making these laws and may not alter or amend them.

The importance of direct democracy as a means to control election regulations extends beyond the particular statutes and constitutional provisions installed by the people rather than the States' legislatures. The very prospect of lawmaking by the people may influence the legislature when it considers (or fails to consider) election-related measures. Turning the coin, the legislature's responsiveness to the people its members represent is hardly heightened when the representative body can be confident that what it does will not be overturned or modified by the voters themselves.

Invoking the Elections Clause, the Arizona Legislature instituted this lawsuit to disempower the State's voters from serving as the legislative power for redistricting purposes. But the Clause surely was not adopted to diminish a State's authority to determine its own lawmaking processes. Article I, § 4, stems from a different view. Both parts of the Elections Clause are in line with the fundamental premise that all political power flows from the people. *McCulloch v. Maryland*, 4 L.Ed. 579 (1819). So comprehended, the Clause doubly empowers the people. They may control the State's lawmaking processes in the first instance, as Arizona voters have done, and they may seek Congress' correction of regulations prescribed by state legislatures.

The people of Arizona turned to the initiative to curb the practice of gerrymandering and, thereby, to ensure that Members of Congress would have "an habitual recollection of their dependence on the people." The Federalist No. 57, at 350 (J. Madison). In so acting, Arizona voters sought to restore "the core principle of republican government," namely, "that the voters should choose their representatives, not the other way around."

Ronald M. George, *The Perils of Direct Democracy: The California Experience*[20]

It is an honor to speak as a representative of the new class of Academy members. I would like to share some thoughts with you on a matter that has been of recent and continued professional concern to me, but that I believe may be of general interest to members of the Academy, because it fundamentally implicates how we govern ourselves. This is the increasing use of the ballot Initiative process available in many states to effect constitutional and statutory changes in the law, especially in the structure and powers of government.

A not-too-subtle clue to my point of view is reflected in the caption I have chosen for these remarks — "The Perils of Direct Democracy: The California Experience." Although two dozen states in our nation permit government by voter Initiative, in no other state is the practice as extreme as in California.

By the terms of its Constitution, California permits a relatively small number of petition signers — equal to at least 8% of the voters in the last gubernatorial election — to place before the voters a proposal to amend any aspect of our Constitution. (The figure is only 5% for a proposed non-constitutional statutory enactment.) If approved by a simple majority of those voting at the next election, the Initiative measure goes into effect on the following day.

The legislature (by two-thirds vote of each house) shares with the voters the power to place proposed constitutional amendments before the electorate. California, however, is unique among all American jurisdictions in prohibiting its legislature, without express voter approval, from amending or repealing even a statutory measure enacted by the voters, unless the Initiative measure itself specifically confers such authority upon the legislature.

The process for amending California's Constitution thus is considerably easier than the amendment process embodied in the United States Constitution, under which an amendment may be proposed either by a vote of two-thirds of each house of Congress or by a convention called on the application of the legislatures of two-thirds of the states. It can be ratified only by the legislatures of (or by conventions held in) three-quarters of the states.

The relative ease with which the California Constitution can be amended is dramatically illustrated by the frequency with which this has

---

[20] Remarks by California's Chief Justice, Ronald M. George, to the American Academy of Arts & Sciences, October 10, 2009 in Cambridge, Massachusetts. Reprinted with permission.

occurred. Only 17 amendments to the United States Constitution (in addition to the Bill of Rights, ratified in 1791) have been adopted since that document was ratified in 1788. In contrast, more than 500 amendments to the California Constitution have been adopted since ratification of California's current Constitution in 1879.

Former United States Supreme Court Justice Hugo Black was known to pride himself on carrying in his pocket a slender pamphlet containing the federal Constitution in its entirety. I certainly could not emulate that practice with California's constitutional counterpart.

One Bar leader has observed: "California's current constitution rivals India's for being the longest and most convoluted in the world.... [W]ith the cumulative dross of past voter initiatives incorporated, [it] is a document that assures chaos."

Initiatives have enshrined a myriad of provisions into California's constitutional charter, including a prohibition on the use of gill nets and a measure regulating the confinement of barnyard fowl in coops. This last constitutional amendment was enacted on the same 2008 ballot that amended the state Constitution to override the California Supreme Court's decision recognizing the right of same-sex couples to marry. Chickens gained valuable rights in California on the same day that gay men and lesbians lost them.

Perhaps most consequential in their impact on the ability of California state and local government to function are constitutional and statutory mandates and prohibitions — often at cross-purposes — limiting how elected officials may raise and spend revenue. California's lawmakers, and the state itself, have been placed in a fiscal straitjacket by a steep two-thirds-vote requirement — imposed at the ballot box — for raising taxes. A similar supermajoritarian requirement governs passage of the state budget. This situation is compounded by voter Initiative measures that have imposed severe restrictions upon increases in the assessed value of real property that is subject to property tax, coupled with constitutional requirements of specified levels of financial support for public transportation and public schools.

These constraints upon elected officials — when combined with a lack of political will (on the part of some) to curb spending and (on the part of others) to raise taxes — often make a third alternative, borrowing, the most attractive option (at least until the bankers say "no").

Much of this constitutional and statutory structure has been brought about not by legislative fact-gathering and deliberation, but rather by the approval of voter Initiative measures, often funded by special interests. These interests are allowed under the law to pay a bounty to signature-gatherers for each signer. Frequent amendments — coupled with the implicit threat of more in the future — have rendered our state government dysfunctional, at least in times of severe economic decline.

Because of voter Initiatives restricting the taxing powers that the legislature may exercise, California's tax structure is particularly dependent upon fluctuating types of revenue, giving rise to a "boom or bust" economic cycle. The consequences this year have been devastating to programs that, for example, provide food to poor children and health care for the elderly disabled. This year's fiscal crisis also has caused the Judicial Council, which I chair, to take the reluctant and unprecedented step of closing all courts in our state one day a month. That decision will enable us to offset approximately one-fourth of the more than $400 million reduction imposed by the other two branches of government on the $4 billion budget of our court system.

The voter Initiative process places additional burdens upon the judicial branch. The court over which I preside frequently is called upon to resolve legal challenges to voter Initiatives. Needless to say, we incur the displeasure of the voting public when, in the course of performing our constitutional duties as judges, we are compelled to invalidate such a measure.

On occasion, we are confronted with a pre-election lawsuit that causes us to remove an Initiative proposal from the ballot because, by combining insufficiently related issues, it violates our state Constitution's single-subject limitation on such measures. At other times, a voter Initiative — perhaps poorly drafted and ambiguous, or faced with a competing or "dueling" measure that passed at the same election — requires years of successive litigation in the courts to ferret out its intended meaning, and ultimately may have to be invalidated in whole or in part.

One thing is fairly certain, however. If a proposal, whatever its nature, is sufficiently funded by its backers, it most likely will obtain the requisite number of signatures to qualify for the ballot, and — if it does qualify — there is a good chance the measure will pass. The converse certainly is true — poorly funded efforts, without sufficient backing to mount an expensive television campaign — are highly unlikely to succeed, whatever their merit.

This dysfunctional situation has led some to call for the convening of a convention to write a new Constitution for California to replace our current 1879 charter, which in turn supplanted the original 1849 document. Yet, although a recent poll reflects that 79% of Californians say the state is moving in the wrong direction, only 33% believe that the state's Constitution requires "major" changes and approximately 60% are of the view that decisions made by Californians through the Initiative process are better than those made by the legislature and the governor.

Add to this mix a split among scholars concerning whether a constitutional convention, if called, could be limited in the subject matter it is empowered to consider. Some argue that a convention would be open to every type of proposal from any source, including social activists and special interest groups. There also is controversy over the most appropriate procedure for selecting delegates for such a convention.

A student of government might reasonably ask: Does the voter Initiative, a product of the Populist Movement that reached its high point in the early 20th century in the mid-west and western states, remain a positive contribution in the form in which it now exists in 21st century California? Or, despite its original objective — to curtail special interests, such as the railroads, that controlled the legislature of California and of some other states — has the voter Initiative now become the tool of the very types of special interests it was intended to control, and an impediment to the effective functioning of a true democratic process?

John Adams — who I believe never would have supported a voter Initiative process like California's — cautioned that "democracy never lasts long.... There is never a democracy that did not commit suicide." The nation's Founding Fathers, wary of the potential excesses of direct democracy, established a republic with a carefully crafted system of representative democracy. This system was characterized by checks and balances that conferred authority upon the officeholders of our three branches of government in a manner designed to enable them to curtail excesses engaged in by their sister branches.

Perhaps with the dangers of direct democracy in mind, Benjamin Franklin gave his much-quoted response to a question posed by a resident of Philadelphia after the adjournment of the Constitutional Convention in 1787. Asked the type of government that had been established by the delegates, Franklin responded: "It would be a republic, if you can keep it." And, as Justice David Souter recently observed in quoting this exchange, Franklin "understood that a republic can be lost."

At a minimum, in order to avoid such a loss, Californians may need to consider some fundamental reform of the voter Initiative process. Otherwise, I am concerned, we shall continue on a course of dysfunctional state government, characterized by a lack of accountability on the part of our officeholders as well as the voting public.

NOTES

1. The State Constitutional initiative was first adopted in Oregon in 1902. Eighteen states now provide for citizens to petition for changes in their state constitutions.

2. The initiative process is referred to as direct democracy, in contrast to representative democracy. When the initiative procedure was challenged

as violating the United States Constitution's guarantee that each state must have a republic form of government, it was held to be a political question for Congress rather than the Supreme Court to decide. *Pacific States Telephone & Telegraph v. Oregon*, 223 U.S. 118 (1912).

3. In *Romer v. Evans*, 517 U.S. 620 (1996), the United States Supreme Court held that an initiated amendment to the Colorado Constitution violated the Equal Protection Clause.

D. CONSTITUTIONAL CONVENTION – REQUIRED FOR COMPLETE REVISION

OPINION OF THE JUSTICES
264 A.2d 342 (Del. 1970)

A question was propounded by the Governor to the Justices of the Supreme Court relating to whether Constitution permitted adoption of amendment or amendments which would revise entire Constitution. The Justices of the Supreme Court were of the opinion that change in Constitution which is mere reorganization, restatement, modernization, abbreviation, consolidation, simplification, or clarification of existing document and which makes no substantial or fundamental change in basic structure of state government can be accomplished by legislative amendment, but changes that do not fall within those lines must be treated as revisions of Constitution which may be accomplished only by constitutional convention, and each situation, as to whether an amendment or revision is involved, must be resolved upon its own facts and circumstances.

Question answered.

[General assembly, while permitted to submit question to electorate as to whether unlimited constitutional convention should be called, may also limit question submitted to electorate so as to ascertain its wishes regarding call of a convention for purpose of revising specified parts of Constitution only. Del.C.Ann.Const. art. 16, § 2.]

To His Excellency Russell W. Peterson Governor of Delaware

Reference is made to your letter dated January 22, 1970, requesting the opinions of the Justices upon the following question:

'Does Article 16, Section 1, of the Delaware Constitution permit the adoption of an amendment or amendments which would revise the entire Constitution?'

As the basis for the question, your letter explains:

Legislation will soon be introduced in the General Assembly which will contain the proposals of the Constitutional Revision Commission set up by former Governor Charles L. Terry, Jr. This proposed revision concerns the entire State Constitution.

It is further stated that the opinions are requested, under 10 Del.C. § 141, in the interest of public information and to enable you to discharge the duties of your office. We assume that the latter reference relates to the fact that the Report of the Constitutional Revision Commission, established by 56 Del.L.Ch. 189, has been presented to you for your consideration and appropriate action, thus bringing your request within the provisions of 10 Del.C. § 141.

The reply to the question requires consideration of the scope and meaning of Article 16, Sections 1 and 2 of the Delaware Constitution:

> Section 1 of Article 16 provides for change of the Constitution by the agreement of two-thirds of all the members elected to each House of two successive General Assemblies, as follows:

> Section 1. Any amendment or amendments to this Constitution may be proposed in the Senate or House of Representatives; and if the same shall be agreed to by two-thirds of all the members elected to each House, such proposed amendment or amendments shall be entered on their journals, with the years and nays taken thereon, and the Secretary of State shall cause such proposed amendment or amendments to be published three months before the next general election in at last three newspapers in each county in which such newspapers shall be published; and if in the General Assembly next after the said election such proposed amendment or amendments shall upon yea and nay vote be agreed to by two-thirds of all the members elected to each House, the same shall thereupon become part of the Constitution.

> Section 2 of Article 16 provides for change of the Constitution by Convention as follows:

> Section 2. The General Assembly by a two-thirds vote of all the members elected to each House may from time to time provide for the submission to the qualified electors of the State at the general election next thereafter the question, 'Shall there be a Convention to revise the Constitution and amend the same?'; and upon such submission, if a majority of those voting on said question shall decide in favor of a Convention for such purpose, the General Assembly at its next session shall provide for the election of delegates to such convention at the next general election. Such Convention shall be composed of forty-one delegates, one of whom shall be chosen from each Representative District by the qualified electors thereof, and two of whom shall be chosen from New Castle County, two from Kent County and two from Sussex County by the qualified electors thereof respectively.

> Section 2 then specifies procedures for the conduct of the business of a Convention.

In our judgment, the problem presented by your question is two-fold: (1) does our Constitution, by Article 16, Sections 1 and 2, distinguish between constitutional 'amendments,' on the one hand, and a constitutional 'revision,' on the other, and (2) if so, what is a 'revision' within the meaning of Section 2?

We are of the opinion that a distinction is made by Art. 16 between 'amendments' to the Constitution under Section 1 and a 'revision' thereof under Section 2.

There is ambiguity in the two terms as used in our Constitution. In a sense, every amendment to the Constitution is a revision in that it is a change therein; but a revision, in the larger sense of the word, may be such a basic alteration of the original document as to surmount entirely the ordinary meaning of the word 'amendment.' The two terms are sometimes used interchangeably in constitutional provisions; in other cases, it is said that they are unrelated and should not be confused one with the other. The ambiguity is pointed up by the use of the two words jointly in the question prescribed for the electorate by Section 2: 'Shall there be a Convention to Revise the Constitution and Amend the same?'

In view of the ambiguity, we look to the Delaware Constitutional Debates of 1897 for insight into the intent of the drafters when they formulated Article 16 of the present Constitution and used the terms we are here called upon to construe.

It is clear from the Debates, we think, that the drafters distinguished between 'amendments', on the one hand, and a 'revision' on the other. This conclusion is impelled by the following considerations:

1) Section 1 is, and throughout its evolution was, confined to amendment, whereas Section 2 refers, and throughout its evolution referred, to revision.

2) Throughout the Debates, the drafters referred to amendments under Section 1 as 'changes' or 'alterations' in the present Constitution, whereas they looked upon a 'revision' under Section 2 as the 'making' or the 'manufacture' of a 'new' Constitution; as the 'framing an organic law for the State.'

3) The drafters discussed at great length the standards to be established for the qualification of delegates to a Constitutional Convention charged with the responsibility of 'revising' the Constitution under Section 2, as compared with the constitutency of a General Assembly vested with the power to make constitutional changes legislatively under Section 1. It was generally agreed by the drafters that a Constitutional Convention should be non-partisan, with the major political parties having approximately equal representation; that it should not be limited entirely to representatives of local areas by Representative or Senatorial Districts but should have delegates at large from each of the Counties to assure getting the best qualified people without regard for residence within the County or party lines. And recurrent throughout the Debates was the thought that a Constitutional Convention, specially elected for its expressed purpose, is more the direct agent of the people for that purpose than is a General Assembly. This concept was and is in accord with authorities on the subject. *E.g., Livermore v. Waite*, 102 Cal. 113, 36 P. 424, 25 L.R.A. 312 (1894); *Jackman v. Bodine*, 43 N.J. 453, 205 A.2d 713, 725-726 (1964). It is also consistent with the arrangement whereunder the work- product of a Convention is not required by Section 2 to be submitted to the people for approval; whereas under Section 1 a proposal by a General Assembly for constitutional change is indirectly

submitted to the people via the general election which must intervene before a successive General Assembly can effectuate the change.

For these reasons, we are of the opinion that the Constitution differentiates between the procedure for adopting a series of legislative 'amendments' under Section 1 of Article 16, and a 'revision' which can be accomplished only by Constitutional Convention under Section 2 thereof.

We come then to the second question: What is a 'revision' which must be accomplished by Convention under Section 2, and how does it differ from a series of 'amendments' which can be accomplished legislatively under Section 1?

A threshold truism is that the mere Number of changes cannot make the difference. Legislative amendments are not limited in number by Section 1; and a 'revision', to which Section 2 is applicable, does not come into being by reason of the mere number of changes or the mere fact that the changes concern the entire Constitution. It would be unreasonable to conclude that a large number of amendatory changes accomplishable piecemeal under Section 1, could not be accomplished simultaneously under that Section. Rather, it is the nature and scope of the changes contemplated that determine whether there is a 'revision' subject to Section 2 or a series of 'amendments' subject to Section 1.

As has been noted heretofore, in discussing the scope and nature of the 'revision' contemplated under Section 2, the drafters had in mind the 'making' of a 'new' Constitution. This concept of a constitutional 'revision', as contrasted with a series of constitutional 'amendments', is in accord with the views and conclusions of the Supreme Court of California in *Livermore v. Waite*, 102 Cal. 113, 36 P. 424 (1894) and *McFadden v. Jordan*, 32 Cal.2d 330, 196 P.2d 787 (1948). We find the definitions in those cases persuasive. A constitutional 'amendment' was defined therein as 'such an addition or change within the lines of the original instrument as will effect an improvement or better carry out the purpose for which it was framed.' A 'revision' on the other hand, was held in McFadden to be the result of proposed changes in the basic governmental plan because the effect thereof 'would be to substantially alter the purpose and to attain objectives clearly beyond the lines of the Constitution as now cast.' In short, to be a 'revision' the result must be to effect a change in the basic philosophy which has cast our government in its present form.

We think those distinctions are supported by reason and authority. A constitutional 'revision' makes substantial, basic, fundamental changes in the plan of government; it makes extensive alterations in the basic plan and substance of the existing document; it attains objectives and purposes beyond the lines of the present Constitution. A 'revision' is more than a mere reorganization, restatement, modernization, abbreviation, consolidation, simplification, or clarification of the existing document.

The latter type of change, making no substantial and fundamental change or alteration in the basic structure of State government, can be accomplished, we think, by legislative amendment under Section 1, as would any other changes that fall 'within the lines of the original instrument' to constitute 'an improvement or better carry out the purpose for which it was framed.' Any change or changes that fall within such lines should be considered, in our opinion, 'amendments' within Section 1; changes that do not fall within those lines must, in our opinion, be treated as 'revisions' within the scope and application of Section 2.

But it is not enough to distinguish a revision from a series of amendments and to ascertain the tests therefor. Each situation must be resolved upon its own facts and circumstances.

The nature and scope of the changes acceptable to the General Assembly are presently unknown. The ultimate action to be taken by the General Assembly on the proposals of the Constitutional Revision Commission remains to be seen. It is to those ultimate changes that the tests of 'amendment' versus 'revision' must be applied. At that stage, and with its final draft of contemplated changes before it, the General Assembly must determine (1) whether it may proceed legislatively under Section 1 because the proposed changes are amendatory; or (2) whether it must proceed by way of Constitutional Convention under Section 2 because the proposed changes are revisory.

When the General Assembly is confronted with that decision, it may be found that some of the changes contemplated are amendatory while others are revisory. In that event, it is our opinion that the Section 1 route may be followed as to the amendatory changes, and the Section 2 route may be simultaneously followed as to the revisory changes. For, in this connection, we are of the opinion that Section 2 permits a partial revision of the Constitution by Convention.

In our view, neither Section 2 nor any other provision of our Constitution prohibits the General Assembly from limiting the question submitted to the electorate so as to ascertain its wishes regarding the call of a Convention for the purpose of revising specified parts of the Constitution only. If the electorate chooses to approve the calling of such limited Constitutional Convention, we are of the opinion that it may do so under Section 2. In such event, the people and not the General Assembly will have limited the work and scope of the Convention; and the authority of such Convention may not exceed the wishes of the people thus expressed. If, on the other hand, the electorate wishes to have the Section 2 question propounded to it by the General Assembly for an unlimited

Constitutional Convention, it may make its wishes known to the legislative candidates at any general election.

It would be unreasonable, in our view, to construe Section 2 otherwise. It could not have been the intent of the drafters to deprive the people of the right and method of making a partial revision of the Constitution. Since a 'revision' can be made only by Convention, and since it is unreasonable to assume that a partial revision is impermissible, it necessarily follows that a partial revision by a limited Convention can be decreed by the electorate, if it wishes, in response to an appropriate question propounded by the General Assembly under Section 2. We find support for this view in *Staples v. Gilmer*, 183 Va. 613, 33 S.E.2d 49 (1945). The Supreme Court of Appeals of Virginia there held that a limited Convention could be called under a constitutional provision almost precisely the same as our Section 2. See also Annotation, 158 A.L.R. 512.

We conclude, therefore, that a decision as to the method of constitutional change must await a final ascertainment of the actual changes to be made and an item-by-item determination of whether they are amendatory or revisory in nature.

The foregoing is the unanimous opinion of the undersigned.

NOTE

In 1776, Delaware held the first convention that was ever called for the sole purpose of writing a state constitution.

E. CONSTITUTIONAL COMMISSIONS

Peter J. Galie and Christopher Bopst, *The Constitutional Commission in New York: A Worthy Tradition*
64 Alb. L. Rev. 1285 (2001)[21]

In 1997, when New Yorkers decisively defeated a constitutionally mandated ballot proposition to convene what would have been the state's fourth constitutional convention in the twentieth century, they placed the fate of constitutional reform with the state legislature. Not until the year 2017 will the question be required to appear on the ballot, and the likelihood of the legislature proposing a convention vote in the interim is remote. New York does not permit amendments to be submitted to the electorate through constitutional initiative, and no constitutional commission has the power to submit amendments directly to the voters; constitutional reform can only emanate from either a constitutional convention or the state legislature. Since 1938, legislatively proposed

---

[21] Reprinted with permission.

amendments have been the only procedure successfully used for revising the state's charter.

Paradoxically, the latest rejection came at a time when many of the state's political actors agreed that systematic constitutional revision was needed. The League of Women Voters, Civil Service Employees Association (C.S.E.A.), American Federation of Labor—Congress of Industrial Organizations (A.F.L.-C.I.O.), National Organization of Women (NOW), and various environmental groups who opposed the calling of a convention in 1997, were, nevertheless, in agreement with proponents of the convention on the need for constitutional reform. Thus, debate has focused on the means for achieving reform. Constitutional conventions, viewed as cumbersome, expensive, and subject to approval by a suspicious, even dangerous, electorate have fallen from favor with citizen groups and politicians. The alternative, the legislature, may not be the ideal agency for providing systematic, regular revision and, in any case, has not been a successful forum for addressing such serious problems as fiscal integrity and state/local relations. Have we reached an impasse? This article examines the use of the constitutional commission, particularly in New York, as a means of achieving constitutional reform.

A study of the constitutional history of New York reveals that the constitutional commission has a long and vital history as a means of proposing meaningful and necessary reform within the state. Some of the most significant constitutional revision in New York has been the product of such commissions, and the most successful commissions were held in the aftermath of constitutional convention defeats.

This article examines the history and tradition of commissions as mechanisms to effectuate constitutional reform in New York, from its origins in the 1870s, when the state was struggling with issues such as corruption, home rule for burgeoning cities, and African-American suffrage, to the present-day, when the state budget process, debt limitations, and social welfare are issues of concern. Each commission will be analyzed, and placed in the historical context from which it emerged. Although a detailed analysis of the results of each commission is outside the scope of this article, an emphasis will be placed on the accomplishments and failures of each commission, as well as each commission's unique contributions to New York's constitutional history. After analyzing the constitutional commission experience of New York State, this article examines the use of constitutional commissions to provide meaningful constitutional reform in several other states, such as Florida, Utah, and Georgia.

1. The New York State Constitutional Commission Experience

Throughout its history, New York has convened ten constitutional commissions. Of these bodies, five were created specifically to prepare for upcoming constitutional conventions, while six were formed to study and propose changes to the existing constitution. As indicated by the appended table, the majority of constitutional commissions were statutorily created, although some were formed by a resolution of one or both houses of the legislature, and others were the product of executive order. The composition of these commissions, both in the number of members and the method of appointment varies. The largest commission was the forty-two member Constitutional Convention Committee of 1937-1938, while the smallest commission was the five member 1914-1915 Constitutional Convention Commission. In marked contrast to constitutional conventions, which typically are composed of over one hundred delegates, six of New York's commissions have had twenty or less members. The maximum amount of funding for an individual commission was $800,000 for the Temporary State Commission on the Constitutional Convention, which was in operation from 1965 through 1967. Although this may appear expensive compared to the earlier commissions, the subsequent convention for which this commission prepared cost taxpayers over six million dollars.

2. The Constitutional Commission Experience in Other States

Resort to the use of constitutional commissions has increased throughout the country since mid-century, and approximately two-thirds of the states have resorted to this procedure in the last thirty years. The composition and function of these commissions varies greatly from state to state. Among the several states achieving considerable success in reforming their state constitutions through constitutional commissions, Florida, Utah, and Georgia provide three different, yet effective, models for constitutional reform using a constitutional commission.

a. Florida

Although Florida has utilized constitutional commissions to effectuate constitutional revision since the 1950s, the Florida Constitution of 1968 represented a unique and historical development in the history of constitutional commissions. In contrast to prior Florida constitutions that had allowed constitutional revision only by legislative amendment or constitutional convention, the new constitution provided an independent constitution revision commission.

The Constitution Revision Commission was mandated to convene in 1978, and every twentieth year thereafter. The thirty-seven member body consists of the attorney general, fifteen members appointed by the governor, nine members each selected by the leaders of both houses of the legislature, and three members chosen by the chief justice of the state supreme court. The chairman of the commission is selected by the governor. When the commission was created, its jurisdiction was plenary, although tax and budget matters were subsequently removed from the province of the body. Proposals from the commission must be filed with the secretary of state at least 180 days before the election, and they do not require legislative approval for ballot placement.

In 1988, Florida voters approved a constitutional amendment that "created a major opportunity to revamp Florida's outdated tax structure." The amendment created a Taxation and Budget Reform Commission with the authority to place proposals on the 1992 ballot without obtaining legislative approval. Unlike its counterpart, the Constitution Revision Commission, the Taxation and Budget Reform Commission is appointed by leaders in only two branches of the government. Taxation and budget processes are the only matters over which the commission has authority, and commission approval of amendments requires a two-thirds vote of the entire body and a majority of each appointed group of members. Sitting legislators are prohibited as voting members of the commission. The body is mandated to meet every ten years, beginning in 1990.

The Florida commissions, the first in history to be afforded the power to submit their proposals directly to the voters, have achieved substantial reform in various areas. The first Constitution Revision Commission submitted many proposals to voters in 1978, recommending a total of eighty-seven constitutional changes to various articles of the constitution. Floridians, unwilling to extensively revise a constitution that had been operating less than ten years, rejected all of the proposals, and even one by a margin of three to one.

Following the rejection of the initial commission's work, the Taxation and Budget Reform Commission in 1992 submitted four proposals to the voters. Of these proposals, one was invalidated by the Florida Supreme Court as violating statutory requirements on clarity of ballot language, and two were ultimately approved by voters. These amendments represented the first time proposals that had been submitted directly by a constitutional commission were approved by voters. In 1998, after several months of meetings and public hearings, the Florida Constitution Revision Commission submitted thirteen proposals to voters, many of which addressed multiple subjects. Of these proposals, twelve were subsequently approved by the voters, validating the effectiveness of the commission as a permanent, constitutionally prescribed device for achieving meaningful constitutional reform.

b. Utah

Like Florida, Utah has established a permanent commission to propose constitutional changes. Unlike the Florida commission, the Utah commission may not make proposals directly to the voters. Instead of meeting at fixed intervals, such as every ten or twenty years, the commission operates continuously, allowing it to address issues in need of reform without additional legislative activity or within the limits of a fixed time period.

Although the composition of the commission contains heavy legislative representation, safeguards have been placed in the enacting legislation to avoid, or at least minimize, partisan conflict. The commission is composed of sixteen members: three are appointed from each house of the legislature by the respective leader of the house, but no more than two of the members appointed from each house may be members of the same political party; three members of the commission are appointed by the governor, and no more than two of them may be from the same political party; the director of the Office of Legislative Research and General Counsel serves as an ex officio member of the commission; and the remaining six commissioners are chosen by the ten existing members. The term of a commission member is six years, and no commissioner may serve for longer than twelve years. The commission selects its own officers.

In addition to conducting a comprehensive examination of the state constitution and making recommendations to the governor and legislature as to specific proposed constitutional amendments to implement the commission's recommendations for constitutional change, the commission is authorized to advise the governor and legislature on any proposed constitutional amendment or revision. The commission is directed to consider recommendations from the governor, members of the state legislature, state agencies, and "responsible members of the public." The commission must publish and distribute an annual report of its studies and recommendations.

The Utah commission, a permanent body combining legislative influence with the expertise of independent members in a non-partisan manner, has achieved considerable success. The commission has made recommendations on, and the voters have approved, amendments concerning several articles, including the legislature, the executive, corporations, election and rights of suffrage, revenue and taxation, education, and the judiciary. The ability of this commission to achieve success in reforming articles that have traditionally been difficult to amend was a testament to the success of the Utah approach.

c. Georgia

Although Georgia has not utilized a permanent constitutional commission to provide systemic reform of its state charter, it has used a constitutional commission to propose a new constitution. The Georgia Constitution of 1877 was ratified as an attempt to deal with the problems of Reconstruction, and resembled a legislative code in its length and prolixity. By 1900, it became apparent that the constitution needed major revision, and by 1943 it had been amended 301 times. Although all seven of Georgia's previous constitutions had been the product of constitutional conventions, fear of an attempt to reapportion representation had prevented the legislature from obtaining the two-thirds vote of the total membership of both houses of the legislature necessary to call a constitutional convention.

In March of 1943, as an alternative to a constitutional convention, which was not politically feasible at the time, the General Assembly enacted a resolution sponsored by Governor Ellis Arnall for the creation of a twenty-three member constitutional commission. Not only did the creation of this commission circumvent the previous problems with elected conventions, as its proposals would be submitted directly to the General Assembly, but this commission was a product of the belief that constitutional revision could be achieved "'more satisfactorily by a small commission...than through a constitutional convention.'" The membership of the commission included:

> the Governor, the President of the Senate, the Speaker of the House of Representatives, three members of the Senate appointed by the President, five members of the House appointed by the Speaker, a justice of the Supreme Court [chosen by the members of that court], a judge of the Court of Appeals [chosen by the members of that court], the Attorney General, the State Auditor, two judges of the Superior Courts, three practicing attorneys-at-law, and three laymen appointed by the Governor. The resolution creating this commission provided that the commission could submit to the general assembly "proposed amendments to the Constitution or...a proposed new constitution.

This commission convened on January 6, 1944, and adjourned on December 9, 1944. However, many of the subcommittees appointed by Governor Arnall, who served as chairman of the commission, met and held public hearings prior to the first full commission meeting. The commission submitted a proposed new constitution in January 1945 to the general assembly. The legislature undertook an extensive study of the document and made several revisions, submitting the new constitution to voters at a special election held on August 7, 1945. At that election, "the new Constitution was approved by a vote of 60,065 to 34,417."

The Georgia Constitution of 1945 represents the first time in American history that a constitution was written by a commission and ratified by popular vote. This action was taken following several unsuccessful attempts to pass a resolution that would have convened a constitutional convention, and represents a method for obtaining a complete revision of the constitution while avoiding the negatives of the convention process.

3. Conclusion

The past quarter century has witnessed the decline of the constitutional convention as a mechanism for achieving constitutional change. Although twenty-six state constitutional conventions were held between 1960 and 1995, thirteen of these were held during the 1960s. Only one state constitutional convention was held between 1988 and 1993. A combination of factors has conspired to make it likely that this trend will continue. Conventions are controversial for a number of reasons: they are viewed as "Pandora's box[es]," creating the possibility of dangerous additions to the constitution; they threaten to upset established relationships between the governing institutions and organized interests; and they are viewed as cumbersome, unwieldy and expensive mechanisms. As an example, the rejected convention in New York in 1997 was projected to cost at least fifty million dollars.

The reluctance to resort to conventions, combined with the inability or unwillingness of state legislatures to propose systematic revision, has left states with few options for meaningful constitutional change. The constitutional commission has the potential to break this constitutional logjam. The commission allows an educated, highly specialized group of persons to analyze the problems of the state in a deliberate and relatively nonpartisan manner. When contrasted with constitutional conventions, which in New York have over 150 delegates, it is not surprising that commissions are often viewed as progressive and deliberate in their work. Moreover, the relatively low cost of a commission compared to a constitutional convention makes using a commission a bargain for constitutional reform.

Constitutional reform commissions have played a significant role in New York's constitutional development, providing expertise and impetus for constitutional conventions, the legislature, and the people in the exercise of their respective powers to revise and amend the constitution. Florida, Utah, and Georgia provide models of constitutional commissions that differ from the traditional commission employed in New York. These varied state experiences, and the history of the commission in New York, suggest that a constitutional commission to undertake a comprehensive evaluation of the constitution and provide recommendations to the legislature for its revision, offer the state its best hope for accomplishing needed constitutional reform.

CHAPTER XVI[1]

THE FRAMING OF STATE CONSTITUTIONS AND THEIR HISTORY

PREFACE

State frameworks of government are the foundation of American constitutional law. The purpose and function of a state constitution has evolved. A knowledge of the origins and history of state constitutions is essential to understanding federalism in the United States.[2] One eminent historian, James Bryce, has said:

> The State Constitutions are the oldest things in the political history of America, for they are continuations and representatives of the royal colonial charters, whereby the earliest English settlements in America were created. ...
>
> They are full of interest; and he [or she] who would understand the changes that have passed over American Democracy will find far more instruction in the study of the state government than of the Federal Constitution. ...
>
> Their interest is all the greater, because the succession of Constitutions and amendments to Constitutions from 1776 till today enables the annals of legislation and political sentiment to be read in these documents more easily and succinctly than in any similar series of laws in any other country. They are a mine of instruction for the natural history of democratic communities.[3]

A. STATE CONSTITUTIONS' NASCENCY

Colonial Interregnum Concerns

The armed conflict between the American colonies and England began on April 19, 1775 at the Battle of Lexington and Concord in Massachusetts. The Second Continental Congress[4] was scheduled to meet

---

[1] This chapter is taken from the thesis written by Randy J. Holland for a Master of Law in the Judicial Process at the University of Virginia School of Law.

[2] *See generally* A.E. Dick Howard, *The Road From Runnymede: Magna Carta and Constitutionalism in America* 203-15 (1968); Gordon S. Wood, The Creation of the American Republic 1776-1787 (1969); Brevard Crihfield & Frank Smothers, *The States in the Federal System*, 34 N.Y.U. L. REV. 1018 (1959); Frank P. Grad, *The State Constitution: Its Function and Form for Our Time*, 54 VA. L. REV. 928 (1968); Thomas C. Grey, *Origins of the Unwritten Constitution: Fundamental Law in American Revolutionary Thought*, 30 STAN. L. REV. 843 (1978); William F. Swindler, *"Rights of Englishmen" Since 1776: Some Anglo-American Notes*, 124 U. PA. L. REV. 1083 (1976); Herbert Wechsler, *The Political Safeguards of Federalism: The Role of the States in the Composition and Selection of the National Government*, 54 COLUM. L. REV. 543 (1954).

[3] James Bryce, 1 The American Commonwealth, 434 (2d rev., ed. New York: Macmillan 1981).

[4] The First Continental Congress adjourned in October 1774.

on May 10, 1775. John Adams, a Massachusetts delegate urged the Continental Congress to do six things: first, recommend that each colony arrest and detain all officers of the King until Boston was free from British martial law; second, recommend that each colony immediately form "Governments for themselves, under their own Authority;" third, declare that the colonies were free and or independent sovereign states; fourth, communicate to the King that the colonies were desirous of resolving all differences; fifth, threaten to ally with France, Spain, and other European powers; sixth, appoint a general to command the army outside of Boston and recognize it as the "Continental Army."[5] Adams' six-part action plan for all of the American colonies made no immediate progress in the Continental Congress.

On June 2, 1775, the provincial Congress of Massachusetts requested that the Continental Congress advise it about exercising the "powers of civil government."[6] The inquiry suggested that Massachusetts contemplated two choices: "it could either accept a constitution drafted by the Continental Congress for all the colonies, or it could draw up its own constitution."[7] Although John Adams spoke in favor of forming new governments for each colony and creating a "Confederacy of States," such ideas were "strange and terrible Doctrines" to a majority of the delegates.[8]

The Continental Congress considered the request from Massachusetts for one week. Its two-part reply was carefully formulated to accommodate those delegates who still hoped for a reconciliation with Britain.[9] First, the Continental Congress declared Parliament's violation of the Massachusetts Charter of 1691 unconstitutional.[10] Second, it advised Massachusetts to hold new elections and to consider the officers of governor and lieutenant governor vacant until the King appointed successors who would adhere to the provisions of the Massachusetts Charter.[11] Those recommendations were acted upon immediately.

---

[5] Willi Paul Adams, The First American Constitutions: Republican Ideology and the Making of the State Constitutions in the Revolutionary Era 51-52 (1980).

[6] *Id.* at 53.

[7] *Id.* (citing 2 JOURNALS OF THE CONTINENTAL CONGRESS, 1774-1789, at 76-78 (Worthington C. Ford et al. eds., 1904-1937)).

[8] *Id.* at 53; 3 Diary and Autobiography of John Adams 351-52 (L.H. Butterfield et al. eds., 1961); 1 Letters of Members of the Continental Congress 106-09 (Edmund C. Burnett ed., 1921-1936).

[9] Willi Paul Adams, The First American Constitutions: Republican Ideology and the Making of the State Constitutions in the Revolutionary Era 54 (1980).

[10] *Id.*

[11] *Id.*

On October 18, 1775, New Hampshire asked the same question that Massachusetts had promulgated to the Continental Congress in May: "How could the administration of justice and other badly neglected governmental functions best be reorganized?"[12] Although the question seemed innocuous, it was intended to be rhetorical by those "who had given up hope for reconciliation with crown and Parliament."[13] As such, it was an effort to force the Continental Congress to squarely confront the issue of independence.

As long as the majority of the delegates in the Congress were not prepared to pursue independence openly, the answers that were sent to the provincial capitals had to be reconcilable with British constitutional law; an unguarded recommendation to draft new constitutions would rightly have been considered as equivalent to declaring independence.[14]

An assemblage of delegates from throughout New Hampshire was convened during the close of 1775 in violation of British law.[15] The colony of New Hampshire adopted a constitution on January 6, 1776.[16] This was the first constitution that had ever been written without approval from the reigning English monarch or Parliament.[17]

Anticipating Independence

In early 1776, a break with England was so inevitable that the American colonies all began to anticipate and debate the parameters of self-governance. A period of interregnum began following the Battle of Lexington and Concord. The remaining vestiges of royal authority were destined to be ephemeral.

On January 9, 1776, a pamphlet entitled *Common Sense* was published in Philadelphia by Thomas Paine, a recently immigrated English tradesman. According to Paine, the proper foundation for successful self-governance was political egalitarianism. Paine urged each colony to form simple republican governments operated by unicameral legislatures and chosen by an expanded electoral franchise.

---

[12] 3 Journals of the Continental Congress, 1774-1789, at 298 (Worthington C. Ford et al. eds., 1904-1937).

[13] Willi Paul Adams, The First American Constitutions: Republican Ideology and the Making of the State Constitutions in the Revolutionary Era 56 (1980).

[14] *Id.*

[15] *Id.*

[16] *Id. at 5.*

[17] *Id.*

Paine described the process of setting forth principles of popular sovereignty in written charters or constitutions as America's coronation of the rule of law. Thomas Paine made the following analogy:

> Let a day be solemnly set apart for proclaiming the charter; let it be brought forth placed on the divine law, the Word of God; let a crown be placed thereon, by which the world may know, that so far as we approve of monarchy, that in America the law is king. For as in absolute governments the king is law, so in free countries the law ought to be king; and there ought to be no other. But lest any ill use should afterwards arise, let the crown at the conclusion of the ceremony be demolished, and scattered among the people whose right it is.[18]

The unique opportunity for self-determination that history had afforded the American colonies was characterized by Thomas Paine as the beginning of a new world:

> The present time, likewise, is that peculiar time which never happens to a nation but once, viz. the time of forming itself into a government. Most nations have let slip the opportunity, and by that means have been compelled to receive laws from their conquerors, instead of making laws for themselves. First, they had a king, and then a form of government;...but from the errors of other nations let us learn wisdom, and lay hold of the present opportunity.... We have every opportunity and every encouragement before us, to form the noblest, purest constitution on the face of the earth. We have it in our power to begin the world over again.[19]

John Adams, like Paine, also described the American colonies' prospect of formulating an ideal political structure in epoch terms:

> You and I, my dear friend, have been sent into life at a time when the greatest lawgivers of antiquity would have wished to live. How few of the human race have ever enjoyed an opportunity of making an election of government...for themselves or their children! When, before the present epocha, had three millions of people full power and a fair opportunity to form and establish the wisest and happiest government that human wisdom can contrive?[20]

Adams responded to Paine's *Common Sense* with an alternative framework for new colonial governments. Adams' pamphlet, *Thoughts on Government*, advocated a system for self-governance that distributed power between a bicameral legislature and a carefully restrained executive. Although Adams contemplated that the paramount power would be vested in a popularly elected lower legislative body, Adams proposed to limit the holding of public office and the exercise of voting rights to landowners.

---

[18] Common Sense, in 1 The Complete Writings of Thomas Paine 29 (Philip S. Foner ed., 1945).

[19] *Id.* at 36-37, 45 (Philip S. Foner ed., 1945).

[20] John Adams, *Thoughts on Government, in* 4 *The Works of John Adams* 200 (Charles Francis Adams ed., 1850-1856).

Thus, in early 1776, Thomas Paine and John Adams identified the theories and framed the issues of state constitutional debates for the next ten years. How would the new governments be structured? Who would participate in the new governments, directly as office holders, and indirectly as voters?

The situation extant in most of the American colonies during the spring of 1776 is depicted in the memoirs of William Moultrie about South Carolina.

> The affairs of the province became too unwieldly for the management of [the provincial] Congress, and the council of safety or general committee: Everything was running into confusion, and although our criminal laws were still of force, yet they were virtually repealed for want of proper officers to execute them, all those under the royal authority being suspended from office, it was therefore thought absolutely necessary to frame a constitution for the purpose of forming a regular system of government, and for appointing public officers for the different departments to put the laws into execution.[21]

On March 26, 1776, a provincial congress inspired by New Hampshire's leadership, as well as by Adams' and Paine's writing, adopted a temporary constitution for the "colony" of South Carolina.

State Constitutions Authorized

As the collective estrangement between the American colonies and the British monarch mounted, the need for stabilizing each colony's internal affairs intensified. In May of 1776, all hope of reconciliation was abandoned. The Second Continental Congress advised the colonies to form new governments.[22] Its resolutions of May 10, 1776,[23] recommended to the respective assemblies and conventions of the "United Colonies":

> where no government sufficient to the exigencies of their affairs, have been hitherto established to adopt such Government as shall, in the Opinion of the Representatives of the People, best conduce to the Happiness and Safety of their Constituents in particular and America in general.[24]

---

[21] William Moultrie, 1 Memoirs of the American Revolution, So Far as It Related to the States of North and South Carolina, and Georgia 125 (1802).

[22] Gordon S. Wood, The Creation of the American Republic 1776-1787, 131-32 (1969).

[23] The resolution was adopted May 10, 1776. A preamble was added on May 15, 1776. Willi Paul Adams, The First American Constitutions: Republican Ideology and the Making of the State Constitutions in the Revolutionary Era 61 (1980). John Adams served with Edward Rutledge of South Carolina and Richard Henry Lee of Virginia on the committee that drafted the resolution. See Gordon S. Wood, The Creation of the American Republic 1776-1787, 131-32 (1969).

[24] Willi Paul Adams, The First American Constitutions: Republican Ideology and the Making of the State Constitutions in the Revolutionary Era 61 (1980).

The American colonies were in agreement that the *sine qua non* of government was consent. There was widespread disagreement, however, about "(1) who is to give consent, (2) to whom is consent given, (3) what act or acts constitute giving consent, and (4) over what range of issues must consent be permanently withheld?"[25]

The Continental Congress considered, but eventually declined to recommend any model format of governance for the states to adopt.[26] It had been impossible to reach an agreement on the format for a model state constitution.[27] The Continental Congress did recommend, however, that the new state constitutions be based on "the authority of the people."[28]

On May 11, 1776, the provincial congress of North Carolina passed several resolutions that comprised "a temporary Civil Constitution."[29] In essence, that "constitution" established a safety council for all of North Carolina. The thirteen member council was charged with exercising all powers of government, consistent with prior legislative enactments, until the provincial congress reconvened.[30]

A Virginia convention gathered at Williamsburg in May of 1776. It adopted a two-fold resolution on May 15, 1776. First, Virginia's delegates in Philadelphia were instructed to move for independence.[31] Second, the Virginia delegates in Williamsburg were directed to appoint a committee "to prepare a DECLARATION OF RIGHTS, and such a plan of government as will be most likely to maintain peace and order in this colony, and secure substantial and equal liberty to the people."[32] In examining these actions by the Virginians gathered in Williamsburg, Professor Howard aptly observed:

---

[25] Donald S. Lutz, Popular Consent and Popular Control: Whig Political Theory in the Early State Constitutions 1-2, 45 (1980).

[26] Robert F. Williams, *State Constitutional Law Processes*, 24 WM. & MARY L. REV. 169 173 (1983).

[27] Willi Paul Adams, The First American Constitutions: Republican Ideology and the Making of the State Constitutions in the Revolutionary Era 56 (1980).

[28] Willi Paul Adams, The First American Constitutions: Republican Ideology and the Making of the State Constitutions in the Revolutionary Era 100 (1980).

[29] Willi Paul Adams, The First American Constitutions: Republican Ideology and the Making of the State Constitutions in the Revolutionary Era 81 (1980).

[30] *Id.*

[31] A.E. Dick Howard, The Road From Runnymede: Magna Carta and Constitutionalism in America, 54 U.VA.L.REV. 816, 820 (1968).

[32] 1 Jefferson Papers 290-91 (Boyd ed.) cited by A.E. Dick Howard, The Road From Runnymede: Magna Carta and Constitutionalism in America, 54 U. VA. L. REV. 816, 820 (1968).

Those members of the 1776 convention steeped in Lockean notions of the social contract might well have considered themselves in a "state of nature" upon the dissolution of the bond with Great Britain. Thus, to declare man's natural rights was a logical step en route to forming a new social compact.[33]

On May 26, 1776, John Adams articulated the proposition and then posed a question to which there was no uniform response: "It is certain, in theory, that the only moral foundation of government is, the consent of the people. But to what extent shall we carry this principle?"[34] On June 3, 1776, John Adams wrote to Patrick Henry that the "natural course and order of things [should be] for every colony to institute a government; for all the colonies to confederate, and define the limits of the continental Constitution; then to declare the colonies a sovereign state, or a number of confederated sovereign states; and last of all, to form treaties with foreign powers."[35] Adams' letter continued, however, with a recognition that there was not enough time for such a logical and orderly progression: "But I fear we cannot proceed systematically, and that we shall be obliged to declare ourselves independent States, before we confederate, and indeed before all the colonies have established their governments."[36]

The provincial congress of New Jersey convened on June 10, 1776. According to its journal entries, a resolution was passed on June 21 to follow the May 15 recommendation of the Continental Congress and to draft a constitution. New Jersey's first constitution was passed like a legislative act and became effective immediately on July 2, 1776.[37]

On June 12, 1776, the provincial congress of Virginia adopted the first declaration of rights that was separate from the text of a state constitution. The Virginia Constitution was ratified on June 29, 1776. Virginia's bifurcated format was frequently replicated in charters that were subsequently adopted by other states. The Virginia Declaration of Rights rejected the British monarchy as a basis for government and instead asserted that "all power is vested in and consequently derived from the people...." Nevertheless, the Virginia Declaration of Rights also included "restatement of English principles—the principles of the Magna Charta,

---

[33] A.E. Dick Howard, *The Road From Runnymede: Magna Carta and Constitutionalism in America*, 54 U. VA. L. REV. 816, 820 (1968).

[34] John Adams to James Sullivan, May 26, 1776, *in* 9 The Works of John Adams 375 (Charles Francis Adams ed., 1850-1856).

[35] Correspondence from John Adams to Patrick Henry, June 3, 1776, *in* 1 Letters of Members of the Continental Congress 47 (Edmund C. Burnett ed., 1921-1936).

[36] *Id.*

[37] Charles R. Erdman, *The New Jersey Constitution of 1776* (Princeton, N.J. 1929).

the Petition of Right, the Commonwealth Parliament, and the Revolution of 1688."[38]

The state constitutions of New Hampshire, South Carolina, New Jersey, and Virginia, were enacted prior to the Declaration of Independence and were all intended to be provisional until the future of the American colonies' relationship with England had been resolved.

B. FIRST STATE CONSTITUTIONAL FORAYS

One noted constitutional scholar, Benjamin Wright, has stated that 1776 must "rank with 1787 as one of the two most significant years in the history of modern constitution-making."[39] The first forays into state constitution-making, after the Declaration of Independence, were completed within six months: Delaware (September 11, 1776); Pennsylvania (September 28, 1776); Maryland (November 8, 1776); North Carolina (December 14, 1776); Georgia (February 4, 1777).[40] Thus, by the end of 1776, eight state constitutions had been adopted and two more had been modified.[41]

Frameworks

Before the substantive content of those state constitutions could be debated, however, it was necessary to establish a process for drafting and adopting the proposed charters of government. The majority of the initial state constitutions were written by state legislatures.[42]

Although the initial state constitutions introduced concepts of representative democracy, they also carried over many provisions from each new state's prior colonial charter or propriety grant. The first state constitutions also perpetuated the individual liberties and property rights that had been afforded to American colonists by the English common law. In lieu of formally adopting state constitutions, however, Connecticut and Rhode Island simply modified their colonial charters. In fact, those states

---

[38] A.E. Dick Howard, *The Road From Runnymede: Magna Carta and Constitutionalism in America* 54 U. VA. L. REV. 823 (1968).

[39] George A. Billias, American Constitutionalism and Europe, 1776-1848, *in* American Constitutionalism Abroad 13-14, 19-23 (George A. Billias ed. 1990).

[40] Robert F. Williams, *The State Constitutions of the Founding Decade: Pennsylvania's Radical 1776 Constitution and its Influences On American Constitutionalism*, 62 TEMP. L. REV. 541 (1989). *See also* Willi Paul Adams, The First American Constitutions: Republican Ideology and the Making of the State Constitutions in the Revolutionary Era 5 (1980). John A. Munroe, History of Delaware, 2d ed. (Newark: University of Delaware Press, 1984).

[41] George A. Billias, American Constitutionalism and Europe, 1776-1848, *in* American Constitutionalism Abroad 13-14, 19-23 (George A. Billias ed. 1990).

[42] *Id.*

functioned under their old charters, with modifications, until 1819 and 1842, respectively.

Two of the most prominent features of the initial state constitutions were written Declarations of Rights and the exaltation of legislative power. With the exception of the unicameral legislature provided for by the first Pennsylvania and Georgia constitutions, the initial state constitutions divided legislative power between upper and lower houses of elected representatives.[43] Membership in the lower houses was expanded through reapportionment, by broadening the base for suffrage eligibility, and by opening the qualifications for office holding.[44] The antecedent models for the upper houses in the first state constitutions were the colonial governor's councils. Therefore, the first state constitutions often authorized the upper house to perform both executive and legislative functions.[45]

The office of governor was profoundly transformed in the first state constitutions. As an instrument for implementing British policy during the colonial period, governors had been vested with prerogative powers that included an absolute veto of legislative acts. In reaction to England's colonial gubanatorial system, the first state constitutions frequently subordinated the executive to the legislature by denying the governor any veto and often providing for the governor to be appointed by the upper house.[46] Thus, the initial state constitutions changed the office of governor to a position that was almost entirely dependent upon and dominated by the newly constituted state legislatures.

Religion and Education

There was a consensus in the American colonies that moral virtue was desirable in public officials and integral to good citizenship. Nevertheless, the first state constitutions reflected diverse approaches to the relationship of church and state, although most included some form of religious test for office holders.[47] The Maryland Constitution of 1776 empowered the

---

[43] The Federalist No. 1, at 3 (Jacob E. Cooke ed., Middletown, Conn.: Wesleyan University Press, 1961).

[44] *See* Donald L. Lutz, Political Participation *in* Paul Finkelman and Stephen E. Gottlieb, eds., Eighteenth Century America Toward a Usable Past: Liberty Under State Constitutions, (Athens: University of Georgia Press, 1991)..

[45] Robert F. Williams, *The State Constitutions of the Founding Decade: Pennsylvania's Radical 1776 Constitution and its Influences on American Constitutionalism*, 62 TEMP. L. REV. 541 (1989).

[46] *Id.*

[47] For a summary of religion provisions in early state constitutions see Morton Borden, *Jews, Turks, and Infidels* (Chapel Hill: University of North Carolina Press, 1984), 11-15; Stephen Botein, "Religious Dimensions of the Early American State," *in* Beyond

legislature with the discretionary authority "to lay a general and equal tax, for the support of the Christian religion."[48] The New Jersey Constitution of 1776 provided that "there shall be no establishment of any one religious sect in this Province, in preference to another."[49] The North Carolina Constitution of 1776 restricted office holding to Protestant Christians, by precluding anyone "who shall hold religious principles incompatible with the freedom and safety of the state."[50] The New York Constitution of 1777 provided for the free exercise of religion to guard against "the bigotry and ambition of weak and wicked priests and princes [who] have scourged mankind."[51]

Several of the initial state constitutions included provisions that provided for the support or establishment of public schools. In the early part of 1776, John Adams had urged the states to provide for public education in their new constitutions.[52] According to Adams, a democratic republic could only be sustained over time by an educated electorate. The North Carolina Constitution of 1776 called for the establishment of "a school or schools."[53] The 1776 Pennsylvania Constitution contemplated the establishment of a public "school or schools" in each county and "one or more universities."[54]

Pennsylvania 1776

A convention to draft Pennsylvania's state constitution was convened at the State House in Philadelphia (Independence Hall) on July 15, 1776.[55] The Pennsylvania Convention adopted a Declaration of Rights on August 16, 1776. Pennsylvania's Declaration of Rights was patterned after Virginia's, but Pennsylvania's Article XII contained one of the broadest statements of speech and press freedom: "The People have a right to freedom of speech, and of writing, and publishing their sentiments; therefore the freedom of the press ought not to be restrained." Article XVI provided: "That the people have a right to assemble together, to consult

---

Confederation: Origins of the Constitution and American National Identity (Richard Beeman, Stephen Botein, and Edward C. Carter II, eds., Chapel Hill: University of North Carolina Press, 1987).

[48] Md. Const. (1776), Declaration of Rights, § 33.

[49] N.J. Const. (1776), § 19.

[50] N.C. Const. (1776), § 32.

[51] N.Y. Const. (1777), § 38.

[52] John Adams, Thoughts on Government (Boston, 1776), *in* American Political Writing, 1:407 (Hyneman and Lutz, ed.).

[53] N.C. Const. § 41, *in* Federal and State Constitutions, 5:2794 (Thorpe, ed.).

[54] Pa. Const. § 44, *in* Federal and State Constitutions, 5:3091 (ed. Thorpe).

[55] *See* R. Brunhouse, The Counter-Revolution in Philadelphia 1776-1790, at 13 (1942).

for their common good, to instruct their representatives, and to apply to the legislature for redress of grievances, by address, petition or remonstrance."

Pennsylvania's Frame of Government also protected various rights. For example, Section 35 specified: "The printing presses shall be free to every person who undertakes to examine the proceedings of the legislature, or any part of government. Thus, Pennsylvania's Declaration of Rights and the Frame of Government operated in tandem to not only guarantee individual rights but to preserve the particular form of republican government that had been established for that state.[56]

The Frame of Government proposed by the Pennsylvania Convention on September 5, 1776, was adopted on September 28, 1776.[57] Pennsylvania's "ultra democratic" 1776 constitution was written by some of Thomas Paine's closest friends; Dr. Thomas Young, Judge George Brigan, and James Cannon.[58] Accordingly, many of the themes advanced by Paine in *Common Sense* were implemented in the 1776 Pennsylvania Constitution.

The unicameral legislature set forth in Section 2 of its Pennsylvania's 1776 Frame of Government was intended to eliminate any element of "aristocracy."[59] It was defended as the logical extension of prior unicameral legislatures in Pennsylvania with origins dating from William Penn's 1701 Charter of Privileges.[60] The lack of restraint on the unicameral legislature in Pennsylvania's 1776 Constitution was an intentional decision to prevent any "undemocratic" restriction on the will of the people's elected representatives.

The commitment to popular sovereignty in the 1776 Pennsylvania Constitution is further illustrated by two other provisions. First, ordinary statutory legislation, as distinguished from constitutional amendments in other states, did not become operative unless approved by two consecutive

---

[56] Robert C. Palmer, Liberties as Constitutional Provisions, 1776-1791, *in* W. Nelson & R. Palmer, Liberty and Community: Constitution and Rights in the Early American Republic 64, 68 (1987).

[57] *See* A. Blaustein & J. Sigler, Constitutions That Made History 20 (1988).

[58] Robert F. Williams, *The State Constitutions of the Founding Decade: Pennsylvania's Radical 1776 Constitution and its Influences on American Constitutionalism*, 62 TEMP. L. REV. 541, 544 (1989); *see also* John Paul Selsam, The Pennsylvania Constitution of 1776 (New York: Octagon Books, 1971).

[59] Robert F. Williams, *The State Constitutions of the Founding Decade: Pennsylvania's Radical 1776 Constitution and its Influences on American Constitutionalism*, 62 Temp. L. Rev. 541 (1989).

[60] Nix & Schweitzer, Pennsylvania's Contributions to the Writing and the Ratification of the Constitution, 112 PA. MAG. HIST. 7 BIOG. 3, 8-9 (1988).

legislative sessions. Second, the legislation that passed the first session had to be published between sessions for the benefit of the voting public.[61]

Pennsylvania's 1776 Constitution, with its unicameral legislature, provided a national focal point for the competing arguments on many of the initial key state constitutional issues. John Adams was especially critical of the Pennsylvania Frame of Government. As Benjamin Rush recalled:

> So great was [Adams'] disapprobation of a government composed of a single legislature, that he said to me upon reading the first constitution of Pennsylvania "The people of your state will sooner or later fall upon their knees to the King of Great Britain to take them again under his protection, in order to deliver them from the tyranny of their own government."[62]

Rush wrote to Adams: "From you I learned to discover the danger of the Constitution of Pennsylvania."[63] One of North Carolina's delegates to the Continental Congress, also a member of the provincial congress working on the North Carolina Constitution, wrote to Samuel Johnson:

> You have seen the constitution of Pennsylvania—the motley mixture of limited monarchy and an execrable democracy—a beast without a head.[64]

Delaware 1776

The constitutional convention was an American innovation and was based on the concept of "the people as a constitutional power."[65] Delaware's 1776 Constitution was the first to be drafted by a convention elected expressly for that purpose.[66] The preamble to Delaware's 1776 Declaration of Rights and Fundamental Rules provided that "all government of right originates from the people, is founded in compact only, and instituted solely for the good of the whole."[67] The initial

---

[61] John Paul Selsam, The Pennsylvania Constitution of 1776 (New York: Octagon Books, 1971).

[62] G. Corner at 142. *See also* D. Hawke, In the Midst of a Revolution 178 (discussion of Adams's dislike for the Pennsylvania Constitution).

[63] Letters of Benjamin Rush 1761-1792, at 114-15 (L. Butterfield ed. 1941), *quoted in* J. Coleman, Thomas McKean: Forgotten Leader of the Revolution 203 n. 56.

[64] Thomas Burke Douglass, *Disillusioned Democrat*, 26 N.C. HIST. REV. 150, 157 (1950).

[65] R.R. Palmer, The Age of Democratic Revolution: The Challenge 215 (Princeton: Princeton University Press, 1959); *see* also Gordon S. Wood, The Creation of the American Republic 1776-1787, at 259-343 (New York: W. W. Norton, 1969).

[66] Donald S. Lutz, Popular Consent and Popular Control: Whig Political Theory in the Early State C Constitutions 1-2 (1980). John A. Munroe, History of Delaware, 2d ed. (Newark: University of Delaware Press, 1984), 69-70.

[67] Declaration of Rights and Fundamental Rules of the Delaware State of 1776, § 1. Many of the first state constitutions included "common good" clauses as "the guiding value for the exercise of legitimate government." Willi Paul Adams, The First American

Constitutions of Georgia, Maryland, and North Carolina were also drafted by conventions. Each of those constitutional conventions, however, also discharged legislative functions.[68]

Delaware's initial constitution was typical of the first state constitutions by differing from the colonial charter it replaced in two important respects: it provided for more legislative and less executive power; and, it was preceded by a Declaration of Rights.[69] The 1776 Delaware Constitution was unique, however, in prohibiting the future importation of slaves.[70] The first constitutions of Delaware, Pennsylvania, and New York had provisions that mandated legislative meetings to be open to the public. Those same state constitutions also required that proceedings of the legislature be published.[71]

Declarations of Rights

A majority of the original thirteen states enacted separate declarations of rights along with their first state constitutions.[72] Some rights were also included within the next state constitutions. The initial separate declarations of rights were frequently written as statements of broad

---

Constitutions: Republican Ideology and the Making of the State Constitutions in the Revolutionary Era 222 (1980). The state constitution adopted by North Carolina in 1776 also was accompanied by a declaration of rights. It began with the proclamation that: "[A]ll political power is vested in and derived from the people only." N.C. CONST. of 1776, *reprinted in* 5 F. Thorpe, American Charters, Constitutions and Organic Laws: 1492-1908, at 2787 (1909); *see also* Md. Const. of 1776, Declaration of Rights art. II; Pa. Const. of 1776, Declaration of Rights art. IV.

[68] Don E. Fehrenbacher, Sectional Crisis and Southern Constitutionalism 84 (Baton Rouge: Louisiana State University Press 1995).

[69] The Declaration of Rights and Fundamental Rules of the State of Delaware was adopted by the convention on September 11, 1776. Shortly thereafter, the first Constitution of the State of Delaware was enacted on September 20, 1776. *See* Gordon S. Wood, *State Constitution-Making in the American Revolution*, 24 RUTGERS L.J. 911, 921 (1993).

[70] 1776 Constitution of the State of Delaware, art. 26.

[71] Del. Const. of 1792, art. 2 §§ 8, 9; N.Y. Const. of 1777, § XV; Pa. Const. of 1776, §§ 13, 14.

[72] *See* Conn. Const. Ordinance of 1776, art. I, *reprinted in* 2 *Sources and Documents of United State Constitutions* 143-44 (William F. Swindler ed., 1973-1979) [hereinafter State Constitutions]; *Del. Declaration of Rights of 1776, reprinted in* 2 State Constitutions, *supra*, at 197-99; *Md. Declaration of Rights of 1776, reprinted in* 4 State Constitutions, *supra*, 372-75; *Mass. Const. of 1780*, pt. I, *reprinted in* 5 State Constitutions, *supra*, at 93-96; *N.H. Const. of 1784*, pt. 1, *reprinted in* 6 State Constitutions, *supra*, at 344-47; *N.C. Const. of 1776, Declaration of Rights, reprinted in* 7 State Constitutions, *supra*, at 402-04; *Pa. Const. of 1776, Declaration of Rights, reprinted in* 8 State Constitutions, *supra*, at 278-79; *Va. Declaration of Rights of 1776, reprinted in* 10 State Constitutions, *supra*, at 48-50.

principles rather than legal codes. They were often articulated in an admonitory fashion, with words like "ought" and "should" rather than "shall" and "will."[73] Examples of such hortatory draftsmanship are: "no man ought to be compelled to give evidence against himself" and "the liberty of the press ought to be inviolably preserved."[74]

Other rights, such as the right to a jury trial, were phrased unequivocally. The English common law form of trial by jury had been transported to the American Colonies through the influence of the common law writers such as Coke, Hale and Blackstone. The American colonies resented royal interference with the right to trial by jury.[75] On October 14, 1774, the First Continental Congress declared:

> That the respective colonies are entitled to the common law of England, and more especially to the great and inestimable privilege of being tried by their peers of the vicinage, according to the course of that law.[76]

The Declaration of Independence stated solemn objections to the King's "depriving us in many cases, of the benefits of Trial by Jury ...."[77] The right to trial by jury was perpetuated as a fundamental component of the judicial system in every new sovereign state. In 1776, ten states allowed juries to decide both the facts and the law.[78] That right was often inserted into the first state constitutions.[79]

Maryland 1776

On July 3, 1776, Maryland's provincial congress acted upon the Constitutional Congress's recommendation of May 15. It decided to elect a new congress "for the express purpose of forming a new Government by the authority of the People only, and enacting and ordering all things for the preservation, safety, and general weal of this Colony."[80]

The members elected to serve in Maryland's convention met during the second week of August in 1776. They sought advice from John

---

[73] See Donald S. Lutz, *Popular Consent and Popular Control: Whig Political Theory in the Early State Constitutions* 67 (Baton Rouge: Louisiana State University Press 1980). (table on the use of shall and ought in state declarations of rights).

[74] Md. Const. of 1776, Declaration of Rights art. XX and XXXVIII.

[75] *Duncan v. Louisiana*, 391 U.S. 145, 152 (1968).

[76] *Id.; see* 2 J. Kent, *Commentaries on American Law* 13 (13th ed. 1884).

[77] *Duncan v. Louisiana*, 391 U. S. 145, 152 (1968). *See also* Vol. 1, *Del.C.* p. 13.

[78] Lloyd E. Moore, The Jury: Tool of Kings, Palladium of Liberty 112 (Cincinnati: W. H. Anderson, 1973); *see, e.g.,* Ga. Const. of 1777, art. XLI, in *Sources and Documents*, 2:448 (Swindler, ed.) ("jury shall be judges of law as well as of fact").

[79] *Id.* ("jury shall be judges of law as well as of fact").

[80] Willi Paul Adams, *The First American Constitutions: Republican Ideology and the Making of the State Constitutions in the Revolutionary Era* 80 (1980).

Dickinson of Pennsylvania about how to avoid ending up with a constitution like Pennsylvania's.[81] A declaration of rights was passed on November 3, 1776. The convention enacted a constitution for Maryland on November 8, 1776. It became effective immediately.[82] As early as 1776, the first constitutions of both Maryland and Delaware provided for amendments pursuant to the approval of two successive legislatures.

North Carolina 1776

In August 1776, the safety council of North Carolina scheduled elections for October 15, 1776. The elected representatives at that time would have not only legislative responsibility but would draft a constitution. North Carolina's new legislature convened on November 12, 1776.

On November 13, 1776, the Fifth Provincial Congress of North Carolina appointed a committee to draft a declaration of rights and a constitution.[83] The committee had the benefit of reviewing John Adam's *Thoughts on Government* and also received copies of constitutions and declarations of rights that had been recently adopted in other states.[84] Those documents, along with two letters of advice from John Adams, had been sent to the committee by William Hooper, North Carolina's delegate to the Continental Congress.[85]

Hooper also wrote a letter of his own to the North Carolina convention. Hooper provided his assessment of the constitutions of Pennsylvania, Delaware, South Carolina and New Jersey. Hooper recommended against a unicameral legislature like Pennsylvania's and against the election of judges, as had been provided for in Rhode Island's Constitution.[86]

---

[81] R. Hoffman, *A Spirit of Dissention: Economics, Politics and the Revolution in Maryland* 170-183, 269 (1973).

[82] Willi Paul Adams, *The First American Constitutions: Republican Ideology and the Making of the State Constitutions in the Revolutionary Era* 81 (1980).

[83] John V. Orth, Symposium: "The Law of the Land": The North Carolina Constitution and State Constitutional Law: North Carolina Constitutional History, 70 N.C. L. REV. 1759, 1760 (1992).

[84] John Adams, Thoughts on Government (Boston, 1776), *in* American Political Writing, 1:407 (Hyneman and Lutz, ed.).

[85] Letter from William Hooper to Fifth Provincial Congress (Oct. 26, 1776), in 10 The Colonial Records of North Carolina 862-70 (William L. Saunders ed., Raleigh, Josephus Daniels, Printer to the State, 1890); Letter from John Adams to William Hooper (ante Mar. 27, 1776), in 4 Papers of John Adams 73-78 (Robert J. Taylor ed., 1979).

[86] Fletcher Green, Constitutional Development in the South Atlantic States, 1776-1860, at 67 (1930).

After some modifications to the committee's drafts, the North Carolina Congress passed the Declaration of Rights on December 17, 1776, and the Constitution on December 18, 1776.[87] The framers of North Carolina's first constitution had drawn selectively upon the constitutional acumen of their contemporaries in other states. In language almost identical to the Maryland Declaration of Rights, North Carolina's Declaration of Rights provided that "the Legislative, Executive, and Supreme Judicial Powers of government ought to be forever separate and distinct from each other."[88] The provisions in the North Carolina Declaration of Rights acknowledging the sovereignty of the people and freedom of religion were patterned after similar provisions in the rights' declarations of Virginia and Pennsylvania, respectively.[89] Similarly, the Georgia and North Carolina constitutions mandated that the legislature establish public schools, was modeled upon an identical provision in the Pennsylvania Constitution.[90] The first constitution of North Carolina also prohibited incarceration for debt after all property of a debtor had been relinquished for the benefit of all creditors.

Unlike Pennsylvania, which had opted for a concentration of power in a unicameral legislature, almost all of the other states concluded that a balance of power between the branches of government was a preferable constitutional framework.[91] Georgia was the only state other than Pennsylvania, and the area known as Vermont, to adopt a unicameral legislature.[92]

Georgia 1777

Georgia adopted a constitution in February of 1777. The form and content of Georgia's Constitution was influenced by Button Gwinnett, one of Georgia's delegates to the Second Constitutional Congress. In 1776, while in Philadelphia, Gwinnett had been exposed to the wide range of the

---

[87] John V. Orth, Symposium: "The Law of the Land": The North Carolina Constitution and State Constitutional Law: North Carolina Constitutional History, 70 N.C. L. REV. 1759, 1761 (1992).

[88] N.C. Const. of 1776, Declaration of Rights, § 4; see MD. CONST. of 1776, Declaration of Rights, § 6.

[89] John V. Orth, Symposium: "The Law of the Land": The North Carolina Constitution and State Constitutional Law: North Carolina Constitutional History, 70 N.C. L. REV. 1759, 1765 (1992).

[90] Id. at 1766-67.

[91] Robert F. Williams, The State Constitutions of the Founding Decade: Pennsylvania's Radical 1776 Constitution and its Influences on American Constitutionalism, 62 TEMP. L. REV. 541 (1989).

[92] Adams, First American Constitutions, 300, 307; James Dealey, Growth of American State Constitutions 37-39 (1915; reprinted New York: Da Capo Press, 1972).

extant state constitutional drafts, pamphlets, and arguments. Benjamin Rush noted that Gwinnet had taken the Pennsylvania Constitution back to Georgia.[93] After the Georgia Constitution of 1777 was adopted, the legislature declared "that all laws of England, statute as well as common, and all laws passed by the general assembly should be in full force and effect as the law of the land."[94]

New York 1777

State constitutional activity continued from the adoption of New York's Constitution later in 1777 until the enactment of New Hampshire's Constitution in 1784. The extended forays into state constitution-making reflected an evolutionary pattern of transition from legislative dominance toward an expanded role for both the executive and judicial branches. The evolution in the adoption of the first state constitutions was also characterized by an introduction of structural changes designed to check and balance the initial state constitutions' tendency to amalgamate power within the legislature.

In early 1777, New York's delegates to the Continental Congress in Philadelphia wrote home about the controversy among Pennsylvanians regarding their Constitution of 1776:

> The unhappy Dispute about their constitution is the fatal Rock on which they have split, and which threatens them with Destruction. We ardently wish that in our own State the utmost Caution may be used to avoid a like calamity. Every wise Man here wishes that the establishment of new Forms of Government had been deferred. ...[95]

New York's 1777 Constitution provided a model based on a blending of governmental powers that appealed to many of those who opposed the Pennsylvania Constitution. Alfred Young described the polar positions that led to what he described as the "middle of the road" New York Constitution of 1777. It is illustrative of the general divergence of opinion concerning state constitutions during the founding decade:

> The [New York] constitution of 1777 retained many "aristocratic" features.... At the same time the constitution made several democratic departures from provincial precedent.... Had extreme conservatives had their way, they would have gotten elections at four-year intervals by voice voting, an upper house indirectly chosen, a governor elected by an upper house, and a governor with

---

[93] Benjamin Rush, The Autobiography of Benjamin Rush 113-14, 153 (G. Corner ed. 1948).

[94] Fletcher Green, Constitutional Development in the South Atlantic States, 1776-1860, at 67 (1930).

[95] Letter from Philip Livingston, James Duane, and William Duer to Abraham TenBroeck (Apr. 19, 1777), *reprinted in* 6 LETTERS FROM THE DELEGATES TO CONGRESS, *supra*, at 686-87.

more of the powers of his royal predecessors. Had the most democratic elements had their way, there would have been taxpayer suffrage, a secret ballot for all elections…annual election of all state officials, and popular election of country and local officials; furthermore the appointive power would have been vested exclusively in the assembly and the governor's veto power would have been eliminated.[96]

The veto provision in the New York Constitution of 1777 subsequently served as a model for the presidential veto in the United States Constitution.[97] The New York Constitution of 1777 did not, however, include a separate declaration of rights.

Vermont 1777

Vermont addressed the issue of drafting a state constitution in 1777, even though it was not yet recognized as an independent sovereign entity. Already estranged from New York, Vermont concluded that the recently enacted New York Constitution of 1777 was a "horrible example." The drafters of the 1776 Pennsylvania Constitution sent copies to representatives of Vermont, who had traveled to Philadelphia to lobby the Second Continental Congress to recognize it as a separate state. A constitution modeled closely after Pennsylvania's was proposed for the geographic area known as Vermont at that time.

South Carolina 1778

The South Carolina Constitution was revised in 1778. The word "State" replaced "colony" and the name of the chief executive became governor rather than president. A bicameral legislature was established. Public offices were established on a rotating basis. And the governor's veto power was eliminated. Popular suffrage was expanded by a reduction in the property requirement, but then contracted by the addition of a religious qualification.[98] The 1778 South Carolina Constitution provided that it could only be amended by a majority vote of both houses following ninety days' notice.

Massachusetts 1780

The 1780 Massachusetts constitution was not only written by a special convention but was submitted for popular ratification.[99] In 1778, the

---

[96] Alfred F. Young, *The Democratic Republicans of New York*: The Origins 1763-1797, at 20-21 (1967).

[97] C. Thach, Jr., *The Creation of the Presidency, 1775-1789*, at 65, 110-16 (E. Douglass, 1955).

[98] Fletcher Green, Constitutional Development in the South Atlantic States, 1776-1860, at 67 (1930).

[99] For a discussion of the process leading to the 1780 Massachusetts Constitution, see generally Cella, *The People of Massachusetts, A New Republic, and the Constitution of*

proposed Massachusetts Constitution was defeated by a popular referendum, in part, because it had been drafted by the legislature rather than a constitutional convention of the people.[100] The 1780 Massachusetts Constitution has been described by Donald Lutz as:

> the most important one written between 1776 and 1789 because it embodied the Whig theory of republican government, which came to dominate state level politics; the 1776 Pennsylvania Constitution was the second most important because it embodied the strongest alternative. The Massachusetts document represented radical Whiggism, moderated somewhat by the form of mixed government if not the actual substance. Pennsylvania Whigs wrote the most radical constitution of the era, one lacking even a bow in the direction of mixed government.[101]

Massachusetts has held several constitutional conventions since 1780 but has never adopted a completely revised constitution. Thus, the 1780 Massachusetts Constitution is still operative today and, as such, is the world's oldest written framework of government.[102] By the close of the Revolutionary War in 1783, every state except Connecticut and Rhode Island had written a new constitution.[103] Prior to the Declaration of Independence, the colonies of Rhode Island and Connecticut were operating as republics, pursuant to their corporate charters. Therefore, those two states "simply confined themselves to the elimination of all mention of royal authority in their existing charters."[104]

C. NEW NATION BEGINS

STATE CONSTITUTIONS REWRITTEN

Following the ratification of the United States Constitution, some of the original thirteen states began to rewrite their constitutions almost

---

1780: The Evolution of Principles of Popular Control of Political Authority, 1774-1780, 14 SUFFOLK U.L. REV. 975 (1980).

[100] E. Morgan, *The Birth of the Republic* 89-90 (1977).

[101] Robert F. Williams, *The State Constitutions of the Founding Decade: Pennsylvania's Radical 1776 Constitution and its Influences On American Constitutionalism*, 62 TEMP. L. REV. 541, 549 (1989) (citing D. Lutz, Popular Consent and Popular Control: Whig Political Theory in The Early State Constitutions 1 (1980); *see also* Alfred Young, The Democratic-Republicans of New York: Their Origins 1763-1797, at 20-21 (1967) (quoting Donald S. Lutz).

[102] Paul C. Reardon, "*The Massachusetts Constitution Marks a Milestone*," 12 Publius: The Journal of Federalism 45-55 (Winter 1982).

[103] *Delaware v. Van Arsdall*, 475 U.S. 673 (1986) (Stevens, J., dissenting).

[104] Gordon S. Wood, State Constitution-Making in the American Revolution, 24 RUTGERS L.J. 133 (1993).

immediately.[105] Fifteen existing states re-wrote their constitutions prior to the Civil War. In exercising their residual sovereign powers, states adopted constitutions that continued to adhere to the same basic principles of republican democracy, but from their own unique perspectives.[106] These documents, for example, reaffirmed each state's commitment to its own declaration of rights and common law traditions.

Georgia 1788

On January 30, 1788, the Georgia legislature decided to call a state constitutional convention after nine states had ratified the proposed Constitution of the United States:

> That they would proceed to name three fit and discreet persons from each county to be convened at Augusta, by the executive, as soon as may be after official information is received that nine states have accepted the federal constitution; and a majority of them shall proceed to take under their consideration the alterations and amendments that are necessary to be made in the constitution of this state, and to arrange, digest and alter the same, in such manner as, in their judgment will be most consistent with the interest and safety, and best secure the rights and liberties to the citizens thereof.[107]

Georgia adopted a new constitution in May 1789. There were several changes in all three branches of government. A bicameral legislature was created to replace the former unicameral house of assembly. Provisions were included for the governor to be elected by the legislature for a term of two years. The 1789 Constitution of Georgia was the first state constitution that required candidates for legislative office to have resided longer in the United States than in the State of Georgia:

> Senators were to be twenty-eight years of age, inhabitants of the United States nine years, citizens of the state three years and of the county six months, and possessed of 250 acres of land or other property worth L250. Members of the lower house of the legislature were to be twenty-one years of age, citizens of the United States seven years, inhabitants of the state two years and of the county three months, and possessed of 250 acres of land or other property worth L150.[108]

---

[105] See, e.g., Del. Const. of 1792; see generally Claudio v. State, 585 A.2d 1278 (Del. 1991).

[106] See, e.g., Del. Const. of 1792; see generally Claudio v. State, 585 A.2d 1278 (Del. 1991).

[107] Stevens, History of Georgia, II, at 388, *quoted in* Fletcher M. Green, Constitutional Development in the South Atlantic States, 1776-1860, at 127 (1930).

[108] Fletcher Green, Constitutional Development in the South Atlantic States, 1776-1860, at 130 (1930).

South Carolina 1790

On March 13, 1789, the legislature of South Carolina passed an act that called for a state constitutional convention to convene at Columbia in May 1790.[109] The new constitution provided for the capital to be moved from Charleston to Columbia. The qualifications for office-holding were changed by reducing the property requirement and eliminating the necessity "of being of the Protestant religion." There were also revisions to the suffrage requirements: a three shilling tax was provided for as an alternative to owning fifty acres of land; and, the religious qualification was deleted.[110] The new South Carolina Constitution also adjusted the powers in each of its three branches of government, provided for freedom of religion, and importuned the legislature to "pass laws for the abolition of the rights of primogeniture, and for giving an equitable distribution of the real estate of interstates."[111] Finally, the new constitution of South Carolina provided for future amendments by: supermajority votes of both houses; a popular vote; and additional supermajority votes of both houses, after an intervening popular election.[112]

D. STATEHOOD ADMISSION REQUIREMENTS

The United States Constitution assigned the process of admitting new states to Congress:

New states may be admitted by the Congress into this Union; but no new State shall be formed or erected within the Jurisdiction of any other State; nor any State be formed by the Junction of two or more States, or Parts of States, without the Consent of the Legislatures of the States concerned as well as of the Congress.[113]

Twenty new states were admitted to the Union prior to the Civil War. The provision in the United States Constitution for admitting new states was initially invoked by Vermont. Vermont became a state in 1791.[114] Vermont's Constitution was the first to eliminate the requirement that a man either own property or pay taxes to be permitted to vote.[115] It enfranchised all free males older than twenty-one who would take the Freeman's Oath. On June 1, 1792, Kentucky was the second state to be admitted to the Union. The Congressional acts admitting Kentucky and

---

[109] *Id.* at 150.

[110] *Id.* at 122.

[111] *Id.* at 124.

[112] *Id.*

[113] U.S. Const. art. IV, § 3.

[114] Act of Feb. 18, 1791, ch. VII, 1 State. 191 (1791).

[115] Vt. Const. of 1793, ch. II, § 21, *in* Sources and Documents, 9:507, 512 (Swindler ed.).

Vermont contained no terms or conditions. Each act provided for admission "as a new and entire member of the United States of America."[116]

When Tennessee was admitted as the third new State, it was declared to be "one of the United States of America," "on an equal footing with the original States in all respects whatsoever."[117] That language has remained substantially the same in all subsequent admission acts.[118]

Enabling Statute Concept

When the first independent territorial requests for statehood were being contemplated, it was a thought that an enabling statute from Congress was a necessary condition precedent to calling for a state constitutional convention.[119] This precedent was established in 1802, when Ohio petitioned Congress for such authorization. That practice was followed by Alabama, Illinois, Indiana, Louisiana, Mississippi, and Missouri. The procedure changed between 1836 and 1848.[120] Wisconsin was admitted following the passage of an enabling act. Arkansas, Florida, Iowa, and Michigan were all admitted to statehood, however, without any prior authorization from Congress to assemble a state constitutional convention. Thereafter, the procedure was not uniform, *e.g.*, California, Kansas, and Oregon organized without the authorization of an enabling act; but Nebraska, Nevada, and Minnesota all received Congressional approval to proceed.[121] Each new state had to have a "Republican form of Government."[122] This requirement had at least two direct affects on the future of constitutions drafted in contemplation of admission to statehood. First, to achieve a "Republican form of Government" the constitutions proposed by many new states were simply adaptations or combinations of provisions in the constitutions of existing states.[123] Second, Congress assumed that public education was "an essential feature of a republican government based upon the will of the people."[124] Therefore, as a

---

[116] *Coyle v. Smith*, 221 U.S. 559 (1911).

[117] *Id.*

[118] *Id.*

[119] Dennis C. Colson, *Idaho's Constitution: The Tie That Binds* 1, 4-6, 220-23 (University of Idaho 1991).

[120] *Id.*

[121] *Id.*

[122] U.S. Const. art. IV § 4.

[123] James Willard Hurst, The Growth of American Law: The Law Makers 336 (Boston: Little, Brown, 1950).

[124] David Tyack, Thomas James, and Aaron Benavot, *Law and the Shaping of Public Education*, 1785-1954, at 20 (Madison: University of Wisconsin Press, 1987).

condition for admission to the Union, Congress frequently insisted that proposed state constitutions include provisions that guaranteed public education.[125] This latter phenomena was simply a perpetuation of the recognition of the need for an educated electorate that began with the Northwest Ordinance of 1787, to wit: "Religion, morality and knowledge, being necessary to good government and the happiness of mankind, schools and the means of education shall be forever encouraged."[126]

One related issue that confronted the writers of state constitutions after 1787 was the propriety of including religion as a component of public education.[127] To varying degrees, the states concluded that moral virtue was a necessary foundation for the institutions of government in a democratic society.[128] Consequently, the articles on public education in many state constitutions often began with preambles or mission statements regarding both civil and moral aims.[129] Throughout the nineteenth century, those aims were often linked inexorably in state constitutions.

Enabling Acts Evolve

The enabling act passed at the close of the nineteenth century for North Dakota, South Dakota, Montana, and Washington is illustrative of how the public school mandate was retained even after sectarian controls were prohibited:

> An act to provide for the division of Dakota into two States and to enable the people of North Dakota, South Dakota, Montana, and Washington to form constitutions and State governments and to be admitted into the Union on an equal footing with the original States, and to make donations of public lands to such States.
>
> ...whereupon the said conventions shall be, and are hereby, authorized to form constitutions and States governments for said proposed States, respectively. The constitutions shall be republican in form ...
>
> And said conventions shall provide, by ordinances irrevocable without the consent of the United States and the people of said States; ...

---

[125] *Id.* at 20-42.

[126] The Federal and State Constitutions, Colonial Charters, and Other Organic Laws of the States, Territories, and Colonies Now or Heretofore Forming the United States of America, 2:961 (Francis N. Thorpe ed., Washington, D.C.: U.S. Government Printing Office, 1909).

[127] *See Pfeiffer v. Board of Education*, 118 Mich. 560, 565 (1898).

[128] Benjamin Rush, Thoughts upon the Mode of Education Proper in a Republic, *in* Essays on Education in the Early Republic 3-23 (Frederick Rudolph ed., Cambridge, Mass.: Harvard University Press, 1965).

[129] David Tyack and Thomas James, *"State Government and American Public Education: Exploring the 'Primeval Forest,'"* 26 History of Education Quarterly 39-69 (1986).

That provision shall be made for the establishment and maintenance of systems of public schools, which shall be open to all the children of said States, and free from sectarian control.[130]

E. STRUCTURES OF GOVERNMENT

State constitutional law, like its federal counterpart, is not limited to issues involving the common law or individual rights. Numerous other areas of law involve the application of state constitutions. The structure and power of state and local governments,[131] the state judicial system,[132] taxation, public finance,[133] and public education[134] are all affected by a state's constitution and its interpretation.

Beginning with several state constitutions that were adopted in the 1790s, e.g., Delaware, Kentucky, and Tennessee, provisions were made "for the legislature to submit the question of calling a Constitutional convention to a vote of the people."[135] If the populace voted in favor of calling a constitutional convention, delegates were elected to that body. Some state constitutional conventions could take definitive action while others were required to submit proposals to amend or replace a constitution to another vote of the electorate.[136]

---

[130] Robert F. Williams, *State Constitutional Law: Cases and Materials* 76-77 (2d ed. 1993) *citing* Chapter 180, *Fiftieth Congress*, Second Session 1889.

[131] John Devlin, *Toward a State Constitutional Analysis of Allocation of Powers: Legislators and Legislative Appointees Performing Administrative Functions*, 66 TEMP. L. REV. 1205 (1993); James E. Herget, *The Missing Power of Local Governments: A Divergence Between Text and Practice in Our Early State Constitution*, 62 VA. L. REV. 999, 1001 (1976); Michael E. Libonati, Intergovernmental Relations in State Constitutional Law: A Historical Overview, 496 ANNALS AM. ACAD. POL. & SOC. SCI. 107 (1988).

[132] Jonathan Feldman, *Separation of Powers and Judicial Review of Positive Rights Claims: The Role of State Courts in an Era of Positive Government*, 24 RUTGERS L.J. 1057 (1993).

[133] Robert F. Williams, Foreword: *The Importance of an Independent State Constitutional Equality Doctrine in School Finance Cases and Beyond*, 24 CONN. L. REV. 675 (1992).

[134] William E. Thro, Note, *To Render Them Safe: The Analysis of State Constitutional Provisions in Public School Finance Reform Litigation*, 75 VA. L. REV. 1639, 1661-70 (1989); Allen W. Hubsch, The Emerging Right to Education Under State Constitutional Law, 65 TEMP. L. REV. 1325 (1992). State constitutions, except for Mississippi, provide for public education.

[135] Don E. Fehrenbacher, Sectional Crisis and Southern Constitutionalism, 87 (Baton Rouge: Louisiana State University Press 1995).

[136] *Id.*

Revising State Constitutions

There were originally two general methods of writing or amending a state constitution: by convention[137] and by legislative action.[138] Amendment by popular initiative was a third method that began to appear in state constitutions, especially at the turn of the century.[139] The initiative has been challenged as a form of pure democracy that "is in contravention of a republican form of government guaranteed to each state by Article IV, Section 4 of the United States Constitution."[140] The United States Supreme Court held that the issue was a non-justiciable political question that was "embraced within the scope of powers conferred upon Congress."[141] The initiative remains operative in many states.

In a majority of states, either the legislature alone or the legislature and a popular referendum can call for a constitutional convention. Some state constitutions either permit a convention to be brought about by an initiative petition or require that the question of having a convention be submitted to the voters at specific periodic intervals.[142] When there is a referendum on the issue of having a constitutional convention, some state constitutions require it to be approved by a majority of those voting in the election, not just a majority of those voting on the question.[143]

State Constitutions More Lengthy

State constitutions are generally more detailed, and therefore, longer than the United States Constitution.[144] Over the years, state constitutions have been rewritten entirely or amended, in part, to include a great variety

---

[137] See Robert J. Martineau, *The Mandatory Referendum on Calling a State Constitutional Convention: Enforcing the People's Right to Reform Their Government*, 31 OHIO ST. L.J. 421 (1970); Robert F. Williams, *Are State Constitutional Conventions Things of the Past? The Increasing Role of the Constitutional Commission in State Constitutional Change*, 1 HOFSTRA L. & POLY'S SYMP. 1 (1996).

[138] See, e.g., Del. Const. art. XVI, § 1.

[139] James W. Hurst, The Growth of American Law: The Law Makers 199-204 (1950). See Thomas E. Cronin, *Direct Democracy: The Politics of Initiative, Referendum, and Recall* (1989); David B. Magleby, Direct Legislation: Voting on Ballot Propositions in the United States (1983); David B. Schmidt, Citizen Lawmakers: The Ballot Initiative Revolution (1989).

[140] Pacific States Telephone and Telegraph v. Oregon, 223 U.S. 188 (1912).

[141] *Id.*

[142] W. Brooke Graves, State Constitutional Law: A Twenty-Five Year Summary, 8 WM. & MARY L. REV. 1, 4 (1966).

[143] *Id.* at 5.

[144] Frank P. Grad, *The State Constitution: Its Function and Form for Our Time*, 54 VA. L. REV. 928 (1968).

of specific matters that could have been enacted by statute.[145] Once a provision is part of a state constitution, it is beyond change by normal, statutory law-making processes.[146]

Legislation enacted into state constitutions reflects the political and social feeling of the time.[147] Several of the recurring subjects addressed in state constitutions relate to suffrage, apportionment, property, economics, slavery, lotteries, banks, corporations, divorces, indebtedness, internal improvements, length of legislative sessions, sinking funds, public credit, and state regulation or performance of services, such as health and education.[148] The original or amended substance of such provisions was often the product of political party or special-interest group conflicts.[149] "In short, state government performed many more of what we think of as the normal tasks of government, while the federal government, especially in the Jacksonian period and after, was more of a caretaker government with only a rudimentary bureaucracy."[150]

Georgia 1798

Georgia convened another constitutional convention in May of 1798. The constitution it adopted at that time was perceived to achieve a better balance of power between Georgia's three branches of government. Certain restrictions were placed upon the legislature, *e.g.*, quorum requirements and recording of votes.[151] The legislature was authorized to establish superior and inferior courts, with the judges of both courts to be elected by the legislature.[152] Several substantive rights provisions were included in the 1798 Georgia Constitution. Incarceration was prohibited

---

[145] Robert F. Williams, *State Constitutional Law Processes*, 24 WM. & MARY L. REV. 169, 202 (1983); *see* Albert L. Strum, *Methods of State Constitutional Reform*, (Ann Arbor: University of Michigan Press1954).

[146] Frank P. Grad, *The State Constitution: Its Function and Form for Our Time*, 54 VA. L. REV. 928, 928-29, 942-43, 945-47, 972-73 (1968); Janet Cornelius, Constitution Making in Illinois 1818-1970, at 42 (Urbana: University of Illinois Press, 1972).

[147] James W. Hurst, The Growth of American Law: The Law Makers, 237-38, 240-46 (1950); *see also* Fletcher Green, Constitutional Development in the South Atlantic States, *1776-1860* (1930); Merrill D. Peterson, Democracy, Liberty & Property: The State Constitutional Conventions of the 1820s (1966).

[148] Michael Heise, *State Constitutions, School Finance Litigation, and the "Third Wave": From Equity to Adequacy*, 68 TEMP. L. REV. 1151 (1995).

[149] *Id.*

[150] Stephen M. Griffin, *American Constitutionalism From Theory to Politics*, p. 34 (Princeton University Press 1996).

[151] Fletcher Green, Constitutional Development in the South Atlantic States, 1776-1860, 124-135 (1930).

[152] *Id.*

for a debtor who had relinquished all property for the benefit of creditors. Several clauses promoted religious freedom. The importation of slaves was prohibited. And, dismembering or killing a slave was punishable as a crime on the same basis as such an act against anyone else.[153]

F. NINETEENTH CENTURY DAWNS

STATE CONSTITUTIONS POPULARIZED

The election of President Thomas Jefferson in 1800 was a significant political change that was indicative of what was happening in many states. There was widespread support for implementing Jeffersonian democracy by invoking the principles of the Declaration of Independence and the Virginia Bill of Rights. The ascendency into power of Jeffersonian Republicans commenced several decades of efforts to amend or revise the provisions in state constitutions, in particular, with regard to suffrage and representation. Georgia, for example, passed a series of amendments to its state constitutions between 1808 and 1824 that provided for the direct popular election of public officials, including the governor, in lieu of legislative appointment.

Connecticut 1818

Connecticut adopted its first operative state constitution in 1818. Its structure of government provided for a traditional separation of powers between the legislature, an executive, and a judiciary. Since the Declaration of Independence, Connecticut had operated in an essentially parliamentary format. The Connecticut Constitution of 1818 also included a bill of rights. Many of the rights written into the 1818 Constitution had well-established common law antecedents in Connecticut.[154]

Jacksonian Influences

The state constitutions that were written or amended in this era characterized by the presidency of Andrew Jackson were frequently influenced by individuals who were interested in issues relating to popular sovereignty.[155] Thus, the state constitutions of that time were often rights-conscious documents.[156] For example, many state constitutions were

---

[153] *Id.*

[154] Ellen A. Peters, *State Constitutional Law: Federalism in the Common Law Tradition*, 84 MICH. L. REV. 583 (1986); Ellen A. Peters, Common Law Antecedents of Constitutional Law in Connecticut, *in* Paul Finkelman and Stephen E. Gottlieb, Toward a Usable Past: Liberty Under State Constitutions.

[155] James A. Henretta, *Foreward: Rethinking the State Constitutional Tradition*, 22 RUTGERS L.J. 819, 819-26, 836-39 (1991). *See also* Merrill D. Peterson, *Democracy, Liberty & Property: The State Constitutional Conventions of the 1820s* (1966).

[156] *Id.*

revised or amended during this era to: expand the right to vote and hold office, by eliminating property requirements and religious tests; substitute popular elections for offices that had been appointed by either the legislature or a governor; and limit or restrict the legislature's right to act on a myriad of subjects.

Nearly all Jacksonian-era state constitutions added or expanded declarations of rights and, as in Delaware's 1831 Constitution, placed them at the beginning of the document.[157] In construing this portion of Delaware's Constitution, one court noted: "Most of the matters mentioned in the first article, are merely declaratory of the doctrines of the common law on the same subjects, formerly affirmed by the [M]agna [C]harta, in the year 1215, and afterwards by the bill of rights, in 1688, as the undoubted rights and liberties of the people of [England]."[158] The corollary to expanding the rights of the populace was often an enlargement of the educational provisions in state constitutions, because of the continuing belief that an informed civil conscience was needed in a democracy to resist challenges of self-interest and demagoguery.[159]

Virginia 1830

Virginia held a state constitutional convention in Richmond from October 5, 1829 until January 15, 1830. Its members included a future President of the United States, John Tyler; two former Presidents, James Monroe and James Madison; and the sitting Chief Justice of the United States, John Marshall. James Monroe was selected as the convention's president. The convention was called for the purpose of broadening the right of suffrage and providing for an equalization of representation.

The revised constitution provided for representation in both houses of the legislature from defined districts and for future reapportionment according to districts every ten years. Suffrage continued to be limited to white males who were at least 21 years of age and who also met various property requirements. The governor's term was increased to three years. A few changes were made to the legislative and judicial articles. The Virginia Bill of Rights was left intact. The revised Virginia Constitution of 1830 was ratified by a popular vote.[160]

---

[157] James A. Henretta, *Foreward: Rethinking the State Constitutional Tradition*, 22 RUTGERS L.J. 819, 819-26, 836-39 (1991).

[158] *Rice v. Foster*, 4 Harr. 479, 488 (Del. 1847).

[159] Daniel Walker Howe, *The Political Culture of the American Whigs* (Chicago: University of Chicago Press, 1979).

[160] Fletcher Green, Constitutional Development in the South Atlantic States, 1776-1860, at 210-224 (1930).

Mississippi 1832

The Mississippi Constitution of 1832 provided for universal suffrage for white males. It also provided for the election of state officials and judges. The purpose of these latter changes was to limit government and make it accountable.[161]

North Carolina 1835

Although many states re-wrote their constitutions completely during this era, it is noteworthy that during the 1835 Constitution Convention, North Carolina "chose to resolve their constitutional dispute by amending the existing document rather than by writing a new instrument."[162] In fact, the legislative act calling for the North Carolina Convention prohibited it initially from revising the bill of rights or any part of the Constitution not mentioned in the act.[163] An additional act was passed in 1834 that gave the convention discretionary power to consider additional subjects including: "the establishment of a tribunal for impeachment; the election of attorney-general for a term of years, the disqualification from office for conviction of crime; the removal of judges by two-thirds vote of the legislature; the limitation of the legislature in special legislation; and provision for future amendments of the constitution.[164]

The convention met at Raleigh on June 4, 1835. The leader of the Jeffersonian party in North Carolina, Nathaniel Macon, was selected as the convention's president. Ultimately, several important amendments were added to the North Carolina Constitution in 1835, for example: both houses of the legislature were limited in number and made more equal in representation; the sessions of the legislature were changed from annual to biennial; the governor would be elected by popular vote rather than by the legislature; and no private act could be introduced without thirty days notice.[165] In accordance with the democratic momentum of the times,

---

[161] Kermit L. Hall, "Mostly Anchor and Little Sail," The Evolution of American and State Constitutions *in* Paul Finkelman and Stephen E. Gottlieb, eds., *Toward a Usable Past: Liberty Under State Constitutions*, 402 (Athens: University of Georgia Press, 1991).

[162] John V. Orth, Symposium: "The Law of the Land": The North Carolina Constitution and State Constitutional Law: North Carolina Constitutional History, 70 N.C. L. REV. 1759, 1770 (1992), citing North Carolina Constitutional Convention, Proceedings and Debates of the Convention of North Carolina, Called to Amend the Constitution of the State, which assembled at Raleigh, June 4, 1835 to which are Subjoined the Convention Act and the Amendments to the Constitution (J. Gales 1836).

[163] Acts of the General Assembly of North Carolina, Session of 1833-34, ch. I, pp. 5-6.

[164] *Id.* at 5-7.

[165] Fletcher Green, Constitutional Development in the South Atlantic States, 1776-1860, at 232 (1930).

another change to the North Carolina Constitution in 1835 expanded the concept of constitutional amendment by extraordinary legislative action to also include submission for popular ratification.[166] After an extended debate, Article 32 of the North Carolina Constitution was amended to substitute the word "Christian" for the word "Protestant." It is interesting to note that the amendment to provide for the popular election of the governor was opposed at the North Carolina convention of 1835 based upon what the opponents viewed as its lack of success in Tennessee.[167]

Georgia 1830s

In 1839, Georgia enacted legislation calling for its second constitutional convention of the decade. Amendments proposed by an 1833 convention had been defeated at the polls. The act which called for the 1839 constitution convention in Georgia, like its predecessor, limited the convention's authority to two subjects: a reduction in the size of the legislature and an equalization of representation. The amendments proposed by the 1839 convention were also rejected by the voters of Georgia. In a letter transmitting that result to the legislature in December 1839, Governor Gilmer stated:

> The amendments to the constitution which were proposed to the people for ratification by the late convention, have been rejected by the most decided expression of public opinion. This is the second time that the people have refused to sanction the proceedings of conventions, held to reform the constitution; and in both instances have probably been induced to the course pursued, by the belief that the amendments offered for their approval, were intended for sectional or temporary party purposes.[168]

Notwithstanding Georgia's two unsuccessful efforts with constitutional conventions in the 1830s, several amendments were made to the Georgia Constitution during that decade by enactments passed in two successive legislative sessions: a limitation on legislative power to grant divorces, except with the concurrence of two special juries (1833); the elimination of property qualifications for legislative office (1834); and a reorganization of the judicial branch (1835).

Rhode Island's Dorr Rebellion

Although many states responded to popular demands for calling constitutional conventions in the 1830s, Rhode Island's legislature refused. In response to the legislature's resistance, an insurgent group held

---

[166] Don E. Fehrenbacher, Sectional Crisis and Southern Constitutionalism, 86 (Baton Rouge: Louisiana State University Press 1995).

[167] Fletcher Green, *Constitutional Development in the South Atlantic States, 1776-1860* (1930).

[168] *Georgia Journal*, December 5, 1839.

an extra-legal state constitutional convention in Rhode Island. Those citizens, who were frustrated by the sitting legislature's intransigence, not only drafted a new constitution but held elections pursuant to its terms. During 1831 and 1832, Rhode Island was in a state of turmoil. The competing claims to legitimacy, by what became two operating governments in Rhode Island, were resolved when vestiges of the Dorr Rebellion reached the United States Supreme Court.[169] That case was an action in trespass. It was an appeal from a Circuit Court of the United States.

The controversy arose from the efforts of the adherents of "the government established by a voluntary convention" to overthrow the established charter government.[170] The defendants asserted that their actions were authorized by the charter government during a period of martial law. The plaintiffs denied the legitimacy of the charter government following the establishment of the voluntary government. The Courts of Rhode Island had decided in favor of the charter government.

Thomas W. Dorr was elected governor pursuant to the state constitution for Rhode Island adopted by those who opposed the charter government. According to Dorr, the charter government had lost is republican character and was subject to being divested of its authority with the adoption of a new constitution by the ultimate sovereign of Rhode Island—its people. The question presented to the United States Supreme Court was which Rhode Island Constitution provided its citizens with a republican form of government as guaranteed to the constituents of every state by the United States Constitution. The United States Supreme Court concluded that question was inherently political in character. It held that whether a state's government was republican in form was a matter that the United States Constitution had committed exclusively to the legislative branch and that the decision of the legislature in that regard was binding upon the judiciary:

> Moreover, the constitution of the United States, as far as it has provided for an emergency of this kind, and authorized the general government to interfere in the domestic concerns of a State, has treated the subject as political in its nature, and placed the power in the hands of that department.

> The fourth section of the fourth article of the Constitution of the United States provided that the United States shall guarantee to every State in the Union a republican form of government, and shall protect each of them against invasion; and on the application of the legislature or of the executive (when the legislature cannot be convened) against domestic violence.

---

[169] *Luther v. Borden*, 7 How. 1 (1849).

[170] Pacific States Telephone & Telegraph Co. v. Oregon, 233 U.S. 118 (1912).

> Under this article of the Constitution it rests with congress to decide what government is the established one in a State. For, as the United States guarantee to each State a republican government, Congress must necessarily decide what government is established in the State before it can determine whether it is republican or not. And when the senators and representatives of a State are admitted into the councils of the Union, the authority of the government under which they are appointed, as well as its republican character, is recognized by the proper constitutional authority. And its decision is binding on every other department of the government, and could not be questioned in a judicial tribunal. It is true that the contest in this case did not last long enough to bring the matter to this issue; and as no senators or representatives were elected under the authority of the government of which Mr. Dorr was the head, congress was not called upon to decide the controversy. Yet the right to decide is placed there, and not in the courts.[171]

This holding would be of great significance following the Civil War. The official position of the Union during the Civil War had been that it was impossible for a state to secede. Therefore, when the conditions of re-admitting the Confederate states to the Union are described, it is more accurate to characterize the process, including the requirement of amending the state constitutions, as establishing conditions precedent to having the Senators and Representatives elected by the Confederate states seated in the United States Congress. In effect, Congress would not recognize the new constitutions of the former Confederate states, as providing a republican form of government, in the absence of compliance with the conditions that had been imposed.

G. ANTEBELLUM STATE CONSTITUTIONS

Special Privilege Limited

One of the recurring themes that influenced the writing or amending of state constitutions after 1840 was the desire to limit special privilege.[172] Efforts to ameliorate that concern resulted in either general or specific prohibitions on the enactment of "special" and "local" legislation.[173] A related fear, that special favors would be granted surreptitiously, was addressed in state constitutions by requirements that the title of every bill state its subject matter clearly and that every bill deal with only one

---

[171] Luther v. Borden, 7 HOW. 1 (1849).

[172] James W. Hurst, The Growth of American Law: The Law Makers 237-38, 240-46 (1950); *see* Michael F. Holt, *The Political Crisis of the 1850s* (1978).

[173] See generally Grace v. Howlett, 283 N.E.2d 474 (Ill. 1972); Vreeland v. Byrne, 370 A.2d 825 (N.J. 1977); Green, A Malapropian Provision of State Constitutions, 24 WASH. U. L.Q. 359 (1939); Horack, Special Legislation: Another Twilight Zone, 12 IND. L.J. 109 (1937); Sidney Z. Karasik, Equal Protection of the Law Under the Federal and Illinois Constitutions: A Contrast in Unequal Treatment, 30 DEPAUL L. REV. 263 (1981).

subject.[174] These same concerns are assuaged in state constitutional requirements designed to ensure full publicity and open deliberation regarding the merits of legislation, *e.g.*, three readings, reference to committee, and requirements for the recording of yea and nay votes.[175]

Manifest Destiny

During the middle of the 1840s, the most compelling national issue became America's Manifest Destiny. In 1845, a New York newspaper editor wrote that it was America's "manifest destiny to overspread and possess the whole of the continent which Providence has given us for the great experiment of liberty and federated self-government entrusted to us."[176] This external national focus was accompanied simultaneously by an interest in revising the internal processes of governing in some of the states that were extant.

Between 1848 and 1852, New Hampshire, Maryland, Virginia, Ohio, Indiana, Michigan, Wisconsin, Kentucky, and Louisiana adopted new state constitutions.[177] Significant amendments were added to constitutions in many states where completely new constitutions were not adopted. Massachusetts and Delaware drafted new constitutions but they were both rejected at the polls in 1853.

Direct Democracy and Legislative Restriction

The state constitutions enacted during this era reflected the popular demand for more direct democracy. The new constitutions provided for the direct popular election of many state and local officials, *e.g.*, judges, auditors, justices of the peace, and sheriffs, who had previously been appointed by governors or legislators.[178] In fact, "by 1861, twenty-four of the thirty-four states selected judges by election rather than by appointment."[179]

The new state constitutions also often restricted the power of legislatures to act in the economic realm. Almost all of the new state

---

[174] *See generally Turnbull v. Fink*, 668 A.2d 1370, 1381-91 (Del. 1995) (Holland, J., dissenting); Millard H. Ruud, *No Law Shall Embrace More Than One Subject*, 42 MINN. L. REV. 389 (1958).

[175] James W. Hurst, The Growth of American Law: The Law Makers 237-38, 240-46 (1950).

[176] Blum, Callon, Morgan, Schlecinger, Staupp and Woodward, The National Experience: A History of the United States 261 (Harcourt, Brace & World, Inc. 1963).

[177] Michael F. Holt, *The Political Crisis of the 1850s* 106 (John Wiley & Sons, Inc. 1978).

[178] *Id.* at 107.

[179] G. Alan Tarr, Constitutional Politics in the States, Contemporary Controversies and Historical Patterns 8 (Greenwood Press, 1996).

constitutions replaced annual sessions of the legislature with biennial sessions. "They also mandated a substantial amount of legislation concerning courts and governmental operations that the ensuing session of the legislature would have to pass to put the constitution into operation."[180] For example, in Indiana, it was reported in early 1852 that "[o]ur legislature is in session and are consuming much time remodeling the laws in unison with the new constitution."[181]

The new state constitutions of this era often imposed specific restrictions on the operations of banks chartered by the legislature. "Even before this period, the Louisiana Constitution of 1845 and the Arkansas Constitution of 1846 had banned the chartering of banks."[182] Accordingly, many of these constitutions resolved what had been major Jacksonian economic issues with regard to banking and currency.[183]

New York 1846

New York held a state constitutional convention in 1846.[184] The debates at that convention were a continuation of the rights-conscious dialogue that had dominated the state for almost two decades. The original 1777 Constitution of New York did not contain a bill of rights. The New York Constitution of 1821 had set forth a list of rights in Article VII. Article I of the 1846 New York Constitution, however, began by setting forth the rights of each "member of this State."[185] "The catalogue of rights in the New York Constitution of 1846 was so comprehensive that subsequent state conventions, in 1867, 1893, and 1915, incorporated it without significant change into the document they proposed for ratification. Only with the convention of 1938, which confronted problems created by the new society of the twentieth century, did New York's politically active classes begin to rethink this long-standing definition of citizens' rights."[186]

The 1846 convention in New York focused on the popular interest of the time in expanding suffrage rights. Ultimately, the concept of universal

---

[180] Michael F. Holt, *The Political Crisis of the 1850s*, p. 107 (John Wiley & Sons, Inc. 1978).

[181] *Id.*

[182] *Id.* at 108.

[183] *Id.*

[184] William B. Bishop and William H. Attree, *Report of the Debates and Proceedings of the Convention for the Revision of the Constitution of New York, 1846* (Albany: Evening Atlas, 1846).

[185] *Id.*

[186] James A. Henretta, *Foreward: Rethinking the State Constitutional Tradition*, 22 RUTGERS L.J. 819, 819-26, 836-39 (1991).

suffrage was not adopted by a majority of the convention's delegates. The right to vote was not extended to women.[187] The prior $250 property qualification for black voters was retained.[188] Article II, Section 1 of the 1846 New York Constitution, however, gave the right to vote to every white male who had been "a citizen for ten days, and an inhabitant of this State for one year."

The 1846 constitutional convention in New York was also confronted with a dilemma that existed in every state at the time: how to reconcile a continuing commitment to popular sovereignty with the influence exercised by an emergence of disciplined political parties. The disproportionate amount of power that had been vested intentionally in the legislative branch of government by the New York Constitution of 1777 was tempered by placing additional checks and more balance in the state constitutional separation of powers.

The 1846 convention decided to retain the gubernatorial veto power that New York had pioneered. Restrictions were added in the state constitution, however, on the governor's age and residency. The convention also decided to attenuate what was perceived to be the influence of a political party caucus by providing for the election of judges.[189] The 1846 New York Constitution did not only reallocate the separation of powers that had previously existed. It extended the authority of the judiciary and restricted the authority of the executive:

> The Constitution of 1846 laid the foundation for judicial protection of private property rights. Article VIII, section 3, explicitly extended to corporations many of the legal rights of "natural persons," thus bringing them under the protection of the due process clause of Article I, section 6. Likewise, Article V, section 8, diminished some of the traditional "police powers" of state governments. It abolished all state offices for "inspecting any merchandise, produce, manufacture, or commodity whatever." This laissez-faire administrative policy was the work of Jacksonian Democrats. It implemented their vision of a negative state by reducing "the patronage of government…[by] 500 officers." It also revealed a new confidence in the market system and in the ability of individual Americans to govern themselves in economics as well as politics.[190]

---

[187] William B. Bishop and William H. Attree, Report of the Debates and Proceedings of the Convention for the Revision of the Constitution of New York, 1846, (Albany: Evening Atlas, 1846).

[188] *Id.*

[189] N.Y. Const. of 1846, Art. VI, §§ 2, 4, 12, 14, 17; *see* Kermit L. Hall, *"The Judiciary on Trial: State Constitutional Reform and the Rise of an Elected Judiciary, 1846-1860,"* Historian 44 (May 1983).

[190] James A. Henretta, "The Rise and Decline of Democratic-Republicanism" Political Rights in New York and the Several States, 1800-1915 *in* Paul Finkelman and Stephen E. Gottlieb, eds., Toward a Usable Past: Liberty Under State Constitutions 77-78 (Athens: University of Georgia Press, 1991).

The 1846 Constitution also mandated the creation of a commission to codify the procedural law of New York. The result was "the origin of the Field codes that replaced common law pleading."[191]

The 1846 Constitution redressed the grievances of the so-called Rent Wars that had taken place during the late 1830s in the Helderberg Mountains. The farmers in that region south of Albany objected to the quitrents that they were required to pay to the descendants of the early Dutch patrons that had dominated land ownership in the Hudson and Mohawk valleys. The 1846 Constitution of New York abolished quitrents, prohibited long term agricultural leases, and provided for "fee simple tenure of allodial land."[192]

The 1846 convention also provided for state constitutional prohibitions on the legislature's authority to extend credit to private persons and limited the legislature's ability to incur public debt.[193] The 1846 New York Constitution also abolished legislative divorce, prohibited lotteries, restricted state indebtedness, and authorized general corporation acts, but prohibited special legislative charters except for banking corporations.[194]

California 1849

The California constitutional convention met in September 1849 at Monterey. The delegates were influenced by the constitutions of other states, in particular, the recently revised New York Constitution and the 1846 Iowa Constitution. Delegate William Gwin distributed copies of the Iowa Constitution and suggested that it be used as a "working standard." Some delegates recommended looking to other state constitutions for guidance, especially the 1846 New York Constitution.

The debates in the California convention, which preceded the final draft, involved a mix of parochial and national concerns: boundaries, suffrage, banking corporation, the rights of free "Negroes," and the expansion of slavery.[195] In the final analysis, "the Iowa and New York Constitutions lay behind virtually every section of the Californians'

---

[191] William M. Wiecek, State Protection of Personal Liberty: Remembering the Future, *in* Paul Finkelman and Stephen E. Gottlieb, eds., Toward a Usable Past: Liberty Under State Constitutions 371, 379-80 (Athens: University of Georgia Press, 1991).

[192] *Id.*

[193] N.Y. Const. 1846, Art. VII.

[194] William M. Wiecek, State Protection of Personal Liberty: Remembering the Future, *in* Paul Finkelman and Stephen E. Gottlieb, eds., Toward a Usable Past: Liberty Under State Constitutions 77-78 (Athens: University of Georgia Press, 1991).

[195] David Alan Johnson, Founding the Far West: California, Oregon, and Nevada, 1840-1890, at 101-04, 108, 120-21, 138-39, 140, 142, 189-90, 192-93 (University of California Press 1992).

document."[196] In fact, some sections of the Iowa Constitution were adopted verbatim.

Maryland 1850-1851

In 1850, Maryland enacted legislation calling for a state constitutional convention. The enabling legislation gave the convention complete power to revise the constitution with one exception: it was not permitted to change the extant state constitutional relationship between master and slave. The enabling legislation also required that the new constitution proposed by the convention had to be submitted to the voters of Maryland for ratification or rejection.[197]

The convention convened at Annapolis on November 4, 1850 and adjourned on May 15, 1851. The revised constitution was approved by Maryland's voters. The prior Maryland Constitution was virtually rewritten. A new Article 41 urged the legislature to encourage knowledge, virtue, literature, science, agriculture, manufacturing, and commerce.[198] The governor's term was increased to four years but his former appointment powers were changed by providing for those offices to be elected. Legislative sessions were limited to a period from January to March of each year. Legislative powers were eliminated or restricted on a diverse range of subjects: divorce, debts, lotteries, the power to charter banks and corporations, and the property rights of married women. The new Maryland Constitution provided for the election of judges and also created the elective office of comptroller.[199]

Virginia 1850-1851

In October 1850, the Virginia "Reform Convention of 1850-51" met in Richmond. It continued its work until August 1, 1851. One of the most important issues debated by the convention was the proper basis for representation.[200] At this time, Virginia was "one of the last two states in the Union to accept free white manhood suffrage."[201] The 1851 Constitution expanded suffrage by making age, residence, and white male citizenship the only requirements for voting. The legislature was

---

[196] Id.

[197] Fletcher Green, Constitutional Development in the South Atlantic States, 1776-1860, at 276 (1930).

[198] Id. at 284.

[199] Id. at 286.

[200] Id. at 290.

[201] Wythe Holt, *Virginia's Constitutional Convention of 1901-1902*, at 1-2, 24-25, 30-31, 104-05, 109, 254 (Garland Publishing, Inc. 1990).

reorganized and it was subjected to specific constitution obligations and restrictions, for example:

> It might restrict the emancipation of slaves, and any freed Negro who remained in the state longer than one year was to lose his freedom. Taxation was to be equal and uniform throughout the state, except that slaves were not to be taxed until 12 years of age, and then only at the rate of $300 per capita. A capitation tax might be laid on white males over 21 years of age equal to the tax on property valued at $200. An equal moiety of this was to be used for primary and free schools. The legislature might bar from office, by law, all persons who engaged in a duel. It could require registration for voting, the registration of births, deaths, and marriages, and the taking of a census five years after each national census. It could also levy taxes on income, salaries, or licenses. Among the prohibitions were the granting of divorces, establishment of lotteries, chartering of churches or religious denominations, pledging the faith or binding the state for the debt of corporations, or contracting any debt for a longer period than 34 years. Should it incur debts it was to set aside annually a sum equal to one per cent above the annual interest to add to the sinking fund. A sinking fund was to be created by setting aside seven per cent of the annual revenue of the state.[202]

With regard to the executive branch of government, the 1851 Virginia Constitution provided for the governor to be popularly elected, created the office of lieutenant governor, and also created a board of public works. The judicial branch was changed to provide terms of office rather than life tenure, selection of the judiciary by popular election, and removal by a concurrent majority of both houses in addition to the traditional impeachment process.[203]

Crime Control Concerns

The state constitutional debates of the 1850s continued to be concerned with traditional American concerns about "due process" protections against government oppression but also introduced what is now characterized as the competing theme of "crime control."[204] For example, Article VII section 17 in the Indiana Constitution of 1851 provided that "the General Assembly may modify or abolish the Grand Jury system." The debates about this proposal reflected a concern about whether faster criminal proceedings would deter crime and how much personal liberty might be affected if criminal proceedings were initiated

---

[202] Fletcher Green, Constitutional Development in the South Atlantic States, 1776-1860, at 295 (1930).

[203] *Id.* at 296.

[204] Herbert Packer, The Limits of the Criminal Sanction (Stanford: Stanford University Press, 1968).

more expeditiously by the filing of informations rather than indictments.[205] Many years later, a provision in the California Constitution that made the grand jury optional was upheld by the United States Supreme Court on the rationale that although the grand jury had once been a guard "against executive usurpation and tyranny" it should not be permitted to undermine or obstruct the "just and necessary discretion of legislative power.[206]

Bible Reading Challenged

The first state supreme court case to address Bible reading in public schools was decided by Maine in 1854.[207] In that case, a Catholic student relied upon the state constitution in refusing to read the King James Bible, as required by the public school's curriculum. The majority opinion affirmed the Catholic student's expulsion and held that the proper forum to resolve the issue was in the legislature rather than the state courts:

> The legislature establishes general rules for the guidance of its citizens. It does not necessarily follow that they are unconstitutional, nor that a citizen is to be legally absolved from obedience, because they may conflict with his conscientious views of religious duty or right. To allow this would be to subordinate the State to the individual conscience. A law is not unconstitutional, because it may prohibit what a citizen may conscientiously think right, or require what he may conscientiously think wrong. The State is governed by its own views of duty. The right or wrong of the State, is the right or wrong as declared by legislative Acts constitutionally passed.[208]

For many decades, thereafter, the religious values of the majority prevailed in most states. In the Cincinnati Bible case, the majoritarian approach resulted in the rejection of a religious challenge to a majority decision to prohibit Bible reading in public schools.[209] More frequently, however, state constitutions either encouraged or permitted religious instruction to promote civic morality and only prohibited "sectarian" uses of the Bible in public schools.[210]

---

[205] *See* David J. Bodenhamer, The Pursuit of Justice: Crime and Law in Antebellum Indiana (New York: Garland, 1986); *see also* Brent E. Dickson, *Lawyers and Judges as Framers of Indiana's 1851 Constitution*, 30 INDIANA L. REV. 397 (1997).

[206] *Hustado v. California*, 110 U.S. 516 (1884).

[207] *Donahoe v. Richards*, 38 Me. 376 (1854).

[208] *Id.* at 376, 410.

[209] *Board of Education of Cincinnati v. Minor*, 23 Ohio St. 211 (1872). *See also Nessle v. Hum*, 1 Ohio N.P. 140 (1894).

[210] *See* Samuel W. Brown, *The Secularization of American Education as Shown by State Legislation, State Constitutional Provisions and State Supreme Court Decisions* (New York: Bureau of Publications, Teachers College, Columbia University, 1912).

Oregon 1857

Oregon held a state constitutional convention in 1857 at Salem. The Oregonian delegates were influenced most strongly by the Indiana Constitution. They also looked for guidance in the state constitutions of Ohio, Michigan, Iowa and Wisconsin.[211]

Nevada 1864

In 1864, Nevada delegates convened in Carson City to write a state constitution. At the time, not only was America in the middle of Civil War but Nevada miners were experiencing an economic crisis. From the outset, the Nevada delegates, "viewed the task before them narrowly, concerned with affirming loyalty to the Union and constructing a charter that would help resolve the economic crisis."[212]

H. ANTEBELLUM INDIVIDUAL RIGHTS

Although state constitutions afforded the primary protection of individual property rights and liberty interests in the antebellum years, the Supremacy Clause was periodically invoked by the United States Supreme Court to reconcile apparently conflicting and often competing interests involving contracts.[213] and matters of interstate commerce.[214] There was one conspicuous area, however, in which state constitutions and statutes were consistently unsuccessful in the face of Federal Constitutional challenges, during the antebellum years. That was the effort of some states to provide individual liberty rights for slaves when their owners asserted federal property protections.[215] Conversely, limitations on the individual liberty of slaves in the constitutions of southern states were upheld. The nadir of this jurisprudence was reached in 1857 by the *Dred Scott* decision.[216]

In *Dred Scott*, the United States Supreme Court held that blacks had never been citizens of the United States. In reaction to that opinion, the Republican controlled legislature of New York proposed an equal suffrage

---

[211] David Alan Johnson, Founding the Far West: California, Oregon, and Nevada, 1840-1890 (University of California Press, 1992).

[212] *Id.*

[213] *Fletcher v. Peck*, 10 U.S. (6 Cranch) 87 (1810); *Dartmouth College v. Woodard*, 17 U.S. (4 Wheat) 518 (1819). Nevertheless, certain economic interests were held to be subject to state law and state constitutions. *E.g., Charles River Bridge & Co. v. Warren Bridge Co.*, 36 U.S. (11 Pet.) 420 (1837).

[214] *Gibbons v. Ogden*, 22 U.S. (9 Wheat) 1 (1824) and *The Passanger Cases*, 48 U.S. (7 How.) 283 (1849).

[215] *Prigg v. Pennsylvania*, 41 U.S. (16 Pet.) 539 (1842).

[216] *Dred Scott v. Sandford*, 60 U.S. (19 How.) 393 (1857).

amendment to the New York Constitution. The *New York Tribune* wrote that the proposed amendment would "carry back the State Constitutions to those principles upon which they were originally established."[217] Although a majority of New Yorkers voted to elect Abraham Lincoln President, a greater majority voted to defeat the proposed equal suffrage amendment to the New York Constitution.[218]

Nevertheless, in 1860, the highest court of New York declined to follow the *ratio decidendi* of *Dred Scott*.[219] The New York Court of Appeals held that slaves, who were brought into the state voluntarily, became free. The United States Supreme Court was never called upon to review that New York decision.

With the advent of the Civil War, the slavery debate moved from the courtroom into the battlefields. Ultimately, the United States Supreme Court never had to reconsider *Dred Scott*. Following the Civil War, that holding was overruled by the Reconstruction Amendments to the United States Constitution.

I. RECONSTRUCTION REVISIONS

CONFEDERATE STATES' CONSTITUTIONS

President Andrew Johnson announced his plans for Reconstruction in two proclamations that were issued on May 29, 1865. At the same time, he appointed William W. Holden as the provisional governor of North Carolina. President Johnson directed Governor Holden to "call a convention to amend the state's prewar constitution so as to create a 'republican form of government' that would entitle North Carolina to its right within the Union."[220] Any person who had not been pardoned by the President's first proclamation was prohibited from voting for delegates to the state constitutional convention. Similar edicts were issued subsequently for the other confederate states. Constitutional conventions began to assemble in the summer of 1865. Mississippi's was the first to convene in mid-August. Initially, President Johnson only wanted the Confederate states to "acknowledge the abolition of slavery and repudiate

---

[217] James A. Henretta, The Rise and Decline of "Democratic-Republicanism" Political Rights *in* New York and the Several States, 1800-1915; Paul Finkelman and Stephen E. Gottlieb, eds., Toward a Usable Past: Liberty Under State Constitutions (Athens: University of Georgia Press, 1991).

[218] See Phyllis F. Field, The Politics of Race in New York: *The Struggle for Black Suffrage in the Civil War Era* (Ithaca: Cornell University Press, 1982).

[219] People v. Lemmon, 20 N.Y. 526 (1860).

[220] Eric Foner, Reconstruction: America's Unfinished Revolution, 1863-1877, at 183 (Harper Collins Publishers, Inc. 1988).

secession."[221] In October, however, President Johnson also directed the seceding states to void debts they had incurred on behalf of the Confederacy. Texas wrote a constitution in 1866. It abolished slavery and nullified secession. In most other regards, it followed the 1845 Constitution that preceded it.

The Reconstruction Act of 1867 set forth the final and definitive requirements for recognition of a state's Congressional delegation after the Civil War.[222] With the exception of Tennessee, the eleven Confederate states were divided into five military districts. The Reconstruction Act provided that a state government could be created and recognized by writing a new state constitution that provided for manhood suffrage and was approved by a majority of registered voters. The other condition precedent to Congressional recognition was ratification of the Fourteenth Amendment.

North Carolina 1868

North Carolina called for a constitutional convention in 1868 at the initiative of the United States Congress.[223] The federally mandated changes were incorporated in the draft of its new state constitution, e.g., "Every citizen of this State owes paramount allegiance to the Constitution and government of the United States."[224] Following the ratification of that new state constitution and the Fourteenth Amendment to the United States Constitution, North Carolina's Senators and Representatives were seated in Congress.[225]

Virginia 1869

In 1868, a convention framed the new Virginia Constitution. It not only prohibited slavery but afforded equal civil and political rights to all citizens.[226] The new Virginia Constitution provided for state funding of a

---

[221] Id.

[222] Id. at 276-77.

[223] John V. Orth, Symposium: "The Law of the Land": The North Carolina Constitution and State Constitutional Law: North Carolina Constitutional History, 70 N.C. L. REV. 1759, 1776 (1992).

[224] N.C. Const., 1878, art. I, § 4, in Sources and Documents of United States Constitutions, 7:415 (William Swindler ed., Dobbs Ferry, N.Y.: Oceana Publications, 1973-78).

[225] John V. Orth, Symposium: "The Law of the Land": The North Carolina Constitution and State Constitutional Law: North Carolina Constitutional History, 70 N.C. L. REV. 1759, 1781 (1992).

[226] Wythe Holt, Virginia's Constitutional Convention of 1901-1902, at 1-2, 24-25, 30-31, 104-05, 109, 254 (Garland Publishing, Inc. 1990).

public school system.[227] The 1869 Virginia Constitution also enacted several provisions that were designed to enhance the democratic process, *e.g.*, secret ballot; annual legislative sessions; expansion of the number of elective offices through the creation of townships; and removal of legislative and executive functions from the county courts.[228] Many of the reforms in what has been characterized as the Virginia "carpetbagger Underwood Constitution" of 1869 have been attributed to the occupation of federal troops.[229]

Texas 1869

Texas wrote another state constitution in 1869. It provided for a centralized state government. It expanded the gubernatorial power of appointment. It introduced a state-financed public school system. It also maintained the bill of rights from the 1845 Texas Constitution, as it had done in 1866.[230]

J. FOURTEENTH AMENDMENT

AFFECTS STATE SOVEREIGNTY

The Fourteenth Amendment fundamentally altered the original balance of power in the United States Constitution, by expanding federal power at the expense of state autonomy.[231] The first section of the Fourteenth Amendment contains prohibitions expressly directed at the states.[232] "No State shall...deny to any person within its jurisdiction the equal protection of the laws."[233] The fifth section of that amendment provides that "[t]he Congress shall have the power to enforce, by appropriate legislation, the provisions of this article."[234]

The Civil War was a cataclysmic alternative to a continuation of the philosophical debate about dual sovereignty and federalism within the United States.[235] That controversy had continued almost unabated since

---

[227] *Id.*

[228] *Id.*

[229] *Id.*

[230] John Walker Mauer, State Constitutions in a Time of Crisis: The Case of the Texas Constitution of 1876, 68 TEX. L. REV. 1615 (1990).

[231] N.C. Const., 1878, art. I, § 4, *in* Sources and Documents of United States Constitutions, 7:415 (William Swindler ed., Dobbs Ferry, N.Y.: Oceana Publications, 1973-78).

[232] City of Rome v. United States, 446 U.S. 156, 179 (1980).

[233] U.S. Const. amend. XIV, § 1.

[234] U.S. Const. amend. XIV, § 5; *see Fitzpatrick v. Bitzer*, 427 U.S. 445, 453 (1976).

[235] *See* Phillip S. Paludan, *The American Civil War Considered as a Crisis in Law and Order*, 77 AMER. HIST. REV. 1021 (1972).

the Constitutional Convention of 1787. Extreme states' rights theorists adhered to the Anti-Federalist view that sovereignty remained vested in the People of each state. For the Federalists, sovereignty resided with the People of the United States as a whole.[236]

Following the Civil War, the Reconstruction Amendments to the United States Constitution strengthened the Federalists' view of popular sovereignty and significantly influenced the operation of dual sovereignty in state constitutions. The states that had attempted to secede from the Union were required to amend their state constitutions in certain respects and to ratify the Fourteenth Amendment as a condition precedent to having their delegations seated in the United States House of Representatives and Senate.

According to Senator Jacob M. Howard of Michigan, the specific purpose of the Fourteenth Amendment was to protect "the personal rights guaranteed...by the first eight amendments of the [United States] Constitution."[237] Until the adoption of the Fourteenth Amendment in 1868, the federal Bill of Rights protected individual rights and liberties solely against encroachment by the federal government.[238] In the *Slaughterhouse Cases* and the *Civil Rights Cases*, the United States Supreme Court held that the Reconstruction Amendments were intended to protect former slaves and their decedents.[239] In 1884, however, the

---

[236] A current majority of the United States Supreme Court appears to adhere to the view that "We the People" means ultimate sovereignty resides with a single national populace rather than with the people of the individual states. See U.S. Term Limits, Inc. v. Thornton, 115 S.Ct. 1842, 1875 (1995) (Kennedy, J. concurring). But see U.S. Term Limits, Inc. v. Thornton, 115 S. Ct. at 1875 (Thomas, J., dissenting, joined by Rehnquist, C.J., O'Connor, J., and Scalia, J.) ("The ultimate source of the Constitution's authority is the consent of the people of each individual State, not the consent of the undifferentiated people of the Nation as a whole."). See Akhil Reed Amar, *Of Sovereignty and Federalism*, 96 YALE L.J. 1425, 1429 (1987).

[237] U.S. Congress, Senate, Globe, 39th Cong., 1st Sess., 2765 (1865-66), *quoted in* Richard C. Cortner, *The Supreme Court and the Second Bill of Rights: The Fourteenth Amendment and the Nationalization of Civil Liberties* 5 (Madison: University of Wisconsin Press, 1981).

[238] Gerald Gunther, Constitutional Law 422-40 (11th ed. 1985); *la*, 32 U.S. (7 Pet.) 243 (1833); *see also* Shirley S. Abrahamson, *Divided We Stand: State Constitutions in a More Perfect Union*, 18 HASTINGS CONST. L.Q. 723, 727-28 (1991); Stanley Mosk, *State Constitutionalism: Both Liberal and Conservative*, 63 TEX. L. REV. 1081, 1081-82 (1985); Stewart G. Pollock, *Adequate and Independent State Grounds as a Means of Balancing the Relationship Between State and Federal Courts*, 63 TEX. L. REV. 977, 979 (1985).

[239] *Slaughterhouse Cases*, 83 U.S. (16 Wall.) 36 (1873), *Civil Rights Cases*, 109 U.S. 3 (1883).

United States Supreme Court held that the Fourteenth Amendment did *not* require states to adhere to the provisions of the Bill of Rights.[240]

The major exceptions to the United States Supreme Court's general refusal to construe the Fourteenth Amendment as imposing national standards of rights or liberties on the states were in cases about private property and liberty of contract. In 1897, the United States Supreme Court held that under the Due Process clause of the Fourteenth Amendment the states could not take private property without just compensation.[241] In 1905, the United States Supreme Court further held that the Due Process clause of the Fourteenth Amendment could be applied to freedom of contract. That same term the Supreme Court reaffirmed its prior holding that the adoption of the Fourteenth Amendment did not make *all* of the Bill of Rights binding upon the States.[242] In 1908, however, the Supreme Court upheld a state law regulating the hours women could work, in the context of a Due Process challenge, as a reasonable restriction on contract rights.[243]

Between 1890 and 1910, a trilogy of cases from three different states relied upon equal protection principles in their state constitutions to invalidate Bible reading in public schools.[244] Those courts concluded that state constitutional principles of equal protection included the formation of a moral conscience. Those states rejected the argument that there should be a unified public conscience and that it should be Christian.[245] Most state supreme courts, however, continued to construe their state constitution as permitting the majority to control the issue of Bible reading in public schools.[246] In 1940, the United States Supreme Court held that the religion clauses of the First Amendment applied to the states by virtue of the incorporation doctrine and the Fourteenth Amendment's expanded protections.[247]

---

[240] *Huratado v. California*, 110 U.S. 516 (1884). The Court reaffirmed this idea in *Maxwell v. Dow*, 176 U.S. 581 (1900), and *Twining v. New Jersey*, 211 U.S. 78 (1908).

[241] Chicago, Burlington & Quincy Railroad Co. v. Chicago, 166 U.S. 226 (1897).

[242] Lochner v. New York, 198 U.S. 45 (1905).

[243] Muller v. Oregon, 208 U.S. 412 (1908).

[244] Weiss v. District Board, 76 Wis. 177 (1890); State ex rel. Freeman v. Scheve, 65 Neb. 853 (1902); People v Board of Educ., 245 Ill.334 (1910).

[245] *Id.*

[246] Alvin W. Johnson, The Legal Status of Church-State Relationships in the United States (Minneapolis: University of Minnesota Press, 1934).

[247] Cantwell v. Connecticut, 310 U.S. 296 (1940).

K. RECONSTRUCTION AND BEYOND

Following the Civil War, the Reconstruction era was marked by popular interest in governmental reform. There was widespread debate not only over the proper role of government in American life, but also its structure and operation. Between 1864 and 1879, thirty-seven new state constitutions were written and ratified.[248] Within that same time period, however, the voters rejected new constitutions that were proposed in Michigan, Nebraska, New York, and Ohio.[249] Delaware Republicans called unsuccessfully for a new constitution in 1874 "as a means of securing the reforms that are so much needed in the organic law of the State, and of keeping pace with the enlightened progress of the age, and with our sister States."[250]

Illinois 1870

The 1870 Illinois Constitution revised the judiciary, strengthened the executive branch, and included several specific prohibitions on the legislature's authority to act. The Illinois Constitution of 1870 also included specific provisions relating to the regulation of: grain elevators and warehouses; as well as freight and passenger railroad tariffs.[251] The rapid expansion of railroads in the three decades after the Civil War gave rise to many regulatory amendments in state constitutions to temper the results that had been yielded by the encouraging effect of earlier state constitutional provisions. With the adoption of a "damage clause," the 1870 Illinois Constitution also introduced an important change in the concept of eminent domain, *e.g.*, compensation for damage, in addition to compensation for a "taking" and the right to have a jury determine the value of the private property owner's loss.[252]

North Carolina 1875

An effort to replace North Carolina's "carpetbagger" constitution of 1868 was defeated in 1870. In 1875, the legislature called for a state constitutional convention. Thirty amendments to the 1868 North Carolina Constitution were proposed and ratified by the voters in 1876. After those amendments were incorporated into the text, it became customary to refer

---

[248] Morton Keller, Affairs of State: Public Life in Late Nineteenth Century America 111 (The Belknap Press of Harvard University 1977).

[249] *Id.*

[250] *Id.* at 112.

[251] Kermit L. Hall, "Mostly Anchor and Little Sail," The Revolution of American and State Constitutions *in* Paul Finkelman and Stephen E. Gottlieb, eds., Toward a Usable Past: Liberty Under State Constitutions 404 (Athens: University of Georgia Press, 1991).

[252] *Id.*

to the amended 1868 constitution as the North Carolina Constitution of 1876.[253]

Segregation and Suffrage

Notwithstanding the enactment of the Reconstruction Amendments to the United States Constitution, provisions for mandatory racial segregation and other requirements that perpetuated racial discrimination were made a part of several state constitutions throughout the balance of the nineteenth century. The Tennessee Constitution of 1870, for example, provided that no school receiving state funds "shall allow white and negro children to be received as scholars together."[254] The "separate but equal" doctrine was approved by the United States Supreme Court in 1896.[255]

The corollary of mandatory segregation in state constitutions was often disfranchisement. Although the Reconstruction Amendments were successful in extending the right of suffrage to blacks, that expansion was frequently curtailed by provisions in state constitutions. In 1898, the United States Supreme Court upheld both the poll tax and the literacy provisions in the 1890 Mississippi Constitution.[256] In 1915, however, the United States Supreme Court decided that the grandfather clauses in several southern state constitutions violated the United States Constitution.[257] Those provisions had exempted the sons and grandsons of white voters during the Civil War from the subsequently enacted property and educational qualifications for voting.

Texas 1875

Texas assembled a state constitutional convention at Austin in August of 1875. The 1876 Texas Constitution was influenced by the agrarian reform movement. The *Grange*, in particular, had a dominant role at the convention.

The Texas convention was not only cognizant but also influenced by national trends in state constitution-making. Accordingly, many new sections were added in an effort to either restrict or limit legislative power. "Eleven of the 18 new sections of the Legislative Article were taken in whole or in part from the Missouri Constitution of 1875 and several others were copied almost verbatim from the Pennsylvania Constitution of 1873,

---

[253] John V. Orth, *Symposium: "The Law of the Land": The North Carolina Constitution and State Constitutional Law: North Carolina Constitutional History*, 70 N.C. L. REV. 1759, 1782 (1992).

[254] Tenn. Const., 1879, art. XI, § 12, *in* Sources and Documents, 9:186 (Swindler, ed.).

[255] *Plessy v. Ferguson*, 163 U.S. 537 (1896).

[256] *Williams v. Mississippi*, 170 U.S. 213 (1898).

[257] *Guinn v. U.S.*, 238 U.S. 347 (1915).

including section 56 that enumerated 29 specific topics of special or local laws that the legislature was prohibited from passing.[258] The 1876 Texas Constitution also provided for the direct election of judges.

Missouri 1876

The Missouri Constitution of 1876 introduced the concept of granting home rule to local municipalities.[259] Home rule authorized local communities to incorporate and operate autonomously within the parameters set by the state constitution. The trend of sharing power within each state between multiple political subdivisions continues today.

California 1879

The 1879 California Constitution was written by a convention that was dominated by Democrats and the Workingman's party.[260] That constitution provided for the regulation of railroads, banks, and mining companies. It also included several anti-Chinese provisions. State funding for public education was restricted to primary schools.[261]

Restricting Political Party Influence

State constitutions enacted during Reconstruction frequently restricted the power of party government within the state legislatures. This was accomplished by giving veto powers to the executive; mandating limits on state debts; requiring budgets to be balanced; regulating the legislative process to deter log-rolling; limiting state interference with local government, *e.g.*, with "ripper clauses,"[262] or home rule charters; giving local government "options" in limited areas, *e.g.*, the sale of alcohol; and as in Delaware's 1897 Constitution, by requiring political balance within the judiciary.[263] Consequently, by the end of the nineteenth century, a generation of state constitutional revisions had circumscribed the authority of the state government in a variety of procedural and substantive ways.

---

[258] Janice C. May, The Texas State Constitution: A Reference Guide, p. 13 (Greenwood Press, 1996).

[259] William F. Swindler, *Missouri Constitutions: History, Theory and Practice*, 23 MISSOURI L. REV. 35-37 (January 1958).

[260] Morton Keller, Affairs of State: Public Life in Late Nineteenth Century America 111-14 (The Belknap Press of Harvard University, 1977).

[261] *Id.*

[262] David O. Porter, *The Ripper Clause In State Constitutional Law: An Early Urban Experiment - Part I*, 1969 UTAH L. REV. 287, 306-11 (1969).

[263] Del. Const. art. IV, § 3.

Omnibus Act 1889

In 1889, four states were admitted to the Union: North Dakota, South Dakota, Montana, and Washington. In February 1889, Congress had authorized each of their state constitutional conventions in an Omnibus Act. Each of these new states' constitutions included sections that not only framed the structure of government but also provided for its administration, primarily by placing limitations on the legislature, the executive, and the judiciary. Each legislature was restricted with regard to special legislation, private legislation, corporations, and public credit. The governors' powers were restricted, *e.g.*, the power of appointment. Each of these four state constitutions modified the jury system and other traditional provisions in the judicial articles of the constitutions in other states. These four constitutions also provided for the election of administrative officers.

Idaho 1889

On July 4, 1889, delegates from the territory of Idaho convened in Boise City to write a state constitution. The Idaho Territory had originally been severed from the Washington territory in 1863 to keep the capital of Washington in Olympia. The Idaho Territory was later divided to create the Montana Territory and the Wyoming Territory. The impetus for statehood in the remaining Idaho Territory was a proposal to subdivide it further by annexing the northern portion to either Washington or Montana and southern Idaho to Nevada. In fact, Congress agreed to annex northern Idaho to Washington in 1887, but the bill was pocket vetoed by President Cleveland.[264]

The Idaho constitutional convention was called by its Territorial Governor Edward A. Stevenson without either an enabling act from Congress or any authorizing action by the territorial legislature.[265] Although there was only limited precedent for such action, there was a sense of urgency in proceeding. The Idaho Constitution has been characterized as "extraordinarily important because it is a charter for the framework of decision."[266] Idaho's Constitution established institutional procedures for reaching decisions within the process of state government. One measure of that success is its continuous operation for more than a century later.[267]

---

[264] Dennis C. Colson, *Idaho's Constitution: The Tie That Binds* 1, 4-6, 220-23 (University of Idaho, 1991).

[265] *Id.*

[266] *Id.*

[267] *Id.*

L. PROGRESSIVE ERA POTPOURRI

TWENTIETH CENTURY BEGINS

As the nineteenth century was drawing to a close, one commentator, James Bryce, noted that state constitutions included many provisions that did not relate to the structure of state governments, *e.g.*, "minute provisions regarding the management and liabilities of banking companies, or railways, or corporations generally.[268] Bryce also remarked on an escalation in the trend to disregard any distinction between those provisions which were properly of constitutional dimensions and those subjects which were better addressed by statutes. "Following the Civil War, Bryce detected a transformation in which not only did state constitutions gradually lose the power to mold conclusively the course of public policies in [internal] areas they once exclusively dominated, but their prestige in relation to the [United States] Constitution also plummeted."[269]

Alabama 1901

"The Alabama Constitution Convention of 1901 was part of a movement that swept the post-Reconstruction South to disenfranchise blacks."[270] John B. Knox was president of the all-white convention. In his opening address to the delegates, he stated: "And what is it that we want to do? Why it is within the limits imposed by the Federal Constitution to establish white supremacy in this State."[271]

Article VIII, Section 182 of the Alabama Constitution of 1901 provided for the disenfranchisement of anyone convicted of certain enumerated crimes and "any crime…involving moral turpitude." In 1985, the United States Supreme Court was called upon to decide "the constitutionality of Article VIII, Section 182 of the Alabama Constitution of 1901" in the context of an allegation that the neutrally written state law produced disproportionate effects along racial lines.[272] The United States Supreme Court held:

> Without deciding whether sec. 182 would be valid if enacted today without any
> impermissible motivation, we simply observe that its original enactment was

---

[268] James Bryce, The American Commonwealth 1:116 (Louis Hacker ed., New York: Capricorn Books, G.P. Putnam's Sons, 1959).

[269] Kermit L. Hall, "Mostly Anchor and Little Sail," The Evolution of American and State Constitutions *in* Paul Finkelman and Stephen E. Gottlieb, eds., Toward a Usable Past: Liberty Under State Constitutions 403 (Athens: University of Georgia Press, 1991).

[270] *Hunter v. Underwood*, 471 U.S. 222 (1985).

[271] 1 Official Proceedings of the Constitution Convention of the State of Alabama 8, May 21st, 1901 to September 3d 1901 (1940).

[272] *Hunter v. Underwood*, 471 U.S. 222 (1985).

motivated by a desire to discriminate against blacks on account of race and the section continues to this day to have that effect. As such, it violates equal protection ....

The record on appeal included "the proceedings before the convention, several historical studies, and the testimony of two expert historians."[273]

Initiative

Thirteen states changed their constitutions between 1898 and 1913 to provide for popular initiatives.[274] Such provision permitted voters to propose state constitution amendments.[275] State constitutional provisions for initiatives were enacted during the same period that nineteen states were authorizing legislation by initiatives and twenty-two states were permitting the electorate to accept or reject specific laws by popular referendum.[276]

Enabling Act Incursions

Congressional efforts to control the provisions of state constitutions as a prerequisite to approval for admission to the Union continued in the twentieth century. For example, on June 20, 1910, Congress passed an Enabling Act that authorized the Territory of New Mexico to form a constitution. When New Mexico subsequently applied for admission to the Union, however, the constitution that it had adopted was not acceptable. The Congress of the United States passed a joint resolution on August 21, 1911, that required the electors of New Mexico to amend its proposed state constitution as a condition precedent to admission. On January 6, 1912, President William Howard Taft issued a Proclamation that:

> in accordance with the provisions of the Act of Congress and the joint resolution of Congress herein named, declare and proclaim the fact that the fundamental conditions imposed by Congress on the State of New Mexico to entitle that State to admission have been ratified and accepted, and that the admission of the State into the Union on an equal footing with the other States is now complete.[277]

In 1911, at about the same time that Congress directed that the proposed constitution for New Mexico had to be amended, the United States Supreme Court upheld a challenge to Oklahoma's refusal to adhere

---

[273] *Id.*

[274] G. Alan Tarr, Constitutional Politics in the States, Contemporary Controversies and Historical Patterns 11 (Greenwood Press, 1996)).

[275] *Id.*

[276] *Id.*

[277] Reprinted in Robert F. Williams, State Constitution Law, Cases and Materials 79-80 (2d ed. Michie, 1993).

to a provision in its Enabling Act subsequent to Oklahoma's admission to the Union.[278] The Oklahoma Enabling Act provided, in part:

> The capital of said State shall temporarily be at the city of Guthrie, and shall not be changed therefrom previous to Anno Domini Nineteen Hundred and Thirteen, but said capital shall after said year be located by the electors of said State at an election to be provided for by the legislature; provided, however, that the legislature of said State, except as shall be necessary for the convenient transaction of the public business of said State at said capital, shall not appropriate any public moneys of the State for the erection of buildings for capital purposes during said period.[279]

Oklahoma was admitted to statehood on November 16, 1907. On December 29, 1910, its legislature passed an act that provided for the immediate removal of the capital from Guthrie to Oklahoma City. That statute was upheld by the Supreme Court of Oklahoma. Upon appeal to the United States Supreme Court, the question before it for review was framed as: "whether the provision of the enabling act was a valid limitation upon the power of the State after its admission, which overrides any subsequent state legislation repugnant thereto."[280] The United States Supreme Court then noted:

> The power to locate its own seat of government and to determine when and how it shall be changed from one place to another, and to appropriate its own public funds for that purpose, are essentially and peculiarly state powers. That one of the original thirteen States could now be shorn of such powers by an act of Congress would not be for a moment entertained. The question then comes to this: Can a State be placed upon a plane of inequality with its sister States in the Union if the Congress chooses to impose conditions which so operate, at the time of its admission?[281]

In analyzing the issue presented, the United States Supreme Court determined that America was "a union of States equal in power, dignity, and authority, each competent to exert that residuum of sovereignty not delegated to the United States by the Constitution itself."[282] This premise led it to hold:

> ...when a new State is admitted into the Union, it is so admitted with all of the powers of sovereignty and jurisdiction which pertain to the original States, and that such powers may not be constitutionally diminished, impaired or shorn away by any conditions, compacts or stipulations embraced in the act under

---

[278] *Coyle v. Smith*, 221 U.S. 559 (1911).

[279] *Id.*

[280] *Id.*

[281] *Id.*

[282] *Id.*

which the new State came into the Union, which would not be valid and effectual if the subject of congressional legislation after admission.[283]

Therefore, the United States Supreme Court held that "by virtue of her jurisdictional sovereignty as a State," Oklahoma was entitled to "determine for her own people the proper location of the local seat of government."[284]

Arizona

President Taft visited the territory of Arizona in October 1909. During speeches in Phoenix and Prescott, he advised its citizens not to model their state constitution after that of Oklahoma, which he apparently described as a "zoological garden of cranks."[285] President Taft encouraged the people of Arizona to make their state constitution a simple framework of fundamental principles. He also urged them implicitly to eschew such progressive spirited features as the initiative and referendum.[286]

The Arizona Enabling Act was signed by President Taft on June 20, 1910. It included several provisions that were intended to be mandatory for inclusion in the Arizona Constitution "by an ordinance irrevocable without the consent of the United States and the people of said State."[287] These mandatory requirements covered a broad range of subjects: religious freedom, polygamy, Indian lands, and the location of the state capital.[288] The Arizona Enabling Act further provided that these provisions in the state constitution could not be amended without the consent of Congress. These mandates became article XX of the Arizona Constitution. Over time, some of these provisions have been ignored or abrogated by the Arizona legislature, while others have been changed by state constitutional amendments that Congress has approved.[289]

Voting Rights

Another aspect of the Oklahoma Constitution was before the United States Supreme Court in 1915.[290] At issue was the grandfather clause for

---

[283] *Id.*

[284] *Id.*

[285] John D. Leshy, *The Making of the Arizona Constitution*, 20 ARIZ. ST. L.J. 1, 31 (1988).

[286] *Id.*

[287] *Id.*

[288] *Id.*

[289] *Id.*

[290] *Guinn v. United States*, 238 U.S. 347 (1915).

voting in Art. 3 section 4A. That section was held to be a violation of the suffrage rights guaranteed by the United States Constitution.[291]

Local Governments

During the twentieth century, there have been significant substantive changes in many state constitutions with regard to local governments. Examples of those amendments include state constitutional provisions for county and municipal home rule. Political subdivisions within a state have also been authorized to levy taxes and issue bonds. The New Jersey Constitution contains some of the more far-reaching language concerning county and municipal governments:

> The provisions of this Constitution and of any law concerning municipal corporations formed for local government or concerning counties, shall be liberally construed in their favor. The powers of counties and such municipal corporations shall include not only those granted in express terms but also those of necessary or fair implication, or incident to the powers expressly conferred, or essential thereto, and not inconsistent with or prohibited by this Constitution or by law.[292]

Other noteworthy provisions affecting the operation of local governments have appeared in the state constitutions of: Missouri (joint performance of certain governmental functions and authorizing contractual arrangements for others); Georgia (county consolidation); and, Oregon (county manager government).[293]

Constitutional Commissions and Limited Conventions

During this century, two methods of amending state constitutions became increasingly popular. First, many states created state constitutional commissions. Those commissions were often comprised of political leaders, legal scholars, and distinguished citizens.[294] One purpose of those commissions has been "to dismantle the archaic institutional remains of participational democracy."[295] A state constitutional commission's final recommendations are submitted to the legislature and/or the public for approval. Second, limited constitutional conventions were called by several states to address or avoid addressing specific issues. The limited

---

[291] *Id.*

[292] W. Brooke Graves, *State Constitutional Law: A Twenty-Five Year Summary*, 8 Wm. & Mary L. Rev. 1, 31 (1966); N.J. Const. art. IV, § 7, Paragraph 11.

[293] *Id.*

[294] *See* Albert L. Sturm and James B. Craig Jr., *State Constitutional Commissions: Fifteen Years of Increasing Use.* 39 State Governance 56-63 (Winter 1966).

[295] Harvey Wheeler, *The Rise and Fall of Political Democracy*, 16 (Center for the Study of Democratic Institutions, Santa Barbara, 1966).

state constitutional convention has also been used to "deal with special situations, more or less of an emergency character."[296]

M. INCORPORATION DOCTRINE'S IMPACT

In 1925, there was a paradigm shift in the operation of America's state and federal jurisprudence. The United States Supreme Court began applying the Bill of Rights to the states by incorporating it into the Fourteenth Amendment through the Due Process Clause. In upholding New York's criminal anarchy statute the United States Supreme Court said: "For present purposes we may and do assume that freedom of speech and of the press—which are protected by the First Amendment from abridgment by Congress—are among the fundamental personal rights and 'liberties' protected by the due process clause of the Fourteenth Amendment from impairment by the States."[297]

Thereafter, the United States Supreme Court continued to hold that other selected provisions of the federal Bill of Rights also afforded protection against state action by virtue of the Due Process Clause of the Fourteenth Amendment.[298] This process is known as the incorporation doctrine.[299] The right to a jury trial is illustrative of the selective incorporation process.

The right to trial by jury has been described as "the morning star of liberty which…revolutionized America and a valuable safeguard to liberty or the very palladium of a free government."[300] The constitutions adopted the original States and "the constitution of every State entering the Union

---

[296] W. Brooke Graves, *State Constitutional Law: A Twenty-Five Year Summary*, 8 WM. & MARY L. REV. 1, 8-9 (1966), *e.g.* New Jersey (1947); Virginia (1945-46); Tennessee (1952-53 and 1959).

[297] *Gitlow v. New York*, 268 U.S. 652, 665-66 (1925).

[298] See Michael Kent Curtis, No State Shall Abridge: The Fourteenth Amendment and the Bill of Rights (Durham: Duke University Press, 1986); Richard Cortner, The Supreme Court and the Second Bill of Rights: The Fourteenth Amendment and the Nationalization of Civil Liberties (Madison: University of Wisconsin Press, 1981).

[299] For discussions regarding the incorporation of the federal Bill of Rights into the Due Process Clause of the Fourteenth Amendment, thereby making them applicable to the states, see Louis Henkin, *"Selective Incorporation" in the Fourteenth Amendment*, 73 YALE L.J. 74 (1963). *See* Richard C. Cortner, The Supreme Court and the Second Bill of Rights: The Fourteenth Amendment and the Nationalization of Civil Liberties (1981); Akhil Reed Amar, *The Bill of Rights and the Fourteenth Amendment*, 101 YALE L.J. 1193 (1992); Michael K. Curtis, *The Fourteenth Amendment and the Bill of Rights*, 14 CONN. L. REV. 237 (1982); Charles Fairman, *Does the Fourteenth Amendment Incorporate The Bill of Rights?* 2 STAN. L. REV. 5 (1949).

[300] The Federalist No. 83, at 582 (Jacob E. Cooke ed. Middletown, Conn.: Wesleyan University Press, 1961).

thereafter, in one form or another," have protected the right to trial by jury in criminal cases.[301] "The guarantees of jury trial in the Federal and State Constitutions reflect a *profound judgment* about the *way* in which law should be enforced and justice administered."[302]

The right to trial by jury is guaranteed by the Sixth and Seventh amendments to the Federal Constitution. Following the adoption of the Fourteenth Amendment to the United States Constitution, the Sixth Amendment right to trial by jury in *criminal* proceedings has been deemed to have been incorporated by the Due Process clause.[303] Accordingly, that Sixth Amendment right now provides protection against state action also. The United States Supreme Court has not yet, however, held that the Seventh Amendment's guarantee of jury trials in *civil* proceedings was made applicable to the states by the adoption of the Fourteenth Amendment.[304] Accordingly, the right to a jury trial in civil proceedings has always been and remains exclusively protected by provisions in the state constitutions.[305] Forty-nine states have state constitutional provisions similar to the Seventh Amendment.[306] Only Louisiana does not have a constitutional provision granting the right to trial by jury.

Federal Constitutional standards, however, set only a minimum level of protection.[307] The declaration of rights or substantive provisions in a state's constitution may, and often do, provide for broader or additional rights.[308] The expansion beyond federally guaranteed individual liberties

---

[301] Duncan v. State of Louisiana, 391 U.S. 145, 153 (1968).

[302] *Id.* (emphasis added). A number of states, for example, now authorize juries of a size less than the common law number of twelve. *Maxwell v. Dow*, 176 U.S. 581 (1900). Several states do not adhere to the common law requirement for unanimous verdict. *Jordan v. Commonwealth*, 225 U.S. 167 (1912); *Fay v. New York*, 332 U.S. 261 (1947); *see, e.g., Note, Trial by Jury in Criminal Cases*, 69 Columbia L. Rev. 419, 430 (1969); *Williams v. Florida*, 399 U.S. 78 (1970).

[303] Duncan v. Louisiana, 391 U.S. 145 (1968).

[304] Minneapolis v. St. Louis R.R. v. Bombolis, 241 U.S. 211 (1916); Walker v. Sauvinet, 92 U.S. 90 (1876).

[305] McCool v. Gehret, 657 A.2d 269, 281 (Del. 1995); Richard S. Arnold, Trial by Jury: The Constitutional Right to a Jury of Twelve in Civil Trials, 22 Hofstra L. Rev. 1 (1993).

[306] J. Kendall Few, In Defense of Trial by Jury, 469-76 (1993).

[307] *See also* William J. Brennan, Jr., *The Bill of Rights and the States: The Revival of State Constitutions as Guardians of Individual Rights*, 61 N.Y.U. L. Rev. 535 (1986); William J. Brennan, Jr., *State Constitutions and the Protection of Individual Rights*, 90 Harv. L. Rev. 489 (1977).

[308] Phyllis W. Beck, *Foreword: Stepping Over the Procedural Threshold in the Presentation of State Constitutional Claims*, 68 Temp. L. Rev. 1035 (1995); Hans A. Linde, *First Things First: Rediscovering the States' Bills of Rights*, 9 U. Balt. L. Rev. 379 (1980); *see also* Stanley Mosk, *State Constitutionalism: Both Liberal and*

by a state constitution is attributable to a variety of reasons: differences in textual language, legislative history, pre-existing state law, structural differences, matters of particular concern, and state traditions.[309]

N. NEW DEAL CHALLENGES

By the time of the Great Depression, many state constitutions had become "super" statutory codes because of multiple amendments over an extended period of time. Ironically, many of the popularly enacted social and economic provisions in state constitutions restricted the states' ability to enact timely statutory solutions to any rapidly developing crisis.[310] Consequently, the federal government was called upon to solve the nation's collective problems. The New Deal legislation, that eventually passed Federal Constitutional muster, responded to the nation's economic distress and caused another paradigm shift in the concept of state sovereignty.[311] The enactment of federal legislation that impacts upon the internal operations of each state and its citizenry has continued unabated since the New Deal era.[312] The provisions in many state constitutions now often compete or conflict with federally created or subsidized programs. It has been noted "that many states which bemoan their loss of power to the Federal Government still cling to constitutional limitations which cripple their own legislatures."[313] In fact, one critic of state constitution-making in the twentieth century has written:

> Changes in state constitutions still are largely directed toward the goals of the Efficiency and Economy movement of two generations ago, concentrating upon professionalization of all branches of government rather than upon improving the responsiveness of state government to widespread popular demands and the major contemporary issues in society.[314]

Conservative, 63 TEX. L. REV. 1081, 1081-82 (1985); John M. Wisdom, *Foreword: The Ever-Whirling Wheels of American Federalism*, 59 NOTRE DAME L. REV. 1063 (1984).

[309] *State v. Williams*, 459 A.2d 641 (N.J. 1983); *State v. Gunwall*, 720 P.2d 808, 811-13 (Wash. 1986). *Commonwealth v. Edmunds*, 586 A.2d 887 (Pa. 1991).

[310] See Kermit L. Hall, "Mostly Anchor and Little Sail," *in* Paul Finkelman and Stephen E. Gottlieb, eds., Toward a Usable Past: Liberty Under State Constitutions 408 (Athens: University of Georgia Press, 1991).

[311] L. Tribe, American Constitutional Law 386 (2d ed. 1988); *see also* Bruce Ackerman, We The People Foundations (Cambridge: Harvard University Press, 1991).

[312] *See United States v. Lopez*, 115 S. Ct. 1624, 1628 (1995).

[313] W. Brooke Graves, *State Constitutional Law: A Twenty-Five Year Summary*, 8 WM. & MARY L. REV. 1, 25 (1966); *see also* W. Brooke Graves, *Concepts of Legislative Power in State Constitutions*, 14 LA. L. REV. 749, 749-763 (1954).

[314] Adrian, *Trends in State Constitutions*, 5 HARV. J. LEGIS. 311, 341 (1968), *quoted in* William F. Swindler, *State Constitutions for the 20th Century*, 50 NEB. L. REV. 577, 577-78 (1971).

This is because the so-called modernization of state constitutions has been tempered by the normal processes of majoritarian partisan politics. Notwithstanding their laudatory intentions, the revisors of many state constitutions have been unable to overcome the temptation "to predetermine decisions with respect of policies and services…by writing specific prohibitions, mandates, or prescriptions into state constitutions."[315] Consequently, many state constitutions continued to be filled with legislative and administrative obstacles that were impervious to statutory solutions.

O. COLD WAR REVISIONS

There was a "wave" of state constitutional revisions between 1945 and 1970. The recurring theme of those revisions was often an effort to modernize the operation of a state's framework of government. These efforts frequently realigned the structure and allocation of power between the political sub-divisions within a state. The focal points were usually related to taxation, public finance, and a shared responsibility for the rendition of intra-state constituent services.

Several state constitutions provided for representation in either one or both houses of its legislature without regard to population.[316] The 1897 Delaware Constitution, for example, not only provided for malapportionment by describing legislative districts with particularity, but also included no mechanism for reappointment.[317] A similar provision in the New Jersey Constitution prevented any state constitutional reform for three decades in this century, until an agreement was reached to exclude reappointment from the agenda of the constitutional convention.[318] In 1964, the United States Supreme Court held that the Fourteenth Amendment's equal protection clause mandated that both houses of bicameral state legislatures had to be apportioned by population.[319]

The constitutions of at least thirteen states were revised between 1963 and 1976.[320] There was a great deal of interest in rewriting state

---

[315] William F. Swindler, *State Constitutions for the 20th Century,* 50 NEB. L. REV. 577, 578 (1971).

[316] *See* Robert G. Dixon, Democratic Representation: Reapportionment in Law and Politics 62-63, chart I (New York: Oxford University Press, 1968).

[317] *See* James Q. Dealey, *Growth of American State Constitutions* 97 (New York: Da Capo Press, 1972).

[318] Robert F. Williams, The New Jersey State Constitution: A Reference Guide 13-16 (Westport, Conn.: Greenwood Press, 1990).

[319] *Reynolds v. Sims*, 377 U.S. 533 (1964).

[320] James A. Henretta, *Foreword: Rethinking the State Constitutional Tradition*, 22 RUTGERS L.J. 819, 836-39 (1991).

constitutions as the decade of the 1960s drew to a close. North Carolina adopted a new (third) constitution in 1971 that was primarily the product of its State Constitution Study Commission. "The text of the new frame of government was that of the 1868 constitution as amended, subjected to rigorous editorial revision," along with some revisions and clarifications.[321] The amendment process was deemed to be most advisable for fundamental reforms.[322]

P. PATTERNS AND MODELS

According to Daniel J. Elazar, there has been a tendency to perpetuate the basic political and cultural values of the majority by reflecting them in state constitutional provisions.[323] Six patterns of state constitutions have been identified and summarized by Elazar in what G. Alan Tarr characterizes as a political-cultural model.[324] The features and characteristics of Elazar's six political-cultural patterns of state constitutions will be described seriatim.[325]

Commonwealth Pattern

According to Elazar, the commonwealth pattern emerged from the state constitutions in and around New England.[326] The philosophic nature of those frameworks of government is to provide definitive guidance for the operation of a civilized society under a republican form of government. The commonwealth pattern is the oldest form of state constitution. Originally characterized by their brevity, the underlying premise is a covenant. The format is to describe the elements of government, while at the same time guaranteeing the preservation of fundamental individual and property rights. The state constitutional commonwealth pattern has demonstrated a capacity for adaptation without the need for wholesale revision. According to Elazar, eight states outside of the New England region have state constitutions based upon the commonwealth pattern.

---

[321] John V. Orth, Symposium: "The Law of the Land": The North Carolina Constitution and State Constitutional Law: North Carolina Constitutional History, 70 N.C. L. REV. 1759, 1791 (1992).

[322] *Id.* at 1792-96.

[323] Daniel J. Elazar, *The Principles and Traditions Underlying State Constitutions, 12 Publius: the Journal of Federalism* 11, 18-22 (1982).

[324] G. Alan Tarr, Constitutional Politics in the States, Contemporary Controversies and Historical Patterns, 4 (Greenwood Press 1996).

[325] Daniel J. Elazar, The Principles and Traditions Underlying State Constitutions, 12 Publius: The Journal of Federalism 11, 18-22 (1982).

[326] *Id.*

Commercial Republic Pattern

The commercial republic pattern of constitution described by Elazar became prevalent in states situated to the south and west of New England.[327] This type of state constitution evolved from a series of compromises. In each state where this pattern emerged, there was a history of commercial development and urbanization, in combination with a citizenry increasingly buoyed by migrants with diverse ethnic heritages. The competition between commercial interests and ethnic ideals resulted in frequent and expansive revisions to the framework of government. The length of the provisions the commercial republic pattern is attributable to the explicit and detailed nature of the solutions to areas of earlier disagreement. The Illinois Constitution is illustrative of the commercial republic pattern.

Southern Contractual Pattern

The southern contractual pattern of state constitution is evidenced, according to Elazar, by frequent changes that are directly attributable to paradigm shifts in social, political, and economic policies.[328] These state constitutions often contained provisions that were normally the subject matter of ordinary legislation. The state constitutional experience of Texas is illustrative: in 1836, a constitution was adopted for the Republic of Texas; in 1845, Texas adopted a new constitution for admission to statehood; it adopted another constitution in 1861, when Texas joined the Confederacy; a fourth constitution was needed before Texas could rejoin the Union in 1866; the fifth Texas Constitution was adopted in 1869, through the efforts of Republican Reconstructionalists; and the sixth Texas Constitution was adopted in 1876. The electorate defeated a proposal and substantially revised constitution for Texas in 1975.

Civil Code Pattern

The civil code pattern described by Elazar is attributed only to the state constitutions of Louisiana.[329] Drawing upon its French legal background, the Louisiana constitutions have resembled the long and detailed civil codes of Europe. Between 1812 and 1982, Louisiana had eleven constitutions. The tenth constitution was adopted in 1921 and had been amended 439 times by 1965. A revised and abbreviated state constitution was adopted for Louisiana in 1974.

---

[327] Id.

[328] Id.

[329] Id.

Frame of Government Pattern

The frame of government pattern is found by Elazar in the state constitutions of the Far West.[330] The primary focus of these documents is to establish a framework of state government. The emphasis in each was upon limited government except for a few specific subjects involving economic development.

Managerial Model

Finally, Elazar depicts the constitutions of Hawaii and Alaska as most approximating the managerial model designed by constitutional reformers in this century.[331] These constitutions provide for broad grants of power to the executive branch and few restrictions on the legislature. They also include provisions that address social legislation, natural resource presentation, and relationships with local political subdivisions. These state constitutions have been analogized to the Hamiltonian managerial model.

Model State Constitution

The National Municipal League published its first Model State Constitution in 1921. During the next fifty years, that Model State Constitution was revised many times and appeared in six editions. The Model State Constitution sets forth both a framework of government and an enumeration of fundamental rights. It has been drawn upon selectively by some states for guidance. This is the "model" that Elazar refers to in his analysis of the constitutions adopted by Alaska and Hawaii.

Historical-Movement Model

Some scholars, other than Elazar, have identified what G. Alan Tarr characterizes as an "historical-movement model" in state constitutions.[332] Unlike Elazar, who looked at the unique aspects of the intra-state politics and culture, those scholars contend that state constitutions reflect the political forces that were prevalent nationally at the time of their adoption.[333] Thus, proponents of the historical movements model in state constitutional-making submit that state constitutional revisions inculcated

---

[330] *Id.*

[331] *Id.*

[332] G. Alan Tarr, Constitutional Politics in the States, Contemporary Controversies and Historical Patterns, 4 (Greenwood Press, 1996).

[333] *See* Albert L. Sturm, *The Development of American State Constitutions*, 12 Publius: The Journal of Federalism 57-98 (Winger 1982); Kermit L. Hall, "Mostly Anchor and Little Sail: The Evolution of American State Constitutions," *in* Paul Finkelman and Stephen E. Gottlieb, eds., Toward a Usable Past: Liberty Under State Constitutions 388-417 (Athens: University of Georgia Press, 1991).

the epic national themes of their time, e.g., Jacksonian democracy, Antebellum concerns, Reconstruction problems, the Progressive movement in the early twentieth century, etc.

Ordinary Politics Model

Another theory of state constitution-making is what Tarr describes as the ordinary-politics model.[334] According to that theory, provisions inserted into state constitutions reflect the ordinary political fluctuations within a state that are an inevitable consequence when the majority in power shifts between parties, regions, or other affiliated interests. To the extent that a group with particular perspectives has the ability to amend the state's constitution, it can enhance the institutionalization of its view more effectively than it could with a statute. Consequently, this model is used to explain why the design of many state constitutions may appear to resemble a patchwork quilt more than a mosaic.

CONCLUSION[335]

The United States Constitution "created a legal system unprecedented in form and design, establishing two orders of government, each with its own direct relationship, its own privity, its own set of mutual rights and obligations to the people who sustain it and are governed by it." State governments became subject to a superior regime of law, established by the people, through a specific delegation of their sovereign power to a national government that was paramount within its delegated sphere. Chief Justice Marshall described the national and state governments as "each sovereign, with respect to the objects committed to it, and neither sovereign with respect to the objects committed to the other."

"From the inception of the American republic, federal and state constitutional traditions have been distinct." The United States Constitution has retained its original character as a document which fixed the basic structure of government and allocated power among its three branches. State constitution-making and amending has been a recurring process within the broader political, social, economic, and historical contexts of time and place.

The goal of American federalism, in the words of the Preamble to the United States Constitution, was to form a "more perfect Union," by

---

[334] *See* Elmer E. Cornwell, Jr., Jay S. Goodman, and Wayne R. Swanson, State Constitutional Conventions (New York: Praeger, 1975); Charles Press, *Assessing Policy and Operational Implications of State Constitutional Change*, 12 *Publius: The Journal of Federalism* 99-111 (Winter 1982).

[335] Taken from Randy J. Holland, *State Constitutions: Purpose and Function*, 69 Temp. L. Rev 989, 1006 (1996).

providing for a division of sovereign power at two levels. In structuring federalism to unite the country, the United States Constitution simultaneously provided for the recognition of the pre-existing format of state governments and strengthened the national government, without concentrating all sovereign power at that level. The result is a deterrence of tyranny, the dual protection of individual liberty, and a division of governmental responsibility in addressing social and economic issues.

The 1787 United States Constitution, as amended, and the succession of state constitutions from 1776 until today, as amended, reflect the history of how democracy has operated within America and each of its United States.

INDEX